Frommer's®

Mexico

17th Edition

by David Baird, Shane Christensen,
Christine Delsol & Joy Hepp

with Maribeth Mellin

WILEY

John Wiley & Sons, Inc.

Published by:
JOHN WILEY & SONS, INC.
111 River St.
Hoboken, NJ 07030-5774

G95.
Q6F92Tf
2011

ISBN 978-1-118-02739-4; ISBN 978-1-118-10529-0 (ebk); ISBN 978-1-118-10530-6 (ebk); ISBN 978-1-118-10531-3 (ebk)

Editor: Michael Kelly, with Jennifer Polland
Production Editor: Erin Amick
Cartographer: Tim Lohnes
Photo Editor: Richard Fox
Production by Wiley Indianapolis Composition Services
Front Cover Photo: Guadalajara, Mexico: Charo cowboy riding horse ©Steve Bly / Getty Images
Back Cover Photo: Waves of Pacific Ocean near Cabo San Lucas ©Val Smirnof / Alamy Images

For information on our other products and services or to obtain technical support, please contact our
Customer Care Department within the U.S. at 877/762-2974, outside the U.S. at 317/572-3993 or fax
317/572-4002.

Wiley also publishes its books in a variety of electronic formats. Some content that appears in print may
not be available in electronic formats.

Manufactured in the United States of America

5   4   3   2   1

CONTENTS

15 Aug. 2011-530

LIST OF MAPS

ABOUT THE AUTHORS

A writer, editor, and translator, **David Baird** has lived several years in different parts of Mexico. Now based in Austin, Texas, he spends as much time in Mexico as possible. **Shane Christensen** has written extensively for Frommer's throughout Mexico, and is also the author of *Frommer's Dubai* and *Frommer's Grand Canyon National Park.* Even though he's a California native, he considers himself an honorary Mexican in heart and soul and returns to Mexico every chance he gets. **Joy Hepp** is a native Californian who has spent most of her life in Mexico and its former territories. She writes about travel, culture, and music for several print and online publications. Author of *Pauline Frommer's Cancún & the Yucatán,* **Christine Delsol** was raised by her Mexican-Chilean grandmother and has been traveling to Mexico for more than 30 years. She has spent most of her career in newspapers, including eight years as a travel editor at the San Francisco Chronicle. She has won an Associated press award, two Lowell Thomas awards, and Mazatlán's Golden Deer Award. **Maribeth Mellin** is the author of *Traveler's Mexico Companion,* which won the country's prestigious Pluma de Plata award, and has covered Mexico and Latin America for dozens of newspapers, magazines, websites, and guides.

HOW TO CONTACT US

In researching this book, we discovered many wonderful places—hotels, restaurants, shops, and more. We're sure you'll find others. Please tell us about them, so we can share the information with your fellow travelers in upcoming editions. If you were disappointed with a recommendation, we'd love to know that, too. Please write to:

Frommer's Mexico, 17th Edition
John Wiley & Sons, Inc. • 111 River St. • Hoboken, NJ 07030-5774
frommersfeedback@wiley.com

ADVISORY & DISCLAIMER

Travel information can change quickly and unexpectedly, and we strongly advise you to confirm important details locally before traveling, including information on visas, health and safety, traffic and transport, accommodation, shopping, and eating out. We also encourage you to stay alert while traveling and to remain aware of your surroundings. Avoid civil disturbances, and keep a close eye on cameras, purses, wallets, and other valuables.

While we have endeavored to ensure that the information contained within this guide is accurate and up-to-date at the time of publication, we make no representations or warranties with respect to the accuracy or completeness of the contents of this work and specifically disclaim all warranties, including without limitation warranties of fitness for a particular purpose. We accept no responsibility or liability for any inaccuracy or errors or omissions, or for any inconvenience, loss, damage, costs, or expenses of any nature whatsoever incurred or suffered by anyone as a result of any advice or information contained in this guide.

The inclusion of a company, organization, or website in this guide as a service provider and/or potential source of further information does not mean that we endorse them or the information they provide. Be aware that information provided through some websites may be unreliable and can change without notice. Neither the publisher or author shall be liable for any damages arising herefrom.

FROMMER'S STAR RATINGS, ICONS & ABBREVIATIONS

Every hotel, restaurant, and attraction listing in this guide has been ranked for quality, value, service, amenities, and special features using a **star-rating system.** In country, state, and regional guides, we also rate towns and regions to help you narrow down your choices and budget your time accordingly. Hotels and restaurants are rated on a scale of zero (recommended) to three stars (exceptional). Attractions, shopping, nightlife, towns, and regions are rated according to the following scale: zero stars (recommended), one star (highly recommended), two stars (very highly recommended), and three stars (must-see).

In addition to the star-rating system, we also use **eight feature icons** that point you to the great deals, in-the-know advice, and unique experiences that separate travelers from tourists. Throughout the book, look for:

special finds—those places only insiders know about

fun facts—details that make travelers more informed and their trips more fun

kids—best bets for kids and advice for the whole family

special moments—those experiences that memories are made of

overrated—places or experiences not worth your time or money

insider tips—great ways to save time and money

great values—where to get the best deals

warning—traveler's advisories are usually in effect

The following **abbreviations** are used for credit cards:

AE	American Express	DISC Discover	V Visa
DC	Diners Club	MC MasterCard	

FROMMERS.COM

Frommer's travel resources don't end with this guide. Frommer's website, **www.frommers. com**, has travel information on more than 4,000 destinations. We update features regularly, giving you access to the most current trip-planning information and the best airfare, lodging, and car-rental bargains. You can also listen to podcasts, connect with other Frommers. com members through our active-reader forums, share your travel photos, read blogs from guidebook editors and fellow travelers, and much more.

THE BEST OF MEXICO

by David Baird, Shane Christensen, Christine Delsol & Joy Hepp

Across Mexico, in villages and cities, and in mountains, tropical coasts, and jungle settings, enchanting surprises await travelers. These might take the form of a fantastic small-town festival, delightful dining in a memorable restaurant, or even a stretch of road through heavenly countryside. Below is a starter list of our favorites, to which you'll have the pleasure of adding your own discoveries.

THE best CULTURAL EXPERIENCES

- **Passing Time in the Plazas & Parks:** All the world may be a stage, but some stages have richer backdrops than others. Town plazas are the place to sit and watch daily Mexican life unfold before your eyes. Alive with people, these open spaces are no modern product of urban planners, but are rooted in the traditional Mexican view of society. Several plazas are standouts: **Veracruz's** famous *zócalo* (chapter 12) features nearly nonstop music and tropical gaiety. One look tells you how important **Oaxaca's** *zócalo* (chapter 11) is to the local citizenry; the plaza is at once remarkably beautiful, grand, and intimate. **Mexico City's** Alameda (chapter 4) has a dark, dramatic history—heretics were burned at the stake here during the colonial period—but today it's a people's park where lovers sit, cotton-candy vendors spin their treats, and the sound of organ grinders drifts over the changing crowd. **San Miguel de Allende's** Jardín (chapter 6) is the focal point for meeting, sitting, painting, and sketching. During festivals, it fills with dancers, parades, and elaborate fireworks. **Guanajuato** and **Querétaro** (chapter 6) have the coziest plazas, and **Mérida's** El Centro (chapter 16), can't be beat on Sundays.
- **Música Popular:** Nothing reveals the soul of a people like music, and Mexico has given rise to various styles, which you can hear in many different settings. You can hear brassy **mariachi** music in the famous Plaza de Garibaldi in Mexico City (chapter 4), under the arches of El Parián in Tlaquepaque, and in other parts of Guadalajara (chapter 8). Or perhaps you want to hear romantic **boleros** sung to the strumming of a Spanish guitar, or what Mexicans call *música tropical* and related *cumbias*, mambos, and cha-cha-chas (chapter 16).

1 Mexico

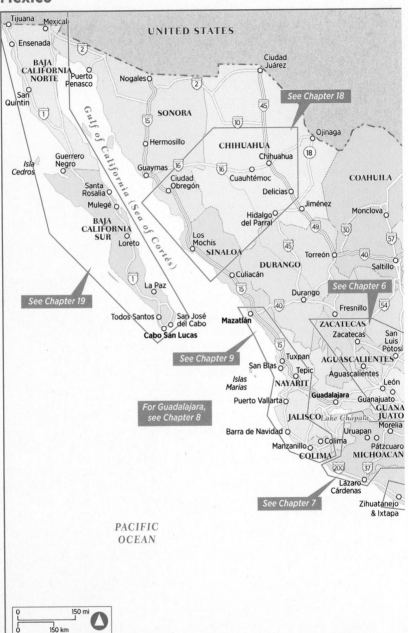

1

1

THE BEST OF MEXICO | The Best Cultural Experiences

UNITED STATES

Piedras Negras

Nuevo Laredo

85
D

Matamoros

Monterrey

NUEVO
LEÓN   85

TAMAULIPAS

Ciudad Victoria

Gulf of Mexico

See Chapter 14

Ciudad Mante

Tampico

SAN LUIS
POTOSÍ

San Miguel
de Allende

QUERÉTARO   Poza Rica

HIDALGO   Papantla

Querétaro   Pachúca

Mexico City   Xalapa

Toluca   TLAXCALA
Tlaxcala

Cuernavaca   Puebla

MORELOS   PUEBLA   Orizaba

Taxco   95   Tehuacán

GUERRERO

See Chapter 5

Acapulco

Oaxaca

OAXACA

Puerto Escondido

Puerto
Ángel   Huatulco

See Chapter 10

See Chapter 11

Tuxpan

See Chapter 12

For Mexico City,
see Chapter 4

See Chapter 16   See Chapter 13

Río Lagartos

Progreso   Valladolid

Celestún   Mérida   180
D   YUCATÁN

Campeche   180

Bay of
Campeche

CAMPECHE

Catemaco

VERACRUZ   TABASCO
Coatzacoalcos   Villahermosa   186

Veracruz

190
D   175

186   Palenque

Salina
Cruz

Gulf of
Tehuantepec

Tuxtla
Gutiérrez   San Cristóbal
de las Casas

CHIAPAS

Comitan

200

GUATEMALA

Tapachula

Isla
Mujeres

Cancún

Playa del   Cozumel
Carmen

Punta
Allen

QUINTANA
ROO

Bacalar   Mahahual
Peninsula

261   186   Chetumal

Escárcega

See Chapter 15

BELIZE   Caribbean
Sea

HONDURAS

EL
SALVADOR

See Chapter 17

- **Regional Folk Dancing:** From the Ballet Folklórico in Mexico City to the Ballet Folclórico in Guadalajara (chapters 4 and 8), or the almost-nightly park dances in **Mérida** (chapter 16), Mexican folk dance events are diverse and colorful expressions of Mexican traditions.

- **Fireworks:** Mexicans share such a passion for fireworks and such a cavalier attitude toward them that it's a good thing the buildings are stone and cement, or the whole country would have burned down long ago. Many local traditions surround fireworks, and every festival includes a display. The most lavish are the large constructions called *castillos*, and the wildest are the *toros* that men carry over their shoulders while running through the streets, causing festivalgoers to dive for cover.

- **Strolling El Malecón:** Wherever there's a seafront road, you'll find *el malecón* bordering it. This is generally a wide sidewalk for strolling, complete with vendors selling pinwheels and cotton candy. In some places, it has supplanted the plaza as a center of town life. The best are in **Puerto Vallarta** and **Mazatlán** (chapter 9), **La Paz** (chapter 19), **Cozumel** (chapter 14), and **Veracruz** (chapter 12).

- **Fútbol Matches:** There are very few people in the world who can match the passion of a serious Mexican *fútbol* (soccer) fan. From dusty rural fields to colossal urban stadiums, you can join *fanáticos* chanting team fight songs. If you have trouble learning the words, all you really need to know is, "Goooooooooooooool."

THE best ARCHAEOLOGICAL SITES

- **Teotihuacán:** It's so close to Mexico City, yet centuries away. You can sense the majesty of the past in a stroll down the pyramid-lined Avenue of the Dead, from the Pyramid of the Sun to the Pyramid of the Moon. Imagine what a fabulous place this must have been when the walls were stuccoed and painted brilliant colors. See "A Side Trip to the Pyramids of San Juan Teotihuacán," p. 126.

- **Monte Albán:** A grand ceremonial city on a mountaintop overlooking the valley of Oaxaca, Monte Albán affords visitors panoramic vistas; a fascinating view of a society in transition, reflected in the contrasting methods of pyramid construction; and intriguing details in ornamentation. See "Road Trips from Oaxaca," p. 417.

- **Palenque:** Like the pharaohs of Egypt, the rulers of Palenque built tombs deep within their pyramids. Imagine the magnificent ceremony in A.D. 683, when King Pacal was entombed in his burial chamber, which lay unspoiled until its discovery in 1952. See "Palenque," p. 632.

- **Uxmal:** No matter how many times we see Uxmal, the splendor of its stone carvings remains awe-inspiring. A stone rattlesnake undulates across the facade of the Nunnery complex, and 103 masks of Chaac—the rain god—project from the Governor's Palace. See "The Ruins of Uxmal," p. 600.

- **Chichén Itzá:** Stand beside the giant serpent head at the foot of El Castillo and marvel at the architects and astronomers who positioned the building so precisely that shadow and sunlight form a serpent's body slithering from peak to earth at each equinox (Mar 21 and Sept 21). See "The Ruins of Chichén Itzá," p. 614.

- **Ek Balam:** In recent years, this is the site where some of Mexico's most astounding archaeological discoveries have been made. Ek Balam's main pyramid is taller than Chichén Itzá's, and it holds a sacred doorway bordered with elaborate stucco figures of priests and kings and rich iconography. See "Ek Balam: Dark Jaguar," p. 624.

THE best BEACH VACATIONS

○ **Puerto Vallarta:** Vallarta exemplifies the beauty of Mexico—a Pacific bay framed by lush mountains, a vibrant colonial town, open-minded culture with an artistic bent, perfect weather, and friendly locals. Spectacularly wide Banderas Bay is graced by 42km (26 miles) of sandy beach. The beaches of Punta Mita, the exclusive development north of Vallarta, offer white-sand, crystalline waters, and coral reefs just offshore. Others around the bay nestle in coves, accessible only by boat. See "Puerto Vallarta," in chapter 9.

○ **Sayulita:** Less than an hour north of Puerto Vallarta, Sayulita is a longboarder's paradise with a chilled-out beach scene. Although tourists descend in droves on the town during vacation periods, the rest of the year Sayulita clings to a bygone era of total beach simplicity and Mexican tranquillity. See p. 301.

○ **Puerto Escondido:** The best overall beach value in Mexico is principally known for its world-class surfing beach, Playa Zicatela. The surrounding beaches and towns all have their own appeal—be they lined with colorful fishing *pangas*, delicious seafood restaurants, or shady palms. Puerto Escondido has unique accommodations at excellent prices, with exceptional budget dining and nightlife. See p. 376.

○ **Ixtapa/Zihuatanejo:** These side-by-side resorts afford beachgoers the best of both worlds: serene simplicity and resort comforts. For travelers seeking to get back to basics, the best and most beautiful beach is Playa La Ropa, close to Zihuatanejo. The wide beach at Playa Las Gatas, with its restaurants and snorkeling sites, is also a great place to play. The high-rise hotels in Ixtapa, on the next bay over from Zihuatanejo, front Playa Palmar, a fine, wide swath of beach. See p. 359.

○ **Cancún:** This man-made resort offers some of the most spectacular beaches anywhere. The powdery white sand is complemented by warm Caribbean waters the color of a Technicolor dream; it's so clear that you can see through to the coral reefs below. You can come here just to relax, but this is also one of the world's most popular entertainment destinations. Cancún offers Mexico's widest selection of beachfront resorts, with more restaurants, nightlife, and activities than any other resort destination in the country. See chapter 13.

○ **Isla Mujeres:** If uninterrupted relaxation is what you're after, Isla Mujeres offers a quintessential laid-back vacation. Most accommodations are small, inexpensive inns, with a few luxury boutique hotels tempting you for at least a night. Bike—or take a golf cart—around the island to explore rocky coves and sandy beaches, or focus your tanning efforts on the wide beachfront of Playa Norte. Here you'll find calm waters perfect for swimming and snorkeling, and beachfront *palapa* restaurants beckoning you for a fresh fish lunch. See chapter 14.

○ **Playa del Carmen:** Stylish and hip, Playa del Carmen has a beautiful beach and a social scene that focuses on the beach by day and the pedestrian-only Quinta Avenida by night, with its assortment of restaurants, clubs, sidewalk cafes, and shops offering all the entertainment you could want. You're also close to the coast's major attractions, including nature parks, ruins, and cenotes (sinkholes or natural wells). Playa is Mexico's fastest-growing city and is becoming homogenized (think Dairy Queen and Starbucks). Enjoy it while it's still a manageable size. See p. 526.

○ **Tulum:** Fronting some of the best beaches on the entire coast, Tulum's small *palapa* hotels offer guests a little slice of paradise far from the crowds and megaresorts. The bustling town lies inland; at the coast, things are quiet, as all these small hotels must generate their own electricity. If you can pull yourself away from the beach, there are ruins to marvel at and a vast nature preserve to explore. See p. 545.

- **La Paz:** This state capital borders a lovely beach, dotted with colorful playgrounds and lively open-air restaurants. Take a cue from the local residents, though, and pass on swimming here in favor of the exquisite beaches just minutes from downtown. La Paz's beaches and the islets just offshore have transformed this tranquil town into a center for diving, sea kayaking, and other adventure pursuits. See p. 714.
- **Los Cabos:** Dramatic rock formations and crashing waves join forces with wide stretches of soft sand and rolling surf breaks. Start at Playa Palmilla and work your way down the Tourist Corridor to the famed Lover's Beach at Land's End. Some beaches are more appropriate for contemplation than for swimming. See p. 682.

THE best ACTIVE VACATIONS

- **Scuba Diving in Cozumel & Along the Yucatán's Caribbean Coast:** The coral reefs off Cozumel, Mexico's premier diving destination, are among the top five dive spots in the world. The Yucatán's coastal reef, part of the planet's second-largest reef system and a national marine park, affords excellent diving all along the coast. Diving from Isla Mujeres is quite spectacular. Especially beautiful is the Chinchorro Reef, 32km (20 miles) offshore from Mahahual or Xcalak. See chapters 14 and 15.
- **Fly-Fishing off the Punta Allen & Mahahual Peninsulas:** Serious anglers will enjoy the challenge of fly-fishing the saltwater flats and lagoons on the protected sides of these peninsulas. See "Sian Ka'an & the Punta Allen Peninsula" and "Mahahual, Xcalak & the Chinchorro Reef" in chapter 15.
- **Hiking & Horseback Riding in the Copper Canyon:** Miles and miles of beautiful, remote, challenging canyon lands are paradise for the serious hiker or rider. Follow a Tarahumara Indian guide, who can take you deep into the canyons to places rarely viewed by tourists. Experienced horseback riders can set up a 12-day ride with **Paraíso del Oso** (p. 666) that tests a rider's skill in mountainous terrain. It has to be the most challenging ride in North America. See chapter 18.
- **Golf in Puerto Vallarta & Los Cabos:** Puerto Vallarta has eight championship courses, including a second Jack Nicklaus Signature course in Punta Mita. Fabulous courses are also within easy driving distance along the Pacific Coast at El Tamarindo, Isla Navidad, and Manzanillo. See chapter 9. The Corridor between San José del Cabo and Cabo San Lucas is one of the world's premier golf destinations, with seven championship courses slated for the area. See chapter 19.
- **Surfing the Pacific Coast:** The world-class break at Zicatela Beach in **Puerto Escondido** is a lure for surfers from around the globe. It challenges the best in the sport each September and October, when the waves peak and the annual surf competitions take place. See chapter 10. Other noted surf breaks in Mexico include **Sayulita, Punta Mita,** and Las Islitas Beach near **San Blas** (all north of Puerto Vallarta); Playa Costa Azul, on the outskirts of **San José del Cabo;** and "Killers" at **Todos Santos Island** in northern Baja. See chapters 9 and 19.
- **Sportfishing in La Paz:** Billfishing for magnificent marlin and sailfish is popular in southern Baja, and La Paz pulls in the most consistent share. See chapter 19. Fishing is excellent in Los Cabos, Mazatlán, Manzanillo, and Zihuatanejo, too. See chapters 9, 10, and 19.
- **Sea Kayaking in the Sea of Cortez:** From Cabo San Lucas to La Paz, and continuing north, the Sea of Cortez is a sea kayaker's dream. Explore its dozens of tiny coves and impressive inlets, under the watchful gaze of sea lions and dolphins. Professional outfitters provide gear, guides, and instruction. See chapter 19.

THE best OF NATURAL MEXICO

o **Michoacán's Million Monarch March:** Mexico is an exotic land, and no place drives this home more than a mountain forest where you stand surrounded by the fluttering wings of millions of monarch butterflies. The setting is the rugged highlands of Michoacán, from mid- to late November through March. See p. 230.

o **Whale-Watching:** Each year between December and April, magnificent humpback and gray whales return to breed and instruct their young in the waters of Banderas Bay, fronting **Puerto Vallarta** (chapter 9), and in **Los Cabos** (chapter 19).

o **Sea Turtle Nesting Beaches:** Between June and November, sea turtles return to the beaches of their birth to lay their eggs in the sand. With poaching and natural predators threatening these species, communities have established protected nesting areas. Many are open for public viewing and participation in egg collection and baby-turtle release. Turtles are found along the Yucatán coast, in Baja Sur, on the Oaxaca coast, in Puerto Vallarta, and on Costa Alegre. See chapters 9, 15, and 19.

o **Technicolor Laguna Bacalar:** The waters of this crystal-clear, spring-fed lake—Mexico's second largest, though it's actually a lagoon—are noted for their vibrant color variations, from pale blue to deep blue-green and turquoise. The surrounding area is known for birding, with over 130 species identified. See p. 561.

o **The Rugged Copper Canyon:** This network of beautiful, remote, and unspoiled canyons is larger than the Grand Canyon in the U.S. It incorporates high waterfalls, vertical canyon walls, mountain forests in the canyon-rim country, and semiarid desert inside the canyons. This is the land of the Tarahumara Indians, who gained their legendary endurance from adapting to this wilderness. See chapter 18.

o **Desert Landscapes in Baja Sur:** The painted-desert colors and unique plant life are a natural curiosity in Los Cabos, where horseback, hiking, and ATV trips explore the area. The arid desert contrasts sharply with the intense blue of the sea surrounding the peninsula. See chapter 19.

THE best PLACES TO GET AWAY FROM IT ALL

o **Tepoztlán:** On the weekends, Tepoztlán's cobblestone streets fill with spirituality seekers, market lovers, and city dwellers, but during the week, travelers find a tranquil, enchanting town that is the embodiment of small-town life in Mexico. In many ways, Tepoztlán is like a town out of a storybook—quaint ice-cream shops, a rock-hewn staircase on the edge of town leading to an ancient pyramid, and wild horses often roaming the streets. See p. 158.

o **Costa Alegre:** Between Puerto Vallarta and Manzanillo, gorgeous boutique hotels cater to the privileged and are ideal for honeymoons or romantic escapes. These resorts sit miles from civilization on secluded, pristine beaches. See "Costa Alegre: Puerto Vallarta to Barra de Navidad," in chapter 9.

o **Punta Mita:** Ancient inhabitants considered this northern tip of the Bay of Banderas sacred ground. Today the point where the Sea of Cortez, the Pacific Ocean, and Banderas Bay meet has evolved into Mexico's most exclusive residential resort development, with the Four Seasons and St. Regis located here alongside two world-class golf courses. The beaches are white and the waters crystalline. See p. 300.

- **The Yucatán's Riviera Maya:** Away from the busy resort of Cancún, a string of quiet getaways, including Paamul, Punta Bete, and Xpu-ha, offer tranquillity on extraordinarily beautiful beaches. For the kind of sleepy fishing village atmosphere—and low prices—that once belonged to Playa del Carmen, pull off the highway at Puerto Morelos. See chapter 15.

- **Laguna Bacalar:** The spring-fed waters of Laguna Bacalar make an ideal place to unwind. South of Cancún, near Chetumal, there's nothing around for miles. If you want adventure, you can paddle a kayak on the lake; follow a birding trail; take a dip in the largest known cenote, Cenote Azul, at the south end of town; or venture to Belize or nearby Maya ruins. See p. 561.

- **Cerocahui:** Up in the high Sierra Tarahumara, far from where the large tours stop, you'll find a peaceful little town surrounding a former mission. Nearby are two small hotels that are even more peaceful—no phones, no crowds, no traffic, just beautiful mountains and canyons clothed in pine forest. See p. 665.

- **Cabo Pulmo:** It's only 97km (60 miles) from the Los Cabos airport to Cabo Pulmo, yet if the mounded Sierra de La Laguna peaks weren't a dead giveaway for Baja, you could be in the South Pacific. Swaying in the shade of a *palapa*-roofed bungalow at Cabo Pulmo Beach Resort, you won't care where you are—you just won't want to leave. Extensive hiking/mountain-biking trails loop through the mountains for those who prefer the peace of the desert. See p. 688.

THE best ART, ARCHITECTURE & MUSEUMS

- **Museo Nacional de Antropología:** The Museum of Anthropology in Mexico City contains riches representing 3,000 years of the country's past. Also on view are fabulous artifacts of still-thriving indigenous cultures. The award-winning building, designed by architect Pedro Ramírez Vázquez, is stunning. See p. 98.

- **Palacio Nacional:** Mexico's national center of government overlooks one of the three biggest public squares in the world (the *zócalo*) and was originally built in 1692 on the site of Moctezuma's "new" palace, to be the home of Hernán Cortez. The top floor, added in the late 1920s, holds a series of stunning Diego Rivera murals depicting Mexico's history. See p. 100.

- **Palacio de Bellas Artes:** The country's premier venue for the performing arts in Mexico City, this fabulous building is the combined work of several masters. The exterior is early-20th-century Art Nouveau covered in marble; the interior is 1930s Art Deco. See p. 104.

- **The Templo Mayor's Aztec Splendor:** The Templo Mayor and Museo del Templo Mayor constitute an archaeological excavation and museum with 6,000 objects on display. They showcase the variety and splendor of the Aztec Empire as it existed in the historic center of what is now Mexico City. See p. 100.

- **Catedral Metropolitana:** This towering cathedral, begun in 1567 and finished in 1788, blends baroque, neoclassical, and *churrigueresque* architecture and was constructed primarily from the stones of destroyed Aztec temples. See p. 106.

- **Santa Prisca y San Sebastián Church:** This baroque church in Taxco, completed in 1758, has an intricately carved facade, an interior decorated with gold-leafed saints and angels, and paintings by Miguel Cabrera, one of Mexico's most famous Colonial-Era artists. See p. 139.

o **Museo de Medicina Tradicional y Herbolaria:** It may not be the largest or most prestigious museum in Cuernavaca, but it certainly is the most quirky. Inside you will find ancient cures to obscure diseases and an inebriation primer. See p. 153.

o **La Parroquia:** In San Miguel de Allende, inspired by European Gothic, but lighter and more cheerful, this fanciful church is like a fiesta captured in stone—especially at night, when it's illuminated. See p. 170..

o **Murals of José Clemente Orozco:** Of the great Mexican muralists of the revolutionary period, Orozco is perhaps the most technical and the most expressive of his generation's concerns. To see his image of Hidalgo bearing down on you from the ceiling of the grand staircase of the Palacio de Gobierno in Guadalajara is to understand what he and his *compañeros* were striving to accomplish. See p. 258.

o **Museo Virreinal de Guadalupe:** Six kilometers (3¾ miles) southeast of Zacatecas in the small town of Guadalupe, this Franciscan convent and art museum holds a striking collection of 17th- and 18th-century paintings by such masters as Miguel Cabrera and Cristóbal de Villalpando. The expressive, dramatic works will fascinate art lovers. See p. 209.

o **Morelia's Cathedral:** Sober lines, balanced proportions, a deft blending of architectural styles, and monumental height—Morelia's cathedral is the most beautiful in the country. It's built of brownish-pink stone that turns fiery rose in the late-afternoon sun. See p. 223.

o **Museo Pantaleón Panduro:** The peoples of Mexico have always placed a high value on pottery as a field of artistic achievement. It's a cultural continuity that spans from pre-Columbian times to the present. This museum in Tlaquepaque is perhaps the greatest single expression of this love for pottery. Its collection holds prized pieces from the yearly national ceramics competition. See p. 260.

o **Museo Antropología de Xalapa:** Along with the finest examples of Olmec and Totonac sculpture and ceramics, this museum includes the best collection of the Olmec megalithic heads. See p. 442.

o **Capilla del Rosario:** In Puebla's church of Santo Domingo, this chapel is a tour de force of baroque expression, executed in molded plaster, carved wood, Talavera tile, and gold leaf. The overall aim is to overpower the senses. See p. 433.

o **Museo de la Cultura Maya:** Chetumal's modern museum, one of the best in the country, explores Maya archaeology, architecture, history, and mythology. It has interactive exhibits and a glass floor that allows visitors to walk above replicas of Maya sites. See p. 563.

THE best SHOPPING

o **Bazar del Sábado in San Angel:** This festive Saturday market in and around Plaza San Jacinto in colonial San Angel, one of Mexico City's more exclusive southern neighborhoods, offers exceptional crafts of a more sophisticated nature than you'll see in most *mercados*. Furnishings, antiques, and collectibles are also easy to find in surrounding shops and street plazas. See p. 118.

o **Polanco, Mexico City:** This fashionable neighborhood is noted for its designer boutiques, formal dress shops, fine jewelers, and leather-goods offerings. Avenida Presidente Masaryk is Mexico City's equivalent of Rodeo Drive in Beverly Hills or the Champs-Elysées in Paris. See p. 116.

- **Calle Colima, Mexico City:** This street has a variety of boutiques and skate shops where the hip *Chilangos* go to procure their outfits for Saturday night or pick out their new sneakers. See p. 116.
- **Contemporary Art:** Latin American art is surging in popularity. Galleries in Mexico City feature Mexico's masters and emerging stars. Oaxaca, Puerto Vallarta, and San Miguel de Allende galleries have excellent selections. See chapters 4, 6, 9, and 11.
- **Taxco Silver:** Mexico's silver capital, Taxco, has hundreds of stores featuring fine jewelry and decorative objects. See p. 134.
- **Talavera Pottery in Puebla & Dolores Hidalgo:** An inheritor of the Moorish legacy of ceramics, Puebla produces some of the most sought-after dinnerware in the world. Tiles produced there adorn building facades and church domes throughout the area. See chapter 12. Dolores Hidalgo, 40km (25 miles) northwest of San Miguel de Allende, has attractive, inexpensive, and less traditional Talavera. See p. 178.
- **San Miguel de Allende's Diverse Crafts:** Perhaps it's the influence of the Instituto Allende art school, but something has made storekeepers here savvy about their merchandise. The stores have fewer typical articles of Mexican handicrafts and more interesting and eye-catching works than in other towns. See p. 165.
- **Pátzcuaro's Fine Crafts:** Michoacán is known for its crafts, and Pátzcuaro is at the center of it all. You can find beautiful cotton textiles, woodcarvings, pottery, lacquerware, woven straw pieces, and copper items in the market, or you can track the object to its source in one of the nearby villages. See p. 231.
- **Decorative Arts in Tlaquepaque & Tonalá:** These two neighborhoods of Guadalajara offer perhaps the most enjoyable shopping in Mexico. Tlaquepaque has attracted sophisticated and wide-ranging shops that sell a wide variety of decorative art. More than 400 artisans have workshops in Tonalá, and you can visit many of them; on market days, wander through blocks and blocks of market stalls to find that one perfect piece. See p. 261.
- **Oaxacan Textiles:** The valley of Oaxaca produces the best weavings and naturally dyed textiles in Mexico; it's also famous for its pottery and colorful, imaginative woodcarvings. See chapter 11.
- **San Cristóbal de las Casas:** Deep in the heart of the Maya highlands, San Cristóbal has shops, open plazas, and markets that feature the distinctive waist-loomed wool and cotton textiles of the region, as well as leather shoes, handsome pottery, amber jewelry, and Guatemalan textiles. Highland Maya Indians sell direct to tourists from their armloads of textiles, pottery, and woodcarvings. See p. 640.
- **Huichol Art in Puerto Vallarta:** One of the last indigenous cultures to remain faithful to their customs, language, and traditions, the Huichol Indians come down from the Sierra Madre to sell their unusual art to Puerto Vallarta galleries. Inspired by visions received during spiritual ceremonies, the Huichol create their art with colorful yarn or beads pressed into wax. See p. 290.

THE best LUXURY HOTELS

- **Condesadf** (Mexico City; www.condesadf.com): The city's trendiest hotel sits in the hip urban neighborhood of Condesa. In an early-20th-century French building, it combines Art Nouveau with contemporary designs and features one of the city's hottest restaurants and rooftop bars. See p. 87.
- **Hotel Four Seasons** (Mexico City; www.fourseasons.com): The standard of excellence in Mexico, and the most classically luxurious option in Mexico City, this

hotel captures serenity and elegance in a palace-style building that surrounds a picturesque courtyard. Bonuses include the gracious staff and unique cultural tours on offer. See p. 84.

○ **W Mexico City** (Mexico City; www.starwood.com/whotels): Stylish and high-tech, this is where the young and cool stay. With its super-*caliente* red hues and lively bar, the W has infused the country's capital with a dose of minimalist urban chic. Luxury extras include expansive bathrooms with circular tubs. See p. 82.

○ **Rosewood** (San Miguel de Allende; www.rosewoodsanmiguel.com): This new resort hotel offers guests the ideal getaway. Spacious rooms with private terraces, surrounded by lush gardens and courtyards, which in turn are surrounded by the colonial charms of San Miguel. Relax at the spa, stroll the cobblestone streets, sip cocktails on the rooftop terrace, and do it all again the next day. See p. 173.

○ **Villa Montaña** (Morelia; www.villamontana.com.mx): The Villa Montaña defines perfection. From the layout of the grounds to the decoration of the rooms, every detail has been skillfully handled. The hotel perches on a ridge that overlooks Morelia; from its terraces, guests can survey the city below. The restaurant is one of the city's best. See p. 228.

○ **Four Seasons Resort Punta Mita** (north of Puerto Vallarta; www.fourseasons.com): This luxury resort offers an unrivaled location in the exclusive Punta Mita beach community with the stellar service characteristic of the chain. A private beach, lazy river pool, expansive spa, and two Jack Nicklaus Signature golf courses are here. See p. 300.

○ **Playa Escondida** (Sayulita; www.playa-escondida.com): This dreamy yet unpretentious resort sits on a secluded beach. Choose among individually designed beachfront casitas, bungalows in the jungle, or imported teak houses from Thailand constructed in a spectacular bird canyon. You won't want to leave. See p. 302.

○ **El Tamarindo Beach & Golf Resort** (btw. Manzanillo and Puerto Vallarta; www.eltamarindoresort.com): Among the world's most exclusive resorts, this breathtaking hotel has just a small selection of casitas hidden amid tropical landscaping or facing the Pacific, as well as a magnificent oceanfront golf course. It's about 1 hour north of Manzanillo along Costa Alegre. See p. 322.

○ **Las Alamandas** (btw. Manzanillo and Puerto Vallarta; www.alamandas.com): The extraordinary Alamandas sits on its own nature preserve, with four private beaches, exquisite gardens, lakes, lagoons, and a bird sanctuary. The guests are all treated like VIPs, which many of them are. See p. 320.

○ **La Casa Que Canta** (Zihuatanejo; www.lacasaquecanta.com): This is one of Mexico's most romantic spots, an unforgettable boutique hotel above Playa La Ropa. *Palapa*-style guest rooms have their own furnished outdoor terraces, many with private plunge pools overlooking the sea. The service, amenities, and cuisine will make you feel like you've landed in heaven. See p. 366.

○ **Amuleto** (Zihuatanejo; www.amuleto.net): With a spectacular view of Zihuatanejo Bay that makes it seem like you're on top of the world, this boutique hotel was designed for people seeking seclusion. Housing only six individually designed suites, Amuleto has a beautiful infinity pool, an outstanding open-air restaurant, and exquisite service. See p. 365.

○ **Ritz-Carlton Cancún** (Cancún; www.ritzcarlton.com): Thick carpets, sparkling glass and brass, and rich mahogany surround guests at this hotel, for years the standard-bearer of luxury in Cancún. The service is impeccable, leaving guests with an overall sense of pampered relaxation. Its restaurants are among the best in the city, and an outstanding culinary center is open to guests and outside visitors. See p. 446.

o **JW Marriott** (Cancún; www.jwmarriottcancun.com): This gorgeous resort affords elegance without pretense, combining classic and Caribbean styling with warm Mexican service. The inviting free-form infinity pool extends to the white-sand beach, and families feel just as comfortable here as romance-seeking couples. The hotel includes a spectacular 3,250-sq.-m (35,000-sq.-ft.) spa. See p. 464.

o **Presidente InterContinental Cozumel** (Cozumel; www.intercontinentalcozumel. com): Surrounded by shady palms, this resort also has the best beach on the island, right in front of Paraíso Reef. Favorite rooms are the deluxe beachside units with spacious patios and direct access to the beach—you can even order romantic in-room dining on the patios, complete with a trio to serenade you. Excellent scuba diving is accessible right in front. See p. 511.

o **Hacienda Xcanatún** (outskirts of Mérida; www.xcanatun.com): With its large, extravagantly designed suites, acres of tropical gardens, a private spa, excellent restaurant, and ample staff, this hotel masters the difficult trick of being compact in size but expansive in offerings. See p. 578.

o **Hacienda Puerta Campeche** (Campeche; www.luxurycollection.com): Not a hacienda at all, but a gorgeous hotel created from several adjoining colonial houses, this is a large property for only 15 rooms. An open area in back features a pool and tropical gardens under ancient crumbling walls. The hotel is beautiful—both in overall layout and design details—and the service is impeccable. See p. 611.

o **Las Ventanas al Paraíso** (Los Cabos; www.lasventanas.com): Stunning in its relaxed elegance, Las Ventanas has a deluxe European spa, excellent gourmet restaurant, and elegantly appointed rooms and suites. From fireplaces and telescopes to private pools and rooftop terraces, each suite offers a slice of heaven. See p. 694.

o **Esperanza** (Los Cabos; www.esperanzaresort.com): This Auberge resort pampers guests in a desert-chic setting, on a bluff overlooking twin coves. Spacious rooms are enhanced by ample terraces, and the resort's spa and dining services make a stay here even more memorable. See p. 694.

THE best INEXPENSIVE INNS

o **Holiday Inn Zócalo** (Mexico City; www.hotelescortes.com): This unique Holiday Inn is one of the city's most charming hotels. Located next to the capital's historic central square, it's decorated in a colonial Mexican style with colorful art, antiques, and handicrafts. See p. 86.

o **Red Tree House** (Mexico City; www.theredtreehouse.com): Mexico City is the second-largest city in the world, so it's easy to feel like a number wherever you are. But life at the Red Tree House features daily breakfasts in a light and airy kitchen and plenty of space to lounge in the courtyard and garden; the inn has an atmosphere where every guest feels at home. See p. 87.

o **Hotel San Francisco Plaza** (Guadalajara; www.sanfranciscohotel.com.mx): This two-story colonial-style hotel is a more agreeable place to stay than lodgings that cost twice the price, and it's every bit as comfortable. See p. 252.

o **Hotel Los Flamingos** (Acapulco; www.hotellosflamingos.com): Once a private club for Hollywood's elite, this hotel will enchant you with its pervasive midcentury charm, funky profusion of hot pink, and breathtaking cliff-top views. See p. 348.

o **Paraíso Escondido** (Puerto Escondido; www.hotelparaisoescondido.net): This eclectic inn is a great bargain, especially for the originality of the decor and the excellent service. It's a short walk to the beach and Puerto's main drag. See p. 381.

o **Misión de los Arcos** (Huatulco; www.misiondelosarcos.com): Just 1 block from the central plaza, this elegant hotel has an all-white facade and intriguing decorative touches that give it an inviting feel. See p. 394.

o **Las Golondrinas** (Oaxaca; www.hotellasgolondrinas.com.mx): We receive more favorable letters about this hotel than about any other in the country. It's small, simple, and colorful, with homey touches of folk art and pathways lined with abundant foliage. See p. 408.

o **Casa Na-Bolom** (San Cristóbal; www.nabolom.org): This beautiful colonial house was once the home and office of Frans and Trudy Blom, and a gathering place for anthropologists interested in the region's various ethnic groups. It is now a museum and library full of materials about the region and its indigenous peoples. Rooms have fireplaces and are decorated in local fashion. See p. 645.

o **Rey del Caribe Hotel** (Cancún; www.reycaribe.com): An inexpensive retreat in downtown Cancún, this hotel has considered every detail in its quest for an organic and environmentally friendly atmosphere. Set in a tropical garden, the Rey del Caribe provides sunny rooms, warm service, yoga and other themed classes, and healthful dining—all a welcome respite from party-hearty Cancún. See p. 470.

o **Cabo Inn** (Cabo San Lucas; www.caboinnhotel.com): This former bordello is the area's best budget inn. Rooms are small but extra clean and invitingly decorated, amenities are generous, and the owner-managers are friendly and helpful. Ideally located, close to town and near the marina, the inn caters to sportfishers. See p. 706.

THE best SPA RESORTS

o **El Santuario Resort & Spa** (Valle de Bravo; www.elsantuario.com): The suites at this spa resort, built into the foot of a quartz mountain, overlook a vast lake. A 1,858-sq.-m (19,999-sq.-ft.) spa offers a wealth of therapies, plus yoga, Pilates, Tai Chi, and meditation classes. See p. 146.

o **Misión Del Sol Resort & Spa** (Cuernavaca; www.misiondelsol.com): This is Mexico's finest spa resort, with every architectural and functional detail designed to soothe body and soul—from meditation rooms and reflexology showers to magnets under your mattress. This sumptuous, full-service spa and fitness center, with delicious vegetarian cuisine, is a heavenly base for personal renewal. See p. 156.

o **Hotel Ixtapan Spa & Golf Resort** (Ixtapan; www.hotelixtapan.com): In operation since 1939, this classic, traditional spa resort has consistently upgraded amenities and services. It's also close to the region's renowned thermal baths. See p. 144.

o **Paradise Village** (Nuevo Vallarta; www.paradisevillage.com): Excellent fitness facilities combined with pampering-yet-affordable spa services make this one of the best all-around spas in Mexico. It actively promotes the beneficial properties of indigenous Mexican spa therapies and natural treatments. See p. 297.

o **Pueblo Bonito Emerald Bay** (Mazatlán; www.pueblobonitoemeraldbay.com): The resort's luxury spa is Mazatlán's best (and most expensive), offering a tempting variety of international spa treatments and more traditional Mexican rituals, as well as massage therapies, body scrubs, and facials. See p. 311.

- **Le Méridien Cancún Resort & Spa** (Cancún; www.meridiencancun.com.mx): The Spa del Mar is a state-of-the-art, 1,400-sq.-m (15,069-sq.-ft.) facility bordering the brilliant Caribbean. It has the most complete spa in the area, with inhalation rooms, saunas, Jacuzzis, cold plunges, Swiss showers, a cascading waterfall whirlpool, and 14 treatment rooms. See p. 466.

- **ME** (Cancún; www.mecancun.travel): The ultrachic Yhi Spa of Cancún's ME hotel overlooks the ocean and offers body glows and exfoliations, aromatherapy massages, body masks, and wraps—this is a place to indulge yourself until you're convinced that you've landed in heaven. See p. 468.

- **The Tides Riviera Maya** (north of Playa del Carmen; www.tidesrivieramaya.com): Small, secluded, and private, the Tides offers extraordinary personal service—some villas come with a major-domo on call—and spa treatments. Rooms are spread throughout the jungle, and there's a beautiful seaside pool and restaurant. See p. 524.

- **Rancho La Puerta** (Baja Norte; www.rancholapuerta.com): One of Mexico's best-known spas, Rancho La Puerta is a spa-vacation pioneer, having opened its doors (at the time, tent flaps) in 1940. A steady stream of guests returns for the constantly expanding facilities, spa services, and outdoor opportunities. See p. 735.

THE best MEXICAN FOOD & DRINK

- **La Opera** (Mexico City; © 55/5512-8959): This legendary cantina, in the style of an opulent European cafe, has attracted illustrious personalities for decades—Pancho Villa shot a still-visible hole through the roof. In the historic center, it doubles as a restaurant, but it's best as a late-afternoon watering hole. See p. 94.

- **El Sacromonte** (Guadalajara; © 33/3825-5447): Various dishes delight the senses with novel tastes and textures and skillful presentation. The menu describes each dish in Spanish couplets. See p. 253.

- **Adobe Fonda** (Tlaquepaque; © 33/3657-2792): Delicious Mexican food is served inside one of those gorgeous decorative arts stores that line Tlaquepaque's Calle Independencia. The point of departure for the food is some uncommon Mexican recipes, which are then given sparkling Italian and Argentine accents. See p. 252.

- **Daiquiri Dick's** (Puerto Vallarta; www.ddpv.com): A Vallarta institution, this beachfront restaurant combines scrumptious Mediterranean cuisine with excellent service and a lovely setting. Come for fresh fish creatively prepared and wash it down with a daiquiri or two. You'll find this casual restaurant as compelling for a romantic occasion as for a fun night out with friends. See p. 282.

- **Trio** (Puerto Vallarta; www.triopv.com): Most locals will tell you Trio is their favorite restaurant in Vallarta, a modest but stylish cafe where chef-owners Bernhard Güth and Ulf Henriksson's undeniable passion for food imbues each of the delicious Mexican and Mediterranean dishes. See p. 279.

- **Le Fort** (Bucerías; www.lefort.com.mx): Diners are treated to a culinary show by acclaimed chef Gilles Le Fort followed by the chance to sit down with him and other guests in a communal gourmet dinner. The prix-fixe menu includes three courses and matching wines, and the table seats 16. See p. 299.

- **Zibu** (Acapulco; ✆ **744/433-3058**): This chic open-air restaurant combines Mexican and Thai architectural and culinary styles to create one of the nation's best dining experiences, including a breathtaking view of the sea. See p. 349.

- **Los Flamingos** (Acapulco; www.hotellosflamingos.com/restaurant.html): If you're in Acapulco on a Thursday, you can enjoy a bowl of pozole, a traditional hominy-and-meat stew. Although you'll find it served at lunchtime throughout town, the best place to savor it is at Los Flamingos' cliff-top restaurant. See p. 348.

- **Mariscos Villa Rica Mocambo** (Veracruz; ✆ **229/922-2113**): Nobody else does seafood the way Veracruz does seafood, and this restaurant is the showcase for the region's cuisine. See p. 449.

- **The Club Grill** (in the Ritz-Carlton Cancún; ✆ **998/881-0808**): Two of the only AAA five-diamond restaurants in all of Mexico sit inside the Ritz-Carlton Cancún, which also operates a world-class culinary center. Consider this jazz and supper club for a special occasion; anything you order will be superb. See p. 472.

- **Labná** (Ciudad Cancún; www.labna.com): In Cancún's old downtown, this authentic Yucatecan restaurant offers deliciously unusual cuisine from the region like lime soup, *poc chuc,* and pork *pibil.* The gracious staff takes good care of diners, ensuring they have an enriching experience. See p. 476.

- **La Pigua** (Campeche; ✆ **981/811-3365**): Campeche's regional specialty is seafood, and nowhere else will you find seafood like this. Mexican caviar, coconut-battered shrimp, and chiles stuffed with shark are just a few of the unique specialties, along with the regional trademark *pan de cazón,* a layered casserole of baby shark. La Pigua's pompano will have you checking flight schedules. See p. 613.

- **Don Emiliano** (downtown San José del Cabo; www.donemiliano.com.mx): Don Emiliano wields farm-fresh ingredients laced with Mexican tradition and emerges from the kitchen with modern delights such as stepped-up *chile en nogada* for Día de Independencia and *lemon atole* with candied pumpkin for Day of the Dead. Don't miss the regular menu, which combines the likes of locally made cheeses with roasted tomatillos and dried hibiscus flowers with beef tenderloin. See p. 691.

- **Palapa Azul** (La Paz; ✆ **612/122-1801**): *Almejas* (clams) can be found everywhere from roadside shacks to gourmet restaurants in Baja Sur and are prepared raw with lime and salsa or baked inside their shells. The best place to enjoy this local treat is Palapa Azul on La Paz's Tecolote beach. The shells are stuffed with cheese, jalapeños, bacon, butter, tomatoes, and a secret ingredient the chef won't reveal. They are then wrapped in aluminum foil and tossed into an oven. The result is delectable and so is the view of the Sea of Cortez you will enjoy. See p. 721.

MEXICO IN DEPTH

by Christine Delsol

Ever since Spanish conquistador Hernán Cortez set sail in 1519 to find a world of gold and riches hidden beyond the sea, curious travelers have been coming to this land in search of the "real" Mexico. Like all timeworn myths, such a place remains just out of reach. Over the years, countless novelists and travel writers have claimed to have found something real while strolling the sun-parched cobblestone streets of Mérida, nesting in the steamy jungles of Chiapas, or swooning in the arms of a Mexican lover.

My grandmother's Mexico was a ranch in California's Central Valley, where her Mexican parents and grandparents carved out a decent, if laborious, life when the land was Mexico's northern outpost. My introduction to the country as a child was a day trip across the border while visiting my uncle in El Paso, Texas; all I can remember is a horrifying bullfight that I am still trying to forget. Was that the real Mexico? Ten years later, I drove the length of the Baja peninsula on the newly completed Hwy. 1 and found dusty crossroads where hastily erected prefab buildings next to *bodeguitas* served as hotels—and then La Paz, with its leafy tropical languor, beguiling *malecón,* and air-conditioned hotels. The real Mexico?

The answer, of course, is all of the above, and more. But my "real Mexico" lies in the generosity of its people, which is extended liberally to visitors. I have been adopted by farm families who gave me tent space under their *palapa* in return for paying a meager sum to share their meals, ushered by an office worker to his family's home for siesta so that we could continue our conversation, and left gape-jawed while watching as a *campesino* scaled a 12m (40-ft.) palm to fell a coconut and hand it to me with a straw after I casually asked what he grows on his farm. I have been stopped by policemen and then escorted to my destination 32km (20 miles) away when I confessed that I was lost. The one constant within this mosaic of experiences is a warmth and compulsion to share, recognizing no regional or economic boundaries and defying hardship, corruption, and natural disaster.

MEXICO TODAY: VIVA LA VIDA

Our art movement is not needed in this country.

–French surrealist artist André Bretón upon visiting Mexico

Despite corrupt politicians, a burdensome bureaucracy, the drug war's bloody undercurrents, and the low wages and swift inflation that the average citizen endures on a daily basis, Mexicans maintain a robust zeal for life with all its idiosyncrasies. A wild sense of humor, an appetite for good food, and the priority placed on friends, family, and fiesta are all essential to life in Mexico today.

Small wonder that magic realism is a popular theme in contemporary Mexican literature. The ghost of Juan Preciado's father floats through his journey like a graveyard breeze in Juan Rulfo's **Pedro Páramo;** the star-crossed lovers in Laura Esquivel's **Like Water for Chocolate** burn down their house with searing love-making. The more time you spend in Mexico, the more such fiction seems based in fact.

When André Bretón arrived here in 1938, his guides included a feisty communist with a unibrow, as famous for her pre-Hispanic wardrobe as for her explicit paintings, and her husband, a frog-faced muralist with a list of sexual conquests as long as his paintbrush. Frida Kahlo and Diego Rivera introduced the French artist to a country of spontaneous 6-hour parades and the newly discovered and mystifying colossal helmeted-head sculptures of the ancient Olmec culture.

If Bretón were to visit today, he would likely find this country no less incredible. Though it is marginally more sedate today, Mexico is still a land where one man can turn the world's attention to the poverty in the steaming southern jungles, never once removing his woolen ski mask; a culture where women dance with flaming candles balanced on their heads; a collection of peoples who affectionately call death "Katrina" and welcome her with flowers, food, and prayer; and a nation where a notorious drug dealer is honored with hit radio songs for escaping prison in a laundry cart. This is the magic that animates the mad and complex Mexican life.

Even everyday activities can be surreal. Naked protesters regularly interrupt traffic on one of the world's busiest avenues, Maya temples serve as the backdrop for train stations, and grown men fly through the air, tethered to a pole, in front of the National Anthropology Museum.

Sundays bring a degree of sanctity, thanks largely to the vast majority of the population that considers itself Catholic. Normally traffic-choked streets and congested plazas are eerily empty on the seventh day, making it virtually impossible to get any work done but wonderful for an aimless stroll.

Lately, news about Mexico tends to be fraught with brazen drug violence and political strife. But Mexicans live by the proverb, *"No hay mal que por bien no venga"*

What's Your Hurry?

A common phrase among Mexicans is *ahorita*, which translates loosely to "a little bit of right now." Depending on the context, it can mean either 5 seconds from now, or a quarter to never. This little phrase illustrates that Mexicans have a different concept of time than their English-speaking neighbors to the north, and that life in Mexico often moves at a slower pace. An imperfect appreciation of this difference can lead to misunderstandings and/or unnecessary frustration. If you're staying in the Sonoran desert in summer and your hotel says the air-conditioning will be fixed *ahorita*, you just might want to pick up a paper fan at the market.

("There is no bad that comes without good"); even these trying times are sure to reveal their own hidden meaning, eventually.

Mexico moves forward despite the saddening current events. In 2011, a year after celebrating the centennial of the Mexican revolution and the bicentennial of the independence movement, Mexico hosted both the Pan American Games and the FIFA U-17 World Cup, spurring renovation and new construction from Monterrey to Puerto Vallarta to Guadalajara to the capital while looking ahead to electing a new government in 2012.

LOOKING BACK: MEXICO HISTORY
Pre-Hispanic Mexicans

The earliest "Mexicans" might have been Stone Age hunter-gatherers from the north, descendants of a race that crossed the Bering Strait and reached North America around 12,000 B.C. A more recent theory points to an earlier crossing of peoples from Asia to the New World. What we do know is that Mexico was populated by 10,000 B.C. Sometime between 5200 and 1500 B.C., these early people began practicing agriculture and domesticating animals.

THE OLMECS & MAYA (THE PRE-CLASSIC PERIOD 1500 B.C.–A.D. 300)

Agriculture eventually supported large communities, with enough surplus to free some people from agricultural work. A civilization emerged that we call the **Olmec**— an enigmatic people who settled the Tabasco and Veracruz coasts. Anthropologists regard them as Mesoamerica's mother culture because they established a pattern for later civilizations, developing basic calendar, writing, and numbering systems; devising principles of urban architecture; and originating the cult of the jaguar and the

IT'S ALL IN THE game

The ancient Maya played a ball game of such importance that ball courts appear in virtually every Maya city (Bonampak is a rare exception). They were laid out in an I shape with sloping walls in the center. Similar ball courts have been found as far south as Nicaragua and as far north as Arizona.

What little we know of this sacred game comes from ancient depictions, the Popol Vuh (the Maya "bible"), and early accounts by the Spanish. The ball was heavy and could inflict injury. Wearing thick padding and protective gear, players formed teams of 2 to 10 members, the object being to propel the ball through a stone ring or other goal using mainly the hips.

We also know the game was part sport and part religious ritual affirming cosmological beliefs. It sometimes involved sacrifice, though whether the winners, the losers, or perhaps prisoners of war lost their heads is unclear. In the Popol Vuh, the hero twins Hunahpu and Xbalanque challenge the lords of the underworld to a ball game, played in part with the head of one brother. Eventually, the twins win and are allowed to return to the world of the living. The ball game, then, might have been one way to cheat the underworld.

sacredness of jade. They likely also bequeathed the sacred ball game found throughout Mesoamerican culture.

A defining feature of the Olmec culture was its colossal carved stone heads, several examples of which reside today in Villahermosa, Tabasco, and Xalapa, Veracruz. These sculptures were immense projects, sculpted from basalt stone mined more than 80km (50 miles) inland and transported to the coast, probably by river rafts. Their rounded, baby-faced look, marked by a peculiar, high-arched lip—a "jaguar mouth"—is an identifying mark of Olmec sculpture.

As Olmec cities began declining, other civilizations rose to the south and north. The **Maya** civilization, developing around 500 B.C. in the late pre-Classic period, perfected the Olmec calendar and developed an ornate system of hieroglyphic writing. North of the Valley of Mexico, a city we know as **Teotihuacán** also began its long life. In the valley of Oaxaca, construction of the Zapotec city of **Monte Albán** began. These cultures would shape the next age of Mesoamerica.

TEOTIHUACÁN, MONTE ALBÁN & PALENQUE: THE CLASSIC PERIOD (A.D. 300–900)

The rise and fall of these three centers of civilization defines this period—the heyday of pre-Columbian Mesoamerican culture and art. Achievements include the pyramids and palaces in Teotihuacán, the ceremonial center of Monte Albán, and the temple complexes and pyramids of Palenque and Calakmul.

The inhabitants of **Teotihuacán** (100 B.C.–A.D. 700), near present-day Mexico City, built a well-organized city that is thought to have had 200,000 inhabitants or more, covering 30 sq. km (12 sq. miles) and built on a grid with streams channeled to follow the city's plan. Led by an industrious and literate ruling class, its wide-ranging influence included the feathered serpent god, Quetzalcóatl, which joined the pantheons of the Toltec, Maya, and other cultures.

Farther south, the **Zapotec,** influenced by the Olmec, raised an impressive civilization in the Oaxaca region. Their principal cities were **Monte Albán,** inhabited by an elite class of merchants and artisans, and **Mitla,** reserved for the high priests.

TOLTECS & AZTEC INVASIONS: THE POST-CLASSIC PERIOD (A.D. 900–1521)

During this period, cultural and social development were replaced by a trend of violent warfare that begat the growth of an empire. The **Toltec** of central Mexico established their capital at Tula in the 10th century. They revered a god known as **Tezcatlipoca,** or "smoking mirror," who later became an Aztec god. Originally one of the barbarous hordes that periodically migrated from the north, they were influenced by remnants of Teotihuacán culture and adopted Quetzalcóatl, who was elevated to a twin god with Tezcatlipoca. The Toltec's large military class was divided into orders symbolized by animals. With as many as 40,000 people at its height, Tula spread its influence across Mesoamerica. But its might was played out by the 13th century, probably because of civil war and battles with northern invaders.

The **Aztecs,** who first served as mercenaries for established cities in the Valley of Mexico, acquired an unwanted, marshy piece of land in the middle of Lake Texcoco for their settlement. It eventually grew into the island city of Tenochtitlán, which lies today beneath the foundations of Mexico City. Through aggressive diplomacy and military action, the Aztecs conquered central Mexico and extended their rule east to the Gulf Coast and south to the valley of Oaxaca.

During this later period, the Maya civilization flourished in northern Yucatán, especially in cities such as Chichén Itzá, Uxmal, and the more recently discovered Ek Balaam.

All Mesoamerican cultures apparently practiced human sacrifice, but the Aztecs brought it to another level. During the 15th century, an estimated 20,000 to 250,000 sacrifices were carried out each year. The victims had usually been taken prisoner during battle and are believed to have accepted their fate with dignity, as sacrifice was seen as both an honorable way to die and a direct ticket to paradise.

Cortez, Moctezuma & the Spanish Conquest

In 1517, the first Spaniards arrived in what is today known as Mexico and skirmished with the Maya off the Yucatán coast. A shipwreck left several Spaniards stranded as prisoners of the Maya. Another Spanish expedition, under **Hernán Cortez,** landed on Cozumel in February 1519. The coastal Maya were happy to tell Cortez about the gold and riches of the Aztec empire in central Mexico. Disobeying his superior, the governor of Cuba, Cortez promptly sailed with his army into the Gulf of Mexico and landed at what is now Veracruz.

Cortez arrived when the Aztec empire was at the height of its wealth and power. **Moctezuma II** ruled over the central and southern highlands and extracted tribute from lowland peoples. His greatest temples were plated with gold and encrusted with the blood of sacrificial captives. A fool, a mystic, and something of a coward, Moctezuma dithered in Tenochtitlán while Cortez blustered and negotiated his way into the highlands, cloaking his intentions. Moctezuma, terrified by the Spaniard's military tactics and technology, was convinced that Cortez was the god Quetzalcóatl making his long-awaited return. By the time he arrived in the Aztec capital, Cortez had accumulated 6,000 indigenous allies who resented paying tribute to the Aztecs. In November 1519, he took Moctezuma hostage to try to leverage control of the empire.

In the middle of Cortez's maneuverings, another Spanish expedition arrived with orders to end Cortez's unauthorized mission. Cortez hastened back to the coast, routed the rival force, and persuaded the vanquished to join him on his return to Tenochtitlán. The capital had erupted in his absence, and the Aztecs chased his garrison out of the city. Moctezuma was killed during the attack—whether by his own men or by the Spaniards is not clear. Cortez laid siege to Tenochtitlán, aided by rival Indians and a devastating smallpox epidemic. When the Aztec capital fell in 1521, all of central Mexico lay at the conquerors' feet, vastly expanding the Spanish empire. The king hastened to legitimize Cortez's victorious pirate expedition after the fact and

THE return OF QUETZALCÓATL

The exact nature of the Toltec influence on the Maya is a subject of debate, but an intriguing myth in central Mexico tells of **Quetzalcóatl** quarreling with the god Tezcatlipoca and being tricked into leaving Tula. Quetzalcóatl heads east toward the morning star, vowing to return. In the language of myth, this could be a metaphor for a civil war between two factions in Tula, each led by the priesthood of a different god. Might the losing faction have migrated to the Yucatán and later ruled Chichén Itzá? Perhaps. What we do know is that this myth of Quetzalcóatl's eventual return became, in the hands of the Spanish, a devastating weapon of conquest.

MALINCHE: MEXICO'S FIRST TOUR guide

When Cortez gained control in present-day Tabasco, the *cacique,* or military chief, presented him with 20 female slaves in an effort to pacify the powerful invader. Among them was **Malinche,** the beautiful daughter of a fallen Aztec chief, whose mother had sold her off after her younger half brother was born, thus denying her the position of rightful heir. In addition to the Aztec's Náhuatl language, she spoke Yucatec Mayan, and her language skills were a boon to Cortez. One member of his entourage was Franciscan Friar Jerónimo de Aguilar, who had been shipwrecked in the Yucatán peninsula in 1511. Unlike the rest of their shipmates, Aguilar and his companion, Gonzalo Guerrero, managed to escape human sacrifice and ended up in friendlier interior territories, where they picked up the local Yucatec Mayan language.

When Cortez came back through the Yucatán in 1519, Guerrero refused to leave his new life as an important chieftain (a statue outside of Chetumal's **Museo de la Cultura Maya** honors him as the symbolic father of the mestizos), but Aguilar joined the party. With Aguilar and Malinche's help, Cortez was able to negotiate with Aztec tribes by translating from Náhuatl to Yucatec Mayan, to Spanish, and vice versa. Malinche eventually learned Spanish—some believe in as little as 3 months—and Aguilar's services were no longer needed.

Malinche proved to be an invaluable asset to Cortez as he toppled the Aztec empire. Eventually, she also became the mother of two of his children, and ironically, finally achieved the status denied her as a young girl. Though many still consider her to be a traitor to her people, she is also credited with being the mother of the **mestizo** (mixed European and indigenous) race.

ordered the forced conversion to Christianity of the new colony, to be called New Spain. By 1540, New Spain included possessions from Vancouver to Panama. In the 2 centuries that followed, Franciscan and Augustinian friars converted millions of Indians to Christianity, and Spanish lords built huge feudal estates with Indian farmers serving as serfs. Cortez's booty of silver and gold made Spain the wealthiest country in Europe.

The Rise of Mexico City & Spanish Colonialism

Cortez set about building a new city upon the ruins of the Aztec capital, collecting the tributes, some of them in labor, that the Indians once paid to Moctezuma. This model for building the new colony backfired over the next century, as the workforce perished from diseases imported by the Spaniards.

Over the 3 centuries of colonial rule, 61 viceroys governed Mexico while Spain became the richest country in Europe from New World gold and silver chiseled out by Indian labor. The Spanish elite built lavish homes filled with ornate furniture and draped themselves in imported velvets, satins, and jewels. Under the new class system, those born in Spain (*peninsulares*) were considered superior to Spaniards born in Mexico (*criollos*). People of other races and the *castas* (Spanish-Indian, Spanish-African, or Indian-African mixes) occupied society's bottom rungs.

Criollo resentment of Spanish rule simmered for years over taxes, royal monopolies, bureaucracy, *peninsulares'* superiority, restrictions on commerce with Spain and other countries, and the 1767 expulsion of the largely criollo Jesuit clergy. In 1808,

Napoleon invaded Spain, deposed Charles IV, and crowned his brother **Joseph Bonaparte.** To many in Mexico, allegiance to France was unthinkable. The next logical step was revolt.

Hidalgo, Juarez & Mexico's Independence

In 1810, **Father Miguel Hidalgo** set off the rebellion with his *grito*, the fabled cry for independence, from his church in the town of Dolores, Guanajuato. With **Ignacio Allende** and a citizen army, Hidalgo marched toward Mexico City. Although he ultimately failed and was executed, Hidalgo is honored as "the Father of Mexican Independence." Another priest, José María Morelos, kept the revolt alive with several successful campaigns before he, too, was captured and executed in 1815.

When the Spanish king who replaced Joseph Bonaparte decided to institute social reforms in the colonies, Mexico's conservative powers concluded they didn't need Spain after all. Royalist **Agustín de Iturbide** defected in 1821 and conspired with the rebels to declare independence from Spain, with himself as emperor. However, internal dissension quickly deposed Iturbide, and Mexico was instead proclaimed a republic.

The young, politically unstable nation ran through 36 presidents in 22 years, during which it lost half its territory in the disastrous **Mexican-American War (1846-48).** The central figure, **Antonio López de Santa Anna,** was flexible enough in those volatile days to portray himself variously as a liberal, a conservative, a federalist, and a centralist. He assumed the presidency no fewer than 11 times and just might hold the record for frequency of exile. He was ousted for good in 1855 and finished his days in Venezuela.

Amid continuing political turmoil, conservative forces, with some encouragement from Napoleon III, resolved to bring in a Habsburg to regain control. With French backing, **Archduke Maximilian** of Austria stepped in as emperor, but ragtag Mexican troops defeated the well-equipped French in a battle near Puebla in 1862 (now celebrated as **Cinco de Mayo**). A more successful second attempt seated Ferdinand Maximilian Joseph as emperor. Maximilian developed a genuine fondness for the Mexican people and upheld such policies as land reforms, religious freedom, and extending the right to vote beyond the landholding class. But

---

A sticky HABIT

Cigar smoking and gum chewing are two pleasures we have the Maya to thank for. Gum, the more innocuous of the two, comes from the sap of a species of zapote tree that grows in the Yucatán and Guatemala. Chewing releases its natural sugars, producing a mild, agreeable taste. The chewing-gum habit spread from the Maya to other cultures and eventually to the non-Indian population. In the second half of the 19th century, a Mexican (said to have been Gen. Santa Anna) introduced gum to the American Thomas Adams, who realized that it could be sweetened further and given other flavors. He marketed chewing gum in the U.S. with great success. Chemists have since figured out how to synthesize the gum, but the sap is still collected in parts of the Yucatán and Guatemala for making natural chewing gum. *Chicle* is the Spanish word, originally from the Náhuatl (Aztec) *tzictli*, and those who live in the forest and collect the sap are *chicleros*. Because the tree takes so long to produce more sap, there is no way to cultivate it commercially, so it is still collected in the wild.

he never overcame the opposition of Mexican extremists or the refusal of many foreign countries, including the United States, to recognize his government. After 3 years of civil war, the French abandoned the emperor, leaving Maximilian to be captured and executed in 1867.

Maximilian's adversary and successor (as president of Mexico) was **Benito Juárez,** a Zapotec Indian lawyer and one of Mexico's greatest heroes. Juárez did his best to unify and strengthen his country before dying of a heart attack in 1872; his plans and visions bore fruit for decades.

Zapata, Pancho Villa & the Mexican Revolution

A few years after Juárez's death, one of his generals, **Porfirio Díaz,** seized power in a coup. He ruled Mexico from 1877 to 1911, a period now called the *Porfiriato*. He maintained his rule through repression and by courting the favor of powerful nations. Generous in his dealings with foreign investors, Díaz became the archetypal *entreguista* (one who sells out his country for private gain). With foreign investment came the concentration of great wealth in a few hands, and social conditions worsened.

In 1910, **Francisco Madero** led an armed rebellion that became the **Mexican Revolution** ("La Revolución" in Mexico; the revolution against Spain is the "Guerra de Independencia"). Díaz was exiled and is buried in Paris. Madero became president, but **Victoriano Huerta,** in collusion with U.S. ambassador Henry Lane Wilson, betrayed and executed him in 1913. Those who had answered Madero's call rose up again—in support of the great peasant hero **Emiliano Zapata** in the south, and the seemingly invincible **Pancho Villa** in the central north, flanked by **Álvaro Obregón** and **Venustiano Carranza.** They eventually expelled Huerta and began hashing out a new constitution.

For a few years, Carranza, Obregón, and Villa fought among themselves; Zapata did not seek national power, though he fought tenaciously for land for the peasants. Carranza, who was president at the time, betrayed and assassinated Zapata. Obregón finally consolidated power and probably had Carranza assassinated. He, in turn, was assassinated when he tried to break one of the tenets of the revolution—no re-election. His successor, Plutarco Elias Calles, learned this lesson well, installing one puppet president after another, until **Lázaro Cárdenas,** elected in 1934, exiled him. At last, the Revolution appeared to have a chance. Cárdenas implemented massive land redistribution, nationalized the oil industry, instituted many other reforms, and gave shape to the ruling political party, which evolved into today's **Partido Revolucionario Institucional,** or **PRI.** Cárdenas is practically canonized by most Mexicans.

A New Democracy

The presidents who followed were noted more for graft than for leadership, and the party's reform principles were abandoned. Ten days before the 1968 Summer Olympics in Mexico City, the government quashed a student demonstration in the Tlatelolco district, killing hundreds of people. Though the PRI maintained its grip on power, it lost its image as a progressive party. Economic progress, particularly in the form of large development projects—most famously a skinny, unpopulated sandbar called Cancún—became the PRI's sole basis for legitimacy.

The government weathered several bouts of social unrest caused by periodic devaluations of the peso. But in 1985, the devastating **Mexico City earthquake**

¡HOLA!

Mexicans place paramount value on family and friends, social gatherings, and living in the present; worrying about the future takes a back seat. They are always ready to meet with friends for a drink or a cup of coffee or attend a family get-together. Social greetings and introductions are their own mini-rituals, and learning all of the intricacies could take a lifetime. The most important courtesy to remember is to acknowledge people individually; a general wave hello to the whole room doesn't cut it. You won't find more amiable people anywhere on Earth, and you can invite the full force of their natural gregariousness by being mindful of some social norms. Here's a start:

Slow Down   The "*mañana* time" stereotype is mostly true. Life obeys slower rhythms, and "on time" is a flexible concept. Arriving 30 minutes to 2 hours late to a party in someone's home is acceptable—in fact, coming at the specified hour would be rude, for your hosts almost certainly will not be ready. Here's the "mostly" part: Dinner invitations are less flexible; arrive within 30 minutes of the appointed hour. And do be on time for business appointments, public performances, weddings, and funerals.

Meet & Greet   Don't short-circuit the hellos and goodbyes; social values trump time efficiency. A Mexican must at least say "¡Buenos días!" even to strangers. When meeting a group of people, each is greeted separately, no matter how long it takes. Handshakes, *abrazos* (embraces), and, among women, kisses abound. Stick to handshakes until your host decides you rate a more intimate greeting. But don't back away from an embrace—that would amount to a rejection of friendship.

Have a Little Respect   Mexicans are lavish with titles of respect, so dispense *señor, señora, and señorita* (Mr., Mrs., Miss) freely. Teachers, lawyers, architects, and other professionals have earned the right to a title: *licenciado* for lawyers (and some other professions requiring a college degree), *maestro* or *maestra* for elementary schoolteachers, *profesor* or *profesora* for secondary or college teachers. Mexicans have two surnames, father's first and mother's second. Both appear on business cards (the mother's name might be abbreviated to an initial), but when addressing people, use just the first (paternal) surname.

Don't Get Huffy   Mexicans are genuinely interested in foreigners. If they stare, it's friendly curiosity. They like to practice their English and will ask about family, friends, money, and other intimate matters. If you are over 30 and have no children, they may express deep concern. Don't take it personally.

Show Some Culture   Mexicans tend to divide the world into the well-raised and cultured (*bien educado*) and the poorly raised (*mal educado*). Don't be shy about trying out your rudimentary Spanish; even the most elementary attempt is appreciated because it shows your interest in the culture. It's no big deal to be categorized as a foreigner, so long as it's a cultured foreigner and not one of the barbarians.

---

brought down many of the government's new, supposedly earthquake-proof buildings, exposing the widespread corruption that had fostered the shoddy construction and triggering heavy criticism of the government's relief efforts.

A political and military **uprising in Chiapas** and the occupation of San Cristóbal de las Casas in 1994 focused world attention on Mexico's profound social problems.

A new political force, the Ejército Zapatista de Liberación Nacional, or EZLN (Zapatista National Liberation Army), skillfully publicized the plight of the peasant.

In the years that followed, opposition political parties gained strength. Facing widespread public discontent at home as well as pressure and scrutiny abroad, the PRI began to concede defeat in state and congressional elections throughout the '90s. Party reformers were able to make changes over the objections of many hard-liners. They instituted a partial system of primary elections to give greater voice to the rank and file. This made for successful campaigns in several states, but in other states the old-style party leaders held on to their right to appoint the official party candidate. Internal strife reached a climax with the 1994 assassination of the party's presidential candidate, Luis Donaldo Colosio. A quick compromise resulted in the nomination of **Ernesto Zedillo** for president. Once in power, Zedillo proved to be a reformer. Over his 6-year term, he steadily led the country toward open and fair elections by strengthening the electoral process, gaining the public's confidence, and getting his own party to accept the possibility of losing power.

VICENTE FOX

In 2000, Zedillo shepherded Mexico's first true elections in 70 years of one-party rule. The winner, by a landslide, was PAN (Partido Acción Nacional) candidate **Vicente Fox,** a former businessman who ran on a platform of economic liberalization and anti-corruption. Many Mexicans voted for him simply to see if their voices would be heard and the PRI would relinquish power.

During Fox's presidency, the three main political parties had to adjust to the new realty of power sharing. The old government party, the PRI, still had a large infrastructure for getting out the vote and still controlled several state governments. Fox's center-right PAN had control of the presidency and most seats in the legislature, while the center-left PRD (Partido de la Revolución Democrática, or Democratic Revolution Party) controlled the government of Mexico City and a few southern states. To their credit, they handled the transition better than expected.

But by the end of Fox's term, Mexico's experiment with pluralistic democracy faced a crisis. Fox hadn't proved to be the master politician that the situation required. His efforts to build a coalition with segments of the PRI foundered, and his government failed to pass most of its initiatives. In the off-year elections of 2004, PAN lost many seats in the legislature and several governorships.

The PRI was in an excellent position for the presidential election of 2006, until party leader Roberto Madrazo sought to become the nominee in 2005 without going through primary elections. His power plays won him the nomination but deeply splintered the party; worse, they reminded voters of the old days when their votes counted for little.

The 2006 Election

Meanwhile, Mexico City mayor **Andrés Manuel López Obrador (AMLO,** for short) was the PRD's clear nominee. He was very popular for creating programs such as a pension for the city's elderly, and he was genuinely interested in helping the poor. Still, there was something unsettling about his habit of taking political opposition personally.

The bitter campaign between AMLO and PAN candidate **Felipe Calderón,** a social conservative and devout Catholic who believes in privatization and market forces, followed by a historically close election in the summer of 2006, was pure political circus. When the elections tribunal finally declared Calderón the winner more than a month later, AMLO refused to recognize the verdict. He launched a protest in grand Mexico City style that clogged the streets and infuriated commuters for a month. Supporters even took over the legislative chambers in an effort to physically prevent Calderón from taking office.

The contretemps diminished AMLO's popularity, and members of his party saw him as a nuisance best forgotten. However, AMLO still has a large following, and the recession brought new currency to his leftist message. He mustered tens of thousands of supporters in 2009 for a rally in Mexico City's *zócalo*, and in January 2010, he announced he would make another run for the presidency in 2012, with Mexico City mayor Marcelo Ebrard as his major rival for the PRD nomination.

THE CALDERÓN PRESIDENCY

Despite the controversy surrounding his election, Calderón quickly asserted his authority. Just 15 days after his December 2006 swearing-in, Calderón sent thousands of troops to his home state of Michoacán to quell the lucrative drug trade. He also created 150,000 temporary jobs and raised military pay.

After his rocky acquisition of power, won with only 35% of the popular vote, Calderón won over more of the public with his no-nonsense approach. Recognizing the PRD campaign's resonance with the poor, he announced programs to boost employment, alleviate poverty, and stabilize the skyrocketing price of tortillas.

His biggest challenge, however, has proved to be the alarming escalation of drug-related violence—a conflagration widely attributed to his crackdown on traffickers who ferry contraband through Mexico on its way to the United States. The violence, directed at journalists and government officials as well as rival drug cartels, is concentrated in five counties along the U.S.–Mexico border and parts of northern and central Mexico.

As 2011 began, Calderón could claim a certain success in his war on the cartels: He succeeded in capturing or killing several high-profile drug lords in 2010 and dismantled several cartel networks in the process. Such victories, however, further upset the balance of power as the organizations attempted to preserve their territory and grab turf from their weakened rivals. The result was the bloodiest year in Mexico's history—more than 11,000 deaths. The gory turf wars have boiled up—though not with the numbers or intensity as in the border areas—in formerly quiet states such as Guerrero, Morelos, Mexico, Colima, and Jalisco.

Opposition to Calderón's strategy has steadily mounted, and 2011 brought new tactics. He deployed more highly trained and better-paid (therefore less susceptible to corruption) federal police to Ciudad Juárez and other key areas. Perhaps more significantly, the legislature approved harsher prison sentences for terrorist acts while acknowledging that cartel violence could be classified as terrorism. Simply characterizing the violence as terrorism raises two interesting possibilities. First, it has the potential to spike the level of outrage among the general population, for whom tolerating cartel activity has long been a given; second, it raises the possibility of increased U.S. involvement in the conflict. Calderón is walking a fine line; he doesn't want the U.S. to storm the border in the name of counterterrorism, nor can he be sure that he, rather than the cartels, will bear the brunt of public outrage.

With the July 2012 presidential election approaching, Calderón is boxed in. Since the July 2009 legislative elections ended his PAN party's majority rule, the rival PRI has gained new strength. He has to reduce the body count, and he's running out of both time and resources. He basically has two choices: Accept U.S. intervention, which carries its own political perils, or give the cartels room to return to a clear division of territory and self-policing. As of this writing, Calderón had not tipped his hand as to which path, if either, he might take to preserve his party's political future.

Drugs & Other Border Issues

For years Mexico's drug traffickers operated in secluded mountain passes along abandoned highways, and from within their own transportation and trade network—much like a hornet's nest, buzzing away in the nation's backyard. As long as politicians and law-enforcement officers stayed out of their way—or, in some cases, aided in their enterprises—they remained out of sight and only occasionally stung an outsider.

When Calderón was elected, he poked a stick into that hornet's nest. His first act as president was to send troops to his home state of Michoacán, where lush mountain slopes support a lucrative marijuana business. Soon afterward, he sent the army into five other areas, most of them border states.

Calderón resorted to military takeovers of local and state police forces because the military is less corrupt than Mexico's law enforcement agencies. Investigations have found that as many as half of all of the country's police officers, who earn only about $5,000 a year, have been deemed incompetent or worse. The number was as high as 9 out of 10 in Baja California Norte. Since 1982, the federal law enforcement system has been reorganized five times, and at least four elite forces have been created in an attempt to combat corruption. The president has implemented such extreme measures as confiscating the guns of 2,300 Tijuana police officers while detectives investigate whether they were used in crimes.

But military personnel are not trained for close contact with civilians, and their heavy-handed tactics have brought accusations of human rights-abuse. Well aware that using the military is far from ideal, Calderón instituted federal police reforms in 2008 with a view to reducing the soldiers' role. The first major step came in January 2010, when he shifted control of Joint Operation Chihuahua from the military to the federal police and sent 2,000 police officers to Ciudad Juárez, the country's deadliest drug war zone. Federal police, who are specifically trained to work with civilians, will operate in high-risk urban areas while the military continues to guard the state's vast expanses of rural desert. If the new strategy succeeds, it could be extended to Mexico's other joint operations.

Despite these efforts—or, some say, because of them—drug violence has escalated. According to security intelligence analyses, the death toll for 2009 was around 7,500, up from 5,700 in 2008 and 2,500 in 2007.

Joaquin Guzman Loera, head of the Sinaloa cartel, is an example of the kind of mastermind authorities face. While feared by citizens and loathed by authorities, Guzman, known as El Chapo ("Shorty"), is lionized by many in his home state, where he is the subject of many a *narco-corrido,* or drug-inspired ballad, and has even had Facebook pages created in his honor. Known for rising from a humble farmer to one of the country's most successful and elusive drug dealers, he enhanced his reputation in 2001 by allegedly bribing guards and escaping prison in a laundry cart. Guzmán made no. 701 on Forbes' 2008 list of the world's richest people, with an estimated net worth of $1 billion.

There are actually two drug wars in Mexico: The battle between the drug lords and the Mexican government, and the fight among competing cartels for lucrative supply routes. It's not that Calderón's efforts have been ineffective; they have taken out some key players, such as Arturo Beltran Leyva, head of the Beltran Leyva Organization operating on the Pacific coast, and his brother Carlos 2 weeks later in December 2009. Such success disrupts the drug runners but in fact spurs more violence as beheaded cartels descend into infighting, other gangs grabs for new territory, and both target journalists and government officials for revenge killings.

Travelers are not likely to see signs of this struggle except in places where the flow of tourists and drugs intersect—mostly along the border, especially in Tijuana, El Paso, Nuevo Laredo, Nogales, and Matamoros. Violence has surged in Michoacán state in the past 2 years, in areas where tourists rarely venture. Even in the most dangerous spots, it's an unspoken tenant among the *narcos* that you don't mess with the tourists. Two important exceptions: Well-to-do Monterrey has recently come under siege, and Acapulco has experienced a spate of grisly incidents that, while not directed at tourists, have impinged on popular tourist areas. Breathless headlines about the slaughter of innocent tourists are rarely followed by reports that the victim was buying or selling drugs, which is usually the case. In fact, many places in Mexico's interior experience less drug violence than U.S. cities, nor are beach resorts likely settings for shootouts between the army and the cartels.

See p. 749 in chapter 20 for more safety-related information.

RELIGION, MYTH & SPIRITUALITY

For more than 150 years, Catholic pilgrims have traveled every Easter to a hill in Mexico City's rough-and-tumble Iztapalapa neighborhood to witness a theatric reenactment of the Crucifixion of Christ. Though many would claim to have always felt a strong spiritual connection to the site, until 2006 the devotees were unaware that ruins from the ancient Teotihuacán culture lay in the earth beneath the actor Jesus' feet. After the discovery of the remains of a 1,500-year-old temple, archaeologists and religious leaders were faced with the quandary of whether to continue with a century-old tradition or risk doing further damage to millennium-old artifacts.

> ## Impressions
>
> "Any contact with the Mexican people, no matter how fleeting, will show that beneath Western forms lie ancient beliefs and customs. These remnants, alive even now, are a testament to the vitality of Mexico's pre-Hispanic cultures."
> —Octavio Paz, *The Labyrinth of Solitude*

This juxtaposition of ancient mythology and modern Catholicism is the perfect metaphor for the history of religion in Mexico. Before Catholicism arrived with the Franciscan order in the late 1500s, there was no specific concept of organized religion, but rather a universal set of beliefs so ingrained in everyday life that they were seen as one entwined experience. While different societies across Mesoamerica worshiped their own specific gods and had local ceremonies, three basic components were universal: a belief in a duality of forces of nature in the universe, reverence for the calendar, and human sacrifice.

Beg, Borrow & Steal

As different societies—the Teotihuacán, Olmec, and Maya—dominated their neighbors, they enforced their own rites and rituals and adopted those of their conquered.

2012: PROPHECY OR CHICKEN LITTLE?

Within the past 10 years, the year 2012—specifically, December 21, 2012—has morphed into a modern doomsday in popular consciousness. History and time have wiped out much of the ancient Maya's writings and scripture, making it near impossible for scholars to determine what the ancient Maya thought about the approaching date. One thing is certain: The predictions of cataclysmic solar storms, magnetic pole reversal, earthquakes, super-volcanoes, a galactic collision, alien invasion, or even the end of the world aren't coming from today's Maya.

Between the scarcity of actual references to the end of the Mesoamerican Long Count Calendar in the few surviving Maya sources, the obliqueness of those references, and the largely self-serving interpretations of contemporary pseudo-scientists and New Age soothsayers, it's rather like a global game of phone tag. December 2012—the date is unspecified—coincides with the end of one 5,125-year cycle of the calendar, used by the classic Maya (A.D. 250-900) but not by contemporary Maya people. Modern interpretations have settled on December 21 primarily because it coincides with the equinox, though the importance of the equinox to the Maya is a matter of debate among serious scholars.

What significance the Maya attached to the end of the Long Calendar cycle is uncertain. They believed an earlier long cycle ended before their time—with no mass destruction—which suggests they expected another cycle to follow. Some inscriptions refer to future events or commemorations to come after completion of the current cycle, so we can safely rule out the end of the world as a Maya prediction.

Rather than fearing this date, those Maya today who recognize it at all regard it as a new dawn: a time for reflection on mankind's failings and an evolution, perhaps a change in consciousness or even a new social order. In some interpretations, the change of time might bring a reawakening of the ancient Maya world, with an appearance of ascending gods to lift the people back up. However much they might have stretched the evidence to make the date jibe with Western astrology and motley spiritual notions, New Agers who deem 2012 the beginning of a new era come closer in spirit to what the evidence suggests. Nowhere does the Western concept of apocalypse appear in surviving Maya inscriptions.

Remodeling that old Cold War–era underground bunker is, to put it mildly, an overreaction—but there's no harm in aspiring to harmony with the universe, and no better place in the world to contemplate the early Maya's complex cosmology than in the heart of their ancient land.

At the height of its power in the 13th century, the Aztec empire was a melting pot of conquered peoples and cultures. They took to wearing the feathered fashions of the tropical nations, Maya lip ornaments, and the colorful clothes of the Totonacs, and their belief system grew to include a vast number of gods and their manifestations, including at least 400 gods of drink and drunkenness.

Much like dominant indigenous tribes before them, the Spaniards were successful in converting the population to Catholicism because they cleverly integrated ancient beliefs into their own theology. They often built churches and shrines directly on top of former holy places; the Catedral Metropolitana in Mexico City's *zócalo* is perhaps the most stunning example, built on the ruins of the Aztecs' greatest temple.

In 1531, Juan Diego Cuauhtlatoatzin, an indigenous Mexican, was walking to a Catholic mass when he witnessed an apparition of the Virgin Mary, who bore a strong resemblance to an Aztec princess. Speaking in his native Náhuatl, she bade him tell the bishop to build her a home on that very site, but when Diego approached the Franciscan Bishop, Juan de Zumárraga, he told him he needed a sign. When Diego returned to relay this to the Virgin, she filled his *tilma*, or cloak, with roses that grew only in Zumárraga's native Spain in order to provide convincing evidence. Today the **Basilica de Guadalupe** is the second-most-visited Roman Catholic holy site in the world, after the Vatican. It was built upon the former site of the Aztec fertility goddess *Tonantzin* (the second-most-important shrine in Mexico, San Juan de los Lagos, occupies the land of a former shrine to the Aztec rain god, *Tlaloc*). The iconic Virgin de Guadalupe is now considered the patron saint of Mexico. Her indelible image, which to this day includes a mantle of roses, along with her prayer, can be seen on everything from key chains to tattoos—she even makes the occasional miraculous appearance in tortillas.

Modern Religion

Catholicism remains the dominant religion in Mexico, with adherents making up 76% of the total population (Protestants trail with 6% while pockets of Muslims, Mennonites, and Jews can be found around the country), and Mexicans continue to incorporate their own ancient traditions with the new. The modern *Día de los Muertos* holiday coincides with the Catholic All Saints' Day, and many of the elements, such as using marigolds and offering food to the dead, are similar to ceremonies held by the Aztecs in late August.

Many growing offshoots of Catholicism are not officially recognized by the church. The Mexico City suburb of Tepito is home to the shrine of *Santa Muerte*, or Saint Death, whose adherents look to her skeletal, scythe-carrying image for protection, not unlike the pre-Hispanic veneration of Mictecacihuatl, queen of the Aztec underworld.

Religion in Mexico thrives and evolves in the country's thousands of shrines, cathedrals, and churches, and the faithful continue to walk and crawl to Iztapalapa every year.

ART & ARCHITECTURE

Ancient Art & Architecture

Art in Mexico begins with one piece, called the Tequixquiac bone. It isn't very big, having been made from the sacrum (hipbone) of an extinct form of camelid that existed in the upper Paleolithic. From this sacrum, some artist sculpted the head of a coyote. The bone was discovered in 1870 in the area of Tequixquiac, north of Mexico City. It's impossible to establish with certainty when the bone was worked by human hand, but given where and how deep it was buried, it might date as far back as 12,000 B.C. A striking piece, it merits special attention, should you visit the National Anthropology Museum in Mexico City, where it's on display.

Aside from a few other artifacts, the record of artistic achievement in Mexico skips forward to the pre-Classic age and the great Olmec and earliest Maya cities. These date from the 3rd millennium before Christ, roughly the same time that cities were growing in Mesopotamia, Egypt, and Peru. Fortunately, the inhabitants left behind a wealth of pottery and stone objects with intriguing images and a clear artistic style.

These are on view in the National Anthropology Museum and the museums of Puebla, Xalapa, and Villahermosa.

The Classic and post-Classic periods left us with much more artwork and better-preserved architecture. Visiting cities such as Teotihuacán, Palenque, or Monte Albán reveals the clear-cut geometry of these spaces and something of what the builders envisioned. To understand the artistic achievement of these civilizations, you must witness the large sculptures that they left behind, such as the massive Aztec calendar stone or the many stelae (large stone monuments) and murals of the Maya. Their thickly textured imagery, meshed into complex allegorical structures, is difficult to understand but visually striking.

After the Conquest

Everything takes an abrupt turn after the conquest. The Spanish were determined to instill in their new subjects an alien belief system, and the Indians, with a highly complex system of their own, had to make sense of things by using what they knew. This clash of beliefs produced a fluid artistic tradition that reconciled contradictory dialectical symbols, but this synthesis took more than a century. The arrival of the baroque style from Europe was a stroke of good fortune. The baroque breadth of scope and possibility, and its lack of emphasis on structure or even consistency, accommodated both symbol systems. Its parallels with pre-Columbian art resonated with Mexican artists, who began producing with a vigor and brilliance that mark the artistic pinnacle of the Colonial Era. Though little of this work survived, good examples include the Capilla del Rosario in Puebla, the altarpieces of Santa Rosa de Viterbo and Santa Clara in Querétaro, the church of Santo Domingo in Oaxaca, and the Sagrario Metropolitano in Mexico City's cathedral.

Postrevolutionary Art & Architecture

The long regime of dictator Porfirio Díaz, which began in 1877 and ended in 1911 with the Mexican Revolution, brought a measure of stability after the near-constant social and economic upheaval following national independence. During these years, known as the Porfiriato, the ruling ideas and art forms came from Europe. A surge in the construction of public buildings took inspiration primarily from French architecture, especially Beaux Arts. Examples include many of the municipal theaters and opera houses throughout the country, such as Bellas Artes in Mexico City and the Palacio Cantón, now housing the Regional Anthropology Museum, in Merida.

La Revolución did as much to give Mexico its own voice as it did to establish the nation's governing institutions. The great Mexican muralists, Diego Rivera, Clemente Orozco, and David Alfaro Siqueiros, were a product of these times, as were painters Frida Kahlo and Rufino Tamayo. All believed art is meant for public enjoyment, not just private collectors, and their styles expressed a quintessentially Mexican sensibility that was artistically revolutionary. The same is true of architects Luis Barragán and Juan O'Gorman, especially the former, who absorbed the ideas of modernist architecture (which, at its heart, is internationalist) and wedded them to warm Mexican colors and an Indian stoicism to create architecture with a strong sense of place.

Contemporary Art & Building

What began during La Revolución continues to this day, as contemporary artists and architects find new ways to express the ever-changing nature of national identity.

Frida & Diego

In Mexico, Frida and Diego are like everyone's beloved yet crazy aunt and uncle who delight everyone at family reunions and threaten each other with the good silver by the end of the night. Painter Frida Kahlo and her husband, muralist Diego Rivera, are among Mexico's most prolific artists, but their tumultuous relationship was often more gut-wrenching than their artwork. During their decade-long marriage/relationship, Diego cheated on Frida with her younger sister, and Frida had an affair with Russian revolutionary Leon Trotsky. Many places where their personal drama played out have now been turned into museums. At least 10 museums feature the artwork of Frida and/or Diego in Mexico City, along with historical sites in Acapulco, Cuernavaca, and Guanajuato and works of art in museums across the country.

Luis Barragán never built anything outside of Mexico, and much of what he built was residential and thus unavailable for public viewing. Yet this didn't hinder the growth of his reputation. In 1980, he was awarded the Pritzker Prize; he died in 1988.

Two architects who have followed in his footsteps, Ricardo Legorreta and Teodoro González de León, have constructed many public buildings both in Mexico and abroad. Legorreta's use of forceful colors and bold lines distinguish his works, including the Public Library of San Antonio (Texas), the Tech Museum of San Jose (California), and the Hotel Camino Real in Mexico City. González de León's work is more futuristic and includes skyscrapers in Mexico City, the Mexican embassy in Berlin, and museums and cultural centers in the U.S.

Gabriel Orozco, an installation artist from Jalapa, Veracruz, is one of Mexico's most prominent artists. He has traveled the world exhibiting his sculptures and conceptual pieces, such as *Homerun*, in which he placed oranges on the windowsills of various apartment buildings. Miguel Calderon, another notable artist, created oil paintings of masked, shirtless savages, featured in the movie *The Royal Tenenbaums*.

One of the most impressive collections of modern Mexican art is the Colección Jumex, owned by Mexican juice magnate Eugenio López Alonso. Every year López opens the gallery, located in the otherwise-nondescript Jumex headquarters in Mexico City, for a well-lubricated event attended by art luminaries from all over the world.

Following in the tradition of the great muralists, many of Mexico's most exciting modern artists go beyond the canvas to present their work. Urban art, or street art consisting of graffiti installations, posters, and even fashion, is exceedingly popular in large cities. A good example of this can be seen at the Mercado Michoacán in Mexico City's Condesa (a neighborhood made up almost exclusively of Art Deco buildings). The bright yellow building is the home to fruit and vegetable vendors on the inside, but its facade features graffiti art by a rotating group of artists.

MEXICO IN POP CULTURE
Books
LITERATURE
It's pulp fiction at heart, but reading Gary Jennings' **Aztec** while traveling in Mexico is a surprisingly rewarding experience. Jennings, an American who wrote the book

while living in San Miguel de Allende, unfurls the tale of Mixtli, a character with an almost omnipotent perspective on the state of Mexico's various indigenous societies in the years just before the arrival of the Spaniards. Jennings gets creative with some of his interpretations, but the important details are historically accurate and provide great cultural context for visiting pre-Hispanic sites.

The earlier novels of Carlos Fuentes, Mexico's preeminent living writer, are easier to read than more recent works; try *The Death of Artemio Cru*. Angeles Mastretta's delightful *Arráncame la Vida (Tear Up My Life)* covers the same subject—Mexican society's values, contradictions, and pleasures after the Revolution from the point of view of a young woman in Puebla. In 2008, a wildly popular cinematic version of the book was released in Mexico and South America. If you want a good idea of period costumes and architecture, tracking down a copy is worth your while. Fuentes has an ironic touch and dips occasionally into the surreal. Mastretta's book is a well-written, straightforward narrative brimming with political gossip.

Another novel covering roughly the same period, but with fewer social observations and more magic realism, is *Like Water for Chocolate,* by Laura Esquivel. This book and the movie of the same title did much to popularize Mexican food abroad.

Guillermo Arriaga, screenwriter for *Amores Perros,* is a brilliant novelist, too. *El Bufalo de la Noche,* about a young man reeling from his best friend's suicide, is available in English. *Retorno 201,* a collection of stories set on the Mexico City street where Arriaga grew up, was published in 2005.

Juan Rulfo, one of Mexico's most esteemed authors, wrote only three slim books before his death in 1986. His second, *Pedro Páramo,* is Mexico's equivalent of Shakespearean tragedy and has never been out of print since its publication in 1955. The short novel of a son's search for his abusive, tyrannical father had a major influence on the magical realism movement. It has been translated twice into English and been made into film several times; Gael García Bernal and Diego Luna are working on a new adaptation.

HISTORY & NONFICTION

For contemporary culture, start with *The Labyrinth of Solitude,* by the Mexican Nobel laureate poet and essayist Octavio Paz. It still generates controversy among Mexicans.

The Life and Times of Mexico, by Earl Shorris, is an in-depth analysis of Mexican history. It's really the only text you'll need to learn the history of the country, from Aztec rituals to the 70-year-rule of the PRI. For a more concise yet still thorough survey of Mexican history, try *A Short History of Mexico,* by J. Patrick McHenry.

For an overview of pre-Hispanic cultures, pick up Michael D. Coe's *Mexico: From the Olmecs to the Aztecs,* Nigel Davies's *Ancient Kingdoms of Mexico,* or Jacques Soustelle's *Daily Life of the Aztecs.* Richard Townsend's *The Aztecs* is a thorough, well-researched examination of the Aztec and the Spanish Conquest. For the Maya, Michael Coe's *The Maya* is probably the best general account. John L. Stephens's classic account of 44 Maya sites, the two-volume *Incidents of Travel in the Yucatán,* is still the most authoritative. Before his expeditions, beginning in 1841, the world knew little about the region and nothing about the Maya.

The best-title prize goes to *Los Angeles Times* columnist Gregory Rodriguez's *Mongrels, Bastards, Orphans and Vagabonds: Mexican Immigration and the Future of Race in America.* Rodriguez's skillful history of race relations in the

Americas provides thought-provoking anecdotes that will have you thinking twice about what it means to be Mexican, American, Mexican-American, American-Mexican, or a citizen of the world.

Mexican Cinema

GOLDEN AGE & CLASSICS

During Mexico's "Golden Age of Cinema" in the 1940s, studios stopped trying to mimic Hollywood and began producing unabashedly Mexican black-and-white films whose stars are still cultural icons in Mexico. **Mario Moreno,** aka Cantinflas, was a comedic genius who personalized the *el pelado* archetype—a poor, picaresque, slightly naughty character trading on his wits alone and getting nowhere. Mexican beauty **Dolores del Río** ended up playing the steamy Latin babe in Hollywood. **Pedro Infante,** the singing cowboy, embodied the ideal of Mexican manhood.

Luis Buñuel's dark *Los Olvidados* (1950) was the Spanish surrealist's third Mexican film, exploring the life of young hoodlums in Mexico City's slums.

THE NEW CINEMA

After a long fallow period, a new generation of filmmakers emerged in the 1990s. The first big **El Nuevo Cine Mexicano** (the New Cinema) hit outside of Mexico was *Like Water for Chocolate* (1992), directed by Alfonso Arau, then author Laura Esquivel's husband. He continues to make films, mainly in Mexico. The second, *Sexo, Pudor y Lágrimas* (1999), by director **Antonio Serrano,** is an unflinching look at the battle of the sexes in Mexico City.

After **Alfonso Cuarón's** debut film, the mordant social satire *Sólo con tu pareja* (1991), scored critical and commercial success in Mexico, he garnered international acclaim with his ironic *Y Tu Mamá También* (2001), which touches on class hypocrisy while following a pair of teenage boys on an impromptu road trip with a sexy older woman. Cuarón has since directed *Harry Potter and the Prisoner of Azkaban* (2004), the science-fiction thriller *Children of Men* (2006), and other international productions. *Gravity,* a space thriller with Sandra Bullock and George Clooney, is due in 2012.

In *Amores Perros* (2000), **Alejandro González Iñárritu** (director of *21 Grams* [2003] and *Babel* [2006]) presents a keen glimpse of contemporary Mexican society through three stories about different ways of life in Mexico City that converge at the scene of a horrific car accident. His Academy Award–nominated *Babel* (2006), another tour de force, features a Mexican border scene that is realistic, exhilarating, and frightening all at once. **Guillermo del Toro's** debut, the dark, atmospheric *Cronos* (1993), won critical acclaim in Mexico. Moving into the international arena, he has directed similarly moody films such as *Hellboy* (2004) and Oscar winner *Pan's Labyrinth* (2006).

As part of a $100-million, five-feature partnership, Cuarón, Iñárritu, and del Toro will each direct his own movie, along with two projects from Colombian director Rodrigo Garcia (*Nine Lives* [2005]) and Cuarón's brother and co-screenwriter of *Y Tú Mama También* (2001), Carlos Cuarón. Each director has experienced crossover success, and at least two of the films will be in Spanish. The first, Carlos Cuarón's *Rudo y Cursi,* reteamed the Mexican dynamic duo Gael García Bernal and Diego Luna and debuted in late 2008. Rodrigo Garcia's star-studded *Mother and Child* opened in May 2010 after premieres at the Toronto and Sundance film festivals. Iñárritu's *Biutiful* brought a best actor award for star Javier Bardem at the 2010 Cannes Film Festival.

Views from the Outside: Films Starring Mexico

Elia Kazan's 1952 classic, *Viva Zapata!,* written by John Steinbeck, stars Marlon Brando as revolutionary Emiliano Zapata. Orson Welles's 1958 film noir *Touch of Evil* (preposterously billing Charlton Heston as a Mexican narcotics agent) looks at drugs and corruption in Tijuana—still compelling, even though it feels sanitized, compared with today's screaming headlines. The adaptation of Carlos Fuentes' novel *The Old Gringo* (1989), a love triangle set during the Mexican Revolution, was filmed with Gregory Peck, Jane Fonda, and a young Jimmy Smits in numerous locations in five Mexican states.

HBO's 2003 flick *And Starring Pancho Villa as Himself,* with Antonio Banderas, is the true story of how revolutionaries allowed Hollywood to film Pancho Villa in battle. *Man on Fire* (2004), with Denzel Washington as a bodyguard hired to protect a little girl, is full of great Mexico City scenes, though the plot is depressing and all too real. Dylan Verrechia's *Tijuana Makes Me Happy* (2005), focusing on Tijuana's humanity rather than its perceived sins, has won awards in Latin America and at U.S. film festivals. Stephen Soderbergh's Academy Award–winning *Traffic* (2000), with Benicio del Toro, has powerful scenes focusing on Tijuana's drug war, while the documentary *Tijuana Remix* (2002) unveils the city's unique and idiosyncratic culture.

Mel Gibson's controversial *Apocalypto* (2006) cast indigenous Maya to depict the Maya empire's waning days; the rainforests of Veracruz state stand in for the lush jungles that must have covered the Yucatán centuries ago. Loosely based on a true story, *Nacho Libre* (2006) is a highly stylized take on Mexican wrestling, shot entirely in rural Oaxaca state. Mexico, most notably an uglified Campeche, stood in for 1950s Cuba in Steven Soderbergh's *Che* (2008), a two-part epic focusing first on the Cuban revolution and then on his attempt to bring revolution to Bolivia; the film won the Cannes best actor award for Benicio del Toro.

Julie Taymor's *Frida* (2002), with Mexican actress Salma Hayek producing and starring, is an enchanting biopic about Frida Kahlo's life and work, from her devastating accident to relationships with Diego Rivera and Leon Trotsky. The exquisite cinematography captures the magic realism evinced in Kahlo's work.

Director **Robert Rodriguez's** breakout film, *El Mariachi* (1992), is set in a small central Mexican town. Made on a shoestring budget, the somewhat cheesy action flick is at least highly entertaining. His *Once Upon a Time in Mexico* (2003) isn't as great, but it's fun to see scenes of San Miguel Allende. Ditto for San Luis Potosí in *The Mexican* (2001), with Brad Pit and Julia Roberts. With *Machete,* his over-the-top 2011 action/gore/humor flick, his aim is clear: to make a Mexican Jean-Claude Van Damme out of star Danny Trejo.

Music

MARIMBA & SON

Marimba music flourishes in much of southern and central Mexico but is considered traditional only in Chiapas and the port city of Veracruz, whose bands travel to such places as Oaxaca and Mexico City, where they play in clubs and restaurants.

Son, a native art form from many parts of Mexico, is played with a variety of string instruments. Ritchie Valens' "La Bamba" popularized one of the most famous forms, *son jarocho,* in the '50s. Often fast paced, with lots of strumming and fancy string picking, it originated in southern Veracruz. Dancing to this music requires a lot of fast, rhythmic pounding of the heels *(zapateado). Jarana,* the Yucatán's principal dance music, is a form of *son jarocho* that adds woodwinds and a sensuous Caribbean beat.

DANZÓN & BOLERO

These musical forms came from Cuba in the late 19th century and gained great popularity, especially in Veracruz and Mexico City. *Danzón* is orchestra music that combines a Latin flavor with a stateliness absent from later Latin music. *Bolero* (or *trova*) is the music mainly of guitar trios, such as Los Panchos. It's soft and romantic, often with a touch of melancholy.

MARIACHI & RANCHERA

Mariachis, with their big sombreros, waist-length jackets and tight pants, embody the Mexican spirit. The music originated from Jalisco state's *son,* arranged for guitars, violins, string bass, and trumpets. Now heard across Mexico—Yucatecan trova music even has mariachi adaptations—and much of the American southwest, it is at its traditional best in Jalisco and its capital, Guadalajara.

The national pride, individualism, and sentimentality expressed in mariachi's kin, *ranchera,* earn it favored status as drinking music. Many Mexicans know the songs of famous composer **José Alfredo Jiménez** by heart.

Mexican-American singer/songwriter **Lila Downs** updated *ranchera* and mariachi for a modern, bicultural audience. Her debut album, *La Cantina,* explored traditional favorites, while her latest, *Shake Away,* features collaborations with famous Latin artists like Mercedes Sosa and Enrique Bunburry.

NORTEÑA, GRUPERA & BANDA

Norteña owes its origins to *tejano* music, coming out of Texas. Mexicans in south-central Texas encountered musicians from the immigrant Czech and German communities of the Texas Hill Country and picked up a taste for polkas and the accordion. Gradually, the music became popular farther south. *Norteña* music tweaked the polka for many of its popular songs and later borrowed from the *cumbia,* slowing the tempo a bit and adding a strong downbeat. It also incorporated the native *corrido,* a type of ballad popularized during the Mexican Revolution (1910–17). *Norteña* became hugely popular in rural northern Mexico though the 1970s, and later generated spinoffs known as *grupera* or *banda,* a style of *norteña* from the area of Sinaloa that replaces the accordion with electric keyboards. *Grupera/banda* is now heard nationwide. **Los Tigres del Norte,** who have released more than 50 albums, are the undisputed kings of banda; other notable groups and artists include **Los Alacranes Musicales** and **Valentín Elizalde.**

ROCK EN ESPAÑOL

Mexican rock forged its identity in the 1980s and exploded during the 1990s with bands such as Jaguares and Molotov out of Mexico City, and Maná, based in Guadalajara. Named for the 1920s cafe in the capital's Centro Histórico, **Café Tacvba** (pronounced *Ta*-cu-ba) has been at it since 1989. Their music is influenced by indigenous Mexican music as much as folk, punk, bolero, and hip-hop. The fast-rising **Yucatán a Go Go**—hailing, despite the name, from central Mexico—fuses a bouncy pop beat to lyrics firmly rooted in cultural tradition.

Latin alternative music, which was born as an alternative to slickly produced Latin pop exemplified by **Ricky Martin** or **Paulina Rubio,** has grown until it has become a genre in itself. Practitioners such as **Panda, División Minúscula,** and **Zoé** have achieved not-so-alternative success.

EATING & DRINKING IN MEXICO

> *Yo soy como un chile verde—picante pero sabroso.*
>
> *I'm like the green chile—spicy but delicious.*
>
> –La Llorona, traditional *corrido*

It can't be a coincidence that on a map, Mexico looks like a giant cornucopia. All the Mexican food you've ever encountered at home has merely been skimmed off the top, leaving all of the interesting, lesser-known fruit at the intriguing bottom of the bounty. Yes, Mexicans eat beans, rice, and tacos, but they also eat complex dishes like the countless variations of *mole,* an intricate sauce that can contain 100 different ingredients and take up to 3 days to prepare; *almejas rellenas,* fresh clam baked in its shell with butter, ham, jalapeños, tomatoes, and onions; and *pozole,* a hearty pork or chicken soup served with radishes, cilantro, avocado, and fried pork rinds as garnish.

Despite a multitude of regional differences, some generalizations can help you navigate. Most Mexican food isn't spicy-hot or piquant when it arrives at the table (though there are exceptions). The *picante* flavor is added with chiles and salsas; you'll never see a table in Mexico without one or both of these condiments. Mexicans don't drown their cooking in cheese and sour cream, a la Tex-Mex, and they use a greater variety of ingredients than most people expect. But the basis of Mexican food is simple—tortillas, beans, chiles, squash, and tomatoes—the same as it was centuries ago before the arrival of the Europeans.

For additional food terms, see chapter 21.

The Staples

TORTILLAS Like the crusty baguette in France, a perfect tortilla can truly round out your meal. **Flour tortillas,** which were developed in northern Mexico and until recently were difficult to find south of Chihuahua, are arguably the most popular north of the border. However, the traditional **corn tortilla,** made from corn cooked in water and lime, ground into *masa* (a grainy dough), patted and pressed into thin cakes, and cooked on a hot griddle known as a *comal,* remains king in most of Mexico. Whether they're sopping up shrimp *molcajetes* in Jalisco or beans and rice in Oaxaca, Mexicans often use tortillas as an alternative to silverware, ripping off large pieces and using them to scoop up food.

SALSA You can usually tell whether you're going to like a restaurant based on its salsa alone—if the cooks are inventive with tomatoes and spices, imagine what they can do with steak. Top marks go to places that bring out a tray with three or more choices, beginning with **pico de gallo,** the most simple and common variety of fresh cilantro, tomatoes, jalapeños, and onions. Another favorite is **salsa chipotle,** which gets its smoky taste from the chipotle chile. **Salsa verde,** made with tomatillos instead of regular red tomatoes, can be tangier and milder. Beyond these three, there are as many salsas as there are colors in the rainbow.

A DEBT OF gratitude

Lost among the laurels heaped upon the ancient Maya for their contributions to science, mathematics, architecture, astronomy, and writing is the wide array of foods these masters of agriculture introduced to the world. It's no exaggeration to say the Maya changed the world's eating habits in the 1500s. Just try to imagine life without:

o **Chocolate** The Maya's "food of the gods," made from the toasted, fermented seeds of the cacao tree, is arguably the New World's greatest gift to civilization. Though Cortez learned of chocolate from the Aztecs, the Maya ate it many centuries earlier and used cacao beans as currency.

o **Vanilla** The elixir from the world's only known edible orchid originally flavored Maya chocolate drinks. Southern Mexico's jungle is the only place the orchid grows wild, pollinated by native stingless bees that produce Maya honey. The prized Tahitian vanilla, from Mexican stock, must be hand-pollinated.

o **Corn** The Popul Vuh, the Maya creation myth, attributes humankind's very existence to this domesticated strain of wild grass, easily the most important food in the Americas. Thousands of years after corn became a dietary staple, the Maya started cultivating it around 2500 B.C. and abandoned their nomadic ways to settle in villages surrounded by cornfields.

o **Chiles** Chiles have been cultivated in the Americas for more than 6,000 years. Blame Christopher Columbus for calling them "peppers," but credit him for their worldwide reach. Southern Mexico's *Capsicum annuum* species, with its many cultivars, is crucial to nearly every fiery cuisine.

o **Tomatoes** Even the Italians had to make do without tomato sauce before Columbus set out for the New World. Precursors originated in Peru, but the tomato as we know it came from the Yucatán, where the Maya cultivated it long before the conquest.

o **Black beans** Archaeological digs indicate the black bean originated in southern Mexico and Central America more than 7,000 years ago. Still the favorite in and around the Yucatán, the black bean spread widely throughout Latin America, the Caribbean, and the southern United States.

o **Avocado** From its origins in southern Mexico, where it was used as an aphrodisiac, the avocado spread to the Rio Grande and central Peru before the Europeans found out about it.

o **Papaya** The large, woody, fastgrowing herb—commonly referred to as a tree—was used to treat stomach ailments. After spreading from southern Mexico, it now grows in every tropical country.

TACOS   Whether it's *tacos al pastor* made with gyro-style spit-grilled meat in Mexico City, or beer-battered shrimp tacos in Ensenada, just about every region has its own take on this quintessential fast food. Anything folded or rolled into a tortilla—sometimes two, either soft or fried—is a taco. *Flautas* and quesadillas (except in Mexico City, where they are a different animal) are species of tacos.

FRIJOLES   Most Mexican households eat beans daily. Pinto beans are predominant in northern Mexico, while black beans are the legumes of choice in the south.

Mexicans add only a little onion and garlic and a pinch of herbs, as beans are meant to be a counterpoint to spicy foods. They also may appear at the end of a meal with a spoonful of sour cream. Fried leftover beans often appear as *frijoles refritos*, a side dish commonly called "refried beans." In fact, they are fried just once; the prefix *re* means "well" (as in "thoroughly"), so a better translation may be "well-fried beans."

TAMALES The ultimate take-out meal, tamales (singular: tamal) developed in pre-Hispanic Mexico and became more elaborate after the Spanish introduced pork and other ingredients. To make a tamal, you mix corn *masa* with lard, beat the batter, add a filling, wrap it, and cook it. Every region has its specialty; in some places, a single *tamal* is big enough to feed a family; in others, they are barely 3 inches long. The most popular *rellenos* (fillings) are pork and cheese, but they might be anything from fish to iguana, augmented by pumpkin, pineapple, rice, or peanuts, and tucked into a blanket of yellow, black, or purple *masa*. Tamales are usually steamed but may be baked or grilled; the jackets are most often dried corn husks or fresh corn or banana leaves but may be fashioned from palm, avocado, or *chaya* (a spinachlike vegetable) leaves.

CHILES Hardly a traditional dish in all of Mexico lacks chiles. Appearing in wondrous variety throughout Mexico, they bear different names depending on whether they are fresh or dried. Chiles range from blazing hot with little discernible taste to mild with a rich, complex flavor, and they can be pickled, smoked, stuffed, or stewed. Among the best-known are the *pimiento*, the large, harmless bell pepper familiar in the U.S.; the fist-sized poblano, ranging from mild to very hot; the short, torpedo-shaped *serrano*; the skinny and seriously fiery *chile de árbol*; the stubby, hot *jalapeño*; the *chipotle*, a dried and smoked jalapeño usually served in *adobo* (vinegar and garlic paste); and the tiny, five-alarm *pequín*.

If you suffer from misadventure by chile, a drink of milk, a bite of banana or cucumber, a spoonful of yogurt, or—if all else fails—a bottle of beer will help extinguish the fire.

Drinks

If you want bottled water, ask for *agua natural* or *agua embotellada* bottled water (*con gas* for carbonated, *sin gas* for still). Coca-Cola and Pepsi are nearly as entrenched in Mexico's drinking habits as tequila, and they taste the way they used to in the U.S., before the makers started adding corn syrup. These and other American *refrescos* outsell Mexican brands such as Manzana, a carbonated apple juice. If you like your soft drinks cold, specify *frío*, or you may get them *clima* (room temperature).

Better yet, treat yourself to **licuados**—refreshing smoothies of fresh fruit (or juice), milk, and ice, sold all over Mexico. (**A note of linguistic caution:** In Spanish, the word for tuna, *atún*, is perilously similar to the word for a small cactus fruit, *tuna*. Make sure you know which one is going in your **licuado**.) **Aguas frescas** ("fresh waters") are lighter drinks made by adding a small amount of fresh fruit juice and sugar to water. Hibiscus, melon, tamarind, and lime are common, but rice, flowers, *tuna*, and other exotic ingredients find their way into these refreshments. And inexpensive, fresh-squeezed juices from every fruit you can name—and a few you can't—are one of Mexico's greatest pleasures.

Coffee, one of Mexico's most important exports, is generally good, but latte addicts beware: Tarted-up coffee isn't Mexico's style. Your basic choices are *café Americano*, the familiar gringo-style brew; espresso and occasionally cappuccino, served in cafes;

Tequila Sun Rising

You can tug on Superman's cape, you can spit into the wind, but don't ever mess with tequila in Mexico. Tequila lovers savor the subtle flavors of the agave spirit and prefer to take it like wine, sip by sip, over the course of an entire meal. They will likely gasp in horror if you throw back a shot of Jose Cuervo like a coed on spring break, and pity you when you wake with a monster hangover.

The makers of tequila—all but one still based in Jalisco—have formed an association to establish standards for labeling and denomination. The best tequilas are 100% agave, made with a set minimum of sugar to prime the fermentation process. These tequilas come in three categories, based on how they were stored: *Blanco* is white tequila aged very little, usually in steel vats; *reposado* (reposed) is aged in wooden casks for between 2 months and a year; *añejo* (aged) has been stored in oak barrels—often reused whiskey barrels from the U.S.—for at least a year. A good way to ease into the world of tequila appreciation is to order a *bandera* (flag), which consists of a shot of tequila and shots of lime and tomato juice. Each glass represents a color in the Mexican flag.

and the widely popular *café con leche,* translated as "coffee with milk" but more accurately described as milk with coffee. Traditional hot drinks are **hot chocolate,** usually made with cinnamon and often some crushed almonds, and *atole,* made from cornmeal, milk, cinnamon, and puréed fresh fruit, often served for breakfast.

Mexico has a proud and lucrative **beer**-brewing tradition that comes from the German immigrants who arrived in the early 1800s. With the exception of Minerva beers out of Guadalajara, Jalisco, you'll be hard-pressed to find any variety beyond amber and light. You will, however, find a variety of beer concoctions, including the **chelada,** beer with lime juice and salt, and its sophisticated cousin, the **michelada,** which may contain hot sauce, Worcester sauce, salt, and lime. The names and recipes vary regionally, so if you're squeamish, ask your waiter.

Tequila's poorer cousins, **pulque** and **mescal,** originated with *octli,* an Aztec agave or maguey drink produced strictly for feasts. Mexicans drank *pulque* (now found mostly in central Mexico's *pulquerías*), made from fermented juice straight from the plant, for more 5,000 years, but it has recently given way to more refined—and more palatable—spirits. The Spanish learned to create serious fire power by roasting the agave hearts and then extracting, fermenting, and distilling the liquids. Thus were born tequila and *mescal. Mescal,* famous for the traditional worm at the bottom of the bottle, is more potent than *pulque* but easier to swallow. Mescal comes from various parts of Mexico and from different varieties of agave. It's available commercially, while *pulque* is found mostly in central Mexico's *pulquerías.* **Tequila** is a variety of mescal produced from the *a. tequilana* Weber species of agave in and around the area of Tequila, in the state of Jalisco. The tequila distilling process is more sophisticated than that of mescal. Once consigned to a stereotype in bad Westerns, the drink has lately acquired a sophisticated aura. A growing coterie of connoisseurs has spotlighted high-quality varieties and is making inroads on the knock-back-a-shot mentality in favor of sipping and swirling as you would with fine Scotch or French cognac.

Markets & Restaurants

Exploring the culinary delights of a *tianguis,* or traditional market, is one of my favorite pastimes. The people-watching is top-notch, and the food stalls harbor creative surprises ranging from strawberry shortcakes covered in fresh cream to juicy cheeseburgers and onion rings. To ensure your chances of getting the healthiest food possible, visit stands that seem to be popular among the locals. Word spreads fast in Mexico, so it doesn't take long for customers to root out the stalls with less than stellar hygiene practices. On the other side of the spectrum, avoid eating at those inviting sidewalk restaurants that you see beneath the stone archways that border the main plazas. These places usually cater to tourists and don't need to count on any return business. But they are great for getting a coffee or beer and watching the world turn.

In most nonresort towns, there are always one or two restaurants (sometimes it's a coffee shop) that are social centers for a large group of established patrons. Over time, they become virtual institutions, and change comes very slowly. The food is usually good standard fare, cooked as it was 20 years ago, and the decor is simple. The patrons have known each other and the staff for years, and the *charla* (banter), gestures, and greetings are friendly, open, and unaffected. If you're curious about Mexican culture, these are fun places to eat in and observe the goings-on.

DINING tips

- Nearly all restaurants and bars that serve middle-class Mexicans use filtered water, disinfect their vegetables, and buy ice made from purified water. If in doubt, look for ice with a rough cylindrical shape and a hollow center, produced by the same kind of machinery across the country. Street vendors and market stalls are less consistent. I've never gotten sick on any of my travels to Mexico, but people who live there say a good way of keeping your stomach happy is by drinking one of the tiny Yakult yogurt drinks found in the dairy section of just about every grocery store or corner market.

- For the afternoon meal, the main meal of the day, many restaurants offer a multicourse daily special called **comida corrida** or **menú del día.** This is the most inexpensive way to get a full dinner.

- In Mexico, you need to **ask for your check;** it is considered rude to present a check to someone who hasn't requested it. If you're in a hurry, ask for the check when your food arrives.

- Tips are about the same as in the U.S. You'll sometimes find a 15% value-added tax on restaurant meals, which shows up on the bill as IVA. This is effectively the tip, which you may augment if you like. Just make sure you're not tipping twice.

- To **summon the waiter,** wave or raise your hand, but don't motion with your index finger, which is a demeaning gesture that may cause the waiter to ignore you. Or if it's the check you want, you can motion to the waiter from across the room using the universal scribbling motion against the palm of your hand.

You'll see multitudes of **taquerías (taco joints)** everywhere in Mexico. These are generally small places with a counter or a few tables set around the cooking area; you see exactly how they make their tacos before deciding whether to order. Most tacos come with a little chopped onion and cilantro, but not with tomato and lettuce. Find one that seems popular with the locals and where the cook performs with *brio* (a good sign of pride in the product). Sometimes a woman will be making the tortillas (or working the *masa* into *gorditas* or *sopes,* if these are also served) right there. You will never see men doing this—this is perhaps the strictest gender division in Mexican society. Men do all other cooking and kitchen tasks, and work with already-made tortillas, but will never be found working *masa*.

WHEN TO GO

Mexico has two principal travel seasons. **High season** begins around December 20, peaks over New Year's, and continues through Easter week (*Semana Santa*); in some places, it begins as early as mid-November. **Low season** is from the day after Easter to mid-December, when prices may drop 20% to 50%. In beach destinations popular with Mexican travelers, such as Veracruz and Acapulco, prices will revert to high season during July and August, the traditional national summer vacation period. Prices in inland cities seldom fluctuate from high to low season, but may rise dramatically during the weeks of **Easter** and **Christmas.** Taxco and Pátzcuaro raise prices during their popular Easter-week celebrations. Along the Caribbean coast, many hotels divide the year into five or six rate periods; high season starts earlier than in the rest of the country and includes the month of August, when many European visitors and Mexican families arrive.

Mexico has two main climate seasons: **rainy** (May to mid-Oct) and **dry** (mid-Oct to Apr). The rainy season can be of little consequence in the dry, northern regions of the country. Southern regions typically receive tropical showers, which begin around 4 or 5pm and last a few hours. Though these rains can come on suddenly and be quite strong, they usually end just as quickly and cool off the air for the evening. **Hurricane season** particularly affects the Yucatán Peninsula and the southern Pacific coast, especially from June through October. If no hurricanes strike, however, the light, cooling winds, especially from September through November, can make it a perfect time to tackle the pre-Hispanic ruins that dot the interior of the peninsula.

Norte **(northern) season** runs from late November to mid-January, when the jet stream dips far south and creates northerly winds and showers in many resort areas. These showers usually last only for a couple of days.

June, July, and August are unrelentingly hot on the Yucatán Peninsula and in most coastal areas, though temperatures rise only into the mid-20s to 32°C (mid-80s to 90°F). Most of coastal Mexico experiences temperatures in the 20s°C (80s°F) in the hottest months. The northern states that border the U.S. endure very high summer temperatures.

Elevation is another important factor. High-elevation cities, such as Mexico City and San Cristóbal de las Casas, can get quite cool. Temperatures can drop near freezing at night in winter, even in San Miguel de Allende and Guanajuato, which are at lower elevations.

Mexican beaches reach uncomfortably hot temperatures, often with high humidity, in summer, and most foreign visitors prefer the Caribbean and Pacific Coasts after the hurricane and rainy seasons end in October. Although the weather may be ideal then, the craziest time to visit Cancún and the Riviera Maya is during the American spring-break period from mid-February into March and April, so avoid this time if you're looking for rest and relaxation. The north of Mexico is unspeakably hot in summer, so it's probably best to avoid extensive travel there at that time. Mexico City is temperate year-round, and the only important difference is whether it's the rainy season or not.

Mexico City's Average Temperatures

	JAN	FEB	MAR	APR	MAY	JUNE	JULY	AUG	SEPT	OCT	NOV	DEC
Avg. High (°C)	21	22	24	25	26	24	23	23	22	22	22	21
Avg. High (°F)	70	72	76	78	79	76	74	74	73	73	72	70
Avg. Low (°C)	7	7	10	11	12	13	13	13	12	11	8	7
Avg. Low (°F)	45	46	50	53	55	57	56	56	55	52	48	45

Cancún's Average Temperatures

	JAN	FEB	MAR	APR	MAY	JUNE	JULY	AUG	SEPT	OCT	NOV	DEC
Avg. High (°C)	27	27	28	29	31	31	32	32	31	30	28	27
Avg. High (°F)	81	82	84	85	88	89	90	90	89	87	84	82
Avg. Low (°C)	19	20	21	22	25	25	25	25	24	23	22	20
Avg. Low (°F)	67	68	71	73	77	78	78	77	76	74	72	69

Acapulco's Average Temperatures

	JAN	FEB	MAR	APR	MAY	JUNE	JULY	AUG	SEPT	OCT	NOV	DEC
Avg. High (°C)	30	30	30	30	31	31	31	31	31	31	31	31
Avg. High (°F)	87	87	87	87	89	89	89	89	89	89	89	88
Avg. Low (°C)	22	22	22	22	24	25	25	25	25	25	23	22
Avg. Low (°F)	72	72	72	73	76	77	77	77	77	77	75	73

Calendar of Events

Religious and secular festivals are a part of life in Mexico. Every town, city, and state holds its own festivals throughout the year commemorating religious and historic figures. Indeed, in certain parts of the country it sometimes feels like the festivities never die down.

For an exhaustive list of events beyond those listed here, see **http://events.frommers. com**, where you'll find a searchable, up-to-the-minute roster of what's happening in cities all over the world.

JANUARY

Año Nuevo (New Year's Day), nationwide. This national holiday is perhaps the quietest day in Mexico. Most people stay home or attend church. All businesses are closed. In traditional indigenous communities, new tribal leaders are inaugurated with colorful ceremonies rooted in the pre-Hispanic past. January 1.

Día de los Reyes (Three Kings' Day), nationwide. This day commemorates the Three Kings' presenting gifts to the Christ Child. Children receive presents, much like they do at Christmas in the United States. Friends and families gather to share the *Rosca de Reyes,* a special cake. Inside the cake is a small doll representing the Christ Child; whoever receives the doll must host a tamales-and-*atole* (a warm drink made of corn dough) party on February 2. January 6.

Feast of San Antonio Abad, Mexico City. This feast is celebrated through the Blessing of the Animals at the Santiago Tlatelolco Church on the Plaza of Three Cultures, at San Juan Bautista Church in Coyoacán, and at the Church of San Fernando, 2 blocks north of the Juárez-Reforma intersection. January 17.

Regional Fair, León, Guanajuato. One of Mexico's largest fairs celebrates the founding of this shoemaking and leather-craft city. The fair features parades, theater, craft exhibits, music, and dance. Month of January.

Día de la Candelaria (Candlemas), nationwide. Music, dances, processions, food, and other festivities lead up to a blessing of seed and candles in a ceremony that mixes pre-Hispanic and European traditions marking the end of winter. Those who attended the Three Kings celebration reunite to share *atole* and tamales at a party hosted by the recipient of the doll found in the Rosca. Celebrations are especially festive in Tlacotalpan, Veracruz. February 2.

Día de la Constitución (Constitution Day), nationwide. This national holiday is in honor of the current Mexican constitution, signed in 1917 as a result of the revolutionary war of 1910. It's celebrated through small parades. February 5.

Carnaval, nationwide. Carnaval takes place the 3 days preceding Ash Wednesday and the beginning of Lent. The cities of Tepoztlán, Huejotzingo, Chamula, Veracruz, Cozumel, and Mazatlán celebrate with special gusto. In some places, such as Veracruz, Mazatlán, and Cozumel, the celebration resembles New Orleans's Mardi Gras, with a festive atmosphere and parades. In Chamula, the event harks back to pre-Hispanic times, with ritualistic running on flaming branches. On Shrove Tuesday, in Tepoztlán and Huejotzingo, brilliantly clad *chinelos* (masked dancers) fill the streets. Transportation and hotels are packed, so it's best to make reservations 6 months in advance and arrive a couple of days ahead of the beginning of celebrations.

Ash Wednesday, nationwide. The start of Lent and time of abstinence, this is a day of reverence nationwide; some towns honor it with folk dancing and fairs.

MARCH

Annual Witches Conference, Lake Catemaco, Veracruz. Shamans, white witches, black witches, and practitioners of Caribbean, Afro, and Antillean ritualistic practices gather on the shores of the lake. Taking place the first Friday night of March every year, the annual gathering is a spectacle of witches, healers, magicians, and wizards.

Benito Juárez's Birthday, nationwide. This national holiday celebrating one of Mexico's most beloved leaders is observed through small hometown celebrations, especially in Juárez's birthplace, Guelatao, Oaxaca. March 21.

Spring Equinox, Chichén Itzá. On the first day of spring, the Temple of Kukulkán—Chichén Itzá's main pyramid—aligns with the sun, and the shadow of the plumed serpent moves slowly from the top of the building down. When the shadow reaches the bottom, the body joins the carved stone snake's head at the base of the pyramid. According to ancient legend, at the moment that the serpent is whole, the earth is fertilized. Visitors come from around the world to marvel at this sight, so advance arrangements are advisable. Elsewhere, equinox festivals and celebrations welcome spring, in the custom of the ancient Mexicans, with dances and prayers to the elements and the four cardinal points. It's customary to wear white with a red ribbon. March 21 (the shadow appears Mar 19–23).

Festival de México en el Centro Histórico (Annual Mexico City Festival), Mexico City. Regarded as one of Latin America's most vibrant celebrations of art and culture, this 2-week festival features diverse events including opera, concerts, theater, art exhibits, dance productions, and gourmet fare. Proceeds go toward the rescue and restoration of the art and architecture of Mexico City's historic downtown area. For a detailed schedule and more information, visit www.festival.org.mx. Mid- to late March, depending on Easter.

APRIL

Semana Santa (Holy Week), nationwide. Mexico celebrates the last week in the life of Christ, from Palm Sunday to Easter Sunday, with somber religious processions, spoofing of Judas, and reenactments of biblical events, plus food and craft fairs. Among the Tarahumara Indians in the Copper Canyon, celebrations have pre-Hispanic overtones. Pátzcuaro, Taxco, and Malinalco hold special celebrations. Businesses close during this traditional week of Mexican national vacations.

If you plan to travel to or around Mexico during Holy Week, make your reservations early. Flights into and out of the country will be full months in advance. Buses to these towns and to almost anywhere else in Mexico will be full, so try arriving on the Wednesday or Thursday before Good Friday. Easter Sunday is quiet, and the week following is a traditional vacation period. Early April.

San Marcos National Fair, Aguascalientes. Mexico's largest fair, first held in 1604, lasts 22 days. About a million visitors come for bullfights and rodeos, as well as *ranchera* music and mariachis. There are craft and industrial exhibits, markets, fireworks, and folk dancing. Mid-April.

MAY

Labor Day, nationwide. Workers' parades countrywide; everything closes. May 1.

Cinco de Mayo, Puebla and nationwide. This national holiday celebrates the defeat of the French at the Battle of Puebla. May 5.

Feast of San Isidro, nationwide. A blessing of seeds and work animals honors the patron saint of farmers. May 15.

Cancún Jazz Festival. Over Memorial Day weekend, the Parque de las Palapas, as well as the area around the Convention Center, has live performances from jazz musicians from around the world. For dates and schedule information, check www.cancun.eventguide.com.

International Gay Festival. This weekend event in Cancún kicks off with a welcome fiesta of food, drinks, and mariachi music. Additional festivities include a tequila party, tour of Cancún, sunset Caribbean cruise, bar and beach parties, and a final champagne breakfast. For information, check www.cancun.eventguide.com.

JUNE

Día de la Marina (Navy Day), various towns. All coastal towns celebrate the holiday, with naval parades and fireworks. June 1.

Corpus Christi, nationwide. This day, celebrated nationwide, honors the Body of Christ (the Eucharist) with processions, Masses, and food. Festivities include performances of *voladores* (flying pole dancers) beside the church and at the ruins

of El Tajín, Veracruz. In Mexico City, children dressed as Indians and carrying decorated baskets of fruit for the priest's blessing gather with their parents before the National Cathedral. *Mulitas* (mules), handmade from dried cornhusks and painted, are traditionally sold outside all churches on that day to represent a prayer for fertility. Dates vary, but celebrations take place on the Thursday following "Holy Trinity" Sunday.

National Ceramics Fair and Fiesta, Tlaquepaque, Jalisco. This pottery center on the outskirts of Guadalajara offers craft demonstrations and competitions, as well as mariachis, dancers, and colorful parades. June 14 to July 14.

Día de San Pedro y San Pablo (St. Peter and St. Paul Day), nationwide. This feast day is celebrated wherever St. Peter is the patron saint; it also honors anyone named Pedro or Peter. It's especially festive at San Pedro Tlaquepaque, near Guadalajara, with mariachi bands, folk dancers, and parades with floats. June 29.

JULY

Guelaguetza Dance Festival, Oaxaca. This is one of Mexico's most popular events. Villagers from the seven regions around Oaxaca gather in the city's amphitheater. They dress in traditional costumes, and many wear colorful "dancing" masks. The celebration dates from pre-Hispanic times. Make advance reservations—this festival attracts visitors from around the world. Go to www.visitmexico.com for more details. Late July.

AUGUST

International Chamber Music Festival, San Miguel de Allende. Held since 1982 in this beautiful town, the festival features international award-winning classical music ensembles. See www.festivalsanmiguel.com for details. July 30 to August 15.

Fall of Tenochtitlán, Mexico City. The last battle of the Spanish Conquest took place at Tlatelolco, ruins that are now part of the Plaza of Three Cultures. Wreath-laying ceremonies there and at the Cuauhtémoc monument on Reforma commemorate the surrender of Cuauhtémoc, the last Aztec king, to Cortez, and the loss of thousands of lives. August 13.

Assumption of the Virgin Mary, nationwide. This day is celebrated throughout the country with special Masses and, in some places, with processions. In Huamantla, flower petals and colored sawdust carpet the streets. At midnight on August 15, a statue of the Virgin is carried through the streets; on August 16 is the running of the bulls. On August 15 in Santa Clara del Cobre, near Pátzcuaro, Our Lady of Santa Clara de Asis and the Virgen de la Sagrado Patrona are honored with a parade of floats, dancers on the main square, and an exposition of regional crafts. Buses to Huamantla from Puebla and Mexico City will be full, and there are few hotels in Huamantla. Plan to stay in Puebla and commute to the festivities. August 15 to 17.

Fiestas de la Vendimia (Wine Harvest Festival), Ensenada, Baja California. This food and wine festival celebrates the annual harvest, with blessings, seminars, parties, and wine tastings. Check out www.visit mexico.com for more details. Mid- to late August.

SEPTEMBER

International Mariachi Festival, Guadalajara, Jalisco. These public concerts of mariachi music include visiting mariachi groups from around the world (even Japan!). Workshops and lectures focus on the history, culture, and music of the mariachi in Mexico. Check www.mariachi-jalisco.com.mx to confirm dates and the performance schedule. August 30 to September 9.

Reto al Tepozteco (Tepozteco Challenge), Tepoztlán, Morelos. This celebration of King Tepoztecatl's conversion to the Catholic religion includes a performance depicting the event. A procession leads toward the Tepozteco Pyramid, where people offer food and beverages. This event includes hypnotic *chinelo* dances, fireworks, and a food festival. September 7 and 8.

Independence Day, nationwide. Celebrates Mexico's independence from Spain with parades, picnics, and family reunions. At 11pm on September 15, the president gives the famous independence *grito* (shout) from the National Palace in Mexico City. At least half a million people crowd into the

zócalo (main plaza), and the rest of the country watches on TV or participates in local celebrations. Tall buildings downtown are draped in the national colors (red, green, and white), and the *zócalo* is ablaze with lights. Many people drive downtown at night to see the lights. Querétaro and San Miguel de Allende, where Independence conspirators lived and met, also celebrate elaborately; the schedule of events is exactly the same in every village, town, and city across Mexico. September 15 and 16.

Fall Equinox, Chichén Itzá. The same shadow play that occurs during the spring equinox is repeated. September 21 and 22.

OCTOBER

Fiestas de Octubre (October Festivals), Guadalajara. This "most Mexican of cities" celebrates for a month with its trademark mariachi music. It's a bountiful display of popular culture and fine arts, and a spectacular spread of traditional food, Mexican beer, and wine. All month.

Festival Internacional Cervantino, Guanajuato. This festival began in the 1970s as a cultural event, bringing performing artists from all over the world to this picturesque village northeast of Mexico City. Now the artists travel all over the republic after appearing in Guanajuato. Check www.festivalcervantino.gob.mx for details. Mid-to late October.

Día de la Raza ("Ethnicity Day," or Columbus Day), nationwide. This day commemorates the fusion of the Spanish and Mexican peoples. October 12.

Feria Nacional del Mole, Mexico City. Just south of Mexico City, thousands of varieties of *mole* will be prepared for sampling and competition. This spicy sauce is a Mexican staple, made of unsweetened chocolate, peppers, and spices, often served with meat or poultry. Between October 1 and 15.

NOVEMBER

Day of the Dead, nationwide. This holiday (Nov 1) actually lasts for 2 days: All Saints' Day, honoring saints and deceased children, and All Souls' Day, honoring deceased adults. Relatives gather at cemeteries countrywide, carrying candles and food, and often spend the night beside graves of loved ones. Weeks before, bakers begin producing bread in the shape of mummies or round loaves decorated with bread "bones." Sugar skulls emblazoned with glittery names are sold everywhere. Many days ahead, homes and churches erect altars laden with bread, fruit, flowers, candles, favorite foods, and photographs of saints and of the deceased. On both nights, costumed children walk through the streets, often carrying mock coffins and pumpkin lanterns, into which they expect money to be dropped.

The most famous celebration—which has become almost too well known—is on Janitzio, an island on Lake Pátzcuaro, Michoacán, west of Mexico City. Mixquic, a mountain village south of Mexico City, hosts an elaborate street fair. At around 11pm on both nights, solemn processions lead to the cemetery in the center of town. Cemeteries around Oaxaca are well known for their solemn vigils, and some for their Carnaval-like atmosphere. November 1 and 2.

Fiestas de Noviembre (November Festivals), Puerto Escondido, Oaxaca. The month's events include the annual Pipeline of Mexico, Zicatela Beach's International Surfing Tournament, the International Sailfish Tournament, and the Coastal Dance Festival. Check local calendars or www.visitmexico.com for details. All month.

Gourmet Festival, Puerto Vallarta, Jalisco. In this culinary capital of Mexico, chefs from around the world join with local restaurateurs to create special menus and host wine and tequila tastings, cooking classes, a gourmet food expo, and other special events. For detailed information, see www.festivalgourmet.com. Dates vary, but the festival generally runs November 12 to 22.

Revolution Day, nationwide. This holiday commemorates the start of the Mexican Revolution in 1910 with parades, speeches, rodeos, and patriotic events. November 20.

Annual Yucatán Bird Festival, Mérida, Yucatán. Bird-watching sessions, workshops, and exhibits are the highlights of this festival designed to illustrate the special role birds play in our environment and in the Yucatán. Visit www.yucatanbirds.org.mx for details. Late November to early December.

National Silver Fair, Taxco. This competition pits Mexico's best silversmiths against some of the world's finest artisans. There are exhibits, concerts, dances, and fireworks. Check local calendars or www.visitmexico.com for details. Late November to early December.

Annual Hot Air Balloon Festival, León, Guanajuato. This is the largest festival in Latin America, with more than 60 balloons and pilots from all over the globe participating. Visit www.festivaldelglobo.com.mx for details. Late November.

DECEMBER

Feast of the Virgin of Guadalupe, nationwide. Religious processions, street fairs, dancing, fireworks, and Masses honor the patroness of Mexico. It is one of the country's most moving and beautiful displays of traditional culture. The Virgin of Guadalupe appeared to a young man, Juan Diego Cuauhtlatoatzin, in December 1531 on a hill near Mexico City. It's customary for children to dress up as Juan Diego, wearing mustaches and red bandannas. One of the most famous and elaborate celebrations takes place at the Basílica de Guadalupe, north of Mexico City, where the Virgin appeared. But every village celebrates this day, often with processions of children carrying banners, and with *charreadas* (rodeos), bicycle races, dancing, and fireworks. In Puerto Vallarta, the celebration begins on December 1 and extends through December 12, with traditional processions to the church for a brief Mass and blessing. In the final days, the processions and festivities take place around the clock. There's a major fireworks exhibition on the feast day at 11pm. December 12.

Festival of San Cristóbal de las Casas, San Cristóbal de las Casas, Chiapas. This 10-day festival in Chiapas includes a procession by the Tzotzil and Tzetzal Indians, *marimba* music, and a parade of horses. December 12 to 21.

Christmas Posadas, nationwide. On each of the 9 nights before Christmas, it's customary to reenact the Holy Family's search for an inn. Door-to-door candlelit processions pass through cities and villages nationwide, especially Querétaro and Taxco. Hosted by churches, businesses, and community organizations, these take the place of the northern tradition of a Christmas party. December 15 to 24.

Fiesta de los Rábanos (Festival of the Radishes), Oaxaca. Local artisans and sculptors set up stalls around the main square to display their elaborate pieces of art—made entirely from radishes! The local crop is used for creating nativity scenes and famous Mexican figures. Balloons and birds crafted from local flowers add even more color. December 23.

Christmas, nationwide. Mexicans often extend this holiday and take vacations for up to 2 weeks before Christmas, returning after New Year's. Many businesses close, and resorts and hotels fill. Significant celebrations take place on December 23 (see above). Querétaro has a huge parade. On the evening of December 24 in Oaxaca, processions culminate on the central plaza. On the same night, Santiago Tuxtla in Veracruz celebrates by dancing the *huapango* and with *jarocho* bands in the beautiful town square. December 24 and 25.

New Year's Eve, nationwide. Like the rest of the world, Mexico celebrates New Year's Eve with parties, fireworks, and plenty of noise. New Year's Eve in Mexico is typically spent with family. Special festivities take place at Santa Clara del Cobre, near Pátzcuaro, with a candlelit procession of Christ; and at Tlacolula, near Oaxaca, with commemorative mock battles. December 31.

LAY OF THE LAND
Geography

Mexico's northern border with the United States runs 3,141km (1,947 miles); the southern border with Guatemala and Belize is less than a third that length, at 1,212km (751 miles). The Pacific Ocean hems in the western and southern coasts, while the Sea of Cortez (or the Gulf of California) is positioned between Baja California and the mainland, forming the world's longest peninsula. In the east, the Gulf of Mexico dominates the north, while the Caribbean Sea flanks the eastern Yucatán Peninsula. In all, the coastline runs 9,330km (5,785 miles).

Northern Mexico is a sprawling, arid region home to two deserts. The larger of the two, *el Desierto Chihuahuense,* sits between the Sierra Madre Occidental in the west and the Sierra Madre Oriental in the east, both extensions of mountain ranges in the U.S. *El Desierto Sonorense* covers most of the Baja peninsula and the northwestern mainland. **Baja California's** mountains run virtually the entire length of the state, about 1,400km (868 miles).

Southwestern Chihuahua is home to the **Copper Canyon,** one of the world's most majestic canyon systems, larger and sometimes deeper than the Grand Canyon in the U.S. The six canyons that make up the **Parque Nacional Barranca del Cobre** are located in the Sierra Tarahumara, traditional home of the indigenous Raramuri (Tarahumara).

The Sierra Madre Occidental begins near the U.S. border and continues 1,250km (775 miles) south, where it merges with the *Cordillera Neovolcánica.* To the east is the Sierra Madre Oriental, stretching 1,350km (837 miles) until also reaching the *Cordillera Neovolcánica.*

The two Sierra Madre ranges frame Mexico's most dominant geographic feature, the *Altiplano.* This group of broad central plateaus reaches from the U.S. border to the Isthmus of Tehuantepec. The southern plateau is home to rolling hills and valleys with some of the best farmland in the country. **Mexico City** and **Guadalajara** are both located in this region, as well as the states of **Jalisco, Puebla, Tlaxcala, Hidalgo,** and **Morelos.**

The Cordillera Neovolcánica extends from the Pacific Ocean to the Gulf of Mexico and includes the active volcanoes Popocatépetl and Volcán de Fuego de Colima, as well as Mexico's other highest peaks: Pico de Orizaba, Iztaccíhuatl, and Paricutín. South of the Cordillera Neovolcánica are other important mountain ranges, including the Sierra Madre del Sur, Sierra Madre de Oaxaca, and Sierra Madre de Chiapas.

The country is positioned on top of three tectonic plates, making Mexico one of the most seismologically active places on Earth, where volcanic eruptions and earthquakes rattle the ground. The last significant eruption was *El Chichon* in **Chiapas** in 1982. A magnitude-8.1 earthquake hit Mexico City in 1985, causing the deaths of thousands and long-term political consequences.

Although surrounded by the sea, Mexico's freshwater resources are unevenly distributed among its 150 rivers. Five rivers—the Usumacinta, Grijalva, Papaloapán, Coatzacoalos, and Pánuco—contain more than half the volume of water in all of the rivers combined. Four of these five rivers are located in southern Mexico, leaving the north, the most populated area, with less than 10% of the country's water resources.

The Isthmus of Tehuantepec, running through southern **Veracruz** and **Chiapas,** marks the smallest distance (200km/124 miles) between the Gulf of Mexico and the Pacific. The northern side of the isthmus is wide and marshy, stretching from Veracruz to the Yucatán. Lush tropical rainforests and dense jungles occupy the Gulf Coastal Plain, Chiapan Highlands, and the southern Yucatán Peninsula. These regions are hot and humid, keeping the region green and teeming with wildlife. Jungle turns to tropical savanna at the end of the peninsula.

Flora & Fauna

Mexico is one of the most biologically diverse places in the world. It is estimated to have between 20,000 and 50,000 species of plants from the northern deserts to the southern jungles. The highest concentrations of species can be found in **Chiapas, Oaxaca,** and **Veracruz.** Mexico also places first in reptile biodiversity, with more than 740 known species; second in mammals, at 526; fourth in amphibians, at 290; and 10th in birds, at 1,150.

Bucking the stereotype of "barren wasteland," Mexico's deserts are some of the planet's most diverse regions. About 6,000 species of desert plants, 90% of them endemic to the deserts of Mexico and the U.S., flourish in the northern deserts. The **Chihuahuan Desert** sustains around 400 cactus species alone, including prickly pears, hedgehogs, living rocks, cory, whitethorn acacia, creosote, and lechuguilla (a type of agave). The sotol, or desert spoon, is used to make a distilled spirit similar to tequila that has become the state drink of Chihuahua.

Certain mammals, birds, amphibians, reptiles, and invertebrates call the northern deserts home. White-tailed deer, pronghorn, coyotes, blacktailed jack rabbits, desert tarantulas, whip scorpions, geckos, and a rich display of butterflies and moths are just a few of the local critters. Finally, the Chihuahuan and Sonoran deserts wouldn't be considered deserts if you couldn't find snakes. King snakes, rat snakes, coral snakes, and many species of rattlesnakes stripe these vast landscapes.

The Sierra Madre mountain ranges support an assortment of trees in Central Mexico. The higher regions of the forests sustain mahogany, zapote, ceiba, oak, cypress, and over 50 different species of pine trees. Within the midrange forests, you will find juniper, piñon (or pinyon) pine, and evergreen oaks. Figs, lianas, orchids, and

Portals to the Underworld

The Yucatán Peninsula is a flat slab of limestone that millions of years ago absorbed the force of the giant meteor thought to have extinguished the dinosaurs. The impact sent shock waves through the brittle limestone, fracturing it throughout and creating an immense network of fissures that drain rainwater away from the surface. You'll notice no bridges, rivers, or watercourses in northern and central Yucatán. The vast subterranean basin stretching across the peninsula is invisible but for the area's many *cenotes*—sinkholes or natural wells that don't exist outside the Yucatán. Many are perfectly round vertical shafts that look like nothing else in nature; others are hidden in caverns that retain a partial roof, often perforated by tree roots. To the Maya, they were passageways to the underworld. Indeed, they look sacred: Quiet, dark, and cool, the opposite of the warm, bright world outside.

bromeliads such as the spiny and silvery Hechtia argentea occupy the lowest slopes of the mountains. The central plateaus (*altiplano*) between the ranges support semi-desert grasslands where yucca and barrel cactus grow.

Central Mexico is also home to the famous agave americana, also known as maguey in Mexico, used to make pulque (similar to tequila) and other useful products. Weber blue agave is the official plant used to make tequila and is mostly grown in the state of Jalisco.

Every winter, hundreds of millions of monarch butterflies wing south to eastern **Michoacán,** where the Oyamel fir forest becomes their winter nest.

The tropical rainforests in the south are covered with dense layers of broadleaf evergreen vegetation and massive deciduous trees joined with palms, marshes, and mangroves. Mexico's fauna is most abundant in these southern *selvas* (jungles). Bats, spider and howler monkeys, the silky anteater, coatimundis, jaguars and jagarundi, the Baird's tapir, numerous species of parrots, macaws, and toucans bring the *selvas* to life. The quetzal bird is also found in the *selvas* and is known for its beautiful colors (*quetzal* comes from the word *quetzalli* in Náhuatl, meaning "large, brilliant tail feather"), as well as its religious symbology in ancient Maya and Aztec beliefs.

The **Yucatán** is more like a tropical savanna, supporting thick grasses mixed with evergreens and shrubs, where ferns, epiphytes, and palms are common. Mangrove swamps and lagoons are an important migratory stop for birds on the North American Migration Flyway, providing habitat for flamingos and herons.

Mexico's ample coasts are home to abundant aquatic life. Just off the Yucatán Peninsula is the **Mesoamerican Reef,** the second-largest reef in the world, after the Great Barrier Reef in Australia. Mexico has about 380 types of freshwater fish and at least 1,300 ocean species. Around 30 different cetaceans live in the seas, from the smallest and most endangered porpoise, the vaquita, to the blue whale, the largest mammal on Earth. Manatees swim in warm coastal waters as well as lagoons. Seven of the world's eight species of sea turtle live in Mexico's waters. Baja California also has an array of marine mammals, including California sea lions, elephant seals, finback whales, humpbacks, blue whales, the California gray whale, and bottle-nosed dolphins.

Despite this abundance, heavy deforestation has endangered many species, including the Mexican bobcat, black howler, jaguar, jagarundi, and quetzal. Both the forests in the north and the rainforests in the south continue to be deforested by logging, farming, and mining. The southern wetlands, in particular, are an important focus of environmental movements in Mexico. Overfishing, poor agricultural practices, infrastructure projects, and salt harvesting threaten reefs and coastal habitats. It's not all bad news: Sea turtle populations, along with other species, are slowly recovering with the help of scientific efforts, grass-roots organizations, and local governments.

RESPONSIBLE TRAVEL

Mexico's ecological diversity is among the broadest of any country in the world, with an abundance of ecosystems ranging from the northern deserts to the central conifer forests, and the southern tropical rainforests. Mexico also supports 111 million people and welcomes more than 20 million visitors each year. Tourism is one of the country's biggest and most lucrative industries, and while tourism has brought jobs and growth to much of Mexico, it has also created and even accelerated many of Mexico's ecological problems. Cancún might be the highest-profile example: Rapidly developed from a rural outpost to an international resort destination, Cancún imported turf from Florida for its golf courses, inadvertently introducing a disease that wiped out the local coconut palms. The region's mangroves, a key habitat for native species and vital to protecting the land from hurricanes and erosion, have also suffered.

However, tourism has also encouraged development of ecological conservation. Mexico is home to seven of the world's eight species of sea turtle, though the entire turtle population was decimated on both coasts as a result of tourism growth and local overfishing. Recent success stories such as Puerto Escondido, in Oaxaca, where sea turtles are now protected by the locals (p. 385), or the Riviera Maya, in the Yucatán, where marine biologists are working with hotels to guard nesting turtles and their eggs, have demonstrated the benefits of linking tourism with local knowledge.

Mexico's people are proud of their land and culture, and through your travels, especially in rural areas, you will likely encounter *ejidos* and *cooperativos,* or local cooperatives, that offer small-scale tourism services—this may be as simple as taking visitors on a boat ride through a lake or as visible as controlling access to archaeological ruins. *Ejidos* will also run tours to popular ecotourism destinations similar to those offered by large travel agencies. When you deal with *ejidos,* everyone you

---

 Biodegradable Sunscreen

Recent scientific studies have shown that the chemicals in commercial sunscreen can do long-term damage to coral reefs, collect in fresh water, and even build up in your own body system. The Riviera Maya, Mexico's Caribbean Coast, receives more than 2.5 million visitors every year, many of them drawn to its rare marine environment—a unique combination of freshwater cenotes and the world's second-largest coral reef. A few ounces of sunscreen multiplied by 2.5 million is equal to a substantial amount of harmful chemicals suspended in the ocean and fresh water. That's why tours to the **Sian Ka'an Biosphere**

Reserve (p. 554) and water parks **Xcaret** (p. 537) and **Xel-Ha** (p. 543) ask that you use only biodegradable sunscreen or wear none at all when swimming in their ocean or cenotes.

The label of a biodegradable sunscreen should state that it is 100% biodegradable (and only 100% will do). You can buy it at the parks, but you'll get a better price from local markets. If you're curious, you can obtain a list of banned chemicals by contacting the parks directly. Buy a supply of biodegradable formula before you go from **www.mexitan.com** or **www.caribbeansol.com**.

encounter will be from the community and you know that your money goes directly back to them. States with a strong network of cooperatives include Chiapas, Oaxaca, Quintana Roo, and Yucatán.

The Mexican Caribbean supports the Great Mesoamerican Barrier Reef, the second-largest reef in the world, which extends down to Honduras. This reef and other marine ecosystems face increasing pressure from sedimentation, pollution, overfishing, and exploitative recreational activities, all newly associated with growing regional tourism. The **Coral Reef Alliance** (**CORAL;** www.coral.org) is an example of an organization that, by teaming up with the **World Wildlife Fund** (**WWF;** www.wwf.org) and **United Nations Environmental Programme** (**UNEP;** www.unep.org), has been working to address threats to the Mesoamerican Barrier Reef and improve environmental sustainability throughout the region. CORAL partners with Mexican Amigos de Sian Ka'an, Conservation International, and the Cozumel Reefs National Park in an effort to build sustainability into mass tourism (such as cruise ships and hotels). CORAL assists marine tourism operators in implementing a voluntary code of conduct for best environmental practices. CORAL is soon to spread its influence to the Yum Balam region of the Yucatán Peninsula, where guidelines for whale shark interactions are greatly needed.

Animal-Rights Issues
BULLFIGHTS
Bullfighting is considered an important part of Latin culture, but before you attend a *correo,* you should know that in all likelihood the bulls (at least four) will ultimately be killed in a gory show. That said, a bullfight is a portal into understanding Mexico's Spanish colonial past, and traditional machismo is on full display. Bullfights take place in towns as different as Tijuana and Puerto Vallarta, and they afford a colorful spectacle like no other, with a brass band playing; the costumed matador's macho stare; men shaking their heads at less-than-perfect swipes of the cape; and overly made-up, bloodthirsty women chanting *"Ole,"* waving their white hankies, and throwing roses, jackets, and hats at the matador's feet. There is also the extremely minuscule chance that if the bull puts up a good enough fight or pierces his horn through the matador's leg, he will be spared for breeding purposes. It does happen, if only rarely. To read more about the implications of attending bullfights, see the website of People for the Ethical Treatment of Animals (PETA) at www.peta.org.

SWIMMING WITH DOLPHINS
The capture of wild dolphins was outlawed in Mexico in 2002. The only dolphins added to the country's dolphin swim programs since then were born in captivity. This law may have eased concerns about the death and implications of capturing wild dolphins, but the controversy is not over. Local organizations have been known to staple notes to Dolphin Discovery ads in magazines distributed in Cancún hotels. Marine biologists who run the dolphin swim programs say the mammals are thriving and that the programs provide a forum for research, conservation, education, and rescue operations. Animal rights advocates maintain that keeping these intelligent mammals in captivity is nothing more than exploitation. Their argument is that these private dolphin programs don't qualify as "public display" under the Marine Mammal Protection Act because the entry fees bar most of the public from participating.

Visit the website of the **Whale and Dolphin Conservation Society** at www.wdcs.org or the **American Cetacean Society,** www.acsonline.org, for further discussion on the topic.

TOURS

Academic Trips & Language Classes

For Spanish-language instruction, **IMAC** (✆ **866/306-5040;** www.spanish-school.com. mx) offers programs in Guadalajara, Puerto Vallarta, and Playa del Carmen. The **Spanish Institute** is affiliated with intensive Spanish-language schools in Puebla (✆ **800/554-2951;** www.sipuebla.com) and Mérida (✆ **800/539-9710;** www.simerida.com).

To explore your inner Frida or Diego while in Mexico, look into **Mexico Art Tours,** 9323 E. Lupine Ave., Scottsdale, AZ 85260 (✆ **888/783-1331** or 480/730-1764; www.mexicanarttours.com). Typically led by Jean Grimm, a specialist in the arts and cultures of Mexico, these unique tours feature compelling speakers who are themselves respected scholars and artists. Itineraries include visits to Chiapas, Guadalajara, Guanajuato, Mexico City, Oaxaca, Puebla, San Miguel de Allende, Veracruz, and the Yucatán—and other destinations. Special tours involve archaeology, architecture, interior design, and culture—such as a Day of the Dead tour.

The **Archaeological Conservancy,** 5301 Central Ave. NE, Ste. 402, Albuquerque, NM 87108 (✆ **505/266-1540;** www.americanarchaeology.com), presents various trips each year, led by an expert, usually an archaeologist. The trips change from year to year and space is limited; make reservations early.

ATC Tours and Travel, Av. 16 de Septiembre 16, 29200 San Cristóbal de las Casas, Chis. (✆ **967/678-2550,** -2557; fax 967/678-3145; www.atctours.com), a Mexico-based tour operator with an excellent reputation, offers specialist-led trips, primarily in southern Mexico. In addition to trips to the ruins of Palenque and Yaxchilán (extending into Belize and Guatemala by river, plane, and bus, if desired), ATC runs horseback tours to Chamula or Zinacantán, and day trips to the ruins of Toniná around San Cristóbal de las Casas; birding in the rainforests of Chiapas and Guatemala (including in the El Triunfo Reserve of Chiapas); hikes to the shops and homes of textile artists of the Chiapas highlands; and walks from the Lagos de Montebello in the Montes Azules Biosphere Reserve, with camping and canoeing. The company can also prepare custom itineraries.

Adventure & Wellness Trips

Mexico Sagaz (Asociación Mexicana de Turismo de Aventura y Ecoturismo) is an active association of ecotourism and adventure tour operators. It publishes an annual catalog of participating firms and their offerings, all of which must meet certain criteria for security, quality, and training of the guides, as well as for sustainability of natural and cultural environments. For more information, contact ✆ **01-800/654-4452** toll-free in Mexico, or 55/5544-7567; www.amtave.org.

Baja Expeditions, 2625 Garnet Ave., San Diego, CA 92109 (✆ **800/843-6967** or 858/581-3311; www.bajaex.com), offers natural-history cruises, whale-watching, sea kayaking, camping, scuba diving, and resort and day trips from La Paz and Loreto, with the kayak trips from Loreto. Small groups and special itineraries are Baja Expeditions' specialty, including an exotic 7-day yoga/massage/kayak expedition to a secluded private island in the bay.

The **California Native,** 6701 W. 87th Place, Los Angeles, CA 90045 (✆ **800/926-1140** or 310/642-1140; www.calnative.com), offers small-group deluxe 7-, 8-, 11-, and 14-day escorted tours through the Copper Canyon. Many trips visit the towns of Batopilas, Urique, and Tejeban, as well as the customary destinations of Creel, El Fuerte, Divisadero, Chihuahua, and Cerocahui. The guides are known throughout the area for their work with the Tarahumara Indians. They also cover Baja and the Yucatán.

Canyon Travel, 900 Rich Creek Lane, Bulverde, TX 78163-2872 (© **800/843-1060** in the U.S. and Canada, or 830/885-2000; www.canyontravel.com), specializes in the Copper Canyon and has a variety of adventures, from easy to challenging. It designs trips for special-interest groups of agriculturists, geologists, rockhounds, and birders. The owner works with the Tarahumara Indians.

Two private companies that run ecotours throughout Chiapas are **Ecochiapas** (Primero de Marzo 30, San Cristóbal de las Casas; © **967/631-7498;** www.eco chiapas.com) and **Latitud 16** (Calle Real de Guadalupe 23, San Cristóbal de las Casas; © **967/678-3909;** www.latitud16.com).

The **Mesoamerican Ecotourism Alliance** (© **800/682-0584** in the U.S.; www.travelwithmea.org) offers award-winning ecotours recognized by *National Geographic* to the Yucatán and Chiapas.

Mountain Travel Sobek, 6420 Fairmount Ave., El Cerrito, CA 94530 (© **888/831-7526** or 510/594-6000; www.mtsobek.com), takes groups kayaking in the Sea of Cortez and hiking in Copper Canyon and Oaxaca. Sobek is one of the world's leading ecotour outfitters.

Natural Habitat Adventures, 2945 Center Green Court, Ste. H, Boulder, CO 80301 (© **800/543-8917** or 303/449-3711; www.nathab.com), offers naturalist-led natural history and adventure tours. Expeditions focus on monarch butterfly-watching in Michoacán, sea turtle– and gray whale–watching in Baja, and hiking through Copper Canyon.

NatureQuest, P.O. Box 22000, Telluride, CO 81435 (© **800/369-3033** or 970/728-6743; www.naturequesttours.com), specializes in the natural history, culture, and wildlife of the Copper Canyon and the remote lagoons and waterways off Baja California. A 10-day hiking trip ventures into rugged areas of the canyon; a less strenuous trip goes to Creel and Batopilas, in the same area. Baja trips get close to nature, with special permits for venturing via two-person kayak into sanctuaries for whales and birds. Special horse-packing adventures are available as well.

Sea Kayak Adventures, P.O. Box 3862, Coeur d'Alene, ID 83816 (© **800/616-1943** or 208/765-3116; www.seakayakadventures.com), features kayak trips in both the Sea of Cortez Loreto Bay National Marine Park and Magdalena Bay, with a focus on whale-watching. This company has the exclusive permit to paddle Magdalena Bay's remote northern waters, and they guarantee gray whale sightings. Trips combine paddling of 4 to 5 hours per day, with hiking across dunes and beaches, while nights are spent camping (as well as staying in a hotel in Loreto). They have added a suite of yoga and spiritual retreats that combine extensive outdoor activity with twice-daily yoga sessions.

Sea Trek Ocean Kayaking Center, P.O. Box 1987, Sausalito, CA 94966 (© **415/332-8494;** www.seatrek.com), has been alternating sea-kayaking trips between Alaska and Baja for 20 years, which has provided them an intimate knowledge of the peninsula's coastline. Eight-day trips depart from and return to Loreto. An optional day excursion to Bahía Magdalena for gray whale–watching is available. Full boat support is provided, and no previous paddling experience is necessary.

Paddling South, P.O. Box 827, Calistoga, CA 94515 (© **800/398-6200** or 707/942-4550; www.tourbaja.com), offers sea-kayaking, mountain bike, and mule-pack tours in the Loreto area. Owner Trudi Angell has guided these trips for more than 20 years. She and her guides offer firsthand knowledge of the area. Kayaking, mountain biking, pack trips, and sailing charters combine these elements with outdoor adventures.

Mexico has more than 120 **golf courses,** concentrated in the resort areas, with excellent options in Mexico City and Guadalajara. Los Cabos, in Baja Sur, has become the country's preeminent golf destination; the Puerto Vallarta area enjoys a growing reputation. For details on courses and events, see chapters 9 and 19. Visitors to Mexico can also enjoy **tennis, racquetball, squash, water-skiing, surfing, bicycling,** and **horseback riding. Scuba diving** is excellent, not only off the Yucatán's Caribbean coast (especially Cozumel), but also on the Pacific coast at Puerto Vallarta and Manzanillo, and off Baja in the Sea of Cortez. **Mountain and volcano climbing** is a rugged sport that allows you to meet like-minded adventurers from around the world. The top peaks are just 80km (50 miles) south of Mexico City—the snowcapped volcanoes Ixtaccihuatl (5,255m/17,236 ft.) and Popocatépetl (5,420m/17,778 ft.). Popocatépetl is an active volcano and has been closed to climbers since a massive eruption in 1994. For information on visiting and climbing the volcanoes, contact **Mountain Guides International** at © 800/766-3396 (www.mountain guidesinternational.com).

Trek America, 16/17 Grange Mills Weir Road, London, SW12 ONE, UK (© **800/873-5872** in the U.S., or 0844/576-1400 in the U.K.; www.trekamerica. com), organizes lengthy, active trips that combine trekking, hiking, van transportation, and camping in the Yucatán.

Veraventuras, Santos Degollado 81-8, 91000 Xalapa, Ver. (© **01-800/712-6572** toll-free in Mexico, or 228/818-9579; www.veraventuras.xalapa.net), offers specially trained guides on well-organized adventures into the state of Veracruz, including rafting through the rapids of the Antigua and Actopan rivers.

Food & Wine Trips

If you're looking to eat your way through Mexico, sign up with **Culinary Adventures,** 6023 Reid Dr. NW, Gig Harbor, WA 98335 (© **253/851-7676;** fax 253/851-9532; www.marilyntausend.com). It runs a short but select list of cooking tours in Mexico. Culinary Adventures features well-known cooks, with travel to regions known for excellent cuisine. Destinations vary each year. The owner, Marilyn Tausend, is the author of *Cocinas de la Familia* (Family Kitchens), *Savoring Mexico,* and *Mexican,* and coauthor of *Mexico the Beautiful Cookbook.*

Volunteer & Working Trips

For numerous links to volunteer and internship programs throughout Mexico involving teaching, caring for children, providing healthcare, feeding the homeless, and doing other community and public service, visit **www.volunteerabroad.com**.

If you're interested in teaching English to Mexican university students in the colonial town of Dolores Hidalgo or Queretaro, **Global Volunteers,** 375 E. Little Canada Rd., St. Paul, MN 55117 (© **800/487-1074;** www.globalvolunteers.org), arranges 2-week programs for a fee.

ProWorld Service Corps, 600 California St., 10th Floor, San Francisco, CA 94108 (© **877/429-6753** or 415/434-5464; www.myproworld.org), organizes rural outreach internships in the areas of health, environment, and economic development, particularly to Oaxaca.

SUGGESTED MEXICO ITINERARIES

by Shane Christensen

3

Mexico's geographic and cultural diversity makes it a fascinating country, a place where Mexicans of wide-ranging descent live amid fertile valleys, spectacular beaches, tropical forests, rugged mountains, and hot deserts. Several of the suggested itineraries described here will take you through visually stunning landscapes and both big-city and small-town Mexico, where the level of development and the way of life sometimes seems to span a century.

Once inside Mexico, travel is best done by plane, bus, or car. A number of low-cost carriers have recently begun flying domestically, significantly reducing the cost of internal flights. Mexico's first-class buses are comfortable and inexpensive—though sometimes slow. Car rental has generally become less expensive, and it's also possible to hire a car and driver—although for greater cost. There is only one true passenger train still operating, which runs along the Copper Canyon to Chihuahua City.

I've tried to keep travel to a minimum in order to maximize time in each destination, so none of these itineraries can be called an exhaustive exploration of Mexico. If you want to see all of the country's most famous sites, however, you can link the central archaeological tour with the Ruta Maya, which would take about 3 weeks. International airports serve major beach resorts, making these convenient gateway points. Remember that it's possible to fly into one airport and out of another, usually without much difference in cost when compared with buying a round-trip ticket in and out of the same airport.

CENTRAL MEXICO'S PRE-COLUMBIAN TREASURES IN A WEEK

Most of Mexico's great archaeological sites, aside from those left by the Maya, lie in the country's center, from Mexico City to the east. This trip takes you to the best of these and to the three most impressive archaeological museums in Mexico. The area in which all of this is located is

Central Mexico's Pre-Columbian Treasures

HIDALGO

MEXICO

Gulf of Mexico

Mexico City

TLAXCALA

Xalapa
6

DISTRITO
FEDERAL

Tlaxcala
4

VERACRUZ

Cholula de
Rivadabia

5
Puebla

Veracruz
7

MORELOS

0   35 mi

0   35 km

PUEBLA

relatively compact. It doesn't require a lot of travel time to cover, unless you add on a side trip to Oaxaca for the ruins of Monte Albán and Mitla.

Days 1, 2 & 3: Mexico City

If you arrive early, go straight to the heart of the nation: Mexico City's *zócalo*, the third-largest public square in the world (p. 114). There, poetically situated between the nation's first cathedral and its National Palace, lie the ruins of the Aztec empire's **Templo Mayor** (p. 100), buried and forgotten until 1978. Dedicate your second day to the **Museo Nacional de Antropología** (p. 98) and **Chapultepec Park** (p. 114). By the third day, you should have adapted to the altitude and will be ready for a day trip to **Teotihuacán** (p. 126), "City of the Gods," where you can explore palaces and pyramids and climb to the summit of the Pyramid of the Sun.

Day 4: Tlaxcala ★

Drive or take a bus to colonial Tlaxcala to view the vivid murals of **Cacaxtla** and the hilltop stronghold of **Xochitécatl** (p. 440). The murals are painted in an intriguing Maya style, with rich symbolism that invites speculation. Stay the night and enjoy the town's slow rhythms and street life. Stroll over to the **Government Palace** (p. 438) to view modern murals of artist Desiderio Hernández Xochitiotzin, which chronicle the history of the Tlaxcaltecans, ancient rivals of the Aztecs.

Days 5 & 6: Puebla ★★★, Cholula & Xalapa

From Tlaxcala, it's a quick car or bus ride to colonial **Puebla** (p. 426). In the afternoon, visit the **Museo Amparo** (p. 434) to see its stunning collection of pre-Hispanic art. The next day, head over to **Cholula** (p. 435) to view the ruins of Mexico's largest pyramid, with the majestic volcano "El Popo" as a backdrop. Visit the local churches of **Tonantzintla** (p. 436) and **San Francisco Acatepec** (p. 436) for their Indian baroque design. From Puebla, it's on to bustling **Xalapa** (p. 441), a 3-hour drive from the dry central plateau to the misty slopes of the Sierra Madre Oriental. Visit the city's wonderful **Museo de Antropología** (p. 442), with a collection of megalithic Olmec heads and expressive Totonac art.

Day 7: Veracruz City ★

Travel to the old port city of **Veracruz** (p. 445). Enjoy a relaxing day in this lively town, with its coffee shops, tropical music, and dance. From here, you can fly out directly or via Mexico City. To extend your trip, consider heading north to the ruins of **El Tajín** (p. 453), or south to **Oaxaca** (p. 398) to Monte Albán and Mitla.

THE BEST OF WESTERN MEXICO IN A WEEK

On this route, you enter Mexico through the León/Guanajuato International Airport and leave from Ixtapa/Zihuatanejo. In between, you're treated to a variety of places and scenes—from the maze of streets and alleyways of the old mining town of Guanajuato, to the stately colonial city of Morelia, to the Indian town of Pátzcuaro, to the modern resort hotels of Ixtapa and Zihuatanejo. From November to March, you can add a day trip from Morelia to a magical place in the mountain forests east of the city where millions of monarch butterflies congregate in a yearly ritual that is one of the most intriguing of nature's mysteries.

Days 1 & 2: Guanajuato & San Miguel de Allende ★★★

These enchanted colonial cities are made for walking. Spend 1 day in each, taking in the sights and sounds of their colorful cobblestone streets, flower-filled plazas, and music-filled cafes and cantinas. If you tire of walking in Guanajuato, contract a taxi for a tour of this university town. The panoramic highway circles the narrow valley where the old town is nestled, and there's an excellent view from the statue of **El Pípila** (p. 183) before descending to the subterranean roads. Consider visiting the bizarre yet intriguing **Museo de Las Momias (Mummy Museum,** p. 186).

In San Miguel de Allende, visit the architecturally stunning **Parroquia** (p. 170), and be sure to stop in some of the marvelous galleries and shops. Most are housed in colonial buildings with beautiful interiors and lovely courtyards. Evenings are a particularly enchanted time to be in San Miguel, when the city is lit by candles and colorful lamps with people on the streets and music everywhere. See p. 178.

Day 3: Morelia ★

Drive or take the bus for the 3-hour trip to **Morelia** (p. 220). Build in time to see the **cathedral** from the vantage point of one of the many cafes and restaurants that front Avenida Madero. Take a tour of the city and enjoy coffee, a drink, or dinner on the terrace of the **Villa Montaña Hotel** (p. 228). In winter you can also make a day trip to view the magnificent **monarch butterflies** (p. 230), or head out to see the dormant volcano **El Paricutín** (p. 242).

Days 4 & 5: Pátzcuaro ★★★ & the Lakeside Villages of the Purépecha

From Morelia, it's only an hour's drive to the picturesque town of **Pátzcuaro** (p. 231) and the heart of the Purépecha homeland. Enjoy a stroll around the two principal plazas of the town, and pay a visit to the **House of Eleven Patios**

(p. 235) and the **Museo de Artes Industrias Populares** (p. 235) for a fascinating examination of the different art forms practiced in the region. On your next day, hire a car or guide to tour the lakeside villages and perhaps take a taxi to the town of **Santa Clara** (p. 240) to watch the coppersmiths at work.

Days 6 & 7: Ixtapa ★ & Zihuatanejo

Zihuatanejo is one of the most appealing beach resorts in Mexico, a small fishing village and luxury getaway that retains its traditional coastal charm. Although I prefer Zihuatanejo to its more artificial neighbor, Ixtapa also offers beautiful beaches, family-friendly resorts, and exciting nightlife. The tollway connecting the central highlands to these resorts will get you there in 4 to 5 hours. Relax for a couple of days and then catch a flight back home. See p. 359.

LOS CABOS TO THE COPPER CANYON

This itinerary offers a great deal of contrast by starting in the resort area of Los Cabos. After immersing yourself in any number of seaside activities, take a short tour of southern Baja that includes bohemian Todos Santos before crossing the Sea of Cortez and boarding a train that climbs up through rugged Sierra Tarahumara, hugging the sides of the Copper Canyon. Stop here to enjoy the beautiful serenity, and then reboard the train heading to Chihuahua, once home to Pancho Villa.

Days 1, 2 & 3: Cabo San Lucas, San José del Cabo & Todos Santos ★★

Take your time enjoying the gorgeous setting of these resort towns and the wideranging activities they offer. Rent a car to drive along the coast, and perhaps visit the town of **Todos Santos** (p. 710) for a feel of the region's character. See p. 682.

Day 4: La Paz ★★ to Los Mochis

Take a bus or *colectivo* to **La Paz** and, from there, to the ferry dock. After a 5-hour voyage, you'll arrive at **Topolobampo** (p. 672), the port area of Los Mochis.

Los Cabos to the Copper Canyon

Days 5 & 6: Bahuichivo & Cerocahui ★★★

The train departs early in the morning and, by late morning, is snaking its way through some of the most beautiful canyon land on the trip. By midday, you reach **Bahuichivo,** where you can get transportation to the town and mission of **Cerocahui.** This is an excellent place for hiking, horseback riding, and driving tours to the overlook of **Cerro Gallego.** See p. 665.

Days 7 & 8: Creel ★

Continue by train to **Creel,** where a car can then take you to the nearby **Copper Canyon Sierra Lodge** (p. 669). Here you can enjoy the peace and quiet of the sierra, visit an old mission, hike to a nearby waterfall, and meet Tarahumara Indian women, who come to sell their pine-needle baskets and other handicrafts. See p. 668.

Days 9 & 10: Chihuahua ★

You'll arrive at night. Use part of the next day to wander the historic downtown area and visit **Pancho Villa's house** (p. 677) before flying back home. See p. 673.

LA RUTA MAYA

This route, which connects the major Maya sites in Mexico, could be done moving frequently over 2 weeks, or more slowly in a month or perhaps broken up into two trips. I've condensed the trip by leaving out Mérida, but you may also want to visit the beautiful Yucatán capital. There's a risk of overdosing on ruins by seeing too many in too short a time, so pick and choose at your own pace. The best mode of travel is by rental car: The highways have little traffic and are, for the most part, in good shape.

Day 1: Arrive in Cancún

After you arrive, head for a swim in the warm waters of the Caribbean, sip a salty margarita at your resort, and dress up for a sunset dinner overlooking the lagoon. Cancún's world-class nightlife beckons if you've got the energy. See chapter 13.

Day 2: Ek Balam ★★★ & Chichén Itzá ★★★

Hop on the modern toll highway that heads toward Mérida and take the exit for Valladolid. Head north, away from town, to visit the ruins of **Ek Balam** (p. 624). Then head back to **Valladolid** (p. 620) for lunch before driving the short distance to **Chichén Itzá** (p. 614). Just outside of Valladolid, stop to see the cenotes of **Dzitnup** and **Sammulá** (p. 623). Farther on is the **Balankanché Cave** (p. 620). When you get to Chichén, check into your hotel, and then go to the **ruins** later in the evening for the sound-and-light show. See p. 615.

Day 3: Uxmal ★★★

Immerse yourself further in the ruins of **Chichén Itzá** in the morning, then continue west on the toll highway toward Mérida, and turn off at Ticopó. Head south toward the town of **Acanceh** (p. 599) and Hwy. 18. Stop to see the small but intriguing ruins in the middle of town, and then proceed down Hwy. 18 to the ruins of **Mayapán** (p. 599). Continue through Ticul to Santa Elena and the ruined city of **Uxmal** (p. 600) for an unforgettable sound-and-light show under the stars.

Day 4: Edzná

Visit **Uxmal** (p. 600) in the morning, then drive back toward Santa Elena, and take Hwy. 261 south to Hopelchén and on to the impressive ruins of **Edzná** (p. 613). Nearby is **Uayamón,** a fancy hacienda-turned-hotel (p. 582). Better still, stay at the sister property in old-town Campeche, **Hacienda Puerta Campeche** (p. 611).

Days 5 & 6: Palenque ★★, Bonampak & Yaxchilán

Take Hwy. 261 to Escárcega, head west on Hwy. 186 toward Villahermosa, and then south on Hwy. 199 to **Palenque** (p. 632), an ancient town with magnificent pyramids. The next day go to the ruins of **Bonampak** and **Yaxchilán** (p. 638).

Days 7 & 8: San Cristóbal de las Casas ★★

Keep south on Hwy. 199 toward otherworldly **San Cristóbal de las Casas** (p. 640). On the way, take a swim at **Misol Ha** (p. 639), and visit the ruins of **Toniná** (p. 639) outside of Ocosingo. From San Cristóbal, go with one of the local guides to see the Maya communities of **San Juan Chamula** and **Zinacantán** (p. 647).

Days 9 & 10: Calakmul & Becán ★★★

Retrace your steps to Escárcega and continue east on Hwy. 186. If you have time, visit the fascinating sculptures of **Balamkú** (p. 570). Settle into one of the hotels in the vicinity of the turnoff for **Calakmul,** one of the prime city-states of the Classic age of the Maya, and not often visited.

The next day, get to **Calakmul** (p. 568) early. Keep your eyes open for wildlife as you drive along the narrow jungle road; all the area surrounding the city is a wildlife preserve. Afterward, continue east on Hwy. 186 to see the ruins of **Becán** (p. 568), a large ceremonial center with impressive temples. Also in the vicinity are **Xpujil** (p. 567) and **Chicanná** (p. 568). Spend the night on the shores of **Lake Bacalar** (p. 561), where you can cool off in its blue waters.

Days 11, 12 & 13: Tulum

Drive north on Hwy. 307 to **Tulum** and settle into one of the small beach hotels there. In the morning, walk through the ruins and take in the spectacular view of the coast. On your last day, you might work on your tan at the beach, or head straight to the airport (25 min. south of Cancún) and depart.

MEXICO CITY

by Joy Hepp

> We wandered in a frenzy and a dream. We ate
> beautiful steaks for forty-eight cents in strange
> tiled Mexican cafeterias with generations of
> marimba musicians standing at one immense
> marimba . . . Nothing stopped; the streets were
> alive all night.
>
> —*On the Road,* Jack Kerouac

To walk down a Mexico City street is to wade through time and space. The ground you are walking on was once likely underwater, the site of a pre-Hispanic marketplace, or an area tread upon by conquistadors. On modern sidewalks indigenous punks rub shoulders with European businessmen, and thinkers and dreamers from all walks of life can find their inspiration.

4

This is quite an ambulatory city. A typical afternoon can involve strolling one of the many plazas or parks, snacking on *cacahuates japonesas,* and people-watching. Parque Mexico and Parque España in the **Condesa** neighborhood are usually bustling with activity on the weekends. Expect to see entire families in matching track suits riding bicycles, 20-somethings showing off fashionable dog breeds, and teenagers smooching on park benches. Most parks are also full of vendors selling local handicrafts such as wooden children's toys or wool scarves and mittens.

Mexico City is a place where the fare being served on the street corner is just as exquisite as the food prepared at upscale restaurants. I had some of the best potato tacos of my life—piled high with salsa and onions and accompanied by a sweet Jaritos soda pop—at a stand under a bridge in **Coyoacán,** and I've tried to distinguish each of the dozens of ingredients of a chicken mole placed upon a white tablecloth at a cafe in the **Roma Norte** neighborhood. Be bold when eating in Mexico City; your taste buds will thank you.

A good place to escape the din of the big city, naturally, is up in the air. Locals often lack a space for a yard, so the wide-open platform of the rooftop or terraza becomes their own personal Shangri-La with plants, wind chimes, and songbirds. Often, hotels try to re-create these places with top-level bars and/or nightclubs. One of the best in the city is at **Condesadf** in Colonia Condesa. If you get a table toward the front, you'll feel like you're at the helm of a ship—the SS *Chillax,* perhaps?

You've undoubtedly heard about Mexico City's pollution. Major steps to improve the air quality (restricted driving, factory closings, emission-controlled buses and taxis) have worked wonders, but the problem persists. On some days you won't notice it (especially during the summer rainy season); on other days it can make your nose run, your eyes water, and your throat rasp. If you have respiratory problems, be very careful; the city's elevation makes matters even worse. Minimize your exposure to the fumes and refrain from walking busy streets during rush hour. Sunday—when many factories close and many cars escape the city—should be your prime outdoor day. Also, in the evenings, the air is often deliciously cool and relatively clean.

One of the most difficult tasks one can face in Mexico City is going home early from a *fiesta*. It doesn't matter if its 8pm or 6am, you will invariably be asked why you are leaving so early and be urged to stay for *una chela mas*. This is a city where you can regularly expect to listen (and sing along) to mariachi music, dance in a posh club, or have an impassioned chat about politics until the sun comes up.

ORIENTATION
Getting There & Departing

BY PLANE   Mexico City's **Benito Juárez International Airport** (www.aicm. com.mx) is something of a small city, where you can grab a bite, have an espresso (including Starbucks), and buy duty-free goods, clothes, books, gifts, and insurance, as well as exchange money and stay in a hotel. It was recently expanded—filled with marble floors, upscale shops, and improved services—and overall has become a much more welcoming airport. (One Japanese traveler, Hiroshi Nohara, liked it so much that he lived in one of the terminals for 117 days in late 2008.) International flights depart from the newer Terminal 2 and from the international section of Terminal 1; domestic flights are accommodated by the rest of Terminal 1.

Guarded **baggage-storage areas** are near Sala D (Gate D; ✆ **55/5786-9048**) near doors 5 and 10. The key-operated metal lockers measure about .5×.5×.5m (1½×1½×1½ ft.) and cost 100 pesos daily. You may leave your items for up to a month.

The Mexico City Hotel and Motel Association offers a **hotel-reservation service** for its member hotels. Look for its booths before you leave the baggage-claim area, or near Gate A on the concourse. Representatives make the call according to your specifications for location and price. If they book a hotel, they require 1 night's payment and will give you a voucher to present at the hotel. Ask about hotels with special deals. **Telephones** (operated by Telmex using prepaid Ladatel cards, available at newsstands and gift shops within the airport) are all along the public concourse.

When departing, be sure to allow at least 45 to 60 minutes' travel time from the Zona Rosa or the *zócalo* (plaza) area to the airport—add about 30 minutes more if you're traveling during rush hour or bad weather. Check in 3 hours before international flights and 2 hours before domestic flights. *Note:* Mexican airlines will usually not let you check in for a domestic flight if it's less than an hour before departure time.

Mexico City & Environs

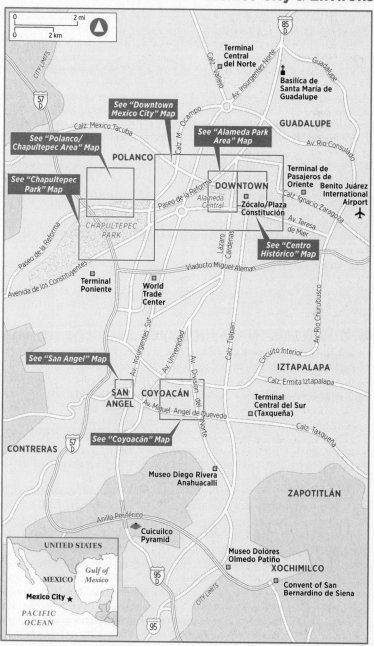

0   2 mi
0   2 km

CITY LIMITS

85
D

Terminal
Central
del Norte

Calz. Vallejo

Av. Insurgentes Norte

Guadalupe

Basílica de
Santa María de
Guadalupe

GUADALUPE

57
D

Calz. Mexico Tacuba

Calz. M. Ocampo

Av. Rio Consulado

See "Downtown
Mexico City" Map

See "Alameda Park
Area" Map

See "Polanco/
Chapultepec Area" Map

POLANCO

Terminal de
Pasajeros de
Oriente

Benito Juárez
International
Airport

See "Chapultepec
Park" Map

Paseo de la Reforma

DOWNTOWN

Alameda
Central

Zócalo/Plaza
Constitución

Calz. Ignacio Zaragoza

CHAPULTEPEC
PARK

Paseo de la Reforma

Lázaro Cárdenas

Av. Teresa
de Mier

See "Centro
Histórico" Map

Avenida de los Constituyentes

Viaducto Miguel Aleman

Terminal
Poniente

World
Trade
Center

Av. Rio Churubusco

Av. Insurgentes Sur

Av. Universidad

Circuito Interior

IZTAPALAPA

Calz. Ermita Iztapalapa

Calz. Tlalpan

See "San Angel" Map

SAN
ANGEL

COYOACÁN

Av. División del Norte

Av. Miguel Angel de Quevedo

Terminal
Central del Sur
(Taxqueña)

Calz. Taxqueña

CONTRERAS

57
D

See "Coyoacán" Map

Museo Diego Rivera
Anahuacalli

ZAPOTITLÁN

Anillo Periférico

Cuicuilco
Pyramid

95
D

Museo Dolores
Olmedo Patiño

XOCHIMILCO

Convent of San
Bernardino de Siena

UNITED STATES

Gulf of
Mexico

MEXICO

Mexico City ★

PACIFIC
OCEAN

CITY LIMITS

95

GETTING TO THE CITY FROM THE AIRPORT Ignore those who approach you in the arrivals hall offering taxis; they are usually unlicensed and unauthorized. **Authorized airport taxis,** however, provide good, fast service. After exiting the baggage-claim area and before entering the public concourse (as well as near the far end of the terminal near Gate A), you'll see a booth marked TAXI. Staff members at these authorized taxi booths wear bright-yellow jackets or bibs emblazoned with TAXI AUTORIZADO (authorized taxi). Tell the ticket seller your hotel or destination; the price is based on a zone system. Expect to pay around 300 pesos for a *boleto* (ticket) to Polanco. Present your ticket outside to the driver. Taxi "assistants" who lift your luggage into the waiting taxi expect a tip for their trouble. Putting your luggage in the taxi is the driver's job. (See also "Taxi Safety Precautions in Mexico City," below.)

The **Metro,** Mexico City's modern subway system, is cheap and faster than a taxi, but it seems to be gaining popularity among thieves who target tourists. If you take it from the airport, be forewarned: As a new arrival, you'll stand out. If you are carrying anything much larger than a briefcase, including a suitcase, don't even bother going to the station—they won't let you on with it. For Metro information, see "Getting Around," later in this chapter.

Here's how to find the Metro at the airport: As you come from your plane into the arrivals hall, turn left toward Gate A and walk through the long terminal, out the doors, and along a covered sidewalk. Soon you'll see the distinctive Metro logo that identifies the Terminal Aérea station, down a flight of stairs. The station is on Metro Línea 5 (Line 5). Follow the signs for trains to Pantitlán. At Pantitlán, change for Line 1 ("Observatorio"), which takes you to stations that are a few blocks south of the *zócalo* and La Alameda park: Pino Suárez, Isabel la Católica, Salto del Agua, and Balderas.

AN ALTERNATIVE TO BENITO JUÁREZ Toluca's **Licenciado Adolfo López Mateos International Airport (TLC)** lies just 52km (32 miles) southwest of Benito Juárez International Airport and has been a convenient alternative for Mexican nationals since it opened in 2002. In 2006 the airport started accommodating a limited amount of international traffic and now **Continental** (𝄢 **800/523-3273** in the U.S., or 01-800/900-5000 in Mexico), **United** (𝄢 **800/538-2929** in the U.S., 01-800/003-0777 in Mexico), and the Mexican airline **Volaris** (𝄢 **866/988-3527** in the U.S., or 01-800/122-8000 in Mexico) offer regular flights from the U.S. Volaris also offers a shuttle service that takes its customers to the Santa Fe financial district. Domestic flights to and from Toluca are often significantly cheaper than comparable flights through Benito Juárez.

To get to the Toluca airport by car from the Mexico City airport, merge onto Viaducto Miguel Alemán, take the exit to North Periférico, and merge onto Constituyentes. Then take the Mexico-Toluca highway. When you arrive in Toluca turn right on to Miguel Alemán Valdez and follow the signs to the airport. Depending on traffic, the drive could take up to 3 hours.

BY CAR Driving in Mexico City is as much a challenge and an adventure as driving in any major metropolis. Here are a few tips. First, ask the rental company whether your license-plate number permits you to drive in the city that day (break the rule and the fine can be well over 10,000 pesos). Traffic runs the course of the usual rush hours—to avoid getting tangled in traffic, plan to travel before dawn. Park the car in a guarded lot whenever possible.

taxi safety precautions
IN MEXICO CITY

There has been a marked increase in violent crime against both residents and tourists using taxis for transportation in Mexico City, concentrated among users of Volkswagen Beetle and *libre* (those hailed off the street) taxis. Robberies of taxi passengers are sometimes violent, with beatings and even murders reported. Victims have included U.S. citizens. Many times the robberies involve taking passengers to an ATM, where they are forced to withdraw whatever limit their card or cards will allow.

If you plan to use a **taxi from the airport or bus stations,** use only an authorized cab with all the familiar markings: yellow car, white taxi light on the roof, and TRANSPORTACION TERRESTRE painted on the doors. Buy your ticket from the clearly marked taxi booth inside the airport or bus terminal—nowhere else. After purchasing your ticket, go outside to the line of taxis, where an official taxi chief will direct you to the next taxi in line. Don't follow anyone else.

In Mexico City, *do not hail a passing taxi on the street.* Most hotels have official taxi drivers who are recognized and regulated by the terminal and city; they are considered safe taxis to use. These are known as **authorized** or *sitio* **taxis.** Hotels and restaurants can call the radio-dispatched taxis. **Official Radio Taxis** (© **55/5590-3325** or 55/5698-5192) are also considered safe. You can hire one of these taxis from your hotel; the driver will frequently act as your personal driver and escort you through your travels in the city. This is a particularly advisable option at night.

All official taxis, except the expensive "turismo" cars, are painted predominantly yellow, orange, or green; have white plastic roof signs bearing the word TAXI; have TAXI or SITIO painted on the doors; and are equipped with meters. Look for all these indications, not just one or two of them. Even then, be cautious. The safest cars to use are sedan taxis (luxury cars without markings) dispatched from four- and five-star hotels. They are the most expensive but worth it—taxi crime in Mexico City is very real.

Do not use VW Beetle taxis, which are frequently involved in robberies of tourists and are nearly phased out of existence. Even though they are the least expensive taxis, you could be taking your life into your hands should you opt to use one. In any case, never get in a taxi that does not display a large 5×7-inch laminated **license card** with a picture of the driver on it; it's usually hanging from the door chain or glove box, or stuck behind the sun visor. *If there is no license, or if the photo doesn't match the driver, don't get in.* It's illegal for a taxi to operate without the license in view. No matter what vehicle you use for transportation, lock the doors as soon as you get in. Do not carry credit cards, your passport, or large sums of cash, or wear expensive jewelry when taking taxis.

The chief thoroughfares for getting out of the city are Insurgentes Sur, which becomes Hwy. 95 to Taxco and Cuernavaca; Insurgentes Norte, which leads to Teotihuacán and Pachuca; Hwy. 57, the Periférico (loop around the city), which is also known as Bulevar Manuel Avila Camacho, to denote street addresses, and goes north and leads out of the city to Tula and Querétaro; Constituyentes, which leads west out of the city past Chapultepec Park and connects with Hwy. 15 to Toluca, Morelia, and Pátzcuaro (Reforma also connects with Hwy. 15); and Zaragoza, which leads east to Hwy. 150 to Puebla and Veracruz.

BY BUS Mexico City has a bus terminal for each of the four points of the compass: north, east, south, and west. However, you can't necessarily tell which terminal serves which area of the country by looking at a map.

Some buses leave directly from the **Benito Juárez airport.** Departures are from a booth located outside **Sala D (Gate D),** and buses also park there. Tickets to Cuernavaca and Puebla each run about 200 pesos, with departures every 45 minutes. Other destinations include Querétaro, Pátzcuaro, and Toluca.

If you're in doubt about which station serves your destination, ask any taxi driver—they know the stations and the routes they serve. All stations have restaurants, money-exchange booths or banks, post offices, luggage storage, and long-distance telephone booths where you can also send a fax.

Each station has a taxi system based on fixed-price tickets to various zones within the city, operated from a booth or kiosk in or near the entry foyer of the terminal. Locate your destination on a zone map or tell the seller where you want to go, and buy a *boleto*. See also the "Taxi Safety Precautions in Mexico City" box above.

Terminal Central de Autobuses del Norte Called "Terminal Norte," or "Central Norte," Avenida de los Cien (100) Metros (© **55/5133-2444** or 55/5587-1552), this is Mexico's largest bus station. It handles most buses coming from the U.S.-Mexico border. It also handles service to and from the Pacific Coast as far south as Puerto Vallarta and Manzanillo; the Gulf Coast as far south as Tampico and Veracruz; and such cities as Guadalajara, San Luis Potosí, Durango, Zacatecas, Morelia, and Colima. You can also get to the pyramids of Teotihuacán and Tula from here. By calling the above number, you can purchase tickets over the phone by charging them to a credit card. The operators can also provide exact information about prices and schedules, but few speak English.

To get downtown from the Terminal Norte, you have a choice: The **Metro** has a station (Terminal de Autobuses del Norte, or TAN) right here, so it's easy to hop a train and connect to all points. Walk to the center of the terminal, go out the front door and down the steps, and go to the Metro station. This is Línea 5 (Line 5). Follow the signs that say DIRECCION PANTITLAN. For downtown, you can change trains at La Raza or Consulado (see the Mexico City Metro map on the inside back cover of this guide). Be aware that if you change at La Raza, you'll have to walk for 10 to 15 minutes and will encounter stairs. The walk is through a marble-lined underground corridor, but it's a long way with heavy luggage. If you have heavy luggage, you most likely won't be allowed into the Metro in the first place.

Another way to get downtown is by **trolleybus.** The stop is on Avenida de los Cien Metros, in front of the terminal. The trolleybus runs down Avenida Lázaro Cárdenas, the *Eje Central* (Central Artery). Or try the Central Camionera Del Norte–Villa Olimpica buses, which go down Avenida Insurgentes, past the university. Just like the Metro, the trolley will not let you board if you are carrying anything larger than a small carry-on suitcase. Backpacks seem to be an exception, but not large ones with frames.

Terminal de Autobuses de Pasajeros de Oriente This terminal is known as **TAPO** (© **55/5786-9341**). Buses going east (Puebla, Amecameca, the Yucatán Peninsula, Veracruz, Xalapa, San Cristóbal de las Casas, and others) and Oaxaca buses, which pass through Puebla, arrive and depart from here.

To get to TAPO, take a Hipodromo-Pantitlán bus east along Alvarado, Hidalgo, or Donceles; if you take the Metro, go to the San Lázaro station on the eastern portion of Line 1 (DIRECCION PANTITLÁN).

Terminal Central de Autobuses del Sur (Taxqueña)   Mexico City's southern bus terminal is at Av. Taxqueña 1320 (© **55/5689-4987**), right next to the Taxqueña Metro stop, the last stop on Line 2. The Central del Sur handles buses to and from Acapulco, Cuernavaca, Guadalajara, Huatulco, Puebla, Puerto Escondido, Taxco, Tepoztlán, Zihuatanejo, and intermediate points. The easiest way to get to or from the Central del Sur is on the Metro. To get downtown from the Taxqueña Metro station, look for signs that say DIRECCION CUATRO CAMINOS, or take a trolley bus on Avenida Lázaro Cárdenas.

Terminal Poniente de Autobuses   The western bus terminal is conveniently located right next to the Observatorio Metro station, at Sur 122 and Tacubaya (© **55/5271-4519**). This is the smallest terminal; it mainly serves the route between Mexico City and Toluca. It also handles buses to and from Ixtapan de la Sal, Valle de Bravo, Morelia, Uruapan, Querétaro, Colima, Ixtapa/Zihuatanejo, Acapulco, and Guadalajara. In general, if the Terminal Norte also serves your destination, you'd be better off going there. It has more buses and better bus lines.

Visitor Information

The Federal District Department provides several information services for visitors. The **Centro Integral de Atención al Turista** (**CIAT**; © 860/640-0597 in the U.S., or 01-800/006-8839, or simply 078, toll-free inside Mexico) offers information in English and Spanish, including maps, a wide selection of brochures, and access to information from the Mexico Secretary of Tourism (SECTUR) website (see below). The office sits in Polanco at Av. President Masaryk 172 (© **55/3002-6300**), at the corner of Hegel. It's open Monday to Friday from 9am to 3pm and Saturday from 9am to 2pm.

SECTUR, Mexico's Secretary of Tourism, developed a website to address safety concerns about travel to this city and other areas in Mexico. SECTUR's website **www.sectur.gob.mx** offers perhaps not-so-objective assessments of destinations, as well as travel safety tips and help with lodging reservations throughout Mexico.

Branches of the **Mexico City Tourist Office** are in the Zona Rosa at Paseo de la Reforma and Florencia (across from the Angel de la Independencia; © **55/5208-1030**), at the TAPO bus terminal (© **55/5784-3077**), and at the airport (© **55/5786-9002**). They're generally open daily from 9am to 6pm. The **Mexico City Secretary of Tourism** website (**www.mexicocity.gob.mx**) includes details on things to do, special events, safety precautions, and tourist services.

The **Mexico City Chamber of Commerce** (© **55/5592-2665**) maintains an information office with a very helpful staff that can sell you detailed maps of the city or country and answer questions. It's conveniently located at Reforma 42—look for the Cámara Nacional de Comercio de la Ciudad de México. It's open Monday through Thursday from 9am to 2pm and 3 to 6pm, Friday from 9am to 2pm and 3 to 5:30pm.

Day and night diversions are listed in the Spanish-language magazine *Tiempo Libre,* which is published each Thursday and is available at hotels and newsstands. It also has a website, **www.tiempolibre.com.mx**. Excellent English-language sources of visitor information are the **Mexico File** (www.mexicofile.com) and **Solutions Abroad** (www.solutionsabroad.com). Current-event information and visitor tips are offered on the excellent site **www.mexicocity.gob.mx**.

People from Oaxaca are referred to as *Oaxaqueños,* the residents of Durango are *Duranguenses,* and those who live in Sinaloa are *Sinaloenses.* What are the residents of Mexico City called? After many years of debate in cantinas across the land, both the Royal Spanish Academy and the Mexican Academy of Language agree that *Chilango* is the proper term to use when referring to people from Mexico City. Theories on the term's origins vary—some wryly joke that it refers to a "body of a *chile,* face of a *chango* (monkey)"—but it's most likely of Náhuatl (Aztec) origin. Like many terms that started out as insults, *Chilango* is now used with pride and affection by many people living in Mexico City. However, *Chilango* can still be considered an insult if it is used by Mexicans in the rest of the country, who often view *Chilangos* as a stuck-up, bourgeois class. In your travels, you'll likely find that discussing one's rancor or adoration for the capital is a lively topic for debate.

Synonyms for *Chilango* include *Defeño,* which refers to the D.F. abbreviation for Distrito Federal, and *Capitalano,* but you'll have more street cred if you use the first term properly.

City Layout

FINDING AN ADDRESS   Despite its size, Mexico City is not hard to get a feel for. The city is divided into 350 *colonias,* or neighborhoods. Taxi drivers are sometimes not aware of the major tourist sights and popular restaurants. Before getting into a taxi, always give a street address, *colonia,* and cross streets as a reference, and show the driver your destination on a map that you carry with you. Some of the most important *colonias* are Colonia Centro (historic city center); Zona Rosa (Colonia Juárez); Polanco (Colonia Polanco), a fashionable neighborhood immediately north of Chapultepec Park; colonias Condesa and Roma, south of the Zona Rosa, where there are many restaurants in quiet neighborhoods; all the Lomas—including Lomas de Chapultepec and Lomas Tecamachalco—which are exclusive neighborhoods west of Chapultepec Park; and San Angel and Coyoacán, the artsy neighborhoods toward the south of Mexico City. In addresses, the word is abbreviated *Col.,* and the full *colonia* name is vital in addressing correspondence.

STREET MAPS   The **CIAT** office (see "Visitor Information," above) generally has several free maps available. Bookstores carry several local map/guides, with greater detail. The best detailed map is the *Guía Roji* (www.guiaroji.com.mx), available at bookstores in Mexico City. It features all the streets in Mexico City and is updated annually. If you're traveling with a smart phone, you can also use an app designed for Mexico City travel. Metrodroid DF is great for Android phones and BusMex and Metromex work on the iPhone.

Neighborhoods in Brief

Colonia Centro This business, banking, and historic center is the heart of Mexico City and includes the areas in and around La Alameda park and the *zócalo,* the capital's historic central square. The Spaniards built their new capital city on top of the destroyed capital of the conquered Aztec, and today it is home to more than 1,500 buildings. In the Centro Histórico—the concentrated historical center within Colonia Centro—you'll find the most historic landmarks, the most important public buildings, the partially unearthed Aztec ruins of the Great Temple, and numerous museums. The area has restaurants, shops, and hotels as well. In recent years, public improvements have spurred the development of a few new hotels here, as well as a surge in nightlife and dining options, with some exquisite bars and clubs located in historic buildings.

A $300-million face-lift was completed in 2003 in honor of the city's 675th anniversary. Mexican telecommunications magnate Carlos Slim Helú, who often, depending on the stock market, is considered the richest person in the world, has also put a lot of money into renovating the area. In addition to a beautification program for the *zócalo,* other elements of the program included the restoration and conversion of more than 80 18th- and 19th-century buildings.

A special corps of police on horseback outfitted in traditional *charro* attire (along with many female police on foot) now patrols the Centro Histórico and Alameda Park. Many speak English, and they have been specially trained in the history and culture of the area they patrol.

Chapultepec Park & Polanco The large residential area west of the city center and Zona Rosa centers on Chapultepec Park. The largest green area in Mexico City, it was dedicated as a park in the 15th century by the Aztec ruler Nezahualcóyotl. Together with the neighboring *colonia* of Polanco (north of the park), this is Mexico City's most exclusive address. With its zoo, many notable museums, antiques shops, stylish shopping, fine dining and nightlife, and upscale hotels, it's an ideal place for discovering contemporary Mexican culture. **Avenida Presidente Masaryk** is the main artery—think of it as the Rodeo Drive or Champs-Elysées of Mexico City. Some of the city's best high-rise hotels are located along the aptly named **Campos Eliseos,** Polanco's version of the Champs-Elysées.

Condesa & Roma These side-by-side bohemian neighborhoods, located just south of the Zona Rosa, are home to some of the city's hippest cafes and bars, from cutting-edge restaurants to offbeat shops, art galleries, and nightclubs. The neighborhoods are also known for their parks and restored Art Deco buildings.

Coyoacán Eight kilometers (5 miles) from the city center, east of San Angel and north of the Ciudad Universitaria, Coyoacán (Koh-yoh-ah-*kahn*) is an attractive, Colonial-Era suburb noted for its beautiful town square, cobblestone streets, fine old mansions, and several of the city's most interesting museums. This was the home of Frida Kahlo and Diego Rivera, and of Leon Trotsky after his exile from Stalin's USSR. With something of a hippie feel, it's a wonderful place to spend the day, but overnight accommodations are almost nonexistent. A fun hippie market takes place here on Sundays.

From downtown, Metro Line 3 can take you to the Coyoacán or Viveros station, within walking distance of Coyoacán's museums. Iztacala-Coyoacán buses run from the center to this suburb. If you're coming from San Angel, the quickest and easiest way is to take a cab for the 15-minute ride to the Plaza Hidalgo. Francisco Sosa, a beautiful cobblestone street surrounded by old aristocratic homes, is the main artery into Coyoacán from San Angel, which you can also walk. Or you can catch the Alcantarilla–Col. Agrarista bus heading east along the Camino al Desierto de los Leónes or Avenida Altavista, near the San Angel Inn. Get off when the bus reaches the corner of Avenida México and Xicoténcatl in Coyoacán.

San Angel Eight kilometers (5 miles) south of the city center, San Angel (Sahn *Ahn-*hehl) was once a weekend retreat for Spanish nobles but has long since been absorbed by the city. It's a stunningly beautiful neighborhood of cobblestone streets and Colonial-Era homes, with several worthwhile museums. This is where the renowned Bazar del Sábado (Saturday Bazaar) is held at Plaza San Jacinto. It's full of artistic and antique treasures and surrounded by excellent restaurants and cantinas—a wonderful place to spend a day. Other attractions in San Angel include a magnificent baroque fountain made of broken pieces of porcelain at the Centro Cultural Isidro Fabela, better known as the Casa del Risco (Plaza San Jacinto 15), and the ethereal Iglesia San Jacinto, a 16th-century church with an exquisite baroque altar, bordering the Plaza San Jacinto.

The nearest Metro station is M.A. de Quevedo (Line 3). From the center of town, take the Metrobus all the way down Insurgentes and get off at the La Bombilla stop and cross to the west side of Insurgentes; continue straight, walking up Avenida La Paz. Cross Avenida Revolucion and walk up Madero to Plaza San Jacinto.

Santa Fe Eight kilometers (5 miles) west of the town center, this is Mexico City's newest and most modern neighborhood. It includes high-tech and multinational companies, banks, Iberro Americana University, and a large shopping complex. Santa Fe looks more like a modern American neighborhood than anywhere else in Mexico City. Many of the capital's well-off young professionals have moved to this area, which has developed a booming restaurant and nightlife scene. To reach Santa Fe, take Avenida Reforma west to the Toluca highway and follow the signs to Santa Fe.

Xochimilco Twenty-four kilometers (15 miles) south of the town center, Xochimilco (Soh-chee-*meel*-coh) is noted for its famed canals and Floating Gardens, which have existed here since the time of the Aztec. Although the best-known attractions are the more than 80km (50 miles) of canals, Xochimilco itself is a Colonial-Era gem: It seems small, with its brick streets, but the streets can become heavy with traffic—it has a population of 300,000. Restaurants are at the edge of the canal and shopping district, and historically significant churches are within easy walking distance of the main square. In the town of Xochimilco, you'll find a busy market, specializing in rugs, ethnic clothing, and brightly decorated pottery.

Xochimilco hosts an amazing number of festivals—more than 400 annually—the most famous of which celebrate the Niñopa, a figure of the Christ Child that is believed to possess miraculous powers. The figure is venerated on January 6 (Three Kings' Day), February 2 (annual changing of the Niñopa's custodian), April 30 (Day of

the Child), and from December 16 to December 24 (*posadas* for the Niñopa). Caring for the Niñopa is a coveted privilege, and the schedule of approved caretakers is filled through 2031. The week before Easter is the Feria de la Flor Más Bella del Ejido, a flower fair when the most beautiful girl with Indian features and costume is selected. For more information and exact dates, contact the **Xochimilco Tourist Office (Subdirección de Turismo),** Pino 36, Barrio San Juan (© **55/5676-8879;** fax 55/5676-0810), next to Domino's Pizza, 2 blocks from the main square. It's open weekdays from 9am to 8pm, and weekends from 10am to 7pm. Attractions in Xochimilco are listed in the section "Southern Neighborhoods," later in this chapter.

To reach Xochimilco, take the Metro to Taxqueña, then the *tren ligero* (light train). From there, take a taxi to the main plaza of the town of Xochimilco. Buses run all the way across the city from north to south to end up at Xochimilco, but they take longer than the Metro. Of the buses coming from the center, the most convenient is La Villa–Xochimilco, which you catch going south on Correo Mayor and Pino Suárez near the *zócalo,* or near Chapultepec on Avenida Vasconcelos, Avenida Nuevo León, and Avenida Division del Norte. Because Xochimilco is located in the far south of the city, it can take a long time to reach in traffic during the workweek. Consider visiting it on the weekend.

Zona Rosa West of the Centro, the "Pink Zone" was once the city's most exclusive residential neighborhood. It has given way to just about every segment of society and offers an array of moderate hotels, antiques and silver shops, casual restaurants, gay bars, and kitsch nightlife venues. Although the Zona Rosa has become increasingly tacky with time, many of the streets here are pedestrian-only, and you will find inviting cafes, ice-cream shops, and shopping plazas along the way. It's a good place to shop or grab a bite, but there are few real historic or cultural attractions within the area. It's not safe to walk in this area at night.

MEXICO CITY fun-derground

Who says you need a lot of money to have a great time while traveling? For the cost of Metro fare (3 pesos!) you can get a true sense of Mexico City's quirkiness. Most major stations are also miniature underground malls, complete with fast food, snack stalls, and shops.

Zócalo station features dioramas and large photographs of the different periods in the history of the Valley of Mexico. The **Pino Suárez** station is home to the preserved ruins of a pyramid dedicated to the Aztec god Ehecatl. In addition to being the god of the wind, Ehecatl was also responsible for the cardinal directions, which is appropriate because Pino Suárez is one of the Metro's most important hubs. Science geeks will not want to miss a trip to the **La Raza** station in the northern part of the city. The "Túnel de la Ciencia" (Tunnel of

Science), a permanent exhibition maintained by the Universidad Nacional Autónoma de México (UNAM), links the platforms for lines 3 and 5 and features giant slides of fractals and embryos as well as a glow-in-the-dark rendition of the universe on the ceiling. Director Paul Verhoeven used the **Insurgentes** station as a backdrop for the 1990 Arnold Schwarzenegger flick *Total Recall*, painting the Metro cars gray in order to portray his vision of the future.

If you find yourself in the company of well-off *Chilangos*—perhaps at a gallery in Polanco or a restaurant in San Angel—mention that you rode the Metro. You'll likely be met with stunned expressions, as many members of the upper class have never set foot underground and will think you're either crazy or brave for trying it.

GETTING AROUND

Mexico City has a highly developed and remarkably cheap public transportation system. It is a shame that the sharp increase in crime and resulting safety concerns have made these less comfortable options for travelers. The Metro, first- and second-class buses, *colectivos,* and Nissan Tsuru *libre* taxis will take you anywhere you want to go for very little money—but visitor warnings about the use of public transportation should be respected. Because *sitio* taxis (official taxis registered to a specific locale or hotel) are relatively inexpensive and the safest way to travel within the city, you are best off using them.

BY TAXI Taxis operate under several distinct sets of rules. *Warning:* Read the box, "Taxi Safety Precautions in Mexico City," p. 67, before using any taxi.

"Turismo" and Sitio Taxis These are by far the safest way to travel within Mexico City. Turismo taxis are unmarked cabs, usually well-kept luxury cars assigned to specific hotels that have special license plates. Although more expensive than the VW Beetle and *libre* taxis (usually Nissan Tsurus), "turismo" taxis, along with radio-dispatched *sitio* taxis, are the safest ones to use. The drivers negotiate rates with individual passengers for sightseeing, but rates to and from the airport are established. Ask the bell captain what the airport fare should be, and establish it before taking off. These drivers are often licensed English-speaking guides and can provide exceptional service. In general, expect to pay around 250 pesos per hour for guided service, and about 15% more than metered rates for normal transportation. Often these drivers will wait for you while you shop or dine to take you back to the hotel, or they can be called to come back and pick you up.

Downtown Mexico City

NORMAL

COLONIA SANTA MARÍA LA RIBERA

GUADALUPE

POLANCO

DOWNTOWN

Chapultepec Park

area of detail

SAN ÁNGEL

COYOACÁN

XOCHIMILCO

0 2 mi
0 2 km

Ribera de San Cosme

Av Insurgentes Norte

Av Jesús

COLONIA BUENAVISTA

Zaragoza

Puente de Alvarado

SAN COSME

(Circuito Interior)

Manuel María Contreras

REVOLUCIÓN

P. Arriaga

15

COLONIA SAN RAFAEL

Serapio Rendón

Av Insurgentes Centro

Plaza de la República

COLONIA TABACALERA

14

I. Ramírez

13

Donato Guerra

Av Parque Via

A. Caso

Reforma Circle

Av Morelos

Villalongin

Jardín del Arte

J Sullivan

Atenas

Gral Prim

Bucareli

Río Tigris

Río Danubio

Río Po

Río Rhin

Río Amazonas

Río Marne

Río Neva

Río Támesis

Cuauhtémoc Circle

Lucerna

Versalles

Río Tiber

Río Sena

Río Lerma

11

Roma

Dinamarca

Berlín

Bruselas

COLONIA CUAUHTÉMOC

Río Boro

Río Guadalquivir

Río Níágara

Río Nilo

Paseo de la Reforma

Niza

Havre

Nápoles

Arcos de Belén

U.S. Embassy

10

Río Mississippi

9

Génova

12

CUAUHTÉMOC

NIÑOS HÉROES

COLONIA JUÁREZ (ZONA ROSA)

Av Chapultepec

Av Cuauhtémoc

Calz Melchor Ocampo

6

Florencia

Varsovia

Amberes

8

Puebla

Niños Héroes

Hamburgo

Praga

Londres

Liverpool

7

INSURGENTES

Oxaca

Orizaba

Jalapa

Puebla

Durango

Parque Alexander Pushkin

COLONIA

5

SEVILLA

Sevilla

Valladolid

Puebla

Sinaloa

Plaza Madrid

Monterrey

Av Oro

Av Insurgentes Sur

Córdoba

Mérida

Colima

Dr. Rafael Lucio

Acapulco

Av Guadalajara

Cozumel

Salamanca

Durango

Medellín

Plaza Río de Janeiro

Orizaba

Tabasco

COLONIA ROMA NORTE

Av Álvaro Obregón

Chihuahua

Guanajuato

Av Veracruz

4

Colima

3

Av Oaxaca

Tonalá

Plaza Luis Cabrera

Sonora

2

LA CONDESA

Parque España

1

Plaza Popocatépetl

Av Yucatán

Zacatecas

Querétaro

HOSPITAL GENERAL

Dr. Pasteur

ATTRACTIONS ●

Lagunilla Market **16**

Mercado de la Merced **17**

Mercado Insurgentes **8**

Monumento a la Revolución/Museo Nacional de la Revolución **14**

Monumento a los Héroes de la Independencia **9**

Museo Nacional de San Carlos **15**

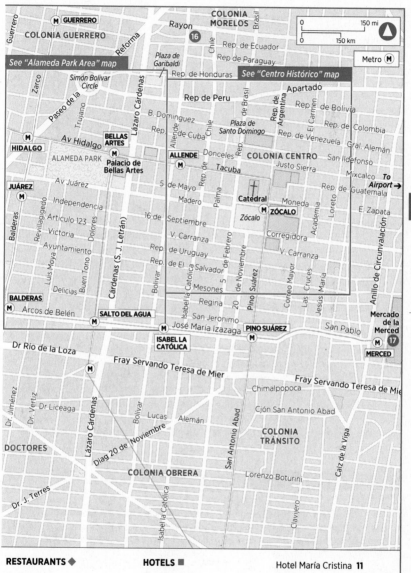

RESTAURANTS ◆

Casa Bell **6**

Cordon Bleu Casa de Francia **12**

Fonda el Refugio **7**

HOTELS ■

Condesa*df* **2**

Embassy Suites **13**

Hostal Condesa Chapultepec **3**

Hotel Four Seasons **5**

Hotel María Cristina **11**

Hotel Sheraton María Isabel **10**

La Casona Hotel-Relais **4**

Red Tree House **1**

Metered Taxis   Most of the classic green VW Beetle cabs have been phased out but their red counterparts as well as *libre* cabs provide low-cost service, but *for safety reasons, you should not use them.* Some *sitio* taxis (radio taxis, which are safe; 🕿 **55/5590-3325** or 55/5698-5192) use meters, while others have set rates. I have used **Intertaxi** (🕿 **55/2603-3268**). They have a fleet of regular cars that don't appear to be taxis from the outside. This is especially safe if you're traveling late at night, when thieves may see taxis as easy targets. Although you may encounter a gouging driver or one who advances the meter or drives farther than necessary to run up the tab, most service is quick and adequate.

BY METRO   The subway system in Mexico City offers a smooth ride for one of the lowest fares anywhere in the world (3 pesos). Twelve lines crisscross the sprawling city. Each train usually has nine cars. The Metro is open Monday to Friday 5am to midnight, Saturday 6am to midnight, and Sunday 7am to midnight.

As you enter the station, buy a *boleto* (ticket) at the glass *taquilla* (ticket booth). Insert your ticket into the slot at the turnstile and pass through; inside you'll see two large signs showing the line's destination (for example, for Line 1, it's OBSERVATORIO and PANTITLÁN). Follow the signs in the direction you want and *know where you're going;* there is usually only one map of the routes, at the entrance to the station. You'll see two signs everywhere: SALIDA (exit) and ANDENES (platforms). On the train, above each door is a map of the station stops for that line, with symbols and names.

CORRESPONDENCIAS indicates transfer points. The ride is smooth, fast, and efficient (although hot and crowded during rush hours). The beautifully designed stations (see the "Mexico City Fun-derground" box above) are clean and have the added attraction of displaying archaeological ruins unearthed during construction. A subterranean passage goes between the Pino Suárez and Zócalo stations, so you can avoid the crowds along Pino Suárez.

The Metro is crowded during the day on weekdays and, consequently, pretty hot and muggy in summer. In fact, you may find it virtually unusable downtown between 4 and 7pm on weekdays, because of sardine-can conditions. At some stations, there are even separate lanes roped off for women and children; the press of the crowd is so great that someone might get molested. Buses, *colectivos,* and taxis are all heavily used during these hours, less so during off hours (such as 10:30am–noon). Avoid the crowds by traveling during off-peak hours, or simply wait a few minutes for the next train.

 The Subway Skinny

The Metro system runs Monday to Friday from 5am to midnight, Saturday from 6am to midnight, and Sunday and holidays from 7am to midnight. Baggage larger than a small carry-on is not allowed on the trains. In practice, this means that bulky suitcases or backpacks will make you persona non grata. On an average day, Mexico City's Metro handles more than five million riders—leaving little room for bags! But in effect, if no one stops you as you enter, you're in.

Watch your bags and your pockets. Metro pickpockets prey on the unwary (especially foreigners) and are very crafty—on a crowded train, they've been known to empty a fanny pack from the front. Be careful, and carry valuables inside your clothing. Women should avoid traveling alone.

Women-Only Buses & Train Cars

In January 2008, Mexico City designated a number of city buses for women only, distinguished by conspicuous pink placards. The popular program was designed to prevent men from groping female passengers—a fairly common problem in the capital's crowded public transportation system. Bus drivers are charged with keeping men off of these buses, and their female passengers are delighted. During peak hours, Mexico City's subway system also designates the first three cars for women and children.

Be prepared to do some walking within the Metro system, especially if you transfer lines. Stations are connected by elevated walkways, corridors with shops or museum-like displays, and escalators.

BY BUS Moving millions of people through this sprawling urban mass is a gargantuan task, but the city officials do a pretty good job of it. Bus stops on the major tourist streets usually have a map posted with the full route description.

Crowding is common during peak hours. The cost is 4 pesos, the U.S. equivalent of 25¢ to 50¢. Although the driver usually has change, try to have exact fare or at least a few coins when you board.

One of the most important bus routes runs between the *zócalo* and the Auditorio (National Auditorium in Chapultepec Park) or the Observatorio Metro station. The route is Avenida Madero or Cinco de Mayo, Avenida Juárez, and Paseo de la Reforma. Buses marked ZÓCALO run this route.

The latest member of the Mexico City transportation family, the **Metrobus** was first introduced in 2006. These buses run in their own designated lanes up and down Avenida Insurgentes and often travel much faster than surrounding traffic. Most of the stops are designed to be convenient for commuters, but you can use it to access Plaza Tres Culturas from the Tlateloco stop, and the luxurious Reforma 222 shopping plaza near the Hamburgo stop; if you get off at Campeche, you'll be just a short walk from Condesa. To board these buses, purchase a smartcard for 15 pesos, which can be recharged for 5 pesos per trip. These buses are generally cleaner and faster than other forms of transportation but can get just as crowded during peak hours.

BY COLECTIVO Also called *peseros* or *microbuses*, these are sedans or minibuses, usually green and gray, that run along major arteries. They pick up and discharge passengers along the route, charge established fares, and provide slightly more comfort and speed than the bus. Cards in the windshield display routes; often a Metro station is the destination. One of the most useful routes for tourists runs from the *zócalo* along **Avenida Juárez,** along **Reforma** to **Chapultepec,** and back again. Board a *colectivo* with a sign saying ZÓCALO, not VILLA. (The Villa route goes to the Basílica de Guadalupe.) Some of the minibuses on this route have automatic sliding doors—you don't have to shut them.

As the driver approaches a stop, he may put his hand out the window and hold up one or more fingers. This is the number of passengers he's willing to take on (vacant seats are difficult to see if you're outside the car).

BY TOURIST BUS A convenient and popular way to see the city is on one of the red double-decker **Turibuses** (*©* **55/5133-2488;** www.turibus.com.mx), which offer separate circuits in the north and south of the city. Each of the double-decker

4

MEXICO CITY | Getting Around

buses seats 75 and offers audio information in five languages, plus street maps. The buses operate from 9am to 9pm, with unlimited hop-on, hop-off privileges after paying 125 pesos for a day pass (145 pesos weekends). The Chapultepec–Centro Histórico route has 25 stops at major monuments, museums, and neighborhoods along the 35km (22-mile) route, which runs from the National Auditorium to the city center (including the *zócalo*) and from there to La Plaza de las Tres Culturas (Square of the Three Cultures), returning via Avenida Reforma toward the posh neighborhood of Polanco and finally to Museo del Niño (Children's Museum). The full circuit takes a little under 3 hours. Another Turibus circuit runs in the city south, taking passengers from La Roma neighborhood south along Avenida Insurgentes to San Angel, Coyoacán, and Tlalpan. Stops include the World Trade Center, Plaza de Toros bullring, Carillo Gil museum, Perisur shopping center, UNAM, and the Frida Kahlo museum, among others. Turibus also offers a route to the pyramids at Teotihuacán (p. 126).

BY RENTAL CAR   If you plan to travel to Puebla (see chapter 12) or a surrounding area, a rental car might come in handy. However, due to high rates of auto theft, I don't recommend renting a car. Taxis and the Metro also eliminate the risk of getting lost in an unsavory area.

If you must rent, be aware that that the least-expensive rental car is a manual-shift without air-conditioning. The price jump is considerable for automatics with air-conditioning. (See also "Getting Around," in chapter 20.) The safest option is to leave the driving to someone else—**Avis** offers chauffeur-driven rental cars at its nine locations in the Mexican capital. The chauffeur is on an 8-hour shift, but the car is available to the customer for 24 hours. For prices and reservations, call Avis (© **800/352-7900** in the U.S., or 01-800/288-8888 in Mexico).

[Fast FACTS] MEXICO CITY

Banks   Banks are usually open Monday through Friday from 9am to 4pm (some later); many offer Saturday business hours, typically from 8am to 3pm. Bank branches at the airport are open whenever the airport is busy, including weekends. They usually offer ATMs and decent rates of exchange. Banks and money-exchange offices line Avenida Reforma. The Centro Histórico downtown also has banks and money-exchange booths on almost every block, as does the Zona Rosa.

Currency Exchange
The alternative to a bank is a currency-exchange booth, or *casa de cambio*. These often offer extended hours, with greater convenience to hotels and shopping areas, and rates similar to bank exchange rates. Usually, their rates are much better than those offered by most hotels. Use caution when exiting banks and currency exchanges, which are popular targets for muggings.

Drugstores   The drug departments at Sanborn's stay open late. After hours, check with your hotel staff, which can usually contact a 24-hour drugstore.

Elevation Remember, you are now at an elevation of 2,239m (7,344 ft.)—over a mile in the sky. There's a lot less oxygen in the air than you're used to. If you run for a bus and feel dizzy when you sit down, it's the elevation. If you think you're in shape but huff and puff getting up Chapultepec Hill, it's the elevation. If you have trouble sleeping, it may be the elevation. If your food isn't digesting, again, it's the elevation. Some people even find themselves getting inebriated more quickly than they would at lower elevations. There is not much you can do to help your body adjust—it takes 3 days or so to adjust to the scarcity of oxygen. Go easy on food and alcohol your first few days in the city.

Embassies & Consulates
Most countries have their embassy in Mexico City. See "Fast Facts," in chapter 20.

Emergencies The Mexico City government has an emergency number for visitors—dial *①* **060** for assistance 24 hours a day; have a local or Spanish speaker help you. **SECTUR** (Secretaría de Turismo; *①* **078;** www.sectur.gob.mx) staffs telephones 24 hours daily to help tourists in difficulty. In case of theft, you can contact **Quejas de Turistas Contra Robos** (*①* **55/5592-2677**). A government-operated service, **Locatel** (*①* **55/5658-1111**), is most often associated with

finding missing persons anywhere in the country. With a good description of a car and its occupants, they'll search for motorists who have an emergency back home.

Hospitals The **American–British Cowdray (ABC) Hospital** is at Calle Sur 136, at the corner of Avenida Observatorio, Col. las Américas (*①* **55/5230-8000;** www.abchospital. com).

Internet Access It is easier to find cybercafes in some resort areas than in Mexico City. However, most hotels that cater to business travelers offer Internet connections in their business centers. The **Internet Café,** Rep. de Guatemala 4, connected to the international youth hostel in the Centro Histórico (*①* **55/5618-1726**), is open daily from 7:30am to 10pm. The price per hour of access is 12 pesos. Many cafes offer free Wi-Fi for customers; just ask for the code and order at least a cup of coffee.

Pollution The rainy season, usually lasting from May to October, has less pollution than the dry season. Mid- to late November, December, and January are noted for heavy pollution. During January, schools may even close because of it, and restrictions on driving that are usually imposed only on weekdays may apply on weekends; be sure to check before driving into or around the city. (See "By Rental Car" under

"Getting Around," above.) Be careful if you have respiratory problems. Just before your visit, call the Mexican Government Tourist Board office nearest you (see "Visitor Information" in chapter 20 for the contact information) and ask for the latest information on pollution in the capital. Minimize your exposure to fumes by refraining from walking busy streets during rush hour. Make Sunday, when many factories are closed and many cars escape the city, your prime outdoor sightseeing day.

Post Office The city's main post office, the gorgeous **Correo Mayor,** is a block north of the Palacio de Bellas Artes on Avenida Lázaro Cárdenas, at the corner of Tacuba. For general postal information, call **FonoPost** (*①* **55/5385-0960**); the staff is very helpful, and a few operators speak English.

If you need to mail a package in Mexico City, take it to the post office called Correos Internacional 2, Calle Dr. Andrade and Río de la Loza (Metro: Balderas or Salto del Agua). It's open Monday through Friday from 8am to noon. Don't wrap your package securely until an inspector examines it. Although postal service is improving, your package may take weeks, or even months, to arrive at its destination.

Restrooms There are few public restrooms. Use those in the larger hotels and in cafes, restaurants, and museums. You might want to carry your own toilet paper and hand soap depending on what neighborhood you're in. Many public restrooms at museums and parks have an attendant who dispenses toilet paper for a "tip" of 5 pesos, in lieu of a usage charge.

Safety Read the "Safety" section in chapter 20 and the "Taxi Safety Precautions in Mexico City" box earlier in this chapter. In response to rising crime, Mexico City has added hundreds of new foot and mounted police officers, and there's a strong military presence. But they can't be everywhere. Watch out for pickpockets. Crowded subway cars and buses provide the perfect workplace for petty thieves, as do major museums (inside and out), crowded outdoor markets and bullfights, and indoor theaters. The "touch" can range from light-fingered wallet lifting or purse opening to a fairly rough shove by two or three petty thieves. Be extra careful anywhere that attracts a lot of tourists: on the Metro, in Reforma buses, in crowded hotel elevators and lobbies, at the Ballet Folklórico, and at the Museo Nacional de Antropología.

Robberies may occur in broad daylight on crowded streets in "good" parts of town, outside major tourist sights, and in front of posh hotels. The best way to avoid being mugged is to not wear any jewelry of value, especially expensive watches. If you find yourself up against a handful of these guys, the best thing to do is relinquish the demanded possession, flee, and then notify police. (You'll need the police report to file an insurance claim.) If you're in a crowded place, you could try raising a fuss—whether you do it in Spanish or English doesn't matter. A few shouts of *"¡Ladrón!"* ("Thief!") might put them off, but that could also be risky. Overall, it's wise to leave valuables in the hotel safe and to take only the cash you'll need for the day, and no credit cards. Conceal a camera in a shoulder bag draped across your body and hanging in front of you, not on the side.

If you think you've been ripped off on a purchase, contact the **consumer protection office (Procuraduría Federal del Consumidor;** ✆ **01-800 /468-8722** or 55/5625-8722; www.profeco. gob.mx).

Telephones Telephone numbers within Mexico City are eight digits; the first digit of the local phone number is always 5. Generally speaking, Mexico City's telephone system is rapidly improving (with new digital lines replacing old ones), offering clear, efficient service. Some of this improvement is resulting in numbers changing. As elsewhere in the country, the telephone company changes numbers without informing the telephone owners or the information operators. Business telephone numbers may be registered in the name of the corporation, which may be different than the name of a hotel or restaurant owned by the corporation. Unless the corporation pays for a separate listing, the operator uses the corporate name to find the number. The local number for **information** is ✆ **040,** and you are allowed to request three numbers with each information call. When dialing a mobile from within the country, dial 044 before the 55.

Coin-operated phones are prone to vandalism; **prepaid Ladatel card–only Telmex phones** have replaced most of them. Ladatel cards are usually available at pharmacies and newsstands near public phones. They come in denominations of 30, 50, and 100 pesos. See "Telephones," under "Fast Facts" in chapter 20, for information on using phones.

Weather & Clothing Mexico City's high altitude means you'll need a warm jacket and sweater in winter and even on some chilly summer nights. The southern parts of the city, such as the university area and Xochimilco, are much colder than the central part. In summer, it gets warm during the day and cool (but not cold) at night. From May to October is the rainy season (this is common all over Mexico)—take a raincoat or rain poncho. People tend to dress somewhat conservatively in Mexico City; neither shorts nor short skirts are common.

WHERE TO STAY

Not only is Mexico City one of the most exciting cities in the world, but it can also be one of the most affordable when it comes to accommodations. For around $75, you can find a double room in a fairly central hotel, including a bathroom and often air-conditioning and TV. Many hotels have their own garages where guests can park free.

The best hotel values concentrate in the downtown **Centro Histórico (historic district),** which has recently undergone a dining and nightlife renaissance. Luxury hotels are mostly in the two most popular areas for mainstream tourism: The Financial District, running alongside Avenida Reforma and near the **Zona Rosa,** attracts predominantly those in the city for business or shopping, whereas **Chapultepec Park** and the **Polanco** neighborhood are ideally located near museums and other cultural attractions. Hotels in these zones not only offer more deluxe accommodations and amenities, but also generally have their own fleets of taxis and secured entrances for guests. The crime rate, though on the decline, is still quite high; visitors should consider staying in the most secure accommodations they can afford.

If you're looking to save a few bucks on accommodations and to meet a few fellow travelers in the process, consider one of the city's budget hostels. The **Hostal Virreyes,** Izazága 8, Colonia Centro Histórico (*C* **55/2141-8087;** www.hostalvirreyes. com.mx; map p. 97), occupies a large, impressive Art Deco building near the Centro Histórico; and **Hostal Condesa Chapultepec,** Cozumel 53-A, Roma Norte (*C* **55/5211-1024;** www.hostelcondesachapultepec.com; map p. 74), a cozy two-story former residence smack between Roma and Condesa, is another great, affordable option. Both offer private rooms in addition to dorm-style accommodations.

Chapultepec Park & Polanco
VERY EXPENSIVE

Casa Vieja ★★★ ⚐ Pure Mexican style and service are the hallmarks of this luxury boutique hotel, a true gem known more to locals than tourists. Once a private residence, Casa Vieja is decorated with bold colors, unique handicrafts, exquisite antiques, and original furnishings. Each individually decorated suite is named after a Mexican artist, such as Frida Kahlo or Diego Rivera, and includes a living and kitchen area, 36-inch TV, spacious bedroom, and large bathroom with Jacuzzi tub. Notwithstanding the lovely decor, the real attraction is the highly personalized, gracious service. Guests receive a welcome drink and fruit basket upon arrival. An intimate rooftop restaurant and lounge serves made-to-order breakfast, lunch, and dinner (not included in the room rate). The only drawback is that in some rooms, you may overhear conversations in the halls and common areas.

Eugenio Sue 45 (a half-block from Av. Presidente Masaryk), Col. Polanco, 11560 Mexico, D.F. www. casavieja.com. *C* **55/5282-0067** or 55/5281-4468. Fax 55/5281-3780. See map p. 83. 10 suites. $300 junior suite; $430 master suite; $950 presidential suite. Rates include continental breakfast. AE, MC, V. Limited free parking. Metro: Polanco. **Amenities:** Bar and cafe w/light meal service; concierge; room service. *In room:* A/C, TV/DVD, hair dryer, kitchenette, minibar, Wi-Fi.

JW Marriott ★★ The JW Marriott is one of the city's most luxurious and expensive hotels, and a number of the city's most important visitors stay here. The refined marble lobby leads past world-class artwork and gorgeous flower displays to a dark-wood library and a piano lounge. The hotel is home to the Club Industriales business center, as well as La Griglia, a beautiful Mediterranean-Italian restaurant. Spacious guest rooms have panoramic city and park views, plush furnishings, and separate showers and tubs with spray jets. The full-service spa includes body and facial treatments, massages, a well-equipped fitness center, and a lovely outdoor pool and Jacuzzi. Executive-level rooms afford premium wines, gourmet food presentations, complimentary pressing and shoeshine, and free Wi-Fi. Impeccable service complements the elegant surroundings, within easy walking distance of Chapultepec Park and Avenida Presidente Masaryk. It's a short drive to the financial center.

Andrés Bello 29 (at Campos Eliseos), Col. Polanco, 11560 Mexico, D.F. www.marriott.com. © **800/228-9290** in the U.S., or 55/5999-0000. Fax 55/5999-0001. See map p. 83. 312 units. $229 and up double; $489 junior suite. AE, DC, MC, V. Valet parking 70 pesos. Metro: Polanco. **Amenities:** 2 restaurants; concierge; executive-level rooms; health club w/spa services and fitness center; Jacuzzi; piano lounge; outdoor pool; room service. *In room:* A/C, TV, hair dryer, minibar, Wi-Fi.

W Mexico City ★★★   This dramatic 26-story business hotel is a sophisticated mixture of style, comfort, and technology. The entry encompasses a series of stepped lounge areas with koi ponds; the trendy four-section Whiskey Bar also features a heated outdoor terrace. Rooms are striking, with cherry-red walls, white feather beds, terrazzo floors, plasma TVs, and a spacious and comfortable work area. Stylish bathrooms have walk-in showers and a hanging hammock; some rooms have a large circular tub. Eight high-ceiling "loft" suites afford views of Chapultepec Park, green-glass showers, and plasma TVs on the ceiling above the beds. Business traveler amenities include nine high-tech conference rooms that seat up to 400, a complete business center, and "cyber rooms" with printers, scanners, and fax. The hotel's full-service spa and health club are excellent. Solea, a fashionable seafood restaurant serving continental Mexican cuisine, offers terrace dining for breakfast or lunch.

Campos Eliseos 252 (corner of Andrés Bello), Col. Polanco, 11560 Mexico, D.F. www.starwood.com/whotels. © **888/625-5144** in the U.S., or 55/9138-1800. Fax 55/9138-1899. See map p. 83. 237 units. $170 and up double; $350 and up suite. AE, MC, V. Valet parking 90 pesos. Metro: Polanco. **Amenities:** Restaurant; 4 bars; concierge; CD and DVD library; room service; full-service spa. *In room:* A/C, plasma TV, hair dryer, minibar, Wi-Fi.

EXPENSIVE

Hotel Camino Real ★★   Although it is aging, the Camino Real remains one of the capital's top spots for business and social entertaining, and frequently sells out. Set amid Mexico's finest museums, it's a work of art in itself. Designed by renowned architect Ricardo Legorreta, the building is a classic example of contemporary Mexican architecture; more than 400 works of art by Mexican masters and other celebrated contemporary artists complement the design. Spacious rooms are brightly colored, with a sitting and desk area and armoires that conceal the TV and minibar. Some rooms could use a renovation. Executive club rooms come with bathrobes; rates here include continental breakfast, evening cocktail hour, and daily newspaper. The hotel houses a branch of China Grill, the 24-hour Bice Bistro, and the first Le Cirque restaurant outside of the U.S. The lobby's Blue Lounge—with waterfall and seating on an acrylic floor over a pool—occasionally features live music.

Mariano Escobedo 700, Col. Anzúrez, 11590 Mexico, D.F. www.caminoreal.com/mexico. © **55/5263-8888.** Fax 55/5263-8889. See map p. 83. 712 units. $170 king double; $399 executive club; $549 fiesta suite. AE, DC, MC, V. Parking 110 pesos for 24 hr. Metro: Chapultepec. **Amenities:** 6 restaurants; popular bar w/live entertainment; concierge; gym; outdoor pool; room service; sauna; steam room. *In room:* A/C, TV, hair dryer, minibar, Wi-Fi.

Hotel Habita ★   Habita deserves credit for helping to modernize the Mexico City hotel scene, even if it's now less trendy than it was a few years ago. A boutique hotel of chic minimalist design, Habita quickly became a preferred hotel in the city's most

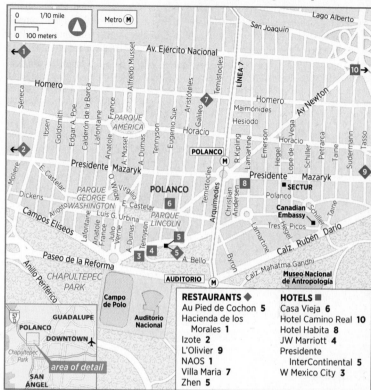

RESTAURANTS ◆
Au Pied de Cochon **5**
Hacienda de los
   Morales **1**
Izote **2**
L'Olivier **9**
NAOS **1**
Villa Maria **7**
Zhen **5**

HOTELS ■
Casa Vieja **6**
Hotel Camino Real **10**
Hotel Habita **8**
JW Marriott **4**
Presidente
   InterContinental **5**
W Mexico City **3**

4

MEXICO CITY | Where to Stay

stylish neighborhood. The white-and-steel room decor is understated, with flatscreen TVs and elegant gray Mexican marble lining the bathrooms from floor to ceiling. Beds are super comfortable, with down comforters and pillows. Located on the rooftop terrace, the hotel's **AREA** (p. 123) bar remains among the city's chic nightspots, despite newer arrivals. The lower level of the terrace features AREA's VIP section, along with a lap pool and small fitness center for guests. Adjacent to the lobby is a designer restaurant and lounge serving fusion cuisine and exotic martinis.

Av. Presidente Masaryk 201, Col. Polanco, 11560 Mexico, D.F. www.hotelhabita.com. ℰ **55/5282-3100.** Fax 55/5282-3101. See map p. 83. 36 units. From $185 superior double; $345 junior suite. AE, MC, V. Free parking. Metro: Polanco. **Amenities:** Restaurant; 2 bars; concierge; small gym; Jacuzzi; rooftop heated pool and solarium; room service; sauna; steam room. *In room:* A/C, TV, hair dryer, minibar, Wi-Fi.

Presidente InterContinental ★★   The buzzing Presidente is a leading destination for business executives and international visitors, a self-contained hotel city in a sleek 42-story building. Situated in the fashionable Polanco neighborhood, the Presidente is a short walk to some of the city's trendiest restaurants and nightlife, and to Mexico City's world-class museums housed in Chapultepec Park. The hotel's excellent restaurants, including the **Palm, Au Pied de Cochon** (p. 90), and **Zhen** (p. 90), are fed by the Presidente's wine cellar, the largest in Latin America.

Contemporary Mexican designs decorate public areas and guest rooms, which are spacious and well appointed with flatscreen TVs and city or park views. Executive club rooms include private check-in service, breakfast, and evening hors d'oeuvres and cocktails; there's also a floor dedicated to rooms with special amenities just for women. The hotel's numerous event salons make this as much of a business as a social center, and the large staff is known for its friendly, professional service.

Campos Eliseos 218, Col. Polanco, 11560 Mexico, D.F. www.ichotelsgroup.com. ℂ **800/424-6835** in the U.S., or 55/5327-7700. Fax 55/5327-7737. See map p. 83. 661 units. $136–$229 double; $329 junior suite. AE, MC, V. Parking $10 per day. Metro: Auditorio. **Amenities:** 5 restaurants; lobby bar w/live entertainment; babysitting; concierge; executive-level rooms; fitness center; room service. *In room:* A/C, TV, hair dryer, minibar, Wi-Fi.

Avenida Reforma
VERY EXPENSIVE

Hotel Four Seasons ★★★   One of the finest hotels in Mexico, the Four Seasons sets the standard for service with a staff noted for gracious manners. In the style of a Colonial-Era palace, its sumptuous guest rooms, restaurant, and bar surround a central courtyard. The luxurious guest rooms have high ceilings, plush bedspreads, Talavera lamps, Indonesian tapestries, and dark-wood furnishings. Most face the courtyard; two deluxe suites have courtyard-facing patios, and most executive suites overlook Avenida Reforma. The hotel offers expert-led private tours to many of the city's historic sites and museums; weekend guests have the option of joining a cultural tour. You won't be able to walk to any tourist attractions from here, but you are within easy driving distance to many of them.

Paseo de la Reforma 500, Col. Juárez, 06600 Mexico, D.F. www.fourseasons.com. ℂ **800/819-5053** in the U.S. and Canada, or 55/5230-1818. Fax 55/5230-1808. See map p. 74. 240 units. $415 and up double. Special weekend packages generally available. AE, DC, MC, V. Valet parking 81 pesos an hour; maximum 273 pesos for 24 hr. Metro: Sevilla. **Amenities:** Restaurant; bar; gym; heated rooftop pool; whirlpool; room service; spa; sauna. *In room:* A/C, TV, hair dryer, Internet, minibar.

EXPENSIVE

Embassy Suites ★★   One of Mexico City's newest and most modern hotels, the Embassy Suites is a welcome addition to what are mostly older hotels on this busy strip of Reforma, part of the capital's financial district. The striking glass high-rise offers two-room suites with living areas including sleeper sofas, dining nooks, and flatscreen TVs; bar areas with microwaves and coffeemakers; marble bathrooms with deep soak tubs; and bedrooms with luxury bedding. The corner and premier rooms are slightly larger than the standards. This is an outstanding value for families and travelers looking for extra space. Guests also enjoy a complimentary cocktail reception and cooked-to-order breakfast along with a 50-peso Starbucks card. This Embassy Suites houses a small but inviting indoor pool and gym, Starbucks, and an Argentine restaurant and bar. Concierge and nightly turndown service (uncommon at Embassy Suites elsewhere) are available.

Paseo de la Reforma 69 (Ignacio Ramirez), 06030 Mexico, D.F. www.embassysuites1.hilton.com. ℂ **800/362-2779** in the U.S., or 55/5061-3000. Fax 55/5061-3001. See map p. 74. 162 units. $99 and up suite. AE, MC, V. Parking 80 pesos. Metro: Hidalgo. **Amenities:** Restaurant; 2 bars; babysitting; concierge; gym; indoor pool. *In room:* A/C, TV, hair dryer, minibar, Wi-Fi.

Hotel Sheraton María Isabel   The Sheraton María Isabel's location in front of the Monumento de la Independencia is ideal: It's next to the U.S. Embassy and across Reforma from the heart of the Zona Rosa. A favorite for business travelers, the updated 1950s-era hotel offers premium amenities in all its rooms. Tower suites, the most deluxe, occupy the 14th through 17th floors and offer private check-in, butler service, and continental breakfast and evening canapés. Some have views of the beautiful Angel of Independence monument in front, and rooms on the 15th floor are specially designed for women travelers. The excellent health club includes two tennis courts, massage services, a fitness center, and small rooftop pool. The **Jorongo Bar** (p. 123), a Mexico City institution, offers some of the best live Mexican music Monday through Saturday from 7pm to 2am. The lobby bar, with its couches and TVs broadcasting in English and Spanish, is a popular gathering place for English-speaking expats and journalists during major events such as the 2008 U.S. presidential election.

Weekend Deals

Traveling business professionals make up most of the clientele of the top hotels, which often offer substantially lower rates Friday through Sunday.

Paseo de la Reforma 325 (at Río Tiber), 06500 Mexico, D.F. www.sheraton.com. ✆ **800/325-3535** in the U.S., or 55/5242-5555. Fax 55/5207-0684. See map p. 74. 755 units. $215 and up double; $250 and up tower suite. AE, MC, V. Covered parking $12. Metro: Insurgentes (6 blocks away). **Amenities:** 2 restaurants; 2 bars; concierge; full-service fitness center; privileges at nearby golf course; outdoor pool; room service; 2 tennis courts. *In room:* A/C, TV, hair dryer, minibar, Wi-Fi.

INEXPENSIVE

Hotel María Cristina This classic choice for budget travelers is conveniently located just a 10-minute walk from the Zona Rosa. Resembling an aged Andalusian palace, the hotel is decorated with wrought-iron chandeliers, mahogany furnishings, and colonial patios and corridors. Standard rooms have one king-size or two double beds, ample closets, and modern bathrooms; the larger deluxe rooms include mini-bars and air-conditioning. The large lobby with overstuffed couches and a fireplace makes for a comfortable meeting place. A grassy courtyard offers lounge chairs for reading or relaxing. The hotel location intersects at Río Neva, on the north side of Reforma.

Río Lerma 31, Col. Cuauhtémoc, 06500 Mexico, D.F. www.hotelmariacristina.com.mx. ✆ **55/5703-1212** or 55/5566-9688. Fax 55/5566-9194. See map p. 74. 150 units. 775 pesos standard double; 990 pesos deluxe double. AE, MC, V. Free guarded parking. Metro: Insurgentes. **Amenities:** Restaurant; bar; private garden. *In room:* A/C (in deluxe rooms only), TV, Wi-Fi (in most rooms).

Centro Histórico & Surrounding Areas
EXPENSIVE

Hilton Mexico City Reforma ★★ Across from Alameda park, this hotel used to be a Sheraton, and after its change is still the most luxurious option in the Historic Center. The striking marble-filled lobby leads to three outstanding restaurants, including the power lunch spot El Cardenal, and a wine bar. Spacious, modern guest rooms have been refurbished and now include Herman Miller chairs, flatscreen televisions, and work desks. Corner rooms are even larger, and suites include kitchenettes and Jacuzzis. Eastern rooms overlook the Alameda and adjacent Palace of Fine Arts; western rooms have city views. The fitness center is one of the best of any hotel in the city, and includes an indoor pool, a sun deck, and limited spa services. Despite the hotel's role as a convention center, the five-star service remains attentive and personalized. You can easily walk from here to the Palace of Fine Arts and the major destinations in the Historic Center.

Av. Juárez 70 (at Balderas), 06010 Mexico, D.F. www1.hilton.com. © **800/445-8667** in the U.S. and Canada, or 55/5130-5300. Fax 55/5130-5285. See map p. 99. 457 units. $99–$325 double; $325 business suite. AE, MC, V. Covered guarded parking $10. Metro: Hidalgo. **Amenities:** 4 restaurants; wine bar; concierge; fitness center; Jacuzzi; heated indoor pool; room service; limited spa services. *In room:* A/C, TV, hair dryer, minibar, Wi-Fi.

MODERATE

Best Western Hotel Majestic ★   A Mexico City institution that visitors should experience at least once, this classic hotel has a prime location facing the *zócalo*—reason enough to stay here. The lobby's glass ceiling is the floor of a sitting area surrounded by guest rooms. The lobby and courtyard are decorated with stone arches and fountains and beautiful tiles. Room furnishings are dated, and renovation plans continually stall. In lower-floor rooms facing Avenida Madero, street noise may be a problem. Guests in rooms that face the *zócalo* will suffer the periodic early morning flag-raising ceremony, complete with marching feet, drums, and bugle. Quieter rooms overlook the courtyard, with its own aviary. The popular La Terraza rooftop cafe/restaurant serves three meals. You can save considerably by booking directly with the hotel and by asking for promotional rates or discounts.

Av. Madero 73, Col. Centro, 06000 Mexico, D.F. www.majestichotel.com.mx. © **55/5521-8600.** Fax 55/5512-6262. See map p. 97. 85 units. $120 and up double; $170 suite. AE, MC, V. Nearby parking $10. Metro: Zócalo. **Amenities:** Restaurant/bar; babysitting; room service. *In room:* TV.

Holiday Inn Zócalo ★★ 💼   Located next to the city's historic central square, this unique Holiday Inn is decorated in colonial Mexican style with colorful art, antiques, handicrafts, and other charming touches. In fact, it's one of the most inviting Holiday Inns I've seen anywhere. Photos of old Mexico City hang in the guest rooms, which have high ceilings, hardwood floors, marble bathrooms, robes, and modern conveniences such as Wi-Fi. Smoke-free rooms are available. The rooftop terrace overlooks the *zócalo,* and the hotel also features a small restaurant, gym, concierge, and travel services. The multilingual staff caters to an international clientele that includes mostly Europeans and Americans.

Av. Cinco de Mayo 61, 06000 Mexico, D.F. www.hotelescortes.com. © **55/5130-5130.** Fax 55/5521-2122. See map p. 97. 105 units. $100 double; $140 suite. AE, MC, V. Free parking. Metro: Zócalo. **Amenities:** Restaurant; bar; concierge; gym; room service. *In room:* A/C, TV, Wi-Fi.

INEXPENSIVE

Hotel Catedral 🔑   This bargain hotel enjoys a stellar location 1 block north of Calle Tacuba on tree-shaded Calle Donceles, half a block from the Templo Mayor, and a block from the Museo San Ildefonso. Guest rooms have purified drinking water from a special tap, over-bed reading lights, and TVs with U.S. cable channels. Some have tub/showers, and others have whirlpool tubs. The furnishings are dated, however. Rooms on the upper floors afford views of the cathedral. On the seventh floor, a terrace with small tables and chairs offers great views. Because heavily trafficked streets surround the hotel, add 45 minutes to your departure time if you leave for the airport from here. In front of the big, marble-embellished lobby lies the bustling restaurant. The cozy bar beyond the reception desk also serves food. Ask for a top-floor room with a view. Breakfast costs $10 extra for a double room.

Calle Donceles 95 (btw. Brasil and Argentina), 06020 Mexico, D.F. www.hotelcatedral.com. © **55/5518-5232.** Fax 55/5512-4344. See map p. 97. 116 units. 550 pesos 1 bed, 765 pesos 2 beds, 995 pesos 3 beds. AE, MC, V. Free parking. Metro: Zócalo. **Amenities:** Restaurant; bar; room service. *In room:* TV, hair dryer, Wi-Fi.

Condesa/Roma

EXPENSIVE

Condesa*df* ★★★   Developed by the same group that brought Hotel Habita to Polanco (see above), Condesa*df* became the city's hottest place to stay after opening in 2005. Housed in a 1928 triangular Beaux Arts building, it features several rooms and bars that open onto a plant-filled interior courtyard. These spaces tend to be popular for small VIP parties and special events, which makes it a perfect place to check in on the local who's who. Interiors were fashioned by the French designer India Mahdavi, and can best be described as "Mexican with a twist"—stone floors, alpaca carpets, and a heavy dose of turquoise accents offset by cream leather sofas. Guest rooms feature high ceilings, balconies or terraces overlooking Parque España, hand-woven rugs, rocking chairs, flatscreen TVs, DVD players, and iPods. A basement "cinema" screening room transforms into a sizzling nightclub Thursday through Saturday nights.

Av. Veracruz 102, Col. Condesa, 06700 Mexico, D.F. www.condesadf.com. ℭ **55/5241-2600.** Fax 55/5241-2640. See map p. 74. 40 units. $210–$400 doubles and suites. AE, MC, V. Free parking. Metro: Insurgentes. Inquire about pets. **Amenities:** 2 restaurants; bar; club; concierge; Jacuzzi; room service. *In room:* A/C, plasma TV/DVD, hair dryer, iPod, minibar, Wi-Fi.

MODERATE

La Casona Hotel-Relais ★★ 🛏   Reminiscent of a small European luxury hotel, this exquisite establishment opened in 1996 in a formerly dilapidated 1923 building. Mexico's National Institute of Fine Arts has since designated it an artistic monument. Modern conveniences such as flatscreen TVs are juxtaposed with antique furniture in the individually decorated guest rooms. Tall interior shutter doors on guest-room windows keep out sound and light at night, and thick glass mutes street noise by day. Oriental-style rugs warm the hardwood floors and black-and-white marble throughout the common areas, decorated with prints of classical composers and fox hunts. A small French-inspired restaurant next to the lobby is a popular gathering spot. The hotel lies 3 blocks south of the Diana Circle on Reforma and 4 longish blocks west of the western edge of the Zona Rosa. More important than decor or location is the excellent service.

Durango 280 (corner of Cozumel), Col. Roma, 06700 Mexico, D.F. www.hotellacasona.com.mx. ℭ **55/5286-3001.** Fax 55/5211-0871. See map p. 74. 29 units. $130–$145 double. Rates include American breakfast. AE, MC, V. Free valet parking. Metro: Sevilla (4 blocks away). **Amenities:** Restaurant; bar; concierge; small gym w/steam room; room service. *In room:* A/C, TV, Wi-Fi.

INEXPENSIVE

Red Tree House ★ 🛏   In a town where corporate hotels and jampacked hostels are the norm, it's rare to find something in between, especially a place as comfortable as the Red Tree House. The original house was built in the 1930s and served as a resting place for visiting artists, writers, and musicians. It got its current name after co-owner Jorge Silva left the red Christmas lights on well into the new year. You will not find a more beautiful bargain than the penthouse, which could double as a studio for a well-off Condesa artist. With a fireplace, stylish living room with leather couches and local artwork, and a separate artist's studio on the patio, the only thing missing is an easel and a gaggle of fabulous friends. All guest rooms have been lovingly decorated with Mexican art and handicrafts; the cheapest rooms share a bathroom. The best part about the Red Tree House is the immediate feeling of welcome. A friendly house golden retriever named Abril greets visitors, and guests gather nightly in the kitchen or garden to chat about current events or travel adventures. The delightful staff can help with everything from arranging taxi pickup to suggesting local dining options.

Culiacán 6, Col. Condesa, 06700, Mexico, D.F. www.theredtreehouse.com. © **55/5584-3829.** See map p. 74. 16 units. $89–$95 double; $120–$165 suite; $230 penthouse. Rates include American breakfast. AE, MC, V. Metro: Partriotismo or Chilpancingo. **Amenities:** Shared computer; shared kitchen; piano. *In room:* A/C, TV/DVD, Wi-Fi.

Near the Airport

MODERATE

Hilton Airport Hotel ★   The Hilton is located inside the expansive Mexico City airport. The lobby bar, Carol's Place, has a great view of the runway, and if the international restaurant happens to be closed, there's 24-hour room service. The staff is attentive and the rooms nicely furnished, though small. Each has an entertainment system with 27-inch TV, pay movies, and video games; work desk with an ergonomic executive chair; and bath amenities by Crabtree & Evelyn. It can't be beat if you have an early morning plane. The Hilton is located on the third level of gate F1, International Arrivals; there's a complimentary shuttle from Terminal 2.

International Mexico City Airport (Sala F1, 3rd floor, door 8), 15260 Mexico, D.F. www1.hilton.com. © **800/445-8667** in the U.S. and Canada, or 55/5133-0505. Fax 55/5133-0500. 129 units. $164 double; $225 executive room. AE, DC, MC, V. Airport parking 300 pesos. **Amenities:** Restaurant; lobby bar; concierge; executive floor; small health club; room service. *In room:* A/C, TV w/pay movies and games, hair dryer, minibar, Wi-Fi.

Santa Fe

MODERATE

Distrito Capital ★★   Leave it to the folks at Grupo Habita—the ones behind exceptional properties like Condesa*df* and Hotel Habita (see above)—to inject a little style into the otherwise stuffed-shirt atmosphere of the Santa Fe financial district. Distrito Capital, styled by Parisian architect Joseph Dirand, occupies the 5th and 25th to 28th floors of a dazzling skyscraper, fit snug among glittering, towering neighbors. The guest rooms have a distinct "big city" feel, and could easily double as galleries, minus the beds. If the vintage furnishings by early modern designers like Charlotte Perriand don't win you over, the floor-to-ceiling city views will. In addition to the on-site restaurant by executive chef Enrique Olvera, a noted restaurant in the building is Cebicheria Peruana La Mar, a delightful Peruvian fusion venture with some of the best ceviche in the city.

Juan Salvador Agraz 37, Col. Santa Fe, 05300, Mexico, D.F. www.hoteldistritocapital.com. © **55/5257-1300.** Fax 55/5257-1355. 30 units. $145–$210 double; $215–$775 suite. AE, MC, V. No Metro access. **Amenities:** Restaurant; bar; gym; library; film projection room; outdoor pool; solarium. *In room:* A/C, iPod docking station, Wi-Fi.

WHERE TO EAT

Dining in Mexico City is sophisticated, with cuisine that spans the globe. From high chic to the standard Mexican *comida corrida* (blue-plate special), the capital offers something for every taste and budget. The **Polanco** area, in particular, has become a place of exquisite dining options, with new restaurants rediscovering and modernizing classic Mexican dishes. The **Centro Histórico** led a resurgence of popular restaurants and bars open for late-night dining and nightlife, which has spread to the

Condesa and **Roma** neighborhoods—which you can easily stroll to find a number of small restaurants and a myriad of cuisines. **San Angel** houses some of Mexico City's finest traditional restaurants. Cantinas, until not so very long ago the privilege of men only, offer some of the best food and colorful local atmosphere.

Everybody eats out in Mexico City, regardless of social class. Consequently, you can find restaurants of every type, size, and price range scattered across the city. Mexicans take their food and dining seriously, so if you see a full house, that's generally recommendation enough. But those same places may be entirely empty if you arrive early—here, remember, lunch is generally eaten at 3pm, with dinner not seriously considered before 9pm.

Note: Many establishments add a "cover" charge of $2 to $4 per person to the bill.

Chapultepec Park & Polanco
VERY EXPENSIVE

Hacienda de los Morales ★★ 📷 MEXICAN HAUTE CUISINE A 16th-century oasis amid one of the world's most populous cities, the Hacienda de los Morales is an enchanted place for special occasions. The Spanish colonial decor includes dark-wood furnishings, stone columns, and domed brick ceilings, with some tables looking out to garden fountains. The entrance patio doubles as an elegant bar, where you will find precious artwork and the original chapel where Spanish aristocrats once prayed. While the Hacienda is a bustling power lunch spot by day, it transforms into a romantic retreat at night. Expertly prepared food includes the best of Mexican dishes, with an excellent selection of meat, fish, and seafood, as well as pastas, crepes, and other selections. A constant stream of weddings and special events takes place in private salons surrounding the gardens. Jacket and tie are suggested for men.

Vázquez de Mella 525 (at Av. Horacio), Col. Polanco. ✆ **55/5283-3054.** www.haciendadelosmorales. com. See map p. 83. Reservations recommended. Main courses 200-400 pesos, plus a nightly per-person cover charge of 45 pesos. AE, MC, V. Daily 1pm-1am. Metro: Polanco.

Izote ★★★ MEXICAN HAUTE CUISINE   Still at the top of the city's superb dining scene, this signature venue of celebrated chef Patricia Quintana pays homage to the best of classic Mexican cooking. There are only 19 tables, and the atmosphere is simple, but what's on your plate will more than compensate. Located on the most upscale street in all of Mexico, it remains one of the capital's most popular restaurants, so reservations are essential, even at lunch. The menu is a compilation of modern versions of pre-Hispanic dishes and draws heavily on indigenous ingredients such as yucca flower, cactus, and *masa* (corn flour). Each dish is a delight. Try traditional Oaxacan *mole*, or lamb barbecued in a banana leaf. Endings are especially sweet here—save room for Tarta Zaachila, a chocolate pastry filled with nuts, accompanied by the traditional *café de olla*, coffee flavored with cinnamon and brown sugar.

Av. Presidente Masaryk 513 (btw. calles Sócrates and Platón), Col. Polanco. ✆ **55/5280-1265.** See map p. 83. Reservations essential. Main courses $25-$40. AE, MC, V. Mon-Sat 1-11:30pm; Sun 1-5:30pm. Metro: Polanco.

L'Olivier ★ BISTRO/COUNTRY FRENCH   This bright, bustling bistro would be reminiscent of an authentic French cafe were it not for the fact that its patrons tend to be business moguls and sophisticated socialites rather than bohemians. The restaurant is particularly buzzing at lunch, and more subdued at night. Although the menu changes seasonally, a regular starter is foie gras with black beans. Main courses range from pâté to soufflé. The lamb chops with mint jelly are delectable, as are the seafood linguine and the lamb couscous. For dessert, leave enough room (and time) for the chocolate soufflé. Service is attentive and efficient.

Masaryk 49-C (at Torcuato Tasso), Col. Polanco. ℂ **55/5545-3133.** See map p. 83. Reservations recommended. Average 500 pesos per person. AE, MC, V. Mon–Sat 1:30–10:30pm; Sun 1:30–6pm. Metro: Polanco.

Zhen ★★ HAUTE CHINESE This Shanghai-based restaurant is one of the capital's top choices for gourmet Chinese cuisine. The contemporary dining room has round tables with revolving centerpieces for sharing, exquisite place settings, and elegant leather chairs. Soft Oriental music plays in the background as the expert servers attentively wait on the tables. Start with pork and masago dim sum or spring rolls with chicken and vegetables. For a main course, I recommend the braised spareribs with aged vinegar, stir-fried snapper with celery, or crispy and delicious Peking duck. Dishes are beautifully presented and full of flavor.

In the Presidente InterContinental (p. 83), Campos Eliseos 218, Col. Chapultepec. ℂ **55/5327-7700.** www.zhen.com.mx. See map p. 83. Reservations recommended. Average cost per person is 500 pesos. AE, MC, V. Tues–Sat 1pm–1am; Sun 1–10pm. Metro: Auditorio.

EXPENSIVE

Au Pied de Cochon ★ FRENCH/BISTRO The *Chilangos* have had a love affair with French bistros over the last several years, and this is a perennial hot spot. A direct import from Paris, this bistro always packs in the city's jet set and fashion-forward for classic cafe fare. Open 24 hours, it's the best late-night dining option in the city. The main dining room is a spirited scene of activity and conversation, in multiple languages. Two service bars offer singles places to dine without feeling "solo," and other tables are packed in together. Pâtés, cheese plates, and exquisite salads are standard starters. The French onion soup and the foie gras are particularly delicious. For the main course, perennial favorites are the steak frites, steamed mussels, and the specialty *pied de cochon* (pigs' feet). There's also a raw bar, an excellent selection of French wines, and an ample choice of tequilas. Desserts are classically French and rich.

In the Presidente InterContinental (p. 83), Campos Eliseos 218, Col. Chapultepec. ℂ **55/5327-7756.** www.aupieddecochon.com.mx. See map p. 83. Reservations recommended. Main courses 200–600 pesos. AE, MC, V. Daily 24 hr. Metro: Auditorio.

NAOS ★★ MEXICAN/SEAFOOD A glass-paneled open kitchen and raw bar serve as the centerpiece of acclaimed chef Monica Patiño's NAOS restaurant in the fashionable Palmas neighborhood. Waiters in black ties and vests provide crisp, attentive service to the food-loving crowd. The contemporary dining room combines glass, marble, and hardwood floors with fascinating, if slightly spooky, wall sketches of *katrinas* (humorous skeleton representations celebrating death). Although the menu spans the gamut, seafood remains the specialty. Consider starting with a tuna carpaccio dressed up with fried capers and a citrus vinaigrette, followed by the mild sea bass prepared with three chiles. Fresh oysters and stone crabs from Baja California are offered, along with numerous creatively prepared fish and seafood dishes.

Palmas 425, Col. Lomas de Chapultepec. ℂ **55/5520-5702.** See map p. 83. Reservations recommended. Main courses 250–500 pesos. AE, DC, MC, V. Mon–Wed 1:30–11pm; Thurs–Sat 1:30pm–midnight; Sun 1:30–6pm. Metro: Auditorio.

MODERATE

Villa Maria ★★ ☺ TRADITIONAL MEXICAN This festive restaurant sits on a residential street of Polanco. A fun crowd comes to drink giant flavored margaritas, listen to mariachi music, and eat delicious Mexican food. The inviting dining room has two floors and is peppered with silly bar sayings such as, "I just joined alcoholics anonymous," and "I'm still drinking, but under a nickname." There are as many locals as expatriates here, and it's as much a refined celebration of Mexican food as of the culture. Tacos are available in every variety (I love the fish tacos with red adobe sauce), as are enchiladas and *mole* dishes. Other excellent suggestions include the red snapper cooked in a tamarind sauce and wrapped in a banana leaf, and the center beef cut served with a creamy tequila sauce. Whatever you order will be delicious, and you're bound to have a great time here. A kids' menu is available.

Homero 704 (at Galileo), Col. Polanco. ℂ **55/5203-0306.** www.villamaria.com.mx. See map p. 83. Reservations recommended. Main courses 95–250 pesos. AE, DC, MC, V. Mon–Sat 1:30pm–midnight; Sun 1:30–7pm. Metro: Polanco.

Zona Rosa & Surrounding Areas

If you're up for a culinary adventure, dine at the student-staffed **Cordon Bleu Casa de Francia,** Havre 15, Zona Rosa (ℂ **55/5208-1868;** www.lcbmexico.com/restaurante.cfm; map p. 74), a training ground for Mexico's up-and-coming chefs. The restaurant occupies two lovely dining rooms inside the Casa de Francia, a French cultural center. The menu varies; it's a great way to sample imaginative variations on classics and local cuisine. Wines by the glass are available. It's open Monday to Saturday from 8:30am to noon and 1:30 to 6pm.

EXPENSIVE

Casa Bell ★ INTERNATIONAL MEXICAN   A longtime favorite of Mexico City's political and business elite, Casa Bell is probably the capital's key power-lunch venue. Expect to find it filled every day by 3pm (peak lunch hour) with political and business leaders. The lovely terrace begins to fill up around 2pm, as birds chirp from strategically placed cages around the patio. Exceptionally well-trained waiters move attentively around the tables as lunch unfolds, and they are likely to recommend dishes such as the duck tacos, *filete Chemite* (filet mignon), or *robalo* (sea bass) prepared any way you like. Diners typically come dressed in suits and tend to linger over their meals and perhaps a few margaritas. Finish off with a delectable pastry from the dessert cart.

Praga 14 (off Paseo de la Reforma), Zona Rosa. ℂ **55/5208-3967.** See map p. 74. Reservations recommended. Average of 420 per person total. AE, MC, V. Daily 1–7pm. Metro: Insurgentes.

MODERATE

Fonda El Refugio ★★ MEXICAN   More than 40 years of tradition have shaped the service, food, and atmosphere here, making this a special place for authentic Mexican dining. It's small and unusually congenial, with a large fireplace decorated with gleaming copper pots and pans. The restaurant manages the almost impossible task of being both refined and informal. The menu runs the gamut of Mexican cuisine, from *arroz con plátanos* (rice with fried bananas) to *enchiladas con mole poblano,* topped with the rich, thick, spicy chocolate sauce of Puebla. For a main course, I recommend the *huachinango a la veracruzana* (Veracruz-style red snapper with tomatoes and olives). Or if you're in a spicy mood, the *chiles poblanos* stuffed with ground beef or cheese. For dessert, opt for the coconut candy or the mouthwatering flan. The tortillas are handmade, and the margaritas are potently delicious. Fonda El Refugio is very popular, especially on Saturday night, so get here early.

Liverpool 166 (btw. calles Florencia and Amberes), Col. Juárez Zona Rosa. ℂ **55/5207-2732** or 55/5525-8128. See map p. 74. Reservations recommended. Main courses 150–250 pesos. AE, MC, V. Daily 1–11pm. Metro: Insurgentes.

Centro Historico & Surrounding Areas

MODERATE

Café Tacuba ★★ MEXICAN   One of the city's most famous restaurants, Café Tacuba dates from 1912 and offers a handsome Colonial-Era atmosphere. Guests are welcomed into one of two long dining rooms, with brass lamps, dark oil paintings, and a large mural of nuns working in a kitchen. The menu is authentic Mexican with traditional dishes, including tamales, enchiladas, chiles rellenos, *mole,* and *pozole.* A wonderful group of medieval-costumed singers entertain Wednesday to Sunday from 2 to 10pm; their sound is like the melodious *estudiantina* groups of Guanajuato accompanied by mandolins and guitars. A trio or quartet plays romantic boleros on Mondays and Tuesdays from 8 to 10pm.

Tacuba 28 (btw. República de Chile and Bolívar), Col. Centro. ⓒ **55/5512-8482** or 55/5518-4950. See map p. 97. Breakfast 50–200 pesos; main courses 80–200 pesos. AE, MC, V. Daily 8am–11:30pm. Metro: Allende.

La Casa de las Sirenas ★ TRADITIONAL MEXICAN   The "house of mermaids," a 16th-century building constructed with rocks from a pyramid, is one of the loveliest restaurants in the historic center. It sits above the famous cantina with the same name (p. 124) and has a wonderful rooftop terrace with a view to the back of the Cathedral and Templo Mayor. The food is as novel as the setting. Start with classic Mexican noodle soup with chicken liver, or perhaps the stuffed crepes with chicken, squash flower, and mushrooms. The best main dishes are beef medallions in a mustard seed sauce, sea bass generously stuffed with shrimp and mushrooms, and Cornish hen served with a mango *mole* sauce. Pair your dish with one of the 250 tequilas on offer. Live music is offered on weekends.

República de Guatemala 32 (behind the Cathedral), Col. Centro. ⓒ **55/5704-3273.** www.lacasadelas sirenas.com.mx. See map p. 97. Reservations recommended. Main courses 220–250 pesos. AE, MC, V. Mon–Sat 11am–11pm; Sun 11am–6pm. Metro: Zócalo.

Restaurant Danubio ★★ SPANISH   Danubio has been a Mexico City tradition since 1936, and it remains an excellent choice for dining in the Historic Center. Photos of celebrity diners line the walls of the classically European-style room. The Basque-inspired menu offers a range of selections emphasizing seafood, and the house specialty is *langostinos* (baby crayfish). Much of the food is prepared on an old coal and firewood stove. Danubio, which lies south of La Alameda, is also noted for its excellent wine cellar.

República de Uruguay 3 (near Bolivar), Alameda. ⓒ **55/5512-0912.** www.danubio.com. See map p. 99. Reservations recommended. Main courses 150–400 pesos. AE, DC, MC, V. Daily 1–10pm. Metro: Bellas Artes or Salto del Agua.

Coyoacán

MODERATE

Corazon de Maguey ★★★ MEXICAN   Forget tacos and margaritas. If you want a true "authentic" Mexican meal—one worthy of the gods—it ought to be accompanied with *chapulines* (dried grasshoppers) and *mezcal* (fermented agave drink). Although this restaurant has undergone quite a few name changes over the years, its food and atmosphere haven't changed. The bold colors and Oaxacan artwork make the idea of washing down a handful of dead insects with a glass of firewater a bit more palatable. The lively restaurant and bar is located off Coyoacán's artsy main square. The *molote de plátano,* an appetizer of puréed plantains and a potent tomato sauce, is worth the trip to the south of the city. In a feat of mixologic genius, the bartenders have

TAKING IT TO THE streets

While Mexico City is home to some of the world's best upscale restaurants, the real culinary adventures can be found sizzling in the street. If you're on a budget, street food can also keep you sustained for cheap. Just about every *colonia* has its own street food *puesto* (stand) of choice. The best way to find good street food is to ask a variety of different residents and note when the same answer repeatedly comes up. If you make it to only one street food purveyor while you're in town, **Tacos Chupacabra** in Coyoacán is your best bet. It's located under the Viaducto Río Churubusco (no phone) near the posh Centro Coyoacán shopping mall. Don't be scared away by the fact that it's located under a freeway bridge. You came to Mexico for the ambience, right? The tacos are delicious, and toppings include everything from spicy mashed potatoes to jalapeño-flavored carrots. The place is always hopping with university students and locals headed to and from the Coyoacán Metro stop. If you're watching your weight, you can order a "Chupas light," which is made with one tortilla instead of two. You can have a feast for less than 50 pesos.

Some other great finds are **Tacos Gus,** on the corner of Michoacán and Amsterdam in Condesa (✆ **044-55/1384-3077;** www.tacosgus.com); **El Califa** (✆ **55/5271-6285**), on Altata 22 in Condesa; **Beatricita** (✆ **55/5511-4213**), on Londres between Florencia and Varsovia in Zona Rosa; or, for a surprisingly rare treat in Mexico City, a big juicy burrito with almond chipotle salsa at the **Los Burritos** stand on the corner of Insurgentes and Havre (✆ **55/5208-8737**).

Mexico City has several other unique street food offerings, which can be found in just about every neighborhood. *Tlacoyos* consist of a thick, oval-shaped blue-corn tortilla stuffed with beans, cheese, or fava beans and topped with cream, lettuce, and any number of meats. Unique to the capital are *tortas de tamal,* which are essentially tamal sandwiches with salsa on top. Another favorite is *elotes,* or corn on the cob served on a stick, popsicle style. If you add all the possible toppings—mayonnaise, cream, Oaxacan cheese, chile, lime, and pepper—you can easily double the weight of your delicious cornsicle. A good place for street food is the *antojitos* (little snacks) market off the main square behind the Guadalupana church in Coyoacán.

created an impressive menu of mezcal-based cocktails, including the Caipirinha Mezcalera, which features mezcal, salt of the worm, lime, orange, and grapefruit juices.

Plaza Jardín Centenario 9-A, Coyoacán. ✆ **55/5554-7555.** www.losdanzantes.com. See map p. 103. Main courses 100–250 pesos. AE, MC, V. Mon–Sun 1:30–11pm.

Cantinas

Cantina La Guadalupana ★★ 🍴 MEXICAN   Opened in 1928, this cantina lies in Coyoacán. From the entrance—off a narrow cobblestone street—to the antiquated bar, a sense of nostalgia permeates the comfortable, jovial cantina. The operation is as traditional as the menu. For those who are only drinking, waiters bring the customary small plates of complimentary snacks (called *botanas*) that range from crisp jicama slices with lime and chile to pigs' feet in a red sauce. It's easy to imagine the communist conversations that must have bounced off the walls here in Frida and Diego's day.

Higuera 2 and Caballo Calco (1 block from the central plaza), Coyoacán. ✆ **55/5554-6253.** See map p. 103. Main courses 70–180 pesos; mixed drinks 30–85 pesos, more for premium tequilas. AE, MC, V. Mon–Sat 1pm–midnight. Metro: Coyoacán.

In Mexico, the preparation and consumption of espresso have been considered an art form for generations. You can find the best coffee in small cafes with a crowd of regulars who congregate to catch up on the local *chisme* (gossip).

Café La Habana, downtown at Bucareli and Morelos (© **55/5546-0255**), is one of the most famous, a long-standing cafe with a rich history—and a reputation for strong coffees, all roasted and ground in-house. Ask the waiter and he'll tell you how Fidel Castro and Che Guevara planned the Cuban revolution while sipping an espresso *cortao*. Strangely, it's Mexican and not Cuban food served here. The cafe is open Monday through Thursday from 7am to 11:30pm, Friday and Saturday from 7am to 1am, and Sunday from 8am to 10pm.

In the Centro Histórico near the Zócalo, **Mumedi,** Francisco I. Madero 74 (© **55/5510-8609**), is a hip designer cafe popular with artists, architects, and graphic designers. Attached to the cafe is a bookstore and gallery featuring contemporary art objects and changing exhibitions. It's open Tuesday through Sunday from 8am to 9pm and Monday from 11:30am to 9pm.

Bohemian-style coffeehouses are in Roma Norte, frequented by artists and trendy urbanites. One of the most popular is **Café de Carlo,** Orizaba 115 between Mérida and Álvaro Obregón (© **55/5574-5647**; Mon–Fri 8am–10pm, Sat 8am–9pm, Sun 9am–5pm). Nearby Álvaro Obregón is a wide boulevard lined with independent coffee shops that each offer their own quirks and charms.

Just north of Roma Norte in the Zona Rosa the sidewalk cafe **Konditori,** Genova 61 (© **55/5511-0722**), is another good option, on a pedestrian-only street. It's open daily 7am to midnight.

The Condesa is another top cafe zone and **El Péndulo,** Nuevo León 115 (© **55/5286-9493**), close to Insurgentes, is a favorite. It combines its cafe setting with a book and music store and tends to draw intellectuals, writers, and students. It frequently hosts live music and poetry readings. It's open Monday through Friday from 8am to 11pm and weekends from 10am to 11pm. Another branch is in the Zona Rosa at Hamburgo 126.

La Opera ★★ 🖼 INTERNATIONAL   La Opera, 3 blocks east of La Alameda, is the most opulent of the city's cantinas. Slide into a dark-wood booth below gilded baroque ceilings, patches of beveled mirror, and exquisite small oil paintings. Or opt for a linen-covered table with a basket of fresh bread. La Opera is the Mexican equivalent of a London gentlemen's club, although it has become so popular for dining that fewer and fewer men play dominoes. Instead, you see people enjoying romantic interludes in cavernous booths—but tables of any kind are hard to find. Service is best if you arrive for lunch, when it opens, or go after 5pm, when the throngs have diminished; the jacketed waiters cater to regulars at the expense of unknown diners. The menu is unimpressive, but the atmosphere and drinks are excellent. Try a margarita or a classic tequila. Specialties include Spanish tapas, Caesar salad, and Veracruz-style red snapper with olives and tomatoes. While you wait for your meal, look to the ceiling for the bullet hole that legend says Pancho Villa left when he galloped in on a horse. The cantina is half a block toward the *zócalo* from Casa de los Azulejos.

Cinco de Mayo 10, Col. Centro. © **55/5512-8959.** See map p. 99. Reservations recommended at lunch. Average price of 350 pesos per person. AE, MC, V. Mon–Sat 1pm–midnight; Sun 1–6pm. Metro: Bellas Artes.

EXPLORING MEXICO CITY

The diversity of Mexico City's attractions springs from its complex history. From simple bustling *mercados* to museums filled with treasures of artistic and historic significance, Mexico City has layers and layers of cultural richness to explore.

Mexico City was built on the ruins of the ancient city of Tenochtitlan. A downtown portion of the city, comprising almost 700 blocks and 1,500 buildings, is designated the Centro Histórico (Historic Center). The area has surged in popularity, and once-neglected buildings are being converted into fashionable shops and restaurants, recalling its former colonial charm.

Remember that this is a major Latin city; dress is more professional and formal here than in other parts of the country. The altitude keeps the temperature mild, which is often a surprise for travelers with preconceptions of Mexico as perpetually hot. In summer, always be prepared for rain, which falls for an hour or two almost daily. In winter, carry a jacket or sweater—stone museums are chilly inside, and when the sun goes down, the outside air gets quite cold. If you want to blend in with the crowd, black is always the new black, especially in the winter.

The Top Attractions

Basílica de Santa María de Guadalupe ★★

Within the northern city limits is the famous Basílica of Guadalupe—not just another church, but the central place of worship for Mexico's patron saint and the home of the image responsible for uniting pre-Hispanic Indian mysticism with Catholic beliefs. It is virtually impossible to understand Mexico and its culture without appreciating the national devotion to Our Lady of Guadalupe. The blue-mantled Virgin of Guadalupe is the most revered image in the country, and you will see her countenance wherever you travel. This is also one of the most important religious sites for Catholics.

The Basílica occupies the site where, on December 9, 1531, a poor Indian named Juan Diego Cuauhtlatoatzin reputedly saw a vision of a beautiful lady in a blue mantle. The local bishop, Zumárraga, was reluctant to confirm that Juan Diego had indeed seen the Virgin Mary, so he asked the peasant for evidence. Juan Diego saw the vision a second time, on December 12, and when he asked the Virgin for proof, she instructed him to collect the roses that began blooming in the rocky soil at his feet. He gathered the flowers in his cloak and returned to the bishop. When he unfurled his cloak, the flowers dropped to the ground and the image of the Virgin was miraculously emblazoned on the rough-hewn cloth. The bishop immediately ordered the building of a church on the spot, and upon its completion, the cloth with the Virgin's image was hung in a place of honor, framed in gold. Since that time, millions of the devout and the curious have come to view the miraculous image that experts, it is said, are at a loss to explain. So heavy was the flow of visitors—many approached for hundreds of yards on their knees—that the old church, already fragile, was insufficient to handle them. An audacious new Basílica, designed by Pedro Ramírez Vazquez, the same architect who designed the breathtaking Museo Nacional de Antropología, opened in 1987.

The miracle cloak hangs behind bulletproof glass above the altar of the new Basilica. Moving walkways going in two directions transport the crowds a distance below the cloak. If you want to see it again, take the people-mover going in the opposite direction; you can do it as many times as you want.

DÍA DE LAS bicis

The traffic-congested streets of Mexico City can be daunting for drivers, let alone travelers who wish to reach their destination on two wheels. However, every Sunday bicycles rule. As part of a program called *Muévete en Bici* (Get Moving on a Bike), the city shuts down the middle lanes of Reforma—from near the entrance of Chapultepec Park to the *zócalo*, although the route can change depending on construction or special events—one of the city's most prominent avenues, so that up to 10,000 cyclists, and their friends the runners, walkers, and even the odd stilt walker, can have free rein of the pavement. The best part is that the route passes by some of the city's most famous monuments and museums, many of which are free to the public on Sundays. The streets are cleared for bicyclists from 8am to 2pm.

In early 2010 the city launched **Eco-Bici** (✆ **55/5005-2424;** www.ecobici. df.gob.mx), a bike-sharing service. With more than 80 stations scattered across **Roma, Condesa, Zona Rosa,** and **Centro Historico,** this is by far the most convenient option for commuters and leisurely riders alike. Although the program was designed with locals in mind, visitors are also welcome to pay the annual fee of 300 pesos at one of the customer service centers—either on Rosas Moreno 152 B. in Colonia San Rafael or Nuevo Leon 78 in Condesa. In exchange you receive an EcoBici card, which grants you access to the red bikes parked at the stations. Simply return the bike when you've finished to any EcoBici station.

In 2002, the pope declared Juan Diego a saint, a very big deal in this predominantly Catholic country; he was the first Mexican to achieve sainthood. The achievement was not, however, without controversy—Juan Diego's images have increasingly taken on a "European" appearance, and native Mexicans insist that Juan Diego be portrayed as the dark-skinned indigenous peasant he was.

To the right of the modern basilica is the Old Basílica, which used to house the cloak. To the back of it lies the entrance to the Basílica Museum, with a very good display of religious art in restored rooms. One of the side chapels, with a silver altar, is adjacent to the museum. Nearby are several gift shops specializing in religious objects and other folk art.

Outside the museum lies a garden commemorating the moment Juan Diego showed the cloak to the archbishop. Numerous photographers with colorful backdrops gather there to capture your visit on film. At the top of the hill, behind a third basilica built in 1950, is the **Panteón del Tepeyac,** a cemetery where big names such as Santa Anna and Velasco are buried. The climb up the steps, though potentially tiring, is worthwhile for the view from the top.

If you visit Mexico City on **December 12,** you will witness the grand festival in honor of the Virgin of Guadalupe. The square in front of the basilica fills with the pious and the party-minded as prayers, dances, and a carnival atmosphere attract thousands of the devout. Many visitors combine a trip to the basilica with one to the **ruins of Teotihuacán,** as both are out of the city center in the same direction.

Plaza de las Américas 1, Villa de Guadalupe. ✆ **55/5577-6022.** www.virgendeguadalupe.org.mx. See map p. 65. Free admission; museum 5 pesos. Daily 6am–8pm. Free guided tours (in Spanish) Fri–Sat noon. Metro: Basílica or La Villa. Signs lead the way along the 15-min. walk to the entrance of the Basílica. No shorts, food, or drinks are allowed inside.

Centro Histórico

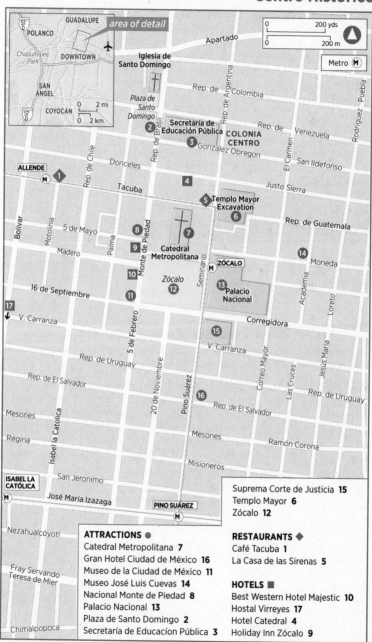

ATTRACTIONS ●
Catedral Metropolitana **7**
Gran Hotel Ciudad de México **16**
Museo de la Ciudad de México **11**
Museo José Luis Cuevas **14**
Nacional Monte de Piedad **8**
Palacio Nacional **13**
Plaza de Santo Domingo **2**
Secretaría de Educacíon Pública **3**
Suprema Corte de Justicia **15**
Templo Mayor **6**
Zócalo **12**

RESTAURANTS ◆
Café Tacuba **1**
La Casa de las Sirenas **5**

HOTELS ■
Best Western Hotel Majestic **10**
Hostal Virreyes **17**
Hotel Catedral **4**
Holiday Inn Zócalo **9**

Museo Frida Kahlo ★★★   Although during her lifetime Frida Kahlo was known principally as the wife of muralist Diego Rivera, today her art surpasses his in popularity. Certainly, the 2002 Salma Hayek movie *Frida* did much to bring this Mexican icon to the attention and appreciation of millions more. Kahlo dedicated her life to both her painting and her passionate, tortured love for her husband. Her emotional and physical pain—her spine was pierced during a serious streetcar accident in her youth—were the primary subjects of her canvases, many of which are self-portraits. Her paintings are now acknowledged as exceptional works of Latin American art and some of the purest artistic representations of female strength and struggle ever created. As her paintings have surged in renown and price, so has interest in the life of this courageous, provocative, and revolutionary woman.

Kahlo was born in this house on July 7, 1910, and lived here with Rivera from 1929 to 1954. During the 1930s and 1940s, it was a popular gathering place for intellectuals. As you wander through the rooms of the cornflower-blue house, you'll get a glimpse of the life they led. Most of the rooms remain in their original state, with mementos everywhere. Tiny clay pots hang about; the names Diego and Frida are painted on the walls of the kitchen. In the studio upstairs, a wheelchair sits next to the easel with a partially completed painting surrounded by brushes, palettes, books, photographs, and other intimate details of the couple's art-centered lives. Much of the movie *Frida* was filmed in this house.

Frida and Diego collected pre-Columbian art, and many of the rooms contain jewelry and terra-cotta figurines from Teotihuacán and Tlatelolco. Kahlo even had a mock-up of a temple built in the garden to exhibit her numerous pots and statues. On the back side of the temple are several skulls from Chichén Itzá. A cafe on the first floor serves light snacks, and the adjacent bookstore offers a full range of Kahlo and Rivera books and other commercialized memorabilia.

Londres 247, Coyoacán. ✆ **55/5554-5999.** www.museofridakahlo.org.mx. See map p. 103. Admission 55 pesos. No cameras allowed. Tues–Sun 10am–5:45pm. Metro: Coyoacán.

Museo Nacional de Antropología ★★★   Occupying approximately 4,100 sq. m (44,132 sq. ft.), Mexico City's anthropology museum is regarded as one of the top museums in the world. It offers the single best introduction to the culture of Mexico.

Inside the museum is an open courtyard (containing the Chávez Morado fountain) with beautifully designed rooms running around three sides on two levels. The **ground-floor rooms** are devoted to history—from prehistoric days to the most recently explored archaeological sites—and are the most popular among studious visitors. These rooms include dioramas of Mexico City when the Spaniards arrived, and reproductions of part of a pyramid at Teotihuacán. The Aztec calendar stone "wheel" occupies a proud place.

Save some time and energy for the livelier and more readily comprehensible **ethnographic rooms** upstairs. This section is devoted to the way people throughout Mexico live today, complete with straw-covered huts, recordings of songs and dances, crafts, clothing, and lifelike models of village activities. This floor, a living museum, strikes me as vital to the understanding of contemporary Mexico because of the importance of pre-Hispanic customs in Mexican village life.

The museum has a lovely, moderately priced restaurant with cheerful patio tables. ***Note:*** Most of the museum is wheelchair accessible; however, assistance will be needed in places.

Paseo de la Reforma y Calzada Gandhi s/n, Chapultepec Polanco. ✆ **55/5553-6266.** www.mna.inah. gob.mx. See map p. 101. Admission 51 pesos; free Sun for residents of Mexico. Still camera 30 pesos, amateur video camera 45 pesos; no tripods or flash permitted. Tues–Sun 9am–7pm. Metro: Auditorio.

Alameda Park Area

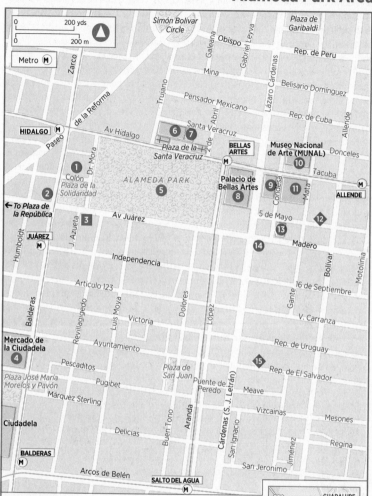

ATTRACTIONS ●

Casa de los Azulejos **13**
Correo (Post Office) **9**
FONART **2**
Juárez Monument **5**
La Torre Latinoamericana **14**
Mercado de la Ciudadela **4**
Museo Franz Mayer **6**
Museo Mural Diego Rivera **1**
Museo Nacional de Arte **10**

Museo Nacional de la Estampa **7**
Palacio de Bellas Artes **8**
Palacio de Minería **11**

RESTAURANTS ◆

La Opera **12**
Restaurante Danubio **15**

HOTELS ■

Hilton Mexico City Reforma **3**

Palacio Nacional and the Diego Rivera Murals ★★ This complex of countless rooms, wide stone stairways, and numerous courtyards adorned with carved brass balconies was once where the president of Mexico worked, and it remains an important site for presidential meetings and events. But it's better known for the fabulous second-floor Diego Rivera murals depicting the history of Mexico. Begun in 1692 on the site of Moctezuma II's "new" palace, this building became the site of Hernán Cortez's home and the residence of colonial viceroys. It has changed much in 300 years, taking on its present form in the late 1920s, when the top floor was added. Just 30 minutes here with an English-speaking guide provides essential background for an understanding of Mexican history. The cost of a guide is negotiable: 150 pesos or less, depending on your bargaining ability.

Enter by the central door, over which hangs the bell rung by Padre Miguel Hidalgo when he proclaimed Mexico's independence from Spain in 1810. Each September 15, Mexican Independence Day, the president of Mexico stands on the balcony above the door to echo Hidalgo's famous *grito* (cry) to the thousands of spectators who fill the *zócalo*. Take the stairs to the Rivera murals, which were painted over a 25-year period. The *Legend of Quetzalcóatl* depicts the famous tale of the feathered serpent bringing a blond-bearded white man to the country. When Cortez arrived, many Aztecs, recalling this legend, believed him to be Quetzalcóatl. Another mural tells of the American Intervention, when American invaders marched into Mexico City during the War of 1847. It was on this occasion that the military cadets of Chapultepec Castle (then a military school) fought bravely to the last man. The most notable of Rivera's murals is the *Great City of Tenochtitlan,* a study of the original settlement in the Valley of Mexico. It showcases an Aztec market scene with the budding city in the background and includes a beautiful representation of Xochiquetzal, goddess of love, with her crown of flowers and tattooed legs.

Diego Rivera, one of Mexico's legendary muralists, left an indelible stamp on Mexico City, his painted political themes affecting the way millions view Mexican history. Additional examples of Rivera's stunning and provocative interpretations are found at the Bellas Artes, the National Preparatory School, the Department of Public Education, the National School of Agriculture at Chapingo, the National Institute of Cardiology, and the Museo Mural Diego Rivera (which houses the mural formerly located in the now-razed Hotel del Prado).

Palacio Nacional, Av. Pino Suárez, facing the *zócalo*. No phone. See map p. 97. Free admission, but visitor tags required; be prepared to show a form of photo identification. Daily 9am–4:30pm, but expect sporadic closings for government events. Metro: Zócalo.

Templo Mayor and Museo del Templo Mayor ★★★ In 1978, workmen digging on the east side of the Metropolitan Cathedral, next to the Palacio Nacional, unearthed an exquisite Aztec stone of the moon goddess Coyolxauhqui. Major excavations by Mexican archaeologists followed, and they uncovered interior remains of the Pyramid of Huitzilopochtli, also called the Templo Mayor (Great Temple)—the most important religious structure in the Aztec capital. What you see are the remains of pyramids that were covered by the great pyramid the Spaniards saw upon their arrival in the 16th century.

At the time of the 1521 conquest, the site was the center of religious life for the city of 200,000. No other museum illustrates the variety and splendor of the Aztec Empire the way this one does. All 6,000 pieces came from the relatively small plot of excavated ruins just in front of the museum. Strolling along the walkways built over

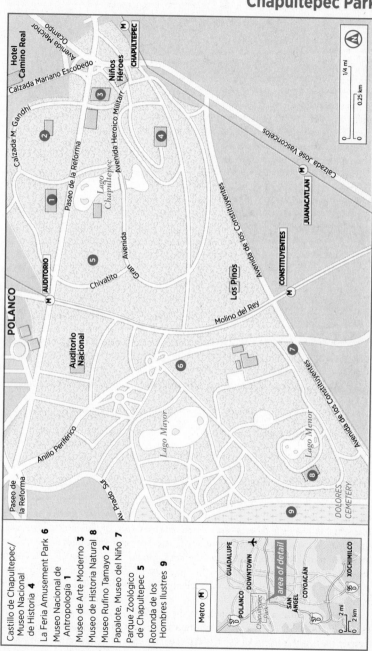

Chapultepec Park

Castillo de Chapultepec/
Museo Nacional
de Historia **4**

La Feria Amusement Park **6**

Museo Nacional de
Antropología **1**

Museo de Arte Moderno **3**

Museo de Historia Natural **8**

Museo Rufino Tamayo **2**

Papalote, Museo del Niño **7**

Parque Zoologico
de Chapultepec **5**

Rotonda de los
Hombres Ilustres **9**

Metro (M)

GUADALUPE

DOWNTOWN

POLANCO

Chapultepec Park

SAN ANGEL

COYOACÁN

XOCHIMILCO

area of detail

0   2 mi
0   2 km

Hotel
Camino Real

Avenida Melchor
Ocampo

Calzada Mariano Escobedo

Niños
Héroes

CHAPULTEPEC

Calzada M. Gandhi

Paseo de la Reforma

Lago
Chapultepec

Avenida Heroico Militar

Gran   Avenida

Chivatito

AUDITORIO

POLANCO

Auditorio
Nacional

Paseo de
la Reforma

Anillo Periférico

Av. Prado Sur

Lago Mayor

Molino del Rey

Los Pinos

Avenida de los Constituyentes

CONSTITUYENTES

JUANACATLAN

Calzada José Vasconcelos

Avenida de los Constituyentes

Lago Menor

DOLORES
CEMETERY

1/4 mi
0.25 km

4

MEXICO CITY | Exploring Mexico City

mighty TENOCHTITLAN

What 16th-century metropolis was home to approximately 200,000 inhabitants, had intricate botanical and zoological gardens filled with thousands of exotic species, and had markets where as many as 40,000 people went to trade a menagerie of goods on a regular basis? London? Nope—there were only 50,000 people living there in 1500. Barcelona? No, sir; the Spaniards had not yet conceived of the concept of botanical gardens. How about Constantinople? Nope. The European soldiers who helped conquer this city said its markets outshone even the Turkish bazaars.

The city in question was called Tenochtitlan, the capital of the mighty Aztec empire. We know the area today as Mexico City.

When the Spanish arrived, they must have felt as though they had landed on another planet; the Aztecs had constructed an entire metropolis on the boggy marshes of Lake Texcoco. The city was intersected by a series of causeways, one of which was 8km (5 miles) long and wide enough for eight horsemen abreast to pass through. Up to 50,000 canoes plied through these causeways and corresponding canals, transporting everything from corn to brightly colored fabrics and obsidian blades. The famous Spanish chronicler Bernal Díaz wrote that "with such wonderful sites to gaze on we did not know what to say, or if this was real that we saw before our eyes," in his account of the siege of Tenochtitlan in *True Story of the Conquest of New Spain.*

Unfortunately, the Spaniards hadn't traveled thousands of miles just to send home pretty postcards—after repeated attacks, famine, and a smallpox epidemic, Tenochtitlan fell on August 13, 1521, and Cuautéhmoc, the last Aztec emperor, was taken prisoner.

If you'd like to get a better feel for Tenochtitlan, the **Museo de la Ciudad de México** (p. 109) has a fine collection of maps and pictographic representations of the time period, and a few farmers still grow their produce using ancient floating garden methods in **Xochimilco** (p. 115).

the site, visitors pass a water-collection conduit constructed during the presidency of Porfirio Díaz (1877–1911), as well as far earlier constructions. Shelters cover the ruins to protect traces of original paint and carving. Note especially the Tzompantli, or Altar of Skulls, a common Aztec and Maya design. Explanatory plaques with building dates are in Spanish.

The Museo del Templo Mayor (Museum of the Great Temple) opened in 1987. To enter it, take the walkway to the large building in the back portion of the site, which contains fabulous artifacts from on-site excavations. Inside the door, a model of Tenochtitlan gives a good idea of the scale of the vast city of the Aztecs. The rooms and exhibits, organized by subject, occupy many levels around a central open space. You'll see some marvelous displays of masks, figurines, tools, jewelry, and other artifacts, including the huge stone wheel of the moon goddess Coyolxauhqui ("she with bells painted upon her face") on the second floor. The goddess ruled the night, the Aztec believed, but died at the dawning of every day, slain and dismembered by her brother, Huitzilopochtli, the sun god.

Seminario 8, off the *zócalo.* ℂ **55/5542-4943.** Fax 55/5542-1717. www.templomayor.inah.gob.mx. See map p. 97. Admission to museum and ruins 57 pesos; free Sun. Video camera permit 35 pesos; no flash photos. Tues–Sun 9am–5pm. Metro: Zócalo.

Coyoacán

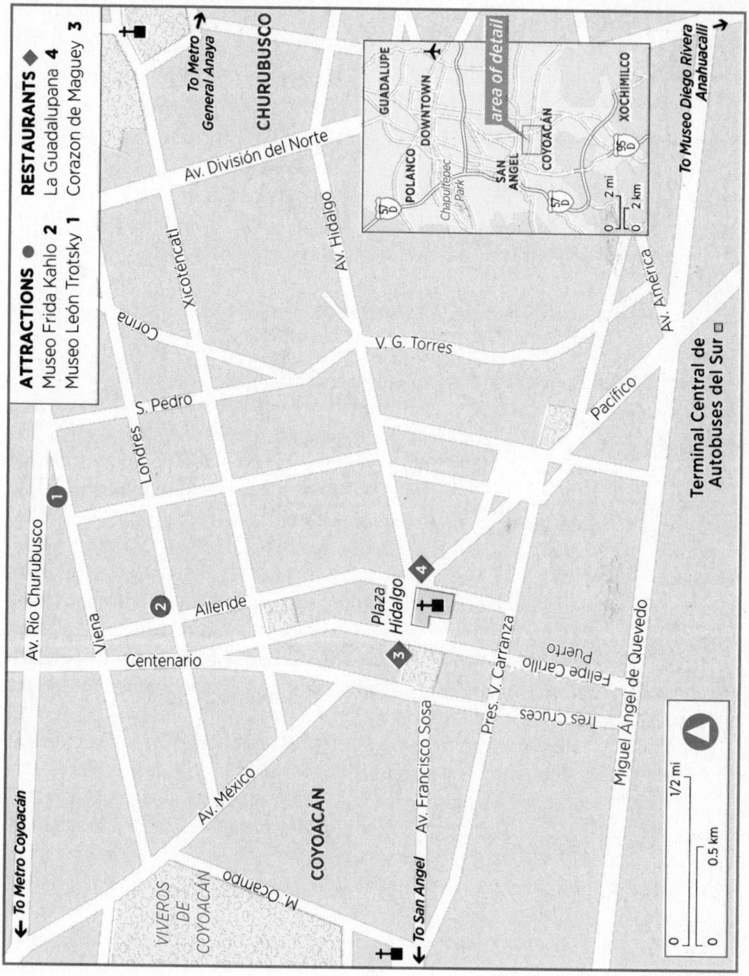
ATTRACTIONS ●
Museo Frida Kahlo 2
Museo León Trotsky 1
RESTAURANTS ◆
La Guadalupana 4
Corazon de Maguey 3
To Metro General Anaya
CHURUBUSCO
Av. División del Norte
Av. Hidalgo
Xicoténcatl
Corina
V. G. Torres
S. Pedro
Londres
Av. Río Churubusco
Viena
Allende
Centenario
Plaza Hidalgo
Av. México
To Metro Coyoacán
VIVEROS DE COYOACÁN
M. Ocampo
COYOACÁN
Av. Francisco Sosa
To San Angel
Pres. V. Carranza
Felipe Carillo Puerto
Tres Cruces
Miguel Ángel de Quevedo
Pacífico
Av. América
Terminal Central de Autobuses del Sur
To Museo Diego Rivera Anahuacalli
area of detail
GUADALUPE
DOWNTOWN
POLANCO
Chapultepec Park
SAN ANGEL
COYOACÁN
XOCHIMILCO
0 2 mi
0 2 km
0 1/2 mi
0 0.5 km

Architectural Highlights

Casa de los Azulejos This "House of Tiles" is one of Mexico City's most precious colonial gems and popular meeting places. Covered in gorgeous blue-and-white tiles, it dates from the end of the 1500s, when it was built for the count of the Valley of Orizaba. According to the oft-told story, during the count's defiant youth, his father proclaimed, "You will never build a house of tiles." A tiled house was a sign of success, and the father was sure his son would amount to nothing. So when success came, the young count covered his house in tiles, a fine example of Puebla craftsmanship. The tiled murals in the covered courtyard, where the restaurant is located, were restored a few years back. Tile craftsmen from Saudi Arabia were brought in to ensure that the technique was true to the original 16th-century work. You can stroll through to admire the interior. Pause to see the Orozco mural, *Omniscience,* on the landing leading to the second floor (where the restrooms are). There's a casual but beautiful Sanborn's Mexican restaurant in the covered patio.

Madero 4, Centro Histórico. *©* **55/5512-7824,** -7882. See map p. 99. Free admission. Daily 6am–1am. Metro: Bellas Artes.

Gran Hotel Ciudad de México Originally a department store, the Gran Hotel boasts one of the most splendid interiors of any downtown building. Step inside to see the lavish lobby, with gilded open elevators on both sides, topped with a breathtaking 1908 stained-glass canopy by Jacques Graber. On the fourth floor, overlooking the *zócalo,* Restaurante Plaza Mayor restaurant is a great stop for a coffee or drink with a view.

Av. 16 de Septiembre 82 at 5 de Febrero. *©* **55/1083-7700.** See map p. 97. Free admission to view the lobby, except on Sun, when the hotel is not open to nonguests. Metro: Zócalo.

Palacio de Bellas Artes ★★ Opulent and dramatic, the Bellas Artes is the masterpiece of theaters in this architecturally rich city. The exterior is early-20th-century Art Nouveau, built during the Porfiriato and covered in Italian Carrara marble. Inside it's completely 1930s Art Deco. Since construction began in 1904, the theater (which opened in 1934) has sunk some 4m (13 ft.) into the soft belly of Lake Texcoco. The Palacio is the work of several masters: Italian architect Adamo Boari, who made the original plans; Antonio Muñoz and Federico Mariscal, who modified his plans considerably; and Mexican painter Gerardo Murillo ("Doctor Atl"), who designed the fabulous Art Nouveau glass curtain that was constructed by Louis Comfort Tiffany in the Tiffany Studios of New York. Made from nearly a million iridescent pieces of colored glass, the curtain portrays the Valley of Mexico, with its two great volcanoes. You can see the curtain before important performances at the theater and on Sunday mornings.

In addition to being a concert hall, the theater houses permanent and traveling art shows. On the third level are famous murals by Rivera, Orozco, and Siqueiros. The controversial Rivera mural *Man in Control of His Universe* was commissioned in 1933 for Rockefeller Center in New York City. He completed the work there just as you see it: A giant vacuum sucks up the riches of the Earth to feed the factories of callous, card-playing, hard-drinking white capitalist thugs—John D. Rockefeller himself among them—while all races of noble workers of the Earth rally behind the red flag of socialism and its standard-bearer, Lenin. Needless to say, the Rockefellers weren't so keen on the new purchase. Much to their discredit, they had it painted over and destroyed. Rivera duplicated the mural here as *Man at the Crossing of the Ways,* to preserve it. For information on tickets to performances of the **Ballet Folklórico,** see "Mexico City After Dark," later in this chapter.

Warning: Avoid taxis parked in front of the Bellas Artes Theater, and call for a radio taxi instead.

Calle López Peralta, east end of La Alameda, Centro Histórico. *©* **55/5512-2593,** ext. 152. www.palacio. bellasartes.gob.mx. See map p. 99. Free admission to view building when performances are not in progress; museum 35 pesos. Tues–Sun 10am–5:30pm. Metro: Bellas Artes.

Palacio de Minería Built in the 1800s, this "mining palace" is one of architect Manuel Tolsá's finest works—considered a masterpiece of Latin American neoclassicism—and one of the capital's handsomest buildings. Formerly the school of mining,

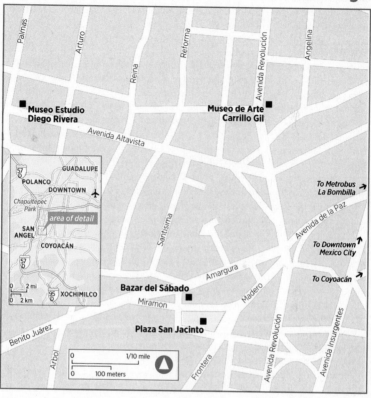

it's occasionally used today for concerts and cultural events (and, in those cases, the patio is often locked off). When it's open, step inside for a look at the patios and fabulous stonework. Guided tours are available.

Tacuba 5, Centro Histórico. © **55/5623-2981.** www.palaciomineria.unam.mx. See map p. 99. Admission 10 pesos; guided tour 25 pesos. Wed–Sun 10am–6pm. Metro: Bellas Artes.

A Cemetery

Rotonda de los Hombres Ilustres   The din of traffic recedes in the serene resting place where Mexico's military, political, and artistic elite are buried. It's more like an outdoor monument museum than a cemetery; the stone markers stand in a double circle around an eternal flame. A stroll here is a trip through who's who in Mexican history. Among the famous buried here are the artists Diego Rivera, David Alfaro Siqueiros, José Clemente Orozco, and Gerardo Murillo; presidents Sebastian Lerdo de Tejada, Valentín Gómez Farías, and Plutarco Calles; musicians Jaime Nunó (author of the Mexican national anthem), Juventino Rosas, and Agustín Lara; and outstanding citizens such as the philanthropist and writer Carlos Pellicer. Stop in the building at the entrance, and the guard will give you a map with a list (in Spanish and English) of those buried here, which includes biographical information.

Constituyentes and Av. Civil Dolores, Dolores Cemetery, Chapultepec Park. See map p. 101. Free admission. Daily 6am–6pm. Metro: Constituyentes.

Churches

Catedral Metropolitana ★★★ The impressive, towering cathedral, begun in 1567 and finished in 1788, blends baroque, neoclassical, and Mexican *churrigueresque* architecture. As you look around the cathedral and the Sagrario (chapel) next to it, note how the building has sunk into the soft lake bottom beneath. The base of the facade is far from level and straight, and when one considers the weight of the immense towers—127,000 tons—it's no surprise. Scaffolding has become almost a part of the structure, in place to stabilize the building. However, much to the credit of Mexico City and its preservation efforts, the Catedral Metropolitana came off the World Monuments Fund's list of 100 Most Endangered Sites in 2000, as a result of an extensive reconstruction of the building's foundation.

In Mexico, the sacred ground of one religion often becomes the sacred ground of its successor. Cortez and his Spanish missionaries converted the Aztec, tore down their temples, and used much of the stone to construct a church on the spots of the temples that preceded it. The church they built was pulled down in 1628 while the present cathedral was under construction. The building today has 5 naves and 14 chapels. As you wander past the small chapels, you may hear guides describing some of the cathedral's outstanding features: the tomb of Agustín Iturbide, placed here in 1838; a painting attributed to the Spanish artist Bartolomé Esteban Murillo; and the fact that the stone holy-water fonts ring like metal when tapped with a coin. Like many huge churches, it has catacombs underneath. The much-older-looking church next to the cathedral is the chapel known as the Sagrario, another tour de force of Mexican baroque architecture built in the mid-1700s.

The Catedral Metropolitana contains many prized works of colonial art in a variety of artistic styles. Jerónimo de Balbas built and carved the Altar de los Reyes (Altar of Kings) and the Altar del Perdón (Altar of Forgiveness) in 1737. For a small donation, a tour of the towers is available (sign up inside the cathedral near the entrance).

As you walk around the outside of the cathedral, you will notice a reminder of medieval trade life. The west side is the gathering place of carpenters, plasterers, plumbers, painters, and electricians who have no shops. Craftspeople display the tools of their trades, sometimes along with pictures of their work. In front of the cathedral, you can buy crystals, gemstones, and herbs, believed to provide special qualities of protection and cure from various afflictions.

Visitors are asked not to tour the cathedral during Mass.

The *zócalo*, on Cinco de Mayo, Centro Histórico. See map p. 97. Free admission. Daily 8am–7pm. Metro: Zócalo.

Convent of San Bernardino de Siena This 16th-century building is noted for its flower petals carved in stone—a signature of the Indians who did most of the work—on 16th-century *retablos* (painted boards), including one of three such altarpieces in the country that were created by pre-Hispanic Indians and that has miraculously been preserved for more than 400 years; most were destroyed by the Spaniards during the conquest and conversion to Christianity. The last Indian governor of Xochimilco, Apoxquiyohuatzin, is buried here. Inside and to the right, the skull over the font is from a pre-Hispanic skull rack, signifying an Indian-Christian mixture of the concept of life and death. Eight lateral *retablos* date from the 16th to the 18th centuries. The fabulous gilt main altar, also from the 16th century, is like an open book, with sculpture and religious paintings. A profusion of cherubic angels decorates columns and borders. Some of the altar paintings are attributed to Baltasar Echave Orio the Elder. Over the altar, above the figure of Christ, is San Bernardino with the *caciques* (local authorities) dressed in clothing with Indian elements, and without shoes.

Pino and Hidalgo (facing the main square), Xochimilco. See map p. 65. Free admission. Daily 8am–8pm. *Tren ligero* (light train): Xochimilco.

Historic Buildings & Monuments

CHAPULTEPEC PARK & POLANCO

Castillo de Chapultepec/Museo Nacional de Historia   This site has been occupied by a fortress since the days of the Aztec, although the present palace wasn't built until 1784. When open, the castle offered a beautiful view of Mexico City. During the French occupation of the 1860s, Empress Carlota (who designed the lovely garden surrounding the palace) could sit up in bed and watch her husband, Maximilian, proceeding down Reforma on his way to work. Later this was the official home of Mexico's president until 1939. In 2004, archaeologists discovered an ancient Teotihuacán settlement behind the landmark. Exhibition halls 1 through 9 have recently undergone remodeling.

Chapultepec Park and Polanco. © **55/5061-9217.** www.castillodechapultepec.inah.gob.mx. See map p. 101. Admission 51 pesos; free Sun. Tues–Sun 9am–5pm. Metro: Chapultepec.

ZONA ROSA & SURROUNDING AREAS

Monumento a la Revolución and Museo Nacional de la Revolución   The Art Deco Monument to the Revolution, in the large **Plaza de la República,** has a curious history. The government of Porfirio Díaz, who was perennially "reelected" president of Mexico, began construction of what was intended to be a new legislative chamber. However, only the dome was raised by the time the Mexican Revolution (1910) put an end to his plans, not to mention his dictatorship. In the 1930s, after the revolutionary turmoil had died down, the dome was finished as a monument. The remains of two revolutionary presidents, Francisco Madero and Venustiano Carranza, were entombed in two of its pillars, and it was dedicated to the Revolution. Later, presidents Plutarco Elías Calles and Lázaro Cárdenas were also buried there. (**Note:** At the time of his death, Calles was buried at La Rotonda de los Hombres Ilustres. His body was then moved to the Monumento a la Revolución by an order of President Díaz Ordaz in 1969. A plaque honoring him still remains at the Rotunda, but his actual body is at the Monumento.)

Beneath the Monument to the Revolution is the **Museo Nacional de la Revolución** (enter directly across from the Frontón). It chronicles the tumultuous years from 1867 to 1917—when the present constitution was signed—in excellent exhibits of documents, newspaper stories, photographs, drawings, clothing, costumes, uniforms, weapons, and furnishings.

Av. Juárez and La Fragua, Plaza de la República s/n, Col. Tabacalera beneath the Monumento a la Revolución. © **55/5566-1902.** See map p. 74. Admission 20 pesos; free Sun. Tues–Sun 9am–5pm. From the Colón Monument on Reforma, walk 2 blocks north on I. Ramírez; the monument looms ahead. Metro: Revolución.

Monumento a los Héroes de la Independencia ★   The Monument to the Heroes of Independence is the most noted of Mexico City's exceptional public sculptures and monuments. The "Angel" is both a landmark and homage to those who lost their lives fighting for independence. It's also a central stage—along with the *zócalo*—for many of Mexico City's celebrations and demonstrations. Set upon a tall marble and Italian granite base, the golden angel is an important and easily discerned guidepost for travelers. A creation of Antonio Rivas Mercado, the 7m-high (23-ft.) gold-plated bronze angel, cast in Florence, Italy, was completed in 1906 at a cost of $2.5 million. The monument's height is 45m (148 ft.). It was renovated in 2006.

Intersection of Paseo de la Reforma, Florencia, and Río Tiber, Reforma/Zona Rosa. See map p. 74. Metro: Sevilla.

Secretaría de Educación Pública   Originally built in 1922 as a convent, this building became the home of the Secretary of Public Education in 1922 and was decorated with a great series of more than 200 Diego Rivera murals, dating from 1923 and 1928, that cover over 1,500 sq. m (16,146 sq. ft.) of wall space. Other artists did a panel here and there, but the Rivera murals are the most outstanding.

República de Argentina 28, near República de Brasil. ② **55/5328-1097.** See map p. 97. www.sep.gob. mx. Free admission. Mon–Fri 9am–5pm. Metro: Allende.

Suprema Corte de Justicia   The Supreme Court of Justice, built between 1935 and 1941, is the highest court in the country. Inside, on the main staircase and its landings, are Orozco murals depicting a theme of justice.

Pino Suárez and Corregidora, Centro Histórico. No phone. See map p. 97. Free admission. Mon–Fri 9am– 5:30pm. Metro: Zócalo.

Other Museums & Galleries
CHAPULTEPEC PARK & POLANCO

Museo de Arte Moderno ★   The Museum of Modern Art is known for having the best permanent exhibition of painters and sculptors from the modern Mexican art movement. It also features some of the most important temporary exhibitions of national and international modern art in the world. Representing the Mexican muralist movement are significant works by the three greats: Diego Rivera (1886–1957), José Clemente Orozco (1883–1949), and David Alfaro Siqueiros (1896–1974). The main building is a round, two-story structure with a central staircase. Two of the museum's four spaces showcase the permanent collection, which also contains works by Mexico's other modern masters—Tamayo, José Luis Cuevas, Alejandro Colunga, Francisco Toledo, and Vladamir Cora. The remaining two spaces house visiting exhibitions. The museum's surrounding gardens exhibit large-scale public sculptures.

Chapultepec Park. ② **55/5553-6233.** www.mam.bellasartes.gob.mx. See map p. 101. Admission 22 pesos; discounts for students and teachers with ID; free Sun. Tues–Sun 10am–5:30pm. Metro: Chapultepec.

Museo de Historia Natural de la Ciudad de Mexico ☺   The 10 interconnecting domes that form the Museum of Natural History contain stuffed and preserved animals and birds; tableaux of different natural environments with the appropriate wildlife; exhibits on geology, astronomy, biology, and the origin of life; and more. It's a fascinating place for anyone with the slightest curiosity about nature, and it's totally absorbing for youngsters.

Chapultepec Park, Section 2. ② **55/5516-2848.** See map p. 101. Admission 22 pesos; free Tues. Tues– Sun 10am–5pm. Metro: Constituyentes.

Museo Rufino Tamayo ★ Oaxaca-born painter Rufino Tamayo not only contributed a great deal to modern Mexican painting, but also collected pre-Hispanic, Mexican, and foreign works, including pieces by Willem de Kooning, Andy Warhol, Salvador Dalí, and René Magritte. Tamayo's pre-Hispanic collection is in Oaxaca, but here you can see a number of his works and the remainder of his collection (unless a special exhibit has temporarily displaced them). A special *noche de jazz* (jazz evening), with a private tour of the museum followed by a small jazz concert, is offered one Wednesday each month; check the website for scheduling.

Paseo de la Reforma s/n (corner of Gandhi), Chapultepec Park. ✆ **55/5286-6519.** www.museotamayo. org. See map p. 101. Admission 15 pesos; free Sun. Tues-Sun 10am-6pm. Metro: Chapultepec or Auditorio.

Papalote, Museo del Niño ☺ The Building of the Pyramids at this interactive children's museum holds most of the more than 350 exhibits, while two films alternate (10 shows daily) in the IMAX building. There's virtually nothing here that children can't touch; once they discover this, they'll want to stay a long time. As they say, adults must be accompanied by children, except on Thursday, when the museum is open until 11pm to give "big kids" a chance to enjoy it themselves. It's probably been a while since you had a chance to play hide-and-seek, run around "musical chairs," crawl through a narrow pitch-black tunnel, or draw animal representations of your friends, but this return to the past is a lot of fun. The patio restaurant offers live jazz during the Thursday adults' night.

Av. de los Constituyentes 268, Chapultepec Park, Section 2. ✆ **55/5237-1700,** -1773. www.papalote. org.mx. See map p. 101. Admission to museum 160 pesos adults, 120 pesos children ages 2-11. 599 pesos family package including IMAX and Digital Dome. Mon-Wed and Fri 9am-6pm; Thurs 9am-11pm; Sat-Sun and holidays 10am-7pm. Metro: Constituyentes.

CENTRO HISTÓRICO & SURROUNDING AREAS

Museo de la Ciudad de México Before you enter the Museum of Mexico City, go to the corner of República del Salvador and look at the enormous stone serpent head, a corner support at the building's base. The stone was once part of an Aztec pyramid. At the entrance, a stone doorway opens to the courtyard of this mansion, built in 1778 as the House of the Counts of Santiago de Calimaya. This classic building became the Museum of the City of Mexico in 1964; it's a must for anyone interested in the country's past. Dealing solely with the Mexico Valley, where the first people arrived around 8000 B.C., the museum contains some fine maps, pictographic presentations of the initial settlements, outlines of the social organization as it developed, and models of several famous buildings. Upstairs is the studio of Mexican Impressionist Joaquín Clausell (1866–1935). There's a good bookstore to the left after you enter.

Pino Suárez 30, Centro Histórico. ✆ **55/5542-0671.** www.cultura.df.gob.mx. See map p. 97. Admission 22 pesos. Tues-Sun 10am-5pm. Metro: Zócalo.

Museo Franz Mayer One of the capital's foremost museums, the Franz Mayer Museum opened in 1986 in a beautifully restored 16th-century building on Plaza de la Santa Veracruz on the north side of La Alameda. The extraordinary 10,000-piece collection of antiques, mostly Mexican objects from the 16th through 19th centuries, was amassed by one man: Franz Mayer. A German immigrant, he adopted Mexico as his home in 1905 and grew rich here. Before his death in 1975, Mayer bequeathed the collection to the country and arranged for its permanent display through a trust with the Banco Nacional. The pieces, mostly utilitarian objects (as opposed to pure art objects), include inlaid and richly carved furniture; an enormous collection of Talavera pottery; gold and silver religious pieces; sculptures; tapestries; rare watches and clocks (the oldest is a 1680 lantern clock); wrought iron; old-master paintings from Europe and Mexico; and 770 *Don Quixote* volumes, many of which are rare editions or typographically unique. There's so much here that it may take two visits to absorb it all. In the central courtyard, a pleasant cafe serves coffee and light snacks.

Av. Hidalgo 45, next to Plaza Santa Veracruz, Col. Guerrero. (*C*) **55/5518-2266**, ext. 251. www.franz mayer.org.mx. See map p. 99. Admission 45 pesos; free Tues. Tues–Fri 10am–5pm; Sat–Sun 10am–7pm. Guided tours by appointment. Metro: Hidalgo or Bellas Artes.

Museo José Luis Cuevas   José Luis Cuevas is one of Mexico's leading contemporary artists, though early in his career, he was considered the *enfant terrible* of Mexican plastic arts. To this day, he can arouse controversy and is known to draw throngs of women wherever he appears. The center that bears his name opened in 1992 and is filled with about 1,000 paintings, drawings, and sculptures donated by Cuevas, including many of his own. Don't miss the Erotic Room, a permanent exhibit of his erotic paintings, photographs, and erotic objects from the artist's personal collection. Housed in the 16th-century Convento de Santa Inés, the museum includes many works by other contemporary Latin American artists, as well as a large collection of Picassos.

Calle Academia 13, 2 blocks northeast of the Palacio Nacional and across from the Academia de San Carlos, Centro Histórico. (*C*) **55/5542-6198**. www.museojoseluiscuevas.com.mx. See map p. 97. Admission 20 pesos. Tues–Sun 10am–5:30pm. Metro: Zócalo.

Museo Mural Diego Rivera   This museum houses Diego Rivera's famous mural *Dream of a Sunday Afternoon in Alameda Park,* which was painted on a wall of the Hotel Prado in 1947. The hotel was demolished after the 1985 earthquake, but the mural, perhaps the best known of Rivera's works, was saved and transferred to its new location in 1986. The huge picture, 15m long and 4m high (49×13 ft.), chronicles the history of the park from the time of Cortez onward. Portrayed in the mural are numerous historical figures. More or less from left to right, but not in chronological order, they include: Cortez; a heretic suffering under the Spanish Inquisition; Sor Juana Inés de la Cruz, a brilliant, progressive woman who became a nun to continue her scholarly pursuits; Benito Juárez, seen putting forth the laws of Mexico's great Reforma; the conservative Gen. Antonio López de Santa Anna, handing the keys to Mexico to the invading American Gen. Winfield Scott; Emperor Maximilian and Empress Carlota; José Martí, the Cuban revolutionary; Death, with the plumed serpent (Quetzalcóatl) entwined about his neck; Gen. Porfirio Díaz, great with age and medals, asleep; a police officer keeping La Alameda free of "riffraff" by ordering a poor family out of the elitists' park; and Francisco Madero, the martyred democratic president who caused the downfall of Díaz, and whose betrayal and alleged murder by Gen. Victoriano Huerta (pictured on the right) resulted in years of civil turmoil.

Plaza de la Solidaridad (at Balderas and Colón), Centro Histórico–Alameda. (*C*) **55/5512-0754.** See map p. 99. Admission 17 pesos; free Sun. Tues–Sun 10am–6pm. Metro: Hidalgo.

Museo Nacional de Arte (Munal)   The National Art Museum's palacelike building, designed by Italian architect Silvio Contri and completed in 1911—a legacy of Europe-loving Porfirio Díaz's era—was built to house the government's Offices of Communications and Public Works. Díaz occupied the opulent second-floor salon, where he welcomed visiting dignitaries. The National Museum of Art took over the building in 1982. Wander through the immense rooms with polished wooden floors as you view the wealth of paintings showing Mexico's art development, primarily covering the period from 1810 to 1950. There's a nice cafe on the second floor.

Tacuba 8, Centro Histórico. ✆ **55/5130-3400,** -3410. Fax 55/5130-3401. www.munal.com.mx. See map p. 99. Admission 33 pesos; free Sun. Tues-Sun 10:30am-5:30pm. Metro: Allende.

Museo Nacional de la Estampa *Estampa* means "engraving" or "printing," and this museum is devoted to understanding and preserving the graphic arts. The beautifully restored 16th-century building holds both permanent and changing exhibits. Displays include those from pre-Hispanic times, when clay seals were used for designs on fabrics, ceramics, and other surfaces. But the most famous works here are probably those of José Guadalupe Posada, Mexico's famous printmaker, who poked fun at death and politicians through his skeleton figure drawings. If your interest in this subject is deep, ask to see the video programs on graphic techniques—woodcuts, lithography, etchings, and the like.

Av. Hidalgo 39 (next door to the Museo Franz Mayer), Centro Histórico-Alameda. ✆ **55/5510-4905.** See map p. 99. Admission 10 pesos; free Sun. Tues-Sun 10am-6pm. Metro: Bellas Artes.

Museo Nacional de San Carlos The San Carlos Museum exhibits 15th- to 19th-century European paintings. The museum was once the Academy of San Carlos, an art school that some of the country's great painters—Rivera and Orozco among them—attended. Architect Manuel Tolsá built the beautiful mansion in the early 1800s; it was later the home of the Marqués de Buenavista. The rooms on the first and second floors hold some of Mexico's best paintings, by both Mexican and European artists. Another gallery holds prints and engravings. In the mansion's elliptical court are displays of 19th-century Mexican statuary and busts by Manuel Vilar and his pupils, and off to one side is a pretty garden court shaded by rubber trees.

Puente de Alvarado 50 (at Arizpe). ✆ **55/5566-8085.** www.mnsancarlos.com. See map p. 74. Admission 28 pesos; free Sun. Wed-Mon 10am-6pm. Walk 5½ blocks west of La Alameda (2½ blocks west of San Fernando Plaza). Metro: Revolución.

SOUTHERN NEIGHBORHOODS

Museo Arqueológico de Xochimilco The building dates from 1904, when it was the pump house for the springs. It houses artifacts from the area, many of them found when residents built their homes. These include 10,000-year-old mammoth bones; figures dating from the Teotihuacán period, including representations of Tlaloc (god of water and life), Ehecatl (god of the wind), Xipe Totec (god of renewal and of plants), and Huehueteotl (god of fire); polychrome pottery; carved abalone; and tombs showing funerary practices. One unique piece is a clay figure of a child holding a bouquet of flowers.

Av. Tenochtitlan and Calle La Planta, Santa Cruz Acalpixcan. ✆ **55/2157-1757.** www.xochimilco.df.gob. mx. Admission 10 pesos; free Sun. Tues-Sun 10am-5pm. From Xochimilco (see "Neighborhoods in Brief," earlier in this chapter), take a cab or microbus to Tulyehualco.

Museo de Arte Carrillo Gil (MACG) Sometimes called the Museo de la Esquina (Corner Museum)—it's at a major intersection on Avenida de la Revolución—this modern gallery features a collection that includes rooms dedicated to the works of José Clemente Orozco, Diego Rivera, David Alfaro Siqueiros, and other Mexican painters. The museum is not accessible by Metro.

Revolución 1608 (at Desierto de los Leónes), Col. San Angel. ✆ **55/5550-6260.** www.museodearte carrillogil.com. See map p. 105. Admission 15 pesos; free Sun. Tues-Sun 10am-6pm.

Museo Diego Rivera Anahuacalli ★ Not to be confused with the Museo Estudio Diego Rivera (see below) near the San Angel Inn, this is probably the most unusual museum in the city. Designed by Rivera before his death in 1957, it's devoted to his works as well as his extensive collection of pre-Columbian art. With over 52,000 pieces, it is the largest private collection displayed in Mexico. Constructed of *pedregal* (the lava rock in which the area abounds), it resembles Maya and Aztec architecture. Anahuacalli means "House of Mexico"; *Anahuac* was the old name for the ancient Valley of Mexico.

In front of the museum is a reproduction of a Toltec ball court, and the entrance to the museum is a coffin-shaped door. Twenty-three display rooms are arranged in chronological order, with thousands of pieces stashed on the shelves, tucked away in corners, and peeking out of glass cases.

Upstairs, in a replica of Rivera's studio, you'll find the original sketches for some of his murals and two in-progress canvases. There's a photo of his first sketch (of a train), done at the age of 3, plus a color photograph of him at work later in life. Rivera studied in Europe for 15 years and spent much of his life as a devoted Marxist. Yet he came through political scrapes and personal tragedies with no apparent diminution of creative energy. A plaque in the museum proclaims him "a man of genius who is among the greatest painters of all time." This is one of the most popular places in Mexico to come for Day of the Dead on November 2.

Calle del Museo 150, Col. San Pablo Tepetlapa. ✆ **55/5617-3797.** www.museoanahuacalli.org.mx. See map p. 65. Admission 20 pesos. Tues–Sun 10am–5pm. Metro: Taxqueña; then *tren ligero* (light train) to Xotepingo; go west on Xotepingo (Museo) 3 short blocks; cross División del Norte and go another 6 blocks.

Museo Dolores Olmedo Patiño ★ Art collector and philanthropist Olmedo left her former home, the grand Hacienda La Noria, as a museum featuring the works of her friend Diego Rivera. At least 137 of his works are displayed here, including his portrait of Olmedo, 25 paintings of Frida Kahlo, and 37 creations of Angelina Beloff (Rivera's first wife), many of them drawings and engravings. Among the notable Kahlo works here is her famed *The Broken Column,* which is considered the artistic embodiment of her physical suffering, the result of a trolley accident that pierced her spine when she was young. Besides the paintings, there are fine pre-Hispanic pieces on display, colonial furniture and other hacienda artifacts, and a collection of folk art. An excellent gift shop and a cafeteria are on the premises. Olmedo was the executor of both the Rivera and Kahlo estates, a close friend and former lover of Diego's, and a rival to Frida. Olmedo died in 2002, recognized as one of the most astute collectors of contemporary Mexican art.

Av. México 5843, Col. La Noria, Xochimilco. ✆ **55/5555-1016** or 55/5555-0891. www.museodolores olmedo.org.mx. See map p. 65. Admission 55 pesos; free on Tues. Tues–Sun 10am–6pm. Metro: Taxqueña; then *tren ligero* (light train) to Xochimilco. Get off at the La Noria station.

Museo Estudio Diego Rivera Here, in the studio designed and built by Juan O'Gorman in 1928, Rivera drew sketches for his wonderful murals and painted smaller works. He died here in 1957. Now a museum, the Rivera studio holds some of the artist's personal effects and mementos, as well as changing exhibits relating to his life and work. (Don't confuse Rivera's studio with his museum, the Anahuacalli; see above.) The museum is not accessible by Metro.

Calle Diego Rivera and Av. Altavista (across from San Angel Inn), Col. San Angel. ✆ **55/5616-0996.** See map p. 105. Admission 11 pesos; free Sun. Tues–Sun 10am–6pm. By taxi, go up Insurgentes Sur to Altavista and make a left.

Museo León Trotsky   During Lenin's last days, Stalin and Trotsky fought a silent battle for leadership of the Communist Party in the Soviet Union. Trotsky stuck to ideology, while Stalin took control of the party mechanism. Stalin won, and Trotsky was exiled to continue his ideological struggle elsewhere. Invited by Diego Rivera, an ardent admirer of his work, he settled here on the outskirts of Mexico City to continue his writings on political topics and communist ideology.

His ideas clashed with those of Stalin in many respects, and Stalin, wanting no opposition or dissension in the world communist ranks, set out to have Trotsky assassinated. A first attempt failed, but it served as a warning to Trotsky; his wife, Natalia; and their household. The house became a veritable fortress, with watchtowers, thick steel doors, and round-the-clock guards, several of whom were Americans who sympathized with Trotsky's philosophies. Finally, a man thought to have been paid, cajoled, or blackmailed by Stalin, directly or indirectly, was able to gain admittance to the house by posing as a friend of Trotsky's and a believer of his political views. On August 20, 1940, he put an ice pick into the philosopher's head. The assailant was caught, and Trotsky died of his wounds shortly afterward. Because Trotsky and Rivera had previously had a falling-out—Trotsky was having an affair with Rivera's wife, Frida Kahlo—Rivera was a suspect for a short time.

You can visit Natalia's study, the communal dining room, and Trotsky's study—with worksheets, newspaper clippings, books, and cylindrical wax dictating records still spread around—as well as the fortresslike bedroom. Some of the walls bear the bullet holes left from the first attempt on his life. Trotsky's tomb, designed by Juan O'Gorman, is in the garden. You can recognize this house by the brick riflemen's watchtowers on top of the high stone walls.

Av. Río Churubusco 410 (btw. Gómez Farías and Morelos), Col. Del Carmen Coyoacán. ⓒ **55/5658-8732** or 55/5554-0687. www.museocasadeleontrotsky.blogspot.com. See map p. 103. Admission 40 pesos. Tues–Sun 10am–5pm. Metro: Coyoacán. From Plaza Hidalgo, go east on Hidalgo 3 blocks to Morelos, then north 8 blocks to Churubusco; the house is on the left.

Outdoor Art/Plazas

Plaza de las Tres Culturas   Three cultures converge here: Aztec, Spanish, and contemporary Mexican. Surrounded by modern office and apartment buildings are large remains of the **Aztec city of Tlatelolco,** site of the last battle of the conquest of Mexico. To one side is the **Church of Santiago.** During the Aztec Empire, Tlatelolco was on the edge of Lake Texcoco, linked to the Aztec capital by a causeway. Bernal Díaz de Castillo, in his *True Story of the Conquest of New Spain,* described the roar from the dazzling market there, and the incredible scene after the last battle of the conquest in Tlatelolco on August 13, 1521—the dead bodies were piled so deep that walking there was impossible. That night determined the fate of the country and completed the Spanish takeover of Mexico. It was also here, in October 1968, that government troops fired on protesters who filled the square, killing hundreds.

View the pyramidal remains from raised walkways over the site. The church, off to one side, was built in the 16th century entirely of volcanic stone. The interior has been tastefully restored, preserving little patches of fresco in stark-white plaster walls, with a few deep-blue stained-glass windows and an unadorned stone altar. Sunday is a good day to combine a visit here with one to the Lagunilla street market (see "Shopping," below), which is within walking distance, south across Reforma.

Lázaro Cárdenas and Flores Magón, Centro Histórico. Metro: Tlatelolco.

Plaza de Santo Domingo 🏛 This fascinating plaza—a wonderful slice of Mexican life—has arcades on one side, a Dominican church on another. A statue of the Corregidora of Querétaro, Josefa Ortiz de Domínguez, dominates the plaza. The plaza is best known for the scribes who compose and type letters for clients unable to do so. Years ago, it was full of professional writers clacking away on typewriters, and a few still ply their trade on ancient electric typewriters among a proliferation of small print shops and presses. Emperor Cuauhtémoc's palace once occupied this land, before Dominicans built their monastery here.

Bordered by República de Venezuela, República de Brasil, República de Cuba, and Palma, Centro Histórico. See map p. 97. Metro: Tacuba.

Zócalo ★★ Every Spanish colonial city in North America was laid out according to a textbook plan, with a plaza at the center surrounded by a church, government buildings, and military headquarters. Because Mexico City was the capital of New Spain, its *zócalo* is one of the grandest, graced on all sides by stately 17th-century buildings. The Plaza de la Constitución, as this square is officially called, is also one of the three biggest public squares in the world.

Zócalo actually means "pedestal" or "plinth." A grand monument to Mexico's independence was planned and the pedestal built, but the project was never completed. Nevertheless, the pedestal became a landmark for visitors, and soon everyone was calling the square the *zócalo*, even after the pedestal was removed. The square covers almost 4 hectares (10 acres) and is bounded on the north by Cinco de Mayo, on the east by Pino Suárez, on the south by 16 de Septiembre, and on the west by Nacional Monte de Piedad. The downtown district—especially north of the Templo Mayor, one of the oldest archaeological sites in the city—is currently undergoing an important restoration project that is renewing much of its colonial charm. Occupying the entire east side of the *zócalo* is the majestic red *tezontle*-stone Palacio Nacional (p. 100), seat of the Mexican national government, and on the northern border is the Catedral Metropolitana (p. 106).

Juárez and 20 de Noviembre, Centro Histórico. See map p. 97. Metro: Zócalo.

Parks & Gardens

Alameda Park Today the lovely tree-filled Alameda Park attracts pedestrians, cotton-candy vendors, strollers, lovers, and organ grinders. Long ago, the site was an Aztec marketplace. When the conquistadors took over in the mid-1500s, heretics were burned at the stake here under the Spanish Inquisition. In 1592, the governor of New Spain, Viceroy Luis de Velasco, converted it to a public park. Within the park, known as La Alameda, is the **Juárez Monument,** sometimes called the **Hemiciclo** (hemicycle, or half-circle), facing Avenida Juárez. Enthroned as the hero he was, Juárez assumes his proper place here in the pantheon of Mexican patriots. European (particularly French) sculptors created most of the other statuary in the park in the late 19th and early 20th centuries.

Av. Juárez and Lázaro Cárdenas. See map p. 99. Free admission. Metro: Bellas Artes.

Chapultepec Park One of the biggest city parks in the world, 220-hectare (543-acre) Chapultepec Park is more than a playground; it's virtually the centerpiece of the city. Besides accommodating picnickers on worn-away grass under centuries-old trees, it has canoes on the lake; jogging and bridle paths; vendors selling balloons, souvenirs, and food; a miniature train; and **Los Pinos,** home of Mexico's president. The park is also home to the **City Zoo** and **La Feria** amusement park. Most important for tourists, it contains a number of interesting museums, including the Museo Nacional de Antropología (p. 98).

Btw. Paseo de la Reforma, Circuito Interior, and Av. Constituyentes. See map p. 101. Free admission. Daily 5am–5pm. Metro: Chapultepec.

Floating Gardens of Xochimilco ★   In Xochimilco are more than 80km (50 miles) of canals known as the Floating Gardens. They consist of two main parts. The first is the tourism-oriented area in the Historic Center of town, where colorful boats called *trajineras* take loads of tourists and locals celebrating a special occasion through a portion of the canals. Lively music, some of it provided by mariachi musicians for hire who board the gondolas, is a staple. Historic buildings, restaurants, souvenir stands, curio sellers, and boat vendors border this area. The other section, north of the center of town, is the ecology-oriented area, or Parque Natural Xochimilco. On Sunday, Xochimilco is jammed; on weekdays, it's nearly deserted. As you enter Xochimilco proper, you will see many places to board boats. Should you miss them, turn along Madero and follow signs that say LOS EMBARCADEROS (the piers).

Southern neighborhood of Xochimilco. ✆ **55/5673-7890.** Admission to area 20 pesos; boat rides 150–180 pesos per boat per hour, which up to 14–18 people may share. Daily 9am–6pm.

UNAM Sculpture Garden   Want to escape the Distrito Federal without getting on a bus? No, it's not a trick question. The campus of the Universidad Nacional Autónoma de México (UNAM) is technically a separate city with its own transportation system, police force, and government, and has therefore escaped much of the sprawl and overdevelopment that plagues the city surrounding it. The grounds are carpeted with lush plants and shaded by tall trees. The best place to get a feel for the university is the sculpture garden located in front of the *Torre de Rectoría*, which is adorned with a three-dimensional mural by socialist painter David Alfaro Siqueiros. The new **Museum Universitario Arte Contemporáneo (MuAC; ✆ 55/5622-6972;** www.muac.unam.mx; admission 30 pesos, free Sun; Wed, Fri, Sat 10am–6pm, Thurs and Sun noon–8pm) sits along the side. The huge green lawn strewn with sculptures by modern Mexican artists among giant lava rock beds is a great place for lounging and people-watching in a university atmosphere; during the week, expect to see everything from lovers holding hands to student violinists rehearsing before class or auditions. On the weekends, families visit with their picnic blankets.

Take the Metrobus to the Ciudad Universitaria stop. Free shuttles run throughout the campus.

Best View

La Torre Latinoamericana   From the observation deck on the 44th floor of this soaring skyscraper, the Latin American Tower, you can take in fabulous views of the entire city. Buy a ticket for the deck at the booth as you approach the elevators. Tokens for the telescope are on sale here, too. You then take an elevator to the 42nd floor, cross the hall, and take another elevator to the 44th floor. An employee will ask for your ticket as you get off.

Eje Central 2 (at Madero and Lázaro Cárdenas), Centro Histórico. ✆ **55/5518-7423.** See map p. 99. Admission 60 pesos adults, 50 pesos children. Daily 9am–10pm. Metro: Bellas Artes.

ORGANIZED TOURS

Mexico City is a great place to explore on your own, and in general this is the easiest and least expensive way to see what you like. But if your time is limited, you may want to acclimate quickly by taking a tour or two.

The many commercial tours include a 4-hour city tour of such sites as the **Metro-politan Cathedral,** the **National Palace,** and **Chapultepec Park and Castle;** a longer tour to the **Shrine of Guadalupe** and nearby pyramids at **Teotihuacán;** and the Sunday tour that begins with the **Ballet Folklórico,** moves on to the **Floating Gardens of Xochimilco,** and may or may not include lunch and the afternoon bullfights. Almost as popular are 1-day and overnight tours to Puebla, Cuernavaca, Taxco, and Acapulco. There are also several nightclub tours. Book through your hotel concierge or tour desk; see also "By Tourist Bus" under "Getting Around," p. 77.

If you want to let your stomach be your guide, consider taking a gastronomic tour. **Eat Mexico** (www.EatMexico.com) is a new tour company founded by American expat food writer Lesley Tellez and her *Chilango* counterpart, Jesica López Sol. Eat Mexico's guides are the perfect stewards to Mexico City's unique local cuisine. If you're squeamish about eating tacos al pastor on a street corner, they'll teach you how to spot the best vendors and even how to administer a squeeze of lime. Other tours include a jaunt around authentic markets in El Centro and a taste of Mexican wine, tequila, and mescal.

SHOPPING

From handicrafts to the finest in designer apparel, Mexico City is a marvelous place for shopping. From malls to *mercados,* to kitschy boutiques, numerous places display fascinating native products and sophisticated goods.

The two best districts for browsing boutiques are on and off **Avenida Presidente Masaryk,** in Polanco, and the **Zona Rosa.** Polanco's shops include Burberrys of London, Christian Dior, Versace, Gucci, Hermès, Louis Vuitton, Giorgio Armani, Tiffany's, and Cartier. Think Beverly Hills's Rodeo Drive, or Paris's Champs-Elysées, and you'll get the picture. The 12 square blocks at the heart of the Zona Rosa are home to antiques shops, boutiques, art galleries, silver shops, and fine jewelers.

For a taste of urban and hip, check out the shops that are sprouting up in **Roma** and **Condesa,** where you'll find the work of independent fashion designers, sneakers in every color of the rainbow, and even a boutique dedicated to *lucha libre.*

Art

If you're looking for a centralized display of street art, visit **Border,** Zacatecas 43, Roma Sur (© **55/5584-7557;** www.border.com.mx).

Exposición Nacional de Arte Popular (FONART) This store is usually loaded with crafts: papier-mâché figurines, textiles, earthenware, colorful candela-bras, hand-carved wooden masks, straw goods, beads, bangles, and glass. The Fonda Nacional para el Fomento de las Artes (FONART), a government organization that helps village craftspeople, operates the store. It's open Monday to Saturday from 10am to 7pm, and Sunday from 10am to 6pm. Juárez 89, Centro Histórico. © **55/5521-0171.** www.fonart.gob.mx. Metro: Hidalgo or Juárez.

López Quiroga Gallery Items include auction-quality works of art by contempo-rary Latin American masters, including Toledo, Tamayo, and Siqueiros. The gallery is not accessible by Metro; take a cab. It's open Monday to Friday from 10am to 7pm and Saturday from 10am to 2pm. Aristóteles 169, Polanco. © **55/5280-1710.** www.lopezquiroga.com.

O.M.R. Gallery This gallery has earned a reputation for discovering and introduc-ing emerging talents and new artists from Latin America. It's open Monday through

Friday from 10am to 3pm and 4 to 7pm, Saturday from 10am to 2pm. Plaza Río de Janeiro 54, Col. Roma. ℰ **55/5511-1179.** www.galeriaomr.com. Metro: Insurgentes.

Pineda Covalin This boutique shop created by two Mexican designers integrates Mexican culture and traditions into its fashionable designs. The beautiful pieces filled with vibrant colors include silk ties and scarves, handbags, shoes, and jewelry. The store's open Monday to Saturday from 9am to 8pm and Sunday from 10am to 2pm. Campos Eliseos 215 (at Galileo), Polanco. ℰ **55/5280-2720.** www.pinedacovalin.com. Metro: Auditorio.

Puro Corazón This high-quality store next to the *zócalo* sells fine arts, crafts, and jewelry from across Mexico. The prices are a good bit higher than they would be where the products were made, but here you get a fabulous selection in one lovely shop. There's also a bookstore, gallery, and traditional Mexican restaurant on-site. The store's open Sunday through Tuesday from 9am to 7pm and Wednesday through Saturday from 9am to 7:30pm. Monte de Piedad 11, Centro Histórico. ℰ **55/5518-0300.** www. arte-mexico.com. Metro: Zócalo.

Books

About the most convenient foreign- and Spanish-language bookstore in Mexico City, with a good selection of guidebooks and texts on Mexico, is **Librería Gandhi,** Av. Juárez 4, near Avenida Lázaro Cárdenas (ℰ **55/2625-0606;** www.gandhi.com.mx), right across from the Bellas Artes. It's open Monday to Saturday from 10am to 9pm, Sunday from 11am to 8pm. The **Museo Nacional de Antropología,** in Chapultepec Park (ℰ **55/5553-1902** or 55/5211-0754; www.mna.inah.gob.mx), also has a fair selection of books on Mexico, particularly special-interest guides. It's open Tuesday through Sunday from 9am to 7pm. Also in Chapultepec, the bookstore **Otro Lugar de la Mancha,** Esopo 11 Chapultepec near Avenida Presidente Masaryk (ℰ **55/5280-4826;** www.lamancha.com.mx), offers a small but outstanding collection of books, music, and art, plus an upstairs cafe in a historic home. It's open Monday through Friday from 8am to 10pm, Saturday and Sunday from 9am to 6pm.

Jewelry

Besides the shops mentioned below, dozens of jewelry stores and optical shops are on Madero from Motolinía to the *zócalo*, in the portals facing the National Palace. **Nacional Monte de Piedad (National Pawn Shop),** also opposite the National Palace, has an enormous jewelry selection. The first Latin American branch of **Tiffany's** is on Avenida Presidente Masaryk in Polanco.

Bazar del Centro Located between La Alameda and the *zócalo,* this Colonial-Era building was the palace of the Counts of Miravalle. It houses shops selling jewelry, precious stones, and silver. It's open Monday through Friday from 10am to 7pm and Saturday from 10am to 3pm. Isabel la Católica 30, Centro Histórico. No phone. Metro: Zócalo.

Tane Located in the ritzy Centro Comercial Santa Fe, this is a branch of one of Mexico's top silver designers, with other locations found only in the best hotels and shopping centers. The quantity of high-quality silver work is enormous. You'll see jewelry, platters, pitchers, plates, cutlery, frames, candlesticks, and even the signature china, by Limoges. There are also branches in the Polanco and San Angel neighborhoods, and at the airport. It's open Monday through Friday from 10am to 7pm and Saturday from 11am to 3pm. Campos Eliseos 218 (at corner of Andrés Bello), Col. Polanco. ℰ **55/5281-0820.** www.tane.com.mx. Metro: Auditorio.

Markets

Bazar del Sábado 📷 Located in San Angel, the charming Colonial-Era neighborhood in the southern part of the city, the "Saturday Market" is my top recommendation for passing a weekend afternoon in Mexico City. The market takes place outside on the Plaza San Jacinto and inside a bazaar building (part of a two-story mansion) next to it. High-quality handicrafts, antiques, art, and Mexican food are all offered here.

In the center of the actual bazaar building is a wonderful Mexican cafe where waiters hustle to serve authentic tacos and frosty margaritas, plus *antojitos* (finger foods) and traditional dishes such as enchiladas. *Marimba* music plays in the background. Dozens of small rooms surrounding the courtyard serve as permanent stalls featuring original decorative art pieces. You'll find blown glass, fine jewelry, papier-mâché figures, masks, and embroidered clothing. The prices are on the high side, but the quality is equally high, and the designs are sophisticated. On adjacent plazas, hundreds of easel artists display their paintings, and surrounding homes abound with antiques, fine rugs, and hand-carved furniture for sale. Members of indigenous groups from Puebla and elsewhere bring their folk art—baskets, masks, pottery, textiles, and so on—to display in the parks. Plan to spend Saturday touring the attractions on the southern outskirts of the city. (See also "San Angel" under "Neighborhoods in Brief," earlier in this chapter.) It's open Saturday from 9am to 6pm. Plaza de San Jacinto, San Angel. Metro: Miguel Angel de Quevado.

Centro Artesanal Buenavista This rather modern building set back off a plaza consists of a number of stalls on two levels, selling everything from leather to tiles. They have some lovely silver jewelry and, as in most non-fixed-price stores, the asking price is high, but the bargained result is often very reasonable. It's open Monday through Saturday from 10am to 5:30pm. Aldama and Eje 1 norte near the Metrobus Buenavista.

Jamaica Flower Market 🏠 The Aztecs may have been violent and downright bloodthirsty, but they adored flowers, almost to the point of worship. The flower markets you'll find around the city are direct descendants of the ones that existed more than 500 years ago. The most splendid of these modern markets is the Jamaica Flower Market in Colonia Jamaica (pronounced Ha-*mai*-ka). It smells like a dream and is an explosion of color. Explore this vast warehouse with vendors selling simple bunches of flowers, to ornate funerary displays. Most business is in wholesale. Around the Day of the Dead, this market receives truckloads of marigolds. Should you have some sort of tulip or geranium emergency, the market is open 24 hours, 365 days a year. Corner of Congreso de la Union and Guillermo Prieto, Colonia Jamaica. Metro: La Viga or Jamaica.

Lagunilla Market This is one of the most interesting and unusual markets in Mexico—but watch out for pickpockets. It's most interesting on Sundays, when the Lagunilla becomes a colorful outdoor market filling the streets for blocks. Arrive around 9am. Vendors sell everything from axes to antiques. The two enclosed sections, on either side of a short street, Calle Juan Salvages, are open all week. They have different specialties: The one to the north is noted for clothes, *rebozos* (shawls), and blankets; the one to the south for tools, pottery, and household goods, such as attractive hanging copper lamps. Here you can find old and rare books, many at a ridiculously low cost, if you're willing to hunt and bargain. Vendors set up shop daily from 10am to 7pm, but bring out the antiques only on Sunday. Tourists will feel safer leaving by sundown. 3 blocks east of Plaza de Garibaldi, at the corner of Francisco Bocanegra. Metro: Allende.

Mercado de la Ciudadela An excellent place to get authentic arts and crafts, this market has hundreds of stalls with arts and crafts from all over Mexico. It's across from the Escuela Nacional de Artes. A few places take credit cards. A lovely park is across the street. It's open daily from 9am to 8pm. Balderas, btw. Reforma and Chapultepec. Metro: Balderas.

Mercado de la Merced This is the city's biggest market and among the most fascinating in the country; the intense activity and energy level are akin to those at Oaxaca's Mercado Abastos Market (see chapter 11). Officially, it's housed in several modern buildings, but shops line the tidy, crowded streets all the way to the *zócalo*.

The first building is mainly for fruit and vegetables; the others contain about what you'd find if a department store joined forces with a discount warehouse—especially housewares, such as hand-held citrus juicers of all sizes, tinware, colorful spoons, and decorative oilcloth. The main market, east of the *zócalo* on Circunvalación between General Anaya and Adolfo Gurrión, is the place to stock up on Mexican spices. The easy 13-block walk from the *zócalo* zigzags past many shops. Or take the Metro; the stop is right outside the market. It's open daily from 7am to 6pm. Circunvalación btw. General Anaya and Adolfo Gurrión. Metro: Merced.

Mercado Insurgentes Mercado Insurgentes is a full-fledged crafts market tucked into the Zona Rosa. Because of its address, you might expect exorbitant prices, but vendors in the maze of stalls are eager to bargain, and good buys aren't hard to come by. It's open Monday through Saturday from 9am to 5:30pm. Londres btw. Florencia and Amberes, Zona Rosa. Metro: Insurgentes.

Nacional Monte de Piedad (National Pawnshop) This building used to be a pawnshop, but now is reserved for the more profitable and saleable jewelry, with a couple of small rooms set aside for art and antiques. Pedro Romero de Terreros, the Count of Regla, an 18th-century silver magnate from Pachuca, donated the present building so that Mexican people could get low-interest loans. It's open Monday through Friday from 8:30am to 6pm, Saturday from 8:30am to 3pm. Corner of Monte de Piedad and Cinco de Mayo, Centro Histórico. www.montepiedad.com.mx. Metro: Zócalo.

Modern Mexico

Chic by Accident This boutique located in a 1920s-era mansion has been featured in the Mexican version of *Architectural Digest* as a place to find unique luxury worthy of furnishing posh penthouses. It operates with interior designers in mind, but curious shoppers can browse for quirky items like a pair of wooden owl-shaped boxes and a 1980s-era neon carpet. The showroom is open Monday through Friday from 10am to 8pm and Saturday from 10am to 2pm. Álvaro Obregón 49, Roma Norte. © **55/5511-1132.** www.chicbyaccident.com. Metro: Cuautéhmoc.

El Hijo Del Santo Fans of *lucha libre* deserve to have a nice quiet place where they can reflect on the beauty of wrestling in tights and shiny masks. Named after one of the most famous names in Mexican *lucha libre* wrestling, this cafe also houses a quirky boutique filled with wrestling merchandise, including official Hijo del Santo silver masks, T-shirts, and artwork. The store's open Monday to Saturday 10am to 9pm. Tamaulipas 219, Condesa. © **55/5515-2186.** www.elhijodelsanto.com.mx. Metro: Patriotismo. There's also a location next to the food court in Terminal 2 of the international airport.

The artists, writers, and fashionistas who find inspiration and party dresses in Roma Norte are only the latest generation of bohemians to do so. In the late 1940s and early 1950s, this neighborhood was the stamping ground of core members of the infamous beat generation, including Jack Kerouac, Allen Ginsberg, and Lucien Carr. In 1951 William S. Burroughs, who took classes in Maya culture at nearby Mexico City College, accidentally killed his wife, Joan, in a William Tell-esque stunt in the building at Medellín 122. Pay homage to the beats by grabbing a bite to eat at the restaurant **Ship Ahoy** (no phone) that currently occupies the infamous lot.

Guru   Guru is a gallery/boutique that regularly features exhibits by new and upcoming artists, and looks like the basement sanctuary you dreamed you had as a teenager. Expect to find one-of-a-kind T-shirts, posters, and postcards by international artists and designers. Unlike most of the upscale galleries, pets are welcome here. The building is bright orange with a giant smiling cartoon head painted on the side. Guru is open Tuesday to Friday noon to 8pm, Saturday noon to 7pm, and Sunday 1 to 6pm. Colima 143, Roma Norte. (C) **55/5533-7140.** www.gurugalleryshop.com. Metro: Cuauhtémoc.

Shelter   If you're a sneakerhead, you'll feel like a kid in a candy store visiting Shelter. This shop is popular with skateboarders and *hip-hoperos* because it's often the only place in Mexico or Latin America to carry exclusive releases by Nike and Adidas. By virtue of authority, the salespeople are extremely knowledgeable about shoe culture. Stop or skate by Monday through Saturday from noon to 8pm. Colima 134, Roma Norte. (C) **55/5208-6271.** www.shelter.com.mx. Metro: Cuauhtémoc.

Sicario   This trendy two-story *tiendita* with floor-to-ceiling windows is a one-stop shop for anyone living the Mexico City urban lifestyle. Shoppers and browsers will find art books and magazines, designer bicycles, and fashion uniform necessities like original screen-print T-shirts. In addition to selling clothing and accessories by local designers, they throw some pretty epic parties and events. Check their website for details. The store is open every day from noon to 8pm. Colima 124, Roma Norte. (C) **55/5511-0396.** www.sicario.tv. Metro: Cuautéhmoc.

MEXICO CITY AFTER DARK

The fiesta is by nature sacred, literally or figuratively, and above all it is the advent of the unusual.

—Octavio Paz, *The Labyrinth of Solitude*

Mexico City is the sort of megalopolis where you can show up at a house party at 11pm on a Monday and find the place already bustling with people. Not only are *Chilangos* master revelers who wouldn't scoff at a midweek party, but they don't put down their beer for a minor inconvenience such as sunrise. On any given night, you can find art gallery openings, new moon ceremonies, crowded dance floors, and independent movie screenings. If you're a night owl, you'll find plenty of fellow *tecolotes*.

The Entertainment Scene

Mexico City boasts a world-class nightlife scene, with hot venues for downing tequila and dancing to music ranging from salsa to house. The **Centro Histórico** downtown has earned a reputation for having a number of hip and edgy bars and clubs concentrated within walking distance. The posh **Polanco** neighborhood is known for its perennially see-and-be-seen dining and bar scene, and in recent years many of the trendiest nightspots have opened in the **Condesa** and **Roma** neighborhoods. Some of the city's most exclusive nightclubs lie in the **Lomas** area. In the south of the city, **San Angel** remains highly popular, although it's a bit of a drive if you're not already staying in that area. Most bars don't even begin to get going until around 10 or 11pm and usually stay open until at least 3am; nightclubs get started after midnight and continue into the wee hours. Many clubs operate only Thursday through Saturday.

For lower-key nightlife and people-watching, outdoor cafes remain a popular option. Those in the neighborhoods of **Polanco** and **Condesa** are among the liveliest. Another tradition is **Garibaldi Square,** where mariachis tune up and wait to be hired, but *be especially careful*—it's now known as much for chronic street crime as for music. The plaza was recently renovated, which will hopefully improve the safety of the neighborhood.

Hotel lobby bars tend to have live entertainment of the low-key type in the late afternoon and into the evening.

Some of the most exciting parties in the city are those sponsored by big-name labels like Nike and Absolut Vodka. These events often have themes, feature performances by well-known DJs, and are perfect if you want to check out the latest outrageous fashions. Check out websites such as **www.trafficodf.com**, **www.diariodefiestas.blogspot.com**, and **www.thecitylovesyou.com** for information about upcoming events.

The Performing Arts

Mexico City's performing arts scene is among the finest and most comprehensive in the world. It includes opera, theater, ballet, and dance, along with concerts of symphonic, rock, and popular music.

For current information on cultural offerings, ***Donde Ir, Tiempo Libre,*** and ***Concierge,*** free magazines found in hotels, are good sources for locating the newest places, though they don't have complete listings of changing entertainment or current exhibits. **Ticketmaster** (© **55/5325-9000**) usually handles ticket sales for major performances.

Note: The majority of the theatrical performances at the Palacio de Bellas Artes and in other theaters around the city are presented in Spanish.

Crime at Night

Leave valuables—especially watches and jewelry—at your hotel, and bring only the cash you will need. While I list Metro stops, these should probably be used only for orientation; take only authorized *sitio* taxis (see the advisory "Taxi Safety Precautions in Mexico City," at the beginning of this chapter). Your hotel can help with these arrangements. If you're really short on cash and are going to head to your destination before 9pm, take the Metro there and hire a taxi for the ride back.

Palacio de Bellas Artes   Although various groups perform around the city, the finest offering is at the Palacio de Bellas Artes, where the famed **Ballet Folklórico de México** performs twice a week. The Ballet Folklórico is a celebration of pre- and post-Hispanic dancing. A typical program includes Aztec ritual dances, agricultural dances from Jalisco, a fiesta in Veracruz, a wedding celebration—all linked with mariachis, marimba players, singers, and dancers.

Because the Bellas Artes books many other events—visits by foreign opera companies, for instance—the Ballet Folklórico occasionally moves. In that case, it usually appears in the **National Auditorium** in Chapultepec Park. Check at the Bellas Artes box office. The show is popular and tickets sell rapidly (especially to tour agencies at twice the cost). The box office is on the ground floor of the Bellas Artes, main entrance. Ballet Folklórico performances are on Sunday at 9:30am and 8:30pm and Wednesday at 8:30pm.

The Fine Arts theater not only offers the finest in performing arts, but is also architecturally worth a visit (see "Exploring Mexico City," earlier in this chapter). It's open Monday through Saturday 11am to 7pm, and Sunday 8:30am to 7pm. Eje Central and Av. Juárez, Centro Histórico–Alameda. © **55/5325-9000.** www.balletamalia.com. Tickets $36–$60. Metro: Bellas Artes.

The Club & Music Scene

This warning can't be reiterated enough: **Take an authorized *sitio* taxi or hire a car for transportation to all nightspots.** Metro stops are given merely as a point of reference.

The double-decker **Turibus** (© **55/5133-2488;** www.turibus.com.mx) now offers nighttime service on Thursday, Friday, and Saturday that runs a circuit through the necessary Mexico City party spots. Hop on and off from 9pm to 1am for 145 pesos.

MARIACHIS

Mariachis often get a bad rap. In movies they're usually portrayed as bumbling nuisances who are masters of ruining romantic moments. So while you're in Mexico, take the opportunity to give them a second listen. Known for their distinctive dress, strolling presentation, and mix of brass and guitars, they epitomize the romance and tradition of the country. They look a little like Mexican cowboys dressed up for a special occasion—tight trousers studded with silver buttons down the outside of the legs, elaborate cropped jackets, embroidered shirts with big bow ties, and grandiose sombrero hats. The dress dates from the French occupation of Mexico in the mid–19th century, as does the name. *Mariachi* is believed to be an adaptation of the French word for marriage; this was the type of music commonly played at weddings in the 15th and 16th centuries. The music is a derivative of *fandango,* which was the most popular dance music of the elite classes in 16th-century Spain. In Mexico, fandango became the peasant's song and dance. Among the most famous mariachi songs are "Mexico Lindo," "El Rey," "Guadalajara," "Cielito Lindo," and "La Cucaracha."

In Mexico City, the mariachis make their headquarters around the **Plaza de Garibaldi,** 5 blocks north of the Palacio de Bellas Artes—up Avenida Lázaro Cárdenas, at Avenida República de Honduras. In its heyday, the plaza was a popular destination for family and tourist gatherings. However, beginning in the 1990s, the plaza became increasingly plagued with petty crime. As deterioration continued, many of the area's legitimate businesses moved on to safer neighborhoods and left many of the seedier characters behind. In 2007 more than a dozen federal and local agencies allocated 90.6 million pesos for the revitalization of the plaza. The inauguration for a new Tequila and Mescal Museum occurred in December 2010. Mexico City Mayor Marcelo Ebrard and the governor of the mescal-producing state, Oaxaca, Gabino Cué, helped celebrate the museum, which is now home to hundreds of forms of distilled agave.

The plaza is liveliest at night, when at every corner guitars are stacked together like rifles in an army camp. Young musicians strut proudly in their outfits, on the lookout for *señoritas* to impress. They play when they feel like it, when there's a good chance to gather some tips, or when someone orders a song—depending on how large your group is, a single song can be anywhere from 10 to 100 pesos and an hour of music anywhere from 200 to 1,000 pesos, but this is negotiable. The most famous cantina on the plaza is **Salón Tenampa,** at Plaza Garabaldi 12 (*©* **55/5526-6176**), which serves traditional Mexican food as well as every type of tequila amid spirited surroundings. It's open daily from 1pm to 3am, and often later on the weekend.

For mariachi music in a more subdued setting, I recommend the following:

Jorongo Bar   Some of city's best mariachi and traditional Mexican music is found in this popular bar, located off the lobby of the Sheraton María Isabel (p. 84). This bar has enjoyed a reputation for outstanding traditional music for decades—it's an institution, with many local regulars. Monday through Saturday from 7pm to 2am (closed Sun), you can enjoy the smooth and joyous sounds for the price of a drink (60–100 pesos) plus cover (150 pesos). Hotel María Isabel Sheraton, Reforma 325, Zona Rosa. *©* **55/5242-5555.** Metro: Insurgentes.

CLUBS & MUSIC BARS

AREA Bar and Terrace at Hotel Habita 🎁   The rooftop bar of this boutique Polanco hotel is among Mexico City's enduring hot spots. Umbrellas top tables, but otherwise, you're under the stars—and, likely, surrounded by a few—among a trendy crowd sipping tequila cocktails and cosmopolitans. Decor is minimalist, of course, with a few white couches. Bar stools set along the railing look out over the city. If you can make it past the bouncer and down the circular stairway to the lower terrace and pool area, you've really arrived—that's the glitzy VIP section, not unlike what you'd find in a rooftop L.A. bar. Music is mainly lounge. It's open Monday to Thursday from 7pm to midnight, and Friday to Saturday until 2am. Hotel Habita (p. 82), Av. Presidente Masaryk 201, Polanco. *©* **55/5282-3100.** Metro: Polanco.

Bengala   Expats, world travelers, and internationally minded Mexicans have made Bengala one of the city's hottest bars, featuring a diverse selection of music and dancing between tables. The 30-somethings crowd comes for live jazz on Tuesday and Thursday nights and a rocking DJ the rest of the week. If you like sweet cocktails, the red-apple martini is the drink of choice. Open Tuesday to Saturday from 8pm to 3am. Sonora 34 (at corner of Puebla), Col. Roma. © **55/5553-9219.** www.bengalabar.com. Metro: Insurgentes.

La Pata Negra   This is the place to go if your toes are burning holes in your dancing shoes. The huge dance floor hosts DJs who play everything from Beastie Boys to Rolling Stones to Café Tacvba, and you can find everyone from 20-something tourists to 30-something bureaucrats shaking it out. Try to arrive early because as the second-story dance floor starts to get crowded around 11pm, the doorman starts handing out numbered tickets to get in. You can grab a drink in the first-floor bar and wait for your number to be called. You know your night is coming to an end when Norteño music starts blaring—an act that is probably intended to clear the dance floor. Don't run away; grab a dance partner and kick up your heels for one last blast. Tamaulipas 30 (at Juan Escutia), Col. Condesa. © **55/5211-5563,** -4678. Not easily accessible by Metro; take a taxi.

Patrick Miller   This "dancetería" certainly isn't for everyone, but if you've got an eye for the quirky and kitschy, come on down. This club opened during the Gloria Gaynor golden days of disco and is named after a popular DJ; you'll quickly discover that sparkly pants, sequined gloves, and decked-out transvestites are still the norm here. But you'll also find plenty of everyday *Chilangos* hoping to get in on the fun. You might think you are entering a large furniture warehouse, but what you get inside is a laser-lit dance floor crowded with circles of people and flamboyant dancers engaged in exaggerated dance-offs in the middle. The only beverage served is beer, but you'll so be fascinated by the retro crowd, you won't even notice the lack of hard liquor. Mérida 17, Col. Roma. © **55/5511-5406.** Metro: Cuautéhmoc.

Rexo   Credited with changing Mexico City's nightlife scene by leading people to Condesa, this Mediterranean restaurant and lounge still rules as one of the city's sexiest spots. A cube walled in by glass, Rexo consists of three contemporary floors, which integrate the restaurant and two stylish bars. The patrons are largely 30-somethings, mostly single, and very fashionable. The club is not easily accessible by Metro. It's open Tuesday 5pm to midnight and Wednesday through Saturday 1:30pm to 2:30am. Saltillo 1 (corner of Nuevo León), Col. Condesa. © **55/5553-5337.**

Zinco   Possibly the coolest jazz club south of the U.S. border, Zinco sits in an old basement vault in the Historic Center. Top performers play in the center of the intimate club, which attracts a crowd that's both cutting edge and unaffected. A full menu is available for those who wish to eat. It's open Wednesday to Saturday from 9pm to 3am. On Wednesday there's no cover, but the rest of the nights prices vary. Motolinía 20 (corner of 5 de Mayo), Centro Histórico. © **55/5512-3369.** www.zincojazz.com. Cover typically starts at 20 pesos and goes up depending on the night's entertainment. Metro: Zócalo.

BARS

The Black Horse   Founded with the idea of introducing funk, jazz, and British rock to the city, the Black Horse often features excellent live musicians. Co-owner Umair Kahn even jumps into the DJ booth when he wants to liven up the joint. In this pub-style bar, Tupac Shakur posters and Borat quotes decorate the walls, and the clientele meander from English to Spanish with ease. Wednesday ladies' night featuring 5-peso drinks is a local favorite. Check the website for upcoming offers and events. Open Tuesday to Sunday from 6pm to 2am. Mexicali 85, near the corner of Tamaulipas, Col. Condesa. © **55/5211-8740.** www.caballonegro.com. Metro: Patriotismo.

La Casa de las Sirenas   This old-school bar serves over 200 types of tequila, one of the widest selections available anywhere (the best of the best are part of the

In a world of global convenience and instant everything, it's rare to find a food or beverage that can truly only be consumed in its native region. Most Mexican beers are imported in some form across the U.S., and heck, salsa is more popular than ketchup. This makes drinking pulque, or octli, a truly "Mexican" experience. The libation is made from the fermented heart of the native maguey plant and loses its unique milky foam after being transported long distances or being left out in the open.

Although public drunkenness was punishable by death in some instances during Aztec reign, pulque was popular with priests and older people, and during religious ceremonies. It was said that if you drank too much you would experience the "dance of 400 rabbits" in your head. Over time it became a drink enjoyed by the masses, until the late 1800s when Eastern Europeans popularized beer. Nowadays pulque is making a comeback, and pulquerias offer daily flavor varieties such as mango, peanut, celery, and honey. **Las Dualistas,** Aranda 28, Centro (✆ 55/1394-0958), is a classic pulqueria that has been around for more than 90 years. The giant Aztec-inspired murals look down upon a crowd of youngsters, artists, and businessmen on break from lunch in el Centro. When I was there, the men's room had no door which only added extra charm. **Pulqueria Los Insurgentes,** Insurgentes 226 (✆ 55/4751-9326; www.lapulqueria. org), in front of Metrobus Durango in the heart of Roma, is a bit more hip. It occupies a Porfirio Diáz–era building. There's a jukebox and a mural of skeletons dancing that takes up an entire wall. They also offer a variety of dishes from around Mexico and host live music events.

selección suprema). It's well known for its friendly bar crowd and ambience, and there's live piano music on weekends. Housed in a 17th-century colonial building, the "House of Mermaids" features a courtyard filled with flowering plants and trees, and lies almost in front of the Templo Mayor in the Centro Histórico. There's also a charming restaurant (p. 92) on the floors above. The bar's open daily 11am to 11pm. República de Guatemala 32, Centro Histórico, behind the cathedral. ✆ **55/5704-3345,** -3273. www. lacasadelassirenas.com.mx. Metro: Zócalo.

Tierra de Vinos Only drinks made with grapes are served in this lively wine bar and restaurant, which offers delicious tapas and other Spanish delights to accompany your wine tasting. The stylish bar has a terrific vibe and one of the city's most impressive wine cellars, with distinct cellars housing bottles from key wine regions around the world. It's open Sunday from 1 to 5pm and Monday to Saturday from 1pm to 1am. Durango 197 (at corner of Oaxaca), Col. Roma. ✆ **55/5208-5133.** Metro: Insurgentes.

Whiskey Bar ★★ The W hotel's multisection bar remains one of the city's most fashionable. It includes the Red Lounge, with its neon tube lamps visible through the lobby windows; the Living Room, with innovative leather booths; the upstairs Cocoa Bar, designated for VIPs; and the outdoor Terrace, which offers blankets for women. The waitstaff, dressed in jet-black attire, serves the sexy, if somewhat elitist, local and international crowd. A DJ spins lounge beats, while customers sip flavored martinis and exotic cocktails. Check for special events on Thursday and Friday. Open until 2am Sunday through Wednesday, until 3am Thursday through Saturday. At the W Mexico City hotel, Campos Eliseos 252, at Andrés Bello. ✆ **55/9138-1800.** Metro: Polanco.

A SIDE TRIP TO THE PYRAMIDS OF SAN JUAN TEOTIHUACÁN ★★★

50km (31 miles) NE of Mexico City

The ruins of Teotihuacán are among the most remarkable in Mexico—indeed, they are among the most important ruins in the world. Mystery envelops this former city of 200,000; although it was the epicenter of culture and commerce for ancient Mesoamerica, its inhabitants vanished without a trace. *Teotihuacán* (pronounced Teh-oh-tee-wa-*khan*) means "place where gods were born," reflecting the Aztec belief that the gods created the universe here.

Occupation of the area began around 500 B.C., but it wasn't until after 100 B.C. that construction of the enormous Pyramid of the Sun commenced. Teotihuacán's rise coincided with the classical Romans' building of their great monuments, and with the beginning of cultures in Mexico's Yucatán Peninsula, Oaxaca, and Puebla.

Teotihuacán's magnificent pyramids and palaces covered about 30 sq. km (12 sq. miles). At its zenith, around A.D. 500, the city counted more inhabitants than contemporary Rome. Through trade and other contact, Teotihuacán's influence was known in other parts of Mexico and as far south as the Yucatán and Guatemala. Still, little information about the city's inhabitants survives: what language they spoke, where they came from, why they abandoned the place around A.D. 700. It is known, however, that at the beginning of the 1st century A.D., the Xitle volcano erupted near Cuicuilco (south of Mexico City) and decimated that city, which was the most prominent of the time. Those inhabitants migrated to Teotihuacán. Scholars believe that Teotihuacán's decline, probably caused by overpopulation and depletion of natural resources, was gradual, perhaps occurring over a 250-year period. In the last years, it appears that the people were poorly nourished and that the city was deliberately burned.

Ongoing excavations have revealed something of the culture. According to archaeoastronomer John B. Carlson, the cult of the planet Venus that determined wars and human sacrifices elsewhere in Mesoamerica was prominent at Teotihuacán as well. (Archaeoastronomy is the study of the position of stars and planets in relation to archaeology.) Ceremonial rituals were timed with the appearance of Venus as the morning and evening star. The symbol of Venus at Teotihuacán (as at Cacaxtla, 80km/50 miles away, near Tlaxcala) appears as a star or half-star with a full or half-circle. Carlson also suggests the possibility that people from Cacaxtla conquered Teotihuacán, as name glyphs of conquered peoples at Cacaxtla show Teotihuacán-like pyramids. Numerous tombs with human remains (many of them either sacrificial inhabitants of the city or perhaps war captives) and objects of jewelry, pottery, and daily life have been uncovered along the foundations of buildings. It appears that the primary deity at Teotihuacán was a female, called "Great Goddess" for lack of any known name.

Today what remains are the rough stone structures of the three pyramids and sacrificial altars, and some of the grand houses, all of which were once covered in stucco and painted with brilliant frescoes (mainly in red). The Toltec, who rose in power after the city's decline, were fascinated with Teotihuacán and incorporated its symbols into their own cultural motifs. The Aztec, who followed the Toltec, were fascinated with the Toltec and with the ruins of Teotihuacán; they likewise adopted many of their symbols and motifs. For more information on Teotihuacán and its influence in Mesoamerica, see chapter 2, "Mexico in Depth."

Teotihuacán

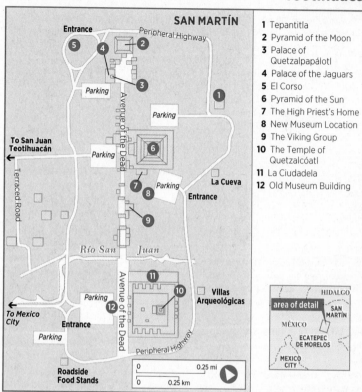

SAN MARTÍN

1 Tepantitla
2 Pyramid of the Moon
3 Palace of Quetzalpapálotl
4 Palace of the Jaguars
5 El Corso
6 Pyramid of the Sun
7 The High Priest's Home
8 New Museum Location
9 The Viking Group
10 The Temple of Quetzalcóatl
11 La Ciudadela
12 Old Museum Building

Entrance
Peripheral Highway
Parking
To San Juan Teotihuacán
Terraced Road
La Cueva
Entrance
Río San Juan
Avenue of the Dead
To Mexico City
Entrance
Villas Arqueológicas
Roadside Food Stands

0   0.25 mi
0   0.25 km

HIDALGO
area of detail
SAN MARTÍN
MÉXICO
ECATEPEC DE MORELOS
MEXICO CITY

4

MEXICO CITY | A Side Trip to the Pyramids of San Juan Teotihuacán

Essentials

GETTING THERE & DEPARTING **By Car** Driving to San Juan Teotihuacán on the toll Hwy. 85D or the free Hwy. 132D takes about an hour. Head north on Insurgentes to leave the city. Hwy. 132D passes through picturesque villages but can be slow due to the surfeit of trucks and buses. Hwy. 85D, the toll road, is less attractive but faster. (See "Getting Around," in chapter 20, for more about the use and cost of toll roads in Mexico.)

By Private Sedan or Taxi If you prefer to explore solo or want more or less time than an organized tour allows, consider hiring a private car and driver for the trip. They can easily be arranged through your hotel or at the Secretary of Tourism (SEC-TUR) information module in the Zona Rosa; they cost about 250 to 300 pesos an hour. The higher price is generally for a sedan with an English-speaking driver who doubles as a tour guide. Rates can also be negotiated for the entire day.

By Bus Buses leave daily every half-hour (5am–10pm) from the Terminal Central de Autobuses del Norte; the trip takes 1 hour and costs about 25 pesos round-trip. When you reach the Terminal Norte, look for the AUTOBUSES SAHAGUN (buses headed in the direction of Sahagun, Hidalgo) sign at the far northwest end, all the way down

127

When you reach the top of the Pyramid of the Sun, you might see people of all ages and entire families jostling to get near a mysterious metal tab, no bigger than your thumbnail, embedded in stone. Many believe that touching it will bring them energy or luck. It turns out that any power the metal might have is in its misconstruction. The metal is actually just a leftover marker from an archaeological excavation and probably hasn't been there for more than 50 years. Don't let this stop you from getting caught up in the excitement. Who knows, maybe you'll get lucky anyway.

to the sign 8 ESPERA. Be sure to ask the driver where you should wait for returning buses, how frequently buses run, and especially the time of the last bus back. **Circuito Pirámides** (📞 **55/5141-1360,** ext. 2000 and 2602; www.circuitopiramides. com.mx) offers guided air-conditioned coach tours to the ruins for 650 pesos for adults and 400 pesos for children, including transportation, entrance, and lunch buffet. Buses depart from the Auditorio Nacional at 9am, Angel de la Independencia at 9:15am, and Zócalo at 9:45am.

ORIENTATION The ruins of Teotihuacán (📞 **59/4956-0276,** -0052) are open daily from 7am to 5pm. Admission is 51 pesos. Using a video camera costs 35 pesos.

A small trolley-train that takes visitors from the entry booths to various stops within the site, including the Teotihuacán museum and cultural center, runs only on weekends, and costs 10 pesos per person.

Remember that you're likely to be doing a great deal of walking, and perhaps some climbing, at an altitude of more than 2,120m (6,954 ft.). Take it slow, bring sunblock and drinking water, and during the summer, be prepared for almost daily afternoon showers.

A good place to start is at the **Museo Teotihuacán ★**. This excellent state-of-the-art museum holds interactive exhibits and, in one part, a glass floor on which visitors walk above mock-ups of the pyramids. On display are findings of recent digs, including several tombs, with skeletons wearing necklaces of human and simulated jawbones, and newly discovered sculptures. Admission is 45 pesos. Using a video camera costs 30 pesos.

The Layout The grand buildings of Teotihuacán were laid out in accordance with celestial movements. The front wall of the **Pyramid of the Sun** is exactly perpendicular to the point on the horizon where the sun sets at the equinoxes (twice annually). The rest of the ceremonial buildings were laid out at right angles to the Pyramid of the Sun.

The main thoroughfare, which archaeologists call the **Calzada de los Muertos (Avenue of the Dead),** runs roughly north to south. The **Pyramid of the Moon** is at the northern end, and the **Ciudadela (Citadel)** is on the southern part. The great street was several kilometers long in its prime, but only a kilometer or two have been uncovered and restored.

Exploring the Teotihuacán Archaeological Site

LA CIUDADELA The Spaniards named the Ciudadela. This immense sunken square was not a fortress at all, although the impressive walls make it look like one. It was the grand setting for the Feathered Serpent Pyramid and the Temple of

Quetzalcóatl. Scholars aren't certain that the Teotihuacán culture embraced the Quetzalcóatl deity so well known in the Toltec, Aztec, and Maya cultures. The feathered serpent is featured in the Ciudadela, but whether it was worshiped as Quetzalcóatl or a similar god isn't known. Proceed down the steps into the massive court and head for the ruined temple in the middle.

The Temple of Quetzalcóatl was covered over by an even larger structure, a pyramid. As you walk toward the center of the Ciudadela's court, you'll approach the Feathered Serpent Pyramid. To the right, you'll see the reconstructed temple close behind the pyramid, with a narrow passage between the two structures.

Early temples in Mexico and Central America were often covered by later ones. The Pyramid of the Sun may have been built up in this way. Archaeologists have tunneled deep inside the Feathered Serpent Pyramid and found several ceremonially buried human remains, interred with precise detail and position, but as yet no royal personages. Drawings of how the building once looked show that every level was covered with faces of a feathered serpent. At the Temple of Quetzalcóatl, you'll notice at once the fine, large carved serpents' heads jutting out from collars of feathers carved in the stone walls. Other feathered serpents are carved in relief low on the walls.

AVENUE OF THE DEAD　　The Avenue of the Dead got its strange and forbidding name from the Aztec, who mistook the little temples that line both sides of the avenue for tombs of kings or priests.

As you stroll north along the Avenue of the Dead toward the Pyramid of the Moon, look on the right for a bit of wall sheltered by a modern corrugated roof. Beneath the shelter, the wall still bears a painting of a jaguar. From this fragment, you might be able to reconstruct the breathtaking spectacle that must have been visible when all the paintings along the avenue were intact.

PYRAMID OF THE SUN　　The Pyramid of the Sun, on the east side of the Avenue of the Dead, is the third-largest pyramid in the world. The first and second are the Great Pyramid of Cholula, near Puebla, and the Pyramid of Cheops on the outskirts of Cairo, Egypt. Teotihuacán's Pyramid of the Sun is 220m (722 ft.) per side at its base—almost as large as Cheops. But at 65m (213 ft.) high, the Sun pyramid is only about half as high as its Egyptian rival. No matter—it's still the biggest restored pyramid in the Western Hemisphere, and an awesome sight. Although the Pyramid of the Sun was not built as a great king's tomb, it is built on top of a series of sacred caves, which aren't open to the public.

The first structure of the pyramid was probably built a century before Christ, and the temple that used to crown the pyramid was completed about 400 years later (A.D. 300). By the time the pyramid was discovered and restoration was begun (early in the 20th c.), the temple had disappeared, and the pyramid was just a mass of rubble covered with bushes and trees.

It's a worthwhile 248-step climb to the top. The view is extraordinary and the sensation exhilarating. On a clear day, you can just barely see downtown Mexico City.

PYRAMID OF THE MOON　　The Pyramid of the Moon faces a plaza at the northern end of the avenue. The plaza is surrounded by little temples and by the Palace of Quetzalpapalotl or Quetzal-Mariposa (Quetzal-Butterfly) on the left (west) side. You have about the same range of view from the top of the Pyramid of the Moon as you do from its larger neighbor, because the moon pyramid is built on higher ground. The perspective straight down the Avenue of the Dead is magnificent.

PALACE OF QUETZALPAPALOTL   The Palace of Quetzalpapalotl lay in ruins until the 1960s, when restoration work began. Today it reverberates with its former glory, as figures of Quetzal-Mariposa (a mythical, exotic bird-butterfly) appear painted on walls or carved in the pillars of the inner court. Behind the Palace of Quetzalpapalotl is the Palace of the Jaguars, complete with murals showing jaguars.

Where to Eat

Vendors at the ruins sell drinks and snacks, but many visitors choose to carry a box lunch—almost any hotel or restaurant in the city can prepare one for you. A picnic in the shadow of this impressive ancient city allows extended time and perspective to take it all in. There is a restaurant called **Las Pirámides** in the new Museo Teotihuacán, which is the most convenient place for a snack or a meal. To the southeast of the Pyramid of the Sun you will find a kitschy joint called **La Gruta** (© **59/4956-0127;** www.lagruta.com.mx). The food is all right, but you'll be more impressed by its cave setting and dinner show featuring regional and folkloric dances.

SILVER, SPAS & SPIRITUAL CENTERS: FROM TAXCO TO TEPOZTLÁN

by Joy Hepp

I t may seem as though the small towns in this region are trying to capitalize on recent trends in travel toward spas and self-exploration, but in reality, they've helped define them. From the restorative properties of thermal waters and earth-based spa treatments to the mystical and spiritual properties of gemstones and herbs, the treasures and knowledge in these towns have existed for years—and in some cases, for centuries.

This is only a sampling of towns south and west of Mexico City. They are fascinating in their diversity, history, and mystery, and make for a unique travel experience, either on their own or combined. They vary in character from mystical villages to sophisticated spa towns, with archaeological and Colonial-Era attractions in the mix. And with their proximity to Mexico City, all are within easy reach by private car or taxi—or by inexpensive bus—in under a few hours.

The legendary silver city of **Taxco,** on the road between Acapulco and Mexico City, is renowned for its museums, picturesque hillside Colonial-Era charm, and, of course, its silver shops. North of Taxco and southwest of Mexico City, over the mountains, are the venerable thermal spas at **Ixtapan de la Sal,** as well as their more modern counterparts in **Valle de Bravo.** Verdant **Cuernavaca,** known as the land of eternal spring, has gained a reputation for its exceptional spa facilities and its wealth of cultural and historic attractions. Finally, **Tepoztlán,** with its enigmatic charms and legendary pyramid, captivates the few travelers who find their way there.

I found that the region as a whole is the perfect place for solo travel. I've never felt alone when visiting Taxco because the locals are so friendly and the whole city is bursting with tiny details. Tepoztlán is a place of reflection, as its spirituality oozes from every rock and New Age shop, and in Cuernavaca you'll find plenty of out-of-town Chilangos to keep you company.

Side Trips from Mexico City

0 _____ 25 mi
0 _____ 25 km

To Querétaro

Ruinas Tula

126

57D

Presa
Huapango

55

MICHOACÁN

15D

Villa del
Carbon

Río Pearl

Atlacomulco

6

55D

← To Guadalajara

MEXICO

55

Río Lerma

134

15

15

Zitacuaro

15

**Ruinas
Calixtlahuaca**

15D

Toluca

PARQUE
NACIONAL
DESIERTO DE
LOS LEONES

**Valle de
Bravo**

Metepec

PARQUE NACIONAL
NEVADO DE TOLUCA

PARQUE
NACIONAL
LAGUNAS DE
ZEMPOALA

Avándaro

Nevado de
Toluca (15,026')

Temascaltepec

55D

55

**Ruinas
Malinalco**

134

Tenancingo

**Ixtapan
de la Sal**

Tonatico

95

UNITED STATES

Gulf of
Mexico

MEXICO

Taxco

95

95D

Mexico City ★

GUERRERO

PACIFIC
OCEAN

95

To Chilpancingo
& Acapulco ↓

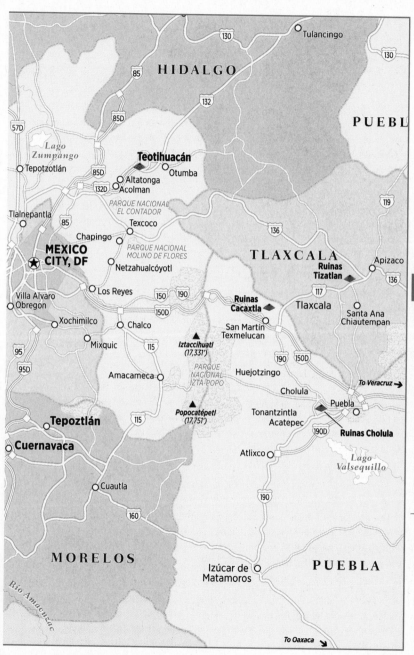

TAXCO: COBBLESTONES & SILVER ★★

178km (110 miles) SW of Mexico City; 80km (50 miles) SW of Cuernavaca; 296km (184 miles) NE of Acapulco

In Mexico and around the world, the town of Taxco de Alarcón—most commonly known simply as Taxco (*Tahs*-koh)—is synonymous with silver. The town's geography and architecture are equally precious: Taxco sits at nearly 1,515m (4,969 ft.) on a hill among hills, and almost any point in the city offers fantastic views.

Hernán Cortez discovered Taxco as he combed the area for treasure, but its rich caches of silver weren't fully exploited for another 2 centuries. In 1751, the French prospector Joseph de la Borda—who came to be known locally as José—commissioned the baroque Santa Prisca Church that dominates Taxco's *zócalo* (Plaza Borda) as a way of giving something back to the town. In the mid-1700s, Borda was considered the richest man in New Spain.

The fact that Taxco has become Mexico's most renowned center for silver design, even though it now mines only a small amount of silver, is the work of an American, William Spratling. Spratling arrived in the late 1920s with the intention of writing a book. He soon noticed the skill of the local craftsmen and opened a workshop to produce handmade silver jewelry and tableware based on pre-Hispanic art, which he exported to the U.S. in bulk. The workshops flourished, and Taxco's reputation grew.

Today most of the residents of this town are involved in the silver industry in some way. Taxco is home to hundreds (some say up to 900) of silver shops and outlets, ranging from sleek galleries to small stands in front of stucco homes. You'll find silver in all of its forms here—the jewelry basics, tea sets, silverware, candelabras, picture frames, and napkin holders.

The tiny one-man factories that line the winding cobbled streets all the way up into the hills supply most of Taxco's silverwork. "Bargains" are relative, but nowhere else will you find this combination of diversity, quality, and rock-bottom prices. Generally speaking, the larger shops that most obviously cater to the tourist trade will have the highest prices—but they may be the only ones to offer "that special something" you're looking for. For classic designs in jewelry or other silver items, shop around, and wander the back streets and smaller venues.

You can get an idea of what Taxco is like by spending an afternoon, but there's much more to this picturesque town than just the Plaza Borda and the shops surrounding it. Stay overnight, wander its steep cobblestone streets, and you'll discover little plazas, fine churches, and, of course, an abundance of silversmiths' shops.

The main part of town is relatively flat. It stretches up the hillside from the highway, and it's a steep but brief walk up. White VW minibuses, called *combis,* make the circuit through and around town, picking up and dropping off passengers along the route, from about 7am until 9pm. These taxis are inexpensive (about 50 pesos from the bus station to most hotels), and you should use them even if you arrive by car, because parking is practically impossible. Also, the streets are so narrow and steep that most visitors find them nerve-racking. Find a secured parking lot for your car, or leave it at your hotel and forget about it until you leave.

Warning: Self-appointed guides will likely approach you in the *zócalo* (Plaza Borda) and offer their services—they get a cut of all you buy in the shops they take you to. Before hiring a guide, ask to see his SECTUR (Tourism Secretary) credentials.

Taxco

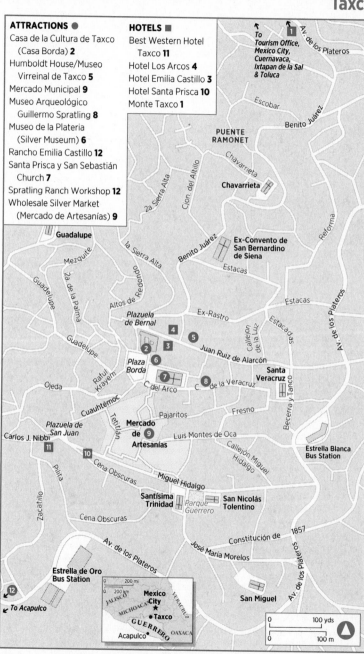

ATTRACTIONS ●

Casa de la Cultura de Taxco
(Casa Borda) **2**
Humboldt House/Museo
Virreinal de Taxco **5**
Mercado Municipal **9**
Museo Arqueológico
Guillermo Spratling **8**
Museo de la Platería
(Silver Museum) **6**
Rancho Emilia Castillo **12**
Santa Prisca y San Sebastián
Church **7**
Spratling Ranch Workshop **12**
Wholesale Silver Market
(Mercado de Artesanías) **9**

HOTELS ■

Best Western Hotel
Taxco **11**
Hotel Los Arcos **4**
Hotel Emilia Castillo **3**
Hotel Santa Prisca **10**
Monte Taxco **1**

The Department of Tourism office on the highway at the north end of town can recommend a licensed guide.

Essentials

GETTING THERE & DEPARTING   **By Car**   From Mexico City, take Paseo de la Reforma to Chapultepec Park and merge with the Periférico, which will take you to Hwy. 95D on the south end of town. From the Periférico, take the Insurgentes exit and merge until you come to the sign for CUERNAVACA/TLALPAN. Choose either *Cuernavaca cuota* (toll) or *Cuernavaca libre* (free). Continue south around Cuernavaca to the Amacuzac interchange, and proceed straight ahead for Taxco. The drive from Mexico City takes about 3½ hours.

From Acapulco, you have two options: Hwy. 95D is the toll road through Iguala to Taxco, or you can take the old two-lane road (Hwy. 95) that winds more slowly through villages; it's in good condition.

See "Getting Around" in chapter 20 for more information about traveling on toll roads and how to estimate toll charges.

By Bus   From Mexico City, buses depart from the Central de Autobuses del Sur station (Metro: Taxqueña) and take 2 to 3 hours, with frequent departures.

Taxco has two bus stations. Estrella de Oro buses arrive at their own station on the southern edge of town. Estrella Blanca service, including Futura executive-class buses, and Flecha Roja buses arrive at the station on the northeastern edge of town on Avenida Los Plateros ("Avenue of the Silversmiths," formerly Av. Kennedy). Taxis to the *zócalo* cost around 20 pesos.

VISITOR INFORMATION   The **State of Guerrero Dirección de Turismo** (©/fax 762/622-2274; www.guerrero.gob.mx) has offices at the arches on the main highway at the north end of town (Av. de los Plateros 1), which is useful if you're driving into town. The office is open Monday to Saturday, 9am to 8pm, and Sunday till 6pm. To get there from the Plaza Borda, take a ZOCALO-ARCOS *combi* and get off at the arch over the highway. As you face the arches, the tourism office is on your right.

CITY LAYOUT   The center of town is the tiny **Plaza Borda,** shaded by perfectly manicured Indian laurel trees. On one side is the imposing twin-towered, pink-stone **Santa Prisca Church;** whitewashed, red-tile buildings housing the famous silver shops and a restaurant or two line the other sides. Beside the church, deep in a crevice of the mountain, is the **wholesale silver market**—the best place to begin your silver shopping, to get an idea of prices for more standard designs. It's open daily from 9am to 7pm. You'll be amazed at the low prices. Buying just one piece is perfectly acceptable, and buying in bulk can lower the per-piece price. One of the beauties of Taxco is that its brick and cobblestone streets are completely asymmetrical, zigzagging up and down the hillsides. The plaza buzzes with vendors of everything from hammocks and cotton candy to bark paintings and balloons.

[FastFACTS] TAXCO

The telephone area code is **762.** The main **post office,** Benito Juárez 6, at the City Hall building (© **762/627-3503**), is open Monday through Saturday from 8:30am to 3:30pm. The older branch of the post office (© **762/622-0501**), open Monday through Friday from 8:30am to 4:30pm, is on the outskirts, on the highway to Acapulco. It's in a row of shops with a black-and-white CORREO sign.

The Taxco campus of the **Universidad Nacional Autónoma de México (UNAM; ℂ 762/622-0124;** www.cepetaxco. unam.mx) houses the Center of Instruction for Foreign Students on the grounds of the Hacienda del Chorrillo, formerly part of the Cortez land grant. Here, students can learn folkloric dancing, Spanish, drawing, composition, and history. Classes are small, and courses generally last 3 months. The school provides a list of accommodations that consist primarily of hotels. More reasonable accommodations for a lengthy stay are available but are best arranged once you're there. At many locations all over town, you'll find notices of furnished apartments or rooms for rent. For information about the school, either contact the Dirección de Turismo (tourist office) in Taxco (see "Visitor Information," above) or write the school directly, at Hacienda del Chorrillo, 40200 Taxco, Gro.

Special Events & Festivals

January 18 marks the annual celebration in honor of Santa Prisca, with public festivities and fireworks displays. **Holy Week ★★** in Taxco is one of the most poignant in the country, beginning Friday of the week before Easter with processions daily and nightly. The most riveting, on Thursday evening, lasts almost 4 hours. Villagers from the surrounding area carry statues of saints, followed by hooded members of a society of self-flagellating penitents, chained at the ankles and carrying huge wooden crosses and bundles of thorny branches. On Saturday morning, the Plaza Borda fills for the **Procession of Three Falls,** reenacting the three times Christ stumbled and fell while carrying the cross.

Taxco's **Silver Fair** starts the last week in November and continues through the first week in December. It includes a competition for silver works and sculptures among the top silversmiths. In late April to early May, **Jornadas Alarconianas** features plays and literary events in honor of Juan Ruiz de Alarcón (1572–1639), a world-famous dramatist who was born in Taxco—and for whom Taxco de Alarcón is named.

Exploring Taxco

Shopping for jewelry and other items is the major pastime for tourists. Prices for silver jewelry at Taxco's shops are about the best in the world, and everything is available, from 10-peso trinkets to artistic pieces that cost hundreds of dollars. In addition to the workshops listed below, there are several standout shops in town, including **TeGo,** Benito Juárez 46 (ℂ 762/622-0615), which features the unique jewelry of designer Teresa Gonzalez. In addition, Taxco is the home of some of Mexico's finest stone sculptors and is a good place to buy masks. However, beware of so-called "antiques"—there are virtually no real ones for sale.

If you purchase a large item during your stay and need help with packaging and/or mailing it, visit **Empaques San David,** Miguel Hidalgo 15 (ℂ 762/622-2036).

SIGHTS IN TOWN

Casa de la Cultura de Taxco (Casa Borda) Diagonally across from the Santa Prisca Church and facing Plaza Borda is the home José de la Borda built for his son around 1759. Now the Guerrero State Cultural Center, it houses a bookstore, library, classrooms, and exhibit halls where period clothing, engravings, paintings, and crafts are on display. The center also books traveling art exhibits, theatrical performances, music concerts, and dance events.

Plaza Borda 1. ☎ **762/622-6617.** Free admission. Tues–Fri 9am–6pm; Sat–Sun 10am–6pm.

Humboldt House/Museo Virreinal de Taxco　Stroll along Ruiz de Alarcón (the street behind the Casa Borda) and look for the richly decorated facade of the Humboldt House, where the renowned German scientist and explorer Baron Alexander von Humboldt (1769–1859) spent a night in 1803. The museum houses 18th-century memorabilia pertinent to Taxco, most of which came from a secret room discovered during a recent restoration of the Santa Prisca Church. Signs with detailed information are in Spanish and English. As you enter, to the right are very rare *túmulos funerios* (painted funerary altars). The bottom two were painted for Charles III of Spain; the top one, with a carved phoenix, was reputedly painted for the funeral of José de la Borda.

Another section presents historical information about Don Miguel Cabrera, Mexico's foremost 18th-century artist. Fine examples of clerical garments decorated with gold and silver thread hang in glass cases, and on the bottom level there's an impressive 17th-century carved wood altar of Dolores. Next to it, a small room is devoted to Humboldt and his sojourns through South America and Mexico.

Calle Juan Ruiz de Alarcón 12. ☎ **762/622-5501.** Admission 20 pesos adults, 15 pesos students and teachers with ID. Tues–Sat 10am–6pm; Sun 10am–4pm.

Mercado Municipal　Located to the right of the Santa Prisca Church, behind and below Berta's, Taxco's central market meanders deep inside the mountain. Take the stairs off the street. In addition to a collection of wholesale silver shops, you'll find numerous food stands, always the best place for a cheap meal.

Plaza Borda. Shops daily 10am–8pm; food stands daily 7am–6pm.

Museo Arqueológico Guillermo Spratling　A plaque in Spanish explains that most of the collection of pre-Columbian art displayed here, as well as the funds for the museum, came from William Spratling (1900–67). You'd expect this to be a silver museum, but it's not—for Spratling silver, go to the Spratling Ranch Workshop (see "Nearby Attractions," below). The entrance floor and the one above display a good collection of pre-Columbian statues and implements in clay, stone, and jade.

Calle Porfirio A. Delgado 1. ☎ **762/622-1660.** Admission 29 pesos adults, free for children 12 and younger; free to all Sun. Tues–Sat 9am–6pm; Sun 9am–3pm. Leaving Santa Prisca Church, turn right and right again at the corner; continue down the street, veer right, then immediately left. The museum will be facing you.

Museo de la Platería　The silver museum holds a small collection of exquisite silver pieces, the most interesting of which is *La Conquista de Anahuac*, in which copper Aztec warriors and silver Spanish conquistadors face off on a chessboard made with black wood and oyster shell. The owner, Antonio Pineda, declined a $1-million offer to sell it. This museum represents his private collection and includes silver pieces from throughout the last century, such as coins, sculptures, jewelry, and crowns. A mural created by a local artist represents the history of Mexico's silver industry.

Plaza Borda 1. ☎ **762/622-0658.** Admission 10 pesos. Tues–Sun 10am–6pm. The museum is located downstairs in the Patio de las Artesanias.

Santa Prisca y San Sebastián Church ★★   This is Taxco's centerpiece parish church; it faces the pleasant Plaza Borda. José de la Borda, a French miner who struck it rich in Taxco's silver mines, funded the construction. Completed in 1758, it's one of Mexico's most impressive baroque churches. The ultracarved facade is eclipsed by the interior, with breathtakingly intricate gold-leafed saints and cherubic angels. The paintings by Miguel Cabrera, one of Mexico's most famous Colonial-Era artists, are the pride of Taxco. Guides, both children and adults, will approach you outside the church offering to give a tour. Make sure the guide's English is passable, and establish whether the price is per person or per tour. Note that flash photos are not allowed.

Plaza Borda. ☏ **762/622-0184.** Free admission. Daily 6:30am–8pm.

NEARBY ATTRACTIONS

The impressive **Las Grutas de Cacahuamilpa** ★, known as the Cacahuamilpa Caves or Grottoes, lie less than a half-hour north of Taxco. Hourly guided tours run daily at the caverns, which house fascinating stalactite and stalagmite formations. To see them, you can join a tour from Taxco (see "Exploring Taxco," above) or take a *combi* from the Flecha Roja terminal in Taxco; one-way is 50 pesos, and admission to the caves is 50 pesos. For more information, see "Sights near Tepoztlán," later in this chapter.

Rancho Emilia Castillo   Don Antonio Castillo was one of hundreds of young men to whom William Spratling taught silversmithing in the 1930s. He was also one of the first to branch out with his own shops and line of designs, which over the years have earned him a fine reputation. Castillo has shops in several Mexican cities. Now his daughter Emilia creates her own noteworthy designs, including decorative pieces with silver fused onto porcelain. After roaming the steep streets of Taxco, a visit to the sprawling hacienda is the perfect way to have the beauty of Guerrero spread out in front of you. The grounds are lush, with a waterfall feeding a stream that runs through the whole property. A tour includes a visit to a workshop where skilled artisans create everything from silver housewares to ceramic figures. Emilia's work is for sale on the ground floor of the Posada de los Castillo, just below the Plazuela Bernal.

8km (5 miles) south of town on the Acapulco Hwy. Also at Plazuela Bernal, Taxco. ☏ **762/622-6901.** If you take a taxi, tell them to drop you off near the crocodile sculpture. Free admission. Workshop Mon–Sat 10am–3pm and 4–6pm; open to groups at other hours by appointment only.

Spratling Ranch Workshop   A trip to William Spratling's hacienda-style home will show you what distinctive Spratling work was all about. Although the prices here are higher than at other outlets, the designs are unusual and considered collectible. There's no store in Taxco, and most of the display cases hold only samples. With the exception of a few jewelry pieces, most items are by order only. Ask about U.S. outlets.

10km (6¼ miles) south of town on the Acapulco Hwy. ☏ **762/622-0026.** Free admission. Call in advance for hours, which vary. The *combi* to Iguala stops at the ranch; fare is 18 pesos.

Where to Stay

MODERATE

Best Western Hotel Taxco ★★   This is the newest and most modern hotel in the town center, with professional service and an international clientele. Rooms are small but very comfortable, with white tiles and bedspreads and Mexican architectural touches. Some have windows (interior rooms do not), and the junior suite has a terrace with views of the surrounding hills. Near the Santa Prisca church, this hotel has a quality Mexican restaurant and access to a nearby pool. The friendly staff will arrange in-room massages upon request. They offer a 10% discount on cash payments.

Carlos J. Nibbi 2, Plazuela de San Juan, 40200 Taxco, Gro. www.bestwesterntaxco.com. ✆ 762/627-6194. Fax 762/622-3416. 23 units. 750 pesos and up double Sun–Thurs; 950 pesos and up double Fri-Sat. AE, MC, V. Free parking. **Amenities:** Restaurant; access to outdoor pool. *In room:* A/C, TV, hair dryer, Wi-Fi.

Monte Taxco ♨ This resort and country club sits atop a hill near the entrance to Taxco coming from Mexico City. A longtime city landmark, it offers golf and tennis, spa services, and access to the mountain's cable car (daily 8am–7pm). Colonial-style rooms are dated but comfortable. Open weekends for dinner only, **Toni's** (see below) has the best city views of any restaurant in Taxco, and you can finish the night at the dance club next door. You'll need to drive or take a taxi to reach the city center.

Fracc. Lomas de Taxco s/n, 40210 Taxco, Gro. www.montetaxcohotel.com. ✆ 762/622-1300. Fax 762/622-1428. 200 units. 1,490 pesos and up double. AE, MC, V. Free parking. **Amenities:** 2 restaurants; bar; dance club; 9-hole golf course; gym; heated outdoor pool; room service; spa services; 3 tennis courts; Wi-Fi. *In room:* A/C, TV, hair dryer.

INEXPENSIVE

Hotel Emilia Castillo ♦ Each room in this delightful small hotel is simply but handsomely appointed with carved doors and furniture; the small tile bathrooms have showers only. Ask for one of the interior rooms, which are much quieter than those facing the street. A high-quality silver shop lies next to the colorful lobby. The hotel does not have parking but instead contracts with a local parking garage.

Juan Ruiz de Alarcón 7, 40200 Taxco, Gro. www.hotelemiliacastillo.com. ✆/fax 762/622-1396. 14 units. $40 double. MC, V. From the Plaza Borda, go downhill a short block to the Plazuela Bernal and make an immediate right; the hotel is a block farther on the right, opposite the Hotel los Arcos (see below). **Amenities:** Wi-Fi. *In room:* TV.

Hotel los Arcos ★ Los Arcos occupies a converted 1620 monastery. The handsome inner patio is bedecked with Puebla pottery and rustic furnishings surrounding a central fountain. Guest rooms are nicely but sparsely appointed, with natural tile floors and colonial-style furniture; the spacious junior suite has two levels. You'll feel immersed in colonial charm and blissful quiet. To find the hotel from the Plaza

Borda, follow the hill down (with Hotel Agua Escondida on your left) and make an immediate right at the Plazuela Bernal.

Juan Ruiz de Alarcón 4, 40200 Taxco, Gro. www.hotellosarcos.net. © **762/622-1836.** Fax 762/622-7982. 21 units. 650 pesos double. No credit cards. **Amenities:** Internet. *In room:* TV, fan.

Hotel Santa Prisca 🐚 The Santa Prisca, 1 block from the Plaza Borda on the Plazuela San Juan, is one of the oldest and best-located hotels in town. Rooms are small but comfortable ("superior doubles" are slightly larger), with standard bathrooms (showers only), tile floors, wood beams, and a colonial atmosphere. For longer stays, ask for a room in the adjacent new addition, where the rooms are sunnier, quieter, and more spacious. A reading area in an upstairs salon overlooks Taxco, as well as a garden patio with fountains.

Cenaobscuras 1, 40200 Taxco, Gro. © **762/622-0080,** -0980. Fax 762/622-2938. 34 units. 500 pesos double; 600 pesos superior double; 700 pesos junior suite. AE, MC, V. Limited free parking. **Amenities:** Breakfast cafe and bar; room service. *In room:* No phone.

Where to Eat

Taxco gets a lot of day-trippers, most of whom choose to dine close to the Plaza Borda. Prices in this area are high for what you get. Just a few streets back, you'll find some excellent, simple *fondas* (taverns) or restaurants.

VERY EXPENSIVE

Toni's ★ STEAKS/SEAFOOD   High on a mountaintop, Toni's is an intimate, classic restaurant enclosed in a huge, cone-shaped *palapa* with a panoramic view of the city. Eleven candlelit tables sparkle with crystal and crisp linen, and piano music accompanies dinner. The menu, mainly shrimp or beef, is limited, but the food is quite good. Try tender, juicy prime roast beef carved at your table, which comes with creamed spinach and baked potato. To reach Toni's, it's best to take a taxi. Note that it's open for dinner on weekends only.

In the Monte Taxco (see above). © **762/622-1300.** www.montetaxcohotel.com. Reservations recommended. Main courses 90–260 pesos. AE, MC, V. Fri–Sun 7–10:30pm.

MODERATE

Cafe Sasha ★★ INTERNATIONAL/VEGETARIAN   One of the cutest places to dine in town, Cafe Sasha is popular with locals and offers a great array of vegetarian options—such as falafel with tabouleh and vegetarian crepes, as well as Mexican and international classics. Try their Thai chicken curry or a hearty burrito. Open for breakfast, lunch, and dinner, it's also a great place for a cappuccino and pastry, or an evening cocktail. The music is hip, and the atmosphere is inviting and chic.

Calle Juan Ruiz de Alarcón 1, just down from Plazuela de Berna. © **762/627-6464.** Breakfast 20–70 pesos; main courses 50–80 pesos. No credit cards. Daily 8am–1am.

El Adobe ★ MEXICAN   This charming restaurant is an eclectic Mexican mix of adobe, brick, and wood with decor that includes regional art, old black-and-white photos of Mexican and American entertainers, and some kitsch memorabilia. There are a number of romantic balcony tables lit with candles and lamps after dark. The hearty fare includes *cecina taxqueña* (thin strip steak served with guacamole), *pollo Guerrero* (chicken cooked with paprika, onion, small potatoes, and guacamole), and enchiladas prepared any way you want. A guitar player/singer performs weekend nights, and brunch is offered on Sunday.

Plazuela de San Juan 13. © **762/622-1416.** Breakfast 30–50 pesos; main courses 55–140 pesos. MC, V. Daily 8am–10:30pm.

El Rincon del Toril LATIN   This festive restaurant combines Mexican, Spanish, Italian, and Argentine cuisines. Delicious steaks are served sizzling hot on the skillet at your table. For a meat-eating extravaganza, order the *parrillada El Toril* for two, which includes *arrachera* beef, ribs, chorizo, and an American steak. Apart from the steaks, the menu offers an enticing selection of fish, chicken, and pasta dishes. The casual and often crowded dining room is brightly decorated with mementos from Mexican bullfights. It leads to an outdoor terrace next to the Plaza Borda. Traditional Mexican music plays cheerfully in the background.

Plaza Borda 3. ✆ **762/627-6207.** Main courses 80–200 pesos. MC, V. Daily 7am–10pm.

La Terraza Café-Bar INTERNATIONAL   One of two restaurants at the Hotel Agua Escondida (on the *zócalo*), the rooftop La Terraza is a scenic spot for a meal or a drink, with tasty food and a great view of the church, town, and surrounding mountains. The diverse menu includes dishes such as breaded veal, grilled pork chops, chicken fajitas, and *mole* enchiladas. Even if you're normally not into desserts, you should seriously think about ordering a delicious crepe or flan here. Frosty margaritas and rich cappuccinos are also on order. During the day, cafe umbrellas shade the sun, and you can stargaze here at night.

Plaza Borda 4. ✆ **762/622-1166.** www.aguaescondida.com/new/english/bar.htm. Main courses 40–100 pesos. MC, V. Daily noon–10:30pm.

Sotavento Restaurant Bar Galería ★★ ITALIAN/INTERNATIONAL   Vibrant Mexican paintings decorate the walls of this stylish restaurant, which offers tables inside, on the balcony, or in the garden patio. The extensive menu features Italian and Mexican dishes—for starters, try the fresh spinach salad with goat cheese and bacon, followed by a large pepper steak. For vegetarians, I recommend the Spaghetti Barbara with poblano peppers, onions, avocado, and cream. Savory crepes are also available.

Benito Juárez 12, next to City Hall. ✆ **762/627-1217.** Main courses 45–150 pesos. MC, V. Tues–Sun 9am–11pm. From the Plaza Borda, walk downhill beside the Hotel Agua Escondida, and then follow the street as it bears left on Agustin de Tulsa (don't go right on Juan Ruiz de Alarcón) about 1 block; the restaurant is on the left just after the street bends left.

INEXPENSIVE

Punta del Cielo INTERNATIONAL   This coffee shop, which is a national chain, is Mexican owned and uses coffee beans from Oaxaca, Chiapas, and Veracruz at a good price. You can't beat the view from this location in Plaza Borda. Several tables are set up on a small patio that overlooks the bustling plaza and the Santa Prisca Church. The rest of the tables are spread throughout the spacious cafe, which has a supply of local newspapers and magazines on hand. After being served your coffee, you're invited to personalize it at a fully stocked flavor bar. They also offer croissants and paninis, which are perfect if you've already had your share of tacos.

Plaza Borda 4. Below Hotel Agua Escondida. ✆ **762/627-2722.** www.puntadelcielo.com.mx. Coffee 17–45 pesos; baguettes and snacks 45–70 pesos. MC, V. If you're leaving the Santa Prisa Church, it will be on your right side after you pass the Casa Borda.

Taxco After Dark

Located upstairs at Plaza Borda 12, **Acerto** (✆ **762/622-0064**) is an enticing all-purpose hangout overlooking the square. It serves as an Internet cafe, sports bar, and restaurant. Taxco's popular, modern dance club, **Windows,** sits high up the mountain in the Monte Taxco (see above; ✆ **762/622-1300**). The entire city is on view, and music runs the gamut from Latin pop to '80s hits. For 30 pesos cover, you can dance away Friday or Saturday night from 9pm to 3am. The club seldom gets crowded.

Completely different in tone is **Bar Berta's** (© 762/622-0172), next to the Santa Prisca Church at Plaza Borda 9. Opened in 1930 by a lady named Berta, who made her fame on a drink of the same name (tequila, soda, lime, and honey), it's the traditional gathering place of the local gentry and tourists. Spurs and old swords decorate the walls. Grab a seat on the balcony overlooking the plaza and church. A Berta (the drink, of course) costs about 55 pesos; rum, the same. It's open daily from 11am to 8pm.

La Concha Nostra (© 762/622-7944), has a local, edgy feel and features live rock music Saturday nights for a 25 pesos cover. It's located upstairs inside the Hotel Casa Grande at Plazuela de San Juan 7 and is open nightly until 1am. If you're looking to get down on the dance floor, **Ibiza Night Club** (© 762/627-1664; www.ibizataxco.com) is the place to go. Located on Av. de los Plateros 137, it hosts local disc jockeys and theme nights; check their website for upcoming events.

IXTAPAN DE LA SAL: A THERMAL SPA TOWN

120km (74 miles) SW of Mexico City

The whitewashed town of Ixtapan de la Sal (not to be confused with Ixtapa, on the Pacific coast) is known for its thermal mud baths—this is an original spa town, with generations of healing traditions. Hotels in Ixtapan (pronounced *Eeks*-tah-pahn) de la Sal tend to fill up on weekends and Mexican holidays, as the town is a popular retreat from Mexico City. Cuernavaca, Taxco, and Toluca are all easy side trips.

Getting There

BY CAR   From Mexico City, take Hwy. 15 to Toluca. In Toluca, Hwy. 15 becomes Paseo Tollocan. Follow Tollocan south until you see signs pointing left to Ixtapan de la Sal. After the turn, continue straight for around 15km (9¼ miles). Just before the town of Tenango del Valle, you have a choice of the free road to Ixtapan de la Sal or the toll road. The free road winds through the mountains and takes 1½ hours. The inexpensive toll road has fewer mountain curves and takes around an hour—it's worth taking. (See "Getting Around" in chapter 20 for more about toll roads and charges.) The toll road stops about 15km (9¼ miles) before Ixtapan; the rest of the trip is on a curvy mountainous drive.

BY BUS   From Mexico City's Terminal Poniente, buses leave for Ixtapan de la Sal every few minutes. Request a bus that's taking the toll road, which cuts the travel time by 30 to 60 minutes, to about 2½ hours. To return, take a bus marked MEXICO DIRECTO, which leaves every 10 minutes and usually stops in Toluca. Buses from here also go to Cuernavaca and Taxco every 40 minutes.

A Public Spa

The **Ixtapan Parque Acuático** (© 55/5254-0500; www.parqueixtapan.com), next to the Hotel Spa Ixtapan, is the town's original public spa and bathhouse. It's not a modern, pampering spa, but a spa in the traditional manner—think Turkish bath. The *balneario* has melded its traditional thermal waters with some features that make it more of an aquatic park. In addition to the large pools of varying temperatures, it offers modern water slides, a slow-moving river, and other attractions. Entrance is 170 pesos for adults, 90 pesos for children between .9m and 1.2m (3–4 ft.) tall; children under .9m (3 ft.) tall enter free. The *balneario* has restaurants, so you can spend the day. The entrance fee gives you access to all of the pools and rides. Lockers are free. The *balneario* is open daily from 8am to 7pm (for the thermal baths); the water park is open daily from 9am to 6pm (for the rides). The traditional spa amenities and services are next door, where you can choose among private thermal water baths, massages, facials, hair treatments, and more. Prices range from 200 to 725 pesos. The spa is open daily from 8am to 8pm during holiday periods; at other times, Monday through Friday from 8am to 8pm, Saturday and Sunday from 7am to 8pm.

Where to Stay & Eat

Hotel Ixtapan Spa & Golf Resort ★ 🍴

The town's famous spa resort sits on 14 manicured and flower-filled hectares (35 acres). In operation since 1939, it feels aged, but unrenovated areas afford guests the nostalgic feel of the original hotel and spa. The resort offers golf, tennis, swimming, and miles of trails for walking, jogging, or biking. It has swimming pools, an outdoor whirlpool, and a host of spa services such as Thai massages and Balinese hot clay treatments. Rooms in the main building are slightly better furnished than the so-called "villa" rooms, but all are fairly basic. There are three restaurants: One features spa cuisine, another serves a more traditional international menu, and the third serves lunch by the pool. Round-trip taxi transportation from the Mexico City airports can be arranged at the time of reservation for around $340 from the Benito Juárez airport and $170 from Toluca, which can be shared by up to four people. Rates for the different packages include full American plan (three meals daily).

Bulevar San Román s/n, Ixtapan de la Sal, 51900 Edo. de México. www.spamexico.com. © **800/638-7950** in the U.S., or 721/143-2440. 220 units, including 45 villas. $120–$150 double. 4-day spa package $665 per person double; 7-day spa package $1,175 per person double; 21-day spa package $2,950 per person double; 28-day spa package $3,930 per person double. Rates include all meals. AE, MC, V. **Amenities:** 3 restaurants; bar; concierge; piano lounge; mountain bikes; private 18-hole golf course; gym; 2 outdoor pools; 2 indoor and 1 outdoor whirlpools; room service; sauna; smoke-free rooms; 2 full-service spas; steam room; 2 tennis courts; hiking trails; Wi-Fi (in lobby). *In room:* A/C, TV.

Marriott Ixtapan de la Sal Hotel & Spa ★★ ☺

The design of this hotel, located at the town entrance, evokes traditional Mexican style while still feeling modern. Built on several levels on the slope of a hill, the Marriott offers sweeping views of the surrounding mountains. Guest rooms are bright and spacious, with tile floors, Mexican accents, and modern amenities, like iHome, LCD TVs, and Wi-Fi. The Tecilli Spa is a full-service luxury spa that offers massages, facials, body wraps, and treatments based on the four elements. This hotel is very kid-friendly, with a go-kart racetrack, soccer fields, tree houses, a playroom designed to look like a jungle, a day care center, and a pirate ship, complete with water slides, at the outdoor pool.

José Maria Morelos s/n, Fracc. Bugambilias. www.marriott.com/hotels/travel/mexix-ixtapan-de-la-sal-marriott-hotel-and-spa. © **888/236-2427** in the U.S., or 721/143-2010. 189 units. $119–$220 double; $199–$309 suite. AE, MC, V. Parking on-site valet $9, $5 daily. **Amenities:** 3 restaurants; bar; children's center and programs; small chapel; concierge; 18-hole golf course nearby; gym; 3 outdoor pools and 1 indoor pool; smoke-free rooms; sauna; spa; tennis courts. *In room:* A/C, TV, hair dryer, Wi-Fi.

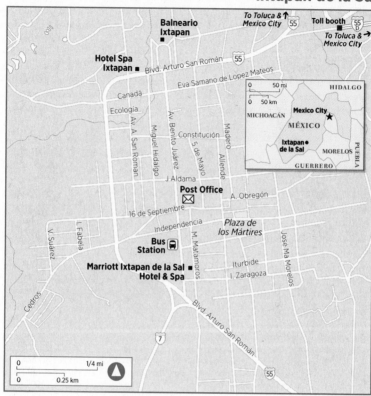

Ixtapan de la Sal

VALLE DE BRAVO & AVÁNDARO: MEXICO'S SWITZERLAND

152km (94 miles) SW of Mexico City

Valle de Bravo has been called the "Switzerland of Mexico." Ringed by pine-forested mountains and set beside a beautiful lake, Valle de Bravo is a 16th-century village with cobblestone streets and colonial structures built around a town plaza. Like San Miguel de Allende, Taxco, and Puerto Vallarta, Valle de Bravo is a National Heritage village; new construction must conform to the colonial style of the original village.

The village's cobbled streets, small restaurants, hotels, spas, and shops are full on weekends—this is a very popular retreat from Mexico City. Some shops and restaurants may be closed weekdays. The crafts market, 3 blocks from the main square, is open daily from 10am to 5pm, and colorfully dressed Mazahua Indians sell their handmade tapestries daily around the town plaza.

Sailing, windsurfing, bass fishing, and water-skiing are popular on the lake. Boats of varying speeds can be rented (along with a driver and water-ski equipment) at the dock for between 200 and 400 pesos per hour; look for the sign that says YATE CRISTAL

145

Y LANCHAS. Excursions from Valle de Bravo include a trip to the nesting grounds of the monarch butterfly between November and February. It can be very rainy and chilly September through December, in addition to the summer rainy season.

The neighboring town of Avándaro, 6km (3¾ miles) away, is a popular place for weekend homes for well-to-do residents of Mexico City.

Getting There

BY CAR From Mexico City, the quickest route is Hwy. 15 to Toluca. In Toluca, Hwy. 15 becomes Paseo Tollocan. Follow Tollocan south until you see signs pointing left to Hwy. 134 and Valle de Bravo, Francisco de los Ranchos, and Temascaltepec. After the turn, continue on Hwy. 142 until Francisco de los Ranchos, where you bear right and follow signs to Valle de Bravo. The drive from here takes 1½ to 2 hours.

BY BUS From Mexico City's Terminal Poniente, buses leave every 20 minutes for the 3-hour journey. First-class buses depart hourly.

Where to Stay

Avándaro Golf and Spa Resort ★ ☺ On 118 hectares (291 acres) amid large estates, lushly forested mountains, and a gorgeous, rolling 18-hole golf course, this resort occupies one of the loveliest settings in Mexico. Rooms come in two categories: large deluxe suites and smaller, less luxurious cabañas. Rooms have fireplaces and terraces or balconies overlooking the grounds. The extensive spa includes hot and cold whirlpools, sauna and steam rooms, and a full range of body and facial treatments. The hotel has two drawbacks: Some of the rooms need upgrading, and large tour groups often stay here. Transportation from Mexico City can be arranged.

Fracc. Vega del Río s/n. Avándaro, 51200 Valle de Bravo. www.hotelavandaro.com.mx. ✆ **726/266-0366;** reservations 55/5280-1532, 5282-0954, 5280-5532, or 5282-0578 in Mexico City. 74 units. $113 double cabaña; $333 deluxe suite. 7-day spa or golf package available. AE, MC, V. **Amenities:** 2 restaurants; bar; children's center; 18-hole golf course; fitness center; 25m (82-ft.) junior Olympic-size pool; hot and cold whirlpools; room service; sauna; spa w/well-trained staff and full range of services; steam rooms; 7 tennis courts. *In room:* TV, hair dryer.

El Santuario Resort & Spa ★★★ Set on the shores of Valle de Bravo's lake, and at the foot of an "energy-conducting" quartz mountain, this resort combines soothing natural surroundings with modern amenities, recreational activities, and spa services. The design includes magnificent use of water, such as infinity pools that seem to fall from the sides of the resort into the lake. The guest suites are built into the mountainside, with panoramic views of the water. Each comes with a private plunge pool. The 1,860-sq.-m (20,021-sq.-ft.) spa offers over 60 therapies in a variety of treatment rooms, including a flotation suite, as well as a cafe, oxygen bar, gym, salon, and studio for yoga, Pilates, meditation, and other mind-body activities. The signature therapy is the Yenecamú—2½ hours of treatments, which, upon request, can be performed on a pontoon boat in the middle of the lake. There's also golf, hiking, watersports on the lake, and other eco-oriented activities to while away the time.

ExHacienda San Gaspar Carretera a Colorines, Km 4.5, 51200 Valle de Bravo. www.elsantuario.com. ✆ **726/262-9100.** 64 suites. 3,600 pesos junior suite on weekdays; 4,400 pesos junior suite on weekends. Spa packages start at 3,200 pesos extra per person, double occupancy for 2 nights, including all meals and selected spa services. Other packages are also available. AE, MC, V. **Amenities:** Restaurant/bar; concierge; outdoor pool w/whirlpools; 9-hole golf course; spa; marina. *In room:* TV, hair dryer, minibar.

Valle de Bravo & Avándaro

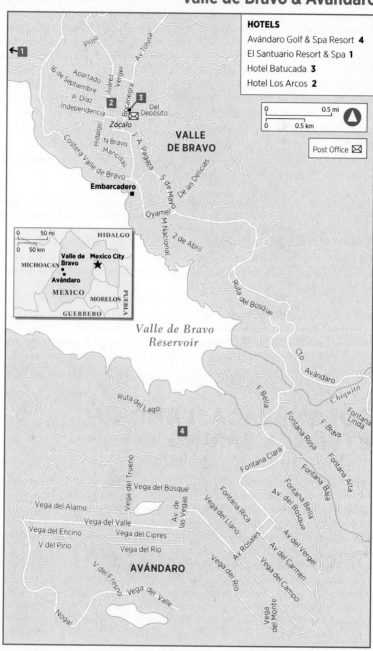

HOTELS

Avándaro Golf & Spa Resort **4**
El Santuario Resort & Spa **1**
Hotel Batucada **3**
Hotel Los Arcos **2**

Post Office ⊠

Hotel Batucada   If you'd like to stay right in the charming town center, this historic option is just 2 blocks from the central square. A handful of guest rooms fill the 300-year-old home and surround a flower-filled courtyard with a trickling fountain and background jazz music. The individually decorated rooms present a warm, colonial feel, with high wood-beam ceilings, rustic wood furnishings, and views of the surrounding mountains. Guests who stay 2 nights or more receive a welcome drink, fruit basket, and free continental breakfast.

Francisco González Bocanegra 207, 51200 Valle de Bravo. www.hotelbatucada.com.mx. © **726/262-0480** or 722/261-4051. Fax 726/262-0586. 9 units. 1,888–2,832 pesos double. Rates include breakfast. AE, MC, V. Free parking. **Amenities:** Restaurant; bar; concierge; room service. *In room:* TV.

Hotel los Arcos ☺   The Hotel los Arcos, close to the main square, affords views of the lake and village. Two stories of rooms on one side and three stories on the other surround a swimming pool. Nineteen rooms have fireplaces, an important feature in winter here. Some rooms have balconies, and most have glass walls with views. This hotel is popular with families.

Francisco González Bocanegra 310, 51200 Valle de Bravo. www.hotellosarcosvb.com. ©/fax **726/262-0042**, -0531, -0168. 24 units. 850–1,207 pesos double. AE, MC, V. **Amenities:** Outdoor pool. *In room:* TV.

Where to Eat

Da Ciro ITALIAN   This wonderful Italian restaurant is a short walk from the town's central square. If you come for lunch, ask for a table on the idyllic outdoor terrace. At night, the dining room transforms into a romantic hideaway, with brick walls, wood-beam ceilings, Tiffany lamps, and floor-to-ceiling windows. Start with a Caprese salad followed by a mouthwatering homemade pizza. The house specialty is pasta, including an incredibly delicious spaghetti Parmesan prepared tableside. Also excellent are risotto with shrimp, *osso buco,* and sea bass stuffed with shrimp in cognac. Like many places in Valle de Bravo, Da Ciro is open only on weekends.

Vergel 201, next to City Hall. © **762/262-0122.** Reservations recommended. Main courses 110–180 pesos. AE, MC, V. Fri–Sat 1pm–midnight; Sun 1–8pm.

CUERNAVACA: LAND OF ETERNAL SPRING ★★★

102km (63 miles) S of Mexico City; 80km (50 miles) N of Taxco

Often called the "land of eternal spring," Cuernavaca is known these days as much for its rejuvenating spas and spiritual sites as for its perfect climate and flowering landscapes. Spa services are easy to find. More important, Cuernavaca exudes a deep sense of connection with its historical and spiritual heritage. Its palaces, walled villas, and elaborate haciendas are home to museums, spas, and extraordinary guesthouses.

Wander the traditional markets and you'll see crystals, quartz, onyx, and tiger's eye amid the trinkets. These stones come from the Tepozteco Mountains—for centuries considered an energy source—which cradle Cuernavaca to the north and east. Mexico begins to narrow here, and several mountain ranges converge. Cuernavaca sits at 1,533m (5,028 ft.) elevation. East and southeast of Cuernavaca are two volcanoes, also potent symbols of earth energy: **Ixtaccihuatl** (the Sleeping Woman) and the recently active **Popocatépetl** (the Smoking Mountain).

Cuernavaca

HOTELS ■
Camino Real Sumiya **7**
Casa Colonial **5**
Hotel Posada María
  Cristina **6**
Las Mañanitas **1**
Misión del Sol Resort
  and Spa **9**

ATTRACTIONS ●
Catedral de Cuernavaca **3**
Cortez Palace **11**
Jardín Borda **2**
Jardín Etnobotánico **8**
Mercado (public market) **10**
Museo de Medicina
  Tradicional y Herbolaria **8**
Museo Casa Robert Brady **4**
Museo de Cuauhnáhuac **11**

To Pirámide de
Teopanzolco
→

To Jardín
de los
Héroes
→

Information ⓘ
Post Office ✉

Cuernavaca, capital of the state of Morelos, is also a cultural treasure, with a past that closely follows the history of Mexico. So divine are the landscape and climate that both the Aztec ruler Moctezuma II and French Emperor Maximilian built private retreats here. Today Cuernavaca remains the most popular weekend getaway for moneyed residents of Mexico City. As a result, the roads between the capital and Cuernavaca are jammed almost every weekend, but you can avoid some of the crowds by traveling early in the morning. Cuernavaca even has a large American colony, plus many students attending the numerous language and cultural institutes.

Emperor Charles V gave Cuernavaca to Hernán Cortez as a fief, and in 1532 the conquistador built a palace (now the Museo de Cuauhnáhuac), where he lived on and off for half a dozen years before returning to Spain. Cortez introduced sugar-cane cultivation to the area, and African slaves were brought in to work in the cane fields, by way of Spain's Caribbean colonies. His sugar hacienda at the edge of town is now the impressive Hotel de Cortez.

After Mexico gained independence from Spain, powerful landowners from Mexico City gradually dispossessed the remaining small landholders, imposing virtual serfdom on them. This condition led to the rise of Emiliano Zapata, the great champion of agrarian reform, who battled the forces of wealth and power, defending the small farmer with the cry of *"¡Tierra y libertad!"* (Land and liberty!) during the Mexican Revolution of 1910.

Today Cuernavaca's popularity has brought an influx of wealthy foreigners and industrial capital. With this commercial growth, the city has also acquired the less desirable byproducts of increased traffic, noise, and air pollution—although still far, far less than nearby Mexico City, which you may be escaping.

Essentials

GETTING THERE & DEPARTING   By Car   From Mexico City, take Insurgentes or Periférico south, which will take you to Hwy. 95D, the toll road on the far south of town that goes to Cuernavaca. From the Periférico, take the Insurgentes exit and continue until you come to signs for Cuernavaca/Tlalpan. Choose either the *Cuernavaca cuota* (toll) or the *Cuernavaca libre* (free) road on the right. The free road is slower and very windy, but more scenic. The toll road costs about 150 pesos.

By Bus   *Important note:* Buses to Cuernavaca depart directly from the Benito Juárez airport in Mexico City. (See "Getting There & Departing: By Bus," p. 68, for details.) The trip takes an hour or longer. The Mexico City Central de Autobuses del Sur exists primarily to serve the Mexico City–Cuernavaca-Taxco-Acapulco-Zihuatanejo route. Pullman de Morelos has two stations in Cuernavaca: downtown, at the corner of Abasolo and Nezahualcóyotl (© **777/312-6063**), 4 blocks south of the

You Wouldn't Know It, But . . .

The city of Cuernavaca has nothing to do with bull's horns, as the direct translation of its name would suggest. The Aztecs were much more succinct when they named their favorite leisurely retreat Cuauhnáhuac (pronounced Kwow-*nah*-wak), or place of the trees. Cortez and his men had trouble getting their tongues around that word, so they just named it after something that sounded similar.

center of town; and Casino de la Selva (© 777/312-9472), less conveniently located at Plan de Ayala 14, near the railroad station.

Autobuses Estrella Blanca (© 777/312-2626; www.estrellablanca.com.mx) depart from the Central del Sur, with four buses daily from Mexico City. They arrive in Cuernavaca at Av. Morelos Sur 329, between Arista and Victoria, 6 blocks north of the town center. Here you'll find frequent buses to Toluca, Chalma, Ixtapan de la Sal, Taxco, Acapulco, the Cacahuamilpa Caves, Querétaro, and Nuevo Laredo.

Estrella de Oro (© 777/312-3055; www.estrelladeoro.com.mx), Morelos 900, serves Iguala, Chilpancingo, Acapulco, and Taxco.

Estrella Roja (© 777/318-5934; www.estrellaroja.com.mx), a second-class station at Galeana and Cuauhtemotzin in Cuernavaca, about 8 blocks south of the town center, serves Cuautla, Yautepec, Oaxtepec, and Izúcar de Matamoros.

VISITOR INFORMATION Cuernavaca's **Municipal Tourist Office** is at Calle Hidalgo 5, next to the Jardin Morelos (Morelos Garden; © 777/314-3920; www. cuernavaca.gob.mx). It's open daily from 9am to 5pm. The **Morelos State Tourism Office** is located on Av. Morelos Sur 187 (© 777/314-3881; www.morelostravel. com). It's open Monday through Friday from 9am to 5pm. There's also a **City Tourism kiosk** (© 777/329-4404) at Morelos Sur 278, beside the El Calvario Church, open daily from 9am to 5pm.

CITY LAYOUT In the center of the city are two contiguous plazas. The smaller and more formal, across from the post office, has a Victorian gazebo (designed by Gustave Eiffel, of Eiffel Tower fame) at its center. This is the **Alameda.** The larger, rectangular plaza with trees, shrubs, and benches is the **Plaza de Armas.** These two plazas are known collectively as the *zócalo* and form the hub for strolling vendors selling balloons, baskets, bracelets, and other crafts from surrounding villages. It's all easygoing, and one of the great pleasures of the town is hanging out at a park bench or table in a nearby restaurant. On Sunday afternoons, orchestras play in the gazebo. At the eastern end of the Alameda is the **Cortez Palace,** the conquistador's residence, now the Museo de Cuauhnáhuac.

Note: The city's street-numbering system is extremely confusing. It appears that the city founders, during the past century or so, imposed a new numbering system every 10 or 20 years. An address given as "no. 5" may be in a building that bears the number "506," or perhaps *"Antes no. 5"* (former no. 5).

[FastFACTS] CUERNAVACA

Area Code The telephone area code is **777.**

Banks Bank tellers (9am–4pm, depending on the bank), ATMs, and *casas de cambio* change money. The closest bank to the *zócalo* is **Bancomer,** Matamoros and Lerdo de Tejada, cater-cornered to Jardín Juárez (across López Rayón from the Alameda).

Drugstore **Farmacias del Ahorro** (© 777/322-2277) offers hotel delivery service, but you must ask the front desk of your hotel to place the order, because the pharmacy requires the name of a hotel employee. It has 12 locations around the city, but the individual pharmacies have no phone. Some are open 24 hours a day, while others are open daily from 7am to 10pm.

Hospital **Hospital Inovamed** is located at Calle Cuauhtémoc 305, Col. Lomas de la Selva (© **777/311-2482,** -2483, -2484).

Internet Access There are several Internet cafes around the city; however, they open and close frequently. Most hotels offer Internet access or can point you in the direction of a place that does.

Post Office The *correo* ((*C*) **777/312-4379**) is on the Plaza de Armas, next door to Café los Arcos. It's open Monday through Friday from 8am to 6pm, Saturday from 10am to 2pm.

Exploring Cuernavaca

On weekends, the whole city (including roads, hotels, and restaurants) fills with people from Mexico City. This makes weekends more hectic, but also more fun. You can spend 1 or 2 days sightseeing pleasantly enough. If you've come on a day trip, you may not have time to make all the excursions listed below, but you'll have enough time to see the sights in town. The traditional *mercado* (**public market**) adjacent to the Cortez Palace is open daily from 10am to 10pm. The colorful rows of stands are a lively place to test your bargaining skills as you purchase pottery, silver jewelry, crystals, and other trinkets. Note that many sights, including the Cuauhnáhuac museum, are closed on Monday.

Catedral de Cuernavaca ★ 📷 As you enter the church precincts and pass down the walk, try to imagine what life in Mexico was like in the old days. Construction on the church, also known as the *Catedral de Asunción de María*, began in 1529, a mere 8 years after Cortez conquered Tenochtitlán (Mexico City) from the Aztec, and was completed in 1552. The churchmen could hardly trust their safety to the tenuous allegiance of their new converts, so they built a fortress as a church. The skull and crossbones above the main door are a symbol of the Franciscan order, which had its monastery here. The monastery is open to the public, on the northwest corner of the church property. Also visible on the exterior walls of the main church are inlaid rocks, placed there in memory of the men who lost their lives during its construction.

Once inside, wander through the sanctuaries and the courtyard, and pay special attention to the impressive frescoes painted on the walls, in various states of restoration. The frescoes date from the 1500s and have a distinct Asian style.

The main sanctuary is stark, even severe, with an incongruous modern feeling (it was refurbished in the 1960s). Frescoes on these walls, discovered during the refurbishing, depict the persecution and martyrdom of St. Felipe de Jesús and his companions in Japan. No one is certain who painted them. In the churchyard, you'll see gravestones marking the tombs of the most devout (or wealthiest) parishioners. Being buried on the church grounds was believed to be the most direct route to heaven.

At the corner of Hidalgo and Morelos (3 blocks southwest of the Plaza de Armas). (*C*) **777/318-4590.** Free admission. Daily 8am–2pm and 4–7pm.

Jardín Borda Across Morelos Street from the cathedral lies the Jardín Borda (Borda Gardens). José de la Borda, the Taxco silver magnate, ordered a sumptuous vacation house built here in the late 1700s. When he died in 1778, his son Manuel inherited the land and transformed it into a botanical garden. The large enclosed garden next to the house was a huge private park, laid out in Andalusian style, with kiosks and an artificial pond. Maximilian took it over as his private summerhouse in 1865. He and Empress Carlota entertained lavishly in the gardens and held concerts by the lake.

The gardens were completely restored and reopened in 1987 as the Jardín Borda Centro de Artes. In the gateway buildings, several galleries hold changing exhibits and

Cuernavaca is known for its Spanish-language schools. Generally, the schools will help students find lodging with a family or provide a list of places to stay. Rather than make a long-term commitment in a family living situation, try it for a week, and then decide. Contact the **Universidad Internacional**, San Jerónimo 304 (Apdo. Postal 1520), 62000 Cuernavaca, Morelos (© **800/932-2068** in the U.S., or 777/317-1087; www.spanish.com.mx); **Instituto de Idioma y Cultura en Cuernavaca** (© **777/317-8947;**

fax 777/317-0455; www.idiomaycultura.com.mx), Privado Narcisso Mendoza #5, Colonia Pradera; or **Universal Center for Language and Social Communication: Innovative Spanish,** J. H. Preciado 171 (Apdo. Postal 1-1826, 62000 Cuernavaca, Morelos; © **777/318-2904** or 312-4902; www.universal-spanish.com). The entire experience, from classes to lodging, can be quite expensive; the school may accept credit cards for the class portion.

large paintings showing scenes from the life of Maximilian and from the history of the Borda Gardens. One portrays the initial meeting between Maximilian and La India Bonita, a local maiden who became his lover.

On your stroll through the gardens, you'll see the little artificial lake on which Austrian, French, and Mexican nobility rowed small boats in the moonlight; rowboats are available to rent. The lake is artfully adapted as an outdoor theater (see website for performance information), with seats for the audience on one side and the stage on the other. Music concerts are often held on Sunday evenings. A cafe serves refreshments and light meals, and a weekend market inside the *jardín* sells arts and crafts.

Av. Morelos Sur 271, at Hidalgo. © **777/312-4789** or 777/318-1038. www.morelosturistico.com. Admission 30 pesos adults, 15 pesos children. Tues–Sun 10am–5:30pm.

Jardín Etnobotánico y Museo de Medicina Tradicional y Herbolaria ★★
This serene museum of traditional herbal medicine, in the south Cuernavaca suburb of Acapantzingo, occupies a former resort residence built by Maximilian, the Casa del Olvido. During his brief reign, the Austrian-born emperor came here for trysts with La India Bonita, his Cuernavacan lover. The building was restored in 1960, and the house and gardens now preserve the local wisdom of folk medicine. The shady gardens are lovely to wander through, and you shouldn't miss the hundreds of orchids growing near the rear of the property.

Matamoros 14, Acapantzingo. © **777/312-5955,** 777/312-3108, or 777/314-4046. www.gobiernodigital.inah.gob.mx, or email jardin.mor@inah.gob.mx. Free admission. Daily 9am–5pm. Take a taxi, or catch combi no. 6 at the mercado on Degollado. Ask to be dropped off at Matamoros near the museum; turn right on Matamoros and walk 1½ blocks; the museum will be on your right.

Museo Casa Robert Brady ★★
This private home and garden–turned–museum houses an eclectic collection of religious, folk, and ethnic art, including pre-Hispanic and colonial pieces; oil paintings by Frida Kahlo and Rufino Tamayo; popular Mexican art; and handicrafts from America, Africa, Asia, and India. Robert Brady, an Iowa native with a degree in fine arts from the Art Institute of Chicago, assembled the collections. The brightly decorated house (tiled with hand-painted Talavera throughout) is a work of art in its own right. Brady lived in Venice for 5 years

5

SILVER, SPAS & SPIRITUAL CENTERS

Cuernavaca

before settling in Cuernavaca in 1960. The wildly colorful rooms remain exactly as Brady left them when he died here in 1986. Admission includes a guide in Spanish; English and French guides are available if requested in advance. A small cafe in the main patio serves refreshments.

Calle Nezahualcóyotl 4 (btw. Hidalgo and Abasolo). ℭ **777/318-8554.** www.bradymuseum.org. Admission 35 pesos. Tues–Sun 10am–6pm.

Museo de Cuauhnáhuac ★ The Palacio Cortez, once home to Mexico's most famous conquistador, is now the Museo de Cuauhnáhuac, devoted to the history of Morelos state. It's also home to a stunning Diego Rivera mural, *The History of Cuernavaca & Morelos,* an unflinching illustrated history of the brutality and treachery of the Spanish Conquest. In one panel, a Spanish soldier holds a hot poker, poised to brand an Aztec prisoner on the neck; behind him, men in armor pour gold pieces into a large trunk while a priest blesses the transaction. True to Rivera's communist faith in the power of the Mexican people, the largest images in the gallery are full-length portraits of Emiliano Zapata, the revolutionary who fought for agrarian reform with the cry, "*¡Tierra y libertad!*" ("Land and liberty!"), and Father José Maria Morelos, a hero of the War of Independence.

On the lower level, the excellent bookstore is open daily from 11am to 8pm. Tour guides in front of the palace offer their services in the museum for about 100 pesos per hour. Make sure you see official SECTUR (Tourism Secretary) credentials before hiring one of these guides. This is also a central point for taxis in the downtown area.

In the Cortez Palace, Leyva 100. ℭ **777/312-8171.** www.morelosturistico.com. Admission 41 pesos; free Sun. Tues–Sun 9am–6pm.

Activities & Excursions

GOLF With its perpetually springlike climate, Cuernavaca is an ideal place for golf. The **Tabachines Golf Club and Restaurant,** Km 93.5 Carr. Mexico-Acapulco (ℭ 777/314-3396; www.tabachines.com), the city's most popular course, is open for public play. Percy Clifford designed this 18-hole course, surrounded by beautifully manicured gardens blooming with bougainvillea, gardenias, and other flowers. The elegant restaurant is a popular place for breakfast, lunch, and especially Sunday brunch. Greens fees are 750 pesos during the week and 2,000 pesos on weekends, with fees reduced by half after 1:30pm. American Express, Visa, and MasterCard are accepted. It's open Tuesday through Sunday from 7am to 6pm.

Also in Cuernavaca is the **Club de Golf Hacienda San Gaspar,** Av. Emiliano Zapata, Col. Cliserio Alanis (ℭ 777/319-4424; www.sangaspar.com), an 18-hole golf course designed by Joe Finger. It's surrounded by more than 3,000 trees and has two artificial lagoons, plus beautiful panoramic views of Cuernavaca, the Popocatépetl and Ixtaccihuatl volcanoes, and the Tepozteco Mountains. Greens fees are 800 pesos on weekdays, 1,400 pesos on weekends (discounted after 2pm); carts cost an additional 450 pesos for 18 holes, and a caddy is 200 pesos plus tip. American Express, Visa, and MasterCard are accepted. Additional facilities include a gym with whirlpool and sauna, pool, four tennis courts, and a restaurant and snack bar. It's open Wednesday through Monday from 7am to 7pm.

LAS ESTACAS Either a side trip from Cuernavaca or a destination on its own, Las Estacas, Km 6.5 Carretera Tlaltizapán–Cuautla, Morelos (ℭ **777/312-4412,** -7610 in Cuernavaca, or 734/345-0350; www.lasestacas.com), is a natural water park. Its clear spring waters reputedly have healing properties. In addition to the crystal-clear

SILVER, SPAS & SPIRITUAL CENTERS

rivers with aquatic ropes, water swings, diving platforms, and hanging bridges, Las Estacas has two pools, wading pools for children, horseback riding, an 18-hole minigolf course, and a diving school. Several restaurants serve such simple food as quesadillas, fruit with yogurt, sandwiches, and *tortas*. Admission is 250 pesos for adults, 154 pesos for children under 1.2m (4 ft.) tall. A small, basic hotel charges 1,580 to 1,900 pesos for a double room; rates include the entrance fee to the *balneario* and breakfast. Cheaper lodging options include a trailer and camping park; you can rent an adobe or straw hut with two bunk beds for 340 pesos. Visit the website for more information. MasterCard and Visa are accepted. On weekends, the place fills with families. Las Estacas is 36km (22 miles) east of Cuernavaca. To get there, take Hwy. 138 to Yautepec, then turn right at the first exit past Yautepec.

PYRAMIDS OF XOCHICALCO ★   This pre-Columbian ceremonial center provides clues to the history of the whole region. Artifacts and inscriptions link the site to the mysterious cultures that built Teotihuacán and Tula, and some of the objects found here would indicate that residents were also in contact with the Mixtec, Aztec, Maya, and Zapotec. The most impressive building in Xochicalco is the Pirámide de la Serpiente Emplumada (Pyramid of the Plumed Serpent), with its magnificent reliefs of plumed serpents twisting around seated priests. Underneath the pyramid is a series of tunnels and chambers with murals on the walls. At the observatory, from April 30 to August 15, you can follow the sun's trajectory as it shines through a hexagonal opening. The pyramids (© **777/374-3090** for information) are 36km (22 miles) southwest of Cuernavaca, open daily from 9am to 6pm. Admission is 51 pesos.

Where to Stay

EXPENSIVE

Camino Real Sumiya ★★   About 11km (6¾ miles) south of Cuernavaca, this unusual resort was once the home of Woolworth heiress Barbara Hutton. Using materials and craftsmen from Japan, she constructed the estate in 1959 for $3.2 million on 12 wooded hectares (30 acres). The main house, a series of large connected rooms and decks, overlooks the grounds and contains restaurants and the lobby. Sumiya's charm rests in its relaxing atmosphere, which is best midweek (escapees from Mexico City tend to fill it on weekends). Guest rooms cluster in three-story buildings bordering manicured lawns. They're simple compared to the main house's striking Japanese architecture. Rooms have subtle Japanese accents, with austere but comfortable furnishings and scrolled wood doors. Some regulars have complained that service has become less personalized under new management.

Interior Fracc. Sumiya s/n, Col. José Parres, 62550 Jiutepec, Mor. www.caminoreal.com/sumiya. © **777/329-9888.** Fax 777/329-9866. 163 units. $145 double; $250 suite. Low-season packages and discounts available. AE, DC, MC, V. Free parking. From the freeway, take the Atlacomulco exit and follow signs to Sumiya. Ask for directions in Cuernavaca if you're coming from there, as the route is complicated. **Amenities:** 2 restaurants; lobby bar; poolside snack bar; concierge; golf privileges nearby; outdoor pool; room service; tennis club; convention facilities w/translation equipment. *In room:* A/C, ceiling fan, TV, hair dryer, minibar, Wi-Fi.

Las Mañanitas   This hotel and garden has been Cuernavaca's most renowned luxury lodging for years. It's also a popular weekend dining spot for affluent visitors from Mexico City. Guest rooms are formal in style, with gleaming polished molding and brass accents, large bathrooms, and rich fabrics. Rooms in the original mansion, called terrace suites, overlook the restaurant and inner lawn; the large rooms in the patio section each have a secluded patio; and those in the luxurious, expensive garden section each have a patio overlooking the pool and emerald lawns. Sixteen rooms have fireplaces, and the hotel also has a heated pool in the private garden of exotic birds, flowers, and trees. Las Mañanitas is one of only three hotels in Mexico associated with the prestigious Relais & Châteaux chain. The restaurant overlooking the peacock-filled gardens is one of the country's premier dining places (see "Where to Eat," below).

Ricardo Linares 107 (5½ long blocks north of the Jardín Borda), 62000 Cuernavaca, Mor. www.las mananitas.com.mx. ② **888/413-9199** in the U.S., or 01-800/221-5299 in Mexico. Fax 777/312-8982. 25 units. Weekdays 2,351–5,264 pesos suite. Rates include breakfast. AE, MC, V. Free valet parking. **Amenities:** Restaurant; airport transfers (for a fee); babysitting; concierge; outdoor pool; room service. *In room:* A/C, TV, hair dryer, Internet.

Misión Del Sol Resort & Spa ★★★ 🎒 You feel a sense of peace from the moment you enter this adults-only hotel and spa, which draws on the mystical wisdom of the ancient cultures of Mexico, Tibet, Egypt, and Asia. Guests and visitors are encouraged to wear light-hued clothes to contribute to the harmonious flow of energy. Architecturally stunning adobe buildings house the guest rooms, villas, and common areas. Group activities, such as reading discussions, a chess club, and painting workshops, take place in the salon. Spacious rooms are designed according to feng shui principles; each looks onto its own garden or stream and has three channels of ambient music. Bathrooms are large, with sunken tubs, and the dual-headed showers have river rocks set into the floor, as a type of reflexology treatment. Beds contain magnets for restoring proper energy flow. Villas feature two separate bedrooms, plus a living/dining area and a meditation room. Spa services include facials, body treatments, and massages, with an emphasis on water-based treatments.

Av. General Diego Díaz González 31, Col. Parres, 62550 Cuernavaca, Mor. www.misiondelsol.com. ② **866/875-0380** in the U.S., or 777/321-0999. Fax 777/320-7981. 42 units, plus 12 villas. $267–$299 deluxe double; $552–$619 2-bedroom villa (up to 4 persons); $651–$732 3-bedroom villa (up to 6 persons). Special spa and meal packages available. AE, MC, V. Free parking. No children 12 and under. **Amenities:** Restaurant; well-equipped gym; basketball; volleyball; daily meditation, yoga, and Tai Chi classes; extensive spa services; 2 tennis courts. *In room:* A/C.

MODERATE

Casa Colonial ★★ 🎒 This splendid inn consists of only 18 guest rooms, individually decorated in a warm colonial style with dark-wood antique furnishings. The rooms surround an idyllic courtyard filled with palms, bamboo, and ficus plants, as well as a shimmering pool. An inviting breakfast patio looks upon the courtyard, which is an intimate setting for weddings and other special events. During the day, the sound of classical music fills the air. The grounds were originally part of the cathedral property, which took up much of the neighborhood. Casa Colonial lies 1 block from the central square and within easy walking distance of all sights in the historic center.

Nezahualcóyotl 37 (at Abasolo), Col. Centro, 62000 Cuernavaca, Mor. www.casacolonial.com. ② **777/312-7033.** Fax 777/310-0395. 18 units. 1,215–1,385 pesos double; 1,495–2,905 pesos suite. AE, MC, V. Limited free parking. **Amenities:** Restaurant; bar; outdoor pool. *In room:* Ceiling fan, TV, minibar.

Hotel Posada María Cristina ★★ The María Cristina's high walls conceal many delights: a small swimming pool, lush gardens with fountains, a good restaurant, and patios. Guest rooms vary in size; all are exceptionally clean and comfortable, with firm beds and colonial-style furnishings. Bathrooms have inlaid Talavera tiles and skylights. Suites are only slightly larger than normal rooms; junior suites have Jacuzzis. La Calandria, the handsome little restaurant, overlooks the gardens and serves excellent meals based on Mexican and international recipes. Even if you don't stay here, consider having a meal. The popular Sunday brunch (160 pesos per person) features live classical music. The hotel is a half-block from the Palacio de Cortez.

Bulevar Juárez 300 (at Abasolo), Col. Centro (Apdo. Postal 203), 62000 Cuernavaca, Mor. www. cuernavacainfo.com/mariacristina.html. ℂ **777/318-5767.** Fax 777/312-9126 or 777/318-2981. 20 units. 1,305–1,877 pesos double; 1,517–2,288 pesos suite. AE, MC, V. Free parking. **Amenities:** Restaurant; bar; outdoor pool. *In room:* Ceiling fan, TV, hair dryer, minibar, Wi-Fi.

Where to Eat

VERY EXPENSIVE

Restaurant Las Mañanitas ★★★ MEXICAN/INTERNATIONAL   The setting
of this hotel garden and restaurant is exquisite, the service superb, and the food better than average. Tables stand on a shaded terrace with a view of gardens, strolling peacocks, and softly playing violinists or a trio playing romantic boleros. Diners have the option of ordering drinks and making their menu selections from chairs in the garden, waiting to take their seats at their tables when their meals are served. The Mexican cuisine with an international flair draws on seasonal produce. They also serve a full selection of fresh seafood, certified Angus beef, lamb chops, baby back ribs, and freerange chicken. Try the zucchini flower soup, filet of red snapper in curry sauce, and black-bottom pie, the house specialty. A tasting menu is also available.

In Las Mañanitas hotel (see above), Ricardo Linares 107 (5½ long blocks north of the Jardín Borda). ℂ **777/362-0000,** ext. 240. www.lasmananitas.com.mx. Reservations recommended. Main courses 200–450 pesos. AE, MC, V. Daily breakfast 8am–noon, lunch 3–6pm, and dinner 6–11pm.

MODERATE

Casa Hidalgo ★★ GOURMET MEXICAN/INTERNATIONAL   Casa Hidalgo
lies in a beautifully restored colonial building across from the Palacio de Cortez. The food is more sophisticated and innovative than that at most places in town. Specialties include chilled mango and tequila soup, smoked rainbow trout, and the exquisite Spanish-inspired Filetón Hidalgo—breaded and stuffed with serrano ham and *manchego* cheese. There are always daily specials, and bread is baked on the premises. Tables on the balcony afford a view of the action in the plaza below.

Jardin de los Héroes 6. ℂ **777/312-2749.** www.casahidalgo.com. Reservations recommended on weekends. Main courses 140–200 pesos. AE, MC, V. Mon–Thurs 1:30–11pm; Fri–Sat 1:30pm–midnight; Sun 1:30–10pm.

Gaia INTERNATIONAL   The dining area at Gaia overlooks a classic Cuernavacan
scene: a fantastically tiled swimming pool and trees and shrubs laced with twinkling lights. The food, however, is far from the usual. The house raviolis are prepared with a rich tomato sauce and garnished with sun-dried tomatoes. The tamarind shrimp is also excellent. The extensive wine menu includes selections from Baja California, and the knowledgeable waitstaff can suggest the perfect complement to your meal. If you're a fan of black-and-white Mexican movies, you'll dig Gaia even more, as it occupies the former home of Mario Moreno, aka Cantinflas, the Mexican equivalent of Charlie Chaplin.

Benito Juárez 102, Col. Centro. ℂ **777/310-0031.** www.gaiarest.com.mx. Main courses 110–380 pesos. AE, MC, V. Mon–Thurs 1–11pm; Fri–Sat 1pm–midnight; Sun 1–6pm.

Restaurant La India Bonita ★★ MEXICAN   Cuernavaca's oldest restaurant is
housed among the interior patios and portals of the restored home—known as Casa Mañana—of former U.S. Ambassador Dwight Morrow. The beautiful setting features

patio tables amid trickling fountains, palms, and flowers. Specialties include *mole poblano* (chicken with a sauce of bitter chocolate and fiery chiles) and the signature *La India Bonita* plate with steak, enchiladas, rice, and beans. There are also several daily specials. A breakfast mainstay is *desayuno Maximiliano,* a gigantic platter of chicken enchiladas with an assortment of sauces. A Mexican folkloric dance show fills the restaurant with colorful energy on Saturday nights from 8 to 9pm.

Morrow 15 (btw. Morelos and Matamoros), Col. Centro, 2 blocks north of the Jardín Juárez. ℅ **777/312-5021.** Breakfast 50-100 pesos; main courses 90-200 pesos. AE, MC, V. Tues-Sat 8am-10pm; Sun-Mon 8am-10pm.

INEXPENSIVE

La Universal ★★ 🍴 MEXICAN/PASTRIES   This is a busy place, partly because of its great location (overlooking both the Alameda and Plaza de Armas), partly because of its traditional Mexican specialties, and partly because of its reasonable prices. It's open to the street and has many outdoor tables, usually filled with older men discussing the day's events or playing chess. These tables are perfect for watching the parade of street vendors and park life. The specialty is a Mexican grilled sampler plate, including *carne asada,* enchilada, pork cutlet, green onions, beans, and tortillas, for 120 pesos. A full breakfast special (110 pesos) for two is served Monday through Friday from 9:30am to 12:30pm. Live music is played weekdays from 3 to 5pm and again from 8 to 10pm.

Guerrero 2. ℅ **777/318-5970.** Breakfast 500-800 pesos; main courses 90-140 pesos; comida corrida 890 pesos. MC, V. Sun-Thurs 9am-11pm; Fri-Sat 9am-1am.

Cuernavaca After Dark

Cuernavaca has a number of cafes right off the Jardín Juárez where people gather to sip coffee or drinks till the wee hours—check out La Universal (see above). Band concerts are held in the Jardín Juárez on Thursday and Sunday evenings. **La Plazuela,** a pedestrian-only stretch across from the Cortez Palace, features cafes, kitsch stores, and live-music bars. It's geared toward a 20-something, university crowd.

TEPOZTLÁN ★★

72km (45 miles) S of Mexico City; 45km (28 miles) NE of Cuernavaca

Tepoztlán is one of the strangest and most beautiful towns in Mexico. Largely undiscovered by foreign tourists, it occupies the floor of a broad, lush valley whose walls were formed by bizarrely shaped mountains that look like the work of some abstract expressionist giant. The mountains are visible from almost everywhere in town; even the municipal parking lot boasts a spectacular view.

Tepoztlán remains small and steeped in legend and mystery—it lies adjacent to the alleged birthplace of Quetzalcóatl, the Aztec serpent god—and comes about as close as you're going to get to an unspoiled, magical mountain hideaway. Eight chapels, each with its own cultural festival, dot this traditional Mexican village. Though the town stays tranquil during the week, escapees from Mexico City descend in droves on the weekends, especially Sunday. Most Tepoztlán residents, whether foreigners or Mexicans, tend to be mystically or artistically oriented—although some also appear to be just plain disoriented. The village wears its New Age heart on its sleeve—homeopathic pharmacies and health-food stores coexist happily alongside Internet cafes, tortilla stands, and satellite-dish companies.

The town is famous throughout Mexico as a symbol of fierce civic pride and independence. In 1994, a multinational firm secretly negotiated a deal to build a Jack Nicklaus golf course and residential development on communally held lands; part of the plan involved construction of a heliport and a funicular to the top of Tepozteco pyramid. When the project came to light, townspeople joined forces, ran the city government out of town (hanging them in effigy), and occupied the *Ayunta-miento* (town hall), sealing off the city limits and repelling state military forces until the developers backed out of the project.

Aside from soaking up the ambience, two things you must do are climb up to the Tepozteco pyramid and hit the weekend folkloric market. In addition, Tepoztlán offers a variety of treatments, cures, diets, massages, and sweat lodges. Some of these are available at hotels; for some, you have to ask around. Many locals swear that the valley possesses mystical curative powers.

If you have a car, Tepoztlán provides a great starting point for traveling this region of Mexico. Within 90 minutes are sights listed in this chapter such as Las Estacas, Taxco, Las Grutas de Cacahuamilpa, and Xochicalco (some of the prettiest ruins in Mexico). Tepoztlán lies 20 minutes from Cuernavaca and only an hour south of Mexico City (that is, an hour once you're able to get out of Mexico City), which—given its lost-in-time feel—seems hard to believe.

Getting There

BY CAR   From Mexico City, the quickest route is Hwy. 95 (the toll road) to Cuer-navaca; just before the Cuernavaca city limits, you'll see the clearly marked turnoff to Tepoztlán on 95D and Hwy. 115. The slower, free federal Hwy. 95D, direct from Mexico City, is also an option and may be preferable if you're departing from the western part of the city. Take 95D south to Km 71, where the exit to Tepoztlán on Hwy. 115 is clearly indicated.

BY BUS   From Mexico City, buses to Tepoztlán run regularly from the Terminal de Sur and the Terminal Poniente. The trip takes an hour.

You can book round-trip transportation to the Mexico City airport through **Marquez Sightseeing Tours** (www.tourbymexico.com/marqueztours) and some hotels. The round-trip is about 2,000 pesos.

Cooking Classes in Tepoztlán

An engaging cooking school called **Cocinar Mexicano** offers weeklong programs in Mexican cuisine. The founder, Magda Bogin, conducts class from her large, sunny outdoor kitchen, tiled in blue-and-white Talavera. Participants study recipes typical of the festival that coincides with their visit. During the Day of the Dead workshop, for example, students learn to make tamales, the traditional dish that families bring to the gravesites of deceased loved ones. For other festivals, the focus is *mole,* a typical fiesta food often made with chocolate and chiles that's arguably the most complex dish in Mexican cuisine. All the programs include a range of contemporary dishes, and participants spend a day of fine dining in Mexico City, where they meet with the country's top chefs. Prices range from $150 for a 1-day class to $2,485 for a 5-day workshop, which includes round-trip transportation from Mexico City and most meals, but not airfare or accommodations. Frommer's readers receive a $100 discount. For more information, visit www.cocinarmexicano.com.

Exploring Tepoztlán

Tepoztlán's **weekend folkloric market** is one of the best in central Mexico. More crafts are available on Saturdays and Sundays, but the market also opens on Wednesdays. Vendors sell all kinds of ceramics, from simple fired-clay works resembling those made with pre-Hispanic techniques, to the more commercial versions of majolica and pseudo-Talavera. There are also puppets, carved-wood figures, and some textiles, especially thick wool Mexican sweaters and jackets made out of *jerga* (a coarse cloth). Very popular currently is the "hippie"-style jewelry that earned Tepoztlán its fame in the '60s and '70s. The market is also remarkable for its variety of food stands selling fruit and vegetables, spices, fresh tortillas, and indigenous Mexican delicacies.

A hike to the **Tepozteco pyramid** is probably one of the most rewarding experiences you will have on your journey in Mexico. The climb is steep and fairly strenuous, especially toward the end, although it is perfectly doable in a few hours and is not dangerous. I once forgot to bring along hiking shoes and bought a pair of plastic *huaraches* at the market, and I managed just fine. That being said, I know it would have been even more enjoyable had I been wearing sneakers. Dense vegetation shades the trail (actually a long natural staircase), which is beautiful from bottom to top. Once you arrive at the pyramid, you are treated to remarkable views and, if you are lucky, a great show by a family of *coatis* (tropical raccoons), who visit the pyramid most mornings to beg for food; they especially love bananas. The pyramid is a *Tlahuica* construction that predates the *Náhuatl* (Aztec) domination of the area. It was the site of important celebrations in the 12th and 13th centuries. The main street in Tepoztlán, Avenida 5 de Mayo, takes you to the path that leads you to the top of the Tepozteco. The 2km (1.2-mile) winding rock trail begins where the name of Avenida 5 de Mayo changes to Camino del Tepozteco. The hike takes about an hour each way, but if you stop and take in the scenery and really enjoy the trail, it can take up to 2 hours each way. Water and drinks are available at the top. The trail is open daily from 9am to 5:30pm and, while the hike is free, the pyramid costs 30 pesos to enter.

Also worth visiting is the **former convent, Dominico de la Navidad.** The entrance to the Dominican convent lies through the religious-themed "Gate of Tepoztlán," constructed with beads and seeds, just east of the main plaza. Built between 1560 and 1588, the convent is now a museum, open Tuesday through Sunday from 10am to 6pm; it costs 10 pesos to enter.

Sights near Tepoztlán

Many nearby places are easily accessible by car. One good tour service is **Marquez Sightseeing Tours,** located in Cuernavaca (www.tourbymexico.com/marqueztours). Marquez has four- and seven-passenger vehicles, very reasonable prices, and a large variety of set tours. The dependable owner, Arturo Marquez Diaz, speaks better-than-passable English and will allow you to design your own tour, including to archaeological sites and museums. He possesses a wealth of knowledge about Mexican language and culture. (Ask him to tell you the joke about the man with two sombreros.) He also offers transportation to and from Benito Juárez airport in Mexico City for approximately 1,700 pesos for up to six people and to and from the Toluca airport for 2,000 pesos for up to six people.

Two tiny, charming villages, **Santo Domingo Xocotitlán** and **Amatlán,** are only a 20-minute drive from Tepoztlán and can be reached by minibuses, which depart regularly from the center of town. There is nothing much to do in these places except wander around absorbing the marvelous views of the Tepozteco Mountains and drinking in the magical ambience.

Las Grutas de Cacahuamilpa ★, the Cacahuamilpa Caves or Grottoes, are an unforgettable system of caverns with a wooden illuminated walkway for easy access. As you pass from chamber to chamber, you'll see spectacular illuminated rock formations, including stalactites, stalagmites, and twisted rock formations with names like Dante's Head, the Champagne Bottle, the Tortillas, and Madonna with Child. Admission for 2 hours is 50 pesos. A guide for groups, which can be assembled on the hour, costs about 100 pesos. The caverns are open daily from 10am to 7pm (last tickets sold at 5pm) and are located 90 minutes from Tepoztlán and 30 minutes from Taxco.

About 50 minutes southeast of Tepoztlán is **Las Estacas,** an ecological resort with a cold-water spring that is said to have curative powers (p. 154). The ruins of **Xochicalco** (see "Cuernavaca: Land of Eternal Spring," earlier in this chapter) and the colonial town of **Taxco** (earlier in this chapter) are easily accessible from Tepoztlán.

Where to Stay

The town gets very busy on the weekends, so if your stay will include Friday or Saturday night, make reservations well in advance. In addition to the choices noted below, consider two other excellent options just outside of town. **Casa Bugambilia ★★★**, Callejón de Tepopula 007, Valle de Atongo (www.casabugambilia.com; © 739/395-0158), is a nine-room hotel property 3km (1¾ miles) outside Tepoztlán. Don't confuse this hotel with Posada Bugambilia, a modest hotel in town. The spacious rooms are elegantly furnished with high-end, carved Mexican furniture, and every room has a fireplace. Doubles average 250 pesos, including breakfast. **Las Golondrinas ★★★**, Callejón de Términas 4 (www.mexonline.com/lasgolondrinas.htm; © 739/395-0649), is a three-bedroom B&B in the area behind Ixcatepec church; it's so far off the beaten track that even cabdrivers have trouble finding the place. Owner Marisol Fernández has imbued the house with her tranquil, down-to-earth charm; the guest rooms open onto a wraparound terrace that overlooks the garden, a small pool, and the Tepozteco Mountains beyond. Doubles cost 1,550 pesos, including breakfast.

Hotel Nilayam Formerly Hotel Tepoztlán, this holistic-oriented retreat lies in a colonial building, but the decor has been brightened up considerably. The gracious, helpful staff offers complete detox programs and a full array of services, including body and facial treatments, reflexology, hot stone and shiatsu massages, yoga, Tai Chi, and meditation. The hotel has a great view of the mountain, and the restaurant features a creative menu of vegetarian cuisine. Spa packages are available.

Industrias 6, 62520 Tepoztlán, Mor. www.nilayam.net. © 739/395-0522. Fax 739/395-0522. 34 units. 1,180–1,420 pesos double. Rates include breakfast. AE, MC, V. Free parking. **Amenities:** Restaurant; outdoor pool; spa services; private *temazcal* (pre-Hispanic sweat lodge). *In room:* TV.

Posada del Tepozteco ★★ This inviting inn has magnificent views overlooking the town and down the length of the spectacular valley. Rooms are tastefully furnished in colonial style. All but the least expensive feature terraces with superb views, and the suites have small whirlpool tubs. The intimate restaurant focuses on healthy and vegetarian dishes. The grounds are exquisitely landscaped, and the atmosphere is intimate and romantic. When you check in, look for the picture of Angelina Jolie behind the reception desk; she stayed here for 3 weeks while filming *Original Sin* in 2001. The hotel reception will arrange in-room massages, and the hotel has a traditional *temazcal* with herbal healing properties. Most rates include breakfast.

Tepoznieves: A Taste of Heaven

Don't leave town without stopping at one of the many **Tepoznieves** locations; Av. 5 de Mayo 21 is one of the most convenient (📞 **739/395-3813; www.tepoznieves.com.mx**). The sublime local ice cream shop's slogan, *"nieve de dioses"* (ice cream of the gods), doesn't exaggerate. Almost 200 types of ice cream and sorbet, made only with natural ingredients, come in flavors that are familiar (vanilla, bubble gum), exotic (tamarind, rose petal, mango studded with *chile piquin*), and off-the-wall (beet, lettuce, corn). It's open daily 8am to 9pm.

Paraíso 3 (2 blocks straight up the hill from the town center), 62520 Tepoztlán, Mor. www.posadadeltepozteco.com. 📞 **739/395-0010.** Fax 739/395-0323. 21 units. 2,260 pesos double; 3,550–4,700 pesos suite. MC, V. Free parking. **Amenities:** Restaurant w/stunning view; small outdoor pool. *In room:* Fan, hair dryer.

Where to Eat

In addition to the two choices listed below, El Chalchi restaurant at the **Hotel Nilayam** (see above) offers some of the best vegetarian fare in the area. It's 3 blocks from the main square, with main courses priced around 60 pesos. Also, visit **Cacao,** Revolucion 9 (📞 **739/395-3770**), a charming chocolaterie, for some of the best bitter hot chocolate you'll ever taste. Imbibe or devour your cacao for 20 pesos and up.

El Ciruelo Restaurant Bar ★★★ GOURMET MEXICAN   This long-standing favorite has beautiful flowering gardens set amid the striking backdrop of the Tepoztlán mountains. The large courtyard is filled with lush potted foliage and topped by a soaring band shell meant to keep patrons dry without obscuring the fantastic view of the mountains. The service is positively charming, and the regional food is divine. House specialties include cilantro soup with almonds, *chalupas* of goat cheese, chicken with *huitlacoche,* and a regional treat: milk-based gelatin with brown sugar. Try to get a seat on the outdoor patio, where a trio often serenades the crowd.

Zaragoza 17, Barrio de la Santísima, in front of the church. 📞 **739/395-1203.** www.elciruelo.com.mx. Dinner 60–200 pesos. AE. Sun–Thurs 1-7pm; Fri-Sat 1-11pm.

Restaurant Axitla ★★★ 🏠 GOURMET MEXICAN/INTERNATIONAL   Axitla is the best restaurant in Tepoztlán. Gourmet Mexican delicacies are made from scratch using the freshest local ingredients. Specialties include chicken breast stuffed with wild mushrooms in a chipotle chile sauce, *chiles en nogada,* pepper steak, grilled octopus, *chile Jarral* (stuffed chile with meat in an avocado sauce), and exceptional *mole.* There are also excellent steaks and fresh seafood. And if the food isn't enough—and, believe me, it is—the enchanted setting will make your meal even more memorable. The restaurant lies at the base of the Tepozteco Pyramid (about a 10-min. walk from the town center), surrounded by 1.2 hectares (about 3 acres) of junglelike gardens that encompass a creek and lily ponds. Memo and Laura, the gracious owners, speak excellent English and are marvelous sources of information about the area.

Av. del Tepozteco, at the foot of the trail to the pyramid. 📞 **739/395-0519.** Lunch and dinner 80-150 pesos. MC, V. Wed-Sun 10am-7pm.

SAN MIGUEL DE ALLENDE & THE COLONIAL SILVER CITIES

by David Baird

Mexico's colonial silver-mining cities—San Miguel, Querétaro, San Luis Potosí, Guanajuato, and Zacatecas—lie northwest of Mexico City in the mountains of the Sierra Madre Occidental. These cities have colonial settings with backdrops of rugged mountains, an ideal climate, local handicrafts, good food, and many memorable vistas.

These cities are close to the Mexican capital by modern standards, but at the time of their founding, this land was the frontier. In pre-Columbian times, the great civilizations of central Mexico never established more than a tenuous sway here. Mountainous and arid, this was the land of the Chichimeca, a large nation of nomadic tribes that occasionally banded together to raid their civilized neighbors to the south. After the Spanish Conquest of the Aztec empire in 1521, the conquistadors turned their attention to this region in search of precious metals. The Chichimecans resisted the encroachers, but epidemic diseases brought from Europe soon decimated the native population. The Spanish established mining cities in quick succession, stretching from Querétaro (established in 1531) north to Zacatecas (1548) and beyond. They found quantities of gold, but silver proved so plentiful that it made Mexico world famous as a land of riches.

For 3 centuries of colonial rule, much of the mines' great wealth went to build urban centers of impressive, enduring architecture. It's wonderful to stroll through these cities and view them, not one building at a time, but in broad views of colonial cityscapes. Of the five cities, four (Guanajuato, Querétaro, Zacatecas, and San Miguel) have been designated World Heritage Sites by UNESCO.

Life in this part of the world is lived at a relaxed pace. If you're of a disposition to handle matters quickly and get things done, try to slow down or you might get frustrated with this region's slower rhythms. Also,

This region of Mexico has largely avoided the violence and mayhem that is occurring in other areas. Travel to these five cities doesn't expose one to heightened risks or the potential disruptions caused by gang conflicts. During the last 2 years there were a few high-profile assassinations and kidnappings in the area, but not the repeated attacks that disrupt the daily life of residents or make them fearful for their safety. Of course, reliable information on the number of kidnappings and extortion cases is notoriously difficult to come by, but one can gauge how bad things are by tapping into the local gossip and by reading the unofficial statements in the local press. When concerns for safety reach a certain point, they find expression, but this was by and large not the case in early 2011. Travelers should still take the usual precautions, especially when driving on the highway. And they need to be aware of recent events, but they don't need to avoid this area on account of what's happening in other parts of the country.

these cities have intimate and close-knit societies. Many people have ancestors who lived here at least a century ago, and they maintain a broad network of kinfolk, friends, and acquaintances. I've walked down streets with locals who would greet every third or fourth person we passed. Often I've had conversations in which I mention someone from a completely different context, only to hear something like, "Oh, he's married to my cousin."

Exploring the Silver Cities

There are two common ways to get here: Fly into Mexico City and take the bus that goes directly from the airport to Querétaro, or fly into the León/Guanajuato airport. Zacatecas, San Luis Potosí, and Querétaro also have international airports that receive a few flights from the U.S. Or you can drive or take a bus from the U.S. border. From Texas, the first of the silver cities you will reach is San Luis Potosí (which, by the way, bills itself to the rest of Mexico as the "Gateway to the United States").

Once in the region, you'll find the roads are good, but not great, and the smaller ones are poorly marked. Driving within these towns can be maddening due to convoluted, narrow streets and bizarre traffic routing (especially in Guanajuato and Zacatecas). If you ever have difficulty navigating into the center of town, simply hail a cab to lead the way. Parking can also be a problem; I have included, when possible, good motels where you can park and leave your car for the length of your visit. If you prefer to travel by bus, you'll find frequent, inexpensive first-class buses connecting all these cities, which are only a few hours apart from each other.

The region has a short rainy season from June through September, which is a good time to come. I also like late fall, winter, and early spring. The hottest month is May (and sometimes early June before the rains arrive). May can also be smoky because it's when many farmers burn the stubble in their cornfields before the spring planting. Wherever you elect to visit, I recommend a stay of at least 3 days per destination—a good part of their charm goes unappreciated if you press too much to see everything.

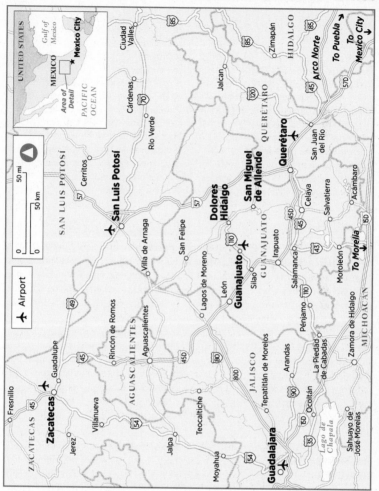

SAN MIGUEL DE ALLENDE ★★★

288km (179 miles) NW of Mexico City; 120km (74 miles) E of Guanajuato; 64km (40 miles) NW of Querétaro

San Miguel de Allende (elevation 1,862m/6,107 ft.) mixes the best aspects of small-town life with the cosmopolitan pleasures of a big city. It is the smallest of the cities covered here and perhaps the most relaxed; a wide variety of restaurants, shops, and galleries makes urbanites feel quite at home. Most of the buildings in the central part of the town date from the Colonial Era or the 19th century; the law requires newer buildings to conform to existing architecture, and the town has gone to some lengths to retain its cobblestone streets.

Living in San Miguel is a large community of Americans: some retired, some attending art or language school, and some who have come here to live simply and follow their creative muses—painting, writing, and sculpting. The center of this community is the public library in the former convent of Santa Ana. It is a good place to find information on San Miguel or just to sit on the patio and read.

A notable aspect of San Migueleña society is the number of festivals it celebrates. In a country that needs only the barest of excuses to hold a fiesta, San Miguel is known far and wide for them. Most of these celebrations are of a religious character and are meant to combine social activity with religious expression. People practice Catholicism with great fervor—going on religious pilgrimages, attending all-night vigils, ringing church bells at the oddest times throughout the night (something that some visitors admittedly might not find so amusing). See "Special Events & Festivals," below.

Because of the easy highway route from Mexico City, San Miguel is popular with weekenders from the capital. Arrive early on Friday or make a reservation ahead of time for weekends, especially long weekends. There's also a squeeze on rooms around the Christmas and Easter holidays and around the feast of San Miguel's patron saint, on September 29.

Essentials

GETTING THERE & DEPARTING **By Plane** The two major airports are the **Benito Juárez International Airport** in Mexico City, 3½ hours away (which has direct bus transportation to nearby Querétaro), and the León/Guanajuato airport, 1½ hours away. See "Orientation" in chapter 4 for details about the Mexico City airport; information about the León/Guanajuato airport is under "Essentials" in the "Guanajuato" section, later in this chapter.

By Car You have a choice of two routes for the 3½-hour trip from Mexico City—a Querétaro bypass or via Celaya. The former is shorter—take Hwy. 57, a four-lane freeway, north toward Querétaro. Past the Tequisquiapan turnoff is an exit on the right marked A SAN MIGUEL. This toll road bypasses Querétaro and crosses Hwy. 57 again north of town. Here it narrows to two lanes and becomes Hwy. 111. Some 30km (19 miles) farther is San Miguel.

From Guanajuato, the quick route is to go south from the city a short distance on Hwy. 110, then east on a secondary, paved road passing near the village of Joconoxtle. For the long but scenic route, which passes through Dolores Hidalgo, go northeast on Hwy. 110 through Dolores, then south on Hwy. 51. If you drive this route, take a break and experience a slice of rural Mexican life near the small community of Santa Rosa, where a few restaurants serve the local *mezcal de la sierra,* a distilled firewater that packs a strong punch and has a forceful aroma of *agave.*

By Bus **From Mexico City airport: AeroPlus** buses (© **55/5786-9357**) leave directly from the airport for Querétaro about every hour or half-hour, depending on the time of day. A one-way ticket costs 256 pesos.

From Mexico City's Central Norte: First-class buses take 4 hours (with one stop in Querétaro). The company ETN (© **01-800/800-0386** in Mexico; www.etn.com.mx) has the best service, with wide seats that recline far back (four buses per day). Primera Plus (© **01-800/375-7587** in Mexico; www.primeraplus.com.mx) has two buses per day. Regular service is handled by Flecha Amarilla, with buses leaving every 40 minutes. Another option is to take a bus to Querétaro and change buses.

From Querétaro: Local buses run to San Miguel every 20 minutes (Flecha Amarilla and Herradura de Plata have alternating departures). If you arrive in Querétaro

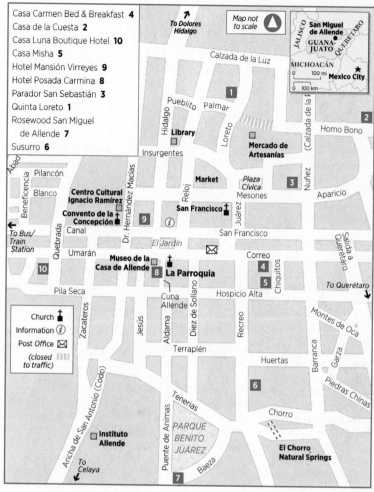

Casa Carmen Bed & Breakfast **4**
Casa de la Cuesta **2**
Casa Luna Boutique Hotel **10**
Casa Misha **5**
Hotel Mansión Virreyes **9**
Hotel Posada Carmina **8**
Parador San Sebastián **3**
Quinta Loreto **1**
Rosewood San Miguel
   de Allende **7**
Susurro **6**

by first-class bus, you'll be in Terminal A. Go out the door, turn right, and walk to Terminal B.

From Guanajuato: ETN has three nonstop superdeluxe buses per day. Primera Plus/Servicios Coordinados has four nonstop buses per day.

To/from Laredo and Nuevo Laredo: Four companies offer an overnight first-class bus to and from Laredo or Nuevo Laredo: **Autobuses Americanos** (© 415/154-8233; www.autobusesamericanos.com.mx/americanos) crosses the border to Laredo, Texas; **Futura** (© 415/152-2237), **Primera Plus** (© 01-800/375-7587 in Mexico), and **Omnibus de México** (© 01-800/765-6636 in Mexico; www.odm.com.mx) go to Nuevo Laredo. The trip takes 12 hours and costs around 900 pesos. From San Miguel, there is one departure per day per

learning at the source: GOING TO SCHOOL IN SAN MIGUEL

San Miguel has several schools for learning Spanish. If you're wishing to take classes, shop around before you travel to San Miguel to find one that's a good fit for you. These schools cater to travelers and often can provide a list of apartments for long-term stays.

Instituto Allende, Calle Ancha de San Antonio 20, 37700 San Miguel de Allende, Gto. (© **415/152-0190;** www. instituto-allende.edu.mx), began in 1950 as a fine-arts school and later added Spanish courses. The main focus is still on the arts, with different classes and workshops offered throughout the year. Spanish students have the option of group and individual classes, short and long term. The school's credits are transferable to many colleges and universities in the United States and Canada; noncredit students are also welcome.

LanguagePoint, 20 de Enero Sur 42, 37750 San Miguel de Allende, Gto. (© **415/152-4115;** www.languagepoint. org), offers instruction and immersion at all levels of competency. With a maximum of three students per instructor, students get a lot of individual attention, and the teaching method leans heavily toward conversation. Emphasis at the basic level is on gaining a working knowledge of everyday Spanish as a basis for further development of language skills.

Warren Hardy Spanish, San Rafael 6, 37700 San Miguel de Allende, Gto. (© **415/154-4017;** www.warrenhardy.

com), is a popular school for those who know little Spanish. Emphasis is on the spoken language, with special focus on the use of verbs. Mr. Hardy has taught Spanish for many years and has designed his own methodology for teaching it, which involves partnering students and using a lot of flashcards. It's best to contact the school through its website. Mr. Hardy's wife, Tuli, answers questions and handles registration.

Academia Hispano Americana, Mesones 4, 37700 San Miguel de Allende, Gto. (© **415/152-0349;** www. ahaspeakspanish.com), has a reputation for offering an intensive language course taught by professional instructors. The focus is on developing communications skills as the foundation for acquiring fluency. Classes are limited to 12 people and usually run much smaller than that. The school has a continuous program of study of 12 4-week sessions for 35 hours a week. Less intensive courses and private lessons are also available.

Habla Hispana, Calzada de la Luz 25, 37700 San Miguel de Allende, Gto. (© **451/152-0713;** www.mexicospanish. com), is a small school with four experienced and dedicated instructors, all locals. Classes are arranged in 4-week courses. Class size is limited to 10 students. The school likes to combine a personal touch with a clearly structured teaching program.

company. The four buses leave San Miguel between 6 and 7pm. Departure times from Laredo and Nuevo Laredo are also around 6 or 7pm.

The **bus station** is 2km (1¼ miles) west of town on the westward extension of Calle Canal. Taxis to town are cheap (30 pesos) and available at all hours.

VISITOR INFORMATION The city's **tourist information office** is in the *ayuntamiento* (city hall) facing El Jardín. The address is Plaza Principal 8, and the phone is © **415/152-0900.** Office hours are Monday through Friday from 8:30am to 8pm, Saturday from 10am to 8pm, and Sunday from 10am to 5:30pm.

CITY LAYOUT Carefully pruned Indian laurel trees shade San Miguel's central square, **El Jardín.** The center of city life, El Jardín is the point of reference for all places in the middle of town and is bounded by Correo (Post Office St.), San Francisco, Hidalgo, and Reloj.

GETTING AROUND Most places in San Miguel are within walking distance, so a car isn't necessary. Buses to outlying villages (La Taboada thermal pool, for example) leave from the little plaza by the *mercado.* Taxis to places inside town should not cost more than 40 pesos, unless ordered from a hotel.

[FastFACTS] SAN MIGUEL DE ALLENDE

Area Code The telephone area code is **415.**

Climate San Miguel can be warm in summer and cold enough for wool clothing in winter, especially at night or during the occasional cold spell.

Communication & Shipping Services Several services offer packing and shipping, mailboxes, and the like. One is **Border Crossings,** Mesones 57-A (at Reloj; 𝒞 **415/152-2497;** fax 415/152-3672), and **Pack 'n' Mail** is at Calle Canal 42 (𝒞/fax **415/152-3191**). Both keep standard office hours: weekdays from 9 or 10am to 6pm, Saturday from 10am to 2pm.

Consular Office A **U.S. Consular Agency** is at Hernández Macías 72, Int. 111 (𝒞 **415/152-2357**). Hours are Monday to Thursday from 9am to 1pm.

Currency Exchange Intercam has three locations: Juárez 27, San

Francisco 4, and Correo 15. Business hours are Monday through Friday from 9am to 5:30pm, Saturday from 9am to 1pm. **CiBanco,** at Juárez and San Francisco, is open Monday through Friday from 9am to 4:30pm. Several banks have cash machines, including one on the corner of the Jardín in the Casa del Conde, and a few on Calle San Francisco.

Drugstore Try the **Farmacia Agundis** (𝒞 **415/152-1198**), Canal 24 at Macías. It's open daily from 9:30am to 1am.

Internet Access Several places offer Internet access around town. These businesses come and go so fast it's not worth listing them. Ask at your hotel for the nearest cybercafe.

Library The **Biblioteca Pública (Public Library),** Insurgentes 25 (𝒞 **415/152-0293;** www.bibliotecasma.com), is a social institution for the resident American

community. It has a good selection of books in Spanish and English. Hours are Monday through Friday from 10am to 7pm, and Saturday from 10am to 2pm. The library also has a very pleasant cafe in the rear patio.

Newspaper An English-language paper, *Atención,* carries local news as well as full listings of what to see and do.

Parking San Miguel is congested, and street parking is scarce. A white pole or sign at the end of a street marks the stopping point for parking (so that other cars can make a turn). Police are vigilant about parking and ticket with glee.

Post Office The *correo,* Calle Correo 16, is open Monday through Friday from 8am to 4:30pm for all services, Saturday from 9am to 1pm.

Special Events & Festivals

San Miguel celebrates 30 to 40 festivals a year. These are just the standouts: January 17 is the **Blessing of the Animals.** In the morning, locals bring their decorated pets and farm animals to the town's churches to be sprinkled with holy water. The first

Friday in March celebrates **Our Lord of the Conquest,** and the day before is filled with music, fireworks, and decorated teams of oxen. After a celebratory Mass, there is dancing by the *concheros* (traditional costumed dancers). Two weeks before Holy Week is the procession of **Our Lord of the Column.** Between then and Easter Sunday are more processions, and altars are set up in honor of **La Virgen Dolorosa.** In May is the **Festival of the Holy Cross.** In June, around Saint Anthony's Day, is the **Fiesta de los Locos (Festival of the Madmen) ★★,** when many dress up in Carnavalesque costumes and go cavorting about the center of town. August begins the preparatory festivals for September 29, the festival of San Miguel's **patron saint.** Parades, fireworks, and band concerts continue throughout September. At the beginning of November is the **Day of the Dead,** followed by the **Christmas fiestas.** In addition to all of this, you have the **Chamber Music Festival** in summer, **Jazz Music Festival** in the fall, and a couple of arts fairs that occur on varying dates.

Exploring San Miguel

It's hard to be bored in San Miguel. The shopping is excellent, and you'll run out of time before you can try all the restaurants. The town is well situated for side trips to Dolores Hidalgo, Querétaro, and Guanajuato. It's popular for Spanish and art classes.

In 2008, UNESCO declared San Miguel and the outlying religious center, Atotonilco, a World Heritage Site (three other cities in this chapter are also designated as such). The colonial architecture tends more toward domestic than monumental and offers much to see—fine courtyards, beautiful interiors, and rich architectural details. Of note are the town's lovely streetscapes, with narrow cobblestone lanes that invite aimless strolling and make it advisable to wear walking shoes with thick soles.

THE TOP ATTRACTIONS

Centro Cultural Ignacio Ramírez (Bellas Artes/El Nigromante) Housed in the former Convento de la Concepción (1755), 2 blocks west of El Jardín, the Centro is a branch of the Palacio de Bellas Artes of Mexico City. The two-story cloister, surrounding an enormous courtyard with large trees and a gurgling fountain, houses art exhibits and classrooms for drawing, painting, sculpture, lithography, textiles, ceramics, dramatic arts, ballet, regional dance, piano, and guitar. A mural by David Alfaro Siqueiros and some of his memorabilia are worth seeing. A bulletin board lists concerts and lectures at this institute and elsewhere in the city. You can also dine in these pleasant surroundings at the restaurant **Las Musas,** which serves pasta, salads, sandwiches, and desserts. Before you leave, take a look at the magnificent dome behind the convent. It belongs to the Iglesia de la Concepción and was designed by the same unschooled architect who designed La Parroquia (see below).

Hernández Macías 75 (btw. Canal and Insurgentes). ⓒ **415/152-0289.** Free admission. Mon–Sat 9am–7pm; Sun 10am–2pm.

La Parroquia ★★★ Looking nothing like any other church in Mexico, La Parroquia has become the emblem of San Miguel. It is an object of great pride for the citizenry and a source of discomfort for architectural purists. Originally built in the colonial style, the church was remade in the late 19th century by a local builder named Zeferino Gutiérrez, who reconstructed the towers and facade. Gutiérrez was unlettered but had seen pictures of Europe's Gothic cathedrals and worked from these alone. I find the finished product fascinating—a highly personal vision of the Gothic style that owes more to the builder's imagination and fancy than to the European churches that were its inspiration. The inside is not nearly so much fun as the outside; the church was looted on several occasions during times of social upheaval, and this kind of art criticism puts a damper on commissioning more paintings and decoration. Still, there are things to see. My favorite, and one often missed, is the crypt beneath the altar. You get to it through a door on the right side. You'll have to seek out the caretaker, who can unlock the door (for a small tip).

South side of El Jardín. No phone. Free admission. Daily 8am–2pm and 5–9pm.

Museo Casa de Allende   The house of San Miguel's most famous son and namesake, the independence leader Ignacio Allende, is a museum. It is of the genre known as *museos regionales* that you will find across Mexico. The objective of these museums is to present a view of the local area from prehistoric times to recent history; to explain what roles the region played in the context of national development; and to illustrate how the great historical movements that swept across Mexico ran their courses at the local level. This museum features a biographical exhibit on Allende, concentrating on his role in the independence movement. It explores the effects that national independence had for San Miguel and the local area. Explanations are in Spanish only, but the artifacts—including fossils, pre-Hispanic pottery, Colonial-Era furnishings, and articles of daily life—and the beauty of the house are worth the price.

Southwest corner of El Jardín. © **415/152-2499.** Admission 37 pesos. Tues–Sun 9am–5pm.

MORE ATTRACTIONS

The **House and Garden Tour ★★**, sponsored by the Biblioteca Pública, is universally enjoyed. The tour opens the doors of some of the city's most interesting colonial and contemporary houses. Tours leave Sunday at 11:30am from the library, Insurgentes 25 (© **415/152-0293**), and last about 2 hours. The tour costs 200 pesos, which goes to support various library projects benefiting the youth of San Miguel.

Bill Levasseur of Casa de la Cuesta Bed and Breakfast has a mask museum called **La Otra Cara de México (The Other Face of Mexico) ★★**. It's a thoughtfully arranged exhibition of masks that provides a lot of cultural context. Masks have played an important role in many of Mexico's native cultures, usually as part of a dance or ritual. Over the years, Bill has collected some great pieces and has filmed dances and performances in which the masks were used. This museum is a treat for both serious collectors and casual travelers. Visits are by appointment (© **415/154-4324**).

A couple of the most enjoyable walks in town are to the lookout point **El Mirador,** especially at sunset, which colors the entire town and the lake beyond, and to **Parque Juárez,** a large and shady park.

NEARBY ATTRACTIONS

Just outside of San Miguel are several hot mineral springs that have been made into bathing spots. They're all just off the road leading to Dolores Hidalgo. **La Taboada, La Gruta,** and **Escondido** lie close to one another, just 8 to 10km (5–6¼ miles) outside San Miguel. La Gruta is perhaps the nicest, but La Taboada has a quiet old hotel reminiscent of an earlier Mexico and makes for a relaxing stay.

Near these hot springs is the sanctuary of **Atotonilco el Grande,** a complex of chapels, dormitories, dining rooms, and a church. UNESCO has declared the complex part of the World Heritage Site for San Miguel. The church was founded in 1740 by Father Luis Felipe Neri Alfaro, an austere mystic. He thought the area in dire need of a religious presence, as many people would gather at the thermal springs to bathe publicly and, in his eyes, licentiously. He commissioned a local artist, Martínez Pocasangre, to paint murals illustrating the instructive verses that Alfaro wrote, with much emphasis on the dangers lying in wait for the human soul. The murals and verses cover the church's ceiling and walls, adding color to an otherwise dark structure.

Father Alfaro built his sanctuary on the spot where he was granted an ecstatic vision of Christ. The location proved providential: Seventy years later, when Father Miguel Hidalgo was in the town of Dolores, he was warned of his imminent capture, so he hastily declared independence and then marched an impromptu army toward San Miguel. En route, he stopped at Atotonilco, where he took the church's image of the Virgin of Guadalupe as his banner, declaring her the protector of the new nation—the first time that she was officially recognized as such.

The church and adjoining buildings still function throughout the year as a religious retreat for people who come from all over the country for a week of prayer, penance, and mortification. These spiritual exercises are conducted in private. You can get to Atotonilco by cab or via the bus marked EL SANTUARIO, at the market. It passes every hour on the hour and goes through Taboada on its way to Atotonilco.

Shopping

San Miguel is a town of artists; you'll find art for sale not only in galleries, but also in restaurants, offices, and just about anywhere there's space in a public area. San Miguel is also a town of artisans working mainly with clay, iron, brass, tin, blown glass, and papier-mâché. And San Miguel is a town of shopkeepers who sell locally produced items as well as folk art and decorative objects from across Mexico. There are so many stores, and they are so different from each other, that a list would not be helpful. The best advice I can give is to explore the streets around the main square. If you're looking for something in particular, ask around. One place that's easily walkable but a bit outside the downtown area is **Fábrica La Aurora,** an old textile mill that's been converted into galleries and shops selling art, furnishings, and antiques. The old factory is an attractive space, with lots of open areas, and includes a restaurant and a cafe. It's a bit north of downtown on Calzada de La Aurora, just past the bridge.

Stores are usually open Monday through Saturday from 9am to 2pm and 4 to 7 or 8pm. Most stores close on Sunday. If you're interested in Talavera pottery, consider going to nearby Dolores Hidalgo (see "A Side Trip to Dolores Hidalgo: Fine Pottery & Shrimp Ice Cream," later in this chapter). Also, you can find some handicrafts and fun knickknacks at the **Mercado de Artesanías (handicrafts market),** but it will require hunting through lots of goods that are either too tacky or not tacky enough. The *mercado* occupies a walkway 3 blocks long that descends from the municipal market past the Hotel Quinta Loreto.

Where to Stay

For longer stays, you might check with the language schools (see "Learning at the Source: Going to School in San Miguel," above) and other bulletin boards around town for lists of apartments or rooms to rent, or check for listings or websites such as **www.internetsanmiguel.com**. Most apartments have kitchens and bedding; some come with maid service. San Miguel is a popular weekend getaway for residents of the capital, and several hotels raise rates on weekends. Secured parking is at a premium; if your hotel doesn't provide it, you'll pay around $12 to $16 daily in a guarded lot. Most places can arrange airport transportation. The rates listed below already include taxes, which are 18%.

VERY EXPENSIVE

Casa Misha ★★★   If so inclined, there are some things that a small hotel can do in providing personal service and privacy that a large hotel cannot match. This is the case at Casa Misha, where the owners, Edward George and Richard Samuel, make a point of offering every assistance and service that their guests might care for, including private dinners, special needs, and custom tours. The property is large (composed of two houses) and affords a variety of common areas in which to relax—intimate patios, grand rooftop terraces with beautiful views, and elegant sitting rooms. You will be surrounded by beauty and serenity. Guest rooms are large and thoughtfully decorated with antiques, rich fabrics, and artwork. Most include a private terrace. For greater privacy, you can rent the two rooms in one house and have it as a private residence.

Chiquitos 15, 37700 San Miguel de Allende, Gto. www.casamisha.com. ℰ **646/688-4862** in the U.S., or 415/152-2021. Fax 415/152-5505. 7 units. $300–$410 double. Rates include full breakfast. AE, MC, V. Valet parking 100 pesos. **Amenities:** Bar; concierge; room service; smoke-free rooms. *In room:* A/C (in 6 units), TV/DVD, CD player, hair dryer, minibar, MP3 docking station, Wi-Fi.

Rosewood San Miguel de Allende ★★★   This new resort opened in February 2011. It's a gorgeous property located a few blocks south of the Jardín. Guest rooms are distributed among three buildings, each three stories tall. The rooms are quite large, the largest in town. Each room has hardwood floors and is furnished and decorated in an uncluttered Mexican-hacienda style, with local accents and French doors leading out to a large and private terrace. All the terraces have views of the extensive gardens, and some of the third-floor suites have views of La Parroquia. Bathrooms are also oversize and come with a large tub and a separate large shower. The common areas are airy and beautiful. Each is oriented to a garden or patio with a pool or fountain. Every time I visit a Rosewood property I'm impressed with the service; they treat you with the same attentiveness and ease, whether you're a lowly travel writer or the king of Morocco.

Nemesio Diez 11 (at Aldama), 37700 San Miguel de Allende, Gto. www.rosewoodsanmiguel.com. ℰ **888/767-3966** in the U.S. and Canada, or 415/152-9700. 67 units. $531–$584 standard and deluxe rooms; $690 rooftop room; $808 and up suite. Rates do not include additional 10% gratuity charge. AE, MC, V. Valet parking $15. Pets 15 lb. and under accepted with restrictions. **Amenities:** 3 restaurants; 2 bars; babysitting; children's program; concierge; fitness room; Jacuzzi; 2 outdoor heated pools; room service; sauna; smoke-free rooms; spa. *In room:* A/C, TV, hair dryer, minibar, MP3 docking station, Wi-Fi.

EXPENSIVE

Casa de la Cuesta ★★   In an upper *barrio* (neighborhood) stands this magnificent house, an example of how colonial architecture can be rethought in modern terms. The entrance to the house is through a passage that opens up to the first of two courtyards. On three sides are structures of different heights, which make use, wherever possible, of rooftop terraces. Most guest rooms encircle the arcaded rear courtyard, with a lot of terraces and common space, much of which has a fine view of the central part of town. Most have fireplaces. Rooms are large and comfortable, with king-size beds, lots of color and detail, and a mix of modern and colonial furnishings. Two rooms come with kitchens. The house is about a 10-minute walk to the center of town, and the return is uphill. Breakfasts are great, and the hosts are helpful and entertaining.

Cuesta de San José 32, 37700 San Miguel de Allende, Gto. www.casadelacuesta.com. ℰ/fax **415/154-4324.** 7 units. $165 double. Rates include full breakfast. AE, MC, V (for deposits). Limited street parking. **Amenities:** Smoke-free rooms. *In room:* Hair dryer, no phone, Wi-Fi.

Casa Luna Boutique Hotel ★★ Casa Luna is visually striking, with lots of color, imaginative decoration, and, here and there, playful touches of Mexican and local handicrafts. It's just the kind of setting to lure you into vacation mode. The house on Calle Quebrada is a large property, designed in hacienda style with verdant patios and handsome common rooms. Guest rooms are large and supplied with a king-size bed or two twins, down comforters, gas fireplaces, and large bathrooms with tub/showers. Several have private patios. Breakfasts are delicious, and cooking classes are sometimes offered. The hotel also has a small ranch just out of town, which is also beautifully designed. It's quite suitable for small groups or get-togethers.

Calle Quebrada 117 (between Umarán and Pila Seca), 37700 San Miguel de Allende, Gto. www.casaluna. com. ℂ **210/200-8758** or 415/152-1117. 14 units. $150–$166 double. Rates include full breakfast. MC, V (for deposits). Limited street parking. Children 15 and younger not accepted. **Amenities:** Bar; Jacuzzi; small outdoor pool; smoke-free rooms. *In room:* Hair dryer, no phone, Wi-Fi.

Susurro ★★ 🏠 Spend any amount of time in places like San Miguel and you realize that the domestic architecture is all about the creation of serene, private spaces. Susurro (which in Spanish describes the sound made by whispering wind and trickling water) has elegant interior spaces, and with only four guest rooms, you'll find plenty of time to enjoy these all to yourself. The soft sounds of flowing water can be heard all around the house. Three of the rooms are large and come with separate terraces. The fourth, the garden room has a lovely patio area in the rear garden. All rooms are beautifully decorated, with either a queen-size or a king-size bed. The house is a few blocks from the main square.

Recreo 78, 37700 San Miguel de Allende, Gto. www.susurro.com.mx. ℂ **310/943-7163** in the U.S., or 415/152-1065. 4 units. $155–$185 double. Rates include full breakfast. AE, MC, V for deposits only; cash only at inn. Limited street parking. Children 12 and younger not accepted. **Amenities:** Plunge pool; smoke-free rooms; Wi-Fi (in half the property). *In room:* TV, hair dryer, no phone.

MODERATE

Casa Carmen Bed & Breakfast Every B&B has its own feel, and this one feels like a friendly Mexican household. It has a pretty little Mexican patio with orange trees and a fountain, and large rooms that are comfortably but simply furnished. English is spoken. All rooms have gas heaters and come with either two twins or one queen-size bed. Of these, the penthouse is perhaps the most comfortable, but the ones in the first courtyard have the most character. Bathrooms vary in size. Breakfast (daily) and the afternoon meal (Mon–Sat) are served in a pleasant dining room; the cooking is good. You can reserve rooms by the day, week, or month, with discounts for extended stays. The location is central, just 2 blocks east of the Jardín.

Correo 31, near Recreo (Apdo. Postal 152), 37700 San Miguel de Allende, Gto. www.casacarmenhotel. com. ℂ/fax **415/152-0844.** 10 units. $126 double; $132–$172 suite. Rates include breakfast and lunch (breakfast only Sun). No credit cards. Limited street parking. Children 13 and younger not accepted. *In room:* No phone.

Hotel Mansión Virreyes Soon after the Mexican Revolution ended, this became the first hotel in San Miguel. The rooms are simply furnished but comfortable. Almost all face the interior courtyard. Half are carpeted, half are tiled. Bathrooms are small to medium. On the top floor are three apartments, which are large and come with kitchenettes. These are usually rented out from January to March.

Canal 19, 37700 San Miguel de Allende, Gto. www.hotelmansionvirreyes.com. ℂ **415/152-3355,** -0851. Fax 415/152-3865. 22 units. Fri–Sun 1,300–1,650 pesos double, 1,950 pesos apt; Mon–Thurs 1,200–1,550 pesos double, 1,700 pesos apt. Rates include full breakfast. MC, V. Free secure parking 4 blocks away. **Amenities:** Restaurant; bar; room service; Wi-Fi (in restaurant/bar). *In room:* Fan, TV.

Hotel Posada Carmina This centrally located hotel is comfortable, beautiful, and well managed. It's a half-block south of the plaza, next to La Parroquia, in a large colonial mansion made from the same stone as the church. The two floors of rooms surround a stately courtyard with orange trees growing around a stone fountain, and bougainvillea and *llamarada* creeping up the walls. Rooms are ample and well furnished. Most of the bathrooms are comfortably sized but simple, with small mirrors (and, in some, little counter space) and plenty of hot water. Light sleepers will find that the bells of La Parroquia prove a nuisance in the front rooms. The new section in back is quieter. Rooms there are midsize, with well-lit bathrooms and firm mattresses.

Cuna de Allende 7, 37700 San Miguel de Allende, Gto. www.posadacarmina.com. *©* **415/152-0458.** Fax 415/152-1036. 24 units. 1,230–1,540 pesos double. Rates include full breakfast. MC, V. Limited street parking. **Amenities:** Restaurant; room service; Wi-Fi (in common areas). *In room:* TV.

INEXPENSIVE

Parador San Sebastián *♦* The San Sebastián is another colonial house–turned–hotel with a central location and comfortable rooms for the price. Standard rooms are simple and vary in size and choice of beds. Pricing is based on bed choices. The lower price is for a double bed or two twins; the higher price is for two doubles. Bathrooms are mostly medium size. Apartments come with a bedroom (double bed), a kitchen, and a living/dining area. Guests can lounge in the chairs on the courtyard and the rooftop terrace. This hotel takes only walk-ins and won't accept reservations.

Mesones 7 (btw. Colegio and Núñez), 37700 San Miguel de Allende, Gto. *©* **415/152-7084.** 30 units. 350–570 pesos double; 500–600 pesos apt. No credit cards. Free parking. *In room:* No phone.

Quinta Loreto *♦* This motel is a good place to stay whether you're traveling by car or not. It has good rooms for the price, a lovely garden, and a friendly atmosphere. Rooms come with ceiling fans and heaters. The cheaper rooms, without phones or televisions, are smaller than the others. Most rooms contain one double and one twin bed. The food is good and the laundry service is a bargain. Make reservations—the Loreto is popular and often books up weeks in advance. Nonguests can come for inexpensive breakfasts and lunches. Quinta Loreto is below the crafts market off Calle Loreto, about 7 blocks from the main square.

Calle Loreto 15, 37700 San Miguel de Allende, Gto. www.quintaloreto.com.mx. *©* **415/152-0042.** Fax 415/152-1304. 40 units. 530–600 pesos double. Weekly and monthly discounts available. AE, MC, V. Free parking. **Amenities:** Restaurant; small outdoor pool. *In room:* Some w/TV and phone, some w/ neither.

Where to Eat

In San Miguel, vegetarians will have no problem—most restaurants have legitimate meat-free main courses. For the best baked goods (pastries, French bread, sandwiches, croissants, and cakes), try **El Petit Four,** Calle Mesones 99. It's open Tuesday through Saturday from 8am to 8pm, Sunday from 8am to 6pm. There's a dining area in the store, or you can take your baked goods with you.

To sample some of the people's food, you might try **Cenaduría La Alborada** at Sollano 11 (*©* **415/513-0577**), by the main square. It's a traditional sort of supper place where you can get a nourishing bowl of *pozole* or a plate of enchiladas. It's open Monday through Saturday from 2pm to 1am. For tacos, try **Los Faroles,** at Ancha de San Antonio 28-C (*©* **451/152-1849**). The owners sell a variety of *tacos de parrilla* (tacos with grilled meats) and *volcanes* (a toasted tortilla topped with meat and cheese).

Another dining option is a 10-minute ride east of town. An Italian chef has taken over a small part of the former **Hacienda de Landeta** and has a "country-kitchen" thing going on there—outdoor dining, chalkboard menu, unhurried personal service (main courses typically 130–240 pesos). Local residents love it. Amid crumbling walls and ancient trees, the setting has a gracious old-world feel to it. The menu always includes fresh pasta, usually a fish dish, and three or four Italian specialties. Chef Andreas personally attends his customers Thursday through Sunday starting around 2pm. He has only a few tables, so make reservations (✆ **415/120-3481**).

MODERATE

Café Ibérico ★★★ TAPAS/PAELLA   The tapas I tried at this restaurant were excellent and included the best fried calamari I've ever eaten. And the paella (either seafood or rabbit with chorizo) is just like what you get in Spain, with a chewy crust on the bottom of the pan. A couple from North Carolina, Tim and Suzanne Inscore, run the place. Tim was trained in Spain and loves to cook. He changes the list of tapas depending on what's available or what he feels like cooking, and he keeps the menu simple. Suzanne takes charge of the desserts, which are excellent. Here they offer weekly specials and a happy hour from 4 to 7pm. If you plan ahead, you can try *lechón al horno* (roast suckling pig) with a 24-hour advanced notice. You can opt to dine outdoors on a large patio or indoors in a dining room with a fireplace. Live music acts perform on Friday (variable) and Saturday (Spanish guitar) evenings.

101 Mesones (between Hidalgo and Hernández Macías). ✆ **415/152-6154.** www.cafeiberico.com.mx. Reservations recommended on weekends. Tapas 30–120 pesos; paella 185–240 pesos. No credit cards. Sun-Thurs 2–10pm; Fri-Sat 2–11pm.

Jackie's San Antonio ★★★ MEDITERRANEAN   This restaurant is somewhat removed from central San Miguel, but it's well worth the taxi ride, since you'll find a view of the neighborhood church of Colonia San Antonio and the spires of La Parroquia from an uncommon perspective. The menu includes some unique dishes, such as duck braised in port and Turkish figs, pork tenderloin with a candied-apple stuffing, or grilled monkfish served with a sweet-pepper aioli. The chef has trained with Mónica Patiño in Mexico City.

Plaza San Antonio 4. ✆ **415/110-2223.** Reservations recommended. Main courses 130–290 pesos. MC, V. Fri-Wed 1pm-midnight; Thurs 6pm-midnight.

Planta Baja ★★ FUSION/MEDITERRANEAN   Planta Baja offers inventive fusion cooking. You could make a dinner of just the appetizers, which include options such as grilled swordfish with roasted sweet peppers, caramelized onion, and balsamic vinegar, or bites of tuna on potato chips with avocado sauce and a sprinkling of onion and cilantro. The shrimp and oyster soup, made at the table, is a popular choice. For a main course, try a stir-fry noodle dish or their delicious spiced salmon. Though the menu changes often, you'll always find a few steaks offered. The dining room has a hedonistic feel from the interesting combination of dramatic colors and muted lighting.

Canal 28. ✆ **415/154-6555.** www.plantabajasanmiguel.com. Reservations recommended on weekends. Main courses 135–212 pesos. AE, MC, V. Daily 1pm-midnight.

The Restaurant INTERNATIONAL   In a colonial courtyard framed in Moorish arches, you can enjoy original dishes by chef Donnie Masterson. The dinner menu changes every couple of weeks, so it's difficult to focus on any particular dish. Mr.

Masterson characterizes his cooking as "global comfort food"—taking the mainstays of the world's cooking (since these days, at least in our dining, we're all globalists) and tweaking them with a few changes in flavors. There's usually something Mexican-inspired on the menu, and at least one Asian dish transformed. Thursday nights feature gourmet hamburgers, which are very popular. Service is good.

Sollano 16. ℂ **415/154-7862.** www.therestaurantsanmiguel.com. Reservations recommended. Main courses 140–240 pesos; lunch 60–100 pesos. MC, V. Tues–Sat 5–10:30pm.

Vivoli Café ★★ ITALIAN   This restaurant should be able to satisfy just about anyone's appetite for Italian food. The menu is large, with a wide variety of pasta, three risottos (including a lively one with three kinds of mushrooms), various pizzas, and many different meat and seafood dishes. On my last visit I enjoyed some tender ravioli followed by pollo piccata cooked perfectly. The dining room is comfortably furnished and softly lit, perfect for a relaxed dining experience.

Hernández Macías 66. ℂ **415/152-0045.** www.vivolicafe.com. Reservations accepted. Main courses 90–250 pesos; pizzas 90–140 pesos. AE, MC, V. Mon–Thurs 12:30–10pm; Fri 12:30–11pm; Sat 11am–11pm; Sun 8am–10pm.

INEXPENSIVE

El Correo ★ MEXICAN   This is a small place right across from the post office. I like the owner's selection, which offers a varied sampling of Mexican standards: *sopes* (little fried *masa* cakes topped with savory meats and veggies); *caldo tlalpeño* (chicken, rice, and vegetable soup; my preference over the tortilla soup, which is what most people come for); and *enchiladas del portal,* which are made in the classic western Mexican style. Other offerings include *mole* and *arrachera a la tampiqueña* (steak with an array of side dishes, such as enchiladas, guacamole, or rice and beans).

Correo 23. ℂ **415/152-4951.** Reservations accepted. Breakfast 50–75 pesos; main courses 68–140 pesos. MC, V. Wed–Mon 8am–10:30pm.

El Pegaso Restaurant & Bar INTERNATIONAL   When you're looking for only a light meal, consider dropping into this place, which is inexpensive, cheerfully lit, and has quick, friendly service. It's popular mainly for the sandwiches, salads, breakfasts, and desserts. You can get anything here from a Reuben sandwich to a tuna melt, to eggs Benedict, to shish kabob.

Corregidora 6 (at Correo). ℂ **415/152-1351.** Breakfast 44–69 pesos; soups, salads, sandwiches 70–96 pesos; main courses 80–135 pesos. MC, V. Mon–Sat 8:30am–10pm.

La Posadita MEXICAN   Mexican food with a view is the draw at this rooftop restaurant near La Parroquia. And the food is creditably executed. I tried a soup and some enchiladas and enjoyed them. The margaritas were good, too—a little small but not watered down. Other popular dishes include the *cochinita pibil,* and the tacos. If you're in the mood for a hearty soup, try the *pozole.* In the evening, ask for a table with a view of the church. There's also plenty of indoor dining.

Cuna de Allende 13. ℂ **415/154-8862.** Main courses 75–150 pesos. No credit cards. Thurs–Tues noon–10pm.

Olé Olé MEXICAN   Festive and friendly, this small restaurant is a riot of red and yellow streamers and bullfight memorabilia. The small menu specializes in grilled main courses—beef or chicken fajitas, shrimp brochettes, and *arrachera* (steak).

Loreto 66 (btw. Insurgentes and Calzada de la Luz). ℂ **415/152-0896.** Main courses 70–130 pesos. No credit cards. Daily 1–9pm.

San Miguel After Dark

To see a calendar of events, find a copy of the local paper, *Atención,* or one of the free monthly periodicals for visitors. Bellas Artes and the Angela Peralta Theater also post announcements of performances around town. Local regulations favor restaurant/ bars over simple bars, so live-music acts often perform in restaurants. Clubs and dance clubs tend to spring up and then die off quickly. A couple of restaurants are popular nightspots: **Tío Lucas** (© 415/512-4996) is a fun place to hear jazz and have a few drinks and perhaps a bite of dinner. It's located at Mesones 105 across from the Teatro Peralta. **Mama Mía,** Umarán 8, between Jesús and Hernández Macías (© 415/152-2063), has a bar area where salsa and jazz bands play on the weekends. There is a cover charge of 40 pesos. In the summer, you can enjoy the late afternoon and early evening from its rooftop terrace. If all you want is a drink and a view, La Azotea Bar, next door to Mama Mía, has a lively rooftop scene all year long.

A Side Trip to Dolores Hidalgo: Fine Pottery & Shrimp Ice Cream

Dolores Hidalgo lies 40km (25 miles) northwest of San Miguel on Hwy. 35. Most people go there to shop at the Talavera pottery companies, but the town itself merits a visit. It remains a quiet, provincial place with a lovely main square and parish church; on the church steps, Father Hidalgo proclaimed the independence of Mexico. The church has a charming facade that, if pressed, I would label late Mexican baroque, but that doesn't do it justice. The interior of the church was plundered at various times but retains a couple of beautiful altarpieces.

The main square has a small-town feel to it. Vendors sell ice cream in exotic flavors—tequila, shrimp, and pulque (a fermented beverage made from agave) are just a few enticing examples—as well as mango, *guanábana,* and other more familiar standbys. It all started 30 years ago on a dare, and then caught on for the notoriety it gave the vendors. Ask for some impossibly bad flavor—such as cilantro–*mescal*– chocolate chip or chicken *mole* swirl—and, without batting an eye, they'll tell you they're fresh out and to come back tomorrow. Most of these ice creams are known as *nieves* and are low in fat; for a richer ice cream, ask for a *mantecado.* If you're hungry, the restaurant El Patio is on the east side of the square.

Dolores has two small museums. The **Casa de Hidalgo** (admission 20 pesos) is filled with letters and historical artifacts having to do with Father Hidalgo and will be of most interest to history buffs. The **Museo de la Independencia** (admission 15 pesos), a more dramatic approach to the theme of independence, also has a small collection of memorabilia of José Alfredo Jiménez, the king of *ranchera* music.

SHOPPING FOR TALAVERA

The **Talavera** pottery produced in Dolores is handsome and colorful, if less traditional than Talavera pottery produced in Puebla. It's also inexpensive and plentiful. You can find all kinds of objects, from sink basins to napkin rings, to hand-painted tiles. The pieces are formed with molds and then painted freehand. Prices here are considerably lower than those in San Miguel. Workshops are usually open from 10am to 6pm but may or may not close for the afternoon meal. Almost all are closed on Sunday.

The first couple of Talavera workshops you'll encounter aren't even in town, but are on the highway just before you get there. **Talavera San Gabriel** (© 418/185-5037) has a warehouse full of large and small decorative objects, including picture frames,

Several tour guides in San Miguel make trips to **Dolores Hidalgo, Guanajuato,** and **Querétaro.** It's a hurried way to see these places, but it can be done. **Leandro Delgado** (📞 415/152-0155; leandrotours@hotmail.com) is an independent guide who is well informed and conscientious. He speaks English, is a good driver, and is familiar with the artisans of Dolores Hidalgo and Guanajuato. Guides offer trips to see the **monarch butterflies,** 5 hours away in the state of Michoacán (see chapter 7). This is an exhausting trip; do it in 2 days, staying overnight in the town of Angangueo, if you can. The season runs from mid- to late November to March.

candlesticks, and ginger jars. And **Talavera Amora** (📞 418/185-9002) has more dinnerware, including the popular blue-and-yellow fish pattern.

Once you get into town, you're best off just asking directions for different stores and factories. There are a lot of shops, and each seems to have a different specialty. At the entrance to the town, on the left side of the first roundabout, is **Hacienda Style** (📞 418/182-2064, or 602/288-9122 in the U.S.). It produces tiles and sink basins and other objects in traditional and contemporary patterns. The factory has a store in San Miguel at Zacateros 83-A (📞 415/154-7962). Another that specializes in decorative objects and tiles is **Talavera Cortés** (📞 418/182-0900), at the corner of Distrito Federal and Tabasco streets. **Azulejos Talavera Vázquez** (📞 418/182-0630) has a large store at the corner of Puebla and Tamaulipas streets. It has a bit of everything, and at that same intersection are a couple of other stores with lots of dinnerware.

GUANAJUATO ★★★

354km (219 miles) NW of Mexico City; 56km (35 miles) SE of León; 93km (58 miles) W of San Miguel de Allende; 208km (129 miles) SW of San Luis Potosí; 163km (101 miles) N of Morelia; 280km (174 miles) SE of Zacatecas

If you're going to Mexico to lose yourself, you'll have no problem doing so on the streets of Guanajuato (Gwah-nah-*whah*-toh). They seem designed for just that purpose as they curl this way and that, becoming alleys or stairways, and intersecting each other at different angles. At times it can seem like the Twilight Zone; I've heard of people hurriedly passing by a curious-looking shop intending to return later, and then never being able to locate it again. To make matters worse, the streets are filled with things that draw your attention away from the business of getting from one place to another. The town is so photogenic that everywhere you look is postcard material. Most buildings, like the streets, are irregular in shape, creating a jumble of walls, balconies, and rooftops meeting at anything but a right angle. The churches are the exception, having regular floor plans, but even they show asymmetry—despite the best efforts of their builders, none have two matching towers, which only adds to their charm.

Founded in 1559, Guanajuato soon became fabulously rich, with world-famous mines (such as La Valenciana, Mineral de Cata, and Mineral de Rayas), which earned their owners titles of nobility. Along with Zacatecas and San Luis Potosí, Guanajuato was one of Mexico's most important mining cities. From the 16th through the 18th centuries, the mines in these towns produced a third of all the silver in the world, and

Guanajuato bloomed with elaborate churches and mansions. Floods plagued the city until it finally diverted the river and turned the old riverbed into a road that winds into the old downtown, with cantilevered houses jutting out high above the cars. The city has also opened an impressive network of tunnels (it is, after all, a mining town).

Still, on the surface, Guanajuato seems like an old Spanish city dumped into a Mexican highland valley (at 2,008m/6,586 ft. elevation). It's one of Mexico's great colonial cities. Picturesque and laden with atmosphere, Guanajuato should be high on your list of places to visit.

Essentials

GETTING THERE & DEPARTING By Plane Air access is good, with frequent flights in and out of the León/Guanajuato (also known as León/Bajío, code BJX) airport, 27km (17 miles) from downtown Guanajuato. The taxi ride costs about 400 pesos. The airport has an ATM, pharmacy, and gift store. It also has rental car counters: **Avis** (☎ 477/713-3003), **Budget** (☎ 477/713-1404), **Hertz** (☎ 477/771-5050), **National** (☎ 477/771-3371), and **Thrifty** (☎ 477/713-8522).

American Airlines' number in Mexico is ☎ 01-800/904-6000, **Continental**'s is ☎ 01-800/900-5000, and **Delta Airlines'** number is ☎ 01-800/123-4710. **Aeroméxico** (☎ 01-800/021-4000) and its affiliate, **Aeroméxico Connect,** fly to and from Los Angeles, Tijuana, Mexico City, Puerto Vallarta, Monterrey, and Ciudad Juárez. **Volaris** (☎ 01-800/122-8000 in Mexico), a discount domestic air carrier, flies to and from Tijuana.

There are airline ticket offices in León and at the airport. In Guanajuato, travel agencies can arrange flight reservations.

By Car From Mexico City, take Tollway 57D north toward Querétaro and follow signs for Tollway 45D west toward Irapuato. This road bypasses the cities of Celaya, Salamanca, and Irapuato, where it turns north. Before Silao, there's a turnoff for Hwy. 110 east. The route is a four-lane road that takes 4½ hours. From San Luis Potosí, the quickest way to Guanajuato is through Dolores Hidalgo (3 hr.).

By Bus The bus station in Guanajuato is 6km (3¾ miles) southwest of town. From **Mexico City's Terminal Norte,** you'll have no trouble finding a *directo* (nonstop bus) to Guanajuato. **Servicios Coordinados/Primera Plus** (☎ **01-800/375-7587** in Mexico) and **Estrella Blanca** (☎ **55/5729-4388**) run express buses (5 hr.). You shouldn't have to wait more than a half-hour. Try to catch one of **ETN**'s (☎ **01-800/800-0386** in Mexico) superdeluxe buses with extra-wide seats that recline far back (10 per day). They're worth the extra money.

From **San Miguel de Allende,** ETN has three nonstop buses; Primera Plus/Servicios Coordinados has nine. These go *vía la Presa* (the short route—1¼ hr.). Don't take buses that go via Dolores Hidalgo. There is also service to Guadalajara (4 hr.), Morelia (usually via Irapuato, 2½ hr.), and elsewhere.

ORIENTATION Arriving by Plane The only transportation from the León/Guanajuato airport, 27km (17 miles) from downtown, is a **private taxi.** You pay for the cab (420 pesos) inside the airport. There is no shuttle service.

Arriving by Car Try not to lose your sanity while finding a place to park. Such a winding, hilly town defies good verbal or written directions. Be alert for one-way streets. Consider parking your car until you leave town, because the frustration of driving in the city could spoil your visit.

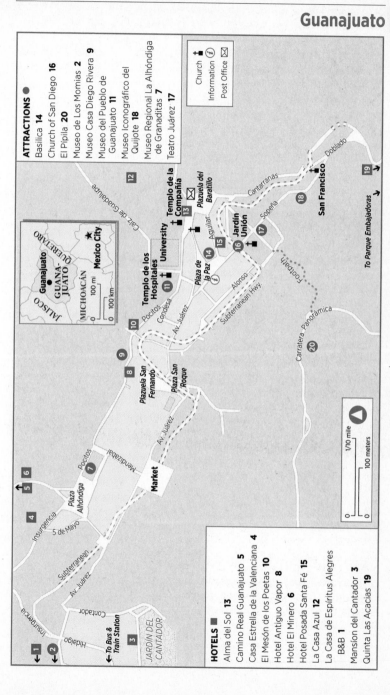

ATTRACTIONS ●

Basilica **14**
Church of San Diego **16**
El Pipila **20**
Museo de Los Momias **2**
Museo Casa Diego Rivera **9**
Museo del Pueblo de Guanajuato **11**
Museo Iconográfico del Quijote **18**
Museo Regional La Alhóndiga de Granaditas **7**
Teatro Juárez **17**

Church ✝
Information ⓘ
Post Office ⊠

HOTELS ■

Alma del Sol **13**
Camino Real Guanajuato **5**
Casa Estrella de la Valenciana **4**
El Mesón de los Poetas **10**
Hotel Antiguo Vapor **8**
Hotel El Minero **6**
Hotel Posada Santa Fé **15**
La Casa Azul **12**
La Casa de Espiritus Alegres B&B **1**
Mansion del Cantador **3**
Quinta Las Acacias **19**

Arriving by Bus   The bus station is about 6km (3¾ miles) southwest of town, on the road to Celaya. Cabs cost about 40 pesos. At night there can sometimes be a scarcity of cabs. Try to schedule your trip to arrive during the day.

VISITOR INFORMATION   The state **tourism office** is at Plaza de la Paz 14, across from the basilica (© **473/732-9492**). The handiest place to get information is at a kiosk in the Jardín Unión. It's staffed daily from 9am to 8pm.

CITY LAYOUT   Guanajuato is a town of narrow streets, alleys, and stairs, and small, picturesque plazas. The hilly terrain and tangle of streets are difficult to represent on a map. You'll soon learn that maps aren't drawn to scale, nor do they show every street and stairway. The best way to get oriented is to visit the overlook at El Pípila (see "The Top Attractions," below), and one by one make out the major landmarks.

The small plaza at the center of the city, **Jardín Unión** (known as the cheese wedge, for its shape), is where students, locals, and visitors gather. Facing the Jardín from the direction of El Pípila are both the **Teatro Juárez** and **Templo de San Diego.** From this plaza, you are within walking distance of many of the major sights.

GETTING AROUND   Walking is the only way to get to know the historic district of this labyrinthine town. For longer stretches, taxis are reasonably priced and abundant, except between 2 and 4pm when office workers are trying to get home for the midafternoon meal. As usual, you should establish the price before setting out.

[FastFACTS] GUANAJUATO

Area Code   The telephone area code is **473.**

Climate   The city has temperatures that are mild in summer, cool in winter, with the occasional freeze at night.

Drugstores   Farmacia Embajadoras is at Paseo Madero 10 (© **473/732-0996**), and **Farmacia La Perla** is at Juárez 146 (© **473/732-1175**).

Emergency & Police   Call © **473/732-0266** for the police.

Hospital   Centro Médico La Presa is at Paseo de la Presa 85 (© **473/731-1074**).

Internet Access   There are several Internet cafes in the downtown area, with a lot of turnover.

Post Office   The *correo,* on the corner of Ayuntamiento and San José, near the Templo de la Compañía,

is open Monday through Friday from 8am to 4:30pm, and Saturday 9am to 1pm.

Seasons   The rainy season is June through September. Occasionally the rain is hard, but mostly it's afternoon showers and presents no problems for travelers. The coldest part of the year is December and January; the hottest is April, May, and some of June, before the rains come.

Special Events & Festivals

Every year in October, the state of Guanajuato sponsors the **Festival Internacional Cervantino (International Cervantes Festival)** ★★, 3 weeks of performing arts from all over the world. In recent years, the festival has featured marionettes from the Czech Republic, the Eliot Feld Ballet from New York, the Kiev Ballet, and a host of Mexican artists. The shows are held in open plazas and theaters all over town. Book rooms well in advance during the festival; if Guanajuato is full, consider staying in San Miguel de Allende.

The main office for the festival is located in Mexico City (© **55/5615-9417;** www. festivalcervantino.gob.mx). The local office is in Plaza San Francisquito 1, 36000 Guanajuato, Gto. (© **473/731-1161**). You can order tickets through **Ticketmaster** in Mexico City (© **55/5325-9000**). Keep your confirmation number; you'll need it to pick up your tickets in Guanajuato. The best time to be at the festival is during the week; on weekends it's absolute madness.

Exploring Guanajuato
THE TOP ATTRACTIONS

El Pípila   This is the best vantage point in Guanajuato for photographs—the entire city unfolds below you, with great views in every direction. A funicular railway runs up the hill from behind the church of San Diego. You can also climb the hill on foot, up a rugged winding pathway. Just look for signs that read AL PÍPILA ("to El Pípila").

The statue is the city's monument to José de los Reyes Martínez, better known as El Pípila. According to the story, El Pípila (if he really existed) was a brave young miner in Father Hidalgo's ragtag army of peasants and workers fighting for Mexican independence. Guanajuato was the first real battle of the war. The royalist forces took up their position inside the Alhóndiga de Granaditas. It seemed impregnable to Hidalgo's army, which lacked artillery. But El Pípila managed to breach the Spanish defenses by tying a flagstone to his back as protection, crawling to the fortress doors, and setting them ablaze. Today El Pípila's statue raises a torch high over the city in everlasting vigilance; the inscription at his feet proclaims AUN HAY OTRAS ALHÓNDIGAS POR INCENDIAR ("There still remain other *alhóndigas* to burn"). Free admission. Daily 24 hr.

> ### Language School
>
> Of the five language schools in Guanajuato, the best known is **Escuela Mexicana**, Potrero 12 (© **473/732-5005**; www.escuelamexicana.com). This school offers small classes for students at various levels of language proficiency, and it has very flexible course scheduling.

Museo Casa Diego Rivera ★★   From the Museo del Pueblo, walk 1½ blocks farther down the street, and you'll find the house where the artist Diego Rivera was born on December 8, 1886. It has been restored and converted into a museum. The first floor is furnished as it might have been in the era of Rivera's birth. Upstairs there's a pretty good collection of his early works. He began painting when he was 10 years old and eventually moved to Paris, where he became a Marxist during World War I. The house contains a few sketches of some of the earlier murals that made his reputation, as well as paintings from 1902 to 1956. The third floor holds a small auditorium for lectures and conferences, and there you'll find a large representation of one of Rivera's most famous murals, *Un Sueño Dominical en la Alameda*. Calle Positos 47. © **473/732-1197.** www.guanajuato.gob.mx/cultura/museos/diego.php. Admission 15 pesos. Tues–Sat 10am–7pm; Sun 10am–3pm.

Museo del Pueblo de Guanajuato ★★   Just north of the Plaza de la Paz is this 17th-century mansion that once belonged to the Marqués San Juan de Rayas. On permanent display is a fascinating collection of Colonial-Era civil and religious pieces gathered by distinguished local muralist José Chávez Morado. As a collector, Chávez Morado had an eye for the macabre, acquiring death portraits, some even eerier portraits of the living, and religious paintings on the subject of mortality. Also in the collection are some paintings by the gifted Hermenegildo Bustos, a portrait artist of the 19th century. A couple of Chávez's murals are also on display; other works by both Bustos and Chávez can be found at La Alhóndiga, down the street. There is a small collection of pre-Hispanic artifacts and several folk-art testimonials dedicated to the miraculous powers of various saints. In 2009 the museum acquired the miniature collection of noted folk art collector Teresa Pomar.

Calle Positos 7. ⓒ **473/732-2990.** www.guanajuato.gob.mx/cultura/museos/pueblo.php. Admission 15 pesos. Tues–Sat 10am–7pm; Sun 10am–3pm.

Museo Iconográfico del Quijote ★ 🎁   There are only a few universal characters in the world of Western literature: Hamlet, Faust, Don Juan, and Don Quixote come to mind. Writers far and wide have taken up these characters and reworked their stories, but Don Quixote has become a favorite subject of artists, including Dalí, Picasso, Miró, Raul Angiano, José Guadalupe Posada, Daumier, José Moreno Carbonero, and Pedro Coronel. This museum, a long block southeast of the Jardín Unión, holds a fascinating collection of art based upon Don Quixote. Particularly forceful are the sculptures and murals, but the sheer variety of forms and thematic treatment is what makes a stroll through this museum so entertaining.

Manuel Doblado 1. ⓒ **473/732-6721.** www.museoiconografico.guanajuato.gob.mx. Admission 20 pesos. Tues–Sat 10am–6:30pm; Sun 10am–2pm.

Museo Regional La Alhóndiga de Granaditas ★★   On the same street as the Rivera Museum, 2 blocks farther down, is La Alhóndiga de Granaditas, which was built between 1798 and 1809 as the town granary—hard to believe, because it is such a beautiful building. The Spanish took refuge here in 1810 when El Pípila (see above) and company captured Guanajuato. A slaughter ensued that Father Hidalgo was unable to stop. This convinced many people who had been leaning toward independence to remain loyal to Spain, although when the Spanish forces under Félix Calleja retook Guanajuato, they exacted a horrible revenge on the locals suspected of collusion. (The exhibits tell the story.) By the next year, the royalist forces triumphed, and the heads of the insurrectionists Hidalgo, Allende, Aldama, and Jiménez adorned the four corners of the building, where they remained until 1821 as a dissuasive reminder.

The old granary now houses a regional museum. Two floors hold exhibits of pre-Columbian artifacts, displays on colonial history, and regional crafts. Adorning the two stairways to the second floor are the murals of José Chávez Morado, who donated his pre-Hispanic art collection to the museum (and whose Colonial-Era collection is in the Museo del Pueblo de Guanajuato, see above). The exhibits take you through the region's Colonial Era and its role in the struggle for independence, all the way up to the Mexican Revolution. Explanatory text is in Spanish only, but the artifacts are interesting.

Mendizábal 6. ⓒ **473/732-1112.** Admission 46 pesos. Use of camera 30 pesos; video camera 60 pesos. Tues–Sat 10am–6pm; Sun 10am–3pm.

Teatro Juárez   Built in 1903 during the opulent era of the Porfiriato, this theater is now the venue for many productions, especially during the Festival Cervantino. The exterior is at odds with its surroundings—Greco-Roman portico adorned with *fin de siècle* bronze lions and lanterns. The interior is eye-catching, with its mix of multiple designs and color combinations. Five tiers of box seats line the walls of the theater, and there's not a bad seat in the house.

Jardín de la Unión. ⓒ **473/732-0183.** Admission 35 pesos. Use of camera 30 pesos, video camera 60 pesos. Tues–Sun 9am–1:45pm and 5–7:45pm.

MORE ATTRACTIONS

The **Church of San Diego,** on the Jardín Unión, stands almost as it did in 1633, when it was built under the direction of Franciscan missionaries. A flood in 1760 nearly destroyed it. The reconstruction was completed in 1786, largely at the expense of the Count of La Valenciana. The pink cantera-stone facade is a fine example of the Mexican baroque.

The **Plazuela del Baratillo,** just behind the Jardín Unión, has a beautiful fountain (a gift from Emperor Maximilian) at its center. You'll always find people sitting around it peacefully, some in the shade and others in the sun. Its name derives from its former role as a weekly *tianguis* (market); vendors would yell *"¡Barato!"* ("Cheap!").

Just west of Baratillo is the **Church of the Compañía.** Built in 1747 by the Jesuit order, it was the biggest of their churches. The *churrigueresque* decoration lightens it somewhat, but the interior, which was restored in the 19th century, is neoclassical. This church was built as part of a Jesuit university, which was founded in 1732 on orders of Philip V. It's the last of 23 universities the Jesuit order built in Mexico. The main building of the **university** is on the same block as the church. Its entrance was rebuilt in 1945 in neoclassical style.

Farther west, between the main street, Juárez, and Calle Positos, are three connected plazas worth seeing: **Plaza San Roque, Jardín de la Reforma,** and **Plaza San Fernando,** where you can sit at one of the outdoor tables and enjoy coffee in a perfectly charming setting. This plaza is an increasingly popular hangout.

NEARBY ATTRACTIONS

The following attractions are all a short distance above the city, and the best way to get to them is by taxi. You can hire one for around 140 pesos per hour. I would recommend taking the panoramic highway around the city, which allows you to pass by La Valenciana, La Cata, and La Raya; each has a mine and a church. The highway circles around to El Pípila. The drive is enjoyable and lasts about an hour, with a couple of stops and a quick drive along the submerged highway to view the houses that are perched above the road.

La Valenciana ★★★   The area around La Valenciana mine holds several attractions, shopping destinations, and a good restaurant. You might want to allot a couple of hours for a visit, but keep in mind that everything closes by 6pm. The star attraction is the magnificent **church of San Cayetano,** built toward the end of the colonial period in an opulent display of Mexican baroque. The interior is dazzling, with gilded carvings and *retablos* (altarpieces). The best time to see it is midafternoon, when sunlight pours through the windows, illuminating the golden carvings.

In the church plaza is an outstanding folk-art store called **Ojo de Venado** (see "Shopping," below), a rock-and-mineral shop, and a mezcal bar, El Fusilado, where you can pop in for something fortifying.

If you walk down toward the rear of the church, you'll come to an old entrance to the mine. A sign reads BOCAMINA SAN CAYETANO. A small cooperative offers (in Spanish only) a half-hour **tour of the mine** (25 pesos) and explains something of its operation. (Zacatecas has a more interesting mine tour.) Across the road from the church is the house of the Count of La Valenciana, which now holds a restaurant, **La Casa del Conde de la Valenciana** (see "Where to Eat," later in this chapter).

La Valenciana silver mine has recently ceased operations. The principal mine opening is a couple of hundred yards west of the house. It's an eight-sided vertical shaft (500m/1,640 ft. deep) surrounded by a tall stone wall in the shape of a crown, with large wooden doors and a miner's chapel at the entrance.

A ranch MUSEUM

Surrounding Guanajuato were more than 150 haciendas of wealthy colonial mine owners. Most are now either in ruins or restored and privately owned, but one has been made into the **Museo Exhacienda San Gabriel de Barrera ★**. About 3km (1¾ miles) from town on the road to Marfil, it's a lovely place noted for its elaborate gardens in different styles (Moorish, English, and Spanish, for example). The hacienda house presents a good picture of the 18th-century life of the *hacendados*. The hacienda still has its requisite chapel (baroque, of course), with a key identifying the various figures depicted in the *retablo*. There is also a state-run shop displaying all the handicrafts produced in the state. The grounds are open daily from 9am to 6pm; admission is 41 pesos. The store's hours are Wednesday through Sunday from 10am to 5pm.

If you keep climbing on the road that runs alongside La Valenciana, you will shortly see the driveway up to Casa de Capelo (see "Shopping," below) and to Cerámica La Cruz. Continue a few miles, and you come to the small town of Santa Rosa, where you can see yet more beautiful ceramics at Mayólica Santa Rosa (see "Shopping," below).

Templo de la Valenciana, Valenciana. Free admission. Daily 9am–6pm.

Museo de Las Momias (Mummy Museum) First-time visitors find this museum grotesque or fascinating, or both: Mummified remains of the dead, some of whom wear tattered clothing from centuries past, are on display. Dryness and the earth's gases and minerals in this particular *panteón* (cemetery) have halted decomposition. Because graveyards have limited space, bodies are eventually exhumed in Mexico to make room for newcomers. Those on display were exhumed between 1865 and 1985. The mummies stand or recline in glass cases, grinning, choking, or staring, while tour guides tell visitors macabre stories (in Spanish) of the fates of some of the deceased. Are they true? *¿Quién sabe?* But it's impossible to resist the temptation to go up and look at them. Next to the mummy museum is a small exhibit called "El Culto a la Muerte" (Worship of the Dead), which is a bad mix of morbid and hokey.

Esplanada del Panteón. ☎ **473/732-0639.** www.momiasdeguanajuato.gob.mx. Admission 50 pesos. Daily 9am–6pm. At the northwest end of town, the steep Esplanada del Panteón leads up to the municipal cemetery.

Templo de Cata Up above the city, perched on the mountain to the north, is this small, elaborate "miners' church." Cata is also the name of the mine nearby and the *barrio* (neighborhood) that surrounds the church. A lovely baroque facade, with just one tower standing, decorates the outside. Until a few years ago, this church held an enormous number of personal testimonials that covered the walls from floor to ceiling. Most of these took the traditional form of small square sheets of tin painted with scenes (in a primitive folk style) and explanatory text describing the miracles performed by the church's Señor de Villaseca. "El Trigueñito" (roughly translated as "the olive-skinned one"), as he is affectionately called, is a popular figure in Guanajuato, especially with miners and truck and taxi drivers. The testimonials were a touching display of the highly personal relationship these people have with El Trigueñito. What has become of all these testimonials is now the question. At first, their removal was supposed to be temporary, but they haven't returned. *¿Quién sabe?*

Carretera Panorámica. Free admission. Daily 9am–5pm.

Shopping

Stores in Guanajuato keep the usual hours—Monday through Saturday from 10am to 2pm and 4 to 8pm. The **Mercado Hidalgo,** or municipal market, is one of the most orderly in Mexico. You can browse on the main floor or watch the action from the raised walkway that encircles it. Aside from food and vegetable stalls, there is a lot of pottery and ceramic ware.

Artesanías Vázquez   Outlet for a Talavera factory in Dolores Hidalgo, this place is small but loaded with the colorful Talavera-style pottery for which Dolores is famous. You'll see plates, ginger jars, frames, cups and saucers, serving bowls, and the like. Open Monday through Saturday from 9am to 9pm; Sunday 10am to 5pm. Cantarranas 8. © **473/732-5231.**

Casa de Capelo   Famous ceramist Javier de Jesús Hernández, known simply as "Capelo," has his workshop high above Guanajuato, past La Valenciana church. Capelo and Cerámica La Cruz have opened galleries downtown at Positos 69 (© **473/732-0612**) and at Ponciano Aguilar 25, in front of the church of La Compañía (no phone). Store hours for both locations are Monday through Saturday 10am to 3pm and 5 to 8pm. If you still want to go to the workshop store, take the highway to Santa Rosa/Dolores Hidalgo and, after la Valenciana, look for a sign on the left pointing to a dirt road that climbs steeply. It's open Monday through Friday from 10am to 6pm. Carretera a Dolores Hidalgo s/n. © **473/732-8964.**

Cerámica La Cruz   The new downtown galleries are listed above. The original store is in the area of La Valenciana, just below Capelo's place. The output is a bit different from Capelo's work. The potters here play a lot with glazes producing crackleware, among other things. Hours are Monday through Friday from 10am to 6pm. Carretera a Dolores Hidalgo s/n. © **473/732-9037.**

The Gorky González Workshop   This prizewinning ceramist has dedicated himself to bringing back the traditional Talavera of Guanajuato. Gorky's son, whose *nom de guerre* is GoGo, is making his own style of ceramics, which is finding favor with some collectors. The workshop is a short cab ride from the historic center. The showroom is open Monday through Friday from 10am to 2pm and 4 to 6pm, Saturday from 10am to 1pm. Call first. Calle Pastita 247 (above the baseball field). © **473/731-0389.**

Mayólica Santa Rosa   This factory store is in the small town of Santa Rosa, on the way to Dolores Hidalgo. It carries high-quality *mayólica* for less money than in Guanajuato. It's open Monday through Friday from 8am to 5pm. On the highway. © **473/739-0572.**

Ojo de Venado   A knowledgeable dealer of folk art, Randy Walz sells a variety of pieces from Guanajuato and other parts of Mexico. He's good at finding unique, highly expressive works. The store is open daily from 10am to 6pm. Plaza la Valenciana. © **473/734-1435.**

Rincón Artesanal   Objects in carved wood, wax, papier-mâché, pewter, and ceramic, produced in different workshops throughout the state of Guanajuato, stock this store. It also carries items from farther afield, including beautiful *catrina calaveras* (skeleton statues in fancy dress) from the state of Michoacán. The woman who owns the place is very helpful. It's open Monday through Saturday from 10am to 8pm; Sunday from 10am to 3pm. Sopeña 5 (1 block east of Jardín Unión). © **473/732-8632.**

Where to Stay

Hotels have high-season rates for Christmas, Easter, and the Festival Cervantino (Oct). High season at moderate and inexpensive hotels also includes July and August, when schools are out and families vacation, and any holiday weekend. During the Festival Cervantino, in October, rooms are virtually impossible to find without a reservation, and even then it's good to claim your room early in the day. Some visitors have to stay as far away as León or San Miguel de Allende. Rates quoted here include the 18% tax.

VERY EXPENSIVE

Camino Real Guanajuato ★★ ☺   Occupying a former hacienda, this Camino Real property is several blocks up the hill from La Alhóndiga. Much of the character of the original hacienda has remained, making this a unique place to stay. You can still make out the old outlines of the original grounds enclosed by a massive stone wall (a big help if you're traveling with kids). Rooms are decorated in an understated, modern style that goes well with the bare stone walls and arcades. The sixth-floor Camino Club rooms have domed ceilings and views of the city. Most rooms are quiet, owing to the large grounds of the hotel (except perhaps for the rooms in the very back, which are closest to the street). In 2010 the hotel completely reconfigured the pool and the sunning area to great effect.

Alhóndiga 100, Col. San Javier, Guanajuato, Gto. www.caminoreal.com.mx/guanajuato. © **800/722-6466** in the U.S. and Canada, or 473/102-1500. Fax 473/732-0626. 105 units. 2,400–2,802 pesos deluxe double; 2,825–3,156 pesos club double; 3,455–3,982 pesos junior suite; 3,942–4,715 pesos master suite. Lower rates are for Mon–Thurs. AE, MC, V. Valet parking 55 pesos. **Amenities:** Restaurant; bar; babysitting; children's programs; club-level rooms; fitness room; large heated outdoor pool; room service; smoke-free rooms. *In room:* A/C, TV, fridge, hair dryer, minibar, Wi-Fi.

Casa Estrella de la Valenciana ★★★   This beautiful modern house, on the mountainside above La Valenciana church, affords a panoramic view of the city and surrounding valley. The American owners have created comfortable, spacious interiors appointed with regional handicrafts and art. All guest rooms have a balcony or terrace; two are handicap accessible. The two superior rooms are large and have special amenities such as a private Jacuzzi (La Valenciana) or a steam locker (La Sirena); each comes with a king-size bed. Another oversize room, the San Bernabé, comes with two queens. The others have either a queen-size or a king-size bed. There is also a two-bedroom casita. Common areas include a living room, an upstairs terrace, and a poolside patio. Another thing to like about this place is the number of extras the owners provide, such as free long distance calls to the U.S., Canada, and the U.K.

Callejón Jalisco 10, Col. La Valenciana 36240 Guanajuato, Gto. www.mexicaninns.com. © **866/983-8844** in the U.S., or 473/732-1784. Fax 562/430-0648 in the U.S. 8 units. $218–$242 standard double; $248–$277 deluxe double; $277–$312 superior double; $500–$555 2-bedroom casita. Rates include full breakfast and beverages. Promotional rates sometimes available. AE, MC, V. Free parking. **Amenities:** Babysitting; Jacuzzi; heated outdoor pool; smoke-free rooms. *In room:* TV, DVD/VCR, hair dryer, Wi-Fi.

Quinta Las Acacias ★★★   The main house dates from the late 19th century, when architecture and design in Mexico were borrowing heavily from Victorian and French (*afrancesado*) styles. It has been painstakingly remodeled. The rooms are decorated and furnished with period furniture, wallpaper, and wainscoting. There are seven period rooms in the house, and in back of the property are larger modern suites, some of which have Jacuzzis. Several of these rooms, including some larger master suites, surround a large cactus garden (it feels more like a cactus forest because these ancient cacti have grown so tall) and afford views of the nearby mountains. Rooms contain one king-size or two queen-size beds and have spacious, well-equipped bathrooms. Breakfast can be served in the dining room, on the terrace, or in the guest's room.

Paseo de la Presa 168, 36000 Guanajuato, Gto. www.quintalasacacias.com.mx. ℰ **888/497-4129** in the U.S., or 473/731-1517. Fax 473/731-1862. 17 units. $224–$265 period room double; $325–$348 suite with Jacuzzi; $425–$449 presidential suite. Rates include full breakfast. AE, MC, V. Free limited parking. Children 11 and younger not accepted. **Amenities:** Restaurant; bar; large outdoor Jacuzzi; room service; smoke-free rooms. *In room:* A/C, TV, hair dryer, Wi-Fi.

EXPENSIVE

Hotel Antiguo Vapor ★   Rooms at this small hotel have all the Mexican character you could wish for, from clay-tile floors to beamed ceilings, to Talavera tile bathrooms. They range in size from medium to large. All are colorful, and most have windows or balconies looking out over the city. For being downtown, the rooms are fairly quiet; there are some interior rooms that would be quite the thing for light sleepers. Room rates vary according to the choice of beds—the most economical have one queen, the most expensive have two doubles, and rooms with king-size beds are in between. Bathrooms are nicely finished and some are quite large. The location is good, close by the Diego Rivera Museum.

Galarza 5, 36000 Guanajuato, Gto. www.hotelavapor.com. ℰ **473/732-3211.** 13 units. 1,450–1,650 pesos medium double; 1,870–2,225 pesos large double; 2,500–2,950 pesos double with Jacuzzi. Higher rates are for holidays and vacation times. Rates include continental breakfast. MC, V. Free guarded parking. **Amenities:** Restaurant; smoke-free rooms. *In room:* TV, hair dryer, Wi-Fi.

La Casa de Espíritus Alegres B&B and Alma del Sol ★★★ ▣   Folk art and atmosphere abound in the idiosyncratic "house of happy spirits," a 16th-century colonial hacienda. Rooms are decorated and furnished in a vivacious and attractive style. Each fulfills the promise of "a skeleton in every closet" (festive *papier-mâché* Day of the Dead bones hang everywhere), and each has its own fireplace. The grounds are so lovely you won't want to leave. Breakfast features Californian and Mexican food. The B&B is 3km (1¾ miles) from downtown (10 min. by taxi).

A smaller downtown property is **Alma del Sol,** across from the grand church of La Compañía. It's partly a museum/gallery of folk textiles and has only four units (two of which are two-bedroom suites) and an open rooftop terrace with a broad vista.

La Exhacienda la Trinidad 1, 36250 Marfil, Gto. www.casaspirit.com. ℰ/fax **473/733-1013.** 15 units. $145–$165 double. Rates include breakfast. MC, V. Free guarded parking. **Amenities:** Smoke-free rooms. *In room:* Hair dryer, no phone, Wi-Fi.

MODERATE

El Mesón de los Poetas   I love hotels that are un-self-conscious expressions of their city, and this is just such a place. Set against a hillside, it makes the most of its space by clever positioning of rooms in an irregular jumble. Following the stairs and walkways that led to my room, I thought for a moment I was trapped in an M. C. Escher drawing. Standard rooms are decorated in Mexican style. They vary in size, and a few come with kitchenettes. The largest hold two double beds or a king. Suites have king-size beds and nicer bathrooms, and the two-bedroom suites, which go for the same price, have a living room with dining table and chairs; a sitting area; and a kitchenette. The hotel is downtown by the Diego Rivera Museum.

Positos 35, 36000 Guanajuato, Gto. www.mesondelospoetas.com. ℰ/fax **473/732-6657,** -0705. 31 units. 1,280 pesos double; 1,750 pesos suite and 2-bedroom suite. Rates are higher during the festival. AE, MC, V. Limited parking. **Amenities:** Smoke-free rooms. *In room:* TV, hair dryer (upon request), Wi-Fi.

Hotel Posada Santa Fé ★   Right on the Jardín Unión, this hotel is for those who want to be in the thick of things from the moment they step out the door. It dates from the 1860s, and the old lobby is a great place to have a drink. Check out the beautiful Talavera wainscoting. Rooms are small, except for the suites and some of the rooms with exterior views. They are, however, attractive, well kept, and comfortable. All come with carpeted floors and tile bathrooms. Standard rooms hold either one double or two twin beds. Exterior-view rooms and suites have larger bathrooms and fancier furniture, and double-glazed windows; most have king-size beds.

Jardín Unión 12, 36000 Guanajuato, Gto. www.posada-santafe.com. ✆ **473/732-0084.** Fax 473/732-4653. 47 units. 1,350–1,525 pesos double; 1,645-2125 pesos double with exterior view; 1,900–2,650 pesos suite. Rates include full breakfast. AE, MC, V. Free valet parking. **Amenities:** Restaurant; bar; whirlpool; room service; smoke-free rooms. *In room:* TV, hair dryer (upon request), Wi-Fi.

INEXPENSIVE

Hotel El Minero 🏷   Only 3 blocks above the Museo Alhóndiga, this four-story hotel (no elevator) has a rare commodity: cheap rooms that aren't ugly or small. Ceramic tile floors, attractive paint jobs, ceiling fans, and cleanliness are the high points. The location is good and the back rooms are quiet, but the lighting is just okay; the bathrooms are small, and the TVs don't add much to the experience of staying here. Most rooms have a double and a single bed.

Alhóndiga 12-A, 36000 Guanajuato, Gto. ✆ **473/732-5251.** Fax 473/732-4739. 20 units. 395–530 pesos double. MC, V. Limited street parking. **Amenities:** Restaurant. *In room:* Fans, TV, no phone.

La Casa Azul   This house is in an upper *barrio* above the Plazuela del Baratillo, which could be good or bad, depending on how you look at it. Staying here would give you an idea of how the locals live, always going up or down through a network of alleys (good?). But staying here means you, too, will be always going up and down (bad?). You decide. It's a steep climb from the plaza to the hotel, but you get to stay in an interesting part of town for not a lot of money. The rooms have character and are well maintained. They are small to medium in size and come with either a double or a king-size bed. There's a rooftop terrace, too. **Note:** Don't stay here if you have a car; the alleys are too narrow.

Carcamanes 57, 36000 Guanajuato, Gto. www.lacasaazul.com.mx. ✆ **473/731-2288.** 6 units. 550–660 pesos double. Rates include continental breakfast in a restaurant on Plaza de la Paz. No credit cards. No parking. *In room:* TV, fridge, no phone.

Mansión del Cantador   For a no-frills hotel, this isn't too bad. It offers large rooms on the Jardín del Cantador for a good price. Being on this square cuts down on noise, and yet it's still close to the market and the Alhóndiga. Most rooms come furnished with two double beds, side tables, and a small desk. They are clean but very plain, and the lighting is basic. In cold weather, ask at the desk for extra blankets. The bathrooms are small but in good repair.

Cantador 19, 36000 Guanajuato, Gto. hmcr84@hotmail.com. ✆ **473/732-6888.** 42 units. 650–750 pesos double. Rates include full breakfast. MC, V. Limited street parking. **Amenities:** Restaurant; Wi-Fi (in lobby). *In room:* TV, hair dryer, no phone.

Where to Eat

Restaurants in the downtown area are improving. In addition to the ones I list below, try an outdoor table at the restaurant of the **Hotel Posada Santa Fé** (see above), which affords a way to enjoy the Jardín de la Unión. The Jardín has a closed, intimate feel; if you want something more open with longer vistas, try the **Plaza de la Paz,** a block away. Here you can sit, have a drink, and perhaps nibble on an appetizer at one of the outdoor cafes in front of Guanajuato's cathedral. If you're in search of coffee, the best in town is at **Café Tal** (© 473/732-6212). It's on Sangre de Cristo, which is the section of the main street running between Jardín Unión and Plaza Embajadoras.

EXPENSIVE

La Casa del Conde de la Valenciana MEXICAN/INTERNATIONAL   Dine in the former home of the Count of La Valenciana, across the street from his other creation, La Valenciana church. You can eat on the patio or in one of the dining rooms. The menu combines old standards and original recipes. For an appetizer, try a fresh salad or refreshing gazpacho served in a bowl of ice. Among Mexico's traditional dishes are such options as a rich chicken *mole* or *enmoladas* (chicken-filled tortillas rolled in *mole*) and a delicate chicken breast *a la flor de calabaza* (in a mild, satisfying cream sauce of blended squash flowers and slices of poblano chile). The shady patio is so relaxing that many linger here over coffee and dessert.

Carretera Guanajuato-Dolores Km 5, opposite La Valenciana church. ©/fax **473/732-2550.** Reservations accepted. Main courses 145–254 pesos. MC, V. Mon–Wed noon–6pm; Thurs–Sat noon–10pm.

MODERATE

El Abue ★ MEXICAN/ITALIAN   A small, comfortable downtown restaurant, El Abue keeps it simple with a small menu that includes a lot of favorites. The cooking is good, and the dining room is pleasant. Dishes include the *sopa azteca* (tortilla soup), the *tostadas yucatecas* with *cochinita pibil,* and enchiladas El Abue (made with a base of chile *guajillo* that's not too spicy). A few standard Italian dishes are usually on the chalkboard, but I would probably stick to the Mexican food. This is a good place for breakfast, too.

San José 14 (at the top of the Plazuela del Baratillo). © **473/732-6242.** www.elabue.com. Reservations accepted. Main courses 95–148 pesos; breakfast 49–74 pesos. MC, V. Daily 8:30am–10:30pm.

El Claustro MEXICAN   Locals like this downtown hole in the wall. Tables are outside on the square or inside in what was once a cellar bodega. Everybody orders the enchiladas (especially the *mineras*) and the *enmoladas,* which make good use of a locally made *mole.* The *pollo con mole* offers another way to enjoy it. Other dishes include various *antojitos.* The Jardín facing Juárez was the site of a convent, but some lonely columns and a section of the facade are all that remain of it.

Jardín de la Reforma 13-B. No phone. Main courses 55–120 pesos. No credit cards. Daily 8am–10pm.

México Lindo y Sabroso ★★★ MEXICAN   This restaurant is a celebration of Mexican cooking; the owners keep to tradition in this quiet Paseo de la Presa neighborhood. You can take a cab and then walk or grab a bus going back down to the city center. The best time to avoid crowds is after 5pm. The surroundings are attractive, and the service is great. You can dine on the front veranda overlooking the street, in an attractive interior patio, or inside in one of the dining rooms. On the menu are many of the dishes that Mexico is known for. The tostadas, the green *pozole,* and the flautas are all great. There are some Yucatecan specialties, such as *cochinita pibil* and *panuchos*—these are delicious, too. Try one of the natural fruit-flavored *aguas frescas.*

Paseo de la Presa 154. © **473/731-0529.** Reservations accepted. Main courses 60–135 pesos. MC, V. Daily 9am–10pm.

THE REDOLENT MEXICAN cantina

If you're curious about Mexican cantinas, swinging saloon doors and all, Guanajuato is a good place to do your fieldwork. You should know, however, that most of these are *men-only* drinking dives.

The town's favorite son is José Alfredo Jiménez, the undisputed master of *ranchera* music. This is the quintessential drinking music (long laments punctuated by classic Mexican yelps) that drives most non-Mexicans screaming from the building. But after downing a few *copitas*, you may warm up to it, and after

asking about Jiménez, you'll probably get a few more drinks on the house. Around the Jardín Unión, a couple of cantinas aren't bad; I always enjoy a few shots at one called **El Incendio (the Fire),** Cantarranas 15. Unlike most cantinas, this place welcomes women. It opens at 10am and closes at 4am. You may be surprised to see an open urinal at the end of the bar. While this is a standard feature in cantinas and part of the, er, authentic flavor, you still may wish to opt for a seat at the opposite end.

Guanajuato After Dark

If city planners had known the **Jardín Unión** would be so popular, they might have made it larger. This tiny plaza, shaded by Indian laurel trees, is the heart of the city and the best hangout. No other spot in town rivals its benches and sidewalk restaurants.

You can catch some worthwhile free **theater** in Plazuela de San Roque at 8pm on Sunday when the university is in session. Students perform short theatrical pieces known as *entremeses* (interludes). These are usually costumed period pieces that rely more on action than dialogue, so you don't need to understand too much Spanish to get the point. The costumes are great and look curiously appropriate in this *plazuela*.

If you're looking for a place just to have a drink, try **La Clave Azul** (© 473/732-1561), at Cantaritos 31. It's a small bar tucked away off Plaza San Fernando, and it's very much a product of its environment. A couple of small, irregularly shaped rooms with rock walls and rustic furniture are connected to each other by narrow stairways. It's a popular spot with the city's bohemians, especially Thursdays and Fridays. Hours are daily 1 to 9 or 10pm (open later on weekends).

More conventional nightspots—such as dance clubs—aren't difficult to find; ask at your hotel. **La Dama de las Camelias,** Sopeña 32 (no phone), is an unpretentious second-floor bar that doesn't get going until late in the evening. The music is all classic recordings of *danzón*, mambo, *son cubano*, and salsa. It opens at 8pm, starts getting busy around midnight, and closes at 4am. **Bar Ocho** (no phone), another salsa bar, is behind the San Diego church at the foot of the hill where El Pípila stands.

SANTIAGO DE QUERÉTARO ★★★

213km (132 miles) NW of Mexico City; 96km (60 miles) SE of San Miguel Allende; 200km (124 miles) S of San Luis Potosí

Querétaro is the most historic city in the region. During the Colonial Era, it was the point of departure for all the expeditions headed into the northern frontier. Later it played a central role in the three wars that forged the Mexican nation: La Independencia, La Reforma, and La Revolución. Downtown Querétaro is lively, pedestrian-friendly, and filled with eye-opening colonial architecture. The local government has

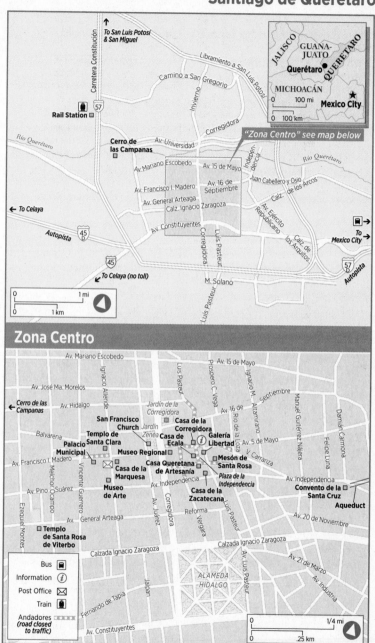

Zona Centro

Bus 🚌

Information ⓘ

Post Office ✉

Train 🚆

Andadores (road closed to traffic)

spruced up the city, keeps it neat with round-the-clock cleaning crews, and provides street vendors with attractive stands, regulating them so that they don't obstruct public streets and walkways. In the evenings, the downtown area fills with people who stroll about the plazas and *andadores* (pedestrian walkways), and eat at one of the restaurants, outdoor cafes, or food stands. The city is only an hour by bus from San Miguel, so it makes an easy day trip. But once you come, you'll be tempted to stay longer and get better acquainted with this lovely city.

The Spanish founded Querétaro in 1531 during their first large-scale expedition into the northern stretches of their new territory. During a skirmish with the Chichimeca, Santiago (St. James) appeared in the clouds. Santiago is the patron saint of Spain and of La Reconquista, the 7-century struggle to recapture all of Spain from the Moors, which had ended barely 40 years earlier. It is no wonder that the Spanish hoped he would again lend a hand in this new struggle for territory. For his appearance, Santiago also became the patron saint of Querétaro. (When you visit the Jardín Zenea at the center of town, look up at the facade of the church of San Francisco, and you will see a depiction of Santiago in battle, lopping off the turbaned head of a Moor.)

While the conquistadors were setting out to conquer lands for the crown, the religious orders were setting out to win souls for Christ. The Franciscans established a large community in Querétaro and eventually a college for the propagation of the faith, the first such institution in the New World. From here, the missionaries set out (always on foot, as the Franciscan Rule forbade riding on horseback or in carriages) to evangelize and establish missions as far away as Texas and California. Among them was Junípero Sierra, who went all the way to California, establishing missions there.

Centuries later, Mexican independence began in Querétaro with the conspiracy of 1810 (of which Father Hidalgo was a member). A little more than 50 years after that, Querétaro was again in the thick of things when Emperor Maximilian made his last stand here and was captured and executed. Another 50 years passed, and the city became the site of the laborious constitutional convention. The document that it produced, the Constitution of 1917, remains the law of the land.

Essentials

GETTING THERE & DEPARTING **By Plane** Most visitors still fly to Mexico City and then take the bus that leaves directly from the airport's main terminal to Querétaro. Look about for an escalator in the E-2 area. Take it up to an elevated concourse, which leads to the bus ticket counters. A one-way ticket costs 256 pesos. Departures are about every half-hour, and the trip takes 3 hours. See "Orientation" in chapter 4 for details about the Mexico City airport.

Querétaro's airport (airport code QRO) has limited international service and is a half-hour from downtown. **Continental ExpressJet** (© **800/231-0856** in the U.S., or 01-800/900-5000 in Mexico) flies to and from Houston. **American Eagle** (American Airlines' subsidiary; © **800/433-7300** in the U.S. or Canada, or 01-800/904-6000 in Mexico) offers daily nonstop service to and from Dallas/Ft. Worth. You can also fly here from the northern Mexican city of Monterrey on **Aeroméxico Connect** (© **01-800/021-4000** in Mexico), which has nonstop daily service.

By Car From Mexico City, take the super toll road Hwy. 57D (2½ hr.). From San Miguel, take Hwy. 111 to Hwy. 57D, and then turn right (1 hr.). From San Luis Potosí, take Hwy. 57D south (2½ hr.). It's now possible to drive between Querétaro and Puebla without passing through Mexico City. A toll road called Arco Norte connects to 57D just south of the turnoff for Tula, Hidalgo and connects to Hwy. 150D near San Martín Texmelucan, west of Puebla. (See "Getting Around" in chapter 20 for more about the use and cost of toll roads in Mexico.)

By Bus   For directions from the Mexico City airport, see "By Plane," above. From Mexico City's northern bus terminal (Central del Norte), buses leave every 15 minutes. Make sure you get a *directo* (nonstop). From San Miguel, second-class buses leave every 20 minutes. The bus station is south of town. Look for a booth in the terminal that sells cab tickets. A cab ride downtown costs about 45 pesos. There are now direct buses to/from Puebla. Futura/Chihuahuenses has nine departures per day. The trip takes 4 hours and costs 335 pesos.

VISITOR INFORMATION   There is a good **tourism information office** at Pasteur Norte 4, just off the Plaza de la Independencia on the north side. It's open daily from 9am to 8pm. The phone numbers are ✆ **888/811-6130** in the U.S., or 442/238-5067; or visit www.venaqueretaro.com. One-hour tours of the city by trolley-style bus are now operated by private companies that also staff the information kiosks in some of the plazas. You can get info from the staff at these kiosks, but you'll also get a pitch to take a bus tour. These concessions are, thus far, on a trial basis. Tourism still offers a self-guided audio walking tour of the *centro histórico*. At the information office, you can rent a digital player for 60 pesos per day, using a credit card voucher for a deposit.

CITY LAYOUT   The heart of downtown is the Jardín Zenea, at the intersection of the main north-south and east-west streets, Corregidora and Madero. Just east is the Plaza de Armas, and farther east are the Convento de la Cruz and the famous aqueduct. West of Jardín Zenea are several plazas, churches, convents, and museums.

[FastFACTS] QUERÉTARO

Area Code   The telephone area code is **442.**

Climate   The average temperature in summer is 24°C (75°F), in winter 13°C (56°F).

Elevation   Querétaro sits at 1,818m (5,963 ft.).

Emergency   The central emergency number (similar to 911) is ✆ **066.**

Hospital   The local hospital is the **Hospital Angeles** (✆ **442/215-5901** or 442/216-2751), at Bernardo del Razo 21, Colonia Ensueño.

Internet Access   Cybercafes and Internet access providers are everywhere in the central historic district.

Parking   To find parking in the downtown area, look for white square signs with the capital letter ᴇ in light blue. There are a couple of places at Pino Suárez 45 and 17. Rates run about 10 pesos for the first hour, and a little less thereafter.

Post Office   The *correo*, Arteaga 5, is open Monday through Saturday from 9am to 2:30pm.

A Stroll Around the Historic Center

In the center of Querétaro, you'll notice right away how many plazas, churches, and convents there are. If you're really observant, you'll see that the plazas are frequently next to the churches. In fact, most of these plazas were formed at the cost of the convents, which lost much of their land to the government during La Reforma. This is true of the town's most important plaza, **Jardín Zenea,** where we will begin. This plaza was part of the atrium of San Francisco Church and Convent, which you see facing the park across Corregidora Street. This park is popular every night, but especially on Sunday, when the municipal band plays dance music of the '40s, '50s, and '60s. Great fun! The old bandstand dates from 1900.

Turn toward **San Francisco Church** to see the depiction of St. James on the facade (mentioned earlier). From the beginning, this church was the most important in town; it remains so today, the more recent cathedral notwithstanding. It and the attached cloister are all that remain of a large complex that included several chapels and an orchard that extended a few blocks east and south. Inside the church, you will see a few interesting remains of baroque decoration. The main altar is a rather uninteresting piece of neoclassicism that replaced what reputedly was a masterpiece of baroque design. This is a common story with churches in Querétaro. Many of the baroque *retablos* escaped the plunderers, only to fall prey to the "improvers," as was the case here.

Next door to the church is the cloister, which now houses the **Museo Regional ★**. It's open Tuesday through Sunday from 10am to 6pm. Admission is 41 pesos. Exhibits include artifacts from pre-Hispanic, colonial, and republican times. The architecture shows common traits of Franciscan design in the simplicity of its lines and decoration, which you can contrast with the rich decoration (caryatids and all) of the former Augustinian convent, now a museum of colonial art (see below). Leaving the museum, turn left and then left again, and you'll be on the pedestrians-only Andador Libertad. This leads to the small Plaza de Independencia or Plaza de Armas, with its carefully pruned Indian laurel trees, outdoor restaurants, and colonial mansions.

At the Plaza de Independencia you'll find **Galería Libertad,** on your right just as you get to the plaza. It's free, and in past visits, I've come upon some entertaining exhibits. At the far end of the plaza is the **Casa de la Corregidora.** As you walk toward it, you will pass on your left the **Casa de Ecala,** a baronial mansion with magnificent balconies and wrought iron, which dates from the 18th century.

"La Corregidora" was the wife of the mayor (*corregidor*) at the beginning of the struggle for independence. Her full name was Doña Josefa Ortiz de Domínguez. She was a member of a secret group of intellectuals bent on liberating Mexico from Spain. As the wife of Querétaro's mayor, she was in a useful position for gathering information. When the group was discovered, she was put under house arrest but still managed to get a warning to Father Hidalgo. He eluded capture and rushed to Dolores, where he gave his famous *grito* (the cry for independence). For her actions, La Corregidora was imprisoned several times between 1810 and 1817. She died several years later, impoverished and forgotten, but was later remembered and became the first woman to appear on a Mexican coin.

The fountain in the middle of the plaza honors Querétaro's greatest benefactor, a Spanish grandee named Don Juan Antonio de Urrutia y Arana, who built a large aqueduct to bring water to the city. This colonial aqueduct is the most famous landmark in the city. To view it, continue east on Andador Libertad. It ends in 1 block, so you must dogleg to the next eastbound street, either Independencia or Carranza. The street gently climbs toward the **church and convent of la Santa Cruz ★★**, where missionaries were trained to evangelize the heathens as far away as California and Nicaragua. The church has one bell tower with an attractive tile dome. It and the convent are Franciscan. The convent continues in operation. You can take a short tour, usually led by an elderly monk, Fray Jesús Guzmán de León, who speaks English. He will show you how the water from the aqueduct arrived here and how it fed a system of fountains known as *cajas de agua* that provided water throughout the old

Walking up Andador Libertad, you will pass under a pergola of bougainvillea. A door on the right leads to the state-run arts-and-crafts outlet **Casa Queretana de Artesanía,** Andador Libertad 52 (© **442/224-3456**). Even though Querétaro is a small state, it has a wide variety of craft traditions. You can see a sampling of these in the three rooms in this part of the store, and in another three rooms that are farther up the walkway. Everything in this store was made in the state. Hours are Tuesday and Wednesday 11am to 1pm and 4 to 7pm, Thursday and Friday 11am to 2pm and 4 to 8pm, Saturday 11am to 8pm, and Sunday 11am to 4pm.

city. From these, the citizens of Querétaro would fill their buckets. He will also show you a thorn tree said to have grown from the walking stick of Friar Antonio Margil de Jesús, a famous missionary who covered vast territories on foot. This thorn tree is considered miraculous because its thorns grow in the shape of the cross. The tour is free, but you may make a contribution to the preservation of the convent and church.

Behind the church is a small plaza from which you can view the aqueduct. Follow the rough stone wall partially covered by the branches of mesquite trees, and you can't miss it. The aqueduct extends across an expanse of bottomland from the hill in front. This feat of engineering required the construction of 74 arches. Work began in 1726 and finished in 1738.

From here, make your way back to the Jardín Zenea. If you go by way of Calle Independencia, you can pop into **La Casa de la Zacatecana** (look for a banner), Independencia 59 (© **442/224-0758**). It presents a vision of what many colonial mansions were like in Querétaro, with period furnishings and decor. Hours are from Tuesday through Sunday 10am to 6pm in winter (11am–7pm in summer). Admission costs 30 pesos. Associated with this house (as with a couple of others in town) is a tale of illicit love, murder, and retribution. Colonial Mexico is a fertile land for Gothic tales.

Back at Jardín Zenea, head west on Calle Madero. At the first corner, just before the street becomes an *andador*, is **La Casa de la Marquesa ★★★**, an opulent colonial residence-turned-hotel. The courtyard lobby has elaborate *mudéjar* style (a Spanish architectural style with Moorish influences) arches and patterned walls.

Cater-cornered from this hotel is the **church and former Convent of Santa Clara ★★★**. Inside the church are six astonishing baroque *retablos* and a choir loft, all gilded and each a self-contained composition. In prominent positions are sculptures and paintings of saints; here and there, the faces of angels appear out of the enveloping, thickly textured ornament. Gazing upon these is like gazing upon a mandala. The juxtaposition of straight lines and multiple facets with overflowing curves that move inward and outward make the *retablos* appear fluid and rigid at the same time. The key to enjoying these *retablos* is not to look for proportion, balance, or an underlying composition, but to look at them as the expression of an ecstatic religious sentiment that rejects these very notions.

For a greater acquaintance with the colonial religious mind, walk south 1 block on Allende. On your right will be the **Museo de Arte ★★★** (© **442/212-3523**), in the former **convent of San Agustín.** Admission is 30 pesos; it's free on Tuesday. The museum is open Tuesday through Sunday from 10am to 6pm. It contains one of the great collections of Mexican colonial art, but the architecture of the former convent

SHOPPING FOR opals

The small state of Querétaro is one of two principal places in the world that mine opals commercially (the other is in southern Australia). The opal is a soft stone noted for its iridescent color. Prices vary depending on size, color, shape, and transparency. A few stores in Querétaro, usually called *lapidarias,* sell locally mined opals and other semiprecious stones. One is the **Lapidaria de Querétaro,** Corregidora Norte 149-A, a few blocks north of Jardín Zenea

(© **442/212-0030**), open Monday through Friday from 10am to 2pm and 5 to 8pm, and Saturday 10am to 3pm. Or stop by **El Artesano,** a shop at Corregidora Norte 42, near the Jardín Zenea. Owner Alfredo Vázquez, who carves miniatures out of opals and other semiprecious stones, speaks mostly Spanish and is a font of information on opals and the trade. He keeps late store hours: 1 to 9pm Monday through Saturday. Also try **Lapidaria Ramírez,** Pino Suárez 98.

alone is worth the price of admission. Highly stylized human forms, complex geometric lines, and vegetal motifs are everywhere. The art is organized by style of painting. The collection has works by Europeans, but its focus is on painters in New Spain, including the most famous of the land.

If you're still in the mood for colonial splendor, walk west 2 blocks on Pino Suárez. After you cross Melchor Ocampo, turn left down a narrow street graced with bougainvillea and you'll come to the **church and former convent of Santa Rosa de Viterbo ★★★**. Like Santa Clara, it is a masterpiece of baroque architecture. On the outside, notice the scroll-shaped flying buttresses (a style that, as far as I know, is unique to Querétaro) and the imaginative tower. Inside, the church is much like Santa Clara, with magnificent gilt *retablos* occupying all available wall space. Also like Santa Clara, the main altar failed to escape the "improvers."

Farther west (a bit too far to walk) is the **Cerro de las Campanas (Hill of Bells),** where Maximilian was executed. You'll find a large, ugly statue of Juárez installed there by the Mexican government to counter a small and sad memorial chapel for Maximilian erected by his brother, Emperor Franz Josef of Austria. Immediately south of downtown is a park called Alameda Hidalgo, which is a lovely setting for a walk.

Where to Stay

Rates below include the 18% tax. Most of the downtown hotels have high and low season. High season is Easter, July, August, December, and any long weekend. The city is a favorite weekend getaway from Mexico City; finding available hotel rooms is much easier during the week.

VERY EXPENSIVE

La Casa de la Marquesa ★★★   Few hotels in Mexico can match this one for sheer colonial opulence. Even if you don't stay here, make a point of walking into the courtyard lobby. Built by the Marqués de Urrutia for his wife, the house, with Moorish arches and tiles, and intricate patterned walls, has an Andalusian feel. Rooms are large, have all the amenities, and are furnished with period pieces and Persian rugs. Bed choices include one queen-size, two queen-size, or one king-size. The least expensive rooms (deluxe) are across the street in another colonial house, La Casa

Azul. The hotel, a member of the Small Luxury Hotels of the World, prides itself on the attention it gives its guests. The location is excellent.

Madero 41, 76000 Querétaro, Qro. www.lacasadelamarquesa.com. © **442/212-0092.** Fax 442/212-0098. 25 units. $212 deluxe double; $248 royal suite; $412 imperial suite. AE, MC, V. Valet parking 80 pesos. **Amenities:** Restaurant; bar; babysitting; concierge; room service; smoke-free rooms; spa. *In room:* A/C, TV (w/DVD in most rooms), hair dryer, Wi-Fi.

EXPENSIVE

Gran Hotel ★★★   The Gran Hotel has a lavish use of space that is decidedly uneconomical (and attention-grabbing for precisely that reason). A grand stairway and cavernous galleries with vaulted ceilings lead the way to your room. The rooms have high ceilings and carpeted floors, and are large and comfortable, with independently controlled air-conditioning and beautifully finished bathrooms. The hotel is set between two plazas, and most rooms have a view of one plaza or the other (with double-glazed windows and French doors). Noise is not a problem, but for the very light sleeper, the hotel has a few interior rooms, which are oversize and come with a few extra amenities for virtually the same price as standard rooms.

Juárez Sur 5 (btw. Jardín Zenea and Plaza Constitución), 76000 Querétaro, Qro. www.granhotel dequeretaro.com.mx. © **442/251-8050.** 42 units. 1,920 pesos interior suite; 2,033–2,150 pesos suite with view; 2,508 pesos executive suite; 3,950 pesos corner suite. AE, MC, V. Valet parking 50 pesos per day. **Amenities:** 3 restaurants; bar; babysitting; membership in local spa; room service; smoke-free rooms. *In room:* A/C, TV, hair dryer, Wi-Fi.

MODERATE

Santa Rosa Hotel ★ ☀   With its large open courtyards, clean lines, and simple stone and iron work, this hotel presents a colonial architecture that contrasts sharply with La Casa de la Marquesa (see above). There are three courtyards, variously holding a pool, a fountain, and a stone trough for watering your horses (a vestige of the original tavern, which served wagon and mule drivers). Rooms are quiet, large, and comfortable, with high ceilings, carpeted floors, and boring furniture and decoration. Standard rooms come with either two doubles or a king-size bed; superior rooms are much larger. Higher rates are for remodeled rooms with air-conditioning. The location, at the southwest corner of the Plaza de Armas, is ideal.

Pasteur 17 Sur (on Plaza de Armas, access from 5 de Mayo), 76000 Querétaro, Qro. www.hotelsanta rosa.com. © **442/224-2623** or 442/227-0600. Fax 442/212-5522. 21 units. 1,462 pesos standard double; 1,968 pesos superior double. AE, DC, MC, V. Valet parking 92 pesos. **Amenities:** Restaurant; bar; babysitting; midsize heated outdoor pool; room service. *In room:* A/C (in 7 rooms), TV, hair dryer, minibar, Wi-Fi.

INEXPENSIVE

Hotel Acueducto ★ ☀   This hotel, owned and managed by the same people behind the Hotel Posada Acueducto (see below), has a number of things going for it. One is that it's a relatively large property for downtown Querétaro. This results in a good bit of space, a nice pool, lots of common areas, and large rooms—all for a bargain price. Standard rooms can have one double, one queen-size, or one king-size bed, and are priced accordingly. All the floors are ceramic tile, including the bathrooms. All rooms have windows opening to the common areas, but none face the street, which means that guests don't hear much in the way of traffic noise. This is a family hotel, but because of the pool, the management doesn't want guests with small children 7 and under. There is a game room and talk of creating an exercise room.

Pino Suárez 11 (btw. Juárez and Allende), 76000 Querétaro, Qro. © **442/224-3083.** 24 units. 600–800 pesos standard double; 950–1,100 pesos oversize double. AE, MC, V. Secure parking ½-block away 20 pesos. **Amenities:** Heated outdoor pool; smoke-free rooms, Wi-Fi (in common areas). *In room:* A/C (not installed in all rooms yet), TV, no phone.

Hotel Posada Acueducto 🍴   You get a good room for the money at this hotel. The rooms are on two floors running along one side of the narrow property. Almost all face a thin strip of patio. Most are in back, in the modern section (slightly preferable). They are mostly medium size with ample bathrooms. The one upstairs in the very back (no. 111) has a king-size bed and a little porch. The lower price listed is for a room with one double bed, the higher price is for a room with a king-size bed; somewhere in between is the price for a room with two beds.

Juárez 64 Sur (btw. Arteaga and Zaragoza), 76000 Querétaro, Qro. 🕿 **442/224-1289.** 15 units. 300–370 pesos double. No credit cards. Street parking. *In room:* A/C, TV, Wi-Fi, no phone.

Hotel Señorial   This is a simple hotel with plainly furnished, medium-size rooms. By and large, they are a little more attractive than the rooms at Posada Acueducto (see above). The carpeting has been replaced with laminate flooring (bathrooms still have tile) in almost all the rooms. The beds (usually two twins or two doubles) are comfortable. Be sure to reserve an even-numbered room; odd-numbered rooms are in the south wing, which has plumbing so noisy you think it will bring down the building.

Guerrero Norte 10-A (corner of Hidalgo), 76000 Querétaro, Qro. www.senorialqro.com. 🕿/fax **442/214-3700.** 63 units. 580–730 pesos double. MC, V. Free secure parking. **Amenities:** Restaurant; room service, smoke-free rooms. *In room:* A/C (in 13 rooms), TV, Wi-Fi.

Mesón del Obispado   For better or worse, this colonial hotel is in the middle of the most popular part of downtown. For better, it's on a pedestrian *andador* and is close to everything. For worse, it's by the Plaza de la Corregidora, which doesn't settle down on weekends until well after midnight. The rooms in front have balconies overlooking the *andador* and are popular with the vacationing crowd that isn't going to bed early anyway. I had a room in back that looked out toward the courtyard of the hotel, and it was perfectly quiet. The rooms are medium to large in size, usually with two double beds or a king. The furniture is plain.

Andador 16 de Septiembre 13, 76000 Querétaro, Qro. www.depuebloenpueblo.com.mx. 🕿 **442/224-2464.** 16 units. 700–840 pesos double. AE, DC, MC, V. Limited street parking. **Amenities:** Restaurant; room service; smoke-free rooms. *In room:* TV.

Where to Eat

In addition to the restaurants listed below, you might want to try the restaurant at the **Mesón de Santa Rosa** (in the Santa Rosa Hotel, see above), on the Plaza de Armas. One local dish I can't recommend is the *enchiladas queretanas*. The problem is that the enchiladas typically come buried in a mountain of salty fresh cheese that completely overpowers the mild sauce. For fancy baked goods, try **Panadería El Globo** (🕿 **442/212-8883**), at Corregidora Sur 41. *Tip:* Late breakfasts are popular on weekends. If you're not eating breakfast at your hotel, you can beat the crowds by showing up at a restaurant by 9am.

EXPENSIVE

El Caserío ★★ SPANISH   The favorite dining spot for Querétaro's well-heeled denizens, El Caserío owes its popularity in part to the stylish, comfortable, no-nonsense dining areas; in part to the cooking and the service, which are both good; and, I suspect, in part to its ample off-street parking (not that common in this city). The menu is broad enough to please a variety of tastes—with steaks cut to order, classic

hot TAMALES

Tamales are a Mexican comfort food that just doesn't taste the same outside Mexico. Restaurants don't usually offer them, and when they do, the tamales are disappointing. Of course, tamales vary a great deal from region to region, but I have a special fondness for those of central Mexico. There are a couple of shops on the same block of Arteaga Street between Allende and Guerrero. Look for a bare white light (the universal sign of tamal vendors). These places offer two styles: I like the traditional ones better than the Oaxacan style because the *masa* tends to be lighter. They usually come with a choice of filling (pork, chicken, or cheese) and kind of sauce (red or green) and there might be cheese with slices of poblano chile *(rajas con queso)*. Two make for a nice breakfast or supper and would run you 20 pesos. These shops also serve flavored *atole*, a hot corn-based beverage.

Mexican soups, and pleasing salads—but Spanish food is the main attraction. Specialties include *lechón segoviano* (roast suckling pig), *pescado a la sal* (fish cooked under a layer of rock salt—allow extra time), and paella. The *crema de tres quesos* (three-cheese soup) and the *pescado a la sidra seca* (fish cooked in a seafood broth with apple cider) are unusual dishes that are worth a try. El Caserío is a long walk from the Jardín Zenea; take a cab.

Constituyentes Poniente 101 (near intersection with Ezequiel Montes). ✆ **442/216-1777.** www.elcaserio.com.mx. Reservations recommended for dinner. Main courses 179-258 pesos. AE, MC, V. Mon-Sat 1pm-midnight; Sun 1-6pm.

San Miguelito ★★ MEXICAN   This restaurant occupies the restored Casa de los Cinco Patios, a famous colonial mansion not far from the main square. The principal patio (which is the main dining area) impresses with the height of its arches and the fine wrought-iron work. It's beautifully lit at night, too. For appetizers, try the *infladitas* (small puffy tostadas topped with Yucatecan-style pork). Most of the main courses are steaks prepared with a variety of sauces. (**Tip:** To request your steak cooked to taste, see "Dining Terminology," in chapter 21.) On one side of the main entrance is the bar **La Viejoteca,** with live music on the weekends. On the other side is **La Antojería,** which serves traditional supper foods—tacos and such. The decor is a folksy and nostalgic take on Mexico. It's a fun place to have a bite and is less expensive than the main restaurant.

Andador 5 de Mayo 39 (btw. Corregidora and Vergara). ✆ **442/224-2760.** Reservations recommended on weekends. Main courses 155-216 pesos. AE, MC, V. Tues-Sat 6-11pm.

MODERATE

Apolonia ★★ NUEVA COCINA   At this restaurant not far from the Plaza de Armas, you can dine on some inventive dishes in attractive surroundings. There's a good selection of soups and salads, including a savory strawberry soup served hot, and a green salad with mango and cashews. The main courses include a chicken breast in a pool of apple/corn/poblano sauce, or shrimp with tequila and roasted cactus leaves. Servings aren't overly large, and the desserts are mostly light dishes.

Andador Libertad 46. ✆ **442/212-0389.** Reservations recommended. Main courses 111-212 pesos. AE, MC, V. Wed-Sun 1:30pm-midnight.

Parrilla Leonesa 🍴 TACOS This place serves the best tacos in the city. Choose from a variety of grilled meats. The popular *parrillada leonesa* grilled combo includes chicken, beef, and pork served on a small brazier on a bed of grilled onions and chile slices, with *queso fundido* on the side. I prefer the smaller taco plates, each of which comes with enough meat for three tacos. Tortillas are handmade. Salsas are fresh. I suggest taking a cab here. *Note:* This place specializes in *tacos de parrilla* (grill). To try another variety of taco—the *tacos de guisos* or *de cazuela* (both casserole tacos)—consider **Tacos del 57** (✆ **442/224-2211**), at Calle del 57 #21; it's 1 block west of Ezequiel Montes, right before you get to the first traffic light (there's no sign).

In the Hotel Flamingo, Constituyentes Poniente 138 (at Av. Technológico). ✆ **442/216-2123.** Taco plates 31 pesos; *parrilladas* 152-184 pesos. AE, MC, V. Mon-Sat 8am-midnight; Sun 8am-11pm.

Restaurante Bar 1810 MEXICAN/INTERNATIONAL This is one of the restaurants on the Plaza de Armas across from the house of La Corregidora. With a large and varied menu, it's the perfect place to enjoy a meal. Your best bet is to stick with traditional Mexican specialties, such as the *mole queretano* or the *chile en nogada*. Saturday and Sunday brunch is popular (8:30am–12:30pm).

Andador Libertad 62 (on the Plaza de Armas). ✆ **442/214-3324.** Reservations not accepted. Main courses 140-200 pesos. AE, MC, V. Mon-Sat 8am-midnight; Sun 8am-10pm.

INEXPENSIVE

Cafetería Bisquets 🍴 MEXICAN This modest restaurant serves inexpensive *comida casera* (home cooking) on a little patio and in adjoining dining rooms. One of the specialties is paper-thin *milanesa* served with green enchiladas on the side. Breakfasts are popular. Avoid the *bisquet*—something like an American biscuit, but larger and heavier—and try the *chilaquiles con pollo y crema* or any of the egg dishes and the *café con leche*. The *menú del día* is a bargain.

Pino Suárez 7 (btw. Juárez and Allende). ✆ **442/214-1481.** Main courses 62-74 pesos; *menú del día* 55-80 pesos. No credit cards. Daily 7:30am-11pm.

Cafetería La Mariposa MEXICAN The favorite thing to order here is the chicken enchiladas (green or red) and for breakfast the *molletes con salsa verde* (a Mexican version of cheese toast, with mashed beans and a fresh chile sauce). The full breakfasts are probably better at Bisquets, but this place makes its own breads and yogurt and is a nice spot for a light meal. The old-time dining room is comfortable (less cramped than at Bisquets). For lunch or dinner, you'll find the Mexican standards.

Angela Peralta 7 (just off Corregidora). ✆ **442/212-1166.** Main courses 54-95 pesos. No credit cards. Daily 8am-9:30pm. From the Jardín Zenea, walk north 2 blocks on Corregidora and turn left.

La Fonda de Santa María 🍴 MEXICAN You can get good cooking for little money at this small restaurant. It's located at the intersection of two andadores. Look for a door leading to a sunken dining room with 12 tables. I really enjoyed the *flautas*, the *sopes*, and the *enmoladas*. There's an economical fixed menu in the afternoon and several larger dishes on the menu if you have an appetite. La Fonda is popular and stays pretty busy, but the service is fast and efficient.

Andador Pasteur Norte 11 (at Andador 16 de Septiembre). ✆ **442/214-4205.** Main courses 95-140 pesos; *antojitos* 26-50 pesos. MC, V. Thurs-Tues 8:30am-10:30pm.

ZACATECAS ★★★

627km (389 miles) NW of Mexico City; 198km (123 miles) NW of San Luis Potosí; 322km (200 miles) NE of Guadalajara; 298km (185 miles) SE of Durango

Zacatecas, like Guanajuato, owes its beauty to the wealth of silver extracted from its mines. The farthest-flung of the silver cities, it still feels like an outpost of civilization. High above the center of town looms a rocky hill with a distinctive crest, which is accessible by cable car. From the summit, you have a panoramic view of the wild and desolate terrain that surrounds the city. The scene makes you realize what a frontier town Zacatecas must have been, and after you have been in town for a few days, you appreciate its present sophistication all the more. You will find surprisingly good museums, beautiful architecture, and good restaurants. The city has gone to the enormous trouble of burying all of its power and telephone cables, which adds greatly to the beauty of the town and makes strolling along the streets a pleasure.

Essentials

GETTING THERE & DEPARTING   By Plane   The airport code for Zacatecas is ZCL. **Volaris** (© **866/988-3527** in the U.S., 01-800/122-8000 in Mexico), a Mexican discount airline, has nonstop flights to/from Los Angeles (twice a week) and Tijuana (daily). **American Airlines** (© **800/433-7300** in the U.S. and Canada, or 01-800/904-6000 in Mexico) flies nonstop to and from Los Angeles. Seats are hard to come by around Christmas, when native Zacatecans fly home in large numbers. **Aeroméxico** (© **800/237-6639** in the U.S., 01-800/021-4000 in Mexico) and its affiliates link Zacatecas to other cities in the country by way of Mexico City.

Taxis from the airport, 29km (18 miles) north of Zacatecas, cost 220 pesos.

By Car   From the south, you can take Hwy. 45D, a toll road, from Querétaro through Irapuato, León, and Aguascalientes (a 6-hr. drive). It's expensive (about 300 pesos) but fast. Hwy. 54 heads northeast to Saltillo and Monterrey (a 5- to 6-hr. drive) and southeast to Guadalajara (a 4½-hr. drive). Hwy. 49 leads north to Torreón (4 hr.) and southeast to San Luis Potosí (3 hr.). Hwy. 45 heads to Durango (4 hr.).

By Bus   Omnibus de México, Estrella Blanca, and their many affiliates handle first-class bus travel to and from Zacatecas. Together they operate 20 buses a day to and from Guadalajara; 20 to and from León (where you would change buses for Guanajuato); 30 buses that go to and from Mexico City, stopping in Querétaro; and 12 per day to and from San Luis Potosí. The **Central Camionera** (bus station) is on a hilltop a bit out of town. The taxi ride costs 35 pesos. You can check schedules and buy tickets from several travel agencies in town. Ask at your hotel.

VISITOR INFORMATION   The downtown office is at Hidalgo 401 at Callejón de la Caja (© **492/924-4047** or 492/925-1277); it's open Monday to Saturday from 9am to 9pm and Sunday from 9am to 5pm. Sometimes there's an information desk outside on Hidalgo.

CITY LAYOUT   Understanding traffic circulation in the middle of town requires an advanced degree in chaos theory. I either walk or let the cabdriver handle it. The city's main axis is Hidalgo. From the **Plaza de Armas (main square),** it goes 8 blocks southwest to the Enrique Estrada Park and Hotel Quinta Real (changing names as it goes); in the opposite direction, it reaches another 8 blocks to the Rafael Coronel Museum (again making a name change). The historical center of town extends several blocks on either side of this 1.5km (1-mile) stretch of Hidalgo.

GETTING AROUND I enjoy walking around Zacatecas, but the terrain is hilly and the air is thin. Cabs are inexpensive and readily available. Their availability declines somewhat between 2 and 4pm, during the midafternoon meal.

[Fast FACTS] ZACATECAS

Area Code The telephone area code is **492.**

Climate It can get very cold in winter here. At other times it can be chilly in the evenings. The weather has been changing and is getting warmer in the summer, to the extent that some upmarket hotels have installed air-conditioning.

Elevation The city is at a lofty 2,485m (8,151 ft.). The air is crisp and cool, but a tad thin for some people.

Emergency & Police The emergency number is 🕾 **066.**

Hospital The two hospitals in town are **Clínica Santa Elena,** Av. Guerrero 143 (🕾 **492/922-6861**), and **Hospital San José,** Cuevas Cancino 208, near the clinic (🕾 **492/922-3892**).

Internet Access Internet cafes are cheap and very popular. Ask at your hotel or get directions from any young person you meet on the street.

Post Office The *correo,* at Allende 111, a half-block from Avenida Hidalgo, is open Monday through Friday from 9am to 3pm, Saturday from 10am to 2pm.

Special Events & Festivals

During Semana Santa (Holy Week), Zacatecas hosts an **international cultural festival** that the town hopes will eventually rival the Festival Cervantino in Guanajuato. Painters, poets, dancers, musicians, actors, and other artists converge on the town.

The annual **Feria de Zacatecas,** which celebrates the founding of the city, begins sometime during the first week of September and lasts for 2 weeks, incorporating the national Fiestas Patrias (independence celebration). Cockfights, bullfights, sporting events, band concerts, and general hoopla prevail. Famous bullfighters appear, and the cheap bullfight tickets go for around 125 pesos.

Exploring Zacatecas

In town you can partake of an old tradition called *callejoneadas.* On Saturday nights, people go strolling and singing with tambourines, drums, and a burro laden with *mezcal* through the winding streets and *callejones* (alleyways) of the city.

Zacatecas remains largely neglected by foreign tourists, though it is popular with Mexicans, so the various sights provide little descriptive material in English.

A STROLL AROUND TOWN

The **Plaza de Armas,** the town's main square on Avenida Hidalgo, is where you'll find the **cathedral ★★★,** with its famous facade. Nowhere else in Mexico is there anything like this; the depth of relief in the carving and wealth of detail create the impression that the images are formed not in stone, but in some softer material, such as cake icing. The cathedral took 23 years to build (1729–52), and the final tower wasn't completed until 1904.

To the left of the cathedral, on the Plaza de Armas, is the 18th-century **Palacio de Gobierno,** where governors lived in colonial times. By the time of Mexico's revolt

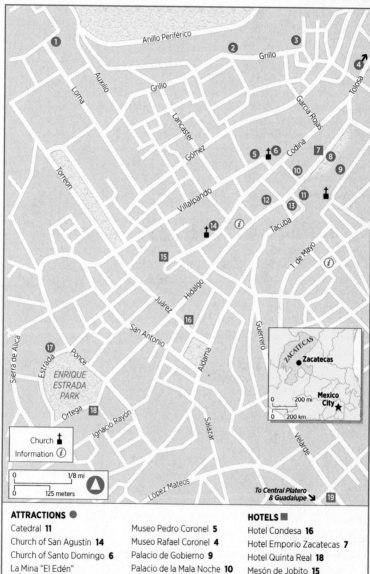

ATTRACTIONS ●

Catedral **11**
Church of San Agustín **14**
Church of Santo Domingo **6**
La Mina "El Edén"
  (front entrance) **1**
  (back entrance) **2**
Mercado Jesús González
  Ortega **13**
Museo F. Goitia **17**

Museo Pedro Coronel **5**
Museo Rafael Coronel **4**
Palacio de Gobierno **9**
Palacio de la Mala Noche **10**
Plaza de Armas **8**
Teatro Calderón **12**
Teleférico Station
  (Cable Car Station) **3**

HOTELS ■

Hotel Condesa **16**
Hotel Emporio Zacatecas **7**
Hotel Quinta Real **18**
Mesón de Jobito **15**
Motel Zacatecas Courts **19**

against Spain in 1810, Don Miguel de Rivera (Count of Santiago de la Laguna) owned it. Since 1834, it's been a government building, inside of which is a modern **mural** (c. 1970) by Antonio Pintor Rodríguez showing the history of Zacatecas. It is a straightforward chronological presentation of history from left to right, except for the center panel, which represents prominent Zacatecans. Below the mural is a stone frieze depicting the economic underpinning that supports society and drives historical events. It flows into the mural's central panel, tying society's leaders to the soil of their motherland.

To the left of the Palacio de Gobierno is the **Residencia de Gobernadores,** with its multicolor stonework. This building is newer than the Palacio and served as the governor's house until 1950. Across the street from the plaza are the **Palacio de la Mala Noche (Palace of the Sleepless Night)** and the Hotel Emporio. The palace's name comes from the mine that brought great wealth to its original owner, Manuel de Rétegui, a philanthropic Spaniard. In case you're thinking that such fine stonework is becoming a lost art, look at the hotel's facade, which was done within the last 40 years.

Climb the small street next to the Palacio de la Mala Noche, and you'll face the massive walls of the **church of Santo Domingo,** which fronts an open space that it shares with the Museo Pedro Coronel (see "Museums," below). This church and the building that houses the museum belonged to the Jesuits, until their expulsion in 1767. Afterward, the Dominicans occupied the church and convent. Inside are some lovely baroque gilt *retablos.*

Two blocks south of Santo Domingo, on Calle Dr. Hierro (a mostly level street that parallels Hidalgo), is another grand church, **San Agustín,** in partial ruins. During the Reform Wars, Zacatecas's liberal leaders kicked out the Augustinian friars, converted the church and convent into a brothel and casino, and destroyed the reportedly beautiful gilt altarpieces. The bishop of Zacatecas promptly excommunicated these Philistines. Twenty years later, a Presbyterian missionary society bought the property and dismantled the ultrabaroque facade that decorated the east door. Again, excommunication for all who aided the missionaries. Now the government has begun restoration of the church and has converted the inside into exhibition space.

Turn and go downhill, and you'll be back on Avenida Hidalgo. Walk back toward the cathedral (left), and you'll pass on your left the **Teatro Calderón** (inaugurated first in 1836 and again in 1891 after a fire). A stately building with lovely stained-glass windows, it is also a favorite spot for people to sit and watch passersby. The opera star Angela Peralta sang here several times in the 1800s. Zacatecas has a flourishing music school, and occasionally it offers performances here. A little farther down Hidalgo, a block before the cathedral on the same side of the street, is the 19th-century **Mercado Jesús González Ortega,** which used to be the town's main market. This pleasant, old-fashioned market now holds small stores selling handicrafts and some regional wines.

Backtrack along Hidalgo, and over the next few blocks you will pass by some lovely buildings and climb up to **Enrique Estrada Park** (the street changes names and becomes Av. General Jesús González Ortega). The **equestrian statue** (1898) portrays none other than the general himself, hero of the Battle of Calpulalpan. Behind it are a gazebo with marvelous acoustics and a pleasant, shady park that is a romantic spot for young couples at night. Beginning at Estrada Park and extending southward are the lovely arches of the **Aqueduct of Zacatecas.** Two of these arches frame the doorway to the Quinta Real Hotel, which you can enter to see the town's old bullring, a lovely sight. Go to the hotel bar and order a margarita—another lovely sight.

A RIDE UP CERRO DE LA BUFA ★★★

To get to the cable car station from the Plaza de Armas, you must climb one of the streets or alleys that lead up the hill that faces the cathedral. But first, glance up to see if the cars are running; if it's windy, they won't be. The first cross-street will be Villalpando or Hierro; go right, and make a left when you get to the Callejón (alley) de García Roja. If you're unaccustomed to the thin air, this is quite a climb. An easier way to get there is to catch bus no. 7, which you can pick up along Juárez, or take a cab. The cable car (© **492/922-5694**) is operated by the state. The ride up to the Cerro de la Bufa is gorgeous, and the view from La Bufa is best in the late afternoon and early evening, when the sun is low in the sky. The cable car normally runs from 10am to 6pm, with a one-way ticket costing 30 pesos. But recently, it has been running at night from Thursday to Saturday 7pm to midnight, with a one-way ticket costing 44 pesos. And the company has opened a panoramic bar at the top that is quite a pleasant place to have a drink. If you're so inclined, there is a nice pedestrian walkway that leads down the hill and back to the city center.

On Cerro de la Bufa is the **Museo de la Toma de Zacatecas,** which will be of most interest to Spanish-speaking history buffs. It displays artifacts and enlarged newspaper articles about the capture of Zacatecas by Pancho Villa. This was a decisive battle of La Revolución, and one of Villa's greatest victories. The museum is in need of investment; admission is 20 pesos. Beside the museum is the beautiful church **La Capilla de la Virgen del Patrocinio,** patroness of Zacatecas. Around the far side of the **La Bufa** is the **Mausoleo de los Hombres Ilustres de Zacatecas,** where many of the city's heroes are entombed.

MUSEUMS

La Mina "El Edén" ★   This mine is a giant gash carved diagonally through the core of a mountain following the trail of a silver vein deeper and deeper underground. To see this gash and think that all the stone and ore that once occupied this space was mined and extracted by hand provokes a sense of wonder. The mine opened in 1586, using forced Indian labor. Accidents, tuberculosis, and silicosis caused the workers' early deaths. The mine was extremely rich, yielding gold, copper, zinc, iron, and lead in addition to silver, but it eventually closed when an attempt to use explosives resulted in an inundation of water in the lower levels. English-speaking guides are available only sporadically, although the tour is eye-opening even for those who don't speak Spanish. A visit also includes a short, unremarkable train ride.

The mine's back entrance is a block from the cable-car terminal. I prefer this entrance because most people start at the main entrance, so you can avoid the crowds. When you get to the ticket office, buy your ticket right then. According to the rules, a tour must begin within 15 minutes after the first ticket is purchased. Often, I've had the guide all to myself (a tip is appreciated). After the tour is over, you can exit by the front entrance, which puts you on Juárez, a few blocks above Hidalgo.

For directions on getting to the front entrance, see La Mina Club, below, under "Zacatecas After Dark."

Cerro Grillo. © **492/922-3002.** Admission 75 pesos (includes train and tour). Daily 10am–6pm.

Museo F. Goitia ★★   Zacatecas has been the homeland for an impressive number of talented artists, most of whom left town to make their names known in Mexico City and abroad. The names of Francisco Goitia, Manuel Felguérez, and the Coronel brothers are well known in Mexico. This small museum pays tribute to them, as well as to other native sons Julio Ruelas and José Kuri Breña. It occupies an impressive one-time residence built as a governor's mansion. The permanent collection is small—five rooms on the first floor—and holds just a few pieces by each artist. The upstairs gallery is used for temporary exhibits.

Enrique Estrada 102, Col. Sierra de Alica. ☎ **492/922-0211.** Admission 30 pesos. Tues–Sun 10am–5pm.

Museo Pedro Coronel ★★ Pedro Coronel, in addition to being an artist, was a collector of inspired tastes. He acquired works from all over the world, but the strongest parts of the collection are the works of European modern masters (Dalí, Picasso, Miró, Kandinsky, Braque, Rouault), pre-Columbian Mesoamerica, and West Africa. Many of the modern pieces are illuminating. Some date from early in the artist's career, and some display a seminal character that points in the direction of later works. This collection is not large; after a while, you drift into the Mesoamerican room—seeing this beautiful stuff so quickly after the modern art gets your mind working out strange and improbable connections. There is no filler here; all of the pieces are outstanding.

Plaza de Santo Domingo. ☎ **492/922-8021.** www.pedrocoronelbienal.com. Admission 30 pesos. Fri–Wed 10am–5pm.

Museo Rafael Coronel ★★★ An unexpected pleasure offered by this mask museum is the gardens and picturesque ruins of the former Franciscan convent, filled with trailing blossoms and framed by crumbling arches and the open sky. Once you step inside the museum, you'll find room after room of bizarre and fantastical masks from all over Mexico. The making and using of masks for ceremonial or ritualistic purposes has been entwined in Mexican culture for millennia. Some of the earliest artifacts we have of the Olmec and Teotihuacán cultures are masks. A visit here only touches on a few aspects of what masks mean for the various peoples of Mexico, but it is fascinating. The museum has more than 4,500 masks. Explanatory text is in Spanish.

One wing of the museum is dedicated to puppets. Dioramas show a bullfight, battling armies, and even a vision of hell. The puppets are some of the hundreds created during the last century by the famous Rosete-Aranda family of Huamantla, Tlaxcala. Also in the museum, to the left after you enter, is the Ruth Rivera room, where some of Diego Rivera's drawings are on display. Ruth Rivera is the daughter of Diego Rivera and the wife of Rafael Coronel.

Calle Chevano (btw. Abasolo and Matamoros). ☎ **492/922-8116.** Admission 30 pesos. Thurs–Tues 10am–5pm.

A SIDE TRIP TO NEARBY GUADALUPE

In the nearby town of Guadalupe, now almost a suburb of Zacatecas, is a large Franciscan convent and evangelical college founded by a famous member of the evangelical college of Querétaro, Fray Antonio Margil de Jesús. It remains an active monastery, but a part of the convent houses a wonderful museum of colonial art, which will impress anyone interested in art and painting of any kind. Some people might skip this one because they suppose colonial art to be staid, scholastic, and full of arcane symbolism. Not true. The paintings, mostly from the 1700s, are by some of the greatest painters of New Spain (colonial Mexico)—Cabrera, Villalpando, Correa, and others. They are detailed, expressive, dramatic, and eye-catching for their use of anachronisms and fantastical themes.

I usually take a taxi (about 50 pesos) and, to save money and chat with locals, grab a city bus for the return. The convent's church has a lovely facade and holds the famous 19th-century Capilla de Nápoles, a chapel with lots of gilding and decoration.

You cannot enter, but you can see it from the ground floor of the church or from the organ loft, which is accessible from the museum.

Convento de Guadalupe/Museo Virreinal de Guadalupe ★★★ To a dedicated museumgoer, seeing these paintings exhibited in galleries with open-air circulation and no climate control is a little unsettling. The museum has about 350 works. On the first floor are over 20 portraits depicting scenes of St. Francis's life. The stairway to the second floor has some large, striking paintings, including Cabrera's *Virgin of the Apocalypse* and Arnáez's *The Triumph of the Sweet Name of Jesus,* which is an amusing propagandistic work showing the victory of Rome over the pagans and the Reformation. Highlights on the second floor include the organ loft, 14 oval paintings by Cabrera, 4 by Villalpando, and the surprising work of a local artist named Gabriel José de Ovalle, who distorts space and deforms human features in a style that seems much more modern than the 1700s. Guides are available for a tour of the museum and to view the Capilla de Nápoles (if the monks aren't celebrating Mass).

Jardín Juárez, Oriente, Guadalupe. ℂ **492/923-2089,** -2386. Admission 41 pesos. Daily 9am–5:30pm.

Shopping

Zacatecan handicrafts include stone-carving, leatherwork, and silver jewelry. Examples can be found in shops inside the old **Mercado González Ortega** on Hidalgo, next to the cathedral. There are a lot of silver jewelry shops in the center of town. A few other stores on Hidalgo and Tacuba sell crafts and antiques. Huichol Indians occasionally sell their crafts around the Plaza Independencia. Zacatecas is well known for its stone carvings. Many architects and builders from the United States come to Zacatecas when they need fancy stonework.

Where to Stay

Zacatecas has a great selection of hotels. Each of the expensive hotels that I've selected has something that sets it apart from the rest. The Quinta Real has the classic old bullring. The Emporio is on the square, and its front rooms have a great view of the Cerro de la Bufa. El Jobito captures the air of an old *vecindad.* In the fall and winter, heat can come in handy. Of the hotels listed here, all but the Condesa have heaters in the rooms, but many hotels in Zacatecas do not. And in the summer, air-conditioning would be nice, but very few hotels have it. Prices quoted here include the 18% tax. Highest rates are for Easter and Christmas holidays and August through September.

VERY EXPENSIVE

Hotel Quinta Real ★★★ Mexico is littered with hotels occupying former mansions, convents, and haciendas, but how many have risen from bullrings? And yet, it's the beauty, not the novelty, that makes this hotel so great. It has won several design awards, undoubtedly because the architects knew enough to leave the beautiful old bullring intact and keep the hotel small enough to be unobtrusive. A few of the arches that remain from the town's colonial aqueduct frame the entrance. From the lobby, you can survey the entire arena. The rooms were built along the outside of the bullring, and their windows open onto a small courtyard. Rooms are large, with well-equipped bathrooms, a writing desk, and a couch. Master suites are one room with a king-size or two double beds; *gran clase* suites are larger, with a sitting area and a whirlpool tub.

Av. Rayón 434, 98000 Zacatecas, Zac. www.quintareal.com. ℂ **866/621-9288** in the U.S. and Canada, or 492/922-9105. Fax 492/922-8440. 49 suites. High season 3,380 pesos master suite, 3,673 pesos *gran clase* suite; low season 3,240–3,680 pesos master suite, 3,360–3,890 pesos *gran clase* suite. The higher rates during low season are for weekends. AE, MC, V. Free secure parking. **Amenities:** Restaurant; bar; babysitting; concierge; golf privileges at local club; fitness center; room service; smoke-free rooms. *In room:* A/C, TV, hair dryer, Internet, minibar.

EXPENSIVE

Hotel Emporio Zacatecas ★★

A comfortable hotel facing the Plaza de Armas, the Emporio is a popular choice with Mexican tourists and businesspeople. The spacious rooms on its six floors are carpeted and well furnished. Rooms in the back are quiet. The rooms in front, mostly junior suites, are sunny and have balconies with good views of the cathedral and Cerro de la Bufa. The ones I like most are those on the fourth floor, which have terraces. These are set back a little and offer more shielding from street noise. These rooms and those on the fifth floor were thoroughly refurbished in 2010. The rooms in back face a small interior patio, complete with gurgling fountain. Most guest rooms offer one king-size or two double beds, and midsize bathrooms.

Av. Hidalgo 703, Col. Centro, 98000 Zacatecas, Zac. www.hotelesemporio.com. ✆ **492/925-6500.** Fax 492/922-6245. 113 units. 1,620–2,250 pesos double; 1,885–2,565 pesos junior suite. AE, MC, V. Sheltered parking 40 pesos. **Amenities:** Restaurant; bar; babysitting; fitness center; room service; sauna; smoke-free rooms. *In room:* TV, hair dryer, Wi-Fi.

Mesón de Jobito ★★

This two-story hotel occupies a traditional *vecindad,* which was a common form of housing for the lower classes in olden days. The buildings ramble back from the entrance, forming private alleys decorated with ornamental plants and flowerpots, and painted in traditional Mexican colors. The hotel feels intimate. Most rooms are large, carpeted, and furnished with queen- or king-size beds. Junior suites are larger and have more flair. Rates vary seasonally and are highest from September to December. The hotel's main restaurant serves great food. The hotel is 5 blocks from the cathedral and a block above Hidalgo.

Jardín Juárez 143, 98000 Zacatecas, Zac. www.mesondejobito.com. ✆/fax **01-800/021-0040** in Mexico, or 492/924-1722. 54 units. 1,330–1,820 pesos double; 1,545–2,020 pesos suite. AE, MC, V. Free valet parking. **Amenities:** 2 restaurants; bar; babysitting; room service; smoke-free rooms. *In room:* A/C, TV, hair dryer, Wi-Fi.

INEXPENSIVE

Hotel Condesa ✦

The good location, well-kept rooms, and economical price are the main attractions here. Many rooms, especially on the lower floors, have been remodeled and have modern furniture, cheerful paint, and new bathroom tile. These rooms have interior views. Rooms on the third floor have new bathrooms. Those facing east overlook Cerro de la Bufa and the market below the hotel. Rooms are small to medium. Most come with one or two double beds.

Av. Juárez 102, 98000 Zacatecas, Zac. www.hotelcondesa.com.mx. ✆/fax **492/922-1160.** 52 units. 590–710 pesos double; 850–960 pesos minisuite. AE, MC, V. No parking. **Amenities:** Restaurant; cafe/bar; babysitting; room service. *In room:* TV, Wi-Fi.

Motel Zacatecas Courts

Rooms have carpeting and comfortable beds. It is a 10-minute walk from the main square. Be sure to get a room in the back, away from the street. Also, ask to have the heat turned on in the room and for extra blankets in winter.

López Velarde 602, 98000 Zacatecas, Zac. ✆ **492/922-0328.** Fax 492/922-1225. 92 units. 752 pesos double. MC, V. Free secure parking. **Amenities:** Restaurant; room service. *In room:* TV.

Where to Eat

Besides the establishments listed below, I've eaten well at the Quinta Real and Mesón del Jobito. The *gordita,* a thick tortilla that is split open and stuffed with any of several cooked fillings, might be considered the state food of Zacatecas, and the most popular *gordita* place is **Gorditas Doña Julia,** which operates three or four locations. The best coffee in town is at **Café San Patrizio,** in the courtyard at Hidalgo 403. It's open from Monday to Saturday from 9am until 10pm.

Café Nevería Acrópolis MEXICAN/COFFEE SHOP   This coffee shop/restaurant with soda fountain is a popular meeting spot for the locals. I like the feel of the place, the breakfasts, the light fare of sandwiches or quesadillas, and the desserts, but for dinner I usually go elsewhere.

Av. Hidalgo and Rinconada de Catedral. ✆ **492/922-1284.** Breakfast 45–75 pesos; main courses 79–115 pesos. MC, V. Daily 8am–10pm.

El Pueblito MEXICAN   I like the menu here. It's not fancy; it's not overreaching. It includes some of my favorite Mexican dishes, and the kitchen does a credible job—*asado de boda, milanesa a la plancha* (home-style breaded steak), *enchiladas zacatecanas,* and lighter fare such as *tacos al pastor* are all good. This is also a comfortable place to take the weight off your feet and enjoy a beer and a guacamole salad. The surroundings are comfortable, attractive, and not too noisy. The nonsensical decor, which I initially found to be off-putting, is actually an homage to the town of Sombrerete, from whence hails the owner.

Hidalgo 802. ✆ **492/924-3818.** Reservations accepted. Main courses 85–148 pesos. MC, V. Wed–Mon 1–11pm.

La Cantera Musical Restaurant Bar ★ MEXICAN/REGIONAL   This restaurant is best known for its regional cooking, especially typical dishes such as *asado de boda* (a pork dish made with cinnamon and *ancho* and *guajillo* chiles) and *mole zacatecano* (a sweet and spicy chicken dish). You can also get a number of Mexican standards. The dining room is attractive. The restaurant is below the Mercado González Ortega, by the cathedral.

Tacuba 2, Centro Comercial El Mercado. ✆ **492/922-8828.** Main courses 95–140 pesos. No credit cards. Mon–Sat 1–11pm; Sun 2–10pm.

Los Dorados de Villa ★★ MEXICAN   If your grandmother were Mexican, this is how you would want her to cook. The green *pozole* is excellent. The enchiladas, which come in many varieties (I recommend the *valentinas* and the *rojas*), are delicious, too. Other menu items include tostadas, tacos, soups, and guacamole. What's for dessert? *Buñuelos,* of course. The name of the place refers to "the golden ones"— Pancho Villa's honor guard. The owner is a collector of memorabilia. Artifacts and reproductions from La Revolución cover the walls of the small dining room. Decorative paper cutouts hang from the ceiling, making the room feel even smaller, but festive, too. Diners need to ring the doorbell to enter; adults only after 8pm.

Plazuela de García 1314. ✆ **492/922-5722.** Reservations recommended. Main courses 73–110 pesos. No credit cards. Mon–Sat 3pm–1am; Sun 3pm–midnight.

Zacatecas After Dark

La Mina Club   Dance music in a mine deep inside the earth—does "Disco Inferno" ring a bell? Whose life could be considered complete without having made the scene here? The entrance is at the end of Calle Dovali. From Hidalgo, walk up Juárez, which turns into Torreón. Just past the Seguro Social building on Avenida Torreón, you'll find Dovali; turn right. Take a cab if you don't want to be so bushed that you can't boogie. The club is open Thursday through Sunday from 9:30pm to 2am. Mina El Edén, Calle Dovali. © **492/922-3727.** Cover 150 pesos.

SAN LUIS POTOSÍ

418km (259 miles) N of Mexico City; 346km (215 miles) NE of Guadalajara; 202km (125 miles) N of Querétaro; 189km (117 miles) E of Zacatecas

San Luis Potosí, a mile high in central Mexico's high-plains region, was among the country's most prosperous mining cities. It's now the largest and most industrial silver city, with a million inhabitants, but you'd never know it if you kept to the historic central district. It has rich colonial architecture and is known for its many plazas. Capital of the state of the same name, San Luis Potosí was named for Louis IX, sainted king of France. *Potosí* is a reference to the rich Bolivian Potosí mines.

Essentials

GETTING THERE & DEPARTING   **By Plane**   The airport code for San Luis Potosí is SLP. **Continental ExpressJet** (© **800/231-0856** in the U.S., or 01-800/900-5000 in Mexico) and **American Eagle** (© **800/433-7300** in the U.S., or 01-800/904-6000 in Mexico) fly to and from Houston and Dallas. Several domestic carriers have flights to Mexico City and other destinations within the country. The **airport** is 11km (6¾ miles) from downtown. A taxi to the city center is 320 pesos.

By Car   From Mexico City, take Hwy. 57D; from Guadalajara, take Hwy. 80. If you're coming from the north, it takes 6 to 7 hours to drive the 536km (332 miles) from Monterrey.

By Bus   The large Central Camionera is 3km (1¾ miles) east of downtown on Guadalupe Torres at Diagonal Sur. Most of the bus travel is through Estrella Blanca and its many affiliates, which occupy the counters to the left as you enter. You can buy a ticket for any of the affiliates from any counter. To the right as you enter are three other first-class bus companies: ETN, Primera Plus, and Omnibus de Mexico.

VISITOR INFORMATION   The **State Tourism Office** (© **444/812-9939,** -9943) is at Manuel Jose Othon 130, to one side of the cathedral. The information office has a helpful staff, a good map of the city and historic district, and lots of brochures. It's open Monday to Friday from 8am to 9pm, Saturday from 9am to 2pm.

CITY LAYOUT   The **Plaza de Armas** is the center of the historic district. All the streets bordering it are pedestrian only. The principal pedestrian street runs north-south in front of the plaza; the southern part (called **Zaragoza**) extends 8 blocks to the Jardín Colón, and the northern part (called **Hidalgo**) runs 5 blocks to the main market. The city also has many plazas and a large downtown park called **La Alameda.** **Avenida Carranza** heads east from the Plaza de Armas, passes by the Plaza de Fundadores, and extends out to the main commercial and residential section of the city. Fronting this street are many banks, clubs, and restaurants.

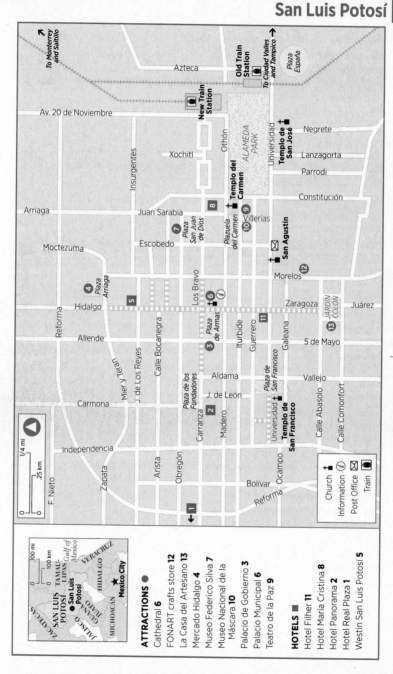

ATTRACTIONS ●

Cathedral **6**
FONART crafts store **12**
La Casa del Artesano **13**
Mercado Hidalgo **4**
Museo Federico Silva **7**
Museo Nacional de la
Máscara **10**
Palacio de Gobierno **3**
Palacio Municipal **6**
Teatro de la Paz **9**

HOTELS ■

Hotel Filher **11**
Hotel María Cristina **8**
Hotel Panorama **2**
Hotel Real Plaza **1**
Westin San Luis Potosí **5**

6 [FastFACTS] SAN LUIS POTOSÍ

Area Code The telephone area code is **444.**

Climate San Luis is on the high plateau more than a mile above sea level, but the weather can get hot during May, June, and sometimes July. In winter it occasionally drops to freezing at night. Rain is rare, with an average total of 14 inches per year; it falls between May and November, mostly in August.

Consular Agency San Luis Potosí has a **U.S. Consular Agency** at Av. Venustiano Carranza 2076-41 (✆ **444/811-7802,** -7803; Mon–Fri 8:30am–12:30pm).

Currency Exchange Four *casas de cambios* near the main post office offer better rates and better service than the banks. Two are in the arcade on Julián de los Reyes, and two are on Mariano Escobedo. This is just a few blocks northeast of the Plaza de Armas. All are open Saturday. The historic district has many ATMs.

Emergency San Luis's central emergency number is ✆ **060.**

Hospital The **Hospital Centro Médico,** Antonio Aguilar 155 (✆ **444/813-3797**), is one of the best in the country.

Post Office The *correos,* Universidad 526-A, is by the church of San Agustín. Hours are Monday through Friday from 8am to 5pm, Saturday 8am to 2pm.

A Stroll Around the Historic Center

San Luis has more streets dedicated solely to the use of pedestrians than any of the other silver cities. The center of town is the **Plaza de Armas,** dating from the mid-1700s and shaded by magnolia and *flamboyán* trees. The **bandstand** in the center of the plaza was built in 1947 (in colonial style), using pink volcanic stone. Free concerts usually begin on Thursday and Sunday at around 7:30 or 8pm. On the west side of the plaza is the **Palacio de Gobierno.** It has been much repaired, restored, and added to through the centuries—the back and the south facade were redone as recently as 1950. The front of the building retains much of the original 18th-century decoration. Upstairs, you'll find the rooms that Juárez occupied when he established his temporary capital here in 1863 and again in 1867. It's worth a peek. You can see it only at designated hours Monday to Friday at 10am, noon, and 2pm. There is a short tour of this room and a couple of others. The tour is free.

Across the plaza from the Government Palace is the **cathedral.** The original building had only a single bell tower; the one on the left was built in 1910 to match, although today the newer tower looks older. The Count of Monterrey built the **Palacio Municipal,** on the north side of the cathedral, in 1850. He filled it with paintings and sculptures, few of which survived the city's stormy history. When the count died in 1890, the palace was taken over by the bishop and, in 1921, by the city government. Since then, it has been San Luis's city hall. On January 1, 1986, it was fire-bombed during a riot. It has been restored and functions again.

East of the plaza is one of the city's most famous squares, **Plazuela del Carmen,** named for the **Templo del Carmen** ★★ church. From the *jardín,* walk east along Madero-Othón to Escobedo. The entire area you see was once part of the extensive grounds of the 18th-century Carmelite monastery. The church has a beautiful and complex facade, in which appear Elijah and Elisha, two prophets in the Old Testament who lived on Mount Carmel and are considered by the Carmelite order as spiritual founders. The other two large figures are St. Theresa of Avila and St. John of the Cross, mystics who, in the 16th century, reformed the order in Spain and founded the congregation of the Discalced Carmelites, who held to stricter vows of poverty than the rest of the order. Inside the church are some beautiful baroque altarpieces.

The **Museo Nacional de la Máscara** (no phone) faces the plaza, too. The museum was closed for several years, and when it reopened in 2009, the number of masks displayed was greatly reduced. These are exhibited in a few rooms on the ground floor, while the upstairs rooms were restored to what they would have looked like in the 1890s, when the house was built. The house is an elegant mix of French architectural styles and holds plenty of features and designs to arrest the eye. Hours are Tuesday through Friday 10am to 6pm, Saturday from 10am to 5pm, and Sunday from 10am to 3pm. The cost of admission is 15 pesos.

Facing the museum from across the plaza is the **Teatro de la Paz,** built in the 1890s, too. It's difficult to get in to view the magnificent old auditorium, but attached to it is the **Sala Germán Gedovius** (© 444/812-2698), with four art galleries. It's open Tuesday through Sunday from 10am to 2pm and 4 to 6pm. Admission is free.

One block north of El Carmen is another plaza called San Juan de Dios. Here you'll find **Museo Federico Silva** (© 444/812-3848). This is a brilliant museum dedicated to the modern sculpture of Federico Silva, one of the masters of contemporary sculpture in Mexico. This museum is necessarily large, as it must accommodate Silva's massive pieces constructed of steel, stone, and concrete, including his modern take on the ancient rain god Tlaloc. The museum is open from Tuesday through Saturday 10am to 6pm, and Sunday 10am to 2pm. Admission is 30 pesos.

One block east of the Plaza del Carmen is a large urban green area known as **La Alameda.** Vendors sell handicrafts, fruit, and all manner of snacks. Facing the park on Negrete is the **Templo de San José,** with lots of ornate gold decorations, huge religious paintings, and *El Señor de los Trabajos,* a miracle-working statue with many *retablos* testifying to the wonders it has performed.

PLAZAS

San Luis Potosí has more plazas than any other colonial city in Mexico. In addition to those mentioned above, the **Plaza de San Francisco** is south of the Plaza de Armas along Aldama, between Guerrero and Galeana. This shady square takes its name from the Franciscan monastery on the south side of the plaza and the church on the west side. The church holds some beautiful stained glass, many Colonial-Era statues and paintings, and a crystal chandelier shaped like a sailing ship.

Another square is **Plaza de los Fundadores (Founders' Square),** at the intersection of Obregón and Aldama, northwest of the Plaza de Armas. Facing it is the **Loreto Chapel,** with its exquisite baroque facade. The adjacent church of **El Sagrario** belonged to the Jesuits before the order was expelled from Mexico.

Shopping

The best shopping in San Luis is at two stores. The state-run store **La Casa del Artesano** (© 444/814-6999), at Jardín Colón 23, has five rooms filled with merchandise from all parts of the state. It's open Monday through Friday from 10am to 8pm and Saturday from 10am to 5pm. The **FONART** crafts store, operated by the federal government (© 444/814-3868), at Morelos 1055, is around the corner from the church of San Agustín. It's open Monday through Friday from 9am to 2pm and 4 to 7pm, Saturday 10am to 5pm. The hand-woven *rebozos* (shawls) from the town of Santa María del Río are what the state is most known for, but the store offers several other crafts, such as the richly colored bags of woven *ixtle* (agave fibers).

Several blocks along the pedestrian Calle Hidalgo north of Jardín Hidalgo, you'll find the city's **Mercado Hidalgo,** and just beyond it, the Mercado República. Look around. You'll find just about anything, including regional products such as baskets, *rebozos* (shawls), and straw furniture. Taken as a whole, the market area in San Luis is one of the most engaging market experiences in Mexico. As you enter the area on Hidalgo, you'll see a good slice of the city's small-business commercial life. Hardware stores, crafts shops, shoe stores, groceries, and taverns line both sides of the street.

A well-loved local candy factory is **Constanzo,** which has several outlets throughout the city, including three on Carranza (including an old-style candy shop at Carranza 325). Most outlets are open Monday through Saturday from 10am to 1:30pm and 4 to 8:30pm.

Where to Stay

There are no luxury hotels in the historic center. Most of them (the María Dolores, Real de Minas, and Holiday Inn) are to the east, where the highway from Mexico City enters the town. The Westin and the Camino Real are to the west, along the highway to Guadalajara. All rates listed below include the 18% tax. Expect higher rates for Easter, Christmas, and in some hotels, August.

EXPENSIVE

Westin San Luis Potosí ★★   Perhaps the loveliest hotel in San Luis, the Westin offers comfort and service in modern surroundings with traditional colonial design elements. The rooms are on three sides of a three-story building enclosing a wide garden courtyard. Stone arcades flank two sides. Rooms are large, carpeted, and sharply designed. They come with the Westin's signature beds, either two full- or one king-size. Bathrooms are large, with marble tiles, and lots of counter space. Suites are even larger and offer a stereo with a CD player and a whirlpool tub. They offer views of the courtyard and are worth the extra money. The center of town is 15 to 20 minutes away by car. Internet rates here can be heavily discounted.

Real de Lomas 1000, 78210 San Luis Potosí, S.L.P. www.westinslp.com.mx. ✆ **800/228-3000** in the U.S., or 444/825-0125. Fax 444/825-0200. 123 units. $185 double; $205 suite. Rates include airport transfers. AE, MC, V. Free valet parking. **Amenities:** 2 restaurants; bar; babysitting; concierge; fitness center; access to nearby health club w/tennis and racquetball; small heated outdoor pool; room service; smoke-free rooms. *In room:* A/C, TV, hair dryer, minibar, Wi-Fi.

MODERATE

Hotel Panorama ★   Aptly named, this downtown hotel is in a 10-story glass building near the Plaza Fundadores. Rooms have floor-to-ceiling views. (As long as you're above the fourth floor, you'll have something to look at, especially to the north or east.) Many years ago, it was *the* hotel in San Luis. Newer, fancier competitors now exist, but none in the downtown area. Rooms vary, but are medium size, and most rooms come with two full-size beds, carpeting, and attractive furniture. Premier rooms (executive level), on the sixth and eighth floors, have better lighting and more attractive furniture.

Av. Carranza 315, 78000 San Luis Potosí, S.L.P. www.hotelpanorama.com.mx. ✆ **444/812-1777.** Fax 444/812-4591. 126 units. 860 pesos double; 1,270 pesos premier double; 1,900–2,500 pesos suite. AE, MC, V. Free secure parking. **Amenities:** Restaurant; cafe; 2 bars; babysitting; executive-level rooms; midsize heated outdoor pool; room service; smoke-free rooms; Wi-Fi (in lobby). *In room:* A/C, TV, hair dryer, Internet.

Hotel Real Plaza 🔥 A modern nine-story hotel 8 blocks from the Plaza de Armas, the Real Plaza offers comfort and quiet at a good price. The midsize rooms are carpeted and the same size as the double in the Hotel Panorama. They are not quite as nice but are comfortable and a good value for the money. Bathrooms are a little larger than at the Panorama, but some rooms have no view. The rooftop pool has a great view and an attractive patio area. In high season, the snack bar offers food and drink service.

Av. Carranza 890, 78250 San Luis Potosí, S.L.P. www.realplaza.com.mx. ℂ **444/814-6969.** Fax 444/814-6639. 268 units. 690 pesos double; 1,800–2,200 pesos suite. AE, MC, V. Free secure parking. **Amenities:** Restaurant; bar; babysitting; fitness center; heated outdoor pool; room service; Wi-Fi (in lobby). *In room:* A/C, TV, hair dryer.

INEXPENSIVE

Hotel María Cristina The María Cristina is in a narrow nine-story building around the corner from the Plaza del Carmen. It's next door to (and often confused with) the Hotel Nápoles. All rooms are small and have a ceiling fan, and most don't offer much of a view. The bathrooms are small, with little counter space. Rooms are quiet, carpeted, and warm in the winter.

Juan Sarabia 110, 78000 San Luis Potosí, S.L.P. www.mariacristina.com.mx. ℂ **444/812-9408.** 74 units. 625 pesos double. MC, V. Free guarded parking. **Amenities:** 2 restaurants; bar; room service. *In room:* Fan, TV.

Where to Eat

Downtown San Luis doesn't have any outstanding restaurant, but you can eat well here, as long as you stick to the local food.

MODERATE

Cielo Tinto MEXICAN This is a beautiful place to dine—just stick to the Mexican dishes, such as the *Chamorro Pibil,* the enchiladas (several kinds), the *arrachera,* and a few other cuts of meat. The restaurant is in a 19th-century house with simple, elegant columns and stonework. There are four dining rooms, each a bit different, and a courtyard with retractable roof. At night the place is lit dramatically.

Carranza 700. ℂ **444/814-0040.** Reservations recommended. Main courses 120–170 pesos. AE, MC, V. Mon–Sat 8am–1:30am; Sun 8am–6pm.

El Callejón de San Francisco ★ MEXICAN If the night air is comfortable, there's no lovelier place for dinner than this restaurant's rooftop terrace, with San Francisco's cupola and bell towers for a backdrop. Even if it's a tad too chilly, you can still enjoy yourself; just ask the waiter for a *jorongo* (hoh-*rohn*-goh), a traditional woolen wrap for the shoulders. There's also a dining room downstairs. The menu has a number of Mexican standards at reasonable prices. The restaurant is on a pedestrian street beside San Francisco church.

Callejón de Lozada 1. ℂ **444/812-4508.** Reservations recommended on weekends. Main courses 98–160 pesos. AE, MC, V. Mon–Fri 6pm–midnight; Sat 2pm–midnight.

La Virreina ★ REGIONAL/MEXICAN Opened in 1959, this restaurant has for years been one of the places Potosinos go to dine when there's something to celebrate. It has the feel of an old-time Mexican restaurant—the staff talks in a soft-spoken, formal manner, the background music is mostly orchestral productions of Mexican favorites from the '60s and '70s, and the tables even have old-fashioned place settings. The kitchen also pays attention to the details missed by others. The *enchiladas potosinas* (ask for them with strips of poblano chile instead of cheese) are the best I've had in San Luis. If you order the *carne asada a la virreina,* you'll get a couple of enchiladas on the side. This dish is a steak topped with a little cheese and a sauce flavored with Mexican sausage. A more moderate option is the pepper steak or the baked fish with blue cheese and bread crumbs.

Av. Carranza 830. © **444/812-3750.** www.lavirreina.com.mx. Reservations accepted. Main courses 105–200 pesos. AE, MC, V. Tues–Sat 1–11pm; Sun–Mon 1–6pm.

INEXPENSIVE

La Parroquia MEXICAN   This is a standard no-frills restaurant with lots of local dishes on the menu. It's got picture windows looking out on Plaza Fundadores, booths upholstered in vinyl, and tables with Formica tops. And yet there's something very Mexican about this place. It attracts lots of office workers for its bargain-priced *menú del día.* Favorite dishes include *tacos arrieros* served with guacamole, *enchiladas huastecas,* and *costillas de cerdo en salsa cascabel* (pork ribs in a dark chile sauce).

Carranza 303. © **444/812-6681.** Reservations not accepted. Main courses 70–144 pesos. 5-course *menú del día* 84 pesos. MC, V. Daily 7am–midnight.

Restaurant Orizatlán ★ HUASTECAN   This colorful restaurant specializes in the traditional Huastecan cooking of eastern San Luis Potosí. If you are hungry, try the *parrillada a la Huasteca.* A large sampling of typical dishes, it includes portions of the *zacahuil,* Mexico's largest tamal. The waiters will keep the Huastecan enchiladas coming until you beg them to stop. Less ambitious eaters can order a la carte. After dinner, the restaurant serves a complimentary home-style cordial made from the fruit of the *jobito* (something similar to a sour plum).

Pascual M. Hernández 240. © **444/814-6786.** Breakfast 45 pesos; main courses 60–120 pesos. AE, MC, V. Mon–Thurs 8am–10pm; Fri–Sat 8am–11pm; Sun 8am–7pm. 8 blocks south of Plaza de Armas on Zaragoza, turn left at Jardín Colón; restaurant is about 30m (98 ft.) down.

San Luis Potosí After Dark

The most popular clubs in town are those where you can sit down to a late supper or drinks, and hear guitarists and vocalists. Most of the music is romantic—*trovas,* or ballads. In the downtown area, a number of bars offer this kind of entertainment, usually on Thursday, Friday, and Saturday nights. They include **La Compañía,** Mariano Arista 350 (© **444/812-9693**); **Restaurant Bar 1913,** Galeana 205 (© **444/812-8352**); and **Café Olé,** Zaragoza 665 (no phone). For more raucous entertainment, try **Los Frailes,** a bar at Callejón de San Francisco 165 (no phone). It offers a mix of pop Mexican music and rock 'n' roll.

MICHOACÁN

by David Baird

West of Mexico City and southeast of Guadalajara lies the state of Michoacán (*Mee*-choh-ah-*kahn*), the homeland of more than 200,000 Tarascan Indians, properly known as the Purépecha. The land is mountainous in the east, north, and center. In the south and west, it drops to a broad coastal plain before it meets the Pacific. The state gets more rain and thus is greener than its neighbors Jalisco and Guanajuato. Many Mexicans consider it the most beautiful state in their country, yet it remains relatively unvisited by foreigners.

High in the mountains, in the northeastern part of the state, a miraculous ritual occurs every year. Millions of monarch butterflies congregate in an isolated highland forest. They are the final link in a migratory chain stretching from Mexico to as far away as Canada and back. During peak season (Dec–Mar), the tree limbs bend under their cumulative weight, and the undulation of so many wings creates a dazzling spectacle (see "Michoacán's Monarch Migration," later in this chapter). In the state's center, highland lakes and colorful Indian towns evoke the Mexico of old. These towns are known for their handicrafts and all-night celebrations on the Day of the Dead. Farther west and south is the famous volcano El Paricutín, the only major volcano born in modern times (1943).

The two most important cities in Michoacán, **Morelia** and **Pátzcuaro,** present contrasting visions of the colonial past. Morelia is a city built of chiseled stone, planned with architectural considerations, and possessed of a clear-cut geometry. Pátzcuaro is all about undulating adobe walls, crooked red-tile roofs, and narrow meandering streets. While the former is proud of its Spanish heritage, the latter remains rooted in its Indian origins.

The native Purépecha are an intriguing people. Where they came from and how they got here we don't know. Their language is unlike any other in Mexico; the closest linguistic connection is with native peoples in Ecuador. Their civilization developed contemporaneously with that of the Aztec, and they successfully defeated Aztec expansionism—the only highland civilization to do so.

As they were not vassals of the Aztec, they didn't simply submit to Spanish rule after the collapse of the Aztec empire. In the history of the conquest and conversion of the Purépecha, two men represent the extremes of Spanish attitudes toward the Indians. One was the conquistador Nuño de Guzmán, a man so rapacious and cruel that he became infamous even among his fellow conquistadors. He was later imprisoned

Travel & the Drug Wars

Over the last few years there has been a simmering conflict between a locally grown drug cartel known as *La Familia* and the army and police. It's a game of cat and mouse that occasionally flares up into large-scale gun battles. The army and police have captured some of the cartel's lieutenants and hampered the cartel's business operations. *La Familia* has retaliated with attacks against police stations and army convoys. In a shootout in December 2010, the army killed one of *La Familia's* two principal leaders. The cartel retaliated with attacks in several parts of the state, and it barricaded state highways with burning vehicles to block army reinforcements. This included all the highways entering the capital city, Morelia. Government forces are predicting that they will soon eradicate the cartel. It seems doubtful, but only time will tell. Meanwhile, life for the locals continues fairly normally. In the cities there are plenty of people out at night in restaurants and bars. But there don't seem to be a lot of tourists. The way things stand now, I would still go to Michoacán, but the U.S. Department of State, in its travel warning dated September 10, 2010, is urging "U.S. citizens to defer unnecessary travel to Michoacán." For the most recent warnings, go to www.travel.state.gov.

in Spain for his crimes. The other was Vasco de Quiroga, a humanist who believed in the ideas of Erasmus and Sir Thomas More. He joined the church late in life and came to Michoacán as the first bishop of the Purépecha, establishing his see, or religious jurisdiction, in Pátzcuaro. Here he strove to build a society of cooperative communities, organizing and instructing each village in the practice of a specific craft. To this day, his organization of crafts among the different villages is largely followed.

Exploring Michoacán

Travel between the major cities of Michoacán takes only an hour or two at most, and public transportation is frequent. You should plan 3 days in **Morelia** (more if you intend to see the butterflies) and a minimum of 3 days in **Pátzcuaro,** but more like a week if you're interested in taking day trips to the lakes and the villages in the region and want to look into the local handicrafts. **Uruapan,** another important town, is an easy day trip from either city, although you may want to stay longer to visit **El Paricutín volcano.** During Easter week or Day of the Dead observances (Nov 1–2), the Plazas Grandes in Pátzcuaro and Uruapan overflow with regional crafts. Reserve rooms in advance for these holidays. With the highway from Ixtapa, it's possible to plan a vacation that combines the colonial cities of Michoacán with quality beach time.

MORELIA ★

312km (193 miles) NW of Mexico City; 365km (226 miles) SE of Guadalajara

The first viceroy of Mexico ordered the founding of the city in 1541 under the name Valladolid. After independence, that name was changed to Morelia to honor the revolutionary hero José María Morelos, who was born here.

Morelia was intended as a bastion of Spanish culture for the region's large population of Indians. The adjective people most frequently use to describe Morelia is *aristocratic.* Indeed, the city's greatest appeal lies in its grand colonial architecture.

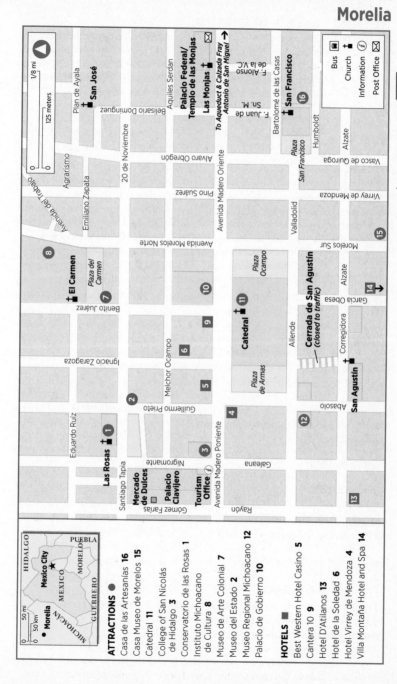

Morelia

Legend
- 🚌 Bus
- ✝ Church
- ⓘ Information
- ⊠ Post Office

Map labels
- Las Rosas ✝ 1
- Mercado de Dulces
- Palacio Clavijero
- Tourism Office ⓘ
- El Carmen ✝ 7
- Plaza del Carmen
- Benito Juárez
- San José ✝
- Plan de Ayala
- Plano de Ayala
- Aquiles Serdán
- Palacio Federal/ Templo de las Monjas
- Las Monjas ⊠
- To Aqueduct & Calzada Fray Antonio de San Miguel →
- F. Alonso de la V.C.
- Bartolomé de las Casas
- San Francisco ✝ 16
- Plaza San Francisco
- Humboldt
- Alzate
- Vasco de Quiroga
- Virrey de Mendoza
- Valladolid
- Morelos Sur
- Catedral ✝ 11
- Plaza de Armas
- Plaza Ocampo
- Cerrada de San Agustín (closed to traffic)
- San Agustín ✝
- Corregidora
- Garcia Obeso
- Alzate
- Allende
- Abasolo
- Galeana
- Rayón
- Santiago Tapia
- Gómez Farías
- Nigromante
- Avenida Madero Poniente
- Avenida Madero Oriente
- Avenida Morelos Norte
- Guillermo Prieto
- Melchor Ocampo
- Ignacio Zaragoza
- Eduardo Ruiz
- Pino Suárez
- Alvaro Obregón
- 20 de Noviembre
- Belisario Domínguez
- Emiliano Zapata
- Agrarismo
- Avenida del Tablao
- Eduardo Ruiz

Scale
- 1/8 mi
- 125 meters

Inset map
- HIDALGO
- PUEBLA
- MORELOS
- GUERRERO
- MICHOACÁN
- MEXICO
- Mexico City ★
- Morelia ●
- 50 mi
- 50 km

ATTRACTIONS ●
- Casa de las Artesanías **16**
- Casa Museo de Morelos **15**
- Catedral **11**
- College of San Nicolás de Hidalgo **3**
- Conservatorio de las Rosas **1**
- Instituto Michoacano de Cultura **8**
- Museo de Arte Colonial **7**
- Museo del Estado **2**
- Museo Regional Michoacano **12**
- Palacio de Gobierno **10**

HOTELS ■
- Best Western Hotel Casino **5**
- Cantera 10 **9**
- Hotel D'Atilanos **13**
- Hotel de la Soledad **6**
- Hotel Virrey de Mendoza **4**
- Villa Montaña Hotel and Spa **14**

Essentials

GETTING THERE & DEPARTING

BY PLANE The airport code for Morelia is MLM. **Continental ExpressJet** (© **800/523-3273** in the U.S., or 01-800/900-5000 in Mexico) has direct flights from Houston. **Volaris** (© **866/988-3527** in the U.S., or 01-800/122-8000 in Mexico), a Mexican discount airline, flies nonstop to/from Los Angeles. A few domestic carriers connect Morelia to other cities in Mexico, principally Mexico City.

Morelia's airport is **Aeropuerto Francisco J. Mújica,** a 45-minute drive from the city center on Km 27 of the Carretera Morelia-Zinapécuaro. A toll road connects the airport to the city and shaves 20 minutes off the drive. Taxis meet each flight. **Budget** has a rental car office (© **800/527-0700** in the U.S. and Canada, or 443/313-3399).

BY CAR The slow route from either Mexico City or Guadalajara is Hwy. 15—a winding and narrow road with beautiful vistas, which can be appreciated at leisure because you inevitably get behind an old truck that can barely climb the mountains. (Morelia sits at an elevation of 1,950m/6,396 ft.) The fast way is the modern **toll highway** that connects Mexico City and Guadalajara. Exit at the turnoff for **Hwy. 43.** It's clearly marked. To Morelia from either city is about 3½ hours and 200 pesos. From Guanajuato (2½ hr.), take this same Hwy. 43. From Morelia to Pátzcuaro (1 hr.), there is **Hwy. 120,** a four-lane road. The toll road from Ixtapa connects to this highway. From Ixtapa to Morelia now takes about 4 hours and costs 200 pesos.

BY BUS Buses to Morelia from Mexico City depart from the Observatorio station. ETN, Pegasso, Primera Plus/Servicios Coordinados, and Autovías all go to Morelia. Make sure to request a *directo* or *via autopista*. The trip takes 4 hours, and there are usually three or four departures every hour. ETN offers the best service. You will arrive at the new **Central Camionera** in the far-northwest side of town. First-class and deluxe bus service to and from Morelia uses Terminal A, and regional service to and from Pátzcuaro uses Terminal B. Service from Guadalajara is also frequent. From Guanajuato, your best bet is Primera Plus and Servicios Coordinados, usually changing buses in Irapuato. From Ixtapa, Autovías has two departures per day; Parhikuni has six. You can buy bus tickets from most travel agencies in town.

ORIENTATION

VISITOR INFORMATION The city government, in association with local guides, has a tourist information kiosk on the Plaza de Armas (main square). It's open Monday through Saturday from 9am to 8pm. The city also operates a website (**www.visitmorelia.com**) and prints a free quarterly magazine with a calendar of events (*La Guía de Morelia*), which is handy.

CITY LAYOUT The heart of the city is the **cathedral,** with the Plaza de Armas on its left (west side) and the Plaza Melchor Ocampo on its right (east side). The wide street passing in front of the cathedral is **Avenida Madero,** the city's main street. It meets the lovely colonial aqueduct 1km (⅔ mile) east of the cathedral. This segment of Madero, along with several blocks to either side, is the old part of town (see "Other Attractions," below.) From the fountain, the **aqueduct** heads southeast toward what has become the fashionable part of town.

GETTING AROUND Taxis are a bargain here. Still, you should settle the fare before you enter the cab.

[FastFACTS] MORELIA

Area Code   The telephone area code is **443.**

Climate   Morelia can be a bit chilly in the morning and evening, especially from November through February.

Emergencies   The local number for emergencies is ✆ **066.**

Hospital   The best in town is the **Sanatorio de la Luz,** Calle Bravo 50, in the Chapultepec Norte neighborhood (✆ **443/314-4568,** -4464, or 315-2966).

Internet Access   You can find Internet service without much effort in the Centro Histórico (Historic District).

Post Office   In the Palacio Federal, on the corner of Madero and Serapio Rendón, 5 blocks east of the cathedral. Hours are Monday through Friday from 8:30am to 4:30pm.

Special Events & Festivals

In April, the **International Guitar Festival** attracts performers from Latin America and Europe. In May, the city holds the **International Organ Festival** (linked to the variable feast day of Corpus Christi). The cathedral has a very large pipe organ that sounds wonderful, and for the festival four organists are invited to give concerts in the cathedral. In October, the city holds its increasingly popular film festival, **Festival Internacional de Cine de Morelia** (www.moreliafilmfest.com). The festival has been attracting the big names of Mexico's film industry, including stars like Salma Hayek and Gael García Bernal. The **International Festival of Music** is held in November, with a series of concerts performed over 2 weeks. Performers come from all over.

The largest civic celebrations are in September, the month of the *fiestas patrias.* **Independence Day** is celebrated on September 15 and 16. Then, on September 29 and 30, Morelia celebrates the **birthday of its favorite son, José María Morelos,** a patriot and revolutionary hero. The second celebration is actually bigger than the first, but both include parades, street parties, and large fireworks displays.

Exploring Morelia

A STROLL THROUGH THE COLONIAL CENTER

Downtown Morelia is a good town for walking. One comes across interesting details on just about any street. The walk outlined below could take an entire day. The museums usually open at 9am; you'll find a lot of places closed on Mondays, holidays, and between 2 and 4pm. For a guided tour of the city, contact the guide mentioned in the section on the monarch butterfly migration ("Michoacán's Monarch Migration," p. 230). He can provide colorful details about the city's history and architecture.

The **cathedral ★★★** is the place to begin. Built with the pink volcanic stone (*cantera* in Spanish) that Morelia is famous for, it's one of the most beautiful cathedrals in Mexico. Notice how Avenida Madero widens as it passes in front of the cathedral, and how a cross street lines up with its facade. Morelia's planners sought to lend prominence to the city's churches by the placement of plazas and the alignment of streets to allow good views. This cathedral took the place of an earlier one; construction began in 1640 and ended in 1745. The new cathedral incorporated the styles of religious architecture already in the city, including *plateresque,* mannerist, and a reserved style of baroque. The cathedral's impressive size and monumental proportions were necessary to place it at the top of the hierarchy of the city's temples,

free-market FORCES

Morelia's **city market** is 5 blocks south of San Francisco in a plain, warehouse-like structure. If you're a veteran market shopper, you'll like this one. It's especially rich in regional manufactures, such as sombreros and huaraches, and has a good produce section where you can stock up on different kinds of dried chiles if you like cooking Mexican food.

To get to the market, go downhill from San Francisco Plaza along Calle Vasco de Quiroga. Just before you get there, you will see a little plaza and the **Templo de las Capuchinas.** It's a precious little baroque church with a gilt *retablo* (altarpiece) inside. Unfortunately, it is often closed; the best time to try is from 8 to 9am and from 5 to 6pm, when the priest opens the church for Mass. Behind the church is the market.

and to make obvious Morelia's superiority to rival Pátzcuaro. The Italian architect who designed it worked closely with the authorities of Morelia's sizable religious community, and he did a masterful job balancing the architectural elements in the facade and shaping the proportions of the towers. The inside is stately, but many of the cathedral's most valuable possessions were plundered. Things to look for include its beautiful **organ ★** with 4,600 pipes (see "Special Events & Festivals," above); the silver baptismal font where Mexico's first emperor, Agustín de Iturbide, was baptized; and the elegant choir with carved wooden stalls. *Tip:* If you're in Morelia on a Saturday, make sure to be around the cathedral when the lights are turned on. This is accompanied by a fireworks display.

Across Avenida Madero from the cathedral is a two-story stone building crowned with finials and fanciful decorations on the corners: the **Palacio del Gobierno,** built in 1732 as a seminary. It now holds sweeping murals depicting the history of Michoacán and Mexico. Some are the work of a well-known local artist, Alfredo Zalce.

As you leave the *palacio,* turn left and walk down Madero for 2 blocks. Turn right at a small church on your right with a tall wrought-iron fence. The name of the street is Vasco de Quiroga. Walk 1 block, and to your left you'll see a broad plaza and the **church and convent of San Francisco ★★**. This is one of the two oldest religious buildings in Morelia. It draws on the Spanish Renaissance architectural style known as *plateresque* (already antiquated by the time of construction) because the builders wanted to accentuate their Spanish heritage. The building is quite striking; it has elegant, Moorish windows on the second floor, borrowed from Spanish Mudéjar architecture. The interior courtyard, unlike any other in Morelia, has a medieval feel. Instead of being broad and open with light arches, it's closed and narrow, with heavy columns set closely together and thick buttressing. The former convent now houses a local **handicrafts museum** with interactive exhibits and some explanatory material in English. It also offers the best shopping in Morelia (see "Shopping," below).

From San Francisco (if you're not going to the market), take the street that lines up with the facade of the church and walk 2 blocks west to Calle Morelos Sur (you'll see Plaza Melchor Ocampo). Turn left. One block down, on the left side, is the **Casa Museo de Morelos,** Morelos Sur 323 (© **443/313-2651**). This is where José María Morelos lived as an adult (there's another Morelos museum in the house where he was born, but it has little of interest). A grand house, with furniture and personal effects that belonged to the independence leader, as well as a period kitchen, this museum is worth a visit. On my last visit it was closed for renovation in preparation for the big bicentennial celebration set for September 2010. The museum is normally open Tuesday through Sunday from 9am to 5pm; admission is 30 pesos.

The next place to see is the **Museo Regional Michoacano ★**, at the intersection of Allende and Abasolo (© **443/312-0407**). To get there, walk uphill the way you came, and then make a left when you get back to Plaza Melchor Ocampo. Walk through the stone arcades behind the cathedral. Continue west to the end of the arcades. Across the street, cater-cornered to the Plaza de Armas, is the Museo Regional Michoacano. It provides a colorful view of the state from prehistoric times to Mexico's Cardenist period of the 1930s. Isidor Huarte, father of Ana Huarte, Emperor Iturbide's wife, originally owned the building, which was finished in 1775. The museum is open Tuesday through Sunday from 9am to 4:45pm. Admission is 37 pesos.

To take a break, sit at one of the outdoor cafes under the stone arches along Avenida Madero. (No need, really, to overexert oneself. Besides, sitting at a table having a little coffee or beer and watching the passersby is a favorite activity of the locals.)

After having your fill of people-watching (or beer or coffee), head west on Madero for a block and you'll come to Calle Nigromante. On the right, you'll see the **College of San Nicolás de Hidalgo,** a beautiful colonial building that claims to house the oldest university in the New World. Founded in Pátzcuaro in 1540 by Vasco de Quiroga, the university moved to Morelia in 1580 and became the University of Michoacán in 1917. On the other corner is another of Morelia's oldest religious structures, the **Iglesia de la Compañía de Jesús,** built by the Jesuits. It's now a picturesque library. Through a doorway to the right of the church is the state's **tourist information office.** Attached to the church is the former convent, now called the **Palacio Clavijero.** To see the arches and rose-colored stone of its broad interior courtyard (the most photographed in Morelia), turn down Nigromante and follow it to the main entrance. The former convent now houses government offices. Once you've seen the *palacio,* continue down the street to the little park. Facing the park is the **Conservatorio de las Rosas,** a former Dominican convent. It became a music school in 1785 and is now the home of the internationally acclaimed **Morelia Boys Choir.** The choir practices on weekday afternoons. If you would like to attend a concert, ask for information inside.

At the other end of the small plaza, facing Calle Guillermo Prieto, is the **Museo del Estado** (© **443/313-0629**). Exhibits include a display on the archaeology and history of the area and a 19th-century apothecary shop. The museum is open Monday

A BRIEF pause FOR THE FOOD cause

Behind the cathedral are two local food vendors that are institutions in the city. One is an ice-cream stand called **Nieves del Correo,** so named because for the first 30 years of its existence, it occupied a bit of sidewalk on Avenida Madero in front of the post office. Now it's in the last doorway under the arches before you get to the pedestrian-only Cerrada de San Agustín. You can't miss it. The specialty is fruit flavors such as mango and mamey. The other option is to enjoy a fruit cocktail known locally as a *gazpacho* (nothing like a gazpacho in Spain). Turn left on the Cerrada and you'll come to **Gazpachos La Cerrada.** Order one and you'll get chopped fruit (mango, pineapple, and jicama) swimming in orange and lime juice with a touch of powdered chile.

through Friday from 9am to 2pm and 4 to 8pm, Saturday and Sunday from 9am to 2pm and 4 to 6pm. Admission is free. Look for, or ask about, concerts and other goings-on.

To visit another interesting museum, continue east on Santiago Tapia 2 blocks to Benito Juárez and turn north (left). The **Museo de Arte Colonial,** Av. Benito Juárez 240 (© **443/313-9260**), is a colonial house with an exhibition of religious art from the 16th to the 18th centuries: three rooms of crucifixes and Christ figures and two rooms of oil paintings, including a couple by Miguel Cabrera. Some of the crucifixes are made from the paste of corn stalks, using a pre-Columbian artistic technique among the Purépecha. The missionaries soon had their Indian converts using it to create the Christ figures and saints that adorn many churches in Mexico. The museum is open Monday through Friday from 10am to 8pm, Saturday and Sunday from 10am to 6pm. Admission is free.

Just around the corner from this museum (turn right as you exit) is the **Plaza del Carmen.** Across the plaza, behind a heavy wrought-iron fence, is the church and former convent of **El Carmen.** The entrance to the convent is on the opposite side of the block from the church, on Morelos Norte. The building is home to the state's **Instituto Michoacano de Cultura** (© **443/313-1320**), which has made this a comfortable and utilitarian destination; you can examine the calendars posted at the entrance to see whether a concert, film, or exhibition is happening during your stay. You can also view the large stone courtyard built in the style often used by the Carmelites. Around the courtyard are a cafe, a large bookstore, and a gallery. Entrance is free. The institute is open daily from 10am to 8pm.

OTHER ATTRACTIONS

On another day you might enjoy exploring Avenida Madero, east from the cathedral. After a couple of blocks, you'll reach the **Templo de las Monjas (Nuns' Temple),** an old church with a unique twin facade and B-shaped floor plan. Beside it is the massive **Palacio Federal,** which houses, among other official bureaus, the post and telegraph offices. Continue on and you'll reach the colonial **aqueduct.** The graceful arches of the aqueduct stretch from here about a kilometer (less than a mile) eastward. A stone walkway, lined with trees and long stone benches, starts from one of the arches in front of the fountain. This is **La Calzada Fray Antonio de San Miguel ★★.** In the 1940s, this walkway was used to shoot some scenes for a Hollywood movie, with Tyrone Power, called *Captains from Castile.* The Calzada leads to the **church of San Diego ★★,** the most ornate church in Morelia; San Diego is also known as **El Santuario de Guadalupe.** It has a colorful interior done in neobaroque. In early December, food stands fill the entire plaza in front of the church, and a festival is held to celebrate the feast day of the Virgin of Guadalupe (Dec 12).

The distance from the cathedral to San Diego is about 1.6km (1 mile). You can take a taxi back or, if you still feel like walking, return by crossing the large plaza with the statue of Morelos on horseback. Go under the aqueduct, and enter Morelia's equivalent of Central Park, known as **El Bosque (The Woods).** Continue west and work your way back to the center of town. If you get turned around, note that if you're walking on level ground, you're parallel to or heading toward Madero; if you're walking downhill, you're heading away from it.

Shopping

Casa de las Artesanías ★★   This place is both a museum and one of the best crafts shops in Mexico. In the showroom, you'll find an array of objects produced in the Indian villages of Michoacán's central highlands, including carved-wood furniture from Cuanajo, pottery from Tzintzuntzan, wood masks from Tócuaro, lacquerware from Pátzcuaro and Uruapan, cross-stitch embroidery from Tarecuato, copperware from Santa Clara, guitars from Paracho, and close-woven hats from Jarácuaro. Straight ahead in the interior courtyard are showcases laden with the best regional crafts. Upstairs, individual villages have sales outlets. Sometimes artisans demonstrate their craft. The shop and museum are open Monday through Saturday from 9am to 8pm, Sunday from 9am to 3pm. Exconvento de San Francisco, Plaza Valladolid. © 443/312-1248.

Mercado de Dulces Along the back of the former Jesuit convent is the sweets market—a collection of stalls selling the typical sweets that Morelia is famous for, such as *ates* (a thick fruit paste), candied fruit wedges, pralines, toasted coconut, and milk candies. The *mercado* is open daily from 7am to 10pm. Behind the Palacio Clavijero, along Valentín Gómez Farías. No phone. From the cathedral, head west on Madero and turn right on Gómez Farías; entrance is a half-block down on the right.

Where to Stay

Rates listed here include the 18% tax. Rates at the inexpensive and moderately priced hotels can go up during Christmas, Easter, Day of the Dead, holiday weekends, and the month of August. In 2010, promotional rates were quite common.

VERY EXPENSIVE

Cantera 10 ★★ High design and a different use of space set this all-suite hotel apart from the competition. Rooms are large, uncluttered, and undivided into sitting rooms/bedroom compartments (with the extrahigh ceilings augmenting the openness). Except where remnants of the original house remain, fixtures and furniture are modern with simple lines, and lighting accentuates the modern feel. There is a certain richness, too, in the textures and colors, the plush mattresses, and the pillow menu. Those who are looking for something different in their surroundings will like this hotel. It's directly across the street from the cathedral.

Benito Juárez 63, 58000 Morelia, Mich. www.canteradiezhotel.com. © **01-800/823-5787** or 443/312-5419. 11 units. 2,660–4,530 pesos suite. Rates include full breakfast. AE, MC, V. Free valet parking. **Amenities:** Restaurant; bar; concierge; massage; room service; smoke-free rooms. *In room:* A/C, TV, hair dryer, minibar, Wi-Fi.

Hotel Virrey de Mendoza ★★ This old-style grand hotel is beautifully kept and impressive, and right on the Plaza de Armas. Most rooms have lots of character—wood floors with area rugs, period furniture, and old-fashioned tile bathrooms with tub/showers. Bed choices include two twins, one full, two queen-size, or one king-size. Standard rooms are midsize; many of the exterior rooms have stone window seats built out from the wall. Two of the exterior rooms have balconies. The suites are large, and master suites have separate sitting rooms. The *suite virreinal* (viceroy suite) is really grand, with a large third-floor terrace that looks out over the Plaza de Armas to the cathedral. Rooms have double-glazed windows, but traffic noise still leaks in.

Av. Madero Poniente 310, 58000 Morelia, Mich. www.hotelvirrey.com. © **866/299-7492** in the U.S., 877/889-2161 in Canada, 01-800/450-2000 in Mexico, or 443/312-0633. 55 units. 2,200 pesos double; 2,620–4,300 pesos suite. Rates include full breakfast. Internet packages sometimes available. AE, MC, V. Free valet parking. **Amenities:** Restaurant; lobby bar; babysitting; room service; smoke-free rooms; Wi-Fi (in lobby). *In room:* A/C (in 11 rooms), TV, hair dryer.

Villa Montaña Hotel and Spa ★★★   High above the city on the Santa María Ridge, this hotel is a small complex of buildings on a hillside, separated by gardens and connected by footpaths. The buildings are at different levels; this, as well as the placement of the entrances, allows for privacy. Rooms are large and impressively furnished, and have working fireplaces. Most come with two doubles or a king-size bed. Bathrooms are large, with tub/showers and lots of counter space. Most of the junior suites have a separate living area and a small terrace with table and chairs. Master suites have a lot of architectural details. The restaurant serves local dishes, and having a drink on the terrace overlooking the city is one of the delights of staying here.

Patzimba 201, Col. Vista Bella 58090 Morelia, Mich. www.villamontana.com.mx. ⓒ **800/925-1737** in the U.S. and Canada, 01-800/963-3100 in Mexico, or 443/314-0231. Fax 443/315-1423. 36 units. $248 double; $342–$419 suite; $543 2-bedroom suite. Prices do not include 7.5% service charge. Internet specials sometimes available. Weekday discounts available. AE, MC, V. Free secure parking. **Amenities:** Restaurant; terrace bar; babysitting; concierge; golf at local country club; fitness room; heated outdoor pool; room service; spa; lighted tennis court. *In room:* TV, hair dryer.

MODERATE

Best Western Hotel Casino ⚑   A colonial hotel without the character of the Hotel de la Soledad, the Best Western should still be considered for its location—across the street from the cathedral—comfort, and price. The owners continue to invest money in improvements and upgrades. They've opened three new rooms on the top floor that are large, sunny, and comfortable. Most rooms are midsize and carpeted. Some second-floor rooms in front have a balcony and view of the cathedral, but they can be noisy. Many rooms have two double beds or one double and one twin.

Portal Hidalgo 229, 58000 Morelia, Mich. www.bestwestern.com. ⓒ **800/528-1234** in the U.S., or 443/313-1328. Fax 443/312-1252. 40 units. $74–$85 double. Balcony suites must be reserved directly from the hotel. AE, MC, V. Free valet parking. **Amenities:** Restaurant; bar; fitness room; room service; smoke-free rooms; Wi-Fi (in lobby). *In room:* TV, hair dryer.

Hotel de la Soledad ★   Past the massive wooden doors of this colonial hotel is a beautiful courtyard, with manicured garden. New ownership has redesigned the common areas and made improvements to the rooms, including new mattresses. By the end of 2011, all guest rooms should be remodeled, with new wiring, windows, and bathrooms. The location is great—1 block north of the cathedral.

Ignacio Zaragoza 90, 58000 Morelia, Mich. www.hsoledad.com. ⓒ **443/312-1888,** -1889. Fax 443/312-2111. 57 units. 1,500–2,000 pesos double; 2,500 pesos suite. Internet specials available. AE, MC, V. Free valet parking. **Amenities:** Restaurant; bar; room service; Wi-Fi in lobby/restaurant. *In room:* TV, hair dryer (on request).

INEXPENSIVE

Hotel D'Atilanos   This is the only decent inexpensive hotel in the downtown area. Two floors of rooms surround a simple patio. The rooms are simply furnished, with one or two double beds, two twins, or one king-size bed (king rooms are more expensive). Most rooms are midsize, but bathrooms are small. I prefer the downstairs rooms, which have high ceilings. Lighting is poor.

Corregidora 465, 58000 Morelia, Mich. ⓒ **443/313-3309** or 443/312-0121. 27 units. 479–580 pesos double. No credit cards. Limited street parking. *In room:* TV.

Where to Eat

Michoacán is known for a dish of slow-cooked pork called *carnitas,* which is sold only in joints that specialize in the dish. Many locals like **Los Tabachines,** in Colonia

Ventura Puente. The address is Laguna de la Magdalena 430. You can eat the *carnitas* there or buy them to go. My favorite place is **Carnitas don Raúl,** at Carpinteros de Paracho 1007, Colonia Vasco de Quiroga. It's best to go around noon.

Cenaduría Lupita ★ ANTOJITOS Translated literally, *antojitos* means "little cravings." This is the traditional supper food of most Mexicans, but they usually eat it at home or in greasy-spoon joints whose cleanliness is dubious. A good-looking, comfortable restaurant that specializes in *antojitos* is a rarity; rarer still is one that does such a good job. Take your pick of *tacos dorados*, tostadas, tamales, *huchepos* (like tamales, but made with fresh corn), and *pozole* prepared Michoacán style.

Sánchez de Tagle 1004 (a half-block off Av. Lázaro Cárdenas). ℂ **443/312-1340.** Antojitos 38-60 pesos. MC, V. Wed-Sat and Mon 7-11pm; Sun 7-10pm.

El Anzuelo ★★ SEAFOOD/STEAKS This simple outdoor restaurant in the modern part of town serves the best seafood in Morelia. It makes the perfect Mexican seafood cocktail and wonderful ceviche. After either of those, you might order *huachinango adobado* (red snapper in a chile-based marinade) or coconut shrimp. If you don't feel like fish, there's filet mignon. The owners are meticulous about food preparation. El Anzuelo is open only in the afternoon. On Sunday, it offers paella, and the restaurant gets very crowded. Take a taxi and keep the address handy.

Av. Camelinas 3180. ℂ **443/314-8339** or 443/324-3237. Reservations recommended on weekends. Main courses 148-240 pesos. AE, MC, V. Daily noon-6pm.

La Casa del Portal REGIONAL This upstairs restaurant is in a beautiful stone mansion facing the Plaza de Armas. The floors, walls, and ceilings of the old house have remained intact. It's good to have so much to observe, as service can be slow. There are several dining rooms, and on occasion the rooftop terrace is open for dining. Most of the furniture comes from the owner's workshop. The restaurant doubles as a sort of factory outlet, and all the furniture is for sale. What's for dinner? The menu includes several regional standards, including some of the best *sopa tarasca* I've had. The *enchiladas del portal* were also good. Other dishes include the *arrachera valladolid*, a skirt steak accompanied by a few Mexican sides.

Guillermo Prieto 30 (cater-cornered from Virrey de Mendoza; entrance is on the side street). ℂ **443/313-4899.** Main courses 88-185 pesos. AE, MC, V. Daily 8:30am-11pm.

Las Trojes STEAKS/REGIONAL A *troje* is the traditional dwelling of the highland Purépecha Indians, constructed of rough-cut wood planks. This restaurant is made of seven connected *trojes*, with windows added for light. For starters, try *sopa tarasca*. Main courses include *cecina*, a good steak *a la tampiqueña* (grilled and served with several Mexican sides); rib-eye; *chistorra* (Spanish-style sausage); and chicken stuffed with cheese en brochette. Take a cab and keep the address handy.

Juan Sebastián Bach 51, Col. La Loma. ℂ **443/314-7344.** Main courses 120-230 pesos. AE, MC, V. Mon-Sat 1pm-midnight; Sun 1-6pm.

Los Mirasoles REGIONAL Los Mirasoles serves regional fare, including *jahuácatas* or *corundas* (a kind of tamal in the form of a triangle without a filling, and served in a chile sauce with bits of pork). They also serve pork ribs marinated in a dark chile sauce spiked with *pulque*. There's a large selection of beer and wine. Service can be slow. The dining rooms are attractive, especially at night.

Av. Madero Poniente 549 (4 blocks west of Plaza de Armas, at León Guzmán). ℂ **443/317-5775.** Reservations recommended on weekends. Main courses 145-255 pesos; seafood/steaks 210-380 pesos. AE, MC, V. Daily 1-11pm.

MICHOACÁN'S monarch MIGRATION

A visit to the winter nesting grounds of the monarch butterfly, high in the mountains of northeast Michoacán, is a stirring experience. It might be the highlight of your trip. The season lasts from mid- to late November to March. Tour operators in Morelia offer a day trip to see the butterflies for 650 to 750 pesos per person. The tour takes 10 to 12 hours and involves hiking up a mountain at a high altitude. You should only do this trip if you're in decent physical condition.

The best time to see the butterflies is on a sunny day, when they flutter through the air in a blizzard of orange and black. At the center of the group, the branches of the tall fir trees bow under their burden of butterflies, whose wings undulate softly as the wind blows through the forest; it's quite a spectacle.

From Morelia, you'll have no difficulty finding a tour; most hotels and all travel agencies can put you in contact with one. I particularly recommend **Luis Miguel López Alanís** (© 443/340-4632). He speaks English, is federally licensed, and belongs to a small cooperative of guides called **Mex Mich Guías** (www.mmg.com.mx). The easiest way to contact him is through the website. Most tours provide transportation, guide, soft drinks, and usually lunch. A good guide is important, if only to answer all the questions that these butterflies and their strange migration provoke.

A few butterfly sanctuaries are open to the public. (The monarchs congregate at nine sites, but five are closed to visitors.) The sites with the best access are **El Rosario** (admission 40 pesos; daily 10am–5 or 6pm) and the newer **Chincua** (same admission and hours as El Rosario). It is less of a drive, but usually more of a walk to the nucleus of the butterfly group—but not always. Throughout the season, the groups shift, moving up and down the mountains and making for a longer or shorter climb. A good guide will lead you to the shorter walk.

If you're driving, take the *autopista* to Mexico City, exit at Maravatío, and go right. Keep right after going through Maravatío and take the narrow two-lane road toward Angangueo. When you get to a T-junction, go right, toward San Felipe. Enter the town of Ocampo and look for a small sign pointing left to get to Rosario, where you will find a parking lot near the trail head. If you want to make this a leisurely trip, spend the night in the nearby town of Angangueo at **Hotel Don Bruno** (© 715/156-0026; 600 pesos double). It's a little overpriced, so ask to see the room before you accept it.

Travel agencies from **San Miguel de Allende** also book monarch tours, which take 1 or 2 days. See chapter 6 for details.

Lu ★★ MEXICAN/REGIONAL   I first met Lucero, the chef at Lu, years ago when she had a small restaurant in a house facing the Calzada. I liked her cooking then, and I really like it now that she's turned her attention to the traditional cooking of her home state of Michoacán. This restaurant is under the *portales* of the Casino Hotel, facing the Plaza de Armas. It's a good place for a relaxing meal, and the food is so delicious and interesting that you'll want to take your time. Some of the dishes are traditional recipes, such as the *churipo* (a stew); others, such as the *sopa tarasca*, have been tweaked a bit; and yet others are completely original, though inspired by the local style of cooking. Of the main courses, the most interesting dishes include a fish cooked in a guava and *guajillo* chile sauce flavored by *hoja santa*, or chicken in a peanut *mole*.

Portal Hidalgo 229. ☎ **443/313-1328.** Main courses 110–165 pesos. Tasting menu 220 pesos, 351 pesos with wine pairing. MC, V. Daily 8am–10pm.

San Miguelito ★★ 🍴 MEXICAN   This is perhaps the most popular restaurant in town, with an inventive menu, attentive service, and a setting loaded with icons of Mexican culture. One part of the main dining room is the Rincón de las Solteronas (the bachelorette corner), where images of Saint Anthony hang upside down—the custom in Mexico when a girl is petitioning him for a boyfriend or husband. Guests are welcome to make a petition; the staff will be happy to show you how. I especially enjoy the appetizers: tacos, *chicharrón de queso* (fried crispy cheese), and other finger foods. The *sopa tarasca* is among the best I've had in restaurants. There are several steak dishes, including one in tequila, *guajillo* chile, and orange sauce. For dessert there's a delicious version of cherries jubilee. Take a cab and keep the address handy.

Av. Camelinas (at Ventura Puente). ☎ **443/324-2300.** Reservations recommended. Main courses 140–220 pesos. AE, MC, V. Mon–Wed 2–11pm; Thurs–Sat 2pm–midnight; Sun 2–5pm.

Morelia After Dark

For nighttime entertainment, check the calendar of events at the **Instituto Michoacano de Cultura** (see "A Stroll Through the Colonial Center," earlier in this chapter). In addition, you can sit at one of the cafes under the stone arches across from the Plaza de Armas to do some people-watching (a very Moreliano thing to do). For dancing, go to **La Casa de la Salsa** (☎ **443/313-9362**), a large dance hall facing Plaza Morelos at the end of the Calzada Fray Antonio de San Miguel. It's open Tuesday through Saturday from 9pm to 3am. It books live music on Friday and Saturday (50-peso cover charge). You can call ahead to reserve a table; the band plays a lot of salsa, merengue, and mambo. If you want live Latin American folk music, a drink, and something to eat, try **Peña Colibrí** (☎ **443/312-2261**), Galeana 36, behind the Virrey de Mendoza. It opens daily at 8pm and closes around midnight.

PÁTZCUARO ★★★

370km (229 miles) NW of Mexico City; 285km (177 miles) SE of Guadalajara; 69km (43 miles) SW of Morelia

Pátzcuaro is perhaps the loveliest town in Mexico. Crooked cobblestone streets, smooth stucco walls painted white with dark red borders, blackened tile roofs that join to form ramshackle rooflines—it is a town meant to be photographed and painted. During the rainy season, when low clouds roll in and curl through the trees, and water drips from the low-slung overhangs, a sweet melancholy descends upon the town.

Pátzcuaro is in the heart of the Purépecha homeland. Beside it is Lake Pátzcuaro (one of the world's highest, at 2,200m/7,216 ft.), whose shores border dozens of Indian villages. In these villages and in town, visitors frequently hear the soft sounds of the Purépechan language in the background as they take in the sights. Although distinct regional costumes are seldom seen today, Indian women still braid their hair with ribbons and wear the blue *rebozos* (long woolen wraps).

Essentials

GETTING THERE & DEPARTING

BY CAR   See "Getting There & Departing" under "Morelia," earlier in this chapter, for information on arriving from Mexico City, Guadalajara, and San Miguel de Allende. From Morelia, there are two routes to Pátzcuaro; the faster is the new four-lane **Hwy. 120,** which passes near Tiripetío and Tupátaro/Cuanajo (see "Side Trips from Pátzcuaro," later in this chapter). The longer route, **Hwy. 15,** takes a little more than an hour and passes near the pottery-making village of Capula and then through Quiroga, where you follow signs to Pátzcuaro (see "Side Trips from Pátzcuaro," later). A taxi from Morelia will cost 250 pesos, a private car and driver a little more, but you travel in a larger, usually newer, vehicle.

BY BUS The bus station is on the outskirts of Pátzcuaro, 5 minutes away by taxi (30 pesos). If you're going anywhere outside of Michoacán, it's best to go to Morelia first. If you're going straight to Mexico City, the Pegaso bus company offers nonstop service. Buses between Morelia and Pátzcuaro run every 10 minutes. To visit any of the lakeside villages or nearby towns, public transportation is an option, but taxis are not that expensive. From the Pátzcuaro bus station, there are buses to Tócuaro and Erongarícuaro every 20 minutes; to Tupátaro and Cuanajo every hour; to Tzintzuntzan and Quiroga every 40 minutes; and to Santa Clara del Cobre every hour. For Ihuatzio, you can pick up a minivan or a bus from the Plaza Chica.

ORIENTATION

VISITOR INFORMATION The **Tourism Office,** Cuesta Buenavista 7 (© **434/342-1214**), near the basilica, is open Monday through Saturday from 9am to 3pm and 4 to 7pm, and Sunday from 9am to 2pm. You may not find someone who speaks English, but the staff members have maps and point you in the right direction. An office on the west side of the Plaza Grande (no phone) keeps the same hours as the main office.

CITY LAYOUT In a way, Pátzcuaro has two town centers, both plazas a block apart. **Plaza Grande,** also called Plaza Principal or Plaza Don Vasco de Quiroga, is picturesque and tranquil, with a fountain and a statue of Vasco de Quiroga. Hotels, shops, and restaurants in Colonial-Era buildings flank this plaza. **Plaza Chica,** also known as Plaza Gertrudis Bocanegra, flows into the market, and around it swirls the commercial life of Pátzcuaro. Plaza Chica is north of Plaza Grande.

GETTING AROUND With the exception of Lake Pátzcuaro, the lookout, the bus station, and hotels on Lázaro Cárdenas, everything is within walking distance. Taxis are cheap. The lake is about 1km (around ⅔ mile) from town; buses make the run every 15 minutes from both the Plaza Grande and the Plaza Chica, going all the way to the *embarcadero* or *muelle* (pier).

[FastFACTS] PÁTZCUARO

Area Code The telephone area code is **434.**

Climate The climate is delightful most of the year, but occasional blustery days bring gusts of chilled air from across the lake, causing everyone to retreat indoors. October through April, it's cold enough for a heavy sweater, especially in the morning and evening. Few hotels have fireplaces or any source of heat in the rooms.

Emergency Dial © **434/349-0209** for emergency assistance or the national emergency number, © **066.**

Hospital The **Hospital Civil Dr. Gabriel García** is at Calle Romero 18 (© **434/342-0285**).

Post Office The *correo,* located a half-block north of Plaza Chica, on the right side of the street, is open Monday through Friday from 10am to 2pm and 4 to 8pm.

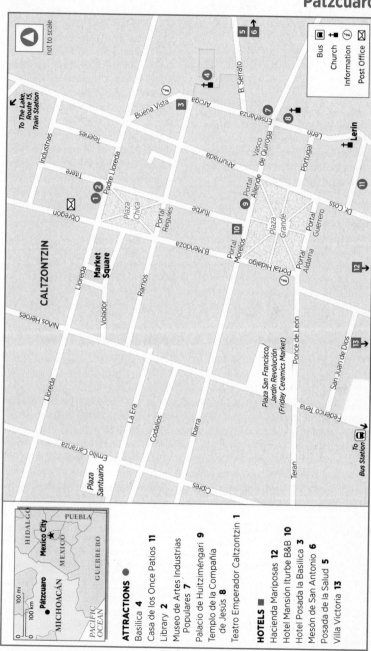

Pátzcuaro

ATTRACTIONS ●
Basílica **4**
Casa de los Once Patios **11**
Library **2**
Museo de Artes Industrias
    Populares **7**
Palacio de Huitziméngari **9**
Templo de la Compañia
    de Jesús **8**
Teatro Emperador Caltzontzin **1**

HOTELS ■
Hacienda Mariposas **12**
Hotel Mansión Iturbe B&B **10**
Hotel Posada la Basílica **3**
Mesón de San Antonio **6**
Posada de la Salud **5**
Villa Victoria **13**

Special Events

The island of **Janitzio** has achieved international celebrity for the candlelight vigil that local residents hold at the cemetery during the nights of November 1 and 2, the Day of the Dead. **Tzintzuntzan,** a village about 15km (9¼ miles) away, also hosts popular festivities, including folkloric dances in the main plaza and in the nearby *yácatas* (pre-Hispanic ruins), concerts in the church, and decorations in the cemetery. If you want to avoid the crowds, skip Janitzio and Tzintzuntzan and go to one of the smaller **lakeside villages or other islands** on the lake that also have extraordinary rituals. The tourism office (see "Visitor Information," above) has a schedule of events for the entire area and publishes an explanatory booklet, *Días de los Muertos.*

> ### Festival Hotel Crunch
>
> Make hotel reservations months in advance for Holy Week or Day of the Dead. Most hotels require a 3-night minimum stay during these events. There are some other less popular festivals in Pátzcuaro and surrounding towns; check with the tourist office to find out if any will occur during your visit.

During the week surrounding **Day of the Dead,** artisans and vendors from all over Michoacán fill the Plaza Grande in Pátzcuaro with regional crafts. **Easter week,** beginning the Friday before Palm Sunday, is special, too. Most activity centers on the basilica. There are processions involving the surrounding villages almost nightly, and in Tzintzuntzan, there's a reenactment of the betrayal of Christ and a ceremonial washing of the feet.

Exploring Pátzcuaro: A Stroll Around Town

The **Plaza Grande** is in the middle of town, surrounded by colonial buildings. A **stone fountain** in the center of the plaza holds a large figure of the beloved Vasco de Quiroga, "Tata Vasco," depicted in a benevolent posture. On the north side of the plaza is the **Palacio de Huitziméngari,** built by the Spaniards for the Tarascan emperor. Local Indian artisans now occupy the slowly deteriorating building.

One long block north is the **Plaza Chica,** crisscrossed by walkways and adorned with the statue of Gertrudis Bocanegra, a heroine of Mexican independence. This is the commercial center of town. On the west side of the plaza are **market** stalls selling pottery, copper, *rebozos, serapes* (a woolen blanket that is sometimes carried over the shoulder), and food. On some days, the stalls extend a couple of blocks up the street. What was once San Agustín church is on the north side of the plaza. The cloister was remodeled in the 20th century and converted into the **Teatro Emperador Caltzontzin,** the municipal theater. The old church is now the **public library;** inside, all the way to the back, you'll find an early work of Juan O'Gorman—a large mural stretching the width and height of the nave.

Don Vasco built the **basilica,** on a hill just east of the Plaza Chica, although he died before it was inaugurated in 1554. It was designated a basilica by papal decree in 1907. Now reconstructed, it has survived many catastrophes, human and natural—from earthquakes to the civil war of the mid–19th century. Be sure to visit the main altar to see the **Virgen de la Salud.** She is a sacred figure to the Indians of this region, who come from the villages to pay homage to her and petition her healing power on the eighth day of each month.

Two blocks south of the basilica is the **Museo de Artes Industrias Populares ★★** (© 434/342-1029). It occupies yet another beautiful colonial building (1540), originally Don Vasco's College of San Nicolás. The rooms, filled with fine examples of regional popular art such as crafts and costumes, open to a central courtyard. The museum guides are well informed. The museum is open Tuesday through Saturday from 9am to 7pm, Sunday from 9am to 4:30pm. Admission is 37 pesos. Behind the museum are some recent excavations of Purépechan ruins.

Of the many old churches in Pátzcuaro, one of the most interesting is the **Templo de la Compañía de Jesús,** just south of the museum. This church was Don Vasco's cathedral before the basilica; afterward, it was given to the Jesuits. The buildings across the street from the church were once part of the complex, containing the hospital, soup kitchen, and living quarters for religious scholars.

The **Casa de los Once Patios (House of Eleven Patios) ★**, between José María Cos and Enseñanza, is another fine achievement of the colonial period. Formerly a convent belonging to the Catherine nuns, today it houses the **Casa de las Artesanías de Michoacán,** with every type of local artistry for sale (see "Shopping," below).

Shopping

Pátzcuaro is one of Mexico's best shopping towns: It has terrific textiles, copper, woodcarvings, lacquerwork, and straw weavings made in the region. Most shops are on the **Plaza Grande** and the streets leading from it to the **Plaza Chica,** the place of choice for copper vendors. There are also a couple of shops on the street facing the basilica. If you're interested in investigating a particular craft, you can find out which village or villages specialize in it, and whether the villages have shops or a market. Tzintzuntzan, Ihuatzio, Cuanajo, Tupátaro, and Santa Clara del Cobre all have shops (see "Side Trips from Pátzcuaro," below).

Casa de las Artesanías de Michoacán/Casa de los Once Patios   This is the best one-stop shopping in the village. Small shops sell textile arts, pottery, and ceramic dishes, lacquerwork, paintings, woodcarvings, jewelry, copper work, and musical instruments (including the famous Paracho guitars). Much of the merchandise was produced in the region. Most shops are open daily from 9am to 2pm and 4 to 6pm. Calle Madrigal de las Altas Torres, btw. Dr. Coss and Lerín. No phone.

Friday Pottery Market 🏪   Early each Friday morning this plaza, 1 block west of the Plaza Grande, fills with vendors of various styles of regionally made pottery, typical for dishes intended for domestic use. There's also a lot of cheap commercially made stuff. This is a market for locals; few tourists seem to hear about it. Prices are low, but you have to really hunt for quality merchandise. Plaza San Francisco, Ponce de León at Federico Teña. No phone.

Galería del Arcángel   Across from the Museo Regional, this store ("the Archangel's Gallery") offers a fine collection of quality regional pottery and hand-carved furniture, plus some of the best crafts from other parts of Mexico. It's open daily from 9:30am to 7pm. Arciga 30. ©/fax **434/342-1774.**

Mantas Típicas ✦   A factory outlet for the company's textile mill, this is one of several textile outlets on the Plaza Grande. Colorful foot-loomed tablecloths, napkins, bedspreads, and bolts of fabric cover the shelves. There's another outlet in the Casa de los Once Patios. It's open daily from 9am to 7pm. Dr. Coss 5. © **434/342-1324.**

Market Plaza   The House of Eleven Patios (see above) should be your first stop, and this your second. The entire plaza fronting the food market holds covered stalls selling crafts, clothing, rugs, *rebozos*, and more. Locally knitted sweaters are a good buy. Streets surrounding the plaza churn with exuberant sellers of fresh vegetables and caged birds. West of Plaza Chica. No phone.

Palacio Huitziméngari   On the north side of the Plaza Grande, in a colonial house, are a few shops run by folk from neighboring towns. Most of the merchandise is pottery and woodcarvings. Open daily from 8am to 10pm. Plaza Grande. No phone.

Telares García Gallardo   This store, on the south side of the Plaza Grande, has a wide selection of wool weavings, including area rugs, throw rugs, and *gabanes* (much like a poncho, heavier than a *serape*). It's open daily from 10am to 7pm. Plaza Vasco de Quiroga 62. ✆ **434/342-6620.**

Where to Stay

In choosing properties, I generally went with those that best reflected in some way the character of the town. Most of these are small properties; a good choice among the large hotels is **La Parroquia,** Plaza Bocanegra 24 (✆ **434/342-2515**). Another option would be to stay in **Casa Santiago,** a small B&B in Ihuatzio, one of the lakeside villages (discussed later). Rates include 18% tax.

EXPENSIVE

Hacienda Mariposas ★★★ ☺   This hotel is a retreat into the Mexican countryside, just outside Pátzcuaro. Located on 5 hectares (12 acres) of forested land above town, the hotel consists of separate or semidetached bungalows. The rooms are big, and the bathrooms are spacious and well equipped. Master suites come with Jacuzzi tubs. Emphasis is on personal attention and ecological practices. The hotel has plenty of educational activities for kids, such as egg collecting and other farm activities, hiking, and pony riding. The entire hotel is smoke-free. Breakfasts feature healthy versions of regional specialties, and there is a separate dining area with a low-fat menu. This is the first hotel in Mexico to be certified as ecological by the Mexican government. Service is attentive, and the spa is a big plus.

Carretera Pátzcuaro–Santa Clara Km 3, 61600 Pátzcuaro, Mich. www.haciendamariposas.com. ✆ **434/342-4728.** 25 units. 1,180 pesos suite; 1,770 pesos junior suite; 2,360 master suite. Rates include full breakfast, horseback rides, spa, and afternoon *antojitos*. AE, MC, V. Free secure parking. **Amenities:** Restaurant; bar; babysitting; children's activities; Jacuzzi; room service; smoke-free rooms; spa; steam room; Wi-Fi. *In room:* CD player and music library, hair dryer, minibar w/organic snacks.

Hotel Mansión Iturbe Bed and Breakfast ★★   Located on the north side of the Plaza Grande, this 17th-century mansion has kept more of its original character than any of the other colonial buildings–turned–hotels. The owners have worked hard to keep the old local touches, such as raised thresholds. Rooms are on the second floor and have the original plank flooring, along with heavy, dark, Spanish-style wooden furniture and fresh-cut flowers. Exterior rooms have double-glazed windows to keep the noise down. Most bathrooms are large. All rooms are smoke-free. The free cocktail hour every night allows guests to make acquaintances and share experiences. Guests have the use of a solarium, a library, and a study. The restaurant, **Doña Paca** (p. 238), and cafe/club, **Viejo Gaucho** (p. 239), are two of this hotel's key amenities.

Portal Morelos 59, 61600 Pátzcuaro, Mich. www.mansioniturbe.com. ✆ **434/342-0368,** -3628. Fax (for reservations only) 434/342-3627. 14 units. 900–1500 pesos double. Rates include full breakfast. Ask about special promotions. AE, MC, V. Free secure parking. **Amenities:** 2 restaurants; 2 bars; smoke-free rooms. *In room:* TV, hair dryer, Wi-Fi.

Hotel Posada la Basílica ★   This colonial-style hotel in a great location across from the basilica has a lovely patio. The rooms, which border the patio on three sides, have tile floors and fireplaces. Seven have small balconies overlooking the street. The restaurant has a fabulous view of the mountains, the tile rooftops, and the lake. Rooms come with one or two double beds.

Arciga 6 (at La Paz), 61600 Pátzcuaro, Mich. www.posadalabasilica.com. 📞 434/342-1108. Fax 434/342-0659. 12 units. 1,500 pesos double; 2,200 pesos suite. AE, MC, V. Free secure parking. **Amenities:** Restaurant; bar; babysitting; room service; Wi-Fi (in common areas). *In room:* TV, hair dryer.

Villa Victoria ★   This small B&B is located in a traditional Pátzcuaro house about 2 blocks from Plaza Grande. The rooms are beautifully decorated with warm colors and local handicrafts. All have fireplaces and heated floors in the bathrooms. Most have a queen-size bed. There's plenty of outdoor space and a beautiful garden. The Canadian owners are in Pátzcuaro for only part of the year.

Navarrete 45, 61600 Pátzcuaro, Mich. www.villavictoriapatzcuaro.com. 📞 434/342-5237. 6 units. $125 double. 2-night minimum stay. No walk-ins. Rates include full breakfast. AE, MC, V (for deposits only); cash only for balance. Street parking. **Amenities:** Babysitting; smoke-free rooms. *In room:* TV, hair dryer, Wi-Fi.

MODERATE

Mesón de San Antonio ★   Retired agronomist Alfredo del Rio Mora runs this small B&B, which retains the feel of a country house in its informality and simple adornment. Nothing cutesy or clichéd is to be found here. The rooms are large and comfortable, and have lots of character, including working fireplaces. The bathrooms are large, too, and well finished.

Serrato 33, 61600 Pátzcuaro, Mich. www.mesondesanantonio.com. 📞/fax 434/342-2501. 7 units. 770–830 pesos double. Rates include continental breakfast. No credit cards. Off-site parking 30 pesos. **Amenities:** Smoke-free rooms. *In room:* TV, no phone, Wi-Fi (in some).

INEXPENSIVE

Posada de la Salud 🦋   This *posada* (inn) offers two floors of quiet, basic rooms built around an attractive courtyard. Rooms are clean and have simple wooden furniture. Two units have fireplaces. Rooms have one double bed, two double beds, two twins, or one twin and one double (the higher price listed below is for two doubles). The location is great—near the basilica, to the right, a half-block down.

Serrato 9, 61600 Pátzcuaro, Mich. www.posadadelasalud.com.mx. 📞 434/342-0058. 12 units. 380–550 pesos double. No credit cards. Limited street parking. *In room:* No phone.

Where to Eat

Restaurants here are okay but not great. I usually try to get by on simple local fare. In the evenings at the Plaza Chica, you can get a meal of chicken with simple enchiladas and heaps of fried potatoes and carrots. Look for a stand called **Don Emilio.** You can also get *buñuelos*, giant cornflakes that drip with cane syrup.

Tip: In the same market area, you can sometimes find good tamales. But if you want tamales in a relaxing setting, have them for breakfast at the restaurant of the **Gran Hotel,** Plaza Bocanegra 6-B (✆ **434/345-0659**), under the arches on the south side of the Plaza Chica. As a rule in Mexico, you don't find fresh tamales in restaurants, but this place is the exception. The other breakfast items, mostly *antojitos*, are good, too.

Another place to eat well and for little money is at a little *fonda* called **Mamá Lupe** (no phone). It serves food in a small patio off Calle Benito Mendoza. Look for a doorway opposite the Bancomer bank offices. It opens around 9am and closes around 6:30pm. In the early afternoon, it offers a good *comida corrida* with three courses and a drink for around 50 pesos.

El Patio MEXICAN/REGIONAL   High ceilings, good lighting, and paintings of local scenes make this a pleasant place to dine. Specialties include *sopa tarasca, trucha salmonada al vino blanco* (farm-raised trout that are fed achiote to give the flesh a salmon color). Standard Mexican dishes include *arrachera a la tampiqueña* (skirt steak with various sides) and more. El Patio is on the south side of Plaza Grande.

Plaza Grande 19. ✆ **434/342-0484.** Breakfast 45-70 pesos; main courses 80-110 pesos. MC, V. Daily 8am-10pm.

El Primer Piso MEXICAN/INTERNATIONAL   El Primer Piso, which means "the first floor" (second floor in American usage), offers a bit of everything but focuses mostly on dishes of its own creation: *pechuga enogada* (chicken breast in walnut cream sauce) with cashews, for instance, and *pescado en salsa negra* (fish in a three-chile vinaigrette). These are good, as are the appetizers. The soups are more conventional—Tarascan, French onion, and Provençal. The restaurant is on the same block as El Patio. Service can be slow.

Vasco de Quiroga 29. ✆ **434/342-0122.** Main courses 115-144 pesos. AE, MC, V. Mon and Wed-Sat 1-10pm; Sun 1-8pm.

Mistongo MEXICAN/INTERNATIONAL   Simple and gracious surroundings reflect the taste of the owner, Susana, an Argentine who was trained formally as an architect but whose heart was always more inclined toward entertaining and cooking. You can enjoy various salads here, Argentine empanadas, grilled fajitas, even Mexican specialties such as chiles rellenos. The menu is simple, and most everything is very fresh. Occasionally, there are performances in the evening.

Dr. Coss 4. ✆ **434/342-6450.** Reservations recommended during holidays. Main courses 100-175 pesos. MC, V. Tues-Sun 1-10:30pm.

Restaurant Doña Paca ★ MICHOACAN   This is a good place to try regional Michoacán cuisine. It serves fish in several ways, including in cilantro sauce, *al mojo de ajo* (this is the most popular way of eating fish in Mexico—it's griddled with tiny toasted bits of garlic), or cooked in herbs. The restaurant also serves a fixed-price menu, which includes a glass of wine. The dining room is comfortable and welcoming. In the afternoon, you can order at the tables outside under the archway.

In the Hotel Mansión Iturbe (p. 236), Portal Morelos 59. ✆ **434/342-3628.** Breakfast 70-110 pesos; main courses 95-140 pesos. AE, MC, V. Daily 8:30-10:30am and 1-8pm. Closed Sun night during low season.

Pátzcuaro After Dark

Pátzcuaro generally closes down before 10pm, so bring a good book or plan to rest up. Late-night-music lovers can go to **Viejo Gaucho** to hear Latin American folk music. The small restaurant serves salads and hamburgers. It's in the Hotel Mansión Iturbe (✆ **434/342-3627;** p. 236); enter from Calle Iturbe. It's open Wednesday through Saturday from 6pm to midnight. Music starts between 8:30 and 9pm.

Side Trips from Pátzcuaro

EL ESTRIBO: A SCENIC OVERLOOK For a good view of the town and the lake, head for the lookout at El Estribo, on the hill 3km (1¼ miles) west of town. Driving from the main square on Calle Ponce de León and following the signs takes 10 to 15 minutes on an unpaved road. Walking up the steep hill will take about 45 minutes. Once you reach the gazebo, you can climb more than 400 steps to the summit of the hill. The gazebo area is great for a picnic; there are barbecue pits and sometimes a couple selling soft drinks and beer.

JANITZIO No visit to Pátzcuaro would be complete without a trip on the lake to one or more of the islands. A hilltop statue of José María Morelos dominates the island of **Janitzio ★★**. The village church is famous for the annual **Day of the Dead** ceremony, held at midnight on November 1. Villagers climb to the churchyard carrying lit candles in memory of their dead relatives and then spend the night in graveside vigil. The long day begins October 30 and lasts through November 2.

The cheapest way to get to Janitzio is by *colectivo* launch, which makes the trip when enough people have gathered to go, about every 20 to 30 minutes from about 7:30am to 6pm. It's best to go during the week when fewer travelers are around. Round-trip fare is 55 pesos; children 4 and younger ride free. A private boat costs around 850 pesos for a trip to Janitzio for 1 hour and then a cruise by the other three islands. Sometimes the cooperative has launches available that are significantly cheaper. The **ticket office** on the pier, or *embarcadero* (✆ **434/342-0681**), is open daily from 8am to 6pm. The pier is 1km (about ⅔ mile) from the main square, and the 5-minute taxi ride costs 30 pesos. At the ticket office, a map of the lake posted on the wall details boat trips to various islands and lakeshore towns. Launches will take you wherever you want to go. Up to 20 people can split the cost.

TZINTZUNTZAN: RUINS & HANDICRAFTS Tzintzuntzan (Tzeen-*tzoon*-tzahn) is an ancient village 15km (9¼ miles) from Pátzcuaro on the road to Quiroga (see "By Bus," under "Getting There & Departing," earlier in this section). In earlier centuries, Tzintzuntzan was the capital of the Purépechan kingdom (a confederation of more than 100 towns and villages). On a hill on the right before you enter town, pyramids, called *yácatas,* remind visitors of the town's past. The village is known for its pottery and woven goods. Several open-air **woodcarving workshops,** full of life-size wooden saints and other figures, are across from the basket market.

There is also an interesting church and former convent that dates from the time of Don Vasco. Parts of the convent have been restored, and there are plans to restore the rest. To get to it you will walk through a wide *atrio* (enclosed area in front of a church) populated by ancient, gnarled olive trees brought from Spain more than 400 years ago. The Franciscan convent is austere, but with a few surprising details, such as the ruins of an intricate ceiling of Moorish design, and building stones etched with non-Christian symbols, which obviously must have been taken from native constructions. The short tour costs 15 pesos and is led by one of the community's members charged with preserving the convent. None of the guides speak English.

LAKESIDE VILLAGES: A PORTRAIT OF INDIAN LIFE For a close-up view of the Purépecha, contact **Kevin Quigley** and **Arminda Flores,** who live in Ihuatzio (see below for contact info). Arminda is Purépecha and can explain much of what you'll see and hear when visiting the villages in the area. Another good guide is **Miguel Angel Nuñez** (© 434/344-0108; casadetierra@hotmail.com). He's a Mexican anthropologist who has lived in the area for years.

SANTA CLARA DEL COBRE: COPPER SMITHERY About 30 minutes away by car, **Santa Clara del Cobre** ★ is a good side trip if you want to purchase copper items or see how copper is worked. Although the copper mines of preconquest times have disappeared, local artisans still make copper vessels using the age-old method of hammering pieces out by hand. They don't work on Sunday and are strict observers of "San Lunes"—taking Monday off to recover from the weekend. On other days, the sound of hammering fills the air. If you want to see someone practicing the craft, go to one of the larger stores and ask if you can visit the *taller* (studio). You can also visit the **Museo del Cobre (Copper Museum),** a half-block from the main plaza at Morelos and Pino Suárez. The museum section of the building displays copper pieces that date to pre-Columbian times. A sales showroom to the left of the entrance features the work of local craftsmen. Admission is 10 pesos. The museum is open Tuesday through Sunday from 10:30am to 3pm and 5 to 7pm.

The **National Copper Fair** is held here each August. It coincides with the **Festival de Nuestra Señora de Santa Clara de Asis** (second week in Aug), with folk dancing and parades. For information, call the tourism office in Morelia.

Buses for Santa Clara leave every few minutes from the Pátzcuaro bus station. If you want to spend the night in town, see "If Pátzcuaro's Packed Solid . . ." on p. 237.

TUPÁTARO & CUANAJO: A HISTORIC CHURCH & HAND-CARVED FURNITURE Just off Hwy. 120 between Morelia and Pátzcuaro is the village of **Tupátaro** (pop. 600), which in Tarascan means "place of reeds."

The village church is the **Templo del Señor Santiago Tupátaro.** It was built in 1775. Indian artists painted the entire wood-plank ceiling with scenes of the life and death of Christ and the Virgin Mary. The gilt *retablo* (altarpiece) is adorned with Solomonic columns and paintings. Santiago (St. James) is in the center of the *retablo,* and the face of the Eternal Father is above him. The symbol of the dove crowns the *retablo.* The church and its ceiling were restored in 1994 by the National Institute of Anthropology and History, which oversees its maintenance. There's no admission charge, and photography is not permitted. The church is open daily from 8am to 5pm. Days of religious significance include the Tuesday of Carnaval week and July 25, which honors Santiago. From Tupátaro, you can get back on Hwy. 120 or take a small road that leads to Cuanajo 8km (5 miles) away. From Cuanajo, a small road leads directly to Pátzcuaro; it's not designated yet by any number.

Cuanajo (pop. 8,000) is a village of woodcarvers who make brightly painted pine furniture. On the road as you enter, and around the pleasant, tree-shaded main plaza, you'll see storefronts with **colorful furniture** inside and on the street. Parrots, plants, the sun, the moon, and faces are carved on the furniture. Furniture is also sold at a **cooperative** on the main plaza. Here you'll also find soft-spoken women who weave tapestries and thin belts on waist looms. Everything is for sale. It's open daily from 9am to 6pm. Festival days in Cuanajo include March 8 and September 8, both of which honor their patron saint, La Virgen María de la Natividad.

IHUATZIO: TULE FIGURES & PRE-HISPANIC ARCHITECTURE This little lakeside village is known for its **weavers of tule figures**—fanciful animals such as elephants, pigs, and bulls, made from a reed that grows on the edge of the lake—and for some pre-Columbian ruins nearby. Kevin Quigley, an American, and Arminda Flores, a Purépechan (✆ **434/344-0880;** www.casasantiagomex.com), rent comfortable rooms to guests at economical rates. Both Kevin and Arminda take people around the area, explaining the local culture, the society, and the local crafts (and Arminda is a good cook). The turnoff to Ihuatzio is a paved road a short distance from the outskirts of Pátzcuaro on the road to Tzintzuntzan.

URUAPAN: HANDICRAFTS & VOLCANOES

61km (38 miles) SW of Pátzcuaro; 105km (65 miles) SW of Morelia

Uruapan has long been a commercial center for western Michoacán. It's a larger, busier town than Pátzcuaro; it's not very pretty, but it's set in some beautiful country. This is a rich agricultural area—the avocado capital of Mexico. Coffee and pistachios are also popular cash crops. Uruapan is useful as a base for some interesting side trips, the most famous of which is to **El Paricutín volcano** and the lava-covered church and village near **Angahuan.** See "Angahuan & El Paricutín Volcano," below.

Essentials

From Morelia, take the modern toll road Autopista Morelia Uruapan. Officially, the road is **Hwy. 14D** or **120** (the same road that heads to Pátzcuaro) but you won't find that on many maps. Buses leave every half-hour from either Terminal A or B of Morelia's bus station (first or second class). Driving will take 1½ hours, and the first-class bus takes a little less than 2 hours.

The **tourist office** (✆ **452/524-0667**) is at Emilio Carranza 20. It's open Monday through Saturday from 9am to 2pm.

The main plaza, **Jardín Morelos/Plaza de los Mártires,** is a long, narrow rectangle running east to west, with the churches and La Huatápera Museum on the north side and a few hotels on the south.

Exploring Uruapan & Beyond

Uruapan's main plaza fills with artisans and craft sellers from around the state before and during **Easter week.** Vendors sell an unbelievable array of wares.

La Huatápera ★, attached to the church on the main square, is a good museum of regional crafts. It occupies a former hospital built in 1533 by Fray Juan de San Miguel, a Franciscan. It's open daily from 10am to 2pm and 4 to 6pm. Admission is free.

For the finest in woven, brilliantly colored tablecloths, bedspreads, and other **textiles,** pay a visit to **Telares Uruapan ★★★** (✆ **452/524-0677,** or -6135), in the **Antigua Fábrica San Pedro,** Calle Miguel Treviño s/n. The old factory makes for an interesting visit, and the colorful fabrics are quite popular. The owners, Bundy and Walter Illsley, came to Mexico in the early '50s and started up a number of rural development projects before deciding to go into the weaving business. In my travels, I come across their distinctive fabrics a lot in establishments across central Mexico. Hours are Monday through Saturday 10am to 7pm.

When you enter the **Parque Nacional Eduardo Ruiz,** a botanical garden 8 blocks west of the main plaza, you'll feel as if you're deep in the Tropics. This semi-tropical paradise contains jungle paths, deep ravines, rushing water, and clear water-falls. The garden is open daily from 8am to 6pm, and there is a small admission fee.

A WATERFALL OUTSIDE URUAPAN

Eight kilometers (5 miles) outside of town is the **Tzaráracua** waterfall. The falls are pretty but not spectacular, and sometimes they smell bad. The real reason to come here is for the walk—a descent that takes you from cool pine forest to warm subtropi-cal vegetation in no time. The return ascent takes 40 minutes, and the trail is good, with handrails in the steeper areas. You can catch a bus from Uruapan's bus station or take a cab, which costs only 75 pesos. Either one will drop you off at the trail head.

ANGAHUAN & EL PARICUTÍN VOLCANO ★★

About 34km (21 miles) from Uruapan is **Angahuan,** a village serving as the point of departure for trips to **El Paricutín volcano.** A taxi costs 200 pesos. The volcano was born in 1943 and grew quickly, eventually enveloping portions of a village in lava. In February 1943, a local man was plowing his cornfield in the valley when the ground began to boil and fissures opened up, emitting steam. At first he tried to plug it up; when that proved impossible, he fled. By that evening, the earth was spitting fire and smoke. Some villagers fled that night; others, days later. The volcano remained active and continued to grow. This was not a violent eruption, but an almost constant belch-ing forth of ash and lava until March 1952, when it ceased as suddenly as it had begun.

USING A GUIDE   Angahuan has a little tourist center that rents cabins and runs a small cafeteria (ⓒ **452/520-8786**). It affords a good view of the volcano and the tower of the **Church of San Juan Parangaricutiro,** which is half-buried in lava. It takes 2½ hours to get to the volcano, because you have to take a roundabout path to get there. The best way to go is with a horse and a guide. A horse costs 200 pesos. A guide costs the same. All the guides are villagers of Angahuan. Some speak English; some don't. But it doesn't make much of a difference; they're mostly there to lead the way, which is circuitous. Many visitors elect to go only as far as the church; it takes 45 minutes one-way, and you don't need a horse.

CLIMBING THE VOLCANO   Allow at least 7 hours from Angahuan. The route to the foot of the volcano makes a big loop around a lava field, before approaching the cone along a "sandy" wash (the texture only seems sandy; it's actually black volcanic cinder). The approach is mostly flat, with some rises toward the end. The only way to climb the crater is on foot; the trek is exhilarating but exhausting because of the footing. It's like climbing a giant pile of loose rock; for every step up, you slide back down a few inches. On the way to the top, you pass by a fumarole. The day I was there, it rained briefly as we were approaching the volcano, which is common (all guides carry rain ponchos for their customers). By the time we got to the fumarole, steam was rising from all the crevasses in the rock. The scene, so barren and vapor-ous, looked primeval. At the top of the cone, the view of the surrounding mountains is splendid, and you can clearly make out the lines of the lava flows on the floor of the valley.

Uruapan

Where to Stay & Eat

The best hotel in town is **Hotel Cupatitzio** (✆ **452/523-2022;** 1,000 pesos double), next to the national park. Its amenities, include a large pool and garden. On the main square, the best option is **Hotel Plaza Uruapan** (www.hotelplazauruapan.com.mx; ✆ **452/523-3599**). Two inexpensive options are the **Hotel Villa de Flores,** Emiliano Carranza 15 (✆ **452/524-2800**), and the slightly less desirable but slightly cheaper **Hotel Nuevo Alameda,** Av. 5 de Febrero 11 (✆ **452/523-3635**). Rooms go for 500 pesos in the former and about 400 pesos in the latter.

The restaurant at the Hotel Plaza is good. Another popular place to eat is **Café Tradicional** (✆ **452/523-5680**), just off the plaza, at Carranza 5-B.

7

MICHOACÁN | Uruapan: Handicrafts & Volcanoes

Uruapan

7

MICHOACÁN | Uruapan: Handicrafts & Volcanoes

Where to Stay & Eat

The best hotel in town is **Hotel Cupatitzio** (✆ **452/523-2022;** 1,000 pesos double), next to the national park. Its amenities, include a large pool and garden. On the main square, the best option is **Hotel Plaza Uruapan** (www.hotelplazauruapan.com.mx; ✆ **452/523-3599**). Two inexpensive options are the **Hotel Villa de Flores,** Emiliano Carranza 15 (✆ **452/524-2800**), and the slightly less desirable but slightly cheaper **Hotel Nuevo Alameda,** Av. 5 de Febrero 11 (✆ **452/523-3635**). Rooms go for 500 pesos in the former and about 400 pesos in the latter.

The restaurant at the Hotel Plaza is good. Another popular place to eat is **Café Tradicional** (✆ **452/523-5680**), just off the plaza, at Carranza 5-B.

243

GUADALAJARA

by David Baird

Guadalajara has two great qualities that appeal to many travelers: a strong Mexican identity, and a big city with big-city pleasures. People who are fond of Mexico and enjoy exploring a different urban scene will love it. One of my favorite things about the city is the ease with which you can move around. Taxis are reasonably priced and numerous; you rarely have to wait more than a minute or two to find one. It takes the fuss out of navigating a big city on your own, and obviates the need to figure out bus routes. Just grab a cab and go.

Guadalajara is a lively town with friendly locals, great food, and lots of options for entertainment. And much of what you'll find here is so very Mexican. Guadalajara is the center of mariachi culture, and, being in the tequila-producing region of Mexico, it's the center of tequila culture as well. The other things that one comes to Mexico to see are present too—colonial architecture, native craft cultures, and shopping galore. Guadalajara really has it all.

It is the second-largest city in the country, with about five million inhabitants. Its altitude (1,590m/5,200 ft.) lends it a mild climate for most of the year. It's a mildly conservative, very Catholic city, quite distinct from Mexico City. And the pace of life here is more relaxed. It's often called the biggest small town in Mexico.

While in Guadalajara, you will undoubtedly come across the word *tapatío* (or *tapatía*). In colonial times, people from the area customarily traded goods in threes, called *tapatíos*. From this practice, the locals came to be called Tapatíos as well; now *tapatío* has come to mean any person, thing, or style that comes from Guadalajara.

ORIENTATION
Getting There & Departing

BY PLANE   Guadalajara's airport (GDL) is a half-hour ride from the city. Taxi tickets, priced by zone, are for sale in front of the airport (235 pesos to downtown).

See "Airline Websites" in chapter 20 for a list of websites for international airlines serving Mexico. Major airlines serving Guadalajara are **AeroMar** (© 01-800/237-6627 in Mexico), **Aeroméxico** (© 800/237-6639 in the U.S., 01-800/021-4000 in Mexico), **Alaska** (© 800/252-7522 in the U.S., 01-800/252-7522 in Mexico), **American** (© 800/433-7300 in the U.S., 01-800/904-6000 in Mexico), **Continental** (© 800/523-3273 in

In the summer of 2010, Mexican soldiers and police cornered one of Mexico's major drug figures, Ignacio Coronel, in a residential zone of Zapopan, a suburb of Guadalajara. He died in the ensuing shootout. This seemed to raise tensions in the city, and in the following month there were some shootings and attacks on the police. Then, on February 2, 2011, the police arrested two leaders of a local gang called La Resistencia. The following day, members of this gang retaliated by coordinating seven attacks in different parts of the city in a 2-hour span. The attackers used grenades, firearms, and incendiary devices, killing two people and wounding several others. A couple attacks were loosely targeted, but mostly this was a show of force meant to create mayhem in the city. A couple of weeks later there was a grenade attack on a local nightclub that killed six people. These attacks have again raised tensions in Guadalajara, but they're probably isolated, and things will return to normal. Still, before you travel to the city, check the news for more developments, and the U.S. Department of State travel page (www.travel.state.gov) to find out if there are any specific travel warnings for the city.

the U.S., or 01-800/900-5000 in Mexico), **Delta** (© 800/241-4141 in the U.S., 01-800/123-4710 in Mexico, or 33/3630-3530), and **United** (© 800/538-2929 in the U.S., 01-800/003-0777 in Mexico, or 33/3616-9489).

Of the smaller airlines, **Azteca** (© 33/3630-4615) offers service to and from Mexico City, and from there to several cities in Mexico. **Allegro** (© 33/3647-7799) operates flights to and from Oakland and Las Vegas via Tijuana.

BY CAR   Guadalajara is at the hub of several four-lane toll roads (called *cuotas* or *autopistas*), which cut travel time considerably but are expensive. From Nogales on the **U.S. border,** follow Hwy. 15 south (21 hr.). From **Tepic,** a quicker route is toll road 15D (5 hr.; 320 pesos). From **Puerto Vallarta,** go north on Hwy. 200 to Compostela; toll road 68D heads east to join the Tepic toll road. Total time is 5½ hours, and the tolls add up to 300 pesos. From **Barra de Navidad,** on the coast southeast of Puerto Vallarta, take Hwy. 80 northeast (4½ hr.). From **Manzanillo,** you might also take this road, but toll road 54D through Colima to Guadalajara (3½ hr.; 260 pesos) is faster. From **Mexico City,** take toll road 15D (7 hr.; 550 pesos).

BY BUS   Two bus stations serve Guadalajara. The old one, south of downtown, is for buses to Tequila and other nearby towns; the new one, 10km (6¼ miles) southeast of downtown, is for longer trips.

The Old Bus Station   For destinations within 100km (62 miles) of town, including the Lake Chapala area, go to the old bus terminal, on Niños Héroes off Calzada Independencia Sur. For Lake Chapala, take **Transportes Guadalajara-Chapala,** which runs frequent buses and *combis* (minivans).

The New Bus Station   The **Central Camionera** is 20 to 30 minutes from downtown (125 pesos by taxi). The station has seven terminals connected by a covered walkway. Each terminal houses bus lines, offering first- and second-class service for different destinations. Buy bus tickets ahead of time from a travel agency in Guadalajara. Ask at your hotel for the closest to you. There are several major bus lines. The best service (big seats and lots of room) is provided by **ETN.**

Visitor Information

The **State of Jalisco Tourist Information Office** is at Calle Morelos 102 (*C* **33/3668-1600,** or -1601; http://visita.jalisco.gob.mx) in the Plaza Tapatía, at Paseo Degollado and Paraje del Rincón del Diablo. It's open Monday through Friday from 9am to 7pm, and Saturday 10am to 2pm. You can get maps, a monthly calendar of cultural events, and good information. Of the **city tourist information booths,** one is in Plaza Liberación (directly behind the cathedral), and another is in Plaza Guadalajara (directly in front of the cathedral). These are open daily from 9am to 1pm and 3 to 7pm. Ask at either of these about free weekend walking tours.

City Layout

The **Centro Histórico (city center),** with all its plazas, churches, and museums, will obviously be of interest to the visitor. The **west side** is Guadalajara's modern, cosmopolitan district. In the northwest corner is **Zapopan,** home of Guadalajara's patron saint. On the opposite side of the city from Zapopan, in the southeast corner, are the craft centers of **Tlaquepaque** and **Tonalá.**

The main artery for traffic from downtown to the west side is **Avenida Vallarta.** It starts downtown as **Juárez.** The main arteries for returning to downtown are **México** and **Hidalgo,** both north of Vallarta. Vallarta heads due west, where it intersects another major artery, **Avenida Adolfo López Mateos,** at **Fuente Minerva** (or simply La Minerva, or Minerva Circle). Minerva Circle, a 15-minute drive from downtown, is the central point of reference for the west side. To go to Zapopan from downtown, take **Avenida Avila Camacho,** which you can pick up on Alcalde; it takes 20 minutes by car. To Tlaquepaque and Tonalá, take **Calzada Revolución.** Tlaquepaque is 8km (5 miles) from downtown and takes 15 to 20 minutes by car; Tonalá is 5 minutes farther. Another major viaduct, **Calzada Lázaro Cárdenas,** connects the west side to Tlaquepaque and Tonalá, bypassing downtown.

The Neighborhoods in Brief

Centro Histórico The heart of the city encompasses many plazas, the cathedral, and several historic buildings and museums. Here, too, are the striking murals of José Clemente Orozco, one of the great Mexican muralists. Theaters, restaurants, shops, and clubs dot the area, and an enormous market rounds out the attractions. All of this is in a space roughly 12 blocks by 12 blocks—an easy area to explore on foot, with several plazas and pedestrian-only areas. To the south is a large green space called Parque Agua Azul.

West Side This is the swanky part of town, with the fine restaurants, luxury hotels, boutiques, and galleries, as well as the American, British, and Canadian consulates. It's a large area best navigated by taxi.

Zapopan Founded in 1542, Zapopan is a suburb of Guadalajara. In its center is the

18th-century basilica, the home of Guadalajara's patron saint, the Virgin of Zapopan. The most interesting part of Zapopan is clustered around the temple and can be explored on foot. It has a growing arts and nightlife scene.

Tlaquepaque This is another suburb that for centuries was a village of artisans (especially potters). It grew into a market center, and in the last 40 years, has attracted designers and artists from across Mexico. Every major form of art and craft is for sale here: furniture, pottery, glass, jewelry, woodcarvings, leather goods, sculptures, and paintings. The shops are sophisticated, yet Tlaquepaque's center retains a small-town feel that makes door-to-door browsing enjoyable and relaxing.

Tonalá This has remained a town of artisans. Plenty of stores sell mostly local products from the town's more than 400 workshops. You'll see wrought iron, ceramics, blown glass, and papier-mâché. A busy street market operates each Thursday and Sunday.

GETTING AROUND

BY TAXI Taxis are the easiest way to get around town. They are quite plentiful. Most have meters, and though some drivers are reluctant to use them, you can insist that they do. There are three rates: for day, night, and suburbia. Typical fares include the following: downtown to the far west side, 70 to 90 pesos; downtown or west side to Tlaquepaque, 70 to 100 pesos; downtown to the new bus station, 90 to 125 pesos; downtown to the airport, 180 to 220 pesos.

BY CAR Familiarize yourself with the main traffic arteries (see "City Layout," above) before you get behind the wheel. Several important freeway-style thoroughfares crisscross the city. **Dr. R. Michel** leads south from the town center toward Tlaquepaque. Use **González Gallo** for the return direction. **Avenida Vallarta** starts out downtown as **Juárez,** heads west past La Minerva, and eventually feeds onto **Hwy. 15,** bound for Tequila and Puerto Vallarta.

BY BUS For the visitor, the handiest route is the **TUR 706,** which runs from the Centro Histórico southeast to Tlaquepaque (10 pesos), the Central Camionera (the new bus station), and Tonalá. You can catch this bus on Avenida 16 de Septiembre. The same bus runs in the reverse direction back to the downtown area.

The **electric bus** is handy for travel between downtown and the Minerva area (5 pesos). It bears the sign PAR VIAL and runs east along Hidalgo and west along the next street to the north, Calle Independencia (not Calzada Independencia). Hidalgo passes along the north side of the cathedral. The Par Vial goes as far east as Mercado Libertad and as far west as Minerva Circle. The city also has a light rail system, **Tren Ligero,** but it doesn't serve areas that are of interest to visitors.

[FastFACTS] GUADALAJARA

Area Code The telephone area code is **33.**

Business Hours Store hours are Monday through Saturday from 10am to 2pm and 4 to 8pm.

Climate & Dress Guadalajara's weather is mostly mild. From November through March, you'll need a sweater in the evening. The warmest months, April and May, are hot and dry. From June through September, the city gets afternoon and evening showers that keep the temperature a bit cooler, but it seems as though the local climate is getting warmer. Dress in Guadalajara is conservative; attention-getting sportswear (short shorts, halters, and the like) is out of place.

Consulates The **American Consular offices** are at Progreso 175 (© **33/3268-2200,** -2100). Other consulates include the **Canadian Consulate,** Mariano Otero 1249, Col. Rinconada del Bosque (© **33/3671-4740**); the **British Consulate,** Calle Jesús Rojas 20, Col. Los Pinos (© **33/3343-2296**); and the **Australian Consulate,** López Cotilla 2018, Col. Arcos Vallarta (© **33/3615-7418**). These offices all keep roughly the same hours: Monday through Friday from 8am to 1pm.

Currency Exchange Three blocks south of the cathedral, on López Cotilla, between Corona and Degollado, are more than 20 *casas de cambio.* Almost all post their rates, which are usually better than bank rates, minus the long lines.

Elevation Guadalajara sits at 1,700m (5,576 ft.).

Emergencies The emergency phone number is © **060.**

Hospitals For medical emergencies, visit the **Hospital México-Americano,** Cólomos 2110 (© **33/3642-7152** or 33/3641-3141).

Internet Access Most of the big hotels have business centers that you can use. There are many Internet cafes in the Centro Histórico.

Newspapers & Magazines Many newsstands sell the two English local papers, the *Guadalajara Reporter* and the *Guadalajara Weekly.*

Police Tourists should first try to contact the Jalisco tourist information office in Plaza Tapatía (© **33/3668-1600**). If you can't reach the office, call the municipal police at © **33/3668-7983.**

Post Office The *correo* is at the corner of Carranza and Calle Independencia, about 4 blocks northeast of the cathedral. Standing in the plaza behind the cathedral, facing the Degollado Theater, walk to the left, and then turn left on Carranza; walk past the Hotel Mendoza, cross Calle Independencia, and look for the post office on the left. It's open Monday through Thursday from 9am to 5pm, Saturday from 10am to 2pm.

Safety Crimes against tourists and foreign students are infrequent and most often take the form of purse snatching. Criminals usually work in teams and target travelers in busy places, such as outdoor restaurants. Keep jewelry out of sight. Should anyone spill something on you, be alert to your surroundings and step away—accidental spills are a common method for distracting the victim.

WHERE TO STAY

Big hotels are apt to offer business discounts, especially if there's no convention in town. Guadalajara's hotels thrive on convention business. Most of the luxury hotels in Guadalajara are on the west side, which has the majority of the shopping malls, boutiques, fashionable restaurants, clubs, and the Expo (convention center). The Centro Histórico is also a good option because there's a lot to do, all in walking distance. And Tlaquepaque is a comfortable place to stay—it's relaxing and is perfect for shoppers; the only drawback is that almost everything shuts down by 7 or 8pm. The rates below are the standard rack rates and include the 19% tax.

Chain hotels not included below are Hilton, Marriott, Camino Real, Howard Johnson, Crowne Plaza, and Best Western. In some of the cheaper, older large hotels, air-conditioning can be a bit feeble.

Very Expensive

Hotel Presidente InterContinental ★★★ This hotel offers the most comprehensive services and amenities in Guadalajara. The health club is a standout. Guest rooms are sharply designed and well appointed, with up-to-date appliances, bathroom fixtures, carpeting, furniture, and lighting. Standard rooms come as "superior" or "deluxe." Superior rooms cost only a little more and have a better view and one or two small improvements in amenities. Club rooms have discreet check-in, are on limited-access hallways, and come with extras. The extra privacy and services are good for Mexican soap opera stars or repeat guests who like having their preferences known in advance. If you're neither of these, opt for one of the other rooms. Suites are large and come with oversize bathrooms with extra fixtures. The lobby bar is popular; during the season, you'll see bullfighters relaxing here after *la corrida*.

Av. López Mateos Sur and Moctezuma (west side), 45050 Guadalajara, Jal. www.intercontinental.com. *(C)* **800/327-0200** in the U.S. and Canada, or 33/3678-1234. Fax 33/3678-1222. 423 units. $215–$222 double; $229–$239 feature or club double; $330 and up suite. Promotional rates available. AE, DC, MC, V. Valet parking 55 pesos. **Amenities:** Restaurant; bar; babysitting; concierge; executive-level rooms; golf at nearby clubs; health club w/saunas, steam rooms, and whirlpools; outdoor heated pool; room service; smoke-free rooms; spa. *In room:* A/C, TV, hair dryer, minibar, MP3 docking station, Wi-Fi.

Quinta Real ★★★ This chain specializes in properties that are suggestive of Mexico's heritage. No glass skyscraper here—two five-story buildings made of stone, wood, plaster, and tile capture the feel of Mexican colonial architecture. Suites vary quite a bit: Eight have brick cupolas, and some have balconies. All are large, with a split-level layout and antique decorative touches. And all come with large, great bathrooms with tub/showers. The "grand-class" suites are larger and come with a few extras, such as a stereo and big bathrooms with Jacuzzi tubs. You can choose between two doubles or one king-size bed. The hotel is 2 blocks from Minerva Circle in western Guadalajara. Ask for a room that doesn't face López Mateos.

Av. México 2727 (at López Mateos, west side), 44690 Guadalajara, Jal. www.quintareal.com. *(C)* **866/621-9288** in the U.S. and Canada, or 33/3669-0600. Fax 33/3669-0601. 76 suites. $275–$300 master suite; $325–$350 grand-class suite. AE, DC, MC, V. Free secure parking. **Amenities:** Restaurant; bar; babysitting; concierge; fitness room; outdoor heated pool; room service; smoke-free rooms; discounts at local day spa. *In room:* A/C, TV, hair dryer, minibar, Wi-Fi.

Villa Ganz ★★★ This small hotel offers the most personal service in Guadalajara. You can relax and have just about any service the city offers brought to the hotel. Or the hotel can provide a car and driver to take you where you need to go. Rooms are big, well furnished, and decorated with flair. Bathrooms are large and well lit. Beds come with down comforters (hypoallergenic option available). The hotel occupies a classic old mansion with a garden and patio in the rear. Rooms facing the garden are the quietest, but those facing the street are set back from the traffic and have double-glazed windows. The common rooms and rear garden are agreeable places to relax.

A sister property, Quinta Ganz, offers furnished apartments by the week for about 1,200 pesos per night. These have mostly the same amenities as the hotel and come with a full kitchen and reduced maid service (3 times a week).

López Cotilla 1739 (btw. Bolivar and San Martín, west side), 44140 Guadalajara, Jal. www.villaganz.com. *(C)* **800/728-9098** in the U.S. and Canada, or 33/3120-1416. 10 suites. $248 junior suite; $310 master suite; $345 grand master suite. Rates include continental breakfast. Internet specials often available. AE, MC, V. Free secure parking. Pets accepted with prior notification. Children 11 and younger not accepted. **Amenities:** Bar; concierge; fitness room; golf and tennis at local club; room service. *In room:* A/C, TV, hair dryer, MP3 stereo, Wi-Fi.

Expensive

Holiday Inn Hotel and Suites Centro Histórico ★★ Of the large downtown hotels, this one has the most comfortable rooms. It is conveniently located near the area's most popular restaurants and just a few blocks from the cathedral. Guest rooms are attractive, if blandly modern with a few Mexican accents, and have comfortable mattresses and good light. The size is good, and the furniture is functional and attractive. Bathrooms in standard rooms are midsize and well equipped, with ample counter space. The suites are larger, with a few more amenities. Room rates include transportation to (but not from) the airport.

Av. Juárez 211, Centro Histórico, 44100 Guadalajara. Jal. www.holiday-inn.com. © **800/465-4329** in the U.S. and Canada, 01-800/009-9900 in Mexico, or 33/3560-1200. 90 units. $125–$170 double; $136–$180 suite; $170–$240 suite with Jacuzzi. AE, MC, V. Free secure parking. **Amenities:** Restaurant; bar; ground transportation; fitness room; room service; smoke-free rooms. *In room:* A/C, TV, hair dryer, minibar, Wi-Fi.

Hotel de Mendoza   On a quiet street next to the Degollado Theater and Plaza Tapatía, 2 blocks from the cathedral, the Mendoza has perhaps the best location of any downtown hotel. The decor would best be described as a stab at old Spanish, with wood paneling and old-world accents. Rooms face the street, an interior courtyard, or the pool. Most standard rooms are midsize; though there are a few larger ones that are split level with laminate floors and exterior windows, which go for the same price. Bed choices are one queen, two full, or two queens. Many of the mattresses here are pretty firm. Bathrooms are midsize, with so-so lighting. Junior suites have an additional sitting area and larger bathrooms, with the recent addition of Jacuzzi tubs.

Carranza 16, Centro Histórico, 44100 Guadalajara, Jal. www.demendoza.com.mx. © **33/3942-5151.** Fax 33/3613-7310. 104 units. 1,687 pesos double; 1,947 pesos junior suite. Discounts sometimes available. AE, MC, V. Secure parking 40 pesos. **Amenities:** Restaurant; bar; fitness room; Jacuzzi; small outdoor pool; room service; smoke-free rooms. *In room:* A/C, TV, hair dryer, Wi-Fi.

Moderate

Hotel Morales ★★   A historic hotel that's attractive and comfortable, the Morales is a good downtown choice. The standard rooms are either *suite sencilla* (one queen-size bed) or *suite doble* (two double beds). The rooms are medium or large and come with laminate floors. The bathrooms are attractive, with ceramic-tile floors, good-looking countertops, and strong showers. The rooms that face the street have balconies with double-glazed windows that do a good job at screening the noise. The imperial suites offer a lot for the money, with superlarge bathrooms equipped with a two-person Jacuzzi tub and a separate shower. All rooms are set around an arcaded lobby holding an attractive bar area. There's live music on Wednesday and Friday evenings.

Av. Corona 243 (corner of Prisciliano Sánchez), Centro Histórico, 44100 Guadalajara, Jal. www.hotel morales.com.mx. © **33/3658-5232.** Fax 33/3658-5239. 64 units. 1,360 pesos double; 1,660 pesos junior suite; 2,140 pesos imperial suite. AE, MC, V. Free sheltered parking. **Amenities:** Restaurant; bar; babysitting; fitness room; room service; smoke-free rooms. *In room:* A/C, TV, hair dryer, Internet.

La Villa del Ensueño ★   This B&B in central Tlaquepaque is a convenient alternative to big-city hotels. A modern interpretation of traditional Mexican architecture, it contains small courtyards and well-tended grounds bordered by old stucco walls, with an occasional wrought-iron balcony or stone staircase. The rooms have more character than most hotel lodgings. Doubles have either two twin or two double beds. The hotel is about 8 blocks from the main plaza.

Florida 305, 45500 Tlaquepaque, Jal. www.villadelensueno.com. © **800/220-8689** in the U.S., or 33/3635-8792. Fax 818/597-0637. 20 units. 1,439 pesos double; 1,636 pesos deluxe double; 1,898 pesos junior suite. Rates include full breakfast and light laundry service. AE, MC, V. Free valet parking. **Amenities:** Bar; indoor/outdoor pool. *In room:* A/C, TV, hair dryer, Wi-Fi.

Old Guadalajara ★★ This downtown bed-and-breakfast in a colonial house is well located, quiet, and beautiful. The rooms reflect the local scene; they speak of Mexico without shouting it. They are large and airy, with high ceilings, tile floors, and comfortable bathrooms. The colonial architecture makes it possible to live without air-conditioning in the warm months, and every room is equipped with a ceiling fan. The central courtyard is cool and shaded by tall bamboo. The common rooms are open to the courtyard and are stocked with material for readers curious about the city. Paul Callahan prepares filling breakfasts for his guests using only natural ingredients.

Belén 236, Centro Histórico, 44100 Guadalajara, Jal. www.oldguadalajara.com. ©/fax **33/3613-9958.** 4 units. $110 double. Rates include full breakfast. AE, MC, V for deposit; no credit cards at B&B. Children 17 and younger not accepted. **Amenities:** Smoke-free rooms. *In room:* Hair dryer, no phone.

Quinta Don José ★★ 🌶 Good value, great location, friendly English-speaking owners—there are a lot of reasons to like this small establishment just 2 blocks from Tlaquepaque's main square. Rooms run the gamut from midsize to extra large. They are comfortable, attractive, and quiet, with some nice local touches. Most of the standard and deluxe doubles have a king-size or two double beds and an attractive, midsize bathroom. A couple of them have small private outdoor spaces. Some of the suites in back come with a full kitchen and lots of space—more than twice the size of the usual suite, with one king-size and one double bed. The breakfasts are good, and recently the owners have installed a full restaurant open for dinner. Some lodgings just have a good feel to them, and this is one of them.

Reforma 139, 45500 Tlaquepaque, Jal. www.quintadonjose.com. © **866/629-3753** in the U.S. and Canada, or 33/3635-7522. 15 units. $105 standard; $119 deluxe; $134–$180 suite. Rates include full breakfast. AE, MC, V. Free secure parking. **Amenities:** Restaurant; bar; free airport transfers; babysitting; heated outdoor pool; smoke-free rooms. *In room:* A/C, TV, hair dryer, Wi-Fi.

Inexpensive

Gran Hotel Los Reyes 🌶 The rooms in this 10-story downtown hotel have good, individually controlled air-conditioning and strong showers, a rarity for budget hotels. The location is downtown near the market (7 blocks from the main square), which is central but in a somewhat decayed part of town. For entertainment, there's a modern multiplex cinema across the street that shows first-run Hollywood movies. Guest rooms are midsize; most have a king-size bed. Those on the mezzanine level are larger and often cost the same. Ask for a room facing away from the busy Calzada Independencia. The rooms on the seventh, eighth, and ninth floors have been totally remodeled and go for the higher price listed below. They are worth the extra money.

Calzada Independencia Sur 168, 44100 Guadalajara, Jal. www.granhotellosreyes.com.mx. © **33/3613-9781.** Fax 33/3614-0367. 181 units. 655–850 pesos double. AE, MC, V. Free valet parking. **Amenities:** Restaurant; outdoor heated pool; room service; smoke-free rooms. *In room:* A/C, TV, Wi-Fi.

Hotel Cervantes ★ 🌶 This six-story downtown hotel offers modern amenities at a good price. The rooms are attractive and midsize. They are decorated and furnished simply and practically, without much fuss. The air-conditioning is not strong. The lower price is for one double bed; the higher price is for a king or two doubles. This is not a noisy hotel, but if you require absolute quiet, request an interior room. The Cervantes is 6 blocks south and 3 blocks west of the cathedral.

Prisciliano Sánchez 442 (corner of Donato Guerra), Centro Histórico, 44100 Guadalajara, Jal. www.hotelcervantes.com.mx. ©/fax **33/3613-6816.** 100 units. 705–745 pesos double; 1,095 pesos suite. AE, MC, V. Free secure parking. **Amenities:** Restaurant; lobby bar; small outdoor heated pool; room service. *In room:* A/C, TV, Wi-Fi.

Hotel San Francisco Plaza ⚜ This colonial-style downtown hotel is both pleasant and a bargain. Most rooms are medium to large and comfortable, with attractive furnishings. All have rugs or carpeting, and most have tall ceilings. The hotel is built around four courtyards, which contain fountains and potted plants. Rooms along Prisciliano Sánchez are much quieter now that the management has installed double windows. Some units along the back wall of the rear patio have small bathrooms. Most rooms have ceramic tile flooring; some have carpeting. The San Francisco Plaza is 6 blocks south and 2 blocks east of the cathedral.

Degollado 267 (corner of Prisciliano Sánchez), Centro Histórico, 44100 Guadalajara, Jal. www.san franciscohotel.com.mx. ✆ **33/3613-8954,** -8971. Fax 33/3613-3257. 76 units. 710-785 pesos double. AE, MC, V. Free parking. **Amenities:** Restaurant; room service. *In room:* A/C, TV, Wi-Fi.

WHERE TO EAT

Guadalajara has many excellent restaurants either for fine dining or for typical local fare. Good local fare can be had in the Centro Histórico, but for fine dining, head to western Guadalajara or, if it's early in the day, to Tlaquepaque. For a quick bite, there are several **Sanborn's** in the city. This is a popular national chain of restaurants known for their *enchiladas suizas* (enchiladas in cream sauce). If you're downtown and looking for baked goods and coffee, go to **El Globo** (✆ 33/3613-9926), an upscale bakery at the corner of Pedro Moreno and Degollado; this chain has a couple more locations around Guadalajara. *Tip:* When taking a taxi, keep the address of the restaurant handy; taxi drivers cannot be relied upon to know where even the most popular restaurants are.

Local dishes include *birria* (goat or lamb covered in maguey leaves and roasted). It comes in a tomato broth or with the broth on the side. Another favorite is the *torta ahogada*, a sandwich with pork bathed in a tomato sauce. The most popular drink here is the *paloma*, which combines tequila, lots of lime juice, and grapefruit soda on ice.

Expensive

Adobe Fonda ★★★ NUEVA COCINA This restaurant shares space with a large store on pedestrian-only Independencia. The dining area is open and airy. Homemade bread and tostadas come to the table with an olive oil–based chile sauce, *pico de gallo*, and *requezón de epazote* (ricotta-like cheese with a Mexican herb). Among the soups are *crema de cilantro* and an interesting mushroom soup with a dark-beer broth. The main courses present some difficult decisions, with intriguing combinations of Mexican, Italian, and Argentine ingredients. The shrimp chile relleno bathed in a creamy sauce flavored with blue cheese is a good choice. Also, there's a filet mignon served in a pool of mild *chile ancho* sauce. Sample the margaritas, too.

Francisco de Miranda 27 (corner of Independencia, Tlaquepaque). ✆ **33/3657-2792.** www.adobe fonda.com. Reservations recommended on weekends. Main courses 150–230 pesos. AE, MC, V. Mon-Fri noon-7pm; Sat 9am-8pm; Sun 9am-7pm.

Chez Nené ★★★ FRENCH In a small and pleasant open-air dining room, you can enjoy a quiet and leisurely meal of delicious French food. After doing just this, I had to meet the owner to see who was behind such work. He turned out to be a French expatriate (whose Mexican wife, Nené, is the restaurant's namesake) with strong ideas about food and dining. Freshness and quality of ingredients are what matter most to him. He goes to the market every day, and from what he finds, creates a daily menu that he puts on a chalkboard. Service is excellent.

Juan Palomar y Arias 426 (continuación Rafael Sanzio, west side). *C* **33/3673-4564.** Reservations recommended on weekends. Main courses 180–280 pesos. AE, MC, V. Tues 4–11pm; Wed-Sat 1–5:30pm and 7:30–11:30pm; Sun 1–6pm.

El Sacromonte ★★★ ALTA COCINA   The food is so exquisite that I try to dine here every time I'm in Guadalajara. El Sacromonte emphasizes artful presentation and design: Order "Queen Isabel's Crown," and you'll be served a dish of shrimp woven together in the shape of a crown and covered in divine lobster-and-orange sauce. Or try quesadillas with rose petals in a deep-colored strawberry sauce. For soup, consider *el viejo progreso* for its unlikely combination of flavors (blue cheese and chipotle chile). The menu features amusing descriptions in verse. The main dining area is a shaded, open-air patio. The restaurant isn't far from the downtown area, on the near west side. Next door is a good steakhouse operated by the same owners.

Pedro Moreno 1398 (corner of Calle Colonias, west side). *C* **33/3825-5447** or 33/3827-0663. www.sacromonte.com.mx. Reservations recommended. Main courses 166–210 pesos. MC, V. Mon-Sat 1:30pm–midnight; Sun 1:30–6pm.

La Matera ★ STEAKS/PIZZA   The steaks are good, and the surroundings are inviting in this two-story open brick structure. The cuts come from the U.S. and Mexico, the lamb from New Zealand, and the wine from all over. La Matera has a decidedly Argentine influence, which of course means Italian influence. Pizzas are a popular menu item; the seafood is beautifully grilled. The bar is downstairs and most of the dining area is upstairs. In good weather it's very pleasant.

Av. México 2891 (west side). *C* **33/3616-1626.** http://lamatera.tripod.com. Reservations recommended on weekends. Steaks 210–360 pesos; pizzas 100–140 pesos. AE, MC, V. Mon-Sat 1pm–midnight; Sun 1–6:30pm.

La Tequila ★★ MEXICAN   Contemporary and traditional Mexican cooking is on the menu in this large, popular restaurant. You'll find dishes such as a pasta stuffed with shrimp and *huitlacoche,* and a *chamorro adobado* (pork shoulder marinated in a chile sauce) wrapped in maguey leaves and cooked in the ground with a wood fire. On my last visit I tried the shrimp in a sweet-and-sour tamarind sauce, as well as tacos "plaza de toros." Both of these were excellent—the tacos were beef tips and bits of Mexican sausage on fresh tortillas served with their own sauce; the shrimp were tangy and different. The bar, too, has started making original concoctions, such as the "tequilibrio." La Tequila can get pretty lively, and the decorative touches, such as trimmed agaves, give the dining areas a regional point of reference. Indoor/outdoor dining areas and a popular upstairs bar make up most of the restaurant.

Av. México 2830 (at Napoleón, west side). *C* **33/3640-3440** or 33/3640-3110. www.latequila.com. Reservations recommended on weekends. Main courses 135–189 pesos. AE, MC, V. Mon-Sat 1pm–midnight; Sun 1–6pm.

Moderate

Hostería del Angel ★★ TAPAS/WINE BAR   Sip wine and munch on a few tapas in this comfortable patio restaurant and wine bar just a few blocks from the basilica in Zapopan. The chef-owner cooked for years in Spain, where he became fascinated with the making of cheeses and deli meats such as Spanish *jamón serrano.* He serves a variety of tapas and popular baguette sandwiches. The menu doesn't do a good job of explaining the dishes, so don't hesitate to ask the waitstaff for explanations. Most of the tapas are under the heading "Por la noche," which also includes sandwiches and the *rotolata*—vegetables and cold cuts surrounded by a thin layer of crispy cheese, which is a house specialty. Acoustic music plays from 9 to 11pm Tuesday through Saturday. The restaurant is a half-block off the pedestrian-only *calzada*, which leads to the plaza in front of the basilica. For breakfast you can get the traditional *molletes*.

5 de Mayo 260, Zapopan (west side). ℂ/fax **33/3656-9516.** www.hosteriadelangel.com. Reservations recommended on weekends. Tapas 55–90 pesos; main courses 109–165 pesos. MC, V. Mon–Sat 9am–midnight; Sun 9am–8pm.

I Latina FUSION   Warehouse chic with a porcine motif (the owner tells me that the pig is a symbol of abundance in Thailand) is the look here. The menu is absurdly small but is supplemented with lots of daily specials. Usually there's a steak of some kind, cooked a bit differently, also some Asian fusion, including at least one noodle dish. This is a good place for people-watching—you get to see a portion of Guadalajara's hip, artsy crowd, who enjoy the antiestablishment surroundings, including the metal and plastic tables and chairs. My main problem is the noise, which at times gets to be too much. If you're looking for quiet dining, go elsewhere. Cabs have a hard time finding this place, despite the fact that it's almost right off of Minerva Circle. It's not that difficult—Inglaterra faces the railroad tracks.

Av. Inglaterra 3128 (west side). ℂ **33/3647-7774.** www.ilatinarest.com. Reservations recommended. Main courses 99–180 pesos. MC, V. Wed–Sat 7:30pm–1am; Sun 2–6pm.

La Fonda de San Miguel 📷 MEXICAN   My favorite way to enjoy a good meal in Mexico is to have it in an elegant colonial courtyard. I love the contrast between the bright, noisy street and the cool, shaded patio. This restaurant is in the former convent of Santa Teresa de Jesús. While you enjoy the stone arches and gurgling fountain, little crisp tacos and homemade bread appear at the table. For main courses, try the shrimp *al tequila,* or perhaps the *chiles en nogada* if it's the season. Traditional *mole poblano* is also on the menu. Wednesday to Saturday, musicians perform from 3 to 5pm and 9 to 11pm.

Donato Guerra 25 (and Pedro Moreno, downtown). ℂ **33/3613-0809.** www.lafondadesanmiguel.com. Reservations recommended on weekends. Breakfast 50–80 pesos; main courses 125–170 pesos. AE, MC, V. Mon 8:30am–6pm; Tues–Sat 8:30am–midnight; Sun 8:30am–9pm.

La Trattoria Pomodoro Ristorante ★ ITALIAN   Good food, good service, and moderate prices make this restaurant perennially popular. The price of pastas and main courses includes a visit to the well-stocked salad bar. Recommendable menu items include the combination pasta plate (lasagna, fettuccini Alfredo, and spaghetti), shrimp linguine, and chicken parmigiana. The Italian owner likes to stock lots of wines from the motherland. The dining room is attractive and casual, with comfortable furniture and separate seating for smokers and nonsmokers.

Niños Héroes 3051 (west side). ℂ **33/3122-1817.** Reservations recommended, but not accepted during holidays. Pasta 80–120 pesos; main courses 95–120 pesos. AE, MC, V. Daily 1pm–midnight.

Mariscos Progreso SEAFOOD   At this outdoor restaurant in Tlaquepaque, the dining area is a rustic, open patio shaded in parts by trees or tile roofs. The tables and chairs are *equipal*—the common rustic, but comfortable, furniture of the region made with leather and rough-cut wood. The seafood cocktails are excellent and not loaded with as much ketchup as in other joints. You can order one of these or a ceviche, which I found fresh on my last visit. The menu includes all the Mexican standards—

fish in toasted garlic butter (*al mojo de ajo*) or with strips of *guajillo* chile (*al ajillo*). Sometimes there's quite a bit of ambience, with mariachis adding to the commotion. At other times, the crowd thins and one can rest peacefully from the exertions of shopping with a cold drink. It's a half-block from El Parián.

Progreso 80, Tlaquepaque. ℂ **33/3639-6149.** Reservations not accepted. Main courses 118–166 pesos. MC, V. Daily 11am–7pm.

Inexpensive

Café Madrid MEXICAN   This little coffee shop is like many coffee shops used to be—a social institution where people come in, greet each other and the staff by name, and chat over breakfast or coffee and cigarettes. Change comes slowly here—the waiters still wear the white jackets with black bow ties, as they did 30 years ago. The coffee and Mexican breakfasts are good, as is the standard Mexican fare served in the afternoon. Most popular dishes include the enchiladas and the *chilaquiles*. The front room opens to the street, with a small lunch counter and another room in the back.

Juárez 264 (btw. Corona and 16 de Septiembre, downtown). ℂ **33/3614-9504.** Breakfast 35–50 pesos; main courses 55–95 pesos. No credit cards. Daily 7:30am–10pm.

La Chata Restaurant REGIONAL/MEXICAN   If you're staying downtown, don't let this place slip off your radar. It does a good job with all the Mexican classics and some regional specialties as well. Unlike most restaurants, this one has the kitchen in front and the dining area in back. For a reasonable sum, you can get a filling bowl of *pozole*. They also offer *flautas, sopes,* quesadillas, and guacamole. There's also traditional *mole* and a couple of combination plates. The chairs are comfortable, and you hang out with lots of locals.

Corona 126 (btw. Juárez and López Cotilla, downtown). ℂ **33/3613-0588.** www.lachata.com.mx. Reservations not accepted. Breakfast 40–60 pesos; main courses 65–119 pesos. MC, V. Daily 8am–midnight.

La Fonda de la Noche ★★ 🍽 MEXICAN   For a host of reasons, this is my favorite place in the city for a simple supper. The limited menu is excellent, the surroundings are comfortable and inviting, the lighting is perfect, and there's a touch of nostalgia for the Mexico of the '40s, '50s, and '60s. It's not far from downtown or the west side; take a cab to the intersection of Jesús and Reforma, and, when you get there, look for a door behind a small hedge. There's no sign. It's a house with five fun dining rooms. Only Spanish is spoken, and the menu is simple. To try a little of everything, order the *plato combinado,* a combination plate that comes with an *enchilada de medio mole,* an empanada called a *media luna,* a *tostada,* and a *sope.* The owner is Carlos Ibarra, an artist from the state of Durango. He has decorated the place with traditional Mexican pine furniture and cotton tablecloths and his personal collection of paintings, mostly the works of close friends. On weekends, La Fonda offers *chiles en nogada.*

Jesús 251 (corner with Reforma, Col. El Refugio). ℂ **33/3827-0917.** Reservations not accepted. Main courses 75–109 pesos. MC, V. Tues–Sun 7:30pm–midnight.

Los Itacates Restaurant ★ 🍴 MEXICAN   *Itacate* is Spanish for lunchbox, and the name implies Mexican home cooking at reasonable prices. Office workers pack the place between 2 and 4pm weekdays, and there's a good crowd on weekend nights, but at other times you'll have no problem finding a table. You can dine outdoors in a shaded sidewalk area, in one of the three dining rooms, or in the terrace in back that overlooks a small playground, which was recently installed. The rooms are brightly decorated, with traditional, painted wood furniture. Specialties include *lomo adobado* and chiles rellenos. *Pollo Itacates* is a quarter of a chicken, two cheese enchiladas, potatoes, and rice. Los Itacates is 5 blocks north of Avenida Vallarta. In the evenings, they serve tacos and other *antojitos*.

Chapultepec Norte 110 (west side). 🕐 **33/3825-1106,** -9551. Reservations accepted. Breakfast buffet 88 pesos; tacos 15 pesos; main courses 62–105 pesos. MC, V. Mon–Sat 8am–11pm; Sun 8am–7pm.

EXPLORING GUADALAJARA

Special Events

Throughout the autumn months Guadalajara hosts a succession of events. In September, when Mexicans celebrate independence from Spain, the city goes all out, with a full month of festivities. The celebrations kick off with the **Encuentro Internacional del Mariachi** (www.mariachi-jalisco.com.mx), in which mariachi bands from around the world play before knowledgeable audiences and hold sessions with other mariachis. Bands come from as far as Japan and Russia. Concerts are held in several venues. In the Degollado Theater, you can hear orchestral arrangements of classic mariachi songs with solos by famous mariachis. You might be acquainted with many of the classics without even knowing it. The culmination is a parade of thousands of mariachis and *charros* (Mexican cowboys) through downtown. It starts the first week of September.

On **September 15,** a massive crowd assembles in front of the Governor's Palace to await the traditional **grito** (shout for independence) at 11pm. The *grito* commemorates Father Miguel Hidalgo's cry for independence in 1810. The celebration features live music on a street stage, spontaneous dancing, fireworks, and shouts of *"¡Viva México!"* and *"¡Viva Hidalgo!"* The next day is the official Independence Day, with a traditional parade; the plazas downtown resemble a country fair and market, with booths, games of chance, stuffed-animal prizes, cotton candy, and candied apples. Live entertainment stretches well into the night.

On **October 12,** a **procession** ★★ honoring Our Lady of Zapopan celebrates the feast day of the Virgin of Zapopan. Around dawn, her small, dark figure begins the 5-hour ride from the Cathedral of Guadalajara to the suburban Basilica of Zapopan (see "Other Attractions," below). The original icon dates from the mid-1500s; the procession began 200 years later. Today, crowds spend the night along the route and vie for position as the Virgin approaches. She travels in a gleaming new car (virginal, in that it must never have had the ignition turned on), which her caretakers pull through the streets. During the months leading up to the feast day, the figure visits churches all over the city. You will likely see neighborhoods decorated with paper streamers and banners honoring the Virgin's visit to the local church.

The celebration has grown into a month-long event, **Fiestas de Octubre,** which kicks off with an enormous parade, usually on the first Sunday or Saturday of the month. Festivities include performing arts, *charreadas* (rodeos), bullfights, art exhibits, regional dancing, a food fair, and a Day of Nations incorporating all the consulates in Guadalajara. By the time this is over, you enter the **holiday season of November and December,** with Revolution Day (Nov 20), the Virgin of Guadalupe's feast day (Dec 12), and several other celebrations.

Downtown Guadalajara

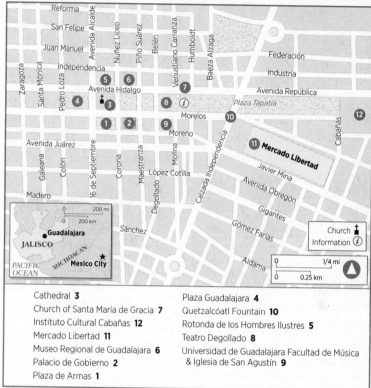

Cathedral **3**

Church of Santa María de Gracia **7**

Instituto Cultural Cabañas **12**

Mercado Libertad **11**

Museo Regional de Guadalajara **6**

Palacio de Gobierno **2**

Plaza de Armas **1**

Plaza Guadalajara **4**

Quetzalcóatl Fountain **10**

Rotonda de los Hombres Ilustres **5**

Teatro Degollado **8**

Universidad de Guadalajara Facultad de Música
 & Iglesia de San Agustín **9**

Downtown Guadalajara

The most easily recognized building in the city is the **cathedral ★**, around which four open plazas form the shape of a Latin cross. Extending eastwards from the plaza behind the cathedral is a long stretch of open area leading all the way to the Instituto Cultural Cabañas. This extension of open space is called **Plaza Tapatía.**

Construction on the cathedral started in 1561 and continued into the 18th century. Over such a long time, it was inevitable that some architectural alteration would be incorporated before the building was ever completed. The result is an unusual facade—an amalgam of several styles, including baroque, neoclassical, and Gothic. An earthquake destroyed the original towers in 1818; their replacements were built in the 1850s, inspired by designs said to have been on the bishop's dinner china. The colors on the towers, blue and yellow, are Guadalajara's official colors. The interior is cavernous and majestic. Items of interest include a painting in the sacristy ascribed to the 17th-century Spanish artist Bartolomé Estaban Murillo (1617–82).

On the cathedral's south side is the **Plaza de Armas,** the oldest and loveliest of the plazas. A cast-iron Art Nouveau bandstand is its dominant feature. Made in France, it was a gift to the city from the dictator Porfirio Díaz in the 1890s. The

GUADALAJARA bus tours

Two companies are now offering bus tours of the city. One is a local company, **Tranvías Turísticos** (no phone), which offers two tours on small buses that look like trolley cars. Get info and buy tickets from the kiosk in Plaza Guadalajara (in front of the cathedral) from 10am until 7pm. There are two routes. One is a circuit through downtown and surrounding neighborhoods. It lasts 1 hour and 10 minutes. The second is a slightly longer tour, going to Tlaquepaque. It lasts 1½ hours. Both cost 90 pesos.

The other company, **Tapatío Tours** (© **33/3613-0887**; www.tapatiotour. com), has modern, bright-red double-decker buses. Its tour goes from downtown to western Guadalajara to Tlaquepaque. The tour costs 100 pesos on weekdays and 120 pesos on weekends. It goes farther out, into western Guadalajara. There are 10 stops; you can get off at any one and catch the next bus when it passes by, which is every 45 minutes to an hour. Catch the bus in the plaza on the north side of the cathedral after 10am.

female figures on the bandstand exhibited too little clothing for conservative Guadalajarans, who clothed them. The dictator, recognizing when it's best to let the people have their way, said nothing.

Facing the plaza is the **Palacio del Gobierno** ★★, a broad, low structure built in 1774. The facade blends Spanish and Moorish elements and holds several eye-catching details. Inside the central courtyard, above the staircase to the right, is a spectacular mural of Hidalgo by the modern Mexican master José Clemente Orozco. The Father of Independence appears high overhead, bearing directly down on the viewer and looking as implacable as a force of nature. On one of the adjacent walls, Orozco painted *The Carnival of Ideologies,* a dark satire on the prevailing fanaticisms of his day. Another of his murals is inside the second-floor chamber of representatives, depicting Hidalgo again, this time in a more conventional posture, writing the proclamation to end slavery in Mexico. The *palacio* is open daily from 10am to 8pm.

In the plaza on the opposite side of the cathedral from the Plaza de Armas is the **Rotonda de los Hombres Ilustres.** Sixteen white columns, each supporting a bronze statue, stand as monuments to Guadalajara's and Jalisco's distinguished sons. Across the street from the plaza, in front of the Museo Regional, you will see a line of horse-drawn buggies. A carriage ride around the Centro Histórico lasts almost an hour and costs 200 pesos for one to four people.

Facing the east side of the rotunda is the **Museo Regional de Guadalajara,** Liceo 60 (© **33/3613-2703**). Originally a convent, it was built in 1701 in the baroque style and contains some of the region's important archaeological finds, fossils, historic objects, and art. Among the highlights are a giant reconstructed mammoth's skeleton and a meteorite weighing 772 kilograms (1,702 lb.), discovered in Zacatecas in 1792. On the first floor, there's a fascinating exhibit of pre-Hispanic pottery and some exquisite pottery and clay figures recently unearthed near Tequila during the construction of the toll road. On the second floor is a small ethnography exhibit of the contemporary dress of the state's indigenous peoples, including the Coras, Mexicaneros, Nahuas, and Tepehuanes. It's open Tuesday through Saturday from 9am to 5:30pm and Sunday from 9am to 4pm. Admission is 45 pesos.

Behind the Cathedral is the Plaza Liberación, with the **Teatro Degollado** (Deh-goh-*yah*-doh) on the opposite side. This neoclassical 19th-century opera house was named for Santos Degollado, a local patriot who fought with Juárez against Maximilian and the French. Apollo and the nine muses decorate the theater's pediment, and the interior is famous for both the acoustics and the rich decoration. It hosts a variety of performances during the year. It's open Monday through Friday from noon to 2pm and during performances.

To the right of the theater, across the street, is the sweet little **church of Santa María de Gracia,** built in 1573 as part of a convent for Dominican nuns. On the opposite side of the Teatro Degollado is the **church of San Agustín.** The former convent is now the **University of Guadalajara School of Music.**

Keep walking east down Plaza Tapatía, and you will arrive at the Instituto Cabañas. You will first pass between a couple of low, modern office buildings. The **Tourism Information Office** is in a building on the right side.

Beyond these office buildings, the plaza opens into a large expanse, now framed by department stores and offices, and dominated by the abstract modern **Quetzalcóatl Fountain.** This fluid steel structure represents the mythical plumed serpent Quetzalcóatl, who figured so prominently in pre-Hispanic religion and culture, and exerts a presence even today.

At the far end of the plaza is the Hospicio Cabañas, formerly an orphanage and known today as the **Instituto Cultural Cabañas ★★**, Cabañas 8 (*©* **33/3818-2800,** ext. 31009). Admission is 70 pesos. This vast structure is impressive for both its size (more than 23 courtyards) and its grandiose architecture, especially the cupola. Created by the famous Mexican architect Manuel Tolsá, it housed homeless children from 1829 to 1980. Today it's a thriving cultural center offering art shows and classes. The interior walls and ceiling of the main building display murals painted by Orozco in 1937. His *Man of Fire,* in the dome, is said to represent the spirit of humanity projecting itself toward the infinite. Other rooms hold additional Orozco works, as well as excellent contemporary art and temporary exhibits.

Just south of the Hospicio Cabañas (to the left as you exit) is the **Mercado Libertad ★**, Guadalajara's gigantic covered central market, the largest in Latin America. This site has been a market plaza since the 1500s; the present buildings date from the early 1950s (see "Shopping," below).

Other Attractions

At **Parque Agua Azul (Blue Water Park),** plants, trees, shrubbery, statues, and fountains create an idyllic refuge from the bustling city. Many people come here to exercise early in the morning. The park is open daily from 7am to 6pm. Admission is 10 pesos for adults, 5 pesos for children.

Across Calzada Independencia from the park, cater-cornered from a small flower market, is the **Museo de Arqueología del Occidente de México,** Calzada Independencia at Avenida del Campesino (no phone). It houses a fine collection of pre-Hispanic pottery from Jalisco, Nayarit, and Colima. The museum is open Tuesday through Friday from 10am to 2pm and 4 to 7pm, Saturday and Sunday 10am to 2pm. There's a small admission charge.

The state-run **Instituto de la Artesanía** (*©* **33/3030-9090**) is just past the park entrance at Calzada Independencia and González Gallo. It exhibits just about every kind of craft produced in the state. (There is also a store—see "Shopping," below.) Hours are Monday to Friday 10am to 4pm, Saturday and Sunday 10am to 2pm.

Also near the park is Guadalajara's rodeo arena, **Lienzo Charro de Jalisco** (*©* **33/3619-0315**). Mexican cowboys, known as *charros,* are famous for their riding and lasso work, and the arena in Guadalajara is considered the big-time. Shows and competitions are every Sunday at noon. The arena is at Av. Dr. R. Michel 577, between González Gallo and Las Palomas.

Basílica de la Virgen de Zapopan ★

A wide promenade several blocks long leads to a large plaza and the basilica. It dates from the 18th-century church and is a combination of baroque and *plateresque* styles. This is the religious center of Guadalajara. On the Virgin's feast day (see "Special Events," above), the plaza fills with thousands of *tapatíos.* The cult of the Virgin of Zapopan practically began with the foundation of Guadalajara itself. She is much revered and the object of many pilgrimages. In the plaza are several stands selling religious figures and paraphernalia. On one side of the church is a museum and store dedicated to the betterment of the Huichol Indians. It is worth a visit. Admission to the Huichol museum is 12 pesos.

Main Plaza, Zapopan (10km/6¼ miles northwest of downtown). No phone. Free admission. Daily 7am–7pm. Museum Mon–Sat 9:30am–1:30pm and 3–6pm; Sun 10am–3pm.

Museo de la Ciudad

This museum would be of interest to those curious about the city's history. It occupies the main house of an 18th-century farm. The permanent collection includes prints from the 18th and 19th centuries, artifacts of daily life from those times, antique weapons, and armor. Descriptive text is in Spanish only.

Independencia 684 (at M. Bárcenas). *©* **33/1201-8712.** 10 pesos. Tues–Sun 10am–4pm.

Museo de las Artes de la Universidad de Guadalajara

Inside the main lecture hall of this building (use entrance facing Juárez) are some more murals by Orozco. On the wall behind the stage is a bitter denunciation of corruption called *The People and Their False Leaders.* In the cupola is a more optimistic work—*The Five-fold Man,* who works to create a better society and better self. The museum (use entrance facing López Cotilla) has a permanent collection of modern art, which includes the works of many local artists.

Juárez 975. *©* **33/3134-1664.** www.museodelasartes.udg.mx. Free admission. Tues–Fri 10am–6pm; Sat–Sun 10am–4pm.

Museo Pantaleón Panduro ★★★

This museum houses a magnificent collection of ceramic works. Collectors and connoisseurs of pottery will love it, but so will casual students of Mexican popular culture and the arts. This could be one of the great museums of Mexico, but I would change a few things to make it perfect. Every year a national competition is held in Tlaquepaque among ceramists from across Mexico. Prizes are awarded in seven categories and a best of show among these. (***Tip:*** The competition is held every June, which is a good time to visit Tlaquepaque.) After the competition, many winning pieces become part of the museum's collection. The virtuosity manifested in some of them will take your breath away. It would be wonderful if they were organized by category, with better explanatory text. But for now, the best thing you can do is cajole someone into showing you around and explaining the pieces on display. The staff is quite knowledgeable, and at least one member speaks English. The museum occupies a third of a large complex that in colonial times housed a religious community. It's now called **Centro Cultural El Refugio,** and it's worth ambling through after you've seen the museum's collection. Some improvements have been made to lighting.

P. Sánchez 191 (at Calle Florida, Tlaquepaque). *©* **33/3639-5656.** Free admission. Tues–Sun 10am–6pm.

SHOPPING

Many visitors to Guadalajara come specifically for the shopping in Tlaquepaque and Tonalá (see below). If you have little free time, try the government-run **Instituto de la Artesanía Jalisciense,** González Gallo 20 at Calzada Independencia (© **33/3030-9090**), in Parque Agua Azul, just south of downtown. This place is perfect for one-stop shopping, with two floors of pottery, silver jewelry, dance masks, glassware, leather goods, and regional clothing from around the state and the country. As you enter, on the right are museum displays showing crafts and regional costumes from the state of Jalisco. The craft store is open Monday through Friday from 10am to 4pm, Saturday and Sunday from 10am to 2pm.

Guadalajara is known for its shoe industry; if you're in the market for a pair, try the **Galería del Calzado,** a shopping center made up exclusively of shoe stores. It's on the west side, about 6 blocks from Minerva Circle, at avenidas México and Yaquis. There is also a section of the street Esteban Alatorre, near Parque Morelos, which has practically nothing but shop after shop of women's dress shoes. It makes for very comfortable shopping.

Women's jewelry is another good that Guadalajara is known for. There are four large buildings filled with jewelry shops on the Plaza Tapatía, by the San Juan de Dios market, also known as Mercado Libertad.

Mariachis and *charros* come to Guadalajara from all over Mexico to buy highly worked belts and boots, wide-brimmed sombreros, and embroidered shirts. Several tailor shops and stores specialize in these outfits. One is **El Charro,** which has a store in the Plaza del Sol shopping center, across the street from the Hotel Presidente InterContinental, and one downtown on Juárez.

To view a good slice of what constitutes the material world for most Mexicans, try the mammoth **Mercado Libertad** ★ downtown. Besides food and produce, you'll see crafts, household goods, clothing, magic potions, and more. Although it opens at 7am, the market isn't in full swing until around 10am. Come prepared to haggle.

Gonvil, a popular bookstore chain, has a branch across from Plaza de los Hombres Ilustres on Avenida Hidalgo, and another a few blocks south at Av. 16 de Septiembre 118 (Alcalde becomes 16 de Septiembre south of the cathedral). It carries few English selections. **Sanborn's,** at the corner of Juárez and 16 de Septiembre, does a good job of keeping English-language periodicals in stock, but most are specialty magazines. For the widest selection of English-language books, try **Sandi Bookstore,** Av. Tepeyac 718 (© **33/3121-0863**), in the Chapalita neighborhood on the west side.

Shopping in Tlaquepaque & Tonalá

Almost everyone who comes to Guadalajara for the shopping has Tlaquepaque (Tlah-keh-*pah*-keh) and Tonalá in mind. These two suburbs are traditional handicraft centers that produce and sell a wide variety of *artesanía* (crafts).

TLAQUEPAQUE

Located about 20 minutes from downtown, **Tlaquepaque** ★★★ has the best shopping for handicrafts and decorative arts in all of Mexico. Over the years, it has become a fashionable place, attracting talented designers in a variety of fields. Even though it's a suburb of a large city, it has a cozy, small-town feel and is a pleasure to stroll through popping into one shop after another. No one hassles you; no one does the hard sell. It's a relaxing, easy-going experience. There are some excellent places to eat (see "Where to Eat," earlier in this chapter), or you can grab some simple fare at **El Parián,** a building in the middle of town that houses a number of small eateries.

A taxi from downtown Guadalajara costs 100 pesos, or you can take one of the TUR 706 buses that make a fairly quick run from downtown to Tlaquepaque and Tonalá (see "Getting Around," earlier in this chapter).

The **Tlaquepaque Tourism Office** (✆ 33/3562-7050, ext. 2320; turismo tlaquepaque@yahoo.com.mx) has an information booth in the town's main square by El Parián. It's staffed from 10am to 8pm daily.

If you are interested in pottery and ceramics, make sure to see the Pantaleón Panduro Museum, listed above. Another is the **Regional Ceramics Museum,** Independencia 237 (✆ 33/3635-5404), which displays several aspects of traditional Jalisco pottery as produced in Tlaquepaque and Tonalá. The examples date back several generations and are grouped according to the technique used to produce them. Note the crosshatch design known as *petatillo* on some of the pieces; it's one of the region's oldest traditional motifs and is, like so many other motifs, a real pain to produce. Look for the wonderful old kitchen and dining room, complete with pots, utensils, and dishes. The museum is open Tuesday through Saturday from 10am to 6pm, Sunday from 10am to 3pm; admission is free.

The following list of Tlaquepaque shops will give you an idea of what to expect. This is just a small fraction of what you'll find; the best approach might be to just wander among the shops. The main shopping is along **Independencia,** a pedestrian-only street that starts at El Parián. It was recently resurfaced in stone and looks pretty sharp. You can go door-to-door visiting the shops until the street ends, and then work your way back on **Calle Juárez,** the next street over, south of Independencia.

 Packing It In

If you need your purchases packed safely so that you can check them as extra baggage, or if you want them shipped, talk to **Margaret del Río.** She is an American who runs a large packing and shipping company at Juárez 347, Tlaquepaque (✆ **33/3657-5652**). Paying the excess baggage fee usually is cheaper than shipping, but it's less convenient.

Agustín Parra So you bought an old hacienda and are trying to restore its chapel—where do you go to find traditional baroque sculpture, religious art, gold-leafed objects, and even entire *retablos* (altarpieces)? Parra is famous for exactly this kind of work, and the store is lovely. It's open Monday through Saturday from 10am to 7pm. Independencia 158. ✆ **33/3657-8530.**

Bazar Hecht One of the village's longtime favorites. Here you'll find wood objects, handmade furniture, and a few antiques. It's open Monday through Saturday from 10am to 2:30pm and 3:30 to 7pm. Juárez 162. ✆ **33/3657-0316.**

Sergio Bustamante Sergio Bustamante's imaginative, original bronze, ceramic, and papier-mâché sculptures are among the most sought-after in Mexico—as well as the most copied. He also designs silver jewelry. This exquisite gallery showcases his work. It's open Monday through Saturday from 10am to 7pm, Sunday from noon to 4pm. Independencia 238 at Cruz Verde. ✆ **33/3639-5519.**

Teté Arte y Diseño Architectural decorative objects—especially hand-wrought-iron hardware for the "Old Mexico" look—are the specialty here. The store also has a large collection of wrought-iron chandeliers. It's open Monday through Saturday from 10am to 7:30pm. Juárez 173. ✆ **33/3635-7347.**

tequila: THE NAME SAYS IT ALL

Tequila is an entertaining (and intoxicating) town, well worth a day trip from Guadalajara. Several taxi drivers charge about 700 pesos to drive you to the town, get you into a tour of a distillery, take you to a restaurant, and haul you back to Guadalajara. A few of them speak English. One recommended driver is **José Gabriel Gómez** (📞 **33/3649-0791;** jgabriel-taxi@hotmail.com); he has a new car and drives carefully. Call him in the evening. Tour companies also arrange bus trips to Tequila; ask at the ticket kiosk of Tranvías Turísticos, mentioned earlier. That company has started a weekend tour to Tequila, taking people to the Cofradía distillery.

Tequila has many distilleries, including the famous brands **Sauza** and **José Cuervo.** All the distilleries—the big, modern ones and the small, more traditional ones—offer tours.

Another approach is to take the **Tequila Express** to the town of Amatitán, home of the Herradura distillery. This excursion is more about having a good time and enjoying some of the things this area is known for than it is about sampling tequila. Serious tequila enthusiasts will be disappointed. There's a nice tour of the distillery, but most of the time is spent watching mariachis and Mexican cowboys perform. The tequila tastings are limited. Everyone has a good time and drinks a fair share, but a trip to the town proper is more informative and offers a greater opportunity for trying different tequilas.

The Tequila Express leaves from the train station on Friday and Saturday, and sometimes on Sunday during vacation and holiday season. It's well organized. You need to be there by 10am. The Guadalajara Chamber of Commerce (Cámara de Comercio), at Vallarta and Niño Obrero (📞 **33/3880-9099**), organizes this trip. Buy tickets ahead of time at the main office; at the small office in the Centro Histórico at Morelos 395; at Calle Colón (no phone); or through Ticketmaster (📞 **33/3818-3800**). Office hours are Monday through Friday from 9am to 2pm and 4 to 6pm. Tickets cost 980 pesos for adults, 500 pesos for children 6 to 12. The tour includes food and drink. It returns to Guadalajara at about 8pm. Travel time is 1¼ hours each way. For more information, see **www.tequilaexpress.com.mx.**

TONALÁ: A TRADITION OF POTTERY MAKING

Tonalá ★★ is a pleasant town 10 minutes from Tlaquepaque. It is without question the largest concentration of artisans in Mexico and was a center of pottery making since pre-Hispanic times. Half of the more than 400 workshops here produce a wide variety of high- and low-temperature pottery. Other local artists work with forged iron, cantera stone, brass and copper, marble, miniatures, papier-mâché, textiles, blown glass, and gesso. This is a good place to look for custom work in any of these materials; you can locate a large pool of craftspeople by asking around a little.

Market days are Thursday and Sunday, when Tonalá reflects Mexico in all its chaotic glory. Expect large crowds and blocks and blocks of stalls displaying locally made pottery and glassware, cheap manufactured goods, food, and all kinds of bric-a-brac. You'll see herb men selling a rainbow selection of dried plants from wheelbarrows, magicians entertaining crowds, and craftspeople spreading their wares on the plaza's sidewalks. All kinds of crafts are for sale, most of which can be found in various parts of Mexico, but every now and then you'll come across something unique, produced by a local artisan. Visiting Tonalá on nonmarket days is easier. You can walk around more easily and find stores and workshops. Tonalá is the place for buying sets of margarita glasses, the widely seen blue-rimmed hand-blown glassware, finely painted *petatillo* ware, and the pottery typically associated with Mexico.

The **Tonalá Tourism Office** (© 33/1200-3912) operates an information kiosk on the town square. It's open Monday to Friday from 9am to 2:30pm.

Tonalá is also the home of the **Museo Nacional de Cerámica,** Constitución 104, between Hidalgo and Morelos (© 33/3284-6000, ext. 1523). The museum occupies most of the **Casa del Artesano,** which promotes local artisans. There is a store to the right just as you enter. You should take time to look through the store and its displays. If there's anything that interests you, ask the staff, who can tell you (in Spanish) about the different methods used to make pottery and other work and show you the difference between original methods and commercial shortcuts. If you like anything in particular they can direct you to the workshop where it was made and tell you of others that make something similar. The museum and store are open Monday through Friday from 9am to 8pm. Admission is free; the fee for using a video or still camera is 85 pesos per camera.

GUADALAJARA AFTER DARK

Mariachis

You can't go far in Guadalajara without coming across some mariachis, but seeing really talented performers takes some effort. Try **Casa Bariachi,** Av. Vallarta 2221 (© 33/3615-0029). In Tlaquepaque, go to **El Parián,** the building on the town square where mariachis serenade diners under the archways.

The Club & Music Scene

Guadalajara, as you might expect, has a lot of variety in entertainment. For the most extensive listing of clubs and performances, get your hands on a copy of *Ocio,* the weekly insert of *Público.* You'll find listings in the back, categorized by type of music. For good mariachis, you should go to Casa Bariachi, mentioned above. Across the street from that club is another called **La Bodeguita del Medio** (© 33/3630-1620), at Av. Vallarta 2320. It offers live old-school Cuban son. The groups come from Cuba and rotate every few months. The place is small, but people were making room to dance. Another thing to do is track down a Cuban diva named **Rosalia,** who lives in Guadalajara. She's a great talent and always has a tight band playing with her as she belts out salsa and merengue tunes.

PUERTO VALLARTA & THE CENTRAL PACIFIC COAST

by Shane Christensen

This stretch of Pacific coastline—with jungle-covered mountains tumbling into the turquoise ocean—provides a breathtaking setting for world-class adventure traveling and exquisite relaxation that is distinctly Mexican in flavor. From Mazatlán through Puerto Vallarta and curving down to Manzanillo, the coast promises and provides a diversity and array of experiences awaiting discovery.

Puerto Vallarta, with its traditional Mexican architecture and gold-sand beaches bordered by jungle-covered mountains, is the second-most-visited resort in Mexico (trailing Cancún). The original town center of Vallarta maintains a small-town charm despite its sophisticated hotels, great restaurants, thriving arts community, active nightlife, and wide variety of ecotourism attractions. **Mazatlán** may be the best resort value in Mexico, luring visitors with excellent fishing, a historic downtown, championship golf facilities, and new residential developments. **Manzanillo** is surprisingly relaxed; even though it's one of Mexico's most active commercial ports, it also offers great fishing, diving, and golf. And along the **Costa Alegre,** between Puerto Vallarta and Manzanillo, pristine coves are home to unique luxury resorts that cater to travelers seeking seclusion. With a little ingenuity, one can discover traditional villages such as **Barra de Navidad** and **Melaque,** which have almost totally escaped commercialization. Quite distinct from the well-known resort towns, they offer a glimpse into the energy and spirit of coastal Mexico outside of traveled tourist corridors—easy-going, friendly, and relaxed.

Puerto Vallarta's unabated growth has continued northward into neighboring Nayarit. With 185 miles of coastline, the **Riviera Nayarit,** as marketing wizards have aptly named it, offers spectacular geography, recreation, and biodiversity. Birdwatchers marvel at the hundreds of species that flock to the region, a collision of jungle and tundra habitats. Small sacred surf spots dot the coastline, including the beginners break in (what used to be) sleepy **Sayulita. Bucerías,** a fishing-village-turned-snowbird-capital, offers charming strolls and an expanding selection of quality restaurants. Next door, exclusive **Punta de Mita** sets the gold standard for luxury accommodations and activities. Majestic vistas, world-class golf courses, a burgeoning sailing community, and thrilling adventure sports round out this gentle and rich slice of Mexico.

PUERTO VALLARTA ★★★

885km (549 miles) NW of Mexico City; 339km (210 miles) W of Guadalajara; 285km (177 miles) NW of Manzanillo; 447km (277 miles) SE of Mazatlán; 239km (148 miles) SW of Tepic

Puerto Vallarta remains my favorite part of this colorful country, for its unrivaled combination of Mexican warmth, international diversity, and artistic charm. Beyond the cobblestone streets, graceful cathedral, bustling *malecón* (boardwalk), and festive *zócalo* (town square), Puerto Vallarta's welcoming atmosphere is complemented by its wealth of natural beauty and man-made pleasures, including hotels of all classes and prices, more than 250 restaurants, and a sizzling nightlife. Cool breezes flow down from the mountains along the Río Cuale, which runs through the city center. Fanciful public sculptures enhance the extensive contemporary arts scene, with the finest galleries in all of Mexico clustered together along a few small and charming blocks. As the most gay-friendly city in Mexico, Vallarta is as open-minded as it is laid-back, and folks from Mexico and the world over have relocated here, in part, for its cosmopolitan and open orientation.

Galleries, boutique shops, and outdoor markets blanket the town's cobblestone streets. You can walk everywhere, pausing along the way at a beachside cafe or on a boardwalk bench. Life here revolves around the ocean, with activities including deep-sea fishing, snorkeling, long-board surfing, and swimming with dolphins. Ecotourism activities abound—sign up for a jungle canopy tour, visit a protected island preserve, or test your sight at bird-watching. Ease yourself into an ocean kayak, watch whales migrating, or put on your scuba gear and dive with giant mantas in Banderas Bay. The range of activities in this earthly heaven is astounding.

Some folks come to Puerto Vallarta for its healing effects. Yoga retreats and fine spas have sprung up all over in recent years. There's something spiritual about a stroll along the *malecón* with its ocean breezes, multihued sunsets, and moonlit views of the bay. Peaceful scenic drives extend north and south of the city along oceanside cliffs and through winding jungle terrain. Those here to rest, read, and relax can choose from 26 miles of beaches, many in pristine coves accessible only by boat and framed by the majestic Sierra Madre mountains.

Dining here is delightful. The fresh fish, locally raised meats, and seasonal ingredients inspire Vallarta's many outstanding chefs, boosting the restaurant scene into one of the country's best. Creative Mexican and international dishes explode with flavor, and service is consistently gracious and warm. Wander through downtown Vallarta for fine sidewalk dining as diverse as the city itself. In Viejo Vallarta, you can enjoy a delicious Mexican meal at a casual eatery steps away from an acclaimed international seafood restaurant. You'll find French, Italian, German, and Asian venues tucked between galleries just on the other side of the Río Cuale.

Nighttime entertainment transforms the *malecón* into a modern Mexican party, where hipsters pack fashionable clubs, dancers swing to salsa, midnight revelers chase back tequila, and celebrations spill into the streets. A number of more chilled-out bars cater to the wine and margarita crowd. Even snowbirds jam to oldies not far from the

Puerto Vallarta: Hotel Zone & Beaches

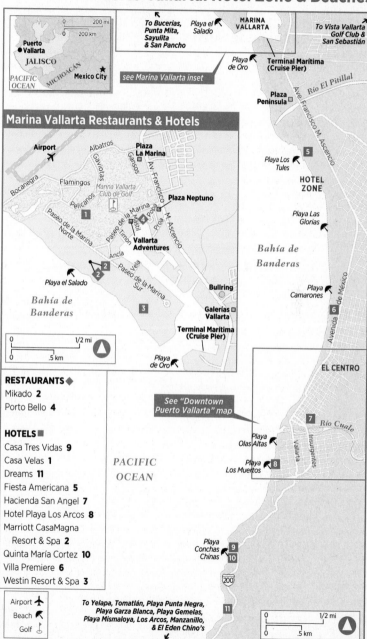

JALISCO

PACIFIC OCEAN

Puerto Vallarta

Mexico City

MICHOACÁN

To Bucerías, Punta Mita, Sayulita & San Pancho

Playa el Salado

MARINA VALLARTA

To Vista Vallarta Golf Club & San Sebastián

see Marina Vallarta inset

Playa de Oro

Terminal Marítima (Cruise Pier)

Río El Pitillal

Plaza Peninsula

Marina Vallarta Restaurants & Hotels

Airport

Albatros

Gaviotas

Plaza La Marina

Gansos

Av. Francisco

Flamingos

Bocanegra

Marina Vallarta Club de Golf

Plaza Neptuno

Paseo de la Marina

Pelícanos

Paseo de la Marina Norte

Timón

Paseo de la Marina

Mástil

Proa

M. Ascencio

Vallarta Adventures

Ancla

Vela

Paseo de la Marina Sur

Bullring

Playa el Salado

Bahía de Banderas

Galerías Vallarta

Terminal Marítima (Cruise Pier)

Playa de Oro

Playa Los Tules

HOTEL ZONE

Playa Las Glorias

Bahía de Banderas

Playa Camarones

Av. Francisco M. Ascencio

Avenida de México

See "Downtown Puerto Vallarta" map

EL CENTRO

Río Cuale

Playa Olas Altas

Insurgentes

Vallarta

Playa Los Muertos

PACIFIC OCEAN

RESTAURANTS ◆
Mikado **2**
Porto Bello **4**

HOTELS ■
Casa Tres Vidas **9**
Casa Velas **1**
Dreams **11**
Fiesta Americana **5**
Hacienda San Angel **7**
Hotel Playa Los Arcos **8**
Marriott CasaMagna
  Resort & Spa **2**
Quinta María Cortez **10**
Villa Premiere **6**
Westin Resort & Spa **3**

Playa Conchas Chinas

To Yelapa, Tomatlán, Playa Punta Negra, Playa Garza Blanca, Playa Gemelas, Playa Mismaloya, Los Arcos, Manzanillo, & El Eden Chino's

Airport ✈
Beach 🏖
Golf ⛳

0   200 mi
0   200 km

0   1/2 mi
0   .5 km

0   1/2 mi
0   .5 km

hottest clubs. The old town is filled with fun-loving gay and gay-friendly bars. As with every aspect of this lively and lovely city, there is something for everyone.

Essentials

GETTING THERE & DEPARTING

BY PLANE International carriers serving Puerto Vallarta include **Alaska Airlines** (© 800/252-7522 in the U.S., or 01-800/252-7522 in Mexico), **American Airlines** (© 800/433-7300 in the U.S., or 01-800/904-6000 in Mexico), **US Airways** (© 800/428-4322 in the U.S., or 01-800/428-4322 in Mexico), **Continental** (© 800/523-3273 in the U.S., or 01-800/900-5000 in Mexico), **Delta** (© 800/241-4141 in the U.S., or 01-800/123-4710 in Mexico), **Frontier** (© 800/432-1359 in the U.S.), and **United** (© 800/538-2929 in the U.S., or 01-800/003-0777 in Mexico).

Aeroméxico (© **800/237-6639** in the U.S., or 01-800/021-4000 in Mexico) flies from Los Angeles, San Diego, Aguascalientes, Guadalajara, La Paz, León, Mexico City, Morelia, and Tijuana.

Major car-rental agencies at the airport, including **Alamo, Avis, Budget, Dollar/Thrifty,** and **National,** are open after flight arrivals. After registering, they will send a shuttle to take you to the nearby car-rental lots. Daily rates start at about $40.

BY CAR The coastal Hwy. 200 is the only choice from Mazatlán (6 hr. north) or Manzanillo (3½–4 hr. south). Hwy. 15 from Guadalajara to Tepic takes 6 hours; to save as much as 2 hours, take Hwy. 15A from Chapalilla to Compostela, bypassing Tepic, and then continue south on Hwy. 200 to Puerto Vallarta. Expect a number of official checkpoints on these highways.

BY BUS The bus station, **Central Camionera de Puerto Vallarta,** is just north of the airport, approximately 11km (6¾ miles) from downtown. It offers overnight guarded parking and baggage storage. Most major first-class bus lines operate from here, including Estrella Blanca, ETN, TAP, Pacifico, Futura, Turistar, Elite, and Primera Plus, with transportation to points throughout Mexico, including Mazatlán (390 pesos), Manzanillo (230 pesos), Guadalajara (350 pesos), Barra de Navidad (185 pesos), and Mexico City (900 pesos). Taxis into town cost approximately $10 and are readily available; public buses operate from 7am to 11pm and regularly stop in front of the arrivals hall.

ORIENTATION

ARRIVING BY PLANE The airport is close to the north end of town near the Marina Vallarta, about 10km (6¼ miles) from downtown. **Transportes Terrestres Puerto Vallarta** minivans and **Aeromovil** taxis make the trip. They use a zone pricing system, with fares clearly posted at the ticket booths. Fares start at $16 for a ride to Marina Vallarta and go up to $28 for the south shore hotels. Federally licensed airport taxis exclusively provide transportation from the airport, and their fares are more than three times as high as city (yellow) taxi fares. A trip to downtown Puerto Vallarta costs between 200 and 250 pesos, whereas a return trip using a city taxi costs only 120 pesos. Only airport cabs may pick up passengers leaving the airport. You can also buy a ticket for a *colectivo* (a shuttle van that goes every 30 min.) at the official taxi stand which, at only 120 pesos to downtown, is the cheapest option.

VISITOR INFORMATION Prior to arrival, a useful source of information and publicity is the **Puerto Vallarta Tourism Board** (© **888/384-6822** in the U.S., or 322/224-1175 in Mexico; www.visitpuertovallarta.com). The office is located in the

Downtown Puerto Vallarta

ATTRACTIONS ●
Gringo Gulch
  (neighborhood) **13**
Isla del Río Cuale **15**
Main Square **6**
Municipal Flea Market **14**
Museo del Cuale **16**
Parish of Nuestra Señora
  de Guadalupe **7**

HOTELS ■
Hacienda San Angel **10**
Hotel Playa Los Arcos **21**

RESTAURANTS ◆

Agave Grill **5**
Archie's Wok **25**
Barcelona Tapas **1**
Café de Olla **22**
Café des Artistes **3**
Café Kaiser Maximilian **21**
Café San Angel **24**

Daiquiri Dick's **20**
El Arrayán **2**
El Planeta Vegetariano **8**
Espresso **19**
Fajita Republic **23**
Hacienda San Angel **10**
La Esquina de Los Caprichos **9**

La Palapa **26**
Las Palomas **4**
Le Bistro **17**
Pomodoro E Basilico **18**
Red Cabbage Café **27**
Trio **12**
Vitea **11**

Hotel Canto del Sol in the Zona Comercial Las Glorias. It's open Monday through Friday from 9am to 7pm. If you have questions after you arrive, visit the downtown **Dirección de Turismo** (municipal tourism office) in the corner of the white City Hall building at Juárez and Independencia (📞 **322/226-8080,** ext. 230), just off the main square. In addition to offering a listing of current events and promotional brochures, the employees can assist with specific questions—there's usually an English speaker on staff. It's open Monday to Saturday from 8am to 8pm, Sunday from 10am to 6pm.

In Marina Vallarta, the **State Tourism Office,** Plaza Marina L 144, 2nd Floor (📞 **322/221-2676,** -2677, -2678), also offers brochures and can assist with specific questions about Puerto Vallarta and other points in the state of Jalisco, including Guadalajara, Costa Alegre, the town of Tequila, and the program that promotes stays in authentic rural haciendas. It's open Monday through Friday from 9am to 5pm.

CITY LAYOUT The seaside promenade, the *malecón*, is a common reference point for giving directions. It's next to **Paseo Díaz Ordaz** and runs north-south through the central downtown area. From the waterfront, the town stretches back into the hills a half-dozen blocks. The areas bordering the **Río Cuale** are the oldest parts of town—the original Puerto Vallarta. The area immediately south of the river, called **Olas Altas** after its main street (and sometimes Los Muertos after the beach of the same name), is home to a growing selection of sidewalk cafes, fine restaurants, espresso bars, and hip nightclubs. In the center of town, nearly everything is within walking distance both north and south of the river. **Bridges** on Insurgentes (northbound traffic) and Ignacio Vallarta (southbound traffic) link the two sections of downtown.

AREA LAYOUT Beyond downtown, Puerto Vallarta has grown along the beach to the north and south. Linking downtown to the airport is **Avenida Francisco Medina Ascencio,** home of many high-rise hotels (in an area called the **Zona Hotelera,** or Hotel Zone), plus several shopping centers with a variety of dining options.

Marina Vallarta, a resort city within a city, lies at the northern edge of the Hotel Zone, just a few minutes from the airport. It boasts excellent hotels, condominiums, and homes; a huge marina with 450 yacht slips; a golf course; restaurants and bars; and several shopping plazas. Because it was originally a swamp, the beaches are somewhat less desirable, with darker sand and seasonal inflows of cobblestones. The Marina Vallarta peninsula faces the bay and looks south to the town of Puerto Vallarta.

Nuevo Vallarta is a planned resort north of the airport, across the Ameca River in the state of Nayarit (about 13km/8 miles north of downtown). It houses a number of all-inclusive hotels, condominiums, and timeshares, and a yacht marina, with a selection of restaurants and shopping. Most hotels here cater to families, with some of the finest beaches in the bay, but guests usually travel into Puerto Vallarta (about $25 a cab ride) for anything other than poolside or beach action. Regularly scheduled public bus service costs about $2 and runs until 10pm.

Bucerías, a small beachside village of cobblestone streets, villas, excellent seafood restaurants, and just a few art galleries and small hotels, sits farther north along Banderas Bay, 30km (19 miles) beyond the airport. Past Bucerías, following the curved coastline of Banderas Bay, you'll find **La Cruz de Huanaxcle,** a new mega marina project, but still an authentic, colorful seaside town. Continue to the end of the road and you'll reach **Punta Mita.** Once a rustic fishing village, it has been artfully developed as an exclusive luxury destination. Although the fishing village still exists, it has been all but eclipsed by the large gated community of Punta Mita that houses private villas, a few world-class resorts, and two championship golf courses. The site of an ancient celestial observatory, it is an exquisite setting, with white-sand beaches and clear waters. The northern shore of Banderas Bay is emerging as the area's most exclusive address for luxury villas and accommodations, and most of greater Puerto Vallarta's growth is in this direction.

The southern coastal highway stretches south from downtown Vallarta in the direction of Manzanillo and the Costa Alegre. Immediately south of town lies the exclusive residential and rental district of **Conchas Chinas.** Ten kilometers (6¼ miles) south, on **Playa Mismaloya** (where *Night of the Iguana* was filmed), lies the Barceló La Jolla de Mismaloya resort. There's no road on the southern shoreline of Banderas Bay, but three small coastal villages are popular attractions for visitors to Puerto Vallarta: **Las Animas, Quimixto,** and **Yelapa,** all accessible only by boat. The tiny, pristine cove of **Caletas,** site of John Huston's former home, is a popular day- or nighttime excursion (see "Boat Tours," later in this chapter). Dreams Resort also lies south of town at Playa Las Estacas.

GETTING AROUND   By Taxi   Taxis are plentiful and relatively inexpensive. Most trips from downtown to the northern Hotel Zone and Marina Vallarta cost 65 to 80 pesos; to or from Marina Vallarta to Mismaloya Beach (to the south) costs 195 pesos. Rates are charged by zone and are generally posted in hotel lobbies. Taxis can also be hired by the hour or day for longer trips. Rates run about 200 pesos per hour, with full-day discounts available—consider this an alternative to renting a car.

By Car   Rental cars are readily available at the airport, through travel agencies, and through the most popular U.S. car-rental services, but unless you're planning a distant side trip, don't bother. Car rentals are relatively expensive, especially because of insurance rates, and parking around town can be very challenging, unless you opt for one of the two new parking garages constructed on either end of the *malecón* zone (at Park Hidalgo to the north, and adjacent to the northern border of the Cuale River to the south). If you see a sign for a cheap car or jeep rental, be aware that these are lures to get folks to attend timeshare presentations. Unless you are interested in a timeshare, stopping to inquire will be a (possibly annoying) waste of your time.

By Bus   City buses, easy to navigate and inexpensive, will serve just about all your transportation needs. They run from the airport through the Hotel Zone along Morelos Street (1 block inland from the *malecón*), across the Río Cuale, and inland on Vallarta, looping back through the downtown hotel and restaurant districts on Insurgentes and several other downtown streets. To get to the northern hotel strip from old Puerto Vallarta, take the ZONA HOTELES, IXTAPA, or LAS JUNTAS bus. These buses may also post the names of hotels they pass, such as Krystal, Sheraton, and others. Buses marked MARINA VALLARTA travel inside this area, stopping at the major hotels there.

Other buses operate every 10 to 15 minutes south to either Mismaloya Beach or Boca de Tomatlán (a sign in the front window indicates the destination) from Constitución and Basilio Badillo, a few blocks south of the river. Buses run generally from 6am to 11pm, and it's rare to wait more than a few minutes for one. The fare is about 7 pesos. You do not have to have exact change; the driver will make change.

By Boat   The *muelle* (cruise-ship pier), also called Terminal Marítima, is where **excursion boats** to Yelapa, Las Animas, Quimixto, and the Marietas Islands depart. It's north of town near the airport, an inexpensive taxi or bus ride from town. Just take any bus marked IXTAPA, LAS JUNTAS, PITILLAL, or AURORA and tell the driver to let you off at the Terminal Marítima. *Note:* Oddly enough, you must pay a nominal federal tax to gain access to the pier—and your departing excursion boat.

Water taxis to Yelapa, Las Animas, and Quimixto leave multiple times per day starting at 10am and continuing until 6pm from the pier at Los Muertos Beach (south of downtown), on Rodolfo Rodríguez next to the Hotel Marsol. A round-trip ticket to Yelapa (the farthest point, which takes about 45 min. each way) costs 250 pesos. The latest return time is usually 4:45pm, but confirm the pickup time with your water taxi captain. Other water taxis to Yelapa depart from Boca de Tomatlán, about 30 minutes south of town by public bus. These can be a better option if you want more flexible departure and return times from the southern beaches. Generally, they leave on the hour for the southern shore destinations, or more frequently if there is traffic. Prices run about $15 round-trip, with rates clearly posted on a sign on the beach. A private water taxi costs about $35 per hour with a 4-hour minimum, allowing you to come and go on your own time. They'll take up to eight people for that price, so often people band together at the beach to hire one. There's also water taxi service from Los Muertos Beach to Paradise Village in Nuevo Vallarta for $12 each way.

[FastFACTS] PUERTO VALLARTA

Area Code The telephone area code is **322.**

Climate It's sunny and warm all year, with tropical temperatures; however, evenings and early mornings in the winter can turn quite cool. Summers are very hot, with an increase in humidity during the rainy season, between May and October. Rains come almost every afternoon in June and July, and are usually brief but strong—just enough to cool off the air for evening activities. In September, heat and humidity are least comfortable and rains heaviest.

Currency Exchange Banks are found throughout downtown and in the other prime shopping areas. Most banks are open Monday through Friday from 9am to 4pm, with shorter hours on Saturday. ATMs are common throughout Vallarta, including the central plaza downtown. They are

becoming the most favorable way to exchange currency, with bank rates plus 24-hour convenience. *Casas de cambio* (money-exchange houses), located throughout town, offer longer hours than the banks, with only slightly lower exchange rates. Most hotels also change money at varying rates.

Drugstores **CMQ Farmacia,** Basilio Badillo 365 (© **322/222-1330**), is open 24 hours and makes free deliveries to hotels between 11am and 10pm with a minimum purchase of $20. **Farmacias Guadalajara,** Emiliano Zapata 232 (© **322/224-1811**), is also open 24 hours.

Embassies & Consulates The **U.S. Consular Agency** office (© **322/222-0069;** http://guadalajara.usconsulate.gov) is located in Nuevo Vallarta at Paseo de los Cocoteros 85, in the

Paradise Plaza, Local L-7, on the second floor. It's open Monday through Friday from 8:30am to 12:30pm. The **Canadian Consulate** (© **322/293-0099,** -0098; 24-hr. emergency line 01-800/706-2900 in Mexico) is located in Plaza Las Glorias, Blvd. Francisco Medina Ascencio 1951, Edificio Obelisco, Loc. 108 (you'll see the Canadian flag hanging from the balcony). It's open Monday through Friday from 9am to 1pm.

Emergencies **Police** emergency, © **060** or **066;** local police, © **322/290-0513,** -0512; intensive care ambulance, **Cruz Roja (Red Cross),** © **322/222-1533** and **San Javier Marina Hospital Ambulance Service** (© **322/226-1010,** ext. 340).

Hospitals The following offer U.S.-standards service and are available 24 hours: **Ameri-Med Urgent Care,** Avenida Francisco Medina Ascencio at Plaza Neptuno,

Loc. D-1, Marina Vallarta (𝄞 **322/226-2080;** www. amerimed.com.mx); **San Javier Marina Hospital,** Av. Francisco Medina Ascencio 2760, Zona Hotelera (𝄞 **322/226-1010**); and **Cornerstone Hospital,** Av. los Tules 136 (behind Plaza Caracol; 𝄞 **322/226-3700**).

Internet Access Most Vallarta hotels have Wi-Fi, and the resorts typically offer business centers. You can also get access at **PV Cafe** (𝄞 **322/223-3308**), located in the old town at Olas Altas 246. It's open daily from 8am to midnight and charges 35 pesos per hour for computer use. Next door, **Café Vayan** (𝄞 **322/222-0092**), at Olas Altas 350, serves tasty breakfasts and snacks with free Wi-Fi. It's open 8am to 11pm.

Newspapers & Magazines *Vallarta Today,* a weekly English-language newspaper (𝄞 **322/225-3323;** www. vallartatoday.com), is a good source for dining, cultural events, retirement information, real estate, and healthy living in Vallarta. The bilingual quarterly city magazine **Vallarta Life-styles** (𝄞 **322/221-0106;** www.virtualvallarta.com) is also very popular. Both are for sale at area newsstands and hotel gift shops. The weekly English-language *Vallarta Tribune* (www. vallartatribune.com) is distributed free throughout town and offers an objective local viewpoint. *PV Mirror* (www.pvmirror.com) is another English-language city paper and online site that offers local news and visitor information.

Post Office The *correo* is at Colombia Street, behind Hidalgo Park, and is open Monday through Friday from 9am to 6pm, Saturday from 9am to 1pm.

Safety Puerto Vallarta enjoys a very low crime rate. Public transportation is safe to use, and Tourist Police (dressed in navy blue and white uniforms) are available to answer questions, give directions, and offer assistance. Most encounters with the police are linked to using or purchasing drugs—so don't (see also "Drugs & Other Border Issues" in chapter 2). **Note:** The tourist police sometimes conduct random personal searches for drugs. If this happens, you are within your rights to request the name of the officer. Report any unusual incidents to the local consular office.

Where to Stay

Beyond a varied selection of hotels and resorts, Puerto Vallarta offers many alternative accommodations. Oceanfront or marina-view condominiums and elegant private villas can offer families and small groups a better value and more ample space than a hotel. For short-term rentals, check out **Costa Vallarta Boutique Villas** (𝄞 **800/728-9098** in the U.S. and Canada, or 01-800/508-7923 in Mexico; www. costavallartaboutiquevillas.com). Office hours are Monday through Friday 9am to 6pm, Saturday 9am to 2pm. Prices start at $100 a night for non-beachside condos and reach into the thousands of dollars for penthouse condos or private villas. This site links to **Mexico Boutique Hotels** (www.mexicoboutiquehotels.com), which is an association of luxury boutique inns across the country, including Hacienda San Angel, El Careyes, Casa de Mita, El Tamarindo, and Verana, reviewed in this chapter. Upon request, the association organizes personalized trips in the region. **Bayside Properties** (𝄞 **322/222-8148;** www.baysidepropertiespv.com) located at Francisco Rodríguez 160, on the corner of Olas Altas, rents condos, villas, and hotels for individuals and large groups, including gay-friendly accommodations. Another reputable full-service travel agency is **Puerto Vallarta Villas** (𝄞 **415/704-0455** in the U.S. or 322/221-5495; www.puertovallartavillas.com). For the ultimate, indulge in a Punta Mita Villa rental within this exclusive resort. Contact **Mita Residential** (𝄞 **877/561-2893** toll-free in the U.S., or 329/291-5300; www.mitaresidential.com).

This section lists hotels from the airport south along Banderas Bay.

MARINA VALLARTA

Marina Vallarta is the most modern and deluxe area of hotel development in Puerto Vallarta. Located immediately south of the airport and just north of the cruise ship terminal, it's a planned development whose centerpiece is a 450-slip modern marina.

In addition to the hotels reviewed below, an excellent choice is **Casa Velas,** on the golf course at Pelícanos 311 (www.hotelcasavelas.com; ℂ **866/529-8813** in the U.S., or 322/226-6688). High-season rates start at $210 per person, all-inclusive.

Marriott CasaMagna Resort & Spa ★★ ☺   Set on a lovely stretch of beach in Marina Vallarta, the family-friendly CasaMagna underwent a $10.7-million renovation in 2008. Guest rooms, all of which are accessed through open-air hallways, were upgraded with contemporary Mexican styling, marble floors, and flower accents, and bougainvillea hangs from each balcony overlooking the pool and bay. Pool activities and beach watersports are offered throughout the day, and there's a luxurious yet reasonably priced spa. Among the many diversions for children is a turtle-preservation program that runs from June to November and provides guests the chance to release baby turtles into the sea. The resort houses four restaurants, including the teppan-yaki-style **Mikado** (see "Where to Eat," below), as well as the colonial-designed Mexican La Estancia. Executive Chef Fred Ruiz offers interactive cooking classes (about $60 per person), beginning with a tour of the hotel's own chile, herb, and cactus garden.

Paseo de la Marina Norte 435, Marina Vallarta, 48354 Puerto Vallarta, Jal. www.puertovallartamarriott. com. ℂ **800/223-6388** in the U.S., or 322/226-0000. Fax 322/226-0060. 433 units. High season $229 and up double, $459–$479 suite; low season $159 and up double, $359–$389 suite. AE, DC, MC, V. Free parking. **Amenities:** 4 restaurants; deli; 3 bars; concierge; golf privileges at Marina Vallarta Golf Club; kids' club; state-of-the-art fitness center and spa w/classes (fee); sauna, steam room, and whirlpool; oceanside pool; room service; 2 lighted grass tennis courts. *In room:* A/C, flatscreen TV, iHome, hair dryer, minibar, Wi-Fi.

Westin Resort & Spa Puerto Vallarta ★★ ☺   Stunning architecture and vibrant colors are the hallmark of this award-winning property. Despite the spacious grounds, the warm service creates the feeling of an intimate resort. Hammocks are strung between the palms closest to the beach, where there are also private beach cabañas. All rooms have ocean-view balconies, "Heavenly" beds, oversize wood furnishings, tile floors, and original art. Eight junior suites and some double rooms have Jacuzzis, and the five grand suites consist of two levels, with spacious living areas. Two floors of rooms make up the Royal Beach Club with VIP services, including a private lounge with continental breakfast and evening drinks included. There's an excellent spa and fitness center, as well as an exclusive beach area with pergolas available for daily rent.

Paseo de la Marina Sur 205, Marina Vallarta, 48354 Puerto Vallarta, Jal. www.starwoodhotels.com/ westin. ℂ **800/228-3000** in the U.S., or 322/226-1100. Fax 322/226-1144. 280 units. $155 and up double. AE, DC, MC, V. Free parking. **Amenities:** 2 restaurants; 3 bars; beach club; concierge; kids' club; golf privileges at Marina Vallarta Golf Club; 2 free-form pools; full-service spa and health club w/sauna and steam room; 3 lighted grass tennis courts; gallery arcade; room service. *In room:* A/C, TV, hair dryer, minibar, Wi-Fi.

THE HOTEL ZONE

The main street running between the airport and town is Avenida Francisco Medina Ascencio. The hotels here offer excellent wide beachfronts with generally tranquil waters for swimming. From here it's a quick 50-peso taxi or bus ride to downtown.

Fiesta Americana Puerto Vallarta ★★ ☺   The Fiesta Americana's towering, three-story, thatched *palapa* lobby is a landmark in the Hotel Zone, and the resort is known for its excellent beach, quality rooms, and friendly service. An abundance of plants, splashing fountains, constant breezes, and comfortable seating areas in the lobby create a casual South Seas ambience. The nine-story terra-cotta building embraces a large beachfront plaza and pool bustling with activities. Marble-trimmed rooms in neutral tones with pastel accents contain carved headboards and comfortable rattan-and-wicker furniture. All have private balconies with ocean and pool views. Beachside massages continue from morning to sunset, and there's a full-service spa.

Av. Francisco Medina Ascencio Km 2.5, 48300 Puerto Vallarta, Jal. www.fiestaamericana.com. ℭ **322/226-2100.** Fax 322/224-2108. 291 units. $150 and up double; $300 and up suite. AE, DC, MC, V. Limited free parking. **Amenities:** 3 restaurants; 3 bars; kids' club; fitness center; large pool w/activities; room service; full-service spa. *In room:* A/C, TV, hair dryer, minibar, Wi-Fi.

Villa Premiere Puerto Vallarta Hotel & Spa ★★   Located a few blocks north of the start of the *malecón*, the Premiere is within walking distance of downtown restaurants, shops, galleries, and clubs. With a first-rate spa and a policy that restricts guests to ages 16 and older, it's a place that caters to relaxation. Rooms are decorated in warm colors with tile floors and light wood furnishings. Deluxe rooms have ocean views, a small seating area with comfortable chairs, and a sizable private balcony. Spa suites offer Jacuzzis in the bedrooms. The stunning bi-level spa is the real attraction of this hotel—scented with aromatherapy and glowing with candlelight, it uses top-notch, 100% natural products, most based on Mexico's natural treasures such as coconut, aloe, and papaya. The Premiere also offers an all-inclusive option.

San Salvador 117, behind the Buenaventura Hotel, Col. 5 de Diciembre, 48350 Puerto Vallarta, Jal. www. premiereonline.com.mx. ℭ **877/886-9176** in the U.S., or 322/226-7001, -7040. Fax 322/226-7043. 83 units. Room only: High season $185–$430 double; low season $135–$370 double. All-inclusive rates are approximately double. AE, MC, V. Limited street parking. Children 15 and younger not accepted. **Amenities:** 3 restaurants; fitness center; yoga classes and meditation workshops; outdoor pool; room service; full spa w/sauna and steam room. *In room:* A/C, TV, hair dryer, minibar, Wi-Fi.

DOWNTOWN TO LOS MUERTOS BEACH

This part of town has undergone a renaissance; economical hotels and good-value guesthouses dominate. Several blocks off the beach, you can find numerous budget inns offering clean, simply furnished rooms; most offer discounts for long-term stays. Many hotels in Viejo Vallarta (the old town, south of the Río Cuale) are gay- and straight-friendly.

Hacienda San Angel ★★★ 🏛   This renowned boutique hotel has a more formal feel than most Vallarta accommodations. Although not on the beach, you'll hardly miss the surf since it offers beautiful vistas of the city and Bay of Banderas. Once the home of Richard Burton, the Hacienda lies just behind Puerto Vallarta's famed church and, in fact, looks somewhat like a church itself (guests can request to stay in Burton's former room, "Celestial"). The inn consists of four rustic colonial villas; the first two are joined to the third villa by a path that winds through a lovely terraced tropical garden with statuary and a fountain. An old chapel across the street offers seven guest rooms decorated in rich colonial furnishings and tapestries; many have antiques and claw-foot tubs. One of the heated pools and deck lie next to the elegant open-air restaurant, and a second sun deck overlooks the church and sea beyond.

Continental breakfast is served outside your suite at the hour you request or in the memorable open-air restaurant (see "Where to Eat," below).

Miramar 336, Col. Centro, 48300 Puerto Vallarta, Jal. www.haciendasanangel.com. (©) **877/815-6594** or 322/222-2692. 19 units. High season $535 and up double; low season $435 and up double. All rates include daily continental breakfast. Rates for the entire Hacienda or separate villas consisting of 3 suites each are also available. AE, MC, V. Very limited street parking. **Amenities:** 3 outdoor pools; en-suite spa services available; assistance with activities and tours; concierge; free Internet. *In room:* A/C, TV/DVD, CD player, hair dryer.

Hotel Playa Los Arcos ★★   This perennially popular hotel has a stellar location in the heart of Los Muertos Beach, central to the Olas Altas sidewalk-cafe action. The lovely four-story structure is U-shaped and faces the ocean. Guest rooms are small but comfortable, and draped in white, with carved wooden furniture. They have balconies that overlook the courtyard pool that virtually extends into the lobby. The hotel grounds include a *palapa* beachside bar with occasional live entertainment, a gourmet coffee shop, and Kaiser Maximilian's gourmet restaurant (see "Where to Eat," later). The hotel is 7 blocks south of the river in the old section of downtown.

Olas Altas 380, 48380 Puerto Vallarta, Jal. www.playalosarcos.com. (©) **800/648-2403** in the U.S., or 322/226-7100. Fax 322/226-7104. 171 units. $120–$150 double; $150–$200 suite. All-inclusive packages available. MC, V. Limited street parking. **Amenities:** Restaurant; lobby bar; outdoor pool; Wi-Fi (in lobby). *In room:* A/C, TV.

SOUTH TO MISMALOYA

Casa Tres Vidas ★★ ⬥   Set on a stunning private cove, Tres Vidas gives you the experience of your own private villa, complete with service staff. It offers outstanding value for the location—close to town, with panoramic views from every room. Each villa has at least two levels and over 460 sq. m (4,951 sq. ft.) of mostly open living areas, plus a private swimming pool, heated whirlpool, and air-conditioned bedrooms. The Vida Alta penthouse villa has three bedrooms, plus a rooftop deck with pool and bar. Vida Sol villa's three bedrooms sleep 10 (two rooms have two king-size beds each). Directly on the ocean, Vida Mar is a four-bedroom villa, accommodating eight. The staff prepares gourmet meals in your villa twice a day—you choose the menu and pay only for the food. Service is consistently excellent.

Sagitario 132, Playa Conchas Chinas, 48300 Puerto Vallarta, Jal. www.casatresvidas.com. (©) **888/640-8100** toll-free in the U.S., or 322/221-5317. Fax 322/221-53-27. 3 villas. High season $900–$950 villa; low season $550–$600 villa. Rates include services such as housekeeping and meal preparation. Special summer 1- or 2-bedroom rates available; minimum 5 nights during high season. AE, MC, V. Limited street parking. **Amenities:** 2 prepared daily meals; concierge; private outdoor pool. *In room:* A/C, TV, Wi-Fi.

Dreams Puerto Vallarta Resort & Spa ☺   The all-inclusive Dreams Resort sits on a beautiful beach with soft white sand in a private cove. Set apart from other properties, with a lush mountain backdrop, it's only a 10-minute ride to town. The hotel consists of two buildings: the 250-room main hotel, which curves gently with the shape of the Playa Las Estacas, and the newer 11-story Club Tower, also facing the beach and ocean. Standard rooms in the aging main building are large; some have sliding doors opening onto the beach, and others have balconies. Preferred Club suites have access to a private lounge, expanded marble bathrooms with upgraded amenities, and balconies with whirlpool tubs. All rooms feature ocean views, vibrant colors, marble floors, and local artwork. The grounds include two swimming pools, a health club, and a spa; activities are offered day and night. The Explorer's Club for Kids (ages 3–12) offers your basic arts and crafts activities and sandcastle contests, as well as your not-so-basic outdoor movies on the beach and weekly campout. Food served in the resort is so-so.

Carretera Barra de Navidad Km 3.5, Playa Las Estacas, 48300 Puerto Vallarta, Jal. www.dreamsresorts. com. © **866/237-3267** in the U.S. and Canada, or 322/226-5000. Fax 322/221-6000. 337 units. All-inclusive rates are per person and include all meals, premium drinks, activities, airport transfers, tips, and taxes. $380 and up double; $540 and up junior suite; $700 and up oceanview suite. AE, DC, MC, V. Free secured parking. **Amenities:** 6 restaurants; 4 bars; pool bar; kids' club; fully equipped health club; yoga; 3 outdoor pools w/daytime activities; room service; shows at night in high season; spa; 2 lighted grass tennis courts; nonmotorized watersports. *In room:* A/C, TV, MP3 players, hair dryer, Internet, minibar.

Quinta María Cortez ★★ 🎁 An eclectic, imaginative B&B on the beach, this is Puerto Vallarta's most original place to stay—and one of Mexico's most memorable inns. Most of the seven large suites, uniquely decorated with antiques, whimsical curios, and original art, have a kitchenette and balcony. Sunny terraces, a small pool, and a central gathering area with fireplace and *palapa*-topped dining area (where an excellent full breakfast is served) occupy different levels of the seven-story house. A rooftop terrace offers another sunbathing alternative—and is among the best sunset-watching spots in town. The quinta sits on a beautiful cove on Conchas Chinas beach. A terrace fronting the beach accommodates chairs for taking in the sunset.

Sagitario 132, Playa Conchas Chinas, 48300 Puerto Vallarta, Jal. www.quinta-maria.com. © **888/640-8100** in the U.S., or 322/221-5317. Fax 322/221-5327. 7 units. High season $170–$320 double; low season $155–$195 double. Rates include breakfast. AE, MC, V. Very limited street parking. Children 17 and younger not accepted. **Amenities:** Concierge; small outdoor pool; Wi-Fi (in common areas). *In room:* A/C, fridge, hair dryer.

YELAPA

Verana ★★★ 📷 Verana is a secluded retreat tucked in the hills overlooking sleepy Yelapa, a natural paradise with spectacular views of the tropical landscape and ocean before it. The adults-only clientele are spread out among eight accommodations ranging from the tranquil two-bedroom "stone house" to the more expensive "tea house" that resembles an enchanted open-air tree house with a private pool. The houses feature king-size beds with mosquito nets, beautiful bathrooms, and private terraces, and while there are no TVs or telephones, Wi-Fi is available. Guests have access to an unforgettable "Jungle Spa," where most of the treatments and programs take place in a tranquil outdoor setting; kayaks; and snorkeling equipment. The European-trained chef prepares exquisite cuisine. Verana is reached via a 30-minute water taxi from Boca de Tomatlán (south of Puerto Vallarta, p. 296) followed by a 10-minute hike up a fairly steep trail from the boat launch (mules can be arranged for people with mobility difficulties). The town of Yelapa lies about a half-hour walk from the inn.

Calle Zaragoza 404, 48304 Yelapa, Jal. www.verana.com. © **866/687-9358** or 310/455-2425 in the U.S., or 322/222-0878. 8 villas. Winter/high season $360–$480 villa per night with 5-night minimum; $750 3-bedroom Casa Grande per night; extra person $70 per night. AE, MC, V. Optional daily breakfast, lunch, and dinner charge $95 per person; alcoholic beverages extra. Shorter stays based on availability. Closed during summer months. Management helps arrange transportation from Puerto Vallarta to Boca. **Amenities:** Restaurant/bar; morning yoga classes; library; outdoor pool; spa w/massage services; snorkeling equipment; kayaks; Wi-Fi. *In room:* No phone.

Where to Eat

Puerto Vallarta has an exceptional dining scene. Over 250 restaurants serve cuisines from around the world, in addition to fresh seafood and regional dishes. Chefs from

France, Switzerland, Germany, Italy, and Argentina have come for visits and stayed to open restaurants. In celebration of this diversity, Vallarta's culinary community hosts a gourmet dining festival each November. Prices below include the 16% IVA tax.

Of the inexpensive local spots, one favorite is **El Planeta Vegetariano,** Iturbide 270, just down from the main church (© **322/222-3073**), serving an inexpensive and delicious vegetarian buffet, which changes for breakfast and lunch/dinner. It's open daily. Breakfast (50 pesos) is served from 8am till noon; the lunch and dinner buffets (75 pesos) are served from noon to 10pm; no credit cards are accepted.

MARINA VALLARTA

Most of the best restaurants in the Marina are in hotels, but a number of quality options line the boardwalk bordering the marina yacht harbor, as well.

Mikado ★ ☺ JAPANESE   Surrounded by koi ponds next to the CasaMagna Marriott, this fun teppanyaki-style restaurant is a favorite among families and celebratory groups. Up to eight people gather around each of the communal tables with a built-in steel grill, as the Mexican-turned-Japanese chef puts on a culinary show of juggling spatulas, flying shrimp, tossed eggs, and steaming onion volcanoes that will delight children and adults alike. Order a la carte or a complete progressive dinner, which includes miso soup and salad along with your choice of chicken, beef, shrimp, or fish prepared flaming in front of your eyes. Each complete dinner is served with steamed or fried rice and fresh grilled vegetables, topped off with green tea and sorbet. Mikado also offers sushi, sashimi, nigiri, and noodle dishes, and there are a few non-teppanyaki tables for those who prefer more private dining.

Paseo de la Marina Norte 435, Marina Vallarta (Marriott CasaMagna). © **322/226-0000.** Reservations recommended. Main courses 179–431 pesos; complete dinner 420–431 pesos. AE, MC, V. Daily 6–11pm.

Porto Bello ★★ ITALIAN   One of the first restaurants in the marina, Porto Bello serves flavorful Italian dishes to the backdrop of docked sailboats and motor yachts. For starters, the fried calamari is delicately seasoned, and the grilled vegetable antipasto could easily serve as a full meal. Signature dishes include fusilli prepared with artichokes, black olives, lemon juice, basil, olive oil, and Parmesan cheese; and sautéed fish filet with white wine, spinach, and arugula. I love the lightly broiled butterfly shrimp served with spaghetti or, for a splurge, the pecan-crusted rack of French lamb. The elegant indoor dining room is air-conditioned, and there's also open-air seating with white linen tables. Porto Bello recently opened a second restaurant in Nuevo Vallarta (© **322/297-6719**), next to the Mayan Palace.

Marina Sol, Loc. 7 (Marina Vallarta *malecón*). © **322/221-0003.** www.portobellovallarta.com. Reservations recommended for dinner. Main courses 195–410 pesos. AE, MC, V. Daily noon–11pm.

DOWNTOWN
Expensive

Café des Artistes/Thierry Blouet Cocina del Autor ★★★ FRENCH/ INTERNATIONAL   The award-winning chef and owner, Thierry Blouet, is both a member of the French Academie Culinaire and a Maitre Cuisinier de France. The Café des Artistes includes the upscale Constantini martini and piano bar and the expensive Thierry Blouet Cocina del Autor dining area. The cafe's menu consists of French gourmet bistro fare, drawing on Chef Blouet's French training and incorporating regional specialty ingredients. Noteworthy entrees include sea bass served with a Swiss chard mousse, and roasted duck glazed with honey, soy, and ginger. At the elegant Cocina del Autor, fashionable diners choose from the fixed-priced tasting menu (prices depend on the number of plates you select, from 4 to 12). Choose any combination of starters, entrees, and desserts. Portions are generally small. For a particularly romantic setting, reserve a table on the lush, candlelit terrace. After dining, you're invited to the cognac and cigar room, an exquisite blend of old adobe walls, flickering candles, and elegant leather chairs. Service is professional, if a bit stiff.

Guadalupe Sánchez 740, corner with Vicario. © **322/222-3228,** -3229, -3230. www.cafedesartistes. com. Reservations recommended. Main courses 210–405 pesos. Cocina del Autor tasting menu 650–1,450 pesos without wine, 1,050–2,100 pesos with wine. AE, DC, MC, V. Daily 6–11:30pm (lounge until 1am).

Moderate

Hacienda San Angel ★★★ MEXICAN   The exquisite beauty of the Hacienda, as well as the city lights and shimmering bay, are proudly displayed for diners at this special location. The menu changes periodically and features Mexican-infused international cuisine. Starters include crispy fried calamari with a selection of sauces; grilled seasonal vegetables in a tomato, olive oil, and basil balsamic vinaigrette; and a shrimp and coconut cream soup accented with brandy. The house specialty is the grilled *Cabreria,* a tender bone-in steak, served with garlic mashed potatoes, a portobello mushroom ragout, and a three-chile sauce. Other standouts include chicken *mole* and the herb-crusted rack of lamb in a green-pepper sauce. Top this memorable dinner off with apple raviolis smothered in butterscotch and almonds. Start the evening by arriving between 7:30 and 9:30pm for a sunset cocktail hour often featuring live mariachi music—you may also enjoy strolling the grounds. Service is wonderful.

Miramar 336, Centro. © **322/222-2692.** www.haciendasanangel.com. Reservations required. Main courses $15–$40, with 20% gratuity added to all checks. AE, MC, V. Daily 6–10pm.

Las Palomas ★ MEXICAN   One of Puerto Vallarta's first restaurants, this is the power-breakfast place of choice—and a popular hangout for everyone else throughout the day. Authentic in atmosphere and menu, it's one of Puerto Vallarta's few genuine Mexican restaurants. Breakfast is the best value. The staff pours mugs of steaming coffee spiced with cinnamon as soon as you're seated. Try classic *huevos rancheros* or *chilaquiles* (tortilla strips, fried and topped with red or green spicy sauce, cream, and cheese, with fried eggs or shredded chicken). Lunch and dinner offer traditional Mexican specialties, such as chiles rellenos, enchiladas, fajitas, and carne asada. The best places for checking out the *malecón* and watching the sunset while sipping an icy margarita are the spacious bar and the upstairs terrace. You may need some drinks to participate in (or even just listen to) the nightly karaoke.

Paseo Díaz Ordaz 610. © **322/222-3675.** www.laspalomaspvr.com. Breakfast 50–125 pesos; lunch and dinner 135–325 pesos. AE, MC, V. Daily 8am–1am.

Trio ★★★ 🍴 INTERNATIONAL   Trio is the darling of Vallarta restaurants, with diners beating a path to the modest but stylish cafe where chef-owners Bernhard Güth and Ulf Henricksson's undeniable passion for food imbues each dish. They call it "Mediterranean food cooked with love," and indeed Trio is noted for its perfected melding of Mexican and Mediterranean flavors and exquisite presentation. Consider starting with the cilantro-ginger-marinated calamari with avocado and a jalapeño salsa. For a main course, I recommend ricotta spinach ravioli with sun-dried tomatoes, or the oven-roasted rabbit with Italian vegetables. These dishes may not be on the menu when you arrive, though—it's a constantly changing work of art. In high season, the rooftop dining area allows for a more comfortable wait for a table or for after-dinner coffee, and a trio plays live music during dinner. Most locals will tell you this is their favorite restaurant in town. The same owners run Vitea (see below).

Guerrero 264. © **322/222-2196.** www.triopv.com. Reservations recommended. Main courses 175–320 pesos. AE, MC, V. Daily 6–11:30pm.

Inexpensive

Agave Grill ★ MEXICAN   Agave Grill has gradually taken over the space at the Casa de Tequila in central downtown. The location is lovely, in a beautiful garden setting within a classic hacienda-style building. Start with fresh salsa made at your table (spiced to your preference), and follow with the *pulpo* (octopus) sautéed to tenderness in a delectable chile and garlic sauce. My favorite main courses include seafood enchiladas, and beef tenderloin prepared with *mole.* For a sweet finish, you'll love the chocolate "tamal" served with homemade vanilla ice cream. All tortillas and savory salsas are handmade. An elegant bar serves Vallarta's most original selection of fine tequilas, many from small distilleries.

Morelos 589. © **322/222-2000.** Reservations not accepted. Main courses 148–298 pesos; chef's tasting menu 300 pesos. MC, V. Mon–Sat noon–11:30pm; Sun 5–11:30pm.

El Arrayán ★★★ 🍴 MEXICAN   The spirited Arrayán, up a steep sidewalk, offers rewarding, authentic Mexican cuisine. The casual open-air dining area surrounds a cozy courtyard, while its exposed brick walls and funky-chic decor showcase a modern view of Mexican classics. Start with an order of delicious ceviche, sumptuous plantain empanadas filled with black beans, or a traditional salad of diced *nopal* cactus paddles with fresh cheese. Favorite main courses include chicken *mole,* chiles rellenos packed with shrimp, and Mexican duck *carnitas* served in an *arrayán*-orange sauce. (*Arrayán,* the namesake of the place, is a small sweet-and-sour fruit native to the region.) Any dish can be made vegetarian. The homemade ice creams and sorbets make for a tasty and refreshing finish to your meal. The full bar offers an extensive selection of original cocktails (check out the "mojo-basil grapefruit mojito"), tequilas, Mexican wines, and nonalcoholic *aguas frescas*—a blended drink of fresh fruit and water. Expect excellent service.

Allende 344, just past Matamoros, on the corner with Miramar. © **322/222-7195.** www.elarrayan.com. mx. Reservations recommended. Main courses 160–230 pesos. AE, MC, V. Wed–Mon 5:30–11pm. Closed Tues.

Tapas, Anyone?

Certainly much of modern Mexico's culture draws on the important influence of Spain, so it only makes sense that Spanish culinary traditions would be evident as well. Of the many options, these are my favorites: the long-standing **Barcelona Tapas**, Matamoros and 31 de Octubre streets (© 322/222-0510), a tapas bar located up a set of stairs on a hillside, with sweeping views of the bay. In addition to tapas and a selection of Spanish entrees, including paella, it offers sangria and a fine selection of wines from noon to 11:30pm. **La Esquina de los Caprichos,** Miramar 402, corner of Iturbide (© 322/222-0911), is a tiny place near Hacienda San Angel known as having the most reasonably priced (35–85 pesos) tapas in town, and perhaps the tastiest. Hours are Monday through Saturday from 8:30am to 10pm; cash only. It closes in August.

Vitea ★★ 🖼INTERNATIONAL　This artistic bistro is run by the acclaimed chef/ owners of Trio, whom many consider to serve Vallarta's best food. It's no surprise then that the fresh, healthy dishes here make Vitea another favorite among locals. Due to strategically placed mirrors on the back wall, every seat has a view of the ocean, while the interior is cheerful and inviting. Starters include succulent shrimp tempura with pumpkinseeds, spicy garlic, and chile or a Greek salad that explodes with flavor. Main courses change regularly and may include barbecue red snapper with wilted spinach, eggplant ravioli with portobello mushrooms, or Angus beef tips sautéed with wine. Dinner selections offer a choice of smaller or larger portions. Lunch offers lighter fare, and breakfast is now served as well.

Malecón no. 2, at Libertad. ⓒ **322/222-8703.** www.viteapv.com. Reservations recommended during peak dining hours. Main courses 155–285 pesos. MC, V. Daily 8am–midnight.

SOUTH OF THE RÍO CUALE TO OLAS ALTAS

South of the river is the densest restaurant area, where you'll find Basilio Badillo. A second main dining drag has emerged along Calle Olas Altas, with a variety of cuisines and price categories. Cafes and espresso bars, generally open from 7am to midnight, line its wide sidewalks, and there are a number of casual seafood eateries open along the beachfront during high season. A wonderful farmers market takes place on Olas Altas Saturdays from 10am to 2pm.

Expensive

Archie's Wok ★★★ 🖼ASIAN/SEAFOOD　Since 1986, Archie's has been legendary in Puerto Vallarta for serving original cuisine influenced by the intriguing flavors of Southeast Asia, and today the restaurant remains as impressive as ever. Archie was Hollywood director John Huston's private chef during the years he spent in the area. Today his family upholds his legacy at this tranquil Asian-inspired retreat, where fountains trickle and table candle lights flicker by night. The Thai Mai Tai and other tropical drinks, made from only fresh fruit and juices, are a good way to kick off a meal, as are the consistently crispy and delicious Filipino spring rolls. The popular Singapore fish filet features lightly battered filet strips in sweet-and-sour sauce; the delicious barbecue pork riblets are baked for 5 hours and then served with a rich oyster sauce. Friday and Saturday from 7:30 to 10:30pm, there's live classical harp and flute in Archie's Oriental garden.

Francisca Rodríguez 130 (a half-block from the Los Muertos pier). ⓒ **322/222-0411.** Main courses 125–225 pesos. MC, V. Mon–Sat 2–11pm. Closed Sept.

Café Kaiser Maximilian ★★ INTERNATIONAL　Designed to resemble a 19th-century Viennese cafe, Kaiser Maximilian presents a distinctly European, not Mexican, atmosphere. It's the prime place to go if you want to combine exceptional food with great people-watching. Austrian-born owner Andreas Rupprechter is almost always on hand to ensure that the service is impeccable and the food delicious. Indoor, air-conditioned dining takes place at cozy tables; sidewalk tables are larger and great for groups of friends. The cuisine merges old-world European preparations with regional fresh ingredients (think Wiener schnitzel with a Mexican touch). Recommended mains include filet of trout with a horseradish crust; rack of lamb wrapped in bacon; and seared scallops with butternut squash purée. The gourmet coffees and desserts made in the adjacent cafe and pastry shop are famous throughout the town: I'd try the warm pecan chocolate bourbon tart if I were you.

Olas Altas 380-B (at Basilio Badillo, in front of the Hotel Playa Los Arcos), Zona Romántica. ℰ **322/223-0760.** www.kaisermaximilian.com. Reservations recommended in high season. Main courses 195–328 pesos. AE, MC, V. Mon–Sat 6–11pm.

Daiquiri Dick's ★★★ PACIFIC RIM/MEDITERRANEAN While Puerto Vallarta is replete with ideal "people-watching" perches, come to Daiquiri Dick's if you want to enjoy some fantastic "food-watching." Each dish is festively prepared, served steaming hot from the kitchen and bursting with color and artistic garnishes. You'll be tempted to try each dish that passes your table. For light fare, try the Asian chicken salad, which blends tender chicken, crunchy vegetables, and a savory ginger sesame dressing. For something more substantial, the barbecue pork spareribs as well as the crispy cornmeal-crusted perch with toasted garlic-ancho chile vinaigrette remain house favorites. Don't forget to order a daiquiri with your meal. The restaurant lies at the northern edge of Viejo Vallarta, set against a lovely section of beach with palm trees wrapped in white lights that provide a warm glow at dinner. Live music accompanies the Sunday brunch, which offers excellent value.

Olas Altas 314. ℰ **322/222-0566.** www.ddpv.com. Main courses 185–265 pesos; Sunday brunch 145 pesos. MC, V. Daily 9am–10:30pm. Closed Sept.

Espresso ITALIAN This popular eatery is one of Vallarta's late-night dining options. The two-level restaurant sits on one of the town's busiest streets—across from El Torito's sports bar—meaning that traffic noise is a factor but not a deterrent. The food is reliable, the service attentive, and the prices reasonable. Owned by a partnership of lively Italians, it serves authentic Italian food, from thin-crust, brick-oven pizza to savory homemade pastas and oven-baked breads. Excellent calzones and *paninis* are also options. I prefer the rooftop garden area for dining, but many patrons gravitate to the air-conditioned downstairs, which features major sports and entertainment events on satellite TV. Espresso also has full bar service and draft beer.

Ignacio L. Vallarta 279. ℰ **322/222-3272.** Entrees 98–189 pesos. MC, V. Daily noon–1am.

Fajita Republic MEXICAN/SEAFOOD/STEAKS Fajita Republic has hit on a winning recipe: delicious food, ample portions, welcoming atmosphere, and low prices. The specialty is, of course, sizzling fajitas, grilled to perfection in every variety: steak, fish, chicken, vegetarian, shrimp, combo, and occasionally lobster. This "tropical grill" also serves sumptuous barbecued ribs, Mexican *molcajetes* with incredibly tender strips of marinated beef filet, and grilled shrimp. Starters include fresh guacamole served in a giant spoon and the ever-popular Maya cheese sticks (breaded and deep-fried). Try an oversize mug or pitcher of Fajita Rita Mango Margaritas.

Basilio Badillo 188, 1 block north of Olas Altas. ℰ **322/222-3131.** Main courses 82–188 pesos. MC, V. Daily 5–11pm.

La Palapa ★★ 🍴 SEAFOOD/MEXICAN This beachside *palapa* restaurant defines enchantment, a decades-old favorite with beautiful amber lamps, candles, and lanterns illuminating the night. With each visit, I've been impressed by the quality of the food and service. For lunch and dinner, seafood is the specialty; dishes include miso Chilean sea bass, pepper-crusted yellowfin tuna, grilled shrimp in coconut and tequila, and—for those looking for a break from seafood—pork tenderloin stuffed with chorizo, pecans, and goat cheese. The Palapa's location on Los Muertos Beach makes dinner especially enticing for moon watching over the bay. The bar opens to the dining area and features acoustic guitars and vocals nightly from 8 to 11pm. The restaurant doubles as a beach club during the day.

Pulpito 103. ☏ **322/222-5225.** www.lapalapapv.com. Reservations recommended for dinner in high season. Breakfast 60–130 pesos; main courses 190–400 pesos. AE, MC, V. Daily 8am–11:30pm.

Moderate

Le Bistro ★★ INTERNATIONAL   I love this place, a French-inspired bistro with a large garden deck set right over the river. Le Bistro's specialty is crepes, with delicious options such as shrimp with broccoli or chicken with squash blossoms. The lunch-and-dinner menu offers fine international cuisine, including filet mignon, duck in a black-berry sauce, and rock Cornish hen stuffed with herbed rice, dried tropical fruit, and nuts, finished in mango-cilantro sauce. Tasty Mexican dishes like crab enchiladas and grilled steak with guacamole are also on order. An extensive wine list and selection of specialty coffees complement the menu, and romantic jazz music plays Thursday through Saturday nights. Le Bistro is also a lovely spot to linger over breakfast.

Isla Río Cuale 16-A (just east of northbound bridge). ☏ **322/222-0283.** www.lebistro.com.mx. Reservations recommended for dinner in high season. Breakfast 48–155 pesos. Main courses 115–275 pesos. AE, MC, V. Mon–Sat 9am–midnight.

Inexpensive

Café de Olla ★★ 🍴 MEXICAN   One of my favorite Vallarta restaurants, the Café de Olla serves up the most consistently delicious Mexican food in town. The atmosphere is simple and festive, and the typically packed dining room is served by a staff that's quick and efficient. Large portions of enchiladas, quesadillas, chiles rellenos, fajitas, and tacos come sizzling hot out of the open kitchen and grill. Although not on the menu, you can also order a terrific seafood platter for two. I recommend an order of fresh, thick guacamole to kick off your meal. The margaritas light up the night. Don't come here for romance or refinement, but do come here for great authentic fare, friendly service, and a fun experience. Only cash is accepted.

Basilio Badillo 168. ☏ **322/223-1626.** Main courses 70–230 pesos. No credit cards. Wed–Mon 9am–11pm. Closed Tues.

Café San Angel ★ CAFE   This eclectic sidewalk cafe is a favorite gathering place from sunrise into the wee hours. For breakfast, choose a three-egg Western omelet, such Mexican classics as huevos rancheros or *chilaquiles,* or a tropical fruit plate. Deli sandwiches, flavorful salads, sweet and savory crepes, and simple Mexican plates like burritos and quesadillas round out the menu. The cafe also serves exceptional fruit smoothies, iced blended coffees, and other coffee drinks. Although service is occasionally slow, keep in mind that this place affords the best people-watching in the area. Bar service and Internet access are available.

Olas Altas 449 (at Francisco Rodríguez). ☏ **322/223-1273.** Breakfast 35–85 pesos; main courses 58–105 pesos. No credit cards. Daily 8am–2am.

Pomodoro E Basilico ★★ ITALIAN   This unobtrusive Italian restaurant is one of Vallarta's best, a delightful table in Vallarta's old town. Choose from Mediterranean salads, fish carpaccios, homemade pastas, and thin-crust pizzas. The hand-tossed pies come as "red" or "white" depending on whether there's a tomato base, with the white pizzas considered more gourmet. My favorite is Patate Provola Pancetta, made with potatoes, Provola smoked cheese, mozzarella, bacon, and rosemary. Daily specialties, including the fish of the day, are listed on a blackboard. The owners hail from Rome, with the mostly Italian staff serving just a dozen al fresco tables. An excellent selection of Italian wines accompanies the simple, delectable menu.

Vallarta 228 (at Lazaro Cardenas), Zona Romántica. ☏ **322/223-6188.** Pizzas and pastas 110–140 pesos, main dishes 120–210 pesos. No credit cards. Tues–Sat 4:30–11:30pm; Sun 6–11:30pm.

Red Cabbage Café (El Repollo Rojo) ★★★ 🎁 MEXICAN   The tiny, hard-to-find cafe is worth the effort—a visit here will reward you with exceptional traditional Mexican cuisine and a whimsical crash course in contemporary culture. The small room is covered wall-to-wall with photographs, paintings, movie posters, and news clippings about the cultural icons of Mexico. Frida Kahlo figures prominently in the decor, and a special menu duplicates dishes she and husband Diego Rivera prepared for guests. Specialties from all over Mexico include *chiles en nogada* (poblanos stuffed with ground beef, pine nuts, and raisins, topped with a sweet walnut cream sauce sprinkled with pomegranates and served cold); intricate chicken *mole* from Puebla; and a hearty Mexican plate with steak, a chile relleno, quesadilla, guacamole, rice, and beans. In addition, the vegetarian menu is probably the most diverse and tasty in town.

Calle Rivera del Río 204A (across from Río Cuale). ✆ **322/223-0411.** www.redcabbagepv.com. Main courses 110–240 pesos. No credit cards. Mon–Sat 5–10:30pm.

Beaches, Activities & Excursions

Travel agencies can provide information on what to see and do in Puerto Vallarta and can arrange tours, fishing trips, and other activities. Most hotels have a tour desk on-site. Of the many travel agencies in town, I highly recommend **Tukari Servicios Turísticos,** Av. España 316 (✆ **322/224-7177;** www.tukari.net), which specializes in ecological and cultural tours. Another source is **Xplora Adventours** (✆ **322/226-6349**), in the Huichol Collection shop on the *malecón*. It has listings of all locally available tours, with photos, explanations, and costs; however, be aware that a timeshare resort owns the company, so part of the information you receive will be an invitation to a presentation, which you may decline. One of the tour companies with the largest—and best-quality—selection of boat cruises and land tours is **Vallarta Adventures** ★★★ (✆ **888/526-2238** in the U.S., or 322/297-1212; www.vallarta-adventures.com). I can highly recommend any of their offerings.

THE BEACHES

For years, beaches were Puerto Vallarta's main attraction. Although visitors today are exploring more of the surrounding geography, the sands are still a powerful draw. Over 42km (26 miles) of beaches extend around the broad Bay of Banderas, ranging from action-packed party spots to secluded coves accessible only by boat.

IN TOWN   The easiest to reach is **Playa Los Muertos** (also known as Playa Olas Altas or Playa del Sol), just off Calle Olas Altas, south of the Río Cuale. The water can be rough, but the wide beach is home to a diverse array of *palapa* restaurants that offer food, beverage, and beach-chair service. The most popular are the adjacent El Dorado and La Palapa, at the end of Pulpito Street. On the southern end of this beach is a section known as "Blue Chairs"—the most popular gay beach. Vendors stroll Los Muertos, and beach volleyball, parasailing, and jet-skiing are all popular pastimes. The **Hotel Zone** is also known for its broad, smooth beaches, accessed through the resorts.

SOUTH OF TOWN   **Playa Mismaloya** is in a beautiful sheltered cove about 10km (6¼ miles) south of town along Hwy. 200. The water is clear and ideal for snorkeling off the beach. Entrance to the public beach is just to the left of the **Barceló La Jolla de Mismaloya** (✆ **322/226-0600**). This is where the *Night of the Iguana,* the movie that made Puerto Vallarta famous with the international jet set, was filmed.

The beach at **Boca de Tomatlán,** just down the road, houses numerous *palapa* restaurants where you can relax for the day—you buy drinks, snacks, or lunch, and you can use their chairs and *palapa* shade. The boat to Verana (p. 296) also goes from here.

The two beaches are accessible by public buses, which depart from Basilio Badillo and Insurgentes every 15 minutes from 5:30am to 10pm and cost about 7 pesos.

Las Animas, Quimixto, and **Yelapa** beaches are the most secluded, accessible only by boat (see "Getting Around," earlier, for information about water-taxi service). They are larger than Mismaloya, offer intriguing hikes to jungle waterfalls, and are similarly set up, with restaurants fronting a wide beach. Overnight stays are available at Yelapa (see "Side Trips from Puerto Vallarta," later in this chapter).

NORTH OF TOWN   The beaches at **Marina Vallarta** are the least desirable in the area, with darker sand and seasonal inflows of stones. The entire northern coastline from Bucerías to Punta Mita is a succession of sandy coves alternating with rocky inlets. For years the beaches to the north, with their long, clean breaks, have been the favored locale for surfers. The broad, sandy stretches at **Playa Anclote, Playa Piedras Blancas,** and **Playa Destiladeras,** which all have *palapa* restaurants, have made them favorites with local residents looking for a quick getaway.

You can also hire a *panga* (small motorized boat) at Playa Anclote to take you to the **Marietas Islands ★★★** just offshore. These uninhabited islands are a great place for bird-watching, diving, snorkeling, or just exploring. Blue-footed booby birds (found only here and in the Galápagos) dawdle along the islands' rocky coast, and giant mantas, sea turtles, and colorful tropical fish swim among the coral cliffs. The islands are honeycombed with caves and hidden beaches—including the stunning Playa de Amor (Beach of Love) that appears only at low tide. Humpback whales congregate around these islands during the winter months, and *pangas* can be rented for a do-it-yourself whale-watching excursion. Trips cost about $40 per hour. You can also visit these islands aboard one of the numerous day cruises that depart from the cruise ship terminal in Puerto Vallarta.

ORGANIZED TOURS

BOAT TOURS   Puerto Vallarta offers a number of boat trips, including sunset cruises and snorkeling, swimming, and diving excursions. They generally travel one of two routes: to the **Marietas Islands,** a 30- to 45-minute boat ride off the northern shore of Banderas Bay, or to **Yelapa, Las Animas,** or **Quimixto** along the southern shore. The trips to the southern beaches make a stop at **Los Arcos,** an island rock formation south of Puerto Vallarta, for snorkeling. Prices range from $45 for a sunset cruise or a trip to one of the beaches with open bar, to $85 for an all-day outing with open bar and meals. Travel agencies sell tickets and distribute information on all cruises.

One of the best outings is a day trip to **Las Caletas ★★**, the cove where John Huston made his home for years. **Vallarta Adventures** (© **888/526-2238** in the U.S., or 322/297-1212; www.vallarta-adventures.com) has done an excellent job of restoring Huston's former home, adding exceptional day-spa facilities, and landscaping the beach, which is wonderful for snorkeling. The trip ($85 per person, $70 for children 4–11) sets out every Monday through Saturday from Nuevo Vallarta at 8:30am or from Vallarta's Maritime Terminal at 9am, and includes a light continental breakfast, buffet lunch, open bar, snorkeling and kayaking equipment, and guided tours.

Whale-watching tours become more popular each year. Viewing humpback whales is almost a certainty from mid- to late November to March. The majestic whales have migrated to this bay for centuries (in the 17th c. it was called "Humpback Bay") to bear their calves. The noted local authority is **Open Air Expeditions,** Guerrero 339 (📞 **322/135-9260;** www.vallartawhales.com). It offers ecologically oriented, oceanologist-guided 4-hour tours on the soft boat *Prince of Whales,* the only boat in Vallarta specifically designed for whale-watching. Cost is $95 for adults, $82 for children 5 to 10, and travel is in a group of up to 12 (there's a discount for booking online). The tour departs at 9:30am.

LAND TOURS Tukari Servicios Turísticos (see "Beaches, Activities & Excursions," above) can arrange an unforgettable morning at **Terra Noble Art & Healing Center ★★** (📞 322/223-0308; www.terranoble.com), a mountaintop day spa and center for the arts where participants can get a massage, *temazcal* (ancient indigenous sweat lodge—available only for groups), or treatment; work in clay and paint; and have lunch in a heavenly setting overlooking the bay. Hotel travel desks and travel agencies, including Tukari, also book popular **Tropical Tour** or **Jungle Tours** ($95), a basic orientation to the area. These excursions are expanded city tours that include the workers' village of Pitillal, the affluent neighborhood of Conchas Chinas, the cathedral, the market, the Taylor-Burton houses, and lunch at a jungle restaurant.

The **Sierra Madre Expedition** is an excellent tour offered by **Vallarta Adventures** (see "Boat Tours," above). The excursion offered Monday through Thursday travels in Mercedes all-terrain vehicles north of Puerto Vallarta through jungle trails, stops at a small town, ventures into a forest for a brief nature walk, and winds up on a pristine secluded beach for lunch and swimming. The $78 outing is worthwhile because it takes tourists on exclusive trails into scenery that would otherwise be off-limits.

STAYING ACTIVE

DIVING & SNORKELING   Underwater enthusiasts, from beginner to expert, can arrange scuba diving or snorkeling through **Vallarta Adventures** (📞 **888/526-2238** in the U.S., or 322/297-1212, ext. 3; www.vallarta-adventures.com), a five-star PADI dive center. You may snorkel or dive at Los Arcos, a company-owned site at Caletas Cove (where you'll dive in the company of sea lions), Quimixto Coves, the Marietas Islands, or the offshore La Corbeteña, Morro, and Chimo reefs. The company runs a full range of certification courses. **Chico's Dive Shop** (📞 **322/222-1895;** www.chicos-diveshop.com), with its main shop at Díaz Ordaz 772–5, near Punto V bar, offers similar diving and snorkeling trips and is also a PADI five-star dive center. Chico's is open daily from 8am to 10pm, with branches at the Barceló, Fiesta Americana, and Playa Los Arcos. You can also snorkel off the beaches at Mismaloya and Boca de Tomatlán; elsewhere, there's not much to see besides a sandy bottom. Expect to pay about $70 for a two-tank boat dive to Los Arcos, and about $30 for a snorkeling trip there.

ECOTOURS & ACTIVITIES   **Open Air Expeditions** (www.vallartawhales.com) offers nature-oriented trips, including birding and ocean kayaking in Punta Mita. **Ecotours de México** (📞 322/222-6606; www.ecotoursvallarta.com), in Marina Vallarta, runs eco-oriented tours, including whale-watching, snorkeling, sea kayaking, hiking, and seasonal (Aug–Dec) trips to a turtle preservation camp where you can witness hatching baby Olive Ridley turtles.

A popular Vallarta adventure activity is **canopy tours.** You glide from treetop to treetop, getting an up-close-and-personal look at a tropical rainforest canopy and the trails far below. Tours depart from the **Vallarta Adventures** (see "Diving & Snorkeling," above) offices in both Marina Vallarta and Nuevo Vallarta at 8am, returning at 2pm. The price ($79 for adults, $55 for children 8–11) includes the tour, bottled water, and light snacks.

A second option is available in the southern jungles of Vallarta, over the Orquidias River, through **Canopy Tours de Los Veranos** (© 877/563-4113 toll-free in the U.S. or 322/223-6060; www.canopytours-vallarta.com). Shuttle locations include the Canopy office (in front of the Pemex Conchas Chinas), in front of Le Kliff Restaurant in Mismaloya, at Hacienda Palma Real in Nuevo Vallarta, or at Collage Disco in Marina Vallarta. Departures are on the hour, from 9am to 2pm. In addition to the 14 cables—the longest being a full 350m (1,148 ft.)—it offers climbing walls and water slides. Price is $79 for adults, or $58 for children ages 6 and older.

FISHING Arrange fishing trips through travel agencies or through the **Cooperativa de Pescadores (Fishing Cooperative),** on the *malecón* north of the Río Cuale, next door to the Rosita Hotel (© 322/222-1202). Fishing charters cost from $300 to over $1,000, depending on the size of the boat and trip duration (4–8 hr.). Smaller boats (7m/24 ft.) can accommodate up to four people, while larger boats (12m/40 ft.) can accommodate up to 10. It's open daily from 8am to 9pm, but make arrangements by phone a day ahead. You can also arrange fishing trips at the Marina Vallarta docks, or by calling **Fishing with Carolina** (© 322/224-7250; www. fishingwithcarolina.com), which uses a 9m (30-ft.) Uniflite sportfisher, fully equipped with an English-speaking crew. There are 4-, 6-, and 8-hour fishing trips starting at about $350 for four people. The waters are filled with marlin, sailfish, dorado (mahi-mahi), and tuna.

GOLF Puerto Vallarta is an increasingly popular golf destination. The Joe Finger–designed private course at the **Marina Vallarta Golf Club** (© 322/221-0073; www.marinavallartagolf.com) is an 18-hole, par-71 course that winds through the Marina Vallarta peninsula and affords ocean views. It's for members only, but most luxury hotels in Puerto Vallarta have memberships for their guests. Greens fees are $130 year-round, and $100 after 2pm. Fees include golf cart, range balls, and tax. A caddy costs about $15 plus tip.

North of town in the state of Nayarit, about 15km (9¼ miles) beyond Puerto Vallarta, is the 18-hole, par-72 **Los Flamingos Club de Golf** (© 329/296-5006; www.flamingosgolf.com.mx). It features beautiful jungle vegetation and is open from 7am to 7pm daily, with a full pro shop and *palapa* restaurant and bar. The daylight greens fee is $140, which drops to $90 after 2pm. It includes the use of a golf cart; hiring a caddy costs $20 plus tip, and club rental is $35 to $45. Free transportation is offered to and from local hotels.

There are two breathtaking Jack Nicklaus Signature courses at the **Punta Mita Golf Club ★★★** (© 329/291-6000; www.fourseasons.com/puntamita/golf). The original Pacifico course features eight oceanfront holes and an ocean view from every hole. The second and more-challenging course, Bahia, intertwines with the original course and also affords stunning seaside holes; its finishing hole is adjacent to the St. Regis Resort. The courses are open only to members or guests staying in the Punta Mita resorts, or to other golf club members with a letter of introduction from their pro. Greens fees are $210 for 18 holes and $135 for 9 holes, including cart but excluding taxes, with (Calloway) club rentals for $60.

Another Jack Nicklaus course is located at the **Vista Vallarta Golf Club** (© 322/290-0030; www.vistavallartagolf.com), along with one designed by Tom

Weiskopf. These courses were the site of the 2002 PGA World Cup Golf Championships. A round costs $196 per person, including cart, or $136 after 2pm. Club rentals are available for $55. A caddy costs about $15 plus tip.

The Robert von Hagge–designed **El Tigre** course at Paradise Village (© **866/843-5951** in the U.S., or 322/297-0773; www.eltigregolf.com), in Nuevo Vallarta, is a 7,239-yard course on a relatively flat piece of land, but the design incorporates challenging bunkers, undulating fairways, and water features on several holes. Greens fees are $150 a round, or $98 if you play after 2pm. Club rentals are $45.

HORSEBACK-RIDING TOURS   Travel agents and local ranches can arrange guided horseback rides. **Rancho Palma Real,** Carretera Vallarta, Tepic 4766 (© **322/222-0501**), has an office 5 minutes north of the airport; the ranch is in Las Palmas, 40 minutes northeast of Vallarta. It is by far the nicest horseback-riding tour in the area. The price ($75; cash only) includes continental breakfast, drinks, and lunch.

Another excellent option is **Rancho el Charro,** Av. Francisco Villa 895 (© **322/224-0114,** or cell 044-322/294-1689; www.ranchoelcharro.com), which has beautiful, well-cared-for horses and a variety of rides for all levels, departing from their ranch at the base of the Sierra Madre Mountains. Rides range in length from 3 to 8 hours, and in price from $62 to $120. Rancho el Charro also has multiple-day rides—check their website for details. **Rancho Ojo de Agua,** Cerrada de Cardenal 227, Fracc. Las Aralias (© **322/224-0607;** www.ranchojodeagua.com), also offers high-quality tours, from its ranch located 10 minutes by taxi north of downtown toward the Sierra Madre foothills. The rides last 3 hours (10am and 3pm departures) and take you up into the mountains overlooking the ocean and town. The cost is $62. Both of the ranches listed above have other tours available, as well as their own comfortable base camp for serious riders who want to stay out overnight.

SWIMMING WITH DOLPHINS   Dolphin Adventure ★★★ (© **888/526-2238** in the U.S., or 322/297-1212; www.vallarta-adventures.com) operates an interactive dolphin-research facility—considered the finest in Latin America—that allows limited numbers of people to swim with dolphins Monday through Saturday at scheduled times. Cost for the **Dolphin Signature Swim** is $129. Reservations are required, and they generally sell out at least a week in advance. **Dolphin Encounter** ($79) allows you to touch and learn about the dolphins in smaller pools, so you're ensured up-close-and-personal time with them. The **Dolphin Kids** program, for children ages 4 to 8, is a gentle introduction to dolphins, featuring the Dolphin Adventure baby dolphins and their mothers interacting with the children participants ($75).

TENNIS   Many hotels in Puerto Vallarta offer excellent tennis facilities; they often have clay courts. The full-service **Canto del Sol Tennis Club** (© **322/226-0123;** www.cantodelsol.com) is at the Canto del Sol hotel in the Hotel Zone. It offers indoor and outdoor courts, a full pro shop, lessons, clinics, and partner matches. Courts cost about $15 per hour.

A STROLL THROUGH TOWN

Puerto Vallarta's streets retain a cobblestone charm that weaves its way through time; they're full of tiny shops, rows of windows edged with curling wrought iron, and vistas of red-tile roofs and the sea. Start with a walk up and down the *malecón*.

Among the sights you should see is the **municipal building** on the main square (next to the tourism office), which has a large Manuel Lepe mural inside in its stairwell. Nearby, right up Independencia, sits the picturesque **Parish of Nuestra Señora de Guadalupe church,** Hidalgo 370 (© **322/222-1326**), topped with a curious crown held in place by angels—a replica of the one worn by Empress Carlota during her brief time in Mexico as Emperor Maximilian's wife. On its steps, women sell religious mementos; across the narrow street, stalls sell native herbs for curing common ailments. Services in English are held each Saturday at 5pm and Sunday at 10am. Regular hours are Monday through Saturday from 7:30am to 8:30pm, Sunday from 6:30am to 7:30pm. Note that the entrance is restricted to those properly attired—no shorts, sleeveless shirts, or cellphones allowed. Three blocks south of the church, head east on Libertad, lined with small shops and pretty upper windows, to the **municipal flea market** by the river. After exploring the market, cross the bridge to the island in the river; sometimes a painter is at work on its banks. Walk down the center of the island toward the sea, and you'll come to the tiny **Museo Arquelogico del Cuale** (no phone; Tues–Sat 10am–2pm and 3–6pm; free admission), which has a small but impressive permanent exhibit of pre-Columbian figurines.

Retrace your steps to the market and Libertad, and follow Calle Miramar to the brightly colored steps up to Zaragoza. Up Zaragoza to the right 1 block is the famous **pink arched bridge** that once connected Richard Burton's and Elizabeth Taylor's houses. In this area, known as **"Gringo Gulch,"** many Americans have houses.

Shopping

For years, shopping in Puerto Vallarta was concentrated in small, eclectic shops rather than impersonal malls. Although plenty of independent stores still exist, it's now home to large, modern shopping centers between the marina and hotel zone areas as well. Vallarta is known for having the most diverse and impressive selection of **contemporary Mexican fine art** outside Mexico City. It also has an abundance of **silver jewelry,** beachwear, and Mexican souvenirs.

THE SHOPPING SCENE

The key shopping areas are central downtown, the Marina Vallarta *malecón,* the popular *mercados,* and the beach—where the merchandise comes to you. Some of the more attractive shops are 1 to 2 blocks in **back of the *malecón.*** Start at the intersection of Corona and Morelos streets—interesting shops spread out in all directions from here. **Marina Vallarta** has two shopping plazas, Plaza Marina and Neptuno Plaza, on the main highway from the airport into town, which offer a limited selection of shops, with Plaza Neptuno primarily featuring home decor shops.

Plaza Peninsula (located on Av. Francisco Medina Ascencio 2485, just south of the cruise ship terminal and north of the Ameca River bridge; no phone number or website), in front of a large waterfront condominium development of the same name, is home to more than 30 businesses, including Vallarta's first **Starbucks,** as well as art galleries, boutiques, and a varied selection of restaurants. The **Galerías Vallarta,** on Av. Francisco Medina Ascencio 2920, adjacent to Walmart and directly across from the cruise ship terminal (✆ **322/209-1520;** www.galeriasvallarta.com.mx), is a large shopping and entertainment mall anchored by the high-end Mexican department store Liverpool. It houses a variety of boutiques, including Levi's, Nine West, and United Colors of Benetton. Among the selections for dining are Chili's, Subway, and Sirloin Stockade. For entertainment, there's a 10-screen movie theater. The mall is open daily from 8am to 2am; most stores are open from 11am to 9pm.

Puerto Vallarta's **municipal flea market** is just north of the Río Cuale, where Libertad and A. Rodríguez meet. The *mercado* sells clothes, jewelry, serapes, shawls, leather accessories and suitcases, papier-mâché parrots, stuffed frogs and armadillos, and, of course, T-shirts. The market is open daily from 9am to 6pm. Upstairs, a **food**

A huichol art PRIMER

Puerto Vallarta offers the best selection of Huichol art in Mexico. Descendants of the Aztecs, the Huichol are one of the last remaining indigenous cultures in the world that has remained true to its traditions, customs, language, and habitat. Huichol art falls into two main categories: yarn paintings and beaded pieces. All other items you might find in Huichol art galleries are either ceremonial objects or items used in everyday life.

Yarn paintings are made on a wood base covered with wax and meticulously overlaid with colored yarn. Designs represent the magical vision of the underworld, and each symbol gives meaning to the piece. Paintings made with wool yarn are more authentic than those made with acrylic; however, acrylic yarn paintings are usually brighter and more detailed because the threads are thinner. It is normal to find empty spaces where the wax base shows. Usually the artist starts with a central motif and works around it, but it's common to have several independent motifs that, when combined, take on a different meaning.

Beaded pieces are made on carved wooden shapes depicting different animals, wooden eggs, or small bowls made from gourds. The pieces are covered with wax, and tiny *chaquira* beads are applied one by one to form designs. Usually the beaded designs represent animals; plants; the elements of fire, water, or air; and certain symbols that give a special meaning to the whole. Deer, snakes, wolves, and scorpions are traditional elements; other figures, such as iguanas, frogs, and any animals not indigenous to Huichol territory, are incorporated by popular demand. Beadwork with many small designs that do not exactly fit into one another is more time-consuming and has a more complex symbolic meaning.

You can learn more about the Huichol at **Huichol Collection,** Morelos 490, across from the sea-horse statue on the *malecón* (✆ **322/223-2141;** open daily 9am–10:30pm). This shop offers an extensive selection of Huichol art in all price ranges, and has a replica of a Huichol adobe hut, informational displays explaining more about their fascinating way of life and beliefs, and usually a Huichol artist at work. However, this is a timeshare sales location, so don't be surprised if you're hit with a pitch for a "free" breakfast and property tour. **Peyote People,** Juarez 222 (✆ **322/222-2302,** or -6268; www.peyotepeople.com; open Mon–Fri 10am–9pm, Sat–Sun 10am–6pm), is a more authentic shop specializing in Huichol yarn paintings and bead art from San Andres Cohamiata, one of the main villages of this indigenous group, high up in the Sierra Madres.

---

market serves inexpensive Mexican meals. An **outdoor market** is along Río Cuale Island, between the two bridges. Stalls sell crafts, jewelry, gifts, folk art, and clothing.

CLOTHING

Vallarta's locally owned department store, **LANS,** has branches downtown at Juárez 867 (✆ **322/226-9100;** www.lans.com.mx) and in both Plaza Peninsula and Plaza Caracol. LANS offers a wide selection of name-brand clothing, accessories, footwear, cosmetics, and home furnishings.

CONTEMPORARY ART

Known for sustaining one of the stronger art communities in Latin America, Puerto Vallarta has an impressive selection of fine galleries featuring quality original works.

Several dozen galleries get together to offer art walks every Wednesday from 6 to 10pm between November and April. Most of the participating galleries serve complimentary cocktails during the art walks. It's a very popular weekly event among the local expat residents.

Ana Romo This contemporary gallery opened in 2009 featuring works of Guadalajara artist Ana Romo. You'll find an impressive selection of abstract paintings, blown-glass vases, and glass sculptures—all at very reasonable prices when compared with galleries featuring art of similar quality. Open Monday through Saturday noon to 2pm and 4 to 9pm. Guadalupe Sanchez 803A, next to Pipila. ✆ **322/223-5666.** www.anaromoart. com.

Corsica Among the best of Vallarta's galleries, Corsica features an exquisite collection of sculptures, installations, and paintings from world-renowned contemporary artists from Mexico. There are two locations—at Guadalupe Sanchez 735 and Leona Vicario 230. Open Monday through Saturday 11am to 2pm and 5 to 10pm. ✆ **322/223-1821.** www.galeriacorsica.com.

Galería des Artistes This stunning gallery features contemporary painters and sculptors from throughout Mexico, Europe, and Latin America, including the renowned original "magiscopes" of Feliciano Bejar. Paintings by Vallarta favorite Evelyn Boren, as well as a small selection of works by Mexican masters, including Orozco, can be found here. There's an impressive new collection of sculptures from Guadalajara as well. It's open Monday to Saturday 11am to 10pm. Just across the street, affiliate **Galería Omar Alonso** exhibits photography by internationally renowned artists. It's also open Monday through Saturday 11am to 10pm. Leona Vicario 248. ✆ **322/222-5587.**

Galería Pacífico Since opening in 1987, Galería Pacífico has been considered one of the finest in Mexico. On display is a wide selection of sculptures and paintings in various mediums by midrange masters and up-and-comers alike. The gallery is a short walk inland from the fantasy sculptures on the *malecón*. Among the artists whose careers Galería Pacífico has influenced are rising talents Alfredo Langarica and Brewster Brockman, renowned sculptor Ramiz Barquet, and David Leonardo. Gallery owner Gary Thompson offers public sculpture walks on Tuesdays at 9:30am in high season. Open Monday through Saturday from 10am to 8pm, Sunday by appointment. Between June and October, check for reduced hours or vacation closings. Aldama 174, 2nd floor, above La Casa del Habano cigar store. ✆ **322/222-1982.** www.galeriapacifico.com.

Galería Uno One of Vallarta's first galleries, the Galería Uno features an excellent selection of contemporary paintings by Latin American artists, plus a variety of posters and prints. In a classic adobe building with open courtyard, it's also a casual, salon-style gathering place for friends of owner Jan Lavender. Open Monday through Saturday from 10am to 8pm. Morelos 561 (at Corona). ✆ **322/222-0908.**

Gallería Dante This gallery-in-a-villa showcases contemporary art including sculptures and paintings against a backdrop of gardens and fountains. Works by more than 100 Mexican and international artists are represented, including the acclaimed Oscar Solis, Guillermo Gomez, Israel Zzepda, Alejandro Colunga, and Tellosa. The gallery, which is the largest in Puerto Vallarta, is open during the winter Monday through Friday from 10am to 5pm, and by appointment. Basilio Badillo 269. ✆ **322/222-2477.** www.galleriadante.com.

CRAFTS & GIFTS

Alfarería Tlaquepaque   Opened in 1953, this is Vallarta's original source for Mexican ceramics and decorative crafts, all at excellent prices. Open Monday through Saturday 9am to 9pm and Sunday from 9am to 3pm in high season, with reduced hours in low season. Av. México 1100. 🕾 **322/223-2121.**

Safari Accents   Flickering candles glowing in colored-glass holders welcome you to this highly original shop overflowing with creative gifts, one-of-a-kind furnishings, and reproductions of paintings by Frida Kahlo and Botero. Open daily from 10am to 11pm. Olas Altas 224, Loc. 4. 🕾 **322/223-2660.**

DECORATIVE & FOLK ART

Banderas Bay Trading Company ★   This shop features fine antiques and one-of-a-kind decorative objects for the home, including contemporary furniture, antique wooden doors, mirrors, Talavera, religious-themed items, original art, hand-loomed textiles, glassware, and pewter. Open Monday to Saturday 10am to 6pm. There's also a *bodega* (warehouse) annex of the shop, with the same hours, located at Constitución 319 (at Basilio Badillo; 🕾 **322/223-9871**). Lázaro Cárdenas 263 (near Ignacio L. Vallarta). 🕾 **322/223-4352.** www.banderasbaytradingcompany.com.

Lucy's CuCu Cabaña 👜   Owners Lucy and Gil Gevins have assembled an entertaining and eclectic collection of Mexican folk art. Each summer they travel through Mexico and personally select the handmade works created by over 200 indigenous artists and artisans. Open Monday through Friday from 10am to 8pm, and Saturday from 10am to 3pm. Basilio Badillo 295 (at Constitución). 🕾 **322/222-1220.**

Olinala   This shop contains two floors of fine indigenous Mexican crafts and folk art, including a collection of museum-quality masks and original contemporary art by gallery owner Brewster Brockman. Open Monday through Friday from 10am to 6pm, Saturday 10am to 2pm. Lázaro Cárdenas 274. 🕾 **322/222-4995.**

Puerco Azul   Set in a space that actually has a former pig-roasting oven, Puerco Azul features a whimsical and eclectic selection of art and home accessories, much of it created by owner and artist Lee Chapman (aka Lencho). Open Monday to Saturday from 10am to 6pm. Constitución 325. 🕾 **322/222-8647.**

Querubines 👜   Owner Marcella García travels across the country to select the items, which include exceptional artistic silver jewelry, embroidered and hand-woven clothing, bolts of loomed fabrics, tin mirrors and lamps, glassware, pewter frames and trays, high-quality wool rugs, straw bags, and Panama hats. Open Monday through Saturday from 9am to 9pm. Juárez 501A (at Galeana). 🕾 **322/223-1727.**

TEQUILA & CIGARS

La Casa del Habano   This fine tobacco shop has certified quality cigars from Cuba, along with humidors, cutters, elegant lighters, and other smoking accessories. It's also a local cigar club, with a walk-in humidor for regular clients. In the back, you'll find comfy leather couches, TV sports, and full bar service. Open Monday through Saturday from noon to 9pm. Aldama 170. 🕾 **322/223-2758.**

La Casa del Tequila ★   Here you'll find an extensive selection of premium tequilas, plus information and tastings. Also available are books, tequila glassware, and other tequila-drinking accessories. The shop has been downsized to accommodate the Agave Grill (see "Where to Eat," earlier in this chapter) in the back. Open Monday through Saturday from noon to 11pm, and Sunday from 4 to 11pm. Morelos 589. 🕾 **322/222-2000.**

Puerto Vallarta After Dark

Puerto Vallarta's spirited nightlife reflects the town's dual nature—part resort, part colonial town. In the past, Vallarta was known for its live music scene, but in recent years the nocturnal action has shifted to DJ clubs with an array of eclectic, contemporary music. Happy hour offering two-for-one drinks usually takes place between 3 and 7pm. A concentration of spirited bars, lounges, and nightclubs line the *malecón*, with more traditional cantinas, sports bars, and gay clubs and bars found south of the Río Cuale in Viejo Vallarta (old town).

PERFORMING ARTS & CULTURAL EVENTS

Truth be told, cultural nightlife beyond the **Mexican Fiesta** is limited. Culture centers on the visual arts; the opening of an exhibition carries considerable social and artistic significance. Puerto Vallarta's gallery community comes together in the central downtown area to present biweekly **art walks** from late October to April, where new exhibits are presented, featured artists attend, and complimentary cocktails are served. Check listings in the daily English-language newspaper *Vallarta Today*, or the events section of **www.virtualvallarta.com**.

FIESTA NIGHTS

Major hotels in Puerto Vallarta feature frequent fiestas for tourists—extravaganzas with open bars, Mexican buffet dinners, and live entertainment. Some are fairly authentic and make a good introduction for first-time travelers to Mexico.

Rhythms of the Night (Cruise to Caletas) ★★ ☉ This is an unforgettable evening under the stars at John Huston's former home at the pristine cove called Las Caletas. The smooth, fast Vallarta Adventures catamaran travels here, entertaining guests along the way. Tiki torches and drummers dressed in native costumes greet you at the dock. There's no electricity—you dine by the light of candles, the stars, and the moon. The evening includes dinner, open bar, and entertainment. The buffet dinner is delicious—steak, seafood, and generous vegetarian options. The entertainment showcases indigenous dances in contemporary style. The cruise departs at 6pm from the Vallarta Adventure Center in Nuevo Vallarta or at 6:30pm from the Puerto Vallarta Maritime Terminal and returns by 11pm. ℂ **888/526-2238** in the U.S., or 322/297-1212. www.vallarta-adventures.com. Cost $89 (includes cruise, dinner, open bar, and entertainment).

THE CLUB & MUSIC SCENE
Restaurants & Bars

Constantini Martini and Piano Bar ★ The most sophisticated martini bar in Vallarta is set in the elegant eatery Café des Artistes (see "Where to Eat," earlier in this chapter). Settle into one of the plush sofas and choose from a fabulous list of champagnes or wines by the glass, signature martinis, and specialty drinks. An ample appetizer and dessert menu makes it appropriate for late-night dining and drinks. Open daily from 6pm to 1am. Guadalupe Sánchez 740. ℂ **322/222-3229.**

La Bodeguita del Medio This authentic Cuban restaurant and bar is known for its casual energy, terrific live Cuban music, and mojitos. It's a branch of the original Bodeguita in Havana (reputedly Hemingway's favorite restaurant there), which opened in 1942. If you can't get to that one, the Vallarta version has successfully imported the essence—and has a small souvenir shop that sells Cuban cigars, rum, and other items. The food is not memorable, so I recommend coming just for drinks and dancing. A Cuban band plays salsa, cumbia, and other tropical rhythms nightly (except Mon) from 10pm to 2am. Kitchen open daily from 11:30am to 1am; bar open until 3am. Paseo Díaz Ordaz 858 (malecón), at Allende. © **322/223-1585.**

Punto V ★ Having replaced Carlos O'Brien's in 2009, Punto V quickly became one of Vallarta's top nightspots. The grand open-air bar and restaurant overlooks the *malecón* and sea, transforming as the night wears on into a sizzling dance club popular with a 30- and 40-something crowd. Crystal chandeliers, faux Greek statues, video screens, and tables and sofas fill the main room; the upstairs sky bar also has daybeds. Live bands often play, too. Open daily from 11am to 3am. Open bar Sunday and Wednesday nights for 450 pesos. Paseo Díaz Ordaz (malecón) 786, at Pípila. © **322/322-1444.**

Z'Tai Z'Tai is a stunning array of spaces that span an entire city block. Enter from the *malecón*, and you'll discover ZBar, an upstairs lounge with chill-out music, backlit orange lighting, bay views, and comfortable banquettes to relax on. Venture farther into this club, and you'll find an expansive open-air garden area that serves cocktails, as well as Asian-inspired dining and snacking options, accompanied by electronic music at a level still appropriate for conversation. There's an enormous selection of wines, but the favorite drink here is their signature cucumber martini. Open daily for food service from 6pm to midnight, with bar service until 2am or later. Valet parking available. Morelos 737, Col. Centro. © **322/222-0306.** www.ztai.com.

Rock, Jazz & Blues

El Faro Lighthouse Bar ★ A circular cocktail lounge at the top of the Marina lighthouse, El Faro is one of Vallarta's most romantic nightspots. Live guitar plays in high season, and the music's not so loud as to interrupt conversations. Drop by at twilight for the magnificent panoramic views, but don't expect anything other than a drink and, if you get lucky, some popcorn. Open daily from 5pm to 1:30am. Royal Pacific Yacht Club, Marina Vallarta. © **322/221-0541,** -0542.

Hard Rock Café Vallarta's iconic Hard Rock Café features live rock music nightly starting at 10:30pm. Standard American fare and bar service are available throughout the day. Packed with rock memorabilia, the Hard Rock also sells merchandise in the adjacent shop. The bar is more popular with tourists than with locals. It's open daily from 11am to 2am. Paseo Díaz Ordaz (malecón) 652 © **322/222-2230.** www.hardrock.com.

Nightclubs & Dancing

A few of Vallarta's clubs charge admission (typically in high season and on weekends), but more generally you pay just for drinks: about 60 pesos for a margarita, 45 pesos for a beer, and a bit more for mixed drinks. Keep an eye out for discount passes frequently available in hotels, restaurants, and other tourist spots. Along with clubs listed below, Carlos 'n Charlie's, Hard Rock Café, and Señor Frog's are also here. Most clubs are open from 10pm to 3am or later.

Collage Club A multilevel monster of nighttime entertainment, Collage includes a pool salon, bowling alley, and the Disco Bar, with frequent live entertainment. It's just past the entrance to Marina Vallarta, air-conditioned, and very popular with a young, mainly local crowd. Calle Proa s/n, Marina Vallarta. © **322/221-0505.** Cover up to 350 pesos, including open bar.

Hilo You'll recognize Hilo by the giant sculptures that practically reach out the front entrance, including somewhat ironic faux-bronze statues of *campesinos* (Mexican farmers). This high-energy club playing extremely loud music ranging from house and electronic to rock remains a favorite with the 20-something set. The later the hour, the more crowded the club becomes. Open daily from 4pm to 6am. Malecón, btw. Aldama and Abasolo sts. © **322/223-5361.** Cover $10 weekends and holidays. No cover weekdays.

Hyde Formerly Christine's, this dazzling club draws a crowd with laser-light shows, pumped-in dry ice, flashing lights, and large-screen video panels. Once a disco—in the true sense of the word—it is now a modern dance club, with techno, house, and hip-hop the primary tunes played. The sound system is amazing, and the mix of music can get almost anyone dancing. Dress code: No tennis shoes or flip-flops, no shorts for men. Open weekends from 10:30pm to 6am. In the Krystal Vallarta hotel, north of downtown off Av. Francisco Medina Ascencio. ✆ **322/224-0202.** Cover $20 men, women free.

J & B Salsa Club This is a popular place to dance to Latin music—from salsa to samba, the dancing is hot and the atmosphere electric. On Fridays, Saturdays, and holidays, the air-conditioned club hosts live bands. Open daily from 8pm to 5am. Av. Francisco Medina Ascencio Km 2.5 (Hotel Zone). ✆ **322/224-4616.** Cover 100 pesos.

La Vaquita A giant dancing cow dominates the bar of this hot addition to the Vallarta club scene. In fact, paintings of flying cows and cattle in any number of amusing poses decorate this raging bar, with couches and daybeds upholstered like spotted cows. A sexy crowd moves to the grooves of the DJ into the wee hours. It's located next to Zoo (see below). Calle Morelos 535 (at Paseo Diaz Ordaz). No phone. Cover 100 pesos.

Mandala The sister club to Hilo is geared toward a slightly more sophisticated crowd. There are giant Buddha sculptures situated throughout the Pan Asian–inspired club, and the three-level bar and dance club has ongoing music video screens and oversize windows overlooking the *malecón*. But there's little meditating here amid the din of house and Latin pop. This place attracts a sleek and suntanned crowd. Open daily from 6pm to 6am. Paseo Díaz Ordaz (malecón) 600 at Abasolo. ✆ **322/223 0966.** Cover 200 pesos.

Roo ★★★ Vallarta's hottest club at press time, Roo attracts a sexy crowd dressed in designer clothes. Giant chandeliers hang over the multilevel nightclub, with a killer sound system, dancing cages, and indoor and outdoor bars. It gets started at 8pm and continues until breakfast time. Expect a line during peak periods, and lots of stolen glances. Morelos 771. ✆ **322/223-3052,** -3053. Cover 200 pesos.

Zoo This is your chance to be an animal and get wild in the night. A giant elephant head emerges out of a jungle-themed mural near the entrance, and the Zoo even has cages to dance in if you're feeling unleashed. This packed club boasts a killer sound system and a hot variety of dance music, including techno, reggae, and rap. Every hour's happy hour, with two-for-one drinks from 5 to 11pm. Zoo opens daily at 5pm and closes around 4am. Paseo Díaz Ordaz (malecón) 630. ✆ **322/222-4945.** www.zoobardance. com. Cover 100 pesos.

A SPORTS BAR

Andale's Andale's is the most happening sports bar in town. The kitschy joint, decorated with an egg carton ceiling, stuffed animals, and comical life-size dolls, attracts a mixed-age English-speaking crowd. Sports play on various screens to the backdrop of classic rock. It's open from 7am to 3am. Olas Altas 425 in the Zona Romantica. ✆ **322/222-1054.** www.andales.com.

GAY & LESBIAN CLUBS

Vallarta has a vibrant gay community with a wide variety of clubs and nightlife options, including special bay cruises and evening excursions to nearby ranches. Most of the gay nightlife happens in so-called *Zona Romantica* (also called *Viejo Vallarta* or old town) on the south side of the Río Cuale, where the busiest street lined with restaurants, cafes, and bars is Olas Altas. The free **Gay Guide Vallarta** (www.gayguidevallarta.com) specializes in gay-friendly listings, including weekly specials and happy hours. Another excellent resource for gay travelers to Puerto Vallarta is www.gogaypuertovallarta.com.

Casanova This small club, decorated with leather sofas, red lights, and disco balls, usually gets going after midnight. There's a small stage featuring strip shows nightly from 11pm to 3am. The club itself is open daily from 10pm until the last customers leave. Lazaro Cardenas 302 (corner of Constituciones). No phone. Cover 100 pesos.

La Noche La Noche is a casual, intimate "neighborhood bar" catering to a gay clientele, with great prices on drinks and a menu of martinis and tequila cocktails. Beers are always two-for-one. Open daily from 6pm to 2am. Lazaro Cardenas 263 (2 doors from Ignacio Vallarta). © **322/222-3364.**

Mañana ★ Located in the Zona Romantica, the town's oldest and most popular gay club offers two dance floors, a pool with a waterfall, and candlelit tables. Weekends bring drag shows and stripteases. Open daily from 10pm to 6am. Venustiano Carranza 290. © **322/222-7772.** www.manana.mx. Cover 200 pesos weekends, 100 pesos weekdays.

Side Trips from Puerto Vallarta

YELAPA: ROBINSON CRUSOE MEETS JACK KEROUAC ★

It's a cove straight out of a tropical fantasy, and only a 45-minute trip by boat from Puerto Vallarta. Yelapa has no cars and one paved (pedestrian-only) road, and it only acquired electricity in the past 10 years. It's accessible only by boat. Its tranquillity, natural beauty, and seclusion make it a popular home for hipsters, artists, writers, and a few expats (looking to escape the stress of the world, or perhaps the law). Yelapa remains casual and friendly—you're unlikely to ever meet a stranger.

To get there, travel by excursion boat or inexpensive water taxi (see "Getting Around," earlier in this chapter). You can spend an enjoyable day, but I recommend a longer stay—it provides a completely different perspective.

Once you're in Yelapa, you can lie in the sun, swim, snorkel, eat fresh grilled seafood at a beachside restaurant, or sample the local moonshine, *raicilla*. The beach vendors specialize in the most amazing pies you've ever tasted (coconut, lemon, or chocolate). You can tour this tiny town or hike up a river to see one of two waterfalls; the closest to town is about a 5-minute walk straight up from the pier. *Note:* If you use a local guide, agree on a price before you start out. Horseback riding, guided birding, fishing trips, and paragliding are also available.

For overnight accommodations, local residents frequently rent rooms, and there's also the rustic **Hotel Lagunita** ★ (www.hotel-lagunita.com; © **322/209-5056, -5055**). Its 29 cabañas have private bathrooms, and the hotel has electricity, a saltwater pool, massage service, an amiable restaurant and bar, the Barracuda Beach lounge and brick-oven pizza cafe, and a gourmet coffee shop. Though the prices are high for what you get, it is the most accommodating place for most visitors. Double rates run up to $120 during high season and up to $90 in the off season. Special rooms are available for honeymooners, for $135 in high season. MasterCard and Visa are accepted. Lagunita is a popular spot for yoga retreats.

If you wish to splurge, look into staying at **Verana** ★★★ (www.verana.com; © **866/687-9358** in the U.S., or 322/222-0878). See "Where to Stay," earlier in this chapter, for details.

If you stay over on a Wednesday or Saturday during the winter, don't miss the biweekly dinner-dance at the **Yelapa Yacht Club** ★ (no phone). Typically tongue-in-cheek for Yelapa, the "yacht club" consists of a cement dance floor and a disco ball, but the DJ spins a great range of tunes, attracting all ages and types. Dinner (80–160 pesos) is a bonus—the food may be the best anywhere in the bay. The menu changes depending on what's fresh. Ask for directions; it's in the main village, on the beach.

NUEVO VALLARTA & NORTH OF VALLARTA: ALL-INCLUSIVES

Many people assume Nuevo Vallarta is a suburb of Puerto Vallarta, but it's a stand-alone destination over the state border in Nayarit. It was designed as a mega resort development, complete with marina, golf course, and luxury hotels. Although it got off to a slow start, it has finally come together, with a collection of mostly all-inclusive hotels catering particularly to families on one of the widest, most attractive beaches in the bay. The biggest resort, Paradise Village, has a full marina and an 18-hole golf course inland from the beachside strip of hotels, plus a growing selection of condos and homes for sale. The Mayan Palace also has an 18-hole course here. The most expensive all-inclusive resort here is **Grand Velas All Suites & Spa Resort** (www. vallarta.grandvelas.com; © **322/226-8000**) at Av. Cocoteros, 98 Sur. The Paradise Plaza shopping center, next to Paradise Village, amplifies the area's shopping, dining, and services. It's open daily from 10am to 10pm. To get to the beach, you travel down a lengthy entrance road from the highway, passing by a few remaining fields (which used to be great for birding) but mostly real estate under construction.

A 26km (16-mile) trip into downtown Puerto Vallarta takes about 30 minutes by taxi, costs about 250 pesos, and is available 24 hours a day. The ride is slightly longer by public bus, which costs 15 pesos and operates from 7am to 11pm.

Marival Resort & Suites   This casual all-inclusive hotel sits at the northernmost end of Nuevo Vallarta. Designed in Mediterranean style, it offers a complete vacation experience, including extensive land sports, watersports, and daytime activities for kids, teenagers, and adults. There are a large variety of room types, ranging from studios to one-, two-, and three-bedroom suites. Rooms and suites have balconies or terraces with garden, pool, or ocean views. The broad white-sand beach is one of the real assets here. The nearby Marival Residences & World Spa is one of Nuevo Vallarta's most luxurious all-inclusive clubs, offering modern condo-like accommodations, an innovative spa, and outstanding dining facilities. This is a better option for those looking for quiet, upscale amenities, and pampering.

Paseo de los Cocoteros and Bulevar Nuevo Vallarta s/n, 63732 Nuevo Vallarta, Nay. www.marival.com. © **877/222-0302** toll-free in the U.S., 322/297-0100, or 322/226-8200. Fax 322/297-0262. 499 units. $210 and up double; $279 and up suite. Rates are all-inclusive. Ask for seasonal specials. AE, MC, V. Free parking. From the Puerto Vallarta airport, enter Nuevo Vallarta from the 2nd entrance; Marival is the 1st resort to your right on Paseo de los Cocoteros. **Amenities:** 6 restaurants; 7 bars; kids' club; 4 outdoor pools and an adults-only whirlpool; spa; 4 lighted tennis courts; beauty salon; extensive watersports, land sports, and daytime activities. In room: A/C, TV, hair dryer, Wi-Fi.

Paradise Village ★   The collection of pyramid-shaped buildings, designed in Maya-influenced style, houses well-designed all-suite accommodations in studio and one-, two-, and three-bedroom configurations. All have sitting areas and kitchenettes, making the resort ideal for families or groups of friends. Truly a village, this self-contained resort set on an exquisite stretch of beach offers a full array of services. The Maya theme extends to both oceanfront pools, with mythical creatures forming water slides and waterfalls. The spa is reason enough to book a vacation here, with treatments, hydrotherapy, massage (including massage on the beach), and fitness and yoga classes. A compelling attraction is the nearby El Tigre golf course (details earlier in this chapter, under "Golf"); their on-site marina continues to draw a growing number of boats and yachts. Paradise Village has begun to feel a bit dated around the edges.

Paseo de los Cocoteros 001, 63731 Nuevo Vallarta, Nay. www.paradisevillage.com. © **866/334-6080** toll-free in the U.S., or 322/226-6770. Fax 322/226-6713. 700 units. $150–$300 junior or 1-bedroom suite; $220–$400 2-bedroom suite; $335–$600 3-bedroom suite. All-inclusive rates available for $89 additional per person. AE, DC, MC, V. Free covered parking. **Amenities:** 3 restaurants; 2 beachside snack bars; kids' club; petting zoo; access to championship golf club w/18-hole course; complete fitness center; basketball court; beach volleyball; 2 beachside pools; lap pool; European spa; 2 tennis courts; watersports center; marina; Wi-Fi in lobby. In room: A/C, TV, hair dryer, minibar.

BUCERÍAS: A COASTAL VILLAGE ★

Only 18km (11 miles) north of the Puerto Vallarta airport and adjacent to Nuevo Vallarta, Bucerías (Boo-seh-*ree*-ahs, meaning "place of the divers") is a trendy coastal town on the Nayarit side of Banderas Bay. Lovely villas, art galleries, and gourmet restaurants line the main street in Bucerías Sur, the gentrified south side of town bustling with expatriates and suburban commuters. Across a walking bridge lies the north side of Bucerías, colloquially referred to as "el pueblo," a traditional fishing village where more of the local population lives.

To reach the town center by car, take the exit road from the highway out of Vallarta and drive down the shaded, divided street that leads to the beach. Turn left when you see a line of minivans and taxis (which serve Bucerías and Vallarta). Go straight ahead 1 block to the main plaza. The beach, with a lineup of restaurants, is a half-block farther. You'll see cobblestone streets leading from the highway to the beach, and hints of villas and town homes behind high walls.

If you take the bus to Bucerías, exit when you see the minivans and taxis to and from Bucerías on the street that leads to the beach. To use public transportation from Puerto Vallarta, take a minivan or bus marked BUCERIAS (they run 6am–9pm). The last minivan stop is Bucerías's town square. There's also 24-hour taxi service.

Exploring Bucerías

Come here for a day trip from Puerto Vallarta just to enjoy the long, wide, uncrowded beach, along with the fresh seafood served at the beachside restaurants or at one of the cafes listed below. On Sundays, many of the streets surrounding the plaza are closed to traffic for a *mercado* (street market)—where you can buy anything from tortillas to neon-colored cowboy hats. There's also an art walk every second Thursday of the month from 7 to 9pm (www.thebuceriasartwalk.com).

Bucerías doesn't offer much in the way of hotels—many people who come here rent condominiums or other vacation properties. One reliable option is the **Hotel Palmeras** (www.hotelpalmeras.com; © 329/298-1288), on Lázaro Cárdenas 35, with simple, comfortable rooms generally under $100, just a block off the beach.

The **Coral Reef Surf Shop,** Heroe de Nacozari 114 (© 329/298-0261), sells a great selection of surfboards and gear, and offers surfboard and Boogie board rentals, and a surf package that includes transport to Punta Mita or La Lancha and a lesson there for $85. Surfboards rent for $20 per day and $100 per week; double that for stand-up paddle boards. The shop is on the main highway heading south out of town.

Where to Eat

In addition to the restaurants mentioned below, many seafood restaurants front the beach. The local specialty is *pescado zarandeado,* a whole fish (usually red snapper) smothered in tasty sauce and slow-grilled, and the ceviche and lobster are excellent here, too. Most fine-dining options here are open only for dinner.

Eva's Brickhouse ★★ INTERNATIONAL   Kent oversees the preparation of the delicious fresh fish and aged steaks while his wife, Eva, takes care of dessert (the Key lime pie, chocolate volcano cake, and carrot cake are all irresistible). Jazz fills the air of the palm-filled outdoor patio, with hanging coconut lamps, Maya-inspired table-cloths, and ribbon-woven flowers with each place-setting. The tender steaks are aged in-house for 14 days and then cooked to order over the mesquite-wood fire; a pep-percorn brandy sauce covers the New York strip. Mahi-mahi (caught locally and served as a thick filet) and sea bass are on the menu, and the flavorful Mediterranean preparation includes shrimp, garlic, tomatoes, onions, peppers, capers, and olives. On Saturdays, Kent slow-roasts pork for 7 hours and serves it with garlic mashed potatoes and homemade apple sauce.

Galeana 15 (at Lázaro Cárdenas). ✆ **329/298-2238.** www.evasbrickhouse.com. Main courses 249–349 pesos. No credit cards. Daily 4–11pm.

Le Fort ★★★ ◎ FRENCH   An evening here begins with champagne smiles as privileged diners watch chef-owner Gilles Le Fort prepare their gourmet meal. The U-shaped bar adjacent to the kitchen accommodates the guests, who sip *kir royales* and nibble on homemade terrine while the master works. Chef Le Fort is the winner of numerous culinary awards, and his warm conviviality is the real secret ingredient of this unusual experience. Once dinner is served in the adjacent open-air dining room, Le Fort and his wife, Margarita, join the table, which seats up to 16. He owns the most extensive wine cellar in the bay—some 2,000 bottles of French and Mexi-can varieties. Three delicious courses are served (the menu is chosen by the first group to reserve for that night), followed by a presentation of fine liquors (available for purchase). I cannot imagine a more creative, social dining experience along this beautiful stretch of coast.

Calle Lázaro Cárdenas 71, 1 block from the Hotel Royal Decameron. ✆ **329/298-1532.** www.lefort.com. mx. Reservations required. Cooking class, 3-course dinner, wines, and recipes $60 per person. MC, V. Daily 8–10:30pm. Closed for a month in summer.

Mark's ★★ 🛍 MEDITERRANEAN   It's worth a special trip to Bucerías just to eat at this open-air patio restaurant. The most popular dinner spot in town, Mark's serves sophisticated cuisine alongside simpler thin-crust pizzas and flatbreads, baked in a brick oven and seasoned with fresh herbs grown in the garden. The bustling kitchen focuses on fresh local and organic products—favorite starters include the roasted beet and apple salad with goat cheese and the tender chicken masala and vegetable spring roll. Among the most tempting entrées are the macadamia-crusted red snapper filet, fresh poached lobster, and grass-fed filet mignon with blue-cheese ravioli. A four-course wine-tasting menu is available for 400 pesos. Multitalented chef Jan Marie (Mark's charming wife and business partner) runs an adjacent boutique (www. janmarieboutique.com), featuring elegant home accessories, art, and gifts. The small restaurant bar televises all major sporting events.

Calle Lázaro Cárdenas 56 (a half-block from the beach). ✆ **329/298-0303.** www.marksbucerias.com. Reservations recommended. Pizza and pasta 175–245 pesos; main courses 210–365 pesos. MC, V. Daily 5–11pm. From the highway, turn left just after bridge, where there's a small sign for Mark's; double back left at next street (immediately after you turn left) and turn right at next corner; Mark's is on the right.

Mezzogiorno ★★ ITALIAN   The owners of this popular oceanfront trattoria built a reputation with their Mezzaluna restaurant in Vallarta and then moved the business to their former home in Bucerías. It's one of the most attractive dining options north of Vallarta, in a sleekly restored home overlooking the bay. Despite the stunning setting, it takes second place to the flavorful dishes. Large, flavorful salads overflow with fresh ingredients—my favorite combines grilled chicken with mixed greens, sun-dried tomatoes, goat cheese, and a currant-balsamic vinaigrette. For main dishes, pasta takes center stage, with bestsellers that include carbonara, fettuccini salmone, and lasagna, as well gnocchi. The black fettuccine topped with shrimp, scallops, and fish is also delicious. A few candlelit tables sit on the beach in high season and offer the best views of all. The restaurant operates a beach club here by day.

Av. del Pacífico 33. ℂ **329/298-0350.** www.mezzogiorno.com.mx. Reservations recommended. Main courses 95–215 pesos. MC, V. Daily 5–11pm (lunch sometimes offered in high season).

PUNTA MITA: EXCLUSIVE SECLUSION ★★★

At the northern tip of the bay lies an arrowhead-shaped, 600-hectare (1,482-acre) peninsula bordered on three sides by the ocean, called Punta de Mita. Considered a sacred place by the Indians, this is the point where Banderas Bay, the Pacific Ocean, and the Sea of Cortez come together. It's magnificent, with quiet beaches and coral reefs just offshore. Stately rocks jut out along the shoreline, and the water is a dreamy translucent blue. Punta Mita has evolved into Mexico's most exclusive development, an enormous gated resort community next to the original little town that to this day has a few authentic restaurants and shops. The luxury community's master plan includes a couple world-class resorts, multimillion dollar villas and residences, and two championship golf courses. You'll find the elegant Four Seasons Resort, St. Regis, and two Jack Nicklaus Signature golf courses here along with plenty of exclusive real estate for sale to the highest bidders.

Casa de Mita ★★ 🎁 This hotel isn't technically in Punta Mita, but it's near enough to convey a sense of the area's relaxed seclusion. It's located on the back road that runs from Punta Mita to Sayulita, on the small, pristine Careyeros Bay. The six rooms and two suites are set in a villa overlooking the exquisite beach. The villa itself is a work of white stucco walls, hand-painted tiles and stone mosaics, thatch and tile roofs, and guayaba-wood balcony detailing. Interiors of the guest rooms are simple and elegant, with touches such as carved armoires, headboards, and doors from Michoacán. Private balconies with ocean views surround the pool, which features canopy daybeds and a small fountain. A big plus here is the delicious dining.

Playa Careyeros, 63734 Punta de Mita, Nay. www.casademita.com. ℂ **866/740-7999** in the U.S., or 329/298-4114. Fax 329/298-4112. 8 units. High season $645–$795 double; low season $505–$635 double. Rates include all meals and drinks. Minimum 3-night stay required. AE, DC, MC, V. Limited street parking. **Amenities:** Restaurant; entertainment room w/TV and DVD; universal gym station; small outdoor pool; spa; tour services, including horseback riding, paddle boarding, and surfing lessons; Wi-Fi. *In room:* A/C, minibar, no phone.

Four Seasons Resort Punta Mita ★★★ The Four Seasons Punta Mita is one of the world's most spectacular resorts, offering refinement, seclusion, and impeccable service. Accommodations lie in three-story casitas surrounding the main building, which houses the stunning open-air lobby, cultural center, restaurants, shopping arcade, and oceanfront infinity pool. Guest rooms offer ocean or garden views from large terraces or balconies. Suites include a private plunge pool, sitting room with a sofa bed, separate bedroom, bar, and a powder room. Rooms are plush and spacious, with a king or two double beds, seating area, and luxurious bathroom. The resort also has an adults-only tranquillity pool, with a sushi and tapas bar surrounded by cabañas available for daily rent, as well as an incredible lazy river pool with inner tubes for kids and adults to float around. The resort rents out magnificent four- and five-bedroom villas with private butlers, and there are two Jack Nicklaus championship golf courses, a full-service spa, and tennis center. Service is unerringly warm and unobtrusive throughout this little paradise, and each of the resort's gourmet restaurants is fantastic.

63734 Bahía de Banderas, Nay. www.fourseasons.com/puntamita. ℂ **800/332-3442** in the U.S., or 329/291-6000. Fax 329/291-6060. 173 units. High season $545–$1,175 double, $1,685–$16,000 suite; low season $375–$925 double, $1,025–$8,750 suite. AE, DC, MC, V. Free valet parking. **Amenities:** 3 restaurants; lobby bar; beachfront bar; horseback riding; children's programs; concierge; cultural center w/ lectures, cooking classes, Spanish classes, dance classes, and other daily activities; full-service fitness center; yoga; Jacuzzi; oceanfront pool; adults-only pool surrounded by private cabañas; lazy river pool; room service; European-style spa; tennis center w/10 courts of various surfaces; watersports equipment; yacht charter. *In room:* A/C, flatscreen TV/DVD, i-Home, hair dryer, Internet, minibar.

St. Regis ★★ Opened in late 2008, this ultraexclusive St. Regis is the first in Latin America, set on a stunning expanse of beach in Punta Mita. Guest rooms and suites are almost hidden amid the 33 two-story casitas spread throughout the property, where palm-filled gardens and three infinity pools compete with the endless ocean for guests' attention. Beautifully appointed rooms incorporate handmade tiles, custom Mexican furnishings, and large marble bathrooms with indoor and outdoor showers. Other features include flatscreen TVs, Remède bath amenities, and the St. Regis signature butler service. Throughout the resort, touches of Provence combine with chic Mexican designs that draw on river stone, marble, onyx, wood, and clay. The resort's spa merits special mention for its pampering service. Although there's a kids' program, the resort targets adults looking for privacy and usually feels very quiet. The three gourmet restaurants give you variety, so you never need to leave the property.

Lote H-4 Carretera Federal 200, Km 19.5, Punta de Mita, 63734, Nay. www.stregis.com/puntamita. ℂ **800/598-1863** in the U.S., or 329/291-5800. Fax 329/291-5801. 120 units. $480 and up double; $1,140 and up suite. AE, DC, MC, V. Free valet parking. **Amenities:** 3 restaurants; 3 bars; babysitting; kids' club; concierge; access to the Jack Nicklaus Signature golf courses Pacífico and Bahía; full-service spa and fitness center; Jacuzzi; Internet room; 3 pools; room service; 8 tennis courts; watersports equipment. *In room:* A/C, flatscreen TV, hair dryer, Internet, minibar.

SAYULITA: A SURFERS' PARADISE

Sayulita sits only 40km (25 miles) northwest of Puerto Vallarta, on Hwy. 200 to Tepic, yet it feels like a world apart. It captures the simplicity and tranquillity of beach life that has long since left Vallarta—but hurry, because it's exploding in popularity. For years, Sayulita has been principally a surfers' destination—the main beach in town is known for its consistent break and long, ridable waves. Visitors and locals who find Vallarta to be too cosmopolitan have started to flock here. Although Sayulita has only 5,800 residents, it swells to nearly 40,000 visitors in high season. You'll now find more real estate offices than surf shops, and more fine-jewelry stores than juice bars, but Sayulita is still holding on to its charms.

An easygoing attitude prevails in this beach town, despite the niceties popping up amid the basic accommodations, inexpensive Mexican food stands, and handmade, hippie-style-bauble vendors. You may encounter a Huichol Indian family that has come down from the Sierra to sell their wares. Yet it's quickly becoming gentrified with new cafes, sleek shops, aromatherapy-infused spas, and elegant villas for rent.

Sayulita is most popular for surfing. Any day, you'll witness a swarm of surfers seeking perfect swells offshore from the main beach. Numerous other surf spots dot the coastline—some more secret than others—and a reliable long-boarders' break can be found at La Lancha and Punta Mita, about half an hour away (most surf shops will organize trips there). Other ocean activities, such as whale watching, fishing, and snorkeling trips, can be arranged through **Riviera Nayarit Magical Tours** (© 329/291-2065), located at the corner of Avenita Revolución and Calle Delfin.

To get to Sayulita, you can rent a car or take a taxi from the airport or downtown Vallarta. The rate is about $70 to get to the town plaza. The taxi stand is on the main square, or you can call for pickup at your hotel. The trip to the airport from Sayulita costs about $60. Guides also lead tours to Puerto Vallarta, Punta Mita, and other surrounding areas, including a Huichol Indian community. There's also a bus that operates between Sayulita and Puerto Vallarta every 15 minutes between 5:30am to 8:15pm for only 25 pesos each way.

Surfing

There are two main surf spots in Sayulita—the most popular is the "point" break fronting the main beach in the village, which is a right long board break. A faster, left break is found just north of the river mouth, in front of the campground. There's also a calmer spot toward the beach's south end where lessons are usually given. Surf instruction and board rentals are available at **Lunazul Surf School** (© 329/291-2009; www.lunazulsurfschool.com), located at Marlin 4, where this street ends at the beachfront. The 90-minute surf lessons cost 450 pesos for individual instruction, or 350 pesos per person for group instruction. This includes a rash guard and hour free board rental after the lesson. Board rentals (including hard and soft short and long boards) through Lunazul are 50 pesos per hour or 200 pesos for the day; you'll need to leave an ID as a deposit. Stand-up paddle boards and Boogie boards are also available. You'll find several other surf schools on the beach during high season. Most surf shops also organize trips to La Lancha, a popular surf spot near Punta Mita with slow-rolling waves perfect for long boarders. Four-hour excursions there cost about $65 per person, including transportation and board rental.

Where to Stay

Along with the hotels listed below, Sayulita has two hostels, a beachside campground, and a number of private homes to rent.

Hotel La Casona ★ ✍ Just half a block from Sayulita's main surfing beach, this cheerful hotel houses nine individually designed rooms decorated in bleached white, terra cotta, and turquoise with colorful Mexican accents. Five rooms—Sky (which has a full ocean view), Amor, Coco, Lily, and Peacock—offer their own balconies with hammocks, and all rooms have private bathrooms with showers only. The communal kitchen and "living lounge" tend to bring guests together, and there are a number of daybeds and couches interspersed throughout the corridors perfect for reading. For breakfast, organic coffee, teas, fresh squeezed orange juice and fruit, granola, and freshly baked muffins are offered. Expect a very friendly vibe here. One drawback: The surrounding streets can be quite noisy, especially in high season.

Calle Delfin 7, 63734 Sayulita, Nay. www.lacasonasayulita.com. © **415/683-3244** in the U.S., or 329/291-3629. 9 units. $75–$140 high season; low season discounts available. Rates include continental breakfast. AE, MC, V. **Amenities:** Massage service; help w/tours and activities; communal kitchen and lounge; Wi-Fi. *In room:* A/C (in some), fan.

Playa Escondida ★★★ ♨ Just above an idyllic beach cove, a handful of uniquely designed bungalows dot the lush tropical grounds of Playa Escondida. A waterfall rains warm water into the oceanfront infinity pool, set next to the *palapa* restaurant and open-air spa. The casual, friendly staff gets to know many of the guests at this gorgeous yet unpretentious resort. It's not the Four Seasons—activities are limited, there are no air conditioners, and Mother Nature sometimes visits the open-air bungalows (which have fans and mosquito nets). But for those who want a peaceful vacation off the beaten track and don't mind sacrificing a bit of commercial convenience for enchanted natural beauty, this place is unforgettable. Choose from among individually designed beachfront casitas, bungalows in the jungle, or imported teak houses from Thailand constructed in a spectacular bird canyon. The open-air spa offers outstanding massages for a great value. Sayulita is a winding 10-minute drive from this splendid resort.

Playa Escondida, 63732 Sayulita, Nay. www.playa-escondida.com. © **805/709-1470** in the U.S., or 329/291-3641. 26 units. High season $220–$475 double; low season $115–$250 double. $100 mandatory fee per guest for food and beverages. AE, MC, V. **Amenities:** Restaurant; bar; oceanfront pool; Jacuzzi; horseback riding; open-air spa; private beach w/watersports equipment; yoga; walking trails; Wi-Fi (in reception and restaurant areas). *In room:* Fan, fridge (full kitchen in houses in bird canyon).

Villa Amor ★★ Resembling an enchanted private villa, Villa Amor is a collection of guest rooms perched on a bluff by the sea. Owner Rod Ingram and his design team carefully crafted each space and individual suite with careful attention to detail. Beach chic rooms may have canopy beds, rattan furnishings, stone floors, original Mexican artwork, and organic bathroom amenities. One- and two-bedroom "villa" suites include fully equipped kitchenettes, plus open-air seating and—in the case of some—private plunge pools. The exterior walls open to breathtaking ocean views all around. Outdoor candlelit tables and the *palapa* bar framed by tiki torches tempt you not to leave the property, even though downtown Sayulita lies just a short walk away. A small private beach sits just in front. Note that many stairs and steep walkways zigzag the property.

Camino Playa Los Muertos s/n, 63732 Sayulita, Nay. www.villaamor.com. © **619/819-5407** in the U.S., or 329/291-3010. Fax 329/291-3018. 34 units. High season $110–$260 1-bedroom villa, $380–$550 2-bedroom villa; $750 3-bedroom villa; low season $55–$130 1-bedroom villa, $190–$275 2-bedroom villa, $375 3-bedroom villa. MC, V. **Amenities:** Restaurant; bar; concierge w/tour services; kayaks; room service; Wi-Fi. *In room:* A/C (in some), fan.

Where to Eat

Fine dining is hard to come by in Sayulita, but you'll find tasty seafood eateries and fish taco stands around town and by the beach. For the best burrito of your life, stop by **Burritos Revolución** just off the main plaza at Revolución 40 (no phone). There's almost always a line here for the cooked-to-order "surf" (marlin, mahimahi, or shrimp) and "turf" (chicken, beef, or carnitas) burritos, and a sign advises you to smile, pay cash, and not ask for any substitutions. This no-nonsense burrito shack is open Tuesday to Sunday from 10am to 6pm. The best fish tacos are made at the aptly named **Sayulita Fish Taco** (© **329/291-3272**), also serving over 200 tequilas at Mariscal 13. **Ruben's Deli** (© **322/183-0692**), located at the corner of Revolución and Delfin, prepares yummy deli sandwiches daily from 10am to 5pm.

Don Pedro's INTERNATIONAL Sayulita's best-known restaurant features an enticing beachfront location, which is the main reason to come here. Choose between an open-air dining area or shaded tables on the beach for breakfast, lunch, or dinner. Although the food quality varies, the grilled artichoke, scallop sushi, and fresh salads are all reliable starters. For main courses, I recommend the thin-crust pizza, fresh fish, and variety of savory pasta and meat dishes, such as the mesquite grilled leg of lamb with couscous. Homemade flatbread accompanies your meal. At night, torches and clay pot fireplaces warm the beachfront tables. In the bar area, TVs broadcast wide-ranging sports events. A Cuban band plays salsa Monday nights.

Marlin 2, on the beachfront. ✆ **329/291-3090.** Main courses 145–285 pesos. MC, V. Daily 8am–10:30pm.

El Costeño SEAFOOD   They say you haven't been to Sayulita if you haven't eaten at El Costeño, the oldest restaurant here dating from 1964. The sandy, sun-drenched eatery right on the main beach invites you to nibble on tortilla chips and ceviche while watching surfers glide across waves just in front. Grab one of the plastic tables and chairs on the large open-air patio or right on the beach—you can come for lunch or an early dinner and sit for as long as you like. Start with an order of guacamole and an outrageously large, potent margarita. The fish tacos are simple and delicious, as are the shrimp quesadillas. Whole fish comes topped with butter, garlic, or spicy "Diablo" sauce, with shrimp and octopus prepared any number of ways. The laid-back waitstaff seems as timeless as the ocean before you, and is never too rushed.

On the main beach. No phone. Dishes 60–110 pesos. No credit cards. Fri–Wed noon–8pm. Closed Thurs.

Restaurant Bar Leyza ★★ 🍴 MEXICAN   Sayulita's most authentic Mexican restaurant sits off the main square and incorporates traditional Huichol dishes, such as *sopes* and *huaraches,* into its creative but no-nonsense menu. Other delectable dishes include chiles rellenos stuffed with shrimp, fish fajitas, *arrachera* beef, chicken *mole,* and enormous combination platters with enchiladas, burritos, and tostadas. There are vegetarian options, too. The perfectly spiced food is cooked in olive oil and served on beautiful ceramic dishes; everything at this family-run restaurant tends to be healthy, cheap, and delicious. Try one of the fresh fruit waters to accompany your meal, and don't miss the hot salsa with fresh tomatoes, chiles, garlic, and shallots. You can sit inside, on the sidewalk patio, or on the rooftop terrace. If you can't get a table here, quality Mexican food is also served next door at Carmelita.

Next to the main square. ✆ **322/100-9373.** Dishes 60–239 pesos. No credit cards. Daily 8am–midnight.

Rollie's ★ INTERNATIONAL   Resident expats love this eclectic restaurant, where the menu welcomes "travelers, strangers, and lovely locals." Known for its good value breakfasts, Rollie's serves, among other items, Adriana's Rainbow (an omelet with cheese, tomatoes, green peppers, and onions) and my personal favorite, Indian Pipe Pancakes. All breakfasts come with lightly seasoned, pan-fried new potatoes. Rollie's also serves dinner, with live music in high season. Specialties include taco salads, paella, and creative hamburgers (such as those with shrimp or mahimahi). An espresso bar opens in the mornings, and terrific Mexican coffee is available all day.

Av. Revolución 58, 2 blocks west of the main square. ✆ **329/291-3567,** -3075. Breakfast 55–75 pesos; dinner 65–135 pesos. No credit cards. Nov–Apr daily 7:30am–noon and 5:30–9pm. Closed for dinner Mon nights; closed May–Oct.

Nightlife

Nightlife in Sayulita is as laid back by night as by day, and much of the action just happens out on the street and around the main square. Locals seem to gravitate to a different locale each night, so when you arrive, ask around to see where the evening's hot spot will be. For salsa in Sayulita, **La Bodeguita del Medio** (✆ **329/291-3866**), located at Av. Revolución 30-A, offers live Cuban music from 8pm until midnight and serves potent *mojitos.* It's open daily from noon to 2am. Housed upstairs under a big *palapa* next to the main plaza, **Calypso** (✆ **329/291-3704**), at

Revolución 44, is a popular bar/restaurant serving consistently high quality Mexican dishes and excellent salads alongside a full collection of tequilas. Traditional Mexican music plays in the background. It's open daily from 5 to 11pm. **Tekari** ⓒ **329/291-3828**), on Calle Manuel Navarrete at the corner of Gaviottas, is basically a big beach shack playing live music weekends and DJ mixes during the week. It's open from 8pm into the wee hours, although the place really gets going after midnight.

MAZATLÁN ★

1,078km (668 miles) NW of Mexico City; 502km (311 miles) NW of Guadalajara; 1,561km (968 miles) SE of Mexicali

In recent years, Mazatlán has shed its image as a spring-break party haven and today attracts mostly families, retirees, and package tourists with an eye for value. Visitors don't step off the plane in Vuitton slacks or Prada heels—you'll be out of place wearing much beyond a bathing suit and sandals. More than any other beach resort in the country, Mazatlán represents the expansive golden beaches, affordable accommodations, and beckoning bars and restaurants that typified Mexico's early appeal to travelers.

The world-class golf scene, luxury-yacht harbor, and myriad watersports activities are largely accessible to even those with a tight budget. Take a short boat ride to **Deer Island,** where you can spend the day swimming, snorkeling, and kayaking. Check out the **cliff divers** near the old lighthouse, and watch the sunset over the long golden beaches. Grab a surfboard and paddle out to the small, consistent waves. Deep-sea fishing for marlin and sailfish is among the best in Mexico. Hiking, bird-watching, and quiet beach walks here will lift your soul.

A trip to Mazatlán forces you to slow down. Get lost among the cobbled streets of the **old town,** where you can absorb the colonial splendor of the 19th-century Italian-style **Teatro Peralta;** meander past restored neoclassical homes resplendent in warm tropical colors; and pause in a traditional cafe for a robust Mexican coffee. Sit in the tree-lined **Plaza Mechado** amid a creative crowd of artists, musicians, and writers.

Mazatlán claims to be the shrimp capital of the world, and whether or not it's true, shrimp of all shapes and sizes comes dressed up in just about every way imaginable on the menu. Don't expect haute cuisine, but foodies will love the fresh, spicy ingredients that accompany grilled fish and succulent seafood. Do expect casual open-air settings with ocean breezes and friendly service.

Mazatlán has its share of clubs and discos—it always seems to be happy hour at **Señor Frog's,** and **Joe's Oyster Bar** attracts an all-day party crowd. But my favorite nightlife is in the old town, where old-school cantinas bring as much warm energy to the night air as the hip modern bars. Enjoy an icy cold *cerveza* at **Café Pacifico** amid the sounds of jazz and vibrant Mexican rhythms swelling from the central plaza. The spring-break party spirit comes back in force for 2 weeks in March for Carnaval celebrations, which in Mazatlán are among the biggest in Mexico.

Essentials

GETTING THERE & DEPARTING

BY PLANE   A number of airlines operate direct or nonstop flights to Mazatlán, though charters predominate. (For contact information, see "Getting There & Departing" under "Puerto Vallarta," earlier in this chapter.) From the United States,

Aeroméxico flies from Los Angeles, Atlanta, Phoenix, and Tucson, via Mexico City. **Alaska Airlines** flies nonstop from Los Angeles and Seattle. **Continental Airlines** flies nonstop from Houston. Check with a travel agent for the latest **charter flights.**

BY BUS First-class and deluxe buses connect Mazatlán to Guadalajara (7 hr.; 430 pesos one-way), Mexico City (16 hr.; 1,000 pesos), Puerto Vallarta (8 hr.; 380 pesos), and other points within Mexico. The main first-class bus company is **TAP** (✆ **01-800/001-1827** toll-free in Mexico; www.tap.com.mx). The bus terminal is located on Hwy. 200 N. Km 1203 (✆ **669/982-1949**).

BY CAR To reach Mazatlán from the United States, take **International Hwy. 15** from Nogales, Arizona, to Culiacán. At Culiacán, change to the four-lane **tollway**—it costs about 200 pesos from here to Mazatlán and is the only road considered safe and in drivable condition. On the tollway, total trip time from the United States to Mazatlán is about 12 hours. Consider an overnight stop, because driving at night in Mexico can be dangerous. **From Puerto Vallarta,** the 560km (347-mile) drive is not easy—the road winds through the mountains and takes about 8 hours, but is in generally good condition. Take **Hwy. 200** north to Las Varas. There it becomes four-lane **Hwy. 68;** follow that until you see a detour for **Hwy. 15.** Take 15 north to Mazatlán.

ORIENTATION

ARRIVING The Rafael Buelna International Airport (airport code: MZT) is 27km (17 miles) southeast of the hotel-and-resort area of town. The following rental car companies have counters in the airport, open during flight arrivals and departures: **Alamo, Avis, Budget, Hertz,** and **National.** Daily rates run $35 and up. A car is desirable for exploring the coast and nearby villages, but it is not essential in Mazatlán.

Taxis and *colectivo* minivans run from the airport to hotels; the airport-chartered taxis cost about 300 pesos, which is significantly more than the *colectivos*, which cost 120 pesos but take up to 12 passengers and, therefore, make multiple stops. Only taxis make the return trip to the airport, which costs 200 to 300 pesos. The **Central de Autobuses** (main bus terminal) is at Jose Angel Ferrusquilla, between the Zona Dorada and downtown.

VISITOR INFORMATION The extremely helpful and professional **State Tourism Office** (✆ **669/981-8883,** -8887; www.vivesinaloa.com), is at Olas Altas Sur 501, near Hotel La Siesta in the historic center. The office is open Monday through Friday from 9am to 5pm; the staff speaks English. To preview what's going on in Mazatlán before you arrive, check the website of the local English-language newspaper *Pacific Pearl* (www.pacificpearl.com), or pick up a copy of the simple publication at various hotels and locations around town. For additional information to help orient you, check *Mazatlán Interactivo* (www.mazatlaninteractivo.com.mx).

CITY LAYOUT Mazatlán extends north from the peninsula port area along Avenida Gabriel Leyva and Avenida Barragan, where the cruise ships, sportfishing boats, and ferries dock. Downtown begins with the historic area of **Viejo Mazatlán (Old Mazatlán)** and **Playa Olas Altas** to the south. A curving seaside boulevard, or *malecón,* extends 27km (17 miles) along the waterfront, all the way from Playa Olas Altas to **Playa Norte,** changing names often along the way. Traveling north, it begins as Paseo Olas Altas and becomes Paseo Claussen parallel to the commercial downtown area. The name changes to Avenida del Mar at the beginning of the Playa Norte area.

Mazatlán Area

Acuario Mazatlán
(Aquarium) **5**

Cathedral of the
Immaculate Conception **6**

El Faro (lighthouse) **13**

El Mirador Lookout Point **12**

Mazatlán Arts and Crafts
Center **1**

Museo Arqueológico
de Mazatlán **9**

Plaza de Toros (bullring) **3**

Plaza Principal **7**

Plazuela Machado **10**

Sea Shell City **2**

Teatro Ángela Peralta **11**

Tourism Office **8**

Valentino's/Punta Camarón **4**

About 6km (3¾ miles) north of downtown lies the Sábalo traffic circle in the **Zona Dorada (Golden Zone),** near the **Punta Camarón,** a rocky outcropping over the water. The Zona Dorada begins where Avenida del Mar intersects Avenida Rafael Buelna and becomes **Avenida Camarón Sábalo,** which leads north through the abundant hotels and fast-food restaurants of the tourist zone. From here, the resort hotels, including the huge El Cid Resort complex, spread northward along and beyond **Playa Sábalo.** The **Marina Mazatlán** (www.marina-mazatlan.com) development has changed the landscape north of the Zona Dorada considerably; hotels, condo complexes, and private residences rise around the marina. Although completion of the extensive project—to comprise the marina, condominiums, and commercial centers—is still years away, the new marina will be the largest on the western seaboard between Los Angeles and Panama, and one of the largest in all of Latin America. This area north of the Marina El Cid is increasingly known as Nuevo Mazatlán. North of here is **Los Cerritos (Little Hills).**

GETTING AROUND

The downtown transportation center for buses, taxis, and *pulmonías* (see below) is on the central Plaza Principal, facing the cathedral.

BY TAXI Eco Taxis are green and red cabs with posted set fares, and generally cost about 50 to 100 pesos per trip. Taxis are easy to flag around town and can also be rented by the hour (200 pesos). Agree on a price in advance. Fares between the Zona Dorada and Old Mazatlán average less than 100 pesos; within the Zona Dorada, you should pay about 50 pesos. It will cost 150 pesos to travel between Emerald Bay and downtown. To request a taxi, call ℭ **669/986-1111** or 669/985-2828.

BY PULMONÍA These open-air VW vehicles resembling overgrown golf carts carry up to three passengers. *Pulmonías* (literally "pneumonias") have surreylike tops and open sides. They're the same price as regular taxis and a quintessential part of the Mazatlán experience.

BY BUS Buses, some with air-conditioning, cover most of the city and are relatively easy to use, although knowing some Spanish is helpful. The SÁBALO CENTRO line runs from the Zona Dorada along the waterfront to downtown near the market and the central plaza; at Avenida Miguel Alemán, the buses turn and head south to Olas Altas. The CERRITOS-JUAREZ line starts near the train station, cuts across town to the *malecón* beside the Zona Dorada, and heads north to Los Cerritos and back. The SÁBALO COCOS line runs through the Zona Dorada, heads inland to the bus station, and goes on to downtown (also stopping at the market) by a back route. The PLAYA SUR line goes to the area where the sportfishing and tour boats depart. Buses run daily from 5:30am to 10:30pm. The fare is 8 pesos.

[FastFACTS] MAZATLÁN

Area Code   The telephone area code for Mazatlán is **669.**

Banks   Most banks are generally open Monday through Friday from 9am to 5pm, and some open from 9am to 2pm on Saturday.

Climate   As the northernmost major beach resort on the mainland, Mazatlán does not get as hot as beach cities farther south. The wettest month is September, and evenings during the winter months can be cool.

Consular Agencies The **Canadian Consular Agency** (☎ **669/913-7320;** Mon–Fri 9:30am–12:30pm) is in the Inn at Mazatlán, Av. Camarón Sábalo 6291. The **U.S. Consular Agency** (☎ **669/916-5889;** Mon–Fri 9am–1pm) is at Avenida Playa Gaviotas 202.

Drugstore **Farmacias Moderno,** German Evers and Hidalgo s/n (☎ **669/985-4545**), is open from 8am to 9pm.

Emergencies Dial ☎ **066.** For medical emergencies, contact the **Sharp Hospital,** Rafael Buelna and Las Cruces (☎ **669/986-5676,** -5678). The **Tourist Police** can be reached at ☎ **669/914-3222.**

Post Office The *correo* is downtown at Benito Juárez and 21 de Marzo, on the east side of the main plaza (☎ **669/981-2121**). Hours are Monday through Friday from 8am to 5:30pm, Saturday from 9am to 1pm.

Where to Stay

The hotels in downtown Mazatlán are generally older and less expensive than those along the beachfront heading north. Room rates rise farther north from downtown. The major areas to stay are the Zona Dorada (Golden Zone), Playa Norte (North Beach), Nuevo Mazatlán (New Mazatlán), Playa Olas Altas, and the downtown seafront.

THE ZONA DORADA & NORTH

The Zona Dorada is an elegant arc of gold sand linked by a palm-lined boulevard and bordered by the most deluxe hotels and elaborate beach houses. A bonus is the sunset view. Many hotels along this beach cut their prices from May through September.

El Cid Resort The grande dame of Mazatlán's resorts, El Cid Resort offers extensive services, outdoor activities, and dining and entertainment options. Both a hotel and a timeshare development, El Cid features three beachside buildings within close distance and a separate hotel at the marina. These include the popular 17-story beachside tower, Castilla; the 28-story, all-suite El Moro Tower (which is mostly for timeshares); and the oldest, lowest-priced building, Granada, near the golf course. El Cid Marina Beach is the newest, most upscale, and most expensive of El Cid's Mazatlán properties, located north of the main El Cid complex on the marina's waterfront. In general, the rooms are not the resort's primary draw (except for at the more luxurious El Cid Marina Beach), although many guest rooms were renovated throughout the complex in 2009 and 2010. The resort's main draw are the activities: The golf and tennis facilities are outstanding, as is the spa. Guests can choose from extensive watersports, adventure and cultural tours, and nature programs.

Av. Camarón Sábalo s/n (btw. Av. Rodolfo T. Loaiza and Circuito Campeador), 82110 Mazatlán, Sin. www. elcid.com. ☎ **866/306-6113** in the U.S., or 669/913-3333. Fax 669/914-1311. 1,320 units. High season $100–$300 double, $200 and up suite; low season $50–$250 double, $175 and up suite. All-inclusive program $270 and up double occupancy, children 3–11 $35. AE, MC, V. Free guarded parking. **Amenities:** 11 restaurants; 8 bars; babysitting; kids' club; concierge; fitness center; 27-hole golf course; 8 outdoor pools (including 1 saltwater pool); room service; spa; 9 tennis courts; watersports equipment. *In room:* A/C, TV, hair dryer, Wi-Fi.

Pueblo Bonito ★★ ☺ The all-suite Pueblo Bonito remains one of my favorite resorts in Mazatlán. The grounds are gorgeous—exotic birds stroll lush lawns, a waterfall cascades into the main pool adjacent to the pool bar, and a row of *palapas* lines the beachfront. The colonial-style suites feature balconies or patios with ocean views; feather-top beds with pillow menus; and architectural touches such as curved ceilings, arched windows, and tiled floors. They come with kitchenettes and ample seating areas, and the extra space makes this a good choice for families or friends traveling together. Much of the action takes place on the beach or around the pool area, and watersports and pool activities enliven the scene throughout the day.

Av. Camarón Sábalo 2121 (Apdo. Postal 6), 82110 Mazatlán, Sin. www.pueblobonito-mazatlan.com. (℃ **800/990-8250** in the U.S., 01-800/990-8250 in Mexico, or 669/989-8900. Fax 669/989-8600. 247 units. High season $230 junior suite; $270 2-bedroom suite (up to 2 adults and 2 children); low season $150 junior suite, $170 2-bedroom suite. AE, MC, V. Free guarded parking; valet parking. **Amenities:** 3 restaurants, including Angelo's (p. 312); 2 bars; babysitting; concierge; gym; 2 large outdoor pools and pool activities; room service; sauna; watersports; whirlpool. *In room:* A/C, TV, Internet.

Villas El Rancho 🏄 Each of the charming, reasonably priced villas is a two-bedroom duplex (one with a king-size bed, the other with two queen-size beds), a fully equipped kitchen, two bathrooms, and a living/dining area. They're decorated with handsome wood furnishings, Mexican handicrafts, and simple artwork. The difference in price depends on your view—garden, pool, or ocean. The small hotel lies on a beautiful stretch of soft-sand beach, immediately to the north of the Zona Dorada. The gardens are lovely, and the laid-back, *palapa*-covered restaurant sits above the bar, making it an ideal spot for catching the sunset. Note that this is also a timeshare resort, so be prepared for a sales pitch if you stay here.

Av. Sábalo-Cerritos 3170, 82110 Mazatlán, Sin. www.elrancho.com.mx. (℃ **888/596-5760** toll-free in the U.S. or 01-800/717-1991 in Mexico. 28 units. High season $135–$200 2-bedroom suite (sleeps up to 6); low season $110–$170 2-bedroom suite (sleeps up to 6). Rates include free airport pickup. AE, MC, V. Free parking. **Amenities:** Restaurant; bar; 2 Jacuzzis; outdoor pool; Wi-Fi (in lobby). *In room:* A/C, TV.

PLAYA NORTE

The waterfront between downtown and the Zona Dorada is Mazatlán's original tourist hotel zone. Moderately priced hotels and motels line the street across from the beach. From May to September, many hotels cut their prices.

Hotel Playa Mazatlán ★ ☺ The most happening place on this stretch of the Zona Dorada, the rustic Hotel Playa Mazatlán (open since 1955) remains enduringly popular with families, tour groups, and regulars who return annually for winter vacations and Semana Santa (Easter Week). The quietest rooms lie in the four-story section surrounding the well-tended interior gardens; those by the terrace restaurant and beach can be noisy. Most rooms are decorated in bright colors, with dark-wood furnishings and colonial accents. The beach is one of the liveliest in town. The hotel hosts a popular Mexican fiesta on Saturday at 7pm and a fireworks display on Sunday. Also at the Hotel Playa Mazatlán, Sendero Mexico (www.senderomexico.com) operates EduVentura, an evolving recreation center that includes waterfalls and ponds, climbing walls, two exciting 120m (400-ft.) zip lines, and more.

Av. Playa Gaviotas 202 Zona Dorada, 82110 Mazatlán, Sin. www.hotelplayamazatlan.com. (℃ **800/762-5816** in the U.S., or 669/989-0555. Fax 669/914-0366. 403 units. $80 and up garden-view double; $100 and up oceanview double; semi-inclusive plans start at $86 per person. AE, MC, V. Free guarded parking. **Amenities:** Restaurant (La Terraza, p. 312); snack bar; bar; gym; 3 outdoor pools; room service; spa and fitness center; 2 outdoor whirlpools; watersports equipment rental. *In room:* A/C, TV, hair dryer, Wi-Fi.

DOWNTOWN SEAFRONT/PLAYA OLAS ALTAS

The old section of Mazatlán spreads around a picturesque beach a short walk from downtown. Movie stars of the 1950s and 1960s came here for sun and surf, and the hotels where they stayed are still here. A few seafront restaurants also remain.

Hotel La Siesta 🔔 The landmark La Siesta occupies a building surrounded by the old mansions of Mazatlán. Inside, three levels encircle a central courtyard; guest rooms facing the ocean have balconies opening to sea breezes and pounding waves. Those at the back of the hotel are quieter but less charming; all have two beds, a table and chair, and small functional bathroom. **El Shrimp Bucket,** once the town's most popular restaurant until the Zona Dorada stole this area's thunder, sits off the courtyard.

Av. Olas Altas 11 Sur, 82000 Mazatlán, Sin. www.lasiesta.com.mx. ✆ **669/981-2640,** -2334. Fax 669/982-2633. 58 units. $40 interior double; $55 oceanview double. AE, MC, V. Street parking. From the deer statue on Olas Altas, go right 1 block. **Amenities:** Restaurant; bar; small pool; limited room service. In room: A/C, TV, Wi-Fi.

NUEVO MAZATLÁN (NEW MAZATLÁN)

New Mazatlán stretches out north of the marina and is the city's newest development area. In addition to Pueblo Bonito Emerald Bay, a Crowne Plaza and an all-inclusive RIU resort have opened in this area. It's about a half-hour drive to the city center from here.

Pueblo Bonito Emerald Bay ★★★ ☺ Mazatlán's most upscale resort sits on a stunning stretch of coastline, undisturbed by much around it. The protected beach area, magnificent free-form infinity pools, and gorgeous landscaped grounds with over 70 types of palms are reason enough to stay here. Outdoor activities abound, and the kids' club offers wonderful programs, involving painting, ceramics, and sand castles. The high-tech spa is Mazatlán's best (and most expensive), offering diverse spa rituals, massage therapies, body treatments, and facials. The generously appointed junior, master, and presidential suites are spread out among 15 buildings, introducing Mexican accents to the neoclassical design. All have kitchenettes, oceanview balconies or terraces, featherbed mattress covers with pillow menus, and lovely bathrooms with designer amenities. As with other resorts in Mazatlán, some of the rooms here are timeshares. La Cordeliere beachfront restaurant serves seafood, and a new bistro offers quality Mexican fare. A free shuttle runs frequently between this resort and Pueblo Bonito, in the Golden Zone.

Av. Ernesto Coppel Compania s/n, Zona Nuevo Mazatlán, 82110 Mazatlán, Sin. www.pueblobonitoemerald bay.com. ✆ **800/990-8250** in the U.S., or 669/989-0525. Fax 669/988-0718. 348 units. High season $260 and up suite; low season $170 and up suite. All-inclusive plans available. AE, MC, V. Free guarded parking. **Amenities:** 3 restaurants; 3 bars, including pool bar; babysitting; kids' club; concierge; fitness center; Jacuzzi; 4 pools including adult pool and multilevel infinity pool w/activities; room service; spa and fitness classes; 2 tennis courts w/instruction available; watersports equipment; Wi-Fi (in deli). In room: A/C, TV, hair dryer, Internet, minibar, kitchen.

Where to Eat

Mazatlán boasts one of the largest shrimp fleets in the world, so it's no surprise that shrimp and seafood are the specialties. Most restaurants are very casual and moderately priced, offering good value. A cheap-eats treat is to stop in one of the many *loncherías* (small establishments that are only for lunch, kind of like a home-cooking place, but not a counter) scattered throughout the downtown area. Here you can get a *torta* (a sandwich on a small French roll) stuffed with a variety of meats, cheeses, tomatoes, and onions, for around $5. Also recommendable is the **Deli 28 Centro,** Belisario Domínguez 1503, Historic Downtown (✆ **669/981-1577**), serving pasta, salads, quality deli meats and cheeses, as well as pizzas. It's open Monday through Saturday from 9am to 11pm.

THE ZONA DORADA
Expensive

Angelo's ★ ITALIAN/SEAFOOD   Even locals consider this northern Italian restaurant one of the best in town, as much for its elegant ambience as for its food. Beveled-glass doors reveal a dining room gleaming with brass, polished wood, and crystal chandeliers, as well as live piano. For an antipasti, consider the pan-fried marinated eggplant with Parmesan cheese followed by a light pasta. Waiters then present diners with fresh fish, veal, and steak (including chateaubriand for two). The formality of the restaurant seems a little out of place given the beach location, but those willing to dress up will appreciate Angelo's for special occasions.

In the Pueblo Bonito hotel (p. 309), Av. Camarón Sábalo 2121. ✆ **669/989-8900.** Reservations required. Main courses 230–530 pesos. AE, MC, V. Tues–Sun 6–11pm.

Papagayo Restaurant ★ INTERNATIONAL   Nestled on the beach at the Inn at Mazatlán, diners at Papagayo enjoy the natural beauty of the sea. Diners can choose beach or open-air patio seating and a view to Las Tres Islas, the three imposing islands just offshore. Chef Vidal offers an extensive international menu, using the freshest fish, fruit, and vegetables. For a treat, order the shrimp CocoLoco, served in a half-pineapple with a coconut and tequila sauce, and wash it down with a rich flavored margarita. If you're overloaded with seafood, the prime rib is a house favorite—and it can be combined with grilled lobster if you prefer to have it both ways. A number of exotic desserts and coffees are prepared tableside here.

The Inn at Mazatlán, Av. Camarón Sábalo 6291. ✆ **669/913-4151.** www.innatmazatlan.com.mx. Main courses 100–240 pesos. AE, MC, V. Daily 7am–11pm.

Pedro y Lola ★★ INTERNATIONAL   Named after legendary *ranchero* singers Pedro Infante and Lola Beltran, this wonderful little restaurant/bar sits on the corner of the Plazuela Machado. Weekends bring live music and performances to the square, when cars are not allowed. The restaurant is housed in the beautifully restored 19th-century Juárez building that once served as the social center of this music-loving city. Inside, the colorful restaurant is decorated with local artwork and has a jazzy feel, but it's even more fun to sit outside on the patio. My favorite dish here is the "Pedro and Lola shrimp" prepared with fresh orange and Cointreau. You can also come just for appetizers or a drink, and the bar stays open until 1am.

Calle Constitución 523. ✆ **669/982-2589.** Main courses 100–200 pesos. AE, MC, V. Daily 6pm–midnight.

Moderate

Jungle Juice CAFE   This festive eatery serves fresh fruit smoothies and juices along with simple, tasty cuisine. Tender rib-eye steaks and delectable shrimps are grilled over mesquite on the patio—two-for-one barbecue specials are often available. Jungle Juice also serves vegetarian dishes and zesty Mexican and American breakfasts. Consider taking a break here during a shopping tour in the Zona Dorada.

Las Garzas 101. ✆ **669/913-3315.** Main courses 70–245 pesos. MC, V. Daily 7am–10pm. Bar daily 6pm–2am. From Pastelería Panamá, take Sábalo and turn right on Las Garzas; it's 1 block down on your right. Heading north on Loaiza, Las Garzas and the Pastelería Panamá are on the right after the Sábalo traffic circle, before the Mazatlán Arts and Crafts Center.

La Terraza ★ MEXICAN/INTERNATIONAL   During the day, diners enjoy a view of the beach and Isla de Venados from the open-air terrace looking right over the ocean. After sundown, candlelit tables, the stars overhead, and the sound of the surging waves serve as the backdrop to live music and dancing from 7pm to midnight. The menu at La Terraza incorporates Mexican and international dishes, with a focus on seafood. Order fish, shrimp, or lobster prepared any way you like. Spicy carne asada, grilled chicken, shrimp kabobs, and surf-and-turf skewers are among the options. The traditional Mexican songs draw a festive crowd of all ages, and it's possible to just come for drinks. Check out the breakfast buffet if you wake up at a reasonable hour.

In the Hotel Playa Mazatlán, Av. Playa Gaviotas 202. © **669/989-0555.** Breakfast 60–120 pesos; Mexican plates 83–138 pesos; seafood and meat 126–247 pesos. AE, MC, V. Daily 7am–11pm. Bar stays open later.

Inexpensive
Pura Vida I ★ VEGETARIAN/HEALTH FOOD   Nearly hidden behind thick plants, Pura Vida has several small seating sections with wood picnic tables and white canvas umbrellas. A perfect morning spot, it specializes in juices and smoothies, from kelp to papaya. The energetic staff serves omelets and whole-wheat pancakes for breakfast, and burgers, purified salads, soups, and Mexican specialties for lunch. There are plenty of vegetarian dishes, such as soy burgers. The veggie and white-chicken sandwiches served on whole-wheat rolls are fabulous.

Bugambilia 100. © **669/916-1010.** Main courses 50–80 pesos. No credit cards. Daily 8am–11pm. From Pastelería Panamá on Sábalo, turn right on Las Garzas, then left 1 block down onto Laguna; the cafe is on your right.

DOWNTOWN & PLAYA NORTE
Moderate
Copa de Leche ★ 🍷 MEXICAN   This nostalgic sidewalk cafe on the waterfront at Playa Olas Altas feels the way Mazatlán must have in the 1950s, and the food is consistently as good as the ocean view. The menu includes *pechugas en nogada* (chicken breast in pecan-and-pomegranate sauce); shrimp *a la plancha* cooked with cheese and white wine; traditional *alambre* (grilled beef cooked with onion, peppers, mushrooms, ham, and bacon); rich seafood soup loaded with squid, shrimp, and chunks of fish; and succulent shrimp with chipotle sauce. Inside, the decor is about as simple as it gets, although the bar is creatively designed using an old wooden boat. Live *música romantica* plays Thursday through Saturday nights.

Av. Olas Altas 1220 A Sur. © **669/982-5753.** Breakfast 40–80 pesos; main courses 70–170 pesos. MC, V. Daily 7am–11pm. From El Shrimp Bucket (at Mariano Escobedo and Olas Altas), turn south and walk half a block down Olas Altas; the cafe is on your left.

El Shrimp Bucket MEXICAN/SEAFOOD   Since 1963, El Shrimp Bucket has reigned as the most popular restaurant in town. Although its luster has been somewhat eclipsed by newer establishments in the Golden Zone, it retains a loyal following and is especially popular for breakfast—when all types of egg dishes are served—and lunch, when many come for sandwiches and salads. The specialty, of course, is Mazatlán's famous shrimp, which can be ordered throughout the day and prepared any way you choose—breaded, beer battered, barbecued, grilled, coconut crusted, or peel-and-eat. The giant Shrimp Boat includes 30 pieces done in different styles, served with rice and fries. Sit inside the festive dining room or on the outdoor terrace, located at the Hotel La Siesta, and enjoy a relaxed meal in this old-time favorite.

In the Hotel La Siesta, Av. Olas Altas 111 (at Mariano Escobedo). © **669/981-6350** or 982-8019. Breakfast 40–85 pesos. Lunch plates 60–100 pesos; seafood and steak 100–375 pesos. AE, MC, V. Daily 7am–11pm.

Activities on & off the Beach

To orient yourself, walk up and enjoy the panoramic view from **El Faro,** the famous lighthouse on the point at the south end of town. It's the second-highest lighthouse in the world (only Gibraltar's is higher), towering 135m (443 ft.) over the harbor. Begin at the end of Paseo Centenario, near the sportfishing docks. There's a refreshment stand at the foot of the hill. Allow about 45 minutes for the climb. The view is nearly as spectacular from the top of **Cerro del Vigía (Lookout Hill),** which is accessible by car from Paseo Olas Altas.

BEACHES   At the western edge of downtown is rocky **Playa Olas Altas,** a lovely stretch of pounding surf not suitable for swimming. Around a rocky promontory north of Olas Altas is **Playa Norte,** which offers several kilometers of good sand beach.

At the Sábalo traffic circle, Punta Camarón juts into the water, and on either side of the point is **Playa Las Gaviotas.** Farther north, **Playa Sábalo** is perhaps the best beach in Mazatlán. The next point jutting into the water is Punta Sábalo, beyond which you'll find a bridge over a channel that flows in and out of a lagoon. Beyond the marina, more beaches stretch all the way to Los Cerritos. Remember that all beaches in Mexico are public property, so you have the right to enjoy the beach of your choice.

Mazatlán is one of only a few resorts in Mexico where surfing is common on central town beaches. The waves are best at **Los Pinos,** north of the fort—known in surfing circles as "the Cannon"—and at Playa Los Gaviotas and Playa Sábalo. Swells are most consistent from May to September. Other notable surf breaks are found at Olas Altos, Cerritos, Isla de la Piedra, and El Camarón, at Playa Norte. The **Mazatlán Surf Center** (© 669/913-1821; www.mazatlansurfcenter.com), in the Zona Dorada, at Camarón Sábalo 500-4, sells gear, rents boards, and offers surf lessons and Billabong day and overnight camps. Lessons cost $65 for 2 hours and include hotel transportation and equipment. Surfboard rentals start at about $25 per day. Boogie boards are widely available for about $15 per day; wet suits rent for $10 per day.

An enticing beach for a day trip lies on **Isla de la Piedra (Stone Island).** From the center of town, board a Circunvalación or Playa Sur bus from the north side of the Plaza Principal for the ride to the boat landing, Embarcadero–Isla de la Piedra. Small motorboats make the 5-minute trip to the island every 15 minutes or so, from 7am to 6pm, for a modest price. When you arrive on the island, walk through the rustic little village to the ocean side, where the pale-sand beaches, bordered by coconut groves, stretch for miles. On Sunday afternoons, the *palapa* restaurants on the shore feature music and dancing, attracting mainly Mexican families.

CRUISES & BOAT RENTALS   The **Kolonahe Sailing Adventure** departs for Isla de Venados (Deer Island) Tuesday through Sunday from Marina El Cid. Reserve through any travel agent or through El Cid (see below). This excursion sails aboard a 15m (49-ft.) trimaran to the island, where guests enjoy a hot Mexican lunch and open bar, plus the use of snorkel equipment, boogie boards, kayaks, and canoes, for a cost of $50 per person. The boat departs at 9:15am and returns at 3:30pm. A 3-hour sunset cruise sets sail on Thursdays at 5pm for a cost of $34 per person.

DEEP-SEA FISHING   Mazatlán claims to be the billfish and shrimp capital of the world, and whether or not it's a valid claim, deep-sea fishing in Mazatlán is generally less expensive than in other parts of Mexico. July and August are the best fishing months, when marlin, sailfish, and dorado (mahimahi) pack the warm Pacific waters. Swordfish, dorado, yellowfin tuna, rooster fish, wahoo, and shark all swim the waters here. If requested, your captain will practice "catch and release." Rates are around $475 per day for a 9m (28-ft.) *lancha* for up to four people and $675 per day for an 11m (36-ft.) cruiser for up to 10 passengers. Rates do not include fishing licenses ($15 per person), drinks, or gratuities. Try the **Aries Fleet** located at the Marina El Cid harbor master's office (© **669/916-3468;** www.elcid.com), or **Escualo Fleet** (© **669/913-0303;** www.escualosportfishing.com) at Marina Mazatlán Pier 10. Locals suggest making fishing reservations for October through January at least 2 weeks in advance; at the very least, do it the minute you arrive in town. You may also choose to rent a *panga* (a small, uncovered fiberglass boat with an outboard motor) at a rate of about $275 per day (6 hr.) for up to four people.

OTHER WATERSPORTS   The best place to arrange scuba diving, snorkeling, or surfing expeditions is the **Aqua Sport Center** (© **669/913-0451;** www.mazatlan-aquasports.com), located at Av. Camarón Sábalo s/n between the Posada Freeman Hotel and El Cid Hotel.

SPECIAL EVENTS IN NEARBY VILLAGES   The weekend of the first Sunday in October, **Rosario,** a small town 45 minutes south on Hwy. 15, holds a **festival honoring Our Lady of the Rosary,** with games, music, dances, processions, and festive foods. From May 1 to May 10, Rosario holds its **Spring Festival.**

In mid-October, the village of **Escuinapa,** south of Rosario on Hwy. 15, holds a **Mango Festival;** call the **Escuinapa Tourism Office** (© **695/953-0019**) or the **State Tourism Office** (© **669/981-8886**) for details.

SPECTATOR SPORTS   There's a bullring (Plaza de Toros) on Rafael Buelna about 1.5km (1 mile) from the Zona Dorada. From December to early April, **bullfights** take place certain Sundays and holidays at 4pm; locals recommend arriving by 3pm. Tickets range from 100 pesos for general admission (ask for the shady side—*la sombra*) to 300 pesos for the front of the shaded section; most travel agencies and tour desks sell advance tickets. Note that the bulls are killed in these events.

At Playa Olas Altas, daring **cliff divers** take to the rock ledges of **El Mirador** and plunge into the shallow, pounding surf below, a la Acapulco. The divers perform sporadically during the day as tour buses arrive near their perch, sometimes diving with torches on Sundays at 7pm. Follow the *malecón* to the esplanade and look for the mermaid statue to find El Mirador.

TENNIS, GOLF & OTHER OUTDOOR SPORTS   Try the **El Cid Resort,** on Camarón Sábalo (© **669/913-3333;** hotel guests have priority). Courts run about $20 per hour. Many larger hotels in Mazatlán also have courts.

Mazatlán is probably the best **golf** value in Mexico. Try the 27-hole course at the **El Cid Resort** (© **669/913-3333**). Nine holes designed by Lee Trevino complement the 18 holes designed by Robert Trent Jones, Jr. It's open to the public, with preference given to hotel guests. Greens fees for nonguests run $80 for 18 holes, plus $20 for the caddy. El Cid guests pay $60, plus $15 for the caddy. A driving range and golf lessons are available. The club's open daily from 7am to 3pm.

Green fees at the **Club Campestre Mazatlán** (© **669/980-1570**) are 250 pesos for 9 holes and 350 pesos for 18 holes; a caddy costs an extra 130 pesos to 180 pesos, and a cart is 150 pesos to 200 pesos, respectively. The club is on Hwy. 15 just outside town, and is open daily from 7am to 3pm.

The **Estrella del Mar Golf Club** (© **800/629-2852** in the U.S., or 669/982-3300; www.estrelladelmar.com) is Mazatlán's best golf course. The 18-hole, 7,004-yard course, also designed by Robert Trent Jones, Jr., stretches along 3km (1¾ miles) of coastline on Isla de la Piedra, a peninsula just south of downtown Mazatlán. There's a PGA pro on staff, a driving range, and lessons available. Greens fees in high season run $110 for 18 holes and $74 for 9 holes, and in low season $75 for 18 holes and $49 for 9 holes; fees include cart, but no caddies are available. It's open daily from 7:30am to sunset. Clubs are available for rent for $35 plus tax.

You can go **horseback riding** on Isla de la Piedra for about 100 pesos. Ask your hotel's travel agent to arrange a **kayaking excursion** on El Verde Camacho Ecological Lagoon, or take a trip to Teacapán for **birding** in one of Mexico's largest estuaries.

Bird-watching tours are offered by **Sendero Mexico** (www.senderomexico. com), an outfitter that also runs sustainable nature excursions and a popular kayaking tour. The birding tours can be arranged in conjunction with a kayak tour, or as a separate trip to the foothills of the Sierra Madres or to the Palmito reserve (located just past Copala on the highway), home to the tufted-jay. In early 2009, Sendero Mexico organized the first **Mazatlán Bird Festival** (www.mazatlanbirdfestival. com).

Exploring Mazatlán

Mazatlán may be best known for its wide, sandy beaches and sporting activities, but visitors who neglect to sample the city's cultural events and attractions are missing out on a multidimensional destination.

MUSEUMS

Acuario Mazatlán ☺ Children and adults interested in the sea will love the Mazatlán Aquarium. With over 200 species of fish, including sharks, eels, and sea horses, it is one of the largest and best in Mexico. Next to the aquarium are a playground and botanical garden, with an aviary and a small crocodile exhibit. Staff feed the sea lions, birds, and fish almost hourly, and there is a scuba demonstration in the morning and a bird show in the afternoon.

Av. de los Deportes 111 (a half-block off Av. del Mar). © **669/981-7815.** www.acuariomazatlan.gob.mx. Admission 75 pesos adults, 50 pesos children 3–11. Daily 9:30am–5:30pm.

Museo Arqueológico de Mazatlán This small, attractive archaeological museum displays pre-Hispanic artifacts and a permanent contemporary art exhibit. From Olas Altas, walk inland on Sixto Osuna 1½ blocks; the museum sits on the right. Art exhibits sometimes take place in the Casa de la Cultura across from the museum.

Sixto Osuna 76 (1½ blocks from Paseo Olas Altas). © **669/981-1455.** Admission 31 pesos, free Sun. Tues–Sun 9am–6pm.

ARCHITECTURAL HIGHLIGHTS

Two blocks south of the central plaza stands the lovely **Teatro Angela Peralta,** Carnaval 1024, Centro (© **669/982-4444;** www.culturamazatlan.com), a national historic monument. Built between 1869 and 1874, the 841-seat Italian-style theater has three levels of balconies, two facades, and, in true tropical style, a lobby with no roof. The theater was named for one of the world's great divas, who, along with the director and 30 members of the opera, died in Mazatlán of cholera in an 1863 epidemic. Some city tours stop here; if you're visiting on your own, the theater is open daily from 9am to 6pm and allows tours for a nominal charge. It regularly schedules folkloric ballets, along with periodic performances of classical ballet, contemporary dance, symphony concerts, opera, and jazz. This theater is the home of Delfos, one of the most important contemporary dance companies in Mexico.

The 20-block historic area near the theater, including the small square **Plazuela Machado** (bordered by Frías, Constitución, Carnaval, and Sixto Osuna), abounds with beautiful old buildings and colorful town houses trimmed with wrought iron and carved stone. On weekends, the streets surrounding the plaza close to cars, giving artists, musicians, vendors, and street performers a chance to set up shop.

The **Plaza Principal,** also called Plaza Revolución, forms the heart of the city, filled with vendors, shoeshine stands, and people of all ages out for a stroll. At its center lies a Victorian-style wrought-iron bandstand with a diner-type restaurant underneath. Be sure to take in the **Cathedral of the Immaculate Conception,** at Calle 21 de Marzo and Nelson, with its unusual yellow-tiled twin steeples and partially tiled facade.

ORGANIZED TOURS

In addition to 3-hour **city tours** ($25), tour operators offer excursions to many colorful and interesting villages nearby, such as Concordia and Copala. Some towns date from the 16th-century Spanish Conquest; others are modest farming or fishing villages. Information and reservations are available at any travel agency or major hotel, and all accept major credit cards. The premier provider of these and other tours is **Pronatours** (✆ 669/916-7720, -3333, ext. 3490; www.elcid.com/pronatours), yet another part of the El Cid megacomplex of activities. In addition to the city tour, they offer a 5-hour Tequila Tour that includes a distillery tour and lunch ($45), a 5-hour sailing excursion to Deer Island (Isla de Venados) that includes kayaking, snorkeling, buffet lunch, and open bar ($50), and a visit to a historic village by the El Quelite river. Three other recommended tour agencies are **Viajes el Sábalo** (✆ 669/986-4930;** www.viajeselsabalo.com); **Olé Tours** (✆ 669/916-6288; www.ole-tours.com); and the sustainable tourism company **Sendero Mexico** (✆ 669/940-8687; www.senderomexico.com), based in the Hotel Playa Mazatlán.

COPALA-CONCORDIA   This popular 6-hour countryside tour stops at several mountain villages where artisans craft furniture and other items. Copala is a historic mining village with a Spanish-colonial church, and it seems all the residents are dedicated to making furniture, bricks, and pottery. The tour ($55), also run by **Pronatours** (see above), includes lunch and soft drinks.

MAZATLÁN JUNGLE TOUR   Some might say that David Pérez's (King David's) **Jungle Tour** (✆ 669/914-1444; www.kingdavid.com.mx) is misnamed, but it's still worthwhile. It consists of a 1½-hour boat ride past a Mexican navy base and Mazatlán's shrimp fleet and packing plants, and into the mangrove swamps to Isla de la Piedra (Stone Island). There's a 3-hour stop at a pristine beach that has what could be the world's largest sand dollars (though fewer and fewer are left). Horseback rides on the beach are available for a modest fee. After the beach stop, feast on *pescado zarandeado* (fish cooked over coconut husks, green mangrove, and charcoal). Tours run from 9am to 3pm Tuesday, Thursday, and Saturday, and cost $45 per person. **Pronatours** (above) offers a similar version of this tour.

Shopping

Mazatlán shopping runs the gamut from precious stones to seashells—with plenty of T-shirts in between. Most stores are open Monday through Saturday from 9 or 10am to 6 or 8pm. Very few close for lunch, and many stores are open on Sunday afternoon. There's also an art walk to a number of galleries from 4 to 8pm on the first Friday of the month between November and May; for details visit www.artwalkmazatlan.com.

La **Zona Dorada** (the **Golden Zone**) is the best area for shopping. There are a number of quality silver shops along Avenida Playa Gaviotas, including **Pacific Jewelry** (© 669/913-3754), at Av. Gaviotas 413. It's open Monday through Saturday from 9am to 8:30pm, and Sunday from 10am to 6pm. For more fine jewelry, seek out **Rubio Jewellers,** in the Costa de Oro Hotel, Av. Camarón Sábalo 710 (© **669/914-3167;** www.rubiojewellers.com). It's open Monday through Saturday from 9am to 6pm, and Sunday from 10am to 1:30pm.

   Sea Shell City (© 669/913-1301), at Av. Playa Gaviotas 407, is exactly what the name implies—more shell-covered decorative items than you ever dreamed could exist, from the tacky to the sublime. It's open daily 10am to 7pm. **Michael Gallery** (© 669/916-7816; www.michaelgallerymexico.com), at Av. Las Garzas 18 off Avenida Camarón Sábalo, has an excellent selection of Tlaquepaque crafts, art, diamonds, and fine silver jewelry. It's open Tuesday to Saturday from 10am to 5:30pm. **Señor Frog's,** which has its main store located next to El Cid resort at Camarón Sábalo s/n (© 669/985-1110; www.senorfrogs.com/mazatlan), is the most popular souvenir store in town, selling Señor Frog's signature shirts, hats, handbags, and beachwear. There are about a dozen branches of Señor Frog's around town. They're open daily from 9am to 11pm.

   The **Centro Mercado** in Old Mazatlán is another kind of shopping experience. Here you'll find women selling fresh shrimp under colorful umbrellas; open-air food stalls; and indoor shops stacked with pottery, clothing, and crafts (mostly of lesser quality). The market opens around 6am and stays open until sundown.

   Small galleries and shops are beginning to appear in Old Mazatlán; one of the nicest is **NidArt Galería,** Av. Libertad 45 and Carnaval (© 669/981-0002, or 985-5991 for after-hours appointments; www.nidart.com), next to the Teatro Angela Peralta. It features changing exhibits of contemporary art. Open Monday through Friday from 10am to 5pm or after hours by appointment.

Mazatlán After Dark

Mazatlán is known for its vibrant Mexican fiestas and equally colorful local bar scene, where dancing on bars, atop tables, and inside cages can be a nightly event. Traditional mariachi groups, *tambora* bands, and live romantic music create a festive mood in many restaurants and hotel bars.

   A free **fireworks** show usually takes place Saturdays at 8pm on the beach fronting the Hotel Playa Mazatlán (p. 310), Av. Playa Gaviotas 202, in the Zona Dorada (© 669/913-5320 or 989-0555). The display is visible from the beach and from the hotel's La Terraza restaurant (p. 312). The same hotel presents Mazatlán's most popular **Fiesta Mexicana** (www.laoriginalfiestamexicana.com), complete with buffet, open bar, folkloric dancing, and live music. Fiestas begin at 7pm on Saturdays; try to arrive by 6pm to get a good table. Tickets are 360 pesos. Pueblo Bonito Emerald Bay (© 669/989-0525) offers a Fiesta Mexicana on Wednesday nights at 6pm in La Cordeliere Restaurant for 300 pesos.

CLUBS & BARS

Café Pacifico   Owned by the popular Mazatlán-based Pacifico brewery, this rustic cafe/bar in the historic center offers a taste of an authentic Mexican cantina. In addition to serving the popular Mexican beer, it serves simple local fare, including steaks. Live music plays on weekend nights. Open Wednesday to Sunday 7pm to 3am. Constitución and Horiberto Frias. © **669/136-0916.**

Joe's Oyster Bar   Beer, cocktails, and tequila, along with oysters and shrimp baskets, are the house specialties at this popular open-air bar. A relaxed beach bar by day, Joe's transforms into a dance party as the night wears on. It's open daily 11am to 2am (until 4am Fri–Sat). On the beachfront at Los Sábalos Hotel, Av. Rodolfo T. Loaiza 100. © **669/983-5333.** Cover 60 pesos weekends, which includes 2 drinks.

Latitud 23   The city's popular recent addition, Latitud 23 is a friendly upstairs bar that plays Mexican hits to a mostly local crowd. Dress is casual, and a simple fusion menu offers pastas, fish and seafood, and simple Mexican dishes. Located a block from the Hotel Playa Mazatlán, Latitud 23 regularly hosts theme nights, occasionally with live music. It's open weekdays from 5pm to midnight, and weekends until 4am. Av. Playa Gaviotas 401 (upstairs), Zona Dorada. © **669/913-1413.**

Señor Frog's   Next to El Cid resort, Señor Frog's remains one of Mazatlán's hottest bar/restaurants, including among locals. Live music rocks the house Thursday through Saturday nights, when the energetic staff leads the festive local and international crowd in song and dance. Other nights a DJ spins beats from inside a transformed VW bus, while hilarious quotes across the walls make for fun table conversation. It's open daily from 11am to 1am, and into the wee hours on weekends. Camarón Sábalo s/n, Zona Dorada. © **669/985-1110.** www.senorfrogs.com/mazatlan. Sat cover 70 pesos.

Valentino's & the Fiestaland Complex   The popularity of **Valentino's** dance club has resulted in its expansion into an array of four nocturnal options. The centerpiece remains Valentino's, dramatically perched on a rocky outcropping overlooking the sea, in an all-white, Moorish-looking complex that you can't miss. Many of the bars here attract a young crowd, although **Bora Bora** is a hip urban beach bar frequented by slightly older young professionals. Open Thursday through Saturday from 9:30pm to 4am (with some clubs occasionally opening Wed and Sun). Punta Camarón, near the Camarón Sábalo traffic circle. © **669/989-1600.** Cover varies.

COSTA ALEGRE: PUERTO VALLARTA TO BARRA DE NAVIDAD ★★★

In my view, the Costa Alegre (also spelled Costalegre) is Mexico's most spectacular coastal area, a 232km (144-mile) stretch that connects tropical forests with a series of dramatic cliff-lined coves and exclusive accommodations. Tiny outpost towns line the coast, while dirt roads trail down to a succession of magical coves with pristine beaches, most of them steeped in privileged exclusivity. The sunset vistas and nighttime stargazing here are incredible—without any light pollution, it feels like you can reach up and grab the stars. Considered one of Mexico's greatest undiscovered treasures, this coast is becoming a favored hideaway for publicity-fatigued celebrities and those in search of natural seclusion. However, don't be surprised to hear about major development plans for this region as the economy recovers.

The area is referred to as **Costa Alegre (Happy Coast)**—the marketer's term—and **Costa Careyes (Turtle Coast),** after the many sea turtles that nest here. It is home to an eclectic array of the most captivating and exclusive places to stay in Mexico, with a selective roster of activities that includes championship golf and polo. Along the line, however, you will encounter the funky beach towns that were the original lure for travelers who discovered the area.

EXPLORING COSTA ALEGRE   Hwy. 200, as it meanders between Puerto Vallarta to the north and Manzanillo to the south, is a beautiful winding road with breathtaking ocean, mountain, and jungle vistas trading places along the way. A handful of Mexican villages dot the route, while most of the beaches are tucked into coves accessible by dirt roads that can extend for a few kilometers. If you drive along this coast, Hwy. 200 is safe and well paved, but it's not lit and parts of it curve through the mountains, making daytime driving preferable. A few buses travel this route, but they stop only at the towns that line the highway; many of them are several kilometers inland from the resorts along the coast. For more information about traveling to this area, visit **www.costalegre.ca**.

Where to Stay & Eat Along Costa Alegre (North to South)

CRUZ DE LORETO'S LUXURY ECO-RETREAT

Hotelito Desconocido 📷   After having been closed and completely renovated, the Hotelito reopened in May 2011 as a luxury eco-resort under new management. The enchanted bungalows, called *palafitos*, offer handcrafted furnishings, richly colored Mexican art, canopy beds, and luxuriously appointed bathrooms with solar-heated showers. Three family-friendly villas are built on stilts with large terraces overlooking the canals, lagoon, and beach. Located 96km (60 miles) south of Puerto Vallarta, Hotelito sits on 40 hectares (100 acres) of private reserve, which includes trails leading past organic gardens and gorgeous Pacific coastline. Among the activities are a holistic spa with a wellness center, yoga program, and aqua gym; a biocenter with programs on marine turtles, indigenous plants, and birds; beachfront horseback riding; an observatory; and a private beach with watersports. The tropical grounds are as serene as they are spectacular, lit up at night by torches, candles, and lanterns. The resort uses renewable energy, including ecofriendly air conditioners in the bungalows, as well as 100% organic food in the gourmet restaurants. The rates include lodging, meals, nonalcoholic beverages, and airport transportation.

Playón de Mismaloya s/n, Cruz de Loreto, 48360 Tomatlán, Jal. www.hotelito.com. 📞 **800/851-1143** in the U.S. and Canada, or 01-800/013-1313 in Mexico. 30 units. High season $580–$1,025 double; low season $485–$855 double. Meal plan high season $160; low season $140. All activities are subject to an extra charge. AE, MC, V. Free parking. Take Hwy. 200 south for 1 hr., turn off at exit for Cruz de Loreto, and continue on clearly marked route on unpaved road for about 25 min. Children allowed in villas but not bungalows. **Amenities:** 2 restaurant/bars; horseback riding; Internet; Jacuzzi; outdoor pool; extensive spa w/yoga and other fitness programs. *In room:* Eco air-conditioning, no phone.

LAS ALAMANDAS: AN EXCLUSIVE LUXURY RESORT

Las Alamandas ★★★ 📷   Almost equidistant between Manzanillo (2 hr.) and Puerto Vallarta (2 hr.) lies one of the world's most exquisite resorts. The privileged guests, served by over 80 employees, enjoy the seclusion of the magnificent grounds, which boast 1,500 acres of gardens, lakes, lagoons, and four stunning private beaches. The owner's commitment to the environment includes a turtle preservation program and bird sanctuary with over 100 species sighted (birding boat tours are available). Palms, jasmine, bougainvillea, and the bright yellow Alamanda flower dominate the landscape. The seven distinctly Mexican villas house 16 suites splashed in pinks, yellows, and blues with brick dome roofs, hand-crafted furniture, regional artwork, tiled verandas, gorgeous ocean or garden views, and many with private Jacuzzis. Activities include a massage and yoga spa, tennis court and gym, mountain

Costa Alegre & Central Pacific Coast

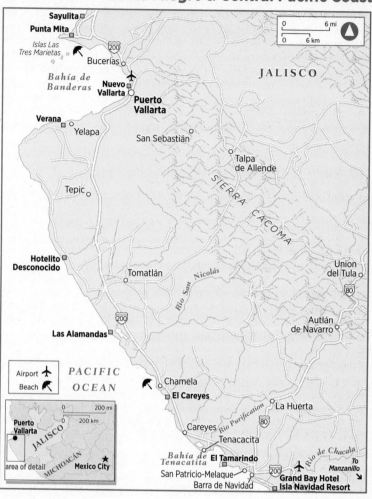

bikes, beach toys, complimentary horseback rides, and rooftop lounge with a telescope. The food here is excellent, with most of the organic products grown right on the property.

Hwy. 200, Km 83 48850 Manzanillo–Puerto Vallarta, Jal. Mailing address: Domicilio Conocido Costa Alegre QUEMARO Jalisco, Apdo. Postal 201, 48980 San Patricio Melaque, Jal. www.alamandas.com. ℘ **888/882-9616** in the U.S. and Canada, or 322/285-5500. Fax 322/285-5027. 16 units. High season $488–$2,070 double; low season $371–$1,499 double. Meal plans $135. AE, MC, V. Free parking. **Amenities:** Restaurant; 2 bars; mountain bikes; horseback riding; concierge; exercise room; 18m (59-ft.) outdoor pool; room service; lighted tennis court; watersports equipment. *In room:* A/C, TV w/DVD/VCR available upon request, minibar.

CAREYES

El Careyes ★   El Careyes sits quietly tucked in a pristine cove between dramatic cliffs. The view over the calm waters, particularly at sunset, is simply magnificent and the resort's primary draw. Most guests come for seclusion, although families also feel welcome here. Room facades are awash in scrubbed pastels and form a U around the center lawn and free-form pool. Palms, banana leaves, and bougainvillea dominate the subtropical landscape. Cheerful, if dated, accommodations face the pool or ocean and come in seven categories, including a number with private plunge pools. Luxurious bathroom amenities, including exfoliating scrubs, use natural local products. The hotel lies roughly 150km (93 miles) south of Puerto Vallarta and 85km (53 miles) north of Manzanillo on Hwy. 200, and is about an hour's drive from the Manzanillo airport (a $110 taxi ride).

Hwy. 200 Km 53.5, 48970 Careyes, Jal. CP. Mailing address: Apdo. Postal 24, 48970 Cihuatlán, Jal. www. elcareyesresort.com. © **888/433-3989** in the U.S. and Canada, or 315/351-0000. Fax 315/351-0100. 51 units. High season $385 double, $575–$1,379 suite; low season $281 double, $448–$936 suite. AE, MC, V. Free parking. **Amenities:** Restaurant; bar; deli; mountain bikes; horseback riding; children's programs (during Christmas and Easter vacations only); large beachside pool; hot and cold plunge pools; room service; spa w/massage rooms, Jacuzzis, steam room, sauna, and fitness center; 2 tennis courts; watersports rentals. *In room:* A/C, TV/DVD, CD player, minifridge, hair dryer, minibar, Wi-Fi.

TENACATITA BAY

Located an hour (53km/33 miles) north of the Manzanillo airport, this jewel of a bay is accessible by an 8km (5-mile) dirt road that passes through a small village set among banana plants and coconut palms. Sandy, serene beaches dot coves around the bay (frolicking dolphins are a common sight), and exotic birds fill a coastal lagoon. Swimming and snorkeling are good, and the bay is a popular stop for luxury yachts. Just south of the entrance to Tenacatita is a sign for the all-inclusive **Blue Bay Los Angeles Locos,** as well as the exclusive **El Tamarindo** resort and golf club. There is no commercial or shopping area, and dining options outside hotels are limited to a restaurant or two that may emerge during the winter months (high season).

El Tamarindo Beach & Golf Resort ★★★ 🎁   The most beautiful resort I know in Mexico, El Tamarindo is a romantic haven amid magnificent jungle surroundings, with exquisite facilities, attentive service, and absolute tranquillity. Enchanted thatched-roof villas feature a wraparound splash pool, hammock, and open-air sitting and dining area that overlooks a private lawn. The bedrooms—with dark hardwood floors and intricately designed furnishings—can be closed off for air-conditioned comfort, but the remaining areas are open to the sea breezes and tropical air. A bottle of wine, fresh fruit, and L'Occitane amenities are included. There are also three luxurious four-bedroom beachfront residences that can accommodate up to eight adults. El Tamarindo boasts a championship 18-hole golf course designed by David Fleming, with 7 oceanside holes and dramatic views. The spa services are exceptional, and the open-air restaurant serves delicious fresh fish. At night, subtle lighting through the jungle and around the casitas transforms El Tamarindo into a truly enchanted retreat. On over 809 hectares (2,000 acres) of nature preserve extending along 3.2km (2 miles) of oceanfront—complete with hiking trails and bird-watching tours—you'll feel as if you've found your own personal bit of heaven here. The laid-back beach town of Barra de Navidad lies 30 minutes away.

Carretera Barra de Navidad–Puerto Vallarta Km 7.5, 48970 Cihuatlán, Jal. www.eltamarindoresort.com. © **866/717-4316** in the U.S., or 315/351-5031. Fax 315/351-5070. 29 casitas. High season $720–$1,875 villa; low season $285–$1,160 villa. Beachfront residences $3,000–$7,995. AE, MC, V. Free valet parking.

From Puerto Vallarta (3 hr.) or the Manzanillo airport (45 min.), take Hwy. 200, and then turn west at the clearly marked exit for El Tamarindo; follow signs for about 25 min. **Amenities:** Restaurant; bar; mountain bikes; kids' club (in high season); high-tech fitness center; beachside pool w/whirlpool; room service; *temazcal* (pre-Hispanic sweat lodge); spa services; 2 clay tennis courts and 1 grass court; watersports equipment; Wi-Fi (in lobby and restaurant). *In room:* A/C, TV, CD player, hair dryer.

Barra de Navidad & Melaque

This pair of rustic beach villages (just 5km/3 miles apart) has been attracting travelers for decades. Only 30 minutes north of Manzanillo's airport and about 100km (62 miles) north of downtown Manzanillo, Barra has cobblestone streets, inexpensive seaside hotels and restaurants, and funky beach charm. All of this lies incongruously next to the superluxurious Grand Bay Hotel, which sits on a bluff across the inlet from Barra.

In the 17th century, Barra de Navidad was a harbor for the Spanish fleet; from here, galleons first set off in 1564 to find China. Located on a crescent-shaped bay with curious rock outcroppings, Barra de Navidad and neighboring Melaque are connected by a continuous beach on the same wide bay. It's safe to say that the only time Barra and Melaque hotels are full is during Easter and Christmas weeks. **Barra de Navidad** has more charm, more tree-shaded streets, better restaurants, more stores, and more conviviality between locals and tourists. Barra is very laid-back; faithful returnees adore its lack of flash. Other than the Grand Bay Hotel, on the cliff across the waterway in what is called Isla Navidad (although it's not on an island), nothing is new or modern. But there's a bright edge to Barra, with more good restaurants and limited—but existent—nightlife.

Melaque, on the other hand, is larger, sun baked, treeless, and lacking in attractions. It does, however, have plenty of cheap hotels available for longer stays, and a few restaurants. Although the beach between the two is continuous, Melaque's beach, with deep sand, is more beautiful than Barra's. Both villages appeal to those looking for a quaint, quiet, inexpensive retreat rather than a modern, sophisticated destination.

Isla Navidad Resort has a manicured 27-hole golf course and the super luxurious Grand Bay Hotel, but the area's pace hasn't quickened as fast as expected. The golf is challenging and delightfully uncrowded, with another exceptional course at nearby El Tamarindo. It's a serious golfer's dream.

ESSENTIALS

GETTING THERE & DEPARTING Regional buses from Manzanillo frequently run up the coast along Hwy. 200 on their way to Puerto Vallarta and Guadalajara. Most stop in the central villages of Barra de Navidad and Melaque. First-class **ETN** buses (www.etn.com.mx) make the 4-hour ride to and from Guadalajara for about 350 pesos each way. From the Manzanillo airport, it's only 30 minutes to Barra, and **taxis** are available. The taxi fare from Manzanillo to Barra is around 450 pesos; from Barra to Manzanillo, 350 pesos. From Manzanillo, the highway twists through some of the Pacific Coast's most beautiful mountains. Puerto Vallarta is 3 hours by **car** and 4 to 5 hours by bus, north on Hwy. 200 from Barra. A taxi from Barra to Puerto Vallarta costs about 1,700 pesos.

VISITOR INFORMATION The **tourism office** for both villages is at Jalisco 67 (btw. Veracruz and Mazatlán), Barra (📞 **315/355-5100;** www.costalegre.com); it's open Monday through Friday from 9am to 5pm and will help with hotel reservations as well as with a general orientation to the towns.

ORIENTATION   In Barra, hotels and restaurants line the main beachside street, **Legazpi.** From the bus station, beachside hotels are 2 blocks straight ahead, across the central plaza. Two blocks behind the bus station and to the right is the lagoon side. More hotels and restaurants are on its main street, **Morelos/Veracruz.** Few streets are marked, but 10 minutes of wandering will acquaint you with the village's entire layout. There's a taxi stand at the intersection of Legazpi and Sinaloa streets. Legazpi, Jalisco, Sinaloa, and Veracruz streets border Barra's **central plaza.**

ACTIVITIES ON & OFF THE BEACH

Swimming and enjoying the attractive beach and bay views take up most tourists' time. You can hire a small boat for a coastal ride or fishing in two ways. Go toward the *malecón* on Calle Veracruz until you reach the tiny boatmen's cooperative, with fixed prices posted on the wall, or walk two buildings farther to the water taxi ramp. The water taxi is the best option for going to Colimilla (5 min.; 30 pesos) or across the inlet (3 min.; 20 pesos) to the Grand Bay Hotel. Water taxis make the rounds regularly, so if you're at Colimilla, wait, and one will be along shortly. At the cooperative, a 30-minute **lagoon tour** costs 300 pesos, with other boat tours available. **Sportfishing** costs 500 pesos per hour for up to four people in a small *panga* (open fiberglass boat).

   Isla Navidad Country Club (© 314/337-9024; www.islanavidad.com) has a 27-hole, 7,053-yard, par-72 **golf course** that is open to the public (daily 7am–7pm). Greens fees are $140 for 18 holes plus tax, $160 for 27 holes plus tax (discounts are available for hotel guests). Prices include a motorized cart. Caddies are available for $30 and rental clubs for $46. The clubhouse is stocked with Cuban cigars and premium tequila.

WHERE TO STAY

Low season in Barra is any time except Christmas and Easter weeks. Except for those 2 weeks, it doesn't hurt to ask for a discount at the inexpensive hotels.

Very Expensive

Grand Bay Hotel Isla Navidad Resort ★★★ ☺   Situated on its own island, this palatial resort spreads out over 480 hectares (1,186 acres) next to a 27-hole golf course. The Spanish-style Grand Bay overlooks the village, bay, and fresh water Navidad lagoon with mountains in the background. The hotel's swimming pools are simply spectacular, and a narrow beach faces the lagoon. Large guest rooms are luxuriously outfitted with marble floors and columns, beautiful bathrooms, hand-carved wood furnishings, and balconies. Outdoor activities abound, and the spa offers an extensive array of facial and body treatments. The hotel is a short water-taxi ride across the inlet from Barra de Navidad. It's worth a visit even if you're not staying here, although the hotel is closed to nonguests at night unless they're coming for dinner.

Circuito de los Marinos s/n, 28830 Isla Navidad, Col. www.wyndham.com. © **877/999-3223** in the U.S., 01-800/849-2373 in Mexico, or 314/331-0500. Fax 314/331-0570. 199 units. $175 and up double; $300 and up suite. AE, DC, DISC, MC, V. Free parking. **Amenities:** 4 restaurants; 2 bars; babysitting; kids' club; concierge; small exercise room; golf club w/pro shop and driving range; 3 outdoor pools, including 1 w/ waterslides and swim-up bar; 27-hole, par-72 golf course; Jacuzzi; marina w/private yacht club; room service; full spa; 3 lighted grass tennis courts. *In room:* A/C, TV, hair dryer, minibar, Wi-Fi.

Moderate

Hotel Alondra   Located next to the church on the main strip of restaurants, shops, and bars, and with a little beach just in front, this place sits in the heart of the action. Guest rooms are spread out in two buildings, one oceanfront called "Casa Club" and

Barra de Navidad Bay Area

the other just across the street. Splashed in hues of blue, yellow, and white, the light-filled rooms feature marble floors and small bathrooms; junior suites have kitchenettes. This hotel, which is especially popular with Canadians, has a small infinity pool in front of the beach, as well as an open-air bar on the fifth floor with a lovely view.

Sinaloa 16, 48987 Barra de Navidad, Jal. www.alondrahotel.com. © **315/355-8373.** 73 units. 1,250–1,340 pesos double; 1,490 pesos oceanview double. MC, V. **Amenities:** Restaurant; bar; outdoor pool; Wi-Fi. *In room:* A/C, TV, kitchenette (in some rooms).

Inexpensive

Hotel Barra de Navidad   At the northern end of Legazpi, this comfortable beach-side hotel remains a favorite among value-seeking visitors. It has friendly management and basic rooms, some with balconies overlooking the beach and bay. Other, less-expensive rooms afford only a street view. Three bungalows offer king-size beds, kitchenettes, and separate sitting areas. A beachside swimming pool lies off the lobby, and there's a popular restaurant here called the Banana Cafe.

Legazpi 250, 48987 Barra de Navidad, Jal. © **315/355-5122.** Fax 315/355-5303. 60 units. 860–1,000 pesos double; 1,550 pesos bungalow. MC, V. Free parking. **Amenities:** Restaurant; bar; outdoor pool. *In room:* A/C and TV in some rooms.

Hotel Cabo Blanco ★ ☺   Located on the point where you cross over to Isla Navidad, the Cabo Blanco is an easy-going option for longer-term stays. Comfortable though basic rooms have tile floors, large tile tubs with showers, and stucco walls. The Cabo Blanco overlooks the canal, and it's a 10-minute walk to the hotel's **Mar y Tierra** beach club (see below), which is open Friday through Sunday. The beamed-ceiling lobby is in its own building; rooms are in hacienda-style buildings surrounded by gardens. The atmosphere is festive, especially during weekends and Mexican holidays, when this hotel tends to fill up. The website has its own theme song celebrating the hotel, and offers all-inclusive packages.

Armada y Bahía de la Navidad s/n, 48987 Barra de Navidad, Jal. www.hotelcaboblanco.com. © **01-800/710-5690** in Mexico, or 315/355-6495, -6496. Fax 315/355-6494. 101 units. 700 pesos double; 1,450 pesos all-inclusive option. AE, MC, V. Limited street parking. **Amenities:** Restaurant; 2 outdoor pools (1 adults only); tennis court. *In room:* A/C, TV.

WHERE TO EAT

Internet is difficult to find in Barra, but one reliable option is **Deli & Espresso** (© **315/107-3995**), at the entrance to the *malecón* next to Hotel Alondra; it offers free Wi-Fi to its patrons, as well as tasty coffees and desserts.

Ambar d'Mare ★★ CREPES/ITALIAN/FRENCH   This cozy beachside restaurant is open to the breezes, and the food is as wonderful as the ambience. The crepes are named after towns in France; the delicious *crêpe Paris,* for example, is filled with chicken, potatoes, spinach, and green sauce. A rich selection of salads and carpaccios are available as starters. Main dishes include grilled fish prepared with olive oil and herbs, lobster kabob in white wine, and beef medallions with a green peppercorn sauce. Pastas and pizzas are also served. Owner Veronique Bourdet's inviting restaurant includes a wine cellar and bar, with live music in high season as well as free Internet. She also rents out a couple of studio lofts—inquire directly with her.

López de Legazpi 150 (corner of Jalisco), across from the church. © **315/355-8169.** Crepes 125–210 pesos; main courses 100–350 pesos. No credit cards. Daily 5pm–midnight.

Mar y Tierra INTERNATIONAL   Hotel Cabo Blanco's beach club is also a popular restaurant and bar, and a great place to spend a day at the beach. Shaded *palapas* and beach chairs dot the sand. Open during the daytime only, the colorful restaurant is decorated with murals of mermaids. Perfectly seasoned shrimp fajitas come in plentiful portions.

In Hotel Cabo Blanco (see above), Legazpi s/n (at Jalisco). © **315/355-5028.** Main courses 120–220 pesos. MC, V. Fri–Sun 10am–6pm.

Restaurant Ramón 🐟 SEAFOOD/MEXICAN It seems that all the English speakers in town eat regularly at Ramón's, where the chips and fresh salsa arrive unbidden, and service is prompt and friendly. The food tastes great, although many options are fried. Try fresh shrimp with french fries, fish and chips, chicken nuggets, fish tacos, or any daily special that features vegetable soup or chicken-fried steak. Ramón, proud of the fried specialties, is often on hand to greet guests.

Legazpi 260. © **315/355-6435.** Main courses 75–150 pesos. No credit cards. Daily 7am–11pm.

Sea Master ★ SEAFOOD Sea Master's creative allure stems from its own private gallery, located at the entrance to the restaurant. Original paintings, artistic lighting, and brilliant colors spill out from the gallery to the cafe and waterfront dining room, and all the tables here afford beautiful sea views. Big, succulent shrimps dominate the menu, with selections such as the "Sea Master pineapple" stuffed with shrimp, cheese, brandy, and Kahlúa, and the "Sea Master roll" with fresh fish filled with shrimp, bacon, nuts, and garlic cream. Filet mignon, rib-eye, and chicken breast are also available. Potent cocktails are poured with double shots, and lounge music plays in the background, except for Thursday nights when the music is live.

Legazpi 146, near the boatmen's cooperative. © **315/107-0889.** Main courses 110–360 pesos. MC, V. Daily 11am–11pm.

BARRA DE NAVIDAD AFTER DARK

When dusk arrives, visitors and locals alike find a cool spot to sit outside, sip cocktails, and chat. Many outdoor restaurants and stores in Barra accommodate this relaxing way to end the day, adding extra tables and chairs for drop-ins. Most of the nighttime action is centered around the walking area near the church. Happy hour typically extends from 4 to 8pm. Closing times depend on the season and mood of the managers.

The colorful **Capri Sunset Bar,** facing the bay at the corner of Legazpi and Jalisco, is a favorite for sunset watching and a game of ocean-side pool or perhaps dancing. **Via Berlin Simona & Niños,** on the second floor of the Hotel Alondra, is another popular watering hole. **Piper Lover,** Legazpi 154 A (© **315/100-9194**), pumps out live blues most nights to a rough-and-tumble crowd.

A VISIT TO MELAQUE (SAN PATRICIO)

For a change of scenery, you may wander over to Melaque (aka San Patricio), 5km (3 miles) from Barra. Its pace is even more laid back, as though it's stuck in time. A few yachts bob in the harbor, and the palm-lined beach is gorgeous. Restaurants and basic bungalows line the beach. You can walk on the beach from Barra or take one of the frequent local buses from the bus station near the main square in Barra for 5 pesos. The bus is marked MELAQUE. To return to Barra, take the bus marked CIHUATLAN. A taxi between the towns costs 50 pesos each way.

WHERE TO STAY & EAT The best hotel in town is **Larios** (© **315/355-8058**), at Calle Av. Primavera 60, just a block from the beach. It has 10 rooms that cost between 500 and 700 pesos per night, depending on if there's a kitchen; cash only. Other motels in town are half that price but far less nice. There are a number of rustic *palapa* **restaurants** on the beach and farther along the bay at the end of the beach.

MANZANILLO ★

256km (159 miles) SE of Puerto Vallarta; 267km (166 miles) SW of Guadalajara; 64km (40 miles) SE of Barra de Navidad

Manzanillo has long been known as a resort town with wide, curving beaches; legendary sportfishing; and a highly praised diversity of dive sites. Golf is also an attraction here. One reason for its popularity could be Manzanillo's enticing tropical geography—vast groves of tall palms, abundant mango trees, and successive coves graced with smooth sand beaches. To the north, mountains blanketed with palms rise alongside the shoreline. And over it all lies the veneer of perfect weather, with balmy temperatures and year-round sea breezes.

Manzanillo is a dichotomous place—it is both Mexico's busiest commercial seaport and a tranquil town of multicolor houses cascading down the hillsides to meet the central commercial area of simple seafood restaurants, shell shops, and salsa clubs. The activity in Manzanillo divides neatly into two zones: the downtown commercial port and the luxury Santiago Peninsula resort zone to the north. A visit to the town's waterfront *zócalo* provides a glimpse into local life. The exclusive Santiago Peninsula, home to the resorts and golf course, separates Manzanillo's two golden-sand bays.

Essentials

GETTING THERE & DEPARTING   By Plane   Alaska Airlines (© 800/252-7522 in the U.S., 01-800/252-7522 in Mexico) offers service from Los Angeles; **Continental** (© 800/523-3273 in the U.S.; 01-800/900-5000 in Mexico) flies from Houston; **AeroMar** (© 01-800/237-6627 toll-free in Mexico; www.aeromar.com.mx) flies to Mexico City; **CanJet** (© 800/809-7777 in the U.S. and Canada; www.canjet.com) flies from select Canadian destinations.

The **Playa de Oro International Airport** is 40km (25 miles) northwest of town. *Colectivo* (minivan) airport service is available from the airport; hotels arrange returns. Make reservations for return trips 1 day in advance. The fare is based on zones and runs 130 pesos to 155 pesos for most hotels. Private taxi service between the airport and downtown area is around 350 pesos. **Alamo** (© 314/334-0124), **Budget** (© 314/333-1445), and **Thrifty** (© 314/334-3282) have counters in the airport open during flight arrivals; they will also deliver a car to your hotel. Daily rates run about $50 to $80. You need a car especially if you plan to explore surrounding cities and the Costa Alegre.

By Car   Coastal Hwy. 200 leads from Acapulco (south) and Puerto Vallarta (north). From Guadalajara, take **Hwy. 54** through Colima into Manzanillo. Outside Colima you can switch to a toll road, which is faster but less scenic.

By Bus   Buses run to Barra de Navidad (1½ hr. north), Puerto Vallarta (5 hr. north), Colima (1½ hr. east), and Guadalajara (4½ hr. north), with deluxe service and numerous daily departures. **ETN** (www.etn.com.mx) is the main bus company. Manzanillo's **Central Camionera** bus station (© 314/336-8035) sits about 12 long blocks east of town.

VISITOR INFORMATION   The **tourism office** (© 314/333-2277; www.vivemanzanillo.com) is on the Costera Miguel de la Madrid 875-A, Km 8.5. It's open Monday through Friday from 9am to 7pm, and Saturday from 10am to 2pm.

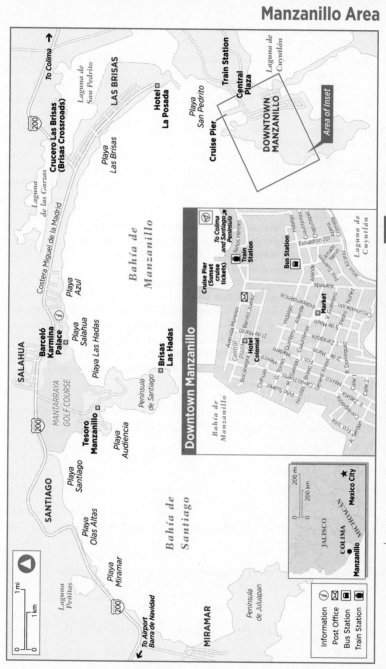

Manzanillo Area

To Colima ↑

Laguna de Cuyutlán

LAS BRISAS

Train Station

Central Plaza

200

Crucero Las Brisas
(Brisas Crossroads)

Hotel La Posada

Playa San Pedrito

DOWNTOWN MANZANILLO

Area of Inset

Cruise Pier

Playa Las Brisas

Laguna de las Garzas

Laguna de San Pedrito

Bahía de Manzanillo

Costera Miguel de la Madrid

Playa Azul

SALAHUA

Barceló Karmina Palace

ⓘ

Playa Salahua

Playa Las Hadas

Brisas Las Hadas

Downtown Manzanillo

Cruise Pier (Sunset cruise tickets)

To Colima and Santiago Peninsula ↗

Viros Héroes

Train Station

Escuadron 201

Bus Station

Hidalgo

Cuauhtémoc

Chapultepec

Colorada

Laguna de Cuyutlán

Avenida Morelos

Central Plaza

Benito Juárez

✉

Independencia

Alameda

Jesús Alcaráz

Circunvalación

Allende

Market

21 de Marzo

Hidalgo

Allende

V. Guerrero

5 de Mayo

Pedro Nuñez

México

Hotel Colonial

Bocanegra

Madero

Cuauhtémoc

Fco. I. Madero

21 de Marzo

Independencia

Bahía de Manzanillo

Coluhs

G. Torres Quintero

J. Zaragoza

México

General Anaya

Camilo Puerto

Calle 1

Pino Suárez

Galindo

Nicolás Bravo

B. Domínguez

Calle 2

Corregidora

E. Zapata

Fco. Villa

A. Serdán

MANTARRAYA GOLF COURSE

Tesoro Manzanillo

Playa Audiencia

Península de Santiago

Bahía de Santiago

SANTIAGO

Playa Santiago

Playa Olas Altas

200

Playa Miramar

Laguna Peñitas

MIRAMAR

Península de Juluapan

To Airport Barra de Navidad ↓

1 mi

1 km

200 mi

200 km

Mexico City ★

JALISCO

COLIMA

MICHOACÁN

Manzanillo ●

ⓘ Information
✉ Post Office
🚌 Bus Station
🚆 Train Station

329

The town lies at one end of an 11km-long (6¾-mile) beach facing Manzanillo Bay and its commercial harbor. The beach has four sections—**Playa Las Brisas, Playa Azul, Playa Salahua,** and **Playa Las Hadas.** At the other end of the beaches is the high, rocky **Santiago Peninsula.** Santiago lies 11km (6¾ miles) from downtown; it's the site of many beautiful homes and the best hotel in the area, Las Hadas, as well as the hotel's Mantarraya Golf Course. The peninsula juts into the bay, separating Manzanillo Bay from Santiago Bay. Playa Las Hadas sits on the south side, facing Manzanillo Bay, and **Playa Audiencia** is on the north side, facing Santiago Bay. The inland town of **Santiago** extends opposite the turnoff to Las Hadas.

Activity in downtown Manzanillo centers on the *zócalo,* known as the Jardín Álvaro Obregón. The plaza has flowering trees, a fountain, and a view of the bay. **Avenida México,** the street leading out from the plaza's central gazebo, is the town's principal commercial thoroughfare. The interesting **Museo de la Perversidad** (© 314/332-5599; www.manzanillomuseo.com) opened in mid-2009 with vivid displays of torture throughout the ages, much of it religiously motivated. The museum is located at Av. Juárez 160, just off the square, and open Monday through Friday from 11am to 8pm, and Saturday and Sunday from 11am to 9pm.

Once you leave downtown, the **Costera Miguel de la Madrid** highway (or just Costera Madrid) runs through the neighborhoods of Las Brisas, Salahua, and Santiago to the **hotel zones** on the Santiago Peninsula and at Miramar.

There are two main lagoons. **Laguna de Cuyutlán** stretches south for miles, paralleling the coast. **Laguna de San Pedrito,** north of the city, parallels the Costera Miguel de la Madrid. Both are good birding sites. There are also two bays. **Manzanillo Bay** encompasses the harbor, town, and beaches. The Santiago Peninsula separates it from the second bay, **Santiago.** Between downtown and the Santiago Peninsula lies **Las Brisas,** a flat peninsula with a long stretch of sandy golden beach, a lineup of inexpensive but run-down hotels, and a few good restaurants.

GETTING AROUND   By Taxi   Taxis in Manzanillo are plentiful. Fares are fixed by zones; rates for trips in town and to more distant points should be posted at your hotel. For example, a taxi ride from Las Hadas to the airport will cost 250 pesos. Daily rates can be negotiated for longer drives outside the Manzanillo area.

By Bus   The *camionetas* (local buses) make a circuit from downtown in front of the train station, along the Bay of Manzanillo, to the Santiago Peninsula and the Bay of Santiago to the north; the fare is 6 pesos. The ones marked LAS BRISAS go to the Las Brisas crossroads, to the Las Brisas Peninsula, and back to town; MIRAMAR, SANTIAGO, and SALAHUA buses go to outlying settlements along the bays and to most restaurants mentioned below. Buses marked LAS HADAS go to the Santiago Peninsula and pass the Las Hadas resort and the Tesoro Manzanillo and Plaza Las Glorias hotels. This is an inexpensive way to see the coast as far as Santiago and to tour the Santiago Peninsula.

[FastFACTS] MANZANILLO

Area Code   The telephone area code is **314.**

Bank   **Banamex,** just off the plaza on Avenida Juárez, downtown (© **314/332-0115**), is open Monday through Saturday from 9am to 4pm.

Hospital   Contact the **Cruz Roja** (**Red Cross;** © **314/336-5770**) or the **General Hospital** (© **314/332-0029**).

Internet Access WWW.CAFE (✆ 314/334-8004; hours vary), is located next to Hotel Pacifico Azul at Blvd. Miguel de la Madrid 1161 and charges 25 pesos per hour.

Police Both the general police and Tourism Police are available by calling ✆ 314/332-1004.

Post Office The *correo,* Dr. Miguel Galindo 30, opposite Farmacia de Guadalajara, downtown (✆ 314/332-0022), is open Monday through Friday from 8:30am to 4pm, Saturday from 9am to 1pm.

Where to Stay

Manzanillo's strip of coastline consists of three areas: **downtown,** with its shops, markets, and commercial activity; **Las Brisas,** the hotel-lined beach area immediately north of the city; and **Santiago,** the town and peninsula, now virtually a suburb, to the north at the end of Playa Azul. Reservations are recommended during the Easter, Christmas, and New Year's holidays.

DOWNTOWN

Hotel Colonial An old favorite, this three-story hotel sits in the central downtown district. Popular for its consistent quality, ambience, and service, it features colonial-style carved doors and windows in the lobby and traditional blue tile. Rooms provide basic comforts with one, two, or three beds, wood furniture, and small bathrooms with showers only. The hotel lies 1 block inland from the main plaza.

Av. México 100 and González Bocanegra 28, 28200 Manzanillo, Col. www.hotelcolonialmanzanillo.com. ✆ 314/332-1080, -0668, -1230. 42 units. 520 pesos double. MC, V. Underground parking. **Amenities:** Restaurant; bar. *In room:* A/C, TV, Wi-Fi.

LAS BRISAS

Hotel La Posada 🔥 This great value inn proudly displays a pink stucco facade leading to a broad tiled patio and beachside swimming pool. Guest rooms incorporate exposed brick walls, tile floors, and simple furnishings with Mexican decorative accents. The atmosphere is casual and informal—help yourself to beer and soft drinks; at the end of your stay, settle up with owners Juan and Lisa Martinez, who will count the bottle caps you deposited in a bowl labeled with your room number. The restaurant, which also welcomes non–hotel guests, is open daily from 8 to 10:30am and noon to 3pm. Stop by for a drink at sunset; the bar's open until 10pm all year. The hotel lies at the end of Las Brisas Peninsula, closest to downtown.

Av. Lázaro Cárdenas 201, Las Brisas (Apdo. Postal 135), 28200 Manzanillo, Col. www.hotel-la-posada. info. ✆/fax 314/333-1899. 23 units. High season 900 pesos double; low season 700 pesos double. Rates include full breakfast. MC, V. Free parking. **Amenities:** Restaurant; bar; Internet kiosk; outdoor pool. *In room:* A/C (in some), ceiling fan.

SANTIAGO

Barceló Karmina Palace ★ ☺ This is my favorite resort in Manzanillo, an all-inclusive getaway with nonstop activities, a beautiful beach and pools, quality restaurants, and an excellent spa and gym. The buildings here are designed to resemble Maya pyramids. Guests check into spacious suites featuring rich wood furnishings, recessed seating areas with pullout couches, two 27-inch TVs, and luxurious bathrooms. Most suites offer terraces or balconies with views of the ocean, overlooking the tropical gardens and swimming pools. Master suites offer spacious sun terraces with private splash pools, plus a full wet bar, refrigerator, and a large living room area. The kids' club provides a host of activities; at night live dance shows and an open-air dance club adjacent to the sea appeal to the adults. Service is not totally personalized, but this is an excellent destination for families looking for an all-inclusive resort.

Av. Vista Hermosa 13, Fracc. Península de Santiago, 28200 Manzanillo, Col. www.barcelokarminapalace. com. (C) **314/331-1313.** Fax 314/331-1340. 324 units. $250 and up double; $430 and up 2-bedroom suite for 4. Rates are all-inclusive. Special packages and Web specials available; ask about seasonal specials. Up to 2 children 7 and younger stay free in parent's room. AE, MC, V. Free parking. **Amenities:** 4 restaurants; 5 bars; nightclub; kids' club; concierge; 9 connected pools; room service; spa w/men's and women's sauna, steam rooms, fitness center; tennis courts; nonmotorized watersports; Wi-Fi (in lobby). *In room:* A/C, TV, hair dryer, minibar.

Brisas Las Hadas Golf Resort & Marina ★ This iconic beachside resort designed in an all-white Moorish style lights up a side of the rocky Santiago peninsula. Rooms are spread over landscaped grounds and overlook the bay; cobbled lanes lined with colorful flowers and palms connect them. The resort is large but maintains an air of seclusion. Views, room size and quality, and amenities differentiate the 10 categories of accommodations. The better rooms feature white-marble floors, sitting areas, and large, comfortably furnished balconies; 12 suites have private pools. The white colonial lobby is a splendid place for a drink in high season. A free-form pool stretches out beside the small beach in front. Pete and Roy Dye designed La Mantarraya, the hotel's 18-hole, par-71 golf course. This is the most famous resort in Manzanillo, but resembles an aging diva in need of a makeover.

Av. de los Riscos s/n, Santiago Peninsula, 28200 Manzanillo, Col. www.brisas.com.mx. (C) **888/559-4329** in the U.S. and Canada, or 314/331-0101. Fax 314/331-0121. 232 units. High season $250 and up double; low season $180 and up double. AE, DC, MC, V. Free guarded parking. **Amenities:** 3 restaurants, including the elegant Legazpi (see "Where to Eat," below); 3 lounges and bars; babysitting; concierge; small exercise room; 18-hole golf course; marina; 2 outdoor pools (1 is adults only); room service; 10 lighted tennis courts; watersports equipment. *In room:* A/C, TV, hair dryer, minibar, Wi-Fi.

Where to Eat
DOWNTOWN
Roca del Mar SEAFOOD   Roca del Mar's menu focuses on seafood and, above all else, shrimp. Start with the tasty shrimp cocktail, shrimp prepared in lemon, or even shrimp dressed up in a coconut. The fish empanadas are a big hit, too. The best main courses include snapper grilled with a hot spice, shrimp fettuccini, and a seafood chile relleno. There's even a shrimp hamburger, unusual as this may be. This outdoor sea-view restaurant is open for breakfast, too.

Bulevar Miguel de la Madrid 2333. (C) **314/336-9097.** Main courses 89–170 pesos. MC, V. Daily 9am–8pm.

PLAYA AZUL
La Toscana ★★ 🍴 SEAFOOD/INTERNATIONAL   You're in for a treat at La Toscana, one of Manzanillo's most popular and consistently reliable restaurants, located on the beach of Playa Azul. You'll pass a decorative pool and waterfall at the entrance to the open-air dining room, where live music plays nightly. Menu items are written on boards scattered throughout the restaurant; to start I recommend the smoked salmon terrine, fresh artichoke, or escargots. Among the grilled specialties are seafood skewers, shrimp imperial wrapped in bacon, red snapper served whole with garlic and butter, sea bass with mango and ginger, and tender fresh lobster. Service is excellent.

Bulevar Miguel de la Madrid 3177. (C) **314/333-2515.** Reservations highly recommended. Main courses 138–350 pesos. MC, V. Daily 6:30pm–midnight.

SANTIAGO ROAD

Bigotes SEAFOOD   Locals flock to this large, breezy restaurant (the name translates as "Mustaches") by the water for the good food and festive atmosphere. Strolling singers serenade diners as they eat fresh fish, shrimp cocktail, seafood soup, or shrimp prepared any number of ways—grilled with butter, garlic, spicy sauces, or simply natural. The signature "Mustache Shrimp" is a hearty portion of coconut shrimp. A lovely beach lies in front of the casual restaurant.

Puesta del Sol 3 (2nd location at Blvd. Costa M. de la Madrid 3157). ⓒ **314/333-1236.** Main courses 136-288 pesos. AE, MC, V. Daily noon-10pm. From downtown, follow the Costera Madrid past the Las Brisas turnoff; the restaurant is behind the Penas Coloradas Social Club, across from the beach.

El Fogón 🎁 MEXICAN   Locals consider this to be the best Mexican restaurant in town, almost hidden in a small garden setting. The menu features a selection of unique and traditional Mexican dishes. *Molcajetes* (meat, seafood, and vegetables grilled in a stone dish) are the house specialty; options include shrimp, beef, and quail. A variety of delicious tacos and fajitas are also served. For those with a large appetite, the *plato mexicano* combines enchiladas, beef fajitas, a chile relleno, and guacamole.

Bulevar Miguel de la Madrid across from Pacifico Azul. ⓒ **314/333-3094.** Main courses 67-159 pesos. MC, V. Daily 8am-midnight. From downtown, follow the Costera Madrid; the restaurant is located just before the Soriana grocery store.

Juanito's MEXICAN/BREAKFAST   It's not easy to find a good breakfast joint in Manzanillo, but this is one. The cheerful American-run eatery attracts Mexicans and tourists in equal numbers. Pancakes, waffles, and French toast are morning favorites, and customers love the fresh-fruit *licuados,* Mexico's version of smoothies. For lunch and dinner, distinctly American fare includes Texas burgers topped with bacon, cheese, and avocado, as well as chili dogs, club sandwiches, fried chicken, and barbecue ribs. Enchiladas, fajitas, and other simple Mexican dishes are also cooked to order. Diners congregate around casual wood tables; be prepared for a short wait on weekends.

Bulevar Miguel de la Madrid Km 14. ⓒ **314/333-1388.** www.juanitos.com. Breakfast $3-$6; main courses $4-$11. AE, MC, V. Daily 8am-11pm.

SANTIAGO PENINSULA

Legazpi ★★ ITALIAN/INTERNATIONAL   This is a top choice in Manzanillo for elegance, service, and outstanding food. The candlelit tables are set with silver and flowers, and enormous bell-shaped windows show off the sparkling bay below. To start, consider the beef filet carpaccio or lobster bisque with a touch of caviar. Homemade pastas include ravioli stuffed with shrimp and crab, and linguine with grilled shrimp and fresh Parmesan. For main courses, the crunchy shrimp with polenta and mango chutney is delicious, as is the "veal mignon" prepared with a shitake mushroom sauce. Top off your meal with one of the decadent flambéed desserts or the Legazpi coffee with brandy, Damiana liqueur, sugar, and cream. The restaurant is open only on weekends, and piano music accompanies dinner.

In the Brisas Las Hadas hotel, Santiago Peninsula. ⓒ **314/331-0101.** Main courses 250-500 pesos. AE, MC, V. Thurs-Sat 6:30-11pm.

Activities on & off the Beach

Activities in Manzanillo revolve around its golden-sand beaches, which sometimes accumulate a film of black mineral residue from nearby rivers. Manzanillo's public beaches provide an opportunity to see local color and scenery. They are the daytime playground for those staying at places off the beach or without pools.

BEACHES **Playa Audiencia,** on the Santiago Peninsula, offers the best swimming as well as snorkeling, but **Playa San Pedrito,** shallow for a long way out, is the most popular beach for its proximity to downtown. **Playa Las Brisas,** located south of Santiago Peninsula as you're heading to downtown Manzanillo, offers an optimal combination of location and good swimming. **Playa Miramar,** on the Bahía de Santiago past the Santiago Peninsula, is popular with bodysurfers, windsurfers, and boogie boarders. It's accessible by local bus from town. The major part of **Playa Azul,** also south of the Santiago Peninsula, drops off sharply but is noted for its wide beach.

BIRDING Birding is good in several lagoons along the coast. As you go from Manzanillo past Las Brisas to Santiago, you'll pass **Laguna de Las Garzas (Lagoon of the Herons),** also known as Laguna de San Pedrito, where many white pelicans and huge herons fish in the water. They nest here in December and January. Directly behind downtown is the **Laguna de Cuyutlán** (follow the signs to Cuyutlán), where you'll usually find birds in abundance; species vary between summer and winter.

DIVING **Underworld Scuba–Scuba Shack** ★★ (© 314/333-3678; www. divemanzanillo.com), located at Blvd. M. de la Madrid Km 15, conducts professional diving expeditions and classes. Many locations are so close to shore that there's no need for a boat. Close-in dives include the jetty, and a nearby sunken frigate downed in 1959 at 8m (26 ft.). Divers can see abundant sea life, including coral reefs, sea horses, giant puffer fish, and moray eels. A two-tank boat dive costs $95 per person ($10 discount if you have your own equipment). "Discover Scuba" for beginners, which starts with instruction in a pool and continues with an ocean dive, costs $85 and lasts about 4 hours total. You can also rent weights and a tank for beach dives for $10. A three-stop snorkel trip costs $45. All guides are certified dive masters, and the shop offers PADI certification classes in intensive courses of various durations. The owner offers a 10% discount on your certification when you mention Frommer's. MasterCard and Visa are accepted.

ESCORTED TOURS Because Manzanillo is so spread out, you might consider a city tour. **Bahías Gemelas Travel Agency** (© 314/333-1000) runs half-day city tours for about $25. Other tours include the daylong Colima Colonial Tour (about $70), which stops at Colima's Archaeological Museum and principal colonial buildings, and passes the active volcano.

FISHING Manzanillo is famous for its fishing, particularly sailfish. Marlin and sailfish are abundant year-round. Winter is best for dolphin fish and dorado (mahimahi); in summer, wahoo and rooster fish are in greater supply. The international sailfish competition is held around the November 20 Revolution Day holiday, and the national sailfish competition is in February. You can arrange fishing through travel agencies or directly at the fishermen's cooperative (© 314/332-1031), located downtown where the fishing boats moor. A 5-hour fishing charter costs about 3,000 pesos for up to eight people.

GOLF The 18-hole **La Mantarraya Golf Course** (© 314/331-0101) is open to nonguests as well as guests of Las Hadas. The compact, challenging 18-hole course designed by Roy and Pete Dye is a beauty, with banana trees, blooming bougainvillea, and coconut palms at every turn. A lush and verdant place (12 of the 18 holes are played over water), it remains a favorite. When the course was under construction, workers dug up pre-Hispanic ceramic figurines where the 14th hole now lies. It is believed to have been an important ancient burial site. The course culminates with its signature 18th hole, with a drive to the island green off El Tesoro (the treasure) beach, in front of the Karmina Palace Resort. Greens fees are 1,950 pesos for 18 holes, 1,070 pesos for 9 holes; cart rental costs 650 pesos for 18 holes and 455 pesos for 9 holes. It's open daily from 7am to 7pm.

SHOPPING   Manzanillo has numerous shops that carry Mexican crafts and clothing, mainly from Guadalajara. Almost all fall on downtown streets near the central plaza. Shopping downtown is an experience—for example, you'll find a shop bordering the plaza that sells a combination of shells, religious items (including shell-framed Virgin of Guadalupe night lights), and orthopedic supplies. The Plaza Manzanillo is an American-style mall on the road to Santiago, and a traditional *tianguis* (outdoor flea market) in front of the entrance to Club Maeva sells clothes, sweets, and souvenirs from around Mexico. Most resort hotels also have boutiques or shopping arcades.

SUNSET CRUISES   The *Antares* (© 314/333-1371; www.antaresmanzanillo. com) departs from Playa Audiencia at different times depending on the season and costs around 360 pesos; buy tickets from a travel agent or your hotel tour desk. The cruise includes drinks, music, and entertainment, and lasts 1½ to 2 hours.

Manzanillo After Dark

Nightlife in Manzanillo varies significantly depending on the season. Clubs and bars change from year to year, so check with your concierge for current hot spots. Some area clubs have a dress code prohibiting shorts or sandals, principally applying to men. For families, a fountain "show of lights" takes place at 8, 9, and 10pm nightly in front of the cruise ship pier.

El **Bar de Félix** (© 314/333-9277), at Costera Miguel de la Madrid 805, is usually open Tuesday through Sunday from 9pm to 3am and has a 100-peso minimum consumption charge. Music ranges from salsa and ranchero to rock and house—it's often the most lively place in town. Next to it, **Nautilus** is a trendy dance club open after 10pm on weekends.

ACAPULCO & THE SOUTHERN PACIFIC COAST

by Christine Delsol and Maribeth Mellin

This region's exotic tropical beaches and rich jungle scenery lured the first modern travelers to Mexico. Although the southern Pacific geography may be uniform, the resorts along this coast couldn't be more varied, ranging from high-energy seaside cities to pristine, primitive coves.

Spanish conquistadors came to this coast for its numerous sheltered coves and protected bays, from which they set sail to the Far East. Centuries later, Mexico's first tourists came for the same natural features, but with a different type of escape in mind.

Over the years, the area developed a diverse selection of resorts. Each is distinct, and there's one for almost any type of traveler. The region encompasses the country's oldest resort, **Acapulco;** its newest, the **Bahías de Huatulco;** and a side-by-side pair of opposites—modern, luxurious **Ixtapa** and the down-to-earth fishing village of **Zihuatanejo.** Between Acapulco and Huatulco lies **Puerto Escondido,** a laid-back beach town rising in tiers above a picturesque bay with world-class waves.

This chapter covers coastal towns in two Mexican states, Guerrero and Oaxaca. Stunning coastline and tropical mountains grace the entire region, but outside the urban centers, few roads are paved. These states remain among Mexico's poorest, despite decades of incoming tourist dollars (and many other currencies). As with some other parts of Mexico, tourism in Guerrero has suffered somewhat from reports of drug-related crime, although this problem has generally not affected the key tourist areas.

Exploring the Southern Pacific Coast

Beach bumming with a frosty piña colada or cold Corona and a big, shady sombrero used to be the stereotype for most travelers to this part of Mexico. Today, ecotourism, adventure tourism, and more culturally oriented travel are siphoning people away from the beach for at least part of their visits. Each beach town in this chapter can serve as a complete vacation. You could also combine several coastal resorts into a single trip or mix the coastal with the colonial—say, Puerto Escondido and Oaxaca (see chapter 11), or Acapulco and Taxco (see chapter 5).

These coastal communities have distinct personalities, but you get the beach wherever you go, whether you choose a city that offers virtually every luxury imaginable or a rustic town providing little more than seaside relaxation.

The largest and most decadent of Mexican resort destinations, **Acapulco** leapt into the spotlight in the late 1930s when movie stars made it their playground. Today, though challenged by other seaside destinations, Acapulco still lures visitors with its glitzy nightlife and sultry beaches (even if the Hollywood celebrities who made it a household name have moved on). Of all the resorts in this chapter, Acapulco has the best airline connections, the broadest range of late-night entertainment, the most savory dining, and the widest range of accommodations. Beaches are generally wide and clean, and although the bay itself remains suspect, it's cleaner than in past years.

Ixtapa and its neighboring seaside village, **Zihuatanejo,** offer beach-bound tourist attractions on a smaller, less hectic scale, attracting travelers with their complementary contrasts—sophisticated high-rise hotels in one, local color and leisurely pace in the other. Their excellent beaches front clean ocean waters. To get there, many people fly into Acapulco, then make the 4- to 5-hour trip north by rental car or bus.

Puerto Escondido, noted for its celebrated surf break, laid-back village ambience, attractive and affordable inns, and nearby nature excursions, is a worthy destination and an exceptional value. It's 7 hours south of Acapulco on coastal Hwy. 200. Most people fly from Mexico City or drive up from Huatulco.

The **Bahías de Huatulco** encompass a total of nine bays—each lovelier than the last—on a pristine portion of Oaxaca's coast. Development of the area has been gradual and well planned, with great ecological sensitivity. The town of **Huatulco,** 130km (80 miles) south of Puerto Escondido, is emerging as Mexico's most authentic adventure-tourism haven. In addition to an 18-hole golf course, cruise ship pier, and a handful of resort hotels, it offers a growing array of soft adventures that range from bay tours to diving, river rafting, and rappelling. Dining and nightlife remain limited, but the setting is beautiful and relaxing.

ACAPULCO

366km (227 miles) S of Mexico City; 272km (169 miles) SW of Taxco; 979km (607 miles) SE of Guadalajara; 253km (157 miles) SE of Ixtapa/Zihuatanejo; 752km (466 miles) NW of Huatulco

In its glitzy heyday in the 1950s, Acapulco was best known as a getaway for Hollywood stars like John Wayne and Frank Sinatra. The glitz and glamour of those days may be long gone, but Acapulco never really lost its sizzle. This Mexican port city's flashy discos are packed nightly, and hotels rise up along miles of sandy beaches that trace beautiful Acapulco Bay for more than 6km (3¾ miles). Mountains ring the city, providing a spectacular backdrop for candlelight dining and the famously fearless La Quebrada Cliff Divers.

No first-time visit is complete without seeing **La Quebrada Cliff Divers** plunge from high cliffs into a narrow gorge, much as they have since 1934. You can see the show from public viewing areas or the terrace at **El Mirador Hotel.** The **Fuerte de San Diego,** built in 1616 to protect Acapulco from pirate attacks, has a museum tracing the port's history. Nearby, the city's *zócalo* (main square) is lined with cafes and shops.

Acapulco's renowned nightlife kicks off around midnight and stays in high gear until the wee hours. Younger crowds flock to the Hotel Zone where rowdy beachside **Paradise/Paraíso** and the cavelike **Baby-O** are favorites. Big, upscale clubs catering

Acapulco Bay Area

To El Mirador,
Pie de la Cuesta,
Iztapa-Zihuatanejo

Av. Constituyentes

Mendoza

Av. Cuauhtémoc

PARQUE
PAPAGAYO

Vasco Nuñez

Guerrero

Escudero Serdán

Río Camarón

Playa Hornos

Playa
Hornitos

La Quebrada

6
7

Market

Zócalo

commercial wharfs

Playa
La Angosta

"Downtown (Old) Acapulco" See Inset

Playa
Manzanillo

Costera M. Alemán

Playa Larga

La Pinzona

5

Av. de la Aguada

Gran Vía Tropical

Peninsula de las Playas

Av. López Mateos

4

*Bahía de
Acapulco*

2

1

3

Playa Caletilla

Playa Caleta

Playa
Roqueta

Isla de la
Roqueta

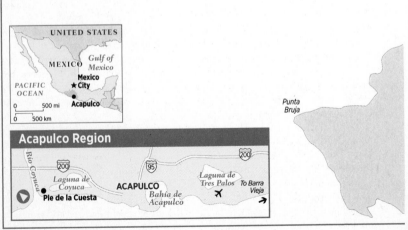

UNITED STATES

MEXICO

Gulf of
Mexico

PACIFIC
OCEAN

**Mexico
★ City**

● **Acapulco**

0   500 mi
0   500 km

Acapulco Region

Río Coyuca

200

95

200

Laguna de
Coyuca

● **Pie de la Cuesta**

ACAPULCO

*Bahía de
Acapulco*

Laguna de
Tres Palos

To Barra
Vieja

Punta
Bruja

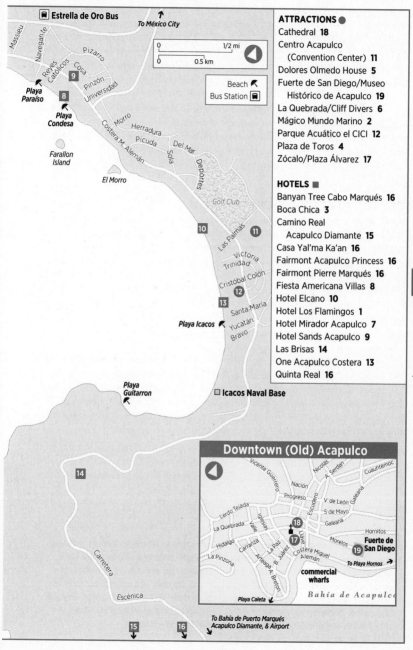

0   1/2 mi
0   0.5 km

Beach ⬈
Bus Station ▣

Massieu
Navegante
Reyes Católicos
Pizarro
Cosa
9
Pinzón
Universidad

Playa
Paraíso
8
Playa
Condesa

Morro
Herradura
Costera M. Alemán
Picuda
Del Mar
Sola

Farallon
Island

El Morro

Deportes

Golf Club

10
11

Las Palmas

Victoria
Trinidad

Cristóbal Colón

13
12

Santa María

Playa Icacos ⬈
Yucatán
Bravo

Playa
Guitarron ⬈

□ Icacos Naval Base

ATTRACTIONS ●
Cathedral **18**
Centro Acapulco
(Convention Center) **11**
Dolores Olmedo House **5**
Fuerte de San Diego/Museo
Histórico de Acapulco **19**
La Quebrada/Cliff Divers **6**
Mágico Mundo Marino **2**
Parque Acuático el CICI **12**
Plaza de Toros **4**
Zócalo/Plaza Álvarez **17**

HOTELS ■
Banyan Tree Cabo Marqués **16**
Boca Chica **3**
Camino Real
Acapulco Diamante **15**
Casa Yal'ma Ka'an **16**
Fairmont Acapulco Princess **16**
Fairmont Pierre Marqués **16**
Fiesta Americana Villas **8**
Hotel Elcano **10**
Hotel Los Flamingos **1**
Hotel Mirador Acapulco **7**
Hotel Sands Acapulco **9**
Las Brisas **14**
One Acapulco Costera **13**
Quinta Real **16**

10

ACAPULCO | Acapulco

Downtown (Old) Acapulco

Vicente Guerrero
Nicolás
A. Serdán
Cuauhtémoc
Nación
V. de León
Galeana
Progreso
Escudero
5 de Mayo
Lerdo Tejada
Iglesias
Valle
Galeana
La Quebrada
Hornitos
Hidalgo
Carranza
La Paz
B. Juárez
Morelos
**Fuerte de
San Diego**
La Pinzona
Artega
A. Breton
Costera Miguel
Alemán
19
To Playa Hornos →
18
17
commercial
wharfs
Bahía de Acapulco

Playa Caleta ↓

14

Carretera

Escénica

15
↓

16
↓

To Bahía de Puerto Marqués
Acapulco Diamante, & Airport

to the chic are on hilltops in Acapulco Diamante, including **Palladium,** with breathtaking bay views, and the multi-leveled **Mandara,** with a mammoth dance floor.

For romance and panoramic views, head for the hills. Overlooking Puerto Marqués, **Zibu** mixes Mexican and Thai influences; try the shrimp in ginger and mango sauce. Set in a hot-pink hillside home, **Su Casa** offers big margaritas and shrimp with garlic and spices. More casual eateries, many specializing in fresh-caught snapper and bass, are packed into the Hotel Zone. Among them, **El Zorrito** serves local fare such as *pozole,* a white hominy stew that's a Thursday lunch tradition in Acapulco.

You can play any number of ways on Acapulco's 19km (12 miles) of beaches, from the south end at oceanfront **Punta Diamante** to the north at low-key **Pie de la Cuesta.** Go scuba diving, set out for some deep-sea fishing for marlin and sailfish, or float above the bay by parasail. Glass-bottom boats depart from **Caletilla** for **Roqueta Island,** where you can snorkel, sun, and hike to an old lighthouse. All kinds of sailing vessels run sunset cruises on the bay and into the open ocean.

Essentials

GETTING THERE & DEPARTING

BY PLANE Phone numbers for major airlines with nonstop or direct service to Acapulco are **Aeroméxico** (© **800/237-6639** in the U.S. and Canada, 01-800/021-4000 in Mexico, or 744/485-1600), **American** (© **800/433-7300** in the U.S. and Canada, 01-800/904-6000 in Mexico, or 744/466-9232), **Continental** (© **800/523-3273** in the U.S. and Canada, 01-800/900-5000 in Mexico, or 744/466-9063), and **Delta** (© **800/241-4141** in the U.S. and Canada, or 01-800/123-4710 in Mexico).

Aeroméxico flies from Guadalajara, Mexico City, Tijuana, and Monterrey; **Inter-Jet** (© **01-800/011-2345**) is a low-cost carrier that flies from Toluca, about an hour from Mexico City; **Volaris** (© **01-800/786-5274**) flies from Toluca and Tijuana. Check with a travel agent about **charter** flights.

The airport (airport code: ACA) is 22km (14 miles) southeast of town, over the hills east of the bay. Private **taxis** are the fastest way to get downtown; they cost 300 to 550 pesos. The major **car-rental** agencies all have booths at the airport. **Milenio** and **Movilaca** have desks at the airport where you can buy tickets for minivan *colectivo* transportation into town (about 100 pesos). You can reserve return service to the airport through your hotel.

BY CAR From Mexico City, take either the curvy toll-free **Hwy. 95D** south (6 hr.) or the scenic **Hwy. 95,** the four- to six-lane toll highway (3½ hr.), which costs around 550 pesos one-way. The free (*libre*) road from Taxco is in good condition; you'll save

---

 Car & Bus Travel Warning Eases

Car robberies and bus hijackings on Hwy. 200, south of Acapulco on the way to Puerto Escondido and Huatulco, used to be common, and you may have heard warnings about the road. The trouble has all but disappeared, thanks to military patrols and greater police protection. However, as in most of Mexico, it's advisable to travel the highways during daylight only. In addition to the still-present risk of unsavory activities, the roads are unlit and animals can wander onto them. Before heading that way, ask locals and the tourism office about the status of the route.

safety

Acapulco has been getting a lot of attention lately, much of it negative. Because it's the most familiar destination in the area, it's often cited as the location of crimes that take place throughout the state of Guerrero. The dreadful stories you hear about gruesome crimes have nothing to do with international tourists and involve disputes between rival drug cartels. We're perfectly comfortable in Acapulco, but we still take precautions. Most important, stick to the known tourist areas around the coastline and don't venture into city neighborhoods, especially not alone. Hotel taxis, though expensive, can be more secure than those on the street. Don't wander around alone at night on the beaches or the streets. Keep your wits about you—it's never wise to wander around inebriated in any city. For up-to-date info on safety issues and complaint forms if you sense something's wrong, check out www.seguridadgro.gob.mx.

around 400 pesos in tolls from there through Chilpancingo to Acapulco. From points north or south along the coast, the only choice is **Hwy. 200,** where you should always try (as on all Mexican highways) to travel by day.

BY BUS   **Estrella de Oro** has two terminals, one in downtown at Av. Cuauhtémoc 14920, and one near the airport in Acapulco Diamante at Blvd. de las Naciones 34. The **Estrella Blanca** terminal (also called Central de Autobuses) is at Av. Cuauhtémoc 1604. **Turistar, Estrella de Oro,** and **Estrella Blanca** have almost hourly service for the 5- to 7-hour trip to Mexico City (380–600 pesos), and daily service to Zihuatanejo (220 pesos). Buses also serve other points in Mexico, including Chilpancingo, Cuernavaca, Iguala, Manzanillo, Puerto Vallarta, and Taxco.

ORIENTATION

VISITOR INFORMATION   The **State of Guerrero Tourism Office** operates the **Procuraduría del Turista** (ⓒ/fax **744/484-4416;** www.guerrero.gob.mx), on the street level of the **Convention Center,** set back from the main Costera Alemán, down a lengthy walkway with fountains. The office offers maps and information about the area, as well as police assistance for tourists; it's open daily from 8am to 11pm. The state also has a public safety website with live chat, Twitter, and informative articles at www.seguridadgro.gob.mx.

CITY LAYOUT   Acapulco stretches more than 6km (3¾ miles) around the huge bay, so trying to take it all in by foot is impractical. The tourist areas are roughly divided into three sections. On the western end of the bay is **Acapulco Viejo (Old Acapulco),** the original town that attracted the jet-setters of the 1950s and 1960s—and today looks as if it's still locked in that era, though a renaissance is projected.

The second section, in the center of the bay, is the **Zona Hotelera (Hotel Zone)** or **La Costera;** it follows the main boulevard, **Costera Miguel Alemán** (or just "the Costera"), as it runs east along the bay from downtown. Towering hotels, restaurants, shopping centers, and strips of open-air beach bars line the street. At the far eastern end of the Costera lie the golf course and the International Center (a convention center). **Avenida Cuauhtémoc** is the major artery inland, running parallel to the Costera.

The third major area begins just beyond the Gran Hotel Acapulco, where the name of the Costera changes to **Carretera Escénica (Scenic Hwy.),** which continues all the way to the airport. The hotels here are lavish, and extravagant private villas, gourmet restaurants, and flashy nightclubs built into the hillside offer dazzling views. The area fronting the beach here is **Acapulco Diamante,** Acapulco's most desirable address.

Street names and numbers in Acapulco can be confusing and hard to find. Many streets are not well marked or change names unexpectedly. Street numbers on the Costera are illogical, so don't assume that similar numbers will be close together.

GETTING AROUND   By Taxi   Taxis are more plentiful than tacos in Acapulco— and practically as inexpensive, if you're traveling in the downtown area. Just remember that you should always establish the price with the driver before starting out. Hotel taxis may charge three times the rate of a taxi hailed on the street, and nighttime taxi rides cost extra, too. Taxis are also more expensive if you're staying in the Diamante section or south. The minimum fare is 25 pesos per ride for a roving taxi in town; the fare from Puerto Marqués to the Hotel Zone is 100 pesos, or 150 pesos into downtown. *Sitio* taxis are nicer cars, but more expensive, with a minimum fare of 450 pesos. Acapulco taxis are easily recognizable by their flashy, blue neon lights.

By Bus   Even though the city has a confusing street layout, using city buses is amazingly easy and inexpensive. Two kinds of buses run along the Costera: pastel color-coded buses and regular "school buses." The difference is the price: New air-conditioned tourist buses (Aca Tur Bus) are 10 pesos; old buses are 5 pesos. Covered bus stops line the Costera, with handy maps on the walls showing routes to major sights and hotels.

The best place near the *zócalo* to catch a bus is next to Sanborn's, 2 blocks east. Buses marked CALETA DIRECTO or BASE-CALETA will take you to the Hornos, Caleta, and Caletilla beaches along the Costera. Some buses return along the same route; others go around the peninsula and return to the Costera. Go for the Directo buses for the fastest service; the others roam through back streets.

For expeditions to more distant destinations, there are buses to **Puerto Marqués** to the east (marked PUERTO MARQUES–BASE) and **Pie de la Cuesta** to the west (marked ZOCALO–PIE DE LA CUESTA). Be sure to verify the time and place of the last bus back if you hop on one of these.

By Car   Rental cars are available at the airport and at hotel desks along the Costera. Unless you plan on exploring outlying areas, trust us, you're better off taking taxis or using the easy and inexpensive public buses.

[FastFACTS] ACAPULCO

Area Code   The telephone area code is **744.**

Climate   Acapulco boasts sunshine 360 days a year, with average daytime temperatures of 27°C (80°F). Humidity varies, with approximately 1.5m (59 in.) of rain per year. June through October is the rainy season, though July and August can be relatively dry. Tropical showers are brief, but rainstorms can last for days, flooding downtown streets.

Consular Agents   The **United States** has an agent at the Hotel Continental Emporio, Costera Alemán 121, Loc. 14 (✆ **744/481-0100**); it's open Monday through Friday from 10am to 2pm. The **Canadian** office is at the Centro Comercial Marbella, Loc. 23 (✆ **744/484-1305**) and is open Monday through Friday from 9am to 5pm.

Currency Exchange   Numerous banks along the Costera are open Monday through Friday from 9am to 6pm, Saturday from 10am to 2pm. Banks and their ATMs generally have the best rates. *Casas de cambio* (currency-exchange booths) along the street may have better rates than hotels.

Drugstores One of the largest drugstores in town is **Farmacía Daisy,** Francia 49, across the traffic circle from the convention center (📞 **744/481-2635**). It's open daily from 9am to 11pm. Sam's Club and Walmart, both on the Costera, have pharmacy services and lower prices on medicine.

Hospital **Hospital Magallanes,** Av. Wilfrido Massieu 2, Fracc. Magallanes (📞 **744/469-0270**), has an English-speaking staff and doctors. For local emergencies, call the **Cruz Roja (Red Cross),** Av. Ruiz Cortines s/n (📞 **065**).

Internet Access Acapulco's hotels have been slow to offer Internet access. Some have Wi-Fi in the lobby only; others have in-room cable service for a fee. If it's important, ask before booking. **Acanet,** Costera Alemán 1632 Int., La Gran Plaza, Loc. D-1

(📞/fax **744/486-8182, -8182**), is open weekdays from 10am to 9pm and weekends from 11:30am to 9pm. Internet access costs about 30 pesos per hour.

Parking It is illegal to park on the Costera at any time. Try parking on side streets or in one of the few covered parking lots, such as in Plaza Bahía or Plaza Mirabella.

Post Office The *correo* is next door to Sears, close to the Fideicomiso office. It's open Monday through Friday from 9am to 5pm, Saturday from 9am to 2pm. Other branches are in the Estrella de Oro bus station on Cuauhtémoc, inland from the Acapulco Qualton Hotel, and on the Costera near Caleta Beach.

Safety Riptides claim a few lives every year, so pay close attention to warning flags posted on Acapulco beaches. Red or black flags warn swimmers to stay out of the water, yellow flags signify caution, and white

or green flags mean it's safe to swim.

As is the case anywhere, tourists are vulnerable to thieves. This is especially true when shopping in a market, lying on the beach, wearing jewelry, or visibly carrying a camera, purse, or bulging wallet. Don't walk on Acapulco's beaches at night. Stick to the tourist areas when exploring.

Telephone Acapulco phone numbers seem to change frequently. The most reliable source for telephone numbers is the **Procuraduría del Turista,** on the Costera in front of the convention center (📞 **744/484-4416**), which has an exceptionally friendly staff. It's open daily from 8am to 11pm.

Tourist Police Policemen in white and light-blue uniforms belong to the Tourist Police (📞 **066** for emergencies, or 744/485-0490), a special corps of English-speaking police established to assist tourists.

Where to Stay

The listings below begin with the most expensive resorts south of town in Diamante and continue along Costera Alemán to the less expensive, more traditional hotels north of town, in the downtown or "Old Acapulco" part of the city. Hotel prices have tended to fall or stay the same in Acapulco in recent years. Inquire about promotional rates or check with the airlines for air-hotel packages. During Christmas and Easter weeks, considered the high season, some hotels double their rates. Low season lasts September through November and April through June; the rest of the year is midseason. The rates below do not include the 17% tax. Private **villas** are available for rent in the hills south of town; staying in one of these palatial homes is an unforgettable experience. **Acapulco Luxury Villas** (📞 **866/403-8322** in the U.S., or 01-800/030-4444 in Mexico; www.acapulcoluxuryvillas.com) handles some of the most exclusive villas.

SOUTH OF TOWN

Acapulco's most exclusive and renowned hotels, restaurants, and villas nestle in the steep forested hillsides here, between the naval base and Puerto Marqués. This area is several kilometers from the heart of Acapulco; you'll pay about 200 pesos round-trip taxi fare every time you venture off the property into town.

Very Expensive

Banyan Tree Cabo Marqués ★★★ Hidden from sight on rugged cliffs overlooking a small inlet, this exclusive resort adds an unparalleled level of luxury to Acapulco's hotel scene. Even the smallest villa (at 2,200 sq. ft.) has an outdoor living area with a horizon pool, couch, and table where room service waiters lay out elegant meals with linen and crystal. Inside the 45 villas, beds, desks, and bathtubs face sky and sea views, and details such as espresso machines and toiletry bags stocked with essentials make these rooms extra special. The Saffron restaurant is one of Acapulco's hottest dining spots and the Thai-inspired spa is beyond divine. Efficient cart drivers whisk guests up and down steep, winding pathways to a lap pool beside the small beach and the spacious main pool by the lobby.

Blvd. Cabo Marqués, Lote 1, Acapulco Diamante 39868 Acapulco, Gro. www.banyantree.com/en/cabomarques. ℂ **800/591-0439** in the U.S., or 744/434-0100. Fax 744/434-0101. 45 units. High season $536–$976 double; low season $524–$884 double. AE, MC, V. Free parking. **Amenities:** 3 restaurants; concierge; gym; 2 pools; room service; spa. *In room:* A/C, TV, DVD, hair dryer, minibar, Wi-Fi.

Quinta Real ★★ Perched on a small cliff with uninterrupted views of the Pacific Ocean, this exclusive retreat is designed for relaxing and getting away from it all. (This is not the place for those looking for entertainment or family-friendly services; for that, we suggest the Fairmont Acapulco Princess, below.) The suites come in different sizes, with California-style furnishings, still-life paintings, extensive use of marble, and light neutral colors. The larger Governor suites have high ceilings, separate living and dining rooms, and terraces with private plunge pools. All rooms were remodeled in 2009. The inviting hotel pool lies just steps from the beach, where there's also a casual seafood restaurant and beach club. Service throughout is impeccable.

Paseo de la Quinta 6, Acapulco Diamante, 39907 Acapulco, Gro. www.quintarealacapulco.com.mx. ℂ **866/621-9288** in the U.S., or 744/469-1500. Fax 744/469-1516. 74 units. 2,830–3,030 pesos suite. AE, MC, V. Free valet parking. **Amenities:** 2 restaurants; lobby bar; airport shuttle; babysitting; beach club; kids' club; concierge; fitness center; 2 outdoor pools (1 for children); room service; spa treatments; tobacco shop; Wi-Fi (in lobby). *In room:* A/C, TV, hair dryer, minibar.

Expensive

Camino Real Acapulco Diamante ★★ Tucked in an almost hidden location on 32 hectares (79 acres) above Playa Puerto Marqués, this relaxing, self-contained resort is an ideal choice for families or for those who want seclusion. It's one of Acapulco's most enticing hotels because of its family-friendly atmosphere, extensive amenities, and beautiful protected cove ideal for swimming. From Carretera Escénica, a handsome brick road winds down to the resort. The hotel lobby features an inviting terrace facing the bay, and the sparkling waterfront pools are the focus of daytime activity. Spacious guest rooms offer balconies or terraces, small sitting areas, marble floors, ceiling fans (in addition to air-conditioning), and bright, colorful decor.

> ### Acapulco, Queen of the Silver Screen
>
> In addition to hosting legendary stars of the silver screen, Acapulco has played a few starring roles. More than 250 films have been shot here, including *Rambo II* (1985), which used the Pie de la Cuesta lagoon as its backdrop.

Carretera Escénica Km 14, Baja Catita s/n, Pichilingue, 39867 Acapulco, Gro. www.caminoreal.com/acapulco. © **866/543-1482** in the U.S., or 744/435-1010. Fax 744/435-1020. 178 units. High season $120 and up double; low season $105 and up double. AE, MC, V. Parking 70 pesos. **Amenities:** 2 restaurants; lobby bar; babysitting; kids' club; health club; 3 outdoor pools (1 for children); room service; tennis court; watersports equipment rentals; Wi-Fi (in lobby). *In room:* A/C, flatscreen TV, hair dryer, Internet, minibar.

Casa Yal'ma Ka'an ★★ 👜

A romantic hideaway 20 minutes south of Diamante, Casa Yal'ma Ka'an is a small ecological retreat with its own ocean beach. Stone paths with little bridges meander past several lookout towers and over lily ponds with palms and flowers, and the beautiful pool lies just steps from the Pacific. In addition to featuring its own beach club, it offers a *temazcal*, a Maya rustic steam bath that will be prepared for you with candles and aromatherapy amenities. Seven individual thatched-roof cottages have king-size beds, rustic wood furnishings, stone bathrooms, and private sitting decks. Gourmet breakfasts are served under a giant *palapa* overlooking the pool and beach, and private romantic dinners can be arranged on the beach. Service throughout is so outstanding it's included in the prestigious Mexico Boutique Hotel collection; children 16 and younger are not allowed.

Carretera hacia Barra Vieja Km 29 L189, 39867 Acapulco, Gro. www.casayalmakaan.com. © **877/278-8018** in the U.S., or 744/444-6389, -6390, -6483. 7 units. High season $384 double; low season $373 double. Rates include American breakfast. No children 16 and under allowed. MC, V. Free parking. **Amenities:** Restaurant; bar; beach club; outdoor pool; sauna; Wi-Fi (in restaurant). *In room:* A/C, TV.

Fairmont Acapulco Princess ★★ ☺

The Princess hotel reigns as Acapulco's most famous resort, with 192 beachfront hectares (480 acres) of tropical gardens, pools, and golf courses. Guest rooms are housed in three 15-story buildings shaped like Aztec pyramids, with modern Mexican decor and terraces with views of the ocean, gardens, or golf course. Five beautiful free-form pools, including a saltwater lagoon dotted with waterfalls, are surrounded by gardens with 750 plant species and swans, flamingos, and other tropical birds. The wide beach offers many watersports activities, and there's an excellent kids' club. The resort also offers tennis, golf, and spa facilities, and enough dining and entertainment options to obviate your need to leave the facility. Chic guest rooms colored in soft blues, cream, and light greens feature 350-count Egyptian cotton sheets, and shuttered windows with sea or garden views. The adults-only Pearl Tower features its own lobby, concierge services, and swimming pool.

Playa Revolcadero s/n, Colonia Granjas del Marqués, 39907 Acapulco, Gro. www.fairmont.com/acapulco. © **800/441-1414** in the U.S., or 744/469-1000. Fax 744/469-1016. 710 units. $214 and up double; $312 and up double in the Pearl Tower. AE, MC, V. Free parking. **Amenities:** 4 restaurants; 5 bars; babysitting; kids' club; concierge; 2 championship golf courses; fitness center; 5 outdoor pools; room service; Willow Stream spa; 8 outdoor lighted tennis courts and 2 indoor tennis courts; watersports activities; Wi-Fi (in common areas). *In room:* A/C, TV, hair dryer, Internet.

Fairmont Pierre Marqués ★★★

The refined Fairmont Pierre Marqués is both more exclusive and more relaxed than the famous Fairmont Princess next door, to which Pierre Marqués guests also have access. It once served as a private home for J. Paul Getty and is today one of Acapulco's most prestigious hotels. Together, the Pierre Marqués and the Princess offer more activities than you are likely to have time for, with three pools alone at the Pierre Marqués, a beautiful beach, championship golf, tennis, and a state-of-the-art spa and fitness center. Luxurious guest rooms include hotel rooms, bungalows with plunge pools, and villas overlooking the pools, tropical gardens, or beach. Fine dining is available here or at the Princess, with a shuttle regularly connecting the two hotels. Service throughout the hotel is outstanding. The Fairmont lies in Diamante, about a 20-minute drive from the center of Acapulco.

Playa Revolcadero s/n, Colonia Granjas del Marqués, 39907 Acapulco, Gro. www.fairmont.com/pierremarques. © **866/540-4481** in the U.S., or 744/435-2600. 229 units. $207 and up double. AE, MC, V. Free parking. **Amenities:** Restaurant; cafe; deli; 2 bars; concierge; championship golf course; health club and spa; 3 outdoor pools; room service; 5 outdoor lighted tennis courts. *In room:* A/C, TV, hair dryer, Wi-Fi.

Las Brisas ★★ 🔲 This local landmark, dating from 1957, is often considered Acapulco's signature hotel. On a hillside with excellent bay views, Las Brisas is known for its tiered pink stucco facade, private pools, and 50 pink jeeps rented exclusively to guests. The retro guest rooms are like separate villas sculpted from a terraced hillside, with panoramic views of Acapulco Bay from a balcony or terrace, as well as a private or semiprivate pool. The upgraded rooms retain the "Las Brisas" style with pink walls, whitewashed wood furnishings, flat-screen TVs, DVD players, and marble bathrooms. Each morning, your continental breakfast arrives in a cubbyhole. In case you tire of your own pool, Las Brisas runs a beach club less than a kilometer (a half-mile) away on Acapulco Bay; continuous shuttle service departs from the lobby. Mandatory service charges cover the shuttle service and all tips.

Apdo. Carretera Escénica 5255, Las Brisas, 39868 Acapulco, Gro. www.brisas.com.mx. © **866/221-2961** in the U.S., or 744/469-6900. Fax 744/446-5328. 251 units. High season $264 shared pool double, $303 private pool double; low season $233 shared pool double, $281 private pool double. Rates do not include $20 per day service charge. Rates include continental breakfast. AE, MC, V. Free parking. **Amenities:** 2 restaurants; deli; concierge; gym; room service; small spa; 4 lighted tennis courts; private beach club w/fresh- and saltwater pools; Wi-Fi (in lobby). *In room:* A/C, TV, DVD, hair dryer, minibar.

COSTERA HOTEL ZONE
Moderate

Fiesta Americana Villas Acapulco ★ The Fiesta Americana is a long-standing favorite in the heart of the beach-bar action. The 19-story structure towers above Condesa Beach, just east and up the hill from the Glorieta Diana traffic circle. The studios, suites, and villas have marble floors and can be loud if you're directly over the pool or street. The higher floors are quieter. Each has a private terrace or balcony. The more expensive rooms feature the best bay views, and all have purified tap water. The location is great for accessing Acapulco's numerous beach activities, shopping, and more casual nightlife.

Costera Alemán 97, 39690 Acapulco, Gro. www.fiestamericana.com. © **800/343-7821** in the U.S., or 744/435-1600. Fax 744/435-1645. 324 units. High season $115–$165 double; low season $102–$115 double. AE, DC, MC, V. Free parking. **Amenities:** 3 restaurants; 3 bars; deli; kids' club; gym; 2 outdoor pools; room service; spa; Wi-Fi. *In room:* A/C, TV, hair dryer.

Hotel Elcano ★★ 🏨 An Acapulco classic, the Elcano is a personal favorite. It offers exceptional service and a prime location—on a broad stretch of beach (on the bay) in the heart of the Hotel Zone. The retro-style, turquoise-and-white lobby and beachside pool area are the closest you can get to a Miami South Beach atmosphere in Acapulco, and its popular open-air restaurant adds to the lively waterfront scene. Rooms are bright, and generally feature classic navy-and-white tile accents with white wicker furniture. The large junior suites, all on corners, have two queen-size beds and huge closets. Studios are small but adequate, with king-size beds and small sinks outside the bathroom area; there are no balconies in the studios. All rooms have purified tap water. Avoid the noisy rooms near the ice machines.

Costera Alemán 75, 39690 Acapulco, Gro. www.hotelelcano.com.mx. ☏**744/435-1500.** 180 units. High season $115 studio, $138 standard double; low season $110 studio, $125 standard double. AE, MC, V. Free parking. **Amenities:** 2 restaurants; bar; babysitting; small workout room; pool; room service. *In room:* A/C, TV, hair dryer, minibar.

Inexpensive

Hotel Sands Acapulco 🗲 ☺

A good option for budget-minded families, this unpretentious 1960s-style motel nestles on the inland side, opposite the giant resort hotels and away from the Costera traffic. Guest rooms have basic furnishings with colorful linens, wall-to-wall carpeting, and tile bathrooms with showers only. The bungalows are smaller and less expensive, but more enticing than the motel rooms because they are surrounded by a small garden. Some units have kitchenettes, and all have a terrace or balcony. The family-friendly motel has a kids' pool and a special play area for youngsters, including *golfito* (minigolf). The rates are reasonable, the accommodations satisfactory, and the location excellent.

Costera Alemán 178, 39670 Acapulco, Gro. www.sands.com.mx. ☏**744/484-2260.** Fax 744/484-1053. 94 units. High season 1,000 pesos double, 800 pesos bungalow; low season 750 pesos double, 550 pesos bungalow. MC, V. Parking 50 pesos. **Amenities:** Babysitting; children's playground w/minigolf; concierge; 2 outdoor pools (including kids' pool); squash court; volleyball. *In room:* A/C, TV, fridge, Wi-Fi.

One Acapulco Costera ★ 🗲

Grupo Posadas, Mexico's largest hotel chain, has a winner with this new line of inexpensive hotels. The sleek seven-story building is located on the Costera near the Convention Center. The entire property is smoke-free, a rarity in this party town, and the rooms are both comfortable and efficient. Travelers appreciate the spacious desks with good lighting and Internet, the clean pool, and the complimentary breakfast served in the Food Corner (open only in the mornings). The One stands out in a neighborhood of older, worn-down hotels.

Costera Alemán 16, 39850 Acapulco, Gro. www.onehotels.com. ☏**744/435-0470.** Fax 744/435-0471. 126 units. From $62 double. MC, V. Indoor parking 70 pesos. **Amenities:** Breakfast cafe; outdoor pool. *In room:* A/C, TV, Wi-Fi.

DOWNTOWN (ON LA QUEBRADA) & OLD ACAPULCO BEACHES

Numerous budget hotels dot the streets fanning out from the *zócalo.* They're among the best values in town, but be sure to check your room first to see that it meets your needs. Several hotels in this area are close to Caleta and Caletilla beaches, or on the back of the hilly peninsula, at Playa la Angosta.

Moderate

Hotel Mirador Acapulco ★

An Acapulco landmark dating from 1934, the Mirador enjoys an unforgettable view of the famous cove where the cliff divers perform. The guest rooms are staggered along the edge of a cliff, with double or queen-size beds and traditional furnishings, small kitchenette areas with minifridge and coffeemaker, and large bathrooms with marble counters. Most have a separate living room, and all are accented with colorful Saltillo tile and other Mexican decorative touches. Ask for a room with a balcony or ocean view. Junior suites have whirlpools. Many guests gravitate to the large, breezy lobby bar as day fades into night on the beautiful cove. La Perla restaurant affords stunning views of the cliff-diving show ($25 minimum during show; menu is a la carte). Nearby is a protected cove with good snorkeling.

Plazoleta Quebrada 74, 39300 Acapulco, Gro. www.miradoracapulco.com. © **866/573-7197** in the U.S., or 744/483-1221. Fax 744/483-8800. 142 units. High season $71–$102 double; low season $54–$77 double. MC, V. **Amenities:** 2 restaurants; lobby bar; Internet; 3 outdoor pools, including 1 rather run-down saltwater pool; room service. *In room:* A/C, TV.

Inexpensive

Boca Chica ★★ ![icon] Acapulco's heyday from the 1950s has been revived at this completely restored classic overlooking Playa Caletilla. The black, white, red, and mint-green color scheme and vintage radios, fridges, and bikes set about give off a playful feel. Minimalist rooms have showers encircled with green plastic curtains near comfy white beds, black string hammocks hanging on balconies, and small desks and shelves of unfinished pine boards. The action takes place poolside and on the sun deck beside the small beach as chic guests lounge beneath black umbrellas and sip cocktails. The excellent open-air restaurant specializes in sushi creations—the burger's great also—along with an extensive sake and mescal menu. The tiny Coco Wash dance club reverberates late into the night. A hip, sexy ambiance prevails; think twice about staying here if you're over 30.

Playa Caletilla, Acapulco Viejo 39868 Acapulco, Gro. www.hotel-bocachica.com. © **744/482-7879.** Fax 744/482-7880. 35 units. $120–$260 double. AE, MC, V. Free limited parking. **Amenities:** 1 restaurant; 2 bars, including dance club; gym; outdoor pool; room service; 24-hour spa; Wi-Fi. *In room:* A/C, TV, DVD, hair dryer, Internet, minibar.

Hotel Los Flamingos ★ ![icon] Perched on a cliff 150m (492 ft.) above Acapulco Bay, this Acapulco landmark once entertained John Wayne, Cary Grant, Errol Flynn, Roy Rogers, and others. The place is a real find in a kitschy, campy sort of way—although the aged rooms are simple and lack modern luxuries, much of the hotel retains the charm of a grand era. Most rooms feature dramatic sea views and a large balcony or terrace, although few have air-conditioning and bathrooms are bare-bones. Thursdays at Los Flamingos are especially popular, with a pozole party and live music by a Mexican band. Even if you don't stay here, at least come for a margarita or "coco loco" cocktail at sunset, admire the black-and-white photos of Hollywood legends, and walk along the dramatic lookout point.

López Mateos s/n, Fracc. Las Playas, 39300 Acapulco, Gro. www.hotellosflamingos.com. © **744/482-0690.** 36 units. High season $65 double, $70 superior double with A/C, $100 junior suite; low season $60 double, $70 superior double with A/C, $80 junior suite. MC, V. Free parking. **Amenities:** Restaurant; bar; outdoor pool; room service; Wi-Fi. *In room:* A/C (in some), TV (in some).

Where to Eat

Diners in Acapulco enjoy stunning views and fresh seafood. The quintessential setting is a candlelit table with the glittering bay spread out before you. If you're looking for a romantic spot, Acapulco brims with such inviting places; most sit along the southern coast, with views of the bay. If you're looking for simple food or an authentic local dining experience, you're best off in Old Acapulco. Cheap, fresh seafood can also be found at any of the simple restaurants in the Barra Vieja neighborhood near Diamante. Many of Acapulco's fine-dining establishments automatically add a small "cover" charge to your bill (which is ostensibly for the bread served when you sit down), which usually amounts to between $2 and $3 per person.

SOUTH OF TOWN: LAS BRISAS AREA

Very Expensive

Baikal ![icon] FUSION/FRENCH/ASIAN Baikal remains the best-known place in Acapulco for an over-the-top dining experience, although you will be paying top dollar for it. The restaurant itself is constructed into the cliff, providing sweeping views of Acapulco Bay's glittering lights. The large dining room, with a two-story ceiling, has comfortable seating. The creative menu combines fusion fare with a dash of Mexican flare. Start with the thinly sliced scallops in chipotle vinaigrette or a terrine of foie gras in a port sauce. Notable entrees include the filet of sole and lobster, pork tenderloin in red wine, or medallions of New Zealand lamb in a sweet garlic sauce. There's also an extensive selection of wines. Baikal has a private VIP dining room, wine cellar, and elegant bar, ideal for enjoying a sunset cocktail or after-dinner drink. It's east of town on the scenic highway just before the entrance to the Las Brisas hotel.

Carretera Escénica 16 and 22. (*) **744/446-6845,** -6867. www.baikal.com.mx. Reservations required. Main courses $21–$90. AE, MC, V. Sun–Thurs 7pm–1am; Fri–Sat 7pm–2am. Closed Mon in summer.

Becco ★★ ITALIAN/SEAFOOD Among the city's most exclusive restaurants, Becco features floor-to-ceiling windows that stretch three floors overlooking the bay. A spiral staircase leads down from the entrance past the cocktail lounge and into the minimalist dining room, which has contemporary cement floors, large white pillars, and refined wood tables and chairs. The multilevel room buzzes with the chatter of Mexico's elite, many on vacation from the capital. The menu involves a rich selection of *antipasti,* including carpaccios, brochettes, and prosciutto with mozzarella; crowd-favorite starters are seared tuna over a bed of arugula and a cone of Parmesan fries. The top pastas are homemade tagliolini with lobster; spaghetti *allo scoglio* loaded with shrimp, calamari, clams, and crayfish; and seafood risotto. The chefs will prepare the fresh catches any way you like. Becco has an extensive Italian wine and champagne selection—all visible through the glass-enclosed cellar.

Carretera Escénica 14. (*) **744/446-7402.** www.beccoalmare.com. Reservations required. Main courses $22–$40. AE, MC, V. Sun–Thurs 7pm–midnight; Fri–Sat 7pm–1am.

Zibu ★★★ SEAFOOD/THAI With a gorgeous view over the sea, Zibu blends Mexican and Thai architectural and culinary styles to create a breathtaking dining experience. The open-air venue is furnished with rattan tables and chairs surrounded by warm lighting of candles, tiki torches, and lamps; an infinity pool separates the restaurant patio from the *palapa*-topped lounge. Consider starting with the sea scallop carpaccio or sea bass tartare, and continue with the shrimp medallions with ginger and mango or grilled fish filet with almonds and soy (there are also meat dishes). You can make a beautiful meal from starters alone, including the shrimp lollipops (shredded shrimp on sugar cane sticks), chilled cucumber soup, and spring rolls with minced pork and crabmeat. Finish with a tropical fruit plate and variety of sorbets. The glass-enclosed wine cellar houses a well-balanced though expensive collection.

> **Dining with a View**
>
> Restaurants with unparalleled views of Acapulco include **Baikal, Becco,** and **Zibu,** in Acapulco Diamante; **El Olvido** along the Costera; **Su Casa** on a hill above the convention center; and the appropriately named **Bella Vista Restaurant** at the Las Brisas hotel, which many consider to have the best view of them all.

Av. Escénica s/n, Acapulco Diamante. (*) **744/433-3058,** -3069. www.zibu.com.mx. Reservations recommended. Main courses $14–$46. AE, MC, V. Daily 7pm–midnight.

COSTERA HOTEL ZONE
Very Expensive

El Olvido ★★ FRENCH/MEXICAN El Olvido gives you all the glittering bay-view ambience of the posh Acapulco Diamante restaurants, without the taxi ride. The menu is one of the most sophisticated in the city, but it's expensive. Start with one of the specialty drinks, such as Olvido, made with tequila, rum, Cointreau, tomato juice, and lime juice. Soups include delicious cold avocado cream, and thick black bean and chorizo. Among the innovative entrees are grilled quails with honey and *pasilla* chiles, tuna steak with goat cheese, and asparagus and beef fillets with anchovy butter. For dessert, try the chocolate fondue or *guanábana* (a tropical fruit) mousse in a rich *zapote negro* (black tropical fruit) sauce. El Olvido sits at the back of the Plaza Marbella shopping center fronting Diana Circle. Dine here at sunset to see how the hills framing the bay glitter with sparkling lights as the sun goes down.

Glorieta Diana traffic circle, Plaza Marbella. ℂ **744/481-0203,** -0256, -0214. www.elolvido.com.mx. Reservations recommended. Main courses $15–$40. AE, MC, V. Daily 6pm–midnight.

Su Casa/Angel and Shelly's ★★ INTERNATIONAL Relaxed elegance and terrific food at reasonable prices are what you get at Su Casa. Owners Shelly and Angel Herrera created this pleasant, breezy, open-air restaurant on the patio of their hillside home overlooking the city. (Angel and Shelly's—previously called La Margarita—is the indoor restaurant below Su Casa that's open during the rainy season.) Both Shelly and Angel are experts in the kitchen and are on hand nightly to greet guests on the patio. The menu changes often. Some items are standard, such as shrimp *a la patrona* in herbs and spices, grilled fish, steak, and chicken. The *pasta el padrino,* with fresh shrimp and crème *chipotle,* is a delicious choice, and those who crave back-home meals can order barbecued ribs. The margaritas are big and delicious. The banana split or any of the flambés make dessert hard to resist.

V. Anahuac 110. ℂ **744/484-4350,** -1261. Fax 744/484-0803. www.sucasa-acapulco.com. Reservations recommended. Main courses $17–$35. MC, V. Daily 6pm–midnight.

Moderate

El Cabrito ★ NORTHERN MEXICAN With its hacienda-inspired entrance, waitresses in white dresses and *charro*-style neckties, and location in the heart of the Costera, this typical Mexican restaurant targets tourists. But its authentic and delicious food makes it a favorite among Mexicans, too—a comforting stamp of approval. Among the specialties are *cabrito al pastor* (roasted goat), *charro* beans, Oaxaca-style *mole,* and *burritos de machaca* (made with shredded beef). A whole *cabrito* is usually being slowly roasted inside the glass-enclosed *parilla*—a sight that can be a turnoff for vegetarians. Bottles of beer are brought to your table in buckets of ice and then poured in frosty cold mugs. El Cabrito lies on the ocean side of the Costera, south of the convention center.

Costera Alemán 1480. ℂ **744/484-7711.** Main courses $8–$20. AE, MC, V. Daily 2pm–midnight.

Inexpensive

El Zorrito ★★ MEXICAN/TACOS If you're looking for quality, no-nonsense Mexican food, El Zorrito is your place. Plastic tables and chairs, a dozen spinning ceiling fans, and photos of famous diners fill the open-air dining space. Waiters with their names printed on the back of their shirts traverse the restaurant with a smile, making sure customers are well fed and attended to. You can watch as homemade tortillas are prepared hot off the *comal* (the cast-iron plate used to make tortillas), and an expert team of cooks works harmoniously in the open kitchen. The food here is spicy and delicious, and the tacos are among the best you'll find. Spot the local elite wolfing down tacos after-hours when the discos close.

Costera Miguel Alemán 212, across from the Costa Club Hotel. © **744/485-7914.** Breakfasts 45-65 pesos; tacos 30-90 pesos; other dishes 70-200 pesos. MC, V. Daily 24 hr.

Ika Tako ★★ 🍴 SEAFOOD/TACOS   These fresh seafood tacos (many served in combinations that include grilled pineapple, fresh spinach, grated cheese, garlic, and bacon) are so tasty that they're addicting. An unusual selection of nine sweet and spicy salsas accompanies them, and there's also an excellent *queso fundido con huit-lacoche* (melted cheese with corn truffle), smoked oyster soup, and, for carnivores, *pastor* and chicken tacos served with french fries. The lighting may be bright, the atmosphere occasionally hectic (even more so when kids fill the play area to the side of the tables), and the service dependably slow, but the tacos are delectable. Consider the *takabrían,* which comes with shrimp, octopus, calamari, pepper, onion, and cheese. You can also order beer, wine, and dessert. This restaurant is across from the Gran Hotel Acapulco.

Costera Alemán 9. © **744/484-9521.** www.ikatako.com. Main courses 55-175 pesos. MC, V. Daily 1pm-1am.

100% Natural ★ ☺ BREAKFAST/HEALTH FOOD   Healthy, delicious, and inexpensive Mexican food fills the plates at this tropical plant–filled restaurant, on the second level of the shopping center across from the Crowne Plaza Hotel. (This chain has five other branches in Acapulco, including another one farther east on the Costera.) If you've overindulged the night before, get yourself back on track here with one of the outstanding breakfast selections, served any time of day, such as whole-wheat pancakes with apple and cinnamon, a vegetarian omelet, or any one of nine fresh-fruit plates. Yogurt shakes, steamed vegetables, and cheese enchiladas are alternatives to the yummy sandwiches served on whole-grain breads. Don't miss one of the fruit *licuados,* blended fresh fruit with your choice of yogurt or milk.

Costera Miguel Alemán 200, across from the Crowne Plaza Hotel. © **744/485-3982.** www.100natural. com. Breakfasts 65-100 pesos; sandwiches 70-100 pesos. AE, MC, V. Open 24 hr.

DOWNTOWN: THE ZÓCALO AREA

The old downtown abounds with simple, inexpensive restaurants serving tasty eats. It's easy to pay more elsewhere for food that's not as consistently good as in this part

If There's Pozole, It Must Be Thursday

If you're visiting Acapulco on a Thursday, indulge in the local custom of *pozole,* a bowl of white hominy and meat in broth, garnished with sliced radishes, shredded lettuce, onions, oregano, and lime, served with crispy tostadas. The traditional version includes pork, but a chicken version has also become a standard. You can also find green pozole, which is made by adding a paste of roasted pumpkin seeds to the traditional pozole base. Green pozole is also traditionally served with a side of sardines. For a singular Acapulco experience, enjoy your Thursday pozole at the cliffside restaurant of the Hotel Los Flamingos (see above). (Some restaurants serve the dish, which takes considerable prep time, the other 6 days of the week.)

of town. To explore, start at the *zócalo* and stroll west along Juárez. After about 3 blocks, you'll come to Azueta, lined with small seafood cafes and street-side stands.

Moderate

La Cabaña de Caleta ★★ 🎁 MEXICAN/SEAFOOD   Imelda Alvarez and her family have been running this Caleta landmark for decades, and it's the best and most popular restaurant on the beach. It's located near Mágico Mundo right on the sand. Families linger over long lunches of ceviche, *campechana* cocktails (with shrimp, octopus, and fish), crepes stuffed with shrimp, and whole snapper grilled with garlic and oil. Bring a large group, order pitchers of lemonade and sangria, and sample as many of the seafood specialties as you can.

Playa Caleta s/n, Old Acapulco. ✆ **744/482-5007.** www.lacabanadecaleta.com. Main courses $8–$25. MC, V. Daily 9am–9pm.

Inexpensive

El Amigo Miguel ★ 🎁 MEXICAN/SEAFOOD   Locals know that El Amigo Miguel is a standout among downtown seafood restaurants—you can easily pay more elsewhere but not eat better. Impeccably fresh seafood reigns; the large open-air dining room, 3 blocks west of the *zócalo,* is usually brimming with seafood lovers. When it overflows, head to a branch across the street, with the same menu. The branch on the Costera at Playa Hornos is a great place for a sunset dinner. Try delicious *camarones borrachos* (drunken shrimp), in a sauce made with beer, ketchup, and bits of fresh bacon—it tastes nothing like the individual ingredients. *Filete Miguel* is a fresh fish filet (often red snapper or sea bass) stuffed with seafood and covered in a wonderful chipotle chile sauce. Grilled shrimp *mojo de ajo* style with garlic and oil, and whole red snapper are served at their classic best. Meat dishes are available as well.

Juárez 31, at Azueta (other locations at Juárez 16 and Costera Miguel Alemán at Playa Hornos). ✆ **744/483-6981.** www.elamigomiguel.com. Main courses $8–$25. MC, V. Daily 10:30am–9pm.

Activities on & off the Beach

Acapulco is known for its great beaches and watersports, and few visitors bother to explore its traditional downtown area. But the shaded **zócalo** (also called Plaza Alvarez) is worth a trip, to experience a glimpse of local life and color. Inexpensive cafes and shops border the plaza. At its far north end is the **cathedral Nuestra Señora de la Soledad,** with blue, onion-shaped domes and Byzantine towers. Though reminiscent of a Russian Orthodox church, it was originally (and perhaps appropriately) built as a movie set, then later adapted into a house of worship. From the church, turn east along the side street going off at a right angle (Calle Carranza, which doesn't have a marker) to find an arcade with newsstands and more shops. The hill behind the cathedral provides an unparalleled view of Acapulco. Take a taxi to the top of the hill from the main plaza, and follow signs to **El Mirador (lookout point).**

Local travel agencies book city tours, day trips to Taxco, cruises, and other excursions and activities. Taxco is about a 3-hour drive inland from Acapulco (see chapter 5 for more information).

BEACHES   Here's a rundown on the beaches, going from west to east around the bay. **Playa la Angosta** is a small, sheltered, often-deserted cove just around the bend from **La Quebrada** (where the cliff divers perform).

South of downtown on the Peninsula de las Playas lie the beaches **Caleta** and **Caletilla.** Separating them is a small outcropping of land that contains the aquarium and water park **Mágico Mundo Marino,** which is open daily from 9am to 6pm

To Swim or Not to Swim in the Bay?

In the past decade, the city has gone to great lengths (and great expense) to clean up the waters off Acapulco. Nevertheless, this is an industrial port that was once heavily polluted, so many choose to stick to their hotel pool. The bay beaches that remain most popular are **Caleta** and **Caletilla**, as well as **Playa Puerto Marqués.**

(© **744/483-1215**) and costs $6 for adults and $3 for children to enter. You'll find thatched-roofed restaurants, watersports equipment for rent, and brightly painted boats that ferry passengers to **Isla Roqueta.** You can rent beach chairs and umbrellas for the day. Mexican families favor these beaches because they're close to several good-value hotels and residential neighborhoods. In the early morning and late afternoon, fishermen pull their colorful boats up on the sand; you can buy the fresh catch of the day and, occasionally, oysters on the half shell.

Pleasure boats dock at **Playa Manzanillo,** south of the *zócalo.* Charter fishing trips sail from here. In the old days, the downtown beaches—Manzanillo, Honda, Caleta, and Caletilla—were the focal point of Acapulco. Today beaches and resort developments stretch along the 6.5km (4-mile) length of the shore.

East of the *zócalo,* the major beaches are **Hornos** (near Papagayo Park), **Hornitos, Paraíso, Condesa,** and **Icacos,** followed by the naval base (La Base) and **Punta del Guitarrón.** After Punta del Guitarrón, the road climbs to the legendary Las Brisas hotel. Past Las Brisas, the road continues to the small, clean bay of **Puerto Marqués,** followed by **Punta Diamante,** about 20km (12 miles) from the *zócalo.* The fabulous Acapulco Princess, the Quinta Real, and the Pierre Marqués hotels dominate the landscape, which fronts the open Pacific.

Playa Puerto Marqués, in the bay of Puerto Marqués, is an attractive area for swimming. The Camino Real and a large residential development are located near here. The water is calm and the bay sheltered. Water-skiing and WaveRunner rentals can also be arranged. Past the bay lies **Revolcadero Beach,** a magnificent wide stretch of beach on the open ocean, where the Fairmont Princess and Pierre Marqués resorts, along with several large timeshare compounds, are found. Past the Hotel Zone, Playa Diamante is lined with fancy villas and condos on the water side and shacks selling groceries and souvenirs on the inland side. This area has become a popular neighborhood for vacation homes.

Other beaches lie farther north and are best reached by car, though buses also make the trip. **Pie de la Cuesta** is 13km (8 miles) west of town. Buses along the Costera leave every 5 or 10 minutes; a taxi costs about 200 pesos. The water is too rough for swimming, but it's great for sunset-watching, especially over *coco locos* (drinks served in fresh coconuts with the tops whacked off) at a rustic beachside restaurant. The area is known for excellent birding and surrounding coconut plantations.

If you're driving, continue west along the peninsula, passing **Coyuca Lagoon** on your right, until almost to the small air base at the tip. Along the way, various private entrepreneurs, mostly young boys, will invite you to park near different sections of beach. You'll also find *colectivo* boat tours of the lagoon offered for about 100 pesos.

BAY CRUISES & ROQUETA ISLAND The waters of Acapulco are dotted with virtually every kind of boat—yachts, catamarans, and trimarans (single- and double-deckers). Cruises run morning, afternoon, and evening. Some offer buffets, open bars, and live music; others just snacks, drinks, and taped music. Prices range from $26 to $50. Cruise operators come and go, and their phone numbers change so frequently from year to year that it's pointless to list them here; to find out what cruises are currently operating, contact any Acapulco travel agency or your hotel's tour desk, and ask for brochures or recommendations.

Boats from Caletilla Beach to **Roqueta Island**—a good place to snorkel, sunbathe, hike to a lighthouse, visit a small zoo, or have lunch—leave every 15 minutes from 9am until the last one returns at 5:30pm for under $10 round-trip. There are also primitive-style glass-bottom boats that circle the bay as you look down at a few fish and watch a diver swim down to the underwater sanctuary of the Virgin of Guadalupe, patron saint of Mexico. The statue of the Virgin—created by sculptor Armando Quesado—was placed there in 1958, in memory of a group of divers who lost their lives at the spot. You can purchase tickets ($5) directly from any boat that's loading.

WATERSPORTS & BOAT RENTALS An hour of **water-skiing** at Coyuca Lagoon can cost as little as $35 or as much as $70.

Scuba diving costs about $80 for 4 hours of instruction, when you book through a hotel or travel agency. Dive trips start at around $70 per person for two-tank dives. One reputable shop is **Acapulco Scuba Center** (℗ **744/482-9474**) on Paseo del Pescador near the *zócalo*. We also recommend **Fish-R-Us** (℗ **877/334-7478** in the U.S., or 744/482-8282; www.fish-r-us.com), which offers shore and boat dives, usually to Roqueta Island. Sunken ships, sea mountains, and cave rock formations are all on display around the area. **Boat rentals** are cheapest on Caletilla Beach, where you can usually find inner tubes, small boats, canoes, paddleboats, and chairs for rent.

For **deep-sea fishing** excursions, go to the boat cooperative's pink building opposite the *zócalo,* or book a day in advance (℗ **744/482-1099**). Charter trips run $200 to $600 for 6 to 7 hours, tackle and bait included, with an extra charge for ice, drinks, and lunch. Credit cards are accepted, but you may get a better deal by paying cash. Boats leave at 7am and return at 2pm. **Fish-R-Us** (see above) also books quality excursions. If you book through a travel agent or hotel, prices start at around $250 for four people.

Parasailing, though not free from risk (the occasional thrill-seeker has collided with a palm tree or even a building), can be brilliant. Floating high over the bay hanging from a parachute towed by a motorboat costs about $35. Most of these rides operate on Condesa Beach, but they also can be found independently operating on the beach in front of most hotels along the Costera.

GOLF & TENNIS The **Acapulco Princess** (℗ **744/469-1000**) course is a rather narrow, level, Ted Robinson design. The adjacent Pierre Marqués course has been completely redesigned by Tripp Davis and rebuilt as the 18-hole **Turtle Dunes Country**

Club, which includes a Lorena Ochoa Golf Academy. The course is the centerpiece for the new Princess Diamante residential development and is open to members only. A morning round of 18 holes at the Princess course costs $150 for guests and $170 for non-guests (discounted rates for afternoon rounds). American Express, Visa, and Master-Card are accepted, and the cart is included in the fee. Tee times begin at 7:30am, and reservations should be made at least a day in advance. Club rental is available for an extra $40. The **Mayan Palace Golf Club,** Geranios 22 (© 744/469-6000 or 744/466-2260), designed by Latin American golf great Pedro Guericia, lies farther east. Greens fees are $110 for visitors, and caddies are available for an additional $20. At the **Club de Golf Acapulco,** off the Costera next to the convention center (© 744/484-0781), you can play 9 holes for $52 and 18 holes for $70, with equipment renting for $10.

The Robert von Hagge–designed course at the exclusive **Tres Vidas Golf Club,** Carretera a Barra Vieja Km 7 (© 744/444-5143), is spectacular. The par-72, 18-hole course, right on the edge of the ocean, has nine lakes, is dotted with palms, and is home to a flock of ducks and other birds. The club is open only to members, guests of members, and guests at Tres Vidas or a few other participating hotels. Greens fees are $200, including cart; a caddy is $20. Also here is a clubhouse with a restaurant (daily 7am–10pm), as well as a pool. American Express, Visa, and MasterCard are accepted.

A few hotels have tennis facilities for guests; the best are at the Fairmont Princess, Mayan Palace, and Las Brisas hotels. The **Fairmont Princess** (© 744/469-1000) also allows nonguests to play for $20 per hour.

RIDING & BULLFIGHTS You can go **horseback riding** along the beach. Independent operators stroll the Hotel Zone beachfront offering rides for about $25 to $45 for 1 to 2 hours. Horses are also commonly found on the beach in front of the Fairmont Acapulco Princess; you go directly to the beach to make arrangements.

Traditionally called Fiesta Brava, **bullfights** are held during Acapulco's winter season at a ring (called Plaza de Toros) up the hill from Caletilla Beach. Tickets purchased through travel agencies cost around $25 to $40 and usually include transportation to and from your hotel. You can also buy a general admission ticket at the stadium for $6.

 Death-Defying Divers

High divers perform at La Quebrada each day at 1, 7:30, 8:30, 9:30, and 10:30pm. Admission to special viewing platforms is 35 pesos for adults, 10 pesos for kids 10 and under. From a spotlit ledge on the cliffs, divers (holding torches for the final performance) plunge into the roaring surf of an inlet that's 7m (23 ft.) wide, 4m (13 ft.) deep, and 40m (131 ft.) below—after praying at a small shrine nearby. Divers climb up the rocks and accept congratulations and gifts of money from onlookers. No visit is complete (even for jaded travelers) without watching the divers at this quintessential Acapulco experience.

To get there from downtown, take the street called La Quebrada from behind the cathedral for 4 blocks. Parking costs 20 pesos.

The public areas have great views, but arrive early, as they quickly fill up. Another option is to watch from the lobby bar of the **Hotel El Mirador.** The bar imposes a $15 cover charge, which includes two drinks. You can get around the cover by dining at the hotel's **La Perla restaurant** ($25 minimum for food during show times). Reservations (© 744/483-1221, ext. 802) are recommended during high season.

A House of Art, Seen from Outside

Of all the exclusive villas and homes in Acapulco, one stands out. Though not as impressive as the villas of Las Brisas, the **home of Dolores Olmedo** in Acapulco's traditional downtown area is a work of art. In 1956, the renowned Mexican artist Diego Rivera covered its outside wall with a mural of colorful mosaic tiles, shells, and stones. The mural, which took 18 months to complete, features Aztec deities such as Quetzalcóatl and Tepezcuincle, the Aztec dog. Rivera and Olmedo were lifelong friends, and Rivera lived in this house for the last 2 years of his life, when he also covered the interior with murals. The home isn't a museum, so you have to settle for a look at the exterior masterpiece. The house is a few blocks behind the Casablanca Hotel, a short cab ride from the *zócalo*, at Calle Cerro de la Pinzona 6.

Be forewarned that this is a true bullfight—meaning things generally do not fare well for the bull. The festivities begin at 5:30pm each Sunday from January to late April.

A MUSEUM & A WATER PARK The original **Fuerte de San Diego,** Calle Hornitos off Costera Alemán, east of the *zócalo* (© **744/482-3828**), was built in 1616 to protect the town from pirate attacks. At that time, the port reaped considerable income from trade with the Philippine Islands (which, like Mexico, were part of the Spanish Empire). The fort you see today was rebuilt after considerable earthquake damage in 1776 and has undergone a series of renovations since. The structure houses the **Museo Histórico de Acapulco (Acapulco Historical Museum)** ★★, with exhibits that reveal the port's role in the conquest of the Americas, Catholic conversion campaigns in the region, and exotic trade with the Orient. Temporary exhibits are also on display. It's one of Mexico's finest museums—and it's air-conditioned. Escape the midday heat here. Admission to the museum costs 35 pesos, free for locals on Sunday. It's open Tuesday through Sunday from 8am to 6pm. To reach the fort, follow Costera Alemán past Old Acapulco and the *zócalo*; the fort is on a hill on the right.

The **Parque Acuático el CICI** ★, Costera Alemán at Colón (© **744/484-1970;** www.cici.com.mx), is a sea-life and water park east of the convention center. It offers guests swimming pools with waves, water slides, and water toboggans, and has a cafeteria and restrooms. The park is open daily from 10am to 6pm. General admission including the dolphin show is 180 pesos, free for children 1 and younger. There are **dolphin shows** (in Spanish) weekdays at 2pm and weekends at 2 and 4pm. There's also a dolphin swim program, which includes 30 minutes of introduction and 30 minutes to 1 hour of swim time. The cost for this option is 990 pesos for the half-hour swim, and 1,350 pesos for the hour; both options include total access to the water park and are available by reservation only. Reservations are required; there is a 10-person maximum for the dolphin swim option. The minimum age is 4 years.

Shopping

Acapulco is not among the best places to buy Mexican crafts, but it does have a few interesting shops, and the Costera is lined with places to buy tourist souvenirs, including silver jewelry, Mexico knickknacks, and the ubiquitous T-shirt.

The shopkeepers aren't pushy, but they'll test your bargaining mettle. The starting price will be steep, and dragging it down may take some time. Before buying silver, examine it carefully and look for ".925" stamped on the back. This supposedly signifies that the silver is 92.5% pure, but the less expensive silver metal called "alpaca" may also bear this stamp. (Alpaca is generally stamped MEXICO or MEX, often in letters so tiny that they are hard to read and look similar to the three-digit ".925.")

Linda de Taxco, located at the Quebrada where the cliff divers perform (© **744/483-3340**), is a large store selling silver and gold pieces, including quality silver from Taxco. It's open Monday through Saturday from 10am to 10pm.

Sanborn's (www.sanborns.com.mx), an excellent department store and drugstore chain, offers an array of staples, including cosmetics, music, clothing, books, and magazines. It also carries high-quality folk art from around Mexico. Its bakery and candy counters are irresistible, and the restaurants serve excellent breakfasts (and other meals). Locations in Acapulco include downtown at Costera Miguel Alemán 209, across from the boat docks (© **744/482-6167**), and one with an outdoor patio by the beach at Costera Miguel Alemán 1226, at the Condo Estrella Tower, close to the convention center (© **744/484-2035**). All are open daily from 7:30am to midnight.

Boutiques selling resort wear crowd the Costera Alemán. These stores carry attractive summer clothing at prices lower than you generally pay in the United States. If there's a sale, you can find incredible bargains. One of the nicest air-conditioned shopping centers on the Costera is **Plaza Bahía,** Costera Alemán 125 (© **744/485-6939,** -6992), which has four stories of shops, movie theaters, a bowling alley, and small fast-food restaurants. The center is just west of the Crowne Plaza Hotel. The bowling alley, **Aca Bol in Plaza Bahía** (© **744/485-0970,** -7464), is open daily from noon to midnight (1am on weekends). Another popular shopping strip is the **Plaza Condesa,** adjacent to the Fiesta Americana Condesa; shops include Guess, Izod, and Bronce Swimwear. **Olvido Plaza,** near the restaurant of the same name, has Tommy Hilfiger and Aca Joe. The enormous glass **Gran Plaza,** Costera Alemán 1632 (© **744/486-6479**), is the Costera's largest, with department stores, 135 shops, Internet cafes, a Starbucks, and a large food court. It's a great place to escape the heat.

The top shopping center in Acapulco is **La Isla,** Blvd. de los Naciones 1813, off the Carretera Escénica close to the airport (© **744/462-1962**). Opened in late 2008, the open-air mall with streams and lush landscaping houses the Mexican department stores Liverpool and Casa Palacio, as well as name-brand stores including Coach, Calvin Klein, DKNY, and Hugo Boss. There's also a cinema and Carlos 'n Charlie's located here, along with other restaurants and entertainment options, and there's free Wi-Fi throughout the property. It's one of the most popular places for locals on weekends, when families stroll about during the day and couples take over the pedestrian pathways and park benches at night.

Acapulco After Dark

SPECIAL ATTRACTIONS   Some major hotels schedule Mexican fiestas and other theme nights that include dinner and entertainment, including the **Mayan Palace** (© **744/469-6000**) on Mondays at 7pm. Local travel agencies will have information.

NIGHTCLUBS & DANCE CLUBS   Acapulco is even more famous for its nightclubs than for its beaches. Because clubs frequently change ownership—and often names—it's difficult to give specific and accurate recommendations. But some general tips will help. Cover charges vary but are almost always higher for men. Drinks can cost anywhere from $5 to $15. Don't even think about going out to one of the hillside dance clubs before 11pm, and don't expect much action until after midnight. But it will keep going until 4 or 5am, and possibly later.

Many dance clubs periodically waive their cover charge or offer some other promotion to attract customers. Look for promotional materials in hotel reception areas, at travel desks or concierge booths, in local publications, and on the beach.

The high-rise hotels have their own bars and sometimes dance clubs. Informal lobby or poolside cocktail bars often offer free live entertainment.

THE BEACH BAR ZONE Prefer a little fresh air with your nightlife? The young, hip crowd favors the growing number of open-air oceanfront dance clubs along Costera Alemán, most of which feature techno or alternative rock. There's a concentration of them between the Fiesta Americana and Grand Plaza hotels. An earlier and more casual option to the glitzy dance clubs, these places include **El Sombrero** (you'll know it when you see it; © 744/484-8230), **Tabú** (no phone), and the pirate-themed **Barbaroja** (© 744/484-5932). These mainly charge a cover (around $10) and offer an open bar. Women frequently drink free or with a lesser charge (men may pay more, but then, this is where the beach babes are). **Paradise/Paraíso** (© 744/484-5988) is the most popular of the bunch and occasionally—such as during spring break—has live bands on the beachfront stage. Most of the smaller establishments do not accept credit cards; when they do, MasterCard and Visa are more widely accepted than American Express.

If you are brave enough—or inebriated enough—there's the **AJ Hackett Bungee Paradise** (named for the kiwi bungee jump inventor) in the midst of the beach bar zone at Costera Alemán 101 (© 744/484-7529). For $60, you get one jump, plus a T-shirt, diploma, and membership. Additional jumps are $20, and your fourth jump is free. For $90, you can jump eight times.

Baby-O ★★★ This longtime Acapulco hot spot is a throwback to the town's heady disco days, although the music is exceptionally contemporary. The 20s-to-40s crowd dances to everything from house to hip-hop and techno. Across from the Days Inn and Hooters, Baby-O has a dance floor surrounded by several tiers of tables and sculpted, cavelike walls, serviced by three bars. Drinks cost 60 to 90 pesos. Three-dimensional laser shows and vapor effects keep the dancing going strong. Service is excellent. This is a high-class dance club attracting a beautiful clientele. It opens at 10:30pm, and you'd be wise to make a reservation. Costera Alemán 22. © 744/484-7474 or 744/481-1035. www.babyo.com.mx. Cover $20 for women, $60 for men.

Carlos 'n Charlie's For fun, danceable music and good food, you can't go wrong with this branch of the Carlos Anderson chain. The most popular spot in the La Isla shopping center, it's great for a late dinner before heading to the discos—or just a fun night of casual drinking and dancing. It's also a good spot to take the kids for lunch or early dinner—the decor is filled with fun distractions. It's open daily from 1pm to 1am. Blvd. de Los Naciones No. 1813, in the La Isla Shopping Center. © 744/462-2104. www.carlosandcharlies.com/Acapulco.

Classico del Mar ★★ One of the newest and hottest clubs in town, Classico is a raging party into the wee hours. A winding mirrored glass entrance leads into this small but trendy *antro* (dance club). Digital screens and candlelit tables surround the illuminated dance floor, where music includes house, hip-hop, and reggaeton mixed by top DJs and blasted over a high-tech sound system. The glittery dance club and outdoor deck sits just in front of Palladium and attracts a young, trendy crowd. The club is open from 10:30pm until whenever the last person leaves—usually around 6:30am—and is closed Mondays and Wednesdays. Carretera Escénica 2, in front of Palladium. © 744/216-2831. www.classicodelmar.com.mx. Cover ranges from $30–$55.

Mandara ★★ 📷   Venture into this chrome-and-neon extravaganza perched on the side of the mountain for a true Acapulco nightlife experience. The plush, dim club has a sunken dance floor and panoramic view of the lights of Acapulco Bay. **Syboney,** in the same building, is a classy piano bar where only the finest singers dare croon for the crowd. The after-hours lounge **Privado,** also in the same building, opens its doors at 4:30am and is most crowded at 6am. Tight and slinky is the norm for women; no shorts for men. The club opens nightly at 10:30pm; fireworks rock the usually full house at 3am, which is when a stylized dance performance takes place on weekends, in the style of Euro clubs. Call to find out if you need reservations; this club tends to be busiest on Fridays. Carretera Escénica, btw. Los Rancheros Restaurant and La Vista Shopping Center. ✆ **744/446-5711,** -5712. www.acapulcomandara.com. Cover starts at $30 for women, $40 for men; includes open bar.

Palladium ★★   This cliffside club reigns as the top spot in town and is found just down the road from Mandara. Generally, it welcomes a younger, rowdier crowd that enjoys the fabulous views and the dancing platforms set in the 50m-wide (164-ft.) glass windows overlooking the bay. Around 3:30am, Silver Man—complete with an Aztec headdress—performs, followed by fireworks outside. Palladium consistently books some of the world's finest DJs, and the music seems to rock the earth below. Ladies pay less on ladies nights (usually Tues and Thurs); special events sometimes command higher covers. Carretera Escénica s/n. ✆ **744/446-5490.** www.palladium.com.mx. Cover averages $30 for women, $40 for men; includes open bar.

NORTHWARD TO ZIHUATANEJO & IXTAPA ★

576km (357 miles) SW of Mexico City; 565km (350 miles) SE of Manzanillo; 253km (157 miles) NW of Acapulco

Side-by-side beach resorts, Ixtapa and Zihuatanejo share geography, but they couldn't be more different in character. Ixtapa is a preplanned resort development, opened in 1971, with modern infrastructure, high-rise hotels, and tourist services, while Zihuatanejo (See-wah-tah-*neh*-hoh)—"Zihua" to the locals—is an authentic yet increasingly tourist-savvy Mexican beach town that has changed slowly with time. The pair offers the intriguing possibility of two vacations in one. Those looking for a package vacation or all-inclusive resort can opt for Ixtapa (Eex-tah-pah) and easily make the quick 6.5km (4-mile) trip to Zihuatanejo to sample the simple life in a *pueblo* by the sea. Those seeking a low-key retreat with Mexican personality should settle in Zihuatanejo, home to simple inns close to the beach as well as some ultraluxury boutique hotels.

The area, with the backdrop of the Sierra Madre and foreground of the Pacific Ocean, provides a broad range of outdoor activities and sun-drenched diversions. Scuba diving, deep-sea fishing, bay cruises to remote beaches, and golf are among the favorites. Nightlife in both towns borders on the subdued, although Ixtapa is livelier during holiday periods.

This dual destination appeals to the traveler looking for a little of everything, from resort-style indulgence to unpretentious simplicity. The two resorts are more welcoming to couples and adults than to families, with a number of places that are off-limits to children 15 and younger—something of a rarity in Mexico.

Essentials

GETTING THERE & DEPARTING

BY PLANE Flights are available year-round from U.S. gateways, but they operate less frequently in the summer. **Aeroméxico** flies daily from Mexico City; **InterJet** flies daily from neighboring Toluca (about an hour from Mexico City). Here are the local numbers of some carriers: **Aeroméxico** (℡ 755/554-2018, -2019), **Alaska Airlines** (℡ 755/554-8457), **Continental** (℡ 755/554-4219), **InterJet** (℡ 01-800/011-2345 toll-free in Mexico), and **US Airways** (℡ 755/554-8634). Ask your travel agent about **charter flights** and packages.

The **Ixtapa/Zihuatanejo airport** (℡ 755/554-2070; airport code: ZIH) is about 11km (6¾ miles) and 15 minutes south of Zihuatanejo. Taxi fares to the Ixtapa Hotel Zone are 350 pesos and to Zihuatanejo centro 300 pesos. **Transporte Terrestre** (℡ 755/554-3298) *colectivos* (minivans) transport travelers to hotels in Ixtapa for 170 pesos and Zihuatanejo for 120 pesos; tickets can be purchased just outside the baggage-claim area. Rental-car agencies with booths in the airport include **Hertz** (℡ 800/654-3131 in the U.S., or 755/554-2952) and **Budget** (℡ 800/527-0700 in the U.S., or 755/553-0397).

BY CAR From Mexico City (about 8–9 hr.), you can take **Hwy. 15** to Toluca, then **Hwy. 130/134** the rest of the way. On the latter road, gas stations are few. Another route is the four-lane **Hwy. 95D** to Iguala, then **Hwy. 51** west to **Hwy. 134.** A new toll road, **Hwy. 37** from Morelia to Ixtapa, cuts an hour off the total trip time.

From Acapulco (4 hr.) or Manzanillo (9 hr.), the only choice is the coastal **Hwy. 200.** You'll pay a 24 peso *cuota* (toll) at Tecpan de Galeana, though unlike other toll roads, it's the same old tope-studded highway. The ocean views along the winding, mountain-edged drive from Manzanillo can be spectacular, although there are many speed bumps along the way that make for slow going. *Warning:* You should not drive this route at night, both because it is dark and curvy and because there are ongoing problems with drug-related crime through the state of Michoacán, where you will encounter numerous military checkpoints.

BY BUS Zihuatanejo has two bus terminals: the **Central de Autobuses Estrella Blanca** (℡ 755/554-3477), Paseo Zihuatanejo at Paseo la Boquita, opposite the Pemex station and IMSS Hospital, from which most lines operate; and the **Estrella de Oro** station (℡ 755/554-2175), a block away. At the Central de Autobuses, several companies offer daily service to and from Acapulco, Puerto Escondido, Huatulco, Manzanillo, Puerto Vallarta, and other cities. At the other station, first-class Estrella de Oro buses run daily to Acapulco.

The trip from Mexico City to Zihuatanejo (bypassing Acapulco) takes 9 hours; from Acapulco, it's 4 to 5 hours. From Zihuatanejo, it's 9 or 10 hours to Manzanillo, and it's an additional 6 hours to Puerto Vallarta.

ORIENTATION

VISITOR INFORMATION The **Ixtapa/Zihuatanejo Tourism Office** (℡ 755/554-2001) sits in the municipal palace on the main square at Av. Zihuatanejo Poniente 21; it's open Monday through Friday from 8am to 6pm and provides basic tourist information. The **Convention and Visitor's Bureau** in Ixtapa is another source of information; it's in the Plaza Zócalo building behind Plaza La Puerta (℡ 755/553-1270; www.travelixtapazihuatanejo.com) and open Monday

ACAPULCO Northward to Zihuatanejo & Ixtapa

Zihuatanejo & Ixtapa Area

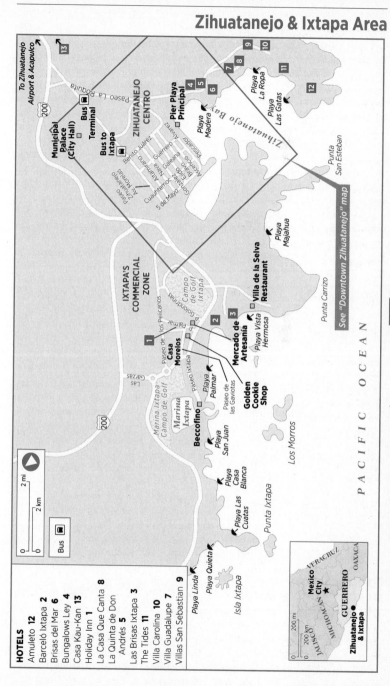

To Zihuatanejo
Airport & Acapulco

Paseo La Boquita

200

Municipal
Palace
(City Hall)

Bus
Terminal

Bus to
Ixtapa

ZIHUATANEJO
CENTRO

Pier Playa
Principal

4
5
6

7
8
9
10

11

12

13

Playa
La Ropa

Playa
Las Gatas

Playa
Madera

Playa Madera

Punta
San Esteban

Zihuatanejo Bay

Benito Juárez

Guerrero
Galeana
Álvaro Obregón

Cuauhtémoc

Altamirano
V. Guerrero
Ascencio
Pescador
Alvarez

N. Bravo
Ejido
5 de Mayo

Paseo
Zihuatanejo

AV. Morelos

See "Downtown Zihuatanejo" map

Playa
Majahua

IXTAPA'S
COMMERCIAL
ZONE

Campo
de Golf
Ixtapa

Villa de la Selva
Restaurant

Punta Carrizo

Paseo de los Pelícanos

Palmar

Bd. Solentiname

Paseo Ixtapa

1

2

3

Mercado de
Artesanía

Playa Vista
Hermosa

Casa
Morelos

Playa
Palmar

Golden
Cookie
Shop

Las Garzas

Marina Ixtapa
Campo de Golf

Marina
Ixtapa

Paseo de las Gaviotas

Beccofino

Playa
San Juan

Playa
Casa
Blanca

200

Playa Las
Cuatas

Punta Ixtapa

Los Morros

PACIFIC OCEAN

2 mi

2 km

Bus

Playa Linda

Playa Quieta

Isla Ixtapa

HOTELS

Amuleto **12**
Barceló Ixtapa **2**
Brisas del Mar **6**
Bungalows Ley **4**
Casa Kau-Kan **13**
Holiday Inn **1**
La Casa Que Canta **8**
La Quinta de Don
Andrés **5**
Las Brisas Ixtapa **3**
The Tides **11**
Villa Carolina **10**
Villa Guadalupe **7**
Villas San Sebastián **9**

VERACRUZ

Mexico
City

GUERRERO

OAXACA

JALISCO

MICHOACÁN

Zihuatanejo
& Ixtapa

200 mi

200 km

361

through Friday from 9am to 2pm and 4 to 7pm. A tourist kiosk on Paseo Ixtapa in front of the plaza is open daily from 10am to 6pm.

CITY LAYOUT The fishing village and resort of **Zihuatanejo** spreads out around the beautiful Bay of Zihuatanejo, framed by downtown to the north and a beautiful long beach and the Sierra foothills to the east. The heart of Zihuatanejo is the waterfront walkway **Paseo del Pescador** (also called the *malecón*), bordering the Municipal Beach. Rather than a plaza, as in most Mexican villages, the town centerpiece is a **basketball court,** which fronts the beach. It's a point of reference for directions. The main road for cars is **Juan Alvarez,** a block behind the *malecón*. Sections of several main streets are designated *zona peatonal* (pedestrian zone).

A cement-and-sand walkway runs from the *malecón* in downtown Zihuatanejo along the water to **Playa Madera.** The walkway is lit at night. Access to Playa La Ropa (Clothing Beach) is by the steep, winding **Camino a Playa La Ropa.** Playa La Ropa and Playa Las Gatas (Cats Beach) are connected only by boat.

A good highway connects Zihua to **Ixtapa,** 6.5km (4 miles) northwest. The 18-hole **Ixtapa Golf Club** marks the beginning of the inland side of Ixtapa. Tall hotels line Ixtapa's wide beach, **Playa Palmar,** against a backdrop of lush palm groves and mountains. Access is by the main street, **Bulevar Paseo de Ixtapa.** On the opposite side of the main boulevard lies a large expanse of small shopping plazas (many with air-conditioned shops) and restaurants. At the far end of Bulevar Ixtapa, **Marina Ixtapa** has excellent restaurants, private yacht slips, and an 18-hole golf course. Condominiums and private homes surround the marina and golf course, and additional exclusive residential areas are rising in the hillsides past the marina on the road to Playa Quieta and Playa Linda. Ixtapa also has a paved bicycle track that begins at the marina and continues around the golf course and beyond Playa Linda.

GETTING AROUND **Taxi** fares are reasonable, but from midnight to 5am, rates increase by 40%. The average fare between Ixtapa and Zihuatanejo is 55 pesos. Within Zihua, the fare runs about 50 pesos; within Ixtapa, it averages 50 to 70 pesos. Radio cabs are available by calling ✆ **755/554-3680,** -3311; however, taxis are available from most hotels. A **shuttle bus** (8 pesos) runs between Zihuatanejo and Ixtapa every 15 or 20 minutes from 5am to 11pm daily but is almost always very crowded with commuting workers. In Zihuatanejo, it stops near the corner of Morelos/Paseo Zihuatanejo and Juárez, about 3 blocks north of the market. In Ixtapa, it makes numerous stops along Bulevar Ixtapa.

The road from Zihuatanejo to Ixtapa is a broad, four-lane highway, so driving between the towns is easier and faster than ever. Street signs are becoming common in Zihuatanejo, and good signs lead in and out of both towns. Both locations have an area called the Zona Hotelera (Hotel Zone), so if you're trying to reach Ixtapa's Hotel Zone, signs in Zihuatanejo pointing to that village's Hotel Zone might be confusing.

[FastFACTS] ZIHUATANEJO & IXTAPA

Area Code The telephone area code is **755.**

Currency Exchange Ixtapa's banks include

Banamex, at the corner of Las Golondrinas (bordering the golf course) and Ixtapa, and **HSBC,** in front of Hotel

Emporio. The most centrally located of Zihuatanejo's banks is **Banamex,** Calle Ejido at Vicente Guerrero.

Banks change money during business hours, generally Monday through Friday from 9am to 4pm, Saturday from 10am to 1pm. **Note:** Banks are persnickety about exchanging U.S. currency; bills with any stray ink marks or the most microscopic tears will be rejected.

Climate Summer is hot and humid, though tempered by sea breezes and brief showers; September is the peak of the tropical rainy season, with showers concentrated in the late afternoons. The coast, while humid, gets less rain than the inland mountains. Dry season is November through May.

Consular Agents The **U.S.** has an office in Ixtapa at the Hotel Fontan,

Boulevard Ixtapa s/n (© **755/553-2100;** Mon–Fri 1–5pm).

Drugstores A branch of **Farmacías Coyuca** (© **755/554-5390**) at Nicolas Bravo and Vincente Guerrero in Zihuatanejo, is open daily from 8am to midnight. Ixtapa has several **FarmaPronto**s (© **755/553-5090**); the most central one faces Paseo de Ixtapa in Plaza La Puerta; it's open Monday through Saturday 8am to 10pm, Sunday 9am to 9pm.

Hospital **Hospital de la Marina Ixtapa** is at Bulevar Ixtapa s/n, in back of the artisans' market (© **755/553-0499**). In Zihuatanejo, there's the **Clinica Maciel,** Las Palmas 12 (© **755/554-2380**), or **Hospital**

Hernández Montejano, Juan Alvarez s/n (© **755/554-5404**). Dial © **065** (Red Cross) from any phone for emergencies.

Internet Access Ixtapa hotels generally have Internet access. Access is cheaper in Zihuatanejo; the most popular is **Zihuatanejo Bar Net,** Agustín Ramírez 2, on the ground floor of the Hotel Zihuatanejo Centro (© **755/554-3661**). High-speed access is 20 pesos per hour; it's open daily 9am to 11pm.

Post Office The *correo* is in the SCT building, Edificio SCT, behind El Cacahuate in Zihuatanejo (© **755/554-2192**). It's open Monday through Friday from 8am to 6pm, Saturday from 8am to noon.

Where to Stay: Zihuatanejo

Some hotels in Zihuatanejo and its nearby beach communities are more economical than those in Ixtapa, while others are far more expensive and exclusive. The term *bungalow* is used loosely—it may mean an individual unit with a kitchen and bedroom, or just a bedroom. It may also be like a hotel, in a two-story building with multiple units, some of which have kitchens. It may be cozy or rustic, with or without a patio or balcony. Accommodations in town tend to be basic, clean, and comfortable.

Playa Madera and Playa La Ropa, separated by a craggy shoreline, are both accessible by road. Prices tend to be higher here than in town, but the value is much better, and people tend to find that the beautiful, tranquil setting is worth the extra cost. The town is 5 minutes away by taxi and 10 to 15 minutes by foot.

Choosing a Hotel in Zihuatanejo or Ixtapa (or Both)

Larger high-rise hotels and all-inclusive resorts dominate accommodations in Ixtapa and on Playa Madera. Package deals for these are readily available online. There are only a few choices in the budget range. If you're looking for lower-priced rooms, Zihuatanejo offers more selection and better values, although it also has some very expensive (and wonderful) boutique hotels. Lodgings in both towns offer free parking. High season generally runs from November 15 to April 30, and low season from May 1 to November 14. The rates quoted below do not include the 17% tax.

IN TOWN

Posada Citlali In this cheerful three-story hotel, small rooms with fans surround a shaded, plant-filled courtyard that holds comfortable rockers and chairs. It's centrally located and a good value for the price, but very basic. Bottled water is in help-yourself containers on the patio. The stairway to the top two floors is narrow and steep.

Vicente Guerrero (near Alvarez), 40880 Zihuatanejo, Gro. ✆ **755/554-2043.** 18 units. 500 pesos double. No credit cards. *In room:* Fan, TV, no phone.

PLAYA MADERA

Madera Beach is a 15-minute walk along the street, a 10-minute walk along the beach pathway, or a cheap taxi ride from Zihuatanejo. Most accommodations are on Calle Eva S. de López Mateos, the road overlooking the beach. Many hotels are set against the hill and have steep stairways.

Moderate

Brisas del Mar This simple but enchanted beach hotel has 30 cheerful suites, all with private terraces overlooking Zihuatanejo Bay. The larger and more expensive units offer separate sitting areas, Jacuzzi tubs, and kitchenettes. Located above Playa Madera, the family-run establishment is known for friendly service, and maid service includes an artistic arrangement of flower petals on the bed. There's direct beach access, a pool, and spa services, including in-room massages upon request. The restaurant and lounge terrace boast a wonderful view of the sea.

Calle Eva S. de López Mateos s/n, Playa Madera, 40880 Zihuatanejo, Gro. www.hotelbrisasdelmar.com. ✆ **755/554-2142.** 30 units. High season $140–$202 double; low season $107–$202 double. MC, V. **Amenities:** Restaurant; bar; Internet; outdoor pool; small spa. *In room:* A/C (in some rooms), TV, hair dryer, minibar.

Inexpensive

Bungalows Ley No two suites are the same at this small complex, one of the nicest on Playa Madera. If you're traveling with a group, you might want to book the most expensive suite (Club Madera); it has a rooftop terrace, outdoor bar and grill, and spectacular view. The simplest of the immaculate units are studios with one king-size bed and a kitchen. Rooms have terraces or balconies just above the beach, and all are decorated in pastel colors. Bathrooms, however, tend to be small and dark, with showers only. The hotel has no pool but leads right to the beach.

Calle Eva S. de López Mateos s/n, Playa Madera (Apdo. Postal 466), 40880 Zihuatanejo, Gro. www.bungalowsley.com. ✆ **755/554-4087.** Fax 755/554-1365. 8 units. 750 pesos double; 1,750 pesos 2-bedroom suite with kitchen (up to 4 persons). Low-season discounts available after 6-night stay. MC, V. Follow Mateos to the right, up a slight hill; it's on your left. *In room:* A/C, TV, kitchenette.

La Quinta de Don Andrés This inexpensive, family-friendly hotel sits just above Playa Madera and is less than a 10-minute walk from the town center. Seven of the ten simply decorated rooms are suites, with separate living areas, bedrooms, kitchens, and air-conditioning. Although they're lacking in decor, the regular rooms are perfectly comfortable and some have panoramic views of the bay. There's a small courtyard pool, and the beach is just down the stairs.

Adelita 11, Playa Madera (Apdo. Postal 466), 40880 Zihuatanejo, Gro. www.laquintadedonandres.com. ✆ **755/553-8213.** 10 units. $100–$150 double; $160–$250 suite with kitchen (up to 4 people). No credit cards. **Amenities:** Outdoor pool. *In room:* A/C (in suites only), TV, fridge, Wi-Fi.

Downtown Zihuatanejo

HOTELS ■
Amuleto **16**
Brisas del Mar **9**
Bungalows Ley **7**
La Casa Que Canta **11**
La Quinta de Don
  Andrés **8**
Posada Citlali **4**
The Tides **14**
Villa Carolina **13**
Villa Guadalupe **10**

RESTAURANTS ◆
Amuleto **16**
Coconuts **3**
Kau-Kan **12**
La Casa Vieja **6**
La Perla **15**
La Sirena Gorda **2**
Nueva Zelanda **1**

ATTRACTIONS ●
Museo de Arqueología **5**

To Ixtapa

Main Bus Terminal

PLAYA LA ROPA

Playa La Ropa is a 20- to 25-minute walk south of town on the east side of the bay, or it's a 50-peso taxi ride.

Expensive

Amuleto ★★   Perched on a hill high above the bay, this intimate boutique hotel was designed for people who want to relax in luxury and exclusivity. Amuleto, which has only six units, has panoramic views of Zihuatanejo Bay that make it seem you're on top of the world. The *palapa*-covered restaurant serves innovative international

365

food and overlooks a small infinity pool framed by the bay. Each bungalow-like unit is individually decorated with Mexican and Asian designs using organic textures and earth colors. The *palapa* suite, for example, features meticulous stone, tile, and wood-work; a bed with 1,000-thread-count Egyptian cotton sheets; a separate sitting area with onyx lamps and bamboo chairs; a rooftop terrace with a hammock surrounded by bougainvillea; and a private plunge pool. The open-air restaurant serves wonderful breakfasts and is open to the public for dinner (p. 369).

Calle Escénica 9, Playa La Ropa, 40880 Zihuatanejo, Gro. www.amuleto.net. © **213/280-1037** in the U.S., or 755/544-6222. Fax 310/496-0286 in the U.S. 6 units. High season $400–$650 double; low season $325–$550 double. $100 extra person. AE, MC, V. No children under 16. **Amenities:** Restaurant; gym; outdoor pool. *In room:* A/C, minibar, Wi-Fi.

La Casa Que Canta ★★★ 📷 "The House that Sings" is a romantic hotel that is regularly rated among the world's top boutique hotels. The striking molded-adobe architecture typifies the rustic-chic Mexican Pacific style. Individually decorated rooms named after Mexican songs have handsome natural-tile floors, unusual painted Michoacán furniture, antiques, and stretched-leather *equipale*-style chairs and tables with hand-loomed fabrics throughout. Each exquisite room has a large furnished terrace with bay views. Most of the spacious units are suites, and 11 of them have private pools. Rooms meander up and down the hillside, and while no staircase is terribly long, there is only one elevator. A "well-being" center offers massage, spa services, and yoga. The hotel's service is remarkably gracious, and you'll find La Casa Que Canta pretty close to heaven.

Camino Escénico a Playa La Ropa, 40880 Zihuatanejo, Gro. www.lacasaquecanta.com. © **888/523-5050** in the U.S., or 755/555-7000, -7026, -7030. Fax 755/554-7900. 25 units. High season $490–$820 double; low season $330–$560 double; 5-night minimum stay required Jan–Apr. AE, MC, V. Children 15 and younger not allowed. **Amenities:** Restaurant (open to outside guests for dinner w/reservation only); bar; fitness center; 2 outdoor pools (1 freshwater, 1 saltwater); room service; spa. *In room:* A/C, hair dryer, minibar.

The Tides ★★ The Tides sits on one of Mexico's most beautiful beaches. Suites feature one or two bedrooms, living areas, large terraces, and private plunge pools. Rooms are decorated with modern Mexican touches and include comfy lounges, CD players, and hammocks that beckon at siesta time. There are 11 beachside suites and one presidential suite. Units that don't overlook the beach surround a fountain-filled lagoon and tropical gardens with enchanting night lighting. Service is first-rate. The Tides allows children only in two-bedroom suites and generally has a quiet feel. The meal plan (breakfast and dinner) is mandatory during holidays and includes an excellent variety of cuisine. In addition to the exquisite beach area, pools, restaurants, and bars, the Tides offers a full-service spa, tennis courts, and massages on the sand.

Playa la Ropa (Apdo. Postal 84), 40880 Zihuatanejo, Gro. www.tideszihuatanejo.com. © **866/905-9560** in the U.S., or 755/555-5500. Fax 755/554-2758. 70 units. High season $500–$550 double; $875–$1,700 suite; low season $355–$385 double, $570–$1,150 suite. Meal plan $100 per person including taxes and tip ($114 and mandatory Dec 19–Jan 5). AE, MC, V. **Amenities:** 2 open-air beachside restaurants; 3 bars; 4 outdoor pools (including 18m/59-ft. lap pool); room service; full-service spa; 2 lighted tennis courts. *In room:* A/C, TV, DVD, hair dryer, iHome, minibar, Wi-Fi.

Moderate

Villa Carolina ★★ 🏠 Located next to the Tides, Villa Carolina is a hidden gem within walking distance of Playa La Ropa. Each beautifully designed suite offers privacy, luxury, and enchantment—for far less than comparable boutique hotels in Zihuatanejo. Garden suites sit on the pool level and have individual patios; the larger upstairs master suites have balconies with hammocks and Jacuzzis. With two levels, the "grand house" is the largest suite, with two bedrooms, two bathrooms, and a private pool. All suites feature open-air sitting areas under palm-thatched roofs with built-in couches, fully stocked kitchens, and satellite TVs with DVD/CD players. Bedrooms and bathrooms mix muted colors and soft Mexican designs with extensive marble, tile, and stonework. Service is gracious and unobtrusive, and hosts Tim and Carolina Conti will help with reservations for restaurants and activities.

Camino Escénico Playa La Ropa s/n, 40880 Zihuatanejo, Gro. www.villacarolina.com.mx. © **755/554-5612.** Fax 755/554-5615. 7 units. High season $219 garden suite, $299 master suite, $350–$550 grand house; low season $169 garden suite, $219 master suite, $290–$450 grand house. MC, V. **Amenities:** Breakfast terrace; bar; outdoor pool; room service. In room: A/C, TV w/DVD/CD player, hair dryer.

Villa Guadalupe ★★   A long wooden staircase descends toward the sea through jungle-like foliage alongside Villa Guadalupe's tiered villas. With adobe walls and *palapa* roofs, the villas seem to blend into the landscape, and Mexican art enhances the magic. Each individually decorated, one-bedroom suite has beach-white furnishings and a private terrace with a spectacular view of Zihuatanejo Bay; the largest suite has its own plunge pool. Service is personalized and friendly, the feel relaxed and intimate. Continental breakfast is served by the small infinity pool, and while there's no dining here, a beautiful restaurant looks over the water just up the hill at the sister Tentaciones Hotel, which offers four more one-bedroom villas for about $75 a night more.

Camino Escénico a Playa La Ropa, 40880 Zihuatanejo, Gro. www.hotelvillaguadalupe.com. © **755/544-8383.** Fax 755/554-3005. 3 suites. High season $230–$355 double; low season $190–$255 double. AE, MC, V. Follow the road leading south out of town toward Playa La Ropa, take the 1st right after the traffic circle, and go left on Adelita. **Amenities:** Breakfast terrace; outdoor pool. In room: TV, minibar.

Villas San Sebastián   On the mountainside above Playa La Ropa, this nine-villa complex offers great views of Zihuatanejo Bay. The one- and two-bedroom villas surround tropical vegetation and a central swimming pool. Each has a kitchenette and a spacious private terrace. The personalized service is one reason these villas come so highly recommended; owner Luis Valle, whose family has lived in this community for decades, is usually available to help guests with any questions or needs.

Bulevar Escénico Playa La Ropa (across from the Dolphins Fountain). www.valleproperties.com/san sebastian. © **755/554-4154.** 9 units. High season $145 1-bedroom villa, $255 2-bedroom villa; low season $98 1-bedroom villa, $165 2-bedroom villa. No credit cards. **Amenities:** Outdoor pool. In room: A/C, TV, kitchenette, Wi-Fi.

PLAYA ZIHUATANEJO
Moderate

Casa Kau-Kan ★★   Casa Kau-Kan is an upscale bohemian oasis on the long, secluded beach of Playa Larga. It's about 20 minutes south of Zihuatanejo on the open Pacific. Spacious bungalow-like accommodations amid palm trees feature private sitting areas, canopied beds with mosquito nets, and bamboo furnishings; four have private terrace pools. Owner Ricardo Rodriguez also runs Kau-Kan restaurant (p. 370), which serves delicious fresh seafood. There's not much to do in the immediate surroundings except tan, swim, eat, read, and enjoy the quiet lazy days, although horseback riding and kite-surfing are available on the beach immediately in front. You should be an experienced swimmer to go in the ocean here, which typically has waves perfect for bodysurfing. Hotel service is friendly and extremely attentive—whether it's a coconut or a cocktail you desire, it'll be right up.

Playa Larga s/n, 40880 Zihuatanejo, Gro. www.casakaukan.com. © **321/206-4131** in the U.S., or 755/554-6226. Fax 755/553-1212. 11 units. High season $120–$235 double; low season $90–$200 double. AE, MC, V. No children younger than 13. **Amenities:** Restaurant; outdoor pool. *In room:* A/C, fridge.

Where to Stay: Ixtapa

EXPENSIVE

Barceló Ixtapa ★★ ✦ ☺ An excellent value and a great choice for families, this grand 12-story all-inclusive resort hotel has an uninteresting exterior that contains bright, handsomely furnished public areas facing Playa Palmar. It's an inviting place to sip a drink and people-watch. Most rooms have balconies with ocean or mountain views. Gardens surround the large pool with a swim-up bar; daytime activities, including a dive center; and a kids' club. Wednesday is Mexican fiesta night.

Bulevar Ixtapa, 40880 Ixtapa, Gro. www.barceloixtapa.com. © **755/555-2000.** Fax 755/553-2438. 340 units. High season $244–$340 double all-inclusive; low season $165–$293 double all-inclusive. AE, DC, MC, V. **Amenities:** 4 restaurants; lobby bar; concierge; fitness room; 3 swimming pools (1 w/Jacuzzi); beachside activities; room service; spa w/massage treatments; 2 tennis courts. *In room:* A/C, TV, hair dryer, minibar, Wi-Fi.

Las Brisas Ixtapa ★ Above high-rise hotels in jungle-like surroundings on a rocky promontory, Las Brisas is notable for its gorgeous private beach cove and striking stepped architecture, designed by renowned architect Ricardo Legorreta. It features large stone and stucco public areas, and though hallways are a bit dim, guest rooms are bright and colorful, with upscale beach decor and oceanview terraces with hammocks, and multitier swimming pools with waterfalls. All rooms face a gorgeous private beach, accessible by an elevator (although enticing, the water is sometimes rough and can be dangerous for swimming). The six master suites come with private pools. Beach Club rooms offer upgraded amenities, complimentary cocktails, and continental breakfast. Internet specials are usually available, and guests receive discounts at a nearby golf course.

Bulevar Ixtapa s/n at Playa Vista Hermosa, 40880 Ixtapa, Gro. www.brisas.com.mx. © **866/221-2961** in the U.S., or 755/553-2121. Fax 755/553-1091. 417 units. High season $264 deluxe double, $303 Royal Beach Club; low season $233 deluxe double, $281 Royal Beach Club. AE, MC, V. **Amenities:** 5 restaurants; 3 bars; babysitting; elevator to secluded beach; executive rooms; fitness center; 4 outdoor pools (1 for adults only, 1 for children); room service; 4 lighted tennis courts w/pro on request. *In room:* A/C, TV, hair dryer, minibar, Wi-Fi.

MODERATE

Holiday Inn ★ ✦ ☺ Call it counterintuitive to bunk in a Holiday Inn in a resort area like Ixtapa, but this one has a lot going for it. If you don't require a room right on the sand—it's 2 long blocks away along a mostly shady street—you can save a bundle and still get most of the amenities offered by the beach high-rises, including a choice of soft or firm pillows and a work desk with what must be the fastest Internet connection in Mexico. Rooms are staid and businesslike but large, well-maintained, and comfortable, with sliding glass doors overlooking the pool and a lovely view of palm trees and hills. This is one place where you'll know you're in Mexico; it's smaller than the beach resorts, and guests are mostly vacationing Mexican families and business travelers. The staff is primarily Spanish-speaking but has enough command of English to take care of business, and everyone is as nice as can be.

Av. Paseo de las Palmas, 40880 Ixtapa, Gro. www.hiixtapa.com. © **888/465-4329** in the U.S., or 755/555-0500. 153 units. High season $95 double; low season $65 double. MC, V. **Amenities:** Restaurant; babysitting; concierge; fitness center; massage room; outdoor pool; room service; Wi-Fi. *In room:* A/C, TV, hair dryer, Internet.

Where to Eat

ZIHUATANEJO

Zihuatanejo's **central market,** on Avenida Benito Juárez, about 5 blocks inland from the waterfront, will whet your appetite for cheap and tasty food. It's best at breakfast and lunch, before the market activity winds down in the afternoon. Look for what's hot and fresh. The market area is one of the coast's best places to shop and people-watch.

Expensive

Coconuts ★★ INTERNATIONAL/SEAFOOD   Located in Zihuatanejo's oldest building, Coconuts has long been a Zihua institution serving fresh, innovative cuisine such as roasted pumpkin and ricotta crepes, bananas flambé for two, and excellent seafood dishes including grilled red snapper and other locally caught fish, prepared with fresh fruit salsa or any way you like. The romantic garden patio, offering seating under cover or under the stars, is as much of a lure as the food. Freshly restored, the historic building was originally the weigh-in station for Zihua's coconut industry in the late 1800s. Expect friendly, efficient service and a large expat clientele.

Pasaje Augustín Ramírez 1 (at Vicente Guerrero). ✆ **755/554-2518,** -7980. www.restaurantcoconuts. com. Reservations recommended. Main courses 190–225 pesos. AE, MC, V. High season daily noon–4pm and 6pm–midnight. Closed late May to Sept (rainy season).

Inexpensive

La Sirena Gorda MEXICAN   For one of the most popular breakfasts in town, head to the fun and unusual Sirena Gorda. "The Fat Mermaid," as it translates into English, serves a variety of eggs and omelets, hot cakes or French toast, and fruit with granola and yogurt. For lunch, the house specialty is seafood tacos—fish, shrimp, or even lobster in a variety of sauces. Daily specials may include blackened red snapper, tuna, or steak. The food is excellent, and patrons enjoy the casual sidewalk-cafe atmosphere. Colorful illustrations and paintings of fat mermaids decorate the walls.

Paseo del Pescador. ✆ **755/554-2687.** Breakfast 55–75 pesos; main courses 75–230 pesos. MC, V. Thurs–Tues 8:30am–10:30pm. Closed Wed. From the basketball court, face the water and walk to the right; La Sirena Gorda is on your right just before the town pier.

Nueva Zelanda MEXICAN   This open-air snack shop serves rich cappuccino sprinkled with cinnamon, fresh-fruit *licuados* (smoothies mixed with water or milk), and pancakes with real maple syrup. The mainstays are *tortas* and enchiladas, and service is friendly and efficient. There's a second location in Ixtapa, in the back section of the Los Patios shopping center (✆ **755/553-0838**), next to Señor Frog's.

Cuauhtémoc 23 (at Ejido). ✆ **755/554-2340.** *Tortas* and sandwiches 35–66 pesos; enchiladas 68 pesos; *licuados* 23–28 pesos; cappuccino 31 pesos. No credit cards. Daily 8am–10pm. From the waterfront, walk 3 blocks inland on Cuauhtémoc; the restaurant is on your right.

PLAYA MADERA & PLAYA LA ROPA
Expensive

Amuleto ★★★ SEAFOOD   This intimate restaurant located in the Amuleto boutique hotel (p. 365) offers a breathtaking view of the sea and town behind it. Just a handful of candlelit tables sit under the open-air *palapa* next to an infinity pool and tropical vegetation. To start, try the tuna tartare with lime, or salmon carpaccio with fresh citrus fruit. Excellent main dishes include grilled mahimahi with caviar and grapefruit; filet mignon, prepared with a rich blue cheese sauce; and lobster and shrimp risotto served with a half-lobster on top. Overseen by Brazilian owners Ricardo Teitelroat and Ticci Tonetto, Amuleto offers outstanding service.

In the Amuleto hotel, Calle Escénica 9, Playa La Ropa, 40880 Zihuatanejo, Gro. ✆ **755/544-6222.** www.amuleto.net. Main courses $20–$35. AE, MC, V. Daily 6–9pm.

Kau-Kan ★★ MEDITERRANEAN/SEAFOOD Candlelit tables and lamps dot this small, romantic open-air restaurant with an unforgettable view of Zihuatanejo Bay. Head chef Ricardo Rodriguez, who also runs the Casa Kau-Kan (p. 367), turns out fresh, meticulously presented dishes. Among the delicious appetizers are eggplant salad with ginger adobo shrimp and mahimahi carpaccio. For a main dish, consider the baked potato stuffed with lobster, or the shrimp prepared in a basil and garlic sauce. Top off your meal with an ambrosial dessert accompanied by one of the aromatic Central American coffees. Reserve a candlelit table and arrive in time for the sunset.

Camino Escénica a Playa La Ropa. ✆ **755/554-8446.** www.casakaukan.com/kaukan. Reservations recommended. Main courses $17–$37. AE, MC, V. Daily 6–10:30pm; open for lunch during high season only. From downtown on the road to La Ropa, Kau-Kan is on the right side of the road past the 1st curve.

Moderate

La Casa Vieja ★ MEXICAN A casual, intimate Mexican restaurant at the entrance to Playa Madera, "The Old House" serves delicious fish and traditional dishes from throughout Mexico, such as *filet a la tampiqueña* (tenderloin steak) and *cochinita pibil* (slow-roasted pork). Fresh fish, prepared any way you like, include tuna, red snapper, and mahimahi. Tiny white lights, twig lamps, and plants decorate the open-air dining room. Service is friendly and relaxed, and soft music plays in the background. The number of Mexicans dining here testifies to the restaurant's quality. Several different kinds of delicious pozole are served on Thursday.

Josefa Ortíz de Domínguez 7. ✆ **755/554-9770.** Main courses $11–$17. MC, V. Mon–Sat noon–10:30pm; Sun 9am–11pm. Restaurant is at the entrance of the road leading into Playa Madera.

Inexpensive

La Perla SEAFOOD Of the many *palapa*-style restaurants on Playa La Ropa, this is the most popular. The combination of plastic tables planted in the sand and simple food served unhurriedly makes La Perla a local tradition. The menu is a mix of Mexican and seafood selections, including delectable seafood ceviches, grilled fish filets, and a 1-kilo (2.2-lb.) grilled or broiled lobster for 450 pesos. Cold beer and cocktails are available whether or not you eat, as are whole coconuts served with a straw and with or without an added kick of gin. Sports are shown throughout the day via satellite TV.

Playa La Ropa. ✆ **755/554-2700.** www.laperlarestaurant.net. Breakfast 35–80 pesos; main courses 100–450 pesos. AE, MC, V. Daily 11am–10pm; breakfast 10am–noon. Near the southern end of La Ropa Beach, take the right fork in the road; look for the sign in the parking lot.

IXTAPA
Expensive

Beccofino ★ NORTHERN ITALIAN At this standout restaurant, owner Angelo "Rolly" Pavia serves the flavorful northern Italian specialties he grew up knowing and loving. The exceptional homemade seafood pastas may include calamari, shrimp, clams, mussels, and crayfish. Ravioli, a house specialty, comes stuffed with beef or seafood. The garlic bread is terrific, and there's an extensive wine list. A popular place in a breezy marina location, the restaurant tends to be loud when it's crowded. It's also a popular breakfast spot.

Marina Ixtapa. ✆ **755/553-1770.** www.zihuatanejo.net/beccofino. Breakfast $7–$18; main courses $14–$25. AE, MC, V. Daily 9am–11:30pm.

Villa de la Selva ★★★ MEXICAN/MEDITERRANEAN   Clinging to the edge of a cliff, this elegant restaurant enjoys the most spectacular sea and sunset view in Ixtapa. Beautiful wood terraces surrounded by a palm- and mango tree-filled jungle look directly over the bay, just steps below. Come early to get one of the best vistas, especially on the lower terrace. (You can make reservations online.) Music from hidden speakers seems to come from the sea. Classically rich dishes are artfully presented. Coconut-pecan encrusted shrimp in a mango-and-chile sauce or tuna carpaccio stand out among the starters. A wonderful main dish is *Filet Villa de la Selva,* red snapper topped with shrimp and hollandaise sauce.

Paseo de la Roca. © **755/553-0362.** www.villadelaselva.com.mx. Reservations recommended during high season. Main courses $16–$35. AE, MC, V. Daily 6–11:30pm winter; 7pm–midnight summer. Closed Sept.

Moderate

Casa Morelos MEXICAN   At this casual place for tasty Mexican seafood, you can order fresh fish with lemon and olive oil, mustard, orange, mango, garlic, or chile. Seafood fajitas, tequila and coconut shrimp, and shrimp enchiladas are delicious, and the fish tacos *al pastor* are the best in the area. The *mar y tierra* is a succulent shrimp and steak dish, while *mar y mar* is shrimp and lobster. You can dine indoors or out.

Centro Comercial La Puerta. © **755/553-0578.** www.casamorelosixtapa.com. Main dishes 100–350 pesos. MC, V. Daily 8am–midnight. Located next to Señor Frog's.

Inexpensive

Golden Cookie Shop ★ PASTRIES/DELI   This German bakery and deli's freshly baked goods beg for a detour, and the organic coffee menu is the most extensive in town. Come for a creative breakfast pancake plate, a hot or cold triple-decker sandwich made with fresh soft bread and your choice of sliced meats (bratwurst and Wiener schnitzel are also served). Nutritional cookies, breads, pastries, and cakes are available, as are vegetarian and low-carb selections.

Los Patios Center, 2nd floor. © **755/553-0310.** Breakfast 60–120 pesos; sandwiches 95–110 pesos; main courses 110–150 pesos. No credit cards. Daily 8am–2pm.

Activities on & off the Beach

The **Museo de Arqueología de la Costa Grande** (© **755/554-7552**) traces the history of the area from Acapulco to Ixtapa/Zihuatanejo (the Costa Grande) from pre-Hispanic times, when it was known as Cihuatlán ("the Land of Women" in the Náhuatl language), through the Colonial Era. Most of its pottery and stone artifacts give evidence of extensive trade with far-off cultures and regions, including the Toltec and Teotihuacán near Mexico City, the Olmec on the Pacific and Gulf coasts, and areas known today as the states of Nayarit, Michoacán, and San Luis Potosí. Local indigenous groups gave the Aztec tribute items, including cotton *tilmas* (capes) and *cacao* (chocolate), representations of which can be seen here. This museum, in Zihuatanejo near Vicente Guerrero at the east end of Paseo del Pescador, easily merits the half-hour or less it takes to stroll through; signs are in Spanish and English, and an accompanying brochure is available in English. Admission is 10 pesos (children 11 and under are free), and it's open Tuesday through Sunday from 10am to 6pm.

THE BEACHES   In Zihuatanejo   At Zihuatanejo's town beach, **Playa Municipal,** local fishermen pull their colorful boats up onto the sand, making for a fine photo op. The small shops and restaurants lining the waterfront are great for people-watching and absorbing the flavor of daily village life. **Playa Madera (Wood Beach),** just east of Playa Municipal, is open to the surf but generally peaceful.

All beaches in Zihuatanejo are safe for swimming. Undertow is rarely a problem, and the municipal beach is protected from the main surge of the Pacific. Beaches in Ixtapa are more dangerous for swimming, with frequent undertow problems.

South of Playa Madera is Zihuatanejo's largest and most beautiful beach, **Playa La Ropa ★★**, a long sweep of sand with a great view of the sunset. Some lovely small hotels and restaurants nestle in the hills; palm groves edge the shoreline. Although it's also open to the Pacific, waves are usually gentle. Beachside restaurants are plentiful, and beach operators rent kayaks, Hobie Cat sailboats, and snorkeling equipment. A taxi from town costs 35 pesos. The name Playa La Ropa (Clothing Beach) comes from an old tale of the sinking of a *galeón* during a storm. The silk clothing it was carrying back from the Philippines washed ashore on this beach.

The best beach for swimming, and for children, is secluded **Playa Las Gatas (Cats Beach),** across the bay from Playa La Ropa and Zihuatanejo. The small coral reef just offshore is a nice spot for snorkeling and diving, and a little dive shop on the beach rents gear. The waters at Las Gatas are exceptionally clear, without undertow or big waves. Open-air seafood restaurants on the beach make it an appealing lunch spot. The PADI-certified **Carlo Scuba** (© **755/554-6003;** www.carloscuba.com) arranges **scuba-diving** and snorkeling trips from here. Kayaks are also available for rent. Small *pangas* or *lanchas* (boats) with shade run to Las Gatas from the Zihuatanejo town pier, a 10-minute trip; the captains will take you across whenever you wish between 8am and 5pm for 40 pesos round-trip. Usually the last boat back leaves Las Gatas at 6:30pm (5:30pm in low season), but check to be sure.

Playa Larga is a beautiful, uncrowded beach between Zihuatanejo and the airport, with several small *palapa* restaurants, hammocks, and wading pools.

In Ixtapa   Ixtapa's main beach, **Playa Palmar,** is a lovely white-sand arc on the edge of the Hotel Zone, with dramatic rock formations silhouetted in the sea. The surf can be rough; use caution, and don't swim when a red flag is posted. There are three public access points to the beach along Paseo de Ixtapa, but several of the nicest beaches in the area are essentially closed to the public. Although by law all Mexican beaches are open to the public, it is common practice for hotels to create artificial barriers (such as rocks or dunes).

Club Med and Qualton Club have largely claimed **Playa Quieta,** on the mainland across from Isla Ixtapa. The remaining piece of beach was once the launching point for boats to Isla Ixtapa, but it is gradually being taken over by a private development. Isla Ixtapa–bound boats leave from the jetty on **Playa Linda,** about 13km (8 miles) north of Ixtapa. Inexpensive water taxis ferry passengers to Isla Ixtapa. Playa Linda is the primary out-of-town beach, with watersports equipment and horse rentals available. **Playa las Cuatas,** a pretty beach and cove a few miles north of Ixtapa, and **Playa Majahua,** an isolated beach just west of Zihuatanejo, are both being transformed into resort complexes. Lovely **Playa Vista Hermosa** is framed by striking rock formations and the Las Brisas hotel high on the hill. All are very attractive beaches for sunbathing or a stroll but have heavy surf and strong undertow. Use caution if you swim here.

WATERSPORTS & BOAT TRIPS   Probably the most popular boat trip is to **Isla Ixtapa** for snorkeling and lunch at the El Marlin restaurant, one of several on the island. You can book this outing as a tour through local travel agencies, or go on your own by taking a boat from Playa Linda. Boats leave for Isla Ixtapa every 10 minutes between 9am and 5pm, so you can depart and return as you like. The round trip is 55 pesos. You'll pass dramatic rock formations and see distant **Los Morros de Los**

Pericos islands, where a great variety of birds nest on the rocky points jutting out into the Pacific. On Isla Ixtapa, you'll find good snorkeling, diving, and other watersports. Gear is available for rent on the island. Be sure to catch the last water taxi back at 5pm, and double-check that time upon arrival on the island.

Local travel agencies can usually arrange day trips to Los Morros de Los Pericos islands for **birding,** though it's less expensive to rent a boat with a guide at Playa Linda. The islands are offshore from Ixtapa's main beach.

Sunset cruises on the sailboat *Picante,* arranged through **Yates del Sol** (© **755/554-2694,** -8270; www.picantecruises.com), depart from the Zihuatanejo town marina at Puerto Mío. The evening cruises last 2½ hours, cost $52 per person, and include an open bar and hors d'oeuvres. There's also a "Sail and Snorkel Adventure" day trip to **Playa Manzanillo** on the very comfortable, rarely crowded sailboat. The 4½-hour trip begins at 10am, costs $74 per person, and includes an open bar and lunch (snorkeling gear $7 extra).

You can arrange **fishing trips** with the **boat cooperative** (© **755/554-2056**) at the Zihuatanejo town pier. They cost $210 to $450, depending on boat size, number of people, trip length, and so on. Most trips last about 7 hours. The cooperative accepts only cash; no credit cards. The price includes soft drinks, beer, bait, and fishing gear, but not lunch. You'll pay more for a trip arranged through a local travel agency. The least expensive trips are on small launches called *pangas;* most have shade. Both small-game and deep-sea fishing are offered. The fishing is adequate, though not on par with that of Mazatlán or Baja. Other trips combine fishing with a visit to the near-deserted ocean beaches that extend for miles along the coast. Sam Lushinsky at **Ixtapa Sportfishing Charters,** 19 Depue Lane, Stroudsburg, PA 18360 (© **570/688-9466;** fax 570/688-9554; www.ixtapasportfishing.com), is a noted outfitter. Prices range from $210 to $445 per day, for 8 to 13m (26–43 ft.) custom cruisers, fully equipped. They accept MasterCard and Visa.

Boating and fishing expeditions from the new **Marina Ixtapa,** a bit north of the Ixtapa Hotel Zone, can also be arranged. As a rule, everything available in or through the marina is more expensive and more Americanized.

Sailboats, sailboards, and other **watersports equipment** are usually available at stands on Playa La Ropa, Playa las Gatas, Isla Ixtapa, and Playa Palmar in Ixtapa. There's **parasailing** at La Ropa and Palmar. **Kayaks** are available for rent at hotels in Ixtapa and some watersports operations on Playa La Ropa. The **Tides** has a beach club in front of the hotel on La Ropa with sailboat, sailboard, and kayak rentals.

The PADI-certified **Carlo Scuba,** on Playa Las Gatas (© **755/554-6003;** www. carloscuba.com), arranges **scuba-diving trips.** Fees start at $65 for a one-tank dive, or $90 for two dives, including all equipment and a drink. This shop has been around since 1962 and is very knowledgeable about the area, which has nearly 30 different dive sites, including walls and caves. Diving takes place year-round, though the water is clearest July to August and November to February, when visibility is 30m (98 ft.) or better. The nearest decompression chamber is in Ixtapa Marina. Advance reservations for dives are advised during Christmas and Easter.

Surfing is particularly good at **Petacalco Beach,** north of Ixtapa. **Swimming with dolphins** is possible at **Delfiniti Ixtapa** (www.delfiniti.com), arranged through any of the hotels or travel agents in town.

GOLF, TENNIS & HORSEBACK RIDING In **Ixtapa,** the **Club de Golf Ixtapa Palma Real** (© **755/553-1062,** -1163), in front of the Barceló Hotel, has an 18-hole course designed by Robert Trent Jones, Jr. The greens fee is $85 for 18 holes, $65 for 9 holes; caddies cost $25 for 18 holes, $20 for 9 holes; electric carts are $35; and club rental is $30. Tee times begin at 7am. The **Marina Ixtapa Golf Course** (© **755/553-1410;** fax 755/553-0825), designed by Robert von Hagge, has 18 challenging holes. The greens fee is $90, carts cost $35, caddies cost $20, and club rental is $35. Discounted rates are available after 1:30pm. The first tee time is 7am. Call for reservations 24 hours in advance. Both courses accept American Express, MasterCard, and Visa. Most hotels offer discounts to the golf courses.

In Ixtapa, the **Club de Golf Ixtapa Palma Real** (© **755/553-1062,** -1163) has lighted **public tennis courts.** Fees are $8.50 an hour during the day, $14 at night. Call for reservations. In Zihuatanejo, the **Tides** (© **755/555-5500**) has lit tennis courts open for $30 an hour; private lessons cost $70 an hour.

For **horseback riding,** the largest local stable is on **Playa Linda** (no phone), offering guided trail rides from the Playa Linda beach (about 13km/8 miles north of Ixtapa). It's just next to the pier where the water taxis debark to Isla Ixtapa. Groups of three or more riders can arrange their own tour, which is especially nice around sunset (though you'll need mosquito repellent). Riders can choose to trace the beach to the mouth of the river and back through coconut plantations, or hug the beach for the entire ride (which usually lasts 1–1½ hr.). The fee is around $40, cash only. Travel agencies in either town can arrange your trip but will charge a bit more for transportation. Reservations are suggested in high season. Another good place to ride is in Playa Larga. There is a ranch on the first exit coming from Zihuatanejo (no phone, but you can't miss it—it is the first corral to the right as you drive toward the beach). The horses are in excellent shape. The fee is about $45 for 1½ hours, and includes transportation to and from your hotel as well as a drink.

Shopping
ZIHUATANEJO

Zihuatanejo has its quota of T-shirt and souvenir shops, but it has also become a better place to buy crafts, folk art, and jewelry. Shops are generally open Monday through Saturday from 10am to 2pm and 4 to 8pm. Many better shops close Sunday, but some smaller souvenir stands stay open, and hours vary.

The **artisans' market** on Calle Cinco de Mayo is a good place to start shopping before moving on to specialty shops. It's open daily from 8am to 9pm. The **municipal market** on Avenida Benito Juárez sprawls over several blocks (about 5 blocks inland from the waterfront), but most vendors hawk the same things—*huaraches*, hammocks, and baskets. On the sand next to the pier is a daily fish market, and just behind it on Paseo del Pescador there's a small seashell market. Spreading inland from the waterfront some 3 or 4 blocks are numerous small shops well worth exploring.

Besides the places listed below, check out **Alberto's,** Cuauhtémoc 12 and 15 (no phone), for jewelry. Also on Cuauhtémoc, 2 blocks down from the Nueva Zelanda Coffee Shop, is a small shop that looks like a market stand and sells beautiful tablecloths, napkins, and other linens; all are handmade in Aguascalientes.

Casa Marina This small complex extends from the waterfront to Alvarez near Cinco de Mayo and houses five intriguing shops, each specializing in handcrafted wares from all over Mexico. Items include handsome rugs, textiles, masks, colorful woodcarvings, and silver jewelry. Café Marina, the small coffee shop in the complex, sells shelves and shelves of used paperback books in several languages. Open daily from 9am to 9pm during the high season, Monday through Saturday 10am to 2pm and 5 to 9pm the rest of the year. Paseo del Pescador 9. © **755/554-2373.**

El Jumil With small fishing boats pulled up on the sand just in front, this store sells coconut shell masks, exotic figurines, indigenous masks (including those used for ceremonial dances from Guerrero), Oaxacan pottery, and other regional art and crafts. There's a 10% discount on all items paid in cash. Open Monday to Saturday from 10am to 9pm. Casa Marina, Paseo del Pescador 9. ✆ **755/554-6191.**

Fruity Keiko Next to Coconuts restaurant (p. 369), this impressive little shop sells gorgeous gifts from across Mexico. Fruity Keiko carries carefully selected crafts and folk art, including some made by Mexico's best present-day artists. There's also a small selection of regional jewelry, handmade dresses, and Talavera pottery. Prices are higher here than if you were in the towns where these goods are actually made. Open Monday through Saturday from 10am to 9pm and Sunday from noon to 8pm. Vicente Guerrero 5-A at Alvarez, opposite the Hotel Citlali. ✆ **755/554-6578.** www.zihuatanejo.net/fruitykeiko.

IXTAPA

Shopping in Ixtapa is not especially memorable, with T-shirts and Mexican crafts the usual wares. Several shops on Bulevar Ixtapa, across from the beachside hotels, sell designer sportswear and most are open daily from 9am to 2pm and 4 to 9pm.

Decoré Ixtapa What used to be small boutique shop selling fine Mexican furniture and decorations at the entrance to the Ixtapa Marina has been demoted to a showroom displaying the company's wood and glass furnishings, onyx lamps, beautiful vases, handbags, and other luxury items. If you see something you like, a sign in the window promises someone will arrive in 2 minutes if you give them a call. Bulevar Ixtapa. ✆ **755/553-3550.** www.decoreixtapa.com.

La Fuente This terrific shop carries gorgeous Talavera pottery, jaguar-shaped wicker tables, hand-blown glassware, masks, tin mirrors and frames, hand-embroidered clothing from Chiapas, and wood furniture. Open daily from 9am to 10pm during high season, daily from 10am to 9pm in low season. Los Patios Center, Bulevar Ixtapa. ✆ **755/553-0812.**

Zihuatanejo & Ixtapa After Dark

With an exception or two, Zihuatanejo nightlife dies down around 11pm or midnight. For a selection of clubs, dance spots, hotel fiestas, special events, and fun watering holes with live music and dancing, head for Ixtapa. Just keep in mind that the shuttle bus stops at 11pm, and a taxi to Zihuatanejo after midnight costs 50% more than the regular price. During the off season (after Easter and before Christmas), hours vary: Some places open only on weekends, while others close completely. In Zihuatanejo, a lively bar showing satellite TV sports is **Bandido's,** at the corner of Cinco de Mayo and Pedro Ascencio in Zihuatanejo Centro, across from the Artisans' Market (✆ **755/553-8072**). It features live salsa music nightly and is open until 2am. There's no cover, and people often come to dance salsa.

THE CLUB & MUSIC SCENE

Many dance clubs stay open until the last customers leave, so closing hours depend upon revelers. Most dance clubs have a ladies' night at least once a week—admission and drinks are free for women.

Christine This long-standing dance club is best known for its midnight light show, which features classical music played on a mega sound system. A semicircle of tables in tiers overlooks the dance floor. The crowd tends to be in their 20s and 30s. No sneakers, flip-flops, or shorts are allowed, and reservations are recommended during high season. Open Thursday to Saturday at 10:30pm. Off-season hours vary. In the NH Krystal Hotel, Bulevar Ixtapa, Ixtapa. ☏ **755/555-0510.** Cover ranges from free–$20.

Señor Frog's   A companion restaurant to Carlos 'n Charlie's, Señor Frog's has several dining sections and a warehouselike bar with raised dance floors. Large speakers play electronic, rock, and Latin music, sometimes prompting dinner patrons to shimmy between courses. The restaurant is open daily from noon to midnight; the bar stays open until 3am. In the La Puerta Center, Paseo de Ixtapa, Ixtapa. ☏ **755/553-2282.** www. senorfrogs.com/ixtapa. Cover charges are around 100 pesos but vary depending on the night.

Zihuablue   One of Zihuatanejo's few nightlife options, Zihuablue opened in late 2007 across from Kau-Kan restaurant. The chic Mediterranean lounge is an open-air oasis with a candlelit bar, small dance floor, canopy beds and sofas, and sand floor. Ambient music fills the air of this small, exclusive retreat, open from 8pm to 2am November through May. Above the lounge is a fine seafood restaurant. Carretera Escénica La Ropa s/n, next to Kau-Kan restaurant. ☏ **755/554-4844.**

HOTEL FIESTAS & THEME NIGHTS

A number of hotels hold Mexican fiestas and other special events that include dinner, drinks, live music, and entertainment for a fixed price (generally $44 from 7–10pm). The **Barceló Ixtapa** (☏ 755/555-2000) stages a popular Wednesday night fiesta; the **Dorado Pacífico** (☏ 755/553-2025), in Ixtapa, hosts a Tuesday night fiesta. Only the Barceló Ixtapa offers them in the off season. Call for reservations, and be sure you understand what the price covers, as drinks, tax, and tip are not always included.

PUERTO ESCONDIDO ★★★

368km (228 miles) SE of Acapulco; 240km (149 miles) NW of Salina Cruz; 80km (50 miles) NW of Puerto Angel

Idyllic Puerto Escondido has been subject to the same inflationary pressures as the rest of Mexico (and the world), so it isn't the dirt-cheap backpacker haven it used to be. Still, it remains the best overall beach value in Mexico, and it retains the same casual beach feel that has drawn people here for decades. Although it has long been known as one of the world's top surf sites, today its appeal is broadening: alternative therapies, great vegetarian restaurants, hip nightlife, affordable hotels and restaurants, and some of Mexico's best coffee shops. It's for those whose priorities include the dimensions of the surf break (big), the temperature of the beer (cold), the strength of the coffee (espresso), and the optimal tanning angle. The young and very aware crowd that comes here measures time by the tides, and the pace is relaxed.

The location of "Puerto," as the locals call it, makes it an ideal jumping-off point for ecological explorations of neighboring jungle and estuary sanctuaries, as well as indigenous mountain settlements. Increasingly, it attracts those seeking both spiritual and physical renewal, with abundant massage and bodywork services, yoga classes, and exceptional and varied healthful dining options.

People come from the U.S., Canada, and Europe to stay for weeks and even months. Expats have migrated from Los Cabos, Acapulco, and Puerto Vallarta seeking what originally attracted them to their former homes—stellar beaches, friendly locals, and reasonable prices. Added pleasures include an absence of beach vendors and timeshare sales, an abundance of English speakers, and terrific, inexpensive dining and nightlife.

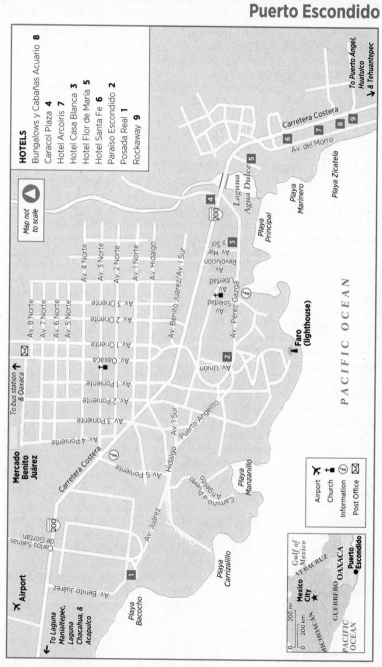

HOTELS

Bungalows y Cabañas Acuario **8**
Caracol Plaza **4**
Hotel Arcoíris **7**
Hotel Casa Blanca **3**
Hotel Flor de María **5**
Hotel Santa Fe **6**
Paraíso Escondido **2**
Posada Real **1**
Rockaway **9**

Map not to scale

Carretera Costera

Av. del Morro

Laguna Agua Dulce

Playa Zicatela

Playa Marinero

Playa Principal

PACIFIC OCEAN

Av. 4 Norte
Av. 3 Norte
Av. 2 Norte
Av. 1 Norte
Av. Hidalgo

Av. 8 Norte
Av. 7 Norte
Av. 6 Norte
Av. 5 Norte

Av. 3 Oriente
Av. 2 Oriente
Av. 1 Oriente

Av. Benito Juárez/Av. 1 Sur

Av. Revolución
Av. Mar y Sol

Av. Libertad
Av. Pérez Gasga
Av. Soledad

Faro (lighthouse)

Av. Oaxaca
Av. 1 Poniente
Av. 2 Poniente
Av. 3 Poniente

Av. Unión

Mercado Benito Juárez

To bus station & Oaxaca

Av. 4 Poniente

Carretera Costera

Av. 5 Poniente

Av. 1 Sur
Hidalgo
Puerto Angelito

Playa Angelito
Playa Manzanillo

Camino a Puerto Angelito

Airport

To Laguna Manialtepec, Laguna Chacahua, & Acapulco

Carlos Salinas de Gortari

Av. Juárez

Av. Benito Juárez

Playa Bacocho

Playa Carrizalillo

To Puerto Angel, Huatulco, & Tehuantepec

Airport ✈
Church ✚
Information ⓘ
Post Office ⊠

Gulf of Mexico
VERACRUZ
MICHOACAN
GUERRERO OAXACA
Puerto Escondido
Mexico City ★
PACIFIC OCEAN

0   200 mi
0   200 km

10

ACAPULCO | Puerto Escondido

This is a real place, not a produced resort. A significant number of visitors are European travelers, and it's common to hear a variety of languages on the beach and in the bars. Puerto Escondido is also a favorite among Mexican college students. Solo travelers will probably make new friends within an hour of arriving. There are still surfers here, lured by the best break in Mexico, but espresso cafes and live music are becoming just as ubiquitous.

The city has been dismissed as a colony of former hippies and settled backpackers, but it's so much more. It's entirely possible that those who favor Puerto are just trying to keep the place true to its name (*escondido* means "hidden") and undiscovered by tourists. Don't let them trick you—visit, and soon, before it, too, changes.

Essentials

GETTING THERE & DEPARTING

BY PLANE   Aerotucán (©/fax **954/582-3461**) operates daily morning flights between Puerto Escondido and Oaxaca (no online reservations; best to go through a travel agent). **Volaris** (© **866/988-3527** in the U.S.), which now has six U.S. gateways and a quasi-codeshare arrangement with Southwest, has been tossing around the idea of adding flights between Oaxaca and Puerto Escondido for more than a year, but the start date keeps getting pushed back.

If flights to Puerto Escondido are booked, another option is flying into **Huatulco** on a scheduled or charter flight. **Interjet** (© **866/285-9525** in the U.S.) flies between Mexico City and Huatulco daily. This is especially viable if your destination is Puerto Angel, which lies between Puerto Escondido and Huatulco. An airport taxi costs about 900 pesos to Puerto Angel, and approximately 1,500 pesos to Puerto Escondido. If you can find a local taxi rather than a government-chartered cab, you can reduce these fares by about 50%, including the payment of a 60 pesos mandatory airport exit tax. There is frequent bus service between the three destinations.

The Puerto Escondido **airport** (airport code: PXM) is about 4km (2½ miles) north of the center of town, near Playa Bacocho. Vans from the airport to town charge 1,300 pesos. The *colectivo* (**minibus**) to hotels costs 40 pesos per person. **Aerotransportes de Pasajeros Turistas de Oaxaca** sells *colectivo* tickets to the airport via **Turismo Dimar Travel Agency** (©/fax **954/582-0737**, -2305), on Avenida Pérez Gasga (the pedestrian-only zone), next to Hotel Casa Blanca. A minibus picks you up at your hotel and costs 50 pesos per person. To get to town for just 45 pesos, catch the second-class "Sur" bus on the street right in front of the airport.

BY CAR   From Oaxaca, **Hwy. 175** via Pochutla is the least bumpy road. The 240km (149-mile) trip takes 5 to 6 hours. **Hwy. 200** from Acapulco is a good road, although stretches of it are dirt only, and numerous speed bumps and army checkpoints may impede progress. It should take about 8 hours to travel. This stretch of road has been the site of numerous car and bus hijackings and robberies at night in recent years—travel only during the day.

From Salina Cruz to Puerto Escondido is a 5-hour drive, past the Bahías de Huatulco and the turnoff for Puerto Angel. The road is paved but can be rutty during the rainy season. The trip from Huatulco to Puerto Escondido takes just over 2 hours; you can easily hire a taxi for a fixed rate of about 550 pesos an hour.

BY BUS   Buses run frequently to and from Acapulco and Oaxaca, and south along the coast to and from Huatulco and Pochutla, the transit hub for Puerto Angel. The main bus station for **Estrella Blanca, Oaxaca Pacífico,** and **Estrella Roja** is the **Central Camionera,** just north of the city center. First-class buses run to Huatulco,

Oaxaca, and Mexico City. Several buses also leave daily for Pochutla, Salina Cruz (5 hr.), and Oaxaca (7 hr. via second-class bus). **Cristóbal Colón** buses (© **954/582-1073**) serve Salina Cruz, Tuxtla Gutiérrez, San Cristóbal de las Casas, and Oaxaca.

Minibuses from Pochutla or Huatulco will let you off anywhere, including the spot where Pérez Gasga leads down to the pedestrian-only zone.

If you're arriving from Oaxaca City, the speediest buses to Puerto Escondido—6 hours away over a tortuous road—leave from the *terminal de segunda clase* (second-class terminal) Armenta y López 721, across from the Red Cross. Two lines serve the route: Pacífico Oaxaca and Estrella del Valle. Many people who go to Puerto Escondido on these buses say that if they had it to do over, they'd fly. Motion sickness is the main reason; there are hundreds of curves through the mountains.

The **Viajes Atlántida** agency, at Armenta y López 621, intersection with La Noria (© **951/514-7077**), offers daily service from Oaxaca City to Pochutla in Suburbans. The Suburbans are faster than the bus. There are 10 runs daily (5–6 hr.; 140 pesos). From Pochutla, you can catch a *colectivo* (Volkswagen van) to Puerto Escondido, Huatulco, or Puerto Angel (which run 1–1½ hr.). You should buy your tickets in advance. The agency is open daily from 5:30am to 11:30pm.

ORIENTATION

VISITOR INFORMATION   A tourist kiosk at the west end of the Adoquín (in the town center) is open Monday through Saturday from 9am to 2pm and 4 to 6pm. Gina, who has been in charge there for 18 years, is quite possibly the most helpful and friendliest tourism officer in all of Mexico. She also has her own part-time business conducting walking tours at 8am every Saturday.

CITY LAYOUT   Looking out on the Bahía Principal and its beach, to your left you'll see the eastern end of the bay, consisting of a small beach, **Playa Marineros,** followed by rocks jutting into the sea. Beyond this is **Playa Zicatela,** unmistakably the main surfing beach. Zicatela Beach has come into its own as the most popular area for visitors, with restaurants, bungalows, surf shops, and hotels, well back from the shoreline. The west side of the bay, to your right, is about 1.5km long (1 mile), with a lighthouse and a long stretch of fine sand. Beaches on this end are not quite as accessible by land, but hotels are overcoming this difficulty by constructing beach clubs reached by steep private roads and jeep shuttles.

The town of Puerto Escondido has roughly an east-west orientation, with the long Zicatela Beach turning sharply southeast. Residential areas behind Zicatela Beach tend to have unpaved streets; the older town, with paved streets, is north of the Carretera Costera (Hwy. 200). The streets are numbered; Avenida Oaxaca divides east *(oriente)* from west *(poniente),* and Avenida Hidalgo divides north *(norte)* from south *(sur).*

South of this is the original **tourist zone,** through which Avenida Pérez Gasga makes a loop. Part of this loop is a paved pedestrian-only zone, known locally as the Adoquín, after the hexagonal bricks used in its paving. Hotels, shops, restaurants, bars, travel agencies, and other services are all here. In the morning, taxis, delivery trucks, and private vehicles may drive here, but at noon it closes to all but foot traffic.

Avenida Pérez Gasga angles down from the highway at the east end; on the west, where the Adoquín terminates, it climbs in a wide northward curve to cross the highway, after which it becomes Avenida Oaxaca.

The beaches—Playa Principal in the center of town and Marineros and Zicatela, southeast of the town center—are connected. It's easy to walk from one to the other, crossing behind the separating rocks. Puerto Angelito, Carrizalillo, and Bacocho beaches are west of town and accessible by road or water. Playa Bacocho is where you'll find the few more expensive hotels.

GETTING AROUND Almost everything is within walking distance of the Adoquín. **Taxis** around town are inexpensive; call © **954/582-0990** for service. It's also easy to hire a boat and possible to walk beside the sea from the Playa Principal to the tiny beach of Puerto Angelito, though it's a bit of a hike.

[Fast FACTS] PUERTO ESCONDIDO

Area Code The telephone area code is **954.**

Currency Exchange Banamex, Bancomer, Banorte, and HSBC all have branches in town, and all will change money during business hours; hours vary, but you can generally find one of the above open Monday through Saturday from 9am to 3pm. ATMs are also available, as are currency-exchange offices.

Note: It has been getting harder to exchange cash in Puerto, and the only place that still cashes traveler's checks is HSBC, from 9am to noon only.

Drugstore **Farmacía de Más Ahorro,** Avenida 1 Norte at Avenida 2 Poniente (© **954/582-1911**), is open from 7am to 3am.

Hospital **Unidad Médico–Quirúrgica del Sur,** Av. Oaxaca 706 (© **954/582-1288**), is the town's

largest hospital, offering 24-hour emergency services and an English-speaking staff and doctor.

Internet Access On Zicatela Beach, **Internet Acuario** is a small, busy Internet service at the entrance to the Bungalows & Cabañas Acuario, Calle de Morro s/n (© **954/582-0788**). It's open daily from 8am to 10pm and charges 15 pesos per hour.

Post Office The *correo,* on Avenida Oaxaca at the corner of Avenida 7 Norte (© **954/582-0959**), is open Monday through Friday from 8am to 4:30pm.

Safety Depending on whom you talk to, you need to be wary of potential beach muggings, primarily at night. Lighting at Playa Principal and Playa Zicatela has caused the crime rate to drop considerably. Local

residents say most incidents happen after tourists overindulge and then go for a midnight stroll along the beach. Puerto is so casual that it's an easy place to let your guard down. Don't carry valuables, and use common sense and normal precautions. Also, respect the power of the magnificent waves here. Drownings occur all too often.

Seasons Season designations are somewhat arbitrary, but most consider high season to be from mid-December to January, around and during Easter week, July and August, and other school and business vacations.

Telephones Numerous businesses offer long-distance telephone service. Many are along the Adoquín; several accept credit cards.

Where to Stay

The rates posted below do not include the 18% tax.

EXPENSIVE

Posada Real ☺ On a cliff top overlooking the beach, the expanse of manicured lawn that backs this all-inclusive hotel is one of the most popular places in town for a sunset cocktail. The smallish standard rooms are less enticing than the hotel grounds (the six "extra large" rooms are preferable for families). A big plus here is Coco's Beach Club, with a 1km (⅔-mile) stretch of soft-sand beach, large swimming pool, playground, and bar with occasional live music. This is a great place for families, and it's open to the public (nonguests pay 120 pesos to enter). The hotel lies 5 minutes from the airport and about the same from Puerto Escondido's tourist zone, but you'll need a taxi to get to town. In high season, it may have vacancies when Puerto Escondido is otherwise fully booked.

Av. Benito Juárez s/n, Fracc. Bacocho, 71980 Puerto Escondido, Oax. www.posadareal.com.mx. ⓒ **800/528-1234** in the U.S., or 954/582-0237. Fax 954/582-0192. 100 units. High season $310 double; low season $123 double. AE, MC, V. Free parking. **Amenities:** 2 restaurants; 2 bars; beach club w/food service; children's playground; 2 outdoor pools; room service; tennis court. *In room:* A/C, TV, hair dryer, Wi-Fi.

MODERATE

Caracol Plaza This hotel sits on a small hill overlooking the bay. Guest rooms feature high ceilings, arched French windows, lovely wood furnishings, and small bathrooms. Ask for a room with a bay view. The large white hotel has a Mexican restaurant and a *palapa* bar with what may be the best sunset-watching spot in all of Puerto Escondido. The friendly staff will help you with your travel plans. The hotel's drawback is that it's across the main highway from the beach and about a 10-minute walk to the Adoquín. At press time, an additional 150 rooms were being constructed.

7a. Oriente s/n y 1a. Sur, Col. Marinero, 71980 Puerto Escondido, Oax. ⓒ **954/582-3814.** 80 units. High season $165 double; low season $149 double. MC, V. Free parking. **Amenities:** Restaurant; bar; outdoor pool; kids' pool. *In room:* A/C, TV, minibar, Wi-Fi.

Hotel Santa Fe ★★★ 📷 The Santa Fe is one of the best values in Mexico, off Hwy. 200 about 1km (⅔ mile) southeast of the town center, at the curve in the road where Marineros and Zicatela beaches join—a prime sunset-watching spot. The three-story hacienda-style buildings surrounding two courtyard swimming pools have clay-tiled stairs, archways, and blooming bougainvillea. Rooms feature large tile bathrooms, colonial furnishings, hand-woven fabrics, and both air-conditioning and ceiling fans. Most have a balcony or terrace, and the master and presidential suites enjoy ocean views. Bungalows are next to the hotel; each has a living room, kitchen, and bedroom with two double beds. The restaurant (see "Where to Eat," below), one of the best on the southern Pacific coast, is supplied by its own farm.

Calle del Morro (Apdo. Postal 96), 71980 Puerto Escondido, Oax. www.hotelsantafe.com.mx. ⓒ **800/712-7057** in the U.S., or 954/582-0170. 61 units, 8 bungalows. High season $158 double, $196 junior suite, $261 suite, $168 bungalow; low season $103 double, $129 junior suite, $210 suite, $112 bungalow. AE, MC, V. Free parking. **Amenities:** Restaurant; bar; babysitting; Internet kiosk; 3 outdoor pools. *In room:* A/C, TV.

Paraíso Escondido ★★ 📷 This eclectic inn is hidden away on a shady street a couple of short blocks from the Adoquín and Playa Principal. It's very popular with families and has a small, intimate feel. A curious collection of Mexican folk art, masks, religious art, and paintings makes this an exercise in Mexican magic realism. An inviting pool—surrounded by gardens, Adirondack chairs, and a fountain—affords a commanding view of the bay. The colonial-style rooms each have one double and two twin beds, tile floors, a small bathroom, and a cozy balcony or terrace with French doors. The suites have much plusher decor than the rooms, with recessed lighting, desks set into bay windows, living areas, and large private balconies overlooking the bay. The penthouse suite has a kitchenette, a tile chessboard inlaid in the floor, and murals adorning the walls—it is the owners' former apartment.

Calle Unión 10, 71980 Puerto Escondido, Oax. www.hotelparaisoescondido.net. ℰ **954/582-0444.** Fax 954/582-2767. 25 units. High season $97 double, $135 suite, $175 penthouse suite; low season $65 double, $75 suite, $95 penthouse suite. MC, V. Free parking. **Amenities:** Restaurant; bar; outdoor pool; wading pool. *In room:* A/C, TV.

INEXPENSIVE

Bungalows y Cabañas Acuario   Facing Zicatela Beach, this surfer's sanctuary offers budget accommodations plus an on-site gym, surf shop, and Internet cafe. The two-story hotel and bungalows surround a pool shaded by great palms. Rooms are small and basic; bungalows offer basic kitchen facilities but don't have air-conditioning. The cabañas lack mosquito nets, so you'll need to cover yourself with bug spray from head to toe. There are several rooms with air-conditioning, which offer a far more comfortable night's sleep. The adjoining retail area has public telephones, money exchange, a pharmacy, an Internet cafe, and a vegetarian restaurant. If you're traveling during low season, once you're there you can probably negotiate a better deal than the rates listed below.

Calle del Morro s/n, 71980 Puerto Escondido, Oax. www.oaxaca-mio.com/bunacuario.htm. ℰ **954/582-0357.** Fax 954/582-1027. 40 units. High season 600 pesos double, 700 pesos double with A/C, 1,100 pesos bungalow; low season 250 pesos double, 300 pesos double with A/C, 450 pesos bungalow. MC, V. Free parking. **Amenities:** Restaurant; well-equipped gym; Internet cafe; Jacuzzi; outdoor pool. *In room:* No phone except in suite and 2 bungalows.

Hotel Arcoiris ★ 🏄   Rooms at the Arcoiris occupy a three-story colonial-style house that faces Zicatela Beach. Each is simple yet comfortable, with a spacious terrace or balcony with hangers for hammocks to rent—all have great views, but the upstairs ones are better (12 units include kitchenettes). Beds come with mosquito nets, and bedspreads were made using beautifully worked Oaxacan textiles. The restaurant/bar runs one of the most popular happy hours in town, daily from 5:30 to 7:30pm, with live music during high season.

Calle del Morro s/n, Playa Zicatela, 71980 Puerto Escondido, Oax. www.hotel-arcoiris.com.mx. ℰ/fax **954/582-2344.** 35 units. High season $63–$90 double, $123–$135 double with kitchen; low season $50–$70 double, $75 double with kitchen. Extra person $4. Rates higher at Easter and Christmas. MC, V. Free parking. **Amenities:** Restaurant; bar; babysitting; gym; outdoor pool; wading pool. *In room:* No phone.

Hotel Casa Blanca ★ 🏄   If you want to be in the heart of the Adoquín, this is your best bet for excellent value and ample accommodations. The courtyard pool and adjacent *palapa* make great places to hide away and enjoy a margarita or a book from the hotel's exchange rack. The bright, simply furnished rooms offer a choice of bed combinations, but all have at least two beds and a fan. Some rooms have both air-conditioning and a minifridge. The best rooms have a balcony overlooking the action in the street below, but light sleepers should consider a room in the back. Some rooms accommodate up to five. This is an excellent and economical choice for families.

Av. Pérez Gasga 905, 71980 Puerto Escondido, Oax. www.hotelcasablanca-oaxaca.com. ℰ **954/582-0168.** 25 units. 420–620 pesos double; 600–900 pesos suite (up to 5 people). MC, V. Limited street parking. **Amenities:** Outdoor pool; smoke-free rooms. *In room:* A/C (in some), fan, TV, minifridge (in some), no phone, Wi-Fi.

Hotel Flor de María ★★   Though not right on the beach, the Flor de María offers a welcoming place to stay. This cheery three-story hotel faces the ocean, which you can see from the rooftop. Built around a garden courtyard, the rooms keep their cool through the heat of the day; each is colorfully decorated with beautiful *trompe l'oeil* still-lifes and landscapes. Rooms have double beds with orthopedic mattresses, and views that vary between the ocean, courtyard, and exterior. On the roof are a small pool, a shaded hammock terrace, and an open-air bar (1–8pm during high season) with cable TV. It's a great sunset spot. The hotel lies about .5km (⅓ mile) from the Adoquín, 60m (197 ft.) up a quiet cobblestone road from Marineros Beach on Calle Marinero at the eastern end of the beach.

Playa Marineros, 71980 Puerto Escondido, Oax. www.mexonline.com/flordemaria.htm. ✆ **954/582-0536.** Fax 954/582-2617. 24 units. High season 500–700 pesos double; low season 400–600 pesos double. Ask about off-season long-term discounts. MC, V. Limited covered parking. **Amenities:** Restaurant (p. 384); bar; small gym; small outdoor pool; Wi-Fi.

Rockaway   Facing Playa Zicatela, this surfer's sanctuary offers very clean, cheap accommodations geared for surfers, including newer hotel-style rooms and older cabañas. Every unit is equipped with a private bathroom, as well as ceiling fan and mosquito net. The good-size swimming pool and *palapa* bar form a popular gathering spot. The cabañas in the older section do not have hot water; those in the newer section feature air-conditioning, hot water, and cable TV. The courtyard has a festive and inviting vibe, with music and laughter lasting well into the night. *Note:* One large cabaña accommodates up to eight people.

Calle del Morro s/n, 71980 Puerto Escondido, Oax. www.hotelrockaway.com. ✆ **954/582-0668.** 14 units. High season 750 pesos double, 650–1,500 pesos cabaña; low season 500 pesos double, 250–1,000 pesos cabaña. No credit cards. Free parking. **Amenities:** Bar; outdoor pool. *In room:* A/C (in some), fans, TV (in some), no phone.

Where to Eat

In addition to the places listed below, a Puerto Escondido tradition is the *palapa* restaurants on Zicatela Beach, for early morning surfer breakfasts or casual dining and drinking at night. One of the most popular is **Los Tíos,** offering very reasonable prices and surfer-size portions. *Note:* Pascal, the French restaurant long recommended for its enchanting location and terrace on the edge of the bay, has been sold and will be a Mexican restaurant by the time you read this.

MODERATE

Restaurant Santa Fe ★★★ 🍴 INTERNATIONAL   The Hotel Santa Fe's beachside restaurant sits under a welcoming *palapa,* with the gentle waves crashing just in front. The excellent fish and seafood selections include crayfish, red snapper, tuna, octopus, and giant shrimp prepared any way you like. More traditional dishes, such as Oaxaca-style enchiladas with homemade tortillas and *mole*, are also available. The restaurant offers numerous vegetarian and vegan selections, including chiles rellenos with cheese, rice, and beans; and breaded tofu with salad and rice. You can request that almost any dish on the menu be made with tofu in place of meat or fish, and they will do it right. The food is served on beautiful hand-painted ceramic ware, and the organic coffee is grown at the hotel's own farm. Elaborate weekend breakfast buffets cost around $13, featuring fresh local specialties. Even if you don't plan to dine, this is an ideal spot to come for a sunset cocktail and perhaps an hors d'oeuvre.

In the Hotel Santa Fe (p. 381), Calle del Morro s/n. ✆ **954/582-0170.** www.hotelsantafe.com.mx. Breakfast $4–$8; main courses $6–$27. AE, MC, V. Daily 7am–10pm.

INEXPENSIVE

Cafecito ★ 🍴 FRENCH PASTRY/MEXICAN   Carmen started with a small bakery in Puerto, and when she opened this cafe years ago on Zicatela Beach, with the motto "Big waves, strong coffee!," it quickly eclipsed the bake shop and now is her main business. It still features all the attractions of her early *patisserie*, with the added attraction of serving full meals all day long under a big *palapa* facing the beach. Giant shrimp dinners cost less than 120 pesos, and creative daily specials are always a sure bet. An oversize mug of cappuccino is 220 pesos and a mango éclair—worth any price—is a steal, at 125 pesos. Smoothies, natural juices, and a variety of coffee selections are available.

Calle del Morro s/n, Playa Zicatela. ℂ **954/582-0516.** Pastries 15-25 pesos; breakfast 45-55 pesos; main courses 35-95 pesos. No credit cards. Daily 6am-10:30pm.

El Jardín ★★ ⏺ ITALIAN This charming restaurant facing Zicatela Beach is popular for its generous use of fresh, healthy ingredients, including lots of olive oil, tomatoes, and Italian vinaigrette. The service is relaxed to extremely slow. The choices are delicious: New York–style pizza, vegetarian sandwiches, crepes, pastas, and large creative salads, such as the *Rey de Reyes*, with spinach, tomato, avocado, pickled eggplant, brown rice, and tofu. Ensalada Caprichosa consists of fresh-cut tomatoes, savory pesto, and salty anchovies atop crisp grilled eggplant slices. There's also a selection of fresh fish and seafood. The extensive menu includes fruit smoothies, Italian and Mexican coffees, herbal teas, and a complete juice bar. The restaurant makes its own tempeh, tofu, pastas, and whole-grain breads. The tiramisu is to die for.

Calle del Morro s/n, Playa Zicatela. ℂ **954/110-5408.** Main courses 60-150 pesos. No credit cards. Daily 8am-11pm.

Flor de María ★★ INTERNATIONAL This open-air dining room near the beach is particularly popular with expats and locals. The menu changes daily but always includes fresh fish, grilled meats, and pasta dishes. Come at opening time to get your choice of table; it fills up in a hurry once the sun sets—even so, the small staff hustles to keep the service prompt. The restaurant sits in the Hotel Flor de María, just steps from the center of town and up a cobblestone road from Playa Marinero at the eastern end of the beach.

In Hotel Flor de María (p. 382), Playa Marinero. ℂ **954/582-0536.** Breakfast 35-50 pesos; main courses 50-165 pesos. No credit cards. Daily 8-11am and 6-9pm (no dinner Tues). Closed May–June and Sept-Oct.

La Galería ★ ITALIAN At the east end of the Adoquín, La Galería offers a satisfying range of eats in a cool, creative setting, with dark-wood beams and contemporary works by local artists on the walls. Specialties include homemade pasta and brick-oven pizza (the five-cheese pizza is especially delicious), but burgers and steaks are also available. Or try something light and refreshing, like the crisp grapefruit and shrimp salad, which visitors and locals alike rave about. Cappuccino and espresso, plus desserts such as apple empanadas with vanilla ice cream, finish the meal. Continental and American breakfasts are available in the morning.

Av. Pérez Gasga s/n. ℂ **954/582-2039.** Breakfast 35-55 pesos; main courses 55-120 pesos. No credit cards. Daily 8am-11pm.

Las Margaritas ★ ⏺ MEXICAN One of the tastiest Mexican restaurants in town, Las Margaritas lies off a busy street, a short drive from the Adoquín. The casual, open-air terrace offers wood tables and chairs, as well as an open kitchen, bar, and tortilla stand, where you can watch as Oaxacan regional dishes are prepared as though you were in a family's home, from empanadas and quesadillas to fish and seafood brochettes, steaks, and *mole* that explodes with flavor.

8 Norte s/n (1 block from the market). ℂ **954/582-0212.** www.oaxaca-mio.com/lasmargaritas.htm. Breakfasts 33-50 pesos; main courses 45-150 pesos. MC, V. Daily 8am-6pm.

Activities on & off the Beach

BEACHES **Playa Principal,** where small boats are available for fishing and tour services, and **Playa Marineros,** adjacent to the town center on a deep bay, are the best swimming beaches. Beach chairs and sun shades rent for about 55 pesos, which may be waived if you order food or drinks from the restaurants that offer them. **Playa Zicatela,** which has lifeguards and is known as the "Mexican Pipeline," adjoins Playa Marineros and extends southeast for several kilometers. The surfing part of Zicatela, with large curling waves, is about 4km (2½ miles) from the town center. Due to the size and strength of the waves (particularly in summer), it's not a swimming beach, and only experienced surfers should attempt to ride Zicatela's powerful waves. Stadium-style lighting has been installed in both of these areas, in an attempt to crack down on nighttime beach muggings. It has diminished the appeal of the Playa Principal restaurants—patrons now look into the bright lights rather than at the sea. Lifeguard service has recently been added to Playa Zicatela, although the lifeguards are known to go on strike. The best beach for learning how to surf is called **La Punta.**

Barter with one of the fishermen on the main beach for a ride to **Playa Manzanillo** and **Puerto Angelito,** two beaches separated by a rocky outcropping. Here, and at other small coves just west of town, swimming is safe and the overall pace is calmer than in town. You'll also find *palapas,* hammock rentals, and snorkeling equipment. The clear blue water is perfect for snorkeling. Local entrepreneurs cook fresh fish, tamales, and other Mexican dishes right at the beach. Puerto Angelito is also accessible by a road that's a short distance from town, so it tends to be busier. You can also take a cab to the cliff above **Playa Carrizalillo** and descend a hundred stone stairs to a calm and secluded swimming beach. **Playa Bacocho** is on a shallow cove (dangerous for swimming) farther northwest and is best reached by taxi or boat than on foot. It's also the location of the Villa Sol Beach Club. A charge of 50 pesos gives you access to pools, food and beverage service, and facilities.

SURFING **Zicatela Beach,** 2.5km (1½ miles) southeast of Puerto Escondido's town center, is a world-class surf spot. A surfing competition in August and Fiesta Puerto Escondido, held for at least 3 days each November, celebrate Puerto Escondido's renowned waves. There is also a surfing exhibition and competition in February, for Carnaval. Gina at the tourist kiosk can supply details. Beginning surfers often start at Playa Marineros before graduating to Zicatela's awesome waves; if you're not a surfer but want to be and you're at Carizalillo, look for Escuela de Surf Oasis. Intermediate surfers do go out at **La Punta,** at the southernmost end of Playa Zicatela, but waves and strong currents make Zicatela dangerous for swimming.

NESTING RIDLEY TURTLES The beaches around Puerto Escondido and Puerto Angel are nesting grounds for the endangered Ridley turtle. In summer, lucky tourists may see the turtles laying eggs or observe the hatchlings trekking to the sea.

Escobilla Beach, near Puerto Escondido, seems to be the favored nesting grounds of the Ridley turtle. In 1991, the Mexican government established the Centro Mexicano la Tortuga, known locally as the **Turtle Museum.** On view are examples of all species of marine turtles living in Mexico, plus six species of freshwater turtles and two species of land turtles. The center (© **958/584-3376;** www.centro mexicanodelatortuga.org) lies on **Mazunte Beach ★**, near the town of the same name about an hour and a half from Puerto Escondido. Hours are Tuesday through Saturday 10am to 6:30pm, and Sunday 10am to 4:30pm; suggested donation is 25 pesos. If you come between July and September, ask to join an overnight expedition

ECOTOURS & OTHER adventurous explorations

An excellent provider of ecologically oriented tour services is **Rutas de Aventura ★**, Hotel Santa Fe (① **954/582-0170;** www.hotelsantafe.com.mx). Gustavo Boltjes speaks fluent English and offers kayak adventures, hiking excursions, and mountain-bike tours. He also leads waterfall hikes, camping trips, and overnight agritourism adventures to learn about local farming and organic coffee production, including trips to a local coffee plantation that has been built upon principles of environmental sustainability. For more, see www.fincalasnieves.com.mx.

Viajes Dimar Travel Agency, on the landward side just inside the Adoquín (① **954/582-2305;** fax 954/582-1551; www.viajesdimar.com; daily 8am–9pm), is another excellent source of information and can arrange all types of tours and travel. Manager Gaudencio Díaz Martinez speaks English and can arrange individualized tours or more organized ones, such as **Michael Malone's Hidden Voyages Ecotours** (www.peleewings.ca/ecco.php). Malone, a Canadian ornithologist, leads dawn and sunset trips in high season (winter) to **Manialtepec Lagoon,** a bird-filled mangrove lagoon about 20km (12 miles) northwest of Puerto Escondido. The kayak tour (750 pesos) includes a stop on a secluded beach for a swim.

One of Dimar's most popular all-day tours offered by both companies is to **Chacahua Lagoon National Park,** about 65km (40 miles) west. It costs $45 with Dimar, $52 with Michael Malone. These are true ecotours—small groups treading lightly. You visit a beautiful sandy spit of beach and the lagoon, which has incredible bird life and flowers, including black orchids. Crocodiles are sometimes spotted here, too. Locals provide fresh barbecued fish on the beach. If you know Spanish and get information from the tourism office, it's possible to stay overnight under a small *palapa,* but bring insect repellent.

An interesting and slightly out-of-the-ordinary excursion is **Aventura Submarina,** Av. Pérez Gasga 601A, in front of the tourism office (① **954/582-2353**). Jorge, who speaks fluent English and is a certified scuba instructor, guides individuals and small groups of qualified divers along the Coco trench just offshore. The price is $60 for a two-tank dive. This outfit offers a refresher scuba course at no extra charge. Jorge also arranges deep-sea fishing, surfing, and trips to lesser-known nearby swimming beaches. **Omar** (① **954/559-4406**) runs dolphin-watching tours in high season.

Fishermen keep their colorful *pangas* (small boats) on the beach beside the Adoquín. A **fisherman's tour** around the coastline in a *panga* costs about 400 pesos, but a ride to Puerto Angelito beaches is only 55 pesos. Most hotels offer or will gladly arrange tours to meet your needs. The waters here are filled with marlin, tuna, and swordfish.

to Escobilla Beach to see mother turtles scuttle to the beach to lay their eggs. The museum is near a unique shop that sells excellent naturally produced soaps, shampoos, bath oils, and other personal-care products. All are packaged by the community as part of a project to replace lost income from turtle poaching. Buses go to Mazunte from Puerto Angel about every half-hour, and a taxi ride is 60 pesos. You can fit this in with a trip to Zipolite Beach (see "A Trip to Puerto Angel: Backpacking Beach Haven," below). Buses from Puerto Escondido don't stop in Mazunte; you can cover the 65km (40 miles) in a taxi or rental car.

The tourism cooperative at **Ventanilla** provides another chance to get up close to the turtles. The villagers here have created their own ecological reserve that encompasses a nearby lagoon, inhabited by crocodiles and dozens of species of birds, and a beach where sea turtles lay their eggs. There's also a great organic restaurant called Maiz Azul. A boat ride to see the crocs costs 50 pesos. Turtles lay their eggs here year-round, although summer is the prime season, so there's always a possibility that a nest is about to hatch. Helping the locals release the eggs is free. Ventanilla is a 30-peso taxi ride from Mazunte or the nearby beaches, but if you're planning to stay past sunset, ask your driver to wait; it's a long walk in the dark to the main highway.

GUIDED WALKING TOURS For local information and guided walking tours, visit the **Oaxaca Tourist Bureau** booth (✆ **954/582-1186;** ginainpuerto@yahoo. com). It's just west of the pedestrian street. Ask for Gina, who speaks excellent English and is incredibly helpful. She provides information with a smile, and many say she knows more about Puerto Escondido than any other person. On her days off, Gina offers walking tours to the market and to little-known nearby ruins. Filled with history and information on native vegetation, a day with Gina promises fun, adventure, and insight into local culture.

A Mixtec ceremonial center was discovered in early 2000, just east of Puerto Escondido, and is considered a major discovery. The site covers many acres with about 10 pyramids and a ball court, with the pyramids appearing as hills covered in vegetation. A number of large carved stones have been found. Situated on a hilltop, it commands a spectacular view of Puerto Escondido and the Pacific coast. The large archaeological site spans several privately owned plots of land and is not open to the public, although Gina has been known to offer a guided walking tour to it.

Shopping

During high season, businesses and shops are generally open all day. During low season, many close between 2 and 4pm.

The Adoquín holds a row of tourist shops selling straw hats, postcards, and T-shirts, plus a few excellent shops featuring Guatemalan, Oaxacan, and Balinese clothing and art. You can also get a tattoo or rent surfboards and boogie boards. Interspersed among the shops, hotels, restaurants, and bars are pharmacies and minimarkets. The largest of these is **El Dragon Store** on Av. Pérez Gasga. It sells anything you'd need for a day at the beach, plus phone (Ladatel) cards and Cuban cigars.

The first surf shop in Puerto Escondido, **Central Surf** (✆ **954/582-2285;** www. centralsurfshop.com), on Zicatela Beach, Calle del Morro s/n, rents and sells surfboards, offers surf lessons, and sells related gear, including custom-made surf trunks. Board rentals usually go for about $10 to $20 per day, with lessons available for $60 for 2 hours. In front of the Rockaway Resort on Zicatela Beach, there's a 24-hour **minisuper** (no phone) that sells the necessities: beer, suntan lotion, and basic food.

Also of interest is **Bazar Santa Fe ★★**, Hotel Santa Fe lobby, Calle del Morro s/n, Zicatela Beach (✆ **954/582-0170**), a small shop that sells antiques, vintage Oaxacan embroidered clothing, jewelry, religious artifacts, and gourmet organic coffee grown on the hotel's own farm. Right next to Central Surf, **Bikini Brazil,** Playa Zicatela, Calle del Morro s/n (✆ **954/582-2555**), you'll find the hottest bikinis under the sun imported from Brazil, land of the *tanga* (string bikini). Another cool beach shop on Playa Zicatela, Calle del Moro s/n, is **Trapos y Harapos** (✆ **954/582-0759**), which sells bathing suits, sandals, and surfboards.

Puerto Escondido After Dark

Sunset-watching is a ritual to plan your days around, and good lookout points abound. At Zicatela, you can watch the sun descend behind the surfers, and at **La Galería,** located on the third floor of the Hotel Arcoiris, you can catch up on local gossip while enjoying a sundowner. It has a nightly happy hour (with live music during high season) from 5:30 to 7:30pm. Other great sunset spots are the **Hotel Santa Fe,** at the junction of Zicatela and Marineros beaches, and the rooftop bar of **Hotel Flor de María.** For a more tranquil, romantic setting, take a cab or walk a half-hour or so west to the cliff-top lawn of the **Hotel Posada Real.**

Puerto's nightlife will satisfy anyone dedicated to late nights and good music. Most nightspots are open until 3am or until customers leave. The Adoquín offers an ample selection of clubs. Favorites include **Wipeout** (© **954/582-2302**), a multilevel club that packs in the crowds until 4am, and **Blue Station,** open from 9pm to 1am.

On Zicatela Beach, **Bar Fly** (no phone) sits upstairs overlooking the beach and features a DJ spinning Latin, retro, and electronic hits. It's open nightly from 9pm to 3am on Calle de Moro s/n. **Casa Babylon** (no phone), a few doors down, is a bohemian beach bar with a book exchange and table games. It's open nightly from 7pm until late and has a hip surfer vibe. There's a movie theater on Playa Zicatela called **Cinemar** (© **954/582-2288**). It's a pretty simple setup consisting of a small bookstore, a large screen, and some beach chairs. It serves up popcorn and movies nightly, and also rents surfboards during the day.

A Trip to Puerto Angel: Backpacking Beach Haven

Seventy-four kilometers (46 miles) southeast of Puerto Escondido and 50km (31 miles) northwest of the Bays of Huatulco lies the tiny fishing port of **Puerto Angel** (*Pwer*-toh *Ahn*-hehl). With its beautiful beaches, unpaved streets, and budget hotels, Puerto Angel is popular with international backpackers and those seeking an inexpensive, and restful vacation. Repeated hurricane damage and the 1999 earthquake took its toll on the village, driving the best accommodations out of business, but the town continues to attract visitors. Its small bay and several inlets offer peaceful swimming and good snorkeling. The village's way of life is slow and simple: Fishermen leave very early in the morning and return with their catch before noon. Taxis make up most of the traffic, and the bus from Pochutla passes every half-hour or so. If you're of a mind to spend a night or two, **La Casa del Encuentro** (zoylayhelmut@yahoo.com), has six simple, well-kept rooms tucked into a lush garden with a small pool across the road from the ocean. To find it, head for the lighthouse, and continue a short distance beyond; look for the sign over a gate on the left.

Important Travel Note

Although car and bus hijackings along Hwy. 200 north to Acapulco have greatly decreased (thanks to improved security measures and police patrols), you're still wise to travel this road only during the day. There are numerous military checkpoints, and the road at points is dirt-only and pothole ridden.

ESSENTIALS

GETTING THERE & DEPARTING   **By Car**   North or south from **Hwy. 200,** look for the signs at Km. 124, just south of the town of Copala, and drive seaward for

7km to Puerto Angel. From Huatulco or Puerto Escondido, the trip should take about an hour.

By Taxi   Taxis are readily available to take you to Puerto Angel or Zipolite Beach for a reasonable price (about 40 pesos to or from either destination), or to the Huatulco airport or Puerto Escondido (about 550 pesos).

By Bus   There are no direct buses from Puerto Escondido or Huatulco to Puerto Angel; however, numerous buses leave Puerto Escondido and Huatulco for Pochutla, 11km (6¾ miles) north of Puerto Angel, where you can pick up a bus to Puerto Angel. If you arrive in Pochutla from Huatulco or Puerto Escondido, you may be dropped at one of several bus stations that line the main street; walk 1 or 2 blocks toward the large sign reading POSADA DON JOSE. The buses to Puerto Angel are in the lot just before the sign.

ORIENTATION   The town center is about 4 blocks long, oriented more or less east-west. There are few signs in the village, and off the main street, much of Puerto Angel is a narrow sand-and-dirt path. The one paved road leads to the navy base on the west end of town, before the creek crossing toward Playa Panteón (Cemetery Beach).

BEACHES, WATERSPORTS & BOAT TRIPS

The golden sands and peaceful village life of Puerto Angel and the nearby towns are all the reasons you'll need to visit. Playa Principal, the main beach, lies between the Mexican navy base and the pier that's home to the local fishing fleet. Near the pier, fishermen pull their colorful boats onto the beach and unload their catch in the late morning while trucks wait to haul it off to processing plants in Veracruz. The rest of the beach seems light-years from the world of work and commitments. Except on Mexican holidays, it's relatively deserted. It's important to note that Pacific coast currents deposit trash on Puerto Angel beaches. The locals do a fairly good job of keeping it picked up, but the currents are constant.

Playa Panteón is the main swimming and snorkeling beach. Cemetery Beach, ominous as that sounds, is about a 15-minute walk from the center, straight through town on the main street that skirts the beach. The *panteón* (cemetery), on the right, is worth a visit, with its brightly colored tombstones and bougainvillea.

In Playa Panteón, some of the *palapa* restaurants and a few of the hotels rent snorkeling and scuba gear and can arrange boat trips, but they tend to be expensive. Check the quality and condition of gear—particularly scuba gear—that you're renting.

Playa Zipolite (See-poh-*lee*-teh) and its village are 6km (3¾ miles) down a paved road from Puerto Angel and about 1½ hours from Puerto Escondido. Taxis charge about 45 pesos from Puerto Angel. You can catch a *colectivo* on the main street in the town center and share the cost.

Zipolite is well known as a good surf break and as a nude beach, although there's more nudity these days at nearby Chambala beach. Although public nudity (including topless sunbathing) is technically illegal, it's allowed here—this is one of only a handful of beaches in Mexico that permits it. This sort of open-mindedness has attracted an increasing number of young European travelers. Most sunbathers concentrate beyond a large rock outcropping at the far end of the beach. Police will occasionally patrol the area, but they are much more intent on drug users than on sunbathers. The ocean and currents are strong (that's why the surf is so good), and a number of drownings have occurred over the years—so know your limits. There are places to tie up a hammock and a few *palapa* restaurants for a lunch and a cold beer.

Hotels in Playa Zipolite are basic and rustic; most have rugged walls and *palapa* roofs. Prices range from $10 to $50 a night.

Traveling north on Hwy. 175, you'll come to another hot surf break and a beach of spectacular beauty: **Playa San Agustinillo.** If you want to stay in San Agustinillo, there are no formal accommodations, but you'll see numerous signs for local guesthouses, which rent rooms for an average of $15 to $25 a night, often with a home-cooked meal included. One of the pleasures of a stay in Puerto Angel is discovering the many hidden beaches nearby and spending the day. Local boatmen and hotels can give details and quote rates for this service.

You can stay in Puerto Angel near Playa Principal in the tiny town, or at Playa Panteón. Most accommodations are basic, older, cement-block style hotels, not meriting a full-blown description. Between Playa Panteón and town are several bungalow and guesthouse setups with budget accommodations.

BAHÍAS DE HUATULCO

64km (40 miles) SE of Puerto Angel; 680km (422 miles) SE of Acapulco

Huatulco has the same unspoiled nature and laid-back attitude as its neighbors to the north, Puerto Angel and Puerto Escondido, but with a difference. Amid the natural splendor, you'll also encounter indulgent hotels and modern roads and facilities.

Pristine beaches and jungle landscapes can make for an idyllic retreat from the stress of daily life—and when viewed from a luxury hotel balcony, even better. Huatulco is for those who want to enjoy the beauty of nature during the day and then retreat to well-appointed comfort by night.

Undeveloped stretches of pure white sand and isolated coves await the promised growth of Huatulco, which lags far behind Cancún, the previous resort planned by FONATUR, Mexico's Tourism Development arm. FONATUR development of the Bahías de Huatulco is an ambitious project that aims to cover 21,000 hectares (51,870 acres) of land, with over 16,000 hectares (39,520 acres) to remain ecological preserves. The small local communities have been transplanted from the coast into Crucecita. The area consists of three sections: **Santa Cruz, Crucecita,** and **Tangolunda Bay** (see "City Layout," below).

Though Huatulco has increasingly become known for its ecotourism attractions—including river rafting, rappelling, and hiking jungle trails—it has yet to develop a true personality. There's little shopping, nightlife, or even dining outside of the hotels, and what is available is expensive for the quality. However, the service in the area is generally very good.

A cruise ship dock in Santa Cruz Bay has given the sleepy resort an important business boost. The dock handles up to two 3,000-passenger cruise ships at a time (passengers are currently ferried to shore aboard tenders). Still being refined is the relatively new 20,000-hectare (49,400-acre) "eco-archaeological" park, **El Botazoo,** at Punta Celeste, where there is a recently discovered archaeological site. Hiking, rappelling, and bird-watching are popular activities there. This new development is all being handled with ecological sensitivity in mind.

If you're drawn to snorkeling, diving, boat cruises, and simple relaxation, Huatulco nicely fits the bill. Nine bays encompass 36 beaches and countless inlets and coves. Huatulco's main problem has been securing enough incoming flights. It relies heavily on charter service from the United States and Canada.

Essentials

GETTING THERE & DEPARTING

BY PLANE Continental (© 800/523-3273 in the U.S. and Canada, or 01-800/900-5000 in Mexico), **American** (© 800/433-7300 in the U.S. and Canada, or 01-800/904-6000 in Mexico), **US Airways** (© 800/428-4302 in the U.S. and Canada, or 01-800/428-4322 in Mexico), and **United** (© 800/538-2929 in the U.S. and Canada, or 01-800/003-0777 in Mexico) offer flights from the U.S. **InterJet** (© 866/285-9525 in the U.S., or 01-800/011-2345 in Mexico) flies daily between Mexico City and Huatulco.

From Huatulco's international airport (airport code: HUX; © **958/581-9007,** -9008), about 20km (12 miles) northwest of the Bahías de Huatulco, private **taxis** charge about $45 to Crucecita, $50 to Santa Cruz or Tangolunda. **Transportes Terrestres** (© **958/581-9014,** -9024) *colectivos* fares are about 100 pesos per person. When returning, make sure to ask for a taxi, unless you have a lot of luggage. Taxis to the airport run 460 pesos, but unless specifically requested, you'll get a Suburban, which costs 600 pesos.

Hertz (© **958/581-9092**), **Europcar** (© **958/581-9094**), and **Thrifty** (© **958/581-9000**) offer car rentals at the airport; Hertz (© **958/581-0588**) and Europcar (© **958/583-4067**) also have in-town locations. Huatulco is spread out and has excellent roads, so you may want to consider a rental car to explore the area.

BY CAR Coastal **Hwy. 200** leads to Huatulco (via Pochutla) from the north and is generally in good condition. The drive from Puerto Escondido takes just over 2½ hours. The road is well maintained—and usually under repair at some point or other—but it's filled with curves and potholes and doesn't have lights, so avoid travel after sunset. Allow at least 6 hours for the trip from Oaxaca City on mountainous **Hwy. 175.**

BY BUS Crucecita has three bus stations, all within a few blocks, but there are none in Santa Cruz or Tangolunda. The **Gacela** and **Estrella Blanca** station, at the corner of Gardenia and Palma Real, handles service to Acapulco, Mexico City, Puerto Escondido, and Pochutla. The **Cristóbal Colón** station (© **958/587-0261**) is at Avenida Riscalillo, Sector T. It serves destinations throughout Mexico, including Oaxaca, Puerto Escondido, and Pochutla. The **Estrella del Valle** station, on Jasmin between Sabali and Carrizal, serves Oaxaca.

ORIENTATION

VISITOR INFORMATION The **State Tourism Office,** or Oficina del Turismo (© **958/581-0176;** www.baysofhuatulco.com.mx), has an information booth in Tangolunda Bay, near the Grand Pacific hotel. It's open Monday through Friday from 8am to 5pm.

CITY LAYOUT The overall resort area is called **Bahías de Huatulco** and includes nine bays. The town of Santa María de Huatulco, the original settlement in this area, is 27km (17 miles) inland. **Santa Cruz Huatulco,** usually called Santa Cruz, was the first developed area on the coast. It has a central plaza with a bandstand kiosk, which has been converted into a cafe that serves regionally grown coffee. It also has an artisans' market on the edge of the plaza that borders the main road, a few hotels and restaurants, and a marina where bay tours and fishing trips set sail. **Juárez** is Santa Cruz's 4-block-long main street, anchored at one end by the Hotel Castillo Huatulco and at the other by the Meigas Binniguenda hotel. Opposite the

Hotel Castillo is the marina, and beyond it are restaurants in new colonial-style buildings facing the beach. The area's banks are on Juárez. It's impossible to get lost, and you can take in almost everything at a glance. This bay is the site of Huatulco's cruise ship dock.

About 3km (1¾ miles) inland from Santa Cruz is **Crucecita,** a planned city that sprang up in 1985, but has taken the shape of a traditional Mexican village, complete with a leafy plaza in the center of town. This is the residential area for the resorts, with neighborhoods of new stucco homes mixed with small apartment complexes. This is where you'll find the area's best and most reasonably priced restaurants, plus some shopping and several less expensive hotels.

Until other bays are developed, **Tangolunda Bay,** 5km (3 miles) east, is the focal point of development. Over time, half the bays will have resorts. For now, Tangolunda has an 18-hole golf course, as well as the Las Brisas, Quinta Real, Barceló Huatulco, Royal, Casa del Mar, and Camino Real Zaashila hotels, among others. Small strip centers with a few restaurants occupy each end of Tangolunda Bay. **Chahué Bay,** between Tangolunda and Santa Cruz, is a small bay with a beach club and other facilities under construction along with houses and a few small hotels.

GETTING AROUND   Crucecita, Santa Cruz, and Tangolunda are too far apart to walk, but **taxis** are inexpensive and readily available. Crucecita has taxi stands opposite the Hotel Grifer and on the Plaza Principal. Taxis are readily available through hotels in Santa Cruz and Tangolunda. The fare between Santa Cruz and Tangolunda is roughly 45 pesos; between Santa Cruz and Crucecita, 35 pesos; between Crucecita and Tangolunda, 35 pesos. To explore the area, you can hire a taxi by the hour (about 200 pesos) or for the day.

There is **minibus service** between towns; the fare is 5 pesos. In Santa Cruz, catch the bus across the street from Castillo Huatulco; in Tangolunda, in front of the Grand Pacific; and in Crucecita, cater-cornered from the Hotel Grifer.

[FastFACTS] BAHÍAS DE HUATULCO

Area Code   The area code is **958.**

Currency Exchange All three areas have banks with ATMs, including the main Mexican banks, Banamex and Bancomer, and HSBC. They change money during business hours, Monday through Friday from 9am to 4pm. Banks line Calle Juárez in Santa Cruz and surround the central plaza in Crucecita.

Drugstores   Farmacía El Centro, just off the central plaza in Crucecita

(📞 **958/587-0232**), is one of the largest drugstores in town. It's open Monday through Saturday from 8am to 10pm and Sunday from 8am to noon. **Farmacía La Clínica** (📞 **958/587-0591**), Sabalí 1602, Crucecita, offers 24-hour service and delivery.

Emergencies   Police emergency (📞 060); **federal police** (📞 958/587-0815); **transit police** (📞 958/587-0186); and **Cruz Roja (Red Cross),** Bulevar Chahué 110 (📞 958/587-1188).

Hospital   Clínica Médico Quirúrgica, Jabali 403 (📞 **958/587-0687,** -0600), is a medical clinic with emergency care run by Dr. Ricardo Carrillo, who speaks English.

Information   Oficina del Turismo, the State Tourism Office (📞 **958/581-0176,** -0177; www.baysofhuatulco. com.mx), has an information module in Tangolunda Bay, near the Campo de Golf. It's open weekdays 8am to 5pm.

Internet Access Crucecita has several Internet cafes. One is at the Terra-Cotta cafe in the Misión de los Arcos, Av. Gardenia 902 (© **958/587-0165**), which, in addition to paid service, is a free Wi-Fi hot spot. Another lies on the ground-floor level of the **Hotel Plaza Conejo,** Av. Guamúchil 208, across from the main plaza (© **958/587-0054**). It's about 15 pesos per hour.

Post Office The *correo,* at Bulevar Chahué 100, Sector R, Crucecita (© **958/587-0551**), is open Monday through Saturday from 8am to 4:30pm.

Where to Stay

Moderate- and budget-priced hotels in Santa Cruz and Crucecita are generally more expensive than similar hotels in other Mexican beach resorts. The luxury hotels have comparable rates, especially when they're part of a package that includes airfare. The trend here is toward all-inclusive resorts, which in Huatulco are an especially good option, given the lack of memorable dining and nightlife options. Hotels that do not front the ocean generally have an arrangement with a beach club at Santa Cruz or Chahué Bay, and offer shuttle service. Low-season rates apply August through November only. Parking is free at these hotels; the 18% tax is not included in the rack rates listed below.

EXPENSIVE

Camino Real Zaashila ★★ ☺   One of the original hotels in Tangolunda Bay, the Camino Real Zaashila sits on a wide stretch of sandy beach secluded from other beaches by small rock outcroppings. It has been renovated with a newly designed *palapa* bar with sit-down check-in. The calm water, perfect for swimming and snorkeling, makes it ideal for families. The white stucco building is Mediterranean in style and washed in colors on the ocean side. The boldly decorated rooms are large and have an oceanview balcony or terrace and a large bathroom with an Italian marble tub/shower. Each of the 41 club rooms on the lower levels has its own private plunge pool and includes buffet breakfast and evening cocktails. The main pool is a free-form design that spans 150m (500 ft.) of beach, with chaises built into the shallow edges. Well-manicured tropical gardens surround it and the guest rooms.

Bulevar Benito Juárez 5, Bahía de Tangolunda, 70989 Huatulco, Oax. www.camino-zaashila.com. © **800/722-6466** in the U.S., or 958/581-0460. Fax 958/581-0468. 120 units. High season $162 and up double; low season $124 and up double, AE, DC, MC, V. **Amenities:** 3 restaurants; lobby bar w/live music; babysitting; kids' club; concierge; Internet; 2 large outdoor pools; outdoor whirlpool; room service; lighted tennis court; watersports. *In room:* A/C, TV, minibar.

Quinta Real ★★★   Double Moorish domes mark this romantic, relaxed hotel, known for its richly appointed cream-and-white decor and complete attention to detail. From the welcoming reception area to the luxurious beach club below, the staff emphasizes excellence in service. The small groupings of suites are built into the sloping hill to Tangolunda Bay and offer spectacular views of the ocean and golf course. Suites on the eastern edge of the resort sit above the highway, which generates some traffic noise. Interiors are elegant and comfortable, with stylish Mexican furniture, original art, wood-beamed ceilings, and marble tub/showers with whirlpool tubs. Balconies have overstuffed seating areas and stone-inlay floors. Eight Grand Class Suites and the Presidential Suite have private pools.

Bulevar Benito Juárez Lt. 2, Bahía de Tangolunda, 70989 Huatulco, Oax. www.quintarealhuatulco.com. mx. © **888/561-2817** in the U.S., or 958/581-0428, -0430. Fax 958/581-0429. 28 units. 2,956 pesos and up suite. AE, MC, V. **Amenities:** 2 restaurants; bar w/stunning view; beach club; concierge; 2 outdoor pools; room service; tennis court. *In room:* A/C, TV, hair dryer, minibar.

MODERATE

Hotel Meicer Palmier Huatulco ★   Huatulco's first hotel retains the charm and comfort that originally made it memorable. Rooms have Mexican-tile floors and colonial-style furniture; French doors open onto tiny wrought-iron balconies overlooking Juárez or the pool and gardens. There's a section with newer rooms that have modern teak furnishings. A nice shady area surrounds the small pool in back of the lobby. The hotel is away from the marina at the far end of Juárez, only a few blocks from the water. It offers free transportation every hour to the beach club at Chahué.

Bulevar Santa Cruz 201, 70989 Santa Cruz de Huatulco, Oax. www.meicerhotels.com/Home_Meicer_Palmier_huatulco.htm. © **958/587-0129.** 165 units. 600–1,200 pesos double. Children 6 and younger stay free in parent's room. MC, V. **Amenities:** Large *palapa*-topped restaurant and bar; shuttle to beach; small outdoor pool. *In room:* A/C, TV, hair dryer.

INEXPENSIVE

Hotel Las Palmas   The central location and accommodating staff add to the appeal of the bright, cheerful rooms at Las Palmas. Located a half-block from the main plaza, it's connected to the popular El Sabor de Oaxaca restaurant (see "Where to Eat," below), which offers room service to guests. The accommodations have tile floors, cotton textured bedspreads, tile showers, and cable TV; most also have balconies. This hotel is partnered with another inexpensive and reliable choice in case this one sells out, featuring similarly comfortable rooms with a bright, open courtyard overlooking El Sabor restaurant.

Av. Guamúchil 206, 70989 Bahías de Huatulco, Oax. © **958/587-0060.** Fax 958/587-0057. 10 units. High season 950 pesos double; low season 500 pesos double. AE, MC, V. *In room:* A/C, TV.

Misión de los Arcos ★★ 🎁   This exceptional hotel, just a block from the central plaza, is similar in style to the elegant Quinta Real—but at a fraction of the cost. The hotel is mostly white, accented with abundant greenery, giving it a fresh, inviting feel. The simple rooms continue the theme, washed in white, with cream and beige bed coverings and upholstery. Each room contains understated accents such as lush potted plants and terra-cotta tile embellishments. At the entrance level, an excellent cafe offers Internet access, Huatulco's regionally grown coffee, tea, pastries, and ice cream. It's open from 7:30am to 11:30pm. The adjacent **Terra-Cotta** restaurant (see below) serves breakfast, lunch, and dinner, and is equally stylish and budget-friendly. Although there's no pool, for 20 pesos, guests can use the Castillo Beach Club (© **958/587-0144**), at Chahué Bay, open daily from 9am to 7pm.

Gardenia 902, Crucecita, 70989 Huatulco, Oax. www.misiondelosarcos.com. © **958/587-0165.** Fax 958/587-1903. 16 units. High season 800 pesos double, 850–1,050 pesos suite; low season 450–500 pesos double, 500–750 pesos suite. Rates increase over Christmas and Easter holiday periods. AE, MC, V. Street parking. **Amenities:** Restaurant; nearby beach club. *In room:* A/C, TV, Wi-Fi.

Where to Eat

El Sabor de Oaxaca ★★★ OAXACAN   This is the best place in the area to enjoy authentic, richly flavorful Oaxacan food, among the best of traditional Mexican cuisine. This colorful restaurant is a local favorite that also meets the quality standards of tourists. A popular item is the mixed grill for two, with an Oaxacan beef filet, tender pork tenderloin, and chorizo (zesty Mexican sausage). If you're feeling adventurous, try the salty grilled *chapulines* (grasshoppers, an Oaxacan specialty).

Generous breakfasts include hearty Oaxacan favorites such as *emoladas*, tortillas generously stuffed with meat fillings and soaked in the zesty traditional *mole* sauce.

Av. Guamúchil 206, Crucecita. ℂ **958/587-0060.** Fax 958/587-0057. Breakfast 55-80 pesos; main courses 80-175 pesos. AE, MC, V. Daily 7am-11pm.

Noches Oaxaqueñas/Don Porfirio ★ SEAFOOD/OAXACAN This dinner show presents the colorful, traditional folkloric dances of Oaxaca in an open-air courtyard reminiscent of an old hacienda (but in a modern strip mall). The dancers perform traditional ballet under the direction of owner Celicia Flores Ramírez, wife of Don Willo Porfirio. House specialties include grilled lobster, shrimp with *mescal* flambéed at the table, and spaghetti marinara with seafood, along with a fountain of seafood that includes shrimp, octopus, and snails, all cooked on hot grills right in front of your table. Meat lovers will enjoy American-style cuts or a juicy *arrachera* (skirt steak). The *Guelaguetza Show* showcases an important annual cultural celebration in Oaxaca. The show normally takes place nightly at 8pm during high season, and Tuesday, Thursday, and Saturday nights at 8pm in low season.

Bulevar Benito Juárez s/n (across from Royal Maeva), Tangolunda Bay. ℂ **958/581-0001.** Main courses 120-250 pesos. AE, MC, V. Daily noon-11pm. Show 130 pesos extra.

Terra-Cotta ★ 🍴 INTERNATIONAL/MEXICAN Located inside the Misión de los Arcos hotel, this stylish yet casual restaurant is best known for breakfast, and it's just as tasty at lunch and dinner. Start the day in this whitewashed, Mediterranean setting with gourmet coffee, fruit salad, and an array of morning favorites, including specials such as French toast stuffed with cream cheese and orange marmalade. Lunch and dinner share the same menu, which offers fajitas, baby back ribs, gourmet tacos, and six different sandwich options. Scrumptious desserts such as caramelized pineapple with coconut ice cream offer a sweet finish.

Gardenia 902, at the Misión de los Arcos (p. 394), in front of Crucecita's central plaza. ℂ **958/587-0165.** www.misiondelosarcos.com. Breakfast 38-78 pesos; lunch and dinner main courses 50-265 pesos. AE, MC, V. Daily 7:30am-11:30pm.

Activities on & off the Beach

Attractions around Huatulco concentrate on the nine bays and their watersports. The number of ecotours and interesting side trips into the surrounding mountains is growing. Though it isn't a traditional Mexican town, the community of Crucecita is worth visiting. Just off the central plaza is the **Iglesia de Guadalupe,** with a large mural of Mexico's patron saint gracing the entire ceiling of the chapel. The image of the Virgin is set against a deep blue night sky and includes 52 stars—a modern interpretation of Juan Diego's cloak.

You can dine in Crucecita for a fraction of the price of eating in Tangolunda Bay, with the added benefit of some local color. Considering that shopping in Huatulco is generally poor, you'll find the best choices here, in the shops around the central plaza. They tend to stay open late, and offer a good selection of regional goods and typical tourist take-homes, including *artesanía*, silver jewelry, Cuban cigars, and tequila. A small free trolley train takes visitors on a short tour of the town.

BEACHES A section of the beach at Santa Cruz (away from the small boats) is an inviting sunning spot. Beach clubs for guests at non-oceanfront hotels are here. In addition, several restaurants are on the beach, and *palapa* umbrellas run down to the water's edge. For about 160 pesos one-way, *pangas* from the marina in Santa Cruz will ferry you to **La Entrega Beach,** also in Santa Cruz Bay. There you'll find a row of *palapa* restaurants, all with beach chairs out front. Find an empty one, and use that restaurant for your refreshment needs. A snorkeling equipment rental booth is about midway down the beach, and there's some fairly good snorkeling on the end away from where the boats arrive.

Between Santa Cruz and Tangolunda bays is **Chahué Bay.** The beach club has *palapas,* beach volleyball, and refreshments for an entrance fee of about 35 pesos. However, a strong undertow makes this a dangerous place for swimming.

Tangolunda Bay beach, fronting the best hotels, is wide and beautiful. Theoretically, all beaches in Mexico are public; however, nonguests at Tangolunda hotels may have difficulty entering the hotels to get to the beach.

BAY CRUISES & TOURS   Huatulco's major attraction is its coastline—a magnificent stretch of pristine bays bordered by an odd blend of cactus and jungle vegetation right at the water's edge. The only way to really grasp its beauty is to take a cruise of the bays, stopping at **Organo** or **Maguey bays** for a dip in the crystal-clear water and a fish lunch at a *palapa* restaurant on the beach.

One way to arrange a bay tour is to go to the **boat-owners' cooperative** (Cooperativo Tangolunda; ✆ **958/587-0081**), located in a white ticket booth with a blue roof near the entrance to the marina. Prices are posted, and you can buy tickets for sightseeing, snorkeling, or fishing. Beaches other than La Entrega, including Maguey and San Agustín, are noted for offshore snorkeling. They also have *palapa* restaurants and other facilities. Several of these beaches, however, are completely undeveloped, so you will need to bring your own provisions. Boatmen at the cooperative will arrange return pickup at an appointed time. Prices run about $25 for 1 to 10 persons to La Entrega, and $50 for a trip to Maguey and Organo bays. The farthest bay is San Agustín; that all-day trip will run $100 in a private *panga.*

Another option is to join an organized daylong bay cruise. Any travel agency can easily make arrangements. Cruises are about $40 per person, plus $5 for snorkeling equipment rental and lunch. One excursion is on the *Tequila,* complete with guide, drinks, and onboard entertainment. Another, more romantic option is the *Luna Azul,* a 13m (43-ft.) sailboat that runs bay tours and sunset sails.

Ecotours are growing in popularity and number throughout the Bays of Huatulco. The mountain areas surrounding the Copalita River are also home to other natural treasures worth exploring, including the **Copalitilla Cascades.** Thirty kilometers (19 miles) north of Tangolunda, at 395m (1,296 ft.) above sea level, this group of waterfalls—averaging 20 to 25m (66–82 ft.) in height—form natural whirlpools and clear pools for swimming. The area is also popular for horseback riding and rappelling.

An all-day **shopping tour** takes you around the area, including Crucecita, to peruse quality handmade arts and crafts, and experience authentic Oaxacan cuisine. Contact **Paraíso Tours** (www.paraisohuatulco.com) for reservations.

Guided **horseback riding** through the jungles and to Conejos and Magueyito beach makes for a wonderful way to see the natural beauty of the area. The ride lasts 3 hours, with departures at 9:45am and 1:45pm, and costs $35 to $45. Contact **Caballo del Mar Ranch** (✆ **958/589-9387**).

Another recommended guide for both **hiking** and **bird-watching** is Laura Gonzalez, of **Nature Tours Huatulco** (✆ **958/583-4047;** lauriycky@hotmail.com). Choices include a hike around Punta Celeste with views of the river, open sea, and forest, for sightings of terrestrial and aquatic birds. The 3½-hour tour can be made in the early morning or late afternoon and costs $45. An 8-hour excursion to the Ventanilla Lagoons takes you by boat through a mangrove to view birds, iguanas, and crocodiles. The cost is $80, including lunch. Tours include transportation, binoculars, specialized bird guide, and beverages.

GOLF & TENNIS The 18-hole, par-72 **Tangolunda Golf Course** (© 958/581-0037) is adjacent to Tangolunda Bay. The greens fee is $80 for 18 holes and $6 for 9 holes; carts cost $34. Tangolunda also has tennis courts as well, for $11 per hour. Tennis courts are also available at the **Barceló** hotel (© **958/581-0055**) for 125 pesos per person per hour and 10 pesos extra for play under the lights.

SHOPPING Shopping in the area is limited and unmemorable. It concentrates in the **Santa Cruz Market,** by the marina in Santa Cruz, and in the **Crucecita Market,** on Guamúchil, a half-block from the plaza. Both are open daily from 10am to 8pm (no phones). Among the prototypical souvenirs, you may want to search out regional specialties, which include Oaxacan embroidered blouses and dresses, and *barro negro*, pottery made from dark clay exclusively found in the Oaxaca region. Also in Crucecita is the Plaza Oaxaca, adjacent to the central plaza. Its clothing shops include **Poco Loco Club/Coconut's Boutique** (© 958/587-0279), for casual sportswear; and **Mic Mac** (© **958/587-0565**), for beachwear and souvenirs. **Coconuts** (© **958/587-0279**) has English-language magazines, books, and music.

Huatulco After Dark

Huatulco has a very limited selection of dance clubs. What clubs there are, seem to change ownership—and names—almost annually. Check with your hotel to see if any new places have opened. A hot spot is **Bar La Crema** (© **958/587-0702;** www.lacremahuatulco.com), in Crucecita (about 4 blocks south of the *zócalo*, at the corner of Bugambilia and La Ceiba), with a lounge atmosphere and a mix of tunes. Nearby is **Café Dublin** (no phone; www.gpshow.com/dublin), Carrizal 504 (1 block east and a half-block south from the *zócalo*), an Irish pub with a book exchange. Both bars open in the evening during high season and stay open as long as the management sees fit; hours are sporadic in low season. The **Tipsy Blowfish** (© **958/587-2844;** www.thetipsyblowfish.com) plays rock music and features televised sports. The bar is open daily from noon to 4am during high season, with limited hours in low season. It's located on Boulevard Tangolunda across from the golf course.

La Papaya (© **958/583-4911**), on Bulevar Chahué, is a popular dance club, open Thursday through Saturday into the wee hours. Each Tuesday, the **Barceló Resort** (© **958/583-1440**) hosts its **Fiesta Mexicana** from 7 to 11pm, featuring folkloric dances, mariachi music, and a buffet of Mexican food and drinks.

OAXACA

by David Baird

The large, southern state of Oaxaca is a fascinating place to visit. Its main draw is its high population of Indians and their vibrant culture and distinct way of viewing things. The Indians belong to several different ethnic groups, each with its own language, and they don't just keep to the villages—you see them everywhere. Over the centuries, their practices, beliefs, and customs have percolated into the local culture at large to such a degree that Indian and non-Indian share a certain worldview that is a bit removed from that held by most Westerners. This is a magical region of Mexico.

In the **central highlands** is a large population of Zapotec and Mixtec Indians surrounding Oaxaca City. It's a land of mountains and valleys checkered with cornfields, at its prettiest during the rainy season (June–Oct), when the corn is green. The villages here are famous for their crafts, and many families now support themselves more by making handicrafts than by growing corn. But growing corn carries much more weight in their ordering of things and is part of who they are.

Their ancestors established agriculture and civilization in these valleys centuries ago. They were the ones who built and rebuilt the magnificent ceremonial center of **Monte Albán** high upon a mountaintop above Oaxaca City. Up there, you'll find an intriguing collection of buildings, ball courts, and plazas with designs distinctive from those of the Maya to the east and the many cultures of central Mexico to the northwest.

But my favorite part of a trip here is visiting the **city of Oaxaca,** a colonial city of stone buildings, plazas, and courtyards. With the pleasures of elegant surroundings, good food, and warm, welcoming people, I find myself very much at home here.

If you're looking for information on Oaxaca's beach resorts—Puerto Escondido and Puerto Angel among them—see chapter 10.

OAXACA CITY ★★★

520km (322 miles) SE of Mexico City; 230km (143 miles) SE of Tehuacán; 269km (167 miles) NE of Puerto Escondido

What you see today when you walk through the historic district of Oaxaca (Wah-*hah*-kah) is largely the product of 3 centuries of colonial society. The city is famous for its green building stone and for its own particular style of colonial architecture—an adaptation to the frequent earthquakes that plagued the city in colonial times and still occasionally shake things

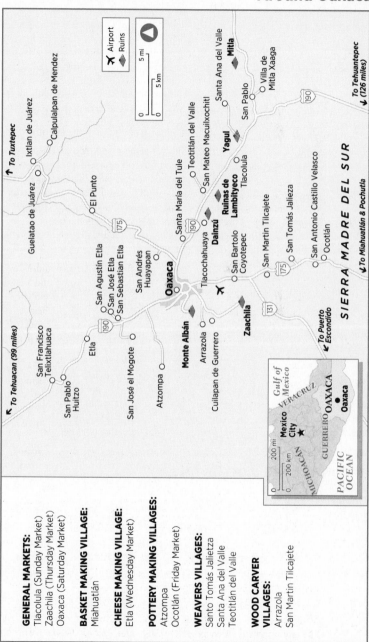

GENERAL MARKETS:
Tlacolula (Sunday Market)
Zaachila (Thursday Market)
Oaxaca (Saturday Market)

BASKET MAKING VILLAGE:
Miahuatlán

CHEESE MAKING VILLAGE:
Etla (Wednesday Market)

POTTERY MAKING VILLAGES:
Atzompa
Ocotlán (Friday Market)

WEAVERS VILLAGES:
Santo Tomás Jalietza
Santa Ana del Valle
Teotitlán del Valle

**WOOD CARVER
VILLAGES:**
Arrazola
San Martín Tilcajete

up. Walls and facades are thick and broad, with heavy buttressing; colonnades are low and spaced closely; and bell towers are squat with wide bases. The overall impression is one of great mass and solidity.

Before the arrival of the Spanish, the central valley of Oaxaca was an important cultural center. Civilization began to take shape 3 millennia before their arrival, when Olmec influence extended into this region from the east sometime around 1500 B.C. This influence shaped the nascent civilization of the Zapotec (the original builders of Monte Albán) who established several cities in the central valleys. The Zapotec civilization flourished with the growth of trade throughout Mesoamerica. The rise of Teotihuacán in central Mexico in the early part of the Classic Period (A.D. 300–900), and the Maya in the highlands of what is now Chiapas and Guatemala created two important sources for commerce in goods and new ideas. This became the golden age of the Zapotec, which lasted until the rise of the neighboring Mixtec in the 9th century. The Mixtec had expansionist policies and through war and diplomacy gained political control over much of the Zapotec homeland before both peoples were humbled by the Aztec and later the Spaniards. To this day, the two principal ethnic groups in Oaxaca remain the Zapotec and Mixtec, whose tonal languages are closely related to each other but far different from the Aztec language Náhuatl.

The city of Oaxaca, originally called Antequera, was founded just a few years after the Spanish vanquished the Aztec. Most of Oaxaca's central valley was granted to Hernán Cortez for his service to the crown. Three centuries of colonial rule followed, during which the region remained calm.

In the years following independence, there was more or less continuous upheaval. From the 1830s to the 1860s, the Liberals and Conservatives fought for control of Mexico's destiny, with the French eventually intervening on the side of the Conservatives. One man, a Zapotec Indian from Oaxaca, led the resistance against the French and played the key role in shaping Mexico's future. He was Benito Juárez, and his handiwork is known to history as *La Reforma*.

Born in the village of Guelatao, north of Oaxaca City, Juárez was adopted by a wealthy Oaxacan family who clothed and educated him in return for his services as a houseboy. He fell in love with the daughter of his benefactor and promised he would become rich and famous and return to marry her. He did all three and became president of the republic in 1861. Juárez is revered throughout Mexico.

Essentials

GETTING THERE & DEPARTING

BY PLANE   The airport (airport code: OAX) gets limited international service. **Continental ExpressJet** (© **800/523-3273** in the U.S., or 01-800/900-5000 in Mexico) has nonstop service to and from Houston. **Volaris** (© **01-800/122-8000** in Mexico) flies to and from Tijuana. **Aeroméxico** (© **800/237-6639** in the U.S., or 951/516-1066) offers flights daily to and from Mexico City through **Aeroméxico Connect,** its regional carrier. **Aerovega** (© **951/516-4982** in Mexico) flies a seven-passenger twin-engine Aero-Commander to and from Puerto Escondido and Bahías de Huatulco once daily (twice if there are enough passengers). Make arrangements for Aerovega at the Monte Albán Hotel facing the Alameda (next to the *zócalo,* or town square). The cost is 1,100 pesos.

BY CAR   It's a 5½-hour drive from Mexico City via the toll roads. Take **Hwy. 150D** east toward Veracruz to Cuacnoapalan, 80km (50 miles) beyond Puebla (250 pesos in tolls), and then south on **Hwy. 150D** to Oaxaca (270 pesos in tolls).

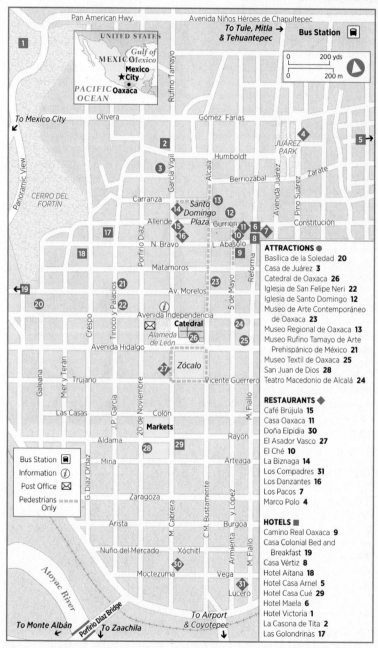

ATTRACTIONS ●
Basílica de la Soledad **20**
Casa de Juárez **3**
Catedral de Oaxaca **26**
Iglesia de San Felipe Neri **22**
Iglesia de Santo Domingo **12**
Museo de Arte Contemporáneo
 de Oaxaca **23**
Museo Regional de Oaxaca **13**
Museo Rufino Tamayo de Arte
 Prehispánico de México **21**
Museo Textil de Oaxaca **25**
San Juan de Dios **28**
Teatro Macedonio de Alcalá **24**

RESTAURANTS ◆
Café Brújula **15**
Casa Oaxaca **11**
Doña Elpidia **30**
El Asador Vasco **27**
El Ché **10**
La Biznaga **14**
Los Compadres **31**
Los Danzantes **16**
Los Pacos **7**
Marco Polo **4**

HOTELS ■
Camino Real Oaxaca **9**
Casa Colonial Bed and
 Breakfast **19**
Casa Vértiz **8**
Hotel Aitana **18**
Hotel Casa Arnel **5**
Hotel Casa Cué **29**
Hotel Maela **6**
Hotel Victoria **1**
La Casona de Tita **2**
Las Golondrinas **17**

peace & politics IN OAXACA

After the political upheaval of 2006 and early 2007, Oaxacan society has gradually returned to what it was, only poorer. The local economy is so dependent on tourism and the sale of artisan goods that the absence of visitors resulted in almost universal impoverishment of the city and the surrounding valleys. The mood is darker, too. Everyone feels that the national government abandoned Oaxaca.

For the last couple of years the situation has been peaceful, and with visitors returning the economy has recovered somewhat. The political scarring, however, is only now beginning to heal. Among the locals I have found a diversity of opinion about who was to blame for the crisis, but almost everyone, regardless of their political philosophy, holds the past governor, Ulises Ruíz, culpable and would like to see him investigated for corruption. In July 2010, the state elected a new governor, Gabino Cué, a former mayor of Oaxaca City, and the candidate of the opposition alliance. Cué is uniquely fitted to be an alliance candidate for he is well known, lacks any strong party identification, and is thought to be more of a pragmatist than

an ideologue. He assumed office on December 1 and immediately began making political gestures indicating an interest in social and political reform.

But in the month before Cue took office, a couple of social activists were assassinated, and a few days later, two thugs who worked for Ruíz's political party, the PRI, were killed. These last two were shot in broad daylight in front of the church of Santo Domingo, one of the prime tourist attractions in the city. It appears that they were executed by the drug gang known as the Zetas, who circulated a flyer explaining the killing as punishment for having extorted money and kidnapped people while claiming to be Zetas. The flyer maintained that normal people would have nothing to fear from the Zetas, and that only corrupt officials and their operatives were in danger.

Of course this adds another dimension to Oaxaca's political situation, but generally things are calm in the city. Petty theft is still prevalent, and lately there has been a rash of *secuestros express*—kidnapping a person for what can be gotten from his or her at an ATM. But by and large, Oaxaca is a safe destination.

BY BUS First-class and deluxe buses to and from Mexico City use the toll road, or *autopista*, and take 6 to 7 hours. A few make a short stop in Nochistlán, which isn't much of a delay. Most buses leave from Mexico City's **TAPO (east) bus station.** There is infrequent service to and from Mexico City's Central del Norte (north), and the Central del Sur (south, also called Taxqueña). No service runs from the Mexico City airport. The **main bus station** in Oaxaca is on Calzada Niños Héroes.

ADO (Autobuses del Oriente) and its affiliates handle the first-class and deluxe bus service. Your options are *primera clase* (ADO), with almost hourly departures and a one-way fare of 426 pesos; *de lujo* (ADO GL), with between three and five departures per day for 510 pesos one-way; and *servicio ejecutivo* (ADO Platino, which used to be called UNO and is still going through rebranding changes), with one to five departures per day for 726 pesos one-way. *De lujo* has the same seats as first class, but more legroom, free soda and bottled water, and separate bathrooms for men and women. *Servicio ejecutivo* has all this plus superwide seats that recline far back. During holidays, you need to reserve a seat. Native Oaxaqueños living outside the state fill the buses for the Day of the Dead, Holy Week, and Christmas. It's possible to reserve seats over the Internet for the higher levels of service, and to check departure times and prices at **www.adogl.com.mx** and **www.uno.com.mx**.

Buses serve Tuxtla Gutiérrez and San Cristóbal de las Casas (four overnight buses); Puebla (10 a day); Veracruz (three a day); Villahermosa (two a day); and Huatulco and Puerto Escondido, on the coast (two a day). It takes 10 hours to reach Puerto Escondido by bus because they go by way of Huatulco.

You can buy your tickets ahead of time at one of the downtown offices of **Ticket Bus.** One is across from the northeast corner of the *zócalo,* at the intersection of Hidalgo and Valdivieso (© 915/516-3820). There's also one at Porfirio Díaz 102-A, just north of calle Independencia (no phone). Office hours are 9am to 9pm, except Sundays, when they open from 11am to 7pm.

If you're coming overland to the city directly from Puerto Escondido or the Oaxacan coast, see p. 404 for information on traveling inland by bus and minivan.

ORIENTATION

ARRIVING BY PLANE   The airport is a 20-minute cab ride south of town. Buy a ticket at the window on your left as you exit the airport. A private cab is 150 pesos; an airport van is 48 pesos per person for downtown locations, more for other areas.

The same company provides service from the town to the airport. **Transportes Terrestres Aeropuerto Oaxaca** (© 951/514-4350), is on the Alameda, in the building facing the cathedral. It doesn't accept phone reservations, so drop by Monday through Saturday from 9am to 2pm or 5 to 8pm to buy your ticket and arrange hotel pickup. The cost is 48 pesos from downtown hotels, 90 pesos and up from outlying hotels, and more if you have extra luggage.

ARRIVING BY BUS   The ADO first-class bus station is a mile north of the center of town. The taxi ride to the city center is 30 pesos. If you're coming from the Pacific coast, you may arrive at the Central Camionera de Segunda Clase (second-class bus terminal), next to the Abastos Market. It's 10 long blocks southwest of the *zócalo.*

VISITOR INFORMATION   A tourist information office (©/fax **951/516-0123**) is at Calle Independencia 607, corner of García Vigil, in front of the Alameda. It shares the building with the Museo de los Pintores, and shares the same hours: Tuesday to Sunday from 10am to 8pm.

CITY LAYOUT   Oaxaca's east-west axis is **Independencia.** When streets cross Independencia or the north-south axis, **Alcalá/Bustamante,** their names change. The city's center is the *zócalo,* a large square surrounded by stone archways, and the **Alameda,** a smaller plaza attached to the northwest part of the *zócalo.* Oaxaca's cathedral faces the Alameda; its Palacio del Gobierno faces the *zócalo.* A few blocks to the north is **Plaza de Santo Domingo.** The area between these open spaces holds most of the historic district's shops, hotels, and restaurants. Two streets that run from Santo Domingo toward the *zócalo—***Alcalá** and **Cinco de Mayo**—are partly closed to traffic.

GETTING AROUND   By Car **Alamo** offices are at 5 de Mayo 203-A (© **951/514-8534**), and 5 de Mayo 315-A (© **951/514-5653**), and at the airport (© **951/511-6220;** alamo.oaxaca@hotmail.com). Rental cars in Oaxaca are expensive, and the process is not exactly streamlined.

By Taxi   If you want to reach some of the outlying villages, I recommend hiring a taxi or signing up for a tour. Most taxi drivers have set hourly rates for touring the Oaxaca valleys. A trustworthy and careful taxi driver who speaks English is **Tomás Ramírez** (© **951/511-5061;** tomasramirez@prodigy.net.mx).

By Bus Buses to the outlying villages of Guelatao, Teotitlán del Valle, Tlacolula, and Mitla leave from the second-class station just north of the Abastos Market. *Colectivos* leave for nearby villages from Calle Mercaderes, on the south side of the Abastos Market.

[FastFACTS] OAXACA

Area Code The telephone area code is **951.**

Consulates The **Canadian Consulate,** Pino Suárez 700-11B (*©* **951/513-3777**), is open daily from 11am to 2pm. The **U.S. Consular Agency** is at Alcalá 407, Int. 20 (*©*/fax **951/514-3054**). Hours are Monday through Friday from 10am to 3pm.

Currency Exchange *Casas de cambio* cluster on the streets at the northeast corner of the *zócalo,* at Alcalá and Valdivieso. These places have short lines and better hours than banks. Several exchange Canadian dollars.

Doctor Dr. Carlos Arnaud Carreño is a reputable internist at Calle Reforma 905 (*©* **951/515-4053**). Hours are Monday through Friday noon to 2pm and 4 to 8pm.

Internet Access Many Internet access services and cybercafes are in downtown. Most are along Alcalá and around the *zócalo* and the Plaza Santo Domingo.

Post Office The *correo* is at the corner of Independencia and Alameda Park. It is open Monday through Friday from 8am to 5pm, Saturday from 9am to 1pm.

Seasons April and May are the hottest, driest months. (Also in May, rural teachers invade the *zócalo* and create havoc in the downtown area while they demonstrate for higher wages.) The rains come in June and improve things considerably. June through March, the city is most enjoyable. High seasons for tourists, when you can expect higher hotel rates, are late July and August (especially around the Guelaguetza), early November (around Day of the Dead), the month of December, and during Easter.

Special Events & Festivals

Oaxaca is famous for its exuberant traditional festivals. The most important ones are **Holy Week,** the **Guelaguetza** in July, **Días de los Muertos** in November, and the **Night of the Radishes** and **Christmas** in December. Make hotel reservations at least 2 months in advance if you plan to visit during these times.

At festival time in Oaxaca, sidewalk stands near the cathedral sell *buñuelos,* a thin, crisp, sweet snack food. It is customary to serve *buñuelos* in cracked or otherwise flawed dishes; after you've finished eating, you smash the crockery on the sidewalk for good luck. Don't be timid! You can wash down the *buñuelos* with hot *ponche* (a steaming fruit punch) or *atole.*

HOLY WEEK During Holy Week, figurines made of palm leaves are sold on the streets. On Palm Sunday, the Sunday before Easter, there are colorful parades. On the following Thursday, Oaxaca residents follow the Procession of the Seven Churches. Hundreds of the pious walk from church to church, praying at each one. The next day, Good Friday, many of the *barrios* (neighborhoods) have *encuentros:* Groups depart separately from the church, carrying religious figures through the neighborhoods, then "encounter" each other back at the church. Throughout the week, each church sponsors concerts, fireworks, fairs, and other entertainment.

FIESTA GUELAGUETZA On the last two Mondays in July, Oaxaca holds the Fiesta Guelaguetza. In the villages of central Oaxaca, a *guelaguetza* ("a gift") is a celebration by a family in need of assistance to hold a wedding or some other event. Guests bring gifts, which the family repays when they attend other *guelaguetzas.* The Fiesta Guelaguetza, begun in 1974, brings dancers from all the state's various ethnic groups to Oaxaca. For many communities, participation has become a matter of intense civic pride, and an opportunity to show people in the state capital and from other ethnic groups the beauty of their traditional clothing and dance. Some 350 different *huipiles* (women's overblouses) and dresses can be seen during the performances. In the afternoon, there is an interpretive dance of the legend of Princess Donají.

The performances take place each Monday from 10am to 1pm in the stadium that crowns the Cerro del Fortín. Admission ranges from free (Section C) to 800 pesos (Section A). Reserve tickets in advance—no later than May—through the State Tourism Office (ⓒ/fax **951/516-0123**). A travel agency may be able to help you. I recommend sections 5 and 6 in Palco (gallery) A for the best seating. The ticket color matches the seat color. You sit in strong sunlight, so wear a hat and long sleeves.

Even if you don't attend the dances, you can enjoy the festival atmosphere that engulfs the city. There are fairs, exhibits, and a lot of gaiety. On the Sunday nights before the Guelaguetza, university students present an excellent program in the Plaza de la Danza at the Soledad church. The production, the *Bani Stui Gulal,* is an abbreviated history of the Oaxaca valley. The program begins at 9pm; arrive early, because the event is free and seating is limited.

DÍAS DE LOS MUERTOS　The Mexican Day of the Dead festival (Nov 1–2) has garnered worldwide attention. It's celebrated across Oaxaca with more passion than in the rest of Mexico, which says quite a lot. Markets brim with marigolds—the flower of the underworld—and every household fills an altar with them and the favorite dishes, drinks, and cigarettes of the deceased. People visit relatives and friends, and anyone who visits is offered food. This is also the time to pay one's respects at the graveyard. Try one of the nocturnal cemetery tours offered around this time; **Hotel Casa Arnel** (ⓒ **951/515-2856**) offers one. Another common form of celebrating is for young men to dress up in macabre outfits and frolic in the streets Carnaval-style.

DECEMBER FESTIVALS　The December festivals begin on the 12th with the **Fiesta de la Virgen de Guadalupe (Festival of the Virgin of Guadalupe)** and continue on the 16th with a *calenda,* or procession, to many of the older churches in the *barrios,* all accompanied by dancing and costumes. Festivities continue on the 18th with the **Fiesta de la Soledad,** in honor of the Virgen de la Soledad, patroness of Oaxaca state. A large fireworks construction known as a *castillo* is erected in Plaza de la Soledad. When it is ignited, look out. December 23 is **La Noche de Rábanos** (the Night of the Radishes), when Oaxaqueños build sculptures out of enormous radishes, flowers, and corn husks. Displays on three sides of the *zócalo* are set up from 3pm on. By 6pm, when the show opens, lines to see the figures are 4 blocks long. It's well organized and overseen by a heavy police presence. On December 24, around 8:30pm, each Oaxacan church organizes a procession with music, floats, enormous papier-mâché dancing figures, and crowds bearing candles, all converging on the *zócalo.*

Where to Stay

High season includes Easter, July, August, early November, and most of December. You should have no difficulty finding a room the rest of the time, and promotional rates are usually available. The prices listed below include the 19% tax. Most evenings are cool enough that you don't need air-conditioning, but for about 60 days a year, mostly from April to June, it comes in handy, and not every hotel has it.

VERY EXPENSIVE

Camino Real Oaxaca ★★★   A magnificent hotel in a 16th-century landmark convent, this is the place to cloister yourself when in Oaxaca. Several beautiful courtyards with age-old walls bring to mind the original purpose of the building. The rooms, however, do not. All are comfortable and have the conveniences you would expect in a hotel of this caliber (no small feat, given the constraints imposed by the infrastructure). Exterior rooms are equipped with noise-reducing windows. Interior rooms with views of the courtyards are more expensive. The main difference between "deluxe" and "club" is the size of the room. Service is good. The location—between the *zócalo* and Santo Domingo on a pedestrian-only street—is ideal.

5 de Mayo 300, 68000 Oaxaca, Oax. www.caminoreal.com/oaxaca. © **800/722-6466** in the U.S. and Canada, or 951/501-6100. Fax 951/516-0732. 91 units. $336–$360 deluxe double; $402–$432 club double; $509 junior suite. Lower rates are for weekdays. AE, MC, V. Valet parking 176 pesos. **Amenities:** Restaurant; 2 bars; babysitting; free membership for guests at local health club; large outdoor pool; room service; smoke-free rooms. *In room:* A/C, TV, hair dryer, minibar, Wi-Fi.

La Casona de Tita ★★   This place is simplicity itself with lots of style, blending colonial and modern themes. The rooms are distributed around a sharply designed central courtyard. They have an uncluttered, cool, and airy feel that quiets the spirit. The bathrooms are large and nicely appointed. The service is personal and attentive. This would be a great choice for anyone interested in the local art scene as the manager is a former museum director with connections to the best-known artists in Oaxaca.

García Vigel 805 (at Cosijopi), 68000 Oaxaca, Oax. www.lacasonadetita.com. © **951/516-1400.** 6 units. High season 2,100–2,800 pesos double, 3,300 pesos suite; low season 1,700–2,600 pesos double, 2,900 pesos suite. Rates include full breakfast. MC, V. Free parking. Children 11 and under permitted only when renting out entire house. **Amenities:** Room service; smoke-free rooms; Wi-Fi. *In room:* A/C, TV, hair dryer, Internet.

EXPENSIVE

Hotel Victoria ★★ 🎁   High above the downtown area, the Hotel Victoria offers that rare combination of actual proximity with the feeling of distance. And you're only a couple of minutes away on the hotel's shuttle bus. The Victoria also has a lovely view. You can enjoy it from a room or suite in one of the main buildings (three stories, no elevator), or you can stay in one of the villas distributed about the grounds, each with its own terrace. Rooms are large and carpeted, and have modern furnishings.

Lomas del Fortín 1, 68070 Oaxaca, Oax. www.hotelvictoriaoax.com.mx. © **951/502-0850.** Fax 951/515-2411. 150 units. 1,785 pesos double; 2,142 pesos villa; 3,094 pesos junior suite. AE, MC, V. Free parking. **Amenities:** Restaurant; bar; babysitting; large outdoor heated pool; complimentary shuttle to downtown; room service; smoke-free rooms. *In room:* A/C, TV, hair dryer, Wi-Fi.

MODERATE

Casa Colonial Bed and Breakfast ★   The casual and comfortable setting created by attentive host Jane Robison promptly sets guests at ease. This is an especially attractive place for first-timers to Oaxaca, who can tap into the owner's knowledge of the area and perhaps even tour some villages with her. The good-size rooms open to a large garden filled with tropical plants and flowers; they are simply but comfortably furnished. Breakfast is cooked to order and includes a large variety of foods. The hotel is 9 blocks from the *zócalo*, a few blocks past La Soledad. Occasionally on Sunday afternoons a small jazz combo plays in the patio. The inn offers a three-meal plan.

Negrete 105 (Apdo. Postal 640), 68000 Oaxaca, Oax. www.casa-colonial.com. © **800/758-1697** in the U.S., or ©/fax 951/516-5280. 15 units. $110 double. Rates include full breakfast. MC, V. Free parking. *In room:* No phone, Wi-Fi.

Hotel Aitana ★ 🎒

This stylish hotel is only 7 blocks from the *zócalo* and 6 blocks from Santo Domingo, but it's about 30m (98 ft.) uphill on a noisy street. All the rooms are away from the street, though, past a courtyard restaurant. They are well lit and beautifully decorated. Most hold two twin beds; a few have either two doubles or a king. Bathrooms are attractive and spacious, with tub/showers.

Crespo 313, 68000 Oaxaca, Oax. www.hotelaitanaoaxaca.com.mx. © **951/514-3788**, -3839. Fax 951/516-9856. 23 units. High season 1,250 pesos double; low season 900 pesos double. Rates include full breakfast. Often the 4th night is free. MC, V. Parking 50 pesos. **Amenities:** Restaurant; bar; room service. *In room:* TV, hair dryer, high-speed Internet.

Hotel Casa Vértiz ★ ⚑

This is a small courtyard hotel in a good location. Rooms are medium size and come with either one or two queen-size beds. They are nicely done, with ceramic tile floor, beamed ceiling, stucco walls, and a few artsy decorations. There's good luggage space. Bathrooms are attractive.

Reforma 404, 68000 Oaxaca, Oax. www.hotelvertiz.com.mx. © **951/516-1700.** 14 units. 950–1150 pesos double. MC, V. Parking nearby 100 pesos. **Amenities:** Restaurant; bar; room service; smoke-free rooms. *In room:* A/C, TV, hair dryer, Wi-Fi.

INEXPENSIVE

Hotel Casa Arnel ⚑ ☺

Less than 1km (about ⅔ mile) from the *zócalo*, this lodging, located in a quiet neighborhood, offers good value. Kids enjoy the garden courtyard with parrots and other birds. From the rooftop terrace, you can admire the view and soak up some sun. Most rooms are plain but comfortable. Across the street are three additional rooms with two double beds (junior suites), plus four furnished, full-service apartments with fully equipped kitchens. Breakfast, at extra cost, is served on the patio. At Christmas, the family involves guests in the traditional Mexican celebrations, or *posadas*, which are held during the 12 nights before Christmas.

Aldama 404, Col. Jalatlaco, 68080 Oaxaca, Oax. www.casaarnel.com.mx. ©/fax **951/515-2856.** 40 units (8 with shared bathroom). $25 double with shared bathroom; $45 double; $75–$80 suite; $450 apt. monthly. Rates go up for Easter, Guelaguetza, Días de los Muertos, and Christmas. No credit cards. Parking $3. *In room:* No phone, Wi-Fi.

Hotel Casa Cué ⚑

A modern hotel 2 blocks from the *zócalo*, Casa Cué has good air-conditioning, good service, and bathrooms with instant hot water. The terrace on top of the three-story building (there's no elevator) has patio furniture and a fine view of the mountains. The midsize standard rooms are attractively furnished and well lit; they contain two twin beds. Junior suites are large and come with a sofa, coffee table, and writing table; most hold two double beds (some have one king and one double). The suites are larger still, with a second bedroom. The market across the street can be a little noisy, but the double-glazed windows do a good job of blocking out the noise.

Aldama 103, 68000 Oaxaca, Oax. www.hotelcasacue.com. ©/fax **951/516-7786.** 23 units. 700 pesos double; 800 pesos junior suite; 1,100 pesos suite. MC, V. Free covered, secure parking. *In room:* A/C, TV, Wi-Fi.

Hotel Maela

This is a family-owned hotel that offers good value: central location (behind Santo Domingo), quiet rooms, and good rates. The owners do a good job of maintaining the property. Rooms are medium to small. Most have one double, two doubles, or one queen-size bed. The staff is helpful.

Constitución 206, 68000 Oaxaca, Oax. www.mexonline.com/maela.htm. ©/fax **951/516-6022.** 26 units. High season 715 pesos double; low season 635 pesos double. No credit cards. Free guarded parking. *In room:* TV, Wi-Fi.

Las Golondrinas ★ This charming one-story hotel has rooms that surround rambling patios with roses, fuchsia, bougainvillea, and mature banana trees. Las Golondrinas (the Swallows) is popular, so make reservations in advance. The simply furnished rooms, with windows and doors opening onto courtyards, all have tile floors and a small desk and chairs. Each holds either one full or two twin beds. A few rooms have a king-size bed and go for a higher price. Breakfast is served in a small tile-covered cafe in a garden setting (50–80 pesos); nonguests are welcome. The hotel is 6½ blocks north of the *zócalo.*

Tinoco y Palacios 411 (btw. Allende and Bravo), 68000 Oaxaca, Oax. www.hotellasgolondrinas.com.mx. © **951/514-3298** or ©/fax 951/514-2126. 26 units. 600 pesos double. No credit cards. No parking. *In room:* No phone, Wi-Fi.

Where to Eat

Oaxacan cooking has a great reputation in Mexico. It makes use of more ingredients from the lowlands than central Mexican cooking. It's known for its *moles* and for a wide variety of chiles, many of which you don't find in other parts of the country. Oaxaca is also known for its *mezcal,* a distillate of the *agave* or maguey plant (a different variety from the blue *agave,* from which tequila is made). This drink has a rougher taste than tequila, and it's commonly drunk with lime and *sal de gusano* (salt with powdered chile and ground-up maguey worms—the same that show up in some bottles of *mezcal*). Any cantina worth its salt will offer *sal de gusano* to its customers.

Restaurateurs here seem bent on providing travelers with something more cosmopolitan than the local cuisine. I'm not sure why. A number of fine-dining places are trying hard and, in my opinion, are overrated. **Casa Oaxaca,** the restaurant (Constitución 104; © **951/516-8889;** www.casaoaxacaelrestaurante.com), gets the best press, but if you're tired of *moles,* then one visit is enough. **Los Danzantes,** Macedonio Alcalá 403 (© **951/501-1184;** www.losdanzantes.com), brings Mexico City chic to Oaxaca. I like what the owners have done with the place, but not with the food. Go for drinks. **La Biznaga,** García Vigil 512 (© **915/516-1800**), usually has the most interesting menu—try it sometime when you feel completely at leisure, because the service is absurdly slow.

Good coffee and espresso are easier to come by these days, but you still have to seek them out. **Café Brújula** (© **951/516-7255;** www.cafebrujula.com), at 409-D García Vigil, serves excellent coffee and light food to go with it, including bagels (a rarity in Mexico that the cafe makes on the premises), sandwiches, and other goodies.

EXPENSIVE

El Ché ★ STEAKS If you need a break from Mexican food, you can have a steak and salad in comfortable surroundings, and wash it all down with a glass of hearty red. The restaurant offers both American and Argentine cuts of beef; the rib-eye and the *churrasco* are the most popular. (To tell them how you'd like it cooked, see our dining guide in chapter 21, p. 768.) The margaritas are good.

5 de Mayo 413. © **951/514-2122.** Reservations recommended during special festivals. Steaks 170–290 pesos. MC, V. Mon–Sat 1–11pm; Sun 1–9pm.

OAXACAN street food

Unless it's during a festival, don't be surprised to find many restaurants empty. Oaxaqueños do not frequent restaurants, but do like eating in market and street stalls. They favor foods such as tacos, tamales, *tlayudas* (12-in. tortillas, slightly dried and chewy, with a number of toppings), and empanadas (in Oaxaca, large tortillas heated on the *comal*—a flat, earthenware pan—or among the coals, with several types of fillings). For adventurous diners, here are my picks for enjoying the people's food.

Empanadas are a morning food, and the best place to eat them is in **La Merced** market (on Murguía, about 10 blocks east of Alcalá), where you'll find a number of food stalls; look for **La Güerita** or **La Florecita.** My favorite empanada is filled with *huitlacoche*.

The following places open only at night: A little *taquería* called **Tacos Sierra** (on corner of Morelos and Alcalá) is a Oaxacan institution. They make simple tacos with pork filling and a spicy salsa, but I can never order enough. It closes when the pork runs out, usually

by 10pm. Don't expect these tacos to come cheap. Another *taquería* is **El Mesón,** which is across from the northeast corner of the *zócalo* at Hidalgo 805. It serves *tacos de la parrilla* (grilled meats) and *de cazuela* (meats and vegetables cooked in a variety of chile sauces).

For *tlayudas*, seek out **El Chepil,** a hole in the wall on Constitución around the corner from Calzada de la República. They come with a number of toppings, and with *tasajo* (dried beef) or *cecina* (pork rubbed with red chile) on the side. If you don't like lard, tell them that you want your *tlayuda sin asiento*. El Chepil also prepares excellent *tostadas*. For **tamales,** find the woman who sets up her little stand on Avenida Hidalgo and 20 de Noviembre, in front of the pharmacy. She often doesn't get there until 7:30pm, but when she does, she quickly draws a crowd. She sells seven flavors, and my favorite is always the last one I've eaten. Given that you're in Oaxaca, though, you might want to ask for a tamal made with *mole negro, mole amarillo,* or *chepil* (an herb).

MODERATE

El Asador Vasco INTERNATIONAL/MEXICAN   Of the restaurants circling the *zócalo*, this is probably the best. It offers the considerable advantage of an upstairs dining area overlooking the *zócalo*. This makes for a more peaceful dinner and a better view. Take your pick of purely Mexican specialties (chiles rellenos, *moles, carne asada*) or dishes with a European twist (snapper filet cooked in olive oil and *guajillo* chile). I can recommend the tortilla soup and the *chile relleno de picadillo*.

Portal de Flores 11. ✆ **951/514-4755.** www.asadorvasco.com. Main courses 110–225 pesos. MC, V. Mon-Sat 1:30–11:30pm; Sun 2–11pm.

Los Pacos OAXACAN   *Moles* are the specialty here. Ask for the *gustación de moles* (a small serving of several sauces) to help you make an educated choice for main course. I like the *negro* and the *rojo moles*. The table sauces are good, too. You can also try one of the other local dishes, such as the *filete al mezcal*, but I would avoid the *botana oaxaqueña* (Oaxacan-style junk food found in restaurants all around town). There's a medium-size dining room as you enter, a couple of tables on the way to the kitchen, and a rooftop terrace that works well for dining in the evening.

Abasolo 121. ✆ **951/516-1704.** www.lospacos.com.mx. Main courses 85–195 pesos. MC, V. Daily noon-10pm.

Marco Polo ★ SEAFOOD Enjoy outdoor dining in an attractive shaded patio. The ceviche tostadas or the seafood cocktails are great starters (if you like your cocktail less tomato-y, tell the waiter you want it *a la marinera*). The specialty is the oven-baked fish (whole or filet), prepared several ways—I like their basic method, with just a *chile guajillo* marinade. For dessert, try the baked bananas. Marco Polo is just north of the central downtown area. Two other locations—downtown at calle 5 de Mayo 103 (✆ **951/514-4360**), and in the Colonia Reforma at Calz. Porfirio Díaz 802 (✆ **951/518-4309**), which also has steaks on the menu—are not as attractive as the main one.

Pino Suárez 806. ✆ **951/513-4308.** Breakfast 40–50 pesos; main courses 90–185 pesos. AE, MC, V. Daily 8am–6pm.

Yu Ne Nisa ★ REGIONAL In the hot lowlands of eastern Oaxaca, an area called the isthmus, you find a different cooking tradition known as *cocina istmeña*. Try sampling some of the region's specialties at this restaurant, located in a residential part of the Colonia Reforma. Start with some *garnachas* for appetizers—little corn patties covered in sauce—and then try a regional specialty such as *gucheguiña*, a lowland *mole*. Seafood plays a big part in *cocina istmeña*. Usually the chef can offer seafood cocktails and soups. She closes occasionally, so call first. Only Spanish is spoken.

Amapolas 1425, Col. Reforma. ✆ **951/515-6982.** www.yunenisa.com. Main courses 70–150 pesos. No credit cards. Daily 1–8pm.

INEXPENSIVE

Doña Elpidia 🏚 OAXACAN The home-style cooking *a la mexicana* is delicious and a real value here. Nothing is a la carte. There's a four-course *comida corrida,* with usually two or three options for the main course, including a *mole*. The house is 5½ blocks south of the *zócalo*, in the untouristy working-class part of the city. Look for a small sign saying only RESTAURANT. Upon entering, you will find some tables in a garden patio and a dining room. Beer and other beverages are extra.

Miguel Cabrera 413 (btw. Arista and Nuño del Mercado). ✆ **951/513-0126.** Fixed-price lunch 50 pesos. No credit cards. Daily 1–6pm.

Itanoni ★ 🏚 MEXICAN/REGIONAL This business began as a specialty tortilla shop. The owner then decided to branch out into making other things. He is dedicated to preserving different forms of native corn and makes use of their varying characteristics in the cooking. The dishes are simple and safe, and include traditional *antojitos* such as tacos, quesadillas, *memelitas,* and tamales. You can get them with a variety of fillings, including bean, fresh cheese, mushrooms, and squash blossoms. Most dishes are cooked on a classic Mexican griddle, nothing is fried here, and you can watch the women as they make your order. This place is well worth the short cab ride from downtown and is a good choice for vegetarians.

Belisario Domínguez 513, Col. Reforma. ✆ **951/513-9223.** www.itanoni.com.mx. Antojitos 11–25 pesos. MC, V. Mon–Sat 10am–4pm; Sun 7am–2pm.

Los Compadres ★ 🍴 OAXACAN This is a people's restaurant in the working-class district south of the *zócalo*. The food is both delicious and safe. It's a bargain, too. The owner and cook, who has been doing her thing for 32 years, cooks for a steady crowd of locals. Everything I had was good, especially the *estofado* (a kind of *mole*), the fresh *huitlacoche* (corn fungus available from June–Oct) quesadillas, and the *sopa de guías* (soup made from zucchini greens). Simpler Oaxacan fare is on the menu, too, such as *tlayudas, tasajo, cecina,* and several kinds of *antojitos.* All lettuce is disinfected. The dining area is an informal, open space with lots of room.

Lucero 109 (btw. Armenta y López and Fiallo). © **951/516-3597.** Main courses 30-70 pesos. No credit cards. Mon-Sat 11am-7pm.

Exploring Oaxaca

With so much sightseeing to do inside and outside Oaxaca, you have to be sure to allow for some idle time in the *zócalo.* In the traffic-free square, you can relax while getting a feel for the town and Oaxacan society. I recommend going in the late afternoon and taking a seat at the outdoor cafe with a good view of the cathedral. You can get a beer or a bowl of the traditional drink of Oaxaca: chocolate. The afternoon light filters through the glossy green leaves of the laurel trees, heightening the color of the cathedral's green stone. As dusk comes, a small drill corps enters stage left and performs a flag-lowering ceremony with much pomp and circumstance. Then the marimba or the municipal band usually strikes up in the central bandstand.

MUSEUMS

Museo de Arte Contemporáneo de Oaxaca   The MACO, 2½ blocks north of the *zócalo,* exhibits the work of contemporary artists, primarily from Oaxaca state (which has produced some of Mexico's most famous painters). It also books traveling exhibitions. A small bookstore is to your right as you enter. The 18th-century building merits a visit for its own sake. It's called the Casa de Cortés, and many locals say that it was built by order of Hernán Cortez after he received the title of Marqués of the Valley of Oaxaca. Records show that it was actually built a century later.

Alcalá 202, btw. Murguía and Morelos. © **951/514-7110.** Admission 20 pesos. Wed-Mon 10:30am-8pm.

Museo Regional de Oaxaca ★★★   Next to the Santo Domingo Church (6 blocks north of the *zócalo*) is the most impressive museum in the city, housed in a former Dominican convent—one of the greatest of colonial Mexico. Construction was largely completed by the early 1600s. The government spent millions to renovate the former convent, and it shows. The stairs, the arches, the cupolas—everywhere you look, are decorative details in stone or in the remnants of Colonial-Era murals. The museum is an ambitious project that displays the course of human development in the Oaxaca valley from earliest times to the 20th century.

The most treasured possessions are the artifacts from Monte Albán's Tomb 7, which was discovered in 1932. The tomb contained 12 to 14 corpses and some 500 pieces of jewelry and art, making use of 3.6 kilograms (8 lb.) of gold and turquoise, conch shell, amber, and obsidian. This is part of a larger collection of artifacts from Monte Albán, which you would do well to see before going up to the ruins. In the many ceramics and carvings, you can see definite Olmec and Teotihuacán influences, yet they display a style different from either culture. Other rooms are dedicated to the present-day ethnographic makeup of Oaxaca and a brief history of the efforts of the Dominican order in the region. Attached to the convent is the Santo Domingo Church (see "Churches," below). From some points on the north side of the convent, you can look down over the botanical garden. Entrance to the garden is by guided tour only (at 1 and 6pm). Sign up at the front desk of the museum the same day of the tour. Two tours a week are in English (100 pesos); ask for info at the front desk.

Gurrión at Alcalá. © **951/516-2991.** Admission 51 pesos. 35 pesos for use of video camera. Tues-Sun 10am-6:15pm.

Museo Rufino Tamayo de Arte Prehispánico de México ★★★ The arti-facts displayed in this museum were chosen "solely for the aesthetic rank of the works, their beauty, power, and originality." The result is a striking collection of pre-Hispanic art. The famed Oaxacan artist Rufino Tamayo amassed the collection over a 20-year period. The artifacts range from the pre-Classic period up to the Aztec, from far northwest Nayarit to southeastern Chiapas: terra-cotta figurines, scenes of daily life, lots of female fertility figures, Olmec and Totonac sculpture from the Gulf Coast, and Zapotec long-nosed figures. The well-displayed works reveal the great variety of styles of pre-Columbian art in Mexico.

Av. Morelos 503, north of the *zócalo* btw. Tinoco y Palacios and Porfirio Díaz. ℂ **951/516-4750.** Admission 40 pesos. Mon and Wed–Sat 10am–2pm and 4–7pm; Sun 10am–3pm. Closed holidays.

Museo Textil de Oaxaca Set in the former monastery of San Pablo, this museum exhibits all manner of textiles. Naturally, there's a partiality for Mexican and Oaxacan works, but exhibits include textiles from around the world and examine the various techniques used in their creation. There are three galleries and a library. Exhibits rotate, but the library always features the works of one or another contemporary Oaxacan artist. One of the latest expositions featured works woven from *izote* (yucca), which is a traditional fiber for weaving in Mexico. The gallery space is in an attractive, well-restored colonial building worth viewing for its own sake.

Hidalgo 917, corner of Fiallo, 2 blocks east of the *zócalo*. ℂ **951/501-1104.** Free admission, donations requested. Tues–Sun 10am–8pm.

CHURCHES

Basílica de la Soledad ★★ The Basílica is the religious center of Oaxaca, and its Virgin is the patroness of the entire state. Adjoining the church is a former convent with a small but charming museum in back. A huge celebration on and around December 18 honors the Virgin, attracting penitents from all over Oaxaca. She is famous for her vestments, which are encrusted with pearls. (Until a few years ago, she had a crown of silver and jewels, which was stolen.) As with most Virgins, there is a story behind her. The short version is that her figure was found in a box on the back of a burro that didn't belong to anyone. The burro sat down on an outcropping of rock and refused to get up. This was the spot where the Virgin revealed herself and, consequently, where the basilica (completed in 1690) was constructed. You can still see the outcropping of rock, enclosed by a cage of iron bars, immediately to your right along the wall as you enter the church.

The concave facade of the church projecting forward from the building is unique in Mexico's religious architecture. The way the top is rounded and the tiers are divided suggests an imitation in stone of the baroque wooden *retablos* (altarpieces) common in Mexican churches. The interior is most impressive, too, but what I really like is the museum, which contains a curious blend of pieces—some museum quality, others mere trinkets that might as well have come from my grandmother's attic.

The Basílica's upper plaza is an outdoor patio and theater (Plaza de la Danza) with stone steps that serve as seats. Here spectators view the Bani Stui Gulal (see "Fiesta Guelaguetza" under "Special Events & Festivals," earlier). When visiting the Basílica, it is traditional to eat ice cream; vendors are in the lower plaza in front of the church.

Independencia at Galeana. No phone. Museum admission by donation. Mon–Sat 9am–2pm and 4–6pm; Sun 11am–2pm. Basílica daily 7am–2pm and 4–9pm.

Catedral de Oaxaca ★★ The cathedral was built in 1553 and reconstructed in 1773. Its elaborate 18th-century baroque facade is an excellent example of the

Oaxacan style. The central panel above the door depicts the assumption of the Virgin. Note the heavy, elaborate frame around the picture and the highly stylized wavelike clouds next to the cherubs—these elements, repeated in other churches in the region, are telltale signs of Oaxacan baroque. An uncommon and quite lovely detail is how the Virgin's cape and its folds are depicted in angular lines and facets. The cathedral's interior is not as interesting as its exterior because it was plundered during the Reform Wars.

Fronting the Parque Alameda. No phone. Free admission. Daily 7am-9pm.

Iglesia de San Felipe Neri This church, 2½ blocks northeast of the *zócalo*, was built in 1636 and displays all the architectural opulence of that period: The altar and nave are covered with ornately carved, gilded wood, and the walls are frescoed. In the west transept and chapel is a small figure of St. Martha and the dragon; the faithful have bedecked her with ribbons in hopes of obtaining her assistance.

Tinoco y Palacios at Independencia. No phone. Free admission. Daily 8am-11pm.

Iglesia de Santo Domingo ★★★ 🖾 Of the 27 churches in Oaxaca, none can equal the splendor of this one's interior. The church was started in the 1550s by Dominican friars and finished a century later; it contains the work of the best artists of that period. Ornate plaster statues and flowers cover the extravagantly gilded walls and ceiling. When the sun shines through the yellow stained-glass window, it casts a golden glow over the interior, like a baroque vision of heaven. As you enter, look up at the ceiling formed by the choir loft to examine the elaborate organizational tree of the Dominican order, which starts with don Domingo de Guzmán, Saint Dominic himself.

Corner of Gurrión and Alcalá. No phone. Free admission. Daily 7am-2pm and 4-11pm.

San Juan de Dios This is the oldest church in Oaxaca, originally built in 1521 or 1522 of adobe and thatch. Construction of the present structure started during the mid-1600s and included a convent and hospital (where the 20 de Noviembre Market is now). The exterior is simple; the interior has an ornate altar and Urbano Olivera paintings on the ceiling. Oaxaqueños especially revere the glass shrine to the Virgin near the entrance, as well as one dedicated to Christ (off to the right). Because it's by the market, 1 block west and 2 blocks south of the *zócalo,* many of the people who visit the church are villagers who have come to Oaxaca to buy and sell.

20 de Noviembre s/n (btw. Aldama and Arteaga). No phone. Free admission. Daily 6am-11pm.

MORE ATTRACTIONS

Besides visiting the places mentioned below, try to get to the **Casa de Cortés,** which houses the Museo de Arte Contemporáneo (see above), and the former convent of **Santa Catalina,** home of the Camino Real Oaxaca (p. 406).

Casa de Juárez This modest museum occupies the house where Benito Juárez first lived when he came to the city as a servant boy. It doesn't have any of his personal effects or any furniture belonging to the house, but it shows how a typical 19th-century household would have looked. An audiovisual presentation of Juárez's life is in Spanish, as is the rest of the museum's explanatory material.

García Vigil 609. ✆ **951/516-1860.** Admission 37 pesos. Tues-Sun 10am-7pm.

Cerro del Fortín To capture Oaxaca in a glance, take a cab to the top of this hill on the west side of town for a panoramic view. It's especially pretty just before sunset. Atop the hill are the statue of Benito Juárez and a stadium built to hold

15,000 spectators. The annual Fiesta Guelaguetza is held here. You can walk to the hill: Head up Díaz Ordaz/Crespo and look for the Escaleras del Fortín (Stairway to the Fortress) shortly after you cross Calle Delmonte; the 218 steps (interrupted by risers) are a challenge, but from the top you can take in distant vistas.

Díaz Ordaz at Calle Delmonte.

Teatro Macedonio de Alcalá This beautiful 1903 Belle Epoque theater, 2 blocks east of the *zócalo,* is still used for performances. It's worth a peek but opens only for concerts, and the management is quite lax about publishing a calendar of events, but sometimes you can find one in the cafe that occupies part of the first floor.

Independencia at Armenta y López. No phone. Open only for events.

Activities

COOKING CLASSES Susana Trilling (© 951/518-7726; www.seasonsofmy heart.com), author of the cookbook *Seasons of My Heart,* operates a cooking school of the same name just outside Oaxaca. In downtown Oaxaca, **Sra. Pilar Cabrera,** owner of La Olla restaurant, gives cooking classes at Libres 205. She can be reached at © 951/516-5704, or at bugambilias2@yahoo.com.mx.

SPANISH CLASSES Oaxaca has about a half-dozen language schools. For total immersion, and with prior notice, most can arrange home stays with a Mexican family. The **Instituto Cultural Oaxaca,** Av. Juárez 909 (Apdo. Postal 340, 68000 Oaxaca, Oax.; © 951/515-3404; www.icomexico.com), has the biggest name and the least flexibility. Besides language skill, classes focus on Oaxaca's history and archaeology. The **Instituto de Comunicación y Cultura,** Alcalá 307–312 (68000 Oaxaca, Oax.; ©/fax 951/516-3443; www.iccoax.com), provides group and private instruction, and uses music, art, and handicrafts to get students into the swing of things. Classes are small. **Becari Language School,** M. Bravo 210 (68000 Oaxaca, Oax.; © 951/514-6076; www.becari.com.mx), was founded in 1994, and I've heard good things from students—lots of flexibility and small classes.

HIKING & BIKING Northwest of the city of Oaxaca is a mountain range known as the Sierra Norte that is cooler and wetter than the valley. The native communities offer guides and simple lodging for active sorts who are interested in seeing yet another side of Mexico. Several ecotourism outfits work with these communities. For information, ask at the State Tourism Office (©/fax 951/516-0123). **Zona Bici,** García Vigil 406 (© 951/516-0953; www.mexonline.com/zonabici.htm), does bike tours on back roads for about 400 pesos for a 4-hour tour.

Shopping

Oaxaca and the surrounding villages are wonderful hunting grounds for handcrafted pottery, woodcarvings, and weavings. The hunt itself may be the best part. Specialties include the shiny **black pottery** for which Oaxaca is famous, **woolen textiles** with the deep reds and purples produced using the natural dye *cochineal,* and highly imaginative *alebrijes* **(woodcarvings).**

SHOPS & GALLERIES

Most of the shops, galleries, and boutiques are in the area between **Santo Domingo** and the *zócalo,* comprising the streets of **Alcalá, 5 de Mayo,** and **García Vigil** and the **cross streets.** Standard hours are Monday to Saturday 10am to 2pm and 4 to 7pm.

Amate Books This shop has perhaps the best selection anywhere of books in English about Mexico. It stocks English-language magazines as well as a number of books about Oaxacan handicrafts. Alcalá 307-2, a few steps from Santo Domingo. ✆ **951/516-6960.** www.amatebooks.com.

Arte Piel This store is an outlet for a local factory that makes leather goods using its own designs. Merchandise includes bags, purses, wallets, belts, and coats. It keeps standard store hours. 20 de Noviembre at Aldama. ✆ **951/501-0219.**

Café Galería Brújula This cafe has opened some gallery space in the back of the establishment for the exhibition of prints, quietly lining up some of the best known print artists in Mexico. García Vigil 409-D. ✆ **951/516-7255.** www.cafebrujula.com.

Casa de las Artesanías de Oaxaca As with MARO (below), this store is one-stop shopping for almost all of the state's many crafts. It has a finer selection of goods, but in some ways it's not as fun shopping here as at MARO. A visit here can help you decide whether to take a trip to some of the craft-making villages in the highland valleys and which villages to go to. Hours are Monday to Saturday 9am to 9pm and Sunday 10am to 6pm. Matamoros 105 at García Vigil. ✆ **951/516-5062.** www.casadelasartesanias.com.mx.

Galería Arte de Oaxaca This gallery represents some of the state's leading contemporary artists and several important artists from other parts of Latin America. It has six rooms of exhibition space and a permanent exhibition of the work of Rodolfo Morales. It's open Monday to Friday from 11am to 3pm and 5 to 8pm, and Saturday from 11am to 6pm. Murguía 105. ✆ **951/514-0910,** -1532. www.artedeoaxaca.com.

Galería Quetzalli The appearance of this modest-looking art gallery behind the Church of Santo Domingo belies the fact that it represents some of the biggest names in Mexican art, such as Francisco Toledo and José Villalobos, as wells as some up-and-coming artists. It has additional exhibition space at the store's "bodega" at Murguía 400, and a contemporary design store at Bravo 109 called Tienda Q. Constitución 104. ✆ **951/514-0030.** www.galeriaquetzalli.com.

Instituto Oaxaqueño de las Artesanías Also known as ARIPO, this government store with a broad range of goods can be a productive stop for exploring Oaxacan handicrafts, but in my opinion the **Casa de las Artesanías** and **MARO** are better stores. Open Monday to Friday from 9am to 7pm and Saturday from 9am to 3pm. It's 2 blocks north of the Benito Juárez house. García Vigil 809 (at Cosijopi). ✆ **951/514-4030.**

La Mano Mágica Come here to see some of the best rug weaving in Oaxaca (by Arnulfo Mendoza) before you head to Teotitlán to see the work of other weavers. In the back rooms, you can find well-chosen pieces of regional folk art. Shipping is available. The store is opposite the Museo de Arte Contemporáneo. Alcalá 203 (btw. Morelos and Matamoros). ✆ **951/516-4275.**

MARO This is the store of Mujeres Artesanas de la Región de Oaxaca, a completely independent cooperative of women artisans with more than 200 member producers. There's lots of variety and lots of inventory displayed in its 20 small showrooms. All the handicrafts of the state are represented, are well priced, and are of high quality. Open daily 9am to 8pm. 5 de Mayo 204 (btw. Murguía and Morelos). ✆ **951/516-0670.**

MARKETS

Oaxaca City has two market areas: one just south of the *zócalo,* and the newer Abastos Market, about 10 blocks west. Both areas bustle with people and are surrounded by small shops selling anything from hardware to leather goods to fabrics.

A few shops specialize in chocolate (not for eating, but for making hot chocolate) and *mole* paste. The neighboring state of Tabasco grows most of the cacao beans used for the chocolate. They are ground with almonds and cinnamon and pressed into bars or tablets. To prepare the drink, you dissolve the chocolate in hot milk or water and beat until frothy. *Mole* paste, which contains chocolate, is used to make the classic Oaxacan dishes *mole negro* and *mole rojo*. A good place to hunt for chocolate and *mole* paste is along Mina Street, on the south side of the 20 de Noviembre Market (see below). Here you'll find **Chocolate Mayordomo** and **Chocolate La Soledad.** Both offer a variety of preparations to fit American and European tastes.

Note: Markets are generally open daily from 8am to 5pm.

Benito Juárez Market One block south of the *zócalo*, this covered market is big and busy; stalls sell vegetables, flowers, medicinal preparation, meats, cheeses, and even clothing. Btw. calles Las Casas, Cabrera, Aldama, and 20 de Noviembre.

Mercado Abastos The Abastos Market is open daily but is most active on Saturday, when Indians from the villages come to town to sell and shop. You'll see dried chiles, herbs, vegetables, crafts, bread, and even burros for sale at this bustling market. 10 blocks west of zócalo, btw. Calle Mercaderes and the periférico.

Mercado de Artesanía Located 1 block south and 1 block west of the 20 de Noviembre Market, this market sells textiles and clothing at cheap prices. I rarely see tourists here. J. P. García and Zaragoza.

20 de Noviembre Market This market is just south of the Benito Juárez Market, across Aldama. There are a lot of food stalls, but also some arts and crafts. On the south side, along Mina, are stores selling chocolate and *mole* paste. Btw. calles Aldama, Cabrera, Mina, and 20 de Noviembre.

Oaxaca After Dark

If you are interested in seeing the region's traditional dances, you can check out the small-scale **Guelaguetza** performed by professional dancers at the Hotel Camino Real on Fridays from 7 to 10pm. The cost (365 pesos) includes a buffet. **La Casa de Cantera** (✆ 951/514-9522; www.casadecantera.com), at Federico Ortiz 104, just off Calzada Porfirio Díaz in the Colonia Reforma, offers something similar. The cover charge of 180 pesos is for the show only, which runs most nights from 8:30 to 10:15pm. Supper costs another 145 pesos, which doesn't include drinks. Call for reservations.

Concerts and dance programs take place all year at the **Teatro Macedonio de Alcalá,** Independencia and Armenta y López. Schedules are often posted by the front doors of the theater. In the early evening, the *zócalo* is a happening place. The municipal brass band and marimba players perform free concerts on alternating nights. As the night wears on, you'll usually find some mariachis hanging about.

Just south of the *zócalo* is a 90-year-old cantina called **La Farola** (✆ 951/516-5352), at 20 de Noviembre 3. Daily from 9:30am to 1:30am it serves *mezcal*, both its own house brand and many others. You can also get beer and other forms of alcohol, of course. It has an original section and a newer section, so you should explore it a bit before you settle down for a drink.

For salsa, go to **La Candela,** Murguía 413 (✆ 951/514-2010), with live music Thursday through Saturday from 10:30pm to 2am. The cover is usually 50 pesos.

ROAD TRIPS FROM OAXACA

The countryside around Oaxaca is dotted with small archaeological sites and villages, and the most important are easy to reach. The landmark ruins in the region are **Monte Albán** (30 min.) and **Mitla** (1 hr.). If you're heading toward Mitla, you can make some interesting stops (see "The Road to Mitla: Ruins & Rug Weavers," below). A number of interesting villages in other directions make good day trips from Oaxaca. The Tourism Office will give you a map that shows nearby villages where beautiful handicrafts are made. The visits are fun excursions by car or bus. If you would like a guided tour of archaeological ruins or crafts villages, contact **Juan Montes Lara.** He is the thinking person's guide to this area, as well as to most of southern Mexico. He speaks English and conducts tours for small groups throughout Oaxaca and Chiapas. He stays pretty busy, so contact him well in advance—the best way is by e-mail (© **951/515-7731;** jmonteslara@yahoo.com).

Many villages have fine small municipal museums. **San José El Mogote,** site of one of the earliest pre-Hispanic village-dweller groups, has a display of carvings and statues found in and around the town, and a display model of an old hacienda. **Teotitlán del Valle** also has a municipal museum; it features displays on the weaving process. Ask at the State Tourism Office for more information.

Monte Albán: Ruins with a View

Had I been the priest-king of a large Indian nation in search of the perfect site on which to build a ceremonial center, this would have been it. **Monte Albán** sits on a mountain that rises from the middle of the valley floor—or, rather, divides two valleys. From here you can see all that lies between you and the distant mountains.

Starting around 2000 B.C., village-dwelling peoples of unknown origin inhabited the Oaxaca valleys. Between 800 and 500 B.C., a new ceramic style appeared, indicating an influx of new peoples, now called Zapotec. Around 500 B.C., these peoples began the monumental exercise of leveling the top of a mountain, where they would build Monte Albán (*Mohn*-teh Ahl-*bahn*).

As you enter the site, you'll see a museum, a shop with guidebooks to the ruins, a cafe, and a craft shop. Video camera permits cost 50 pesos. The site is open daily from 8am to 6pm. Admission to the ruins is 51 pesos. Licensed guides charge 200 pesos per person for a walking tour.

Very little of the original structures remain; they've either been obscured beneath newer construction or had their stones reused for other buildings. A center of Zapotec culture, Monte Albán was also influenced by contemporary cultures outside the valley of Mexico. You can see Olmec influence in the early sculptures; more recent masks and sculptures reflect contact with the Maya. When Monte Albán was at its zenith in A.D. 300, it borrowed architectural ideas from Teotihuacán. By around A.D. 800, the significance of Monte Albán in Zapotec society began to wane. Although most likely never completely abandoned, it became a shadow of its former grandeur. At the beginning of the 13th century, the Mixtec appropriated Monte Albán. The Mixtec, who had long coexisted in the area with the Zapotec, began expanding their territory. At Monte Albán, they added little to the existing architecture; however, they seem to have considered it an appropriate burial ground for their royalty. They left many tombs, including **Tomb 7,** with its famous treasure.

Monte Albán centers on the **Gran Plaza,** a man-made area created by flattening the mountaintop. From this plaza, aligned north to south, you can survey the Oaxacan valley. The excavations at Monte Albán have revealed more than 170 tombs, numerous ceremonial altars, stelae, pyramids, and palaces.

Begin your tour of the ruins on the eastern side of the Great Plaza at the I-shaped **ball court.** This ball court differs slightly from Maya and Toltec ball courts, in that there are no goal rings, and the sides of the court slope. Also on the east side of the plaza are several **altars** and **pyramids** that were once covered with stucco. Note the sloping walls, wide stairs, and ramps; all are typical of Zapotec architecture and reminiscent of the architecture of Teotihuacán. The building, slightly out of line with the plaza (not on the north-south axis), is thought by some to have been an observatory; it was probably aligned with heavenly bodies rather than with points of the compass.

The south side of the plaza has a large **platform** that bore several stelae, most of which are now in the National Museum of Anthropology in Mexico City. A good view of the surrounding area can be had from the top of this platform.

The west side has more ceremonial platforms and pyramids. Atop the pyramid substructure are four columns that likely supported the roof of the temple at one time.

The famous building of **Los Danzantes (The Dancers),** on the west side of the plaza, is the earliest known structure at Monte Albán. This building is covered with large stone slabs that have distorted naked figures carved into them (the ones you see are copies; the originals are protected in the site museum). There is speculation about who carved these figures and what they represent, although there is a distinct resemblance to the Olmec baby faces at La Venta, in Tabasco state. The distorted bodies and pained expressions might connote disease. Clear examples of figures representing childbirth, dwarfism, and infantilism are visible. Because of the fluid movement represented in the figures, they became known as Los Danzantes—merely a modern label for these ancient and mysterious carvings.

The **Northern Platform** is a maze of temples and palaces interwoven with subterranean tunnels and sanctuaries. Take time to wander among the reliefs, glyphs, paintings, and friezes along the lintels and jambs, as well as the walls. In this section of the ruins, you are likely to see vendors discreetly selling "original" artifacts found at the site. These guys come from the nearby town of Arrazola, where the fabrication of "antiquities" is a long-standing cottage industry. I like to buy a piece occasionally and pretend I'm getting the real thing just to get an opportunity to talk with them.

Leaving the Great Plaza, head north to the **cemetery** and **tombs.** If you have a day to spend at Monte Albán, be sure to visit some of the tombs, which contain magnificent glyphs, paintings, and stone carvings of gods, goddesses, birds, and serpents. Lately, the tombs have been closed to the public, but check anyway. Of the excavated tombs, the most famous is **Tomb 7,** next to the parking lot. It yielded some 500 pieces of gold, amber, and turquoise jewelry, as well as silver, alabaster, and bone art objects. This amazing collection is on display at the Museo Regional de Oaxaca (p. 411).

To get to Monte Albán, take a bus from the Hotel Rivera del Angel, at Mina 518 between Mier y Terán and Díaz Ordaz. **Transportadora Turística, Arqueología e Historia (© 951/516-0666)** makes hourly runs to the ruins. A round-trip ticket costs 40 pesos. Additional buses usually run during high season. If this company isn't running vans, you can buy a ticket with the competition, **Autobuses Turisticos** (© **951/516-5327**), at Mina 505, just down the block. They use buses and charge the same for a round-trip ticket. If you're driving from Oaxaca, take Calle Trujano out of town. It becomes the road to Monte Albán, which is about 10km (6¼ miles) away.

Tomb 7

↑ To Oaxaca

Ticket Office & Museum

Parking Area

Tomb 172

Building X

Tomb 110

Tomb 104

Tomb 118

Tomb 103

Building B

Northern Platform

Sunken Patio

Ball Court

Gran Plaza

Building G

Mound II

Building IV

Pyramid (Building P)

Building H

Building I

Palace

Building L

Altar

Building J

Danzantes

Gran Plaza

Building Q

Building M

Mound III

Stela 1

South Platform

0   330 feet
0   100 meters

The Road to Mitla: Ruins & Rug Weavers

East of Oaxaca, the Pan American Highway (Hwy. 190) leads to Mitla and passes several important archaeological sites, markets, and craft villages.

Many little stops dot this route, and some are a bit off the highway, so I recommend hiring a taxi, renting a car, or signing up with a small tour rather than using local bus transportation. If you take a tour, ask which sites it includes. To get to the highway, go north from downtown to Calzada Niños Héroes and turn right. This feeds directly on to the highway. All the sites are listed in order, from west (Oaxaca) to east (Mitla).

SANTA MARÍA DEL TULE'S 2,000-YEAR-OLD TREE   Santa María del Tule is a small town 8km (5 miles) outside Oaxaca. It's famous for the immense **El Tule Tree**, an *ahuehuete* (Montezuma cypress, akin to the bald cypress) standing in a churchyard just off the main road. Now over 2,000 years old, it looks every bit its age, the way large cypresses do. However, this one is the most impressive tree I've ever seen for the sheer width of its trunk and canopy. It is said to have the broadest trunk of any tree in the world. When the tree was younger, the entire region around Santa María del Tule was marshland; in fact, the word *tule* means "reed." Now the water table has dropped, so to protect the tree, a private foundation waters and takes care of it. The admission fee of 5 pesos goes toward these efforts.

IGLESIA DE SAN JERÓNIMO TLACOCHAHUAYA Six kilometers (3¾ miles) farther along, you'll see a sign pointing right; go less than another kilometer (about a half-mile) into town. This church is the next stop. Inside the church are an elaborately carved altar and a crucifix fashioned out of a ground paste made from the corn plant. The murals decorating the walls were the work of local artists of the 18th century and are a sweet mix of Spanish and Indian aesthetics. Make a point of seeing the beautifully painted baroque organ in the choir loft. The church is usually open daily from 10am to 2pm and 4 to 8pm.

DAINZÚ'S ZAPOTEC RUINS Three kilometers (1¾ miles) farther, visible from the highway (26km/16 miles from Oaxaca), you'll see a sign pointing to the right. It's less than 1km (⅔ mile) to the ruins, which were first excavated in the 1960s. Dainzú is a pre-Classic site that dates from between 700 and 600 B.C. Increasingly sophisticated building continued until about A.D. 300. The site occupies the western face of a hill, presumably for defense. The main building is a platform structure, its walls decorated with carvings resembling Monte Albán's Danzantes. These carvings are now in a protective shed; a caretaker will unlock it for interested parties. These figures show Olmec influence but differ from the Danzantes because they wear the trappings of the "ballgame," which likely make them the earliest representations of the ballgame in Mexico. A partially reconstructed ball court sits below the main structure. The site provides an outstanding view of the valley. Admission is 31 pesos.

TEOTITLÁN DEL VALLE'S BEAUTIFUL RUGS The next major turnoff you come to is 2km (1¼ miles) farther along, 3km (1¾ miles) from the highway. This is Teotitlán, famous for weaving and now an obviously prosperous town, to judge by all the current development. This is where you'll want to go for rugs, and you'll find no shortage of weavers and stores. Most weavers sell out of their homes and give demonstrations. The prices are considerably lower than in Oaxaca City.

The church in town is well worth a visit. The early friars used pre-Hispanic stones to build the church and then covered them with adobe. When the townspeople renovated the church, they rediscovered these stones with carved figures and now proudly display them. You'll see them in odd places in the walls of the church and sacristy. Teotitlán also has a small community museum, opposite the artisans' market and adjacent to the church. The museum has an interesting exhibit on natural dye-making, using herbs, plants, and *cochineal* (a red dye derived from insects).

For a bite to eat, consider the **Restaurant Tlamanalli,** Av. Juárez 39 (© **951/524-4006**), run by three Zapotec sisters who serve Oaxacan cuisine. Its reputation attracts lots of foreigners. It's on the right on the main street as you approach the main part of town, in a red brick building with black wrought-iron window covers. It's open Monday through Friday from 1 to 4pm. A bit farther on, there's another nice restaurant on the left where the main street intersects with the town center.

LAMBITYECO'S RAIN GOD Getting back to the highway and continuing eastward, in 3km (1¾ miles), you'll see a turnoff on the right for the small archaeological site of Lambityeco. Of particular interest are the two beautifully executed and preserved **stucco masks** of the rain god Cocijo. At Lambityeco, a major product was salt, distilled from saline groundwater nearby. Admission is 31 pesos.

TLACOLULA'S FINE MARKET & UNIQUE CHAPEL Located 30km (19 miles) from Oaxaca (1.5km/1 mile past Lambityeco), Tlacolula is in *mezcal* country, and along the road from here to Mitla, you'll see a couple of small distilleries and distillery outlets advertising their product. Stop by any one to taste their wares. *Mezcal* is distilled from a species of agave different from that of tequila. Most *mezcal* has a very strong smell and may or may not come with a worm in the bottle. Many of these small distilleries flavor their *mezcal* in much the same way that Russians flavor vodka.

Sunday is market day in Tlacolula, with rows of textiles fluttering in the breeze and aisle after aisle of pottery and baskets. If you don't go on market day, you won't have to compete with crowds. The **Capilla del Mártir** of the parochial church is a stunning display of virtuosity in wrought iron. The doorway, choir screen, and pulpit, with their baroque convolutions, have no equals in Mexico's religious architecture. Also eye-catching (to say the least) are the graphic, almost life-size sculptures of the Twelve Apostles in their various manners of martyrdom. A few years ago, a secret passage was found in the church, leading to a room that contained valuable silver religious pieces. The silver was hidden during the Mexican Revolution in 1910; the articles are now back in the church.

YAGUL'S ZAPOTEC FORTRESS Yagul, a fortress city on a hill overlooking the valley, is 2km (about 1½ miles) farther on down the highway. You'll see the turnoff to the left; it's less than 1km (about ⅔ mile) off the road. The setting is spectacular, and, because the ruins are not as fully reconstructed as those at Monte Albán, you're likely to have the place to yourself. Bring a picnic.

The city was divided into two sections: the fortress at the top of the hill and the palaces lower down. The center of the palace complex is the plaza, surrounded by four temples. In the center is a ceremonial platform, under which is the **Triple Tomb.** The door of the tomb is a large stone slab decorated on both sides with beautiful hieroglyphs. The tomb may be open for viewing; if there are two guards, one can leave the entrance to escort visitors.

Look for the beautifully restored, typically Zapotec **ball court.** North of the plaza is the **palace** structure built for the chiefs of the city. It's a maze of rooms and patios decorated with painted stucco and stone mosaics. Visible here and there are ceremonial mounds and tombs decorated in the same geometric patterns found in Mitla. The panoramic view of the valley from the fortress is worth the rather exhausting climb.

Admission is 31 pesos. Still cameras are free, but use of a video camera costs 35 pesos. The site is open daily from 8am to 5:30pm. It's just a few kilometers farther southeast to Mitla. The turnoff comes at a very obvious fork in the road.

MITLA'S LARGE ZAPOTEC & MIXTEC SITE Mitla is 4km (2½ miles) from the highway; the turnoff terminates at the **ruins** by the church. If you've come here by bus, it's less than 1km (about ⅔ mile) up the road from the dusty town square to the ruins; if you want to hire a cab, there are some in the square.

The Zapotec settled Mitla around 600 B.C., and it became a Mixtec bastion in the late 10th century. This city was still flourishing at the time of the Spanish Conquest, and many of the buildings were used through the 16th century.

Tour groups often bypass the **town of Mitla,** but it is worth a visit. The University of the Americas maintains the **Museum of Zapotec Art** (previously known as the Frissell collection). It contains some outstanding Zapotec and Mixtec relics. Admission is 35 pesos and includes admission to the ruins. Be sure to look at the Leigh collection, which contains some real treasures. The museum is in a beautiful old hacienda.

You can easily see the most important buildings in an hour. Mixtec architecture is based on a quadrangle surrounded on three or four sides by patios and chambers, usually rectangular. The chambers are under a low roof, which is excellent for defense but makes the rooms dark and close. The stone buildings are inlaid with small cut stones to form geometric patterns.

There are five groups of buildings, divided by the Mitla River. The most important buildings are on the east side of the ravine. The **Group of the Columns** consists of two quadrangles, connected at the corners with palaces. The building to the north has a long chamber with six columns and many rooms decorated with geometric designs. The most common motif is the zigzag pattern, the same one seen repeatedly on Mitla blankets. Human and animal images are rare in Mixtec art. In fact, only one **frieze** has been found (in the Group of the Church, on the north patio). Here you'll see a series of figures painted with their name glyphs.

Admission to the site is 37 pesos. Use of a video camera costs 35 pesos. Entrance to the museum is included in the price. It's open daily from 8am to 5pm.

Outside the ruins, vendors will hound you. The moment you step out of a car, every able-bodied woman and child for miles around will come charging over with shrill cries and a basket full of bargains—heavily embroidered belts, small pieces of pottery, fake archaeological relics, and cheap earrings. Offer to pay half the price the vendors ask. A modern handicrafts market is near the ruins, but prices are lower in town.

South of Monte Albán: Arrazola, Cuilapan & Zaachila

Though the two roads to these towns are unnumbered, they are clearly signposted along the way.

ARRAZOLA: WOODCARVING CAPITAL   Arrazola lies in the foothills of Monte Albán, about 24km (15 miles) southwest of Oaxaca. The tiny town's most famous resident is **Manuel Jiménez,** the septuagenarian grandfather of the resurgence in woodcarving as folk art. Jiménez's polar bears, anteaters, and rabbits carved from copal wood are shown in galleries throughout the world; his home is a magnet for folk-art collectors. Now the town is full of other carvers, all making fanciful creatures painted in bright, festive colors. Little boys will greet you at the outskirts offering to guide you to individual homes for a small tip. Following them is a good way to get to know the town, and after a bit you can take your leave of them.

If you're driving to Arrazola, take the road out of Oaxaca City that goes to Monte Albán, then take the left fork after crossing the Atoyac River and follow the signs for Zaachila. Turn right after the town of Xoxo and you will soon reach Arrazola. You can also take a bus from the second-class station near the Abastos Market.

CUILAPAN'S DOMINICAN MONASTERY   Cuilapan (Kwi-*lah*-pan) is about 15km (9¼ miles) southwest of Oaxaca. The Dominican friars inaugurated their second **monastery** here in 1550. Parts of the convent and church were never completed due to political complications in the late 16th century. The roof of the monastery has fallen in, but the cloister and the church remain. The church, which is still in use, is being restored. There are three naves with lofty arches, large stone columns, and many frescoes. It is open daily from 10am to 6pm; entry is 31 pesos, with an additional cost of 35 pesos for use of a video camera. The monastery is visible on the right a short distance from the main road to Zaachila, and there's a sign as well. The bus from the second-class station stops within a few hundred feet of the church.

ZAACHILA: MARKET TOWNS WITH MIXTEC TOMBS   Farther on from Cuilapan, 24km (15 miles) southwest of Oaxaca, Zaachila (Sah-*chee*-lah) has a **Thursday market;** baskets and pottery are sold for local household use, and the produce market is always full. Also take note of the interesting livestock section and a **mercado de madera (wood market)** just as you enter town.

Behind the church is the entrance to a small **archaeological site** containing several mounds and platforms and two interesting tombs. The artifacts found here now reside in the National Museum of Anthropology in Mexico City, but **Tomb 1** contains carvings that are worth checking out.

At the time of the Spanish Conquest, Zaachila was the last surviving city of the Zapotec rulers. When Cortez marched on the city, the Zapotec offered no resistance, and he formed an alliance with them. This outraged the Mixtec, who invaded Zaachila shortly afterward. The site and tombs are open daily from 9am till 4pm, and the entrance fee is 31 pesos.

In Zaachila is a great outdoor restaurant called **La Capilla** (© **951/528-6115**). It's large and set up to handle lots of people, but often there will be only a few tables occupied. It's a peaceful, attractive setting, and the cooking is delicious. You can enjoy all manner of regional specialties, including *moles, tlayudas,* special roasted chicken, and *barbacoa* on Sundays. You also get handmade tortillas and fresh fruit drinks (made with filtered water and ice). La Capilla is open daily 10am to 7pm. It's located just off the highway at Km 14.5.

To return to Oaxaca, your best option is to line up with locals to take one of the *colectivos* on the main street across from the market. If you're driving, see the directions for Arrazola, above.

South Along Highway 175

SAN BARTOLO COYOTEPEC'S POTTERY   San Bartolo is the home of the famous **black pottery** sold all over Oaxaca. It's also one of several little villages named Coyotepec in the area. Buses frequently operate between Oaxaca and this village, about 15km (9¼ miles) south on Hwy. 175. In 1953, a native woman named Doña Rosa invented the technique of smoking the pottery during firing to make it black and rubbing the fired pieces with a piece of quartz to produce a sheen. Doña Rosa died in 1979, and her son, **Valente Nieto Real,** carries on the tradition. Watching Valente change a lump of coarse clay into a work of art with only two crude plates (used as a potter's wheel) is an almost magical experience. The family's home and factory is a few blocks off the main road; you'll see the sign as you enter town. It's open daily from 9am to 5:30pm.

You can buy black pottery at many shops on the little plaza or in the artists' homes. Villagers who make pottery often place a piece of their work near their front door, by the gate, or on the street. It's their way of inviting prospective buyers to come in.

SAN MARTÍN TILCAJETE: WOODCARVING VILLAGE   San Martín Tilcajete, about 15km (9¼ miles) past San Bartolo, is home to **woodcarvers** who produce *alebrijes*—fantastical, brightly painted animals and imaginary beasts—much like those produced in Arrazola. You can wander from house to house viewing the amazing collections of hot-pink rabbits, bright-blue twisting snakes, and two-headed Dalmatians.

SANTO THOMÁS JALIETZA   About 2km (1¼ miles) beyond San Martín, you'll see a sign on the left for this village of **weavers** who use backstrap looms. The village cooperative runs a market in the middle of town. Prices are fixed; you'll find the greatest variety of goods on Friday.

OCOTLÁN Twenty minutes farther on Hwy. 175 brings you to this fairly large market town. This city is notable for a few reasons: One is the **Aguilar sisters** (Josefina, Guillermina, Irene, and Concepción) and their families, who produce red clay pottery figures that are colorful, sometimes humorous, and prized by collectors. You'll see their row of home-workshops on the right as you enter, with pottery figures on the fence and roof. (Don't go around town asking for the Aguilar family. Most of the town's inhabitants are named Aguilar.)

Ocotlán is also the home of **Rodolfo Morales,** a painter who, upon becoming rich and famous, took an active role in aiding his hometown with renovation projects. Two projects worth visiting are the parish church and former convent. Inside the convent, you can see some of the original decorations of the Dominicans. The noticeable sheen of the stucco walls is produced using the viscous innards of the *nopal* cactus. The convent is now a community museum.

Friday is market day in Ocotlán, and the town fills with people and goods. It's a very good market where you can find a variety of things at reasonable prices.

North of Oaxaca

GUELATAO: BIRTHPLACE OF BENITO JUÁREZ High in the mountains north of Oaxaca, this lovely town has become a living monument to its favorite son, Benito Juárez. Although usually peaceful, the town comes to life on **Juárez's birthday** (Mar 21). The museum, statues, and plaza all attest to the town's obvious devotion to the patriot. A second-class bus departs from Oaxaca's first-class station six times daily. There are also several departures from the second-class station. The trip takes at least 2 hours, through gorgeous mountain scenery. Buses return to Oaxaca every 2 hours until 8pm.

EASTWARD FROM MEXICO CITY: PUEBLA & VERACRUZ

by David Baird

E l Oriente is what Mexicans call this region stretching from the central valley of Mexico east to the Gulf. It includes the states of Puebla, Tlaxcala, and Veracruz, and has much to recommend it. For adventure travelers, it offers excellent white-water rafting, challenging climbs that include Mexico's highest mountain—a dormant volcano called the Pico de Orizaba—and scuba diving along Veracruz's coastal reefs. For culture, the region has three fascinating ruins, excellent museums and historical sites, and great food and architecture.

Puebla and **Cholula** have the ideal highland climate, beautiful colonial churches and palaces, incredible food, and a strong local culture. The ruins in the area feature the startlingly vivid pre-Columbian murals of Cacaxtla and the New World's largest man-made structure, the great pyramid of Cholula. Farther east you'll find the magnificent anthropology museum in **Xalapa,** and the ruins of **El Tajín.** Finally, you get to the coast and the old port of **Veracruz,** a fun town for music, dancing, and nightlife, and for soaking up the easygoing way of life of the Tropics.

PUEBLA & CHOLULA ★★★
128km (79 miles) E of Mexico City; 285km (177 miles) W of Veracruz

Puebla and Cholula sit in a broad valley that lies between mountain ranges and snowcapped volcanoes. The valley is 2,150m (7,052 ft.) above sea level and has a mild climate and fertile soils. Puebla was founded by the Spanish in early colonial times; Cholula's origins date from the earliest civilizations of Mexico. Until the Spanish arrived, it had displayed a remarkable continuity for an ancient city in central Mexico. It seems never to have been sacked and abandoned in the manner of Teotihuacán or Tula or many other cities. And although it was a large city, it was never the capital of an empire. Rather, it seems to have been a religious center.

The Spanish chroniclers noted that it had 365 temples, one for each day of the year. But none of this remains today, as the city was sacked and destroyed during the Spanish Conquest. Only the Great Pyramid still stands.

Though these two cities—one Indian, one Spanish—have recently grown together into one metropolitan area, they still remain worlds apart. Puebla has a large historic center with magnificent architecture, including so many convents, churches, and public palaces that it has been named a UNESCO World Heritage Site. Its architecture differs from that of the rest of Mexico in the extensive use of painted tiles, gold leaf, and molded plaster. Facades and exterior walls are commonly surfaced with clay and Talavera tiles to hide or lend color to the dark gray-black building stone. Cholula, on the other hand, has an architecture that reflects humility and simplicity and has nothing of the grandiose about it. The building materials are of the simplest sort, and the churches, houses, and plazas are unassuming in size and design, with an inherent Indian quality in their most expressive elements.

There are several reasons to visit this part of the world: to sample the food for which Puebla is famous, to take in the colonial architecture, to gaze upon the volcanoes, to explore the Great Pyramid, and to visit the Talavera workshops. Depending on how much you want to do, you could stay here anywhere from 3 days to a week.

Essentials

GETTING THERE & DEPARTING **By Plane** Puebla has an international airport (code PBC), but most air travelers fly into Mexico City because it has more flights. From the Benito Juárez airport in Mexico City, you can take an express bus directly to Puebla. Buses leave every half-hour and cost 180 pesos. They will arrive at either the main bus station (CAPU) or the small downtown bus station. **Continental ExpressJet** (© **800/523-3273** in the U.S., or 01-800/900-5000 in Mexico) has a direct flight connecting Puebla and Houston. A taxi to downtown costs 235 pesos.

By Car From Mexico City the quickest route is **Hwy. 150D.** It's a four-lane toll road that continues on to Veracruz. From Mexico City the tolls add up to 120 pesos; from Veracruz they add up to 350 pesos. From Xalapa, take **Hwy. 140** west to the intersection with 150D.

If you're coming from Querétaro, there's a recently constructed road that bypasses Mexico City and Texcoco, making for a much shorter trip by avoiding city traffic. Completed in September 2009, its official name is **El Arco Norte.** It connects with the Autopista México-Querétaro just south of the turnoff for Tula and stretches east and then south before joining up with the Autopista México-Puebla near San Martín Texmelucan. Tolls add up to about 250 pesos, which is well worth it.

By Bus The ride from **Veracruz** to Puebla takes 3½ hours and costs around 300 pesos. From **Mexico City,** it takes 2 hours and costs 130 pesos. Several bus lines have regular departures from Mexico City's **TAPO bus station,** as frequently as every 15 minutes. You can also catch a bus to Puebla directly from the **Mexico City airport** (see "By Plane," above). There is good bus service between Puebla and Oaxaca (4½ hr.) and now, with the new bypass that circumvents Mexico City, there is direct bus service between Querétaro and Puebla (4 hr.).

You'll probably arrive at a large **bus station,** known by its acronym, CAPU. To get to downtown Puebla, look for a booth marked TAXI AUTORIZADO. Taxi service to almost anywhere in Puebla costs 60 pesos. Many buses to and from the Mexico City airport use the small downtown **Estrella Roja station,** at Calle 4 Poniente 2110.

Puebla

ATTRACTIONS ●

Biblioteca Palafoxiana **24**
Callejón de los Sapos
  (Alley of the Frogs) **21**
Casa de Alfeñique **6**
Casa de Cultura **24**
Casa de los Muñecos **12**
Cathedral **17**
Exconvento de
  Santa Mónica **5**
Exconvento de Santa Rosa **4**
Iglesia de Santo Domingo **7**
Mercado de Artesanías
  (El Parián) **9**

Museo Amparo **23**
Museo Bello y González **15**
Museo Nacional
  del Ferrocarril **3**

RESTAURANTS ◆

Casa de los Muñecos **12**
Celia's Café **20**
Ekos **11**
Fonda de Santa Clara **16**
La Conjura **22**
Mesones Sacristía **19**
Mi Ciudad **1**

HOTELS ■

Estrella de Belem **10**
Hotel Camino Real Puebla **26**
Hotel Colonial **18**
Hotel La Quinta Luna **2**
Hotel Posada San Pedro **8**
Hotel Puebla Plaza **25**
Hotel Royalty **13**
La Casona de la
  China Poblana **11**
Mesones Sacristía **19**
NH Puebla **14**

cinco de mayo & THE BATTLE OF PUEBLA

In the United States, Cinco de Mayo is often compared to the Fourth of July, but it's not Mexican Independence Day. The date commemorates the Battle of Puebla, on May 5, 1862, which resulted in a memorable victory against foreign invaders.

At the time, Napoleon III of France was scheming to occupy Mexico. A well-trained and handsomely uniformed army of 6,000, under the command of General Laurencez, landed in Veracruz with the objective of occupying Mexico City. In its path were 4,000 ill-equipped Mexicans under Gen. Ignacio Zaragoza. Despite the odds, the Mexicans won

resoundingly. The French were humiliated and suffered their first defeat in nearly a half-century at the hands of the penniless, war-torn republic of Mexico.

For Mexico, it marked the nation's first victory against foreign attack, and the battle remains a matter of national pride. Never mind that by the following year the French were in possession of both Puebla and Mexico City. Today the Cinco de Mayo holiday is an enduring symbol of Mexico's sense of patriotism.

On a trip to Puebla, you can visit the forts of Guadalupe and Loreto, where the battle took place, just north of the old part of the city.

VISITOR INFORMATION The **State Tourism Office** (© 222/777-1519, -1520) is at Calle 5 Oriente 3, across from the cathedral. The office is open Monday through Saturday from 8am to 8pm, Sunday from 9am to 2pm. The city's tourism office is under the archway that runs along Palafox y Mendoza in front of the *zócalo* (Portal Hidalgo 14; © 222/404-5047). It's open Monday through Friday 9am to 8pm, with shorter hours on the weekends. The staff at the state office is much more helpful.

CITY LAYOUT Puebla's streets are laid out on a Cartesian quadrant. Two main avenues serve as the x- and y-axes, but instead of separating the positive from the negative numbers, they separate odd from even. The role of x-axis is played by **Avenida Reforma/Palafox.** North of it are even-numbered streets; south of it are odd-numbered streets. The north-south axis (y-axis) is **5 de Mayo/16 de Septiembre.** East of it are even-numbered streets, and west are odd-numbered. So if someone tells you that some place is at the intersection of calles 6 and 10, you know it's in the northeast quadrant. Street names also include a direction—*norte, sur, oriente, poniente* (north, south, east, west). So if someone tells you that a church is on Calle 7 Oriente, then you know what part of town it's in: *Oriente* tells you that it's the eastern portion of an east-west street, and the odd number indicates that it's south of Palafox. Each main axis changes names after it passes the center point of the city. Don't count on taxi drivers to know where restaurants, hotels, or attractions are located; keep addresses handy.

[Fast FACTS] PUEBLA

Area Code The telephone area code is **222**.

Drugstores Pharmacies are almost as common as churches. They usually close around 9pm but take turns staying open late *(de turno)*. **Farmatodo** (© 222/248-1302) delivers to downtown hotels until 10pm. **Farmacias Guadalajara** (© 222/246-0052) has a 24-hour location at the corner of 11 Sur and Paseo Bravo.

Emergency   The emergency number is ✆ **066.**

Hospital   **Beneficiencia Española** is at 19 Norte 1001 (✆ **222/232-0500**).

Internet Access   There are several Internet access businesses downtown.

Post Office   The *correo* is around the corner from the State Tourism office, on Avenida 16 de Septiembre. Hours are Monday through Friday from 8am to 6:30pm, and Saturday 9am to 4pm.

Where to Stay

Except for two small properties in Cholula, all these establishments are in Puebla's city center. Staying in Cholula is a bit more relaxing because it still feels like a small town. From late March through May, the area can experience heat waves. Consider getting a room with air-conditioning for those months. Prices quoted include the 18% tax.

VERY EXPENSIVE

Hotel Camino Real Puebla ★★   This hotel, in the 16th-century former convent of the Immaculate Conception, is a nicely restored colonial gem. Courtyards spill into more courtyards, and remnants of polychromed Colonial-Era frescoes are everywhere, even in the guest rooms, which are decorated handsomely with period-style paintings and furniture. There is considerable variation in size and amenities. Most have clay tile or stone floors and beamed ceilings. Upstairs rooms are generally preferable. The hotel is 2½ blocks south of the *zócalo*.

Calle 7 Poniente 105 (btw. Calle 3 Sur and Av. 16 de Septiembre), Centro Histórico, 72000 Puebla, Pue. www.caminoreal.com/puebla. ✆ **800/722-6466** in the U.S., or 222/229-0909, -0910. Fax 222/232-9251. 84 units. 3,050 pesos deluxe double; 3,615 pesos superior deluxe double; 4,305–5,000 pesos suite. AE, DC, MC, V. Valet parking 50 pesos. **Amenities:** Restaurant; bar; babysitting; exercise room; room service; smoke-free rooms. *In room:* A/C, TV, hair dryer, Internet, minibar.

La Casona de la China Poblana ★★★   According to the owners of this property, La China Poblana resided here toward the end of her life. This could be true; the house is across the street from the Jesuit church that was her favorite. Whatever the truth, the important thing is that this house is a great place to reside now. Rooms are comfortable and surprisingly quiet, and can be made completely dark thanks to the restoration of the Colonial-Era wooden doors that close over the balcony windows. This is one of those revealing details that indicate the level of effort put into the restoration. All the rooms are upstairs. The style of decor varies from modern to colonial to eclectic, but all the rooms have flair. In general, rooms are large and have tile or wood floors.

Calle 4 Norte 2 (at Palafox y Mendoza), 72000 Puebla, Pue. www.casonadelachinapoblana.com.mx. ✆/fax **01-800/122-7662** in Mexico, or 222/242-5621. 10 units. 2,223 pesos luxury double; 2,632 pesos junior suite; 3,744 pesos and up suite. Rates include full breakfast. AE, MC, V. Free secured parking. No children 11 and under. **Amenities:** Restaurant (Ekos, p. 432); bar; concierge; membership in local heath club; room service; smoke-free rooms. *In room:* A/C, TV w/DVD, hair dryer, minibar, Wi-Fi.

EXPENSIVE

Estrella de Belem ★★★   This hotel in Cholula is a block from the entrance to the pyramid. Rooms are an attractive mix of old and modern, except for one master suite decorated exclusively with 1890s furnishings and details. All rooms have heated floors and large bathrooms; master suites come with two-person Jacuzzi tubs and king-size beds. Junior suites come with a queen-size bed. The rooftop pool with terrace is a big plus, as are the elaborate breakfasts. This property is completely smoke-free.

Av. 2 Oriente 410, 72760 Cholula, Pue. www.estrelladebelem.com.mx. ☏ **222/261-1925.** Fax 222/261-1725. 6 units. 1,888 pesos junior suite; 2,478 pesos master suite. Rates include full breakfast. AE, MC, V. Free secure parking. No children. **Amenities:** Bar; rooftop pool; spa. *In room:* A/C, TV, hair dryer, Wi-Fi.

Hotel La Quinta Luna ★★★ This boutique hotel in Cholula is simple and elegant. The seven rooms are all off a large garden courtyard. They are spacious and comfortable, and the windows are double-glazed for quiet. The bathrooms are modern and each is finished differently, but they are all large and well arranged. The service is attentive, and the food at the little restaurant is quite good.

Calle 3 Sur 702, 72760 Cholula, Pue. www.laquintaluna.com. ☏ **800/728-9098** in the U.S. and Canada, or 222/247-8915. Fax 222/247-8916. 7 units. 1,950 pesos double; 2,250 pesos junior suite; 2,715 pesos and up suite. AE, MC, V. Free valet parking. **Amenities:** Restaurant; bar; concierge; room service; smoke-free rooms; spa; Wi-Fi in the reading room. *In room:* TV w/DVD, hair dryer, minibar.

Mesones Sacristía ★★★ This hotel is a fun adaptation of a colonial house in an excellent location in downtown Puebla, near the church of La Compañía. Despite basic modern amenities, the interiors still feel like a step back in time. For instance, the doors haven't been resized, and in a couple of rooms you have to bow slightly to enter. (This feature of colonial architecture enamored the great modern Mexican architect Luis Barragán, who saw the act of bowing as you enter a room as an aspect of colonial religious life.) In the courtyard, a restaurant and popular nightspot serves Poblano specialties. A guitarist or a trio performs romantic songs and ballads until about 11pm. The hotel offers packages for guests interested in cooking lessons or Talavera.

Calle 6 Sur 304, Callejón de los Sapos, 72000 Puebla, Pue. www.mesones-sacristia.com. ☏/fax **222/232-4513** or 222/242-3554. 8 units. 1,880–2,223 pesos double. Rates include full breakfast. AE, MC, V. Free secure parking. **Amenities:** Restaurant; bar; babysitting; access to local health club; room service. *In room:* A/C, TV, hair dryer, Wi-Fi.

MODERATE

Hotel Posada San Pedro ★ ☺ This convenient and comfortable downtown hotel is a better bargain than others in the neighborhood. Spacious rooms come with plain wooden furniture, and midsize bathrooms. A remodeling job in 2010 improved the mattresses and, in some of the rooms, updated the furniture. There is a well-manicured courtyard with a small pool, surrounded by four stories of rooms. It's a family hotel, with afternoon videos for the kids, and child-care service can be provided if requested with sufficient advance notice.

Calle 2 Oriente 202, 72000 Puebla, Pue. www.hotelposadasanpedro.com.mx. ☏ **01-800/712-2808** in Mexico, or 222/891-5700. Fax 222/246-5376. 80 units. 1,065 pesos double; 1,500 pesos suite. Special Internet rates available. AE, MC, V. Free covered parking. **Amenities:** Restaurant; bar; babysitting; outdoor heated pool; room service; smoke-free rooms. *In room:* A/C, TV, hair dryer.

NH Puebla ★★ This hotel in the center of town offers reasonably priced lodging in modern, uncluttered rooms. The overall feel of the place is quiet and soothing. Guest rooms come furnished with deep, comfortable mattresses, soft lights, and a muted color scheme. The modern bathrooms with frosted glass counters are a comfortable size. The junior suites are reasonably priced. The NH is just the place to relax after a busy day walking around this city, which can at times overwhelm the senses.

Calle 5 Sur 105 (at 3 Poniente), 72000 Puebla, Pue. www.nh-hotels.com. ☏ **800/400-0064** in the U.S. and Canada, or 222/309-1919. 128 units. $94–$146 double; $109–$161 deluxe double; $115–$176 junior suite. AE, MC, V. Valet parking $3. **Amenities:** Restaurant; bar; babysitting; concierge; fitness room; small heated outdoor pool; room service; smoke-free rooms. *In room:* A/C, TV, hair dryer, minibar, Wi-Fi.

INEXPENSIVE

Hotel Colonial   This four-story hotel (with elevator) has a great location on the walkway in front of the church of La Compañía. The rooms are ample and attractive. Try to avoid units along Calle 3, which can be noisy from traffic below. The furnishings are simple, but the rooms are attractively decorated. Standard rooms usually contain two twin or double beds. Bathrooms are basic but very clean.

Calle 4 Sur 105 (at 3 Oriente), 72000 Puebla, Pue. www.colonial.com.mx. ✆ **222/246-4612.** Fax 222/246-0818. 67 units. 670–980 pesos double. AE, MC, V. Parking 100 pesos per day. **Amenities:** Restaurant; room service; smoke-free rooms; Wi-Fi (in common areas). *In room:* TV.

Hotel Puebla Plaza   The Puebla Plaza is almost in the shadow of the cathedral. Rooms are small to midsize, with small bathrooms. Most have one double or two twin beds. Reserve a room in back to avoid the commotion in the front courtyard and at the restaurant next door. The lower prices apply to rooms with one double bed. Of the inexpensive hotels listed here, this is my last choice; the others are better maintained.

Calle 5 Poniente 111, 72000 Puebla, Pue. www.hotelpueblaplaza.com.mx. ✆ **01-800/926-2703** in Mexico, or 222/246-3175. Fax 222/242-5792. 48 units. 550–650 pesos double. AE, MC, V. Secure parking 40 pesos. **Amenities:** Wi-Fi (in common areas). *In room:* TV.

Hotel Royalty 🍴   This hotel on Puebla's main square is a sweet deal. You get the central location, yet the rooms are pretty quiet. They are small to medium in size (there's a good bit of variation) with laminate or carpeted flooring and either two double or two twin beds. Most of the junior suites have balconies or at least windows with views of the square. Some of these have larger beds yet don't cost much more.

Portal Hidalgo 8, 72000 Puebla, Pue. www.hotelr.com. ✆ **01-800/638-9999** in Mexico, or 222/242-4740. 45 units. 620 pesos double; 1,250 pesos junior suite. Rates include full breakfast except on Sun. AE, MC, V. No parking. **Amenities:** Restaurant; bar; room service; smoke-free rooms. *In room:* TV, mini-bar, Wi-Fi.

Where to Eat

Puebla is known throughout Mexico for *mole poblano,* a spicy sauce with more than 20 ingredients, including chocolate. Another regional specialty, *pipián,* is similar to *mole* but based on ground, toasted pumpkinseeds. July through September is the season for *chiles en nogada,* and the city goes crazy for them. You'll see them as daily specials on all the menus. This is a dish of contrasts involving a poblano chile; a spicy-sweet filling made of pork, chicken, and sweetmeats; and a walnut cream sauce.

In addition to the restaurants listed below, try the one in the **Mesones Sacristía** (see above). I've enjoyed the *mole* there. Also, I've eaten well in the museum restaurant at the **Casa de los Muñecos.** It has a good reputation and a menu that features several local foods. For a steak, try **Chimichurri** (✆ **222/249-1534**), at the corner of Avenida Juárez and Calle 27 Sur, in the restaurant district (take a cab).

VERY EXPENSIVE

La Conjura ★★★ SPANISH   Perhaps it's odd to eat Spanish food in this city known for its Mexican cuisine, but this restaurant is special. It plays with combinations of old- and new-world ingredients, such as tapas of *chistorra* (Spanish sausage) cooked with a small amount of *guajillo* peppers, or a shrimp dish with locally made goat cheese and passion-fruit sauce. The menu changes daily, with offerings of seafood, lamb, and beef. If they have *arroz negro con calamares* (rice with squid cooked in the squid's ink), give it some consideration, or the *huachinango en alberino* (snapper in a scented wine sauce topped with mussels, clams, and shrimp). The small, attractive dining room with its low, vaulted ceiling was formerly a bodega.

Calle 9 Oriente 201. ✆ **222/232-9693.** Reservations recommended. Tapas 40-150 pesos; main courses 200-430 pesos. AE, MC, V. Sun-Tues 2-6pm; Wed-Sat 2-11pm.

EXPENSIVE

Ekos ★★ NUEVA COCINA   This restaurant, located in the sheltered courtyard of a boutique hotel, La Casona de la China Poblana (p. 429), offers a beautiful and relaxing place for dinner and/or drinks. Most of the dishes are original and incorporate traditional Mexican ingredients. Dishes come and go, depending on the season, but a representative example would be salmon cooked in a hibiscus sauce with a dusting of crumbled pumpkinseeds. The kitchen produces its own *mole*, which is a little different from the traditional recipes. It's served over a chicken breast stuffed with zucchini blossoms. You can also count on delicious soups and fresh ceviche.

Calle 4 Norte 2. ✆ **222/242-5621,** ext. 115. Reservations recommended. Main courses 125-210 pesos. AE, MC, V. Sun-Tues 8am-6pm; Wed-Sat 8am-11pm.

MODERATE

Celia's Café 🏮 REGIONAL/MEXICAN   This restaurant near the Callejón de Los Sapos is also the store for Talavera Celia. Everything served here is on handmade dishes from the factory. The restaurant's regional specialties are quite good, including *pipián* and *mixiotes*. Prices are low, and the service is great. The dining experience is informal and friendly. In the evenings musicians show up, and the scene becomes bohemian as regulars sing along to old favorites until 11pm or even midnight—but you must show up by 9pm before they lock the door to keep out any late arrivals.

Calle 5 Oriente 608. No phone. Main courses 50-135 pesos. MC, V. Daily 9am-9pm.

Fonda de Santa Clara 🍴 REGIONAL   This is one of those restaurants invariably associated with a particular city. For many people, it is the automatic choice in Puebla, but this fame has resulted in a decline in quality. However, the service is still good, the Talavera dining room is well worth seeing, and the *mole* is worth trying. Many visitors walk away happy, especially those who don't harbor high expectations.

Calle 3 Poniente 307. ✆ **222/242-2659.** www.fondadesantaclara.com. Main courses 70-120 pesos lunch, 90-160 pesos dinner. AE, MC, V. Daily 9am-10pm.

Mi Ciudad ★★ MEXICAN   They serve some excellent renditions of all of Puebla's traditional dishes here, including stellar *pipián verde* and chiles rellenos. Situated in the center of Puebla's restaurant and club district along Avenida Juárez, Mi Ciudad is either a short cab ride or a long walk from downtown. The menu is large and varied. Two soups, *chile atole* and *sopa poblana,* are excellent choices. By special request, they will prepare half-portions of either *mole* and *pipián* or *pipián rojo* and *pipián verde.* They also offer steaks and seafood prepared in a variety of ways. The dining room decor makes lots of references to Puebla. An attractive bar area with full food service is to the left as you enter. Another location is in the Zona Dorada, at the corner of 31 Oriente and 14 Sur (✆ **222/245-4556**).

Av. Juárez 2507. ✆ **222/231-5326.** Reservations recommended. Main courses 85-155 pesos. AE, DC, MC, V. Daily 1pm-midnight.

Exploring Puebla

Puebla is a city full of stories and anecdotes that color the colonial houses and convents of the historic district. For historical tours of the city or a tour of the surrounding

> ## La China Poblana: Princess, Slave, Mystic, Icon
>
> In Puebla you'll notice the iconic figure of "La China Poblana" virtually everywhere. She was a historical figure whose life would make for a great opera. She was a young princess from India (not China) who was captured by Portuguese pirates, sold into slavery, and shipped to Mexico on a Manila galleon in the 17th century. Eventually, she was sold to a rich family of Puebla. This family, impressed with the woman's simplicity and spirituality, adopted her. Thus freed from domestic chores, she delved into a life of religious devotions, mixing elements of her native beliefs with Catholicism. She gradually gained fame as a mystic who led an austere life of prayer and became revered by the population of the city. At her death, she was interred in the church of the Compañía, but church authorities later moved her remains when a cult began to form around them. Her form of dress has become the standard folkloric outfit of the city.

area, you might want a guide. One I can recommend is **Carlos Rivero Tours** (© **222/304-2855;** www.riveros.com.mx). He speaks English, knows his city, and is very capable. For a quick sightseeing tour of the city, you can hop on one of the buses that park on the street between the *zócalo* and the cathedral (Calle 3 Oriente). Tours are in Spanish, depart every half-hour, and cost 40 pesos. Or you can climb on to one of the new **Turibus** (www.turibus.com.mx) open-air double-decker buses, with narrative in several languages. Your ticket (110 pesos) is valid for the entire day and allows you to get off at any location and board the next bus that comes along. The circuit of both buses includes a quick view of the site where the Battle of Cinco de Mayo was fought. Both also offer tours to Cholula, but just on the weekends.

CHURCHES

If you were to stop to examine every church you pass in Puebla, you would be in for a long stay. Still, it is something I enjoy doing, even with the smaller churches. Many have simple, austere interiors that express a sweetness and humility that I like. But three churches in the Puebla's historic district require special mention.

The **cathedral ★★★**, completed in 1649, has the tallest bell towers in Mexico. Its dark-stone exterior and severe *Herrerian* (Spanish Renaissance) design lend it a lugubrious appearance that may befit a cathedral but takes a little while to warm up to. The inside is worth a peek. Near the front doors, you can usually find guides (or they'll find you) who offer a short tour.

The **Iglesia de Santo Domingo ★★★**, on the corner of 5 de Mayo and 4 Poniente, was originally part of a Dominican monastery completed in 1611. Lining the walls of the nave are some exquisite baroque altars. In the left transept you'll find the **Capilla del Rosario,** built in 1690. It is a masterpiece of gold leaf and plaster convolutes dedicated to the Virgin of the Rosary. Some observers point to it as the epitome of Mexican baroque architecture. Note, too, the intricate Talavera wainscoting.

The massive **church of La Compañía,** built by the Jesuits, is where La China Poblana worshiped and was briefly entombed. Look to the right of the church doorway, and you'll see a curious bit of text in Talavera. It marks the date of the execution of a con man who arrived in Mexico on a boat from Spain carrying papers identifying him as a *visitador* (papal emissary and inspector). He was wined and dined by the bishops in the capital and in Puebla, and lived the good life for several weeks before being found out. As the text notes, he was executed, and his head was hung above the doorway. The message, I guess: It's not nice to fool the mother church.

Near Cholula are two other impressive churches: Tonantzintla and San Francisco Acatepec. See more about them below.

MUSEUMS

In addition to the museums listed below, a couple of smaller attractions are worth visiting: The **Biblioteca Palafoxiana ★** is an impressive colonial library, the collection of the famous 17th-century bishop who went on to become viceroy, Juan Palafox y Mendoza. The library is on the second floor of the Casa de Cultura, next to the state tourism office. The **Casa de Alfeñique** is a colonial mansion and a landmark known for its exterior plaster decoration, reminiscent of cake icing; the museum collection, a hodgepodge of things Poblano, is fun if you have time. It's at the intersection of calles 4 Oriente and 6 Norte. The **Casa de los Muñecos,** Calle 2 Norte 4, is more important for its exterior than for the museum collection inside. The large grotesques that adorn the late-18th-century facade are said to be caricatures of the town council, though this story is apocryphal.

Exconvento de Santa Mónica After independence, a long political struggle ensued between the national government and the Church. It climaxed in the Reform Wars of the 1850s, when the liberal government instituted several anticlerical measures, including expropriation of the convents. The nuns at Santa Mónica discreetly walled up their doors and kept functioning as a religious community with the aid of their neighbors and the blind eye of local officials. They survived with little assistance from the outside as, over the years, the convent slowly crumbled around them. Then in 1934 (during another political feud btw. church and state), a local official "discovered" them. This history makes for an interesting visit: Displays include the contents of this and two other clandestine convents confiscated at the same time. These nuns weren't sitting on great treasures—most of the paintings are poor representatives of their era—but you will find a rare set of paintings on velvet predating Elvis or poker-playing dogs. Don't miss the crypt, the chapel, and the upper and lower *coros* (choirs). This museum was closed for restoration work for part of 2009 and 2010. **Note:** In the church next door is the much-revered image of *Nuestro Señor de las Maravillas* to the left as you enter. He is an important and popular saint in Puebla, and there's often a crowd of worshipers surrounding him.

Calle 18 Poniente 103. ✆ **222/232-0178.** Admission 30 pesos. Tues–Sun 9am–6pm.

Exconvento de Santa Rosa ★ Unlike Santa Mónica, this former convent was unable to postpone confiscation and served variously as barracks, hospital, and public housing. It's now the home of the **Museo de Arte Popular.** It can be seen only by tour, which includes a visit to the kitchen where *mole* was invented, and a large display of the crafts practiced in the state. If you enjoy handicrafts, don't miss this place, but the experience varies greatly depending on the knowledge of the tour guide. I've had good guides; I've had bad guides. Unfortunately, the best don't speak English. Tours take 1 hour and usually start on the hour.

Calle 3 Norte 1203. ✆ **222/232-7792.** Admission 25 pesos. Tues–Sun 10am–5pm (last tour at 4pm).

Museo Amparo ★★★ The finest museum in the city, the Museo Amparo (named for the deceased wife of the founder) has a brilliant collection of pre-Columbian pieces from across Mexico, beautifully displayed and intelligently organized. Its collections of colonial and modern art are good, and the museum gets traveling exhibitions, which usually don't require an additional admission charge. The collection of *arte virreinal* (colonial art) is on the second floor and includes decorative objects and furniture. It is exhibited in the restored living quarters of the original mansion. The interiors are from the *Porfiriato* (1880–1910), with the elaborate decoration of that period. Inexpensive audio tours of the pre-Columbian collection are available. Or you can hire an English-speaking guide for the entire museum (180 pesos). Signs are in Spanish and English.

Calle 2 Sur 708. ℂ **222/229-3850.** www.museoamparo.com. Admission 35 pesos adults, 25 pesos children 3-12 and students; free Mon. Wed–Mon 10am–6pm.

Museo Bello y González ★★   Located near the corner of Calle 3 Sur and Calle 3 Poniente, a block west of the *zócalo,* this museum houses a fine collection of 17th-, 18th-, and 19th-century art, furniture, and antiques from all over the world. Many of the Oriental objects in the museum were brought over in colonial times on a Manila galleon. Viewing the house is another reason for seeing the place. There are several beautiful rooms. My favorite room is almost completely covered in Talavera tile, and the display cabinets are filled with Talavera from various centuries. The museum is named for José Luis Bello y González, the father of Mariano Bello, the man who gathered this collection. Admission includes a guided tour (in English or Spanish).

Calle 3 Poniente 302. ℂ **222/232-9475.** Admission 30 pesos. Tues–Sun 10am–5pm.

Museo Nacional del Ferrocarril   This museum exhibits several train engines and cars in a large open space, including both steam and diesel locomotives, a baggage car, passenger cars, a dining car, a Pullman coach, and a caboose. You can board several of these, but a couple of the best are off-limits. Some of the cars serve double-duty as gallery space for photos and artwork relevant to railroads.

Calle 11 Norte and Calle 12 Poniente. ℂ **222/774-0100.** Admission 10 pesos. Tues–Sun 9am–5pm.

Exploring Cholula
VOLCANOES & PYRAMIDS

On the western outskirts of Puebla is the small town of **Cholula,** which offers a good vantage point for viewing the volcanoes, Popocatépetl and Ixaccihuatl. These volcanoes separate the Valley of Mexico from the Valley of Puebla. The best time for viewing them is on a clear morning in the winter or early spring, when the snowcaps would be at their largest.

In pre-Columbian times, Cholula was a large city—the religious capital of highland Mexico. The Spanish razed the hundreds of temples that stood here, and we know little about them. But the **Great Pyramid** still exists, the largest pyramid in the New World. At first glimpse, it looks more like a hill crowned by a church (Nuestra Señora de los Remedios). All the surfacing of the pyramid was removed in earlier times, but you can readily make out the geometry of the stepped platform, which rises from the ground in four levels. One face of the pyramid has been partially reconstructed. Tunnels dug by archaeologists give you an idea of how the thing was built. From atop the neighboring platform (if the guards allow you to climb it), you can get a view of the volcano with the church in the foreground. The entrance fee for the Cholula pyramid is 41 pesos; the site is open daily from 9am to 5:30pm. Tour guides charge 150 pesos per person and can be located at the entrance to the main tunnel.

While you're in Cholula, you might want to walk around the town's center. A restaurant under the stone archway bordering the *zócalo* offers a decent, inexpensive meal. It's called **Los Tulipanes.**

TONANTZINTLA & SAN FRANCISCO ACATEPEC

A perfect complement to this trip is a visit to the church of **Tonantzintla** ★★★, just to the south. Leave the town on Bulevar Miguel Alemán, which becomes the road to Tonantzintla. Less than 1.5km (1 mile) ahead, the church is within plain sight of the road. It's famous for its jewel-box interior, executed in an endearing style of Indian baroque. It has mesmerized many visitors, including R. Gordon Wasson, who saw in its manifold imagery allusions to a secret mushroom cult. If this visit hasn't quenched your appetite for visiting churches, proceed a bit farther down the road and you will imperceptibly cross into the neighboring community of **San Francisco Acatepec** ★★. Its church is also along the road and stands out for its stunning tile facade.

Shopping

Talavera ★★★ is a type of majolica earthenware fashioned into dishes, tiles, and decorative objects. It traces its origins back to the Moors, who introduced it into Spain in the 9th century, setting up workshops in the town of Talavera. From there, artisans took the practice to Puebla in the 16th century—hence the name.

It's no exaggeration to say that Talavera is the face of Puebla. Its widespread use as facing for buildings is the most distinctive characteristic of the local architecture. You see it almost anywhere you look. And you'll definitely see it anywhere you shop. But the best and most expensive Talavera is produced by a dozen factories in Puebla and Cholula, all members of an association that sets standards and certifies manufacturers. To be officially certified, a workshop must use only the traditional methods and ingredients (no commercial ceramic mix or glazes); practically everything must be done by hand. There's no restriction on artistic taste, just the methods for making Talavera. So there's a good bit of variety from one workshop to another. The genuine article is not cheap, so you should look around in the showrooms until you learn how to discern the knockoffs from the real stuff and find a style you prefer over others.

If you're interested in watching people make Talavera, consider a workshop tour. **Uriarte Talavera,** Calle 4 Poniente 911 (© **222/232-1598**), charges 50 pesos for its tour. The factory has an impressive facade made completely of Talavera. And inside you'll see some great pieces displayed. There's one factory in the Parián area—**Talavera Armando,** at Calle 6 Norte 408 (© **222/232-6468**). If enough people are around, they'll get a free tour. One factory, **Talavera Celia** (© **222/242-3663**), has a shop/restaurant downtown, at Calle 5 Oriente 608, that serves meals on its own Talavera (see the review for Celia's Café, above). Inquire there about touring the workshop, which isn't too far from downtown. **Talavera de la Luz** specializes in large maps and panoramic views rendered in Talavera tiles. It has shown some of its largest pieces in museums in the United States. Unfortunately, it doesn't open very much.

The **Mercado de Artesanías (El Parián)** is a pedestrian-only, open-air shopping area just east of Calle 6 Norte between calles 2 and 6 Oriente. You'll see rows of neat brick shops selling inexpensive crafts and souvenirs. The shops are open daily from 10am to 8pm. Bargain to get a good price. While you're in this area, you can take a look at the **Teatro Principal.**

For antiques browsing, go to **Callejón de los Sapos (Alley of the Frogs),** about 3 blocks southeast of the *zócalo* near Calle 4 Sur and Calle 7 Oriente. Wander in and out; there's good stuff, large and small. Shops are generally open daily from 10am to 2pm and 4 to 6pm. On Saturday mornings, there's a flea market in the little square. If you're there in the afternoon, stop by **La Pasita,** across Calle 5 from the Plaza de los Sapos, to taste homemade cordials and browse through the owner's humorous collection of Mexicana. The owner keeps flexible hours and only opens if the mood strikes him. Start with a *pasita*, then work your way up to a China Poblana—a layered cordial of red, white, and green liqueurs.

If you're out walking around Puebla, you might amble over to a short stretch of Calle 6 Oriente between 4 Norte and 5 de Mayo. It has a few picturesque candy shops selling famous local sweets, such as *camotes* (sweets made from yams in various flavors), which are very popular with Mexicans but are not to my taste. There's also a Victorian-era shopping mall made of wrought iron, which has been fixed up nicely: Ex-Mercado La Victoria, which is behind Santo Domingo.

Puebla After Dark

Mariachis play daily from 6pm on **Plaza de Santa Inés,** Calle 11 Poniente and Calle 3 Sur. They stroll through the crowds that gather at the sidewalk cafes. Another square where you can hear live music is **Plaza de los Sapos,** Calle 7 Oriente near Calle 6 Sur. In the courtyard of the **Mesón Sacristía de la Compañía,** Calle 6 Sur 304, a singer/guitarist entertains with popular ballads until 11pm.

Along Avenida Juárez, there are several popular bars and clubs. When the weather is agreeable, one of my favorite places for drinks is the rooftop bar of the **NH Puebla** hotel (p. 430) at the corner of calles 3 and 5. It offers a great view. **Teorema,** Reforma 540, near Calle 7 Norte (② **222/242-1014**), is a good coffee shop and bookstore that features guitarists and folk singers every evening. It's open daily from 9:30am to 2:30pm and 4:30pm to midnight.

TLAXCALA ★

120km (74 miles) E of Mexico City; 40km (25 miles) N of Puebla

Tlaxcala is the capital of Mexico's smallest state (also named Tlaxcala) and a Colonial-Era city that is much slower paced than Puebla. It's close enough to be visited in a day trip from Puebla, but I enjoy spending the night and getting to know the city at leisure. In some respects, life in Tlaxcala reminds me of an older Mexico with slower rhythms and life lived day by day. To understand Tlaxcala and its inhabitants, one must go back 500 years, to before the conquest, when the Tlaxcaltecan federation of city-states was the bitter rival of the Aztec Empire, and both were locked in a mortal struggle that the Tlaxcaltecans were losing. Along come the conquistadors. And Cortez, crafty Spaniard that he was, played on this enmity to enlist the Tlaxcaltecan warriors in his siege of the Aztec capital, Tenochtitlán, now Mexico City. As a reward for being the first and foremost allies of the Spanish, the Tlaxcaltecan people received special rights and privileges and a certain level of independence.

To this day, 500 years after the fact, locals express a latent defensiveness for having befriended the invading forces and betrayed the New World. It surfaces frequently in conversations with visitors, sometimes surprisingly quickly. Serving to mitigate these feelings of guilt is the martyred figure of Xicoténcatl, a Tlaxcaltecan prince who rebelled against the Spanish and became a symbol of cultural resistance, much the same way as the Aztec prince Cuauhtémoc did. Another peculiarity that sets locals apart is that their worldview is still shaped by the ancient rivalry, so that they conceive of Tlaxcala and Mexico City as the two poles of a national axis, with both cities in possession of a set of complementary cultural figures arranged in pairings. Thus, as with Xicoténcatl and Cuauhtémoc, you have **La Virgen de Ocotlán** opposite La Virgen de Guadalupe, and so forth.

This fascinating history, local culture, and the relaxed pace of life here make for pleasant exploration. Tlaxcala retains its small-town atmosphere and overall low prices. *Tip:* It's best to visit Tlaxcala during the week because it has become a week-end getaway for city dwellers.

Essentials

GETTING THERE & DEPARTING A taxi ride from Puebla takes 30 to 40 min-utes and costs 280 pesos. The bus takes an hour, costs 18 pesos, and leaves every 15 to 30 minutes from a station on 6 Poniente, between 11 Norte and 13 Norte.

VISITOR INFORMATION Tlaxcala's **tourist information office** is at the intersection of avenidas Juárez and Lardizábal (© **01-800/509-6557** in Mexico, or 246/465-0900). Office hours are daily 9am to 7pm. On Friday, Saturday, and Sunday, it sponsors small bus tours of the city (in Spanish) that cost 20 pesos. It also offers a Sunday tour of the Cacaxtla site. Inquire at the office.

[FastFACTS] TLAXCALA

The telephone area code is **246**. Most hotels have Internet access, but there is also **free Wi-Fi** on the main square, though it often isn't working. A number of small Internet cafes can be found within a couple blocks of the *zócalo*. The **post office** is on the main square beside the Hotel Posada San Francisco and is open from 9am to 5pm Monday through Friday.

Exploring Tlaxcala

Two blocks from the main plaza is a classic old bullring, still in use, and across from it is the old **Templo de San Francisco,** supposedly the site where the Tlaxcalan chiefs were baptized. The church is noted for the elaborately inlaid Moorish ceiling below the choir loft. A painting inside the Chapel of the Third Order shows the baptism of the chiefs. To the right of the Templo is the former convent, now a museum containing early paintings and artifacts from nearby archaeological sites.

The **Government Palace ★★**, on the handsome, tree-shaded *zócalo,* contains vivid murals by a local artist, Desiderio Hernández Xochitiotzin, who died in 2007. The murals illustrate the city's history and are definitely worth a visit. The expanded **Museo de Artesanías** (© **246/462-2337**), on Sánchez Piedras between Lardizábal and Primera de Mayo, showcases the state's wide-ranging crafts and customs. Here local artisans give visitors demonstrations in such crafts as embroidery, weaving, and *pulque*-making (juice of fermented *agaves*). The museum is open Tuesday through Sunday from 10am to 6pm; admission is 6 pesos.

Less than 1km (⅔ mile) from the town center is the **Santuario de Ocotlán ★★**, constructed after Juan Diego Bernardino claimed to have seen an apparition of the Virgin Mary on that site in 1541. Baroque inside and out, it has elaborate interior decorations of carved figures and curling gilded wood that date from the 1700s. The carvings are attributed to Francisco Miguel Tlayotehuanitzin, an Indian sculptor who labored for more than 20 years on the building's decoration.

EXPLORING THE CACAXTLA ARCHAEOLOGICAL SITE ★★★

Cacaxtla (pronounced Kah-*kahsh*-tlah) is perhaps Tlaxcala's main attraction. It's a pre-Hispanic hilltop site 19km (12 miles) southwest of the city with some of the most vivid murals in Mexico. The site was uncovered in 1975. What the archaeologists

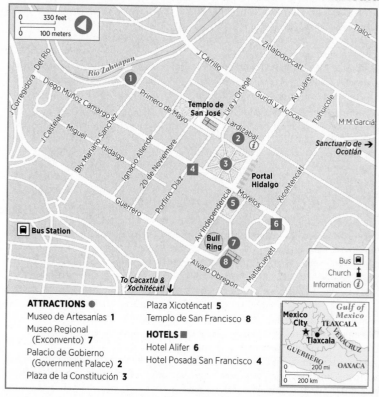

ATTRACTIONS ●
Museo de Artesanías **1**
Museo Regional
  (Exconvento) **7**
Palacio de Gobierno
  (Government Palace) **2**
Plaza de la Constitución **3**

Plaza Xicoténcatl **5**
Templo de San Francisco **8**

HOTELS ■
Hotel Alifer **6**
Hotel Posada San Francisco **4**

found—vivid murals in red, blue, black, yellow, and white, showing Maya warriors (from the Yucatán)—revolutionized our understanding of settlement patterns in central highland Mexico. Since then, more murals and at least eight construction phases have been uncovered.

Scholars attribute the influence of the site to a little-known tri-ethnic group (Náhuatl, Mixtec, and Chocho-Popoloca) known as Olmec-Xicalanca, from Mexico's Gulf Coast. Among the translations of its name, "merchant's trade pack" seems most revealing. Like Casas Grandes, north of Chihuahua City and Xochicalco between Cuernavaca and Taxco, Cacaxtla appears to have been an important crossroads for merchants, astronomers, and others in the Mesoamerican world. Its apogee, between A.D. 650 and 900, corresponds with the abandonment of Teotihuacán, the decline of the Classic Maya civilization, and the emergence of the Toltec culture at Tula.

How those events affected Cacaxtla isn't known. The principal **mural** is a vividly detailed victory scene, with triumphant dark-skinned warriors wearing jaguar skins, and the vanquished dressed in feathers and having their intestines extracted. Numerous symbols of Venus (a half-star with five points) found painted at the site have led archaeoastronomy scholar John Carlson to link historical events such as wars, captive taking, and ritual sacrifice with the appearance of Venus; all of this was likely undertaken in hope of ensuring the continued fertility of crops.

The latest mural discoveries show a wall of corn plants from which human heads sprout, next to a merchant whose pack is laden with goods. The murals flank a grand **acropolis** with unusual architectural motifs. A giant steel roof protects the grand plaza and murals.

Xochitécatl is a small ceremonial center on a hilltop overlooking Cacaxtla, about 1km (⅔ mile) to the east and in plain sight of Cacaxtla. It was probably inhabited, at least in the classical period, by the same people living in Cacaxtla. A curious **circular pyramid** stands atop this hill, 180m (590 ft.) above the surrounding countryside. Beside it are two other **pyramids** and three massive **boulders** (one about 3m/9¾ ft. in diameter), which were hollowed out for some reason. Hollowed boulders appear to have been restricted to the Puebla-Tlaxcala valley. Excavation of the Edificio de la Espiral (spiral pyramid), dated between 1000 and 800 B.C. (middle formative period), encountered no stairways. Access is thought to have been by its spiral walkway. Rounded boulders from the nearby Zahuapan and Atoyac rivers were used in its construction. Cone-shaped platforms in this part of Mexico are thought to have been dedicated to Ehecatl, god of the wind. The base diameter exceeds 55m (180 ft.); it rises to a height of 15m (49 ft.).

The stepped and terraced **Pyramid of the Flowers** was started during the middle formative period. Modifications continued into colonial times, as exemplified by faced-stone and stucco-covered adobe. Of the 30 bodies found during excavations, all but one were children. Little is known about the people who built Xochitécatl. Evidence suggests that the area was dedicated to Xochitl, goddess of flowers and fertility. The small **museum** contains pottery and small sculpture, and a **garden** holds larger sculpture. From the top of the hill you are afforded an excellent view of Popocatépetl and, on a clear day, can make out the snowcap of the Pico de Orizaba.

Admission to both sites is 42 pesos, plus 35 pesos for a video or still camera. Both sites are open daily 9am to 5pm. To get there and back in a taxi, you will have to contract the taxi on an hourly basis (100 pesos per hour) so that he'll wait for you. Before doing that, ask at the tourism office to find out if any set tours to Cacaxtla are running.

Where to Stay & Eat in Tlaxcala

Tlaxcala has several restaurants beneath the stone arches (*portales*) on the east side of the *zócalo*. One of them, **Los Portales** (no phone) has handmade corn tortillas all day and makes good breakfasts. Just across the small Plaza Xicoténcatl, at Calle Independencia 7-A, is **Tirol** (© **246/462-3754**), a restaurant serving several regional specialties and traditional dishes.

Hotel Alifer The Alifer's rooms are medium size and simply furnished. Most have carpeting; some have tile floors. The rooms are a little worn but are clean and comfortable. The poor lighting is the only other thing that I can complain about, which is saying quite a lot for a hotel in this price range with this kind of location. The price varies by number and size of beds.

Morelos 11, 90000 Tlaxcala, Tlax. www.hotelalifer.com.mx. © **246/462-5678,** -3062. 40 units. 435–620 pesos double. MC, V. Free parking. **Amenities:** Restaurant. *In room:* TV, Wi-Fi.

Hotel Posada San Francisco de Tlaxcala This hotel is in a 19th-century mansion facing the town's main square called La Casa de Piedra (House of Stone). Most guest rooms are in the back of the property in two modern buildings fronting a large pool that is shaded by a roof. The rooms are attractive and comfortable. Almost all have been remodeled in the last couple of years. Most have carpeting, but some have tile floors and area rugs. Five rooms in the *zona antigua* have more character but are smaller. They are in one of the original buildings and are grouped around a small stone patio.

Plaza de la Constitución 17, 90000 Tlaxcala, Tlax. © **246/462-6022.** Fax 246/462-6818. 68 units. 1,270 pesos double; 1,870 pesos suite. AE, MC, V. Free parking. **Amenities:** Restaurant; bar; outdoor heated pool; room service; tennis court. *In room:* TV, Wi-Fi.

XALAPA ★

102km (63 miles) NW of Veracruz; 203km (126 miles) NE of Puebla

Xalapa (pronounced Hah-*lah*-pa and sometimes spelled "Jalapa," which lent its name to the famed jalapeño pepper) is a highland city in the middle of Mexico's prime coffee-growing area and the capital of the state of Veracruz. Less than 2 hours from the port of Veracruz, it's a hilly city, crisscrossed by narrow, winding streets and alleys. A fine, misty rain known as *chipi chipi* often floats in the air, cloaking the views in a vaporous shroud. When the sky is clear, you can sometimes make out in the distance the snowcapped peak of Pico de Orizaba (also known as Citlaltépetl), an extinct volcano that is Mexico's tallest peak, at 5,747m (18,850 ft.).

Xalapa is a university town and has the best music school in the country, which is part of the University of Veracruz. It's easy to come across chamber music and symphony concerts. Xalapa also has an excellent anthropology museum that is second only to Mexico City's monster of a museum. And for active types, there's first-rate white-water rafting nearby.

Essentials

GETTING THERE & DEPARTING   Veracruz, 1½ hours away, has the closest major airport. If you're **driving** from Veracruz, take Hwy. 180 to Cardel, and then go west on Hwy. 140. From Papantla, you can avoid the mountains by taking Hwy. 180 south to Cardel. From Mexico City and Puebla, there's a turnoff for Hwy. 140 on the toll highway to Veracruz (Hwy. 150D). Fog is common and dangerous between Perote and Xalapa. The trip by bus to or from Papantla takes 4 hours.

The **bus station** (CAXA) is 2.5km (1½ miles) east of the town center off Calle 20 de Noviembre. Taxis are downstairs, and prices are controlled. Tickets to downtown cost around 35 pesos. Buses run to Veracruz every 20 to 30 minutes and to Puebla 15 times a day. You can buy tickets downtown at the same information booth in front of the city hall where tourism has a staff person. Hours are Monday through Saturday 8am to 9pm.

Being Alert

I regard Xalapa as a generally safe place to visit, but there was a prolonged gun battle here in January 2011 between the army and drug cartel members. Xalapa hasn't seen much violence before this, and though information is hard to come by, it seems that kidnappings are uncommon here. On the other hand, other parts of the state not far from Xalapa have seen violence. The police chiefs of three small towns of central Veracruz have been killed, and there have been shootouts, kidnappings, and assassinations in the port city of Veracruz. Before you plan a visit, check the U.S. Department of State website (www.travel.state.gov) for travel warning updates.

VISITOR INFORMATION   Go to the **tourist information booth** in front of the Ayuntamiento (city hall), across from the Plaza Juárez. Hours are Monday through Friday from 9am to 3pm.

CITY LAYOUT   Xalapa is a hilly town with streets that defy order. In the center of town is the large **Plaza Juárez,** where on a clear day the Pico de Orizaba is visible to the southwest. Across the street (north) from the plaza is the Ayuntamiento (city hall); east is the Palacio del Gobierno (state capitol). The cathedral is across (north) from this.

GETTING AROUND   Most of the recommended hotels and restaurants (see "Where to Stay" and "Where to Eat," below) are within easy walking distance of the central Plaza Juárez. Taxis in Xalapa are inexpensive, as are city buses. Because streets in the center of town are busy and narrow, cabs aren't allowed to stop just anywhere. Sometimes you have to look for a TAXI sign. Otherwise, try to hail a cab in a place that permits traffic to pass. If you would like a guide to give you a tour of the city or the surrounding region, contact José Ernesto Hernández (see "River Rafting," below).

[Fast FACTS] XALAPA

The telephone **area code** is ✆ **228.** The city is 1,430m (4,690 ft.) above sea level. The **climate** is humid and cool, for the most part. It can be warm from March to early May. The light *chipi chipi* rain comes and goes at any time of year. The rainy season is May through July and can bring strong downpours.

Exploring Xalapa

For information on cultural events, go to **El Agora,** a cultural center with a coffee shop beneath the Plaza Juárez (reached by steps on the south side of the plaza). Look for posters announcing upcoming concerts. There's usually something going on. Also look in the local paper, *Diario de Xalapa,* or in the *Cartelera,* a monthly publication of the Instituto Veracruzano de Cultura.

Museo de Antropología de Xalapa ★★★   This museum exhibits excellent examples of the megalithic heads and other monumental sculptures made by the Olmec—better than those in Mexico City or in Villahermosa. The collection of Totonac pieces, from the highly stylized smiling faces to the unadorned, realistic sculptures of faces and heads, is the best anywhere. The museum is laid out in order from earliest to latest cultures, from the Olmec—the mother culture of Mesoamerican civilization—to the post-Classic civilizations of Veracruz. Explanatory text is in Spanish. Bilingual guides are available. A taxi runs about 35 pesos.

Av. Xalapa s/n. ✆ **228/815-4952,** -0708. www.uv.mx/max. Admission 50 pesos, free for children 11 and younger. Tues–Sun 9am–5pm.

Museo de El Lencero   Occasionally called the Museo de Muebles (Furniture Museum), this country estate 14km (8¾ miles) southeast of the town center was for 14 years (1842–56) the home of Antonio López de Santa Anna, the 11-time president of Mexico. Here he retreated from the world, though on occasion he opened his doors to receive notable visitors. Furniture from Mexico, Europe, and Asia fills the rooms, illustrating the cosmopolitan tastes of Mexico's upper classes during the 19th century.

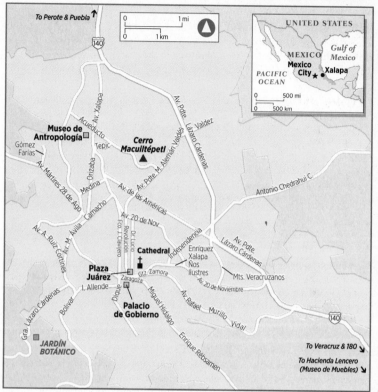

Among the notable pieces is the leader's bed, embellished with the national emblem (an eagle holding a serpent in its beak). The grounds are lovely and shaded by ancient trees. The grand house overlooks a spring-fed pond.

Carretera Xalapa-Veracruz Km 10. No phone. Admission 40 pesos; free guided tours (in Spanish only) on request. Tues–Sun 10am–5pm. Bus: Banderilla–P. Crystal–Lencero from Av. Lázaro Cárdenas to village of El Lencero or nearby spot along the highway. Drive or take a taxi (125 pesos) about 10km (6¼ miles) south of town on Hwy. 140 toward Veracruz, past the country club; watch for the signs on the right.

RIVER RAFTING

Close by Xalapa are three popular rivers for rafting and a number of rafting companies that can accommodate you. No experience is necessary. If you're planning ahead, contact José Ernesto Hernández at **Eco Expediciones** (☎ **228/812-1176;** www. ecoexpediciones.net). He is the most trusted guide in the area.

Where to Stay

Mesón del Alférez ★★   In most other parts of Mexico, rooms such as these, in a thoroughly renovated colonial house, would go for much more money. Most rooms are spacious and beautifully decorated. Standard rooms come with one double bed or one queen, suites with a choice of two doubles or one king. Rooms are colonial in style, accented by bright colors and stone. In some, a loft creates extra space. Two smaller rooms in front get noise from the street. Additional rooms around the corner in a modern house, Balcones del Alférez, are comfortable, modern, and a little quieter.

Sebastián Camacho 2, corner of Zaragoza, 91000 Xalapa, Ver. www.pradodelrio.com. ℂ/fax **228/818-0113.** 17 units. 750 pesos standard double; 930 pesos suite. Rates include continental breakfast. MC, V. Free secure parking 1 block away. **Amenities:** Restaurant; room service; smoke-free rooms. *In room:* TV, hair dryer, Wi-Fi.

Posada del Cafeto 🦯 This well-managed, comfortable hotel has three stories of rooms surrounding a tidy garden. Furnishings and decor are simple and attractive: clay tile floors, white plaster walls with cheerful accents, and rustic wood furniture. Each room is slightly different. Some are small, but all have ample bathrooms. Bed choices include one double, two twins, a twin and a double, or two doubles for a higher rate.

Canovas 8, 91000 Xalapa, Ver. www.pradodelrio.com. ℂ **228/817-0023.** 32 units. 540–600 pesos double; 850 pesos suite. Rates include continental breakfast. MC, V. No parking. **Amenities:** Cafe (breakfast); Wi-Fi (in lobby). *In room:* TV, hair dryer.

Where to Eat

Callejón del Diamante is an alley near the cathedral, with a half-dozen inexpensive restaurants that cater to office workers and students. One, **La Sopa,** offers a daily blue-plate special for 50 pesos. The restaurant at the **Mesón del Alférez** hotel (see above) serves traditional Mexican food and some regional dishes. At night you can get some delicious tamales at **Tamales y Atoles Doña Adelina** (ℂ **228/841-0317**) at Ursula Galván 108 (3 blocks west of the Parque Juárez). Each tamal goes for 14 to 20 pesos, and they are big enough that two would make a meal.

Churrería del Recuerdo MEXICAN This is a popular place for supper, and I've eaten well here. The traditional supper fare is *antojitos*—enchiladas, *gorditas,* and tamales, which you can wash down with *tepache* (fermented pineapple drink). You might want to try the *churros,* best described as the Spanish equivalent of doughnuts, but crispy and usually eaten with hot chocolate. The restaurant is across from the Hotel Xalapa; take a cab (35 pesos from downtown). On my last visit service was very slow.

Victoria 158. ℂ **228/841-4961.** *Antojitos* 50–70 pesos. No credit cards. Daily 6pm–midnight.

La Casona del Beaterio MEXICAN The restaurant occupies a colonial house near the main square. It offers outdoor and indoor dining in an attractive setting. The menu is large and varied but highlights grilled cuts of beef, some marinated in *adobo* (a mix of chiles and spices). Also on the menu are plenty of Mexican standards, including *sopa azteca* (tortilla soup), *pechuga poblana* (chicken breast cooked in a poblano chile cream sauce), and enchiladas. Among the main courses is a platter of traditional dishes called *cazuelitas mexicanas,* which allows you to sample a bit of several things. La Casona is 2 blocks east of Parque Juárez on the south side of the street. Live music begins at 9pm from Thursday through Saturday.

Zaragoza 20. ℂ **228/818-2119.** Breakfast 50–60 pesos; *comida corrida* Mon–Sat 70 pesos; main courses 65–220 pesos. AE, MC, V. Tues–Sun 8am–midnight; Mon 8am–10pm.

VERACRUZ CITY ★

Veracruz has a reputation as a town with a rich history but little to show for it. True enough, since much of that history involved sackings by pirates; heavy bombardment by three different foreign powers (including once with the French in the wonderfully named French Pastry War); and epidemics of malaria, yellow fever, and cholera. One may not want to preserve such a history, even when those same events didn't destroy the city. For this reason, and for the character of the natives, Veracruz (unlike Puebla) is better suited to cafegoers than museumgoers. With the exception of the old fort of San Juan de Ulúa and perhaps the aquarium, the museums can be missed. Come here for the feel of the Tropics, the balmy air, and the carefree attitude of the locals.

Veracruz brings to mind other Gulf and Caribbean port cities—part New Orleans, part Maracaibo. Things such as schedules are managed rather loosely, even by Mexican standards. You won't find punctuality and order here. Instead, you relax: You get your coffee in the morning at the Café de la Parroquia, you stroll down the *malecón* (boardwalk), you take in the party scene at the *zócalo* (town square) at night. It's a simple life. The city attracts a lot of Mexicans, who come here to take a break from the social constraints of their hometowns. In many parts of Mexico, for instance, a woman walking into a bar by herself would be frowned upon; not here.

Music is important to Veracruz. Specific to the port city are *marimba, danzonera,* and *comparsa* (carnavalesque) music. Just south of the city begins the Jarocha region of the state, whose music is rhythmic, with sexually suggestive lyrics that depend on double meanings. This is the home of "La Bamba," popularized by Ritchie Valens. In the northern part of the state is the Huasteca region. Its music, the *huapango huasteco,* involves a violin, a couple of strumming guitars, and harmonized singing.

Cortez first landed a bit north of where the port is now, and his name for the place gives you an idea of what was on his mind: Villa Rica de la Vera Cruz ("Rich town of the true cross"). In colonial times, the Spanish galleons sailed for Spain from here, loaded with silver and gold. Pirates repeatedly attacked, and on one occasion, captured the city. The citizens defended themselves, constructing a wall around the old town and a massive fort, San Juan de Ulúa. The walls are gone now, but the fort remains.

Essentials

GETTING THERE & DEPARTING By Plane   Continental (© 800/523-3273 in the U.S., or 01-800/900-5000 in Mexico) has nonstop service to and from Houston. **Aeroméxico** (© 800/237-6639 in the U.S., 01-800/021-4000, 229/935-0283, or 229/34-1534) and its affiliates offer service to and from Mexico City and other domestic destinations.

12

EASTWARD FROM MEXICO CITY: PUEBLA & VERACRUZ

Veracruz City

Public Insecurity

Lately, local attitudes have been slightly less carefree, as the violence raging in the bordering states of Tamaulipas and Nuevo Leon has spilt over into this state. The principal cause of the violence is a gang war between two formerly allied criminal organizations— the Zetas and the Gulf Cartel. Travelers haven't been targeted, but there have been shootouts in the street including one in the modern hotel zone to the south of downtown. You should exercise caution when visiting this port city.

The **airport** is 11km (6¾ miles) from the town center. Getting there by **taxi** costs 150 pesos. Major rental car agencies with counters at the airport and locations in downtown hotels include **Avis** (☎ **800/331-1212** in the U.S., or 229/931-1580), **Dollar** (☎ **800/800-4000** in the U.S., or 229/935-5231), and **National** (☎ **800/328-4567** in the U.S., or 229/931-7556).

By Car   From Mexico City (6 hr.) and Puebla (3½ hr.), take the *autopista* **(toll Hwy. 150D)** into Veracruz. From Xalapa (1½ hr.), take **Hwy. 140** to coastal toll **Hwy. 180** south.

By Bus   The **ADO** first-class bus station is 20 blocks south of the town center on Díaz Mirón between calles Orizaba and Molina. There is frequent service to Mexico City, Puebla, Xalapa, and other cities. Taxis wait in front of the terminal; the trip to the center costs around 30 pesos. You can buy a bus ticket downtown at the **Ticket Bus** agency (☎ **01-800/702-8000** in Mexico), at the corner of Mario Molina and Independencia. It's open Monday through Saturday from 10am to 6pm.

VISITOR INFORMATION   The **tourism office** (☎/fax 229/200-2071) is downtown by the *zócalo,* on the ground floor of the Palacio Municipal (City Hall). It's open Monday through Friday from 9am to 8pm, Sunday from 10am to 6pm.

CITY LAYOUT   Downtown Veracruz is a jumble of streets. The social center of town is the *zócalo,* or town square (formally Plaza de Armas), where you'll find the tourism office. Two short blocks away is another landmark, *el malecón,* a long promenade fronting the harbor. Starting at the *malecón* and running south along the coast is **Bulevar Avila Camacho,** known as *el bulevar.* It connects downtown to Veracruz's hotel and restaurant zone, which stretches along the coast all the way to the one-time village of **Boca del Río.**

GETTING AROUND   Taxis are plentiful and inexpensive. Getting from the downtown area to the restaurant and hotel district to the south takes 5 to 10 minutes.

[Fast FACTS] VERACRUZ

Area Code   The telephone area code is **229.**

Climate   Veracruz is hot and humid most of the year, but the hottest months are May and June. In the winter, strong winds, known as *nortes,* occasionally bring cool, even chilly, weather.

Drugstore   **Farmacía Las Torres,** Av. Díaz Mirón 295, at Cañonero Tampico (☎ **229/923-5807**), is open daily 24 hours.

Emergencies   Dial ☎ **060.**

High Season   The peak tourist times are Carnaval, Easter, July and August, and December. Veracruz is more popular with Mexicans than with foreigners.

Hospital   The **Hospital de María** is at Alacio Pérez 1004, between Carmen Serdán and 20 de Noviembre (☎ **229/931-3626** or -3619).

Post Office   The *correo,* on Avenida de la República near the Maritime Customs House, is open Monday through Saturday from 8am to 4pm.

Where to Stay

Most hotels have high- and low-season rates. High-season rates apply during Carnaval, Easter, July and August, December, and long weekends. Low season is the rest of the year. Prices quoted include the 18% tax.

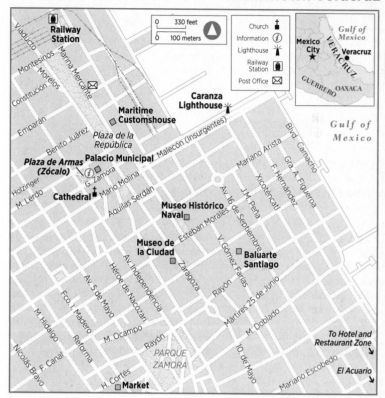

VERY EXPENSIVE

Fiesta Americana Veracruz ★★ ☺   Veracruz's most resortlike hotel is six stories high and very long, stretching out across a wide beachfront. Spacious and decorated in muted colors, most rooms have either terraces or balconies, and all have ocean views. Each contains two full beds or one king. It's on the Playa Costa de Oro, one of Veracruz's nicest beaches, but there is also a large and inviting pool area, with an ample shaded section.

Bulevar Avila Camacho s/n, 94299 Boca del Río, Ver. www.fiestamericana.com. © **800/343-7821** in the U.S. and Canada, or 229/989-8989. Fax 229/989-8909. 233 units. 2,500–2,890 pesos double; 3,250–4,110 pesos junior suite. AE, DC, MC, V. Free parking. **Amenities:** 2 restaurants; poolside snack bar; bar; babysitting; children's activities; concierge; health club; 2 large pools (1 indoor); 2 whirlpools; room service; smoke-free rooms; spa; lighted tennis court; watersports. *In room:* A/C, TV, hair dryer, minibar, Wi-Fi.

EXPENSIVE

Gran Hotel Diligencias ★★★   With the best rooms and service in the downtown area, and located across from the *zócalo,* this hotel beats all the competition. Standard rooms are large, quiet, and comfortable. Bathrooms are large and attractive, and the mattresses are plush. There is a beach club south of town where guests can go for free. Transportation is not provided, but getting there by taxi is easy.

Independencia 1115, 91700 Veracruz, Ver. www.granhoteldiligencias.com. ℰ **01-800/505-5595** in Mexico, or 229/923-0280. 120 units. High season 2,100–2,420 pesos double; low season 1,650 pesos double. AE, MC, V. Free valet parking. **Amenities:** Restaurant; bar; babysitting; fitness center; Jacuzzi; outdoor pool; room service; smoke-free rooms. *In room:* A/C, TV, hair dryer, Wi-Fi.

Hotel Lois ★   Good location, good service, and a wide variety of amenities for the price are the biggest reasons for staying here. The Lois is located on the coast between downtown and the Boca del Río hotel zone. It's a modern 10-story building. Rooms are competitively priced and comfortable. They are midsize, with two double beds or one king. The lighting, though not great, is better than at other hotels in this price range. The suites are larger, with larger bathrooms, and some have Jacuzzi tubs. The large pool area on a third-floor terrace affords a good view of the coastline and the Isla de Sacrificios directly offshore. The hotel bar has live music 2 nights a week.

Calzada Ruiz Cortines 10, 94294 Boca del Río, Ver. www.hotellois.com.mx. ℰ **01-800/712-9136** in Mexico, or 229/937-8290. Fax 229/937-8089. 122 units. High season 1,400 pesos double, 1,800–2,000 pesos suite; low season 1000–1,200 pesos double, 1,300–1,500 pesos suite. AE, MC, V. Free secure parking. **Amenities:** Restaurant; bar; babysitting; health club w/sauna and Jacuzzi; large outdoor pool; room service; squash courts. *In room:* A/C, TV, Wi-Fi.

Hotel Mocambo ★★ ☺   The Mocambo, built in 1932, was the city's first resort hotel, host to presidents and movie stars during the 1940s and 1950s. It's on the beach in the hotel zone south of downtown. No bunched rooms and boxy corridors here. The Mocambo makes luxurious use of space, with wide, breezy walkways and terraces that overlook the ocean, the gardens, and the coconut palms. The architecture is simple and of the period. The hotel may show its age, but it echoes Mexico's age of glamour with stylish touches such as the Art Deco indoor pool and an elevated promenade. Most of the simply furnished rooms are large, with sea views and tile floors. My favorites are those on the upper floors, which have balconies. The grounds and a small play area are fenced in so that kids can't escape, and there's a water slide at the pool.

Calzada Ruiz Cortines 4000, Boca del Río (Apdo. Postal 263), 94290 Veracruz, Ver. www.hotel mocambo.com.mx. ℰ **229/922-0205.** Fax 229/922-0212. 104 units. High season 1,850–2,130 pesos double; low season 1,150–1,400 pesos double. AE, MC, V. Free guarded parking. **Amenities:** 2 restaurants; 2 bars; babysitting; gym w/sauna and steam room; 2 pools (1 indoor); whirlpool; room service; smoke-free rooms; spa; tennis court; Wi-Fi (in lobby). *In room:* A/C, TV.

MODERATE

Hotel Colonial   Two hotels sit next door to each other on the *zócalo:* the Hotel Colonial (which isn't so colonial) and the Hotel Imperial (which isn't so imperial). In terms of rooms, services, and price, they are much the same—comfortable, but not fancy. The location is great: You can enjoy the music and party atmosphere in the *zócalo* and then retire to your room (preferably an interior one). The Colonial has two sections. Rooms in the new section are worth getting. Rooms in the old section are dark and worn. The Imperial's rooms are nicer than the Colonial's old section but aren't quite equal to the new section. Still, I think of these hotels as interchangeable. If you can't get a room at the Colonial, try the Imperial (ℰ **229/932-1204;** www. hotelimperialveracruz.com). Lower rates below are for the old section.

Miguel Lerdo 117, 91700 Veracruz, Ver. www.hcolonial.com.mx. ℰ **229/932-0193.** Fax 229/932-2465. 178 units. High season 900–1,000 pesos double, 1,200 pesos balcony room; low season 630–700 pesos double, 850 pesos balcony room. AE, MC, V. Covered guarded parking 30 pesos. **Amenities:** Sidewalk cafe and bar; indoor pool; room service. *In room:* A/C, TV, Wi-Fi.

Where to Eat

If you want to have seafood with the locals, go to the city fish market on Landero y Coss around the corner from the *malecón*. Facing the street are several small restaurants. Find the one called **La Cría.**

EXPENSIVE

Restaurant El Cacharrito ★★★ STEAKS   Midway between downtown and the Boca del Rio hotel zone is this family-run steakhouse. The steaks are expertly cooked and served Argentine style. They should be eaten Argentine style, too, meaning you should wash them down with lots of red wine. You'll find a large wine list for the purpose. The *bife de chorizo* (rib-eye) is the most popular cut. Also, you might want to try the Argentine empanadas, one of the salads, or the *jugo de carne,* a rich and satisfying essence of beef. Another specialty is the grilled octopus, which is amazingly tender, with just the right hint of smoke. The upstairs dining room is large with a high ceiling. Another location in Mocambo, across from the Hotel Mocambo, serves more seafood.

Bulevar Ruiz Cortines Lote 37-38. ℂ **229/935-7288.** Reservations recommended. Steaks 240-450 pesos. AE, MC, V. Daily 2-11pm.

Mariscos Villa Rica Mocambo ★★★ SEAFOOD   This establishment prides itself on cooking Veracruz style. The menu includes all the seafood standards, plus a few dishes that are harder to come by in Mexico, let alone north of the border. Consider a classic *campechana* seafood cocktail with lots of fresh lime and finely minced *chile serrano,* followed by *pampano al acuyo* (pompano cooked in a sauce of green herbs). Other possibilities include conch filet *al ajillo* (with toasted strips of *guajillo* peppers), and *steak de camarón a la naranja* (shrimp pressed together and cooked in orange sauce). Service is excellent. Look for an open-air thatched structure below the Mocambo hotel.

Calzada Mocambo 527. ℂ **229/922-2113.** Main courses 175-270 pesos. AE, MC, V. Daily noon-10pm.

INEXPENSIVE

Gran Café de la Parroquia ★★ 📷 MEXICAN/COFFEE   More than a coffeehouse, La Parroquia is an institution. Making the scene here for morning or afternoon coffee is mandatory on any trip to Veracruz. The action takes place in a large, bustling dining area facing the *malecón*. There's nothing fancy about it; the furniture is simple, and there's a minimum of decoration. The thing to order is *café lechero.* You'll get a couple of ounces of strong, dark coffee in a glass. Add sugar, if desired, and stir, clinking your spoon against the glass. This will attract the attention of the waiter who circulates with the kettle of steaming milk. Don't be shy. The sound of clinking glass rings throughout the dining room. The cafe also offers pastries and decent breakfasts, but some of the main courses disappoint.

Av. Gómez Farías 34. ℂ **229/932-2584.** Breakfast 35-60 pesos; coffee 24-30 pesos; main courses 55-140 pesos. AE, MC, V. Daily 6am-midnight.

Gran Café del Portal 🍴 MEXICAN   In the *portales* facing the front door of the cathedral is this dependable restaurant with good prices and local color. In the evenings, a parade of strolling troubadours, harpists, marimba players, and shoeshine men passes by. For the midafternoon meal, the *comida corrida* provides lots of food at a reasonable price. Avoid the overcooked pasta and most beef dishes, which are tough. The exception is the tenderized *milanesa,* which is recommendable. For seafood, ask the waiter what's freshest. The enchiladas and the soups are good, and the *flan napolitano* could feed a family of four.

Independencia at Zamora. ☎ **229/931-2759.** Main courses 85–220 pesos; *comida corrida* Mon–Sat 62–95 pesos, Sun 115–130 pesos. MC, V. Daily 7am–midnight.

Samborcito ★ 🍴 REGIONAL   Samborcito is simple eating at its best. The name pokes fun at Sanborn's, the oldest, best-known chain of restaurants in Mexico. Classic dishes include *picadas* (*masa* pancake with cheese and sauce—a Veracruz tradition), puffy *gordas* (puffy soft tortilla with black-bean paste and flavored with the toasted leaf of the aguacatillo—not spicy), and the *empanada de picadillo*. Tamales are available on weekends. The food is served under a long thatched roof, and there's live music on weekends. Samborcito is near downtown; a cab will run about 20 pesos.

16 de Septiembre 727. ☎ **229/931-4388.** Breakfast 35–55 pesos; *antojitos* 25–65 pesos; main courses 80–160 pesos. MC, V. Daily 7am–7:30pm.

Exploring Veracruz

The **zócalo** ★★★ is the social hub, where locals hang out in the cafes chatting with friends while the *marimbas, Jarocha* bands, and mariachis make a lively scene, playing well into the night. Bordering the *zócalo* are the **cathedral** and the **Palacio Municipal (City Hall).** There always seems to be some kind of performance on the square: exhibitions of *danzón* (see "Music, Dance & Carnaval," below), clown acts, band concerts, and comedy sketches.

One block east is the **Plaza de la República,** a long plaza where you'll find the **post office,** the old **Customs house,** and the civil registry, all built around the turn of the 19th century. On the north side is the old train station, **Estación de Ferrocarriles,** with its remarkable yellow-and-blue tile facade. From the east side of this plaza, you can board a bus to Veracruz's most famous tourist attraction, the fortress of **San Juan de Ulúa.** Around the corner from the south side of the plaza is the *malecón* (boardwalk), where you can take a boat ride or have coffee at the city's most popular gathering spot, **El Café de la Parroquia.**

Turibus (www.turibus.com.mx) runs sightseeing buses around the downtown area and then south along the shore past the hotel zone, all the way to the township of Boca del Rio. Explanations are given in several languages, including English. You buy a ticket on board the bus (120 pesos), which entitles you to get off at any of the 20 stops and catch any later bus that same day. Schedules and hours of operation vary depending on the season. You can get details from the tourism office (see above).

MUSIC, DANCE & CARNAVAL

Hang out in the *zócalo*, and you'll be serenaded with *danzonera, marimba, Jarocha,* mariachi, and *norteño* music playing to a large crowd of Veracruzanos who've stopped to drink and chat with friends. On Tuesday, Thursday, and Saturday, a band plays in front of the Palacio Municipal for couples dancing the *danzón*. It's a stately affair: They alternate between dancing perfectly erect in a slow rumbalike fashion and promenading arm in arm while the women wave their fans. The *danzón* came to Veracruz from Cuba in the 1890s; today you won't often see it elsewhere.

If you would like to see more styles of traditional dance, inquire at the tourism office in the *zócalo* (see above) about performances by the **Ballet Tradiciones de México.** Several times throughout the year, the company appears at the **Teatro Clavijero** (☎ **229/931-0574** or 229/932-6693 for reservations). Tickets cost 50 to 80 pesos. The shows are fun and colorful.

In the week before Ash Wednesday, Veracruz explodes with **Carnaval,** one of the best in Mexico. By local tradition, Carnaval begins with the ritual burning of "ill humor" and ends with the funeral of "Juan Carnaval." Visitors flood in from all over the country, packing the streets and hotels.

Carros alegóricos (floats) are made with true Mexican flair—bright colors, papier-mâché figures, flowers, and live entertainment. Groups from neighboring villages dance in peacock- and pheasant-feathered headdresses. Draculas, drag queens, and women in sparkling dresses fill the streets. The parades follow Bulevar Avila Camacho; most of the other activities center in the *zócalo* and begin around noon, lasting well into the night.

On the Sunday before Ash Wednesday, the longest and most lavish of the Carnaval parades takes place on the *malecón.* Parades on Monday and Tuesday are scaled-down versions of the Sunday parade (ask at the tourist office about these routes); by Wednesday, it's all over.

THE TOP ATTRACTIONS

El Acuario ★ ☺   For most Mexican visitors, the aquarium is one of the city's major attractions. The largest aquarium in Latin America, with numerous tanks, large and small, displaying a multitude of marine environments, el Acuario can hold its own with American public aquariums. The doughnut-shaped reef tank gives the illusion of being surrounded by the ocean and its inhabitants. The large shark tank also impresses.

Plaza Acuario Veracruzano, Bulevar M. Avila Camacho. ✆ **229/931-1020.** www.acuariodeveracruz. com. Admission 80 pesos adults, 40 pesos children 2–11. Daily 9am–7pm.

Fort of San Juan de Ulúa ★★★   Built to ward off pirates and foreign invasions, the fortress was enlarged throughout the colonial period until it became the massive work you see today. After independence, it served as a prison noted for its harsh conditions and for the famous people incarcerated there, among them Benito Juárez. It's a formidable example of colonial military architecture, with crenelated walls projecting straight up some 11m (36 ft.) from the water's edge, and bastions at each corner. Inside is a large courtyard, with wide ramps along the inside walls, storehouses, barracks, and old prison cells. English-speaking guides are available at the entrance. A cab from downtown will cost 50 pesos.

Recinto Portuario s/n ✆ **229/938-5151.** Admission 50 pesos. Tues–Sun 9am–4:30pm.

MORE ATTRACTIONS

Baluarte Santiago   Built in 1635, this bastion is all that remains of the wall and fortifications that encircled the city. It was one of the nine original bastions protecting the wall. A small collection of pre-Hispanic gold jewelry, recovered several years ago by a fisherman along the coast just north of Veracruz, is on permanent display here.

Calle Canal and 16 de Septiembre. ✆ **229/931-1059.** Admission 41 pesos. Tues–Sun 10am–4:30pm.

Museo de la Ciudad   This small city museum is on the ground floor of a 19th-century building. The exhibits concern the history of the city and its social evolution from colonial times to the present. Text and audio are in Spanish; most of the exhibits are photos or dioramas.

Zaragoza 397. ✆ **229/200-2236.** Free admission. Tues–Sun 10am–6pm. From the Palacio Municipal, walk 5 blocks south on Zaragoza; it's on the right.

Museo Histórico Naval   This museum occupies the old naval academy. Exhibits concern the history of navigation, including nautical paraphernalia, the history of the naval academy, and Mexico's struggles with other countries. In the courtyard, the foundations of the old wall that used to encircle the city are visible. As you enter, look for uniformed guides, who will show you around free.

Mariano Arista btw. Landero y Coss and Gómez Farías. No phone. Free admission. Tues–Sun 10am–5pm.

OTHER THINGS TO SEE & DO

BEACHES   Veracruz has beaches, but they mostly have brown sand, and the Gulf water is a dull green. The nearest true beach is at the **Villa del Mar,** a little way down *el bulevar,* followed by **Costa de Oro** and then **Mocambo** beach.

BOAT TRIPS   Boats tour the harbor (most narration is in Spanish only), around the tankers and ships docked in the port and San Juan de Ulúa fortress, and out to the Isle of Sacrifices. Departures are sporadic (depending on the weather and demand) from the *malecón* in front of the Hotel Emporio. The cost is 120 pesos for adults and 50 pesos for children ages 2 to 8.

EXCURSIONS   Popular day-trip destinations include **La Antigua;** the Totonac ruins at **Zempoala; Xalapa,** the state capital and home of an excellent anthropology museum; and the archaeological site at **El Tajín.** For prices and reservations, contact **VIP Tours** (© 229/922-3315 or -1918) or **Centro de Reservaciones de Veracruz** (© 229/935-6422).

SCUBA DIVING   Divers can explore a series of reefs and shipwrecks south of town toward Boca del Río. Contact **Dorado Divers** (© 229/931-4305; www.doradobuceo.com) at Avila Camacho 865. Or try **Mundo Submarino** (© 229/980-6374; www.mundosubmarino.com.mx) at Avila Camacho 3549.

SHOPPING   Veracruz excels in one category of shopping and no other. It has sublimely **tacky souvenirs,** which make perfect payback for coworkers who have burdened you with white elephants. On the *malecón* across from Café de la Parroquia, you'll find a long row of small souvenir shops that constitute Veracruz's version of San Francisco's Fisherman's Wharf. Another place of interest (not so much for buying as for looking) is the **city market** at the corner of Madero and Cortez.

Veracruz After Dark

The first thing that always comes to mind with Veracruz is the scene on the *zócalo,* which on a weekend can go on until the wee hours of the morning. The evening shows presented by the municipal government can be quite good. I've seen some great dance troupes perform *jarocho.*

Rincón de la Trova (no phone) is a small bar downtown with a real local feel, where on weekends you can hear live groups play *son montuno,* an old-style Latin tropical music. It's at Plazuela de la Campana, which is simply the widening of the pedestrian-only Callejón Lagunilla between Arteaga and Serdán. Live music is Thursday through Saturday. Friday and Saturday, there's a 35-peso cover.

There are several dance clubs to choose from. Most play Latin music and are in or near the hotel zone. One with good acts is **La Casona de la Condesa** (© 229/933-5451), at Bulevar Avila Camacho 2014.

EL TAJÍN & PAPANTLA
The Ruins of Zempoala

Headed north on Hwy. 180 toward Papantla, you'll pass by the village of **Antigua,** 22km (14 miles) north of the port of Veracruz. It's not very well known today, but for 75 years beginning in 1525, it was the main port used by the Spanish. The village is known locally for its seafood restaurants and is especially popular on weekends.

Continuing north, you come to the ruins of **Zempoala,** 40km (25 miles) north of Veracruz. The ruins are surrounded by lush foliage. Though not as large as the site of El Tajín, they're still noteworthy. Zempoala was the principal city of the Totonac at the time of the Spanish Conquest. The name means "place of the 20 waters," for the several creeks that meander by the site.

Zempoala is a late post-Classic city. Most of the buildings date from the 14th century. The Great Temple is constructed in the Aztec style. The Temple of Quetzal-cóatl, the feathered serpent god, is also of central Mexican design, and the Temple of Ehecatl, god of the wind, is (as usual) round. On weekends and during vacation months, you're likely to find a group of the famous *voladores* (flyers) from Papantla performing their acrobatic ritual (see the "The Ruins of El Tajín," below).

Admission to the archaeological site is 45 pesos; it's open daily from 9am to 5pm. A video camera permit costs 35 pesos.

El Tajín & Papantla

El Tajín (Ehl Tah-*heen*) is among the most important archaeological sites in Mexico. It has a large ceremonial center with several pyramids, platforms, and ball courts, some in the architectural styles of other cultures (Olmec, Teotihuacán, Maya) and some in the city's own unique style. It was probably built and inhabited (at least, in its last stages) by the Totonac Indians, who still live in this region. The Totonac culture is most famous for the "dance" of the *voladores,* a pre-Columbian religious ritual in which four men are suspended from the top of a tall pole while another beats a drum and plays a flute while balancing himself at the top.

The major stopover for seeing these ruins is **Papantla,** a hilly city of 165,000 in the coastal lowlands 225km (140 miles) north of Veracruz. In many respects, it's a typical Mexican town, with lots of clay-tile roofs, a jumble of small shops, and a lively street scene. It's best known for producing vanilla beans. Vanilla is native to Mexico and was used principally to flavor a beverage made with cacao, also indigenous to Mexico.

ESSENTIALS

GETTING THERE & DEPARTING   **By Car**   If you're driving from the south, follow the coastal road, **Hwy. 180,** from Veracruz. From Xalapa, it's best to do the same: Drive down to the coast and then north.

By Bus   The quaint **ADO station** (© 784/842-0218) is at the corner of Venustiano Carranza and Benito Juárez, 4 blocks below the main square. Almost all buses are *de paso* (originating elsewhere), so departure times can be a little earlier or later than the schedule says. Taxis pass in front of the station frequently.

CITY LAYOUT   Easily visible from many parts of town, the parish church and the Hotel El Tajín are at the top of a hill. This is where you'll find the *zócalo.*

GETTING AROUND Taxis are available around the central plaza, and **city buses** go to the ruins of El Tajín (see below). Almost everything worth seeing is within easy walking distance of the central plaza.

SPECIAL EVENTS The **Feast of Corpus Christi,** the ninth Sunday after Easter, is part of a very special week in Papantla. Well-known Mexican entertainers perform, and the native *voladores* make special appearances. Lodging is scarce during this week, so be sure to book ahead.

[FastFACTS] EL TAJÍN

The telephone **area code** is **784.** The **climate** is steamy for most of the year, except for a few occasions in winter when a north wind blows.

EXPLORING PAPANTLA & EL TAJÍN

In Papantla, the shady *zócalo* built of ceramic tile is where couples and families come in the evenings to sit or stroll. The large wall below the church facing the *zócalo* is covered with the image of El Tajín and a modern depiction of Totonac carved reliefs.

THE RUINS OF EL TAJÍN The city lies among some low hills clothed in thick tropical forest. The views are lovely, but climbing on the pyramids is forbidden; your best view is from a high terrace that supports the Tajín Chico buildings toward the back. The city is divided into **Tajín Viejo** and **Tajín Chico**—the old and new sections. Of the 150 buildings identified at the site, 20 have been excavated and conserved, resurrecting their forms from what were grass-covered mounds. At least 12 ball courts have been found, of which 6 have been excavated. The most impressive structure, in the old section, is the **Pyramid of the Niches,** which is a unique stone-and-adobe pyramid with 365 recesses extending to all four sides of the building. The pyramid was formerly covered in red-painted stucco, and the niches were painted black. Try to imagine how that must have looked. Near the Pyramid of the Niches is a restored **ball court** with beautiful carved reliefs depicting gods and kings.

The most important building in the Tajín Chico section is the **Temple of the Columns.** A stairway divides the columns, three on either side, each decorated with reliefs of priests and warriors and hieroglyphic dates. Many mounds remain unexcavated, but with the reconstruction that has been done so far, it's becoming easier to visualize the ruins as a city.

In a clearing near the museum, a group of local Totonac Indians called *voladores* **(flyers)** performs the acrobatic and religious ritual. This is a traditional, solemn ceremony that dates back centuries. The Totonac perform the unusual ritual in honor of the four directions of the earth. There's no set schedule for performances; the sound of a slow-beating drum and flute signals that the *voladores* are preparing to perform. Five flyers, dressed in brightly colored ceremonial garments and cone-shaped hats with ribbons and small round mirrors, climb to a square revolving platform at the top of a 25m (82-ft.) pole. Four of the five flyers perch on the sides of the platform and attach themselves by the waist to a rope, while the fifth stands atop the pole and plays an instrument called a *chirimía.* The instrument is a small bamboo flute with a deerskin drum attached. The performer plays the three-holed flute with his left hand and beats the drum with his right hand. When the time is right, the four flyers fall backward, suspended by the rope, and descend as they revolve around the post.

The small but impressive **museum** is worth seeing as well. A small snack and gift shop and small restaurant are across from the museum. Admission to the site and museum is 50 pesos. The fee to use a personal video camera is 35 pesos. If you look like a professional photographer, the authorities will ask you to get a permit from the **Instituto Nacional de Antropología e Historia** in Mexico City. If you watch a performance of the *voladores,* one of them will collect an additional 25 pesos from each spectator. The site is open daily from 9am to 5pm.

To El Tajín from Papantla, taxis charge about 225 pesos, but it's easy to take a local bus. Look for buses marked CHOTE/TAJIN, which run beside the town church (on the uphill side) every 15 minutes beginning at 7am. Buses marked CHOTE pass more frequently and leave you at the Chote crossroads; from there, take a taxi for around 50 pesos. From Veracruz, take Hwy. 180 to Papantla, then Route 127, a back road to Poza Rica that runs through El Tajín.

SHOPPING   There are two markets in Papantla, both near the central plaza. **Mercado Juárez** is opposite the front door of the church. **Mercado Hidalgo** is 1 block downhill on the same street. The former has more food stalls, where you can order a bowl of *zacahuil,* a typical dish of the region. The latter has locally made baskets; vanilla extract; *Xanath,* a locally produced vanilla liqueur; and whole vanilla beans.

WHERE TO STAY

Hotel Provincia Express   Opened in 1990, this hotel is a good choice in a place with meager selections. Rooms are nicely furnished, with tile floors, and hold a king-size or two double beds. The medium-to-small bathrooms have showers. On occasion, it takes awhile for water to heat up, but it will. Nos. 1 to 6 have small balconies overlooking the *zócalo.* Others, toward the back, are windowless and quiet, and are reached through a tunnel-like hallway.

Enríquez 103, 93400 Papantla, Ver. provinciaexpress_papantla@hotmail.com. ✆ **784/842-1645.** Fax 784/842-4213. 20 units. 515–685 pesos double. MC, V. Free secure parking a half-block away. **Amenities:** Cafe; room service; Wi-Fi (in lobby). *In room:* A/C, TV.

WHERE TO EAT

In the morning, numerous stands at the Mercado Juárez offer the local specialty, *zacahuil* (a huge tamal cooked in a banana leaf). In Papantla, the *zacahuil* is cooked in enough liquid to be served in a bowl. Look around until you see a cook with a line of patrons—that's where you'll get the best *zacahuil.*

Plaza Pardo MEXICAN   This upstairs restaurant facing the main plaza serves Mexican standards and a couple of regional dishes. A few tables are on a balcony looking out over the *zócalo,* church, and giant statue of the *volador.* Specialties include *bocales* (small *gorditas* with different fillings), enchiladas, and *mole.*

Enríquez 105-altos. ✆ **784/842-0059.** Breakfast 28–50 pesos; sandwiches 28–50 pesos; main courses 52–85 pesos. No credit cards. Daily 7:30am–11pm.

CANCÚN

by Shane Christensen

Powdery white sand and a Caribbean sea the color of blue Curaçao—believe the brochures about Cancún. No matter how high-rise this city gets with all-inclusive megaresorts and supermalls, the beach puts it on the map—and no hurricane or swine flu has swept it away. Get up from your poolside lounge and discover why millions flock to this sun-drenched destination—turtle-spotting off Isla Mujeres, discovering Chichén Itzá's iconic Maya pyramid, and swaying to reggaetón in the Hotel Zone's tequila-slamming bars.

While it's tempting just to laze on **Playa Langosta's** bleached sand, life beyond Cancún's beaches beckons with adventure. Scuba dive or snorkel off the islands of **Isla Mujeres** and **Cozumel,** both with quieter waters than Cancún. The enigmatic culture of the Maya comes alive at nearby **Tulum's** seafront ruins. Or take a day trip to the pyramid temples of **Chichén Itzá** and jungly **Uxmal.** Kids in tow? Let them swim with dolphins in **Xel-Ha** eco–theme park's gigantic natural aquarium.

Cancún's glossy malls, such as **Plaza Las Americas** and **Plaza Kukulcán,** have an American flavor with their brand-name stores, cinemas, and food courts. **La Isla Shopping Village,** though, has Venetian-style canals and a spectacular aquarium. For a more Mexican experience, root around downtown **El Centro** for crafts, fresh produce, and authentic street chow. Pick up unique gifts from handmade sombreros to hammocks or huaraches (sandals) and artisan silver jewelry.

Tuck into sizzling **fajitas** in party-mad Tex-Mex joints or **fresh shrimp and lobster** while being serenaded by mariachis in the seafront restaurants in the **Zona Hotelera.** Food is cheaper and the atmosphere more authentically Mexican in **El Centro,** where locals eat incendiary **tacos, enchiladas** with chocolate-chile *mole* sauce, and succulent **tamales** (corn dough studded with meat or beans, wrapped in a banana leaf or corn husk). For an inexpensive snack, graze the food stalls in **Parque Las Palapas.**

Nightlife here is loud, sexy, and relentless. Hop (or crawl) from a pool party to a pumping open-air club. Forget about quiet cantinas—Cancún is about pulsating dance clubs with theme shows and party favors. Many of the monster clubs, from **The City** to **CoCo Bongo,** lie within the same block, routinely turning the area into a sidewalk party. In El Centro's clubs playing bouncy *cumbia* music, sip tequila in a refreshing margarita or slam it with lime and salt.

A BRIEF HISTORY OF cancún

Due to Cancún's ideal mix of elements—its transparent turquoise sea, powdery white sand, and immense potential for growth—a group of Mexican government computer analysts targeted the town for tourism development in 1974, transforming it from a deserted beach area to a five-star resort. Since then, Cancún has sustained the devastations of hurricanes and other powerful tropical storms, only to emerge stronger and more irresistible. In the wake of Hurricane Wilma, which tore through the Yucatán peninsula in 2005, wreckage rapidly gave way to exacting renovations, luxurious upgrades, and brand-new destinations. However, the double whammy of the worldwide economic crisis and worries caused by swine flu has not made for an easy time in Cancún in the past couple of years. Hotels, restaurants, and tourist services across the board have suffered here, just as they have elsewhere in the region. With a struggling economy and more budget-minded travelers, Cancún's resorts have been moving increasingly to all-inclusive options, which typically include lodging, meals, domestic drinks, and a variety of discounts on activities.

Cancún embodies Caribbean splendor and the exotic joys of Mexico, but even a Western traveler feeling apprehensive about visiting foreign soil will feel completely at ease here. English is spoken and dollars accepted; roads are well paved and lawns manicured. Some travelers are surprised to find that Cancún is more like a U.S. beach resort than a part of Mexico. Indeed, signs of Americanism are rampant. U.S. college students continue to descend in droves during spring break—which, depending on your perspective, may be reason to rush headlong into the party or stay far, far away during this season. One astonishing statistic suggests that more Americans travel to Cancún than to any other foreign destination in the world. Indeed, almost three million people visit annually—most of them on their first trip to Mexico.

ORIENTATION
Getting There

BY PLANE If this is not your first trip to Cancún, you'll notice that the **airport's** (www.cancun-airport.com) facilities and services continue to expand. Most international flights, including those to and from the U.S. (except for JetBlue and AirTran, which use Terminal 2), now go through the new Terminal 3, which has money-exchange services, duty-free shops, restaurants, medical services, an express spa, and even a welcome bar serving beer and margaritas just outside the terminal. **Aeroméxico** flies to Cancún through Mexico City. In addition to these carriers, many **charter** companies—such as Apple Vacations (www.applevacations.com) and Funjet (www.funjet.com)—travel to Cancún; these package tours make up as much as half of arrivals by U.S. visitors. Note that as of August 2010 **Mexicana** and **Click Mexicana** stopped operating indefinitely.

Interjet (© **866/285-9525** in the U.S., or 01-80/0011-2345 in Mexico; www.interjet.com.mx) and **Volaris** (© **866/988-3527** in the U.S.; www.volaris.com.mx) are two regional carriers that fly to Cancún from Mexico City. Domestic flights generally use Terminal 1, and flights to and from other destinations in Latin America use

Terminal 2. **Mayair** (© **998/881-9413;** www.mayair.com.mx) flies between Cancún and Cozumel.

The following major international carriers serve Cancún: **Alaska** (© 800/426-0333 in the U.S.; www.alaskaair.com), **American** (© 800/433-7300 in the U.S.; www.aa.com), **Continental** (© 800/231-0856 in the U.S.; www.continental.com), **Delta** (© 800/221-1212 in the U.S.; www.delta.com), **Frontier** (© 800/432-1359 in the U.S.; www.frontierairlines.com), **JetBlue** (© 800/538-2583 in the U.S.; www.jetblue.com), **Spirit** (© 800/772-7117 in the U.S.; www.spiritair.com), **United** (© 800/241-6522 in the U.S.; www.united.com), and **US Airways** (© 800/428-4322 in the U.S.; www.usairways.com).

Most major car-rental firms have outlets at the airport, so if you're renting a car, consider picking it up and dropping it off at the airport, to save on airport-transportation costs. Another way to save money is to arrange for the rental before you leave home. If you wait until you arrive, the daily cost will be around $50 to $75 for a compact vehicle. Major agencies include **Alamo, Avis, Budget, Hertz, National,** and **Thrifty.** The Zona Hotelera (Hotel Zone) lies 10km (6¼ miles)—a 20-minute drive—from the airport along wide, well-paved roads.

The rate for a **private taxi** from the airport is $60 to Ciudad Cancún (downtown) or the Hotel Zone. The return trip with an airport taxi is discounted by 50%. The **Green Line** and **Taxi by Hertz** both run shuttles from the airport into town approximately every 20 minutes. Buy tickets, which cost about $15, from the booth to the far right as you exit the airport. These services accept U.S. dollars, though you'll get a more favorable rate if you pay in pesos. **Local bus** transportation on ADO ($4) goes from the airport to Ciudad Cancún. From there, you can take another bus for less than a dollar to Puerto Juárez, where passenger ferries leave to Isla Mujeres regularly. There is no shuttle service returning to the airport from Ciudad Cancún or the Hotel Zone, so you'll have to take a taxi, but the rate will be much less than for the trip from the airport. (Only federally chartered taxis may take fares *from* the airport, but any taxi may bring passengers *to* the airport.) Ask at your hotel what the fare should be, but expect to pay about half what you paid from the airport to your hotel.

BY CAR   From Mérida or Campeche, take **Hwy. 180** east to Cancún. This is mostly a winding, two-lane road that branches off into the express **toll road 180D** between Izamal and Nuevo Xcan. Nuevo Xcan is approximately 40km (25 miles) from Cancún. Mérida is about 320km (199 miles) away.

BY BUS   Cancún's **ADO bus terminal** (© **01-800/702-8000** in Mexico; www.ado.com.mx) sits in downtown Ciudad Cancún at the intersection of avenidas Tulum and Uxmal. All out-of-town buses arrive here. Buses run to Playa del Carmen, Tulum, Chichén Itzá, other nearby beach and archaeological zones, and other points within Mexico. ADO buses also operate between the airport and downtown.

Visitor Information

The **Cancún Municipal Tourism Office** is downtown at Avenida Nader at the corner of Avenida Cobá (© **998/887-3379**). It's open Monday through Friday from 9am to 4pm. The office lists hotels and their rates, as well as ferry schedules. For information prior to your arrival in Cancún, visit the Convention Bureau's website, **www.cancun.travel**. The state tourism website is in Spanish, at www.qroo.gob.mx.

Pick up copies of the free booklet *Cancún Tips* (www.cancuntips.com.mx), and a seasonal tabloid of the same name.

City Layout

There are really two Cancúns: **Ciudad Cancún (Cancún City)** and **Isla Cancún (Cancún Island).** Ciudad Cancún, on the mainland, is the original downtown area, where most of the local population lives. It's home to traditional restaurants, shops, and less expensive hotels, as well as pharmacies, dentists, automotive shops, banks, travel and airline agencies, and car-rental firms—all within about 9 square blocks. The city's main thoroughfare is **Avenida Tulum.** Heading south, Avenida Tulum becomes the highway to the airport and to Tulum and Chetumal; heading north, it intersects the highway to Mérida and the road to Puerto Juárez and the Isla Mujeres ferries.

Isla Cancún is a sandy strip 22km (14 miles) long, shaped like a 7. It's home to the famed **Zona Hotelera,** or Hotel Zone (also called the Zona Turística, or Tourist Zone), connected to the mainland by the Playa Linda Bridge at the north end and the Punta Nizuc Bridge at the southern end. Between the two areas lies Laguna Nichupté. Avenida Cobá from Cancún City becomes Bulevar Kukulcán, the island's main traffic artery. Cancún's international airport is just inland from the south end of the island.

FINDING AN ADDRESS   Cancún City's street-numbering system is a holdover from its early days. Addresses are still given by the number of the building lot and by the *manzana* (block) or *supermanzana* (group of blocks). The city is relatively compact, and the downtown commercial section is easy to cover on foot.

On the island, addresses are given by kilometer number on Bulevar Kukulcán or by reference to some well-known location. In Cancún, streets are named after famous Maya cities. Boulevards are named for nearby archaeological sites, Chichén Itzá, Tulum, and Uxmal.

Getting Around

BY TAXI   Taxi prices in Cancún are clearly set by zone, although keeping track of what's in which zone can take some doing. The minimum fare within the Hotel Zone is 90 pesos per ride, making it one of the most expensive taxi areas in Mexico. In addition, taxis operating in the Hotel Zone feel perfectly justified in having a discriminatory pricing structure: Local residents pay about half of what tourists pay, and prices for guests at higher-priced hotels are about double those for budget hotel guests—these are all established by the taxi union. Rates should be posted outside your hotel; if you have a question, all drivers are required to have an official rate card in their taxis, though it's generally in Spanish. Taxi drivers will accept dollars, though at a less favorable rate than pesos.

Within the downtown area, the cost is about 25 pesos per cab ride (not per person); within any other zone, it's 70 to 110 pesos. It'll cost about 180 pesos to travel between the Hotel Zone and downtown. Settle on a price in advance, or check at your hotel. Trips to the airport from most zones cost about 280 pesos (up to four people). Taxis can also be rented for 250 pesos per hour for travel around the city and Hotel Zone. If you want to hire a taxi for an all-day tour, for example to Chichén Itzá or along the Riviera Maya, expect to pay about 3,500 pesos total—many taxi drivers feel that they are also providing guide services.

BY BUS   Bus travel within Cancún continues to improve and is increasingly popular. In town, almost everything lies within walking distance. **Ruta 1** and **Ruta 2** (HOTELES) city buses travel frequently from Puerto Juárez on the mainland to the beaches along Avenida Tulum (the main street) and all the way to Punta Nizuc at the far end of the Hotel Zone on Isla Cancún. **Ruta 8** buses go to Puerto Juárez/Punta Sam for ferries to Isla Mujeres. They stop on the east side of Avenida Tulum. All these city buses run between 6am and 10pm daily. Buses also go up and down the main strip of the Hotel Zone day and night. Public buses have the fare painted on the front; at press time, the fare was 12 pesos.

BY SCOOTER   Scooters are a convenient but dangerous way to cruise through the very congested traffic. Rentals start at about $30 for a day, not including insurance, and a credit card voucher is required as security. You should receive a crash helmet (it's the law) and instructions on how to lock the wheels when you park. Make sure the vehicle is in adequate condition and has been serviced. Also read the fine print on the back of the rental agreement regarding liability for repairs or replacement in case of accident, theft, or vandalism, and make sure you have adequate insurance coverage in case of an accident.

[FastFACTS] CANCÚN

Area Code   The telephone area code is **998.**

ATMs & Banks   Most banks sit downtown along Avenida Tulum and are usually open Monday through Friday from 9am to 3pm, although some are open later and even half the day on Saturday. Many have ATMs for after-hours cash withdrawals. In the Hotel Zone, you'll find an HSBC bank in Kukulcán Plaza that's open Monday through Saturday from 9am to 7pm.

Consulates   The **U.S. Consular Agent** is in the Plaza Caracol 2, Bulevar Kukulcán Km 8.5, 2nd level, 320–323 (© **998/883-0272;** http://merida.us consulate.gov); open Monday through Friday from 8am to 1pm. The **Canadian Consulate** is in the Centro Empresarial, Bulevar Kukulcán Km 12 (© **998/883-3360;** www.mexico.gc.ca); open Monday through Friday from 9am to 1pm. The **United Kingdom** has a

consular office at the Royal Sands Hotel (© **998/881-0100;** http://ukinmexico.fco. gov.uk/en); open Monday through Friday from 9am to 3pm. Irish, Australian, and New Zealand citizens should contact their embassies in Mexico City.

Crime   Car break-ins are a frequent crime here, especially around the shopping centers in the Hotel Zone. Rapes and sexual assault are serious concerns. Most have taken place at night or in the early morning.

Currency Exchange
Cancún has many *casas de cambio* (exchange houses). Downtown merchants are eager to change cash dollars, but island stores don't offer very good exchange rates. Hotels usually change money as well, but rates vary. Avoid changing money at the airport as you arrive, especially at the first exchange booth you see—its rates are less favorable than those of any in town

or others farther inside the airport. Dollars are widely accepted throughout Cancún.

Drugstores   Across the street from Señor Frog's in the Hotel Zone, at Bulevar Kukulcán Km 9.5, **Farmacías del Ahorro** (© **998/892-7291**) is open 24 hours. Plenty of drugstores are in the major shopping malls in the Hotel Zone and are open until 10pm. In downtown Cancún, **Farmacía Cancún** is located at Av. Tulum 17 (© **998/884-1283**). It's open Monday to Saturday from 9am to 10pm, and Sunday from 10am to 10pm. You can stock up on over-the-counter and many prescription drugs without a prescription.

Emergencies   The local **Red Cross** (© **998/884-1616**) is open 24 hours on Avenida Yaxchilán between avenidas Xcaret and Labná, next to the Telmex building.

Hospital   **Galenia Hospital** is one of the city's most modern, offering full emergency and other services with excellent care, at Av. Tulum, SM 12, at Nizuc (📞 **998/891-5200;** www.hospitalgalenia.com). **AMAT,** Av. Nader 13, SM 2, at Avenida Uxmal (📞 **998/887-4422**), is a small emergency hospital with some English-speaking doctors open 24 hours. Desk staff may have limited command of English. **U.S. Air Ambulance** (Global Ambulance) service is available by calling 📞 800/948-1214 in the U.S., or 01-800/305-9400 in Mexico (www.usairambulance.net).

Internet Access All of **Kukulcán Plaza,** Bulevar Kukulcán Km 13, offers free Wi-Fi. You'll need to pick up a password at Customer Services, near the main entrance. Also in Kukulcán Plaza, **Cyber Terrace** offers computers with Internet access for 60 pesos per hour. There's a cafe here,

and it's open daily from 10am to 10pm. Most hotels now have Internet access, and five-star hotels have business centers.

Luggage Storage & Lockers Hotels will generally tag and store luggage while you travel elsewhere.

Newspapers & Magazines Most hotel gift shops and newsstands carry English-language magazines and English-language, Mexican-edition newspapers, such as *USA Today. Cancún Tips* (www.cancuntips.com.mx) is an entertainment magazine that offers descriptions of local activities, maps, and tourist information.

Police Dial 📞 **066** for the police in an emergency. Cancún also has a fleet of English-speaking tourist police to help travelers. Dial 📞 **998/885-2277.**

Post Office The main *correo* lies at the intersection of avenidas Sunyaxchen

and Xel-Ha (📞 **998/884-1418**). It's open Monday through Friday from 9am to 4pm, and Saturday from 9am to noon for the purchase of stamps only.

Seasons High season runs from December 15 to April; low season extends from May to December 15, when prices drop 10% to 30%. Some hotels are starting to charge high-season rates during June and July, when Mexican, European, and school-holiday visitors often travel, but rates may still be lower than in winter months.

Weather The day's are hot and, in summer, very humid. The rainy season runs May through October. August to November is hurricane season, which brings erratic weather. November through February can be partly cloudy, windy, and occasionally rainy. Evenings can get cool.

WHERE TO STAY

Island hotels—almost all of them offering modern facilities and English-speaking staff—line the beach like concrete dominoes. The water on the upper end of the island facing Bahía de Mujeres is placid, while beaches lining the long side of the island facing the Caribbean are subject to choppier water and crashing waves on windy days. (For more information on swimming safety, see "Beaches, Watersports & Boat Tours," later in this chapter.) Be aware that the farther south you go on the island, the longer it takes (20–30 min. in traffic) to get back to the "action spots," which are primarily between the Plaza Flamingo and Punta Cancún on the island and along Avenida Tulum on the mainland.

Following Hurricane Wilma's devastation, the news item that received the most coverage was the destruction of Cancún's famed white-sand beaches. Immediately following the storm, literally all of the sand was washed away from the northern border of Isla Cancún, and from Punta Cancún. The Mexican government has made a series of efforts to pump the dislocated sand back to the beach. The southern beaches of Isla Cancún actually benefited from the storm, and now have especially wide beachfronts.

In all price categories, Cancún's hotels generally set their rates in dollars, so they are immune to variations in the peso. Travel agents and wholesalers always have air/hotel packages available. Cancún also has numerous all-inclusive properties, which allow you to take a fixed-cost vacation. Note that the price quoted when you call a hotel's reservation number may not include Cancún's 14% tax. Prices can vary considerably throughout the year and have dropped considerably during the global financial crisis, so it pays to consult a travel agent or shop around.

In the wake of the international economic crisis, hotels and resorts here have increasingly turned to all-inclusive concepts, either in full or as an option. This puts an emphasis on quantity of consumption at lower prices, but with quality sometimes sacrificed. This means a dip in service, programs, and amenities, particularly at hotels that have dramatically reduced prices. Some of the more expensive hotels have struggled to survive in this environment, and more changes to Cancún's hotel landscape are likely.

Almost all major hotel chains have real estate on Cancún Island (the "Hotel Zone"). The reality is that Cancún is so popular as a **package destination** from the U.S. that prices and special deals are often the deciding factor for consumers rather than loyalty to any one hotel brand. Ciudad Cancún offers independently owned, smaller, less expensive lodging. For condo, home, and villa rentals, check with **Cancún Hideaways** (www.cancun-hideaways.com; ✆ 817/522-4466), an American company specializing in luxury properties, downtown apartments, and condos, as well as air/hotel packages—many at prices much lower than comparable hotel stays.

The hotel listings in this chapter begin on Cancún Island and finish in Cancún City (the real downtown), where bargain lodgings are available. Unless otherwise indicated, parking is free at Cancún's hotels. Prices given below do not include Cancún's 14% tax.

Isla Cancún

VERY EXPENSIVE

Fiesta Americana Grand Coral Beach ★★★ ☺ This grand coral-colored resort sits on Punta Cancún, offering relative seclusion despite lying within easy walking distance of the Hotel Zone's key entertainment. It's one of the top-rated resorts in Mexico and attracts an international clientele for good reason. In front, the whitest sand beach glides into emerald waters, where the surf is calm and perfect for swimming. Yet you may feel tempted not to leave the beautiful multitiered pools with waterfalls, fountains, swim-up bars, and lush surroundings. The all-suites hotel includes junior suites with sunken sitting areas, whitewashed furniture, marble bathrooms, and soothing California colors. Guests staying in Grand Club suites enjoy access to a private rooftop lounge, exclusive check-in, continental breakfast, hors d'oeuvres, and beverages. Service throughout this luxury property is gracious and attentive, and the magnificent lobby is embellished with elegant dark-green granite and fresh flowers. The Fiesta Kids Activities include nonstop games, contests, and

Downtown Cancún

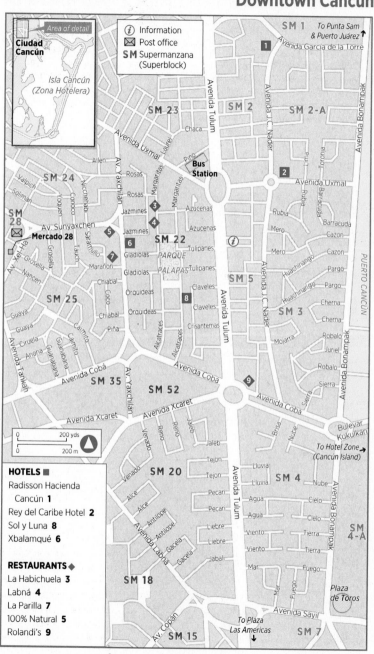

Area of detail

Ciudad Cancún

Isla Cancún
(Zona Hotelera)

ⓘ Information
✉ Post office
SM Supermanzana
(Superblock)

SM 1 — To Punta Sam & Puerto Juárez ↑

Avenida Garcia de la Torre

SM 23

SM 2

SM 2-A

Avenida Tulum

Avenida J.C. Nader

Avenida Bonampak

Chaca

Avenida Uxmal

Laurel

Pino

Allen

Av. Yaxchilán

Rosas

Margaritas

Bus Station

SM 24

Valpich

Nichehabin

Soliman

Conoco

Yoquen

Rosas

Jazmines

Margaritas

Azucenas

Avenida Uxmal

Rubia

Rubia

Barracuda

Toronja

Lima

SM 28 ✉ **Mercado 28**

Av. Sunyaxchen

Sarumullo

Tauch

Jazmines

Azucenas

Mero

Barracuda

Av. Yei-Ha

Grosella

SM 22

Tulipanes

Mero

Cazon

Av. Yei-Ha

Nancen

Marañon

Gladiolas

PARQUE PALAPAS

Tulipanes

ⓘ

SM 5

Huachinango

Cazon

Pargo

SM 25

Chiabal

Coco

Gladiolas

Orquideas

Claveles

Huachinango

Pargo

Guaya

Chiabal

Piña

Orquideas

Claveles

Avenida J.C. Nader

Cherna

Guaya

Ciruela

Cairmito

Alcatraces

Alcatraces

Crisantemas

SM 3

Cherna

Avenida Tankah

Anona

Guanabana

Guanabana

Avenida Coba

Avenida Coba

Mojarra

Robalo

Juriel

Avenida Bonampak

SM 35

Av. Yaxchilán

SM 52

Robalo

Sierra

Avenida Xcaret

Avenida Coba

Avenida Xcaret

Venado

Reno

Reno

Jaleb

Brisa

Nube

Sierra

Bulevar Kukulkán

0 — 200 yds
0 — 200 m

Venado

Jaleb

Tejon

Lluvia

To Hotel Zone (Cancún Island) →

HOTELS ■

Radisson Hacienda Cancún **1**

Rey del Caribe Hotel **2**

Sol y Luna **8**

Xbalamqué **6**

SM 20

Alce

Alce

Tejon

Pecari

Pecari

Avenida Tulum

Lluvia

Agua

Agua

Viento

SM 4

Nube

Cielo

Cielo

Tierra

Avenida Bonampak

Antilope

Antilope

Liebre

Liebre

Viento

Tierra

SM 4-A

RESTAURANTS ◆

La Habichuela **3**

Labná **4**

La Parilla **7**

100% Natural **5**

Rolandi's **9**

SM 18

Avenida Labná

Gacela

Gacela

Jabali

Mar

Mar

Fuego

Fuego

Plaza de Toros

Av. Copan

SM 15

To Plaza Las Americas ↓

Avenida Sayil

SM 7

shows for the little ones, and there are daylong sports and social activities planned for adults as well.

Bulevar Kukulcán Km 9.5, 77500 Cancún, Q. Roo. www.fiestamericanagrand.com. © **800/343-7821** in the U.S., or 998/881-3200. Fax 998/881-3288. 602 units. High season $300 and up double, $400 and up club-floor double; low season $200 and up double, $300 and up club-floor double. AE, MC, V. **Amenities:** 5 restaurants; 4 bars; babysitting; kids' club; concierge w/multilingual staff; concierge floor; fitness center; outdoor pool w/swim-up bars; room service; sauna; boutique spa; watersports. *In room:* A/C, flatscreen TV, hair dryer, minibar, MP3 docking station, Wi-Fi.

Hilton Cancún Golf & Spa Resort ★★ ☺   Full of energy, this is a grand resort in every sense of the word. The Hilton Cancún sits on 100 hectares (247 acres) of prime beachside property, which means every room has a sea view (some have both sea and lagoon views). And there's an 18-hole, par-72 golf course across the street. Like the sprawling resort, guest rooms are spacious and decorated in minimalist style. The Beach Club villas are the largest and best-located rooms, and come with continental breakfast and an evening cocktail hour. This Hilton is a kid-friendly hotel, with one of the island's best children's activity programs, children's pool, and babysitting. The spectacular multisection swimming pool stretches out to the gorgeous beach. The Hilton is especially appealing to golfers because it's one of only two in Cancún with an on-site course (the other is the Meliá). Greens fees for guests during high season are $79 for 9 holes, $129 for 18 holes (low season and twilight discounts offered), and come with use of a cart. The Wellness Spa includes oceanfront massage cabañas, yoga, and aromatherapy. This Hilton has a friendly vibe and excellent service.

Bulevar Kukulcán Km 17, Retorno Lacandones, 77500 Cancún, Q. Roo. www.hiltoncancun.com. © **800/548-8690** in the U.S., or 998/881-8000. Fax 998/881-8080. 426 units. High season $159 and up double, $259 and up suite; low season $129 and up double, $249 and up suite. AE, DC, MC, V. **Amenities:** 5 restaurants; 2 bars; babysitting; kids' club; concierge; golf clinic; golf course across the street; 10 interconnected outdoor pools w/swim-up bar; 2 whirlpools; room service; wellness spa and fully equipped gym; 2 lighted tennis courts; watersports. *In room:* A/C, flatscreen TV, CD/MP3 player, hair dryer, minibar, Wi-Fi.

JW Marriott ★★★   This remains my favorite resort in Cancún, a refined oasis that offers exceptional service without pretense. Despite its many touches of elegance, the JW is friendly and even family-friendly—although more families stay at the neighboring and less expensive Marriott CasaMagna (p. 468). From the beautifully decorated marble and flower-filled lobby to the luxurious oceanview guest rooms, the resort combines classic and Caribbean styling with warm Mexican service. Guest rooms feature exquisite marble bathrooms with separate tub and shower, private balconies, flatscreen TVs, bathrobes and slippers, and twice-daily maid service. The breathtaking infinity pool meanders through the property and overlooks the sea. A spectacular 3,252-sq.-m (35,004-sq.-ft.) spa includes an indoor pool and Jacuzzi, high-tech fitness center, and full range of massages, body scrubs and polishes, facials, and healing water treatments. **Gustino** (p. 473) is the hotel's outstanding Italian restaurant, while **Sedona Grill** (p. 474) combines Southwestern U.S. and Caribbean flavors.

Bulevar Kukulcán Km 14.5, 77500 Cancún, Q. Roo. www.jwmarriottcancun.com. © **800/223-6388** in the U.S., or 998/848-9600. Fax 998/848-9601. 448 units. High season $350 and up double; low season $200 and up double. AE, DC, MC, V. **Amenities:** 3 restaurants; deli; lobby bar and pool bar; access to kids' club at Marriott CasaMagna; concierge; club floor w/special amenities and complimentary cocktails; expansive outdoor pool; dive pool w/waterfalls; indoor pool; 3 whirlpools; room service; sauna; full-service spa w/fitness center and aerobics studio; steam room. *In room:* A/C, flatscreen TV, hair dryer, minibar, Wi-Fi.

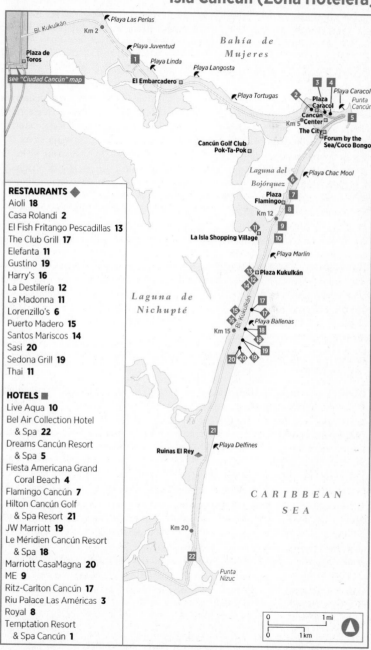

Isla Cancún (Zona Hotelera)

Bl. Kukulkán
Km 2
Playa Las Perlas
Playa Juventud
Plaza de Toros
see "Ciudad Cancún" map
Playa Linda
El Embarcadero
Playa Langosta

Bahía de Mujeres

Playa Tortugas
Playa Caracol
Punta Cancún
Plaza Caracol
Cancún Center
The City
Forum by the Sea/Coco Bongo

Cancún Golf Club Pok-Ta-Pok

Laguna del Bojórquez
Playa Chac Mool
Plaza Flamingo
Km 12

La Isla Shopping Village

Playa Marlin

Plaza Kukulkán

Laguna de Nichupté

Playa Ballenas
Km 15
Bl. Kukulkán

Ruinas El Rey
Playa Delfines

Km 20

Punta Nizuc

CARIBBEAN SEA

RESTAURANTS ◆
Aioli **18**
Casa Rolandi **2**
El Fish Fritango Pescadillas **13**
The Club Grill **17**
Elefanta **11**
Gustino **19**
Harry's **16**
La Destilería **12**
La Madonna **11**
Lorenzillo's **6**
Puerto Madero **15**
Santos Mariscos **14**
Sasi **20**
Sedona Grill **19**
Thai **11**

HOTELS ■
Live Aqua **10**
Bel Air Collection Hotel & Spa **22**
Dreams Cancún Resort & Spa **5**
Fiesta Americana Grand Coral Beach **4**
Flamingo Cancún **7**
Hilton Cancún Golf & Spa Resort **21**
JW Marriott **19**
Le Méridien Cancún Resort & Spa **18**
Marriott CasaMagna **20**
ME **9**
Ritz-Carlton Cancún **17**
Riu Palace Las Américas **3**
Royal **8**
Temptation Resort & Spa Cancún **1**

0   1 mi
0   1 km

Le Méridien Cancún Resort & Spa ★★ Frequented by Europeans familiar with this fine chain of hotels, Le Méridien is among Cancún's most inviting luxury options. The elegant lobby, featuring original artwork, fresh flowers, and subtle lighting, creates a sense of intimacy that extends throughout the hotel. Guest rooms are generous in size, with small balconies overlooking the pool; due to the hotel's design, they do not have full ocean views. Each has a large marble bathroom with a separate tub and glassed-in shower. The resort's **Spa del Mar** is one of Mexico's most complete European spa facilities, with more than 4,570 sq. m (49,191 sq. ft.) of services dedicated to your body and soul. It consists of an extensive fitness center, full-service salon, selection of treatment rooms, men's and women's steam rooms, saunas, whirlpools, and cold plunge pools. **Aioli** (p. 471) is the splendid fine-dining restaurant connected to the lobby. The hotel staff offers calm, personalized service. An all-inclusive option is now offered, as well.

Retorno del Rey Km 14, Zona Hotelera, 77500 Cancún, Q. Roo. www.starwoodhotels.com/lemeridien. ℂ **800/543-4300** in the U.S., or 998/881-2200. Fax 998/881-2201. 213 units. $230 and up double. Ask about all-inclusive and special spa packages. AE, DC, MC, V. Small dogs accepted with prior reservation. **Amenities:** 2 restaurants; bar; babysitting; supervised children's program w/clubhouse, play equipment, and wading pool; concierge; 3 cascading outdoor pools; whirlpool; room service; spa; 2 lighted championship tennis courts; watersports. *In room:* A/C, flatscreen TV, CD player, hair dryer, minibar, Wi-Fi.

Live Aqua ★ The all-inclusive Live Aqua is one of the most stylish resorts in the Hotel Zone—New Age music emanates from each corner, behind every palm tree, and around the eight tempting pools. The spa is outstanding, with indoor and outdoor treatments that incorporate the best techniques from around the globe. All of the soothing guest rooms face the ocean and have iHome sound systems, luxury bath amenities, and artisan soaps. I don't remember the last time I slept in such a comfortable bed; Egyptian cotton sheets share company with a plush collection of form-fitting pillows. The only thing calling you out of bed is likely to be the clear blue skies, deep turquoise waters, and brilliant white sand outside your window—as well as the fact that everything is included, except for some spa services. Top international chefs oversee the three gourmet restaurants.

Bulevar Kukulcán Km 12.5, 77500 Cancún, Q. Roo. www.feel-aqua.com. ℂ **800/343-7821** in the U.S., or 998/881-7600. Fax 998/881-7635. 371 units. High season $500 and up double; low season $350 and up double. All-inclusive. AE, MC, V. **Amenities:** 3 gourmet restaurants; 3 bars; beach club; 8 outdoor pools; room service; sauna; boutique spa and gym; 2 tennis courts; yoga and other fitness activities. *In room:* A/C, flatscreen TV w/DVD, hair dryer, minibar, MP3 docking station, Wi-Fi.

Ritz-Carlton Cancún ★★★ ☺ The exclusive Ritz-Carlton fronts a gorgeous white-sand beach, having recently added a significant stretch of sand as part of Cancún's $71-million beach recovery project. Rooms and public areas overlook the pools and beach and offer the low-key elegance that's a hallmark of the Ritz chain—think plush carpets; chandeliers; fresh flowers; and rooms with marble baths, fluffy featherbeds, and 400-count bed linens. Several features will enhance your stay, including a fabulous culinary center offering themed gourmet cooking classes, as well as wine and tequila tastings. A group of specially designed "Itzy Bitzy Ritz Kids" guest rooms offer baby-friendly amenities and conveniences. In addition to the daytime Kids Camp, the Ritz offers a "Kids' Night Out" program that allows parents to steal away for the evening. The beachfront Kayantá Spa bases many of its treatments on traditional Maya rituals and therapies. The resort's oceanfront restaurant, **Casitas,** is the only beachside dining spot in Cancún, where you can dine on steakhouse fare in candlelit cabañas. The hotel's primary restaurant, **The Club Grill,** is reviewed in the "Where to Eat" section, below; **Fantino** is similarly outstanding and focuses on Mediterranean cuisine; and the **Dance Floor at the Lobby** (p. 484) is a refined space for an evening out. The resort itself, as well as The Club Grill and Fantino, another Ritz-Carlton restaurant, have received AAA five diamonds.

Retorno del Rey 36, off Bulevar Kukulcán Km 13.5, 77500 Cancún, Q. Roo. www.ritzcarlton.com. ✆ **800/241-3333** in the U.S. and Canada, or 998/881-0808. Fax 998/881-0815. 365 units. May 1–Dec 21 $319–$489 double, $439 and up club floor and suites; Dec 22–Jan 3 $799 and up double, $1,679 and up club floor and suites; Jan 4–Apr 30 $549–$629 double, $769 and up club floor and suites. Ask about all-inclusive, spa, and weekend packages. AE, MC, V. **Amenities:** 6 restaurants; lounge w/sushi bar; babysitting; Kids Camp; concierge; club floors; fully equipped fitness center; 2 outdoor pools (heated in winter); room service; spa; Cliff Drysdale tennis center w/3 lighted tennis courts. *In room:* A/C, TV, CD player, hair dryer, minibar, Wi-Fi.

Riu Palace Las Américas ★ ☺ One of Cancún's original all-inclusives, the Riu Palace is part of a family of Riu resorts known for their grand, opulent style. This is the smallest of them and the most over-the-top, steeped in pearl-white Greco architecture. It looks more like it belongs on the Las Vegas strip than next to the Caribbean Sea, but then again, no one ever said Cancún had a consistent style. The location is prime—near the central shopping, dining, and nightlife centers, and just a 5-minute walk to the Convention Center. All rooms are spacious junior suites with an ocean or lagoon view, separate seating area with sofa or sofa bed, and a balcony or terrace. Eight have Jacuzzis. The beautiful central pools overlook the ocean and a small stretch of beach. Riu Palace offers guests virtually 24 hours of all-inclusive snacks, meals, and beverages. Activities include watersports, daytime entertainment for adults and kids, live music and shows at night, and access to other Riu hotels in Cancún. The hotel's European opulence stands in contrast to the mostly informal North American guests.

Bulevar Kukulcán Km 8.5, Lote 4, 77500 Cancún, Q. Roo. www.cancun.riu.com. ✆ **888/666-8816** in the U.S., or 998/891-4300. Fax 998/891-4301. 372 units. High season $320 and up double; low season $250 and up double. Rates are all-inclusive, and a 2-night stay may be required. AE, MC, V. **Amenities:** 6 restaurants; 5 bars; access to golf and tennis; fitness center; 2 outdoor pools; room service; spa; non-motorized watersports, including introductory scuba lessons; Wi-Fi (in lobby). *In room:* A/C, TV, hair dryer, minibar.

Royal ★★ This adults-only all-suites hotel is my favorite of Cancún's all-inclusive establishments, offering a level of services and amenities unmatched almost anywhere. From the stunning infinity pools and gorgeous beach to the gourmet restaurants and sophisticated spa, the owners have spared no expense. The elegant marble lobby looks out one side to the Caribbean and the other to the lagoon, with sit-down check-in and a champagne welcome. All of the innovative suites feature flatscreen TVs with CD/DVD players, marble bathrooms with rain showers, two-person Jacuzzis, and oceanview balconies with hammocks. Swim-up master suites have semiprivate plunge pools facing the resort's pool and beach; guests in the top-category suites enjoy "Royal Service," which includes upgraded amenities, Bose stereo systems, pillow menus, the ability to preselect your suite online, and, incredibly, free use of a Mini Cooper. The Maya-inspired oceanview spa includes a massage room, Jacuzzi, sauna, traditional *temazcal* steam bath, massage waterfall, and state-of-the-art fitness center. Actually, the range of services is almost hard to believe, except that you will be paying top dollar for it. The all-inclusive package includes gourmet meals, premium drinks, and evening entertainment.

Bulevar Kukulcán Km 11.5, 77500 Cancún, Q. Roo. www.realresorts.com. ☎ **800/760-0944** in the U.S., or 998/881-7340. 288 units. $500 and up double. Rates are all-inclusive. AE, DC, MC, V. No children 15 and younger. **Amenities:** 6 restaurants; 8 bars; concierge; well-equipped fitness center; expansive outdoor pool; room service; sauna; full-service spa; steam room. *In room:* A/C, flatscreen TV, CD/DVD player, hair dryer, minibar, Wi-Fi.

EXPENSIVE

Dreams Cancún Resort & Spa ☺
The all-inclusive Dreams Resort enjoys one of the island's most idyllic locations at the tip of Punta Cancún. The setting is casual and family friendly. Bright colors and strategic angles define the design, which now looks somewhat dated relative to Cancún's newer establishments. Choose from two sets of rooms: those in the 17-story club section with ocean views and extra services and amenities, and those in the pyramid overlooking the dolphin-filled lagoon. The all-inclusive concept here includes meals, 24-hour room service, and premium-brand drinks, as well as the use of all resort amenities, nonmotorized watersports, theme-night entertainment, and tips. Unfortunately, service at the resort is inconsistent.

Bulevar Kukulcán, 77500 Punta Cancún (Apdo. Postal 14), Cancún, Q. Roo. www.dreamsresorts.com. ☎ **866/237-3267** in the U.S., or 998/848-7000. Fax 998/848-7001. 376 units. $350 and up double. Rates are all-inclusive. AE, DC, MC, V. **Amenities:** 5 restaurants; 5 bars; babysitting; bikes; kids' club; Spanish and cooking classes; fitness center w/steam bath; private saltwater lagoon w/dolphins and tropical fish; 2 outdoor pools; lighted tennis court; ocean trampoline; watersports including kayaks, catamarans, paddleboats, snorkeling equipment, and scuba lessons; beach volleyball; yoga. *In room:* A/C, TV w/DVD/CD player, hair dryer, minibar.

Marriott CasaMagna ★★★ ☺
This picture-perfect Marriott resort is one of the most enticing family destinations in Cancún. Entering through a half-circle of Roman columns, you'll pass through a domed foyer to a wide, lavishly marbled lobby filled with plants and shallow pools. It looks out to the sparkling pool and enormous whirlpool at the edge of the beach. Guest rooms are decorated with Mexican-Caribbean furnishings and have balconies facing the sea or lagoon. The Marriott caters to family travelers (up to two children stay free with parent), and the supervised children's program is one of the best of any resort here. That said, the resort never feels overrun by kids, and young couples will also have a wonderful time. Among the many places to dine, the most fun is the *teppanyaki*-style (cook-at-your-table) Mikado Japanese restaurant. Service throughout the resort is excellent. Guests can also pay to use the more luxurious JW Marriott spa next door, although the one here is already quite impressive.

Bulevar Kukulcán Km 14.5, 77500 Cancún, Q. Roo. www.marriott.com. ☎ **800/228-9290** in the U.S., or 998/881-2000. Fax 998/881-2085. 450 units. $180 and up double; $300 and up suite. Ask about family packages and all-inclusive options. AE, MC, V. **Amenities:** 5 restaurants (including Sasi, p. 474); lobby bar w/live music; babysitting; concierge; health club; outdoor pool and whirlpool; room service; spa; 2 lighted tennis courts. *In room:* A/C, flatscreen TV, hair dryer, minibar.

ME ★
The now all-inclusive ME hotel by Meliá brings to Cancún a level of minimalist chic with an atmosphere befitting a trendy nightclub more than a beach resort. Bathed in hues of beige and mauve, with polished marble, onyx lamps, and modern artwork, the hotel creates its own fashion statement—and the hip clientele reflects it. The modern lobby feels a bit like an urban cocktail lounge, with designer bars and chill-out music filling the space. Guest rooms have distinctive contemporary furnishings, plasma TVs, MP3 players, and marble bathrooms with rain showers and Aveda bath products; half look to the Caribbean Sea and the other half to the lagoon. The super-stylish Yhi Spa overlooks the ocean and offers body glows and exfoliations,

aromatherapy massages, body masks, and wraps. The Beach House restaurant appears sunken into the main pool and joins the beach in front. The "Complete ME" all-inclusive package includes food and drinks.

Bulevar Kukulcán Km 12, 77500 Cancún, Q. Roo. www.me-cancun.com. ℰ **877/954-8363** in the U.S., or 998/881-2500. Fax 998/881-2501. 448 units. $400 and up double. Rates are all-inclusive. AE, MC, V. **Amenities:** 3 restaurants; 2 bars; beach club; concierge; concierge floor; fitness center; Internet cafe; 3 outdoor pools; whirlpool; full-service luxury spa. *In room:* A/C, flatscreen TV, hair dryer, minibar, MP3 player, Wi-Fi.

MODERATE

Bel Air Collection Hotel & Spa ★ ✦

This minimalist beachfront hotel attracts the young, hip, and hot—making this hotel into something you'd expect to find in Miami, standing in direct contrast to the nearby all-inclusive megaresorts. Of the hotel's 156 rooms, nearly half face the ocean; the rest face the lagoon. Guest rooms are modern and spacious, with white and red decor. There's an asymmetrical infinity pool that seems to spill over onto the turquoise Caribbean Sea, with guests lazing around it on comfortable mattresses while lounge music plays in the background. The Collection Spa offers a variety of moderately priced services, including a chocolate facial. Guests receive a welcome cocktail, morning coffee, and afternoon tea. *Note:* This Bel Air is a 15-minute ride from the center of the Hotel Zone, and children 11 and under are not allowed, so if you're looking for privacy and peace, this is the place for you.

Bulevar Kukulcán Km 20.5, 77500 Cancún, Q. Roo. www.belaircollection.com. ℰ **998/885-0236.** Fax 998/885-2144. 156 units. High season $150 and up double; low season $100 and up double. All-inclusive option available. AE, MC, V. No children 11 and under. **Amenities:** 2 restaurants; sushi bar; 2 bars; concierge; exercise room; Jacuzzi; infinity outdoor pool; room service; spa; Wi-Fi (in lobby). *In room:* A/C, satellite TV/DVD, hair dryer, minibar.

Flamingo Cancún ☺

The Flamingo seems to have been inspired by the dramatic, slope-sided architecture of the Dreams Cancún, but it's considerably smaller and less expensive (guests can opt out of the all-inclusive package, which includes three meals and domestic drinks). With two pools and a casual vibe, it's also a friendly, accommodating choice for families. The bright guest rooms—all with balconies—border a courtyard facing the interior swimming pool and *palapa* pool bar. Some, but not all, of the rooms have been remodeled in recent years. The Flamingo lies in the heart of the island hotel district, opposite the Flamingo Shopping Center and close to other hotels, shopping centers, and restaurants.

Bulevar Kukulcán Km 11, 77500 Cancún, Q. Roo. www.flamingocancun.com. ℰ **998/848-8870.** Fax 998/883-1029. 260 units. $85–$145 double. All-inclusive option available. AE, MC, V. **Amenities:** 2 restaurants; 2 bars; kids' club; fitness center; 2 outdoor pools; room service; Wi-Fi (in lobby). *In room:* A/C, TV, hair dryer, minibar.

Temptation Resort & Spa Cancún

This adults-only (21 and over) getaway is a spirited all-inclusive resort favored by those looking for significant social interaction. Although it's not advertised as such, the hotel is widely known for its popularity with "swingers." By day, pool time is all about flirting, seducing, and getting a little wacky with adult games such as teasing time and a dirty jokes contest. The main pools are top-optional. Note that tops are also optional on the beach in front, which has calm waters for swimming. Come night, theme dinners, shows, a DJ, and other live entertainment keep the party going. The small, somewhat dated rooms are housed in two sections, with quiet rooms in one and "sexy" rooms, complete with red lighting, in another. Surrounded by acres of tropical gardens, this moderate hotel lies at the northern end of the Hotel Zone, close to the major shopping plazas, restaurants, and nightlife. It reminds me of a Carnival Cruise, but on land.

Bulevar Kukulcán Km 3.5, 77500 Cancún, Q. Roo. www.temptationresort.com. © **877/485-8367** in the U.S., or 998/848-7900. Fax 998/848-7994. 384 units. High season $179 per person per night double occupancy; low season $139 per person per night double occupancy. Rates include food, beverages, and activities. AE, MC, V. Guests must be at least 21 years old. **Amenities:** 6 restaurants; 5 bars; exercise room w/daily classes; marina; 3 outdoor pools; 7 whirlpools; limited room service; snorkeling and scuba lessons; spa; nonmotorized watersports. *In room:* A/C, TV, hair dryer, Wi-Fi.

Ciudad Cancún

You won't find much in the way of authentic Mexican charm in the Hotel Zone, although you can get a glimpse of it in Ciudad Cancún, where most of the local population lives. You'll find good value hotels, a number of outstanding traditional restaurants, and some excellent shopping here.

MODERATE

Radisson Hacienda Cancún ★ 🍴 This is the top hotel in downtown Cancún, and one of the best values in the area. The business-friendly Radisson offers all the expected comforts of the chain, yet resembles a hacienda with the distinct manner of Mexican hospitality. Guest rooms surround a warm, rotunda-style lobby with a cool onyx bar, as well as lush gardens and an inviting pool area. All have brightly colored fabric accents; views of the garden, the pool, or the street; and a small sitting area and balcony. The hotel lies within walking distance of downtown Cancún.

Av. Nader 1, SM2, Centro, 77500 Cancún, Q. Roo. www.radissoncancun.com. © **800/395-7046** in the U.S., or 998/881-6500. Fax 998/884-7954. 248 units. $100 and up double; $120 and up junior suite. AE, MC, V. **Amenities:** Restaurant; lobby bar; small gym; outdoor pool w/adjoining bar and separate wading area for children; limited room service; sauna; lighted tennis courts; Wi-Fi (in lobby). *In room:* A/C, TV, hair dryer.

Rey del Caribe Hotel ★★ 🎒 This acclaimed ecofriendly hotel is a unique oasis where every detail works toward establishing harmony with the environment. You might easily forget you're in the midst of downtown Cancún in the tropical garden setting, with blooming orchids and other flowering plants. The lovely grounds include statues of Maya deities, hammocks, and a tiled swimming pool. Yoga, as well as special classes on astrology, tarot, and other subjects, is periodically offered. The on-site spa offers facial and body treatments. Guest rooms, renovated in recent years, are large and sunny, with a kitchenette and your choice of one king-size or two full-size beds; some have a terrace. The extent of ecological sensitivity is impressive—ranging from the use of collected rainwater to waste composting. Recycling is encouraged, and solar power is used wherever possible.

Av. Uxmal SM 24 (corner of Nader), 77500 Cancún, Q. Roo. www.elreydelcaribe.com. © **998/884-2028.** Fax 988/884-9857. 31 units. High season $85 double; low season $65 double. Rates include breakfast. MC, V. **Amenities:** Airport transfer $20; Jacuzzi; outdoor pool; spa. *In room:* A/C, TV, kitchenette, Wi-Fi.

INEXPENSIVE

Sol y Luna 🍴 This simple but cheerful hotel next to the Parque Las Palapas has 11 individually decorated rooms on three floors with small balconies, and mosaic-trimmed bathrooms with showers only. A tiny bridge crosses the small pool at the entrance. Come here if you want to explore the downtown and experience Cancún's more local flavor, but don't expect much in the way of service or amenities. The hotel sits up one flight of stairs, just above a tapas and wine bar.

Calle Alcatraces 33, at Parque Las Palapas, 77500 Cancún, Q. Roo. © **998/887-5579.** www.hotel solylunacancun.com. 11 units. 600–800 pesos double. AE, MC, V. Street parking. **Amenities:** Restaurant/bar; outdoor pool; Wi-Fi. *In room:* A/C, TV, fridge.

Xbalamqué ★ Creatively designed to resemble a Maya temple, this downtown hotel features a lovely pool and waterfall, full-service spa, and authentic Mexican cantina. Live music plays evenings in the bookstore/cafe adjacent to the lobby. Guest rooms and 10 junior suites have rustic furnishings with regional touches, colorful tilework, and small bathrooms with showers. Ask for a room overlooking the ivy-filled courtyard. A tour desk is available to help you plan your vacation activities, and the spa offers some of the best rates of any hotel in Cancún. The small theater offers programs on weekends for children and adults alike.

Av. Yaxchilán 31, Sm. 22, Mza. 18, 77500 Cancún, Q. Roo. www.xbalamque.com. © **998/884-9690.** Fax 998/884-9690. 99 units. $75 double; $85 suite. AE, MC, V. **Amenities:** Restaurant; cafe; cantina; bar; outdoor pool; spa; Wi-Fi. *In room:* A/C, TV.

WHERE TO EAT

A wide range of dining options spanning Mexican, American, European, and Asian cuisines dot Cancún's Hotel Zone and downtown, with some of Mexico's top restaurants located right here. Restaurants divide into roughly three categories: expensive and international in resort hotels; independent establishments along the lagoon (with great sunset views); and inexpensive Mexican eateries in El Centro (Cancún City). One cheap, reliable Mexican chain in the Hotel Zone serving tasty meals, including breakfasts, is **Vips,** across from the Convention Center. The establishments listed below are typically locally owned, one-of-a-kind restaurants or exceptional selections at area hotels. Many schedule live music. Unless otherwise indicated, parking is free.

One unique way to combine dinner with sightseeing is aboard the **Lobster Dinner Cruise** (© **998/849-4748;** www.thelobsterdinner.com). Cruising around the tranquil, turquoise waters of the lagoon, passengers feast on steak and lobster dinners accompanied by wine. Cost is $89 per person for the surf-and-turf menu. The two daily departures are from the Aquatours Marina (Bulevar Kukulcán Km 6.5). A sunset cruise leaves at 5pm during the winter and 5:30pm during the summer; a moonlight cruise leaves at 8pm winter, 8:30pm summer. Another, albeit livelier, lobster dinner option is the **Captain Hook Lobster Dinner Cruise** (© **998/849-4451;** www. pirateshipcancun.com), which is similar, but with the added attraction of a pirate show involving two 28m (92-ft.) replicas of 18th-century Spanish galleons, making this a fun choice for families. The steak option costs $90 per person, and the lobster (or steak and lobster) option is $100 per person, including open bar. It departs at 7pm from El Embarcadero at Playa Linda, and returns at 10:30pm.

Isla Cancún

VERY EXPENSIVE

Aioli ★★ FRENCH Le Méridien's signature restaurant offers French and Mediterranean gourmet specialties in an exquisite French setting. Wrought-iron chandeliers, hand-painted Talavera vases, original artwork, and candlelit tables define the elegant dining room. To start, the foie gras medallions and caramelized figs with a cherry brandy sauce is the clear winner, although the Caesar salad tossed with jumbo shrimp is a worthy competitor. Favorite mains include the red snapper with a Spanish sausage risotto, and tender rack of lamb with couscous. The in-house pastry chef (whose dessert preparation you can watch in action) creates decadent sweets—I recommend the rich "Fifth Element" with chocolate and a berry sauce. Live music accompanies the highly attentive service.

In Le Méridien Cancún Resort & Spa (p. 466), Retorno del Rey Km 14. © **998/881-2200.** Reservations recommended. No sandals or tennis shoes; men must wear long pants. Main courses 250–420 pesos. AE, MC, V. Daily 6:30am–11pm.

The Club Grill ★★★ INTERNATIONAL The Ritz-Carlton's Club Grill is one of Mexico's top-ranked restaurants. In a resort town that's increasingly going with the all-inclusive concept, this jazz and supper club stands out as an outstanding hotel restaurant open to the wider public. The gracious service starts in the anteroom, with its elegant seating and superb selection of cocktails and wines. It continues in the candlelit dining room, with shimmering silver and crystal. French-inspired appetizers include caramelized scallops, escargot, and sautéed foie gras. Among the excellent mains, you'll find roasted duck with chipotle, herbed rack of lamb, crispy organic chicken breast, and filet mignon accented with foie gras. Finish with a pistachio crème brûlée or chocolate fondant. Guests seeking an even more gastronomically rich experience can sign up for the chef's table or take a gourmet cooking class at the hotel's renowned Culinary School.

In the Ritz-Carlton Cancún (p. 466), Retorno del Rey 36, Bulevar Kukulcán Km 13.5. © **998/881-0808.** Reservations required. No sandals or tennis shoes; men must wear long pants and collared shirts. Main courses 390–640 pesos. AE, DC, MC, V. Tues–Sun 7–11pm.

Lorenzillo's ★★ ☺ SEAFOOD This longtime Cancún favorite hasn't changed much over the years. Lobster remains the star, and part of the appeal is plucking your dinner right out of the giant lobster tank set in the lagoon. Twinkle lights line the dock between Lorenzillo's and Limoncelle, the waterfront Italian restaurant next door, creating a magical reflection off the water. When Lorenzillo's main dining room is packed, a wharf-side bar handles the overflow. To start, I recommend *El Botin,* which consists of two soft-shell crabs breaded and fried to perfection. In addition to lobster (prepared in any of 20 different ways), you can also choose from shrimp stuffed with cheese and wrapped in bacon, the *Pescador* (Caribbean grouper prepared to taste), and steak and seafood combinations. Desserts include the tempting crêpes suzette, prepared tableside. Climb into the large built-in wine cellar for a tasting of one of the 280 labels, from 16 countries, with some very high-end bottles available by the glass. Lorenzillo's is as popular with families as it is with couples looking for lagoon-side romance.

Bulevar Kukulcán Km 10.5. © **998/883-1254.** www.lorenzillos.com.mx. Reservations recommended. Main courses 280–580 pesos. AE, MC, V. Daily 1pm–midnight.

EXPENSIVE

Casa Rolandi ★★★ SWISS/ITALIAN French-trained chef-owner Danielle Muller has taken the reins and redesigned both the dining space and the menu of Casa Rolandi. Famous personalities, from international actors to Mexican presidents, have dined here over the years, and Casa Rolandi remains one of Cancún's best tables. The core dishes are Swiss-Italian, although monthly thematic festivals—featuring, for example, seafood, venison, or asparagus—infuse the menu with creative selections using seasonal ingredients. The carpaccios, ceviches, and seared scallops make for excellent starters. Among my favorite main courses are veal cheeks in wine served over polenta, suckling pig served *pibil*-style (wrapped in banana leaves with achiote and spices), fresh seafood *tagliolini* draped in black ink, and salt-crusted red snapper. Finish with the sublime tiramisu accompanied by Kahlua and coffee. Service remains personalized and friendly, and an urban-chic cigar and wine lounge, **Very Wine,** sits upstairs (p. 485). Casa Rolandi remains open later than most Hotel Zone restaurants.

Bulevar Kukulcán Km 8.5, in Plaza Caracol. © **998/883-2557.** www.rolandi.com. Reservations recommended. Main courses 178–415 pesos. AE, MC, V. Sun–Wed 1pm–midnight, Thurs–Sat 1pm–2am.

Elefanta ★★ INDIAN   A partner restaurant to Thai (p. 475), Elefanta is one of the trendiest spots on Cancún's dining scene. The exotic waterfront space has two open kitchens overseen by an Indian chef—one for cooking in the clay tandoor oven, and the other for curries. The kitchens focus on fish, shrimp, and chicken dishes; this is also one of the few places in Cancún serving a substantial selection of quality vegetarian plates. Dishes can be ordered on regular or half-size plates and are perfect for sharing with friends or family. Elefanta's chill-out music is coordinated with Thai, next door, and a DJ here spins hot mixes Thursday through Saturday nights. If you're in the mood for a cocktail, try one of the 30 exotic martinis.

La Isla Shopping Village, Bulevar Kukulcán 12.5. © **998/176-8070.** Reservations recommended during high season. Main courses 200–400 pesos. AE, MC, V. Daily 6–11:30pm.

Gustino ★★★ ITALIAN   JW Marriott's signature restaurant Gustino offers romantic Italian dining unsurpassed in Cancún. The exquisite dining room boasts a gorgeous centerpiece candle display, floor-to-ceiling windows looking out to a lazy man-made lagoon and the beach beyond, and live saxophone. The meal begins with a heaping basket of fresh-made Italian breads, including a flavorful basil and tomato focaccia. For an antipasto, the unusual pear carpaccio with Parmesan nuggets and caramelized grapes tastes sublime, as do the sautéed shrimp in a white wine sauce with capers and roasted celery crouton. I also love the warm tossed spinach salad, topped with pancetta, mushrooms, sun-dried tomatoes, and walnuts. Expertly prepared main dishes include open lasagna with lobster and black olives, and roasted loin of venison with a stuffed potato croquette. The menu, which changes seasonally, features other homemade pastas and succulent steak and seafood selections. Gustino houses a wine cellar with an excellent variety of international grapes. Service is outstanding.

In the JW Marriott (p. 464), Bulevar Kukulcán Km 14.5. © **998/848-9600.** www.gustinorestaurant.jwmarriottcancunrestaurants.com. Reservations required. Main courses 205–585 pesos. AE, DC, MC, V. Daily 6–11pm.

Harry's ★★ STEAK   Situated adjacent to the Nichupté Lagoon, this recent arrival to Cancún's dining scene is the Hotel Zone's top steakhouse. The dining room and waterfront terrace combine local stone and wood with burnt orange marble and large expanses of glass to create a sense of California chic. The attentive waitstaff brings to your table a tempting selection of different cuts of beef, as well as a presentation from the raw bar. The New York strips, rib-eyes, and other cuts of beef are broiled in a 1,700°F (927°C) oven, while the fish and seafood are grilled on a *parilla*. A la carte selections blend Mexican and Asian influences, with fascinating results such as lobster pozole, crab wontons with spicy plum sauce, and jasmine rice balls with tuna steak. Don't expect a kids' menu here: Even the Kobe beef burger is so big (and expensive) it could feed a family. A selection of over 500 international and Mexican boutique wines accompanies the menu. This is also one of the few restaurants in Cancún serving kosher options.

Bulevar Kukulcán Km 14.2. ⓒ **998/840-6550.** www.harrys.com.mx. Reservations recommended. Main courses 320–1,100 pesos. AE, MC, V. Daily 1pm–1am.

La Madonna ★ SWISS/ITALIAN   This architecturally dazzling restaurant and bar emerges unexpectedly from La Isla Shopping Village like an Italian Renaissance showroom along the canal. Inside, the dining room resembles one of the mystical international Buddha Bars, with an enormous replica of the Mona Lisa looking over the dazzled clientele. La Madonna offers authentic Italian and Swiss cuisine, including antipasti, pasta, grilled fish, steak, and fondues. Main dishes include chicken in limoncello sauce, saffron risotto, and the veal chop in prosciutto sauce. For dessert, request the tableside flambéed strawberries. Many people come just for dessert and drinks (p. 485).

La Isla Shopping Village, Bulevar Kukulcán 12.5. ⓒ **998/883-2222.** www.lamadonna.com.mx. Reservations recommended. Main courses 155–800 pesos. AE, MC, V. Daily noon–1am.

Puerto Madero ★★★ ARGENTINE/SEAFOOD/STEAK   A tribute to the famed Puerto Madero of Buenos Aires, this trendy restaurant has earned a reputation for its steak and fish as well as its unique urban atmosphere. Overlooking the Nichupté Lagoon, the decor re-creates a 20th-century dock warehouse similar to what you'd find in the real Puerto Madero, with dark woods, exposed brick, visible pipes, and a marble-lit bar. A wall of glass separates the bustling dining room from the patio, where smoking is allowed. Puerto Madero offers an extensive selection of prime-quality beef cuts (not authentically Argentine, but tasty nevertheless), local and imported fish, seafood, and pasta. For a more traditional Argentine starter, the crispy tuna-filled empanada comes with a delectable *chimichurri* dipping sauce. Excellent mains include blue or yellowfin tuna, black cod laced with hazelnut butter, and creative pastas like crab tortellini smothered in white Parmesan sauce. The Alaskan king crab tail, fried tempura-style, remains one of my favorites. Service is gracious and warm, and the wine and champagne list extensive.

Marina Barracuda, Bulevar Kukulcán Km 14. ⓒ **998/885-2829.** -2830. www.puertomaderorestaurantes.com. Reservations recommended. Main courses 170–740 pesos. AE, MC, V. Daily 1pm–1am.

Sasi ★★ THAI   One of two outstanding Thai restaurants in Cancún—and the more family-friendly of the two—Sasi sparkles under a series of *palapas* lit by soft onyx lamps. To start, try ordering the Sasi Sampler, which comes with a selection of shrimp, pork, beef, and chicken dumplings presented in a *domburi* basket. Main courses include stir-fried rice plates with chicken or shrimp, two versions of pad Thai, and a variety of curries prepared with toasted herbs and jasmine rice. Those looking for spicy options will find worthy contenders in the *tom yang goong* shrimp soup and the chicken and shrimp green curry. Dishes arrive carefully prepared and artfully presented, and the bartender mixes among the best martinis I've found in this city. The wait staff is Mexican, and the service every bit as gracious as you'd find if you were in Thailand.

In the Marriott CasaMagna (p. 468), Bulevar Kukulcán Km 14.5. ⓒ **998/881-2092.** www.sasi-thai.com. Reservations recommended. Main courses 140–240 pesos. AE, MC, V. Daily 5:30–11pm.

Sedona Grill ★★ SOUTHWEST   Sedona Grill successfully adapts French culinary techniques to Southwestern American cuisine. The result is exceptional, with fresh Mexican Caribbean ingredients infusing the original menu. Start with a light shrimp ceviche served with mango, Key lime, and Navajo fry bread, or the roasted corn bisque filled with country flavor. Excellent mains include the *chimichurri* red snapper served with chile-lemon risotto, the "tequila sunrise" penne pasta with hickory-smoked chicken, and the thick seared filet mignon so tender it almost cuts through like butter. The high-ceiling dining room, created with subtle Southwestern decor, looks out to the JW Marriott pools and Caribbean Sea.

In the JW Marriott (p. 464), Bulevar Kukulcán Km 14.5. 🕐 **998/848-9600.** www.sedona.jw marriottcancun.com. Reservations required. Main courses 160–450 pesos. AE, DC, MC, V. Daily 6:30am–11pm.

Thai ★★★ 📷 THAI This exotic restaurant and lounge reminds me of Southeast Asia rather than the edge of a Mexican shopping plaza. The stunning outdoor setting includes thick foliage and bamboo, with private *palapas* (open-air huts, each with its own table, sofa, and flickering candles) constructed like tiny islands over the expansive lagoon. Unobtrusive service, soft red and blue lighting, and Asian chill and lounge music contribute to the chic ambience. Classic Thai specialties such as roasted duck breast in coconut red curry, spicy shrimp soup with lemon grass and mushrooms, glass noodle salad, chicken satay, and chicken and shrimp curries and stir-fries are served alongside unusual cocktails to the beautiful crowd. A DJ works the stylish lounge on weekends. Thai opens at sunset.

La Isla Shopping Village, Bulevar Kukulcán Km 12.5. 🕐 **998/176-8070.** www.thai.com.mx. Reservations recommended during high season. Main courses 230–495 pesos. AE, MC, V. Daily 6pm–1am.

MODERATE

La Destilería 😊 MEXICAN To experience Mexico's favorite export on a relaxed lagoon-side deck, this is your place (keep an eye out for Tequila, the lagoon crocodile who often comes to visit). La Destilería is more than a tequila-inspired restaurant; it's a minimuseum honoring the "spirit" of Mexico with over 150 brands of tequila, including some treasures that never find their way across the border. A tequila tour takes place at various times between 1 and 5pm daily, and patrons can always order tequila "samplers" at their tables. No surprise, the margaritas are among the island's best. You'll also find a creative Mexican menu, with everything from quesadillas with zucchini flower, cheese, and poblano pepper to *arrachera* beef fajitas served in a hot *molcajete* pot with chorizo, black beans, and avocado. Live mariachi music plays nightly from 8 to 9pm, and there's a kids' playroom and menu with tacos, chicken, and fish.

Bulevar Kukulcán Km 12.65, across from Kukulcán Plaza. 🕐 **998/885-1086,** -1087. www.ladestileria. com.mx. Main courses 135–300 pesos. Tequila tour 85 pesos. AE, MC, V. Daily 1pm–midnight.

INEXPENSIVE

El Fish Fritanga Pescadillas MEXICAN/SEAFOOD Simple beach chairs and tables sit in the sand among beached fishing boats and a small dock. Just below La Destilería, Pescadillas—as it's known to locals—offers friendly service, refreshing (and promptly served) beverages, and tasty snacks. Munch on any number of appetizers, such as tostadas packed with sizzling fish, shrimp, or octopus, or snappy, lemon-drenched ceviches of all kinds. Chicken and pasta are available for more conventional palates, but I'd recommend diving into the "aphrodisiac lobster," grilled to perfection with fragrant cloves of garlic and butter. Alongside the octopus, shrimp, and fish specialties are sizzling platters of fajitas served with rice and beans, and the best salsa I've had on the island. This is a fun, casual place for lingering over a snack and drinks, and perfect for sunsets over the lagoon.

Bulevar Kukulcán Km 12.73. 🕐 **998/840-6216.** Main courses 70–180 pesos. AE, MC, V. Daily 1pm–midnight.

Santos Mariscos MEXICAN/SEAFOOD   Silver stars dangle from the 9m (30-ft.) ceiling of this cheerful seafood cantina, decorated with local art on rustic adobe walls. A small patio provides outside seating, where you can dazzle your taste buds with chips and strawberry jalapeño salsa accompanied by an ice-cold *cerveza*. Order tacos packed with seafood, chicken, or beef, or try one of the *cazuelos* (casseroles of seafood slow-cooked with local spices and garlic). The best part of this local eatery is its unpretentious and good-natured feel.

Bulevar Kukulcán Km 12.73. © **998/840-6300.** Main courses 59–145 pesos. AE, MC, V. Daily 11am–11pm.

Ciudad Cancún

EXPENSIVE

La Habichuela ★★ 📷 SEAFOOD   In a musically accented garden setting with flowering white-lit hibiscus trees, this longtime favorite remains downtown's most elegant table. For an unforgettable culinary adventure, order crème of *habichuela* (string bean) soup; giant shrimp in any number of sauces, including Jamaican tamarind, tequila, or ginger and mushroom; and exotic Maya coffee prepared tableside with Xtabentun (a strong, sweet, anise-based liqueur). Grilled seafood and steaks are excellent, and the menu includes luscious ceviches, Caribbean lobsters, an inventive seafood "parade," and shish kabob flambé with shrimp and lobster or beef. For something divine, try *cocobichuela,* lobster and shrimp in sweet curry served in a coconut shell with rice and topped with fruit. Top it off with one of the boozy butterscotch crepes. La Habichuela now has a second branch in the Hotel Zone called **La Habichuela Sunset** at Bulevar Kukulcán Km 12.6 (© **998/840-6280**), which features giant windows overlooking the lagoon and is close to La Isla Shopping Village. It's open daily from noon to midnight.

Margaritas 25. © **998/884-3158.** www.lahabichuela.com. Reservations recommended in high season. Main courses 157–400 pesos. AE, MC, V. Daily noon–midnight.

MODERATE

Labná ★★ YUCATECAN   Coming for a meal at Labná is like a very special trip to a Yucatecan home, a place that serves delicious Maya food and treats you like a friend. Specialties include a sublime lime soup, *poc chuc* (marinated, barbecue-style pork), chicken or pork *pibil* (sweet and spicy barbecue sauce served over shredded meat wrapped in banana leaves), and appetizers such as *papadzules* (tortillas stuffed with boiled eggs in a pumpkin-seed sauce). The Labná Special is a sampler of four typically Yucatecan main courses, including *poc chuc,* while another specialty of the house is baked suckling pig, served with guacamole. The refreshing Yucatecan beverage, *agua de chaya*—a blend of sweetened water and the leaf of the *chaya* plant, to which sweet Xtabentun liquor (a type of anise) can be added for an extra kick—is also served here. The vaulted-ceiling dining room is decorated with a mural of a pre-Hispanic Yucatecan scene, as well as with black-and-white photographs of Mérida, the capital of the Yucatán, dating from the 1900s. A local trio occasionally plays.

Margaritas 29, next to Cristo Rey church and La Habichuela restaurant. © **998/884-3158.** www.labna.com. Reservations recommended. Main courses 80–200 pesos. AE, MC, V. Daily noon–10pm.

La Parilla ★★ MEXICAN   A downtown institution, La Parilla is a celebration of Mexican folklore featuring a colorful open-air dining room, nightly mariachi music, and a rich menu promising excellent food. You'll find authentic dishes from the garden and the Caribbean, as well as Mexican specialties such as *mole* enchiladas or grilled Aztec steak wrapped in cactus leaves and stuffed with onions. There are also tacos of every variety (*pastor* is the specialty), sumptuous grilled steaks and seafood, and Maya treats such as *poc chuc*. This is a place to eat, drink, and be merry, and tequila samplers are available for those willing to risk a hangover tomorrow morning. One drawback: There are fans but no air-conditioning, so take a cold shower before you come here on a hot night.

Av. Yaxchilán 51. ℰ **998/287-8118.** Main courses 150–350 pesos. AE, MC, V. Daily 11:30am–1:30am.

INEXPENSIVE

100% Natural ★ BREAKFAST/HEALTH FOOD   If you want a healthy reprieve from an overindulgent night—or just like your meals as fresh and natural as possible—this favorite national chain is your oasis. No matter what your dining preference, you owe it to yourself to try a Mexican tradition, the fresh-fruit *licuado*. These tropical smoothies combine fresh fruit, ice, and water or milk. More creative combinations may mix in yogurt, granola, or other goodies. 100% Natural serves more than just quality drinks—there's a bountiful selection of healthy Mexican plates and terrific sandwiches served on whole-grain bread, with options for vegetarians. Breakfast is delightful and the attached bakery features all-natural baked goods such as chocolate croissants and apple-cinnamon muffins. There are several 100% Natural locations in town, including branches at Playa Chac-Mool, in front of Señor Frog's, and downtown.

Av. Sunyaxchen 63. ℰ **998/884-0102.** www.100natural.com.mx. Main courses 50–190 pesos. AE, MC, V. Daily 7am–11pm.

Rolandi's ☺ ITALIAN   At this patio restaurant-bar and pizzeria known for dependable Italian delights, you can choose from an enticing selection of antipasti and salads, calzones, and baked dishes, such as roast beef, garlic shrimp, and tender chicken. There are also almost two dozen delicious, if greasy, wood-oven pizzas (individual size) ranging from simple to exotic. Why not try the deliciously spicy "Fiesta Mexicana" pizza with tomato, cheese, Mexican sausage, and jalapeños, or the "Pizza del Patron" with tomato, mascarpone cheese, arugula, and Parma ham? A Cancún institution since 1979, Rolandi's has additional branches in Cozumel and Isla Mujeres (see chapter 14). It's as popular with locals as it is with tourists.

Av. Cobá 12. ℰ **998/884-4047.** www.rolandi.com. Reservations recommended. Pasta 112–135 pesos; pizza and main courses 99–172 pesos. AE, MC, V. Daily 12:30pm–12:30am.

BEACHES, WATERSPORTS & BOAT TOURS

THE BEACHES   Cancún recently added significant stretches of sand to its beaches as part of a $71-million beach recovery project to counter the amount of sand eroded by various storms in recent years. Big hotels dominate the best stretches of beach. All of Mexico's beaches are public property, so you can use the beach of any hotel by walking through the lobby or directly onto the sand. Be especially careful on the east-facing beaches fronting the open Caribbean, where the undertow can be quite strong. By contrast, the waters of **Bahía de Mujeres** (Mujeres Bay), at the north end of the island, are usually calm and ideal for swimming. Get to know

Cancún's water-safety pennant system, and make sure to check the flag at any beach or hotel before entering the water. Here's how it goes:

White	Excellent
Green	Normal conditions (safe)
Yellow	Changeable, uncertain (use caution)
Black or **red**	Unsafe—use the swimming pool instead!

In the Caribbean, storms can arrive and conditions can change from safe to unsafe in a matter of minutes, so be alert: If you see dark clouds heading your way, make for the shore and wait until the storm passes.

Playa Tortuga (Turtle Beach), Playa Langosta (Lobster Beach), Playa Linda (Pretty Beach), and Playa Las Perlas (Beach of the Pearls) are some of the public beaches. At most beaches, you can rent a sailboard and take lessons, ride a parasail, or partake in a variety of watersports. There's a small but beautiful portion of public beach on Playa Caracol, by the Xcaret Terminal. It faces the calm waters of Bahía de Mujeres and, for that reason, is preferable to those facing the Caribbean.

WATERSPORTS   Many beachside hotels offer watersports concessions that rent rubber rafts, kayaks, and snorkeling equipment. On the calm Nichupté Lagoon are outlets for renting **sailboats, jet skis, sailboards,** and **water skis.** Prices vary and are often negotiable, so check around.

DEEP-SEA FISHING   You can arrange a shared or private deep-sea fishing charter at one of the numerous piers or travel agencies. Prices fluctuate widely depending on the length of the excursion (there's usually a 4-hr. minimum), number of people, and quality of the boat. Marinas will sometimes assist in putting together a group. Charters include a captain, a first mate, bait, gear, and beverages. Rates are lower if you depart from Isla Mujeres or from Cozumel—and, frankly, the fishing is better closer to those departure points.

SCUBA & SNORKELING   Known for its shallow reefs, dazzling color, and diversity of life, Cancún is one of the best places in the world for beginning scuba diving. Punta Nizuc is the northern tip of the **Gran Arrecife Maya (Great Mesoamerican Reef),** the largest reef in the Western Hemisphere and one of the largest in the world. In addition to the sea life along this reef system, several sunken boats add a variety of dive options. Inland, a series of caverns and cenotes (wellsprings) are fascinating venues for the more experienced diver. Drift diving is the norm here, with popular dives going to the reefs at **El Garrafón** and the **Caves of the Sleeping Sharks**—although be aware that the famed "sleeping sharks" have departed, driven off by too many people watching them snooze.

A variety of hotels offer resort courses that teach the basics of diving—enough to make shallow dives and slowly ease your way into this underwater world of unimaginable beauty. One preferred dive operator is **Scuba Cancún,** Bulevar Kukulcán Km 5 (© **998/849-7508;** www.scubacancun.com.mx), on the lagoon side. Full open-water PADI certification takes 3 days and costs $410. A half-day resort course for beginners with theory, pool practice, and a one-tank dive at a reef costs $88. Scuba Cancún is open daily from 7am to 8pm. For certified divers, Scuba Cancún also offers PADI specialty courses and diving trips in good weather to 18 nearby reefs, as well as to cenotes (9m/30 ft.) and Cozumel. The average dive is around 11m (36 ft.), while advanced divers descend farther (up to 18m/59 ft.). Two-tank dives to reefs around Cancún cost $68, and one-tank dives cost $54; those to farther destinations cost $140. Discounts apply if you bring your own gear. Dives usually start around

9:30am and return by 1:30pm. Snorkeling trips cost $29 and leave daily at 1:30 and 4pm for shallow reefs about a 20-minute boat ride away.

The largest dive operator is **Aquaworld,** across from the Meliá Cancún at Bulevar Kukulcán Km 15.2 (© **998/848-8300;** www.aquaworld.com.mx). It offers resort courses and diving at a reef barrier—including a visit to an underwater sculpture project designed to promote the growth of coral reef and marine life—as well as snorkeling, parasailing, jet-ski "jungle tours," fishing, day trips to Isla Mujeres and Cozumel, and other watersports activities. Aquaworld has the **Sub See Explorer,** a boat with picture windows beneath the surface. The vessel doesn't submerge—it's an updated version of a glass-bottom boat—but it does provide nondivers with a worthwhile peek at life beneath the sea.

BOB Submarines (© 998/849-7284) offers an unforgettable underwater experience involving individual propelled "submarines" with breathing observation bubbles (BOBs). This is like scuba diving, but easier. The shop sits at El Embarcadero next to Playa Linda, and a boat takes groups from there to a nearby reef where the BOBs are deployed into the water. These personal minisubs let you discover the Caribbean at 6m (20 ft.) below the surface with a big air bubble over your head (supported by oxygen tanks) and operate much like a very slow scooter would. The tours include instruction, soft drinks, and a 30-minute assisted dive (with videos and photos of the dive available at extra cost). The price is $85 per person and the minimum age is 12, with departures at 9 and 11:30am and 2pm. The same company also offers WaveRunner jungle tours.

Besides snorkeling at **El Garrafón Natural Park** (see "Boating Excursions," below), travel agencies offer an all-day excursion to the natural wildlife habitat of **Isla Contoy,** which usually includes time for snorkeling. The island, 90 minutes past Isla Mujeres, is a major nesting area for birds and a treat for nature lovers. You can call any travel agent or see any hotel tour desk to get a selection of boat tours to Isla Contoy. Prices range from $50 to $80, depending on the length of the trip, and generally include drinks and snorkeling equipment.

The Great Mesoamerican Reef also offers exceptional snorkeling opportunities. In Puerto Morelos, 37km (23 miles; p. 517) south of Cancún, the reef hugs the coastline for 15km (9⅓ miles). The reef is so close to the shore (about 460m/1,500 ft.) that it forms a natural barrier for the village and keeps the waters calm on the inside of the reef. The water here is shallow, from 1.5 to 9m (5–30 ft.), resulting in ideal conditions for snorkeling. Stringent environmental regulations implemented by the local community have kept the reef here unspoiled. Only a select few companies are allowed to offer snorkel trips, and they must adhere to guidelines that will ensure the reef's preservation. **Cancún Mermaid** (© **998/273-4257;** www.cancunmermaid. com), in Puerto Morelos, is considered the best—it's a family-run ecotour company that has operated in the area since the 1970s. It's known for highly personalized service. The 8-hour tour typically takes snorkelers to two sections of the reef, spending about an hour in each area. When conditions allow, the boat drops off snorkelers and then follows them along with the current—an activity known as "drift snorkeling," which enables snorkelers to see as much of the reef as possible. The trip costs $95, which includes boat, snorkeling gear, life jackets, a light lunch, bottled water, sodas, and beer, entrance to the park, and round-trip transportation to and from Puerto Morelos from Cancún hotels. Departures are Monday through Saturday at 9am. Reservations are required at least 1 day in advance; MasterCard and Visa are accepted.

JET-SKI/FAST BOAT TOURS Several companies offer the thrilling **Jungle Cruise,** in which you drive your own small speedboat (called a *lancha*) or WaveRunner rapidly through Cancún's lagoon and mangrove estuaries out into the Caribbean Sea and a shallow reef. The excursion lasts about 2½ hours and costs $60 to $80, including snorkeling equipment. Many people prefer the companies offering two-person boats rather than WaveRunners, since they can sit side by side rather than one behind the other.

Jungle Cruise operators and names offering excursions change often. To find out what's available, check with a local travel agent or hotel tour desk. The popular **Aquaworld,** Bulevar Kukulcán Km 15.2 (*𝒞* **998/848-8300**), calls its trip the Jungle Tour and charges $66 for the 2½-hour excursion, which includes 30 minutes of snorkeling time. It even gives you a free snorkel and has the WaveRunner-style one-behind-the-other seating configuration. Multiple departures happen daily from 9am to 4:30pm. If you'd prefer a side-by-side boat so that you and your partner can talk or at least look at each other, try **Blue Ray,** Bulevar Kukulcán Km 13.5, next to Mambo Café (*𝒞* **998/885-1108**), which charges $66, with departures every hour between 9am and 3pm. Expect to get wet, and wear plenty of sunscreen. If you just want to rent a WaveRunner, Aquaworld offers them for $45 per half-hour or $82 per hour.

Boating Excursions

ISLA MUJERES The island of **Isla Mujeres,** just 13km (8 miles) offshore, is one of the most pleasant day trips from Cancún. At one end is **El Garrafón Natural Park,** which is good for snorkeling. At the other end is a captivating village with small shops, restaurants, and hotels, and **Playa Norte,** the island's best beach. If you're looking for relaxation and can spare the time, it's worth several days. For complete information about the island, see chapter 14.

There are four ways to get there: **public ferry** from Puerto Juárez, which takes between 15 and 20 minutes; **shuttle boat** from Playa Linda or Playa Tortuga, an hour-long ride, with irregular service; **water taxi** (more expensive, but faster), next to the Xcaret Terminal; and daylong **pleasure-boat cruises,** most of which leave from the Playa Linda pier.

The inexpensive but fast Puerto Juárez **public ferries** ★ lie just a few kilometers from downtown Cancún. From Cancún City, take the Ruta 8 bus on Avenida Tulum to Puerto Juárez. The air-conditioned **Ultramar boats** (*𝒞* **998/843-2011;** www.granpuerto.com.mx) cost 80 pesos per person each way and take 15 to 20 minutes. Departures are every half-hour from 6:30am to 8:30pm and then at 9:30, 10:30, and 11:30pm. Ultramar also runs ferries between Isla Mujeres and El Embarcadero at Playa Linda, in the Hotel Zone. The cost is $15 round-trip. Upon arrival, the ferry docks in downtown Isla Mujeres near all the shops, restaurants, hotels, and Playa Norte. You'll need a taxi to get to El Garrafón park at the other end of the island. You can stay as long as you like on the island and return by ferry, but be sure to confirm the time of the last returning ferry.

Pleasure-boat cruises to Isla Mujeres are a favorite pastime. Modern motorboats, yachts, sailboats (including the "Sea Passion" catamaran), and even old-time sloops—more than 25 boats a day—take swimmers, sun lovers, snorkelers, and shoppers out on the translucent waters. Some tours include a snorkeling stop at El Garrafón, lunch on the beach, and a short time for shopping in downtown Isla Mujeres. Most leave at 9:30 or 10am, last about 5 or 6 hours, and include continental breakfast, lunch, and rental of snorkel gear. Others, particularly sunset and night cruises, go to beaches away from town for pseudo-pirate shows and include a lobster dinner or Mexican buffet (p. 471). If you want to actually see Isla Mujeres, go on a morning cruise, or travel on your own using the public ferry from Puerto Juárez. Prices for the day cruises run around $80 per person. Reservations aren't necessary.

An all-inclusive entrance fee of $69, $50 for children to **Garrafón Natural Reef Park ★★** (© **998/849-4748;** www.garrafon.com), includes transportation from Playa Langosta in Cancún; meals; open bar with domestic drinks; access to the reef; and use of snorkel gear, kayaks, inner tubes, life vests, the pool, hammocks, and public facilities and showers (but not towels, so bring your own). There are also nature trails and several on-site restaurants.

Other excursions go to the **reefs** in glass-bottom boats, so you can have a near-scuba-diving experience and see many colorful fish. However, the reefs are some distance from the shore and are impossible to reach on windy days with choppy seas. They've also suffered from over-visitation, and their condition is far from pristine. **Atlantis Submarine** (© **987/872-5671;** www.atlantisadventures.com) takes you close to the aquatic action. Departures vary, depending on weather conditions. Prices are $99 for adults, $59 for children ages 4 to 12. The submarine descends to a depth of 30m (98 ft.). Atlantis Submarine departs daily at 9am, 11am, and noon; the tour lasts about 40 minutes. The submarine departs from Cozumel, so you need to either take a ferry to get there or purchase a package that includes round-trip transportation from your hotel in Cancún. Reservations are recommended.

OUTDOOR ACTIVITIES & ATTRACTIONS

DOLPHIN SWIMS On Isla Mujeres, you have the opportunity to swim with dolphins at **Dolphin Discovery ★★** (© **998/877-0207** or 998/849-4757; www.dolphindiscovery.com). Groups of eight people swim with two dolphins and one trainer. Swimmers view an educational video and spend time in the water with the trainer and the dolphins before enjoying 15 minutes of free swimming time with them. Reservations are recommended (you can book online), and you must arrive an hour before your assigned swimming time, at 10:30am, 12:15pm, 2:15pm, or 3:30pm. The cost is $129 per person for the Dolphin Royal Swim. There are less expensive programs that allow you to learn about, touch, and hold the dolphins (but not swim with them) starting at $69. Ferry transfers from Playa Langosta in Cancún are available.

La Isla Shopping Village, Bulevar Kukulcán Km 12.5, has an impressive **Interactive Aquarium** (© **998/883-0411;** www.aquariumcancun.com.mx), with dolphin swims and shows and the chance to feed a shark while immersed in the water in an acrylic cage. Guides inside the main tank use underwater microphones to point out the sea life, and even answer your questions. Open exhibition tanks enable visitors to touch a variety of marine life, including sea stars and manta rays. The educational program and dolphin swim costs $85 and the shark-feeding experience runs $60. The entrance fee to the aquarium is $10, and it's open daily from 9am to 6pm.

GOLF & TENNIS The 18-hole **Cancún Golf Club at Pok-Ta-Pok** (© **998/883-0871;** www.cancungolfclub.com), located at Bulevar Kukulcán Km 7.5, is a Robert Trent Jones II design on the northern leg of the island. Greens fees run $175 for 18 holes in high season, $145 in low season, including breakfast or lunch and golf cart (discounted fees after 2pm), with clubs renting for $45. A caddy costs $20 plus tip. The club is open daily from 6:30am to 5pm.

The **Hilton Cancún Golf & Spa Resort** (© **998/881-8016;** www.hilton cancun.com) has a championship 18-hole, par-72 course around the Ruinas Del Rey. Greens fees during high season for the public are typically $179 for 18 holes and $99 for 9 holes; Hilton Cancún guests pay discounted rates of $129 for 18 holes, or $79 for 9 holes, which includes a golf cart. Low-season and twilight discounts are available. Golf clubs and shoes are available for rent. The club is open daily from 6am to 6pm and accepts American Express, MasterCard, and Visa. The **Gran Meliá Cancún** (© **998/881-1100**) has a 9-hole executive course; the greens fee is $35. The club is open daily from 7am to 3pm (last tee time is 1pm).

The first Jack Nicklaus Signature Golf Course in the Cancún area is at the **Moon Palace Spa & Golf Club** (© **998/881-6000;** www.palaceresorts.com), along the Riviera Maya. The $260 greens fee ($160 for twilight) includes cart, snacks, and drinks.

SHOPPING

Aside from the surrounding natural splendor, Cancún is known throughout Mexico for its diverse shops and festive malls catering to international tourists. Visitors from the United States may find apparel more expensive in Cancún, but the selection is much broader than at other Mexican resorts. Numerous duty-free shops offer excellent value on European goods. The largest is **Ultrafemme,** Av. Tulum, SM 25 (© **998/884-1402**), specializing in imported cosmetics, perfumes, and fine jewelry and watches. The downtown Cancún location offers slightly lower prices than branches in Plaza Caracol, La Isla, and Kukulcán Plaza. It's open Monday to Saturday from 9:30am to 9pm and Sunday from 2 to 9pm.

Handicrafts are more limited and more expensive in Cancún than in other regions of Mexico because they are not produced here. They are available, though; the best **open-air crafts market** is Mercado 28 in Cancún City. A less enticing open-air market in the Hotel Zone is **Coral Negro,** Bulevar Kukulcán Km 9.5, next to Plaza Dady'O, open daily from 7am to 11pm. **Plaza La Fiesta,** next to the Cancún Center (© **998/883-4519**), is a large Mexican outlet store selling handicrafts, jewelry, tequila, leather, and accessories. It's open daily from 7am to midnight.

Cancún's main venues are the **malls**—not quite as grand as their U.S. counterparts, but close. All are air-conditioned, sleek, and sophisticated. Most lie on Bulevar Kukulcán between Km 7 and Km 12. Kukulcán Plaza and La Isla offer the most extensive parking garages.

The **Kukulcán Plaza** (© **998/885-2200;** www.kukulcanplaza.com) houses hundreds of shops, restaurants, and entertainment. It has a bank, a bowling alley, several crafts stores, a Play City with gambling machines, a liquor and tobacco store, several bathing-suit specialty stores, music stores, a drugstore, a leather-goods shop (including shoes and sandals), and a store specializing in silver from Taxco. U.S. eateries include Häagen-Dazs and Ruth's Chris Steak House, and there's an extensive food court. The adjacent Luxury Avenue complex features designer labels such as Cartier, Coach, Fendi, Louis Vuitton, Salvatore Ferragamo, and Ultrafemme. The mall is open daily from 8am to 10pm, until 11pm during high season. Assistance for those with disabilities is available upon request, and wheelchairs, strollers, and lockers are available at the information desk.

The long-standing **Plaza Caracol** (© 998/883-1038; www.caracolplaza.com) is one of Cancún's less glamorous malls, although it houses among other things, Casa Rolandi (p. 472) restaurant and its Very Wine lounge. It's just before you reach the Convention Center as you come from downtown Cancún, and is open daily from 10am to 10pm.

Most people come to entertainment-oriented **Forum by the Sea,** Bulevar Kukulcán Km 9 (© 998/883-4425; www.forumbythesea.com.mx), for the food and fun, choosing from Hard Rock Cafe, Carlos 'n' Charlie's, Rainforest Cafe, and CoCo Bongo, plus an extensive food court. Shops include Diesel, Harley-Davidson, Massimo Dutti, Señor Frog's, Sunglass Island, and Zingara Beachwear and Swimwear. The mall is open daily from 10am to midnight (bars remain open later).

One of Mexico's most appealing malls is the **La Isla Shopping Village,** Bulevar Kukulcán Km 12.5 (© 998/883-5025; www.laislacancun.com.mx), a wonderful open-air complex that borders the lagoon. Walkways lined with quality shops and restaurants cross little canals (boat rides are even offered through the canals), and an attractive boardwalk lines the lagoon itself, as well as an interactive aquarium and dolphin swim facility (p. 481). Shops include Bulgari, Guess, Nautica, Nine West, Puma, Tommy Hilfiger, Ultrafemme, and Zara, as well as a large Mexican handicrafts store called Casa Mexicana and an iStore selling Apple products. Among the dining choices are Johnny Rockets, Chili's, Italianni's, Planet Hollywood, the romantic Thai restaurant (p. 475), and the new Elefanta (p. 473). You will also find a movie theater, video arcade, and several bars, including La Madonna (p. 474).

CANCÚN AFTER DARK

Cancún's party reputation is not confined to spring break—the action here continues year-round. While the revelry often begins by day at the beach, the sun-drenched crowd heads at happy hour to the rocking bars located along the Hotel Zone, which often serve two-for-one drinks at sunset. Hotels play in the happy hour scene, with special drink prices to entice visitors and guests from other resorts. Come night, the hottest centers of action are also along Kukulcán, and include **Plaza Dady'O, Forum by the Sea,** and **La Isla Shopping Village.** These entertainment plazas transform into true spring break madness for most of March and April.

The Club & Music Scene

Clubbing in Cancún is a favorite part of the vacation experience and can go on each night until the sun rises over that incredibly blue sea. Several big hotels have nightclubs or schedule live music in their lobby bars. At the clubs, expect to stand in lines on weekends, pay a cover charge of about $40 with open bar, or $15 to $25 without open bar; and then pay $8 to $10 for a drink. Some of the higher-priced clubs include live entertainment. The places listed in this section are air-conditioned and accept American Express, MasterCard, and Visa.

Numerous restaurants, such as **Carlos 'n' Charlie's, Hard Rock Cafe,** and **Señor Frog's,** double as nighttime party spots, offering wildish fun at a fraction of the price of more costly clubs.

Grupo Dady offers a package deal enticing clubbers to party in all five of its neighboring bars, including Dady'O, Terresta, UltraClub, Dady Rock, and Dos Equis Bar. It costs $45 to $55 per person depending on the night and includes open bar; buy tickets at any of the Grupo Dady bars.

If you have been drinking when you're ready to go back to your accommodations, take public transportation or have someone with you rather than drive or get in a taxi alone.

Bling ★★ This is one of the coolest nightspots in Cancún, featuring a chic outdoor terrace overlooking the lagoon. A fashionable 30-something crowd congregates amid sofas under the stars, a killer sound system, and flowing cocktails. A sushi and sashimi bar and some Mediterranean dishes are also offered. This upscale lounge is considerably more sophisticated than Cancún's typical frat-style bars, and it's open daily from 6pm to 2am. Bulevar Kukulcán Km 13.5. © **998/840-6014.**

The City ★★ One of Cancún's hottest and largest nightclubs, The City features nine bars over three floors with progressive electronic music spun by visiting DJs from New York, L.A., and Mexico City (the DJ station looks like an airport control tower). This is where celebrities come to party when they're in town. You actually need never leave, as The City is a day-and-night club. The Playa Cabana beach club opens at 10am and features beach cabañas, a pool, and food and bar service with frequent activities, pool parties, and bikini contests. The Terrace Bar, overlooking the action on Bulevar Kukulcán, serves food and drinks all day long. For a relaxing evening vibe, the Lounge features comfy couches, chill music, and an extensive menu of martinis, snacks, and desserts. Open from 10:30pm to 4am, the 743-sq.-m (7,998-sq.-ft.) nightclub features a one-million-watt sound system, stunning light shows, and several VIP areas. Bulevar Kukulcán Km 9.5. © **998/848-8380.** www.thecitycancun.com. Cover $25; $45 with open bar.

CoCo Bongo ★★★ Continuing its reputation as the hippest venue in town, CoCo Bongo combines an enormous dance club with extravagant theme shows: Think flying acrobats, bar-top conga lines, soap bubbles, and confetti streamers. It has no set dance floor—you dance anywhere, and that includes on the tables, on the bar, and even on the stage with the occasional live band. This place regularly packs in as many as 1,800 people—you have to experience it to believe it. Despite its capacity, lines are long on weekends and in high season. The music alternates between Caribbean, salsa, house, hip-hop, techno, and classics from the '70s, '80s, and '90s. Open from 10:30pm to 3:30am, CoCo Bongo draws a hip young crowd. Plaza Forum by the Sea, Bulevar Kukulcán Km 9.5. © **998/883-5061.** www.cocobongo.com.mx. Weekend cover $60 with open bar; $50 weekdays with open bar.

Dady'O This is a popular rave among the young and brave, with frequent long lines. Grupo Dady offers a package deal that includes open bar and entrance to all five of its neighboring bars (see above), and this is the granddaddy of them. It opens nightly at 10pm and has a giant dance floor and awesome light system. Bulevar Kukulcán Km 9.5. © **998/883-3333.** www.dadyo.com. Cover $20–$25.

Dady Rock Bar and Club The offspring of Dady'O, Dady Rock opens at 8pm and goes as long as any other nightspot, offering a combination of live rock bands and DJs spinning grooves, along with a Tex-Mex menu, open bar, and dancing. Bulevar Kukulcán Km 9.5. © **998/883-3333.** www.dadyrock.com.mx. Cover $20–$25.

The Dance Floor at the Lobby ★ CoCo Bongo it's not, but for socialites who want a more refined dance than what they'll find along Cancún's party row, the Ritz-Carlton's lobby bar offers a good place to start. A DJ spins beats to the small but energetic dance floor on weekends, while patrons choose from flavored margaritas, creative martinis, and single-malt whiskeys. It's open daily from 5pm to midnight. Ritz-Carlton Cancún (p. 466), Retorno del Rey 36, off Bulevar Kukulcán Km 13.5. © **998/881-0808.**

La Madonna With more than 150 creative martini selections accompanied by ambient music, La Madonna also offers authentic Swiss-Italian cuisine, as well as delicious desserts (p. 474). Enjoy your red mandarin, lychee, or green apple martini or glass of wine elbow to elbow with Cancún's beautiful people on the outdoor patio. Cognac and cigars are served upstairs, and there's an international wine selection. Bossa nova and lounge music are the norm. It's open daily from noon to 1am. La Isla Shopping Village, Bulevar Kukulcán Km 12.5. ℂ **998/883-2222.** www.lamadonna.com.mx.

Very Wine ★ This chic urban wine bar sits on the upper level of Casa Rolandi (p. 472), a calm place to come for a predinner drink or nightcap. The gourmet bar has a fine wine and liquor selection, including wines by the glass, and also offers an extensive tapas selection (and the full menu at Rolandi's), fondues, and desserts, as well as cigars. This is a refined alternative to Cancún's more raucous bars and clubs, and affords wonderful sunset views over the lagoon. It's open from 1pm until the last customer leaves. Plaza Caracol, Bulevar Kukulcán Km 8.5. ℂ **998/883-1817.**

The Performing Arts

Several hotels host **Mexican fiesta nights,** including a buffet dinner and a folkloric dance show; admission with dinner and open bar costs about 550 pesos, unless you're at an all-inclusive resort that includes this as part of the package. Check out the show at **Hacienda Sisal** (ℂ **998/848-8220**), located at Bulevar Kukulcán Km 13.5, which is offered Tuesday and Thursday nights starting at 6pm.

ISLA MUJERES & COZUMEL

by Shane Christensen

These two Caribbean islands are among the most peaceful beach destinations in Mexico, both easy jaunts from Cancún and the Riviera Maya. Although day-trippers and cruise-ship visitors come ashore during high season, the islands never feel overrun. Come evening, the uncrowded streets and relaxed energy of the residents exemplify the enduring tranquillity of the islands. Neither Isla Mujeres nor Cozumel is particularly large, and they each still have that small island feel—with pristine beaches, bumpy roads that don't go far, a welcoming remoteness, and a seemingly timeless setting.

14

Fish-shaped **Isla Mujeres** lies 13km (8 miles) northeast of Cancún, a quick boat ride away but what feels like a world removed from its glittery neighbor. Despite this proximity, I consider Isla Mujeres a little-known gem filled with historic and rustic charm. During pre-Hispanic times, Maya women would cross over to the island to make offerings to the goddess of fertility, Ixchel. More than 40 sites containing shrines remain around the island, and archaeologists still uncover the small dolls that were customarily part of those offerings. Hotels range from rustic to boutique, and the value of accommodation and dining are among the best one can find in this part of Mexico. Passenger ferries travel to Isla Mujeres from Cancún's Puerto Juárez and the Hotel Zone's Embarcadero at Playa Linda; car ferries leave from Punta Sam.

Larger than Isla Mujeres and farther from the mainland (19km/12 miles off the coast from Playa del Carmen), **Cozumel** has its own mini-international airport. Life here revolves around two major activities: scuba diving and cruise ships making a port of call. Yet a strong sense of family and community continues to prevail here. There are less than 100,000 people on the island, a couple thousand of whom are Americans and the rest of whom are mostly Maya, Yucatecan, and Mexican from elsewhere in the country. There's just one town, San Miguel de Cozumel; to the north and south lie resorts. The rest of the shore is deserted and predominantly rocky, with a scattering of small sandy coves that you can have all to yourself. Because Cozumel remains a frequent stop on the cruise ship circuit, the town's waterfront is lined with jewelry stores and duty-free and souvenir shops.

Unfortunately, there's no way to travel directly between Cozumel and Isla Mujeres, but you can get from one to the other by traveling via Cancún and Playa del Carmen.

ISLA MUJERES ★★★

13km (8 miles) NE of Cancún

Only a quick boat ride from the swarming beaches of Cancún, Isla Mujeres feels like a different world. Bathed in the warm waters of the Caribbean Sea, the sleepy island attracts visitors who prefer a laid-back lifestyle focused around the beach and watersports such as diving and snorkeling. The name translates as "the island of women," but few islanders agree on the origin. While Isla Mujeres has a healthy nightlife, relaxed *isleños* frown upon spring break antics; if you're looking for parties, stick to Cancún.

Playa Norte, which runs along the northernmost edge of town, is a picture-perfect Caribbean dream, ideal for relaxing with a cool beverage or wading in the waist-deep water. For stunning views across the turquoise waters to Cancún, head to **Playa Lancheros,** on the southern side of the island. Enjoy the spectacular sunset from the **Casa Rolandi** restaurant, on the waterfront of the Villa Rolandi resort.

Fans of ancient cultures can tour the crumbling Maya temple at the southernmost tip of the island, thought to be dedicated to Ixchel, goddess of fertility. Wander through the multicolored sculpture garden, or venture just beyond to the **Cliff of the Dawn.** The views from the cliff are extraordinary, and you can walk along pathways nearly down to the water's edge. Get up close to sea turtles at the **Tortugranja,** a sea turtle sanctuary that contains several enclosures to protect the marine reptiles. Bypass the Isla's downtown T-shirt stores in favor of boutiques where you can shop for Mexican artworks ranging from Day of the Dead skeletons to sea-glass jewelry.

The island's culinary specialty is seafood, best enjoyed at a beach restaurant such as **Zazil Ha,** where you can sink your feet into the sand by day and dine by tiki torch at night. A local favorite dish of Maya origin is *Tikinxic*—whole fish marinated in achiote and sour oranges, then wrapped in a banana leaf and cooked in an earthen oven. While tequila isn't made on the island, it's the most popular spirit here, especially when included in freshly made margaritas.

Divers and snorkelers have a wealth of sites to discover off Isla Mujeres. The preferred spot for diving is the **Caves of the Sleeping Sharks,** once famous as a meeting point for slow-moving sharks. Snorkelers prefer the calm, shallow water of the island's western side, with Lighthouse and Manchones being the best spots to see the coral reef. On a day trip to **Isla Contoy,** a national park with mangrove lagoons, you'll spot dozens of more than 150 species of birds.

Essentials

GETTING THERE & DEPARTING **Puerto Juárez,** just north of Cancún, is the dock (☎ **998/877-0382**) for passenger ferries to Isla Mujeres. **Ultramar** (☎ **998/843-2011;** www.granpuerto.com.mx) has fast boats leaving every half-hour from "Gran Puerto" in Puerto Juárez, making the trip in 15 minutes. There is storage space for luggage and the fare is 80 pesos each way. These boats operate daily, starting at 6:30am and usually ending at 11:30pm (check beforehand for latest schedules). They might leave early if they're full, so arrive ahead of schedule. Pay at the ticket office or on board if the ferry is about to leave.

Note: Upon arrival by taxi or bus in Puerto Juárez, be wary of pirate "guides" who tell you either that the ferry is canceled or that it's several hours until the next ferry. They'll offer the services of a private *lancha* (small boat) for about 450 pesos—and it's nothing but a scam. Small boats are available and, on a co-op basis, charge 200 to

350 pesos one-way, based on the number of passengers. They take about 50 minutes and are not recommended on days with rough seas. Check with the ticket office—the only accurate source for information.

On your return to Puerto Juárez, you'll see taxi fares posted by the street where the taxis park, so be sure to check the rate before agreeing to a taxi for the ride back to Cancún. Rates generally run 120 to 150 pesos, depending upon your destination. Moped and bicycle rentals are also readily available as you depart the ferry. This small complex also has public bathrooms, luggage storage, a snack bar, and souvenir shops.

Isla Mujeres is so small that a vehicle isn't necessary, but if you're taking one to the island, you'll use the **Punta Sam** port a little beyond Puerto Juárez. The 40-minute car ferry (© **998/877-0065**) runs five or six times daily between 8am and 8pm, year-round except in bad weather. Times are generally as follows: Cancún to Isla 8 and 11am and 2:45, 5:30, and 8:15pm; Isla to Cancún 6:30 and 9:30am and 12:45, 4:15, and 7:15pm. Always check with the tourist office in Cancún to verify this schedule. Cars should arrive an hour before the ferry departure to register for a place in line and pay the posted fee, which is 185 pesos per car. A gas pump is at Avenida Rueda Medina and Calle Abasolo, northwest of the ferry docks.

From the Hotel Zone, ferries to Isla Mujeres also depart from **El Embarcadero** at Playa Linda, but they're less frequent and slightly more expensive than those from Puerto Juárez. There are up to eight scheduled departures per day to Isla Mujeres, depending upon the season. Adult fares are $15 round-trip. A **Water Taxi** (© **998/886-4270**) to Isla Mujeres operates from the Embarcadero (just off Bulevar Kukulcán Km 4 on the northern tip of the Hotel Zone/Isla Cancún).

To get to Puerto Juárez or Punta Sam from **Cancún,** take any Ruta 8 city bus from Avenida Tulum. From the Cancún airport, take the shuttle bus to the pier (160 pesos).

VISITOR INFORMATION The **City Tourist Office** (© **998/877-0767,** -0307; www.isla-mujeres.net/tourism/home.htm) is at Av. Rueda Medina 130, just across the street from the pier. It's open Monday through Friday from 9am to 4pm, closed on Saturday and Sunday. *Islander* is a free publication with local information, advertisements, and event listings.

ISLAND LAYOUT Isla Mujeres is about 8km (5 miles) long and 4km (2½ miles) wide, with the town at the northern tip. "Downtown" is a compact 4 blocks by 6 blocks, so it's very easy to get around. The **passenger ferry docks** are at the center of town, within walking distance of most hotels, restaurants, and shops. The street running along the waterfront and in front of the ferry docks is **Avenida Rueda Medina,** commonly called the *malecón* (boardwalk). The **Mercado Municipal (town market)** is by the post office on **Calle Guerrero,** an inland street at the north edge of town, which, like most streets in the town, is unmarked.

GETTING AROUND A popular form of transportation on Isla Mujeres is the electric **golf cart,** available for rent at many hotels or rental shops for 180 pesos per hour or 600 pesos for 24 hours. Prices are set the same at all rental locations. **El Sol Golf Cart Rental,** Av. Benito Juárez Mza. 3 no. 20 (corner of Matamoros; © **998/877-0791**), is one good option in the town center. The golf carts don't go more than 30kmph (19 mph), but they're fun. Anyway, you aren't on Isla Mujeres to hurry. Many people enjoy touring the island by *moto* **(motorized bike or scooter).** **Gomar** (© **998/877-0604**), at the corner of Madero and Hidalgo, rents reliable scooters. Fully automatic versions are available for 100 pesos per hour, 250 pesos for 8 hours, or 450 pesos for 24 hours. They come with helmets and seats for two people. There's only one main road with a couple of offshoots, so you won't get lost.

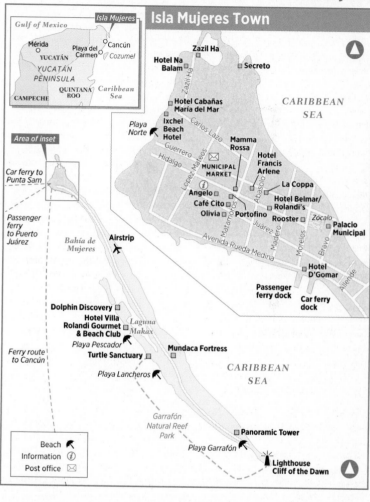

Isla Mujeres Town

Be aware that the rental price does not include insurance, and any injury to yourself or the vehicle will come out of your pocket. **Bicycles** are also available for rent at some hotels for about 35 pesos an hour or 120 pesos per day, usually including a basket and a lock.

Tricycle taxis are the least expensive and easiest way to get to your hotel if it's in town. From the ferry pier to any of the downtown hotels will cost about 20 to 30 pesos. If you ask the guys, they'll say, "Oh, whatever you care to give." I will let them haul my bags and lead the way while I walk.

If you prefer to use a taxi, rates are about 25 pesos for trips within the downtown area, or 50 pesos for a trip to the southern end of Isla. You can also hire them for about 100 pesos per hour. Regular taxis are always lined up in a parking lot to the right of the pier, with their rates posted. The number to call for taxis is ☎ 998/877-0066.

[FastFACTS] ISLA MUJERES

Area Code The telephone area code is **998.**

ATMs & Banks Isla has only one bank, **HSBC Bank** (*(C)* **998/877-0005**), across from the ferry docks. It's open Monday through Friday from 8:30am to 6pm, and Saturday from 9am to 2pm. It has ATM machines.

Currency Exchange Isla Mujeres has numerous *casas de cambio,* or currency exchanges, along the main streets. Most of the hotels listed here change money for their guests, although often at less favorable rates than the commercial enterprises.

Drugstore **YZA Farmacia** (*(C)* **998/886-6035**), located at the corner of Juárez and Morelos, stays open 24 hours.

Hospital The **Hospital de la Armada** is on Avenida Rueda Medina at Ojón P. Blanco (*(C)* **998/877-0001**), less than a kilometer (⅗ mile) south of the town center. It will treat you only in an emergency. Otherwise, the **Hospital Integral** is on Avenida Guerrero, a block before the beginning of the *malecón* (*(C)* **998/877-0117**).

Internet Access **Europa Computer Internet,** at Abasolo between Hidalgo and Juárez, offers Wi-Fi and computers for 20 pesos per hour.

Post Office The *correo* is at Calle Guerrero 12 (*(C)* **998/877-0085**), at the corner of López Mateos, near the market. It's open Monday through Friday from 9am to 4pm.

Seasons Isla Mujeres's high season runs December through May. Some hotels raise their rates in August, and some raise their rates beginning in mid-November. Low season runs from June to mid-November.

Beaches & Outdoor Activities

BEACHES & SWIMMING **Playa Norte** ★★★, which extends around the northern tip of the island, is perhaps the world's best municipal beach—a gorgeous swath of fine white sand and calm, translucent turquoise-blue water that stays shallow far off the shore. It's just a short walk to the beach from the ferry and downtown hotels. Watersports equipment, beach umbrellas, and lounge chairs are widely available for rent. This is a terrific place for swimming and snorkeling. Areas in front of restaurants usually cost nothing if you use the restaurant as your headquarters for drinks and food, and the best of them have hammocks and swings from which to sip your piña coladas.

Garrafón Natural Reef Park ★★ (p. 490) offers beautiful snorkeling areas, but there's also a nice stretch of beach on either side of the park for those who want to avoid the expensive entrance fee. The **Beach Club Garrafón de Castilla,** located right next to the park, has a wonderful swimming area, snorkeling equipment for rent, and a beachside snack shop. The entrance fee is 50 pesos. **Playa Lancheros** sits on the Caribbean side of Laguna Makax and is another lovely swimming beach. Local buses travel to Lancheros from downtown.

There are no lifeguards on duty on Isla Mujeres, which does not use the system of water-safety flags employed in Cancún and Cozumel. The bay between Cancún and Isla Mujeres is calm, with warm, transparent waters ideal for swimming, snorkeling, and diving. The east side of the island facing the open Caribbean Sea is typically rougher, with much stronger currents.

FISHING For a day of fishing, ask at the **Sociedad Cooperativa Turística** (the boatmen's cooperative), on the right side of the pier off Avenida Rueda Medina (*(C)* **998/877-1363**; open daily 8am–8pm), next to Mexico Divers and Las Brisas restaurant. Four hours of fishing costs $280 for up to eight people, which typically includes lunch and drinks. Year-round you'll find bonito, mackerel, kingfish, and amberjack. Sailfish and sharks (hammerhead, bull, nurse, lemon, and tiger) are in good supply in April and May. In winter, larger grouper and jewfish are prevalent.

SCUBA DIVING   Most of the dive shops on the island offer the same trips for similar prices, including reef, drift, deep, and night dives: One-tank dives cost about $45 to $65; two-tank dives about $55 to $75. **Squaloadventures,** Madero 10 between Hidalgo and Guerrero (© 998/877-0607; www.squaloadventures.com), is a full-service shop that offers dive packages and certifications. Another respected dive shop is **Carey Dive Center,** at Matamoros 13A and Rueda Medina (© 998/877-0763; www.careydivecenter.com). Both offer 2-hour snorkeling trips for about $25.

Cuevas de los Tiburones (Caves of the Sleeping Sharks) is Isla's most renowned dive site—but the name is slightly misleading, as shark sightings are rare these days. Two sites where you could traditionally see the sleeping sharks are the Cuevas de los Tiburones and La Punta. The sharks have mostly been driven off, and a storm collapsed the arch featured in a Jacques Cousteau film showing them. However, the caves survive. Other dive sites include a **wreck** 15km (9⅓ miles) offshore; **Banderas** reef, between Isla Mujeres and Cancún, where there's always a strong current; **Tabos** reef on the eastern shore; and **Manchones** reef, 1km (⅔ mile) off the southeastern tip of the island, where the water is 4.5 to 11m (15–36 ft.) deep. **The Cross of the Bay** is close to Manchones reef. A bronze cross, weighing 1 ton and standing 12m (39 ft.) high, was placed in the water between Manchones and Isla in 1994, as a memorial to those who have lost their lives at sea.

SNORKELING   One of the most popular places to snorkel is **Garrafón Natural Reef Park ★★** (p. 490). **Manchones** reef, off the southeastern coast, is also good. It's just offshore and accessible by boat. You can snorkel around *el faro* (the lighthouse) in the **Bahía de Mujeres** at the southern tip of the island. The water is about 2m (6½ ft.) deep. Boatmen will take you for around 250 pesos per person if you have your own snorkeling equipment or 300 pesos if you use theirs.

YOGA   Increasingly, Isla is becoming popular among yoga enthusiasts. The trend began at **Hotel Na Balam ★★** (p. 494; © 998/881-4770; www.nabalam.com), which offers *ashtanga, vinyasa,* and hatha flow yoga classes weekday mornings under its large poolside *palapa,* complete with yoga mats and props. The hotel also offers yoga vacations featuring respected teachers and a more extensive practice schedule; call for more information. Individual yoga classes cost $12, with discounts available for multiple classes. Another yoga center is **Elements of the Island** (© 998/274-0098; www.elementsoftheisland.com). The cafe and adjacent apartments are located at Juárez 64, between López Mateos and Matamoros.

Attractions

DOLPHIN DISCOVERY ★★   You can swim with dolphins (© 998/849-4748 or -4757; www.dolphindiscovery.com) at the "Dolphinario," located midway along the island near Villa Rolandi (on the side of Isla Mujeres facing Cancún). Groups of up to eight people swim with two dolphins and a trainer. Swimmers view an educational video and spend time in the water with the trainer and the dolphins before enjoying swimming time with the dolphins. Reservations are necessary, and you must arrive an hour before your assigned swimming time, at 10:30am, 12:15pm, 2:15pm, or 3:30pm. The cost is $129 per person for the Dolphin Royal Swim. There are less expensive programs that allow you to learn about, touch, and hold the dolphins (but not swim with them), starting at $79 ($69 for kids). The park is open from 10am to 5pm, and the fee includes lunch and open bar.

TURTLE FARM ★★   Years ago, fishermen converged on the island nightly from May to September to capture turtles when they would come ashore to lay eggs. Then a concerned fisherman, Gonzalo Chale Maldonado, began convincing others to spare the eggs, which he protected. It was a start. Following his lead, the fishing ministry founded the **Centro de Investigaciones Pesqueras** to find ways to protect the species and increase the turtle populations. Although the local government provides some assistance, most of the funding comes from private-sector donations. Since the center opened, tens of thousands of young turtles have been released, and local schoolchildren have participated, helping to educate a new generation. Releases are scheduled from May to October, and visitors are invited to take part. Inquire at the center.

Three species of sea turtles nest on Isla Mujeres. An adult green turtle, the most abundant species, is 1 to 1.5m (3⅓–5 ft.) long and can weigh 204kg (450 lb.). At the Tortugranja, as the Turtle Farm is called in Spanish, visitors walk through the indoor and outdoor turtle pool areas, where the creatures paddle around. Turtles are separated by age, from newly hatched up to 1 year. People who come here usually end up staying about an hour, especially if they opt for the guided tour, which I recommend. They also have a small gift shop. The sanctuary is on a spit of land jutting out from the island's west coast. The address is Carretera Sac Bajo no. 5; you'll need a taxi to get there. Admission is 30 pesos; the shelter is open daily from 9am to 5pm. For more information, call © **998/877-0595.**

GARRAFÓN NATURAL REEF RESORT ★★   Garrafón (© **998/849-4748;** www.garrafon.com) sits at the southern end of the island. Once a public national underwater park, Garrafón is now operated by Dolphin Discovery and has myriad water activities that include snorkeling, kayaks, a dive platform, and swimming. Although the tropical fish are dazzling to see, most of the reef has sadly died. The pricey ecopark also offers a swimming pool, zip line, bicycle tour, restaurant and bar, beach chairs, shaded hammocks, changing rooms with showers and lockers, and gift shop. Admission costs $69 ($50 for children under 12); the all-inclusive package includes round-trip transportation between Cancún and Isla Mujeres, buffet lunch, domestic open bar, and use of snorkeling equipment and kayaks (admission for walk-ups is $59). The park stays open daily in high season from 10am to 5pm. In low season, it may close a couple of days per week.

Just south of Garrafón, the small **Caribbean Village** has colorful clapboard buildings that house cafes and shops displaying folk art. You can have lunch or a snack here and stroll around before heading on to Sculptured Spaces and the Maya ruins.

Walking toward the southern tip of the island, you'll find **Sculptured Spaces,** a sculpture garden with pieces donated to Isla Mujeres by internationally renowned sculptors. Among Mexican sculptors represented are José Luis Cuevas and Vladimir Cora. A small **Maya ruin** dedicated to the fertility goddess Ixchel rests here, as well (p. 493). There's a 30-peso entrance fee for the garden and Maya ruin; a lighthouse is also located here. It's open daily from 9am to 5pm.

The **Cliff of the Dawn** ★★★ lies just beyond the sculpture garden, at the southeasternmost point of Mexico. The cliff has extraordinary views, and pathways leading to nearly the water's edge. The cafe and restrooms on-site are open from 9am to 5pm, but you can enter at any time; if you make it there to see the sunrise, you can claim you were the first person in Mexico that day to be touched by the sun.

ISLA CONTOY ★ Try to visit this pristine uninhabited island, 30km (19 miles) by boat from Isla Mujeres. It became a national wildlife reserve in 1981. The 6km-long (3¾-mile) island is covered in lush vegetation and harbors 70 species of birds, as well as a host of marine and animal life. Bird species that nest on the island include pelicans, brown boobies, frigates, egrets, terns, and cormorants. Flocks of flamingos arrive in April. Most excursions troll for fish (which will be your lunch), anchor en route for a snorkeling expedition, skirt the island at a leisurely pace for close viewing of the birds without disturbing the habitat, and then pull ashore. While the captain prepares lunch, visitors can swim, sun, follow the nature trails, and visit the fine nature museum, which has bathroom facilities. The trip from Isla Mujeres takes about 45 minutes each way and can be longer if the waves are choppy. Because of the tight-knit boatmen's cooperative, prices for this excursion are the same everywhere: $60 for adults; half-price for children under 9 (cash only). You can buy a ticket at the **Sociedad Cooperativa** (© 998/877-1363), on Avenida Rueda Medina, next to Mexico Divers and Las Brisas restaurant. Trips leave at 9am and return around 4pm. Boat captains should respect the cooperative's regulations regarding ecological sensitivity and boat safety, including the availability of life jackets for everyone on board. If you're not given a life jacket, ask for one. Sodas, beer, and snorkeling equipment are usually included in the price, but double-check before heading out.

A MAYA RUIN ★★ Just beyond the lighthouse, at the southern end of the island, lie the remains of a small Maya temple. Archaeologists believe it was dedicated to the moon and fertility goddess Ixchel. The location, on a lofty bluff overlooking the sea, is worth seeing and makes a great place for photos. It is believed that Maya women traveled here on annual pilgrimages to seek Ixchel's blessings of fertility.

A PIRATE'S FORTRESS Almost in the middle of the island is a large building purported to have been a pirate fortress. A slave trader who arrived here in the early 19th century claimed to have been the pirate Mundaca Marecheaga. He set up a business selling slaves to Cuba and Belize, and prospered here. According to island lore, a charming local girl captivated him, only to spurn him in favor of a local.

Shopping

Shopping is a casual activity here. Several shops, especially concentrated on Avenida Hidalgo, sell Saltillo rugs, onyx, silver, Guatemalan clothing, blown glassware, masks, folk art, crafts, beach paraphernalia, and T-shirts in abundance. Prices are lower than in Cancún or Cozumel.

Where to Stay

You'll find plenty of hotels in all price ranges on Isla Mujeres. The rates listed below do not include the 14% room tax. They also do not apply to the brief Christmas/New Year's season, when many hotels charge extra. High season runs from December through May and sometimes includes August. Low season is the rest of the year.

For private home rentals or longer-term stays, contact **Mundaca Travel and Real Estate** on Isla Mujeres (www.mundaca.com.mx; © 866/646-0536 in the U.S., or 998/877-0025), or book online with **Isla Beckons** property rental service (www.islabeckons.com). Another helpful website is www.travelyucatan.com.

VERY EXPENSIVE

Hotel Villa Rolandi Gourmet & Beach Club ★★★ 📷 Villa Rolandi is a romantic escape on a little sheltered cove with a pristine white-sand beach. Each of the luxurious suites has a large terrace or balcony with private whirlpool overlooking the sea. The bathrooms have Molton Brown products and enticing showers with multiple shower heads that convert into steam baths. Breakfast is served in the oceanfront restaurant or in bed, delivered to the room through a small portal. The spa offers an outdoor Thalasso therapy whirlpool and beachside massages. The owner is a Swiss-born restaurateur who made a name for himself with his restaurants on Isla Mujeres and in Cancún. You can eat exceedingly well at **Casa Rolandi** (p. 496) without having to go off property, which is reached directly by yacht from Cancún's Embarcadero (provided complimentary by the resort) or via a 20-minute drive from town.

Fracc. Lagunamar, SM 7, Mza. 75, Locs. 15 and 16, 77400 Isla Mujeres, Q. Roo. www.villarolandi.com. ⓒ **800/525-4800** in the U.S., or 998/999-2000. Fax 998/877-0100. 35 units. High season $357 and up double, $438 and up junior suite; low season $290 double, $323 junior suite. Rates include full American breakfast. No children 12 and under. AE, MC, V. **Amenities:** Restaurant (see "Where to Eat," below); airport transfer via van (for a fee) and yacht (included); concierge; cooking classes; small fitness room; saltwater Jacuzzi; kayaks; 2 infinity pools; room service; spa. *In room:* TV, hair dryer, minibar, Wi-Fi.

EXPENSIVE

Hotel Na Balam ★★★ 🏨 This ecologically friendly hotel on Playa Norte promises a piece of Maya heaven on the beach, which is one of the most beautiful anywhere. Bleached white rooms lie in three sections separated only by sand, palms, and flowers; some face the beach and others lie in a garden setting with a swimming pool. They're individually decorated with a king-size or two double beds, folk art, and terrace or balcony with hammocks. Master suites feature additional amenities, including small pools with hydromassage. The older section is well kept and surrounds a lush inner courtyard and Playa Norte. The beautiful turquoise cove in front of the hotel makes for perfect swimming and snorkeling. Na Balam's restaurant, **Zazil Ha,** remains one of the island's most popular (see "Where to Eat," below), and the beachside bar and lounge is a beautiful spot for sunsets.

Zazil Ha 118, 77400 Isla Mujeres, Q. Roo. www.nabalam.com. ⓒ **998/881-4770.** Fax 998/877-0446. 32 units. High season $226–$253 double, $313 and up junior suite; low season $129–$145 double, $180 junior suite. Children 11 and under stay free. AE, MC, V. **Amenities:** Restaurant; bar; diving and snorkeling trips available; spa; Wi-Fi; yoga (for a fee). *In room:* A/C, hair dryer, minibar, no phone.

Secreto One of the Caribbean's top-rated resorts in the last decade, this boutique hotel oozes a chic Mediterranean feel. Twelve suites overlook an infinity pool, Jacuzzi, and the open sea. Located on the northern end of the island, Secreto lies within walking distance of town, yet feels removed enough to make for an idyllic retreat. Tropical gardens surround the exquisite pool, and an outdoor living area offers large couches and small dining areas. Guest rooms are contemporary, featuring lots of space, simple and bold design lines, individual balconies, and rich amenities. Nine suites include king-size beds, while the remaining three have two double beds.

Sección Rocas, Lote 1, 77400 Isla Mujeres, Q. Roo. www.hotelsecreto.com. ⓒ **998/877-1039.** Fax 998/877-1048. 12 units. $250–$300 double. Extra person $25. One child 4 and younger stays free in parent's room. Rates include continental breakfast. AE, MC, V. **Amenities:** Bar; outdoor pool; watersports equipment/rentals (diving and snorkeling). *In room:* A/C, TV/DVD, fridge, hair dryer, minibar, MP3 docking station.

MODERATE

Hotel Cabañas María del Mar ★ This good choice for simple beach accommodations sits on the beautiful Playa Norte. The older two-story section behind the reception area and beyond the garden offers nicely outfitted rooms facing the beach. All have two single or double beds, refrigerators, and oceanview balconies. Twenty-two single-story cabañas closer to the reception area are decorated in a rustic Mexican style. The third section, El Castillo, sits beside Buho's beach bar and restaurant. All rooms are "deluxe," though some are larger than others. The five rooms on the ground floor have large patios and king-size beds. Upstairs rooms offer small balconies, and most have ocean views. The central courtyard contains a small pool.

Av. Arq. Carlos Lazo 1 (on Playa Norte, a half-block from the Hotel Na Balam), 77400 Isla Mujeres, Q. Roo. www.cabanasdelmar.com. © **998/877-0179.** Fax 998/877-0213. 73 units. High season $125–$145 double; low season $75–$100 double. MC, V. **Amenities:** Restaurant; bar; outdoor pool. *In room:* A/C, TV, fridge.

Ixchel Beach Hotel ☺ This moderately priced "condohotel" enjoys a privileged location on Playa Norte. Most of the comfortable if indistinctive rooms in the two white-washed towers offer balconies with ocean and pool views; the suites also have kitchens and DVD players. Especially popular with families, Ixchel sits right on an idyllic stretch of beach with lounge chairs and umbrellas and nearby access to watersports. The swimming pool and bar sit adjacent to the beach, and the hotel lies less than a 10-minute walk from the ferry dock and town center.

Calle Guerrero at Playa Norte, 77400 Isla Mujeres, Q. Roo. www.ixchelbeachhotel.com. ©/fax **998/999-2010.** 117 units. High season $175–$205 double, $265 suite; low season $99–$119 double, $155 suite. AE, MC, V. **Amenities:** Restaurant; bar; direct beach access; small gym; outdoor pool; Wi-Fi. *In room:* A/C, TV, kitchen (in all but standard rooms).

INEXPENSIVE

Hotel Belmar ★★ Right in the center of Isla's entertainment district, this charming three-story hotel (no elevator) sits above the usually packed Rolandi's restaurant. The simple, attractive rooms come with tile floors, whitewashed furniture, and either a king bed or two twins or two doubles. The rooms are well maintained and have quiet air-conditioning. One large suite features a sitting area, large patio, and whirlpool. Though I had little trouble with noise from the restaurant in my third-floor room, light sleepers might want to look elsewhere. A full breakfast is included.

Av. Hidalgo 110 (btw. Madero and Abasolo, 3½ blocks from the passenger-ferry pier), 77400 Isla Mujeres, Q. Roo. www.rolandi.com. © **998/877-0430.** Fax 998/877-0429. 11 units. High season 813 pesos double, 1,425 pesos suite; low season 563 pesos double, 1,425 pesos suite. Rates include full breakfast (up to 200 pesos). AE, MC, V. **Amenities:** Restaurant/bar (see "Where to Eat," below); room service; Wi-Fi. *In room:* A/C, fan, TV.

Hotel D'Gomar ⚑ This very simple hotel sits at the bottom of the inexpensive range; it's comfortable but don't expect any thrills. Rooms have two double beds and a wall of windows affording gentle breezes. The higher prices are for air-conditioned rooms with refrigerators. The four-story hotel has no elevator, and is conveniently located cater-corner from the ferry pier (look right). The name of the hotel is the most visible sign on the "skyline."

Rueda Medina 150, 77400 Isla Mujeres, Q. Roo. ©/fax **998/877-0541.** 20 units. High season 550 pesos double; low season 350–450 pesos double. MC, V. *In room:* A/C (in some), fan, TV, fridge (in some), no phone.

Hotel Francis Arlene ★   The Magaña family operates this neat little two-story inn built around a shady courtyard. It's bright, cheerful, and well managed, and features attractive common spaces. For these reasons, it gets a lot of return guests and remains especially popular with families and seniors. Some rooms have ocean views, and many are remodeled or updated each year. They are comfortable, with tile floors, tiled bathrooms, balconies or patios, and a very homey feel. Standard rooms include a coffeemaker and a refrigerator; top-floor rooms come with kitchenettes and offer an ocean view. Ten rooms have only a ceiling fan and are the lowest-priced doubles.

Guerrero 7 (5½ blocks inland from the ferry pier, btw. Abasolo and Matamoros), 77400 Isla Mujeres, Q. Roo. www.francisarlene.com. ✆/fax **998/877-0310,** -0861. 24 units. High season $60–$75 double, $90 top-floor double; low season $50–$65 double, $80 top-floor double. MC, V. *In room:* A/C (in some), fridge, kitchenette (in some), no phone.

Where to Eat

At the **Municipal Market,** next to the post office on Avenida Guerrero, obliging, hardworking women operate several food stands. When you're in the mood for an ice cream, stop by **La Coppa** (no phone), at Hidalgo and Abasolo, where you can choose from among 18 natural flavors of Italian gelato. It's open daily from 10am to midnight.

EXPENSIVE

Casa Rolandi ★★★ ITALIAN/SEAFOOD   The Villa Rolandi's restaurant is the best on the island, a stunning open-air setting gazing across the sea to Cancún and serving exquisitely prepared fresh seafood, meats, and homemade pasta. The restaurant takes advantage of an open kitchen and brick oven to transform Caribbean lobster, fish filets, shrimp brochettes, rack of lamb, suckling pig, and other creatively prepared dishes into delectable meals. Dinners include hot baked bread that leaves the oven looking like a puffer fish—with black olives and a dash of olive oil it's an irresistible temptation, but don't fill up! The light fish filet baked in that magical oven with a white wine, lemon, and parsley sauce comes out tasting almost like lobster. This is a great place to enjoy the sunset. Breakfast selections, which come with complimentary fresh fruit and French toast, include spicy omelets and creative egg dishes, and Mexican specialties such as *chilaquiles rojos.*

On the pier of Villa Rolandi (p. 494), located in the center of the island, Lagunamar SM 7. ✆ **998/999-2000.** Reservations necessary. Main courses 197–446 pesos. Breakfast 76–120 pesos. AE, MC, V. Daily 7am–10:30pm.

MODERATE

Angelo ITALIAN   An Italian restaurant in the town center, Angelo offers a selection of antipasti, pasta, grilled seafood, and wood-oven-baked pizzas. The Sardinian-born owner instills his menu with the flavors of his homeland, including a rich tomato sauce. Consider starting with a bowl of seafood soup or black mussels au gratin and continuing with the grilled shrimp kabobs or seafood pasta in an olive oil and white-wine sauce. The open-air restaurant includes an inviting sidewalk terrace and lies across the street from a casual Cuban restaurant also owned by Angelo.

Av. Hidalgo 14 (btw. Lopez Mateos and Matamoros). ✆ **998/877-1273.** Main courses 89–298 pesos. MC, V. Daily 4pm–midnight.

Mamma Rosa ★ ITALIAN   Mamma Rosa serves mouthwatering pizzas and homemade pasta to happy patrons seated at candlelit sidewalk tables. The most extravagant pizza is the Diamante smothered with lobster, mozzarella, and tomatoes. For pasta, I recommend the simple meat lasagna or tortellini with ricotta cheese and spinach. The filet of grouper makes for a perfect main course, unless you're in the mood for an Angus steak with green pepper. Lots of olive oil is used in the light, Mediterranean-inspired cooking. Accompany your meal with an Italian wine and finish with the rich tiramisu. Waiters here speak Italian and little Spanish or English.

Av. Hidalgo 10 (at Matamoros). © **998/200-1969.** Pizzas and pasta 75–220 pesos; main courses 105–220 pesos. MC, V. Daily 4–11pm.

Olivia ★★ MEDITERRANEAN   This intimate dinner spot combines Greek, Turkish, and Moroccan influences in one tempting menu by the Balkan family owners. To start, the Greek tapas features eggplant salad, *tzaziki,* and marinated green olives served with fresh Parmesan bread. Delicious mains prepared in the open kitchen include moussaka with ground beef and eggplant baked in a creamy béchamel sauce; I also like the Moroccan-style fish filet slowly cooked in a red sauce with lime, garlic coriander, and chickpeas served over couscous. The candlelit dining room leads out to an equally enchanted courtyard with tiki torches and luminarias. Soothing lounge music plays in the background.

Av. Matamoros (corner of Juárez). © **998/877-1765.** www.olivia-isla-mujeres.com. Main courses 80–270 pesos. MC, V. Tues–Sat 5–9:30pm.

Portofino SEAFOOD/STEAK   Opened in late 2010, Mamma Rosa's sister restaurant is owned by the same northern Italian family, with a staff that hails mostly from Florence. The white dining room splashed with hues of blue opens to candlelit sidewalk dining. Steak and seafood dominates the menu, and despite the restaurant's Italian heritage, no pizza or pasta is prepared in the chef's open kitchen. There's no better meat selection than the *parillada mixta,* an extravagant platter for two with grilled chicken, *arrachera* beef, Italian sausage, and meat kabobs. For seafood, the jumbo shrimp braised with Italian olive oil, garlic, and parsley is simply delicious. If you're in a celebratory mood, pop open a bottle of *prosecco* to accompany your meal (there's also an impressive Italian wine list). Service is warm and distinctly Italian.

Av. Hidalgo, next to the youth hostel. © **998/190-0713.** Main courses 95–195 pesos. MC, V. Daily 4–11pm.

Rolandi's ITALIAN/SEAFOOD   This casual Italian eatery is an Isla institution, and usually the most crowded place in town. The thin-crust pizzas and calzones feature wide-ranging ingredients—from traditional tomato, cheese, ham, and oregano to more exotic seafood selections. A wood-burning oven imparts the signature flavor of the pizzas, as well as fish kabobs, baked chicken, and roast beef. The extensive menu offers a wealth of salads and appetizers, plus an ample array of homemade pasta dishes, steaks, fish, and desserts. Rolandi's also serves tasty breakfast items such as sweet and savory crepes, spicy omelets, flour and corn tortilla quesadillas, richly filled croissants, and fresh fruit plates. The restaurant sits adjacent to the Hotel Belmar (p. 495), with a patio courtyard and sidewalk tables along Avenida Hidalgo.

Av. Hidalgo 10 (3½ blocks inland from the pier, btw. Madero and Abasolo). © **998/877-0430.** Reservations recommended. Breakfast 30–60 pesos; main courses 99–172 pesos. AE, MC, V. Daily 7am–11:30pm.

Rooster ★★★ CAFE   Mexican chef Sergio Carrillo opened this upscale eatery in 2010, and it's quickly become one of the island's most popular tables. Wake up to a creative omelet, *huevos rancheros, chilaquiles,* steak and eggs, or the "Rooster Vegetariano" with poached eggs, spinach, feta cheese, and tomatoes. Customers rave about the lobster Benedict, as well (ask for it even if you don't see it on the menu). Creative salads and sandwiches mark the lunch menu, along with turkey sausage tacos and "burritas" flavored with Black Forest ham, chipotle cream cheese, sliced avocado, and salsa. The "Rooster at Night" dinner menu changes seasonally and may feature specialties like roasted duck, *osso bucco,* and surf and turf. Most tables sit outdoors, and service is friendly and relaxed.

Calle Hidalgo 1, at Plaza Isla Mujeres. ✆ **998/274-0152.** Reservations recommended for dinner. Breakfast 55–120 pesos; sandwiches 85–90 pesos; dinner 130–250 pesos. No credit cards. Daily 7am–3pm and 6–10pm (dinner only Wed–Sat).

Zazil Ha ★★ SEAFOOD Here you'll find some of the island's tastiest Mexican and international cuisine served at tables on the sand among palms and gardens. Come night, candlelit tables sparkle underneath the open-air *palapa.* Specialties include stuffed calamari with fish and scallops, the fresh fish filet *al pastor* served with grilled pineapple, fish and shrimp "meatballs," and green risotto with seafood or vegetables. A tasty rib-eye steak is also on the menu. The delicious breads are baked in-house. Between the set meal times, you can order all sorts of enticing snacks, such as tacos and sandwiches, ceviche, nachos, and vegetable and fruit drinks. A chill-out bar and lounge sits next door.

At the Hotel Na Balam (at the end of Playa Norte, almost at the end of Calle Zazil Ha; p. 494). ✆ **998/877-0279.** www.nabalam.com. Reservations recommended. Breakfast 60–120 pesos; main courses 130–220 pesos. AE, MC, V. Daily 7:30am–10:30pm.

INEXPENSIVE

Café Cito CAFE At this adorable, Caribbean-blue corner restaurant you can begin the day with flavorful coffee and a croissant, fried eggs, or a waffle (this is the only place in town where you can enjoy breakfast until 2pm). Terrific crepes come with yogurt, ice cream, fresh fruit, or *dulce de leche* (caramel sauce made from goat's milk), as well as ham and cheese. The cafe is not open for dinner.

Calle Matamoros 42, at Juárez. ✆ **998/877-1470.** Crepes 38–76 pesos; breakfast 40–60 pesos; sandwiches 35–50 pesos. No credit cards. Daily 7:30am–2pm.

Isla Mujeres After Dark

Those in a party mood may want to start at the beach bar and lounge of the **Na Balam** hotel on Playa Norte, which serves tapas and creative cocktails to a cool crowd. **Jax Bar & Grill,** on Avenida Rueda Medina, close to Hotel Posada del Mar, is a Texas-style sports bar offering live music nightly. **Las Palapas Chimbo's** restaurant on the beach becomes a jammin' dance joint with a live band from 9pm until whenever. Farther along the same stretch of beach, **Buho's,** the restaurant/beach bar of the Cabañas María del Mar, has its moments as a popular, low-key hangout, complete with swinging seats under a giant beachfront *palapa.* If you want to sample one of nearly 100 tequila brands on a relaxing sidewalk terrace, stop by **Fayne's,** located at Av. Hidalgo 12 and open nightly from 7pm to midnight or later. It offers excellent live music and dancing that usually gets going after 10pm. Also in the town center at Av. Hidalgo 17, **El Patio** has tables in the sand ("the only beach on this street," as they say) with live music nightly, including guitar, saxophone, and reggae. It's open Monday to Saturday from 7pm to midnight or later.

COZUMEL ★★★

70km (43 miles) S of Cancún; 19km (12 miles) SE of Playa del Carmen

Although otherwise a sleepy little Caribbean island, Cozumel's clear waters and exquisite coral reefs make it a world-famous destination for snorkeling and scuba diving. Far quieter than neighboring Cancún, without highways, high-rises, or construction projects, the only town on the island is San Miguel. Avenida Rafael Melgar lazily runs through it, the main waterfront road that includes a boardwalk with casual restaurants and a chilled-out nightlife. Staying in town is fun and convenient. Alternatively, several peaceful dive resorts are along the island's western coast.

Cozumel is 45km (28 miles) long and 18km (11 miles) wide, and lies just 19km (12 miles) from the mainland. Most of the terrain is flat and clothed in a low tropical forest. Tall reefs line the **southwest coast,** creating towering walls that offer divers a fairytale seascape to explore. The water on the protected side, the **western shore,** stays as calm as an aquarium, unless a front is blowing through. The rougher, wild **Eastern shore** remains more lightly traveled for those preferring to wander off the beaten path. **Chankanaab National Park,** along the southwestern shore of the island, offers beautiful sightseeing and sunning spots.

Come to Cozumel to sink your toes into the same dreamy white sand and turquoise waters that Cancún offers, but without its commercialism or party atmosphere. Put on a snorkel mask to peek underwater near the **lighthouse,** even if you don't dive here. Explore the crocodile-filled **Faro Celerain** ecological reserve and drive through the inland jungle on the way to the Maya ruins at **San Gervasio.**

Carnaval

Carnaval (similar to Mardi Gras) is Cozumel's most colorful fiesta. It begins the Thursday before Ash Wednesday, with daytime street dancing and nighttime parades on Thursday, Saturday, and Monday (the best).

Dining in Cozumel is not particularly sophisticated, with Italian and Mexican predominating. Caribbean-caught **seafood** fills restaurant menus (with **lobster** in abundance), while traditional Yucatán influences bring zest to chicken and pork by infusing them with *mole,* achiote, and garlic. For a more refined dining experience, the island's few resorts offer the best options.

Scuba diving in Cozumel is the finest in the Western Hemisphere, with a tremendous diversity of reefs, caves, and canyons teeming with tropical fish and coral. The colors of the underwater life here shimmer with resplendence, and the biodiversity is breathtaking. Whether one is a novice toying with the idea of a beginner dive, or an expert seeking new underwater frontiers, don't leave Cozumel without submersing yourself below the surface.

Essentials

GETTING THERE & DEPARTING

BY PLANE   During high season, several more international commercial flights fly in and out of Cozumel's airport (CZM) than in low season, including a few flights from northern U.S. cities. Airlines include **Aeroméxico, American, Continental, Delta, Frontier, United,** and **US Airways.** You might also inquire about buying a ticket on one of the charter flights in high season. Some packagers, such as **Fun Jet**

(www.funjet.com), will sell you just a ticket. But look into packages, too. Several of the island's independent hotels work with packagers.

BY FERRY Passenger ferries run to and from Playa del Carmen. **México Waterjets** (© 987/872-1508; www.mexicowaterjets.com) and **Ultramar** (© 998/881-5890; www.granpuerto.com.mx) offer departures almost every hour in the morning and about every 2 hours in the afternoon. The schedules change according to seasons but generally start at 7am and continue until 9 or 10pm. The trip takes 30 to 45 minutes, depending on conditions, and costs about 160 pesos one-way. The boats are air-conditioned. In Playa del Carmen, the ferry dock is 1½ blocks from the main square. In Cozumel, the ferries use Muelle Fiscal, the town pier, a block from the main square. Luggage storage at the Cozumel dock costs 20 pesos per day.

The car ferry that used to operate from Puerto Morelos now uses the Calica pier just south of Playa del Carmen. The fare for a standard car is 555 pesos. **TransCaribe** (© 987/872-7688; www.transcaribe.com.mx) has six departures daily; check the website for exact scheduling. The ferry docks in Cozumel at the **Muelle Internacional** (the **International Pier,** which is south of town near La Ceiba Hotel).

BY BUS If you plan to travel on the mainland by bus, purchase tickets in advance from the ticket office for **ADO buses** called **Ticket Bus** on the municipal pier (open while the ferries are running). Another is on Calle 2 Norte and Avenida 10 (© 987/872-1706). Hours are from 8:30am to 9:30pm daily. ADO buses make the 1-hour trip from Cancún airport to Playa del Carmen (and back) throughout the day for 110 pesos; you can easily catch the ferry to Cozumel from Playa.

ORIENTATION

ARRIVING Cozumel's **airport** is a 5-minute drive from downtown. **Transportes Terrestre** provides hotel transportation in multipassenger vans. Buy your ticket as you exit the terminal. To hotels downtown, the fare is 47 pesos per person; to hotels along the north and south shore, 78 pesos. A private taxi to downtown costs 110 pesos. Passenger ferries arrive at the Muelle Fiscal, the municipal pier, by the town's main square. Cruise ships dock at the **Punta Langosta** pier, several blocks south of the Muelle Fiscal, and at the **International Pier,** which is at Km 4 of the southern coastal road. A third cruise-ship pier is the **Puerta Maya** near the International Pier.

VISITOR INFORMATION The **Municipal Tourism Office** (© 987/869-0212; www.cozumel.gob.mx), located at Plaza del Sol, also has information booths at the International Pier and Punta Langosta Pier. It's open 8am to 3pm Monday to Friday.

CITY LAYOUT San Miguel's main waterfront street is **Avenida Rafael Melgar.** Running parallel to Rafael Melgar are *avenidas* numbered in multiples of five—5, 10, 15. **Avenida Juárez** runs perpendicular to these, heading inland from the ferry dock. Avenida Juárez divides the town into northern and southern halves. The *calles* (streets) that parallel Juárez to the north have even numbers. The ones to the south have odd numbers, except for Calle Rosado Salas, which runs between calles 1 and 3. *Note:* Vehicles on the *avenidas* have the right of way.

ISLAND LAYOUT One road runs along the western coast of the island, which faces the Yucatán mainland. It has different names. North of town, it's **Santa Pilar** or **San Juan;** in the city, it is **Avenida Rafael Melgar;** south of town, it's **Costera Sur.** Hotels stretch along this road north and south of town. The road runs to the southern tip of the island (Punta Sur), passing **Chankanaab National Park.**

Cozumel

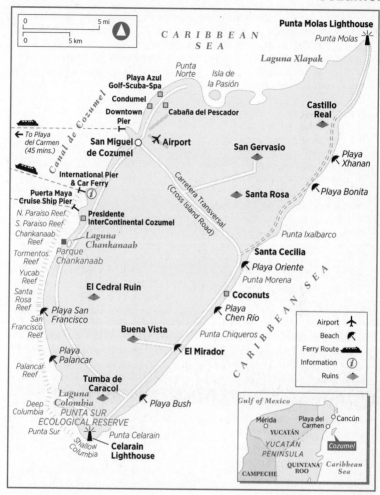

Avenida Juárez (and its extension, the **Carretera Transversal**) runs east from the town across the island. It passes the airport and the turnoff to the ruins of San Gervasio before reaching the undeveloped ocean side of the island. It then turns south and follows the coast to the southern tip, where it meets the Costera Sur.

GETTING AROUND   You can walk to most destinations in town, and it's very safe. Getting to outlying hotels and beaches requires a taxi, rental car, or moped.

Car rentals are about $45 for a VW bug and $60 for a Jeep Wrangler. **Avis** (② 987/872-0099) and **Hertz** (② 987/871-6783) have counters in the airport. Other major rental companies have offices in town, including **Thrifty** (② 987/869-2957) at Juárez 181, between avenidas 5 and 10 Norte. Rentals are easy to arrange through your hotel or at any of the many local rental offices.

AN all-inclusive vacation IN COZUMEL

Booking a room at an all-inclusive resort should be done through a vacation packager. Booking through the hotel usually doesn't make sense, even with frequent-flier mileage to burn, as discounts offered by most packagers are so deep. I include websites to find out more info about the properties, but don't expect to find clear info on rates. The game of setting rates with these hotels is complicated and always in flux.

Two all-inclusives are north of town: **El Cozumeleño** (www.elcozumeleno. com) and the **Meliá Cozumel** (www.sol melia.com). Both occupy multistory modern buildings and have attractive rooms. El Cozumeleño is the larger of the two resorts and has the nicest hotel pool on the island. It's best suited for active types. The Meliá is quieter and offers golf discounts for the nearby golf course. The Cozumeleño's small beach has to be replenished with sand periodically. The Meliá's beach is long, narrow, and pretty, but occasionally seaweed washes up, which doesn't happen on the rest of the island's coast. The advantages of staying in these two are the proximity to town, with its restaurants, clubs, movie theaters, and so on, and the fact that most rooms at these hotels come with views of the ocean.

The **Cozumel Palace** (www.palace resorts.com) is right on the water on the southern fringes of town, occupying the property that used to be Plaza las Glorias. Despite the location, it doesn't have a beach. But that's not so bad. The water is usually so calm on Cozumel's west shore that swimming here is like swimming in a pool, and you can snorkel right out of the hotel.

Of the all-inclusives to the south, my favorites are the **Occidental** resort (**Grand Cozumel** and **Allegro Cozumel;** www.occidentalhotels.com) and the **Iberostar Cozumel** (www.iberostar.com). These are "village" style resorts with two- and three-story buildings, often with thatched roofs, spread over a large area at the center of which is the pool and activities area. Rooms at the Grand Cozumel are larger and more attractive than the all-inclusives in the south. Like the Occidental chain, Iberostar has several properties in the Mexican Caribbean. This one is the smallest. I like its food and service and the beauty of the grounds. The rooms are attractive and well maintained. At these places you're close to a lot of dive sites, but you're somewhat isolated from town, and you don't have many rooms with ocean views.

An excellent adults-only all-inclusive is the **Wyndham Cozumel Resort and Spa** (www.wyndham.com), which boasts the largest beach of any island resort. And then there's the friendly **Hotel Cozumel & Resort** (formerly the Costa Club; www.hotelcozumel.com.mx), which lies within easy walking distance of the town. The **Fiesta Americana Cozumel All-Inclusive** (www.fiesta mericana.com), on a pristine stretch of beach off the road toward Chankanaab, features an excellent dive center next to the oldest and largest coral reef in the hemisphere.

Moped rentals are readily available and cost 250 to 500 pesos for 24 hours, depending upon the season. If you rent a moped, be careful. Riding a moped made a lot more sense when Cozumel had less traffic; now it involves a certain amount of risk as taxi drivers and other motorists have become more numerous and pushier. Moped accidents easily rank as the greatest cause of injury in Cozumel. Before renting one, inspect it carefully to see that all the gizmos—horn, light, starter, seat, mirror—are in good shape. I've been offered mopeds with unbalanced wheels, which made them unsteady at higher speeds, but the renter quickly exchanged them upon my request. You are required to stay on paved roads. It's illegal to ride a moped without a helmet outside of town (subject to a 300 peso fine).

Cozumel has lots of **taxis** and a strong drivers' union. Fares are standardized—there's no bargaining. Here are sample fares for two people (there is an additional charge for extra passengers to most destinations): island tour, 800 pesos; town to southern Hotel Zone, 100 to 200 pesos; town to northern hotels, 50 to 70 pesos; town to Chankanaab, 120 pesos for up to four people; in and around town, 50 pesos.

[FastFACTS] COZUMEL

Area Code The telephone area code is **987.**

ATMs, Banks & Currency Exchange The island has several banks and *casas de cambio*, as well as ATMs. Most places accept dollars, but you usually get a better deal paying in pesos.

Climate From October to December, there can be strong winds all over the Yucatán, as well as some rain. June through October is the rainy season.

Consulates The **U.S. Consular Agent** is in the Villa Mar Mall in the Plaza, Parque Juárez between Av. Juárez and 5th Av. Norte (☎ **987/872-4574**); open Monday through Friday from noon to 2pm.

Hospital Médica San Miguel (☎ **987/872-0103**) works for most things and includes intensive-care facilities. It's on Calle 6 Norte between avenidas 5 and 10. **Centro Médico Cozumel** (☎ **987/872-9400**) is an alternative. It's at the intersection of Calle 1 Sur and Avenida 50.

Internet Access Several cybercafes are in and about the main square. If you go just a bit off Avenida Rafael Melgar and the main square, prices drop. **Modutel,** Av. Juárez 15 (at Av. 10), offers good rates. Hours are Monday through Saturday from 10am to 8pm.

Post Office The *correo* is on Avenida Rafael Melgar

at Calle 7 Sur (☎ **987/872-0106**), at the southern edge of town. It's open Monday through Friday from 9am to 3pm, Saturday from 9am to noon.

Recompression Chamber Cozumel has three *cámaras de recompresión*. The best are **Buceo Médico Mexicano,** staffed 24 hours, at Calle 5 Sur 21-B, between Avenida Rafael Melgar and Avenida 5 Sur (☎ **987/872-2387,** -1430); and the **Hyperbaric Center of Cozumel** (☎ **987/872-3070**), at Calle 6 Norte, between avenidas 5 and 10.

Seasons High season is from Christmas to Easter and August.

Exploring the Island

For **diving** and **snorkeling,** you have plenty of dive shops to choose from. For **island tours, ruins tours** on and off the island, **evening cruises,** and other activities, go to a travel agency, such as **InterMar Cozumel Viajes,** Calle 2 Norte 101-B, between avenidas 5 and 10 (☎ **01-800/122-7423** in Mexico; www.intermar.com. mx). Office hours are Monday through Saturday from 8am to 8pm, Sunday from 9am to 5pm.

WATERSPORTS

SCUBA DIVING Cozumel is the number-one dive destination in the Western Hemisphere. Don't forget your dive card and dive log. Dive shops will rent you scuba gear but won't take you out on a boat until you show some documentation. If you have a medical condition, bring a letter signed by a doctor stating that you've been cleared to dive. A two-tank dive trip costs about $70 to $90; some shops offer an additional one-tank dive for a modest additional fee. A lot of divers save some money by buying a dive package with a hotel. These usually include two dives a day.

Diving in Cozumel is drift diving, which can be a little disconcerting for novices. The current that sweeps along Cozumel's reefs, pulling nutrients into them and making them as large as they are, also dictates how you dive here. The problem is that it pulls at different speeds at different depths and in different places. When it's pulling strong, it can quickly scatter a dive group. The role of the dive master becomes more important, especially with choosing the dive location. Cozumel has a lot of dive locations. To mention but a few: the famous **Palancar Reef,** with its caves and canyons, plentiful fish, and sea coral; the monstrous **Santa Rosa Wall,** famous for its depth, sea life, coral, and sponges; the **San Francisco Reef,** with a shallower drop-off wall and fascinating sea life; and the **Yucab Reef,** with its beautiful coral.

For Experienced Divers

Bring proof of your diver's certification and your log. Underwater currents can be strong, and many of the reef drops are quite steep, so dive operators want to make sure divers are experienced.

Finding a dive shop in town is even easier than finding a jewelry store. Cozumel has more than 50 dive operators, including: **Aqua Safari,** which has a location on Av. Rafael Melgar 429 at Calle 5 (© 987/872-0101; www.aquasafari.com). **Dive Paradise** (© 987/872-1007; www.diveparadise.com), next to the Naval Base at 602 R.E. Melgar, has been in business over 25 years and offers dive training at all levels. **Liquid Blue Divers** (© 987/869-2812; www.liquidbluedivers.com) arranges tours by appointment and provides high-quality service to small groups. **Scuba Du** (© 987/872-9505; www.scubadu.com), based at the Presidente Inter-Continental resort (p. 511), offers excellent diving excursions, refresher courses, and all levels of diving certification.

SNORKELING   Most resorts offer snorkeling equipment, and many dive shops do, as well. Even though you won't see a lot of the more delicate structures, such as fan coral, you will still see plenty of sea creatures and enjoy the clear, calm water of Cozumel's protected west side. When contracting for a snorkel tour, stay away from the companies that cater to the cruise ships. Those tours are crowded and not very fun.

BOAT TRIPS   Travel agencies and hotels can arrange boat trips, a popular pastime on Cozumel. Choose from evening cruises, cocktail cruises, glass-bottom boat cruises, and other options. A real submarine tour is offered by **Atlantis Submarines** (© 987/872-5671; www.atlantisadventures.com). The tour includes 40 minutes at up to 30m (98 ft.) beneath the surface of the Chankanaab protected marine park (total excursion time is 1½ hours). It costs $89 per adult, $59 for kids ages 4 to 12. This is a superior experience to the **Sub See Explorer** offered by **AquaWorld** (www.aquaworld.com.mx), which is really just a glorified glass-bottom boat. You can make reservations online and get a bit of a discount.

FISHING   The best months for fishing are March through June, when the catch includes blue and white marlin, sailfish, tarpon, and swordfish. The least expensive option would be to contact a boat owner directly. A reliable operator offering deep-sea fishing and bonefishing in Cozumel is **Aquarius Fishing** (© 987/872-1092; www.aquariusflatsfishing.com), located at Avenida 20 Sur between Calle 3 Sur and Calle Rosado Salas. The cost for an 8-hour excursion is $385 for up to two anglers, and $100 more for each additional angler.

San Miguel de Cozumel

Information ⓘ
Pedestrians only ▦▦▦▦
Post office ✉

To Airport

Bulevar Aeropuerto Internacional

Calle 14 Norte

To Hotels North

Calle 12 Norte

Calle 10 Norte

Calle 8 Norte

Museo de Cozumel

Calle 6 Norte

Calle 4 Norte

Calle 2 Norte

Channel

Carretera Transversal

Plaza Cozumel

Avenida Benito Juárez

ⓘ Plaza del Sol

To Playa del Carmen

Calle 1 Sur

Cozumel

Avenida Rafael Melgar

Market ☐

Calle Dr. Adolfo Rosado Salas

Calle 3 Sur

Calle 5 Sur

Calle 7 Sur

Recompression Chamber

✉ Plaza Punta Langosta

To Hotels South & Cruise/Car Pier

Calles Morelos

Calle Hidalgo

5 Avenida Norte · 10 Avenida Norte · 15 Avenida Norte · 20 Avenida Norte · 25 Avenida Norte · 30 Avenida Norte · 35 · 40 Avenida Norte

5 Av. Sur · 10 Av. Sur · 15 Avenida Sur · 20 Avenida Sur · 25 Avenida Sur · 30 Avenida Sur · 35 Avenida Sur · 40 Avenida Sur

0   200 yds
0   200 m

14

ISLA MUJERES & COZUMEL | Cozumel

RESTAURANTS ◆
Comida Casera Toñita **10**
El Amigo Mario **14**
French Quarter **11**
Guido's **4**
Kinta **8**

La Choza **12**
La Cocay **3**
Pancho's
  Backyard **2**
Restaurant del Museo **5**
Zermatt **7**

HOTELS ■
Hacienda San Miguel **1**
La Casona Real **9**
Suites Vima **6**
Vista del Mar **13**

San Miguel de Cozumel

COZUMEL ISLAND

505

CHANKANAAB NATIONAL PARK & FARO CELERAIN ECOLOGICAL RESERVE (PUNTA SUR)

Chankanaab National Park ★ (www.cozumelparks.com), off the Carretera Costera Sur at Km 9, is the pride of many islanders. In Mayan, Chankanaab means "little sea," which refers to a beautiful landlocked pool connected to the sea through an underwater tunnel—a sort of miniature ocean. Snorkeling in this natural aquarium is not permitted, but the park itself has a beach for sunbathing and snorkeling. Arrive before 9am to stake out a chair and *palapa* before the cruise-ship crowd arrives. The snorkeling is also best before noon. The park has bathrooms, lockers, a gift shop, several snack huts, a restaurant, and a *palapa* for renting snorkeling gear.

You can also swim with dolphins here. **Dolphin Discovery** (© 800/293-9698 in the U.S.; www.dolphindiscovery.com) has several programs for experiencing these sea creatures. These are popular, so plan ahead—you should make reservations well in advance. The surest way is through the website—make sure to pick the Cozumel location, as there are a couple of others on this coast. There are three different programs for swimming with dolphins. The Dolphin Royal Swim costs $129 and features close interaction with the beautiful swimmers. There are also swim-and-snorkel programs for under $100 that get you in the water with these creatures. The park is open daily from 9am to 5pm and lies south of town, just past the Fiesta Americana Hotel. Taxis run constantly between the park, the hotels, and town (about 100 pesos from town for up to four people).

Faro Celerain Ecological Reserve (admission $10), also called Punta Sur, is an ecological reserve at the southern tip of the island that includes the Columbia Lagoon. A number of crocodiles make the lagoon their home, so swimming is not only a bad idea, it's not allowed. The only practical way of going out to the lighthouse, which lies 8km (5 miles) from the entrance, is to rent a car or scooter; there's no taxi stand, and usually few people. At the entrance to Punta Sur, you'll find a reggae beach bar and a sea turtle nesting area. The lovely beaches just in front are kept as natural as possible, but be cautious about swimming or snorkeling here depending on the winds and currents. Regular hours are daily 9am to 6pm. If you have a rental car, getting here is no problem, and this is usually a great place to get away from the crowds and have a lot of beach to yourself. Occasionally, boat tours of the lagoon are offered. Ask at the information office.

Cenote Diving on the Mainland

A popular activity in the Yucatán is cave diving. The peninsula's underground **cenotes** (seh-*noh*-tehs)—sinkholes or wellsprings—lead to a vast system of underground caverns. The gently flowing water is so clear that divers seem to float on air through caves complete with stalactites and stalagmites. If you want to try this but didn't plan a trip to the mainland, contact **Yucatech Expeditions,** Avenida 5, on the corner of Calle 3 Sur (©/fax **987/113-7044;** www.yucatech.net), which offers all-day cenote tours as well as cave dive training. The cenotes lie 30 to 45 minutes from Playa del Carmen, and a dive in each cenote lasts around 45 minutes. Dives are within the daylight zone, about 40m (131 ft.) into the caverns, and no more than 18m (59 ft.) deep. Open water certification and at least five logged dives are required. For those without diving certifications, a cenote snorkeling tour is also offered.

14

Cozumel

ISLA MUJERES & COZUMEL

506

ANATOMY OF the coral reef

Corals are polyps, tiny animals with hollow, cylindrical bodies that attach by the thousands to hard surfaces of the sea floor. The polyps extract calcium carbonate from the seawater to create hard, cup-shaped skeletons that assume an endless variety of shapes and sizes. These massive limestone structures shelter nearly one-fourth of all marine life. The soft, delicate polyps retreat into their skeletons during the day, but their protruding tentacles can be seen when they feed at night.

Two distinct types of coral formations dominate Cozumel's waters. Bases of the less developed platform reefs, such as Colombia Shallows, Paradise, and Yucab, are rarely more than 9 to 15m (30–49 ft.) in depth. Edge reefs are more complex structures built up over many millennia, and their layered structures peak high above the edge of the drop-off, extending as much as 55m (180 ft.) below the surface. These are found mostly in the south; examples include Palancar, Colombia Deep, Punta Sur, and Maracaibo.

BEACHES

Along both the west and east sides of the island you'll see signs advertising beach clubs. A "beach club" in Cozumel can mean just a *palapa* hut that's open to the public and serves soft drinks, beer, and fried fish. It can also mean a recreational beach with the full gamut of offerings, from banana boats to parasailing. They also usually have locker rooms, a pool, and food. The biggest of these is **Mr. Sancho's** (© 987/112-1933; www.mrsanchos.com), south of downtown San Miguel at Km 15 on the main road between the Reef Club and Allegro Resort. It offers a restaurant, bar, massage service, and motorized and nonmotorized watersports. Quieter versions of beach clubs are **Playa San Francisco** (no phone) and **Paradise Beach** (www.paradise-beach-cozumel.com), next to Playa San Francisco. All of these beaches are south of Chankanaab Park and easily visible from the road. Several have swimming pools with beach furniture, a restaurant, and snorkel rental. They cost about $12 to enter.

Once you get to the end of the island, the beach clubs become simple places where you can eat, drink, and lay out on the beach. **Paradise Cafe** is on the southern tip of the island across from Punta Sur Nature Park, and as you go up the eastern side of the island you pass **Playa Bonita, Chen Río,** and **Punta Morena.** Except on Sunday, when the locals head for the beaches, these places are practically deserted. Most of the east coast is unsafe for swimming because of the surf. The beaches tend to be small and occupy gaps in the rocky coast.

ISLAND TOURS

Travel agencies can arrange a variety of tours, including horseback, Jeep, and ATV tours. Taxi drivers charge 800 pesos for a 3-hour tour of the island, which most people would consider only mildly amusing, depending on the driver's personality. The best horseback tours are offered at **Rancho Palmitas** (no phone), on the Costera Sur highway, across from the Occidental Cozumel resort. Rides can be from 1 to 2½ hours long and cost about 350 pesos.

OTHER ATTRACTIONS

MAYA RUINS A popular island excursion is to **San Gervasio** (100 B.C.–A.D. 1600). Follow the paved transversal road to Km 7.5, and you'll see the well-marked turnoff about halfway between town and the eastern coast. For what you see, it's a bit overpriced. Entrance is 70 pesos; camera permits cost an additional 50 pesos. A small tourist center at the entrance sells handicrafts, cold drinks, and snacks. The ruins are open daily from 7am to 4pm.

When it comes to Cozumel's Maya ruins, getting there is most of the fun—do it for the mystique and for the trip, not for the size or scale of the ruins. The buildings, though preserved, are crudely made and would not be much of a tourist attraction if they were not the island's principal ruins. More significant than beautiful, this site was once an important ceremonial center where the Maya gathered, coming even from the mainland. The important deity was Ixchel, the goddess of weaving, women, childbirth, pilgrims, the moon, and medicine. Although you won't see any representations of Ixchel at San Gervasio today, Bruce Hunter, in his *Guide to Ancient Maya Ruins,* writes that priests hid behind a large pottery statue of her and became the voice of the goddess, speaking to pilgrims and answering their petitions. Ixchel was the wife of Itzamná, the sun god.

Guides charge about $35 for a tour for one to six people. Seeing it takes 30 to 60 minutes. Taxi drivers offer transportation for about $50, which includes the driver waiting for you outside the ruins.

A HISTORY MUSEUM　The **Museo de la Isla de Cozumel ★**, Avenida Rafael Melgar between calles 4 and 6 Norte (© **987/872-1475**), is more than just a nice place to spend a rainy hour. On the first floor, an exhibit illustrates endangered species, the origin of the island, and its present-day topography and plant and animal life, including an explanation of coral formation. The second-floor galleries feature the history of the town, artifacts from the island's pre-Hispanic sites, and Colonial-era cannons, swords, and ship paraphernalia. It's open daily from 9am to 5pm (but closes at 4pm on Sun). Admission is 36 pesos. There's also a gift shop and a picturesque rooftop cafe that serves breakfast and lunch (p. 514; you don't need to pay admission to eat here, unless you plan to visit the museum, too).

GOLF　Cozumel has an 18-hole course designed by Jack Nicklaus. It's at the **Cozumel Country Club** (© **987/872-9570;** www.cozumelcountryclub.com.mx), north of San Miguel. Greens fees are $169 for a morning tee time, including cart rental and tax. Afternoon tee times cost $105. Tee times can be reserved 3 days in advance. A few hotels have special memberships with discounts for guests and advance tee times; guests at Playa Azul Golf and Beach Club pay no greens fees, but the cart costs $25.

Trips to the Mainland

CHICHÉN ITZÁ, TULUM & COBÁ　Travel agencies can arrange day trips to the ruins of **Chichén Itzá ★★★**. The ruins of **Tulum ★**, overlooking the Caribbean, and **Cobá ★**, in a dense jungle setting, are closer and cost less to visit. A trip to both Cobá and Tulum begins at 8am and returns around 6pm. A shorter, more relaxing excursion goes to Tulum and the nearby nature park of Xel-Ha.

PLAYA DEL CARMEN & XCARET　Going on your own to the nearby seaside town of **Playa del Carmen** and the **Xcaret** nature park is as easy as a quick ferry ride from Cozumel (for ferry information, see "Getting There & Departing," earlier in this chapter). For information on Playa and Xcaret, see chapter 15. Cozumel travel agencies offer an Xcaret tour that includes the ferry ride, transportation to the park, and the admission fee.

Shopping

If you're looking for silver jewelry or other souvenirs, go no farther than the town's coastal avenue, Rafael Melgar. Along this road, you'll find one store after another selling jewelry, Mexican handicrafts, and other souvenirs and duty-free merchandise. The most impressive is **Los Cinco Soles** (© **987/872-0132;** www.loscincosoles. com), on the waterfront at 8 Norte, adjacent to Pancho's Backyard restaurant (p. 514). There are also some import/export stores in the Punta Langosta Shopping Center in the southern part of town in front of the cruise-ship pier. Prices for serapes, T-shirts, and the like are lower on the side streets off Avenida Melgar.

Where to Stay

I've grouped Cozumel's hotels by location—**north** of town, **in town,** and **south** of town. The prices quoted are public rates and do not include the 14% tax. High season is from December to Easter. Expect rates from Christmas to New Year's to be still higher than the regular high-season rates quoted here. Low season is the rest of the year, though a few hotels raise their rates in August, when Mexican families go on vacation.

All of the beach hotels in Cozumel, even the small ones, have deals with vacation packagers. Keep in mind that some packagers will offer last-minute deals to Cozumel with hefty discounts; if you're the flexible sort, keep an eye open for these.

Most hotels have an arrangement with a dive shop and offer dive packages. These can be good deals, but if you don't buy a dive package, it's quite okay to stay at one hotel and dive with a third-party operator—any dive boat can pull up to any hotel pier to pick up customers. Most dive shops won't pick up from the hotels north of town.

In addition to the hotels listed below, another reliable option is the **Fiesta Americana All-Inclusive Dive Center** (www.fiestamericana.com; © **987/872-9600**), located on Carretera Chankanaab Km 7.5, which is popular with families and has its own dive center. As an alternative to a hotel, you can try **Cozumel Vacation Villas and Condos,** Av. Rafael Melgar 685 (btw. calles 3 and 5 Sur; www.cozumel-villas. com; © **800/224-5551** in the U.S.), which offers accommodations by the week.

NORTH OF TOWN

Carretera Santa Pilar, or San Juan, is the name of Avenida Rafael Melgar's northern extension. All the hotels lie close to each other on the beach side of the road a short distance from town and the airport.

Very Expensive

Playa Azul Golf-Scuba-Spa ★   This quiet hotel is perhaps the most relaxing of the island's properties. It's smaller than the others, and an excellent choice for golfers; guests pay no greens fees, only cart rental ($30). The hotel's small beautiful beach with shade *palapas* has a quiet little beach bar. All three categories of guest rooms have ocean views. The units in the original section are suites—very large, with oversize bathrooms with showers. The new wing has mostly standard rooms that are comfortable and large. The corner rooms are master suites with large balconies and Jacuzzis overlooking the sea. If you prefer lots of space over having a Jacuzzi, opt for a suite in the original building. Rooms contain a king-size or two double beds; some suites offer two convertible single sofas in the separate living room. The hotel also offers deep-sea- and fly-fishing trips.

Carretera San Juan Km 4, 77600 Cozumel, Q. Roo. www.playa-azul.com. © **987/869-5160.** Fax 987/869-5173. 51 units. High season $200 double, $250 suite; low season $150 double, $185 suite. Rates include unlimited golf and full breakfast. AE, MC, V. Free guarded parking. **Amenities:** 2 restaurants; 3 bars; dive shop; unlimited golf privileges at Cozumel Country Club; medium-size pool; room service; snorkeling equipment; spa. *In room:* A/C, TV, fridge, hair dryer, Wi-Fi.

Expensive

Condumel Condobeach Apartments 🗝

If you want some distance from the crowds, consider lodging here. It's not a full-service hotel, but in some ways, it's more convenient. The one-bedroom waterfront apartments are designed and furnished in practical fashion—airy, with sliding glass doors that face the sea and allow for good cross-ventilation (especially in the upper units). They also have ceiling fans, air-conditioning, and two twin beds or one king-size. Each apartment has a separate living room and a full kitchen with a partially stocked fridge, so you don't have to run to the store on the first day. There's a small, well-tended beach area (with shade *palapas* and a grill for guests' use) that leads to a low, rocky fall-off into the sea.

Carretera Hotelera Norte s/n, 77600 Cozumel, Q. Roo. www.condumel.com. ✆ **987/872-0892.** Fax 987/872-0661. 10 units. High season $142 double; low season $120 double. Dive packages available. No credit cards. *In room:* A/C, kitchen, no phone, Wi-Fi.

IN TOWN

Staying in town is not like staying in the town on Isla Mujeres, where you can walk to the beach. The oceanfront in town is too busy for swimming, and there's no beach, only the *malecón*. Prices are considerably lower, but you'll have to drive or take a cab to the beach; it's pretty easy. English is spoken in almost all of the hotels.

Moderate

Hacienda San Miguel ★ 🗝

This is a peaceful hotel built in Mexican colonial style around a large garden courtyard. The property is well maintained and the service is good. It's located a half-block from the shoreline on the town's north side. The large guest rooms offer rustic Mexican furnishings and fully equipped kitchens. Most of the studios have a queen-size bed or two doubles, while the junior suites have more living area and a queen-size as well as a twin bed. The two-bedroom suite comes with four double beds. For this hotel, high season runs from January to August; low season is from September to December, excluding the holiday season.

Calle 10 Norte 500 (btw. Rafael Melgar and Av. 5), 77600 Cozumel, Q. Roo. www.haciendasanmiguel. com. ✆ **866/712-6387** in the U.S., or 987/872-1986. Fax 987/872-7043. 11 units. High season $94 studio, $106 junior suite, $154 2-bedroom suite; low season $72 studio, $84 junior suite, $114 2-bedroom suite. Rates include continental breakfast and free entrance to Mr. Sancho's beach club. MC, V. Guarded parking on street. *In room:* A/C, TV, hair dryer, kitchen, no phone, Wi-Fi.

Vista del Mar ★

This boutique hotel sits on the town's shoreline boulevard. Guest rooms are bright and cheerfully decorated with bamboo furnishings. The rooms in front offer ocean views with wrought-iron balconies. Those in back go for slightly less than the oceanview rooms and overlook a small pool. This hotel is operated by the same people who run Hacienda San Miguel, and it has the same high season/low season split, with higher rates for Carnaval and Christmas time.

Av. Rafael Melgar 45 (btw. calles 5 and 7 Sur), 77600 Cozumel, Q. Roo. www.hotelvistadelmar.com. ✆ **888/309-9988** in the U.S., or 987/872-0545. Fax 987/872-7036. 20 units. High season $110 double; low season $78–$90 double. Discounts sometimes available. AE, MC, V. Limited street parking. **Amenities:** Bar; Jacuzzi; outdoor pool. *In room:* A/C, TV, fridge, hair dryer, free local calls, Wi-Fi.

Inexpensive

La Casona Real 🗝

Five blocks from the waterfront, this cheerful two-story hotel is a bargain for those wanting a hotel with a pool. The simple rooms are small to medium in size, with a king or two double beds, good air-conditioning, and colorful

Mexican decor. A courtyard with an oval pool is on the west side of the building, and some rooms have views of the pool while others look toward the town (and are a bit noisier). Families can make good use out of the one-bedroom suite, which has a futon in the living room, full kitchen, and cable TV with a DVD player.

Av. Juárez 501, 77600 Cozumel, Q. Roo. www.hotel-la-casona-real-cozumel.com. ℂ **987/872-5471.** 12 units. $50–$55 double; $80 suite. No credit cards. Limited street parking. **Amenities:** Medium-size outdoor pool. *In room:* A/C, TV, no phone.

Suites Vima 🦋   This three-story hotel sits 4 blocks from the main square. It offers large, plainly furnished rooms for a good price. The lighting is okay, the showers are good, and every room comes with its own fridge, which for island visitors can be a handy feature. The rooms are fairly quiet. Choose between two doubles or one king-size bed. There is no restaurant, but there is a pool and lounge area. As is the case with other small hotels on the island, the staff at the front desk doesn't speak English. This is one of the few hotels in town that doesn't use high season/low season rates.

Av. 10 Norte btw. calles 4 and 6, 77600 Cozumel, Q. Roo. ℂ **987/872-5118.** 12 units. 500 pesos double. No credit cards. Limited street parking. **Amenities:** Tiny outdoor pool. *In room:* A/C, fridge.

SOUTH OF TOWN

The hotels in this area tend to be more spread out and farther from town than hotels to the north. Some are on the inland side of the road; some are on the beach side, which means a difference in price. Those farthest from town are all-inclusive properties. The beaches tend to be slightly better than those to the north, but all the hotels have swimming pools and piers from which you can snorkel, and all of them accommodate divers. Head south on Avenida Rafael Melgar, which becomes the coastal road **Costera Sur** (also called Carretera a Chankanaab).

Very Expensive

Presidente InterContinental Cozumel ★★★   The best resort in Cozumel, the Presidente spreads out across a magnificent stretch of coast with only distant hotels for neighbors. Guests enjoy Egyptian cotton sheets, marble bathrooms, Mexican artwork and onyx lamps, Maya-inspired turndown service, and complimentary tea or coffee in the morning. Beachfront "reef" rooms and suites occupy the resort's most exclusive section and include 24-hour butler service and hammocks. There's a full-service spa here, and a pyramid of iguanas out by the pool that is thrilling for children to see. The excellent poolside dive shop (**Scuba Du,** p. 504) offers introductory and one- and two-tank dives as well as certification programs in the clear turquoise sea just in front. A long stretch of sandy beach, dotted with *palapas* and palm trees, fronts the entire hotel, and the sunsets are amazing. Alfredo di Roma serves excellent Italian food.

Costera Sur Km 6.5, 77600 Cozumel, Q. Roo. www.intercontinentalcozumel.com. ℂ **800/327-0200** in the U.S., or 987/872-9500. Fax 987/872-9528. 220 units. High season $330 pool view, $398 ocean view, $582 and up beach front and suite; low season $257–$291 pool view, $302–$358 ocean view, $370–$504 beach front and suite. Internet specials sometimes available. AE, MC, V. Free valet parking. **Amenities:** 3 restaurants; 4 bars; babysitting; 24-hr. butler service in reef section; kids' club; concierge; dive shop; deep-sea fishing trips; access to golf club; putting green; 2 outdoor pools, including adults-only pool; room service; full-service spa with salon and fitness center; 2 lighted tennis courts; watersports; yoga. *In room:* A/C, flatscreen TV w/pay movies, hair dryer, minibar, MP3 docking station, Wi-Fi.

Where to Eat

The island offers a number of tasty restaurants. Taxi drivers will often steer you toward restaurants that pay them commissions; don't heed their advice.

Zermatt (© 987/872-1384), a nice little bakery selling homemade breads and desserts, is on Avenida 5 at Calle 4 Norte. It's open Monday to Saturday from 7am to 8:30pm. For inexpensive local fare during the day, I like **Comida Casera Toñita** (© 987/872-0401), at Calle Rosado Salas 265 between avenidas 10 and 15. Hours are Monday to Saturday from 9am to 6pm. For morning tacos of *cochinita pibil* (traditionally a breakfast item), go to **El Amigo Mario** (© 987/872-0742), on Calle 5 Sur, between Francisco Mújica and Avenida 35. The doors close at 12:30pm.

EXPENSIVE

Cabaña del Pescador (Lobster House) ★★ LOBSTER   The story's a little strange, but brothers Fernando and Enrique, who no longer speak with each other due to a business dispute, run adjacent restaurants both called the Lobster House. They have slight differences in decor, but both restaurants are excellent. Fresh lobster is weighed, then grilled or boiled with a hint of spices, and served with melted butter or garlic, accompanied by sides of rice, vegetables, and bread. Does lobster require anything more? Lobster is the only thing on the menu at Fernando's restaurant, but Enrique will also cook up steaks, shrimp, or fish. The setting is pure tropical—a pair of thatched bungalows bordering a pond with lily pads and reeds, traversed by a small footbridge. The open-air rooms flicker with the glow of candles and are furnished with rustic tables and chairs. The restaurants ramble around quite a bit, so explore until you find the spot most to your taste. Finish with the signature Key lime pie.

Carretera Santa Pilar Km 4 (across from Playa Azul Hotel). No phone. Reservations not accepted. Lobster (by weight) 250–400 pesos. No credit cards. Daily 6–10:30pm.

French Quarter ★★ SOUTHERN   Owner Mike Slaughter brings his Louisiana roots to this downtown favorite where you can order Southern and Creole classics, such as jambalaya and étouffée, or the daily catch blackened, grilled, or stuffed. The restaurant also serves Black Angus beef, and a filet mignon with red-onion marmalade that's delicious. I appreciate the uniqueness of the menu, but the dishes are pricey. Some more traditional Mexican entrees have been added. The downstairs bar attracts locals and expats, especially for sports events. Sunday is American football night.

Av. 5 Sur 18. © **987/872-6321.** Reservations recommended during Carnaval. Main courses 80–300 pesos. AE, MC, V. Wed–Mon 5–10:30pm.

Guido's ★★ MEDITERRANEAN   The inviting terrace, with director's chairs and rustic wood tables, makes this a restful place in daytime and a romantic spot at night. The kitchen blends Mediterranean, Italian, and Swiss influences. The specialties are oven-baked pizzas and homemade pastas, including lasagna with a Bolognese and béchamel sauce, ravioli stuffed with spinach and beef, and spaghetti with shrimp, garlic, olive oil, and Parmesan. My favorite main courses include sautéed grilled shrimp and the spinach-stuffed chicken breast. The other item people love here is the *pan de ajo*—a house creation of fresh bread prepared with olive oil, garlic, and rosemary. In addition to an impressive wine list, pitchers of sangria are available.

Av. Rafael Melgar, btw. calles 6 and 8 Norte. © **987/872-0946.** Reservations recommended. Main courses 162–312 pesos; pizzas 150–174 pesos. AE, MC, V. Mon–Sat 11am–11pm; Sun 3–9:30pm.

La Cocay ★★★ MEDITERRANEAN/SEAFOOD   La Cocay, which means "firefly" in Mayan, serves the most original cooking on the island. The intimate dining room and outdoor courtyard, glittering with white lights wrapped around a sprawling palm tree, create an alluring atmosphere. For an appetizer, the empanadas with goat cheese and caramelized apples make for excellent tapas, as do the figs with prosciutto. For a main course, try the 8-ounce filet mignon, roasted stuffed chicken breast, or mixed grilled seafood served with Spanish rice. Give special consideration to the daily specials and the wonderful chocolate torte. It takes a little extra time to prepare, so order it early. The wine list offers excellent selections from South America.

Calle 8 Norte 208 (btw. avs. 10 and 15). © **987/872-5533.** www.lacocay.com. Reservations recommended. Main courses 130–350 pesos. AE, MC, V. Mon–Sat 5:30–11pm.

MODERATE

Coconuts ★★ 🏠 SEAFOOD   This fun-filled beach restaurant and bar sits on the highest point in Cozumel, which really isn't saying much but nevertheless offers a magnificent view of the Caribbean. Coconuts is open only during the day and has no electricity—running only a daytime generator using solar power. Grab a plastic table in the sand or a seat under the open-air *palapa* and check out the proverbs around you. One says, "Beer: so much more than just a breakfast drink," while another advises, "What happens at Coconuts stays at Coconuts." If you do nothing else here, please order the mixed seafood ceviche. It's just too delicious. There are also sumptuous shrimp quesadillas, the freshest guacamole, and all kinds of tacos and fajitas.

Carratera Oriente Km 43.5. No phone. www.coconutscozumel.com. Main courses 100–180 pesos. No credit cards. Daily 10am–6pm.

El Moro ★ 🌶 REGIONAL   El Moro is an out-of-the-way place that has been around for a long time and has always been popular with the locals, who come for the food, the service, and the prices—but not the decor, which is orange, orange, orange, and Formica. Get there by taxi, which will cost a couple of bucks. Portions are generous. Any of the shrimp dishes use the real jumbo variety when available. For something different, try the *pollo Ticuleño,* a specialty from the town of Ticul, a layered dish of tomato sauce, mashed potatoes, crispy baked corn tortillas, and fried chicken breast, topped with shredded cheese and green peas. Chicken is prepared a half a dozen additional ways, too. Other specialties include enchiladas and fresh seafood prepared many ways, plus grilled steaks and sandwiches.

75 Bis Norte 124 (btw. calles 2 and 4 Norte). © **987/872-3029.** Main courses 50–150 pesos. MC, V. Fri–Wed 1–11pm.

Kinta ★★ CARIBBEAN   An excellent example of Mexican creativity, this chic restaurant blends tropical decor with a cool urban style. Chill-out music fills the air of the lush garden terrace decorated with palms, tiny white lights, and a pond. Chef Kris Wallenta, who previously worked at Guido's and trained at New York's French Culinary Institute, has created a menu celebrating contemporary Mexican cuisine. I recommend the "Mexikanissimo" to start—crispy warm *panela* cheese over a green tomato sauce with herbs. Then order a chile relleno—a poblano pepper with vegetable ratatouille and cheese, baked and cooked over red sauce with a chipotle cream. The filet mignon with *huitlacoche* (corn mushroom), mashed potatoes, and poblano pepper sauce is terrific, too. Service is slow on busy nights, so come for a leisurely evening.

Av. 5 148B (btw. calles 2 and 4 Norte). © **987/869-0544.** Main courses 150–225 pesos. MC, V. Tues–Sun 5:30–11pm; closed Mon.

La Choza ★ MEXICAN/YUCATECAN   A favorite among locals, La Choza is an open-air restaurant with well-spaced tables under a tall thatched roof. Platters of poblano chiles stuffed with shrimp, grilled *brochetas* (kabobs), and *pollo en relleno negro* (chicken in a sauce of blackened chiles) are all delicious. Be sure to add some of the zesty table sauces and guacamole to your meal. Breakfasts are tasty here, as well.

Rosado Salas 198 (at Av. 10 Sur). © **987/872-0958.** Reservations accepted for groups of 6 or more. Breakfast 50 pesos; main courses 110-170 pesos. AE, MC, V. Daily 7:30am-10pm.

Pancho's Backyard ★★★ MEXICAN   Despite its popularity with visitors, the number of locals also eating here attests to Pancho's authenticity. Owned by father and son duo Pancho and Panchito, this charming open-air restaurant surrounded by palms, banana trees, and fountains occupies one of the town's original buildings. Cuisine here focuses on traditional Mexican fare—corn, beans, vegetables, and rice—with a healthy selection of chicken and fish plates. My favorite is the mahi-mahi filet topped with an almond, mango, orange, and pineapple *pico de gallo*. Home-made tortilla chips are served with fresh tomato and onion salsa, as well as a bowl of extraordinarily spicy habanero sauce. Crisply dressed waiters wearing white *guay-aberas* with blue bandanas offer friendly, efficient service. There's also an outstanding artisan store, Los Cinco Soles, here (p. 509).

Av. Melgar 27 at Calle 8 Norte. © **987/872-2141.** www.panchosbackyard.com. Lunch $7-$17; dinner $13-$19. AE, MC, V. Mon-Sat 10am-11pm; Sun 6-11pm.

INEXPENSIVE

Restaurant del Museo BREAKFAST/MEXICAN   The museum's rooftop restaurant and cafe remains my favorite place in San Miguel for breakfast or lunch (weather permitting). It offers a serene ocean view, removed from the traffic noise below and sheltered from the sun above. Breakfasts include *huevos rancheros* with corn tortillas, fried eggs, and salsa, Mexican and American omelets, fresh fruit platters, and pancakes. The Spanish menu offers even more choices than the English menu. Simple lunch dishes include sandwiches and enchiladas, while the Mexican platter for two, with chicken and beef tacos, enchiladas, nachos, quesadillas, and guacamole, ensures you won't go home hungry.

Av. Rafael Melgar (corner of Calle 6 Norte). © **987/872-0838.** Breakfast 55-75 pesos; lunch main courses 64-110 pesos. No credit cards. Daily 7am-2pm.

Cozumel After Dark

Most of the music and dance venues are along Avenida Rafael Melgar. **Carlos 'n' Charlie's** (© **987/869-1648**), which is in the Punta Langosta shopping center, is practically next to **Señor Frog's** (© **987/869-1650**). Punta Langosta lies just south of Calle 7 Sur. The **Hard Rock Cafe** (© **987/872-5271**) is also on Avenida Rafael Melgar, at no. 2, just north of the municipal pier, and remains open until 2am or later with live music on weekends.

In town, there are a few Latin music clubs. These open and close with every high season, prospering when people have cash in their pockets, but closing down when the flow of tourism stops bringing in money. Calle 1 Sur between avenidas 5 Sur and 10 Sur is a pedestrian walking street with a number of local bars, some with live music.

For sports events, the most popular watering hole for locals and expats remains the **French Quarter** (p. 512), open Wednesday to Monday from 5pm to midnight. On Sunday evenings, the place to be is the main square, which usually has a free concert and lots of people strolling about and visiting with friends. Various cafes and bars surround the square.

San Miguel's **movie theater** is Cinépolis, the modern multicinema in the Chedraui Plaza Shopping Center at the south end of town. It mainly shows Hollywood movies. Most of these are in English with Spanish subtitles *(película subtitulada)*; before buying your tickets, make sure the movie hasn't been dubbed *(doblada)*.

THE RIVIERA MAYA & THE SOUTHERN CARIBBEAN COAST

by Christine Delsol & Maribeth Mellin

15

You've heard it more times than you can count: "endless stretch of pristine beach" . . . "soft white sand caressed by turquoise waves" . . . So let's get right to what you really need to know. The Yucatán's Caribbean coast reaches 380km (236 miles) from Cancún to Chetumal, at the Belize border. The northern coast, from Cancún to Tulum and down the Punta Allen peninsula, has been dubbed the Riviera Maya; the southern half, the Costa Maya. In between is the vast Sian Ka'an Biosphere Reserve.

The Riviera Maya, mixing soft, white-sand beaches with Maya ruins and the second-longest coral reef in the world, has grown from a secret escape into a thriving tourist corridor vying with Cancún for visitors. The most popular town, Playa del Carmen, is Mexico's fastest-growing city, bustling with a hip street and beach scene and trendy nightlife. Still, most of the coast retains a laid-back calm. Whether you lounge in the sun with a margarita at a beach bar or snorkel in the protected waters of a cenote, there's no wrong choice in the Riviera Maya.

The region's greatest geological asset is the Great Mesoamerican Reef, which extends south to Honduras and protects most of the Caribbean coast from harsh currents and waves. The best beaches are usually found where the reef is far from shore. **Playa del Carmen's** beaches, such as **Playa El Faro,** are among the area's most beautiful, with soft sand and minimal surf. Beach clubs offer lounge chairs for rent, festive music, and restaurant service, making it easy to linger. Lined with small hotels, **Tulum's** uninterrupted beaches are ideal for getting away from the crowds and strolling on the sand. Head to **Paamul's** wide, curving beach for a relaxing swim in the warm turquoise water.

A single highway connects many of the coast's major sites, making it easy to enjoy the region's history and nature off the beach. Visitors interested in Maya archaeology should head to **Tulum** or **Cobá** for stunning ancient structures. Go caving in Akumal's **Aktun Chen,** with a forest of stalactites and stalagmites leading to a deep pool. Stroll down Playa del Carmen's **Quinta Avenida** for the best shopping, from Brazilian bikinis to *huipiles*—the traditional embroidered dresses worn by Maya women. A trip to **Xcaret** park invites you to commune with native flora and fauna and experience Mexico's folkloric music and dance.

Simple beachfront restaurants along the coast combine wiggling your toes in the sand with enjoying freshly caught fish and conch. Playa del Carmen has a thriving restaurant scene off the beach. At **Yaxché,** dive in to **Maya specialties** such as *cochinita pibil,* pork marinated in achiote and sour orange, wrapped in a plantain leaf and baked. *Panuchos,* a Yucatecan snack, are fried tortillas filled with black beans, topped with meat and pickled red onions—the perfect bite-size accompaniment for an icy beer. Finish your meal with a Café Maya, made from a local liqueur, **Xtabentun.**

Scores of contented visitors hardly leave their happy perch on the powdery sand. But the shoreline is merely the first act; the main event is the Caribbean's gorgeous aquamarine water, and its easy-to-find places to snorkel and dive with lots of fish and other sea creatures. The world's second-largest coral reef is in the Riviera Maya's front yard. Scuba diving and snorkeling are superb, especially along the reefs just off the shores of **Puerto Morelos** and at Akumal's **Laguna Yal-Ku.** The region's cenotes (water-filled sinkholes) connect to form the world's largest underground river system, with crystal-clear water for snorkelers and swimmers to enjoy. You'll also find jungle, caverns, and mangroves; the latter are now protected by the federal government, which is slowly helping the coastline return to its more natural state.

PUERTO MORELOS & VICINITY
Between Cancún & Playa del Carmen

The coast directly south of the Cancún airport has several roadside attractions, all-inclusives, small cabaña hotels, and some spa resorts. Much of the latest development targets the well-heeled traveler—small boutique hotels and astonishingly luxurious all-inclusives. The agreeable town of **Puerto Morelos** lies midway along this 51km (32-mile) stretch of coast between the airport and Playa del Carmen.

ROADSIDE ATTRACTIONS

Just south of the Puerto Morelos turnoff is **Jardín Botánico Dr. Alfredo Barrera** (© 998/206-9223; www.ecosur.mx/jb/YaaxChe). Opened in 1990 and named after a biologist who studied tropical forests, this botanical garden is the largest swath of undeveloped land along the coast, save for the Sian Ka'an Biosphere Reserve (p. 554). Ceiba trees, sacred to the Maya, stand tall amid bromeliads, ferns, orchids, small archaeological sites, a reconstructed Maya residential home, and a *chiclero* camp. Biology students working here are happy to share details (it helps to speak Spanish). Spider monkeys, nearly extinct along the coast, frolic here along with tropical birds. The park is open Monday to Saturday from 9am to 5pm; admission 100 pesos. Wear sturdy walking shoes and insect repellent.

Kids are more likely to enjoy the interactive zoo **CrocoCun** ★ (© 998/850-3719; www.crococunzoo.com), 1.6km (1 mile) north of Puerto Morelos. Formerly a crocodile farm, it now runs a captive breeding program that has helped to restore the reptiles' population in Cancún's Nichupté Lagoon. Currently, it protects all animals native to the Yucatán; those in residence include iguanas, spider monkeys, a boa constrictor, and immense tarantulas. A guided tour with one of the knowledgeable and enthusiastic veterinary students who volunteer here lasts 1½ hours. Again, wear bug repellent. Open daily from 9am to 5pm. Entrance fees are high, as are most roadside attractions on this coast: 276 pesos adults, 168 pesos children 6 to 12, free for children 5 and younger.

SPA RESORTS ★★★

Several resorts with first-rate spas are clustered between Puerto Morelos and the Cancún airport. They're actually more convenient for quick getaways than those along Cancún's Hotel Zone, and all offer airport transfers for the 15- to 20-minute commute. Rates quoted below are for high season, but don't include the often-exorbitant holiday periods. These hotels are mostly all-inclusive (there are few other dining choices nearby). Some add a 10% or 15% service charge.

Ceiba del Mar ★★   Closest to the town of Puerto Morelos, this peaceful resort consists of seven three-story buildings along a landscape of gardens, ponds, and pools. Rooms are large, with a terrace or balcony complete with hammocks. Bathrooms have both showers and tubs, some with an ocean view. Service is attentive and unobtrusive—exemplified by the morning coffee and juice quietly slipped into a niche by the door. The spa's excellent therapists quickly assess each client's needs and preferences. I try to spend at least 1 night here after my travels through the Riviera Maya for a preflight massage.

Av. Niños Héroes s/n, 77580 Puerto Morelos, Q. Roo. www.ceibadelmar.com. © **877/545-6221** in the U.S., or 998/872-8060. Fax 998/872-8061. 88 units. High season $430–$516 deluxe and junior suite, $602 and up master suite; low season $229–$275 deluxe and junior suite, $431 and up master suite. Spa and dining packages available. AE, MC, V. Free parking. **Amenities:** 2 restaurants; 2 bars; babysitting; bikes; concierge; dive shop w/watersports; state-of-the-art gym w/sauna, steam room, whirlpool, and Swiss showers; 2 outdoor pools (1 heated); room service; spa; Wi-Fi. *In room:* A/C, TV/VCR, CD player, hair dryer, minibar, MP3 docking station.

Zoëtry Paraíso de la Bonita ★★   A luxurious all-inclusive, all-suites hotel as well as a serious wellness center with the region's most extensive thalassotherapy spa, this resort offers a bit of everything. Macaws squawk and lovebirds coo in an indoor aviary. Drinks are served in the library amid celeb photos, shared computers, and plush sofas. Guest suites, all with ocean view, are decorated around global themes—guests reside in Bali, India, or Africa. The over-the-top design combines sunken marble tubs, beds so puffy short people have to hop to get on, and stone carvings jutting from lintels. Ground-floor rooms have a plunge pool; upstairs rooms have balconies. Sculptures of Chinese dragons and Maya deities are spread through hallways and gardens between the two restaurants, pool, and outdoor cocktail lounge.

Carretera Cancún–Chetumal Km 328, Bahía Petempich, 77710 Q. Roo. www.zoetryparaisodelabonita.com. © **888/496-3879** in the U.S., or 998/872-8300. Fax 998/872-8301. 90 units. High season $1,000 and up suite; low season $800 and up suite. Rates include ground transfer and meals, drinks, and some activities. AE, MC, V. Free valet parking. No children 11 and under. **Amenities:** 2 restaurants; 2 bars; concierge; 2 Jacuzzis; 4 outdoor pools; room service; spa; lighted tennis court; watersports. *In room:* A/C, TV/DVD, hair dryer, minibar, Wi-Fi.

Puerto Morelos

Puerto Morelos remains a quiet fishing village, perfect for lying on the white-sand beach and reading, with the occasional foray into snorkeling, diving, windsurfing or kayaking. This was the coast's boomtown 100 years ago, when its port shipped hard-

The Yucatán's Upper Caribbean Coast

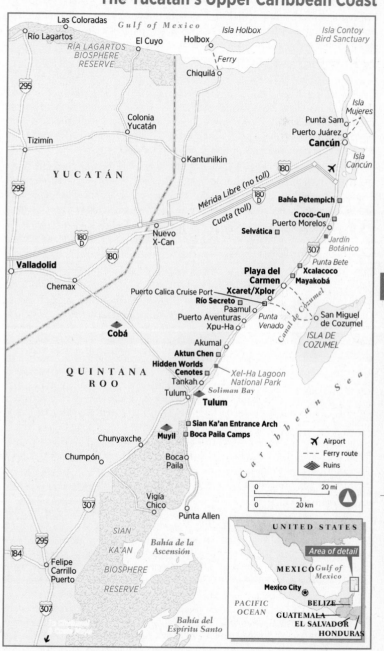

Gulf of Mexico

Las Coloradas
Río Lagartos
El Cuyo
Holbox
Isla Holbox
Isla Contoy
Bird Sanctuary

RÍA LAGARTOS
BIOSPHERE
RESERVE

Ferry

Chiquilá

Isla
Mujeres

Punta Sam
Puerto Juárez
Cancún

Isla
Cancún

295

Colonia
Yucatán

Tizimín

Kantunilkin

Y U C A T Á N

Mérida Libre (no toll)

Bahía Petempich

Croco-Cun
Puerto Morelos

295

Cuota (toll)

Selvática

Jardín
Botánico

Nuevo
X-Can

180
D

307

Punta Bete

Valladolid

180

**Playa del
Carmen**

Xcalacoco
Mayakobá

Chemax

Puerto Calica Cruise Port
Xcaret/Xplor
Río Secreto
Paamul
Puerto Aventuras
Xpu-Ha

Punta
Venado

**San Miguel
de Cozumel**

Cobá

Akumal
Aktun Chen
**Hidden Worlds
Cenotes**

**ISLA DE
COZUMEL**

**Q U I N T A N A
R O O**

Tankah
Tulum

Xel-Ha Lagoon
National Park

Soliman Bay

Tulum

Chunyaxche

Muyil

Sian Ka'an Entrance Arch
Boca Paila Camps

Chumpón

Boca
Paila

C
a
r
i
b
b
e
a
n

S
e
a

✈ Airport
- - - Ferry route
≋ Ruins

Vigía
Chico

Punta Allen

0   20 mi
0   20 km

307

295

**SIAN
KA'AN
BIOSPHERE
RESERVE**

Bahía de la
Ascensión

184

Felipe
Carrillo
Puerto

307

Bahía del
Espíritu Santo

UNITED STATES

Area of detail

MEXICO Gulf of
Mexico

Mexico City ✹

PACIFIC
OCEAN

BELIZE

GUATEMALA
EL SALVADOR
HONDURAS

wood and *chicle* to the U.S. and Europe. Today, the biggest attraction is its small-town atmosphere and easy pace.

Puerto Morelos' section of the Great Maya Reef is designated a national park. The reef is close to the surface and easy to snorkel, and it protects the coast from storm surges. The government-maintained beaches are great, and the water is shallow, calm, and clear, with sea grass growing on the bottom.

Puerto Morelos brims with foreign tourists at times during the high season, but low season is so low that many businesses close for the season, earning it the affectionate nickname, Muerto Morelos (*muerto* means "dead").

ESSENTIALS
Getting There
BY CAR Puerto Morelos is at Km 31, about a half-hour from Cancún. You'll need to exit the highway onto the frontage road and then turn left under the overpass.

BY BUS Buses from Cancún to Tulum and Playa del Carmen usually stop here, but be sure to ask in Cancún if your bus makes the Puerto Morelos stop. Buses stop at the highway, and you'll need to get a taxi (20 pesos) for the ride to the center of town.

EXPLORING IN & AROUND PUERTO MORELOS
The biggest draw is the **coral reef ★★★** rising directly in front of the village to top out just a couple of feet below the water's surface. Divers have nothing over snorkelers here; everyone gets a close-up of the convoluted passages and large caverns burgeoning with fish and sea flora. Restrictions on fishing and boating make this the coast's most pristine patch of coral. Several dive shops in town offer snorkeling tours and gear rentals, but my choice is the local **fishing cooperative ★** (© 998/121-1524) at the foot of the pier. Its 22-member fishing families are national park–certified guides who rotate tour gigs to supplement their income. The fixed fee is 300 pesos for a 2-hour trip that visits two snorkeling sites. Tours leave approximately every half-hour, Monday through Saturday from 9am to 3pm. During whale shark season, the manager, Paco González, also runs tours to Isla Holbox (p. 625) on his day off.

Dive shops around town charge $45 to $50 for one-tank dives; PADI certification costs $350 to $400. One of the best is **Almost Heaven Adventures** (©/fax 998/871-0230; www.almostheavenadventures.com), on Javier Rojo Gómez a block north of the plaza. Enrique Juárez, in business for 15 years, holds groups to five divers and is known for thorough briefings and attentive boat crews. Also recommended: **Dive In Puerto Morelos** (© 998/206-9084; www.diveinpuertomorelos.com) and **Wet Set Diving Adventure** (© 998/871-0198; www.wetset.com).

The small, modern **central plaza** is less beguiling than the adjacent sea walk, but it is the fulcrum of local life and brims with a fine variety of restaurants. On the south side, **Alma Libre** (© 998/252-2207; www.almalibrebooks.com) sells more English-language books than any other bookstore in the Yucatán. The owners, Canadians Joanne and Rob Birce, stock everything from beach reads to English classics, cookbooks to volumes on Maya culture, as well as regional maps. The store also acts as a book exchange, tourist information center, and vacation rental agency. It is open daily, 10am to 3pm and 6 to 9pm, November through April; closed in the off season.

About a block south of the plaza on Javier Rojo Gómez, the local artisans' cooperative runs **Hunab Kú market,** a collection of *palapa* stands selling hammocks, hand-embroidered clothes, jewelry, blankets, ceramics, and other local handicrafts. The wares are high quality, and there are some bargains. Vendors don't hustle you, and it's worth a stroll just for the parklike setting. The market is open daily from 9am to 8pm.

driving THE RIVIERA MAYA

Driving along this coast isn't difficult, but it takes eagle-eyed attention, especially for first-timers. With only one highway, you can't get too lost unless you miss the signs for your hotel. Hwy. 307 traces the coastline for 380km (236 miles) from Cancún to Chetumal, a 4½-hour trip by car. The section between Cancún's airport and Tulum is now a four-lane divided highway with speed limits up to 110kmph (68 mph). It takes about 2 hours to drive the 130km (81 miles) from Cancún airport to Tulum.

Turnoffs can be from either the right or the left lane; if you miss the one you want, go a bit farther and circle back. You're not allowed to stop on the highway to make a left turn, but there are several short left-turn lanes at many points across the road from major resorts. It is impossible to overemphasize just how dangerous this highway can be, especially during high season when you've got locals speeding to work, tour buses clogging the lanes, truck and bus drivers barreling along, and confused or distracted tourists changing lanes on whim. Speed limits are clearly posted and change constantly. Keep an eye out for speed signs, especially around towns and resorts. Lots of drivers ignore speed limits, often to their chagrin. The police have become ever more sophisticated at ticketing speeders and are especially vigilant around stoplights and one-way streets. Several overpasses have been constructed (or are under construction) over the busiest intersections at Puerto Morelos, Puerto Aventuras, and Playa del Carmen, which greatly reduce the danger and traffic congestion. Be aware, however, the roadwork is constant on this highway and can almost double your expected drive time.

All that said, it's hard to imagine traveling around the Riviera Maya without a rental car. So many wonderful places to explore are right beside the highway and along side roads leading to the beach and jungle. First-class gas station plazas with minimarts and fast-food spots are becoming a common sight. Attendants pump the gas (be sure they don't overfill the tank) and will check your oil. Make sure you receive the right change, and tip attendants if they provide extra services. As long as you study your maps in advance and keep your wits about you, driving allows freedom for serendipitous discoveries.

Always carry plenty of drinking water when driving along the coast. Most hotels offer a couple of small bottles in the room upon arrival, then charge close to $2 for each new bottle. Having at least one half-gallon bottle in the car and a reusable water bottle cuts down on expense and waste.

Six blocks north of the plaza in a residential district, the 2-year-old **Little Mexican Cooking School** ★★ (© 998/251-8060; www.thelittlemexicancooking school.com) has been a resounding success. Classes, offered October through July, begin with a continental breakfast, an introduction to modern Mexican cuisines, and an overview of traditional ingredients. With students' help, the chef demonstrates five to seven dishes that make up the grand finale, a *comida fuerte,* or full Mexican late lunch. Sessions last about 5 hours and cost $90.

On Wednesday and Friday, you can get a good massage and wraps at the **Jungle Spa** ★★ (© 998/208-9148; www.mayaecho.com), a short distance west of Hwy. 307. This is a cooperative endeavor by Maya women who have been trained to incorporate current spa techniques into traditional Maya healing massage. Full-body massages cost $40 for 1 hour, $60 for 1½ hours—a fraction of what nearby hotels charge—and the money directly supports local Maya families. Appointments are available Tuesday through Saturday and occasionally on Sunday. The women also perform a traditional Maya dance and sell unique handicrafts at their Sunday Jungle Market, held from mid-December to Easter Sunday.

Selvática (✆ **866/552-8825** in the U.S., or 998/847-4581; www.selvatica.com.mx), operating out of offices in Cancún, offers guests a little jungle adventure, with 2.5km (1½ miles) of zip lines strung up in the forest canopy 19km (12 miles) west of Puerto Morelos. The program also includes biking and swimming in cenotes. In high season, you should make reservations a month in advance. The cost ($99 adults/$49 children for the basic 5-hr. tour) includes transportation, activities, a light lunch, locker, and all equipment.

WHERE TO STAY

For condo rentals, see the website of Alma Libre books (above).

Carmen Hacienda   The former Hacienda Morelos is a good beachfront alternative to one of the all-inclusives outside of town—just don't expect resort-level service. Rooms, all facing the ocean, are smallish and basic but refurbished, and bathrooms have plenty of hot water and good pressure. The hotel's main virtues are the ocean views and expansive beachfront patio. Aquanuts, the on-site dive shop, earns consistently high marks. The restaurant is expensive and slow—all the more reason to sample the many restaurants around the square, just a block away. (The incredible deals touted on the huge sign that seems to be always posted outside the hotel door, unfortunately, are *para quintanaroenses*—for Quintana Roo residents only.)

Av. Rafael E. Melgar no. 5, 77580 Puerto Morelos, Q. Roo. www.carmeninn.com/en/puerto-morelos. ✆ **998/871-0448.** 30 units. High season $125–$150 double; low season $50–$55 double. AE, MC, V (through PayPal). Free off-street parking. **Amenities:** Restaurant; dive shop; outdoor pool. *In room:* A/C, TV, fridge (in some), patio (with ground-floor rooms).

Club Marviya ★   Guest rooms in the original Club Marviya occupy the second floor of a converted mansion on the town's main street, where small terraces offer terrific views and refreshing breezes. Mexican style and color infuse the airy contemporary rooms, which have firm beds and ceramic tile floors. A large communal kitchen and lounge encourage socializing, and the hospitable owners often schmooze with guests in the covered courtyard during the evening. Around the corner, the same owners offer nine newly renovated studios geared toward longer stays (but available by the night). Neither property has air-conditioning, but sea breezes suffice most of the year. They are 3 blocks from the main square and 1 block from the best beach in town.

Av. Javier Rojo Gómez (at Ejército), SM2, 77580 Puerto Morelos, Q. Roo. www.marviya.com. ✆ **998/871-0049.** 15 units. High season $110 double with breakfast; low season $75 double with breakfast, $60 without breakfast; high season $125 studio without breakfast; low season $80 studio without breakfast. Weekly/monthly rates available. MC, V. **Amenities:** Bikes; communal kitchen/lounge; on-site massage therapist; sailboard and kayak rentals; Wi-Fi (in lobby). *In room:* Ceiling fans, fridge.

Hotel Ojo de Agua ☺   This family-run hotel's perch on the town's best stretch of beach, 2 long blocks from the main square, would be enough to recommend it, but it also has a good dive shop, watersports, and a popular beach restaurant. Utilitarian rooms are brightened by rattan furniture and bold paint. Studios with kitchenettes and small yards come with one king-size bed or a double and two twins—they have ceiling fans but no air-conditioning—and are well-suited for families. The beach's excellent snorkeling includes the undersea cenote for which the hotel is named.

Av. Javier Rojo Gómez 16, SM2, M 2, 77580 Puerto Morelos, Q. Roo. www.ojo-de-agua.com. © **998/871-0027.** 36 units. High season $70–$80 double, $100 studio; low season $60–$70 double, $90 studio. AE, MC, V. **Amenities:** Restaurant; dive shop; outdoor pool. *In room:* A/C (in some), kitchen (in some).

Posada El Moro ★★★ ☺ One of the town's most appealing hotels, a half-block off the town square, also happens to be a great deal. Renting a room is akin to ordering dim sum: Add $10 a night for air-conditioning, $5 more for TV, and another $5 for a kitchenette. French-paned sliding doors and windows flood the rooms with natural light, and the tile bathrooms are sparkling clean. Simple, cheery furnishings include queen-size beds with nearly perfect mattresses, plus a futon. Junior suites also have a single bed; full suites have two double beds, a futon, and a kitchenette. The pretty, compact garden has a small pool perfect for kids, and the rooftop has an oceanview *palapa.* The amiable family that runs the place creates a homey atmosphere.

Av. Javier Rojo Gómez, SM2, M 5, Lote 17 (north of José Morelos), 77580 Puerto Morelos, Q. Roo. www. posadaelmoro.com. ©/fax **998/871-0159.** 31 units. High season $60–$80 double, $90 suite; low season $50–$70 double; $80 suite. Rates include continental breakfast. MC, V. Limited free parking. **Amenities:** Small outdoor pool. *In room:* A/C (in some), TV (in some), Wi-Fi.

WHERE TO EAT

Most of Puerto Morelos's restaurants are on or around the main square. These include **Doña Triny's** for Mexican and Yucatecan standards; **Los Pelícanos** for seafood; **David Lau's** for Asian food; enduring local favorite **Hola Asia** for Chinese, Japanese, and Thai; **El Pirata** if you have kids (for its large menu); and **Le Café d'Amancia** for coffee, pastries, and addictive smoothies.

John Gray's Kitchen ★★★ INTERNATIONAL Definitely a splurge, and worth it. After chef John Gray elevated the Club Grill at the Ritz-Carlton Cancún to iconic status, he cooked his way around the world before settling in Puerto Morelos in 2002. He's since opened restaurants in Playa del Carmen and Cancún, but he still captains the kitchen here most nights. The menu changes with market offerings and Gray's mood; don't be surprised if he bursts out of the kitchen to scribble fresh swordfish and clams on the menu just as you've made up your mind. Pick out three appetizers, such as crab cakes with a Mexican twist or ambrosial baked red chile cauliflower, and split them among two people for a very haute meal at a bargain price. Newcomer **La Suegra,** just north of the square near the lighthouse, is owned by Gray's mother-in-law. The food is good, if a bit expensive, and it has a full bar, but its greatest virtue is the two-level deck overlooking the ocean.

Av. Niños Heroes, Lote 6 (north of Av. José Morelos). © **998/889-9800.** www.johngrayrestaurant group.com. Reservations recommended. Main courses $12–$29. MC, V. Mon–Sat 6–11pm.

Posada Amor ★ BREAKFAST/YUCATECAN Puerto Morelos's oldest restaurant, now run by the founder's son, has patrons who have been eating here for nearly 30 years. The *palapa*-roofed dining room, a half-block south of the plaza, is a great place for a complete breakfast or the bargain-priced Sunday breakfast buffet. A few sidewalk tables are perfect for nighttime. The dinner menu focuses on fresh seafood and Yucatecan-influenced dishes.

Avs. Javier Rojo Gómez and Tulum. © **998/871-0033.** Main courses 48–200 pesos; breakfast 45–70 pesos. AE, MC, V. Daily 7am–10pm.

Resorts South of Puerto Morelos

The beaches, bays, mangrove lagoons, and jungles between Puerto Morelos and Tulum are constantly undergoing transformation. Punta Maroma, home to the coast's first exclusive hideaway, now has several resort and residential compounds. Massive all-inclusives loom above beaches where campgrounds once thrived. Mayakobá, a master-planned resort just north of Playa del Carmen, is a fine example of an ecologically responsible development, though some other resorts use the land without much thought to conservation. This area is packed with adventures and attractions.

EXPENSIVE

Grand Velas ★★★   From afar, this irresistible resort looks massive and imposing. But the small, Mexican-owned Velas hotel chain has merged all-inclusive with all the luxuries of the area's finest hotels. Suites are clustered in three categories—the adults-only Grand Class, family-friendly Ambassador Suites, and Master Suites located amid jungle vegetation. The first two all have ocean views; jungle suites are located beside the spa and convention center and have the most amenities for business travelers, including large desks facing canals and jungle. The restaurants are top-notch: The Cocina de Autor has won numerous accolades thanks to its creative Spanish chefs, as has the French restaurant Piaf. You could spend hours in the spa's hydrotherapy area ($50 for a full day or free with spa treatment), with its bubbling jets, gushing water spouts, "experience showers," saunas, and cushy lounge chairs. The service is impeccable, even keeping kids' clubs open until 11pm to give parents a chance to enjoy romantic evenings.

Carretera 307 Km 62, Playa del Carmen, 77710 Q. Roo. www.rivieramaya.grandvelas.com. (℡ **866/335-4640** in the U.S. and Canada, or 984/877-4414. 481 units. $518 and up double. Rates include meals, drinks, and gratuities. AE, MC, V. Free valet parking. **Amenities:** 8 restaurants; 3 bars; butler service; children's programs; concierge; fitness center; 3 outdoor pools; room service; spa; watersports. *In room:* A/C, fan, TV/CD/DVD, hair dryer, MP3 docking station, Wi-Fi.

Hacienda Tres Rios ★★★   An ecofriendly all-inclusive may seem a contradiction in terms, but this property proves a resort can pamper guests and still care for nature. Its 132-hectare (326-acre) nature park incorporates lush jungle, mangrove forests, and coastal dunes, plus plant nurseries, 10 cenotes, and the three rivers for which the hotel is named. Ecoconsciousness is emphasized everywhere. Buffet food is arranged in small individual portions rather than huge bowls and platters; recycling bins are located in all departments; and air-conditioning, heating, and lighting all encompass custom-designed operating systems to reduce water and power consumption. The hotel was built on raised pilings to maintain the surface water's natural flow, and pathways wind through vegetation past meandering rivers and a large pool area. Rooms are elegant and comfortable, the restaurants are very good, and the tours offered throughout the park, including a highly lauded SenseAdventure tour, are great fun.

Carretera 307 Km 54, 77760 Q. Roo. www.haciendatresrios.com. (℡ **866/921-6984** in the U.S. and Canada, or 984/877-2400. 273 units. $700 and up double. Rates include meals, drinks, and gratuities. AE, MC, V. Free valet parking. **Amenities:** 5 restaurants; 4 bars; children's programs; fitness center; 2 outdoor pools; room service; spa; watersports. *In room:* A/C, fan, TV/CD/DVD, hair dryer, Wi-Fi.

The Tides Riviera Maya ★★   The smallest resort in this area once held sway over a private white beach. New hotels and neighborhoods have risen all around it, but the Tides (formerly Ikal del Mar) has 2.5 hectares (6¼ acres) of waterfront property and is all about privacy and tranquillity. A family-friendly all-inclusive smack on the south side takes the privacy out of long beach walks. Thirty well-separated villas—each with a view of jungle, little pool, and outdoor shower—are connected by sparsely lit paths through vegetation. The large villas blend with the setting, using louvered shutters, crocheted hammocks, and minimal decorations in a modern, spare style. The bathrooms have two showers (the private pools are perfect for long soaks). Thoughtful touches include a lady's silk headband and straw hat, special scents, a selection of hand-cut soaps, and room service wherever you wish. The bar and restaurant, overlooking an inviting pool, make for an attractive common area. And, of course, there's the ecospa with *temazcal* surrounded by jungle.

Playa Xcalacoco, Carretera Cancún–Tulum, 77710 Q. Roo. www.tidesrivieramaya.com. © **866/332-1672** in the U.S. and Canada, or 984/877-3000. Fax 713/528-3697. 33 units. High season $700 and up double; low season $585 and up double. Rates include full breakfast. AE, MC, V. Free secure parking. No children 17 and under except during some holidays. Pets under 6 pounds permitted. **Amenities:** Restaurant; 2 bars; concierge; 2 Jacuzzis; large outdoor pool; room service; spa; steam bath; watersports. *In room:* A/C, TV/DVD, hair dryer, minibar, MP3 docking station, Wi-Fi.

MODERATE

Azul Fives ★ ☺ Kids are greeted with milkshakes while parents get sparkling wine when checking in at this family-friendly all-inclusive. Toys are everywhere, from the lobby to the suites, which are also equipped with cribs, changing tables, strollers, bottle warmers, and baby-size robes. The amazing Kid's Club and play programs were designed with Fisher-Price, and include all sorts of colorful toys and games. Older kids hang out in the video game room, complete with beanbag chairs, while adults rejuvenate in the luxurious spa (kids' treatments available). Both European and all-inclusive plans are available. The Gourmet Inclusive concept includes specialty restaurants, premium liquors, all sorts of activities, and nightly entertainment. The stylish suites work well for honeymooners, who get an instant crash-course in family dynamics. Children under 3 stay free; those 3 to 12 get a 50% discount when sharing a room with parents. Though it's just 10 minutes to Playa del Carmen, taxis cost $15 each way.

Predio El Limonar Fracc. 2, 77710 Xcalacoco, Municipio de Solidaridad, Q. Roo. www.karismahotels.com. © **888/280-8810** in the U.S. and Canada, or 984/877-2750. 360 units. $285 and up double European Plan; $470 double all-inclusive. AE, MC, V. Free parking. **Amenities:** 4 restaurants; 5 bars; Kid's Club; gym; 3 outdoor pools; spa; watersports. *In room:* A/C, TV/CD/DVD, hair dryer, Wi-Fi.

Petit Lafitte Hotel ★ One kilometer (⅔ mile) south of the original, venerable Posada Lafitte, this hotel has the same easygoing attitude that permeated the old one. In relative isolation, you get all the amenities of a relaxing vacation. The three-story building, with 30 rooms, is surrounded by 17 bungalows. Spacious, attractive rooms are larger than those in the original property but have a similar beach-hotel simplicity. The staff came from the old property, so service remains personal and attentive.

Carretera Cancún–Tulum Km 63 (Punta Bete), 77710 Playa del Carmen, Q. Roo. www.petitlafitte.com. © **800/538-6802** in the U.S. and Canada, or 984/877-4000. 47 units. High season $200–$285 double; low season $170–$285 double. Rates include breakfast and dinner. MC, V. Free guarded parking. **Amenities:** Restaurant; bar; outdoor pool. *In room:* A/C, TV, hair dryer, minibar, Wi-Fi.

Mayakobá Residential Golf & Spa Resort

One of the most impressive ecologically sensitive developments I've seen, **Mayakobá** (www.mayakoba.com) incorporates three upscale hotels (two reviewed below) and a championship golf course into more than 607 hectares (1,500 acres) of healthy mangroves, lagoons, cenotes, and beaches. The compound's concept is unusual—it's a beach resort with precious few oceanview rooms. Instead, the hotels line a series of freshwater canals. It takes some getting used to, but the idea works.

Guests travel about in electric boats and golf carts and may use the restaurants, spas, and other facilities in all three hotels. Some have trouble with the jungle setting—bug repellent is a must, especially at dusk, and swimming is forbidden in the canals. I've spotted small crocodiles in the canals and have been assured they're removed to more suitable homes on Mayakobá's wild side. The **El Camaleón** golf course, designed by Greg Norman, is an Audubon-certified bird reserve—and a challenge for the pros competing in Mexico's only PGA tournament in late February/early March. You must have a reservation to get past the gates of this extremely private development. Consider booking a meal or spa treatment at one of the hotels to take a look around.

Fairmont Mayakobá ★★ ☺ Families, groups, and recluses are all happy with Mayakobá's first resort. Active types head for the beach, pool island, 24-hour gym, or golf course. Sybarites spend hours at the Willow Stream Spa. Dining choices range from a gourmet deli to lagoon-side breakfast buffets to two excellent formal restaurants. Rooms come in 13 categories, including a suite on its own island. All open out to gardens, lagoons, or the sea. Wooden shutter doors close off sleeping areas or can be open to nature. Befitting the eco setting, rooms have cans for recyclable materials and the spa uses soaps and lotions made at a local co-op.

Carretera Cancún–Tulum Km 298, 77710 Playa del Carmen, Q. Roo. www.fairmont.com/mayakoba. ✆ **800/435-2600** in the U.S. and Canada, or 984/206-3000. 401 units. High season $409–$659 casita, $809 and up signature casita; low season $219–$469 casita, $299 and up signature casita. AE, MC, V. Free guarded parking. **Amenities:** 3 restaurants; 3 bars; fitness center; 5 outdoor pools; spa; watersports. *In room:* A/C, fan, TV/CD, hair dryer, Internet, minibar.

Rosewood Mayakobá ★★★ Privacy is the hallmark of this pricey resort designed with sail-like roofs on open-air spaces taking full advantage of the natural setting. Classy two-story suites face mangrove-backed lagoons and have awe-inspiring sea views from rooftop pools and sundecks. Overwater decks and plunge pools are almost totally hidden, though motorized boats sometimes pass by when ferrying new guests around the property. Beachfront suites are a bit less secluded. Interiors have sliding shuttered doors connecting bedrooms, spacious closet areas, and outdoor showers and tubs buried in foliage. Private butlers and housekeepers anticipate your needs. Guests linger over breakfasts at Casa del Lago, tequila tastings and ceviches at the Agua Azul bar, and Mexican cuisine at Punta Bonita.

Carretera Cancún–Tulum Km 298, 77710 Playa del Carmen, Q. Roo. www.rosewoodmayakoba.com. ✆ **800/435-2600** in the U.S. and Canada, or 984/875-8000. 128 units. High season $790 and up lagoon-view suite, $1,350 and up oceanview suite; low season $590–$850 lagoon-view suite, $1,050 and up oceanview suite. AE, MC, V. Free guarded parking. **Amenities:** 3 restaurants; 3 bars; fitness center; 3 outdoor pools; spa; watersports. *In room:* A/C, fan, TV/CD/DVD, hair dryer, Internet, minibar, MP3 docking station.

PLAYA DEL CARMEN ★★★

32km (20 miles) S of Puerto Morelos; 70km (43 miles) S of Cancún; 10km (6¼ miles) N of Xcaret; 13km (8 miles) N of Puerto Calica

Young adventuresome travelers have long been attracted to the eclectic beach scene in Playa del Carmen. Though it's no longer an idyllic village, it remains a laid-back beach town at its core, with a variety of unique hotels, restaurants, and stores. Architecture incorporates elements of native building (rustic clapboard walls, thatched

Playa del Carmen

RESTAURANTS ◆
Casa Mediterránea **10**
El Oasis **2**
La Casa del Agua **13**
Las Mañanitas **11**
La Tarraya Restaurant/Bar **14**
Los Carboncitos **12**
Media Luna **4**
Super Carnes H C de Monterrey **15**

HOTELS ■
Deseo Hotel + Lounge **5**
El Taj Condo Hotel **3**
Hotel Lab Nah **9**
Hotel Lunata **6**
Jardín de Marieta **7**
La Tortuga **1**
Playa Maya **8**

Beach
Lighthouse
Post office
Pedestrians Only

roofs, rough-hewn wood), though cheap-looking commercial architecture and chain restaurants and shops have intruded. Playa retains the feel of a cosmopolitan getaway with a counterculture ethos and a distinctly European feel—many beachfront hotels are run by Europeans, topless sunbathing (illegal in Mexico) is nonchalantly tolerated, and tacos don't dominate the menus. Ages-old Maya culture and a colorful underwater world await beyond the resorts.

This bustling town is fronted with several beaches popular with families, scenesters, and fishermen alike. Bury your toes in white sand and sip an umbrella drink, stopping occasionally to frolic in Playa's turquoise water. You can dive or snorkel through the cenotes (underwater caves) at **Hidden World Cenotes,** spend an afternoon fishing or boating at the **Puerto Aventuras** marina, or arrange for a horseback ride on the beach through **Rancho Punta Venado.**

Playa makes a great base for exploring the Riviera Maya's central coast. Delve into Maya culture with a drive south to the limestone ruins of the ancient cities of **Tulum** and **Cobá.** A short ferry ride to the nearby island of **Cozumel** puts you in putting distance of the 18-hole Cozumel Country Club golf course—just watch out for the blue crabs and crocodiles that also make it their home. Take a day trip to nature park **Xel-Ha** and swim with dolphins.

527

Make the most of Playa's international mix and feast on Argentine steak one day and noodles the next. For a taste of old Playa, try Yucatecan *Tikinxic* fish with achiote and bitter-orange sauce cooked in a banana leaf, in a casual setting right on the beach. Maya cuisine gets an innovative twist in such dishes as cream of *chaya* soup with the local version of spinach and white wine.

Playa's **La Quinta** (Quinta Avenida) is the city's social magnet at night, with browse-worthy shops and plenty of bars and restaurants studding the pedestrian promenade. Sample the best of Mexico's national spirit—tequila, naturally—or call into **Blue Parrot,** a local institution known for its live rock acts and diverse crowd, with a beachside location for good measure. If you brought your dancing shoes, Playa's most popular dance clubs are clustered around the intersection of La Quinta and Calle 12.

Essentials

GETTING THERE & DEPARTING

BY PLANE   Fly into Cancún and take a bus directly from the airport (see "By Bus," below), or fly into Cozumel and take the passenger ferry.

BY CAR   Hwy. 307 is the only highway that passes through Playa. The highway divides as you approach from Cancún. The two main arteries into town are Avenida Constituyentes, which works well for destinations in northern Playa, and Avenida Juárez, which leads to the town's main square and ferry pier. Keep to the inside lanes that permit turning left at any of the traffic lights; otherwise you will have to continue past Playa until you get to the turnaround, then double back, staying to your right.

BY FERRY   Air-conditioned passenger ferries to Cozumel leave from the pier, 1 block from the main square. There is also a car ferry to Cozumel from the Calica pier just south of Playacar. The schedule changes with demand. You can usually count on hourly departures in the morning and late afternoon—just like rush hour on land. Ferries typically depart every 2 hours around midday. For more information about both ferries, see "Getting There & Departing" in the Cozumel section of chapter 14.

BY TAXI   Taxi fares from the Cancún airport are about 650 to 750 pesos one-way.

BY BUS   **Autobuses Riviera** offers service from the Cancún airport about 10 times a day between 8:10am and 8pm. Cost is about $7 one-way. Ticket counters are located outside customs at Terminals 2 and 3. At either terminal, you can also pay the driver, in either pesos or U.S. dollars. For a higher fee ($10 to Playa, $4 to Cancún) you can also reserve your seat online at www.cancun-airport.com/public-buses.htm or by calling © **800/317-1921** in the U.S. and Canada. A representative outside the terminal will escort you to the bus. From the downtown Cancún bus station, buses depart almost every 30 minutes and cost 40 pesos.

ORIENTATION

ARRIVING   Playa has two **bus** stations. Buses from Cancún and places along the coast, such as Tulum, arrive at the Riviera bus station at the corner of Juárez and Quinta Avenida, by the town square. Buses from interior destinations arrive at the ADO station on Avenida 20 between calles 12 and 14.

A word of caution: Most "information" stands along Quinta Avenida are associated with timeshare and vacation ownership properties. The salespeople are usually generous with information, hoping you'll agree to a sales tour. Some tourists are wise to this and willingly give up a morning in exchange for free car rental, tours, or other perks. If your time is tight, however, steer clear.

CITY LAYOUT The main street, **Avenida Juárez,** leads to the town square from Hwy. 307. On the way, it crosses several numbered avenues running parallel to the beach, all of which are multiples of five. The east-west streets parallel to Juárez are in multiples of two. A wonderful bike path along Avenida 10 provides fairly safe passage for *tricilcos* (bike taxis) and cyclists.

Quinta Avenida (Fifth Avenue), often simply "La Quinta," runs 1 to 2 blocks inland from the beach and is the most popular street in the Riviera Maya. It's closed to traffic from Avenida Juárez to Calle 12 (and some blocks beyond, in the evening). However, taxis and drivers are allowed to access hotels on side streets. Hotels, restaurants, shops, clubs, and chains like Starbucks and Dairy Queen line La Quinta and its side streets. **Avenida Constituyentes** delineates the newest part of rapidly growing Playa. Several excellent international restaurants and pricey condo developments are located here.

Playacar, a golf-course development with private residences and several resort hotels, is located just south of Avenida Juárez.

[Fast FACTS] PLAYA DEL CARMEN

Area Code The telephone area code is **984.**

ATMs & Banks Playa has several banks and ATMs.

Currency Exchange Many *casas de cambio* or currency-exchange houses are close to the pier or along Quinta Avenida at Calle 8.

Doctor For serious medical attention, go to **Hospiten** (© 984/803-1002), on Hwy. 307 at the second Playacar exit, just south of Sam's Club.

Drugstore The **Farmacía del Carmen,** Avenida Juárez between avenidas 5 and 10

(© **984/873-2330**), is open 24 hours.

Internet Access Internet cafes are all over town; most have fast connections. Most hotels have Wi-Fi, at least in public areas.

Parking Parking on the street in Playa is tough, as spots are hard to come by and police are quick to ticket violators. The Estacionamiento México, at avenidas Juárez and 10 (where the entrance is located) is open daily 24 hours and charges 20 pesos per hour, 120 pesos per day. There's also a 24-hour lot a few blocks from the pier on

Avenida 10 and Calle 3 Sur. Very few hotels have on-site parking, but some can get you reduced rates at nearby lots.

Post Office The *correo,* on Avenida Juárez, 3 blocks from the plaza, is on the right past the Hotel Playa del Carmen and the launderette.

Seasons The main high season is from mid-December to Easter. Mini high seasons are in August and around Thanksgiving. Low season is all other months, though many hotels further divide these into several micro seasons.

Exploring Playa del Carmen

Playa del Carmen is best enjoyed from a lounge chair on the sand or during an evening strolling **Quinta Avenida ★★**, paralleling the beach for 20 blocks north from the ferry pier. The area around the ferry terminal, predictably, is rife with trinket emporiums and chain eateries, but right around the plaza you'll find a small church with an ocean view and vendors selling sliced fruit and tasty tacos. Heading north, the avenue mellows into bistros, cool bars, sweet clothing shops, and sophisticated restaurants.

Playa's most active pursuits revolve around simply enjoying the good life. The hippest **sandy beaches** for swimming, sunning, and people-watching are north of Avenida Constituyentes; Central Playa's beach is more popular with local families and fishermen, and is home to several inexpensive hotels and restaurants. The best stretch of sand in this area, offering a breather from encroaching hotels, is Playa El Faro, between calles 8 and 10. The most beautiful beach, though—and unfortunately the most crowded—extends from Constituyentes north for 5 blocks to Las Mamitas and Kool beach clubs, between calles 28 and 30. Its gradually deepening waters and breaking waves farther out provide ample fodder for water play. The sublime sands farther north are increasingly being squeezed by condo developments.

Playa's offshore reef offers decent **diving,** though it doesn't compare to Cozumel (p. 499) or Puerto Morelos (p. 517). Its primary virtue, which has earned it scores of dive shops, is access to Cozumel and a chain of inland cenotes. Reef dives generally cost $45 to $50 for one tank and $70 to $75 for two; two-tank cenote trips are around $110 to $120. Prices for Cozumel trips vary more and are noted below. (Cozumel dives almost always require you to take the ferry on your own and board the dive boat on the island.) Dedicated divers should look for the discounted multidive deals and dive/hotel packages offered by many shops. **Buceo Cyan Ha** (✆ 984/803-2517; www.cyanha. com), one of the first shops in Playa and still one of the most respected, has a second site at the Petit Lafitte Hotel (p. 525). **Tank-Ha Dive Center** (✆ 984/873-0302; www.tankha.com) takes divers to Cozumel directly from Playa. **Yucatek Divers** (✆ 984/803-2836; www.yucatek-divers.com) specializes in cenote diving and in dives for people with disabilities. They also run snorkel trips to Isla Holbox north of Cancún from June to September, when whale sharks migrate just off the island's shores. The entire trip takes about 12 hours (including at least 3 hours travel each way) and costs $220. The **Abyss Dive Center** (✆ 984/873-2164; www.abyssdiveshop. com) has its own hotel. You won't go wrong with any of these.

The best **snorkeling** spots are not along Playa's shore but at Moché reef to the north and Inna reef to the south. Most dive shops offer guided snorkeling tours for $35 to $45, or $55 to $65 for cenote snorkeling. Before you book, ask whether gear is included, the size of your group, how long the trip will last, and how many reefs or cenotes you'll visit. Small boats docked up and down the beach also offer snorkeling tours for a little less than dive-shop prices, and they'll launch as soon as you show up.

Countless **watersports** outfitters line the beach and La Quinta, offering excursions inland to cenotes, ruins, and adventure parks. Banana boating, tubing, and jet-skiing are just a few of the (pricey) watersports you can enjoy in Playa's calm waters.

Playa makes a great base for excursions up and down the Riviera Maya. It's easy to shoot out to Cozumel on the ferry, drive south to the nature parks and the ruins at Tulum and Cobá, or drive north to Cancún. Directly south of town is the Playacar development, which has a golf course, several large all-inclusive resorts, and a residential development. My favorite outfitter for unusual trips is **Alltournative** (✆ 800/507-1092 in the U.S., or 984/803-9999; www.alltournative.com; p. 553), on La Quinta between calles 12 and 14.

Shopping

Playa is the Caribbean coast's retail heart, and meandering Quinta Avenida and its side streets to ferret out the latest boutiques and shops makes a fine late-afternoon diversion. Once you get past the ferry terminal area, low-key, locally owned shops vie for your vacation dollar with high-end clothing, Cuban cigars, specialty tequila, handicrafts, jewelry, and beach wear. Credit cards are widely accepted. Abundant folk art and boutiques are concentrated between calles 4 and 10; Calle Corazón, a leafy pedestrian area between calles 12 and 14, has art galleries, restaurants, and still more boutiques.

Some favorite shops along La Quinta, south to north: **De Beatriz Boutique,** Calle 2, west of Quinta Avenida (© **984/879-3272**), a little side-street shop selling locally designed *manta* (Mexican cotton) clothing; **Caracol,** between calles 6 and 8 (© **984/803-1504**), with tasteful and unique textiles, crafts, and clothing from throughout Mexico; **La Calaca,** between calles 12 and 14 (© **984/873-0174**), for its wondrous variety of wooden masks, quirky carvings of angels, devils, and skeletons, and *alebrijes* (the famous Oaxacan carved, whimsically painted animals); **Rosalia,** between calles 12 and 14 (© **984/803-4904**), for fabulous textiles from Chiapas, including embroidered *huipiles* and inexpensive shawls, scarves, and bags; **Casa Tequila,** at Calle 16 (© **984/873-0195**), for its impressive selection of fine silver jewelry as well as 100 types of specialty tequila (you sample before you buy); and **Ah Cacao,** at Constituyentes (© **984/803-5748**; www.ahcacao.com), for its intense and rare *criollo* chocolate, the Maya's "food of the gods," in bars, cocoa, or roasted beans—the cafe's fudgy mochas, frappes, and chocolate shots will ruin you for Starbucks.

North of Constituyentes, artists display their works along Quinta Avenida, wine bars abound, and shops offer high-quality clothing, folk art, and shoes. This section is often used for art shows and festivals. **La Sirena,** at Calle 26 (© **984/803-3422**), offers trendy folk art with *calaca* (skull), *lucha libre,* and Frida Kahlo themes.

Paseo del Carmen, at the south end of Quinta Avenida, has acquired a collection of interesting shops, galleries, and restaurants. **InArt** (© **984/803-3968**; www.inartmexico.com), a jewelry gallery that also sells gorgeous, unique silver pieces embedded with Mexican semiprecious gems and stones, is worth the trip in itself.

Where to Stay

Playa's many affordable small hotels give you a better feel for the town than staying in one of the resorts in Playacar. Don't hesitate to book a place that's not on the beach. Town life here is much of the fun, and staying on the beach has its disadvantages—in particular, noise from a couple of beach bars. Beaches are public property in Mexico, and you can lay out your towel anywhere you like. At some beach clubs in north Playa, for a small sum or the price of a meal, you have use of lounge chairs and towels.

When tourism is slow you can score some great walk-in offers. Promotional rates and packages pop up online as well. Reservations are essential around holidays, however. Rates listed below include the 12% hotel tax, but not the rates around Christmas and New Year's, which soar well beyond the standard high-season rates.

EXPENSIVE

Deseo Hotel + Lounge ★★　The lounge serves as lobby, restaurant, bar, and pool area all at once. It's a raised open-air platform with bar, pool, self-serve kitchen, and daybeds for sunning or sipping an evening drink when the action is in full swing. It's filled with a hip Mexico City clientele during national holidays and is popular with the 20 to 50 set. Guest rooms are comfortable, original, and striking, but they don't tempt one to stay indoors—no TV, no cushy armchair. Their simplicity gives them an almost Asian feel, heightened by nice touches such as sliding wood-and-frosted-glass doors. The bottom of each bed has a little drawer that slides out with a night kit containing incense, earplugs, and condoms.

The owners also operate the cleverly styled **Hotel Básico** (www.hotelbasico.com; ✆ **984/879-4448**). It's a fun mix of industrial and '50s styles, built with concrete, plywood, and plastics. As with Deseo, the common areas are not wasted space.

Av. 5 (at Calle 12), 77710 Playa del Carmen, Q. Roo. www.hoteldeseo.com. ✆ **984/879-3620.** Fax 984/879-3621. 15 units. $199–$233 lounge view double; $222–$255 balcony double; $278–$311 suite. Rates include continental breakfast. AE, MC, V. No parking. No children 17 and under. **Amenities:** Bar; Jacuzzi; small rooftop pool; room service. *In room:* A/C, hair dryer (on request), minibar.

El Taj Condo Hotel ★   Condos and vacation villas are popular with regulars staying a week or more. This lovely Bali-inspired complex on a semiprivate beach has a wide range of accommodations, from penthouses with ocean views to one-bedroom units with kitchenettes. The 63 condos are housed in two complexes, one across the street from the beach. Varying amenities include private hot tubs, full gourmet kitchens, and outdoor terraces with grills. Pools flow amid lush plants at both properties, and there's an excellent beach club restaurant called Indigo and a full gym and spa nearby. The same company manages several adjacent condo hotels, giving guests a wide range of choices. Rates are determined by number of bedrooms, type of amenities, and views, and are lower when booked by the week.

Av. 1 Norte (btw. calles 12 and 14), 77710 Playa del Carmen, Q. Roo. www.condohotelsplayadelcarmen. com. ✆ **866/479-2738** in the U.S. and Canada, or 984/879-3919. 63 units. High season $305–$825; low season $255–$685. AE, MC, V. Free parking. **Amenities:** Restaurant; bar; gym; 2 outdoor pools; spa. *In room:* A/C, fan, TV/CD/DVD, hair dryer, kitchen or kitchenette, Wi-Fi.

MODERATE

Hotel Lunata ★★ 🗝   In the middle of Playa, there isn't a more comfortable or more attractive place to stay than this small hotel on Quinta Avenida. Rooms offer character and polished good looks. The few standard rooms are midsize and come with a queen-size or a double bed. Large deluxe rooms come with a king-size bed and small fridge; junior suites come with two doubles. The well-designed bathrooms have good showers. Rooms facing the street have double-glazed glass doors opening to a balcony. When they're shut, the street noise is not bothersome, but light sleepers should ask for a room facing the garden.

Av. 5 (btw. calles 6 and 8), 77710 Playa del Carmen, Q. Roo. www.lunata.com. ✆ **984/873-0884.** Fax 984/873-1240. 10 units. High season $129 double, $159–$179 deluxe and junior suite; low season $110 double, $125–$145 deluxe and junior suite. Rates include continental breakfast. AE, MC, V. Secure parking $5. No children 10 and under. **Amenities:** Bikes; watersports. *In room:* A/C, fan, TV, fridge (in some), hair dryer (on request), Wi-Fi (in some).

La Tortuga ★★★   You'll have a hard time staying anywhere else when you can get amiable service, a variety of rooms, and all the amenities you need at these digs. The word's out and travelers fill the rooms—though there's usually a good choice for returning guests. Some rooms edge the sinuous pool; others have tiny balconies overlooking rooftops. Suites have whirlpool tubs, balconies, and extras like irons and robes. All rooms have coffee machines and alarm clocks. The cozy living-room space by the pool has a bar, a book exchange, and comfy couches, and its El Bistro restaurant is very good. Guests have a private entrance to the Zen Eco Spa next door.

Av. 10 (at Calle 14), 77710 Playa del Carmen, Q. Roo. www.hotellatortuga.com. ✆ **984/873-1484.** 51 units. $160–$269 double; $266–$306 suite. Rates include reduced-rate parking at an indoor lot, breakfast, and beach passes. MC, V. **Amenities:** Restaurant; bar; outdoor pool; Wi-Fi. *In room:* AC, fan, TV, Jacuzzi (in suite), minibar, MP3 docking station (in suite).

Playa Maya ★ 🖤 There are plenty of reasons to choose this over other beach hotels in downtown Playa—good location, good price, comfortable rooms, and friendly, helpful management, to name a few. But what really sets it apart is that you enter the hotel from the beach. This seemingly inconsequential detail sets the mood and creates a little separation from the busy street. What's more, the design blocks out noise from nearby bars and neighboring hotels. Rooms are large, with midsize bathrooms. A couple units have private garden terraces with Jacuzzis; others have balconies facing the beach. High-season rates here extend from Christmas through August, and minimum stays are required.

Zona FMT (btw. calles 6 and 8 Norte), 77710 Playa del Carmen, Q. Roo. www.playa-maya.com. ✆ **984/803-2022.** 20 units. High season $150–$200 double; low season $100–$180 double. Rates include continental breakfast. MC, V. Limited street parking. **Amenities:** Restaurant; bar; Jacuzzi; outdoor pool; room service. *In room:* A/C, TV, fridge, hair dryer, Wi-Fi.

INEXPENSIVE

Hotel Lab Nah 🖤 Good rooms in a central location for a good price are the main attraction at this economy hotel in the heart of Playa. Windows in the cheapest rooms face Quinta Avenida, allowing in some noise—mostly of late-night bar hoppers. It's not a big problem, but it's worth the money to get one of the partial-oceanview standards with balcony on the third floor, which are quieter and larger. Garden-view rooms directly below the ocean-views are just as large and quiet, but not quite as fixed up. The largest unit, a rooftop *palapa*, is good for three or four people.

Calle 6 (and Av. 5), 77710 Playa del Carmen, Q. Roo. www.labnah.com. ✆ **984/873-2099.** 33 units. High season $57–$79 double, $102–$110 rooftop *palapa;* low season $50–$69 double, $85–$93 rooftop *palapa.* Rates include continental breakfast. MC, V. Limited street parking. **Amenities:** Small outdoor pool. *In room:* A/C, hair dryers (in some), no phone.

Jardín de Marieta 👭 Besides the reasonable rates, this pleasant, quirky place is appealing for its central, yet half-hidden location in a small, quiet interior property with no street frontage on La Quinta. Rooms vary a good bit, but most are large, bright, and cheerful. Four rooms have kitchenettes adequate for simple meals. Most rooms encircle a tree-shaded patio with a few shops and a restaurant.

Av. 5 Norte 173 (btw. calles 6 and 8), 77710 Playa del Carmen, Q. Roo. www.jardindemarieta.com. ✆ **984/873-0224.** 10 units. High season $60–$100 double; low season $40–$80 double. No credit cards. Limited street parking. **Amenities:** Restaurant. *In room:* A/C, TV, fridge, kitchenette (in some), no phone, Wi-Fi.

Where to Eat

For a delicious Veracruz-style breakfast in pleasant, breezy surroundings, try the upstairs terrace restaurant of the **Hotel Básico,** at Quinta Avenida and Calle 10 Norte. For fish tacos and inexpensive seafood, try **El Oasis,** on Calle 12, between avenidas 5 and 10 (no phone). For *arrachera* (fajita) tacos, the place to go is **Super Carnes H C de Monterrey** (✆ **984/803-0488**), on Calle 1 Sur between avenidas 20 and 25.

EXPENSIVE

La Casa del Agua ★★ EUROPEAN/MEXICAN Excellent food in inviting surroundings. Instead of obtrusive background music, you hear the sound of falling water. The German owners do a good job with seafood—try the grilled seafood for two. For a mild dish, try chicken in a scented sauce of fine herbs accompanied by fettuccine; for something heartier, there's a tortilla soup listed as "Mexican soup." A number of cool and light dishes are appetizing for lunch or an afternoon meal, such as avocado stuffed with shrimp and flavored with a subtle horseradish sauce on a bed of alfalfa sprouts and julienne carrots—a good mix of tastes and textures. For dessert, try the chocolate mousse. This is an upstairs restaurant under a large and airy *palapa* roof.

Av. 5 (at Calle 2). ✆ **984/803-0232.** Reservations recommended in high season. Main courses 165–280 pesos. MC, V. Daily 10am–midnight.

Yaxché ★★★ YUCATECAN   The menu at this Playa standout employs native foods and spices to present elaborate regional cooking unlike the usual offerings at Yucatecan restaurants. The sleek decor at this two-story location enhances the artsy section of La Quinta, while the food retains its ancient origins. Excellent examples are a cream of *chaya* (a native leafy vegetable similar to spinach) and an *xcatic* chile stuffed with *cochinita pibil*. The classic Mexican-style fruit salad with lime juice and dried powdered chile is another favorite. Seafood dishes are fresh and well prepared.

Av. 5 (at Calle 22). ✆ **984/873-3011.** Reservations recommended in high season. Main courses 134–279 pesos. AE, MC, V. Daily noon–midnight.

MODERATE

Casa Mediterránea ★ ITALIAN   Tucked away on a quiet little patio off Quinta Avenida, this small, homey restaurant serves excellent Italian cuisine. Maurizio Gabrielli and Maria Michelon routinely greet customers and make recommendations. Maurizio came to Mexico to enjoy the simple life, and it shows in the restaurant's welcoming, unhurried atmosphere. The menu is mostly northern Italian, with several dishes from other parts of Italy. The lobster is prepared beautifully. There are daily specials, too. Pastas (except penne and spaghetti) are made in-house, and none are precooked. Try fish and shrimp ravioli or *penne alla Veneta*. There are several wines, mostly Italian, to choose from.

Av. 5 (btw. calles 6 and 8; look for the Hotel Marieta sign). ✆ **984/876-3926.** Reservations recommended in high season. Main courses 120–220 pesos. No credit cards. Wed–Mon 2–11pm.

La Cueva del Chango ★★ HEALTH FOOD/MEXICAN   Good food in original surroundings with a relaxed attitude makes this quirky place enduringly popular (expect a wait on weekend mornings). True to its name (The Monkey's Cave), the place is cavelike and has wicker and fabric monkeys hanging about. You'll enjoy great juices, blended fruit drinks, salads, soups, Mexican specialties with a natural twist, and handmade tortillas. The fresh fish is delicious, and the warm *panella* cheese with tortillas is divine. Mosquitoes can sometimes be a problem at night, but the management has bug spray on hand.

Calle 38 (btw. Av. 5 and the beach). ✆ **984/147-0271.** Main courses 80–140 pesos. No credit cards. Mon–Sat 8am–11pm; Sun 8am–2pm.

Media Luna ★★ FUSION   The inventive menu here favors grilled seafood, sautés, and pasta dishes. Everything is fresh and prepared beautifully. Try the tasty pan-fried fish cakes with mango and honeyed hoisin sauce, or the black pepper–crusted fish. And keep an eye on the daily specials. For lunch, you can get sandwiches and salads, as well as black-bean quesadillas and crepes.

Av. 5 (btw. calles 12 and 14). ✆ **984/873-0526.** Breakfast 40–60 pesos; sandwich with salad 50–70 pesos; main courses 80–150 pesos. No credit cards. Daily 8am–11:30pm.

CHOOSING AN all-inclusive IN THE RIVIERA MAYA

All-inclusive resort rooms far outnumber those in regular hotels in the Riviera Maya. And the trend continues to dominate new construction, along with vacation-ownership developments. Most folks are familiar with the AI (short for all-inclusive) concept—large hotels that work with economies of scale to offer lodging, food, and drink all for a single rate. Some AIs offer convenience and low rates good for families with many mouths to feed. Because they are enclosed areas, they make it easy for parents to watch their children. The system works well for multiple-generation family reunions and group meetings, and seasonal deals offer amazingly cheap getaways.

All-inclusive resorts aren't for everyone; think of it as a cruise vacation on land. Colored bracelets designate various AI plans, which usually include all buffet meals, drinks of varying quality, specialty restaurants (some with an additional charge), elaborate pool areas with activities, evening entertainment, and so on. Some charge extra for use of golf courses, spas, and fitness centers. If you decide all-inclusive is the way to go, choose a resort whose amenities suit your desires. This type of all-inclusive is best booked through a vacation packager or travel agent. Their air and AI packages usually beat anything you can get by booking your own flight and room, even if you have frequent-flier miles to burn. In a recent comparison of package prices with the cost of separate direct air and hotel bookings, for example, a couple could save an average of more than $100 a night through BookIt. com, which offers a particularly good range of all-inclusive resorts among its deals.

I came to understand and appreciate this type of vacation while staying at the **Iberostar** (www.iberostar.com) complex on Paraíso Beach north of Playa del Carmen. The enormous compound includes five hotels in all price ranges, a golf course, shopping center, nightclubs, spacious beach, and terrific spa. A tram travels between the resorts. (Guests at the higher-end hotels can use the amenities at all hotels.) Despite the size, I never felt overwhelmed.

With several resorts of varying quality and style, **Karisma Hotels + Resorts** (www.karismahotels.com) merits attention. Their Azul resorts have a partnership with Fisher-Price and their Kid's Clubs are amazing. Their adults-only Dorado resorts pamper grownups with spas and gourmet restaurants. Some have Gourmet Inclusive plans offering all the amenities you expect in upscale resorts, all included in the rate.

Another all-inclusive concept offers beyond-luxurious resorts with fabulous suites, spas, pools, and beaches along with exceptional gourmet dining. Daily rates can soar beyond $1,000 per person per day. But more and more resort companies are moving in this direction, and big spenders have outstanding options. The **Grand Velas Riviera Maya** (p. 524) excels in this category. The pricey **Royal Hideaway Playacar** (www. royalhideaway.com) is acclaimed as an idyllic wedding and honeymoon setting. The exclusive resorts sometimes have some odd rules, though. For example, specialty restaurants at one resort require men to wear closed-toe dress shoes—even dressy leather sandals are verboten. Be sure you know such things before you go.

INEXPENSIVE

Las Mañanitas 🌶 MEXICAN   The set-price breakfast is a steal here—around $8 for eggs scrambled with tomatoes, chiles, and onions, with toast, coffee, and OJ. Tables fill with hotel and shop workers in early morning. Travelers wander in around 9am and continue claiming tables under the piñatas through lunch. In the evening, diners observe the action from sidewalk tables as they feast on fresh fish, a bountiful grilled meat platter for two, pasta, and meats. The vibe is low-key and the waiters friendly.

Av. 5 (btw. calles 4 and 6). ✆ **984/873-0114.** Main courses 89–189 pesos. MC, V. Daily 7am–midnight.

La Tarraya Restaurant/Bar 🌶 SEAFOOD/YUCATECAN   THE RESTAURANT THAT WAS BORN WITH THE TOWN, proclaims the sign. The wood hut doesn't look like much, but there are tables right on the beach, and the owners are fishermen. The catch of the day is so fresh it's practically wiggling. If you haven't tried the Yucatecan specialty *Tikinxic*—fish with achiote and bitter-orange sauce, cooked in a banana leaf—this is a good place to start.

Calle 2 Norte. ✆ **984/873-2040.** Main courses 50–100 pesos; whole fish 100 pesos per kilo (2.2 lb.). No credit cards. Daily noon–9pm.

Los Carboncitos ★ MEXICAN   Among the top choices at this simple sidewalk hangout are the tacos, with *arrachera* (beef) or *al pastor* (pork) served with a great salsa selection. I also recommend the chicken soup (*caldo xochitl*) and the traditional pozole. For seafood, try the shrimp al chipotle or the shrimp kabobs. Sides include fried crispy cheese (*chicharrón de queso*) and guacamole, and the beer is always icy cold.

Calle 4 (btw. avs. 5 and 10). ✆ **984/873-1382.** Main courses 80–138 pesos; order of tacos 74–89 pesos. No credit cards. Daily 9am–1am.

Playa del Carmen After Dark

It seems as if everyone in town is out strolling La Quinta until midnight; there's pleasant browsing, dining, and drinking available at any number of establishments. Wild and crazy **CoCo Bongo** (✆ **984/803-5939**) presents a must-see show with flying acrobats, strutting rock star impersonators, and an array of dancers, followed by long nights of impassioned dancing among the guests. It's at Avenida 10 and Calle 12. On the beach, the **Blue Parrot** (✆ **984/873-0083**) at Calle 12 attracts a mixed crowd with its live rock acts and nightly fire show on the beach. Just to the south is **Om** (no phone), which gets a younger crowd with louder musical acts.

Alux (✆ **984/110-5050**) is a club occupying a cave with two dramatically lit chambers and several sitting areas. The local conservancy group approved all the work. The club books music acts and usually charges no cover. The bar is cash only and is open Tuesday to Sunday from 7pm to 2am. Take Avenida Juárez across to the other side of the highway—2 blocks down on your left.

Though they technically close around sunset, several beach clubs north of Avenida Constituyentes (at the foot of calles 30 to 36) book live acts occasionally.

SOUTH OF PLAYA DEL CARMEN

A succession of small communities, resorts, and nature parks flank a 56km (35-mile) stretch of highway leading south from Playa del Carmen. This section covers them from north to south. Renting a car is the best way to move around here. The best buses might do is get you close to your destination; from the highway, it can be a hot walk to the coast. Another option is to hire a car and driver.

Beyond Paamul, you'll see signs for this or that cenote or cave. The Yucatán has thousands of cenotes, and each is slightly different (p. 538). These turnoffs are less visited than the major attractions and can make for a pleasant visit.

Punta Venado: Horseback Riding

A few places along the highway offer horseback rides. The best of these, **Rancho Punta Venado,** is just south of Playa, past the Calica Pier. This ranch is the least touristy—though it does cater to groups—and the owners take good care of the horses. It has a nice stretch of coast with a sheltered bay and offers horseback riding ($60 for 75 min. or $79 for a package including snorkeling), ATV expeditions to caves and cenotes ($55 for one person, $90 for two), and other activities. Transportation from Cancún, Playa del Carmen, and Tulum is available for an extra fee. Use of the beach club is included in tour prices, or you can use the facilities for $20. Make arrangements in advance so that they can schedule you on a day when they have fewer customers. The turnoff for the ranch is 2km (1¼ miles) south of the Calica overpass near Km 279. For more info call ℭ **984/803-5224** or go to www.puntavenado.com.

Río Secreto: Wondrous Cavern

More spiritual than commercial, this community-based ecopark teaches visitors about Maya beliefs regarding the "underworld" as they explore a 600m-long (1,969-ft.) cavern hidden from view for centuries. As the story goes, a local *campesino* was chasing a meaty lizard into the brush and under a rock pile. The *campesino* followed, digging through rocks, until he heard a splash. The lizard, it seemed, had discovered a hiding place. Digging a bit farther, the man found the entrance to a cave filled with stalactites and stalagmites. Local naturalists discovered a dazzling series of chambers with rock formations dating back 2.5 million years. The area was declared a nature reserve and opened to the public in April 2008.

Avoiding the Cruise-Ship Crowds

Fewer ships arrive on weekends than on weekdays, which makes the weekend a good time for visiting the coast's major attractions.

Visitors must be accompanied by guides and wear short wetsuits and helmets as they walk and swim through the cavern. At times, it is so dark you feel like you're totally blind. Other times, sunshine streams through holes in the roof, illuminating the blue and pink striations caused by mineral-rich water dripping over earth-toned stone. An occasional swim through an emerald green pool adds to the fun, as does the guide's banter and knowledge. From donning your wetsuit to downing a filling lunch after the 90-minute underground tour, it will take about 3½ hours. Hot showers and lockers are available. The basic tour without transportation costs $59. Call ahead for reservations. Río Secreto is located off Hwy. 307, 5 minutes south of Playa del Carmen (between Xcaret and the Calica Port). For more info, call ℭ **877/357-4242** in the U.S., or 984/877-2377, or go to www.riosecretotours.com.

Xcaret: Tribute to the Yucatán

A billboard in distant Guadalajara's airport reads in Spanish, "And when visiting Xcaret, don't forget to enjoy the pleasures of the Riviera Maya, too." An exaggeration, yes, but a point well taken: Xcaret (Eesh-ca-*ret*) is the biggest attraction in these parts

The Yucatán Peninsula's land surface is a thin limestone shelf jutting out like a footprint between the Gulf of Mexico and the Caribbean Sea. Rainwater seeps through the surface into cenotes, freshwater sinkholes that dot the underground world. Some cenotes are like small wells. Others are like giant green ponds with high rock walls—tempting sights to would-be Tarzans. Cenotes often provide access to magical caves where sunlight from holes in the land's surface glimmers on icicle-like stalactites and stalagmites. The Riviera Maya is filled with these formations, and it seems every farmer and landowner has posted a sign offering access to their pools and caverns for a few pesos. Some are actually blasting the ground in search of cenotes, unfortunately. More elaborate parks include underground rivers and cenotes among their many attractions. Several, including Xcaret, Hidden Worlds, Río Secreto, and Aktun Chen, are described in this chapter. Dozens of smaller cenotes and caves deserve your attention as well, and entry costs much less than at the big parks. Adventuresome types should seek out newly opened sites marked with rustic wooden signs. Below are a few cenotes accessible from Hwy. 307. Most have bathrooms, are open daily from about 8 or 9am until 5 or 6pm, and charge about 30 to 50 pesos.

Cenote Azul (approximately 2km/1¼ miles south of Puerto Aventuras, just south of Ecopark Kantun Chi): Situated close to the highway with several large pools, Cenote Azul has a fun jump-off point on a section of overhanging rock, and a wooden lounging deck jutting over the water. Walkways along the edge make it easier to get in and swim with the abundant catfish.

Gran Cenote (about 3km/1¼ miles west of Tulum on the road to Cobá): Divers are especially fond of this aptly named bottomless, crystal-clear cenote leading to caverns that seem to have no end. Snorkelers can follow the dive lights into caves close to the surface and see fantastic rock formations. Since it's off the main highway, this fabulous cenote is less popular with groups and feels like it's buried in jungle.

Jardín del Edén (1.6km/1 mile north of Xpu-Há, just south of Cenote Azul):

and even has its own resort. Thousands visit every week; stay away if you like solitude. Xcaret samples everything the Yucatán—and the rest of Mexico—has to offer, and action junkies take full advantage of the pricey admission fee.

The activities include scuba and snorkeling; cavern diving; hiking through tropical forest; horseback riding; an underwater river ride; swinging in a hammock under palms; and meeting native Maya people. Exhibits include a bat cave; a butterfly pavilion; mushroom and orchid nurseries; and a petting aquarium. Native jaguars, manatees, sea turtles, monkeys, macaws, and flamingos are also on display. The best folk art museum in Mexico is housed in the Hacienda Henequenera, a traditional Yucatecan hacienda with rooms decorated as if a family lived there. The Cava, an amazing underground wine cellar, displays bottles from Mexico's many excellent wineries and offers wine tastings with advance reservations; the dining rooms look like somewhere major global negotiations would take place. The Hacienda and Cava both offer guided tours; book them when purchasing your entrance tickets. The evening show celebrates Mexico in music and dance, and the costumes and choreography are unequaled anywhere in Mexico.

"El Edén" is one of my favorite cenotes because it's run by an accommodating family and has lots of rocky outcroppings where you can lounge in the warm sun after the freezing water leaves you covered in goose bumps. There's plenty of room along the edges of the cenote, which looks like a huge swimming pool. Shrieks fill the air as daredevils attempt swan dives from a high jump-off point. Snorkelers and divers find plenty of tropical fish and eels.

Manatí (Tankhah, east of the highway 10km/6¼ miles north of Tulum): The large, open lagoon near Casa Cenote restaurant is part of a long underwater cave system that ends at the sea. Fresh water bubbling up into ocean waters creates significant but not dangerous currents that attract a great variety of saltwater and freshwater fish. The cenote was named for the manatees that used to show up occasionally; the shy creatures have disappeared as the region has gained popularity.

Xunaan ha (outside of Chemuyil, 12km/7½ miles south of Akumal): Gaining popularity because of its sense of authenticity, this one is reached by winding through a Maya village and growing town that is home to locals who work in and around Akumal. Signs point to the small cenote nearly hidden in the jungle, where you can swim, float, or snorkel with schools of fish and the occasional freshwater turtle. Be prepared: no bathrooms here.

Most dive shops along the Riviera Maya offer cenote and reef diving and snorkeling. Recommended outfitters that specialize in cenotes include **Yukatek Divers** (✆ 984/803-2836; www.yucatek-divers.com) and **Go Cenotes** (✆ 984/803-3924; www.gocenotes.com), both in Playa del Carmen, and **Cenote Dive Center** (✆ 984/871-2232; www.cenotedive.com) and **Xibalba Dive Center** (✆ 984/871-2953; www.xibalbadivecenter.com) in Tulum. Rates start at $55 for a snorkel tour and $120 for two-tank cavern dives, which take place in open cenotes where you are always within reach of air and natural light; cave diving requires advanced technical training and specialized gear, and is more expensive.

15

THE RIVIERA MAYA & THE COAST

South of Playa del Carmen

Xcaret is 10km (6¼ miles) south of Playa del Carmen; you'll know when you get to the turnoff. It's open daily from 8:30am to 9pm. Basic admission prices are $69 for adults, $35 for children 5 to 12; many activities and facilities cost extra. The Xcaret at Night rate is a good deal at $49 for adults and $25 for children. You enter the park after 3pm and have plenty of time to play and explore before the night show. All-inclusive tickets start at around $100. Xcaret is now offering deluxe tours to Chichén Itzá and Valladolid. The tour has drawn rave reviews and costs about $100 adult, $50 children. Discounted rates for all Xcaret tickets are available online. For more info, call ✆ 998/883-0470 or visit www.xcaret.net.

The people who created Xcaret have another park called **Xplor** (✆ 998/849-5275; www.xplor.travel) next door. The adventure park has a zip line, four-wheel-drive track, and an underground river ride. Admission is $99 for adults, $49 for children (8 or over); you get a 10% discount for booking online 3 days in advance.

Four kilometers (2½ miles) south of the entrance to Xcaret is the turnoff for **Puerto Calica,** the cruise-ship pier. Passengers disembark here for tours of Playa, Xcaret, the ruins, and other attractions on the coast.

Paamul: Seaside Getaway ★

About 15km (9⅓ miles) beyond Xcaret and 25km (16 miles) from Playa del Carmen is Paamul (also written Pamul), which in Mayan means "a destroyed ruin." The exit is clearly marked. You can enjoy the Caribbean in relative quiet here. The water at the out-of-the-way beach is wonderful, but the shoreline is rocky.

Scuba-Mex (© 888/871-6255 in the U.S., or 984/875-1066; www.scubamex. com) is a fully equipped PADI- and SSI-certified dive shop next to the cabañas. Using two boats, the staff takes guests on dives 8km (5 miles) in either direction. If it's too choppy, the reefs in front of the hotel are also good. The cost for a one-tank dive with rental gear is $39. They also have multidive packages and certification instruction and offer accommodations in four bedrooms in a beach house for $80 per night.

Cabañas Paamul ★   Paamul works mostly with the trailer crowd, but there are also 12 modern "junior suites" near the water's edge. They are spacious and comfortable, and come with a kitchenette and two queen beds. Trailer guests have access to 12 showers and separate bathrooms for men and women. Laundry service is available nearby. The *palapa* restaurant is open to the public, and customers are welcome to use the beach, which is rocky on this stretch of the coast. Prices vary according to season.

Carretera Cancún–Tulum Km 85. www.paamul.com. © **984/875-1053** or 612/353-6825. 13 units; 200 trailer spaces (all with full hookups). $100–$150 junior suite. RV space with hookups $30 per day, $600 per month. Ask about discounts for stays longer than 1 week. No credit cards. Free parking. **Amenities:** Restaurant; bar; dive shop; outdoor pool. *In room:* A/C, TV, kitchenette.

Puerto Aventuras: Dolphins & Shipwrecks

Five kilometers (3 miles) south of Paamul and 104km (65 miles) from Cancún, Puerto Aventuras is a condo/marina development with a 9-hole golf course on Chakalal Bay. At its center is a collection of restaurants bordering a dolphin pool that offer Mexican and Italian food, steaks, and pub grub. The major attraction is swimming with the dolphins in a highly interactive program; make reservations well in advance with **Dolphin Discovery** (© 998/849-4757; www.dolphindiscovery.com). The surest way is through the website.

Puerto Aventuras has the region's only maritime museum, **Museo Sub-Acuatico CEDAM ★** (© 984/873-5000; www.puertoaventuras.com/services.html). This is a compelling display of coins, weapons, gold dentures, clay dishes, and other items from colonial-era shipwrecks. All were recovered by members of the "Explorations and Water Sports Club of Mexico" (CEDAM), a group of former World War II frogmen. Most of the artifacts came from a Cuban ship that foundered near Akumal in 1741. Other displays include Maya offerings dredged from the peninsula's cenotes, finds from local archaeological sites, vintage diving equipment, and early photos of cenote explorations. The museum is on the second floor of a pink building near the entrance.

Puerto Aventuras is also popular for boating and deep-sea fishing. **Capt. Rick's Sportfishing Center** (© 888/449-3562 in the U.S., or 984/873-5195; www.fish yucatan.com) will combine a fishing trip with some snorkeling, which makes for a leisurely day. The best fishing on this coast is from March to August.

Puerto Aventuras has a few hotels, but most residential development is condos and homes. The most prominent hotel, the **Omni Puerto Aventuras** (© 888/444-6665 in the U.S., or 984/875-1958), is nice but pricey, starting around $200 per night.

Xpu-Ha: Sublime Beach

Three kilometers (1¾ miles) beyond Puerto Aventuras is **Xpu-Ha** (eesh-poo-hah) ★★★, a wide bay lined by a broad, beautiful sandy beach. Much of the shore is filled with private houses and condos, along with a few all-inclusive resorts. The beach is one of the best on the coast and is long enough to accommodate hotel guests, residents, and day-trippers without feeling crowded.

Al Cielo ★ This is a good choice if you want a small hotel on the beach where you can go native. The four rooms (two upstairs, two down) occupy a large thatched building right on the beach. The restaurant is popular, but the rooms are rustic and simple. If you're looking for more amenities, this won't be for you.

Carretera Cancún-Tulum Km 118, 77710 Xpu-Ha, Q. Roo. www.alcielohotel.com. © **984/840-9012.** 4 units. $212–$258 double. Rates include full breakfast. MC, V. Free secure parking. No children. **Amenities:** Restaurant; bar; Hobie cat; room service. *In room:* Fan, hair dryer, no phone, Wi-Fi.

Esencia ★★★ No other property on this coast epitomizes leisure and escape more than Esencia. The hotel includes a few rooms in a villa and guesthouse built as a private getaway for an Italian duchess. Families spread out in the two-story cottages surrounded by lush plants and gardens. Every room throughout the property has lots of space, lots of beauty, lots of privacy, and an air of serenity (decorations are tastefully minimalist, like three oranges on a driftwood tray). Of course, the magnificent beach includes private day beds under A-framed thatch shades. Service is personal and understated (a service fee is added to the room rate) and the food is outstanding. If the spa were any more relaxing, it would be an out-of-body experience.

Predio Rústico Xpu-Ha, Fracc. 16 y 18, L. 18, 19 (exit Xpu-Ha-2), 77710 Xpu-Ha, Q. Roo. www.hotelesencia. com. © **877/528-3490** in the U.S. and Canada, or 984/873-4830. 29 units. High season $569 and up double or suite; low season $479 and up double or suite. Rates include full breakfast. Internet specials sometimes available. AE, MC, V. Free valet parking. **Amenities:** Restaurant; 2 bars; babysitting; concierge; Jacuzzi; 2 outdoor pools; room service; spa. *In room:* A/C, TV/DVD, hair dryer, Internet, minibar.

Akumal: Beautiful Bays & Cavern Diving

Continuing south on Hwy. 307 for 2km (1¼ miles), the turnoff for Akumal ("Place of the Turtles") is marked by a traffic light. The ecologically oriented tourism community is spread among four bays, with two entrances off the frontage road parallel to the highway. The main entrance, labeled Akumal, leads to hotels, rental condos, and vacation homes. Take the Akumal Aventuras entrance to the Grand Oasis all-inclusive hotel and more condos and homes. No waterside road connects the two, so you'll need to know which exit to take. A white arch delineates the main entrance to the tourism community (years ago, the original residents were moved across the highway to a fast-growing town where many workers and business owners reside). Just before the arch are a couple of grocery stores and a laundry service. Just inside the arch, to the right, is the **Hotel Akumal Caribe.** If you follow the road to the left and keep to the left, you'll reach Half Moon Bay, lined with two- and three-story condos, and eventually

---

In Case of Emergency

The Riviera Maya, south of Puerto Aventuras, is susceptible to power failures that can last for hours. Gas pumps and cash machines shut down when this happens, and once the power returns, they attract long lines. It's a good idea to keep a reserve of gas and cash.

Yal-ku Lagoon, a snorkeling park. To rent a local condo, contact **Akumal Vacations** (www.akumalvacations.com; © **800/448-7137** in the U.S.) or **Loco Gringo** (www.locogringo.com).

Both bays have sandy beaches with rocky or silt bottoms. This is a popular diving area and home to Mexico's original diving club. Three dive shops are in town and at least 30 dive sites are offshore. The **Akumal Dive Shop** (© **984/875-9032;** www.akumal.com), one of the oldest and best dive shops on the coast, offers cavern-diving trips and courses in technical diving. The friendly owner and dive masters know all the secret spots in the area and can offer all sorts of insider tips. It and **Akumal Dive Adventures** (© **888/425-8625** in the U.S., or **984/875-9157**), at the Vista del Mar hotel on Half Moon Bay, offer resort courses as well as full open-water certification.

Modern sculptures punctuate gardens beside the clear **Yal-ku Lagoon,** which is about 700m (2,297 ft.) long and 200m (656 ft.) at its widest. You can paddle around comfortably in sheltered water and see fish and turtles. It's a perfect place to learn how to snorkel and let kids swim about safely. Of course, there are many spots along the bays where you can snorkel for free, but this little park is an easy, relaxing outing. It's open daily from 8am to 5:30pm. Admission is 80 pesos for adults, 45 pesos for children 3 to 14.

The gentle crescent of **Akumal Bay,** washing a wide, soft beach shaded by coconut palms, is one of the few places where you'll often be surprised by a sea turtle swimming along with you. During nesting season (May–July), visit **Centro Ecológico Akumal ★★★** (© **984/875-9005;** www.ceakumal.org) in the morning to sign up for that evening's 9pm turtle walk (Mon–Fri). You'll help staff search for new nests, protect exhausted mothers making their way back to sea, and remove eggs to hatcheries where they can incubate safely.

WHERE TO STAY

Rates below are for two people and include taxes. During the holidays, most hotels and condo rentals charge higher rates than those listed.

Hotel Akumal Caribe ★★ ☺   The first accommodations on Akumal Bay were simple thatch-roofed cabañas beside a gorgeous beach. Since then, the property has morphed into a casual resort with 40 tile-roofed bungalows spread about dense gardens. Simply and comfortably furnished, with kitchenettes, spacious showers, and jugs of purified water, the bungalows are great for a night or a week. The 21 rooms in the three-story beachside hotel have kitchenettes, and fancier furnishings. The hotel also has a freshwater pool (open to all guests). They also book condos and four villas with multiple bedrooms and a shared pool on Half Moon Bay. The property's best asset is its placement at the edge of beautiful Akumal Bay. Visiting its restaurants and shops will get you past the guards, who turn nonguests away.

Carretera Cancún–Tulum (Hwy. 307) Km 104. www.hotelakumalcaribe.com. © **800/351-1622** in the U.S., 800/343-1440 in Canada, or 915/584-3552. 70 units. High season $120–$134 bungalow, $149 double; low season $89 bungalow, $99–$119 double. Rates include full breakfast. Low-season packages and reduced Web rates available. AE, MC, V. Free parking. **Amenities:** 2 restaurants; bar; babysitting; seasonal children's activities; dive shop; large outdoor pool. *In room:* A/C, Internet (in some), kitchenette (in some), no phone (in some).

Vista del Mar Hotel and Condos ★ 🗝   This beachside property rents hotel rooms at good prices and large, fully equipped condos that you can rent by the day or week. The lovely, well-tended beach in front of the hotel has chairs and umbrellas. The on-site dive shop eliminates the hassle of organizing dive trips. Hotel rooms are small and contain either a queen-size or a double and a twin bed. The condos consist of a well-equipped kitchen, a living area, two or three bedrooms, and up to three bathrooms. All have balconies or terraces facing the sea and are furnished with hammocks. Several rooms come with whirlpool tubs.

Half Moon Bay, 77760 Akumal, Q. Roo. www.akumalinfo.com. © **888/425-8625,** 505/992-3333 in the U.S., or 984/875-9060. 27 units. High season $90–$110 double, $160–$290 condo; low season $75–$95 double, $110–$175 condo. MC, V. Limited free parking. **Amenities:** Restaurant; bar; dive shop; small outdoor pool; watersports. *In room:* A/C, TV, CD player, fridge, kitchenette (in condos), no phone (in some).

WHERE TO EAT

Akumal has about 10 places to eat, and a convenient grocery store, **Super Chomak** (with an ATM), by the arch. A collection of businesses just inside the arch includes a bakery and coffeehouse. At the Hotel Akumal Caribe, **Lol-Ha** serves good breakfasts and dinners and has free Wi-Fi, and the **Palapa Snack** bar dishes out everything from ice cream cones to burgers with poblano chiles and avocado. Tell the guards at the hotel's entrance that you're there for a meal and they'll direct you to special parking areas—and they don't notice if you take some time to wander along the hotel's beautiful beach.

La Buena Vida SEAFOOD/REGIONAL   This beach restaurant is just plain fun. Where else can you scale a *mirador* (crow's nest) to dine while under the influence of the best view of Half Moon Bay? The menu is varied and the fare excellent, especially the Maya chicken, *Tikinxic* fish (grilled after marinating in achiote and sour orange), and other regional specialties. Afterward, belly up to swings at the sand-floored bar, which blends its own unique cocktails and serves a barrage of special tequilas.

Half Moon Bay beach (btw. Akumal and Yal-ku Lagoon). © **984/875-9061.** www.akumalinfo.com/restaurant.htm. Main courses 80–285 pesos. MC, V. Daily 11am–1am.

Turtle Bay Cafe & Bakery ★ AMERICAN   Yummy pancakes with pecan maple syrup, fried eggs with hash browns, and eggs Benedict with Canadian bacon satisfy the expats dining beneath the palms. More adventuresome eaters go for *huevos rancheros* or a breakfast burrito with eggs, corn, and mushrooms. Lunches are equally tempting—you can even get a lentil burger—and cool smoothies and pastries are served throughout the day. Dinner might start with coconut shrimp and move on to crab cakes over mashed potatoes or a bodacious steak sandwich with caramelized onions. There's free Wi-Fi and plenty of friendly folks conversing with travelers.

Plaza Ukana. © **984/875-9138.** Main courses 88–180 pesos. MC, V. Daily 7am–3pm; Tues–Fri 6–9pm.

Xel-Ha: Snorkeling & Swimming ★★

A little over 3km (2 miles) south of Akumal you'll see the turnoff for **Aktun Chen ★★** (© **984/109-2061;** www.aktunchen.com). This is one of Yucatán's best caverns, with lots of geological features, good lighting, several underground pools, and large chambers, all carefully preserved. It has thrived under management by the local community rather than outside tour companies. The cavern tour takes about 90 minutes and requires a lot of walking, but the footing is good. It costs $26 for adults and $14 for children. Other choices are snorkeling in a cenote ($21 adults and children), or soaring above the jungle on zip lines ($38 adults and children). There is also a zoo with spider monkeys and other local fauna; some critters are allowed to run about freely. Aktun Chen is open from 9am to 4pm daily (closed Christmas and New Year's days). The turnoff is to the right, and the cave is about 4km (2½ miles) from the road.

Thirteen kilometers (8 miles) south of Akumal is **Xel-Ha** ☺ (© **998/884-9422** in Cancún, 984/873-3588 in Playa, or 984/875-6000 at the park; www.xelha.com. mx). The centerpiece is a large, beautiful lagoon where freshwater and saltwater meet. You can swim, float, and snorkel in beautifully clear water surrounded by jungle. A small train takes you to a drop-off point upriver, and you float back down on water moving calmly toward the sea. With no waves or currents to pull you around, snorkeling here is more comfortable than in the open sea, and the water has several species of fish, including rays.

The park rents snorkeling equipment and underwater cameras. Platforms allow nonsnorkelers to view the fish. Even better, use the park's Snuba gear—a contraption that allows you to breathe through 6m (20-ft.) tubes connected to scuba tanks floating on the surface. It rents for about $45 for an hour. Like Snuba but more involved is sea-trek, an elaborate plastic helmet with air hoses that allows you to walk around on the bottom, breathing normally, and perhaps help to feed the stingrays.

The dolphin area offers several interactive programs. A 1-hour swim costs $134 plus park admission; a shorter program costs $100. Make reservations at least 24 hours in advance by calling © **998/883-0524.**

Other attractions include a plant nursery; an apiary for the local stingerless bees; and a lovely path through the tropical forest bordering the lagoon. Admission includes use of inner tubes, life vest, shuttle train to the river, and changing rooms and showers. (Though not listed on the website, the park often discounts admission on weekends.) Xel-Ha is open daily from 8:30am to 6pm. Parking is free. Admission is $40 adults and $30 children ages 5 to 11; children younger than 5 enter free. An all-inclusive option includes all rentals plus food and beverages: $79 adults, $39 children. (These prices are not discounted.) The park has five restaurants, two ice-cream shops, a store, and an ATM. Bring biodegradable sunblock.

Signs clearly mark the turnoff to Xel-Ha, close to the ruins of Tulum. A popular day tour from Cancún or Playa combines the two. If you're traveling on your own, the best time to enjoy Xel-Ha without the crowds is during the weekend from 9am to 2pm.

About 2km (1¼ miles) south of Xel-Ha is **Hidden Worlds Cenotes ★★★** (© **984/877-8535;** www.hiddenworlds.com), which offers an excellent opportunity to snorkel or dive in a couple of nearby caverns. The caverns are part of a vast network that makes up a single underground river system. The water is crystalline (and cold), and the rock formations impressive. These caverns were filmed for the IMAX production *Journey into Amazing Caves.* The main form of transportation is "jungle mobile," with a guide tossing out information and lore about the jungle plant life you see. You'll be walking some, so take shoes or sandals. If you've toured caverns before, floating through gives you an entirely different perspective. For divers, a one-tank dive is $80, two tanks $100. The owners have also installed a 180m (591-ft.) zip line on the property, a zip-line roller-coaster-style ride called Avatar, and a Skycycle that has you riding a recumbent bike over the tree tops. They now offer full-day packages that include several activities.

Soliman Bay: Secluded Beauty

Jashita ★★   The latest contender for luxury travelers opened in September 2010 on the secluded Bahía de Soliman near Tankah. The setting couldn't be better. A reef protects the bay from winds, creating a shallow pool filled with sea creatures. The snorkeling and kayaking are fabulous on both sides of the reef, and gear for both sports is at hand for free. Elegantly minimalist, the 15 rooms and suites have terraces with plunge pools, platform beds dressed in crisp linens and puffy lightweight covers for chilly winter nights, and plasma TVs with SKY service (great music channels). Top-floor suites claim awe-inspiring views of the sea, lagoons, and seemingly endless vegetation, but the sun shines brightly through high windows beneath the peaked thatch roof. Two private villas are also available for rent. Indonesian statues and furnishings decorate the serene Sahara restaurant, where the entire Marchiorello family competes to create divine seafood soup, pastas, and fish.

Bahía Punta Soliman, Q. Roo. www.jashitahotel.com. © **984/804-8097.** 15 units. High season $190–$580 double; low season $140–$450 double. AE, MC, V. Free parking. **Amenities:** Restaurant; bar; outdoor pool; Wi-Fi. *In room:* A/C, TV/DVD, CD player, hair dryer, minibar.

Tankah Bay: Bubbling Cenote

Tankah Bay (about 3km/1¾ miles from Hidden World Cenotes) has a handful of rental houses and condos. The most interesting hotel in the area is **Casa Cenote** (www.casacenote.com; © **998/874-5170**). Its underground river surfaces at a cenote in the back of the property, then goes underground and bubbles up into the sea just a few feet offshore. Casa Cenote has seven beach bungalows. The double rate runs from $125 to $175, depending on the season (excluding holidays) and includes breakfast. A few simple rustic cabins with shared bath and kitchen go for $125 in high season and $75 low season. The American owner provides kayaks and snorkeling gear and can arrange dives, fishing trips, and sailing charters.

TULUM ★★★

Tulum (130km/81 miles from Cancún) is best known for its archaeological site, a walled Maya city of the post-Classic age perched dramatically on a rocky cliff overlooking the Caribbean. The coastline south of the site is packed with *palapa* hotels and upscale retreats for a well-heeled crowd seeking a "rustic" hideaway.

This stretch of incredible white beaches has become the unofficial center of the Tulum Hotel Zone—a collection of about 30 small hotels stretching from the Tulum ruins south to the entrance to the Sian Ka'an Biosphere Reserve. Hotels here rely on freshwater deliveries and rain tanks, and most generate their own electricity. Wi-Fi is available in public areas in many hotels and in some hotel rooms, and cell service is usually good.

The official town of Tulum is bisected by Hwy. 307, where it intersects the road to Cobá. The commercial center sprawls along both sides of Hwy. 307 for about 20 blocks jam-packed with gas stations, auto repair shops, drugstores, banks, markets, tour offices, and eateries. Two *glorietas* (traffic circles) slow the traffic through town; frontage roads allow access to parking spaces and driveways. Restaurants and hotels pop up along side streets around the municipal building and concrete plaza. Anyone who thinks of Tulum as a charming pueblo hasn't been here for a few years. The growth is astounding and shows no sign of slowing.

ORIENTATION A rental car will make everything much easier. From the north, you pass the entrance to the ruins before you enter town. When you come to an intersection with a traffic light, the highway to the right leads to the ruins of Cobá (p. 551). Turn left to reach Tulum's beach Hotel Zone, beginning about 2km (1¼ miles) away; the road sign reads BOCA PAILA. When you come to a T junction, there will be hotels in both directions. If you turn left (north), you'll be heading toward the back entrance to the ruins. If you take a right, you'll pass a long line of small hotels until you reach the entrance to Sian Ka'an.

In the town of Tulum, Hwy. 307 widens and is called Avenida Tulum. A particularly handy resource is the travel agency/communications/package center called **Savana** (© **984/871-2081**), on the east side of Avenida Tulum between calles Orion and Beta. Most of the staff speaks English and can answer questions about tours and calling home.

Exploring in & Around Tulum

The main attractions in this area are Tulum's archeological site and the biosphere reserve at Sian Ka'an, but there are enough other diversions to keep you busy for a week or more. Expeditions to explore natural wonders are available through **CESiaK ★** (© **984/871-2499**; www.cesiak.org). Excellent guides lead kayak tours in Sian Ka'an's canals, lagoons, and reefs for $45 (self-guided tours are also available for $20 single, $30 double). Sunset bird-watching tours are offered during migration season, December to May, for $70. **Mexico Kan Tours** (© **984/140-7870**; www.mexicokantours.com) at Avenida Tulum and Centauro Sur in downtown Tulum uses local guides for boat tours through Sian Ka'an's Maya canals to Punta Allen. The full-day tour includes snorkeling and lunch for $125.

The diving and snorkeling are fabulous as well, with coral reefs and cenotes aplenty. **Halocline Diving** (© **984/120-6402**; www.halocline-diving.com) at Orion Sur and Andromeda in downtown Tulum offers two-tank ocean dives for $75; snorkeling tours cost $25. Two-tank cenote dives cost $110, including transportation. Certified cave divers can explore dark cavern systems for $160 for two tanks.

Kiteboarding (also called kite-surfing) is hugely popular in Tulum, and the sea is dotted with bright kites when winds are blowing. **Extreme Control** (© **984/745-4555**; www.extremecontrol.net) was one of the first operators in Tulum, and has a full-scale facility at El Paraiso Beach Club near the back entrance to the ruins, another facility at Cabañas Tulum, and a shop at the intersection of Avenida Tulum and the road to Cobá in downtown Tulum. Their introductory kiteboarding lesson costs $52. They also rent paddleboards, kayaks, and wave kayaks and surfboards. **Mexico Kan Tours** (above) operates a kiteboarding school at the Ocho Tulum hotel.

Tulum's eclectic mix of locals and expats operates coffee bars, gelato shops, produce markets, and souvenir shops along Avenida Tulum and the beach road. The outstanding folk art shop **Mixic,** selling items collected throughout Mexico, has a branch across the road from Zamas hotel. **Shalom,** a high-end clothing boutique and folk art shop, also has branches in downtown and on the beach.

 Getting to the Beach

If you're staying elsewhere but want some beach time in Tulum, the easiest way is to drive to El Paraíso (© **984/113-7089**; www.elparaisohoteltulum.com) about 1km (⅔ mile) south of the ruins (take a left at the T junction). This is a great place with a long, broad beach that is pure sand, and access is free. The owners have a restaurant on the sand and make money by selling food and drink, so they ask you not to bring your own. They've also opened an 11-room hotel with A/C and plasma TVs; rates range from $85 to $155 depending on season and demand. A few tents are available for camping. For true isolation, check out the small hotels in Sian Ka'an and Punta Allen.

Exploring the Tulum Ruins

Thirteen kilometers (8 miles) south of Xel-Ha are the ruins of Tulum, a Maya fortress-city on a cliff above the sea. They are open daily from 7am to 5pm in winter, 8am to 6pm in summer. It's best to arrive before 9:30am, when the crowds start showing up. At the entrance, you'll find artisans' stands, a bookstore, a museum, a restaurant, several large bathrooms, and a ticket booth. It's about a 5-minute walk from the entrance to the archaeological site. Admission is 51 pesos. If you want to ride the shuttle from the visitor center to the ruins, it's another 15 pesos. Parking is 30 pesos. A video camera permit costs 41 pesos. Licensed guides at the stand next to the path to the ruins charge 200 pesos for a 45-minute tour in English, French, or Spanish for up to four people. In some ways, they are performers who will tailor their presentation to the responses they get from you. Some will try to draw connections between the Maya and Western theology, and they will point out architectural details that you might otherwise miss.

By A.D. 900, the end of the Classic period, Maya civilization had begun its decline, and the large cities to the south were abandoned. Tulum is one of the small city-states that rose to fill the void. It came to prominence in the 13th century as a seaport, controlling maritime commerce along this section of the coast, and remained inhabited well after the arrival of the Spanish. The primary god here was the diving god, depicted on several buildings as an upside-down figure above doorways. Seen at the Palace at Sayil and Cobá, this curious, almost comical figure is also known as the bee god.

The most imposing building in Tulum is a large stone structure above the cliff called the **Castillo** (castle). A temple as well as a fortress, it was once covered with stucco and paint. In front of the Castillo are several unrestored palace-like buildings partially covered with stucco. Tourists swim and sunbathe on the **beach** below, where the Maya once came ashore.

The **Temple of the Frescoes,** directly in front of the Castillo, contains interesting 13th-century wall paintings, though entrance is no longer permitted. Distinctly Maya, they represent Chaac, the rain god, and Ixchel, goddess of weaving, women, the moon, and medicine. The cornice of this temple has a relief of Chaac's head; from a slight distance, you can make out the eyes, nose, mouth, and chin. Notice the remains of the red-painted stucco—at one time all of Tulum's buildings were painted bright red.

Much of what we know of Tulum at the time of the Spanish Conquest comes from the writings of Diego de Landa, third bishop of the Yucatán. He wrote that Tulum was a small city inhabited by about 600 people who lived in platform dwellings along a street and supervised the trade traffic from Honduras to the Yucatán. Though it was a walled city, most inhabitants probably lived outside the walls, leaving the interior for the ceremonial structures and residences of governors and priests. Tulum survived for about 70 years after the conquest before finally being abandoned. Because of the great number of visitors this site receives, it is no longer possible to climb all of the ruins. In some cases, visitors are asked to remain behind roped-off areas.

Where to Stay

Tulum's beaches are among the most gorgeous on the coast, soft white sand, small coves, and clear aquamarine sea for swimming, kite-surfing, kayaking, and snorkeling. In the past, humble cabaña hotels and campgrounds dotted the coastline. Today, at least 30 small hotels claim any available space and a confounding collection of signs lines the narrow road. The drive can be confusing for first-timers trying to dodge bicyclists, pedestrians, and delivery trucks. The beach's popularity has driven prices into the stratosphere, and you'll have a hard time finding a room for less than $100 per night in high season. Several hotels now have A/C, 24-hour electricity, Wi-Fi, and freshwater pools, and old favorites such as Ana y Jose have grown into full-scale resorts.

There's still a rustic feel to Tulum's beach area, though, and many beach hotels don't accept credit cards (though there's now an ATM on the beach road). Most use generators for electricity and rely on trucks to deliver fresh water. With the under-$100-a-night room on the beach approaching extinction, budget travelers are better off staying in town and making day trips to the beach. The good news is that the town's supply of comfortable and increasingly sophisticated hotels has been steadily growing.

ON THE BEACH
Very Expensive

Ana y José ★★   This *palapa* hotel gets fancier each year. A reception area on the inland side of the road is built to eventually include a bridge over the road to the seaside rooms and suites decked out with marble countertops, marble tile floors, and furnished wooden terraces. Rooms range from garden- and poolview doubles with soaring *palapa* ceilings to pricey oceanfront suites with private pools. All have hammocks swinging near the door. Accoutrements include a spa and wedding planners (ceremonies on the excellent white-sand beach are very popular). Ana y José is 6.5km (4 miles) south of the Tulum ruins.

Carretera Punta Allen Km 7 (Apdo. Postal 15), 77780 Tulum, Q. Roo. www.anayjose.com. ✆ **998/880-5629.** Fax 998/880-6021. 23 units. $303–$447 double. AE, MC, V. Free parking. **Amenities:** Restaurant; outdoor pool; spa. *In room:* A/C, fan.

Cabañas Tulum ★★   This old favorite underwent a complete makeover in 2010. Front-row rooms right on the sand with a sea view from the bed are the priciest, but you'll be happy with a room in the two-story second row when the winds blow sand around. Perfectly functional and simple, the rooms have 24-hour electricity and A/C at night; ceiling fans and open windows are fine in winter. The rates are much higher than at the old rundown property, but are heavily discounted with early booking or 4-night stays and include excellent full breakfasts. The owners are building a fancier 16-room hotel with a pool next door and have added a great restaurant, El Bistro, to the beach's restaurant scene. Ziggy's Beach Club, a longtime favorite, has been spruced up with beach beds, tables in the sand, a full bar, and a branch of Extreme Control kiteboarding center.

Carretera Punta Allen Km 7, 77780 Tulum, Q. Roo. www.cabanastulum.com. ✆ **866/550-6878** in the U.S. and Canada, or 984/151-8754. 16 units. High season $155–$175 double; low season $129–$149 double. MC, V. Free parking. **Amenities:** Restaurant; bar; kiteboarding; yoga. *In room:* A/C, fan, Wi-Fi.

Moderate

Posada Dos Ceibas ★   Of all the places along this coast, this is closest to the way hotels in Tulum used to be: simple, quiet, and ecological without being pretentious. This is a good choice for a no-fuss beach vacation. Bright yellow, blue, and pink cottages are spread throughout dense vegetation. Simply furnished rooms come with ceiling fans and most have private patios or porches with hammocks. Prices vary with room size and are high for what you get. The grounds are well tended. The solar-generated electricity kicks in at 6pm. The hotel is near the entrance to Sian Ka'an and is more private than those bunched together to the north.

Carretera Tulum–Boca Paila Km 10, 77780 Tulum, Q. Roo. www.dosceibas.com. ✆ **984/877-6024.** 8 units. High season $75–$170 double; low season $60–$110 double. MC, V. **Amenities:** Restaurant; Wi-Fi (in restaurant); yoga. *In room:* No phone.

Inexpensive

Don Diego de la Playa ★   An offshoot of the hugely popular Don Diego de la Selva in town, this simple little ecohotel is buried in palms beside a quiet swath of sand. The least expensive accommodations are in Bedouin tents with wooden floors. Their small net windows catch some breeze, but not enough to keep you cool on sweltering summer nights. Two cement cabañas with thatch roofs are more comfortable. All rooms share common bathrooms with hot-water showers.

Carretera Punta Allen Km 4.5, 77780 Tulum, Q. Roo. www.dtulum.com. ✆ **984/114-9744.** 6 units. High season $75–$95 tent, $95–$125 cabaña; low season $60–$75 tent, $76–$95 cabaña. No credit cards. Limited parking. **Amenities:** Restaurant. *In room:* Fan, no phone.

IN TOWN

Don Diego de la Selva ★★   The combination of a wild garden setting and easy town and beach accessibility keeps guests coming back to this stylish hotel and restaurant. It feels like you're in the jungle with all the benefits of civilization—24/7 electricity; immaculate rooms; a large, clear swimming pool; and a huge *palapa* restaurant that attracts diners from town and the beach. The gregarious French owners serve drinks and mingle with guests each night, and the concierge dotes on you like a loving nanny. Eight spacious, air-conditioned rooms open to garden patios with chairs and hammocks. Rooms boast orthopedic mattresses, hot showers with skylights, thick towels, and simple, elegant furnishings. Two large bungalows come with queen-size beds and are cooled by ceiling fans. Room rates include a filling breakfast with fresh fruit and a different cake baked every morning.

Av. Tulum, Mza. 24 Lote 3 (1km/⅔ mile south of ADO bus station), 77780 Tulum, Q. Roo. www.dtulum. com. ✆ **984/114-9744.** 10 units. $95 double with A/C; $75 double with fan. Rates include continental breakfast. MC, V. Parking lot. **Amenities:** Restaurant; bar; shared fridge; outdoor pool. *In room:* A/C (in some), fan, Wi-Fi.

Posada Luna del Sur ★★ 🗝   Guests have been known to linger well past their planned departure date at this convenient, comfortable inn. Jugs of purified water, coffeemakers, utensils, and refrigerators make each room feel like home. Ground-floor rooms open to palms, bougainvillea bushes, and banana trees; those on the second story have balconies. The bright decor combines modern sinks and furnishings with Mexican tiles and folk art. Dozens of produce stands, grocery stores, and restaurants are within walking distance, and the beach is a 10-minute drive away.

Calle Luna Sur 5, 77780 Tulum, Q. Roo. www.posadalunadelsur.com. ✆ **984/871-2984.** 12 units. High season (3-night minimum) $80 double; low season (2-night minimum) $70–$75 double. High-season rates include hot breakfast. No credit cards. Limited covered parking. No children 15 and under. **Amenities:** Rooftop dining area; Wi-Fi. *In room:* A/C, fan, TV, fridge.

Where to Eat

Tulum's dining scene is surprisingly sophisticated, given its laid-back beach vibe. The variety is best in town, where classy restaurants, rowdy bars, and bare-bones taco stands crowd together along Avenida Tulum and side streets. Many beach hotels have great food as well, though the prices are sometimes appallingly high. Several markets and grocery stores provide do-it-yourself supplies.

Cetli ★★★ 🍴 MEXICAN   You'd think chef Claudia Pérez Rívas would be a culinary star in Mexico City or New York, but she's applying her considerable talents to create *alta cocina mexicana* (gourmet Mexican cuisine) in a gorgeous old home in downtown Tulum. She grinds spices and herbs in stone *metates* for authentic *moles* (sauces with multitudinous ingredients), places grilled shrimp atop a bed of *huitlacoche* (a savory corn mushroom), and stuffs chicken breasts with *chaya* (similar to spinach). Linen-covered tables are spaced far enough apart for quiet conversation, though diners tend to share opinions and recommend favorites. Dining here is both a pleasure and a culinary adventure.

Calle Polar Poniente at Calle Orion Norte, downtown Tulum. ✆ **984/108-0681.** Main courses 170–210 pesos. No credit cards. Thurs–Tues 5–10pm.

Don Cafeto's ★ MEXICAN   The first place to go for home-style *huevos rancheros* or *camarones mojo de ajo* (grilled shrimp with oil and garlic) is this sometimes noisy, always interesting cafe. The coffee's strong, the margaritas are perfectly mixed, and the salsas range from mild to *muy picante*. Background music varies from marimbas to mariachis to romantic guitars, and the waiters are always friendly and patient with non-Spanish speakers. It's like a dependable diner, but with far more interesting cuisine.

Av. Tulum btw. calles Centauro and Orion, downtown Tulum. ✆ **984/871-2207.** Main courses $8–$15. MC, V. Daily 7am–11pm.

El Asadero ★★ 🍴 STEAKHOUSE   In a part of the world where fresh seafood is revered, carnivores will find refuge in perfectly prepared rib-eye, T-bone, and New York steaks cooked on a grill by the front door. The husband-and-wife team who run this unassuming place out of their home also fire up *arrachera* flank steak, sausage, and chicken. Prices are in line with the setting—bare plastic tables arranged in what looks like it might have once been a garage—but the food would do linen tablecloths proud. For lighter appetites, they also conjure wonderful stuffed potatoes and tacos, and vegetarians will enjoy *nopal* (roast cactus) concoctions and sautéed vegetables.

Av. Satelite Norte btw. Sagitario and 2 Poniente, downtown Tulum. ✆ **984/128-6258.** Main courses 60–170 pesos. No credit cards. Daily except Wed 6:30–10pm.

El Camello ★★ 🍴 SEAFOOD   Fishermen deliver their daily catch to a sidewalk *pescadería* where it's quickly cleaned and passed on to the kitchen next door. There, cooks prepare seafood cocktails, whole fried fish, and other simple dishes for amazingly low prices. Waiters rush about the crowded dining room and along the sidewalk as lines of eager diners wait to claim a simple plastic table. Freshly fried chips arrive almost immediately, followed by chilled beers, *limonada*, and bowls of yummy beans. I ordered a medium-sized *ceviche mixto* on my first visit and could barely eat a third of the portion. I returned the next day for *pulpo* (octopus) with *guajillo* chiles and was sad to leave Tulum without trying the shrimp with garlic. It's on the south side of town as Avenida Tulum becomes Zamná. They may close early if all the fish is gone.

Av. Zamná. btw. Kukulcán and Palenque, downtown Tulum. No phone. Main courses 80–120 pesos. No credit cards. Daily 11am–7pm.

¡Que Fresco! ★★ AMERICAN/MEXICAN   Start the day with fragrant coffee from Chiapas, homemade bread and marmalade, and yogurt with papaya, all served at a bright yellow table on the sand beside a gorgeous beach. Snack on crisp chips and salsas with midday margaritas, and dine on grilled shrimp or filet mignon after dark. Why leave? Well-deserved rave reviews cover the walls at the Zamas hotel's barefoot cafe, and I've yet to see an unhappy diner even when the place is packed.

Carretera Punta Allen Km 5 on the beach. ✆ **415/387-9806** in the U.S. Main courses $7–$15. No credit cards. Daily 7am–10pm.

COBÁ RUINS ★★★

168km (104 miles) SW of Cancún

Older than most of Chichén Itzá and much larger than Tulum, Cobá was the eastern Yucatán's dominant city before A.D. 1000. The site is widely spread out, with thick forest growing between the temple groups. Rising high above the forest canopy are tall, steep pyramids of the Classic Maya style. Of the major sites, this one is the least reconstructed, with mounds that are sure to be additional structures still covered in vines and roots. Since they have been left in the condition in which they were found, most of the stone sculptures are worn down and impossible to make out. But the structures themselves, the surrounding jungle, and the twin lakes are impressive and enjoyable. The forest canopy is higher than in the northern part of the peninsula, and the town of Cobá is much like those in Yucatán's interior.

Cobá is my favorite easy escape from the action on the coast. Spending a night here gives you a chance to roam through the archaeological site in early morning when birds chatter, butterflies hover over flowers, and trees shade solitary trails. In the evening, you can easily spot turtles and crocodiles in the lake and graceful white egrets fishing for their dinners. Locals walk along the lakeside and gather outside their simple homes, chatting and watching children run about. I often wish I could spend several nights in this peaceful enclave.

Essentials

GETTING THERE & DEPARTING   By Car   The road to Cobá begins in Tulum and continues for 65km (40 miles). Watch out for *topes* (speed bumps) and potholes. The road has been widened and repaved and should be in good condition. Close to the village of Cobá, you will come to a triangle; be sure to follow the road to Cobá and not Nuevo Xcan or Valladolid. The entrance to the ruins is a short distance down the road past some small restaurants and the large lake.

By Bus   Several buses a day leave Tulum and Playa del Carmen for Cobá. Several companies offer bus tours.

Exploring the Cobá Ruins

The Maya built many intriguing cities in the Yucatán, but few as grand as Cobá ("water stirred by wind"). Much of the 67-sq.-km (26-sq.-mile) site remains unexcavated. Scholars believe Cobá was an important trade link between the Caribbean coast and inland cities. A 100km (62-mile) *sacbé* (raised road) through the jungle linked it to Yaxuná, once an important Maya center 50km (31 miles) south of Chichén Itzá. This is the Maya's longest-known *sacbé,* and at least 50 shorter ones lead from here. An important city-state, Cobá flourished from A.D. 632 (the oldest carved date found here) until after the rise of Chichén Itzá, around 800. Then Cobá faded in importance and population until it was finally abandoned.

Once at the site, keep your bearings—you can get turned around in the maze of dirt roads in the jungle. Branching off from every labeled path, you'll see unofficial narrow paths into the jungle, used as shortcuts by locals. These are good for birding, but be careful to remember the way back.

The **Grupo Cobá** holds an impressive pyramid, **La Iglesia (the Church).** Take the path bearing right after the entrance. Resist the urge to climb the temple; the view is better from El Castillo in the Nohoch Mul group farther back.

Return to the main path and turn right, passing a sign pointing to the restored *juego de pelota* (**ball court**). Continuing for 5 to 10 minutes, you'll come to a fork in the road, where you'll notice jungle-covered, unexcavated pyramids to the left and right. At one point, a raised portion of the *sacbé* to Yaxuná is visible as it crosses the pathway. Throughout the area, carved stelae stand by pathways or lie forlornly in the underbrush. Although protected by crude thatched roofs, most are weatherworn enough to be indiscernible.

The left fork leads to the **Nohoch Mul Group,** which contains **El Castillo.** Except for Structure 2 in Calakmul, this is the tallest pyramid in the Yucatán, out-reaching El Castillo at Chichén Itzá and the Pyramid of the Magician at Uxmal. From the top, you can see unexcavated, jungle-cloaked pyramids poking through the forest canopy all around. Climbing the Castillo was forbidden for a short time as archaeologists determined that all the traffic wasn't disturbing the pyramid's inner temples. Climbing resumed in late 2009.

The right fork (more or less straight on) goes to the **Conjunto Las Pinturas,** whose main attraction is the **Pyramid of the Painted Lintel,** a small structure with traces of its original bright colors above the door. You can climb up for a close look.

Admission is 51 pesos, free for children younger than 12. Parking is 50 pesos, and video camera permits 41 pesos. The site is open daily from 8am to 5pm, sometimes longer. ***Note:*** Visit Cobá in the morning or after the heat of the day has passed. Mosquito repellent, drinking water, and comfortable shoes are imperative. Bicycles are available for rent for $3 per hour at a stand just past the entrance. You can also hire a *triciclo* with driver to carry you around the site; rates start at $10. Clever *triciclo* drivers also park at Nohuch Mul to carry hot, tired passengers back to the entrance.

Where to Stay & Eat

Cobá offers a few hotels, restaurants, and markets, and food choices abound at stands near the entrance when the archaeological site is open. Prices are refreshingly realistic, and the locals enjoy chatting with travelers. A few truly rustic hostelries offer hard mattresses and cold-water showers for budget travelers, and a couple of hotels are on the road to Tulum. Making reservations is difficult, as phone and Internet service is spotty, but it's a good idea to give it a shot during high season.

El Bocadito 🏷 Cobá's longtime family-run hotel is always changing as the owners add air-conditioning and TVs to some rooms while keeping others bare-bones basic. The adjacent large restaurant (popular with groups at lunch) sits on the main road through town, right where buses to Playa del Carmen depart. Bathrooms in the cheapest rooms are so small that the seatless toilet is practically in the cold-water shower, and the single beds take up nearly all the space. Size and comfort levels gradually increase with the rates, up to the four rooms with TVs and one with air-conditioning. Guests gather at picnic tables beneath banana and orange trees in a narrow courtyard or in the Internet cafe with several communal computers. It's hard to make reservations, since phone and Internet service is unreliable.

On main road through Cobá town. www.cancunsouth.com/bocadito. © **985/852-0052** or 984/876-3738. 9 units. Rates start at $10 double. MC, V (10% charge). **Amenities:** Restaurant. *In room:* A/C (in one), fan (in some), Internet (for a fee).

Villas Arqueológicas Cobá ★★ 🛍 Lovingly maintained for several decades, this peaceful compound facing the lake is removed from town on a private road. Its cool blue pool, good restaurant, attentive service from faithful local workers, and a

A Day in the Life of a Maya Village

In the tropical forest near Cobá, a village of 27 families exists much as their long-ago ancestors did, living in round thatch huts with no electricity, indoor plumbing, or paved roads, gathering plants in the jungle for medicinal and other uses on their way to dip into a hidden cenote, appealing to the gods for successful crops. And every day, the people of Pac Chen open their homes to as many as 80 tourists who want to know what Maya village life is in the 21st century.

The only way to visit Pac Chen is on trips with **Alltournative** (© **877/437-4990** in the U.S., or 984/803-9999; www.alltournative.com), an ecotour company that works with villagers to help them become self-sustaining. Farming continues, but tourism income allows them to survive without burning their land to squeeze out the last remaining nutrients.

The arrangement is a boon to tourists, too. On your own, it would be pretty well impossible to walk into a Maya village and be ushered through the jungle and lowered into a cenote or to glide through the forest canopy on a zip line, kayak a lagoon full of birds, eat lunch cooked by village women, and receive a copal-incense blessing from a village elder for a safe trip home. The Maya Encounter tour costs $119 for adults and $95 for children.

---

superb library make it the best choice close to the ruins. The rooms have a double and a single bed in semiprivate niches, a small bathroom with hot-water shower, a sink outside the bathroom door, and dreadful lighting. Bougainvillea, palms, and ferns flourish in the central courtyard, shading the pool and dining terraces. The restaurant's Mexican/Continental food is very good, if a bit overpriced (meal plan available for $20). An excellent library contains tomes on the Maya, archaeology, and Mexican art—and a pool table for guests bored by the lack of activities after dark.

West of the ruins beside the lake. www.villasarqueologicas.com.mx. © **984/206-7001.** 43 units. $60–$125 double. MC, V. Parking lot. **Amenities:** Restaurant; bar; outdoor pool; room service; tennis court; Wi-Fi (in public areas). *In room:* A/C, hair dryer.

SIAN KA'AN & THE PUNTA ALLEN PENINSULA ★★★

Just past Tulum's last cabaña hotel is the entrance arch to the vast (526,000-hectare/1.3-million-acre) **Sian Ka'an Biosphere Reserve.** This inexpressibly beautiful tract of wild land is the domain of howler monkeys, ocelots, crocodiles, jaguars, tapirs, sea turtles, and thousands of species of plants. The Mexican government created this reserve in 1986; the following year, the United Nations declared it a World Heritage Site. Sian Ka'an protects 10% of Quintana Roo's land mass, including almost one-third of the Caribbean coastline, from development. Another 319,000 hectares (788,266 acres) of land was added to the reserve in 2010.

The entrance to the Punta Allen Peninsula, a small portion of the reserve, is one of two main entrances to the reserve; the other is from the community of Muyil off Hwy. 307 south of Tulum, where you take a boat down canals built by the Maya to the Boca Paila lagoon.

Legends still swirl about the 4 hours it takes to drive the 50km (31 miles) over potholes, ruts, and rivulets to the town of Punta Allen at road's end. In fact, the road has been much improved, though it is still dirt, still pockmarked to varying degrees, and subject to weather-related conditions. Guards at the entrance gate are fond of declaring it's now a 1-hour trip, and no doubt that's true for the locals who sailed past me in my rented compact sedan. Driving cautiously after a stretch of rainy weather, it took me a little less than 2 hours. Those driving four-wheelers or other robust vehicles should plan to spend about 1½ hours on the road.

If you don't fancy yourself a road warrior, you can drive through the entrance arch in Tulum (entry 25 pesos per person) and continue south about 4km (2½ miles) to where a beach comes into view, pull over, and spread out your beach towel.

The Punta Allen Peninsula

As you drive the skinny peninsula, which separates the Boca Paila Lagoon from the sea, you'll find no trails leading into the jungle and much of the coastal side of the road is fenced off. But you can swim or snorkel off the beaches that come into view. Guided tours are the only way to see most of the reserve. Otherwise, there is no practical way to visit Sian Ka'an except by car.

THE SIAN KA'AN BIOSPHERE RESERVE ★★★

Maya life in ancient times remains essentially a mystery, but there's no wondering why they named this land Sian Ka'an (See-*an* Caan), Mayan for "where the sky is born." Sunrise here truly is like witnessing the birth of a day.

The reserve encompasses most of the ecosystems that exist on the entire Yucatán Peninsula: medium- and low-growth jungles, beaches, savannas, marshes, freshwater and brackish lagoons, cenotes, underground rivers, and untouched coral reef. Numerous archaeological sites have also been found within its borders.

More than 2,000 people, most of them Maya, live in Sian Ka'an. All are original residents of the area, or their descendants. Tours to the reserve are often led by locals, who grew up nearby in homes occupied for countless generations. They'll almost never consult a field guide; their knowledge about the birds, the plants, the water, and the ruins are simply a part of their lives.

To access the reserve beyond the road, arrange for a tour in Tulum. Two organizations in particular keep their groups small and work only through the local people.

Anatomy of a Biosphere Reserve

Unlike its national parks, which focus on historical and aesthetic features, Mexico's biosphere reserves were created purely to protect its last natural ecosystems. Recognition by UNESCO (United Nations Educational, Scientific and Cultural Organization) requires that the biosphere contain at least 10,000 hectares (24,711 acres), at least one pristine area of biological diversity, and threatened or endangered endemic species.

Mexico pioneered the zoning system that allows some carefully managed tourism. The core area—the heart of the reserve—is limited to scientific research and is surrounded by a buffer zone that allows only conservation-related activity. On the periphery, a transition zone permits sustainable use of natural resources to benefit local communities, as CESiaK's tours do. Biosphere reserves allow original residents to remain; local people, in fact, are recruited to research, monitor, and manage the ecosystem while developing sustainable activities such as ecotourism.

THE RIVIERA MAYA & THE COAST | Sian Ka'an & Punta Allen

SLEEPING where the sky is born

To see the sun rise in Sian Ka'an as the Maya did, you can stay in CESiaK's **Boca Paila Camps** ★★, 4km (2½ miles) past the entrance arch. The ecolodge's tent cabins are tucked into the edge of the jungle on a clean, white beach, raised on platforms to avoid interfering with the sand's natural processes. The fine linens and solid wood furniture make it feel less like camping, but when night falls and you're stumbling around by candlelight, it feels plenty rustic. Guests share scrupulously clean bathrooms with composting toilets, housed in buildings whose rooftop lookouts grant views of the sea and lagoon that give "panoramic" new meaning—you'll actually see the curvature of the earth. Deluxe tent cabins with one queen and ocean or lagoon views are $80 to $100. Meals are extra. The camp has no electricity—guests get battery-powered lamps—but wind and solar power provide hot water. Things do not always run perfectly smoothly: The restaurant, which is reasonably priced and turns out better meals than it has any right to in this remote location, sometimes runs out of ingredients for a popular menu item, and one time I was assigned to a tent that was already occupied (and quickly reassigned). But this place makes Tulum's vaunted sands look like Panama City Beach in springtime—and its staff knows the reserve's plants, animals, and local culture backward and forward.

The **Centro Ecológico Sian Ka'an,** or CESiaK, with an office on Hwy. 307 just south of Tulum ruins turnoff (© **984/871-2499;** www.cesiak.org), is a nonprofit group supporting the reserve with education and community development programs. Its popular all-day canal tour ($77 per person, including lunch and tax), includes a guided walk through coastal dunes and jungle and a boat trip across two brackish lagoons where freshwater cenotes well up from under the ground. Boats follow a narrow channel through mangroves to a small temple where Maya traders stopped to make offerings and ask for successful negotiations. You'll don life jackets and float part of the way in the currents of a freshwater lagoon and snorkel in a cenote before the day is over. Other tours include a sunset bird-watching trip and single- and multiday fly-fishing packages. Tours depart from the CESiaK center at the Boca Paila Camps, 4km (2½ miles) south of the reserve entrance.

Community Tours Sian Ka'an, Avenida Tulum between calles Centauro and Orión (© **984/114-0750;** www.siankaantours.org), is a local guides' cooperative that runs snorkeling, birding, and adventure tours into the biosphere. They formerly worked within the Sian Ka'an Visitor Center, but that structure has fallen into disrepair. The guides now run their tours out of Muyil, where they are attempting to create an eco-oriented visitor center. Their "Forest and Float" canal tours ($99 per adult, $70 child) begin with a visit to the Muyil archaeological site and enter the reserve from that side. Transportation is available from Riviera Maya hotels for an extra charge.

THE ROAD TO PUNTA ALLEN

About 11km (6¾ miles) past the arch, you'll come to the **Boca Paila Fishing Lodge** (www.bocapaila.com). Not for the general traveler, it specializes in weeklong, all-inclusive packages for fly-fishers. The peninsula is so narrow here that you see the Boca Paila lagoon on one side and the sea on the other. In another 3km (1¾ miles), you will be flooded by false hope when you reach a smooth, concrete roadway—this is the foot of the Boca Paila Bridge, which spans the inlet between the ocean and the lagoon, and the pavement disappears as quickly as it appeared. You'll often see people fishing off the sides. This is a good place to stop and stretch your legs while taking in ethereal water views from either side.

After the bridge, it's mostly deserted coastline until you get to Punta Allen. About 8km (5 miles) before you do, you'll come to **Rancho Sol Caribe** (www.solcaribe-mexico.com), with four comfortable cabañas and the stunning beach it has all to itself.

Punta Allen

Punta Allen, the peninsula's only town, is a lobster fishing village on a palm-studded beach perched between Ascension Bay and the Caribbean Sea. About 100 families survive by lobster fishing and, increasingly, tourism; many of the young men now are expert fly-fishing guides.

Isolated and rustic, this is very much the end of the road. The town has a lobster cooperative, a few sand streets with modest homes, and a lighthouse. The generator, when it's working, comes on for a few hours in the morning and a few more at night. Your cellphone won't work here, and no one takes credit cards. Without the help of a friendly local, it's a challenge to figure out when any of the businesses are open.

This is slowly beginning to change. The few lodges that bravely set up shop here 10 or 15 years ago have acquired some upstart young neighbors, and 80 more guest rooms have been approved (no telling how long they might take to materialize). For now, unless you're a fishing enthusiast, there's not a lot to do in Punta Allen except kick back, snorkel a little, and eat your fill of fresh seafood.

Cuzan Guesthouse　One of the town's original fishing lodges, this collection of basic, *palapa*-roofed wood cabañas on a sandy beach also has one of the town's best restaurants and a full bar. Despite the increasing competition, it has a loyal following. Cuzan's bread and butter is its all-inclusive fishing packages, but it will rent a cabaña to anyone interested in passing some time in Punta Allen. The guesthouse also offers a variety of birding, snorkeling, and other boat tours.

Apdo. Postal 24, Felipe Carrillo Puerto, 77200 Q. Roo. www.flyfishmx.com. ✆ **983/834-0358.** 12 units. $50–$110 cabañas. No credit cards. *In room:* No phone.

Serenidad Shardon　This retreat on the coastal road just south of town—we're talking about the equivalent of 3 or 4 blocks—can put you in a three-bedroom beach house or one of two sweet, private cabañas, all with private bathrooms, contemporary decoration, and views of the Caribbean from decks or windows. The amiable owner can also set you up with tours and think of a dozen other ways to make sure you are happy.

Beach road south of town square. www.shardon.com. ✆ **616/827-0204** in the U.S., or 984/876-1827. 3 units. $150–$200 cabañas; $350 beach house ($250 lower floor only). No credit cards. *In room:* No phone.

En Route to the Lower Caribbean Coast

About 25km (16 miles) south of Tulum on Hwy. 307, a sign points to the small but interesting ruins of **Muyil** (take bug spray), on the western edge of Sian Ka'an. The principal ruins are a small group of buildings and a plaza dominated by the Castillo. It's one of the Caribbean coast's taller structures but is more interesting for the unique, solid round masonry turret at the top. A Maya canal enters the biosphere reserve and empties into a lake; more canals then continue to the saltwater estuary of Boca Paila. The local community offers a boat ride through these canals and lakes. The 3½-hour tour includes viewing some otherwise inaccessible ruins, snorkeling the canal, and floating in its current.

Felipe Carrillo Puerto (pop. 60,000) is the first large town on the road to Chetumal. The town was a rebel stronghold during the War of the Castes and home to the millenarian cult of the "Talking Cross." A sizable community of believers still practices its own brand of religion and commands the town's respect. Of primary interest to travelers, however, are Carrillo Puerto's two gas stations, a market, a bus terminal, and a bank next to the gas station in the center of town, which has an ATM. From Carrillo Puerto, Hwy. 184 goes into the peninsula's interior and eventually to Mérida, making it a turning point on the "short circuit" of the Yucatán Peninsula.

MAHAHUAL, XCALAK & THE CHINCHORRO REEF

Tourism has been late to arrive on the quiet southern half of the Caribbean coast. The recently dubbed Costa Maya is tucked under the Sian Ka'an Biosphere Reserve on a wide peninsula jutting out from the mainland. It remained largely unnoticed—except by fly-fishers—while resorts gobbled up the beaches of Cancún and the Riviera Maya over the past few decades.

Lying 354km (220 miles) from Cancún's airport and more than 48km (30 miles) from the highway, the Costa Maya's beaches might never see Riviera Maya–scale development, but changes have already come since Carnival Cruise Line and government tourism officials brought a huge cruise port to the tiny fishing village of Mahahual (sometimes spelled Majahual) in 2001. New roads have cut the trip to the even smaller and more remote village of Xcalak (Eesh-kah-*lahk*)—the Mexican Caribbean's southernmost settlement—from 4 hours to less than one. Luxury developments are rumored to be on the drawing boards, but tourism officials vow to abandon the Cancún/Riviera Maya model by integrating the local population into restrained development of small, ecofriendly hotels and nature tours.

Information, please

Good, up-to-date information about the Costa Maya is still scarce, though you can get decent overviews at www. mahahual.com and www.xcalak.info. For the latest goings-on, sign up for the detailed and gossipy newsletter from Mayan Beach Garden in Mahahual (p. 559).

So far, the Costa Maya remains a landscape of mangrove marshes, low jungle, and long stretches of palm-fringed, white-sand beaches. Affordable bungalows and small restaurants serving fresh-caught fish await visitors drawn to the region's cenotes, Maya ruins, and incomparable snorkeling and diving.

ORIENTATION About 45 minutes south of Felipe Carrillo Puerto, a few kilometers past the town of Limones at a place called El Cafetal (there's a gas station before the turnoff), you reach the clearly marked turnoff for Mahahual and Xcalak. It's 50km (31 miles) on a good paved road to the coast at Mahahual. The turnoff for the new road to Xcalak comes 2km (1¼ miles) before you reach Mahahual, at a military checkpoint. Xcalak is 55km (34 miles) to the south, less than an hour's drive.

DIVING the chinchorro reef

The **Chinchorro Reef Underwater National Park,** about 30km (19 miles) off this coastline, is by most accounts the largest coral atoll in the Northern Hemisphere, at 38km (24 miles) long and 13km (8 miles) wide. Its coral formations, massive sponges, and abundant sea life are certainly among the most spectacular. The oval reef is as shallow as 1m (3⅓ ft.) at its interior and as deep as 900m (2,953 ft.) at its exterior. It's invisible from the ocean side and has doomed scores of ships. Contrary to popular misconception, diving the 30 or so **shipwrecks** that decorate the underwater landscape is prohibited—they are protected by the Banco Chinchorro Biosphere. However, the reef offers at least a dozen stellar dive sites.

And most wrecks, including the famous **40 Cannons** on the northwest side, are quite shallow and can be explored by snorkeling. The west side of the reef is a wonderland of walls and coral gardens.

The number of divers who have tried to dive Chinchorro Reef and never got there is kind of a running joke along the Costa Maya. It can be a challenge to get to the reef, partly because of fickle sea conditions and partly because of the strict limit on permits. **XTC Dive Center** (✆ **983/839-8865;** www.xtcdivecenter. com) in Xcalak specializes in trips to Chinchorro—the company's name stands for "Xcalak to Chinchorro." XTC also offers a lineup of dives to local reefs and cenotes.

Mahahual

The cruise ship pier (north of the road entering town) has given Mahahual a split personality. The port has grown into a tourist zone with a beach club, shopping mall, and tour companies offering dozens of excursions, and a minicity with its own suburb of homes and apartments has sprouted nearby. A Señor Frog's opened in late 2010, not far from the Hard Rock Cafe—what else is there to say? On port days, the town's packed-sand main street brims with tipsy, sunburned passengers who elect beach time over bus tours, only to empty at night and return to somnolence.

Your best bet is to stay in the lower Mahahual area (or repair to Xcalak). Frankly, Mahahual isn't the most appealing town even when devoid of cruise passengers, though it has acquired some good hotels and fine restaurants, and the new *malecón* (seafront promenade) makes for a pleasant walk along a fine white beach. Beach areas north and south of town, on the other hand, are the stuff of dreams. Most of the town's hotels and services line the sand road running through town and south along the coast.

In addition to the always-reliable hotels below, the newer **Matan Ka'an** (www. matankaan.it) and **El Caballo Blanco** (www.hotelelcaballoblanco.com; ✆ **983/126-0319**) offer bright, air-conditioned rooms starting at $60 and $80, respectively.

Balamkú Inn on the Beach ★★★ This comfortable, friendly place on the coast road south of town rents large, breezy rooms in stylish one- and two-story thatched bungalows distributed across 110m (361 ft.) of dazzling white beach on a stretch of pristine reef. They have comfortable mattresses, large attractive bathrooms, and louvered windows that let you control the breeze. All have terraces facing the beach. The friendly, environmentally minded Canadian owners derive enough energy from wind to provide 24-hour power without using a generator. Even more impressive, they rely

The Yucatán's Lower Caribbean Coast

on a large rainwater collection system and route shower and sink wastewater to nourish the wetlands, and use a composting waste system instead of polluting septic tanks—they not only allow but urge guests to flush paper down the toilet.

Carretera Costera Km 5.7, Mahahual, Q. Roo. www.balamku.com. ✆ **983/839-5332.** 10 units. High season $90 double; midseason $85 double; low season $80 double. Rates include full breakfast. AE, MC, V for deposits; no credit cards at hotel. Free guarded parking. **Amenities:** Restaurant (breakfast and lunch; Sun dinner); bar (afternoons); airport transfer; kayaks and snorkeling gear. *In room:* No phone, Wi-Fi.

Mayan Beach Garden Inn ★★ Simple but well-furnished, whitewashed rooms have huge, cushy beds with incredible mosaic headboards and are elevated to take in sea views at this longtime favorite. A lovely stretch of soft beach near a shallow section of the unspoiled reef; friendly, helpful staff; owners who will show you every prime snorkeling spot and undiscovered Maya site in the area; and fantastic food add up to an extraordinary stay. Three oceanview rooms and three beachfront cabañas (one a suite sleeping four) are available; all have large covered decks with hammocks and lounge chairs. Solar power provides 24-hour electricity, but some appliances will run only when the backup generator is running; make sure you get the schedule.

Camino Costera Km 20.5, Mahahual, Q. Roo. www.mayanbeachgarden.com. © **983/132-2603.** 6 units. High season $91–$117 double, $135–$147 suite; low season $72–$96 double, $127 suite. 3-night minimum in high season. Rates include full breakfast; all-inclusive packages available. **Amenities:** Restaurant/bar; kayaks (with cabañas). *In room:* AC (in some, at night), kitchenettes (in some), Wi-Fi.

Xcalak

Quintana Roo's last stand before the channel marking Mexico's border with Belize, **Xcalak** (Eesh-kah-*lahk*) is a former military outpost that had a population as large as 1,200 before the 1958 hurricane washed most of the town away; now it has about 600 permanent residents. Fly-fishers started coming in the 1980s and are still pulling prizes out of the water. The town oozes shabby charm, but the real lure is the inns just beyond town that offer a little patch of paradise safe from anything resembling a crowd.

You'll likely eat most of your meals wherever you stay, but don't miss the **Leaky Palapa ★★★** (no phone; www.leakypalaparestaurant.com) in town. The two women who run the place do wonderful things with the best local ingredients available from day to day. The short but varied menu applies traditional preparation to all manner of contemporary dishes, from 100 to 300 pesos. Reservations recommended. Open November to May, Saturday to Tuesday from 5 to 10pm.

Costa de Cocos Dive & Fly-Fishing Resort ★ Freestanding cabañas sit around a large, attractive sandy beach graced with coconut palms. Co-owner Ilana Randal epitomizes a "life is too short" philosophy that makes you feel all is right with the world. Comfortable cabañas have one king- or queen-size bed or two doubles; one is a two-bedroom unit with two bathrooms. They have plenty of cross-ventilation, ceiling fans, hot water, and good mattresses. Wind and solar power provides 24-hour electricity. Activities include kayaking, snorkeling, scuba diving, and fly-fishing. The resort has experienced English-speaking fishing guides and a dive instructor. The casual restaurant/bar, which offers good home-style cooking—pizza is a popular recent addition—is open late.

Carretera Mahahual–Xcalak Km 52, Q. Roo. www.costadecocos.com. © **983/839-8537.** 16 units. High season $90 double; low season $84 double. Dive and fly-fishing packages available by e-mail request. Rates include breakfast buffet. AE, MC, V (through PayPal). Free parking. **Amenities:** Restaurant; bar; dive shop; watersports. *In room:* No phone, Wi-Fi.

Sin Duda Villas ★★ There's a reason half of this B&B's guests are repeat customers. It's a bit of a haul on the bouncy beach road, but the beautiful beach, homey accommodations, and sociable owners are worth the drive. White sand and turquoise sea is the front yard for three standard rooms, one studio, and two two-bedroom apartments. All open onto the beach and are fan-cooled and comfortably furnished. A roof deck offers dazzling 360-degree views of jungle, lagoon, and sea. The owners are voracious readers, and a bright, well-stocked guest kitchen doubles as a library. Self-serve snorkel gear, kayaks, and bicycles are provided—just be sure to pack it in before cocktail hour with the owners, which often turns into the evening's entertainment.

Beach road 8km/5 miles north of town. www.sindudavillas.com. © **415/868-9925** in the U.S. (messages only). 6 units. High season $90–$130 double; low season $75–$114 double. Rates include light breakfast. AE, DISC, MC, V (through PayPal). Free parking. **Amenities:** Bikes; kayaks; communal kitchen; snorkel gear; Wi-Fi in living room by request. *In room:* No phone.

LAGUNA BACALAR ★★★

104km (65 miles) SW of Felipe Carrillo Puerto; 37km (23 miles) NW of Chetumal

On a sunny day, you will see why Laguna Bacalar is nicknamed *Lago de los Siete Colores* (Lake of the Seven Colors): The white sandy bottom turns the crystalline water pale turquoise in shallow areas, morphing to vivid turquoise and through a spectrum to deep indigo in the deeper center. Colors shift with the passing of the day, making a mesmerizing backdrop.

Considered Mexico's second-largest lake, Bacalar is actually a lagoon, with a series of waterways leading eventually to the ocean. Fed not by surface runoff but by underground cenotes, it is almost 50km (31 miles) long. You'll glimpse the jewel-toned water long before you reach the town of Bacalar, about two-thirds of the way down, where you must go for swimming or kayaking.

The town of Bacalar is quiet and traditional, though it seems every year brings a new cadre of expats looking for a different kind of life. There's not a lot of action in town, but you shouldn't miss the **Fuerte San Felipe Bacalar,** built in 1733 to protect the Spanish from the pirates and Maya rebels who regularly raided the area. Admission is 52 pesos. Overlooking the lake on the eastern edge of the central plaza, the fort houses an excellent museum devoted to regional history, with a focus on the pirates who repeatedly descended upon these shores.

As if to prove the water gods smile upon Bacalar, Mexico's biggest and deepest cenote is less than 2km (1¼ mile) south of town, at Km 15. Measuring 185m (607 ft.) across, **Cenote Azul** is surrounded by lush flowers and trees, and filled with water so clear that you can see 60m (197 ft.) down into its nearly 91m (299-ft.) depth.

Some lovely inns dot the lagoon's western shore, which makes Bacalar an appealing alternative base to Chetumal for exploring the Maya ruins in the nearby Río Bec area.

ORIENTATION   Driving south on Hwy. 307, the town of Bacalar is 1½ hours beyond Felipe Carrillo Puerto, clearly marked by signs. If you're driving north from Chetumal, it takes about a half-hour. Buses going south from Cancún and Playa del Carmen stop here, and there are frequent buses from Chetumal.

Where to Stay

You can stay quite comfortably in Bacalar for very little money. My favorite inn is **Amigos B&B Laguna Bacalar ★★** (www.bacalar.net; ✆ **987/872-3868**), with five rooms of various sizes and configurations overlooking the water on Avenida Costera, about 1.6km (1 mile) south of the plaza. Doubles are 700 pesos including breakfast, 600 to 700 without. A little closer to the center of town on the same road, the endearingly quirky **Casita Carolina** (www.casitacarolina.com; ✆ **983/834-2334**), offers three units in a converted family home that share a common living room and kitchen, and three separate casitas scattered through a large, grassy garden sloping to the lake's shore. The owner, who lives on-site, hosts an artist's retreat every February. Prices range from 300 to 600 pesos, making this a great value. If you want to really get away from it all, **Villas Ecotucán** (www.villasecotucan.info; ✆ **983/120-5743**) commands about 40 hectares (99 acres) of largely undeveloped land and focuses on the outdoors; its five spacious *palapa*-roofed cabañas (made out of native materials from the property) and two suites have separate sitting rooms and rent for 650 pesos. They also offer more jungle walks, swimming, and kayaking tours than you could go through in a week. Ecotucán is 5km (3 miles) north of town and 1km (⅔ mile) off Hwy. 307; look for the tall, rainbow-colored tree, flags, and welcome sign.

For a bit of luxury, the all-suites **Villas Bakalar** ★ (www.villasbakalar.com; ⓒ **983/835-1400**) on Avenida 3, a couple of blocks north of the plaza, has 15 new and modern one- and two-bedroom suites, starting at 1,130 pesos, set in a veritable botanical garden of native flora—a passionate interest of the owner. It's a block from the shore but has sweeping lake views. And the well-known **Rancho Encantado** ★ (www.encantado.com; ⓒ **877/229-2046** in the U.S., or 983/839-7900) near Hwy. 307 north of town, rents 12 large white stucco cottages scattered over a shady lawn beside the lake, surrounded by native trees, orchids, and bromeliads. It charges $135 to $160 in high season, $65 to $85 in low season.

Where to Eat

I've had good, simple meals on the town square, and great dinners at the more upscale **Los Aluxes** (ⓒ **983/152-5608**) on Avenida Costera, south of Amigos B&B. **Restaurante Cenote Azul** (ⓒ **983/834-2460;** www.cenoteazul.com), with its vantage point overlooking the cenote, wouldn't even have to serve decent food to attract a following, but it does, and with great variety. While you're there, you can swim in the cenote (as long as you aren't wearing lotions or deodorant), or simply watch others take the plunge.

CHETUMAL

251km (156 miles) S of Tulum; 37km (23 miles) S of Laguna Bacalar

Quintana Roo's capital and second-largest city (after Cancún), Chetumal (pop. 210,000) is a tourist destination only in the sense that it's the gateway to Belize, Tikal (Guatemala), and the Río Bec ruins (p. 564). It has little to offer a tourist, with the one huge exception: the best museum devoted to Maya culture outside of Mexico City. The federal government is rebuilding the rundown zoo on Avenida Insurgentes at Andrés Quintana Roo into the modern, highly interactive **Biouniverzoo,** devoted to native species. The first phase opened in December 2010 with such exhibits as a cenote populated by bats. As you descend into the cenote, glass viewing walls allow an up-close look at the blind catfish that live deep within the underground water. Signs are in Mayan, Spanish, and English. Reactions from locals attending the opening were generally favorable, but there is much more work to be done on the project, which aims to create Mexico's best zoo. Biouniverzoo is open Wednesday to Sunday 9am to 5pm; admission is 150 pesos adults, 80 pesos ages 3 to 12; younger kids are free.

Essentials

GETTING THERE & DEPARTING

BY PLANE   Mexicana's suspension of operations, along with its regional carrier, **Click,** leaves Chetumal (airport code CTM) with no service from the U.S. The Mexican airline **Interjet** (ⓒ **866/285-9525** in the U.S.; www.interjet.com.mx) flies there through its Mexico City hub from a dozen airports all over Mexico. The airport is west of town, just north of the entrance from the highway.

BY CAR   Chetumal is just over 3 hours from Tulum. If you're continuing to Belize, be aware that rental companies don't allow you to take their cars across the border. To get to the ruins of Tikal in Guatemala, you must go through Belize to the border crossing at Ciudad Melchor de Mencos.

BY BUS   The main bus station (✆ **983/832-5110**) is 20 blocks from the town center on Insurgentes at Avenida Héroes. Buses go to Cancún, Tulum, Playa del Carmen, Puerto Morelos, Mérida, Campeche, Villahermosa, and Tikal, Guatemala.

To Belize: Buses depart from the Lázaro Cárdenas market, most often called Mercado Nuevo (Héroes and Circuito). Ask for **Autobuses Novelo,** which has local service throughout the day (140 pesos) and several express buses per day (185 pesos).

VISITOR INFORMATION

The **State Tourism Office** (✆ **983/835-0860**) is at Calzada del Centenario 622, between Comonfort and Ciricote. It's open Monday to Friday from 9am to 6pm.

ORIENTATION

The telephone **area code** is **983.**

Traffic enters the city from the west on Hwy. 186 and feeds onto Avenida Obregón into town. Stay on Obregón and don't take the exit veering left for Avenida Insurgentes (unless you're looking for the zoo or the huge Plaza Las Americas mall). You'll cross Avenida Héroes, the main north-south street through downtown.

A Museum Not to Miss

Museo de la Cultura Maya ★★★   This sophisticated museum unlocks the complex world of the Maya through interactive exhibits and genuine artifacts. Watch a slide show explaining medicinal and domestic uses of plants with their Mayan and scientific names, or write your birth date in Maya glyphs. One of the most fascinating exhibits describes the Maya's ideal of personal beauty, which prompted them to deform craniums, scar the face and body, and induce *estrabismo,* or cross-eyed vision.

An enormous screen flashes aerial images of more than a dozen Maya sites from Mexico to Honduras. Another large television shows the architectural variety of Maya pyramids and how they were probably built. A walk on a glass floor takes you over representative ruins in the Maya world. The museum is built around a stylized three-story ceiba tree, which the Maya believed connected Xibalba (the underworld), Earth, and the heavens, and each floor corresponds to those levels of the Maya cosmos. Try to see the museum before you tour the Río Bec ruins; signs are in Spanish and English.

Av. Héroes s/n (btw. Colón and Gandhi, 8 blocks from Av. Obregón, just past the Holiday Inn). ✆ **983/832-6838.** Admission 55 pesos. Tues–Sat 9am–7pm; Sun 9am–2pm.

Where to Stay

Bacalar, about 30 minutes away, is a more appealing base for exploring this region, but if you do need to stay over in the capital, here are a couple of serviceable hotels.

Hotel Holiday Inn Chetumal Puerta Maya   This modern hotel is a reliable if not inspiring option. It has the best air-conditioning in town and is only a block from the museum. Most rooms are midsize and come with one king-size or two double beds. Bathrooms are roomy and well lit.

Av. Héroes 171, 77000 Chetumal, Q. Roo. www.holidayinn.com. ✆ **800/465-4329** in the U.S., or 983/835-0400. 85 units. $70–$95 double. AE, MC, V. Free secure parking. From Av. Obregón, turn left on Av. Héroes, go 6 blocks, and look for the hotel on the right. **Amenities:** Restaurant; bar; fitness room; midsize outdoor pool; room service. *In room:* A/C, TV, Wi-Fi.

Hotel Los Cocos   Renovated rooms are positively sleek, bathrooms are scrupulously clean, and the small but inviting pool is in the middle of a lush garden.

Courtyard-facing rooms are the most pleasant. The open-air restaurant, popular with museum visitors, does a good job with Mexican favorites. This three-story hotel is 2 blocks south of the museum.

Av. Héroes 134 (corner of Chapultepec), 77000 Chetumal, Q. Roo. www.hotelloscocos.com.mx. 𝄐 **983/832-0920.** 176 units. 912–1,026 pesos double. AE, MC, V. Off-street parking. **Amenities:** Restaurant; bar; Internet terminal; 2 outdoor pools; room service. *In room:* A/C, TV, fridge.

Where to Eat

For local atmosphere on a budget, try **Restaurante Pantoja,** on the corner of calles Ghandi and 16 de Septiembre (𝄐 **983/832-3957**), 2 blocks east of the Museum of Maya Culture. It offers a cheap daily special, good green chile enchiladas, and Yucatecan specialties. It's open Monday to Saturday from 7am to 7pm. To sample excellent *antojitos,* the local supper food, try **El Buen Gusto,** on Calzada Veracruz across from the market (no phone). A Chetumal institution, it serves excellent *salbutes* and *panuchos,* tacos, and sandwiches. It's open from the morning until 2pm and again from about 7pm to midnight. Many locals prefer **La Ideal** next door, which has delicious *tacos de pierna* (soft tacos with thinly sliced pork shoulder) and *agua de horchata* (water flavored with rice, vanilla, and toasted pumpkin seed).

Onward from Chetumal

The Maya ruins of Lamanai, in Belize, are an easy day trip if you have transportation (not a rental car). You can explore the Río Bec route (see below) directly west of the city by taking Hwy. 186.

SIDE TRIPS TO MAYA RUINS FROM CHETUMAL

A few miles west of Bacalar and Chetumal begins an area of Maya settlement known to archaeologists as the Río Bec region. Numerous ruins stretching well into the state of Campeche are intriguing for their heavily stylized, lavishly decorated architecture. Excavation has brought restoration, but these cities have not been rebuilt to the degree found at Uxmal and Chichén Itzá. Buildings here often were in such great shape that reconstruction was unnecessary.

Nor have these sites been cleared of jungle growth like the marquee ruins mentioned above. Trees and vines grow in profusion, creating the feel of lost cities. In visiting them, you can imagine what John Lloyd Stephens and Frederick Catherwood must have felt when they traipsed through the Yucatán in the 19th century. The entire route is rich in wildlife; you might see a toucan, a grand curassow, or a macaw hanging about, while orioles, egrets, and several birds of prey are common. Gray fox, wild turkey, *tesquintle* (a bushy-tailed, plant-eating rodent), the coatimundi (raccoon kin with long tapered snout and tail), and armadillos inhabit the area in abundance. Several bands of spider and howler monkeys circulate Calakmul and the surrounding jungle.

THE ROUTE Halfway between Bacalar and Chetumal is the well-marked turnoff for Hwy. 186 to Escárcega (about 20km/12 miles from either town). This same road leads to Campeche, Palenque, and Villahermosa. A couple of gas stations are en route, including one in the town of Xpujil. Carry plenty of cash, as credit cards are rarely accepted in the area.

The Río Bec sites lie varying distances off this highway. You pass through a checkpoint at the Campeche state border; guards might ask for your travel papers or simply inquire where you've been and where you are going before waving you on. Rarely, they will want to inspect your trunk or even your luggage. You can divide your sightseeing into several day trips from Bacalar or Chetumal, or you can spend the night in this area and see more the next day. If you get an early start, you can easily visit a few of the sites mentioned here in a day.

Opening Hours

The archaeological sites along the Río Bec (except for Calakmul, which has its own opening days and hours) are open daily 8am to 5pm.

Evidence, especially from Becán, shows that these ruins were part of the **trade route** linking the Caribbean coast at Cobá to Edzná and the Gulf Coast, and to Lamanai in Belize and beyond. A great number of cities once thrived here, and much of the land was dedicated to cultivating maize. All of this has been swallowed by the dense jungle blanketing the land from horizon to horizon.

The following sites are listed in east-to-west order, the way you would see them driving from the Caribbean coast, ideally after visiting the Museo de la Cultura Maya (p. 563) in Chetumal to gain some context. If you want a guide to show you the area, **Dan Griffin** (merida07forever@yahoo.com) is based in Mérida but is studying archaeology with the University of Leicester and works on archaeology and anthropology projects all over the Yucatán Peninsula. You might meet him guiding for Río Bec Dreams (p. 565), but he also leads independent tours focusing on lesser-known sites and on bird-watching. Another good choice is **Luis Téllez** (📞 **983/832-3496;** www.mayaruinsandbirds.com) in Chetumal. He's knowledgeable, speaks English, and drives safely and well. He's acquainted with archaeologists excavating these ruins, knows the local wildlife, and guides many tours for birders.

Entry to each site is 31 to 49 pesos. Informational signs are in Mayan, Spanish, and English. Few if any refreshments are available, so bring your own water and food. All the principal sites have toilets.

FOOD & LODGING   The only town in the Río Bec region offering basic tourist services is Xpujil, which doesn't have much else going for it. Of the basic affordable hotels in town, the best food and lodging is at **Restaurant y Hotel Calakmul** (📞 **983/871-6029**), which rents air-conditioned doubles with TV for 600 pesos. They have tile floors, private bathrooms with hot water, and good beds. The restaurant is reliable and is open daily from 6am to midnight. Main courses cost 45 to 120 pesos.

A rental car opens up some better options. Just beyond Xpujil, across from the ruins of the same name, is **Chicanná Eco Village** at Carretera Escárcega–Chetumal Km 144 (www.chicannaecovillageresort.com; 📞 **981/811-9192**). Its 42 comfortable, nicely furnished rooms are distributed among several two-story thatched bungalows. They offer doubles or a king-size bed, ceiling fans, a large bathroom, and screened windows. Pathways through manicured lawns and flower beds link the bungalows to one another and to the restaurant and swimming pool. Doubles go for 1,200 pesos.

Río Bec Dreams ★★, Carretera 186, Escárcega–Chetumal Km 142 (www.riobecdreams.com; 📞 **983/126-3526**), 11km (6¾ miles) west of Xpujil just past Becán, rents "jungalows"—small, wooden cabins on stilts—scattered through a tropical forest. They have good screens and such niceties as curtains, tile counters, hand-painted sinks, porches, and very comfortable beds with mosquito netting, for 550 pesos a night. Cabins have wash basins, but guests share spotless bathrooms (the one unit with private bathroom costs 700 pesos). Rates are for a 2-night minimum stay; for 1 night, add 50 pesos. Three large cabañas with screened-in porches and private bathrooms rent for 1,000 pesos (one bedroom) to 1,150 pesos (two bedrooms), with a 2-night minimum stay. For all its rusticity, the hotel provides Wi-Fi. The Canadian owners have lived in the area a long time and are devoted students of Río Bec architecture who guide tours of the ruins; tours run from short excursions to smaller ruins for 250 pesos to all-day treks through Calakmul for 1,500 pesos. The owners are a wonderful resource and good companions around the open-air bar. The restaurant is easily the best in the area.

Dzibanché & Kinichná

The turnoff, 37km (23 miles) from the highway intersection, is well marked; another 23km (14 miles) brings you to the ruins. Ask about the condition of the road before setting out. These unpaved roads can go from good to bad pretty quickly, but this is an important enough site that road repair is generally kept up. Dzibanché (or Tzibanché) means "place where they write on wood"—obviously not the original name, which remains unknown. It dates from the Classic period (A.D. 300–900) and was occupied for around 700 years. Exploration began here in 1993, and the site opened to the public in late 1994. Scattered over 42 sq. km (16 sq. miles) are several groupings of buildings and plazas; only a small portion is excavated.

TEMPLES & PLAZAS Two large adjoining plazas have been cleared. The most important structure yet excavated is the **Temple of the Owl** in the main plaza, Plaza Xibalba. Archaeologists found a stairway descending from the top of the structure and deep into the pyramid to a burial chamber (not open to visitors), where they uncovered some beautiful polychromatic lidded vessels, one of which has an owl painted on the top handle with its wings spreading onto the lid. White owls were messengers of the underworld gods of the Maya religion. Also found here were the remains of a sacrificial victim and what appear to be the remains of a Maya queen, which is unique in Maya archaeology.

Opposite the Temple of the Owl is the **Temple of the Cormorant,** named after the bird depicted on a polychromed drinking vessel found here. Archaeologists also found evidence here of an interior tomb similar to the one in the Temple of the Owl, but excavations have not yet begun. Other magnificently preserved pottery pieces found during excavations include an incense burner with an almost three-dimensional figure of the diving god attached to the outside, and another incense burner with an elaborately dressed representation of the god Itzamná attached.

Situated all by itself is **Structure VI,** a miniature rendition of Teotihuacán's style of *tablero* and *talud* architecture. Each step of the pyramid is made of a *talud* (sloping surface) crowned by a *tablero* (vertical stone facing). Teotihuacán was near present-day Mexico City, but its influence stretched as far as Guatemala. At the top of the pyramid, a doorway with a wooden lintel is still intact after centuries of weathering. This detail gave the site its name. Date glyphs for the year A.D. 733 are carved into the wood.

Another nearby city, **Kinichná** (Kee-neech-*nah*) is about 2.5km (1½ miles) north. The road leading there becomes questionable during the rainy season, but an Olmec-style jade figure was found there. It has a large acropolis with five buildings on three levels, which have been restored and are in good condition. Fragments of the original stucco are visible.

Kohunlich ★

Kohunlich (Koh-*hoon*-leech), 42km (26 miles) from the turnoff for Hwy. 186, dates from around A.D. 100 to 900. Turn left off the road, and the entrance is 9km (5⅔ miles) farther. Enter the grand, parklike site, cross a large, shady ceremonial area flanked by four large pyramids, continue walking straight ahead.

Just beyond this grouping you'll come to Kohunlich's famous **Pyramid of the Masks** under a thatched covering. Six stucco heads, more than 2.4m (8 ft.) tall, flank the giant staircase. Dating from around A.D. 500, each is slightly different but all are elongated and wear a headdress with a mask on its crest and a mask on the chin piece—essentially masks within masks. The carving on the pupils suggests a solar connection, possibly with the night sun that illuminated the underworld. It's speculated that masks covered much of the facade of this building, which was built in the Río Bec style with rounded corners, a false stairway, and a false temple on the top. At least one theory holds that the masks are a composite of several rulers at Kohunlich.

In the buildings immediately to the left after you enter the site, recent excavations uncovered two intact pre-Hispanic skeletons and five decapitated heads that were probably used in a ceremonial ritual. To the right, follow the shady path through the jungle to another recently excavated plaza. The fine architecture and the high quality of pottery found there suggests this complex housed priests or rulers. Scholars believe overpopulation led to Kohunlich's decline.

Xpujil

Xpujil (Eesh-poo-*heel*; also spelled Xpuhil), meaning either "cattail" or "forest of kapok trees," flourished between A.D. 400 and 900. This small, well-preserved site is easy to get to; look for a highway sign pointing right (north). The entrance is just off the highway; the main structure is a 180m (591-ft.) walk farther. Along the path are some *chechén* trees, recognizable by their blotchy bark. Don't touch; they are poisonous and can cause blisters. On the right, a platform supports a restored two-story building with a central staircase on its eastern side. Remnants of a decorative molding and two galleries are connected by a doorway. About 90m (295 ft.) farther you come to **Structure I,** the site's main structure—a rectangular ceremonial platform 2m (6½ ft.) high and 50m (164 ft.) long supporting the palace, decorated with three tall towers shaped like miniature versions of the pyramids in Tikal, Guatemala. These towers are purely decorative, with false stairways and temples that are too small to serve as such. The effect is beautiful. The building holds 12 rooms, which are now in ruins.

Becán ★★★

Becán (Beh-*kahn*) is about 7km (4⅓ miles) beyond Xpujil, visible on the right side of the highway. Becán means "moat filled by water," and it was in fact protected by a moat spanned by seven bridges; the city is a stellar (and rare) example of Maya fortification; dirt from digging the moat was piled up to create a fortified wall around the city. The extensive site dates from the early Classic to the late post-Classic (600 B.C.– A.D. 1200) period. Although it was abandoned by A.D. 850, ceramic remains indicate that there may have been a population resurgence between 900 and 1000, and it was still used as a ceremonial site as late as 1200. Becán was an administrative and ceremonial center with political sway over at least seven other cities in the area, including Chicanná, Hormiguero, and Payán.

The first plaza group you see after you enter was the center for grand ceremonies. From the highway, you can see the back of **Structure I,** a pyramid with two temples on top. Beyond and in between the two temples you can see the temple atop **Structure IV,** opposite Structure I. When the high priest exited the mouth of the earth monster in the center of this temple (which he reached by way of a hidden side stairway that's now partially exposed), he would have been visible from well beyond the immediate plaza, where it's thought that commoners had to stand. The back of Structure IV is believed to have been a civic plaza where rulers sat on stone benches. The second plaza group dates from around A.D. 850 and has perfect twin towers on top. Under the platform supporting the towers are 10 rooms that are thought to be related to Xibalba (Shee-*bahl*-bah), the underworld. Earth-monster faces probably covered this building (and appeared on other buildings as well). Remains of at least one ball court have been unearthed. Next to the ball court is a well-preserved figure in an elaborate headdress behind glass, excavated not far from where he is now displayed. The markings are well defined, displaying a host of details.

Chicanná

Slightly over 1.5km (1 mile) beyond Becán, on the left side of the highway, is Chicanná, which means "house of the mouth of snakes." Trees loaded with bromeliads shade the central square surrounded by five buildings. **Structure II,** the site's outstanding building, features a monster-mouth doorway and an ornate stone facade with more superimposed masks. As you enter the mouth of the earth monster, you are on a platform configured as the monster's open jaw, with stone teeth on both sides. Again you find a lovely example of an elongated building with ornamental miniature pyramids on each end, typical of Río Bec architecture.

Calakmul ★★★

This area is both a massive Maya archaeological zone, with at least 60 sites, and a 70,000-hectare (172,974-acre) rainforest designated in 1989 as the Calakmul Biosphere Reserve, including territory in both Mexico and Guatemala. The best way to see Calakmul is to spend the night at Xpujil or Chicanná and leave early in the morning for Calakmul. If you're the first to drive down the narrow access road to the ruins (1½ hr. from the highway), you'll probably see plenty of wildlife. On my last trip to the ruins, I saw two groups of spider monkeys swinging through the trees on the outskirts of the city and a group of howler monkeys sleeping in the trees in front of Structure II. I also saw a couple of animals that I couldn't identify, and heard the growl of a jungle cat that I wasn't able to see.

The site is open Tuesday to Sunday from 7am to 5pm. The rainy season, when the place is soaked, is from June to October.

THE ARCHAEOLOGICAL ZONE   Since 1982, archaeologists have been excavating the ruins of Calakmul, which date from 100 B.C. to A.D. 900. It's the largest of the 60 known Río Bec sites. Nearly 7,000 buildings have been discovered and mapped. At its zenith, at least 60,000 people may have lived around the site, but by the time of the Spanish Conquest in 1519, less than 1,000 lived there. Arriving at a large plaza filled with trees, you immediately see several stelae; Calakmul contains more of than 100—more than any other site—but they are much more weathered and indistinguishable than the stelae of Palenque or Copán in Honduras. Looters have cut the face off of some. By Structure XIII is a stele of a woman thought to have been a ruler that dates from A.D. 652.

Some structures here are built in the Petén style characteristic of Guatemala, with extraordinarily high crested structures, steep staircases, and false facades. Others are typical Río Bec style. **Structure III** must have been the residence of a noble family. Its design is unique and quite lovely; it retains its original form, never having been remodeled. Offerings of shells, beads, and polychromed tripod pottery were found inside. **Structure II** is the tallest pyramid in the Yucatán, at 54m (177 ft.). From the top, you can see the outline of the ruins of El Mirador, 50km (31 miles) across the forest in Guatemala. Two stairways ascend along the sides of the pyramid's principal face in the upper levels, with masks further breaking up the space.

Temple IV charts the line of the sun from June 21, when it falls on the left (north) corner; to September 21 and March 21, when it lines up in the east behind the middle temple on the top of the building; to December 21, when it falls on the right (south) corner. Numerous jade pieces, including spectacular masks, were uncovered here, most of which are on display in the Museum of Mayan Culture in Campeche (p. 610). **Structure VII** is largely unexcavated except for the top, where, in 1984, the most outstanding jade mask yet to be found at Calakmul was uncovered. In their book *A Forest of Kings,* Linda Schele and David Freidel tell of wars among the Calakmul, Tikal, and Naranjo (the latter two in Guatemala), and how Ah-Cacaw, king of Tikal (120km/75 miles south of Calakmul), captured King Jaguar-Paw in A.D. 695 and later Lord Ox-Ha-Te Ixil Ahau, both of Calakmul.

CALAKMUL BIOSPHERE RESERVE   Set aside in 1989, this is the peninsula's only high forest, a rainforest that annually records as much as 5m (16 ft.) of rain. The tree canopy is higher here than in the forest of Quintana Roo. It lies very close to the border with Guatemala, but, of course, there is no way to get there. Among the plants are cactus, epiphytes, and orchids. Endangered animals include the white-lipped peccary, jaguar, and puma. So far, more than 250 species of birds have been recorded. At present, no overnight stay or camping is permitted. If you want a tour of a small part of the forest and you speak Spanish, you can inquire for a guide at one of the two nearby *ejidos* (cooperatives). Some old local *chicleros* (the men who tap sapodilla trees for their gum) have expert knowledge of flora and fauna and can take you on a couple of trails.

> **A Driving Caution**
>
> Numerous curves in the road obscure oncoming traffic (what little there is).

The turnoff on the left for Calakmul is located 53km (33 miles) from Xpujil, just before the village of Conhuas. There's a guard station there where you pay 40 pesos per car. From the turnoff, it's an hour's drive on a paved one-lane-road. Admission to the site is 41 pesos.

It's advisable to take with you some food and drink and, of course, bug spray.

Balamkú ★★

Balamkú (Bah-lahm-*koo*), just off Hwy. 186 about 5km (3 miles) west of Conhuas, is easy to reach and worth the visit. A couple of buildings in the complex were so well preserved that they required almost no reconstruction. Inside the **Temple of the Four Kings,** covered by a later pyramid built over it, is one of the largest stucco friezes in the Maya world. The three major figures—looters made off with a fourth before the frieze was discovered in 1990 and protected—are a rabbit, an alligator, and a crocodile, flanked by many carvings of animals, mythological beings, and kings. The concept behind this temple is life and death, and figures of men sit in the gaping maws of crocodiles and toads as they descend into the underworld. On each stucco figure's head are the eyes, nose, and mouth of a jaguar, followed by the full face of the human figure, then a neck formed by the eyes and nose of another jaguar, and an Olmec-like face on the stomach, with its neck ringed by a necklace. Now the frieze is under lock and key, and visitors must ask the caretaker to let them view the unique art. Much of the original painting remains, so flash photography is not allowed.

MÉRIDA, THE MAYA INTERIOR & CHICHÉN ITZÁ

by Christine Delsol

Long before Cancún was a glimmer in some computer programmer's eye, all roads led to Mérida. The great "White City"—still the region's cultural heart and soul—presided over a peninsula rich with legacies of colliding civilizations. The trove of ancient cities left behind by that cataclysm has enticed visitors ever since New York writer John Lloyd Stephens and illustrator Frederick Catherwood ventured south to investigate rumors of lost cities in the jungle.

The splendors of the ancient Maya world are still the Yucatán's biggest draw beyond the Caribbean coast. **Chichén Itzá,** every bit as wondrous as its coronation as a "new" Wonder of the World suggests, has many worthy companions. **Uxmal, Edzná, Cobá, Calakmul,** and several smaller ancient cities are still infused with a quiet, ancient spirit that seems to be losing ground daily in the glare of Chichén Itzá's celebrity status.

The thoughtful visitor, though, will soon learn the Maya heartland is far more than a living museum revealing an extraordinary culture—it is the evolution of that civilization. Whether you stay in a restored hacienda and indulge in a massage from the granddaughter of a Maya shaman, attend Mérida's weekly *Vaquería* with traditional Yucatecan cowboy music and dancing, or visit a village whose people live in thatch-roof huts and still speak the Yucatec Mayan language, you'll find past and present converging as they do nowhere else.

The best way to see the Yucatán is by car. The terrain is flat, highways are well maintained and hypnotically straight, and traffic beyond the cities is light. Secondary roads are narrow and sometimes rough, though a flurry of road projects has improved a good percentage of them in the past couple of years. Add about 30% to the time you think any particular trip should take—not only will you miss a lot by speeding through, you will also run afoul of innumerable *topes* (*toh*-pehs), or speed bumps. These might be a rope across the road, a concrete island, or a row of metal half-spheres that will eat your undercarriage for breakfast. Most have warning signs, but sometimes they appear out of nowhere—or the signs might appear but the *topes* do not. You *will* slow down, either to ease over the *topes* or to ask around for a repair shop.

Renting a car (p. 577) isn't cheap, but some promotional deals are available, especially in low season. And some of your most memorable experiences will be in places not easily reached by bus. Plenty of buses serve major towns and ruins, but service to smaller towns and ruins, and the haciendas, is sparse. Autobuses del Oriente (ADO) controls most of the first-class bus service and does a good job with the major destinations. Second-class buses go to some out-of-the-way places, but they make countless stops and often aren't air-conditioned; they are best for short distances. If you don't want to rent a car, a few tour operators take small groups to more remote ruins, cenotes, and villages. Alternatively, hiring a taxi for a half- or full day can be less expensive than renting a car.

The Yucatán is hot country; always travel with a hat, sunblock, mosquito repellent, and water. November to February are the coolest months, April to June the hottest. Thunderstorms moderate temperatures from July to October. More tourists visit the interior in winter, but the high season/low season distinction is far less pronounced than on the Caribbean coast.

Between tramping through ruins, swimming in the cool, clear waters of a cenote (natural underground pools), staking out your own private beach, or spotting flamingos in an estuary, you won't lack for diversions. But the greatest pleasure is simply slowing down, lazing in a town square, eating regional food prepared with centuries-old techniques, and making conversation with the proud, gentle people whose ancestors created the ancient empires we admire today.

MÉRIDA: GATEWAY TO THE MAYA HEARTLAND ★★★

1,440km (895 miles) E of Mexico City; 320km (199 miles) W of Cancún

Mérida, capital of the state of Yucatán, has been the peninsula's lodestar since the Spanish Conquest, yet many visitors treat it merely as a base camp for forays to the surrounding ruins. Though "The White City" (named after its limestone buildings) endures the traffic and noise common to many colonial cities, its vibrancy, eye-popping architecture, and kind, dignified people are what you remember. The heady brew of ancient and modern is at its most piquant in the bustling, genial historic center, and the Meridanos' celebratory proclivities are infectious. This is the best place to shop for regional specialties, such as hammocks, Panama hats, *guayabera* shirts, and embroidered *huipiles*, the colorful native blouses. Mérida enjoys a remarkable bounty of bed-and-breakfasts and beautifully restored colonial homes, many of which are available for vacation rentals. Expatriates have been flocking to the city in recent years—not only retirees but young couples with boundless energy to explore and show off their adopted home. In the midst of this cultural explosion, you never have to look far to find a festival, concert, theater production, or art exhibition.

Essentials

GETTING THERE & DEPARTING

BY PLANE **Aeroméxico** (© 800/237-6639 in the U.S., or 01-800/021-4000 in Mexico; www.aeromexico.com) flies nonstop to and from Miami and Mexico City and has expanded its connecting flights from other U.S. cities since Mexicana suspended operations. **Continental** (© 800/523-3273 in the U.S.; www.continental.com), in the process of merging with United, flies nonstop to and from Houston. American, Delta, and Alaska also serve Mérida through code shares, usually at higher

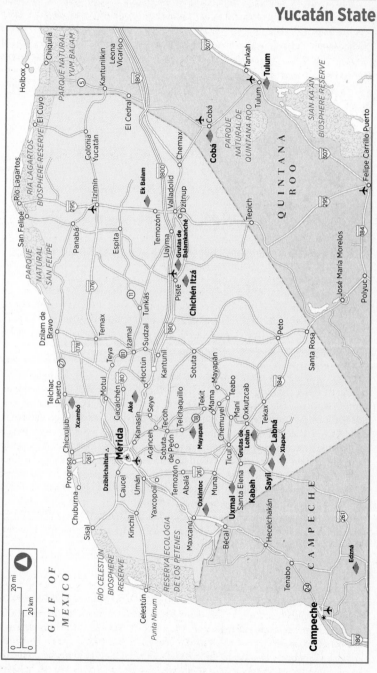

fares. The Mexican discount carrier **Volaris** (*©* **866/988-3527** in the U.S.; www. volaris.com.mx) flies to Mérida through Mexico City, and offers connecting flights from Chicago, Las Vegas, Los Angeles, San Francisco, and San Jose. Another Mexican budget line, **VivaAerobus** (*©* **01-81/8215-0150** in Mexico; www.vivaaerobus. com), flies to Mérida from Guadalajara, Mexico City, and Monterrey and has connecting flights from Houston and Las Vegas.

BY CAR   Hwy. 180 is the old *carretera federal* (federal highway) between Mérida and Cancún. The trip takes about 6 hours on a good road that passes through many Maya villages. A four-lane divided *cuota*, or *autopista* (toll road) parallels Hwy. 180 and begins at the town of Kantunil, 56km (35 miles) east of Mérida. For a toll of 368 pesos each way, you avoid the tiny villages and their not-so-tiny speed bumps. Coming from the direction of Cancún, Hwy. 180 feeds into Mérida's Calle 65, which passes 1 block south of the main square.

Coming from the south (Campeche or Uxmal), you enter the city on Avenida Itzáes. To get to the town center, turn right on Calle 59 (the first street after the zoo).

A *periférico* (loop road) circles Mérida, making it possible to skirt the city. Directional signs into the city are generally good, but lapping the city on the loop requires vigilance.

BY BUS   Mérida is the Yucatán's transportation hub. Of its five bus stations, two offer first-class buses and the other three provide local service to nearby destinations. The larger first-class station, **CAME,** is on Calle 70, between calles 69 and 71 (see "City Layout," below). The ADO bus line and its affiliates operate the station, which is also used by other long-distance lines. All the windows sell first-class tickets except for the last couple to the right, which sell tickets for ADO's deluxe services. ADO-GL is a small step up from first class, while UNO has superwide seats with lots of leg room. Unless it's a long trip, go for the bus with the most convenient departure time. Tickets can be purchased in advance; ask the agent for ticket options and departure times for the route you need.

To and from Cancún: You can pick up a bus almost every hour at the Came; some lines also collect passengers at the Fiesta Americana Hotel on Calle 60 at Avenida Colón, across from the Hyatt; you can buy a ticket in the hotel's shopping arcade at the **Ticket Bus** agency (which also takes reservations at www.ticketbus.com.mx) or at the Elite ticket agency. Cancún is 4 hours away; a few buses stop in **Valladolid.** If you're downtown, you can purchase tickets from the agency in Pasaje Picheta, a mall next to the Palacio de Gobierno on the main square.

To and from Chichén Itzá: Three buses per day (2½-hr. trip) depart from the CAME. Tour operators in Mérida hotels also offer day trips.

To and from Playa del Carmen, Tulum, and Chetumal: From the CAME, there are at least 10 departures per day for Playa del Carmen (5 hr. away), six for Tulum (6 hr.), and eight for Chetumal (7 hr.).

To and from Campeche: The CAME station has about 40 departures per day. It's a 2½-hour trip.

To and from Palenque and San Cristóbal de las Casas: There are three departures a day from the Came to San Cristóbal and four to Palenque. Minor thefts have been reported on buses to Palenque, so don't take second-class buses; check your luggage so that it's stowed in the cargo bay; and put your carry-on in the overhead rack, not on the floor.

The main **second-class terminal, TAME,** is around the corner from the CAME on Calle 69, between calles 68 and 70.

To and from Uxmal: Four buses per day leave from the second-class terminal. (You can pick up a tour through most hotels, travel agents, or tour operators in town.)

To and from Progreso and Dzibilchaltún: Transportes AutoProgreso offers service to and from its downtown station at Calle 62 no. 524, between calles 65 and 67. The trip to Progreso takes an hour by second-class bus.

To and from Celestún: Buses depart every hour from the Noroeste second-class station on Calle 67 at Calle 50.

To and from Izamal: Frequent buses leave from the Autobuses del Centro station (second class) on Calle 46 between calles 65 and 67, as well as from the Noroeste.

To and from Río Lagartos: Second-class buses leave from the Noroeste terminal.

To and from Isla Holbox: An Oriente bus makes the trip from the TAME station at 11:30pm, arriving in Chiquilá (ferry terminal) at 5am; Noroeste departs in the morning and arrives late in the afternoon.

ORIENTATION

ARRIVING BY PLANE   Mérida's airport is 13km (8 miles) from the city center on the southwestern outskirts of town, near the entrance to Hwy. 180. The airport has desks for rental cars, hotel reservations, and tourist information. Taxi tickets to town (150 pesos) are sold outside the airport doors, under the covered walkway.

VISITOR INFORMATION   The city and state **tourism offices** have different resources; if you can't get the information you're looking for at one, go to the other. The city's visitor information office (© **999/942-0000,** ext. 80119) is on the ground floor of the Ayuntamiento building, facing the main square on Calle 62. Look for a glass door under the arcade. Hours are Monday to Saturday from 8am to 8pm, and Sunday from 8am to 2pm. The staff offers a free walking tour of the area around the main square at 9:30am, Monday through Saturday. The state operates two downtown tourism offices, both open daily from 8am to 9pm. One is the **Teatro Peón Contreras,** facing Parque de la Madre (© **999/924-9290**), and the other on the main plaza in the **Palacio de Gobierno** (© **999/930-3101,** ext. 10001), immediately to the left as you enter. It also has information booths at the airport and the CAME bus station.

Keep your eye out for the free monthly magazine *Yucatán Today;* it's packed with information about Mérida and the rest of the region.

CITY LAYOUT   Downtown Mérida's grid layout is typical of the Yucatán: Even-numbered streets run north and south; odd-numbered streets run east and west. The numbering begins on the north and the east sides of town, so if you're walking on an odd-numbered street and the even numbers of the cross-streets are increasing, you are

 House Hunting

Address numbers bear little relation to a building's physical location, so addresses almost always include cross-streets. In "Calle 60 no. 549 × 71 y 73," for example, the "×" is shorthand for the word *por* (meaning "by"), and *y* means "and." So this address is on Calle 60 between calles 71 and 73. This tidy system disappears outside of downtown, where street numbering gets erratic (to say the least). It's important to know the name of the *colonia* (neighborhood) where you're going. This is the first thing taxi drivers will ask you.

heading west; likewise, if you are on an even-numbered street and the odd-numbered cross-streets are increasing, you are going south. Most downtown streets are one-way.

Mérida's main square is the busy **Plaza Grande,** bordered by calles 60, 61, 62, and 63. Calle 60, the *centro's* (downtown's) central artery, runs in front of the cathedral and connects the main square with several smaller plazas, some theaters and churches, and the University of Yucatán, just to the north. Handicraft shops, restaurants, and hotels are concentrated here. Around the plaza are the cathedral, the Palacio de Gobierno (state government building), the Ayuntamiento (town hall), and the Palacio Montejo. The plaza always has a crowd, and it overflows on Sundays, when surrounding streets are closed for an enormous street fair. (See "Festivals & Events in Mérida," below.) The teeming market district is a few blocks to the southeast.

festivals & events IN MÉRIDA

Many Mexican cities offer weekend concerts in parks and plazas, but Mérida surpasses them all by offering performances every day of the week. Unless otherwise indicated, admission is free.

Sunday From 9am to 9pm, the *centro* stages a fair called *Mérida en Domingo* (Mérida on Sunday). The plaza and a section of Calle 60 extending to Parque Santa Lucía close to traffic. Parents stroll with their children, taking in the food and drink booths, the lively little flea market and used-book fair, children's art classes, and educational booths. At 11am, musicians play everything from jazz to classical and folk music in front of the Palacio del Gobierno, while the police orchestra performs Yucatecan tunes in Parque Santa Lucía. At 11:30am, you'll find bawdy comedy acts at Parque Hidalgo, on Calle 60 at Calle 59. After a midafternoon lull, the plaza fills up again as people walk around and visit with friends. Around 7pm in front of the Ayuntamiento, a large band starts playing mambos, rumbas, and cha-chas with great enthusiasm; you may see 1,000 people dancing in the street. Afterward, folk ballet dancers reenact a typical Yucatecan wedding inside.

Monday At 9pm in front of Palacio Municipal, performers dance and play *Vaquería regional* (traditional cowboy music) to celebrate the *Vaquerías* feast, which was associated originally with the branding of cattle on the haciendas.

Performers include dancers with trays of bottles or filled glasses balanced on their heads—a sight to see.

Tuesday At 9pm in Parque Santiago, Calle 59 at Calle 72, the Municipal Orchestra plays Latin and American big-band music from the 1940s.

Wednesday At 9pm, the University of Yucatán Ballet Folklórico performs in the Teatro Peón Contreras, Calle 60 at Calle 57. Admission is 50 pesos. Auditorio Olimpio, on the Calle 62 side of the plaza, hosts guitar *trovas* (boleros or ballads) and other live music and theater performances, free of charge.

Thursday At 9pm in Parque Santa Lucía, the Serenata Yucateca presents regional music, dance, and spoken-word performances.

Friday At 9pm in the courtyard of the University of Yucatán, Calle 60 at Calle 57, the University of Yucatán Ballet Folklórico performs typical Yucatecan dances.

Saturday At 8pm in the park at Paseo de Montejo and Calle 47, *Noche Mexicana* features traditional Mexican music and dance performances with craft booths and food stands selling great *antojitos* (finger foods), drinks, and ice cream. At 9pm, Calle 60 closes between Plaza Grande and Calle 53 for *En El Corazón de Mérida,* a festival featuring several live bands joined by stilt walkers, mariachis, and crafts and food stands.

Mérida's most fashionable district is the wide, tree-lined boulevard **Paseo de Montejo** and its surrounding neighborhood. The Paseo de Montejo parallels Calle 60 and begins 7 blocks north and a little east of the main square. It has trendy restaurants, modern hotels, bank and airline offices, and a few clubs. The boulevard is known for its stately mansions built during the henequén boom times. Near Montejo's intersection with Avenida Colón, you'll find the Hyatt and the Fiesta Americana hotels.

GETTING AROUND   By Car   In general, reserve a car in advance to get the best weekly rates during high season (Nov–Feb); in low season, renting a car after you reach Mérida may yield better deals from local rental companies that offer promotional deals that you can get only if you are there. Always ask if the price quote includes the IVA tax and insurance coverage. Practically everybody offers free mileage. For tips on saving money on car rentals, see the "Getting Around" section in chapter 20. Rental cars are generally a little more expensive (unless you find a promotional rate) than similar rentals in the U.S., though less than in Cancún. If your visit will be primarily in Mérida except for a couple of day trips, you'll do better to rent for a day or two, which also spares you the high cost of Mérida's parking lots. These *estacionamentos* often charge one price for the night and double that if you leave your car for the following day. Many hotels offer free parking, but make sure that includes daytime hours.

By Taxi   Taxis are easy to come by and much cheaper than in Cancún, usually 30 to 60 pesos around town and 100 to 120 to the outskirts.

By Bus   City buses are a little tricky to figure out but aren't needed often because almost everything of interest is within walking distance of the main plaza. The most useful buses run between downtown and Paseo de Montejo, which is a bit of a hike from the plaza. Catch an "Itzimná" bus on Calle 59, between calles 56 and 58, to visit points along the boulevard. You can also take a *colectivo* (minibus) heading north on Calle 60. Most take you within a couple of blocks of Paseo de Montejo. The *colectivos* or *combis* (usually painted white) line up along the side streets next to the plaza and fan out in several directions along simple routes.

[FastFACTS] MÉRIDA

Area Code   The telephone area code is **999.**

Business Hours   Generally, businesses are open Monday to Saturday from 10am to 2pm and 4 to 8pm.

Consulates   The **American Consulate** is at Calle 60 no. 338-K between calles 29 and 31 (☏ **999/942-5700**), 1 block north of the Hyatt hotel (Col. Alcalá Martín). Office hours are Monday to Friday from 9am to 1pm.

Currency Exchange   I prefer *casas de cambio* (currency exchange offices)

over banks. Mérida has plenty; one called **Cambios Portales,** Calle 61 no. 500 (☏ **999/923-8709**), is on the north side of the main plaza in the middle of the block. It's open daily from 8:30am to 8:30pm. There are also many ATMs; one is on the south side of the same plaza.

Drugstore   Farmacía Yza, Calle 63 no. 502-A, between calles 60 and 62 (☏ **999/924-9510**), on the south side of the plaza, is open 24 hours.

Hospitals   Mérida has several good hospitals, the best of which is **Centro Médico de las Américas,** Calle 54 no. 365 between 33-A and Avenida Pérez Ponce. The main phone number is ☏ **999/926-2611;** for emergencies, call ☏ **999/927-3199.** You can also call the **Cruz Roja (Red Cross)** at ☏ **999/924-9813.**

Internet Access   You hardly have to walk more than a couple of blocks to find an Internet access provider; rates hover around 15 pesos per hour. Most hotels provide free Wi-Fi, and the city has installed free Wi-Fi in more than 50 city parks, including the Plaza Grande, Parque San Juan, Parque de las Américas, and Parque Zoológico del Centenario.

Police   Mérida has a special body of English-speaking police to assist tourists. They patrol the downtown area and Paseo de Montejo, wearing white shirts with a POLICIA TURISTICA patch on the sleeve. Their

phone number is
© **999/942-0060.**

Post Office   The *correo* is near the market at the corner of calles 65 and 56, with its own entrance separate from the new city museum. It's open Monday to Friday from 8am to 7pm, Saturday from 9am to 1pm.

Seasons   Mérida has two high seasons, but they aren't as pronounced as on the Caribbean coast. One is in July and August, when Mexicans take their vacations,

and the other is between November 15 and Easter Sunday, when winter-weary Canadians and Americans flock to the Yucatán.

Weather   From November to February, the weather can be pleasantly cool and windy. In other months, it's just plain hot, especially during the day. Rain can occur any time of year, especially during the rainy season (July–Oct), and usually comes in the form of afternoon tropical showers.

Where to Stay

Mérida soothes the budget, especially if you've come from the Caribbean resorts. Though winter is the most popular time, the stream of visitors is steadier than on the coast, so many hotels don't have high- and low-season rates. That said, promotional rates are more plentiful during low season. Large trade shows can fill the hotels, so reservations are a good idea. Rates quoted here include the 17% tax (always ask if the price includes tax). Most hotels in Mérida offer at least a few air-conditioned rooms, and some also have pools. But many inexpensive places haven't figured out how to provide a comfortable bed; either the mattresses are hard or the bottom sheet is too small to stay tucked in. Hotels in Mérida that don't have their own parking lots have arrangements with nearby garages, letting you park for a fee. If you can find a parking space on the street, cars are generally safe from vandalism. Some hotels offer free parking, but sometimes it's free only at night, with a charge incurred during the day.

VERY EXPENSIVE

Hacienda Xcanatún ★★★   This magnificent example of the Yucatán's converted haciendas was built in the mid–18th century at the edge of present-day Mérida and later became one of the region's most important henequén (sisal) plantations. Restoration with handcrafted local hardwood, wrought iron, marble, and stone has resuscitated its original luster and then some: The capacious bathrooms have double-sized, carved-stone waterfall tubs, and its Casa de Piedra, occupying the old machinery house, is one of Mexico's top-rated restaurants. Fountains and a bridged stream grace the extensive, jungle-like gardens, and the spa's ancient Maya healing techniques use local plants and flowers. The hacienda offers private guided cultural tours.

Carretera Mérida–Progreso Km 12, Mérida, Yuc. www.xcanatun.com. © **888/883-3633** in the U.S. and Canada, or 999/930-2140. Fax 999/941-0319. 18 units. $265–$340 double; $300–$382 deluxe suites; $330–$417 master suites. Rates include breakfast. Ask about Best Available Rate promotion. AE, MC, V. Free parking. No children under 12 without prior arrangement. **Amenities:** Restaurant; 2 bars; concierge; private day-trip program; garden; golf privileges at nearby Jack Nicklaus course; 2 outdoor pools; spa; Wi-Fi on patios, in restaurant, and lobby. *In room:* A/C, hair dryer, minibar, outdoor whirlpool tubs (in suites).

Hotel Indigo Mérida Hacienda Misné ★★   This is a rarity among the region's hacienda hotels: a country estate located within Mérida's city limits, operated by the family who bought it for a summer home years before it became a hotel in 2007. It's

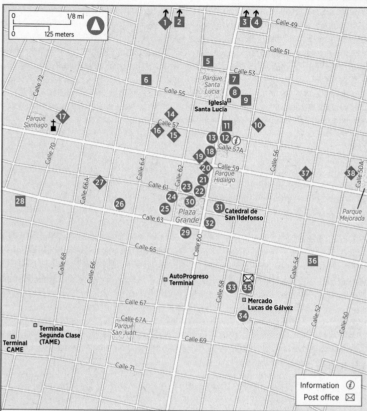

Information ⓘ
Post office ✉

ATTRACTIONS ●
Bazaar de Artesanías **34**
Casa del Alguacil **23**
Casa de las Artesanías **26**
Cathedral **31**
Centro Cultural Olimpo **24**
Iglesia de Jesús **18**
Iglesia de Santa Lucía **8**
Museo de Arte
  Contemporáneo **32**
Museo de la Ciudad **35**
Palacio Cantón/Museo
  Regional de Antropología **4**
Palacio de Gobierno **22**
Palacio Montejo **29**
Palacio Municipal **25**
Plaza Mayor Grande **30**
Portal de Granos **33**

Teatro Ayala **21**
Teatro Peón Contreras **12**
Universidad de Yucatán **13**

RESTAURANTS ◆
Alberto's Continental **16**
Amaro **19**
Café Alameda **10**
Casa de Frida **27**
Eladio's **37**
El Portico del Peregrino **14**
La Chaya Maya **15**
La Flor de Santiago **17**
Restaurante Kantún **1**
Restaurante Los
  Almendros **38**
Vito Corleone **20**

HOTELS ■
Casa Álvarez **5**
Casa del Balam **11**
Casa Santiago **28**
Fiesta Americana Mérida **3**
Hotel Dolores Alba **36**
Hotel Maison Lafitte **7**
Hotel Marionetas **2**
Hotel MedioMundo **6**
Luz en Yucatán **9**

579

a beauty, with long red-tiled colonnades stretching along vast gardens peppered with ponds and fountains. The family strives to preserve the hacienda's original character while creating luxurious modern rooms within the traditional exteriors. Some even have private sitting pools. It's about a 15-minute drive from downtown, just off Calle 65 (the road to and from Cancún) about .5km (less than ⅓ mile) from the *periférico*. The neighborhood's confounding street-numbering system makes it tricky to find the first time; look for a tree in the middle of the road on Calle 6B at Calle 65.

Calle 19 no. 172 (at Calle 6B), Fracc. Misné 1, 97173 Mérida, Yuc. www.haciendamisne.com.mx. © **999/940-7150.** Fax 999/940-7160. 50 units. $145–$510 double. See website for promotional rates. AE, DC, DISC, MC, V. Free parking. **Amenities:** Restaurant; bar; concierge; library; 2 outdoor pools; room service; spa. *In room:* A/C, TV, CD player, hair dryer, MP3 player, Wi-Fi.

Rosas y Xocolate ★   Paseo de Montejo claimed a spot of its former grandeur when two of its long-abandoned mansions emerged after a 3-year transformation into this boutique hotel. Despite the restored antiques, ornate "rugs" created from fantastic original and reproduction pasta tiles and walls restored with a *chukum* resin technique borrowed from ancient Maya architects, the vibe is cool, sleek, and modern, with all the amenities and technology to back it up. (Lighting in public areas, from the courtyard to room corridors to the rooftop Moon Lounge's spiral staircase, however, might be a bit too noir—if not hazardous—for those lacking perfect night vision.) A delightful design twist: Double-height ceilings enclosing tubs and showers are open to the sky. Why "Xocolate," you ask? The hotel has an on-site Belgian chocolatier, and the spa makes liberal use of the "food of the gods" to invoke its mood-elevating and aphrodisiac properties. This hotel, whose restaurant won a loyal following before the hotel opened, could well become Mérida's marquee property.

Paseo de Montejo no. 480 at Calle 41, 97000 Mérida, Yuc. www.rosasandxocolate.com. © **999/924-2992.** 17 units. $200–$265 double; $300–$650 suite. MC, V. **Amenities:** Restaurant; 2 bars; concierge; library; 2 outdoor pools; room service; spa. *In room:* A/C, TV/DVD, CD player, minibar, MP3 docking station, Wi-Fi.

EXPENSIVE

Casa del Balam ★★★ 📷   Even with a king-size bed and massive wooden furniture, suites in the original owners' bedrooms of this onetime colonial mansion, converted in 1968, have space enough to do cartwheels. Those overlooking Calle 60 have heavy cedar doors opening onto the street and windows onto the lush courtyard dining room, where piano strains waft up at times. Standard rooms in the newer annex are more modest but supremely comfortable, with tile floors and wrought-iron headboards honoring the colonial atmosphere. The plaza is just 2 blocks away, and staff members treat you like their favorite niece or nephew.

Calle 60 no. 488 at Calle 57, 97000 Mérida, Yuc. www.casadelbalam.com. © **800/624-8451** in the U.S. and Canada, or 999/924-8844. 51 units. $86–$117 double; $96–$146 honeymoon suite; $110–$187 master suite. AE, DISC, MC, V. Free parking. **Amenities:** Restaurant; bar; babysitting; concierge; golf club access; outdoor pool; room service; spa services; Wi-Fi. *In room:* A/C, TV, hair dryer, minibar.

Casa San Angel ★   It's hard to guess which draws more people in to this lovely, family-run former converted mansion—the exuberant, largely *trompe l'oeil* jungle that serves as lobby and lounge, or the hotel's own bakery shop, piled high with delectable treats. Colorful guest rooms are roomy and uncluttered but well furnished. The lobby is an appealing place to have dessert and coffee even if you aren't staying here. You can also browse the hotel's two gift shops, 100 Percent Mexico and Pineda Covalin, whose fine handicrafts from all over Mexico and elegant silk accessories are a huge step beyond the typical souvenir trinkets. ***One caveat:*** The hotel is blessedly quiet most of the time, but it's right next to the staging ground for *Noche Mexicana* on Saturdays—one of Mérida's free weekly cultural celebrations. The best way to get around the noise problem is to step outside and join in the fun.

Paseo de Montejo no. 1 at Calle 49, 97000 Mérida, Yuc. www.hotelcasasanangel.com. © **999/928-1800.** 15 units. $140 double; $180–$211 suite. Rates include full breakfast. AE, MC, V. Free parking. No children 14 and under. **Amenities:** Restaurant; outdoor pool. *In room:* A/C, filtered water, Wi-Fi.

Fiesta Americana Mérida   This six-story hotel on Paseo de Montejo, built in the *fin-de-siècle* style of the old mansions along the boulevard, is the grand dame of Mérida's luxury chain hotels. Guest rooms around the soaring lobby with its stained-glass ceiling face outward and have views of one of the avenues. Rooms are comfortable and large, with innocuous modern furnishings and decorations in light, tropical colors. The floors are tile and the bathrooms large and well equipped. The hotel was built with local materials and at least a nod to Mexican design—far preferable to the cookie-cutter Hyatt across the street, and the service is more attentive.

Av. Colón 451, corner of Paseo de Montejo, 92127 Mérida, Yuc. www.fiestaamericana.com.mx. © **800/343-7821** in the U.S. and Canada, or 999/942-1111. Fax 999/942-1112. 350 units. $129–$135 double; $179 executive level; $244 junior suite. AE, DC, MC, V. Free secure parking. **Amenities:** 2 restaurants; bar; babysitting; children's programs; concierge; executive-level rooms; health club w/saunas, men's steam room, whirlpool; midsize outdoor pool; room service; tennis court. *In room:* A/C, TV w/pay movies, hair dryer, Internet, minibar.

Hotel Marionetas ★   This quiet, attractive B&B, 6 blocks north of the main square, has a comforting feel. Sofi (Macedonian) and Daniel (Argentine) are engaging, interesting people and attentive innkeepers who have created a lovely space with common areas in front, rooms in back, and a lush garden/pool area in between. Each room is different, but all have handmade tile floors, liberal use of bold but not overbearing color, and large, colonial-style windows and doors.

Calle 49 no. 516 (btw. calles 62 and 64), 97000 Mérida, Yuc. www.hotelmarionetas.com. © **999/928-3377.** 8 units. $88–$105 double; $105–$120 suite. Rates include full breakfast. 2-night minimum stay. MC, V. Free secure parking for compact cars. No children 9 and under. **Amenities:** Small outdoor pool. *In room:* A/C, TV, fridge, hair dryer, Wi-Fi.

MODERATE

Casa Santiago ★★★   This B&B's four recently remodeled guest rooms open off the wide central corridor of a lovely colonial home. With the gregarious manager, Vince, living on-site, it offers an ideal blend of comfort and privacy, traditional detail, and modern style. Casa Santiago is part of a compound that includes Casa Feliz, whose two large, newly restored rooms are available individually when the entire house isn't rented, and Casa Navidad, with one more guest room. Each has its own distinct theme, but all have the original pasta tile floors (made in Mérida for centuries with a technology brought over from Spain), handmade furniture, and some of the most comfortable mattresses in Mexico. Its Parque Santiago neighborhood is 5 easy blocks from the main plaza. Guests have use of the house's immaculate, modern kitchen.

Calle 63 no. 562 (btw. calles 70 and 72), 97000 Mérida, Yuc. www.casasantiago.net. © **314/266-1888** in the U.S. and Canada, or 999/928-9375. 7 units. $59–$125 double. Rates include full breakfast. No credit cards (PayPal for deposits). Limited free parking. No children 13 and under. **Amenities:** Common kitchen; phone for local calls; 2 outdoor pools. *In room:* A/C, Wi-Fi.

Hotel Maison Lafitte ★   This three-story hotel has modern, attractive rooms and tropical touches such as wooden window louvers and light cane furniture. Rooms are medium to large, with midsize bathrooms that have great showers and good lighting.

Most come with either two doubles or a king-size bed. Rooms are quiet and overlook a pretty little garden with a fountain, though a few don't have windows.

Calle 60 no. 472 (btw. calles 53 and 55), 97000 Mérida, Yuc. www.maisonlafitte.com.mx. ✆ **800/538-6802** in the U.S. and Canada, or 999/928-1243. Fax 999/923-9159. 30 units. High season 950 pesos; low

haciendas & HOTELS

During the colonial period, **haciendas** in the Yucatán were isolated, self-sufficient fiefdoms. Mostly they produced food-stuffs—enough for the needs of the owners and peasants, plus a little extra that the owners could sell for a small sum in the city. The owners, though sometimes politically powerful, were never rich.

This changed in the 19th century, when the expanding world market created high demand for henequén—more commonly known in the U.S. as sisal—an agave cactus fiber that was used to bale hay. Haciendas shifted to henequén production en masse, and the owners became wealthy as prices and profits climbed through the end of the 19th century and into the 20th. Then came the bust. Throughout the 1920s, prices and demand fell, and no other commodity could replace sisal. The haciendas entered a long decline, but by then, henequén cultivation and processing had become part of local culture.

Visiting a hacienda is a way to understand what the golden age was like. **Sotuta de Peón** (p. 593) has been refurbished and operates much as in the old days—a living museum involving an entire community. At another, **Yaxcopoil** (p. 598), you can wander about the shell of a once-bustling estate and take in the faded splendor.

Today another boom of sorts has brought haciendas back, this time as hotels, retreats, and country residences. The hotels convey an air of the past—elegant gateways, thick walls, open arches, and high ceilings—and extravagant suites and personal service make guests feel like lord and master of their little islands of order and tranquillity in a sea of chaos.

Six of the region's hacienda hotels are pure luxury. The most opulent is **Hacienda Xcanatún ★★★** (p. 578) on the outskirts of Mérida, off the highway to Progreso.

Four more luxury hotels are owned by Roberto Hernández, one of Mexico's richest men, and are affiliated with Starwood Hotels (www.luxurycollection.com; ✆ **800/325-3589** in the U.S. and Canada). They are restored to their original condition, and they are quite beautiful. **Temozón** (p. 584), off the highway to Uxmal, is the most magnificent. **Uayamón ★★★**, located between the colonial city of Campeche and the ruins of Edzná, is perhaps the most romantic, with its exterior preserved in a state of arrested decay. **Hacienda San José Cholul ★** is east of Mérida toward Izamal, and picturesque **Santa Rosa** lies southwest of Mérida, near the town of Maxcanú. Packages are available for staying at more than one of these haciendas. All offer personal service, activities, and spas.

Another luxury hotel, **Hacienda Misné ★★** (p. 578), is within Mérida city limits and is run by the family who once used it as a summer home.

One of the more affordable options on the eastern outskirts of Mérida on the highway to Cancún is **Hacienda San Pedro Nohpat** (p. 584).

Two more haciendas can be leased by small groups for retreats and vacations: **Hacienda Petac** (www.haciendapetac. com; ✆ **800/225-4255** in the U.S., or 999/911-2601) and **Hacienda San Antonio** (www.haciendasananantonio.com.mx; ✆ **999/910-6144**). Both have beautiful rooms, common areas, and grounds.

season 896 pesos. Rates include full breakfast. AE, MC, V. Free limited secure parking for compact cars. **Amenities:** Restaurant; bar; outdoor pool; room service. *In room:* A/C, TV, hair dryer, minibar, Wi-Fi.

Hotel MedioMundo ★ ⛟
Bright colors and lush gardens distinguish this quiet courtyard hotel, 3 blocks north of the main plaza. The simple, beautiful rooms have their original tile floors. The English-speaking owners have invested their money in the right places, going for pillow-top mattresses, good lighting, quiet air-conditioning, lots of space, and good bathrooms with strong showers. What they didn't invest in were TVs, which adds to the serenity. The eight rooms with air-conditioning cost $10 more, but all units have windows with good screens and get ample ventilation. A generous breakfast is served in one of the two attractive courtyards.

Calle 55 no. 533 (btw. calles 64 and 66), 97000 Mérida, Yuc. www.hotelmediomundo.com. ✆/fax **999/ 924-5472.** 12 units. $75–$90 double. MC, V. Limited street parking. No children 7 and under. **Amenities:** Small outdoor pool; Wi-Fi (in public areas). *In room:* A/C (in some), no phone.

Luz en Yucatán ★★★ ⛟ ✦
Behind a deceptively plain wall next to Santa Lucia Church, this inn offers a dizzying variety of rooms, suites, studios, and apartments in the main building (rumored to have been Santa Lucia's convent) and tucked into the garden around the pool. Every unit is different, thoughtfully decorated with Mexican arts and crafts, and the place is full of nooks and crannies for visiting or lounging. A large kitchen and dining room that seats 12 at a beautiful wooden table are available for guests in rooms without kitchens. The beds are among the best in Yucatán. The amiable and knowledgeable manager, who lives on-site, delights in taking guests under his wing. Oh, and did we mention the free bar cart?

Calle 55 no. 499 (btw. calles 60 and 58), 97000 Mérida, Yuc. www.luzenyucatan.com. ✆/fax **999/924- 0035.** 15 units. $50–$74 double; $64–$69 studio with kitchen; $74–$94 apt. Weekly and monthly discounts. No credit cards. Discounted parking in secure lot $5 a day. **Amenities:** Communal kitchen and dining room; outdoor pool; Wi-Fi. *In room:* A/C, TV, fridge.

INEXPENSIVE

Casa Alvarez Guest House ★ ⛟ ☺
Many guests come to this inn, 4 blocks from the plaza, for extended stays with the kind and hospitable owners. Each spacious room is different, all featuring light but vivid colors and a variety of wooden, iron, and painted headboards. Larger rooms have air-conditioning and command the higher prices. The eat-in kitchen where guests may prepare their own meals is stocked with coffee, tea, spices, and sometimes breakfast food and invariably becomes a social center. The owners go out of their way to keep children happy.

Calle 62 no. 448 at Calle 53, 97000 Mérida, Yuc. www.casaalvarezguesthouse.com. ✆ **999/924-3060.** 8 units. 450–550 pesos. No credit cards. Free parking. **Amenities:** Kitchen for guests' use; Wi-Fi in public areas. *In room:* A/C (in some), fan, TV, fridge, Wi-Fi (in some).

Hotel Dolores Alba ✦
Cheerful, comfortable rooms offer respite from a busy and not very pleasant street 3½ blocks from the main square. It's a good deal for an inviting swimming pool, good air-conditioning, and free parking. The newer three-story section (with elevator) surrounding the courtyard offers spacious, more stylish rooms with good-size bathrooms. Beds (two doubles or one double and one twin) have supportive mattresses, usually in a combination of one medium-firm and one medium-soft. All rooms have windows or balconies looking over the pool. An old mango tree shades the front courtyard. The older rooms in this section are decorated with local crafts and have small bathrooms. The family that owns the Hotel Dolores Alba outside Chichén Itzá manages this hotel; you can make reservations at one hotel for the other.

Calle 63 no. 464 (btw. calles 52 and 54), 97000 Mérida, Yuc. www.doloresalba.com. ☎ **999/928-5650.** Fax 999/928-3163. 100 units. 475 pesos double. Internet specials available. MC, V (with 8% surcharge). Free guarded parking. **Amenities:** Restaurant; bar; outdoor pool; room service. *In room:* A/C, TV.

Where to Stay Outside of Mérida

Hacienda San Pedro Nohpat ★★ ☺ 🍴 The large, comfortable rooms, vast lawn and gardens, and large pool and hot tub make an ideal retreat in a tiny town just off Hwy. 180 about 1.6km (1 mile) from Mérida's *periférico*. Rooms retain their sometimes grandiose hacienda flourishes but are furnished for contemporary travelers. Four of the rooms opening onto the large, clean swimming pool sleep four to six people and are set up with families in mind, including space for a child's crib. Children love the menagerie, including dogs, cats, burros, and birds, that wander the grounds. The Canadian owner, a font of local knowledge, is a master at organizing weddings at the picturesque hacienda for half of what hotels and haciendas typically charge.

Chichén Km 8, Mérida, Yuc. www.haciendaholidays.com. ☎ **999/988-0542.** 11 units. $95–$155. Rates include full breakfast. MC, V. **Amenities:** Restaurant; library; outdoor pool. *In room:* AC, TV/VCR (in some), Jacuzzi (in some).

Hacienda Temozón ★★★ This magnificent 17th-century estancia presides over 37 hectares (91 acres) of subtropical gardens and cenotes, 39km (24 miles) from Mérida. Built in 1655 by Don Diego de Mendoza, Temozón was the region's most productive livestock ranch in the early 18th century, then the top sisal producer in the late 1800s. Meticulously restored in 1997, it's now a Starwood property employing local workers and using organic produce from nearby farms in the restaurant. Spacious Spanish colonial–style rooms have 5.5m (18-ft.) ceilings with exposed rafters, fans, and thick whitewashed walls; Spanish-tile floors and baths; hammocks positioned to catch natural breezes; tropical hardwood furniture; and large, cushy beds with white linens adorned daily with fresh flowers. Suites have tubs, private terraces, and plunge pools. The Casa del Patrón suite has accommodated many global heads of state.

Carretera Mérida–Uxmal, Km 182, 97825 Temozon Sur, Yuc. www.haciendasmexico.com/temozon. ☎ **800/325-3589** in the U.S. and Canada, or 999/923-8089. Fax 999/923-7963. 28 units. $350–$450 double; $439–$590 suite. AE, MC, V. **Amenities:** Restaurant; free airport transfers; bikes; horseback riding; concierge; health club; outdoor pool; room service; spa; outdoor tennis court. *In room:* AC, fan, CD player, Internet, MP3 docking station.

Where to Eat

The people of Mérida are traditionalists when it comes to food. Certain dishes are associated with a particular day of the week. In households across the city, Sunday would feel incomplete without *puchero* (a kind of stew). On Monday, at any restaurant that caters to locals, you are sure to find *frijol con puerco* (pork and beans). Likewise, you'll find *potaje* (potage) on Thursday; fish, of course, on Friday; and *chocolomo* (a beef dish) on Saturday. These dishes are heavy and slow to digest; they are for the midday meal and not suitable for dinner. What's more, Meridanos don't believe seafood is a healthy supper food; seafood restaurants close by 6pm unless they cater to tourists. The preferred dinner food is turkey, best served in the traditional *antojitos—salbutes* (small, thin rounds of *masa* fried and topped with meat, onions, tomatoes, and lettuce) and *panuchos* (*salbutes* with the addition of bean paste)—and turkey soup.

Mérida also has a remarkable number of Middle Eastern restaurants. A large influx of Lebanese immigrants around 1900 has exerted a strong impact; Meridanos think of kibbe almost the way Americans think of pizza. Speaking of pizza, if you want to get some to take back to your hotel, try **Vito Corleone,** on Calle 59 between calles 60 and 62. Its pizzas have a thin crust with a slightly smoky taste from the wood-burning oven.

Downtown Mérida is well endowed with good midrange and budget restaurants, but the best upscale restaurants are in outlying districts. For something special, treat yourself to a meal at **Hacienda Xcanatún** (p. 578), whose French-trained chef excels at a fusion of French, Caribbean, and Yucatecan dishes.

EXPENSIVE

Alberto's Continental ★ LEBANESE/YUCATECAN   There's nothing quite like dining here at night in a softly lit room or on the wonderful old patio framed in Moorish arches. Elegant *mudejar*-patterned tile floors, simple furniture, and a gurgling fountain create a romantic mood, though prices are on the expensive side. For supper, you can choose a sampler plate of four Lebanese favorites, or traditional Yucatecan specialties, such as *pollo pibil* or fish Celestún (bass stuffed with shrimp), and finish with Turkish coffee.

Calle 64 no. 482 (at Calle 57). ✆ **999/928-5367.** Reservations recommended. Main courses 80-220 pesos. AE, MC, V. Daily 1-11pm.

Casa de Frida ★★ MEXICAN   This colorful restaurant serves fresh, healthful classics such as *mole poblano* and *chiles en nogada.* The *mole* is good, as is the interesting *flan de berenjena* (a kind of eggplant timbale). This is a comfortable, no-nonsense place with fuchsia pink walls and peacock blue trim, a la Frida. The menu's breadth will satisfy any appetite.

Calle 61 no. 526 (at Calle 66). ✆ **999/928-2311.** Reservations recommended. Main courses 100-130 pesos. No credit cards. Mon-Fri 6-10pm; Sat noon-5pm and 6-10pm; Sun noon-5pm.

El Pórtico del Peregrino ✋ INTERNATIONAL   The *berenjenas al horno* here—layers of eggplant, chicken, and cheese baked in tomato sauce—are kind of a hybrid of lasagna and moussaka that seems to personify Mérida's Italian and Lebanese influences. This unassuming entree is just as delectable as it was 10 years ago, and the small, vine-covered patio is one of the sweetest dining areas in Mérida. The higher-priced meat and fish dishes, though—even the traditional specialties—no longer seem to have the zip that one expects in the Yucatán.

Calle 57 no. 501 (btw. calles 60 and 62). ✆ **999/928-6163.** Main courses 70-175 pesos. AE, MC, V. Daily noon-midnight.

MODERATE

Amaro VEGETARIAN/YUCATECAN   This peaceful courtyard restaurant, with walls providing gallery space for local art, lists some interesting vegetarian dishes, such as *crema de calabacitas* (cream of squash soup), apple salad, and avocado pizza. It also offers a few fish and chicken dishes; you might want to try the Yucatecan chicken. The *agua de chaya* (*chaya* is a spinachlike vegetable that has sustained the Maya through the centuries) is refreshing on a hot afternoon. All desserts are made in-house.

Calle 59 no. 507 Interior 6 (btw. calles 60 and 62). ✆ **999/928-2451.** Main courses 50-90 pesos. MC, V. Daily 11am-2am.

El Príncipe Tutul Xiú ★★ 🍴 YUCATECAN   Authentic regional specialties from a limited menu are served in a Yucatecan village atmosphere by staff in traditional Maya dress. The owner of the original restaurant in the town of Maní opened this location in response to persistent pressure from Meridanos. Try the famous *sopa de lima* and one of the six typical main courses, such as *pavo escabeche,* served with great handmade tortillas. Meat is cooked over a charcoal grill. The flavored waters, such as *horchata* or *tamarindo,* are especially good here. It's a short taxi ride from downtown, and to return you can pick up a local bus that passes by the restaurant.

Calle 123 no. 216 (btw. calles 46 and 46b), Colonia Serapio Rendón. ✆ **999/929-7721.** Main courses 58 pesos. MC, V. Daily 11am-7pm.

La Chaya Maya ★★ YUCATECAN   Women in traditional Maya garb slap torti-llas onto the grill in an open space in the dining room of this spotless, comfortable restaurant devoted to Yucatecan cooking made with ultrafresh ingredients. I can't imagine skipping the cream of *chaya.* You'll find traditional dishes that rarely grace restaurant menus, such as *mucbil pollo* (chicken tamale casserole), traditionally served for Day of the Dead, and *sikil p'aak,* an earthy paste of ground squash seeds, tomatoes and chiles served with the complimentary chips. The friendly, professional staff does a better job than most with large groups, too.

Calle 57 no. 481 (at Calle 62). ✆ **999/928-4780.** Main courses 60–90 pesos. No credit cards. Daily 7am-11pm.

Restaurante Kantún ★★ 🐟 SEAFOOD   This modest restaurant serves the fresh-est seafood for incredibly low prices. The owner-chef is always on the premises taking care of details. The menu includes excellent ceviche and seafood cocktails, and fish cooked to order with delicate seasonings and sauces, including such specials as the *especial Kantún,* lightly battered and stuffed with lobster, crab, and shrimp. The dining room is air-conditioned, the furniture comfortable, and the service attentive.

Calle 45 no. 525-G (btw. calles 64 and 66). ✆ **999/923-4493.** Reservations recommended. Main courses 60–120 pesos. MC, V. Daily noon-8pm (occasionally closed Mon).

Restaurante Los Almendros YUCATECAN   As the first place to offer tourists such Yucatecan specialties as *salbutes, panuchos* and *papadzules, cochinita pibil,* and *poc chuc,* this place is an institution. That doesn't mean it produces the best of these dishes, but the food is good and reliable. Photographs on the menu make it a good place to try Yucatecan food for the first time. It's 5 blocks east of Calle 60, facing the Parque de la Mejorada. A newer branch in the Fiesta Americana hotel offers a less traditional but more inspiring setting, and the service is better.

Calle 50A no. 493 at Calle 57. ✆ **999/928-5459.** Reservations recommended Sun. Main courses 60–100 pesos. AE, MC, V. Daily 10am-11pm.

INEXPENSIVE

Café Alameda MIDDLE EASTERN/VEGETARIAN   This simple and informal place (metal tables, plastic chairs) is a good place to catch a light meal. The trick is figuring out the Spanish names for popular Middle Eastern dishes. Kibbe is *quebbe bola* (not *quebbe cruda*), hummus is *garbanza,* and shish kabob is *alambre.* I leave it to you to figure out what a spinach pie is called (and it's excellent). Café Alameda is a treat for vegetarians, and the umbrella-shaded tables on the patio are perfect for morning coffee and *mamules* (walnut-filled pastries).

Calle 58 no. 474 (btw. calles 55 and 57). ✆ **999/928-3635.** Main courses 22–58 pesos. No credit cards. Daily 8am-5pm.

Eladio's ★ YUCATECAN   Locals have come to this open-air restaurant since 1952 to relax, drink very cold beer, and snack on Yucatecan specialties. Five of these restaurants are now scattered about the city; this one is the closest to the historic center. You can order a beer and enjoy *una botana* (a small portion that accompanies a drink—in this case, usually a Yucatecan dish), or order from the menu. *Cochinita,* *poc chuc,* and *relleno negro* (turkey flavored with burnt chiles) are all good. You'll often be treated to live music. The restaurant is 3 blocks east of Parque de la Mejorada.

Calle 59 (at Calle 44). © **999/923-1087.** Main courses 40–85 pesos. AE, MC, V. Daily noon–9pm.

La Flor de Santiago YUCATECAN   This is an old-world, atmospheric place with a loyal clientele. The dining area is classic—fans spinning under a high ceiling, dark wood furniture, one wall lined by bakery cases for fresh treats from a wood-fired stove. The service, though friendly, can be classically slow, too. It's especially popular for breakfast, but I like to stop in for one of its Yucatecan specialties on the way to the weekly big-band dancing in Parque Santiago across the street.

Calle 70 no. 478 (btw. calles 57 and 59). © **999/928-5591.** *Comida corrida* 40 pesos; main courses 40–75 pesos. No credit cards. Daily 7am–11pm.

Exploring Mérida

Most of Mérida's attractions are within walking distance from downtown. One easy way to see more of the city is on the popular, open-air **Carnavalito City Tour Bus.** It leaves Santa Lucia Park (calles 60 and 55) at 10am and 1, 4, and 7pm (no 7pm tour on Sun). The guided tour costs 75 pesos per person and lasts 2 hours. A national company, **Turibus** (www.turibus.com.mx), operates modern, bright-red, double-decker buses that provide earphones with a recorded narrative in English and five other languages. You can ride the entire circuit in less than 2 hours, or hop off at any stop to explore at will and grab the next bus to continue. Pick them up in front of the cathedral, or at any scheduled stop, every half-hour. The tour costs 100 pesos. Another sightseeing option is a *calesa* (horse-drawn carriage), best at night or on Sunday morning when traffic is light. A 45-minute ride around central Mérida costs 250 pesos. You can usually find *calesas* beside the cathedral on Calle 61.

PLAZA GRANDE ★★★   Downtown Mérida has a casual, relaxed feel. Buildings lack the severe baroque and neoclassical features that characterize central Mexico; most are finished in stucco and painted light colors. Mérida's many gardens, where plants are allowed to grow in wild profusion, add to the languid tropical atmosphere. The city's plazas are a slightly different version of this aesthetic: Unlike the highland plazas with their carefully sculpted trees, Mérida's squares are typically built around large trees that are left to grow as tall as possible.

The natural starting point for exploring Mérida, the plaza is a comfortable and informal place to gather with friends. Even when no orchestrated event is in progress, the park is full of people strolling or sitting on benches and talking. Big as Mérida is, the plaza bestows a personal feel and sense of community. Mérida's oldest buildings, beautiful in their scale and composition, surround the square.

The most prominent, the fortresslike **cathedral**—which was in fact designed as a fortress as much as a place of worship—is the oldest on the continent, built between 1561 and 1598. Much of the stone in its walls came from the ruined buildings of the Maya city of T'hó (sometimes Tiho). The original finish was stucco, and some of its remnants cling to the bare rock. Inside, decoration is sparse, all smooth white stone, with a conspicuous absence of gold adornments seen in many of Mexico's cathedrals. The most notable item is a picture of Ah Kukum Tutul Xiú, chief of the Xiú people, visiting the Montejo camp to make peace; it hangs over the side door on the right.

To the left of the main altar is a small shrine with a curious figure of Christ that replicates one recovered from a burned-out church in the town of Ichmul. In the 1500s a local artist carved the original figure from a miraculous tree that was hit by lightning and burst into flames—but did not char. The statue later became blistered in the church fire at Ichmul, but it survived. In 1645, it was moved to Mérida, where the locals attached great powers to the figure, naming it *Cristo de las Ampollas* (Christ of the Blisters). It did not, however, survive the sacking of the cathedral in 1915 by revolutionary forces, so a new figure was modeled after the original. Take a look in the side chapel (daily 8–11am and 4:30–7pm), which contains a life-size diorama of the Last Supper. The Mexican Jesus is covered with prayer crosses brought by supplicants asking for intercession.

Next door to the cathedral is the old bishop's palace, now converted into the city's contemporary art museum, **Museo de Arte Contemporáneo Ateneo de Yucatán ★** (© 999/928-3258; www.macay.org), or **MACAY.** The palace was confiscated and rebuilt during the Mexican Revolution in 1915. The museum entrance faces the cathedral from the reconstructed walkway between the two buildings called the Pasaje de la Revolución. The 17 exhibition rooms display work by contemporary artists, mostly from the Yucatán. (The best known are Fernando García Ponce and Fernando Castro Pacheco, whose works also hang in the government palace described below.) Nine rooms hold the museum's permanent collection; the rest are for temporary exhibits. It's open Wednesday to Monday from 10am to 6pm, until 8pm Friday and Saturday. Admission is free.

As you move clockwise around the plaza, **Palacio Montejo** is on the south side. The heavy, elaborate decoration around the doorway and windows is carved in the Spanish *plateresque* architectural style, but the content is very much a New World creation. Conquering the Yucatán was the Montejo family business, begun by the original Francisco Montejo and continued by his son and nephew, both also named Francisco Montejo. Francisco Montejo El Mozo ("The Younger") began construction of the house in 1542. Bordering the entrance, figures of conquistadors stand on the heads of vanquished Indians—borrowed, perhaps, from the pre-Hispanic custom of portraying victorious Maya kings treading on their defeated foes. The conquistadors' quixotic posture and somewhat cartoonish expressions make them less imposing than the Montejos might have intended. A bank now occupies the building, but you can enter the courtyard, view the garden, and imagine what home must have been like for the Montejos and their descendants, who lived here as recently as the 1970s. (Mérida society keeps track of Montejo's descendants, as well as those of the last Maya king, Tutul Xiú.)

In stark contrast to the severity of the cathedral and Casa Montejo is the light, unimposing **Ayuntamiento** or **Palacio Municipal (city hall).** The exterior dates from the mid–19th century, an era when a tropical aesthetic tinged with romanticism began asserting itself across coastal Latin America. On the second floor, you can see the city council's meeting hall and enjoy a view of the plaza from the balcony. Next door to the Ayuntamiento is the **Centro Cultural de Mérida Olimpo.** Built in 1999, it follows the lines of the historic building it replaced, but inside it is a large, modern space that hosts art exhibits, films, and lectures. It houses the **Arcadio Poveda Ricalde Planetarium** on the lower level and also holds concert and gallery space, a bookstore, and a lovely courtyard. A comfortable cafe is under the arches.

Cater-corner from the Olimpo is the old **Casa del Alguacil (Magistrate's House).** Under its arcades is something of an institution in Mérida: the **Dulcería y Sorbetería Colón,** an ice cream and sweet shop that will appeal to those who prefer lighter ice creams. A spectacular side doorway on Calle 62 bears viewing, and across the street is the **Cine Mérida,** with two movie screens showing art films and one stage for live performances. Returning to the main plaza, down from the ice cream store, is a **shopping center** of boutiques and convenience food vendors called **Pasaje Picheta.**

At the end of the arcade is the **Palacio de Gobierno (state government building) ★**, dating from 1892. Large murals by Yucatecan artist Fernando Castro Pacheco, completed between 1971 and 1973, decorate the courtyard walls with scenes from Maya and Mexican history. The painting over the stairway depicts the Maya spirit with ears of sacred corn, the "sunbeams of the gods." Nearby is a painting of musta-chioed President Lázaro Cárdenas, who, in 1938, expropriated 17 foreign oil companies and was hailed as a Mexican liberator. The long, wide upstairs gallery holds more of Pacheco's paintings, which have an almost photographic double-exposure effect. The palace is open Monday to Saturday from 8am to 8pm, Sunday from 9am to 5pm (and often later). A small tourism office is to the left of the entrance.

A few blocks from Plaza Grande in the market district, on Calle 56 between 65 and 65A, the **Museo de la Ciudad (City Museum) ★** has moved into the grand old post office building. An exhibit outlining Mérida's history includes explanatory text in English. Hours are Tuesday to Friday from 8am to 8pm, Saturday and Sunday from 8am to 2pm. Admission is free.

CALLE 60 Heading north from Plaza Grande up Calle 60, you'll see many of Mérida's old churches and squares, as well as stores selling gold-filigree jewelry, pot-tery, clothing, and folk art. A stroll along this street leads to the Parque Santa Ana and continues to the fashionable boulevard Paseo de Montejo and its **Museo Regional de Antropología (Anthropology Museum).**

The **Teatro Daniel Ayala Pérez,** on the left between calles 61 and 59, sometimes schedules interesting performances. On the right side is the small Parque Cepeda Peraza, more often called **Parque Hidalgo,** named for 19th-century Gen. Manuel Cepeda Peraza. It was part of Montejo's original city plan. Small outdoor restaurants front hotels on the park, making it a popular stopping place at any time of day—for locals, tourists, and hammock vendors alike. Across Calle 59 is the **Iglesia de Jesús,** or El Tercer Orden (the Third Order). Built by the Jesuits in 1618, it has the richest interior of any church in Mérida, making it a favorite spot for weddings. If you look at the church's west wall carefully, you'll find stones that still bear Mayan inscriptions from their previous life. The entire block on which the church stands belonged to the Jesuits, who are known for being great educators. The school they left behind after their expulsion became the Universidad de Yucatán.

On the other side of the church is the **Parque de la Madre,** with a copy of Renoir's statue of the *Madonna and Child.* Beyond the park is the **Teatro Peón Contreras,** an opulent theater designed by Italian architect Enrico Deserti. The theater is noted for its Carrara marble staircase and frescoed dome. National and international performers appear here often; check the schedule inside for perfor-mances taking place during your stay. In the southwest corner of the theater, facing the Parque de la Madre, is a **tourist information office.** Across Calle 60 is the main building of the **Universidad de Yucatán.** The Ballet Folklórico performs in its flag-stone courtyard on Friday nights.

A block farther north, across from **Iglesia de Santa Lucía** (1575), is **Parque Santa Lucía.** Bordered by an arcade on the north and west sides, this square was where early visitors first alighted from the stagecoach. The park holds a used-book market on Sundays and hosts popular entertainment several evenings a week, includ-ing a performance of Yucatecan songs and poems on Thursday nights.

Four blocks farther up Calle 60 is **Parque Santa Ana;** turn right to get to the beginning of Paseo de Montejo in 2 blocks.

Maya scholars, Spanish teachers, and archaeologists from the United States are among the students at the **Centro de Idiomas del Sureste,** Calle 52 no. 455 (btw. calles 49 and 51; 📞 **999/923-0954; www.cisyucatan.com.mx**). The school has two other locations: the Norte campus in Colonia México and the Poniente campus in Colonia García Ginerés. Students live with local families or in hotels; sessions running 2 weeks or longer are available for all levels of proficiency and areas of interest.

The older **Benjamin Franklin Institute** (📞 **999/928-6005; www.benjamin franklin.com.mx**), which claims Mérida's longest-running Spanish program for English speakers, also has many satisfied customers with its somewhat more formal and structured program. The choice depends on what kind of a student you are.

PASEO DE MONTEJO   The Paseo de Montejo, a broad, tree-lined boulevard modeled after Paris's Champs-Elysées, runs north-south starting at Calle 47, 7 blocks north and 2 blocks east of the main square. In the late 19th century, Mérida's upper crust (mostly plantation owners) decided the city needed something grander than its traditional narrow streets lined by wall-to-wall town houses. They built this monumentally proportioned boulevard and lined it with mansions. It came to a halt when the henequén industry went bust, but numerous mansions survive—some in private hands, others as offices, restaurants, or consulates. Today this is the fashionable part of town, home to restaurants, trendy dance clubs, and expensive hotels.

Of the surviving mansions, the most notable is the Palacio Cantón, a Beaux Arts confection that houses the **Museo Regional de Antropología ★★** (Regional Anthropology Museum; 📞 **999/923-0557**), Mérida's most impressive museum. Enrico Deserti, the architect of the Teatro Peón Contreras, designed and built this between 1909 and 1911, during the last years of the Porfiriato. It was the home of Gen. Francisco Cantón Rosado, who enjoyed his palace for only 6 years before his death. For a time, the mansion served as the governor's official residence.

A visit to the museum offers the irony of one of Mérida's most extravagant examples of European architecture housing a tribute to the ancient civilization the Europeans did their best to extinguish. The exhibition of pre-Columbian cultures covers the Yucatán's cosmology, history, and culture, with a special focus on the inhabitants' daily life. Displays illustrate such strange Maya customs as tying boards to babies' heads to create the oblong shape that they considered beautiful, and filing or perforating teeth to inset jewels. Drawings and enlarged photos of several archaeological sites illustrate various styles of Maya dwellings. Captions for the permanent displays are mostly in Spanish, but it's a worthwhile stop even if you barely know the language for the background it provides for explorations of Maya sites. The museum is open Tuesday to Saturday from 8am to 8pm, Sunday from 8am to 2pm. Admission is 41 pesos.

Ecotours & Adventure Trips

The Yucatán Peninsula has been enjoying a recent explosion of companies that organize nature and adventure tours. One well-established outfit with a great track record is **Ecoturismo Yucatán,** Calle 3 no. 235, Col. Pensiones (📞 **999/920-2772;** fax 999/925-9047; www.ecoyuc.com). Alfonso and Roberta Escobedo create itineraries to meet your special or general interest in the Yucatán or southern Mexico. Alfonso has been creating adventure and nature tours for more than a dozen years. Specialties include archaeology, birding, natural history, and kayaking. The company also offers day trips that explore contemporary Maya culture and life in villages in the Yucatán. Package and customized tours are available.

Mayan Ecotours, Calle 80 no. 561 × 13-1, Col. Pensiones 6a Etapa (② 999/987-3710; www.mayanecotours.com), also comes highly recommended. The young company specializes in low-impact visits to unspoiled natural areas and pueblos absent from tourist maps. A new Mayan Life tour combines swimming in a cenote, weaving jipijapa (palm leaves that Panama hats are made of) the traditional way—in a cave—and a home cooking lesson in a Maya village. Custom tours are also available.

For a personal guided tour around Mérida or as faraway as Calakmul, call **Dan Griffin** (p. 565), whose home is in Mérida.

Shopping

Mérida is known for hammocks, *guayaberas* (lightweight men's shirts worn untucked), and Panama hats. Local baskets and pottery are sold in the central market. Mérida is also the place to pick up prepared adobo, a pastelike mixture of ground achiote seeds (annatto), oregano, garlic, and other spices used as a marinade for such dishes as *cochinita pibil* (pit-baked pork).

Hordes of people come to Mérida's bustling **market district,** a few blocks southeast of the Plaza Grande, to shop and work. It is by far the most crowded part of town. Behind the former post office (at calles 65 and 56, now the city museum) the oldest part of the market is the **Portal de Granos (Grains Arcade),** a row of maroon arches where grain merchants once sold their goods. Just east, between calles 56 and 54, is the market building, **Mercado Lucas de Gálvez.** The city built a new municipal market on the south side of this building, but has had difficulty persuading the market vendors to move. When they do, the city plans to tear down the Lucas de Gálvez and replace it with a plaza. If you can abide the chaos, you can find anything inside from fresh fish to flowers to leather and other locally made goods. A secondary market is on Calle 56, labeled **Bazaar de Artesanías (crafts market)** in big letters. Still another crafts market, **Bazaar García Rejón,** lies a block west of the main market on Calle 65 between calles 58 and 60.

The English-language bookstore **Amate Books** (② 999/924-2222), Calle 60 453-A, by Calle 51, includes some English titles in its large selection of books. Hours are Tuesday through Sunday from 10:30am to 8:30pm. **The Librería Dante,** Calle 59 between calles 60 and 62 (② 999/928-3674), has a small selection of English-language cultural-history books on Mexico.

CRAFTS

Casa de las Artesanías ★   This state-run store, occupying the front of a restored monastery, sells a wide selection of crafts, 90% of which come from the Yucatán. The quality of work is higher than elsewhere, as are the prices. The monastery's back courtyard is used as a gallery, with rotating exhibits on folk and fine arts. It's open Monday to Saturday from 10am to 8pm, Sunday from 10am to 2pm. Calle 63 no. 513 (btw. calles 64 and 66). ② **999/928-6676.**

Miniaturas   This fun little store is packed to the rafters with miniatures, a traditional Mexican folk art form that has been evolving into social and political satire, pop art, and bawdy humor. The owner collects these hand-crafted items from around Mexico and offers plenty of variety, from traditional miniatures such as dollhouse furniture and *arboles de vida* (trees of life), to popular cartoon characters and old movie posters. Hours are Monday to Saturday from 10am to 8pm. Calle 59 no. 507A-4 (btw. calles 60 and 62). © **999/928-6503.**

GUAYABERAS

Instead of sweltering in business suits in Mérida, businessmen, bankers, and bus drivers alike wear the *guayabera,* a loose-fitting shirt decorated with narrow tucks, pockets, and sometimes embroidery, worn over the pants rather than tucked in. Mérida is famous as the best place to buy *guayaberas,* which can go for less than 150 pesos at the market or for more than 650 pesos custom-made; a linen *guayabera* can cost about 800 pesos. Most are made of cotton, although other materials are available. The traditional color is white.

Most shops display ready-to-wear shirts in several price ranges. *Guayabera* makers strive to outdo one another with their own updated versions of the shirt. When shopping, here are a few things to keep in mind: When Yucatecans say *seda,* they mean polyester; *lino* is linen or a linen/polyester combination. Look closely at the stitching and such details as the way the tucks line up over the pockets; with *guayaberas,* details are everything.

Guayaberas Jack   The craftsmanship here is good, the place has a reputation to maintain, and some of the salespeople speak English. Prices are as marked. This will give you a good basis of comparison if you want to hunt for a bargain elsewhere. If the staff does not have the style and color of shirt you want, they will make it for you in about 3 hours. This shop also sells regular shirts and women's blouses. Hours are Monday to Saturday from 10am to 8pm, Sunday from 10am to 2pm. Calle 59 no. 507A (btw. calles 60 and 62). © **999/928-6002.**

HAMMOCKS

Natives across tropical America used hammocks long before Europeans reached the New World, and they are widely used throughout Latin America. They come in many forms, but none as comfortable as the Yucatecan hammock, which is woven with cotton string in a fine mesh. While we might think of a hammock as garden furniture to laze in for an hour or two, they are beds for most Yucatecans, who generally eschew mattresses. Hotels that cater to Yucatecans always provide hammock hooks in the walls because many guests travel with their own.

A good shop will gladly hang a hammock for you to test-drive. Look to see that there are no untied strings. The woven part should be cotton, it should be made with fine string, and the strings should be so numerous that when you get in it and stretch out diagonally (the way you're meant to sleep in them), the gaps between the strings remain small. Don't pay attention to descriptions of a hammock's size; they have become practically meaningless. Good hammocks don't cost a lot of money (250–350 pesos). Superior hammocks are made with fine crochet thread—*hilo de crochet*—and be prepared to pay as much as 1,200 pesos.

You can also see what street vendors are offering, but you have to know what to look for, or they are likely to take advantage of you.

Hamacas El Aguacate   El Aguacate sells hammocks wholesale and retail. It has the greatest variety and is the place to go for a really fancy or extra-large hammock. A good hammock is the no. 6 in cotton; it runs around 340 pesos. The store is open Monday to Friday from 8:30am to 7:30pm, Saturday from 8am to 5pm. It's 6 blocks south of the main square. Calle 58 no. 604 (at Calle 73). © **999/928-6429.**

Tejidos y Cordeles Nacionales   This place near the municipal market sells only cotton hammocks, priced by weight—a pretty good practice because hammock lengths are fairly standardized. The prices are better than at El Aguacate, but quality control isn't as good. My idea of a good hammock is one that weighs about 1.5kg (3⅓ lb.) and runs about 270 pesos. Calle 56 no. 516-B (btw. calles 63 and 65). © **999/928-5561.**

PANAMA HATS

Another useful and popular item is this soft, pliable hat made from the fibers of the jipijapa palm in several towns south of Mérida along Hwy. 180, especially Becal, in the neighboring state of Campeche. Hat makers in these towns work inside caves so that the moist air keeps the palm fibers pliant.

Jipi hats come in various grades determined by the pliability, softness, and fineness of the fibers and closeness of the weave. A fine weave gives the hat more body and helps it to retain its shape. You'll find Panama hats for sale in several places, but often without much selection. One of the market buildings has a hat store: Walk south down Calle 56 past the post office; just before the street ends in the marketplace, turn left into a passage with hardware stores at the entrance. The fourth or fifth shop is **Casa de los Jipis.**

Mérida After Dark

For nighttime entertainment, see the box "Festivals & Events in Mérida," p. 576, or check out the theaters noted here.

Teatro Peón Contreras, Calle 60 at Calle 57, and **Teatro Ayala,** Calle 60 at Calle 61, feature a wide range of performing artists from Mexico and around the world. **Centro Cultural de Mérida Olimpo,** on the main square, schedules frequent concerts; and **Cine Mérida,** a half-block north of the Olimpo, has two screens for showing classic and art films, and one live stage.

Mérida's club scene offers everything from ubiquitous rock/dance music to some one-of-a-kind spots. Most of the dance clubs are in the big hotels or on trendy Paseo de Montejo, such as the ever-so-cool **El Cielo Lounge** at Prolongación Montejo and Calle 25. For dancing, a small cluster of clubs on Calle 60, around the corner from Santa Lucía, offers live rock and Latin music. For salsa, go to **Mambo Café** in the Plaza las Américas shopping center.

SIDE TRIPS FROM MÉRIDA

Hacienda Sotuta de Peón ★

What started out as one man's hobby has grown into one of the best living museums you'll ever see. If you've passed one of the Yucatán's elegantly decaying haciendas and wondered what it was like during its heyday, here's your chance to find out. The owner didn't just restore the buildings, he put the entire hacienda into working order and is now turning out 10 to 15 tons of henequén per month.

You can arrange transportation from any of Mérida's hotels by calling **Hacienda Sotuta de Peón** at © **999/941-8639** or going to www.haciendatour.com. Be sure to get precise directions if you plan to take your own car. After a welcome drink and a tour of the beautiful main house, you'll visit the henequén fields via mule-drawn "trucks," or carts. You get to see harvesting and, later, processing at the *casa de máquinas,* and learn how to spin the fiber into twine. You'll also learn about the culture surrounding henequén production, visiting one of the workers in his traditional Maya home. Bring your bathing suit because you'll have time for a swim in a cenote on the property. You can also sample fine regional cooking in a restaurant on the premises. Admission is 300 pesos per adult, 150 pesos per child; transportation is 200 pesos extra. Packages are available that combine entrance fee, transportation from Mérida, and a meal. The hacienda is open daily, with tours at 10am and 1pm.

Izamal ★★

Izamal, about 80km (50 miles) east of Mérida, presents one of Mexico's most vivid juxtapositions of three cultures: Ancient pyramids surround one of the largest monasteries the Spanish ever built in Mexico, while contemporary Maya artisans do a brisk trade in their traditional crafts.

The entire city center glows with ocher-yellow paint—the market, all the colonial buildings, and the massive Franciscan convent of **San Antonio de Padua ★★★** for which Izamal is best known. Walking along the colonnades high over the plaza, you know why priests believed they were close to God. The porticoed atrium, reputedly second in size only to the Vatican's, presents a sound-and-light show Monday to Saturday at 8:30pm. Admission is 84 pesos; headphones with English narration cost another 30. Bishop Fray Diego de Landa, who would became infamous for his brutal *auto-da-fé* at Maní—burning all the native scripts and later trying to rectify his deed by writing down all he could remember of Maya ways—leveled a pyramid here to build the monastery and church. Inside is a beautifully restored altarpiece and, among many statues, the Nuestra Señora de Izamal, brought from Guatemala in 1652 and still drawing pilgrims every August to climb the staircase on their knees to plead for miracles.

The **Centro Cultural y Artesanal ★★**, opened just a few years ago in a colonial building across the square from the convent, provides an excellent introduction to Izamal's abundance of handicrafts. A beautiful and highly informative exhibition (20 pesos) displays many examples of crafts produced throughout Mexico. The shop sells top-quality hammocks, clothing, and other work of local artists. The center also has a spa and a cafe in the interior courtyard. Follow up with a self-guided tour, available at the center, of folk art workshops in town. A good way to reach them is by *victoria,* the horse-drawn buggies that serve as taxis here.

Izamal is superimposed over a pre-Hispanic city and remnants of ancient Maya structures emerge through the layer of contemporary life—forming a retaining wall or the foundation for a church, or as a derelict but recognizable pyramid looming over the town. The largest of the four Maya pyramids enduring in the city center, **Kinich Kakmó** on Calle 28 at Calle 25 (daily 8am–8pm; free admission), measures 200×180m (656×591 ft.)—by many accounts, the Yucatán's largest pre-Hispanic building. Impressing with sheer size rather than fine architecture, it looks like an oddly symmetrical hill, but if you climb the restored stairways on its south face to the temple at the top, you can enjoy the odd sensation of looking down on the lofty convent building and taking in leafy mounds on the landscape for miles in every direction—undoubtedly more vestiges of Maya structures. The original city could have tucked the Izamal of today into its pocket.

The easiest way to get to Izamal from Mérida is to take Hwy. 180 toward Cancún. At Km 68, follow the signs for the *cuota* (toll road) until just past the Kantunil turnoff. Before you reach the toll plaza, the exit for Izamal will be on the left. You'll head north, passing through the villages of Xanaba and Sudzal, for 7.7 km (4¾ miles) to Izamal.

Izamal, which had meager lodging options only a few years ago, is enjoying a bit of a boom. Long-standing favorite **Macan ché Bed and Breakfast,** in the middle of town at Calle 22 no. 305 between calles 33 and 35 (www.macanche.com; ✆ **988/954-0287**), recently opened a second house suited for families and long-term stays as well as a new building with four quirky, highly designed rooms. Rates range from $42 to $52 for rooms, $90 to $135 for a house. Just east of the city center, on Calle 18 between calles 33 and 35, an Austrian entrepreneur has turned a ranch into **Hotel Rancho Santo Domingo** (www.izamalhotel.com; © **988/967-6136**). Bright, modern rooms in a tropical garden house go for $60 to $80, including breakfast, tax, and some refreshments. A small Maya-style house with *palapa* roof rents for $35 to $50, and a larger house is $110 to $130. A spa and a bar were in the works at press time.

Celestún National Wildlife Refuge: Flamingos & Other Waterfowl

On the Gulf Coast west of Mérida, Celestún is the gateway to a wildlife reserve harboring one of North America's only two flamingo breeding colonies (the other is Ría Lagartos, p. 624). The long, shallow estuary, where salty Gulf waters mix with freshwater from about 80 cenotes, is sheltered from the open sea by a skinny strip of land, creating ideal habitat for flamingos and other waterfowl. This *ría* (estuary) is shallow (.3–1m/1–3⅓ ft. deep) and thick with mangroves. You can ride a launch through an open channel just .5km (⅓ mile) wide and 50km (31 miles) long to see flamingos dredging the shallows for small crustaceans and favorite insects. You might also see frigate birds, pelicans, spoonbills, egrets, sandpipers, and other waterfowl. At least 15 duck species have been counted. Nonbreeding flamingos remain year-round; breeding birds take off around April to nest in Ría Lagartos, returning to Celestún in October.

The old days of approaching a fisherman under the bridge to negotiate a trip to the flamingos are over. Immediately to the left after you cross the bridge into town is a modern visitor center with a small museum, snack bar, clean bathrooms, and a ticket window. Tour prices are fixed at about 750 pesos for a 75-minute tour for up to six people. You can join others or hire a boat by yourself. In addition to flamingos, you'll see mangroves close up, and you might stop for a swim in a cenote. It's a pleasant ride through calm waters on wide, flat-bottom skiffs with canopies for shade. *Don't ask boatmen to get closer to the flamingos than they are allowed to.* If pestered too much, the birds will abandon the area for another, less-fitting habitat.

Celestún is an easy 90-minute drive from Mérida. (For bus info, see "Getting There & Departing: By Bus," p. 574.) Leave downtown on Calle 57, which ends just past Santiago Church and doglegs onto Calle 59-A. After crossing Avenida Itzáes, it becomes Jacinto Canek; continue until you see signs for Celestún Hwy. 178. After Hunucmá, the road joins Hwy. 281. Continue to the bridge, and you are in Celestún.

WHERE TO STAY

Casa de Celeste Vida ★★ ✦ 🎁   This newish guesthouse, 1.5 km (1 mile) north of town on a quiet, unspoiled beach that stretches for miles, hits the perfect balance between comfort and economy, seclusion and convenience. Two studios and a one-bedroom apartment have ocean views, kitchens stocked with utensils and food staples, and use of bikes, kayaks, and outdoor grills. The amiable Canadian owners, who live on-site, gladly arrange tours and sometimes even accompany guests on errands in town. They are highly tuned in to local culture and provide enormous insights into the lives of local fishermen and their families.

Calle 12 49-E, Celestún, Yuc. www.hotelcelestevida.com. © **988/916-2536.** 3 units. $75 studio; $100 apt. Weekly/monthly rates available. AE, DISC, MC, V. Free parking. **Amenities:** Bikes; kayaks; kitchen; Wi-Fi.

Hotel Eco Paraíso Xixim   This resort draws accolades for its ecological practices, such as composting, reusing treated wastewater, and developing barely more than 1% of its 25 hectares (62 acres). The 5km (3 miles) of unsullied beach are sublime. The *palapa*-roof bungalows are exquisitely private and generally comfortable. For its five-star rating and its rates, though, I expect more consistent cleaning standards and restaurant service. And if you don't relish bouncing over 11km (6¾ miles) of potholes whenever you want to explore, you are captive to the resort's services. This hotel is best for well-off travelers looking to cosset themselves away for a week.

Antigua Carretera a Sisal Km 10, 97367 Celestún, Yuc. www.ecoparaiso.com. ✆ **988/916-2100.** Fax 988/916-2111. 15 units. High season $276 double; low season $250 double. Rates include breakfast. AE, MC, V. Free parking. **Amenities:** Restaurant; bar; outdoor pool. *In room:* Hair dryer.

Dzibilchaltún: Maya Ruins & Museum

This small archaeological site can be a quick day trip or part of a longer trip to the Yucatán's Gulf Coast. It stands 14km (8⅔ miles) north of Mérida along the Progreso road, 4km (2½ miles) east of the highway. Take Calle 60 out of town and follow signs for Progreso and Hwy. 261. Turn right at the sign for Dzibilchaltún, which also reads UNIVERSIDAD DEL MAYAB; the entrance is a few miles farther. If you don't want to drive, take one of the *colectivos* lined up at Parque San Juan.

Dzibilchaltún was founded about 500 B.C., flourished around A.D. 750, and began its decline long before the conquistadors arrived. Since their discovery in 1941, more than 8,000 buildings have been mapped, but only about a half-dozen have been excavated. The site covers almost 15 sq. km (5¾ sq. miles); of greatest interest are the buildings surrounding two plazas next to the cenote and a third connected by a *sacbé* (causeway). At least 25 stelae have been found in Dzibilchaltún, which means "place of the stone writing."

Start with the **Museo del Pueblo Maya** (it closed in early 2010 for repairs and renovation but should be open by the time you read this), which exhibits artifacts from sites around the Yucatán and provides fairly thorough bilingual explanations. Displays include a beautiful plumed serpent from Chichén Itzá and a finely designed incense vessel from Palenque. The museum moves on to artifacts specifically at Dzibilchaltún, including the curious dolls that gave the site's main attraction its name. Another exhibit covers Maya culture through history, including a collection of *huipiles,* the woven blouses worn by Indian women. From here, a door leads out to the site.

You first encounter the *sacbé*. To the left is the **Temple of the Seven Dolls,** whose doorways and the *sacbé* line up with the rising sun at the spring and autumnal equinoxes. To the right are the buildings grouped around the Cenote Xlacah, the sacred well, and a complex of buildings around **Structure 38,** the **Central Group** of temples. Yucatán's State Department of Ecology has added nature trails and published a booklet (in Spanish) of birds and plants seen along the mapped trail.

The site is open daily from 8am to 5pm (museum closes at 4pm). Admission is 107 pesos, including the museum; children under 13 free.

Progreso, Uaymitun & Xcambó: Gulf Coast City, Flamingo Lookout & More Maya Ruins

Puerto Progreso is Mérida's refuge when the weight of summer heat descends on the city. And though it doesn't occur to most U.S. travelers, it is also a gateway to the trove of undiscovered white sands and mangrove-lined estuaries. Except for the vacation homes within easy reach of Mérida, most of the Yucatán's 378 seafront kilometers

(235 miles)—stretching from near Isla Holbox to Celestún—belongs to some scattered fishing villages, a lot of flamingos, and an increasing number of American and Canadian expats and snowbirds.

Progreso has been the Yucatán's main port of entry since the 1870s, when henequén shipped all over the world. Today, it's a major stop for cruise ships. The cruise business has allowed the city to spruce up the *malecón*, its 16-block seaside promenade that skims past well-groomed, white-sand beaches. Though the water is green and murky compared with the Caribbean, it's clean, and good for swimming. Fancy restaurants have been added (many sell good seafood), and vendors now ply their wares on the beach, but it's still pretty quiet most of the time. The 7km (4⅓-mile) pier, which seems to disappear in the distance, became the world's longest when a new section was added to accommodate cruise ships, which dock twice a week. The sea is so shallow here that large ships cannot get any closer to shore.

From Mérida, buses to Progreso leave from the AutoProgreso terminal (p. 575) every 15 minutes or so, taking almost an hour and costing 26 pesos. If you drive, take Paseo Montejo or Calle 60 north; either funnels you onto Hwy. 261 leading to Progreso.

If you have time, a drive east on the coastal road toward Telchac Puerto will reveal the other side of the Yucatán's coast. The shoreline along Hwy. 27 from Chuburna to the village of Dzilam de Bravo is dubbed La Costa Esmeralda (the Emerald Coast), after the clear, green Gulf waters. First up: the sleepy beach town of **Chicxulub,** about 8km (5 miles) east of Progreso. To winter-phobic northerners, it's a bit of paradise. To scientists, it's the site of a buried impact crater, about 161km (100 miles) in diameter, left by a meteor that smashed into Earth 65 million years ago; it is blamed for extinguishing the dinosaurs and probably created the Yucatán's cenotes. Less than 10km (6¼ miles) farther, in **Uaymitun,** a large wooden tower looming on the right is an observation post for viewing a new colony of flamingos that migrated from Celestún. Binoculars are provided free of charge. You might also spot some of the rosy birds about 20 minutes down near the turnoff for the road to Dzemul.

The road to Dzemul also leads to the small but intriguing Maya site of **Xcambó,** which was (and still is) a salt production center. Archaeologists have reconstructed the small ceremonial center, including several platforms and temples. A rough-hewn Catholic church, complete with altar, flowers, and statues, rises from some of the ruins. Admission is free.

You can continue on the same road through the small town of Dzemul to Baca, where you can pick up Hwy. 176 back to Mérida or Progreso, or you can return to the coast road and continue east until it ends in **Dzilam de Bravo,** final resting place of "gentleman pirate" Jean Lafitte. On the way, you'll pass through **Telchac Puerto,** which holds little interest unless you're hungry for some decent seafood, and the appealing village of **San Crisanto,** where a group of fishermen will paddle you through shallow canals in the mangroves to an array of newly accessible cenotes (40 pesos).

WHERE TO STAY

Hotel Yakunah ★★ ☺ This beautiful former colonial home is owned by a generous, outgoing Dutch family who have turned it into an expat gathering place as well as an exemplary B&B. The quiet location is a 10-minute walk from the Progreso city center but right across the street from the beach. Spacious rooms have a romantic air, with large beds, pasta tile, and armoires. Gleaming tiled bathrooms have large showers. A two-bedroom garden apartment with fully equipped kitchen and private terrace is also available. Co-owner Gerben Hartskeerl is a talented chef who turns out breakfasts and dinners (extra charge) that will spare you the tribulations of finding a restaurant.

Calle 23 no. 64 (btw. calles 48 and 50), Col. Ismael García, Progreso, Yuc. www.hotelyakunah.com.mx. ⓒ **969/935-5600.** 7 units. 750–850 pesos double; 1,400 pesos 2-bedroom casita. Rates include light breakfast; extra charge for full breakfast. Minimum stay 2 nights. MC, V. **Amenities:** Restaurant; bar; library; outdoor pool; smoke-free rooms. *In room:* A/C, TV, Wi-Fi.

En Route to Uxmal

Two routes go to Uxmal, about 80km (50 miles) south of Mérida. The most direct is Hwy. 261, via Umán and Muna. Hwy. 18 is a longer, more scenic road sometimes called the Convent Route. You might also make the trip to Uxmal as a loop by going one way and coming back the other, with an overnight stay at Uxmal. Arriving at Uxmal in late afternoon, you could attend the evening sound-and-light show, and see the ruins the next morning while it is cool and uncrowded.

Both roads will lead you to the central square in one small village after another, and many lack signs to point you in the right direction. Get used to poking your head out the window and saying, *"Buenos días. ¿Dónde está el camino para . . .?"* ("Good day. Where is the road to . . .?") You might have to ask more than one person before you get back on track. Streets in these villages are full of children, bicycles, and animals, so drive carefully, and learn to recognize unmarked *topes* from a distance.

Churches on these routes don't keep strict hours but are open daily from roughly 10am to 1pm and 4 to 6pm, so you might want to plan for lunch and a visit to a ruin midday. Ruins are open daily from 8am to 5pm.

HWY. 261: YAXCOPOIL & MUNA From downtown Mérida, take Calle 65 or 69 west and then turn left on Avenida Itzáes, which feeds onto the highway. To save some time by looping around the busy market town of Umán, take the exit for Hwy. 180 to Cancún and Campeche, and follow signs toward Campeche. Keep going south on Hwy. 180 until it intersects with Hwy. 261 and take the Uxmal exit.

You'll soon come to the town and **Hacienda Yaxcopoil** (Yash-koh-po-*eel*; ⓒ **999/ 900-1193;** www.yaxcopoil.com), 32km (20 miles) south of Mérida. The ruined hacienda, immediately identifiable by its double Moorish arches, has been preserved but not restored, making for an eerie but particularly vivid trip back in time. Tours take in the *casa principa*, with its large lounges and drawing rooms, the extensive gardens, a small Maya museum, and the henequén factory. It's open Monday to Saturday from 8am to 6pm, and Sunday 9am to 5pm. Admission is 50 pesos.

The hacienda is no secret, but few travelers seem to know you can stay overnight in the **Casa de Visitas ★★★**, a guesthouse behind the manor house that is not open to the public. It is roomy, with a sitting and dining room, and charming, with a patterned tile floor and colonial-style furniture. After 6 p.m., it's just you, the entire empty hacienda, the deep starry sky, and the utter silence. It's a unique experience that I look forward to repeating, but it's not for travelers whose comfort level requires a front desk ready to snap to attention at any hour of the day or night. The guesthouse rents for $60 a night; another $20 per person gets you a homemade tamale dinner and a hearty breakfast, delivered and served by a local woman in town.

South of Yaxcopoil, the little market town of **Muna** (65km/40 miles from Mérida) sells excellent **reproductions of Maya ceramics,** created by artisan Rodrigo Martín Morales, who has worked 25 years to replicate the ancient Maya's style and methods. As you enter Muna, watch for two large ceiba trees on the right side of the road, with handicraft and food stalls in a small plaza under the branches. Turn right, and in about 45m (148 ft.) the **Taller de Artesanía Los Ceibos** (ⓒ **997/971-0036**) will be on your left. The family works in the back, and only Spanish is spoken. The store is open from 9am to 6pm daily. Uxmal is 15km (9⅓ miles) beyond Muna.

HWY. 18: THE CONVENT ROUTE

From downtown Mérida, take Calle 63 east to Circuito Colonias and turn right, then look for a traffic circle with a small fountain and turn left. This feeds onto Hwy. 18 to Kanasín (Kah-nah-*seen*) and then Acanceh (Ah-kahn-*keh*). In **Kanasín,** the highway divides into two; go to the right, and the road curves to flow into the next parallel street. Pass the market, church, and main square on your left, and then stay to the right when you get to a fork.

Shortly after Kanasín, the upgraded road now bypasses a lot of villages. Follow the sign pointing left to **Acanceh.** Across the street from and overlooking Acanceh's church is a restored pyramid. On top, under a makeshift roof, are some stucco figures of Maya deities. The caretaker will guide you up to see them and give you a little explanation (in Spanish). Admission is 25 pesos. A few blocks away, at some other ruins called **El Palace de los Stuccoes,** a stucco mural was found in mint condition there in 1908. Exposure deteriorated it somewhat, but it is sheltered now. You can still distinguish the painted figures in their original colors. To leave Acanceh, head back to the highway on the street that passes between the church and the plaza.

The next turnoff will be for **Tecoh,** on the right side. Its ornate and crumbling parish church and convent sit on the base of a massive pre-Columbian ceremonial complex that was sacrificed to build the church. The three carved *retablos* (altarpieces) inside are covered in gold leaf and unmistakably Indian in style. About 9km (5⅔ miles) farther on, you come to the ruins of Mayapán, the last of the great city-states.

MAYAPÁN ★

Founded, according to Maya lore, by the man-god Kukulkán (Quetzalcóatl in central Mexico) in about A.D. 1007, Mayapán quickly established itself as northern Yucatán's most important city. For almost 2 centuries, it was the capital of a Maya confederation of city-states that included Chichén Itzá and Uxmal. Sometime before 1200, Mayapán attacked and subjugated the other two cities, leading to a revolt that eventually toppled Mayapán. It was abandoned during the mid-1400s.

The walled city, considered the last great Maya capital, extended out at least 4 sq. km (1½ sq. miles), but the ceremonial center is quite compact. Several buildings bordering the principal plaza have been reconstructed, including one that looks eerily like Chichén Itzá's El Castillo (and also named El Castillo) and another much like the observatory. Excavation has uncovered murals and stucco figures that provide more grist for the mill of conjecture: atlantes (supporting columns in the form of a human figure), skeletal soldiers, macaws, entwined snakes, and a stucco jaguar. With some 4,000 mounds, and only half a dozen in different stages of restoration, Mayapán shows the full spectrum of ruins in their original discovered state, some in midtransformation and others in stages of advanced restoration. Well worth a stop.

The site is open daily from 8am to 5pm. Admission is 41 pesos. Use of a personal video camera is 45 pesos.

Where to Stay

Hotel Na' Lu'um ★ 🍴 Whether you need a place to stay because you've run out of steam while exploring the Puuc or Convent routes, or you're looking for a tranquil retreat in the heart of the Mundo Maya, this ecohotel will fit the bill. Spacious *palapa*-roofed cabañas fit unobtrusively into the well-tended gardens and surrounding natural landscape. Their rustic Maya design uses clay and wood to keep them cool and windows in every direction to pull in cross-breezes. Inside, they offer every modern comfort and a few unusual touches, such as a pull-out clothesline in the oversized shower. The hotel restaurant, which is becoming a popular roadside stop on the way to the Mayapán ruins, specializes in regional dishes and is very good. On Saturdays, the hotel opens the *temazcal* for Maya-style ritual steam cleansings.

Carretera Mérida–Chetumal Km 22.9 (before Mayapán archaeological zone), Libramiento Tecoh, Yuc. www. naluumtm.com. © **999/195-6294.** 10 units. 900–950 pesos double. Rates include full breakfast. AE, MC, V. Free parking. **Amenities:** Restaurant; jogging track; outdoor pool; *temazcal. In room:* No phone.

FROM MAYAPÁN TO TICUL   About 20km (12 miles) after Mayapán, take the highway for **Mama** on your right, and the narrow road quickly enters town. Some parts of this village are quite pretty. The main attraction is the church and former convent, with several fascinating *retablos* sculpted in a native form of baroque. Colonial-age murals and designs were uncovered and restored during the restoration of these buildings. You can peek at them in the sacristy. From Mama, continue on about 20km (12 miles) to Ticul, a large (for this area) market town with a couple of simple hotels.

TICUL

Best known for the cottage industry of *huipil* (native blouse) embroidery and the manufacture of women's dress shoes, Ticul is both an exciting stop and a convenient place to wash up and spend the night. It's also a center for large-scale pottery production—most of the widely sold sienna-colored pottery painted with Maya designs is made here. If it's a cloudy, humid day, potters may not be working (part of the process requires sun drying). They still welcome visitors to purchase finished pieces.

Ticul is only 20km (12 miles) northeast of Uxmal, making a good alternative to the expensive hotels at the ruins, especially if you want to do the Puuc Route one day and the Convent Route the next. On the main square is the **Hotel Plaza,** Calle 23 no. 202, near Calle 26 (www.hotelplazayucatan.com; © **997/972-0484**). It's a modest but comfortable 30-room hotel. A double room with air-conditioning costs 340 pesos. A 5% charge applies to payments made by credit card (MasterCard and Visa accepted). Get an interior room to avoid noise from Ticul's lively plaza. From Ticul, you can head straight for Uxmal via Santa Elena, or loop around the Puuc Route (p. 604) the long way to Santa Elena.

FROM TICUL TO UXMAL   Follow the main street (Calle 23) west through town. Turn left on Calle 34 and drive 15km (9⅓ miles) to Santa Elena; it will be another 15km (9⅓ miles) to Uxmal. In Santa Elena, by the side of Hwy. 261, is a clean restaurant with good food, **El Chaac Mool,** and on the opposite side of the road the **Flycatcher Inn B&B** (see listing, below).

THE RUINS OF UXMAL ★★★

80km (50 miles) SW of Mérida; 19km (12 miles) W of Ticul; 19km (12 miles) S of Muna

The ceremonial complex of Uxmal (Oosh-*mahl*) is one of the masterworks of Maya civilization. Expansive and intricate facades of carved stone make it strikingly different from all other Maya cities. Unlike other sites in northern Yucatán, such as Chichén Itzá and Mayapán, Uxmal isn't built on a flat plane, but incorporates the varied elevations of the hilly landscape. And then there is the strange and beautiful oval-shaped Pyramid of the Magician, unique among the Maya. The great building period took place between A.D. 700 and 1000, when the population probably reached

25,000. After 1000, Uxmal fell under the sway of the Xiú princes (who may have come from central Mexico). In the 1440s, the Xiú conquered Mayapán, and not long afterward, the age of the Maya ended with the arrival of the Spanish conquistadors.

Close to Uxmal, four smaller sites—**Sayil, Kabah, Xlapak,** and **Labná**—can be visited in quick succession. With Uxmal, these ruins (p. 604) are collectively known as the **Puuc Route.**

Essentials

GETTING THERE & DEPARTING   By Car   The two main routes to Uxmal from Mérida are described in "En Route to Uxmal," above. *Note:* There's no gasoline at Uxmal.

By Bus   See "Getting There & Departing" (p. 572) for information about bus service between Mérida and Uxmal. To return, wait for the bus on the highway at the entrance to the ruins. To see the sound-and-light show, sign up with a tour operator from Mérida.

ORIENTATION   Entrance to the ruins is through the visitor center where you buy tickets (two per person; hold on to both). It has a restaurant; toilets; a first-aid station; shops selling soft drinks, ice cream, film, batteries, and books; a state-run Casa de Artesanía (crafts house); and a small museum, which isn't very informative. The site is open daily from 8am to 5pm. Admission to the archaeological site is 166 pesos, including the evening sound-and-light show. Bringing in a video camera costs 45 pesos and parking is 10 pesos. If you're staying the night in Uxmal, consider getting to the site late in the day, viewing the sound-and-light show that evening and visiting the ruins the next morning before it gets hot. (Make sure the ticket vendor knows what you intend to do, and keep the ticket.)

Guides at the entrance of Uxmal give tours in several languages, charging $40 for a single person or a group. The guides frown on it, but you can ask other English speakers if they'd like to join you in a tour and split the cost. As at other sites, the guides vary in quality but will point out areas and architectural details you might otherwise miss. The 45-minute **sound-and-light show** begins each evening at 7pm during standard time and 8pm during daylight saving. It's in Spanish, but you can rent headsets for 25 pesos that narrate the program in several languages. It's part Hollywood, part high school, but the lighting of the buildings is worth the effort to see it. After the show, the chant *"Chaaac, Chaaac"* will echo in your mind for weeks.

A Tour of the Ruins

THE PYRAMID OF THE MAGICIAN ★★   As you enter the ruins, note a *chultún,* or cistern, where Uxmal stored its water. Unlike most of the major Maya sites, Uxmal stands about 30m (98 ft.) above sea level, so it has no cenotes to supply freshwater from the subterranean rivers. The city's inhabitants depended on rainwater, and consequently venerated the rain god, Chaac, with unusual devotion.

Rising in front of you is the Pirámide del Adivino, the city's tallest structure at 38m (125 ft.). The name comes from a myth about a magician-dwarf who reached adulthood in a single day after being hatched from an egg and built this pyramid in one night. It is built over five earlier structures. The pyramid has an oval base and rounded sides. You are looking at the east side. Walk around the left, or south, side to see the main face on the west side. The pyramid was designed so that the east side rises less steeply than the west side, which shifts the crowning temples to the west of the central axis of the building, causing them to loom above the plaza below. The temple doorway is heavily ornamented, characteristic of the Chenes style, with 12 stylized masks representing Chaac.

THE NUNNERY QUADRANGLE To get from the plaza to the large Nunnery Quadrangle, walk out the way you walked into the plaza, turn right, and follow the wall of this long stone building until you get to the building's main door—a corbeled arch that leads into the quadrangle. You'll be in another plaza, bordered on each side by stone buildings with elaborate facades. The 16th-century Spanish historian Fray Diego López de Cogullado gave the quadrangle its name when he decided its layout resembled a Spanish convent.

The quadrangle does have a lot of small rooms, about the size of a nun's cell. Poke your head into one to see the shape and size, but they don't warrant much exploration, being long ago abandoned to the swallows that fly above the city. No interior murals or stucco work have been found here, at least not yet. The richness of Uxmal lies in the stonework on its exterior walls.

The Nunnery is a stunning example. The first building that catches your eye when you enter the plaza is the north building in front of you. It is the tallest, and the view from the top includes all the city's major buildings, making it useful for the sound-and-light show. The central stairway is bordered by doorways supported by rounded columns, a common element in Puuc architecture. Remnants of the facade on the second level show elements used in the other three buildings and elsewhere in the city: a crosshatch pattern and a pattern of square curlicues, called a step-and-fret design, and the vertical repetitions of the long-nosed god masks—found so often on the corners of Uxmal's buildings that they have been dubbed "Chaac stacks." Though the facades of these buildings share these and other common elements, their composition varies. On the west building, long, feathered serpents are intertwined at head and tail. A human head stares out from a serpent's open mouth. There are many interpretations of this motif, repeated elsewhere in Maya art, and that's the trouble with symbols: They are usually the condensed expression of multiple meanings, so any one interpretation could be true, but only partially true.

THE BALL COURT Leaving the Nunnery the same way you entered, you will see a ball court straight ahead. What Maya city would be without a ball court? This one is a particularly good representative of the hundreds found elsewhere in the Maya world. It even has a replica of one of the stone rings the players aimed at, using their knees, hips, and maybe their arms to strike a solid rubber ball (the Maya knew about natural rubber and extracted latex from a couple of species of rubber trees). Spectators are thought to have observed the game from atop the two structures.

THE GOVERNOR'S PALACE Continuing south, you come to the large raised plaza supporting the Governor's Palace, which runs north and south. The surface area of the raised plaza measures 140×170m (459×558 ft.), and it is raised about 10m (33 ft.) above the ground—quite a bit of earth moving. Most of this surface is used as a ceremonial space facing the front (east side) of the palace. In the center is a double-headed jaguar throne, which is seen elsewhere in the Maya world. From here, you get the best view of the building's remarkable facade. Like the other palaces here, the first level is smooth and the second is ornate. A series of Chaac masks moves diagonally across a crosshatch pattern. Crowning the building is an elegant cornice projecting slightly outward from above a double border, which could be an architectural reference to the original crested thatched roofs of the Maya. Human figures adorned the main doors, though only the headdress of the central figure survives.

THE GREAT PYRAMID Behind the palace, the platform descends in terraces to another plaza with a large temple, known as the Great (or Grand) Pyramid, on its south side. On top is the Temple of the Macaws, for the repeated macaw image on the face of the temple, and the ruins of three other temples. The view from the top is extraordinary.

THE DOVECOTE This building is remarkable, in that roof combs weren't a common feature of temples in the Puuc hills, although Sayil's El Mirador has one of a very different style.

Where to Stay

Flycatcher Inn B&B ★★ 🔥 This pleasant bed-and-breakfast is 15 minutes southeast of Uxmal in the village of Santa Elena, just off Hwy. 261. Spacious rooms are attractive and quiet, and they come with pillow-top orthopedic mattresses and decorative ironwork made by one of the owners, Santiago Domínguez. His wife, Kristine Ellingson, is from the Northwest but has lived in Santa Elena for years and has voluminous information on travel and local culture to share with guests. The large, attractive grounds include a recently discovered little Maya ruin along the nature trail that runs through the property. The inn's new Owl's Cottage, a secluded house with a small kitchen and large living/dining room, is designed for longer stays.

Carretera Uxmal–Kabah, 97840 Santa Elena, Yuc. www.flycatcherinn.com. ✆ **997/102-0865.** 8 units. $55–$65 double; $75 suite; $70–$85 cottage. Weekly/monthly rates available. 4-night minimum for Owl's Cottage. Rates include full breakfast. No credit cards. Free secure parking. Not set up to accommodate young children. *In room:* A/C.

Hacienda Uxmal ★★ The Hacienda is the oldest hotel in Uxmal. Located just up the road from the ruins, it was built for the archaeology staff. Large, airy rooms exude a feel of days gone by, with patterned tile floors, heavy furniture, and louvered windows. Room nos. 202 through 214 and 302 through 305 are the nicest of the superiors. Larger corner rooms are labeled A through F and come with Jacuzzi tubs. A handsome garden courtyard with towering royal palms, a bar, and a pool adds to the air of tranquility. A guitar trio usually plays on the open patio in the evenings.

Carretera Mérida–Uxmal Km 80, 97844 Uxmal, Yuc. www.mayaland.com. ✆800/235-4079 in the U.S., or 997/976-2012. Fax 987/976-2011. 82 units. High season $164–$185 double, $238–$249 superior; low season $110–$140 double, $144–$196 superior. AE, MC, V. Free guarded parking. **Amenities:** Restaurant; bar; 2 outdoor pools. *In room:* A/C, TV, hair dryer (upon request), minibar.

Villas Arqueológicas Uxmal ★ 🔥 Still the best value among the hotels clustered around the ruins' entrance, the Villas and its sister properties have new owners who have added some polish, though the food seems blander than before. A basic two-story quadrangle around a garden patio and pool is admirably prettied up by lush vegetation, Maya statues, and a paint job with a semblance of traditional style. At guests' disposal are a tennis court, a library, and an audiovisual show on the ruins in English, French, and Spanish. Each of the small, modern rooms has a double and a twin bed fit into spaces that are walled on three sides (very tall people should look elsewhere). Ask about rates for half-board (breakfast plus lunch or dinner) or full board (three meals).

Ruinas Uxmal, 97844 Uxmal, Yuc. www.islandercollection.com. ✆ **987/872-9300,** ext. 8101. 43 units. High season $69–$82 double; low season $59 double. AE, MC, V. Free guarded parking. **Amenities:** Restaurant; bar; outdoor pool; tennis court; Wi-Fi (in public areas). *In room:* A/C, hair dryer, Wi-Fi (in some).

Where to Eat

You can eat well at the hotel restaurant of the **Lodge at Uxmal** if you order the Yucatecan specialties, which are fresh and well prepared. In Santa Elena, the **Pickled Onion** offers a menu of mostly Mexican dishes with a few international twists; the food is good, and the owner's hospitality is legendary. The *palapa* restaurants by the highway as you approach the ruins from Mérida are a mixed bag. They do a lot of business with bus tours, so the best time to try them is early afternoon.

THE PUUC MAYA ROUTE

South and east of Uxmal are several other ancient Maya cities, small and largely unexcavated but worth visiting for their unique architecture.

Kabah is 28km (17 miles) southeast of Uxmal via Hwy. 261 through Santa Elena, and only 2km (1¼ miles) farther to Sayil. Xlapak is almost walking distance (through the jungle) from Sayil, and Labná is just a bit farther east. A short drive beyond Labná brings you to the caves of Loltún. Oxkutzcab is at the road's intersection with Hwy. 184, which you can follow west to Ticul or east all the way to Felipe Carrillo Puerto. If you aren't driving, a daily bus from Mérida (p. 572) goes to all these sites, with the exception of Loltún.

Puuc Maya Sites

KABAH ★   From Uxmal, head southwest on Hwy. 261 to Santa Elena (1km/⅔ mile), then south to Kabah (13km/8 miles). The ancient city lies along both sides of the highway. Turn right into the parking lot.

The outstanding building at Kabah, to the right as you enter, is the **Palace of Masks,** or Codz Poop ("rolled-up mat"), named for its decorative motif. Its Chenes-style facade is completely covered in a repeated pattern of 250 masks of Chaac, each with curling remnants of the god's elephant trunk–like nose. It is unique in all of Maya architecture. For years, parts of this building lay lined up in the weeds like pieces of a puzzle awaiting assembly. Sculptures from this building are in the anthropology museums of Mérida and Mexico City.

Just behind and to the left of the Codz Poop is the **Palace Group** (also called the East Group), with a fine Puuc-style colonnaded facade. Originally, it had 32 rooms. On the front are seven doors, two divided by columns—a common feature of Puuc architecture. Across the highway is what was once the **Great Temple,** and beyond

---

 Seeing the Puuc Maya Sites

These sites are undergoing excavation and reconstruction, and some buildings may be roped off when you visit. The sites are open daily from 8am to 5pm. Admission ranges from 37 to 43 pesos for each city (except Xlapak, which is free) and 95 pesos for Loltún. Loltún has tours at 9:30 and 11am, and 12:30, 2, 3, and 4pm. Even if you're the only person there when a tour is scheduled, the guide must give you a tour, and he can't charge you as if you were contracting his services for an individual tour (though sometimes they try). Use of a video camera at any time costs 45 pesos; if you visit Uxmal the same day, you pay only once for video permission and present your receipt as proof at each ruin.

that is a **great arch.** It was much wider at one time and may have been a monumental gate into the city. A *sacbé* linked this arch to Uxmal. Compare this corbeled arch to the one at Labná (below), which is in much better shape.

SAYIL   About 4km (2½ miles) south of Kabah is the turnoff (left, or east) to Sayil, Xlapak, Labná, Loltún, and Oxkutzcab. The ruins of **Sayil** ("place of the ants") are 4km (2½ miles) along this road.

Sayil is famous for **El Palacio ★★.** With more than 90 rooms, the palace is impressive for its size alone. Climbing is not permitted, but the facade that makes this a masterpiece of Maya architecture is best appreciated from the ground. It stretches across three terraced levels, and its rows of columns give it a Minoan appearance. The upside-down stone figure known to archaeologists as the Diving God, or Descending God, over the doorway on the second level is the same motif used at Tulum a couple of centuries later. The large circular basin on the ground below the palace is an artificial catch basin for a *chultún* (cistern); this region has no natural cenotes (wells) for irrigation.

In the jungle beyond El Palacio is **El Mirador,** a small temple with an oddly slotted roof comb. Beyond El Mirador, a crude stele (tall, carved stone) is carved with a fertility god burdened with a phallus of monstrous proportions. Another building group, the Southern Group, is a short distance down a trail that branches off from the one heading to El Mirador.

XLAPAK   Xlapak (*shla*-pahk) is a small site with one building; it's 5.5km (3½ miles) down the road from Sayil. The Palace at Xlapak bears the masks of the rain god Chaac. If you're running out of steam, this is the one to skip.

LABNÁ   Labná, dating from between A.D. 600 and 900, is 30km (19 miles) from Uxmal and only 3km (1¾ miles) past Xlapak. The entrance has a snack stand and toilets. Descriptive placards fronting the main buildings are in Spanish, English, and German.

As soon as you enter you'll see **El Palacio,** a magnificent Puuc-style building on your left that is much like the one at Sayil, but in poorer condition. Over one doorway is a large, well-conserved mask of Chaac with eyes, a huge snout nose, and jagged teeth around a small mouth that seems on the verge of speaking. Jutting out on one corner is a highly stylized serpent's mouth from which pops a human head with an unexpectedly serene expression. From the front, you can gaze out to the enormous grassy interior grounds flanked by vestiges of unrestored buildings and jungle.

From El Palacio, you can walk on a reconstructed *sacbé* leading to Labná's **corbeled arch.** At one time, there were probably several such arches through the region. This one has been extensively restored, although only remnants of the roof comb are visible. It was once part of a more elaborate structure now lost to history. Chaac's face occupies the corners of one facade, and stylized Maya huts are fashioned in stone above the two small doorways. You can pass through the arch to reach **El Mirador** or El Castillo. Towering above a large pile of rubble, the remains of a pyramid, is a singular room crowned with a roof comb piercing the sky.

LOLTÚN   The caverns of Loltún are 31km (19 miles) past Labná on the way to Oxkutzcab, on the left side of the road. One of the Yucatán's largest and most fascinating cave systems, they were home to the ancient Maya and were used as a refuge during the War of the Castes (1847–1901). Inside are statues, wall carvings, paintings, *chultunes* (cisterns), and other signs of Maya habitation. Guides will explain much of what you see, though their English isn't always easy to understand.

The admission price includes a 90-minute tour. These begin daily at 9:30 and 11am, and 12:30, 2, 3, and 4pm. The floor of the cavern can be slippery in places; take a flashlight if you have one.

To return to Mérida from Loltún, drive the 7km (4⅓ miles) to Oxkutzcab. From there, you can take the slow route through Maní and Teabo, which will allow you to see some convents and return by Hwy. 18, known as the "Convent Route" (p. 599). The other option is to head toward Muna to hook up with Hwy. 261 (p. 598).

Oxkutzcab

Oxkutzcab (Ohsh-kootz-*kahb*), 11km (6¾ miles) from Loltún, is the center of the Yucatán's fruit-growing region. Oranges abound. The tidy village of 21,000 centers on a beautiful 16th-century church and the market. **Su Cabaña Suiza** (no phone) is a dependable restaurant in town. The last week of October and first week of November is the **Orange Festival,** when the village turns exuberant, with a carnival and orange displays in and around the central plaza.

En Route to Campeche

From Oxkutzcab, head back 43km (27 miles) to Sayil, and then drive south on Hwy. 261 to Campeche (126km/78 miles). After crossing the state line, you'll pass through the towns of Bolonchén and Hopelchén, both of which have gas stations. The drive is pleasant, and there's little traffic. Watch carefully for directional traffic signs in these towns to stay on the highway. From Hopelchén, Hwy. 261 heads west. After 42km (26 miles), you'll find yourself at Cayal and the well-marked turnoff for the ruins of the city of Edzná (p. 613), 18km (11 miles) farther south. If you're taking this route to Campeche, this could be the time to see this tranquil, underappreciated ancient city.

CAMPECHE ★★

251km (156 miles) SW of Mérida; 376km (234 miles) NE of Villahermosa

Campeche, capital of the state of the same name, is a splendidly restored colonial city that is woefully overlooked by travelers. All the historic center's facades have been repaired and painted, electrical and telephone cables moved underground, and the streets paved to resemble cobblestone. Several period films have been shot here, including *Che,* Steven Soderbergh's epic two-part biography of Che Guevara.

Those who do come to Campeche often are on their way to the ruins at Palenque (chapter 17) or the Río Bec region (chapter 15), or they are accidental wanderers by nature. In truth, Campeche is not geared to foreign tourism the way Mérida is—though it is catching up—so expect less English translation at museums, ruins, and services. Also, expect less in the way of nightlife, except on weekend nights when the main square becomes one huge street party.

Campeche's history is laden with drama. The conquistadors arrived in 1517, when Francisco de Córdoba landed here while exploring the coast and stayed just long enough to celebrate Mass. Native resistance thwarted attempts to settle here until Montejo the Younger gained a foothold in 1540.

In the 17th and 18th centuries, pirates repeatedly sacked the city. The list of attackers reads like a who's who of pirating. On one occasion, several outfits banded together under the famous Dutch pirate Peg Leg (the likely inspiration for many a fictional one-legged sailor) and captured the city. Campechanos, tired of hosting pirate parties, erected walls around the city, with *baluartes* (bastions) at critical points.

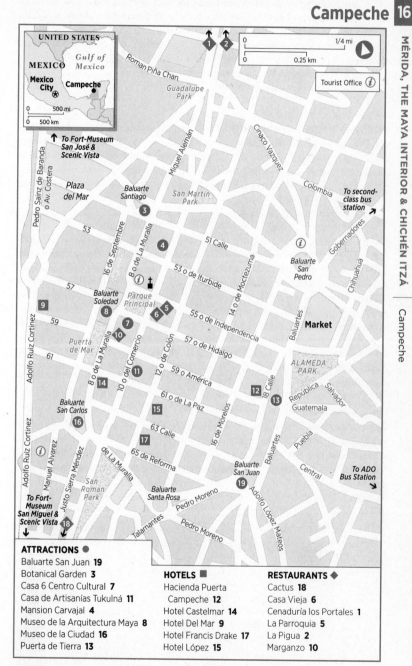

ATTRACTIONS ●

Baluarte San Juan **19**
Botanical Garden **3**
Casa 6 Centro Cultural **7**
Casa de Artisanías Tukulná **11**
Mansion Carvajal **4**
Museo de la Arquitectura Maya **8**
Museo de la Ciudad **16**
Puerta de Tierra **13**

HOTELS ■

Hacienda Puerta
  Campeche **12**
Hotel Castelmar **14**
Hotel Del Mar **9**
Hotel Francis Drake **17**
Hotel López **15**

RESTAURANTS ◆

Cactus **18**
Casa Vieja **6**
Cenaduría los Portales **1**
La Parroquia **5**
La Pigua **2**
Marganzo **10**

For added security, they built two forts, complete with moats and drawbridges, on the hills flanking Campeche. Four gates breached the wall, two of which still stand: the Puerta de Mar (Sea Gate) and the Puerta de Tierra (Land Gate). The pirates never cared to return, but in Mexico's stormy political history, the city did withstand a couple of sieges by different armies. The wall was razed in the early 1900s, but the bastions and main gates remain, along with the two hilltop fortresses. Most of the bastions and both forts now house museums.

Essentials

GETTING THERE & DEPARTING   **By Plane**   Aeroméxico (© 800/237-6399 in the U.S., 01-800/021-4000 in Mexico, or 981/816-6656; www.aeromexico.com.mx) flies once daily to and from Mexico City. Campeche's **airport** is several kilometers northeast of the town center, and you'll have to take a taxi into town (about 100 pesos).

By Car   Hwy. 180 goes south from Mérida, passing near the basket-making village of Halacho and near Becal, known for its Panama-hat weavers. The trip takes 2½ hours. The longer way from Mérida is along Hwy. 261 past Uxmal.

When driving from Campeche to Mérida via Hwy. 180, go north on Avenida Ruiz Cortines, bearing left to follow the water (this becomes Av. Pedro Sainz de Baranda, but there's no sign). Follow the road as it turns inland to Hwy. 180, where you turn left (there's a gas station at the intersection).

To go from Campeche to Edzná and Uxmal, drive north on either Ruiz Cortines or Gobernadores and turn right on Madero, which feeds onto Hwy. 281. To go south to Villahermosa, take Ruiz Cortines south.

By Bus   ADO (© 981/811-9910; www.ticketbus.com.mx) offers first-class *de paso* (passing through) buses to Palenque (6 hr.; 266 pesos) four times a day and two or three times per hour to Mérida (2½ hr.; 152 pesos) around the clock. The ADO **bus station** is on Avenida Patricio Trueba at Avenida Casa de Justicia, almost 2km (1¼ miles) from the Puerta de Tierra. The second-class bus station, with service to nearby cities and to Mérida, is at Avenida Gobernadores and Calle 45 (also called Calle Chile on the east side of Gobernadores).

INFORMATION   The **State of Campeche Office of Tourism** (© 981/811-9229; fax 981/816-6767; www.campeche.travel) is in Plaza Moch-Couoh, Avenida Ruiz Cortines s/n (btw. calles 63 and 65). Hours are daily 8am to 4pm and 6 to 9pm. This is one of the state buildings between the historic center and the shore. Tourist information offices are also in the bastions of Baluarte San Pedro (daily 9am–1pm and 5–9pm) and in Casa 6 (daily 9am–9pm). The city's **Tourism and Culture Office** (© 981/811-3989) is on Calle 55 between calles 10 and 8; open daily 9am to 9pm.

CITY LAYOUT   By far the most interesting feature of the city is the restored old part, most of which once lay within the walls. Originally, the seaward wall was at the water's edge, but land has been gained from the sea between the old walls and the coastline. This is where you'll find most of the state government buildings, built in glaringly modernist style around **Plaza Moch-Couoh:** buildings such as the office tower **Edificio de los Poderes (Judicial Building)** or **Palacio de Gobierno (headquarters for the state of Campeche),** and the futuristic **Cámara de Diputados (Chamber of Deputies),** which looks like a cubist clam.

Campeche's street-numbering system is typical of the Yucatán, except that numbers of the north-south streets increase as you go east instead of the reverse.

GETTING AROUND   Most recommended sights, restaurants, and hotels are within walking distance of the old city, except for the two fort-museums. Campeche isn't easy to negotiate by bus, so take taxis for sights beyond walking distance—they are inexpensive.

[FastFACTS] CAMPECHE

Area Code   The telephone area code is **981.**

ATMs   More than 10 cash machines are around the downtown area.

Internet Access   Plenty of places to check e-mail are in town—just look for signs with the words INTERNET or CYBERCAFE.

Post Office   The *correo* is in the Edificio Federal, at Avenida 16 de Septiembre and Calle 53 (✆ **981/816-2134**), near the Baluarte de Santiago; it's open Monday to Saturday from 7:30am to 8pm.

Exploring Campeche

With beautiful surroundings, friendly people, and an easy pace of life, Campeche is made for walking. Its more than 1,000 refurbished facades and renovations, grand mansions, monumental buildings, and ornate churches can be sampled in half a day or savored, along with a few day trips, over a week.

INSIDE THE CITY WALLS

The natural starting point is the modest but exceedingly pretty *zócalo,* or **Parque Principal** ★, bounded by calles 55 and 57 running east and west, and calles 8 and 10 running north and south. On Saturday nights and Sundays, streets close down and bands tune up in the gazebo. People set up tables in the streets, and an exuberant street party ensues. Construction of the **cathedral** on the north side, whose crown-shaped bell towers dominate the square, began in 1650 and was finally completed 150 years later. A pleasant way to see the city is to take the *tranvía* (trolley) tour leaving the plaza approximately every hour between 9am and 1pm and 5 to 9pm. The cost is 80 pesos for a 45-minute tour.

Baluarte San Juan   The city's smallest bastion holds an exhibition on the history of the baluartes and an old underground dungeon. The only remaining chunk of the old city wall connects San Juan with the Puerta de Tierra. The short walk between the two offers incomparable views of the new as well as the old city.

Calle 18 btw. calles 8 and 10. No phone. Free admission. Tues–Sun 8am–7:30pm.

Botanical Garden   The Jardín Botánico Xmuch'haltún is a riot of some 250 species of exotic and common plants, including an enormous ceiba tree, in a tiny courtyard surrounded by the stone walls of the last bastion Campeche built (Baluarte de Santiago).

Av. 16 de Septiembre and Calle 49. No phone. Free admission. Mon–Sat 9am–9pm; Sun 9am–4pm.

Casa 6 Centro Cultural ★★   Some rooms in this remodeled colonial house are decorated with period furniture and accessories. The traditional stucco and terra-cotta kitchen is arranged just as many Campechanos use them today. The patio of mixtilinear arches supported by simple Doric columns is striking. The front of the house is now a cultural center with a patio restaurant and a bookstore focusing on Campeche's history. One bedroom has been turned over to exhibition space.

Calle 57 no. 6. ✆ **981/816-1782.** Free admission. Daily 9am–9pm.

Mansion Carvajal ★   Another remarkable colonial mansion, built by one of the Yucatán's wealthiest *hacendados* in the early 19th century, has been put to more prosaic contemporary use for state offices but is open to the public on weekdays. It is most famous for its massive Carrara marble stairway, curving to the open, light-filled second story as if ascending to the heavens. Surrounded by pale mint-green walls punctuated by white columns and sinuous Moorish arches, you feel like you're standing on a colossal·tiered wedding cake. Art Nouveau curlicues in the iron railings and black-and-white checkerboard floors are, well, the icing on the cake.

Calle 10 btw. calles 51 and 53. No phone. Free admission. Mon–Fri 8am–2:45pm.

Museo de la Ciudad   The Museo de la Ciudad, or city museum, with the Baluarte de San Carlos, deals primarily with the design and construction of the fortifications. A model of the city shows how it looked in its glory days and provides a good overview for touring within the city walls. There are several excellent ship models as well. All text is in Spanish.

Circuito Baluartes and Av. Justo Sierra. No phone. Admission 31 pesos. Tues–Sat 8am–8pm; Sun 9am–1pm.

Museo de la Arquitectura Maya   The Baluarte de la Soledad, next to the Sea Gate, houses the Maya Stele Museum. Four rooms of Maya artifacts recovered from throughout the state, including columns from Edzná, provide an excellent overview of Maya writing, sculpture, and architecture. Many of the stelae are badly worn, but line drawings beside the stones allow you to appreciate their former design.

Calle 57 and Calle 8, opposite Plaza Principal. No phone. Admission 31 pesos. Daily 9am–5:45pm.

Puerta de Tierra ☺   The Land Gate, unlike the reconstructed Sea Gate at the opposite end of Calle 59, is the original, and is connected to the last remaining patch of the old city wall. A small museum displays portraits of pirates and the city founders. The 1732 French 5-ton cannon in the entryway was discovered in 1990. On Tuesday, Friday, and Saturday at 8pm, it holds a light-and-sound show, as long as enough people buy tickets. A variation on the popular shows at the archaeological sites, this reenacts pirate tales with blazing cannons and flashing lights. A little over the top, but fun, and kids are enthralled.

Calle 59 at Circuito Baluartes/Av. Gobernadores. No phone. Free admission to museum; show 52 pesos adults, 15 pesos children younger than 11. Daily 9am–9pm.

OUTSIDE THE WALLS: SCENIC VISTAS

Fuerte–Museo San José el Alto   This fort is higher and has a more sweeping city and coastline views than Fuerte San Miguel—its sloping lawns are a popular picnic spot—but it houses only a small exhibit of 16th- and 17th-century weapons and scale miniatures of sailing vessels. The rogue's gallery of pirates is irresistible. Take a cab; you will pass an impressive statue of Juárez on the way.

Av. Morazán s/n. No phone. Admission 31 pesos. Tues–Sun 9:30am–5:30pm.

Fuerte–Museo San Miguel ★★   For a good view of the city and a great little museum, take a cab up to Fuerte–Museo San Miguel, a small fort with a moat and a drawbridge. Built in 1771, it was the most important of the city's defenses. Gen. Santa Anna captured it when he attacked Campeche in 1842. The **Museum of Mayan Culture** was renovated in 2000 and is worth seeing. Artifacts are organized around central issues in Maya culture. The room devoted to Maya concepts of the afterlife displays a captivating *in situ* burial scene with jade masks and jewelry from

Maya tombs at Calakmul. Another room explains Maya cosmology, one depicts war, and another explains the gods. The history of the fort has its own exhibits.

Ruta Escénica s/n. No phone. Admission 34 pesos. Mon 9am–3pm (fort only); Tues–Sun 9am–5:30pm; Sun 8am–noon.

Malecón ★★ Not everything Campeche has to offer is lodged in the past. The flurry of renovation also lined about 3km (1¾ miles) of the waterfront with this broad, palm-lined sea walk, encompassing fountains, cannons, exercise stations, gardens, and monuments. The jogging and bike path bustles with energetic locals in the cool of early morning and late-night hours. Join them as the day's heat breaks for a sunset you won't soon forget.

Shopping

Casa de Artesanías Tukulná This store, run by a government family-assistance agency, occupies a restored mansion and sells top-quality examples of everything that is produced in the state, from textiles to clothing to furniture. An elaborate display of regional arts and crafts in the back includes a hammock in the making and a replica of a mud-walled Maya house. Calle 10 no. 333 (btw. calles 59 and 61). © **981/816-9088.** Mon–Sat 10am–8pm.

Where to Stay

Rates quoted include the 17% tax.

VERY EXPENSIVE

Hacienda Puerta Campeche ★★★ This beautiful and original hotel was created from several adjoining colonial homes, just inside the Puerta de Tierra in Campeche's colonial center. There is a tropical garden in the center and a pool that runs through the ruined walls of one house. Rooms are colonial with flair—large with old tile floors, distinctive colors, and beamed ceilings. "Hacienda" is in the name to make it apparent that this is connected to the hacienda properties managed by Starwood hotels (p. 582).

Calle 59 no. 71 (btw. Calles 16 and 18), 24000 Campeche, Camp. www.luxurycollection.com. © **800/ 325-3589** in the U.S. and Canada, or 981/816-7508. Fax 999/923-7963. 15 units. High season $335–$510 superior double, $415 and up suite; low season $207–$390 superior double, $279 and up suite. AE, MC, V. Free guarded parking. **Amenities:** Restaurant; 2 bars; airport transfer; babysitting; concierge; outdoor pool; room service; spa. In room: A/C, TV, fridge, hair dryer, Internet, minibar.

EXPENSIVE

Hotel Del Mar ★ It's your typical concrete rectangle, but rooms in this modern four-story hotel are large, bright, and comfortably furnished. All have balconies facing the Gulf of Mexico. The beds (two doubles or one king-size) are comfortable. The Del Mar is on the main oceanfront boulevard, between the coast and the city walls. You can make a reservation here to stay in the Río Bec area, or you can buy a package that includes guide and transportation.

Av. Ruiz Cortines 51 (at Calle 59), 24000 Campeche, Camp. www.delmarhotel.com.mx. ©/fax **981/811-9191.** 164 units. $90 double. AE, MC, V. Free parking. **Amenities:** 2 restaurants; bar; babysitting; gym w/ sauna; large outdoor pool; room service. In room: A/C, TV, hair dryer.

MODERATE

Hotel Castelmar ★★ ☺ This remarkable transformation of a one-time flophouse was restored in 2006. Pillars, archways, and tall wooden doors are reminiscent of Puerta de Campeche. The original floor plans and tiles (different patterns in each room) remain, and rooms are all shapes and sizes. But the bathrooms, swimming pool, and sun deck are new. I like the rooms with double doors opening onto a tiny balcony overlooking the street, though some people find them too noisy. It's a great *centro histórico* (historical district) location, two blocks from the *zócalo*.

Calle 61 no. 2 (btw. calles 8 and 10), 24000 Campeche, Camp. www.castelmarhotel.com. ✆ **981/811-1204.** Fax 702/297-6826. 22 units. 750 pesos double; 850 pesos superior double; 1,050 pesos junior suite. AE, MC, V. Free parking. **Amenities:** Concierge; outdoor pool; sun deck. *In room:* A/C, TV, hair dryer (on request), Wi-Fi.

Hotel Francis Drake ★ ⌀   This three-story hotel in a quiet *centro histórico* location has comfortable, midsize rooms with upscale touches not often seen at the rates they charge. The rooms are attractive, with tile floors and one king-size bed, two doubles, or two twins. The modern marble bathrooms have large showers. Suites are larger and better furnished than the standard rooms. Service is attentive, if not particularly warm by Campeche standards. The small restaurant, with a whimsical sky scene painted in the ceiling coves, serves fine examples of local dishes at very reasonable prices.

Calle 12 no. 207 (btw. calles 63 and 65), 24000 Campeche, Camp. www.hotelfrancisdrake.com. ✆ **981/811-5626,** -5627. 24 units. 795 pesos double; 905 pesos junior suite; 1,030 pesos suite. AE, MC, V. Limited free parking. **Amenities:** Restaurant; concierge; room service. *In room:* A/C, TV, hair dryer, minibar.

INEXPENSIVE

Hotel López ⌀   Unique among the historic center's hotels, the López is all Art Deco verve, with curlicued ironwork swooping around layers of curved walkways above an oval-shaped, open-air courtyard. The 1950 building was rehabilitated several years ago, now with gleaming tile bathrooms, a new waterfall pool, and a small cafe. Guest rooms are small and not nearly as stylish as the public areas, but they are comfortable enough and clean. It's the best hotel in its price range.

Calle 12 no. 189 (btw. calles 61 and 63), 24000 Campeche, Camp. www.hotellopezcampeche.com.mx. ✆ **981/816-3344.** 48 units. 500 pesos. MC, V. **Amenities:** Outdoor pool. *In room:* A/C, TV, Wi-Fi.

Where to Eat

Campeche is a fishing town, known for its fresh seafood, but restaurants also offer classic Yucatecan pork, chicken, turkey, and beef dishes. Campeche also has its own regional cuisine, fusing Spanish dishes, recipes brought by pirates from all over the world, and the region's own exotic fruits and vegetables. Make a point to try the number-one specialty, *pan de cazón* (baby shark casserole)—a stack of tortillas layered with baby shark and refried beans, then smothered with tomato sauce. For an inexpensive introduction to Campechano cuisine, sample the home-cooked food served in stalls around the *zócalo* on weekend evenings.

MODERATE

Cactus MEXICAN/STEAKS   If seafood isn't to your taste, or you've just had enough, this steakhouse is a favorite with the locals. The rib-eyes are good, as is everything but the *arrachera*, which is the same tough cut of meat used for fajitas.

Av. Malecón Justo Sierra. ✆ **981/811-1453.** Main courses 120–250 pesos. No credit cards. Daily 7am–2am.

Casa Vieja ✋ INTERNATIONAL/MEXICAN   Casa Vieja has gotten a little, well, old. While the blend of Yucatecan and Cuban food still holds interest, there's been a drop in effort. But this is still the city's prettiest dining space, in an upstairs arcade overlooking the main square. Stick with simple regional dishes, and if you're lucky, they'll be on the upswing in that mysterious cycle of quality through which so many restaurants operate.

Calle 10 no. 319. © **981/811-8016.** Main courses 60-160 pesos. No credit cards. Tues-Sat 8:30am-midnight; Sun 4pm-midnight.

La Pigua ★★★ SEAFOOD   The dining area is an air-conditioned version of a traditional Yucatecan cabin, but with walls of glass looking out on green vegetation. Sure to be on the menu is fish stuffed with shellfish, which I recommend. If you're lucky, you'll also find pompano in a green sauce seasoned with a peppery herb known as *hierba santa*. Other standouts are coconut-battered shrimp with applesauce and chiles rellenos with shark. Service is excellent, and the accommodating owner can have your favorite seafood prepared in any style you want.

Av. Miguel Alemán no. 179A. © **981/811-3365.** Reservations recommended. Main courses 120-260 pesos. AE, MC, V. Daily 1-9pm. From Plaza Principal, walk north on Calle 8 for 3 blocks; cross Av. Circuito by the botanical garden where Calle 8 becomes Miguel Alemán; the restaurant is 1½ blocks farther, on the right.

Marganzo ★ SEAFOOD   The menu veers toward the expensive side if you indulge in the seafood—its specialty—but if you stick to the Yucatecan dishes such as *poc chuc* and *pollo pibíl*, you'll eat quite well for 75 pesos or so. If you spring for seafood, whitefish filled with seafood is a local favorite. Either way, you'll leave satisfied; the kitchen knows what it's doing. Though it isn't the bargain it used to be, breakfast is still the most popular meal here.

Calle 8 no. 267 (in front of the Sea Gate). © **981/811-3899.** www.marganzo.com. Main courses 82-228 pesos. MC, V. Daily 7am-11pm.

INEXPENSIVE

Cenaduría los Portales ★ ANTOJITOS   This is a traditional Campechano supper place, a small restaurant under the stone arches facing the Plaza San Francisco in the *barrio* (neighborhood) of San Francisco. This is the oldest part of town, but it lies just outside the walls to the north. Start with the *horchata* (a sweet, milky-white drink made, in this case, with coconut). Try the delicious turkey soup and the *sincronizadas* (tostadas) and *panuchos*.

Calle 10 no. 86, Portales San Francisco. © **981/811-1491.** *Antojitos* 4-15 pesos. No credit cards. Daily 6pm-midnight.

La Parroquia MEXICAN   This local hangout offers good, inexpensive fare. It's best for breakfasts and the afternoon *comida corrida*, which might offer pot roast, meatballs, pork, or fish, with rice or squash, beans, tortillas, and fresh fruit–flavored water. Service can be slow.

Calle 55 no. 9. © **981/816-2530.** Breakfast 50 pesos; main courses 50-130 pesos; *comida corrida* (noon-3pm) 45-55 pesos. MC, V. Daily 24 hr.

Side Trips from Campeche

EDZNÁ ★★

Don't skip **Edzná** just because you've seen Chichén Itzá, Uxmal, or other famous ruins. There are several reasons to see this city. The area was populated as early as 600 B.C., with urban formation by 300 B.C. Edzná grew impressively, displaying considerable urban-planning skills. It has an ambitious and elaborate canal system that must have taken decades to complete, but would have allowed for a great expansion in agricultural production and therefore, concentration of population.

   Another construction boom began around A.D. 500, during the Classic period—the city's most prominent feature, the **Great Acropolis,** was started then—and rose to its height as a grand regional capital between A.D. 600 and 900. This was a crossroads between cities in present-day Chiapas, Yucatán, and Guatemala, and influences from all those areas appear in the city's elegant architecture.

Sitting atop the Great Acropolis are five main pyramids, the largest being the much-photographed **Pyramid of Five Stories.** It combines the features of temple platform and palace. Maya architecture typically consists of palace buildings with many vaulted chambers or solid pyramidal platforms with a couple of interior temples or burial passages. The two types of construction are mutually exclusive—except here. Such a mix is found only in the Puuc and Río Bec areas, and in only a few examples there. None are similar to this, which makes this pyramid a bold architectural statement.

Each of the Acropolis's four lesser pyramids is constructed in a different style, and each is a pure example of that style. It's as if the city's rulers were flaunting their cosmopolitanism, showing that they could build in any style they chose but preferred creating their own, superior architecture.

West of the Acropolis, across a large open plaza, is a long, raised building whose purpose isn't quite clear. But its size, as well as that of the plaza, makes you wonder just how many people this city actually held to necessitate such a large public space. Other major structures to explore include the **Platform of the Knives,** where flint knives were recovered, and the **Temple of the Big Masks,** flanked by twin sun-god faces with protruding crossed eyes (a sign of elite status).

To reach Edzná, take Hwy. 261 east from Campeche to Cayal, then Hwy. 188 south for 18km (11 miles). Buses from Campeche leave from a small station behind Parque Alameda, which is next to the market. Plan to spend an hour or two. The site is open daily from 8am to 5pm. Admission is 111 pesos, including the evening light-and-sound show, plus 45 pesos if you use a video camera.

CALAKMUL & RÍO BEC

If you're interested in seeing the ruins along the Río Bec route, see "Side Trips to Maya Ruins from Chetumal," in chapter 15. **Calakmul ★★★** (p. 568) is an important site, with the tallest pyramid in the Yucatán peninsula; Balamkú and other Río Bec sites are well worth seeing while you're in the area. You can get information and book a tour in Campeche, or rent a car. Calakmul is too far away for a day trip.

From the Calakmul area, it's easy to cross over the peninsula to Yucatán's southern Caribbean coast. Then you can head up the coast and complete a loop of the peninsula.

THE RUINS OF CHICHÉN ITZÁ ★★★

179km (111 miles) W of Cancún; 120km (75 miles) E of Mérida; 138km (86 miles) NW of Tulum

The fabled ruins of Chichén Itzá (Chee-*chen* Eeet-*zah*) are by far the Yucatán's best-known ancient monuments. Sadly, its coronation as a "New World Wonder" has made the great city harder to appreciate. Still, walking among these stone temples, pyramids, and ball courts gives you a feel for this civilization that books cannot approach, and there's no other way to comprehend the city's sheer scale. The ceremonial center's plazas would have been filled with thousands of people during one of the mass rituals that occurred here a millennium ago—and that is the saving grace for hordes of tourists that now flow through every day.

Much of what is said about the Maya (especially by tour guides) is merely educated guessing. We do know the area was settled by farmers as far back as the 4th century A.D. The first signs of an urban society appear in the 7th century in construction of stone temples and palaces in the Puuc Maya style, found in the "Old Chichén" section of the city. In the 10th century (the post-Classic Era), Chichén Itzá came under the rule of the Itzáes, who arrived from central Mexico by way of the Gulf Coast. They may have been a mix of highland Toltec Indians, who built the city of Tula in central Mexico, and lowland Putún Maya, a thriving population of traders. Following centuries brought Chichén Itzá's greatest growth. The style of the grand architecture built during this age clearly reveals Toltec influence.

The new rulers might have been refugees from Tula. A pre-Columbian myth from central Mexico tells of a fight between the gods Quetzalcóatl and Tezcatlipoca that forced Quetzalcóatl to leave his homeland and venture east. In another mythic tale, the losers of a war between Tula's religious factions fled to the Yucatán, where they were welcomed by the local Maya. Over time, the Itzáes adopted more and more the ways of the Maya. Sometime at the end of the 12th century, the city was captured by its rival, Mayapán.

Though it's possible to make a day trip from Cancún or Mérida, staying overnight here or in nearby Valladolid makes for a more relaxing trip. You can see the light show in the evening and return to see the ruins early the next morning when it is cool and before the tour buses start arriving.

Essentials

GETTING THERE & DEPARTING   By Car   Chichén Itzá is on old Hwy. 180 between Mérida and Cancún. The fastest way to get there from either city is to take the *autopista* (or *cuota*). The toll is 78 pesos from Mérida (1½ hr.), 267 pesos from Cancún (2½ hr.). From Tulum, take the highway leading to Cobá and Chemax, which connects to Hwy. 180 a bit east of Valladolid. Exiting the *autopista*, turn onto the road to Pisté. In the village, you'll reach a T junction at Hwy. 180 and turn left to the ruins; the entrance is well marked. On the same highway a few kilometers beyond, you'll come to the Hotel Zone exit at Km 121 (first, you'll pass the eastern entrance to the ruins, which is usually closed).

By Bus   First-class buses run from Mérida's CAME station nearly every hour, and some first-class buses to Cancún and Playa also stop here. Cancún and Valladolid also have first-class service. Day trips to Chichén Itzá are also widely available from Mérida, Cancún, and Playa del Carmen (and almost any destination in the Yucatán).

AREA LAYOUT   The village of **Pisté,** where most of the budget hotels and restaurants are located, is about 2.5km (1½ miles) west of the ruins. Public buses can drop you off here. Another budget hotel, the Dolores Alba (p. 619) is on the old highway 2.5km (1½ miles) east of the ruins. Three luxury hotels are situated right at Chichén Itzá's entrance.

Exploring the Ruins

The site occupies 6.5 sq. km (2½ sq. miles), requiring most of a day to see it all. The ruins are open daily from 8am to 5pm, service areas from 8am to 10pm. Admission for foreigners is 166 pesos, free for children 11 and younger. A video camera permit costs 45 pesos. Parking is extra. *You can use your ticket to reenter on the same day.* The **sound-and-light show** (worth seeing as you're being charged for it anyway), is held at 7pm fall and winter, or 8pm spring and summer. The narrative is in Spanish, but headsets are available for rent in several languages. The real reason for seeing the show is the lights, which show off the beautiful geometry of the city.

The large, modern visitor center at the main entrance consists of a museum, an auditorium, a restaurant, a bookstore, and bathrooms. Licensed guides who speak

English or Spanish usually wait at the entrance and charge around 450 pesos for one to six people (there's nothing wrong with approaching a group of people who speak the same language and offering to share a guide). You can also see the site on your own, but the guides can point out architectural details you might miss on your own.

Chichén Itzá has two parts: the central (new) zone, which shows distinct Toltec influence, and the southern (old) zone, with mostly Puuc architecture. The most important structures are in New Chichén, but the older ones are also worth seeing.

EL CASTILLO   As you enter from the tourist center, the icon of Yucatán tourism, the magnificent 25m (82-ft.) El Castillo (also called the Pyramid of Kukulkán) is straight ahead across a large, open grassy area. It was built with the Maya calendar in mind. The four stairways leading up to the central platform each have 91 steps, which, added to the platform, totals the 365 days of the solar year. The 18 terraces flanking the stairways on each face of the pyramid add up to the number of months in the Maya religious calendar. The terraces contain a total of 52 panels, representing the 52-year cycle when the solar and religious calendars reconverge. The pyramid, now closed to climbers, is aligned so that the **spring** or **fall equinox** (Mar 21 or Sept 21), triggers an optical illusion: The setting sun casts the terraces' shadow onto the northern stairway, forming a diamond pattern suggestive of a snake's geometric designs. As it meets the giant serpent's head at the bottom, the shadow appears to slither down the pyramid as the sun sets, a phenomenon that brings hordes of visitors every year. (The effect is more conceptual than visual, and frankly, the ruins are much more enjoyable on other days when they are less crowded.)

Like most Maya pyramids, El Castillo was built over an earlier structure. A narrow stairway at the western edge of the north staircase leads inside to a sacrificial altar-throne—a red jaguar encrusted with jade. The stairway is open from 11am to 3pm and is cramped, usually crowded, humid, and uncomfortable. A visit early in the day is best. Photos of the jaguar figure are not allowed.

JUEGO DE PELOTA (MAIN BALL COURT)   Northwest of El Castillo is Chichén's main ball court, the largest and best preserved anywhere, and only one of nine ball courts built in this city. Carved on both walls are scenes showing Maya figures dressed as ball players and decked out in protective padding. A headless player kneels with blood shooting from his neck; another player holding the head looks on.

Players on two teams tried to knock a hard rubber ball through one of the two stone rings placed high on either wall, using only their elbows, knees, and hips. According to legend, losers paid for defeat with their lives. However, some experts say the victors were the only appropriate sacrifices for the gods. Either way, the game, called *pok-ta-pok*, must have been riveting, heightened by the ball court's wonderful acoustics.

THE NORTH TEMPLE   Temples stand at both ends of the ball court. The North Temple has sculptured pillars and more sculptures inside, as well as badly ruined murals. The acoustics of the ball court are so good that from the North Temple, a person speaking can be heard clearly at the opposite end, about 135m (443 ft.) away.

TEMPLE OF JAGUARS   Near the southeastern corner of the main ball court is a small temple with serpent columns and carved panels showing warriors and jaguars. Up the steps and inside the temple, a mural chronicles a battle in a Maya village.

TZOMPANTLI (TEMPLE OF THE SKULLS)   To the right of the ball court, the Temple of the Skulls obviously borrows from the post-Classic cities of central Mexico. Notice the rows of skulls carved into the stone platform; when a sacrificial victim's head was cut off, it was impaled on a pole and displayed with others in a tidy row. Also carved into the stone are pictures of eagles tearing hearts from human victims. The word "Tzompantli" is not Mayan, but comes from central Mexico.

PLATFORM OF THE EAGLES Next to the Tzompantli, this small platform has reliefs showing eagles and jaguars clutching human hearts in their talons and claws, as well as a human head emerging from the mouth of a serpent.

PLATFORM OF VENUS East of the Tzompantli and north of El Castillo, near the road to the Sacred Cenote, is the Platform of Venus. In Maya and Toltec lore, a feathered monster or a feathered serpent with a human head in its mouth represented Venus. This is also called the tomb of Chaac-Mool, for the figure that was discovered "buried" within the structure.

SACRED CENOTE Follow the dirt road (actually an ancient *sacbé,* or causeway) leading north from the Platform of Venus for 5 minutes to get to the great natural well that may have given Chichén Itzá (the Well of the Itzáes) its name. This well was used for ceremonial purposes, and the bones of both children and adult sacrificial victims were found at the bottom.

Edward Thompson, who was the American consul in Mérida and a Harvard professor, purchased the ruins of Chichén early in the 20th century and explored the cenote with dredges and divers. He uncovered a fortune in gold and jade, most of which ended up in Harvard's Peabody Museum of Archaeology and Ethnology—a matter that disconcerts Mexican classicists to this day. Excavations in the 1960s yielded more treasure, and studies of the recovered objects show that the offerings came from throughout the Yucatán and even farther away.

TEMPLO DE LOS GUERREROS (TEMPLE OF THE WARRIORS) The Toltec influence is especially evident on the eastern edge of the plaza. Due east of El Castillo is one of Chichén Itzá's most impressive structures, the Temple of the Warriors, named for the carvings of warriors marching along its walls. The temple and the rows of almost Greco-Roman columns flanking it are also called the Group of the Thousand Columns, and recall the great Toltec site of Tula. A figure of Chaac-Mool sits at the top of the temple (visible only from a distance now that the temple is closed to climbers), surrounded by impressive columns carved in relief to look like enormous feathered serpents. South of the temple was a square building that archaeologists call **El Mercado (The Market);** a colonnade surrounds its central court.

The main Mérida-Cancún highway once ran straight through the ruins of Chichén, and though it has been diverted, you can still see the great swath it cut. South and west of the old highway's path are more impressive ruined buildings.

TUMBA DEL GRAN SACERDOTE (TOMB OF THE HIGH PRIEST) Past the refreshment stand to the right of the path, the Tomb of the High Priest shows both Toltec and Puuc influence. The 9m (30-ft.) pyramid, with stairways on each side depicting feathered serpents, bears a distinct resemblance to El Castillo. Beneath its foundation is an ossuary (a communal graveyard) in a natural limestone cave, where skeletons and offerings have been found.

CASA DE LOS METATES (TEMPLE OF THE GRINDING STONES) This building, the next one on your right, is named after the Maya's concave corn-grinding stones.

TEMPLO DEL VENADO (TEMPLE OF THE DEER) Past Casa de los Metates is this fairly tall, though ruined, building. The relief of a stag that gave the temple its name is long gone.

CHICHANCHOB (LITTLE HOLES) This temple has a roof comb with little holes, three masks of the rain god Chaac, three rooms, and a good view of surrounding structures. It's one of Chichén's oldest buildings, built in the Puuc style during the late Classic period.

EL CARACOL (THE OBSERVATORY) One of Chichén Itzá's most intriguing structures is in the old part of the city. From a distance, the rounded tower of El Caracol ("The Snail," for its shape), sometimes called The Observatory, looks like any modern observatory. Construction of this complex building with its circular tower was carried out over centuries, acquiring additions and modifications as the Maya's careful celestial observations required increasingly exact measurements. Quite unlike other Maya buildings, the entrances, staircases, and angles are not aligned with one another. Four doors lead into the tower and a circular chamber, where a spiral staircase leads to the upper level. The slits in the roof are aligned with the sun's equinoxes. Astronomers observed the cardinal directions and the approach of the all-important spring and autumn equinoxes, as well as the summer solstice.

On the east side of El Caracol, a path leads north into the bush to the **Cenote Xtoloc,** a natural limestone well that provided the city's daily water supply. If you see lizards sunning there, they may well be *xtoloc,* the species for which this cenote is named.

TEMPLO DE LOS TABLEROS (TEMPLE OF THE PANELS) Just south of El Caracol are the ruins of a *temazcalli* (a steam bath) and the Temple of the Panels, named for the carved panels on top. A few traces remain of the much larger structure that once covered the temple.

EDIFICIO DE LAS MONJAS (EDIFICE OF THE NUNS) This enormous nunnery is reminiscent of the palaces at sites along the Puuc route. The new edifice was built in the late Classic period over an older one. To prove this, an early 20th-century archaeologist put dynamite between the two and blew away part of the exterior, revealing the older structures within. Indelicate, perhaps, but effective.

On the east side of the Edifice of the Nuns is **Anexo Este (annex),** constructed in highly ornate Chenes style with Chaac masks and serpents.

LA IGLESIA (THE CHURCH) Next to the annex is another of Chichén's oldest buildings, the Church. Masks of Chaac decorate two upper stories; a close look reveals armadillo, crab, snail, and tortoise symbols among the crowd of Chaacs. These represent the Maya gods, called *bacah,* whose job it was to hold up the sky.

AKAB DZIB (TEMPLE OF OBSCURE WRITING) Beloved of travel writers, this temple lies east of the Edifice of the Nuns. Above a door in one of the rooms are some Mayan glyphs, which gave the temple its name because the writings are hard to make out. In other rooms, traces of red handprints are still visible. Reconstructed and expanded over the centuries, Akab Dzib might be the oldest building on the site.

CHICHÉN VIEJO (OLD CHICHÉN) For a look at more of Chichén's oldest buildings, constructed well before the time of Toltec influence, follow signs from the Edifice of the Nuns southwest into the bush to Old Chichén, about 1km (⅔ mile) away. Be prepared for this trek with long trousers, insect repellent, and a local guide. Attractions here include the **Templo de los Inscripciones Iniciales (Temple of the First Inscriptions),** with the oldest inscriptions discovered at Chichén, and the restored **Templo de los Dinteles (Temple of the Lintels),** a fine Puuc building. Some of these buildings are being restored.

Where to Stay

The expensive hotels in Chichén all occupy beautiful grounds, are close to the ruins, serve decent food, and have toll-free reservations numbers. They do a brisk business with tour operators—they can be empty one day and full the next. From these hotels, you can easily walk to the back entrance of the ruins, next to the Hotel Mayaland. **Hotel Chichén Itzá** (www.mayaland.com; ✆ 998/887-2495) is the best of several inexpensive hotels just west of the ruins in the village of Pisté, which has little else to recommend it. Another option is to stay in the colonial town of Valladolid (p. 620), 40 minutes away.

EXPENSIVE

Hacienda Chichén Resort ★★   The smallest and most private of the hotels at the ruins' entrance is also the quietest. A one-time hacienda that served as headquarters for the Carnegie Institute's excavations in 1923, the bungalows built for institute staff residences now house one or two units with a dehumidifier, a ceiling fan, and good air-conditioning. The floors are ceramic tile, ceilings are stucco with wood beams, and walls are adorned with carved stone. Trees and tropical plants fill manicured gardens that you can enjoy from your private porch or from the terrace restaurant, which occupies part of the original main house. Standard rooms come with a queen-size, two twin, or two double beds; suites have king-size beds.

Zona Arqueológica, 97751 Chichén Itzá, Yuc. www.haciendachichen.com. ✆ **985/851-0045.** (Reservations office in Mérida: ✆ 877/631-4005 in the U.S., or 999/920-8407.) 28 units. High season $165–$180 double, $200–$280 suite; low season $120 double, $135–$180 suite. Promotional rates available. AE, MC, V. Free guarded parking. **Amenities:** Restaurant; 2 bars; large outdoor pool; spa. *In room:* A/C, hair dryer, minibar, no phone.

MODERATE

Villas Arqueológicas Chichén Itzá ★ ☺   Similar to its sister property at Uxmal, this hotel is built around a courtyard and pool and is a happy compromise between low-budget lodging and the more lavish hotels nearby. It's by far the best deal if you want to stay near the entrance to the ruins (a 5- to 10-min. walk on a peaceful road). The grounds are lush with two massive royal poinciana trees and bougainvillea-draped walls. Rooms are modern, clean, and quite comfortable, unless you're 1.9m (6 ft. 2 in.) or taller—each bed is in a niche, with walls at the head and foot. Most rooms have one double bed and a twin bed, and Islander has added a few suites. You can also book a half- or full-board plan.

Zona Arqueológica, Carretera Mérida–Valladolid Km 120, 97751 Chichén Itzá, Yuc. www.islander collection.com. ✆ **985/856-6000.** Fax 985/856-6008. 45 units. $59–$84 double; $121–$173 suite. Rates include continental breakfast. Half-board (breakfast plus lunch or dinner) $20 per person; full board (3 meals) $35 per person. AE, MC, V. Free parking. **Amenities:** Restaurant; bar; large outdoor pool; tennis court; Wi-Fi (in public areas). *In room:* A/C, hair dryer.

INEXPENSIVE

Hotel Dolores Alba 🍃   This longtime budget favorite is of the motel variety, and it is a bargain for what you get: two pools (one fed by a natural spring); hammocks hanging under *palapas*; and large, comfortable rooms with some colorful hacienda-style accents that come with two double beds. The restaurant serves good meals at moderate prices. The hotel provides free transportation to the ruins and the Cave of Balankanché during visiting hours, though you will have to take a taxi back. It is located on the highway 2.5km (1½ miles) east of the ruins (toward Valladolid).

Carretera Mérida–Valladolid Km 122, Yuc. www.doloresalba.com. ✆ **985/858-1555.** (Reservations: Hotel Dolores Alba, Calle 63 no. 464, 97000 Mérida, Yuc.; ✆ 999/928-5650; fax 999/928-3163.) 40 units. 600 pesos double. MC, V (8% service charge). Free parking. **Amenities:** Restaurant; bar; 2 outdoor pools; room service. *In room:* A/C, TV, no phone.

Where to Eat

This area has no great food, but it has plenty of adequate food; simple choices are the best. The restaurant at the ruins' visitor center serves decent snack food. The hotel restaurants mostly do a fair job, though they are more expensive than they should be. In the village of Pisté, you can try the **Hotel Chichén Itzá** or one of the restaurants along the highway that cater to the bus tours (best during early lunch or regular supper hours, when the buses are gone).

Other Attractions in the Area

Ik-Kil is a large, deep cenote on the highway across from the Hotel Dolores Alba, 2.5km (1½ miles) east of the main entrance to the ruins. Getting down to the water's edge requires navigating many steps, but they are easier to manage than those at Dzitnup. The view from both the top and the bottom is dramatic, with lots of tropical vegetation and curtains of hanging tree roots stretching all the way to the water's surface. The best swimming is before 11:30am, when bus tours begin to arrive. These tours are the main business of Ik-Kil, which also has a restaurant and souvenir shops. The cenote is open from 8am to 6pm daily. Admission is 70 pesos.

The **Cave of Balankanché** is 5.5km (3½ miles) from Chichén Itzá on the road to Valladolid and Cancún. Taxis will make the trip and wait. The entire excursion takes about a half-hour, but the walk inside is hot and humid. This is the tamest of the Yucatán's cave tours, with good footing and the least amount of walking and climbing. It includes a cheesy and uninformative recorded tour. The highlight is a round chamber with a central column that resembles a large tree. The cave became a hideout during the War of the Castes, and you can still see traces of carving and incense burning, as well as an underground stream that supplied water to the refugees. Outside, meander through the botanical gardens, where nearly everything is labeled with common and botanical names.

Admission is 70 pesos, 5 pesos for children 6 to 12 (younger than 6 not admitted). Use of a video camera costs 45 pesos (free if you bought a video permit in Chichén earlier in the day). Tours in English are at 11am and 1 and 3pm, and, in Spanish, at 9am, noon, and 2 and 4pm. Double-check these hours at the main entrance to the Chichén ruins.

VALLADOLID

40km (25 miles) E of Chichén Itzá; 160km (99 miles) SW of Cancún; 98km (61 miles) NW of Tulum

Valladolid (pronounced Bah-yah-doh-*leed*) is a small colonial city halfway between Mérida and Cancún. One of the first Spanish strongholds and crucible of the War of the Castes, the city still has handsome colonial buildings and 19th-century structures that make it a pleasant place to bask in the real Yucatán. People are friendly and informal, and the only real challenge is the heat. The city's economy is based on commerce and small-scale manufacturing. It's close to a couple of famous cenotes, the intriguing ruins of Ek Balam, Ría Lagartos' nesting flamingos, and the sandy beaches of Isla Holbox (p. 625). It's closer to Chichén Itzá than Mérida is, making it a good alternative base for exploring.

Essentials

GETTING THERE & DEPARTING   By Car   From Mérida or Cancún, you can take either the Hwy. 180 *cuota* (toll road) or the Hwy. 180 *libre* (free). The toll is 233 pesos from Cancún and 135 pesos from Mérida. The *cuota* passes 2km (1¼ miles) north of the city; the exit is at the crossing of Hwy. 295 to Tizimín. **Hwy. 180 *libre*,** passing through a number of villages (with their requisite *topes*) takes significantly longer. Both 180 and 295 lead straight to downtown. Leaving is just as easy: From the main square, Calle 41 turns into 180 E. to Cancún; Calle 39 heads to 180 W. to Chichén Itzá and Mérida. To take the *cuota* to Mérida or Cancún, take Calle 40 (see "City Layout," below).

By Bus   Buses leave throughout the day for Mérida (134 pesos) and Cancún (82 pesos). You can also get several buses a day to Playa del Carmen (96 pesos) and Tulum (64 pesos). To get to Chichén Itzá, take a second-class bus, which leaves at least every hour. The recently remodeled bus station is at the corner of calles 39 and 46.

VISITOR INFORMATION   The small **tourism office** is in the Palacio Municipal, open Monday to Friday from 8am to 9pm, Saturday and Sunday 9am to 9pm.

CITY LAYOUT   Valladolid's layout is the standard for towns in the Yucatán: Streets running north-south are even numbers; those running east-west are odd numbers. The main plaza is bordered by Calle 39 on the north, 41 on the south, 40 on the east, and 42 on the west. The plaza is named Parque Francisco Cantón Rosado, but everyone calls it **El Centro.** Taxis are easy to come by.

Exploring Valladolid

Before it became Valladolid, the city was a Maya settlement called Zací (Zah-*kee*), which means "white hawk." The old name lives on in the cenote in a small park at the intersection of calles 39 and 36. The long but easily navigable stepped trail at **Cenote Zací ★** leads past caves, stalactites, and hanging vines that give the place a prehistoric feel, but the cenote's partially open roof lightens the atmosphere. It's a fine place to cool off, whether you jump in for a swim, dangle your feet in the water and let the fish nibble your toes, or just walk down to escape city heat and noise. After several trips to both, I find Zací more peaceful and just as pretty as the famous cenotes outside of town (p. 623). The park, which has a large *palapa* restaurant overlooking the cenote, is free; entry to the cenote is 15 pesos.

Ten blocks southwest of the main square is the Franciscan monastery of **San Bernardino de Siena ★★**, dating from 1552. The monastery complex was sacked during the War of the Castes but a fine baroque altarpiece and some striking 17th-century paintings remain. Most of the compound was built in the early 1600s; a large underground river is believed to pass under the convent and surrounding neighborhood, which is called Barrio Sisal. ("Sisal," in this case, is a corruption of the Mayan phrase *sis-ha*, meaning "cold water.") The *barrio* has been extensively restored and is a delight. For a real treat, walk there along the **Calzada de los Frailes (Walkway of the Friars) ★**. From the corner of calles 41 and 46, follow Calle 41A, the cobblestone street running diagonally to the southwest, about 1km (⅔ mile) to the monastery. The road is lined by huge clay planters and passes elegantly painted colonial homes.

Valladolid's **main plaza** is the town's social center and a thriving market for Yucatecan dresses. The square was renovated in the winter of 2009–10, and all of the lush old shade trees were preserved. The old-world benches and *confidenciales* (S-shaped chairs inviting friends or lovers to chat or nuzzle face-to-face), were either replaced or repainted. Although the buildings flanking the square were repainted, new lighting was added, and walking paths were repaved, the square still retains its old colonial feel.

On the plaza's south side is the imposing cathedral, **Iglesia de San Gervasio** (sometimes called Parroquia de San Servacio). Its thick stone walls weren't enough to stop the Maya rebels who sacked it in 1847, touching off the War of the Castes. Vallesoletanos, as the locals are known, believe most all cathedrals in Mexico point east, and they cherish a local legend to explain why theirs points north—but don't believe a word of it. On the east side, the municipal building, **El Ayuntamiento,** is the repository for dramatic paintings outlining the peninsula's history, including a wonderful depiction of a horrified Maya priest foreseeing the arrival of Spanish galleons. On Sunday nights, beneath the stone arches of the Ayuntamiento, the municipal band plays *jaranas* and other traditional music of the region.

For an overview of arts and crafts from surrounding Maya villages, find the pink, fortresslike building that houses **Museo San Roque** on Calle 41 between calles 38 and 40. Signs are in Spanish, but the displays mostly speak for themselves. Ancient stone masks, pottery, and bones unearthed at nearby Ek Balam (p. 624) are also on exhibit. The museum is open Monday through Saturday, 9am to 9pm. Entry is free.

Shopping

The **Mercado de Artesanías de Valladolid (crafts market),** at the corner of calles 39 and 44, gives you an overview of the local merchandise. Perhaps the town's primary handicraft is embroidered Maya dresses, which you can buy here or from women around the main square. **Yalat,** on Calle 39 at Calle 40, looks like a gallery but sells unique folk art from throughout Mexico, specializing in the Yucatán.

Valladolid is in cattle country, making it a good place to buy inexpensive, locally made leather goods such as huaraches (sandals) and bags. On the main plaza is a small shop above the municipal bazaar. A good sandal maker has a shop called **Elios,** Calle 37 no. 202, between calles 42 and 44 (no phone). An Indian named **Juan Mac** makes *alpargatas,* the traditional Maya sandal, in his shop on Calle 39, 1 block from the main plaza near Calle 38 (across from the Bar La Joya). There's no sign, but the door jamb is painted yellow. Juan Mac is working there most mornings. Most of his output is for locals, but he's happy to knock out a pair for visitors.

Where to Stay

Aside from lodging listed below, Valladolid's best budget hotels are **Hotel San Clemente,** on Calle 42 between calles 41 and 43 (www.hotelsanclemente.com.mx; ✆ **985/856-3161;** 448 pesos per night; MasterCard, Visa) and **Hotel Zací,** Calle 44 between calles 37 and 39 (✆ **985/856-2167;** 468 pesos; no credit cards).

For something a bit different, you can stay in a small ecohotel in the nearby village of Ek Balam, close to the ruins, at **Genesis Retreat Ek Balam** (www.genesisretreat. com; ✆ **985/858-9375;** 488–599 pesos; no credit cards). The Canadian owner, Lee Christie, takes guests on village tours that unveil daily life for the contemporary Maya. She rents simple cabañas (with shared or private bathrooms) surrounding a lovely pool and a restaurant.

Casa Quetzal ★ The landlady, Judith Fernández, is a gracious Mexican woman who moved to Valladolid to slow down. She has created airy, attractive lodging in the refurbished Barrio Sisal, within easy walking distance of the main square. Emphasis is on comfort and service—good linens and mattresses, quiet air-conditioning, and a large and inviting central courtyard. English is spoken, and Sra. Fernández has lined up a good guide you can contract to take you to outlying areas.

Calle 51 no. 218, Barrio Sisal, 97780 Valladolid, Yuc. www.casa-quetzal.com. ℂ/fax **985/856-4796.** 8 units. $65–$80 double; $85 junior suite; $90 casita. Rates include full breakfast. No credit cards. Free secure parking. **Amenities:** Babysitting; small outdoor pool; room service; spa. *In room:* A/C, TV, no phone, Wi-Fi.

El Mesón del Marqués ★★ Originally an early-17th-century house, the doyen of Valladolid's plaza has grown by adding new construction in back. All the rooms (most with two double beds) are quite comfortable, though the new buildings don't have the wow factor of the original porticoed courtyard, which drips with bougainvillea and hanging plants and is mostly occupied by the restaurant (see "Where to Eat," below). The pretty, fairly large pool is another modern addition. The hotel is on the north side of the plaza, opposite the church.

Calle 39 no. 203 (btw. calles 40 and 42), 97780 Valladolid, Yuc. www.mesondelmarques.com. ℂ **985/ 856-2073.** Fax 985/856-2280. 90 units. 700–1,000 pesos double; 1,341–1,460 pesos junior suite. AE, MC, V. Free secure parking. **Amenities:** Restaurant; bar; outdoor pool; room service. *In room:* A/C, TV, Wi-Fi.

Where to Eat

Valladolid is not a hotbed of haute cuisine, but the regional specialties are reliably good. **Hostería El Marqués** ★★, at the Hotel El Mesón del Marqués, turns out the best food in town—Yucatecan classics and international dishes—in an achingly romantic setting. Also on the main square, friendly, informal **Las Campanas** serves tasty food for reasonable prices. Locals like to visit over a meal at the stalls in the **Bazar Municipal,** next door to the Mesón del Marqués; I like them for a quick, cheap breakfast or a huge tumbler of fresh-squeezed orange juice when the heat gets to me (you can also take it to go in a plastic bag with a straw).

Side Trips from Valladolid

CENOTES DZITNUP & SAMMULÁ

The **Cenote Dzitnup** (also known as Cenote Xkekén) is 4km (2½ miles) west of Valladolid off Hwy. 180 toward Chichén Itzá. It's said to be the most photographed cenote in the Yucatán, and it's easy to see why. The deep, glassy, blue water, beneath a thicket of stalactites and ropy tree roots straining for a drink, is a spectacle to behold. The beautiful pictures, however, don't reveal the treacherous stone steps, the unrelenting humidity even on an otherwise comfortable day (wear contacts instead of glasses, which will be constantly fogged), and the somewhat claustrophobic feeling if you're there with a crowd (which is most of the time). It's an awesome sight, to be sure, and you should see it at least once. Bring a suit and take a swim; it will revive you for the climb back out.

> **Cenote Etiquette**
>
> If you swim in a cenote, be sure you don't have creams or other chemicals on your skin—including deodorant. They damage the habitat of the small fish and other organisms living in the water. No alcohol, food, or smoking is allowed.

The cenote is open daily from 7am to 7pm; admission is 52 pesos. If it's crowded, you can go for a swim about 90m (295 ft.) down the road on the opposite side in a smaller, less developed but also beautiful cenote, **Sammulá.**

EK BALAM: DARK JAGUAR ★★★

About 18km (11 miles) north of Valladolid, off the highway to Río Lagartos, are the spectacular ruins of **Ek Balam,** which, owing to a certain ambiguity in Mayan, may mean "black jaguar," "dark jaguar," or "star jaguar." Though tourists have yet to catch on, these ruins could prove to be a more important discovery than Chichén Itzá. Archaeologists began work only in 1997, and their findings have Maya scholars all aquiver. Built between 100 B.C. and A.D. 1200, the smaller buildings are architecturally unique—especially the large, perfectly restored **Oval Palace** (also sometimes called La Redonda or Caracol).

The imposing central pyramid, known as **El Torre ★★** or the Acropolis, is about 160m (525 ft.) long and 60m (197 ft.) wide. At more than 30m (98 ft.) high, it easily surpasses El Castillo in Chichén Itzá. To the left of the main stairway, archaeologists have uncovered a large ceremonial doorway of perfectly preserved stucco work. Designed in the Chenes style associated with Campeche, it forms an astonishingly elaborate representation of the gaping mouth of the underworld god. Around it are several beautifully detailed human figures, including what appear to be winged warriors. Known as Mayan Angels, they are unique in Maya architecture. Excavation inside the pyramid revealed a long chamber (so far closed to the public) filled with hieroglyphic writing that suggests the scribes probably came from Guatemala. The script revealed the name of one of the city's principal kings—Ukit Kan Le'k Tok', whose tomb was uncovered about two-thirds of the way up the pyramid. Climb to the top and you see untouched ruins masquerading as overgrown hills to the north, and the tallest structures of **Cobá,** 50km (31 miles) to the southeast.

Also visible are the Maya's *sacbeob,* or raised causeways, appearing as raised lines in the forest. More than any of the better-known sites, Ek Balam inspires a sense of mystery and awe at the scale of Maya civilization and the utter ruin to which it fell.

A new road runs from the highway to the ruins. Take Calle 40 north out of Valladolid to Hwy. 295 and go 20km (12 miles) to a large marked turnoff. Ek Balam is 13km (8 miles) from the highway; admission is 31 pesos, 45 pesos per video camera. The site is open daily from 8am to 5pm.

RÍA LAGARTOS NATURE RESERVE ★

About 80km (50 miles) north of Valladolid (40km/25 miles north of Tizimín) on Hwy. 295, Ría Lagartos is a 50,000-hectare (123,553-acre) refuge established in 1979 to protect the largest nesting flamingo population in North America. The nesting area is off-limits, but you can see plenty of flamingos, as well as many other species of waterfowl, on an enjoyable boat ride around the estuary.

Río Lagartos, at the west end of the

 A Matter of Timing

You'll see some flamingos any time of year (and probably ducks, hawks, cranes, cormorants, and osprey as well). But to see great rosy masses of them, go between April and October. After the birds complete their courtship rituals in Celestún, they fly to Ría Lagartos to nest, lay their eggs, and prepare their young for the return journey in October.

estuary, is the place to get boats to the flamingos. Misnamed by Spaniards who mistook the long, narrow *ría* (estuary) for a *río* (river), it's a small fishing village of about 3,000 people who make their living from the sea and from the occasional tourist who shows up to see the flamingos. Colorful houses face the *malecón* (oceanfront street), and brightly painted boats dock here and there.

When you drive into town, keep going straight until you get to the shore. Where Calle 10 intersects with the *malecón,* near a modern church, is a little kiosk where the guides can be found (no phone). You can book a 2-hour tour, which costs about 750 pesos for two to three people. The guides also like to show you the evaporation pools used by the local salt producer at Las Coloradas (a good source of employment for the locals until it was mechanized) and a freshwater spring bubbling out from below the saltwater estuary.

The best time to see flamingos is in the early morning, so you might want to stay overnight in town. Río Lagartos has a few simple hotels, the best of which is **Hotel Villa de Pescadores** (✆ **986/862-0020**) on the waterfront. Another option is **Hotel San Felipe** (✆ **986/862-2067**) in the pleasant fishing village of San Felipe, 9km (5⅔ miles) to the west.

ISLA HOLBOX ★

A sandy strip of an island off the northeastern corner of the Yucatán Peninsula, Isla Holbox (pronounced Hohl-*bosh*) is in Quintana Roo, and is actually closer to Cancún than Valladolid. But, unless Cancún tourists take a boat tour, they have to drive almost to the Yucatán border to get to the road north. Given the challenges of driving in Cancún, it makes sense to visit Holbox from the Yucatán side.

Holbox was a half-deserted fishing village in a remote corner of the world before tourists started showing up for the beach. Now it's a semiprosperous little community that makes its livelihood from tourist services, employment at the beach hotels, and tours. It's most popular with visitors from May to September, when more than a hundred **whale sharks ★★★** congregate in nearby waters to feed on the plankton and krill churned up by the collision of Gulf and Caribbean waters. Whale sharks are much larger than other sharks, reaching as much as 18m (59 ft.), and they filter their food much as baleen whales do. These peaceable giants swim slowly along the surface of the water and don't seem to mind the boat tours and snorkelers that come for the thrill of swimming alongside them. That said, they can do some mischief if you annoy them.

Besides swimming with whale sharks, most tourists come to Holbox to laze on the broad beach of fine-textured sand. The water, though, is not the amazing blue of the Caribbean but a murkier green. Diving, snorkeling, sportfishing, and nature tours of **Laguna Yalahu,** the shallow lagoon separating Holbox from the mainland, are the primary other diversions. It's not a place for Type-A types.

Posada Mawimbi (www.mawimbi.net; ✆ **984/875-2003**), starting at $75 to $90 a night depending on season, hits the best balance between price and comfort among the beach hotels in town. **Casa Sandra** (www.casasandra.com; ✆ **984/875-2171**) charges $227 and (way) up in low season, $274 and up in high season, but travelers who want only the best will find it here, along with air-conditioning, a rarity in Holbox. Just beyond town, **Villas Delfines,** which has an office in Cancún (www.villasdelfines.com; ✆ **998/884-8606**), is an ecohotel charging $90 to $150 in low season, $120 to $180 high season, for thatched-roof beach bungalows.

From Valladolid, take Hwy. 180 east for about 90km (56 miles) toward Cancún; turn north after Nuevo Xcan at the tiny crossroads of El Ideal. Drive nearly 100km (62 miles) north on a state highway to the tiny port of Chiquilá, where you can park your car in a secure parking lot; walk 180m (591 ft.) to the pier, and catch the ferry to the island. It runs 10 times per day and costs 70 pesos per person. When you arrive in the village, you can contract with one of the golf-cart taxis for a ride to your hotel.

Visiting the Whale Sharks of Isla Holbox

In 2002, Mexico's whale sharks were designated an endangered species. The government, along with environmental groups, closely monitors their activity and the tours that visit them off Isla Holbox. Several restrictions apply to how tours are run, and all tour operators must abide by them. See details of the restrictions, and learn more about the whale sharks, at www.domino.conanp.gob.mx/rules.htm.

Whale shark tours are kept small; just two people at a time are allowed to snorkel with the sharks. Tours typically cost around $80 to $100 per person and last 4 to 6 hours. Many hotels or outfitters on the island can arrange a tour.

TABASCO & CHIAPAS

by David Baird

The states of Tabasco and Chiapas, in southernmost Mexico, are largely covered in jungle and rainforest. In pre-Classic times (before A.D. 300) a large part of this area was homeland to Mexico's "mother culture," the Olmec, who in many ways gave form to the cultural development of the civilizations that would come afterward. And in both pre-Classic and Classic times (A.D. 300–900) this was the homeland of the Maya, whose descendants still populate the region. The ruins that these people left behind, as well as the villages of the present-day Maya, attract many visitors to this region: the giant stone heads of the Olmec, the ancient ceremonial centers of the Maya, such as Palenque and Toniná, and the living Maya cultures of both highland and lowland Chiapas.

The lowland jungle with its high canopy offers a tremendous variety of flora and fauna. Placid lakes dot the land and provide the only open vistas in this densely packed landscape. The mountainous central highlands of Chiapas are also thickly forested and often shrouded in mist. Rivers, including Mexico's two largest, the Grijalva and the Usumacinta, cut their way down to the lowlands, through rugged canyons and tumbling waterfalls. And the cool mountain air feels refreshing after the heat and humidity of the lowlands.

Tabasco is a small, oil-rich state along the Gulf Coast. The capital, **Villahermosa,** is the main port of entry into this region. It has a boomtown feel and an intriguing history. But the large state of **Chiapas** holds the greater number of attractions. In its eastern lowland jungle is the ancient ceremonial center of **Palenque.** Near the border with Guatemala are the smaller but dramatic sites of **Yaxchilán** and **Bonampak.** Between these lowlands and the central highlands are many waterfalls and rapids as well as the ruins of **Toniná.** Located high in the mountains and surrounded by Indian communities is the colonial city of **San Cristóbal de las Casas,** with its beautiful old town and market center.

VILLAHERMOSA

142km (88 miles) NW of Palenque; 469km (291 miles) SW of Campeche; 160km (99 miles) N of San Cristóbal de las Casas

Villahermosa (pop. 600,000) is the capital of Tabasco state and its largest city. It lies in a shallow depression about an hour's drive from the Gulf

In the past 6 years, one or another part of Tabasco has been inundated by flooding every year. This flooding has caused lengthy delays for travelers trying to get from Veracruz to the Yucatán or vice versa. In some cases it's taken weeks to clear the highway. Most of the flooding has occurred in Villahermosa and the western part of the state, so check the forecast before heading down to Tabasco.

Coast, at the confluence of two rivers: the Grijalva and the Carrizal. This location makes the city susceptible to flooding. The land is marshy, with shallow lakes scattered here and there. For most of the year it's hot and humid.

Oil has brought money to this town and raised prices. Villahermosa is one of the most expensive cities in the country and contrasts sharply with inexpensive Chiapas. Though there's a lot of money, it's all being pulled to the modern western sections surrounding a development called Tabasco 2000. This area, especially the neighborhoods around the **Parque–Museo La Venta,** is the most attractive part of town, dotted by small lakes. The historic center has been left to decay. It's gritty, crowded, and unpleasant. The main reason to be downtown is for the cheap hotels.

Two names that you will likely see and hear are Carlos Pellicer Cámara and Tomás Garrido Canabal. The first was a mid-20th-century Tabascan poet and intellectual. The best known of Mexico's *modernista* poets, he was a fiercely independent thinker. Garrido Canabal, socialist governor of Tabasco in the 1920s and 1930s, was even more fiercely independent. He wanted to turn the conservative, backwater state of Tabasco into a model of socialism and fought for many socialist causes. But his anticlericalism campaigning is what he is most remembered for today. He went so far as to name his son Lucifer and his farm animals Jesus and the Virgin Mary.

Essentials

GETTING THERE & DEPARTING

BY PLANE Villahermosa's airport (airport code: VSA) is the main port of entry into this region. **Continental ExpressJet** (© **800/525-0280** in the U.S., or 01-800/900-5000 in Mexico; www.continental.com) has direct service to/from Houston on a regional jet. **Aeroméxico** (© **800/237-6639** in the U.S., or 01-800/021-4000 in Mexico; www.aeromexico.com) and its subsidiaries have direct flights to and from Mexico City, Monterrey, Mérida, and Veracruz. Mexican discount carrier **VivaAerobus** (© **01-81/8215-0150** in Mexico; www.vivaaerobus.com) has a direct flight to/from Monterrey. Another domestic discount carrier, **Interjet** (© **866/285-9525** in the U.S., or 01-80/0011-2345 in Mexico; www.interjet.com.mx), has flights to and from Mexico City.

BY CAR Hwy. 180 connects Villahermosa to Campeche (6 hr.). Hwy. 186, which passes by the airport, joins Hwy. 199 to Palenque and San Cristóbal de las Casas. The road to Palenque is a good one, and the drive takes 2 hours. Between Palenque and San Cristóbal, the road enters the mountains and takes 4 to 5 hours. On any of the mountain roads, conditions are apt to worsen during the rainy season from May to October.

BY BUS The **bus station** is at Mina and Merino (© **993/312-8900;** www.ticketbus.com.mx), 3 blocks off Hwy. 180. There are eight nonstop buses per day to/from Palenque (2½ hr.). There are eight nonstop buses per day to Mexico City (10 hr.), six deluxe services on **ADO-GL,** and two superdeluxe on **UNO.** To/from Campeche, eight buses travel nonstop per day (7 hr.); some of these go on to Mérida.

ORIENTATION

ARRIVING Villahermosa's **airport** is 16km (10 miles) east of town. The trip takes between 20 and 30 minutes. Once you cross the bridge over the Río Grijalva, turn left to reach downtown. Taxis to downtown cost 180 pesos.

Parking downtown can be difficult; it's best to find a parking lot. Use one that's guarded round-the-clock.

VISITOR INFORMATION The **State Tourism Office** (© **993/316-5122,** ext. 229) has two information booths: The one at the **airport** is staffed daily from 10am to 5pm; the one at **Parque–Museo La Venta** (next to the park ticket counter) is staffed Monday to Friday from 9am to 1pm.

CITY LAYOUT The downtown area, including the pedestrian-only **Zona Luz,** is on the west bank of the Grijalva River. About 1.5km (1 mile) upstream (south) is **CICOM,** an academic organization with the large archaeology museum named for the poet Carlos Pellicer Cámara. The **airport** is on the east side of the river. Hwy. 180 passes the airport and crosses the river just north of downtown, becoming **Bulevar Ruiz Cortines.** To get to the downtown area, turn left onto **Madero** or **Pino Suárez.** By staying on Ruiz Cortines you can reach the city's biggest attraction, the Parque–Museo la Venta. It's well marked. Just beyond that is the intersection with **Paseo Tabasco,** the heart of the modern hotel and shopping district.

GETTING AROUND Taxis are your best way to get around town. Villahermosa is rare for being a Mexican city without a capable public transportation system.

[FastFACTS] VILLAHERMOSA

The telephone **area code** is **993.** There aren't a lot of *casas de cambio,* but you can exchange money at the airport, the hotels, and downtown banks on calles Juárez and Madero. ATMs are plentiful.

Exploring Villahermosa

Downtown Villahermosa is poor and decaying, while the modern western part of the city is picturesque in places because the land is broken up by lots of shallow lakes. I don't recommend budgeting much time for the city. The two major attractions, the **Parque–Museo La Venta** and the **Museo Regional de Antropología Carlos Pellicer Cámara** (which is closed—see below) can be seen in a day.

If you're bound and determined to get to know the city, take a stroll about the pedestrian-only Zona Luz in the old city center, and you'll see signs that investment might be returning to the downtown area. Outside the Zona Luz, things get more unpleasant, with lots of traffic and crowds of pedestrians. You can walk south along the banks of the Grijalva until you come to a pedestrian bridge with an observation tower. That's the highlight. You won't miss much by keeping away.

Museo Regional de Antropología Carlos Pellicer Cámara This museum on the west bank of the river about 1.5km (1 mile) south of the town center was wrecked in the flood of 2007. It has remained closed ever since, while it awaits the completion of its new home. The new, larger structure is on the same site as the original. It was scheduled to open in late 2010, but construction has stopped, and the funds have dried up. When it does reopen, the museum's permanent collection of pre-Columbian sculpture and pottery is well worth a visit. It focuses on the cultures of the region—Olmec and Zapotec—but also includes pieces from other parts of Mexico.

CICOM Center, Av. Carlos Pellicer Cámara 511. © **993/312-6344.** Admission 45 pesos. Tues–Sun 9am–5pm.

Parque–Museo La Venta ★★   The Olmec created the first civilization in Mexico and developed several cultural traits that later would be adopted by all subsequent civilizations throughout Mesoamerica. In addition to their monumental works, they carved small, exquisite figurines in jade and serpentine, which can be seen in the Museo Regional de Antropología (see above). This *parque-museo* occupies a portion of a larger park named after Tomás Garrido Canabal, which includes a serene lake, a zoo, a natural history museum, and a lot of green space with several walkways frequented by joggers. Once inside the *parque-museo*, a trail leads you from one sculpture to the next. Most of the pieces are massive heads or altars. These can be as tall as 2m (6½ ft.) and weigh as much as 40 tons. The faces seem to be half adult, half infant. Most have highly stylized mouths with thick fleshy lips that turn down (known as the "jaguar mouth," this is one of the identifying characteristics of Olmec art). At least 17 heads have been found: 4 at La Venta, 10 at San Lorenzo, and 3 at Tres Zapotes—all Olmec cities on Mexico's east coast. The pieces in this park were taken from La Venta, a major city during the pre-Classic period (2000 B.C.–A.D. 300). Most were sculpted around 1000 B.C. without the use of metal chisels. The basalt rock used for these heads and altars was transported to La Venta from more than 113km (70 miles) away. It is thought that the rock was transported most of the distance by raft. Most of these pieces were first discovered in 1938. Now all that remains at La Venta are some grass-covered mounds that were once earthen pyramids. An exhibition area at the entrance to the park does a good job of illustrating how La Venta was laid out and what archaeologists think the Olmec were like.

As you stroll along, you will see labels identifying many species of local trees, including a grand ceiba tree of special significance to the Olmec and, later, the Maya. A few varieties of local critters scurry about, seemingly unconcerned with the presence of humans or with escaping from the park. Allow at least 2 hours for wandering through the jungly sanctuary and examining the 3,000-year-old sculpture. *Note:* Don't forget the mosquito repellent.

Bulevar Ruiz Cortines s/n. © **993/314-1652.** Admission 40 pesos. Tues–Sun 8am–4pm.

Where to Stay

Hotel rooms in Villahermosa are a little pricier than in other Mexican cities. Rates listed below include the 18% tax. Rates can go up during conventions, but there is no high-season/low-season split. Most hotels have live music on weekends. This makes it difficult to sleep in several of the inexpensive downtown hotels. The only inexpensive hotel I could find that didn't have this problem is listed below.

VERY EXPENSIVE

Hyatt Villahermosa ★★   I like this property more than the Camino Real (which is the other top hotel in the city), for its better location and service. A short walk away is the Parque–Museo La Venta. The rooms have a sleek, modern design with sharp-looking furnishings, fixtures, and accents. This is true of the bathrooms as well, which are large and made to feel larger by the use of sliding doors and minimal clutter. The remodeled pool area is a good place to relax in the heat of the afternoon.

Av. Juárez 106, 86000 Villahermosa, Tab. www.villahermosa.regency.hyatt.com. © **800/233-1234** in the U.S., or 993/310-1234. Fax 993/315-1963. 206 units. $150–$210 double; $265–$335 Regency Club room; $330–$375 junior suite. Weekend rates often discounted. AE, DC, MC, V. Free guarded parking. **Amenities:** Restaurant; 2 bars (1 w/live music, 1 sports bar); concierge; concierge-level rooms; well-equipped exercise room; outdoor pool and wading pool; room service. *In room:* A/C, TV, hair dryer, Internet (58 pesos per day), minibar.

EXPENSIVE

Best Western Hotel Maya Tabasco This hotel is centrally located between the downtown area and the modern western section. It's close to the Parque–Museo La Venta, the bus station, and the city's principal restaurant district. Rooms are larger than the norm. Most have ceramic tile floors and are simply furnished. Midsize bathrooms are attractive and have good counter space. A lush pool area separates the hotel from the hotel's bar, which gets fairly good live talent.

Bulevar Ruiz Cortines 907, 86000 Villahermosa, Tab. www.hotelmaya.com.mx. © **800/528-1234** in the U.S. and Canada, or 993/358-1111, ext. 822. Fax 993/358-1118. 151 units. 1,270 pesos double; 1,975 pesos junior suite. AE, MC, V. Free guarded parking. **Amenities:** Restaurant; bar; airport transfer; large outdoor pool; room service. *In room:* A/C, TV, hair dryer, Wi-Fi.

INEXPENSIVE

Hotel Plaza Independencia ⚑ The Plaza Independencia is the only hotel in this price range with a pool and enclosed parking. It's downtown, by the pedestrian bridge, and not far from the Anthropology Museum. Rooms are a little small but are better lit than the norm. End rooms, whose numbers end in 01, 02, 14, and 15, have balconies and are generally preferable.

Independencia 123, 86000 Villahermosa, Tab. www.hotelesplaza.com.mx. © **993/312-1299**, -7541. Fax 993/314-4724. 90 units. 755 pesos double. AE, MC, V. Free secure parking. **Amenities:** Restaurant; bar; small outdoor pool; room service; Wi-Fi (in common areas). *In room:* A/C, TV, hair dryer, minibar.

Where to Eat

Like other Mexican cities, Villahermosa has seen the arrival of U.S. franchise restaurants, but as these things go, I prefer the Mexican variety: **Sanborn's,** Av. Ruiz Cortines 1310, near Parque–Museo La Venta (© **993/316-8722**), and **VIPS,** Av. Fco. I. Madero 402, downtown (© **993/312-3237**). Both usually do an okay job with traditional dishes such as enchiladas or *antojitos*.

Jangada ★★ SEAFOOD My favorite restaurant here is an all-you-can-eat seafood buffet. Start with a small glass of delicious seafood broth and an appetizing empanada of *pejelagarto*, a freshwater fish for which Tabasco is famous. The salad and cold seafood bar offers a seafood salad of freshwater lobster, different kinds of ceviche, and seafood cocktails made to order. There's a variety of soups—especially good is the shrimp-and-*yuca* chowder. And then, of course, there are the main dishes, including charcoal-grilled *pejelagarto* (mild taste—light and almost nutty), and fish kabobs. Jangada is in the fancy western part of town in La Choca neighborhood. It closes early, but next door is a good Brazilian-style steakhouse (Rodizio) that stays open until 9pm.

Paseo de la Choca 126, Fracc. La Choca. © **993/317-6050.** 365 pesos per person, excluding drinks and dessert. AE, DC, MC, V. Daily 12:30–7pm.

Los Tulipanes REGIONAL/SEAFOOD/STEAKS Los Tulipanes is an old-school Mexican restaurant downtown, next to the Pellicer Museum of Anthropology. The food is good if you stick to the Mexican dishes and steer clear of the international.

Before you order, *tostones de plátano macho*—mashed and fried plantain crisps—are brought as an appetizer. Included on the menu are such Mexican specialties as chiles rellenos, tacos, and enchiladas. Dishes that are out of the ordinary include *tortilla de maíz nuevo* (oversize tortilla made with fresh corn and stuffed with shrimp or other seafood). For breakfast, the *tamales de chipilín* (an herb) are quite good.

CICOM Center, Periférico Carlos Pellicer Cámara 511. © **993/312-9209,** -9217. Main courses 90–210 pesos; Sun buffet 212 pesos. MC, V. Mon–Sat 8am–7pm; Sun 12:30–7pm.

PALENQUE ★★

142km (88 miles) SE of Villahermosa; 229km (142 miles) NE of San Cristóbal de las Casas

The ruins of Palenque look out over the jungle from a tall ridge that juts out from the base of steep, thickly forested mountains. It is a dramatic sight colored by the mysterious feel of the ruins themselves. The temples here are in the Classic style, with high-pitched roofs crowned with elaborate combs. Inside many are representations in stone and plaster of the rulers and their gods, which give evidence of a cosmology that is—and perhaps will remain—impenetrable to our understanding. This is one of the grand archaeological sites of Mexico.

Eight kilometers (5 miles) from the ruins is the town of Palenque. There you can find lodging and food, as well as make travel arrangements. Transportation between the town and ruins is cheap and convenient.

Essentials

GETTING THERE & DEPARTING

BY CAR   Hwy. 186 from Villahermosa should take about 2 hours. Drive only during the day. You may encounter military roadblocks that involve a cursory inspection of your travel credentials and perhaps your vehicle. The 230km (143-mile) trip from San Cristóbal to Palenque takes 5 hours and passes through lush jungle and mountain scenery. Take it easy, and watch out for potholes and other hindrances.

BY BUS   ADO/Cristóbal Colón (© **916/345-1344**) has regular service to and from Villahermosa and San Cristóbal, as well as Campeche (six per day, 5 hr.), Villahermosa (nine per day, 2 hr.), Mérida (two per day, 9 hr.), and Playa del Carmen (once per day, 12 hr.). The station is located on Avenida Juárez between the town center and La Cañada.

ORIENTATION

VISITOR INFORMATION   The downtown tourism office is a block from the main square at the corner of Avenida Juárez and Abasolo. It's open Monday to Saturday from 9am to 9pm, Sunday from 9am to 1pm. There's no phone at the downtown office. To get info over the phone, call the tourism office's business office (© **916/345-0356**).

CITY LAYOUT   Avenida Juárez is Palenque's main street. At one end is the **plaza;** at the other a traffic circle adorned with a monument imitating the iconic figure of a Maya head, which was discovered at the ruins. To the right of the statue is the entrance to La Cañada; to the left is the road to the ruins, and straight ahead past the statue is the highway to Villahermosa. The distance between the town's main square and the monument is about 1.5km (1 mile).

La Cañada is a restaurant and Hotel Zone tucked away in the forest. Aside from the main plaza area, this is the best location for travelers without cars, because the town is within a few blocks, and the buses that run to the ruins pass right by.

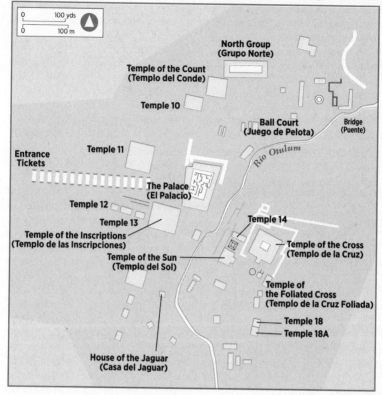

Palenque Archaeological Site

0   100 yds
0   100 m

North Group (Grupo Norte)

Temple of the Count (Templo del Conde)

Temple 10

Ball Court (Juego de Pelota)

Bridge (Puente)

Río Otulum

Entrance Tickets

Temple 11

The Palace (El Palacio)

Temple 12

Temple 13

Temple 14

Temple of the Inscriptions (Templo de las Inscripciones)

Temple of the Cross (Templo de la Cruz)

Temple of the Sun (Templo del Sol)

Temple of the Foliated Cross (Templo de la Cruz Foliada)

Temple 18

Temple 18A

House of the Jaguar (Casa del Jaguar)

17

TABASCO & CHIAPAS | Palenque

GETTING AROUND   The cheapest way to travel to the ruins is on the white vans (*colectivos*) that run down Juárez every 10 minutes from 6am to 6pm. The buses pass La Cañada and hotels along the road to the ruins, and can be flagged down at any point, but they may not stop if they're full. The cost is 10 pesos per person.

[FastFACTS] PALENQUE

The telephone **area code** is **916.** As for the **climate,** Palenque's high humidity is downright oppressive in the summer, especially after rain showers. During the winter, the damp air can occasionally be chilly in the evening. Rain gear is handy at any time of year. **Internet service** and **ATMs** are easily available.

Exploring Palenque

The reason to come here is the ruins; although you can tour them in a morning, many people savor Palenque for days. There are no must-see sights in town.

PARQUE NACIONAL PALENQUE ★★★

A **museum and visitor center** sits not far from the entrance to the ruins. Though it's not large, the museum is worth the time it takes to see; it's open Tuesday to

Sunday from 10am to 5pm and is included in the price of admission to the ruins. It contains well-chosen and artistically displayed exhibits, including jade from recently excavated tombs. Text in Spanish and English explains the life and times of this magnificent city. New pieces are sometimes added as they are uncovered in ongoing excavations.

The **main entrance,** about 1km (⅔ mile) beyond the museum, is at the end of the paved highway. There you'll find a large parking lot, a refreshment stand, a ticket booth, and several shops. Among the vendors selling souvenirs are often some Lacandón Indians wearing white tunics and hawking bows and arrows.

Admission to the ruins is 76 pesos. The fee for using a video camera is 50 pesos. Parking at the main entrance and at the visitor center is free. The site and visitor center shops are open daily from 8am to 4:45pm.

TOURING THE RUINS Pottery shards found during the excavations show that people lived in this area as early as 300 B.C. By the Classic period (A.D. 300–900), Palenque was an important ceremonial center. It peaked around A.D. 600 to 700.

When John Stephens visited the site in the 1840s, the ruins that you see today were buried under centuries of accumulated earth and a thick canopy of jungle. The dense jungle surrounding the cleared portion still covers unexcavated temples, which are easily discernible in the forest even to the untrained eye. But be careful not to drift too far from the main path—there have been a few incidents where tourists venturing alone into the rainforest were assaulted.

Of all Mexico's ruins, this is the most haunting, because of its majesty; its history, recovered by epigraphers; and its mysterious setting. Scholars have identified the rulers and constructed their family histories, putting visitors on a first-name basis with these ancient people etched in stone. You can read about it in *A Forest of Kings,* by Linda Schele and David Freidel.

As you enter the ruins, the building on your right is the **Temple of the Inscriptions,** named for the great stone hieroglyphic panels found inside. (Most of the panels, which portray the family tree of King Pacal, are in the National Anthropological Museum in Mexico City.) This temple is famous for the crypt of King Pacal deep inside the pyramid, but the crypt is closed to the public. The archaeologist Alberto Ruz Lhuillier discovered the tomb in the depths of the temple in 1952—an accomplishment many scholars consider one of the great discoveries of the Maya world. In exploratory excavations, Ruz Lhuillier found a stairway leading from the temple floor deep into the base of the pyramid. The original builders had carefully concealed the entrance by filling the stairway with stone. After several months of excavation, Ruz Lhuillier finally reached King Pacal's crypt, which contained several fascinating objects, including a magnificent carved stone sarcophagus. Ruz Lhuillier's own gravesite is opposite the Temple of the Inscriptions, on the left as you enter the park.

Just to your right as you face the Temple of the Inscriptions is **Temple 13.** Archaeologists recently discovered the burial of another richly adorned personage, accompanied in death by an adult female and an adolescent. Some of the artifacts found there are on display in the museum.

Back on the main pathway, the building directly in front of you is the **Palace,** with its unique tower. The explorer John Stephens camped in the Palace when it was completely covered in vegetation, spending sleepless nights fighting off mosquitoes. A pathway between the Palace and the Temple of the Inscriptions leads to the **Temple of the Sun,** the **Temple of the Foliated Cross,** the **Temple of the Cross,** and **Temple 14.** This group of temples, now in various stages of reconstruction, was built by Pacal's son, Chan-Bahlum, who is usually shown on inscriptions with six toes.

Chan-Bahlum's plaster mask was found in Temple 14 next to the Temple of the Sun. Archaeologists have begun probing the Temple of the Sun for Chan-Bahlum's tomb. Little remains of this temple's exterior carving. Inside, however, behind a fence, a carving of Chan-Bahlum shows him ascending the throne in A.D. 690. The panels depict Chan-Bahlum's version of his historic link to the throne.

To the left of the Palace is the North Group, also undergoing restoration. Included in this area are the **Ball Court** and the **Temple of the Count.** At least three tombs, complete with offerings for the underworld journey, have been found here, and the lineage of at least 12 kings has been deciphered from inscriptions left at this site.

Just past the North Group is a small building (once a museum) now used for storing the artifacts found during restorations. It is closed to the public. To the right of the building, a stone bridge crosses the river, leading to a pathway down the hillside to the new museum. The rock-lined path descends along a cascading stream, where giant ceiba trees grow. Benches are placed along the way as rest areas, and some small temples have been reconstructed near the base of the trail. In the early morning and evening, you may hear monkeys crashing through the thick foliage by the path; if you keep noise to a minimum, you may spot wild parrots as well. Walking downhill (by far the best way to go), it will take you about 20 minutes to reach the main highway. The path ends at the paved road across from the museum. The *colectivos* (minibuses) going back to the village will stop here if you wave them down.

Where to Stay

English is spoken in all the more expensive hotels and about half of the inexpensive ones. The quoted rates include the 18% tax. High season in Palenque is limited to Easter week, July and August, and December. Palenque gets most of its visitors through bus tours, which originate in Cancún; if you want to avoid running into large groups, pick a small hotel.

EXPENSIVE

Chan-Kah Resort Village ★   This is a pretty property located between the town and the ruins. It's a grouping of comfortable bungalows, called casitas, surrounded by tropical forest. Staying here offers a measure of privacy and quiet in the tropical surroundings. The grounds are well tended, and an inviting freshwater pool is fed by a stream that runs through the property. The bungalows are spacious, and each comes with its own terrace and two rocking chairs. The master suites are two-bedroom bungalows. Christmas prices are higher than those quoted here, and you may be quoted a higher price if you reserve a room in advance from outside Mexico. Room service is pricey.

Carretera Las Ruinas Km 3, 29960 Palenque, Chi. www.chan-kah.com.mx. © **916/345-1100.** Fax 916/345-0820. 73 units. 1,455 pesos casita; 3,861 pesos master suite. Promotional rates Sept–Nov. MC, V. Free guarded parking. **Amenities:** Restaurant; bar; 3 outdoor pools (1 large w/natural spring); room service; Wi-Fi (in common areas). *In room:* A/C, TV, hair dryer.

MODERATE

Hotel Ciudad Real   Though not fancy, this hotel does the important things right—the rooms are ample, quiet, well lit, and comfortably furnished. Most units hold two double beds; a few have king-size beds. All rooms have a small balcony, which, in the best case, overlooks tropical vegetation. When making a reservation, specify the hotel in Palenque (there's also a Ciudad Real in San Cristóbal). It's at the edge of town in the direction of the airport. Though it works with bus tours, as other large hotels do, this hotel works well for individual travelers who have their own car.

Carretera a Pakal-Na Km 1.5, 29960 Palenque, Chi. www.ciudadreal.com.mx. ⓒ **916/345-1343,** or 967/678-4400 for reservations. 72 units. High season 1,375 pesos double, 1,695 pesos junior suite; low season 940 pesos double, 1,200 pesos junior suite. Internet discounts sometimes available. AE, MC, V. Free secured parking. **Amenities:** Restaurant; bar; outdoor pool and children's pool; room service; Wi-Fi (in lobby and restaurant). *In room:* A/C, TV, hair dryer.

Hotel La Aldea 🗲   This hotel on the way to the ruins enjoys the same lush surroundings as the more expensive Chan-Kah Resort Village, but it's smaller and most often quieter. It is a family-owned hotel, designed and managed by an architect. The rooms show that a good deal of thought went into making them attractive and functional. They are in a collection of free-standing bungalows set on rising ground (mostly two rooms per bungalow). A few of the rooms (no. 10 in particular) have great views of the surrounding forest. All rooms are large, with good space for luggage. Each has an outdoor sitting area. In terms of layout and decor, I like them better than those in the neighboring Chan-Kah Village.

Carretera Las Ruinas Km 2.8, 29960 Palenque, Chi. www.hotellaaldea.net. ⓒ/fax **916/345-1693.** 28 units. 1,225 pesos double. Low season discounts of 20%–30%. MC, V. Free secured parking. **Amenities:** Restaurant; bar; outdoor pool; Wi-Fi (in common areas). *In room:* A/C, no phone.

Hotel Maya Tulipanes   This attractive hotel tucked away in the Cañada is a good choice for its location and management. Service and upkeep are both good. Rooms are medium to large and come with a queen-size, a king-size, or two double beds. Tropical vegetation adorns the grounds, along with some reproductions of famous Maya architecture. The hotel has an arrangement with a sister hotel at the ruins of Tikal, in Guatemala. The travel agency operates daily tours to Bonampak and other attractions.

Calle Cañada 6, 29960 Palenque, Chi. www.mayatulipanes.com.mx. ⓒ **916/345-0201,** -0258. Fax 916/ 345-1004. 74 units. High season 1,265 pesos double; low season 880–1,100 pesos double. Internet packages available. AE, MC, V. Free secured parking. **Amenities:** Restaurant; bar; ground transportation to/ from Villahermosa airport; outdoor pool; room service. *In room:* A/C, TV, hair dryer, Wi-Fi.

Misión Palenque ★   This is the most attractive and comfortable property in town, and it offers the best service of any hotel in the area. Rooms are medium size, furnished with light, modern furniture. Bathrooms are spacious, with ample counters and good lighting. The rooms are quiet thanks to the extensive grounds, which separate it from the rest of the town. In one corner of the property, a natural spring flows through an attractive bit of jungle, where the hotel has installed the spa. Part of the spa is a *temazcal*, or sweat lodge. There's also a mud bath along with the more common elements. The hotel is a few blocks east of the town's main square.

Periférico Oriente s/n, 29960 Palenque, Chi. www.hotelesmision.com.mx. ⓒ **916/345-0241,** or 01-800/900-3800 in Mexico. Fax 916/345-0300. 156 units. 1,190 pesos double; 2,925 pesos junior suite. AE, MC, V. Free guarded parking. **Amenities:** Restaurant; babysitting; exercise room; Jacuzzi; outdoor pool and wading pool; room service; spa; 2 tennis courts. *In room:* A/C, TV, hair dryer (on request), Wi-Fi.

INEXPENSIVE

Hotel Xibalba   This budget hotel recently expanded to handle larger groups, but the price is still right. You can ask for a room in back if a group is being noisy. The medium-to-small rooms are basic but clean, with functioning air-conditioning, which is not always the case at the budget level. The upstairs units are a little smaller than the downstairs units. Most of the beds have firm mattresses. Check out the full-size replica of Pacal's sarcophagus lid on the premises.

Where to Stay & Eat in Palenque

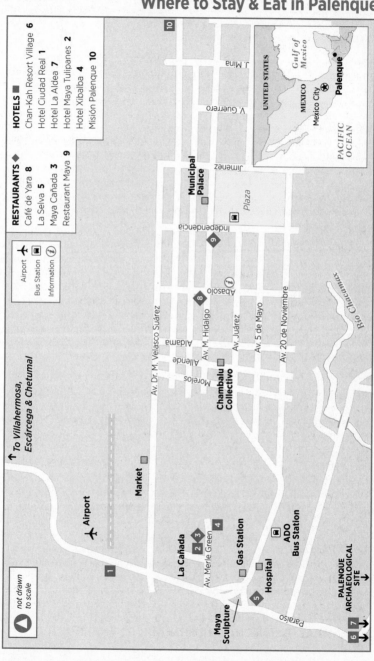

RESTAURANTS ◆
Café de Yara **8**
La Selva **5**
Maya Cañada **3**
Restaurant Maya **9**

HOTELS ■
Chan-Kah Resort Village **6**
Hotel Ciudad Real **1**
Hotel La Aldea **7**
Hotel Maya Tulipanes **2**
Hotel Xibalba **4**
Misión Palenque **10**

Airport ✈
Bus Station ■
Information ℹ

not drawn to scale

↑ To Villahermosa, Escárcega & Chetumal

Airport ✈

Market

Av. Dr. M. Velasco Suárez

La Cañada

Av. Merle Green

Gas Station

Maya Sculpture

Hospital

ADO Bus Station

Paraíso

PALENQUE ARCHAEOLOGICAL SITE →

Chambalu Collectivo

Morelos

Allende

Aldama

Av. M. Hidalgo

Av. Juárez

Av. 5 de Mayo

Av. 20 de Noviembre

Abasolo

Independencia

Jiménez

Municipal Palace

Plaza

V. Guerrero

J. Mina

Río Chacamax

UNITED STATES

Gulf of Mexico

MEXICO

Mexico City

Palenque

PACIFIC OCEAN

Calle Merle Green 9, Col. La Cañada, 29960 Palenque, Chi. www.hotelxibalba.com. ☎ **916/345-0392.**
Fax 916/345-0411. 35 units. 550-780 pesos double. MC, V. Free parking. **Amenities:** Restaurant; bar;
Wi-Fi. *In room:* A/C, TV, no phone.

Where to Eat

Palenque and, for that matter, the rest of backwater Chiapas, are not for gourmets.
Who'd a thunk? I had an easy time eliminating a number of restaurants that didn't
even seem to be keeping up the appearance of serving food. But the situation has
been improving, and you can at least get some decent Mexican food.

MODERATE

La Selva INTERNATIONAL/MEXICAN   At La Selva (the jungle), you dine under
a large, attractive thatched roof beside well-tended gardens. The menu includes
seafood, freshwater fish, steaks, and Mexican specialties. The most expensive thing
on the menu is *pigua*, freshwater lobster caught in the large rivers of southeast
Mexico. These can grow quite large—the size of small saltwater lobsters. This and
the finer cuts of meat have been frozen, but you wouldn't want otherwise in Palenque.
I liked the fish stuffed with shrimp, and the *mole* enchiladas. La Selva is on the
highway to the ruins, near the statue of the Maya head.

Carretera Palenque Ruinas Km .5. ☎ **916/345-0363.** Main courses 177-235 pesos. MC, V. Daily
11:30am-11:30pm.

INEXPENSIVE

Café de Yara MEXICAN   A small, modern cafe and restaurant with a comforting,
not overly ambitious menu. The cafe's strong suit is healthful salads (with disinfected
greens) and home-style Mexican entrees, such as the beef or chicken *milanesa* or
chicken cooked in a *chile pasilla* sauce. It also offers decent tamales. In the evenings
it occasionally offers live music.

Av. Hidalgo 66 (at Abasolo). ☎ **916/345-0269.** Main courses 68-105 pesos. MC, V. Daily 7am-11pm.

Restaurant Maya and Maya Cañada ★ MEXICAN   These two are the most consistently good restaurants in Palenque. One faces the main plaza from the corner of
Independencia and Hidalgo, the other is in La Cañada (☎ **916/345-0216**). Menus differ a bit, but much is the same. Both do a good job with the basics—good strong, locally
grown coffee and soft, pliant tortillas. The menu offers a combination of Mexican standards and regional specialties. If you're in an exploratory mood, try one of the regional
specialties such as the *mole chiapaneco* (dark red, like *mole poblano,* but less sweet) or any
of the dishes based on *chaya* or *chipilín* (mild-flavored local greens), such as the soup with
chipilín and *bolitas de masa* (corn dumplings). If you want something more comforting, go
for the chicken, rice, and vegetable soup, or the *sopa azteca.* The plantains stuffed with
cheese and fried Mexican style are wonderful. Waiters sometimes offer specials not on
the menu, and these are often the thing to get. You can also try *tascalate,* a pre-Hispanic
drink made of water, *masa,* chocolate, and achiote, and served room temperature or cold.

Av. Independencia s/n (at Hidalgo). ☎ **916/345-0042.** Breakfast 50-80 pesos; main courses 58-159
pesos. MC, V. Daily 7am-11pm.

Road Trips from Palenque

BONAMPAK & YAXCHILÁN: MURALS IN THE JUNGLE

Intrepid travelers may want to consider the day trip to the Maya ruins of Bonampak and
Yaxchilán. The **ruins of Bonampak** ★, southeast of Palenque on the Guatemalan

border, were discovered in 1946. The site is important for the vivid and well-preserved **murals** of the Maya on the interior walls of one temple. Particularly striking is an impressive battle scene, perhaps the most important painting of pre-Hispanic Mexico.

Several tour companies offer a day trip. The drive to Bonampak is 3 hours. From there you continue by boat to the **ruins of Yaxchilán ★**, famous for its highly ornamented buildings. Bring rain gear, boots, a flashlight, and bug repellent. All tours include meals and cost about 1,000 pesos. No matter what agency you sign up with, the hours of departure and return are the same. You leave at 6am and return at 7pm.

Try **Viajes Na Chan Kan** (✆ **916/345-2154;** chiapastour@hotmail.com), at Hidalgo 5 across from the main square. It offers all the usual side trips as well as ecological and cultural tours to outlying Indian communities.

WATERFALLS AT MISOL HA & AGUA AZUL

Misol Ha is 20km (12 miles) from Palenque, in the direction of Ocosingo. It takes about 30 minutes to get there, depending on the traffic. The turnoff is clearly marked; you'll turn right and drive another 1.5km (1 mile). The place is absolutely beautiful. Water pours from a rocky cliff into a broad pool of green water bordered by thick tropical vegetation. There's a small restaurant and some rustic cabins for rent for around 500 pesos per night, depending on the size of the cabin. The place is run by the *ejido* cooperative that owns the site, and it does a good job of maintaining the place. To inquire about the cabins, call ✆ **916/345-1506.** Admission for the day is 25 pesos.

Approximately 44km (27 miles) beyond Misol Ha are the **Agua Azul** waterfalls— 270m (886 ft.) of tumbling falls with lots of water. There are cabins for rent here, too, but I would rather stay at Misol Ha. You can swim either above or below the falls, but make sure you don't get pulled by the current. You can see both places in the same day or stop to see them on your way to Ocosingo and San Cristóbal. Agua Azul is prettiest after 3 or 4 consecutive dry days; heavy rains can make the water murky. Check with guides or other travelers about the water quality before you decide to go. The cost to enter is 30 pesos per person. Trips to both of these places can be arranged through just about any hotel.

OCOSINGO & THE RUINS OF TONINÁ

By the time you get to Agua Azul, you're halfway to Ocosingo, which lies halfway between Palenque and San Cristóbal. So instead of returning for the night to Palenque, you can go on to Ocosingo. It's higher up and more comfortable than Palenque. It's a nice little town, not touristy, not a lot to do other than see the ruins of Toniná. But it is a nice place to spend the night so that you can see the ruins early before moving on to San Cristóbal. There are about a half-dozen small hotels in town; the largest is not the most desirable. I would stay at the **Hospedaje Esmeralda** (✆ **919/673-0014**) or the **Hotel Central** (✆ **919/673-0024**), on the main square. Both of these are small and simple, but welcoming. The restaurant in front of Hotel Central has good cooking.

RUINS OF TONINÁ ★★   The ruins of Toniná (the name translates as "house of rocks") are 14km (8⅔ miles) east of Ocosingo. You can take a cab there and catch a *colectivo* to return. The city dates from the Classic period and covered a large area, but the excavated and restored part is all on one steep hillside that faces a broad valley. This site is not set up to handle lots of tourists (and doesn't really receive many). There is a good bit of climbing involved, and some of it is a little precarious. This is not a good place to take kids. Admission is 47 pesos.

This complex of courtyards, rooms, and stairways is built on multiple levels that are irregular and asymmetrical. The overall effect is that of a ceremonial area with multiple foci instead of a clearly discernible center. It affords beautiful and intriguing perspectives from just about any spot.

As early as A.D. 350, Toniná emerged as a dynastic center. In the 7th and 8th centuries, it was locked in a struggle with rival Palenque and, to a lesser degree, with faraway Calakmul. This has led some scholars to see Toniná as more militaristic than its neighbors—a sort of Sparta of the Classic Maya. Toniná's greatest victory came in 711, when, under the rule of Kan B'alam, it attacked Palenque and captured its king, K'an Joy Chitam, depicted on a stone frieze twisted, his arms bound with rope.

But the single most important artifact yet found at Toniná is up around the fifth level of the acropolis—a large stucco frieze divided into panels by a feathered framework adorned with the heads of sacrificial victims (displayed upside down) and some rather horrid creatures. The largest figure is a skeletal image holding a decapitated head—very vivid and very puzzling. There is actually a stylistic parallel with some murals of the Teotihuacán culture of central Mexico. The other special thing about Toniná is that it holds the distinction of having the last ever date recorded in the long count (A.D. 909), which marks the end of the Classic period.

SAN CRISTÓBAL DE LAS CASAS ★★★

229km (142 miles) SW of Palenque; 80km (50 miles) E of Tuxtla Gutiérrez; 74km (46 miles) NW of Comitán; 166km (103 miles) NW of Cuauhtémoc; 451km (280 miles) E of Oaxaca

San Cristóbal is a colonial town of white stucco walls and red-tile roofs, of cobblestone streets and narrow sidewalks, of graceful arcades and open plazas. It lies in a green valley 2,100m (7,000 ft.) high. The city owes part of its name to the 16th-century cleric Fray Bartolomé de las Casas, who was the town's first bishop and spent the rest of his life waging a political campaign to protect the indigenous peoples of the Americas.

Surrounding the city are many villages of Mayan-speaking Indians who display great variety in their language, dress, and customs, making this area one of the most ethnically diverse in Mexico. San Cristóbal is the principal market town for these Indians, and their point of contact with the outside world. Most of them trek down from the surrounding mountains to sell goods and run errands.

Several Indian villages lie within reach of San Cristóbal by road: **Chamula,** with its weavers and unorthodox church; **Zinacantán,** whose residents practice their own syncretic religion; **Tenejapa, San Andrés,** and **Magdalena,** known for brocaded textiles; **Amatenango del Valle,** a town of potters; and **Aguacatenango,** known for embroidery. Most of these "villages" consist of little more than a church and the municipal government building, with homes scattered for miles around and a general gathering only for church and market days (usually Sun).

Many Indians now live on the outskirts of town because they've been expelled from their villages over religious differences. They are known as *los expulsados.* No longer involved in farming, they make their living in commerce and handicrafts. Most still wear traditional dress, but they've adopted Protestant religious beliefs that prevent them from partaking in many of their community's civic and religious celebrations.

The influx of outsiders hasn't created in most Indians a desire to adopt mainstream customs and dress. It's interesting to note that the communities closest to

RESTAURANTS ◆

El Edén **4**
Emiliano's Moustache **14**
La Casa del Pan Papalotl **8**
La Paloma **15**
Namandí **13**
Normita's **18**
Restaurant Tuluc **17**

ATTRACTIONS ●

Casa Na-Bolom **9**
Catedral **5**
Museo del Ambar **12**
Museo Templo y Convento Santo Domingo **2**
Palacio de las Bellas Artes **21**
Templo de San Cristóbal **22**

HOTELS ■

Casa de los Arcángeles **16**
Casa Felipe Flores **10**
Hotel Casa Mexicana **3**
Hotel Casavieja **7**
Hotel Don Quijote **6**
Hotel Palacio de Moctezuma **19**
Hotel Posada La Media Luna **20**
Mansión de los Angeles **11**
Parador San Juan de Dios **1**

✝ Church
▦ Pedestrian Only
✉ Post Office

☐ ADO Bus Station

UNITED STATES
Gulf of Mexico
MEXICO
Mexico City ★
PACIFIC OCEAN
San Cristóbal de las Casas

San Cristóbal are the most resistant to change. The greatest threat to the cultures in this area comes not from tourism, but from the action of large market forces, population pressures, environmental damage, and poverty. The Indians aren't interested in acting or looking like the foreigners they see. They may steal glances or even stare at tourists, but mainly they pay little attention to outsiders, except as potential buyers for handicrafts.

You may see or hear the word *Jovel,* San Cristóbal's Indian name, incorporated often in the names of businesses. You'll hear the word *coleto,* used in reference to someone or something from San Cristóbal. You'll see signs for *tamales coletos, pan coleto,* and *desayuno coleto* (Cristóbal breakfast).

Essentials

GETTING THERE & DEPARTING

BY PLANE The local airport is little used, and the closest airport with regular service is in Tuxtla Gutiérrez (p. 654).

BY CAR From Palenque (5 hr.), the beautiful road provides jungle scenery, but portions of it may be heavily potholed or obstructed during rainy season. Check with the local state tourism office before driving. From Tuxtla Gutiérrez, the 1½-hour trip winds through beautiful mountain country.

BY TAXI Taxis from Tuxtla Gutiérrez to San Cristóbal cost around 650 pesos.

BY BUS The **ADO** station (which also handles the affiliates Altos, Cristóbal Colón, and Maya de Oro) is at the corner of Insurgentes and Bulevar Juan Sabines, 8 blocks south of the main square. This company offers service to and from Tuxtla (12 buses per day), Palenque (almost every hour), and several other destinations: Mérida (two buses per day), Villahermosa (two buses per day), Oaxaca (two buses per day), and Puerto Escondido (two buses per day). To buy a bus ticket without going down to the station, go to the **Ticket Bus** agency, Real de Guadalupe 24 (*C* **967/678-8503**). Hours are Monday to Saturday from 7am to 10pm.

The best cheap way to get to and from nearby Tuxtla Gutiérrez is by microbus, 16-seat buses that depart every 5 to 15 minutes from the small bus station across the street from the ADO bus station. The company is called **Omnibuses de Chiapas** (no phone). Look for white buses that say *omni* or *expreso* on the front. The fare is 38 pesos and the trip takes an hour. There are also vans making the run every 15 to 30 minutes. They can be found just off Juan Sabines by the bus station. You'll have to ask someone to point them out to you because there isn't a sign. The problem with these is that they pack too many passengers in them for comfort.

ORIENTATION

ARRIVING To get to the town square from the highway, turn on to **Avenida Insurgentes** (at the traffic light). From the bus station, the main plaza is 8 blocks north up Avenida Insurgentes (a 10-min. walk, slightly uphill). Cabs are cheap and plentiful.

VISITOR INFORMATION The **Municipal Tourism Office** (℃/fax **967/678-0665**) is in the town hall, west of the main square. It's open daily from 9am to 9pm. Check the bulletin board here for apartments, shared rides, cultural events, and local tours.

CITY LAYOUT San Cristóbal is laid out on a grid; the main north-south axis is **Insurgentes/Utrilla,** and the east-west axis is **Mazariegos/Madero.** All streets change names when they cross either of these streets. The *zócalo* (main plaza) lies where they intersect. An important street to know is **Real de Guadalupe,** which runs from the plaza eastward to the church of Guadalupe; located on it are many hotels and restaurants. The market is 7 blocks north of the *zócalo* along Utrilla.

Take note that this town has at least three streets named Domínguez and two streets named Flores. There are Hermanos Domínguez, Belisario Domínguez, and Pantaleón Domínguez; and María Adelina Flores and Dr. Felipe Flores.

GETTING AROUND Most of the sights and shopping in San Cristóbal are within walking distance of the plaza.

Urbano **buses** (minibuses) take passengers between town and the residential neighborhoods. All buses pass by the market and central plaza on their way through town. Utrilla and Avenida 16 de Septiembre are the two main arteries; all buses use the market area as the last stop. Any bus on Utrilla will take you to the market.

Colectivos to outlying villages depart from the public market at Avenida Utrilla. Buses late in the day are usually very crowded. Always check to see when the last or next-to-last bus returns from wherever you're going, and then take the one before that—those last buses sometimes don't materialize, and you might be stranded.

Rental cars come in handy for trips to the outlying villages and may be worth the expense when shared by a group, but keep in mind that insurance is invalid on unpaved roads. Try **Optima Car Rental,** Av. Mazariegos 39 (℃ **967/674-5409**). Office hours are daily from 9am to 1pm and 5 to 8pm. You'll save money by arranging the rental from your home country; otherwise, a day's rental with insurance will cost around 700 pesos for a VW Beetle with manual transmission, the cheapest car available.

THE zapatista movement & CHIAPAS

In January 1994, Indians from this area rebelled against the Mexican government over health care, education, land distribution, and representative government. Their organization, the **Zapatista Liberation Army,** known as EZLN (Ejército Zapatista de Liberación Nacional), and its leader, Subcomandante Marcos, became symbols of the struggle for social justice. Times have changed. The situation has long since quieted, and there is no longer any talk of armed revolt. Subcomandante Marcos has become a social critic and commentator, and the EZLN has become an independent political organization not tied to any particular party. Even the town's graffiti reflects the new mood, with political exhortations disappearing in favor of the more artsy, more obscure scribblings, resembling the graffiti in the U.S.

Scooters can be rented from **Croozy Scooters** (☏ 967/631-4329), at Belisario Domínguez 7-A. Passport and 500 pesos deposit required.

Bikes are another option for getting around the city; a day's rental is about 140 pesos. **Los Pingüinos,** Av. Ecuador 4-B (☏ **967/678-0202;** pinguinosmex@yahoo. com), offers bike tours out-of-town. Tours in the valley around San Cristóbal last 4 to 6 hours and cost 300 to 400 pesos. It's open daily from 10am to 2:30pm and 4 to 7pm.

[FastFACTS] SAN CRISTÓBAL DE LAS CASAS

Area Code   The telephone area code is **967.**

ATMs   San Cristóbal has a number of ATMs.

Currency Exchange There are at least five *casas de cambio* on Real de Guadalupe, near the main square, and a couple under the colonnade facing the square. Most are open until 8pm, and some are open Sunday.

Doctor   Try **Dr. Roberto Lobato,** Av. Belisario Domínguez 17, at Calle Flavio A. Paniagua (☏ **967/ 678-7777**). Don't be unsettled by the fact that his office is next door to Funerales Canober.

Internet Access   Internet cafes are everywhere.

Parking   Use the underground public lot in front of the cathedral, just off the main square on 16 de Septiembre. Entry is from Calle 5 de Febrero.

Post Office   The *correo* is at Crescencio Rosas and Cuauhtémoc, a block south and west of the main square. It's open Monday to Friday from 8am to 7pm, Saturday from 9am to 1pm.

Spanish Classes   The **Centro Bilingüe,** at the Centro Cultural El Puente, Real de Guadalupe 55, 29250 San Cristóbal de las Casas,

Chi. (☏ **800/303-4983** in the U.S., or ☏/fax 967/678-3723), offers classes in Spanish and can arrange home stays for their students.

Weather   San Cristóbal can be chilly when the sun isn't out, especially during the winter. It's 2,100m (7,000 ft.) above sea level. Most hotels are not heated, although some have fireplaces. There is always a possibility of rain, but I would avoid going to San Cristóbal from late August to late October, during the height of the rainy season.

Exploring San Cristobal

San Cristóbal is a lovely town in a lovely region. A lot of people come for the beauty, but the main thing that draws most visitors here is the highland Maya. They can be seen anywhere in San Cristóbal, but most travelers take at least one trip to the outlying villages to get a close-up of Maya life.

Casa Na-Bolom ★ This is the old headquarters of anthropologists Frans and Trudy Blom, who made this area their home and their passion. It became a gathering place for those studying in the region. Frans Blom (1893–1963) led many early archaeological studies in Mexico, and Trudy (1901–93) was noted for her photographs of the Lacandón Indians and her efforts to save them and their forest homeland. A room at Na-Bolom contains a selection of her Lacandón photographs, and postcards of the photographs are on sale in the gift shop (daily 9am–2pm and 4–7pm). The house is now a museum. A tour covers the displays of pre-Hispanic artifacts collected by Frans Blom; the cozy library, with its numerous volumes about the region and the Maya (weekdays 10am–2pm); and the gardens Trudy Blom started for the ongoing reforestation of the Lacandón jungle. The tour ends with a showing of *La Reina de la Selva,* an excellent 50-minute film on the Bloms, the Lacandón, and Na-Bolom.

The 17 guest rooms, named for surrounding villages, are decorated with local objects and textiles. All rooms have fireplaces and private bathrooms. Prices (museum admission included) are 1,110 pesos for a double; 1,520 pesos for a suite.

Even if you're not a guest here, you can come for a meal, usually an assortment of vegetarian and other dishes. Just be sure to make a reservation at least 2½ hours in advance, and be on time. The colorful dining room has one large table, and the eclectic mix of travelers sometimes makes for interesting conversation. Breakfast costs 75 pesos; lunch and dinner cost 200 pesos each. Dinner is served at 7pm. Following breakfast (8–10am), a guide not affiliated with the house offers tours to San Juan Chamula and Zinacantán (see "The Nearby Maya Villages & Countryside," below) on every day but Monday.

Av. Vicente Guerrero 33, 29200 San Cristóbal de las Casas, Chi. ℂ **967/678-1418.** Fax 967/678-5586. www.nabolom.org. Group tour and film 50 pesos. Tours daily 11:30am (Spanish only) and 4:30pm.

Catedral San Cristóbal's main cathedral was built in the 1500s. Make note of the interesting beamed ceiling and a carved wooden pulpit.

Calle 20 de Noviembre at Guadalupe Victoria. No phone. Free admission. Daily 7am-6pm.

El Mercado Once you've visited Santo Domingo (see listing below), meander through the San Cristóbal town market and the surrounding area. Every time I do, I see something different to elicit my curiosity.

By Santo Domingo church. No phone. Mon-Sat 8am-7pm.

Museo del Ambar If you've been in this town any time at all, you know what a big deal amber is here. Chiapas is the third-largest producer of amber in the world, and many experts prefer its amber for its colors and clarity. A couple of stores tried calling themselves museums, but they didn't fool anybody. Now a real museum moves methodically through all the issues surrounding amber—mining, shaping, and identifying it, as well as the different varieties found in other parts of the world. It's interesting, it's cheap, and you get to see the restored area of the old convent it occupies. There are a couple of beautiful pieces of worked amber that are on permanent loan—make sure you see them. In mid-August, the museum holds a contest for local artisans who work amber; they do remarkable work.

Exconvento de la Merced, Diego de Mazariegos s/n. ℂ **967/678-9716.** Admission 20 pesos. Tues–Sun 10am-2pm and 4-7:30pm.

Museo Templo y Convento Santo Domingo Inside the front door of the carved-stone facade is a beautiful gilded wooden altarpiece from 1560, walls with saints, and gilt-framed paintings. Attached to the church is the former Convent of Santo Domingo, now a small museum about San Cristóbal and Chiapas. It has changing exhibits and often shows cultural films. It's 5 blocks north of the *zócalo,* in the market area.

Av. 20 de Noviembre. ℂ **967/678-1609.** Free admission to church; museum 44 pesos. Museum Tues-Sun 9am–6pm; church daily 10am–2pm and 5–8pm.

Palacio de las Bellas Artes Bellas Artes periodically hosts dance events, art shows, and other performances. The schedule of events is usually posted on the door if the Bellas Artes is not open. A public library is next door. Around the corner, the Centro Cultural holds concerts and other performances; check the posters on the door to see what's scheduled.

Av. Hidalgo, 4 blocks south of the plaza. No phone.

Templo de San Cristóbal For the best view of San Cristóbal, climb the seemingly endless steps to this church and *mirador* (lookout point). A visit here requires stamina. There are 22 more churches in town, some of which also demand strenuous climbs.

At the very end of Calle Hermanos Domínguez.

HORSEBACK RIDING

The **Casa de Huéspedes Margarita,** Real de Guadalupe 34, can arrange horseback rides for around 175 to 220 pesos, including a guide. The excursions are around 4½ hours long. Reserve your steed at least a day in advance. Possible places to visit might include San Juan Chamula, some nearby caves, or some of the outlying hills, depending upon interest.

THE NEARBY MAYA VILLAGES & COUNTRYSIDE

The Indian communities around San Cristóbal are fascinating worlds unto themselves. If you are unfamiliar with these indigenous cultures, you will understand and appreciate more of what you see by visiting them with a guide, at least for your first foray out into the villages. Guides are acquainted with members of the communities and are viewed with less suspicion than newcomers. These communities have their own laws and customs—and visitors' ignorance is no excuse. Entering these communities is tantamount to leaving Mexico, and if something happens, the state and federal authorities will not intervene except in case of a serious crime.

The best guided trips are the locally grown ones. Two operators go to the neighboring villages in small groups. They charge about the same price (175 pesos per person), use minivans for transportation, and speak English. They do, however, have their own interpretations and focus.

Pepe and Ramiro leave from **Casa Na-Bolom** (see above) for daily trips to San Juan Chamula and Zinacantán at 10am, returning to San Cristóbal between 2 and 3pm. They look at cultural continuities, community relationships, and religion.

Alex and Raúl can be found in front of the cathedral between 9:15 and 9:30am. They are quite personable and get along well with the Indians in the communities. They focus on cultural values and their expression in social behavior, which provides a glimpse of the details and the texture of life in these communities (and, of course, they talk about religion). Their tour is very good. They can be reached at ℂ **967/678-3741** or chamul@hotmail.com.

For excursions farther afield, see "Road Trips from San Cristóbal," later in this chapter. Also, Alex and Raúl can be contracted for trips to other communities besides Chamula and Zinacantán; talk to them.

CHAMULA & ZINACANTÁN   A side trip to the village of San Juan Chamula will get you into the spirit of life around San Cristóbal. Sunday, when the market is in full swing, is the best day to go for shopping; other days, when you'll be less impeded by eager children selling their crafts, are better for seeing the village and church.

The village, 8km (5 miles) northeast of San Cristóbal, has a large church, a plaza, and a municipal building. Each year, a new group of citizens is chosen to live in the municipal center as caretakers of the saints, settlers of disputes, and enforcers of village rules. As in other nearby villages, on Sunday local leaders wear their leadership costumes, including beautifully woven straw hats loaded with colorful ribbons befitting their high position. They solemnly sit together in a long line somewhere around the central square. Chamula is typical of other villages, in that men are often away working in the "hot lands," harvesting coffee or cacao, while women stay home to tend the sheep, the children, the cornfields, and the fires.

Don't leave Chamula without seeing the **church interior.** As you step from bright sunlight into the candlelit interior, you enter what is sacred space for the Chamula. The air is heavy with the smell of copal, a native incense. Pine needles and lit candles cover the tile floor. Saints line the walls, and people kneel before them, praying aloud while passing around bottles of Pepsi-Cola. Shamans are often on hand, passing eggs over sick people or using live or dead chickens in a curing ritual. The statues of saints are similar to those you might see in any Mexican Catholic church, but beyond sharing the same name, they mean something completely different to the Chamulas. Visitors can walk carefully through the church to see the saints or stand quietly in the background.

Just to the south, in Zinacantán, a wealthier village than Chamula, you must sign a strict form promising *not to take any photographs* before you see the two side-by-side **sanctuaries.** Once permission is granted and you have paid a small fee, an escort will usually show you the church, or you may be allowed to see it on your own. Floors may be covered in pine needles here, too, and the rooms are brightly sunlit. The experience is an altogether different one from that of Chamula. You may be approached by children who will offer to show you to their home where their female relatives will most likely be weaving or working at some other craft.

AMATENANGO DEL VALLE   About an hour's ride south of San Cristóbal is Amatenango, a town known mostly for its **women potters.** You'll see their work in San Cristóbal—small animals, jars, and large water jugs—but in the village, you can visit the potters in their homes. Just walk down the dirt streets. Villagers will lean over the walls of family compounds and invite you in to select from their inventory. You may even see them firing the pieces under piles of wood in the open courtyard or painting them with color derived from rusty iron water. The women wear beautiful red-and-yellow *huipiles,* but if you want to take a photograph, you'll have to pay. To get here, take a *colectivo* from the market in San Cristóbal. Before it lets you off, be sure to ask about the return-trip schedule.

AGUACATENANGO   This village, 16km (10 miles) south of Amatenango, is known for its **embroidery.** If you've visited San Cristóbal's shops, you'll recognize the white-on-white and black-on-black floral patterns on dresses and blouses for sale. The locals' own regional blouses, however, are quite different.

TENEJAPA   The **weavers** of Tenejapa, 28km (17 miles) northeast from San Cristóbal, make some of the most beautiful and expensive work you'll see in the region. The best time to visit is on market day (Sun and Thurs, though Sun is better). The Tenejapa weavers taught the weavers of San Andrés and Magdalena—which accounts for the similarity in their designs and colors. To get to Tenejapa, try to find a *colectivo* in the very last row by the market, or hire a taxi. On Tenejapa's main street, several stores sell locally woven regional clothing, and you can bargain for the price.

THE HUITEPEC CLOUD FOREST   Pronatura, Calle Pedro Moreno 1 (✆ 967/ 678-5000), a private, nonprofit, ecological organization, offers environmentally sensitive tours of the cloud forest. The forest is a haven for **migratory birds,** and more than 100 bird species and 600 plant species have been identified here. Guided tours run from 9am to noon Tuesday to Sunday. Guided birding trips and general nature tours cost 70 to 100 pesos per person. Make reservations a day in advance. To reach the reserve on your own, take the Chamula road north; the turnoff is at Km 3.5. The reserve is open Tuesday to Sunday from 8am to 3pm.

Shopping

Many Indian villages near San Cristóbal are noted for **weaving, embroidery, brocade work, leather,** and **pottery,** making the area one of the best in the country for shopping. You'll see beautiful woolen shawls and skirts, colorful native shirts, and magnificently woven *huipiles,* which often come in vivid geometric patterns. A good place to find textiles as well as other handicrafts, besides what's mentioned below, is in and around Santo Domingo and the market. The stalls and small shops in that neighborhood make for interesting shopping. Working in leather, the craftspeople are artisans of the highest caliber. Tie-dyed *jaspe* from Guatemala comes in bolts and is made into clothing. The town is also known for **amber,** sold in several shops; two of the best are mentioned below.

For the best selection of new and used books and reading material in English, go to **La Pared,** Andador Eclesiásticos 13 (✆ 967/678-6367). The owners keep a large collection of books on the Maya, and Mexico in general, both fiction and nonfiction. Hours are Monday through Saturday 10am to 7:30pm.

CRAFTS

El Encuentro   The owner has been in business for more than 50 years and has quite a list of local artisans who sell her merchandise. She specializes in textiles, but also sells other forms of handicrafts, such as work made with agave fibers, forged iron, carved wood, or shaped tin. The store is open Monday to Saturday from 9am to 8pm. Calle Real de Guadalupe 63-A (btw. Dugelay and Colón). ✆ **967/678-3698.**

La Galería   This art gallery beneath a cafe shows the work of national and international painters. Also for sale are paintings and greeting cards by Kiki, the owner, a German artist who has found her niche in San Cristóbal. There are some Oaxacan rugs and pottery, plus unusual silver jewelry. It's open daily from 10am to 9pm. Hidalgo 3. ✆ **967/674-7273.**

Lágrimas de la Selva   "Tears of the Jungle" sells amber and amber jewelry, offering the best variety, quality, and artistry in San Cristóbal. It's not a bargain hunter's turf, but if you want to see high-quality amber visit this place or Piedra Escondida, listed below. Often you can watch the jewelers in action. Open Monday through Saturday from 10am to 8pm, Sunday from noon to 8pm. Hidalgo 1-C (half-block south of the main square). ✆ **967/674-6348.**

Piedra Escondida   This is another excellent choice for out-of-the-ordinary amber and jewelry. Open daily from 8:30am to 8pm. 20 de Noviembre 22. No phone.

Tienda Chiapas   This showroom has examples of every craft practiced in the state. It is run by the government in support of Indian crafts. You should take a look, if only to survey what crafts the region practices. It's open Monday to Friday from 9am to 9pm, Saturday 10am to 8pm, and Sunday 10am to 2pm. Niños Héroes at Hidalgo. ✆ **967/678-1180.**

TEXTILES

El Telar   "The Loom" sells textiles all handmade in San Cristóbal, and most are from the store's workshop, which you can visit in the northwest part of town, next to the hotel Rincón del Arco. It specializes in textiles made on large floor looms. Open Monday to Saturday from 9am to 2pm and 4 to 8pm. Calle 28 de Agosto 3 (next door to Hotel Casa Mexicana). ✆ **967/678-4422.** www.eltelar.com.mx.

Plaza de Santo Domingo   The plazas around this church and the nearby Templo de Caridad fill with women in native garb selling their wares. Here you'll find women from Chamula weaving belts or embroidering, surrounded by piles of loomed woolen textiles from their village. Their inventory includes Guatemalan shawls, belts, and bags. There are also some excellent buys on Chiapanecan-made wool vests, jackets, rugs, and shawls, similar to those at Sna Jolobil (described below), if you take the time to look and bargain. Vendors arrive between 9 and 10am and begin to leave around 3pm. Av. Utrilla. No phone.

Sna Jolobil   Meaning "weaver's house" in Mayan, this place is in the former convent (monastery) of Santo Domingo, next to the church of Santo Domingo. Tzotzil and Tzeltal craftspeople operate the cooperative store, which has about 3,000 members who contribute products, help run the store, and share in the moderate profits. You'll find some elegant *huipiles* and other weavings; prices are high, as is the quality. It's open Monday to Saturday from 9am to 2pm and 4 to 6pm; credit cards are accepted. Calzada Lázaro Cárdenas 42 (Plaza Santo Domingo, btw. Navarro and Nicaragua). ✆ **967/678-2646.**

Unión Regional de Artesanías de los Altos   Also known as J'pas Joloviletic, this cooperative of weavers is smaller than Sna Jolobil (described above) and not as sophisticated in its approach to potential shoppers. It sells blouses, textiles, pillow covers, vests, sashes, napkins, baskets, and purses. It's near the market and worth looking around. Open Monday to Saturday from 9am to 2pm and 4 to 7pm, Sunday from 9am to 1pm. Av. Utrilla 43. ✆ **967/678-2848.**

Where to Stay

Among the most interesting places to stay in town is the seminary-turned-hotel-and-museum **Casa Na-Bolom** (p. 645).

Hotels in San Cristóbal are inexpensive. You can do tolerably well for $50 to $70 per night per double. Rates listed here include taxes. High season is Easter week, July, August, and December.

EXPENSIVE

Parador San Juan de Dios ★★   This is San Cristóbal's handsomest property. It's in the north end of town in some 17th-century farm buildings. The rooms are large, plush, and distinctive, with something of the air of the old adobe and stone buildings. Most have fireplaces and period pieces mixed with a few modern comforts.

Bathrooms are large and beautifully finished. In the suites they include Jacuzzi tubs. Most rooms also come with their own stone terraces (and in some cases two terraces), which afford views of the extensive grounds. The hotel is a long walk or short taxi ride from the main square. In 2011, the hotel opened a small spa and a large gallery exhibiting traditional works of art from the region.

Calzada Roberta 16, Col. 31 de Marzo, 29229 San Cristóbal de las Casas, Chi. www.sanjuandios.com. ✆/fax **967/678-1167**, -4290. 12 units. High season 1,800 pesos double, 3,300–6,000 pesos suite; low season 1,600 pesos double, 2,200–6,000 pesos suite. AE, MC, V. Free secure parking. **Amenities:** Restaurant; bar; room service; Wi-Fi (in common areas). *In room:* TV, hair dryer, Internet.

MODERATE

Casa de los Arcángeles 🗡 The owner of a large courtyard restaurant decided to convert the rooms surrounding the courtyard into hotel rooms. This kind of afterthought is often a recipe for disaster, but it works in this case. The rooms, each with a queen-size bed, are large, comfortable, attractive, and well priced. The restaurant closes early so noise isn't a factor, and the location just south of the main square is excellent.

Cuauhtémoc 4, 29200 San Cristóbal de las Casas, Chi. casadelosarcangeles@hotmail.com. ✆ **967/678-1531**, -1936. 7 units. 1,250 pesos double. Rates include full breakfast. MC, V. Free parking. **Amenities:** Restaurant; bar. *In room:* TV, hair dryer, minibar.

Casa Felipe Flores ★ This beautifully restored colonial house is the perfect setting for getting a feel for San Cristóbal. The patios and common rooms are relaxing and comfortable, and their architectural details are so very *coleto*. The guest rooms are nicely furnished and full of character and are heated in winter. The owners, Nancy and David Orr, enjoy sharing their appreciation and knowledge of Chiapas and the Maya.

Calle Dr. Felipe Flores 36, 29230 San Cristóbal de las Casas, Chi. www.felipeflores.com. ✆/fax **967/678-3996**. 5 units. $95–$125 double. Rates include full breakfast. 10% service charge. No credit cards. Limited street parking. **Amenities:** Library. *In room:* No phone.

Hotel Casa Mexicana ★ This colonial hotel with well-manicured courtyards offers attractive, comfortable lodging. The management is attentive and keeps the property looking sharp. Service is great. The standard rooms are carpeted and come with two double beds or one king-size. They have good lighting, electric heaters, and spacious bathrooms. Across the street in another colonial house are several suites that are much larger and have distinctive clay tile floors and larger bathrooms. The hotel handles many tour groups; it can be quiet and peaceful one day, full and bustling the next.

28 de Agosto 1 (at General Utrilla), 29200 San Cristóbal de las Casas, Chi. www.hotelcasamexicana.com. ✆ **967/678-1348**, -0698. Fax 967/678-2627. 55 units. High season $110 double, $150 junior suite, $180 suite; low season $90 double, $140 junior suite, $170 suite. AE, MC, V. Free secure parking 1½ blocks away. **Amenities:** Restaurant; bar; babysitting; room service; sauna. *In room:* TV, hair dryer, Wi-Fi.

Hotel Casavieja This old colonial house retains some of its original creakiness, at least in the original section. Most of the rooms, however, are in the new section, where construction has been faithful to the original design in essentials such as wood-beam ceilings. Half the rooms have carpeted floors, and half have tile or laminate flooring. Rooms are medium size and not brightly lit. Some have smallish bathrooms.

María Adelina Flores 27 (btw. Cristóbal Colón and Diego Dugelay), 29200 San Cristóbal de las Casas, Chi. www.casavieja.com.mx. ✆/fax **967/678-6868**, -0385. 40 units. 830–1,200 pesos double; 1,100–1,350 pesos junior suite. Internet specials often available. AE, MC, V. Free parking. **Amenities:** Restaurant; bar. *In room:* TV, Wi-Fi.

Mansión de los Angeles   This colonial hotel is clean and attractive. Guest rooms are medium size and come with either a single and a double bed or two double beds. They are more attractive, warmer, and better lit than most hotels in this town. They are also quiet. Some of the bathrooms are small. Most rooms have windows that open onto a pretty courtyard with a fountain. The rooftop sun deck is a great siesta spot.

Calle Francisco Madero 17, 29200 San Cristóbal de las Casas, Chi. www.hotelmansiondelosangeles.com. ℭ **967/678-1173**, -4371. 20 units. 630–900 pesos double. AE, MC, V. Limited secure parking 5 blocks away. *In room:* TV, Wi-Fi.

INEXPENSIVE

Hotel Don Quijote 🔥   Rooms in this three-story hotel (no elevator) are small yet quiet, carpeted, and well lit, but a little worn. All have two double beds with reading lamps over them, tiled bathrooms, and plenty of hot water. There's complimentary coffee in the mornings.

Cristóbal Colón 7 (near Real de Guadalupe), 29200 San Cristóbal de las Casas, Chi. ℭ **967/678-0920.** Fax 967/678-0346. 25 units. 280–370 pesos double. MC, V. Free parking 1 block away. *In room:* TV.

Hotel Palacio de Moctezuma   The rooms in this three-story hotel have windows facing one of the two courtyards. They are quiet, minimally furnished, carpeted, and poorly lit. Most are medium size and come with two double beds, but a few are large. On the third floor is a solarium with comfortable tables and chairs and a city view.

Juárez 16 (at León), 29200 San Cristóbal de las Casas, Chi. ℭ **967/678-0352**, -1142. Fax 967/678-1536. 48 units. 300–500 pesos double. MC, V. Free limited parking. **Amenities:** Restaurant. *In room:* TV, hair dryer, Wi-Fi.

Hotel Posada La Media Luna 🔥   A modern two-story hotel in the downtown area with medium-size, attractive rooms for a good price. The bathrooms are larger than the norm, and the staff is helpful and friendly, and some speak English.

Hermanos Domínguez 5, 29200 San Cristóbal de las Casas, Chi. www.hotel-lamedialuna.com. ℭ **967/ 631-5590.** 11 units. 400–500 pesos double. MC, V. **Amenities:** Restaurant. *In room:* TV, no phone, Wi-Fi.

Where to Eat

San Cristóbal is not known for its cuisine, but you can eat well at several restaurants. For baked goods, try the **Panadería La Hojaldra,** Insurgentes 14 (ℭ **967/678-4286**). It's a traditional Mexican bakery that's open daily from 8am to 9:30pm.

MODERATE

El Edén ★ INTERNATIONAL   This is a small, quiet restaurant inside the Hotel El Paraíso where the food and service are consistently good, better than in most restaurants in San Cristóbal. The steaks are tender, and the margaritas are especially dangerous (one is all it takes). Specialties include Swiss cheese fondue for two, Edén salad, and brochettes.

In the Hotel El Paraíso, Av. 5 de Febrero 19. ℭ **967/678-5382.** Breakfast 35–55 pesos; main courses 60–150 pesos. AE, MC, V. Daily 8am–10:30pm.

La Paloma ★ INTERNATIONAL/MEXICAN   La Paloma I particularly like in the evening because the lighting is so well done. For starters, I enjoyed the quesadillas Mexico City–style (small fried packets of *masa* stuffed with a variety of fillings). Don't make my mistake of trying to share them with your dinner companion—it will only lead to trouble. Mexican classics include *albóndigas en chipotle* (meatballs in a thick chipotle sauce), Oaxacan black *mole,* and a variety of chiles rellenos. Avoid the *prof-iteroles.* Live music nightly 9 to 10:30pm.

Hidalgo 3. ☎ 967/678-1547. Main courses 120–165 pesos. MC, V. Daily 9am–midnight.

INEXPENSIVE

Emiliano's Moustache 🍴 MEXICAN/TACOS   Like any right-thinking traveler, I initially avoided this place on account of its unpromising name and some cartoonlike figures by the door. But a conversation with some local folk overcame my prejudice and tickled my sense of irony. Sure enough, the place was crowded with *coletos* enjoying the restaurant's popular *comida corrida.* You can choose from a menu of taco plates (a mixture of fillings cooked together and served with tortillas and a variety of hot sauces). Live music Thursday through Saturday.

Crescencio Rosas 7. ☎ **967/678-7246.** Main courses 70–90 pesos; taco plates 40–50 pesos; *comida corrida* 48 pesos. No credit cards. Daily 8am–midnight.

La Casa del Pan Papalotl VEGETARIAN   This place is known for its vegetarian lunch buffet with salad bar. The vegetables and most of the grains are organic. Kippy, the owner, has a home garden and a field near town where she grows vegetables. She buys locally grown, organic red wheat for her breads. These are all sourdough breads, which she likes because she feels they are easily digested and have good texture and taste. The pizzas are a popular item. The restaurant shares space with other activities in the cultural center El Puente, which has gallery space, a language school, and cinema.

Real de Guadalupe 55 (btw. Diego Dugelay and Cristóbal Colón). ☎ **967/678-7215.** Main courses 50–70 pesos; pizzas 50–140 pesos; lunch buffet 60–75 pesos. No credit cards. Mon–Sat 9am–10pm (lunch buffet 2–5pm).

Namandí INTERNATIONAL/REGIONAL   If you're looking for a light meal or snack this place is the perfect choice. Excellent-quality, fair-trade coffee and delicious Mexican items such as enchiladas or tostadas. The crepes are excellent, but if you want to sample local fare, try the tamales, which were delicious and different. The restaurant space is modern, light, and airy.

Mazarriegos 16. ☎ **967/678-8054.** Crepes, salads, and sandwiches 45–75 pesos; breakfasts 35–50 pesos. MC, V. Mon–Sat 8am–11:30pm; Sun 8:30am–11pm.

Normita's MEXICAN   Normita's is famous for its *pozole,* a chicken and hominy soup to which you add extra ingredients at the table. It also offers cheap, short-order Mexican mainstays. This is a "people's" restaurant; the open kitchen takes up one corner of the room, the rest of which is filled with simple tables and chairs.

Av. Juárez 6 (at Dr. José Flores). No phone. Breakfast 30–40 pesos; *pozole* 35 pesos; tacos 30 pesos. No credit cards. Daily 7am–11pm.

Restaurant Tuluc 🍴 MEXICAN/INTERNATIONAL   The owner hails from Puebla, but learned the restaurant business in Germany and Belgium. The house specialty is *filete Tuluc,* a beef filet wrapped around spinach and cheese served with fried potatoes and green beans; while not the best cut of meat, it's certainly priced right. The *tampiqueña* steak, served with a plethora of sides, is certainly good and filling. The Chiapaneco breakfast is a quartet of juice, toast, two Chiapanecan tamales, and coffee. Lighter favorites include the sandwiches and enchiladas.

Av. Insurgentes 5 (btw. Cuauhtémoc and Francisco León). ☎ **967/678-2090.** Breakfast 35–50 pesos; main courses 68–85 pesos; *comida corrida* (served 2–5pm) 65 pesos. No credit cards. Daily 7am–10pm.

COFFEEHOUSES

Because Chiapas-grown coffee is highly regarded, it's not surprising that coffeehouses proliferate here. Most are concealed in the nooks and crannies of San Cristóbal's side streets. Try **Café La Selva,** Crescencio Rosas 9 (© **967/678-7244**), for coffee served in all its varieties and brewed from organic beans; it is open daily from 9am to 11pm. A more traditional-style cafe, where locals meet to talk over the day's news, is **Café San Cristóbal,** Cuauhtémoc 1 (© **967/678-3861**), between Hidalgo and Insurgentes. It's open daily 7:30am to 10pm, Sunday from 9am to 9pm.

San Cristóbal After Dark

San Cristóbal is blessed with a variety of nightlife, both resident and migratory. There is a lot of live music, surprisingly good and varied. The bars and restaurants are cheap. And they are easy to get to: You can hit all the places mentioned here without setting foot in a cab. Weekends are best, but on any night you'll find something going on.

Almost all the clubs in San Cristóbal host Latin music of one genre or another. **El Cocodrilo** (© **967/678-1140**), on the main plaza in the Hotel Santa Clara, has acoustic performers playing Latin folk music (*trova, andina*) from 9 to 11pm daily. Relax at a table in what usually is a not-too-crowded environment. After that, your choices vary. One of the two most popular bars is **Café Bar Revolución** (© **967/678-6664**), on the pedestrian-only 20 de Noviembre at 1 de Marzo. It has two live acts every night—usually blues, reggae, Latin, or rock, and always rock on Saturday nights. Usually it winds down around midnight. For Latin dance music, there's a club on the corner of Madero and Juárez, called **Latino's** (© **967/678-9972**)—good bands playing a mix of salsa, merengue, and *cumbia*. On weekends it gets crowded, but it has a good-size dance floor. There's a small cover on weekends. The place is dark and has a bit of an urban edge to it. For a relaxing place to have a drink, try the bar at the **Hotel Posada Real de Chiapas.** It's across the street from Latino's. There's a piano player on Saturdays, and soft recorded music the rest of the week.

Road Trips from San Cristóbal

For excursions to nearby villages, see "The Nearby Maya Villages & Countryside," earlier in this chapter; for destinations farther away, there are several local travel agencies. But first you should try **Alex and Raúl** (p. 646). You can also try **ATC Travel and Tours,** Calle 5 de Febrero 15, at the corner of 16 de Septiembre (© **967/678-2550;** fax 967/678-3145), across from El Fogón restaurant. The agency has bilingual guides and reliable vehicles. ATC regional tours focus on birds and orchids, textiles, hiking, and camping.

Strangely, the cost of the trips includes a driver but not necessarily a bilingual guide or guided information of any kind. You pay extra for those services, so when checking prices, be sure to flesh out the details.

CHINCULTIC RUINS, COMITÁN & MONTEBELLO NATIONAL PARK

Almost 160km (99 miles) southeast of San Cristóbal, near the border with Guatemala, is the **Chincultic** archaeological site and **Montebello National Park,** with 16 multicolored lakes and exuberant pine-forest vegetation. Seventy-four kilometers (46 miles) from San Cristóbal is **Comitán,** a pretty hillside town of 40,000 inhabitants known for its flower cultivation and a sugar cane–based liquor called *comiteco*. It's also the last big town along the Pan-American Highway before the Guatemalan border.

The Chincultic ruins, a late Classic site, have barely been excavated, but the main **acropolis,** high up against a cliff, is magnificent to see from below and is worth the walk up for the view. After passing through the gate, you'll see the trail ahead; it passes ruins on both sides. More unexcavated tree-covered ruins flank steep stairs leading up the mountain to the acropolis. From there, you can gaze upon distant Montebello lakes and miles of cornfields and forest. The paved road to the lakes passes six lakes, all different colors and sizes, ringed by cool pine forests; most have parking lots and lookouts. The paved road ends at a small restaurant. The lakes are best seen on a sunny day, when their famous brilliant colors are optimal.

Most travel agencies in San Cristóbal offer a daylong trip that includes the lakes, the ruins, lunch in Comitán, and a stop in the pottery-making village of Amatenango del Valle. If you're driving, follow Hwy. 190 south from San Cristóbal through the pretty village of Teopisca and then through Comitán; turn left at La Trinitaria, where there's a sign to the lakes. After the Trinitaria turnoff and before you reach the lakes, there's a sign pointing left down a narrow dirt road to the Chincultic ruins.

TUXTLA GUTIÉRREZ

82km (51 miles) W of San Cristóbal; 277km (172 miles) S of Villahermosa; 242km (150 miles) NW of Ciudad Cuauhtémoc on the Guatemalan border

Tuxtla Gutiérrez (altitude 557m/1,827 ft.) is the commercial center of Chiapas. Coffee is the basis of the region's economy, along with recent oil discoveries. Tuxtla (pop. 350,000) is a business town, and not a particularly attractive one. Most travelers simply pass through Tuxtla on their way to San Cristóbal, the Sumidero Canyon, or Oaxaca.

Essentials

GETTING THERE & DEPARTING

BY PLANE Tuxtla's airport (airport code: TGZ) is 45 minutes south of the city. There is taxi service at the airport. With the separate closings of **Aviacsa** and **Mexicana,** air service has declined, but the void has been partially filled by **Aeroméxico** (© **800/237-6639** in the U.S., or 01-800/021-4000 in Mexico; www.aeromexico. com) and two domestic discount airlines: **VivaAerobus** (© **01-81/8215-0150** in Mexico; www.vivaaerobus.com) and **Interjet** (© **866/285-9525** in the U.S., or 01-80/0011-2345 in Mexico; www.interjet.com.mx). But no matter which you choose, you'll be flying in and out of Mexico City.

BY CAR From Oaxaca, you'll enter Tuxtla by Hwy. 190. From Villahermosa, or Palenque and San Cristóbal, you'll enter at the opposite end of town on the same highway from the east. In both cases, you'll arrive at the large main square at the center of town, La Plaza Cívica.

From Tuxtla to Villahermosa, take Hwy. 190 east past the town of Chiapa de Corzo; soon you'll see a sign for Hwy. 195 north to Villahermosa. To San Cristóbal and Palenque, take Hwy. 190 east. The road is beautiful but tortuous. It's in good repair to San Cristóbal, but there may be bad spots between San Cristóbal and Palenque. The trip from Tuxtla to Villahermosa takes 8 hours by car; the scenery is beautiful.

The Chiapas Highlands

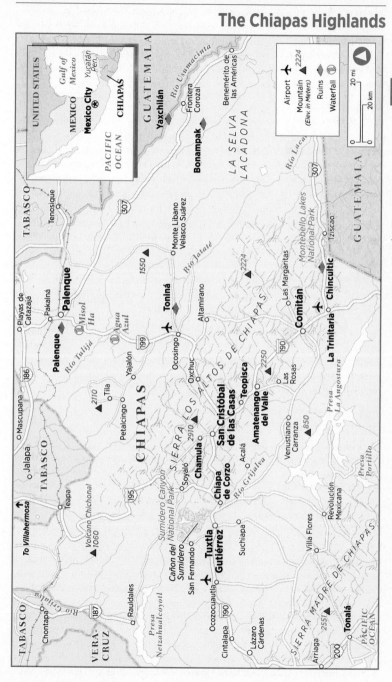

BY BUS   The **ADO bus station** (✆ **961/612-2624**) is 1.6km (1 mile) northwest of the city center on Avenida 5 Norte Poniente, at the Plaza del Sol. There are eight buses a day to Villahermosa, three or four buses a day to Oaxaca, and five to Palenque. There's usually no need to buy a ticket ahead of time, except during holidays. Small buses (microbuses) to San Cristóbal leave every 5 to 15 minutes from the station at the intersection of Avenida 4 Sur and Calle 15 Oriente.

ORIENTATION

ARRIVING   There is taxi service from the airport to town (220 pesos) and taxi service at the bus station.

VISITOR INFORMATION   Information desks are on the main square and on Avenida Central across from Parque de la Marimba. They are open daily from 9am to 2pm and from 4 to 8pm. Some staff speak English and can provide good maps.

CITY LAYOUT   Tuxtla is laid out on a grid. The main street, **Avenida Central,** is the east-west axis and is the artery through town for Hwy. 190. West of the central district, it's called **Bulevar Belisario Domínguez,** and in the east, it's **Bulevar Angel Albino Corzo. Calle Central** is the north-south axis. The rest of the streets have names that include one number and two directions. This tells you how to get to the street. For example, to find the street 5 Norte Poniente (5 North West), you walk 5 blocks north from the center of town and turn west. To find 3 Oriente Sur, you walk 3 blocks east from the main square and turn south. When people indicate intersections, they can shorten the names because it's redundant.

GETTING AROUND   Taking taxis is the easiest way to get around in this city. They are plentiful and easy to come by. **Buses** to all parts of the city converge upon the Plaza Cívica along Calle Central.

[FastFACTS] TUXTLA GUTIERREZ

The telephone **area code** is **961.** If you need medical help, the best **clinic** in town is Sanatorio Rojas, Calle 2 Sur Poniente 1847 (✆ **961/611-2079** or 961/612-5414).

Exploring Tuxtla

Miguel Alvarez del Toro Zoo (ZOOMAT)   Located in the forest called El Zapotal, ZOOMAT is one of the best zoos in Mexico. The collection of animals and birds indigenous to this area gives the visitor a tangible sense of what the wilds of Chiapas are like. The zoo keeps jaguars, howler monkeys, owls, and many more exotic animals in roomy cages that replicate their home terrain; the whole zoo is so deeply buried in vegetation that you can almost pretend you're in a natural habitat. Unlike at other zoos I've visited, the animals are almost always on view.

Bulevar Samuel León Brinois, southeast of downtown. No phone. General admission 20 pesos. Tues-Sun 9am–5:30pm. The zoo is about 8km (5 miles) southeast of downtown; catch a bus along Av. Central and at the Calzada.

Shopping

The government-operated **Instituto Marca Chiapas,** Bulevar Domínguez 2035 (✆ **961/602-9800**), endeavors to support artisans and promote the crafts from all parts of the state. The store is subsidized, making the prices here quite reasonable. The two stories of rooms feature an extensive collection of crafts grouped by region and type from throughout the state of Chiapas. It's open Monday to Saturday from 9am to 8pm and Sunday from 10am to 2pm.

Where to Stay

The center of the hotel industry is out of town, west to Hwy. 190. You'll notice the new motel-style hotels, such as the **Hotel Flamboyán, Palace Inn, Hotel Laganja,** and **La Hacienda.**

Camino Real Tuxtla Gutiérrez ★★   Bold modern architecture is the hallmark of the Camino Real chain, and this one is no exception, with stark lines, bright colors, and subtle references to the Maya culture and the local region. The center of the hotel is open-air and filled with a spot of jungle, a small cascade, and tropical birds flying freely about. This is a relaxing hotel; walking to and from your room, you hear bird song and splashing water. Guest rooms have two doubles or a king, are carpeted, and are comfortably furnished. Bathrooms are large.

Bulevar Domínguez 1159, 29060 Tuxtla Gutiérrez, Chi. www.caminoreal.com. ✆ **800/7-CAMINO** (722-6466) in the U.S. and Canada, or 961/617-7777. Fax 961/617-7779. 210 units. 2,400 pesos double; 2,850 pesos and up suite. Internet promotions often available. AE, MC, V. Free secured parking. **Amenities:** 2 restaurants; bar; babysitting; concierge; executive floor; health club and spa; outdoor pool; room service. *In room:* A/C, TV, hair dryer, minibar, Wi-Fi.

Hotel María Eugenia   This is a centrally located, well-managed property with plain, medium-size rooms. The white walls and white ceramic tile make them seem even plainer, but clean and uncluttered. Beds have comfortable mattresses and come as either two doubles or one king. There is good space for luggage.

Av. Central Oriente 507, 29000 Tuxtla Gutiérrez, Chi. ✆ **961/613-3767,** or 01-800/716-0149 in Mexico. 83 units. 880 pesos double. AE, MC, V. Free guarded parking. **Amenities:** Restaurant; bar; outdoor pool; room service. *In room:* A/C, TV, Wi-Fi.

Where to Eat

For a full sit-down meal, you can try local Chiapan food at **Las Pichanchas,** Av. Central Oriente 837 (✆ **961/612-5351**). It's festively decorated and pretty to look at. The emphasis is on meat, with several heavy dishes on the menu. I would recommend the *filete simojovel* (a thin steak in a not-spicy chile sauce) or the *comida grande,* which is beef in a pumpkinseed sauce. Eating here is a cultural experience, but I usually prefer to head over to the **Flamingo,** 1 Poniente Sur 168, just off Avenida Central (✆ **961/612-0922**), which serves standard Mexican dishes: enchiladas, *mole,* roast chicken. The restaurant is owned by a Spaniard, who also owns an elegant steakhouse called El Asador Castellano, which is on the west side of town. Take a taxi.

If all you want is tacos, there are several good places around the **El Parque de la Marimba.** This plaza has free *marimba* music nightly and is enjoyable. There you'll find a couple of local taco restaurants bordering the plaza, such as **Parrilla Suiza** and **El Fogón Norteño.** Both have good grilled tacos. The Parque de la Marimba is on Avenida Central Poniente, 8 blocks west of the main square.

Chiapa de Corzo & the Sumidero Canyon

The real reason to stay in Tuxtla is to take a boat trip through the **Canyon of El Sumidero ★★.** The canyon is spectacular, and the boat ride is fun. Boats leave from the docks in **Chiapa de Corzo,** a colonial town of about 50,000 inhabitants that bumps up to Tuxtla. To get there, take a taxi or hop on the bus operated by Transportes Chiapa-Tuxtla (Av. 1 Sur btw. calles 5 and 6 Oriente). Buses leave every couple of minutes and cost 9 pesos. The ride takes a half-hour. Ask to get off at the main square *(parada del parque)*. The two main boat cooperatives have ticket booths under the archways bordering the square. But you don't have to look for these; just go straight to the boats at the pier *(embarcadero)* 1½ blocks below the square.

As you pass the church of Santo Domingo, you'll see a large **ceiba** tree shading the churchyard. In better circumstances these trees get even larger than this, but this one has taken up an interesting position in front of the church. The Maya felt that these trees embodied the connection between the heavens, the world of men, and the underworld because they extend into all three realms.

The **two cooperatives** (the reds and the greens identified by the color of their boats) offer the same service. They work together sharing passengers and such. Boats leave as soon as at least 12 people show up. The interval can be up to an hour or as short as 10 minutes, depending on the season. The cost is 190 pesos. The ride takes 2 hours. This river is the Grijalva, which flows to the Gulf of Mexico from Guatemala and is one of Mexico's largest. Besides the canyon vistas, you're likely to see some crocodiles and other things of interest. The boat's pilot explains a few things in Spanish, but much of what he says adds little to the tour. At the deepest point in the canyon, our pilot said the walls stretch up vertically 1,000m (3,281 ft.) above the water, which in turn is about 100m (328 ft.) deep at that point. I wasn't about to double-check this statement—all I know is that the view was really something. There are some interesting things happening on the walls; water seeps out in places, creating little micro-environments of moss, grass, and mineral deposits. One of these places is called the Christmas Tree, for its form. Our boat glided slowly by as a fine mist fell on us from the plants.

The boats operate from 8am to 4pm. They are fast, and the water is smooth. The best times to see the canyon are early or late in the day, when the sun is at an angle and shines on one or the other of the canyon walls. The boats are necessarily open, so you should take an adjustable cap or a hat with a draw string or some sunscreen. A pair of earplugs would come in handy, too.

If you'd rather stay in Chiapa de Corzo than Tuxtla, check out the simple but nice hotel off the main square: **Hotel Los Angeles,** at Av. Julián Grajales 2 (© **916/616-0048**). It offers rooms with or without air-conditioning for 400 to 500 pesos per night.

THE COPPER CANYON

by David Baird

W hen people talk about the Copper Canyon (la Barranca del Cobre), they are referring to a section of the Sierra Madre of northwestern Mexico known as the Sierra Tarahumara (after the indigenous people who live there). To appreciate the Copper Canyon, it's best not to think of it as a variation on the Grand Canyon. Geologically they are not alike. This area is much newer, having formed through violent volcanic uplifting. The topography is more varied, creating the existence of microclimes in the Sierra Tarahumara that provide a far greater range of flora and fauna. And the local Indian cultures, especially the Tarahumara, are nothing like the Native Americans that live near the Grand Canyon.

How one experiences the canyons is very different. Winding through the Copper Canyon is one of the most remarkable railways in the world: the famed **Chihuahua al Pacífico (Chihuahua to the Pacific)** railway. Acclaimed as an engineering marvel, the 624km (387-mile) railroad has 39 bridges—the highest is more than 300m (984 ft.) above the Chinipas River, and the longest is about .5km (⅓ mile) long—and 86 tunnels, including one that stretches more than 1.5km (1 mile) long. It climbs from **Los Mochis,** at sea level, up nearly 2,425m (7,954 ft.) through some of Mexico's most magnificent scenery—thick pine forests, jagged peaks, and shadowy canyons—before descending to the city of **Chihuahua.**

Exploring the Copper Canyon

PLANNING YOUR TRIP The principal airports for the region are Los Mochis and Chihuahua, the two terminal points of the railroad. Connecting flights are available out of both cities, which makes entry into the region fairly easy. But once you arrive, you have to take precautions. Los Mochis is in the state of Sinaloa, home to two violent drug cartels. Chihuahua is the capital of the most violent state in the country, home to one cartel, and disputed territory in the drug wars. Carjackings are not uncommon in both places, making it much safer to fly into this area and move around town by taxi and in daylight. Taking the train through the Copper Canyon is still relatively safe, but getting off and hiking through the area is now a bit more iffy.

troubled times IN CHIHUAHUA & SINALOA

Conflicts between drug gangs, and the Mexican government's attempts to eradicate them, have led to increased violence in parts of the states of Chihuahua and Sinaloa. The violence has taken the form of killings, kidnappings, and carjackings. The U.S. Department of State (www.travel.state.gov) has issued a travel warning for the Mexican border area that specifically mentions Ciudad Juárez, Chihuahua City, and the Copper Canyon. It doesn't say not to go to the area, but it urges travelers to practice caution and avoid traveling at night. The Mexican government has sent in the military to aid federal and local police. Checkpoints can now be found on many area roads. If you decide to go to the Copper Canyon, be prepared to find added security in and around the cities and on the highways. Don't travel in a way that will make you a target. That means don't drive a personal vehicle, especially a pickup or SUV, which are highly desired by gangs, and don't travel alone into areas of the canyon that are too far off the beaten path.

The canyon lands are prime growing areas for marijuana. This didn't used to be a source of anxiety for tour operators. And travelers driving or hiking through the canyons didn't used to be a concern for the local growers. But violence in the region has escalated, there have been shootings in some of the small towns, and everyone's nerves are on edge. Travelers through the canyon should consider limiting their outings to areas that are seen primarily as tourist destinations.

It used to be the case that going in high season meant planning an itinerary well in advance, including reserving both train tickets and hotel rooms. Now, with the decrease in travel to the region, limited hotel space is less of a problem. You can make arrangements on your own or go through a travel agent or tour operator. (For tips, see "Choosing a Package or Tour Operator," below.) It's possible to buy train tickets as you need them and make last-minute reservations or no reservations at all. There is a small risk that you might run into a large group that has taken all the hotel rooms, but in most locations now, somebody usually has an inexpensive cabin for rent. The most plentiful lodging is to be found in Creel.

WHEN TO GO There are two high seasons for the Sierra: from mid-October to mid-November and March through April. These months are the most popular because of the likelihood of moderate temperatures—but even in these months, temperatures in the bottom of the canyon will be warm. Most canyon visitors stay up in the rim country. To avoid the crowds and get cheaper prices, I suggest **going in August or September** (the rainy season). During that time, barring drought, you'll find occasional afternoon thundershowers (very pretty in the canyon land), green vegetation, flowing water, and comfortable temperatures up along the rim. In the winter, temperatures at the bottom of the canyons are actually moderate. **Avoid the Sierra from late April through June.** This is the driest part of the year, with chronic water shortages in many of the towns and hotels; the vegetation is brown, and the canyons can be hazy.

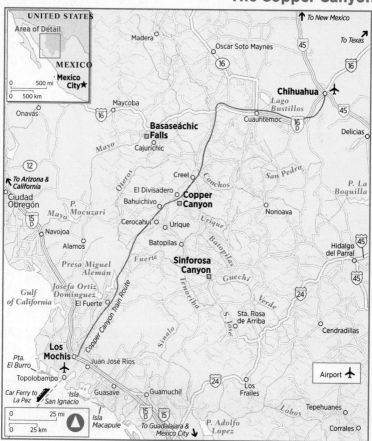

THE COPPER CANYON TRAIN & STOPS ALONG THE WAY

The Train

First-class service between Chihuahua and Los Mochis operates daily in both directions. Departure times are listed below. Second-class trains also run daily. They stop more frequently than the first-class trains and are slower. First-class service has undergone major improvements. The passenger cars have been revamped, with clean bathrooms that work and improved seating and windows. (They already were air-conditioned in summer and heated in winter.) In addition, the train makes fewer

Which Direction Should I Travel?

For sightseeing, **Los Mochis,** the western terminus, is the better starting place: The most scenic part of the 15- to 16-hour journey comes between **El Fuerte** and **Bahuichivo/Cerocahui,** which you are guaranteed to see in daylight if you come from Los Mochis. The train that starts in Chihuahua often gets to this area in darkness. This chapter lists the stops in order from Los Mochis to Chihuahua.

stops than before. The owner, **Ferromex** (www.ferromex.com.mx), invested heavily in improving the tracks, making delays due to landslides less frequent. It has also spruced up some of the local stations.

The train makes 12 stops; the 5 of principal interest to travelers are described in detail below. The schedule is a word problem that would gratify any high school algebra teacher: Two trains depart from opposite ends of the line (Chihuahua and Los Mochis) at the same time (6am) to meet at point *x*. So that you don't have to solve for *y*, I've included the "official" schedule below.

Train Departure Times

FROM LOS MOCHIS		FROM CHIHUAHUA	
Los Mochis	6am	Chihuahua	6am
El Fuerte	9am	Creel	11:35am
Bahuichivo/Cerocahui	1:10pm	El Divisadero	1:30pm
Barrancas	2:25pm	Barrancas	2pm
El Divisadero	2:35pm	Bahuichivo/Cerocahui	3:15pm
Creel	4:50pm	El Fuerte	7:20pm
Chihuahua (arrives)	10:25pm	Los Mochis (arrives)	10:25pm

Actual times vary. The locals at each stop are well attuned to train times, so it's good to ask them. The stops are short except at **El Divisadero,** where you have 20 minutes to get out and walk down the steps to the overlook for a spectacular panorama of the canyon, and perhaps time to buy a trinket or a taco from one of the many vendors.

DELAYS Travelers may have to contend with delays because of landslides, minor derailments, or maintenance projects. Traveling in this region requires some flexibility and patience. In case of a major service interruption, you can travel on a highway that parallels the railway from Chihuahua as far as Cerocahui, but the final stretch from Cerocahui to El Fuerte is not much of an option because it requires four-wheel-drive.

BUYING A TICKET The train offers no rail pass; you must buy a ticket for a particular day, point of departure, and destination. This is not usually a problem during the off season. You can buy a ticket for the first leg of your trip when you get to Los Mochis or Chihuahua, and then buy the rest each time you board the train. You're not going to have a guaranteed seat, but there's usually abundant seating during this part of the year. If you have an itinerary, you'll have guaranteed seating throughout the trip. You may not get to choose which seat, but that's a minor issue. Should you deviate from your itinerary, you can buy a new ticket at the local station or aboard the train. The cost of a ticket for the entire trip one-way is 1,981 pesos.

18

THE COPPER CANYON — The Copper Canyon Train & Stops Along the Way

To reserve tickets ahead of time, call the railway directly (© **888/484-1623** in the U.S. and Canada, or 614/436-7212). A few days before your trip, you will need to call again to reconfirm your reservations. Then you can buy the tickets at the station the morning of your departure with cash or credit card (MasterCard or Visa). For more information, see **www.chepe.com.mx**. If you actually want to purchase tickets ahead of time, you can do so from a local travel agency in Chihuahua or Los Mochis. To start out in Chihuahua, contact **Turismo al Mar** (© **614/410-9232** or 614/416-5950); from Los Mochis, contact **Viajes Araceli** (© **668/815-5780;** fax 668/815-8787; ventasaracely@viajearacely.com) or **Viajes Flamingo** (© **668/812-1613;** fax 668/812-0046; www.mexicoscoppercanyon.com). Travel agencies outside of Mexico sell tickets only as part of a package that includes transportation to the region and hotel accommodations. A wide variety of packages and custom trips are available. Look into these carefully before you book (see "Choosing a Package or Tour Operator," below).

LODGING If you spend a night at any spot en route, you'll have roughly 24 hours to explore, unless you're heading back in the direction from which you came. Drivers from

choosing A PACKAGE OR TOUR OPERATOR

A number of tour operators and packagers offer trips to the Copper Canyon. You can purchase your package through a travel agency; those that do frequent business with Copper Canyon trips have better knowledge of what's out there. Keep in mind that the travel agent may try to steer you toward one package over another because it pays a higher commission. The industry breaks down into the following categories:

Bus Tours Some outfits run buses from El Paso to Chihuahua or Tucson to Los Mochis, and then put their customers on the train. The usual length of stay in the Sierra is 2 nights before returning by bus to the U.S. These tours involve a lot of sitting on a bus or train, but they are the least expensive.

Train Tours   Sierra Madre Express has stopped running trains into the Copper Canyon from Tucson, Arizona, probably as a result of the economic downturn— perhaps, too, because of the bad press that Chihuahua is getting.

Standard Packages This option merely bundles airfare, train tickets, and lodging. Hotels in the canyon send drivers to

meet the train, so getting to your hotel is not hard once you're in the canyon. With these tours, you can have more time in the canyon, but once you're there, it's up to you to line up activities.

Custom Tour Operators These outfits sell fixed package tours through travel agents only because it simplifies the agent's job. If you eliminate the middle person and call any of the outfits directly, you might be able to arrange a custom trip. Travel through these companies generally allows you more time in the canyon and a better experience. Some assemble small groups with a guide; some allow you to travel by yourself and supply you with contacts in different locations. As the number of people visiting the Sierra increases, these companies are taking people deeper into the mountains to get away from the effects of mass tourism. Two reliable operators are **California Native,** 6701 W. 87th Place, Los Angeles, CA 90045 (© **800/926-1140** in the U.S.; www.calnative.com), and **Native Trails,** 613 Querétaro, El Paso, TX 79912-2210 (© **800/884-3107** in the U.S.; www.nativetrails.com).

Going Solo on Foot: Not a Good Idea

If you're planning to hike in the Copper Canyon, it's a good idea to have company, especially someone who knows the area and speaks Spanish. To be on the safe side, don't go too far from the main parts of the canyon.

all canyon hotels pick up guests from the train station; if you don't have a reservation, ask a driver about room availability. Rates for hotels in both of these towns usually include meals. The number of rooms is limited, and with groups of 40 or 50 people going through the Sierra, a hotel can be empty one day and full the next. When hotels are full, you'll notice a decline in service in the dining room, or you'll have to wait in line at the buffet even if you're not part of the group. Overbooking rooms also seems to be a problem with some of the large hotels, though it's not common enough that you should worry about it. In Creel, you find the greatest variety of accommodations and restaurants. This is also where most of the economical hotels are.

CLIMATE Los Mochis and El Fuerte are warm year-round. Chihuahua can be warm in summer, windy at almost any time, and freezing in winter. The canyon rim may experience freezes from November through March; the bottom of the canyon may occasionally get cool enough for a sweater. In the other half of the year, it's hot below and cool above.

Stop 1: El Fuerte ★

El Fuerte is on the coastal plain before the foothills of the Sierra Madre. With its charming cobblestone streets and handsome colonial mansions, it is the prettiest town along the train route. At only 80m (262 ft.) above sea level, it is most comfortable in winter. The town owes its origin to silver mining, and its existence in recent times to booming agriculture. From the late 18th century onward, the town has been under the control of a few families, and to this day, much of the real estate in and about the center of town remains in their hands. The town's plaza is quaint and handsome, with a 19th-century bandstand surrounded by graceful palms. One way to see the town is to take a taxi from Los Mochis and pick up the train the next day. An added advantage to this plan is that it allows you an extra hour in bed. The train station is a few kilometers from town. El Fuerte may look quiet, but there have been killings here, too, though this is by no means a common occurrence. You'll have a hard time getting anyone to talk about what happened, so don't raise the subject with them. I consider this place safer than Los Mochis.

EXPLORING THE TOWN Possible activities include visiting nearby villages, birding, fishing for black bass and trout, and hunting for duck and dove. Hotels can arrange guides and all equipment if they're contacted in advance.

Money-Changing: Be Prepared

Be sure to start the journey with adequate funds, because exchanging money outside of Creel is almost impossible; even credit cards are good only at the expensive hotels. I won't use a credit card at some of the hotels listed in this chapter because they use radio communication to the main office to confirm a card—hardly a secure system.

WHERE TO STAY & EAT

In addition to the restaurants at the hotels mentioned here, more inexpensive restaurants are on and near the central plaza.

Hotel El Fuerte ★   This is a charming inn loaded with character. Rooms have double or king-size beds, tiled bathrooms, and colonial furnishings. The courtyard and common areas are shady and cool. During high season, this hotel occasionally books up with tour groups, but it's a good option for the rest of the year.

Montesclaro 37, 81820 El Fuerte, Sin. www.hotelelfuerte.com.mx. Ⓒ **698/893-0226.** Fax 698/893-1246. 49 units. 766–935 pesos double. AE, MC, V. Free parking. **Amenities:** Restaurant; bar; Jacuzzi; room service; smoke-free rooms, Wi-Fi (in lobby). *In room:* A/C, TV, hair dryer, no phone.

Hotel La Choza   Two stories of rooms are arranged around a modern courtyard/parking lot. The upstairs rooms are nicer, as they come with a *bóveda* ceiling, but all are comfortable and colorfully decorated and have nice, midsize bathrooms. Most have two double beds.

Cinco de Mayo 101, 81820 El Fuerte, Sin. www.hotellachoza.com. Ⓒ/fax **698/893-1274,** -1503. 36 units. 850 pesos double. MC, V. Free secure parking. **Amenities:** Restaurant; bar/dance club; outdoor pool; room service. *In room:* A/C, TV, no phone, Wi-Fi.

Hotel Posada del Hidalgo ★★   This handsome hotel is one of the Balderrama properties and can be booked through the central reservations office in Los Mochis. It, too, can fill up fast with tour groups. The mansion section, with open arcades around a central patio, belonged to silver barons in the 18th century; there's even a carriage ramp from its days as a stagecoach stop. There are three courtyards, each in a different style, with bougainvillea and tall palm trees. The guest rooms are nicely finished with attractive tile or hardwood floors, attractive furniture, and good bathrooms. All have two double beds.

Hidalgo 101, 81820 El Fuerte, Sin. www.hotelposadadelhidalgo.com. Ⓒ **888/528-8401** in the U.S. (to the Balderrama Hotels & Tours in Los Mochis), or 698/893-1194 in El Fuerte. Fax 698/893-1194. 68 units. 1,430 pesos double. AE, MC, V. Free parking. **Amenities:** Restaurant; bar; Jacuzzi; outdoor pool; spa. *In room:* A/C, hair dryer, no phone.

Río Vista Lodge 🛅   Free-spirited owner Chal Gámez has done it his way in this small hotel on a hilltop above the town. The common areas and rooms hold fanciful murals, artifacts of Yaqui and Mayo Indians, decorations from northern Mexico, and a few things reminiscent of the Old West. The outdoor dining area is a lovely place to gaze at the river or watch the swarms of hummingbirds that feast at Chal's feeders. These birds seem little bothered by the proximity of humans—you can even put your hand under the feeder and be fanned by their wings. Meals are simple but good.

Cerro de la Pilas s/n, 81820 El Fuerte, Sin. hotelriovista@hotmail.com. Ⓒ/fax **698/893-0413.** 32 units. 600 pesos double. MC, V. Free parking. **Amenities:** Restaurant. *In room:* A/C, hair dryer, no phone.

Stop 2: Bahuichivo & Cerocahui ★★★

This is the first train stop in canyon country. **Bahuichivo** is merely the train depot and didn't exist before the railroad's construction. The village of **Cerocahui** (elevation 1,670m/5,478 ft.) dates from before the Colonial Era. It's home to 600 people and is in a valley about 10km (6¼ miles) from the train stop. The road is unpaved, so the trip takes about 30 minutes. The most dramatic part of the train ride is the section between El Fuerte and Bahuichivo.

EXPLORING CEROCAHUI Built around a humble mission church, Cerocahui is little more than rambling unpaved streets and 100 or so houses. It enjoys a wonderful view of the mountains, but you have to take an excursion to get real canyon vistas. All hotels can arrange horseback rides to nearby waterfalls and other scenic spots, as well as trips to **Cerro Gallego,** a famous lookout point with a beautiful vista of Urique Canyon. It's possible to see the waterfall on arrival, schedule the Gallego trip for the next morning, have lunch, and still make the train. I like the quiet of Cerocahui, however, and recommend staying here as long as you can, provided you like hiking or horseback riding. There are a number of secluded places, both near and far, to visit. One possible trip is a hike to the mining town of **Urique** at the bottom of the Urique Canyon (one of several canyons that make up the Copper Canyon), and then a car ride back up. There are a few simple but comfortable hotels where you can stay for between 350 and 450 pesos a night. The nicest is **Hotel Barrancas Urique** (© **635/456-6076**). It can provide you with a guide if want to hike more. The rooms come with fans, but the hotel might install air-conditioning units in a couple of the rooms.

WHERE TO STAY & EAT

Rates for doubles in the two hotels listed below include all meals for two people and transportation to and from the train station. The Paraíso del Oso is less than a kilometer (about ⅔ mile) short of the village. The mission is in Cerocahui proper. In the town, you can find simple lodging for a fraction of the cost of the other places. There are also some cabins for rent up above town. They go for 600 pesos for two people and include transportation from the train station. You can reserve a cabin through Río Vista Lodge (see above) or by calling © **635/456-5257** and saying you want a cabin in Cerocahui (the staff speaks English).

Hotel Misión Cerocahui ★ Established years ago, the Hotel Misión is right on the town's little plaza. Guest rooms have hot water and electricity. They are decorated in Mexican country style (with tile floors, wood-burning stoves, and kerosene lanterns) and are comfortable. The lobby and restaurant area surrounds a large rock fireplace, where a local guitarist and singer sometimes entertain in the evenings. Food service is inconsistent; it's been good and bad in the past. The hotel offers several tours, including rides to Cerro Gallego, Urique, and the local waterfalls. There are also hiking, mountain-biking, and horseback-riding trips.

Domicilio Conocido, Cerocahui. www.hotelmision.com. © **888/528-8401** in the U.S. (to the Balderrama Hotels & Tours in Los Mochis), or 635/456-5294, -5017. 38 units. 2,572 pesos double. Rates include meals. AE, MC, V. Free parking. **Amenities:** Restaurant.

Paraíso del Oso ★ 📷 Paraíso del Oso sits in a sheltered hollow with a backdrop of impressive stone palisades less than a kilometer (about ⅔ mile) from the town. Owner Doug Rhodes is an avid horseman and takes guests for rides that can last anywhere from 3 hours to more than a week. Rooms come with two double beds and ranch furniture. They are comfortable, with wood-burning stoves and plenty of hot water. Solar-generated electricity fuels such vital services as refrigeration, while lanterns provide light. This and the utter solitude of the area are charming traits that make you feel more in touch with the Sierra than you would at the big canyon hotels along the railroad tracks. The inn has a cash bar, a small but good library, Wi-Fi, and topographical maps of the area.

Cerocahui. www.mexicohorse.com. © **800/884-3107** or 915/833-3107 in the U.S., or 614/421-3372. Fax 614/421-3372. (Reservations: Paraíso del Oso, P.O. Box 31089, El Paso, TX 79931.) 21 units. $185 double. Rates include meals. MC, V. Free parking. **Amenities:** Bar; library; Wi-Fi. *In room:* No phone.

Stops 3 & 4: Barrancas/El Divisadero ★★

Between Bahuichivo and here, the train stops at San Rafael to change crews. By the time it arrives at these two stops, it's at the highest part of its journey. Many packages include at least a night here for soaking up the great views of the canyons. Two nights would be better if you want to spend some time in the mountains.

Barrancas and El Divisadero are less than 3km (1¾ miles) apart. Coming from Los Mochis, you'll arrive at Barrancas first. At this stop, drivers from the **Hotel Mirador, Hotel Rancho,** and **Mansion Tarahumara** meet passengers. Then the train takes you to El Divisadero (elevation 2,240m/7,347 ft.), where you'll find the **Hotel Divisadero-Barrancas,** taco stands (at train time), and a **spectacular view of the canyon.** The train stops for 20 minutes—time to walk down the steps to the lookout to enjoy the view and purchase one or two mementos from the Tarahumara Indians, who sell sweet-smelling pine-needle baskets, homemade violins, and wood and cloth dolls. Hotels arrange various excursions, including a visit to a cave-dwelling Tarahumara family, hiking, and horseback riding. All hotels listed below offer free secure parking.

The state of Chihuahua has plans to build an adventure park in this part of the canyon, specifically the area below El Divisadero. In 2010 it inaugurated **cable car service** from the rim down 345m (1,150 ft.) into the canyon. The cable car system is Swiss built and offers spectacular views of the canyon. Each car holds up to 50 passengers. The trip, down or up, lasts about 8 minutes and costs $20 per person. Thrill seekers can pay $50 to take a network of zip lines to get to the lower cable car station, getting there in a more roundabout way. There are plans to gradually add more services, and activities such as mountain biking trails, and there is even talk of building another, smaller cable car that goes all the way to the bottom of the canyon.

WHERE TO STAY & EAT

Hotel Divisadero-Barrancas ★★   This location, on the edge of the canyon over-look, provides the most spectacular view of any hotel in the canyon. The restaurant has a large picture window, perfect for sitting and gazing at the canyon. The rooms are in four sections. The newest section (nos. 35–48) is a two-story building perched on the edge of the canyon. These rooms have sliding glass doors that open on to balconies with a view. The bathrooms are midsize and modern. The new rooms are probably the quietest, but I also like the original section (room nos. 1–10). These are made of logs and stones and are more rustic, which for me is a good part of their appeal.

El Divisadero. www.hoteldivisadero.com. ℂ 888/232-4219 in the U.S. and Canada, or 635/578-3060. (Reservations: Av. Mirador 4516, Apdo. Postal 661, Col. Residencial Campestre, 31238 Chihuahua, Chih.; ℂ 614/415-1199; fax 614/415-6575.) 52 units. High season $220 double; low season $180 double. Rates include meals and 2 tours. AE, MC, V. **Amenities:** Restaurant; bar.

Hotel Mirador ★★ 🖸   The Mirador sits on the edge of the canyon 5 minutes up the mountain from its sister hotel, the Hotel Rancho (see below). Every room has a dramatic balcony that seems to hang right over the cliff's edge. The views are breath-taking. Rooms have attractive decorations and furniture, with bold Mexican color combinations; most have two double beds. Each room has its own heater. The common areas are also comfortable and attractive.

El Divisadero. www.mexicoscoppercanyon.com/mirador. ℂ 635/578-3020. (Reservations: Hotel Santa Anita, Apdo. Postal 159, 81200 Los Mochis, Sin.; ℂ 800/896-8196 in the U.S.) Fax 668/812-0046. 65 units. 2,895 pesos double. Rates include meals. AE, MC, V. **Amenities:** Restaurant; bar; transporta-tion to and from train station. *In room:* Hair dryer, no phone.

Hotel Rancho   The train stops in front of this inn. Rooms are comfortable, with two double beds and a wood-burning iron stove. As in other lodges, meals are a communal affair in the cozy living and restaurant area, and the food is good. You can rent horses or hike to the Tarahumara caves and to the rim of the canyon, where a more expensive sister hotel, the Hotel Mirador (see above), has a beautiful restaurant and bar with a magnificent view. This hotel sometimes accommodates overbooking at its sister hotel.

El Divisadero. www.mexicoscoppercanyon.com/rancho. © **635/578-3020.** (Reservations: Hotel Santa Anita, Apdo. Postal 159, 81200 Los Mochis, Sin.; © 800/896-8196 in the U.S.) Fax 668/812-0046. 25 units. 2,572 pesos double. Rates include meals. AE, MC, V. **Amenities:** Restaurant; bar; transportation to and from train station. *In room:* Hair dryer, no phone.

Mansion Tarahumara ★   The Mansion Tarahumara spreads across a mountainside above the train stop at Posada Barrancas. The cabin rooms offer more privacy and space than the hotel rooms, but not direct views of the canyon. Made of stone and wood, each room has a big fireplace, a wall heater, and two double beds. The castle-like structure, which is the first thing that catches the guest's eye, houses the restaurant and bar. It offers views from its big windows and good food from its kitchen.

El Divisadero. www.hotelmansiontarahumara.com.mx. © **635/578-3030.** (Reservations: Mansion Tarahumara, Calle Juárez 1602-A, Col. Centro, 31000 Chihuahua, Chih.; © 614/415-4721; fax 614/416-5444.) 60 units. $165 double. Rates include meals. MC, V. **Amenities:** Restaurant; bar; Jacuzzi; heated outdoor pool; spa; transportation to and from train station; tours. *In room:* No phone.

Stop 5: Creel ★

This rustic logging town with a handful of paved streets offers the most economical lodgings in the canyon. Creel (rhymes with "feel") is also the starting point for some of the best side trips of the region. Creel sits at an elevation of 2,210m (7,249 ft.); its population of around 6,000 makes it the largest town in the canyon area.

ESSENTIALS

GETTING THERE & DEPARTING   By Train   See the chart on p. 662 for "official" arrival and departure times.

By Car   From Chihuahua, follow the signs to La Junta until you see signs for Hermosillo. Follow those signs until you see signs to Creel (left). The trip takes about 4 hours on a paved road.

By Bus   Estrella Blanca (© **614/429-0219** in Chihuahua) has five trips to Chihuahua per day. The trip takes 4 hours and costs 277 pesos. This is cheaper and faster than the train but less secure. In the past, the bus has been stopped.

ORIENTATION   The train station, around the corner from the Mission Store and the main plaza, is in the heart of the village and within walking distance of all lodgings except the Copper Canyon Sierra Lodge. Look for your hotel's van waiting at the station (unless you're staying at the Casa de Huéspedes Margarita, which is only 2 blocks away). There's one main street, **López Mateos,** and almost everything is within a couple of blocks.

[Fast FACTS] CREEL

The **area code** is 635. Electricity is available 24 hours daily in all Creel hotels. (In other parts of the canyon, electricity is sporadic or not available.) Creel has one ATM, one bank, and one *casa de cambio*. The best sources of information are the Mission Store and the hotels. Several businesses and many of the hotels offer long-distance **telephone** service; look for LARGA DISTANCIA signs or ask at your hotel.

EXPLORING CREEL

You'll occasionally see the Tarahumara as you walk around town, but mostly, you'll see rugged logging types and tourists from around the world.

Several stores around Creel sell Tarahumara arts and crafts. The best is **Artesanías Misión (Mission Crafts)**, which sells quality merchandise at reasonable prices; all profits go to the Mission Hospital run by Father Verplancken, a Jesuit, and benefit the Tarahumara. Here you'll find dolls, pottery, woven purses and belts, drums, violins (an instrument borrowed from the Spanish), bamboo flutes, bead necklaces, bows and arrows, cassettes of Tarahumara music, woodcarvings, baskets, and heavy wool rugs, as well as an excellent supply of books and maps relating to the Tarahumara and the region. It's open daily from 10am to 1pm, and Monday through Saturday from 3 to 6pm. It's beside the railroad tracks on the main plaza.

WHERE TO STAY & EAT

Though a small town, Creel has several places to stay, all with free parking. A lot of the hotels cater to backpackers. It's advisable to make reservations during high season.

For meals, there are several places to eat in Creel, but no standouts. Aside from the restaurants at the hotels, you might want to try one of the establishments on López Mateos, such as the **Caballo Bayo, Tío Molcas,** or **Verónica's.**

Expensive

Copper Canyon Sierra Lodge ★★ 🛏 About 20 minutes (22km/14 miles) southwest of Creel, the Sierra Lodge has everything you hope for in a mountain lodge—rock walls, beamed ceilings, lantern lights, and wood-burning stoves; in other words, rustic charm and no electricity. Its out-of-town location is a great starting point for self-guided hikes and walks in the mountains to the Cusárare Waterfalls. This hotel has a sister lodge in Batopilas, which is beautiful and runs a little cheaper per room.

Apdo. Postal 3, 33200 Creel, Chih. www.coppercanyonlodges.com. ℂ **800/648-8488** in the U.S. 22 units. $145 double. Rates include meals. MC, V for deposits. *In room:* No phone.

The Lodge at Creel Each of this Best Western hotel's cheerfully decorated cabins holds four units, built completely of pine, including the furniture. Most have two double beds, and some have their own porches. Their construction, decor, and layout remind me of old-style motels that you find next to U.S. national parks. The lobby, next to the dining area, has a phone for guests' use and a small gift shop. The hotel offers 3-night backpacking trips to the bottom of the canyon, among other tours, for 4 to 10 people. The on-site restaurant serves all three meals. The van meets all trains.

Av. López Mateos 61, 33200 Creel, Chih. www.thelodgeatcreel.com. ℂ **877/844-0409** in the U.S., or 635/456-0071. Fax 635/456-0082. 38 units. 1,350 pesos double. AE, MC, V. **Amenities:** 2 restaurants; bar; fitness room; Jacuzzi; room service; sauna; smoke-free rooms; Wi-Fi (in half the hotel). *In room:* TV, hair dryer, no phone.

Moderate

Hotel Parador de la Montaña This is the largest hotel in town, located 4 blocks west of the plaza. The comfortable rooms have two double beds, high wood-beamed ceilings, central heating, tiled bathrooms, and thin walls. Guests congregate in the restaurant, bar, and lobby, which has a roaring fireplace. The hotel caters to groups and offers some 10 overland tours, priced from 300 to 800 pesos.

Av. López Mateos s/n, 33200 Creel, Chih. www.hotelparadorcreel.com. ℂ **635/456-0023.** Fax 635/456-0085. (Reservations: Calle Allende 1414, 31300 Chihuahua, Chih.; ℂ 614/415-5408.) 50 units. 834 pesos double. AE, MC, V. **Amenities:** Restaurant; bar; tours. *In room:* TV, no phone.

Inexpensive

Hotel Nuevo   The Nuevo has two sections: the older one, across the tracks from the train station and next to the restaurant and variety store, and newer log cabañas in back. Rooms are small to midsize and not as attractive as the higher-priced (and carpeted) cabañas. Half the rooms have TVs. The nice hotel restaurant is open from 8:30am to 8pm, and the small general store carries local crafts as well as basic supplies. Ask at the store about rooms.

Francisco Villa 121, 33200 Creel, Chih. © **635/456-0022.** Fax 635/456-0043. 27 units. 420–650 pesos double. MC, V. **Amenities:** Restaurant; general store. *In room:* TV (in some), no phone.

NEARBY EXCURSIONS

Close by are several canyons, waterfalls, a lake, hot springs, Tarahumara villages and cave dwellings, and an old Jesuit mission. Ten kilometers (6¼ miles) north of town is an ecotourism complex, **San Ignacio de Arareko** (© **635/456-0126**). It has a lake, hiking and biking trails, horses, cabins, and a crafts shop, all run by indigenous peoples of the *ejido* (cooperative). **Batopilas,** an 18th-century silver-mining town at the bottom of the canyon, requires an overnight excursion. You can ask for information about these and other things to do at your hotel, or go by the office of the **3 Amigos** (© **635/456-0179;** www.amigos3.com), at Av. López Mateos 46 in downtown Creel. These guys rent pickups with crew cabs or mountain bikes and can give you maps and advice on where to go, depending on your interests.

From Creel, you can drive to **El Divisadero** (see "Stops 3 & 4: Barrancas/El Divisadero," above, for details) on a recently paved road. The trip takes about an hour.

ORGANIZED TOURS   Hotels offer 2- to 10-hour organized tours that cost between 300 and 900 pesos per person (four-person minimum). All tour availability depends on whether a group can be assembled; your best chance is at the **Hotel Parador de la Montaña.**

Basaseáchic Falls

This is an exhausting day tour to what is billed as the tallest single cascade in North America. The best time to go is during the rainy season, from July to September. The tour costs around 750 pesos per person and takes about 11 hours. Driving time is 4 hours one-way, and the strenuous hike to the bottom and back up takes 3 hours—not a lot of time to be by the falls. Another option is to stay in one of the simple accommodations that have opened near the falls, if you can get transportation back the next day. Ask around Creel.

Batopilas

You can make an overnight side trip from Creel to the old silver-mining town of Batopilas, founded in 1708. It's 7 to 9 hours from Creel by town bus, 5 hours by sport utility vehicle, along a narrow, winding dirt road through some of the most spectacular scenery in the Copper Canyon. In Batopilas, which lies beside a river at the bottom of a deep canyon, the weather is tropical, though it can get cool in the evenings. You can visit a beautiful little church and do several walks, including one to **Misión Satevó,** a ruined mission church that dates from the early 18th century. The place has many colorful little details: The dry-goods store is a veritable time capsule, cobblestone streets twist past whitewashed homes, miners and ranchers come and go on horseback, and the Tarahumara frequently visit. A considerable number of pigs, dogs, and herds of goats roam at will—this is, after all, Chihuahua's goat-raising capital.

GETTING THERE From Creel, take the **bus** from the Restaurant Herradero, López Mateos s/n, three doors past the turnoff to Hotel Plaza Mexicana. It goes to Batopilas on Tuesday, Thursday, and Saturday, leaving Creel at 7am and arriving midafternoon. Tickets are sold at the restaurant. Several Suburban-type **vans** offer transportation. One leaves on Monday, Wednesday, and Friday at 10:30am and arrives midafternoon. Both bus and van return the following day. There are no bathrooms, restaurants, or other conveniences of civilization along the way, but the bus may stop to allow passengers to stretch and find a bush.

WHERE TO STAY & EAT Batopilas has a few little restaurants and inns. There are no telephones, though, so don't expect to make reservations. One night probably isn't enough for a stay here, since you arrive midafternoon and must leave at 7am or 10:30am the next day. The staff at the Hotel Parador de la Montaña (see above) in Creel provides information about vacancies at the basic, comfortable, 10-room **Hotel Mary** (formerly Parador Batopilas). All rooms have private bathrooms and cost around 250 pesos per night. There are also the rustic **Hotel Batopilas** and **Hotel Las Palmeras,** with five or six rooms each; if all else fails, you can probably find a family willing to let you stay in an extra room.

Restaurants in Batopilas are informal about their schedules, so bring along some snacks and bottled water to tide you over; snacks are available at the general store. The place to eat in Batopilas is **Doña Mica's,** facing a little plaza tucked behind the main square. Ask anyone for directions (everyone knows her). She serves meals on her front porch surrounded by plants, but it's best to let her know in advance when to expect you. On short notice, she can probably rustle up some scrambled eggs.

LOS MOCHIS: THE WESTERN TERMINUS

202km (125 miles) SW of Alamos; 80km (50 miles) SW of El Fuerte; 309km (192 miles) SE of Guaymas; 416km (258 miles) NW of Mazatlán

Los Mochis, in Sinaloa State, is a coastal city of 350,000 founded in 1893 by Benjamin Johnson of Pennsylvania. It is a prosperous city in a fertile agricultural area but holds little of interest for the visitor. The most important aspects of the city are that it is a boarding point for the train, it has an airport, and it is connected to La Paz, Baja California, by ferry, and to the U.S. border by highway.

Essentials

GETTING THERE & DEPARTING **By Plane** Aeroméxico/Aerolitoral (© 800/ 237-6639 in the U.S., or 668/815-2570 for reservations) has direct service from Phoenix, Chihuahua, Hermosillo, Mazatlán, and La Paz. The airport is 21km (13 miles) north of town; transportation is by *combi* (collective minivan) or airport taxi (125 pesos).

By Train The first-class **Chihuahua al Pacífico (Copper Canyon train)** runs between Los Mochis and Chihuahua once daily, departing at 6am.

By Car Coastal Hwy. 15 is well maintained in both directions leading into Los Mochis.

By Ferry A ferry plies the waters between La Paz and Topolobampo, the port for Los Mochis carrying passengers, vehicles, and cargo. The company, **Baja Ferries**

(© **668/817-3752,** -3864; www.bajaferries.com), uses a large and dependable ship; disruption of ferry service is uncommon.

By Bus   Buses serve Los Mochis, however marginally. Most are *de paso*—passing through. All bus stations are downtown, within walking distance of the hotels. The **first-class station** is near Juárez at Degollado 200. From here, Elite buses go to and from Tijuana, Monterrey, Nogales, and Ciudad Juárez. Auto-transportes Transpacíficos, in the same station, serves Nogales, Tijuana, Mazatlán, Guadalajara, Querétaro, and Mexico City. A lot of travelers who arrive in Los Mochis prefer to go directly to El Fuerte, spend the night there, and then catch the train. There are two places to catch the bus to El Fuerte (1½–2 hr.). The first is at the **Mercado Independencia;** the bus stops at the corner of Independencia and Degollado. The other is at the **corner of Cuauhtémoc and Prieto,** near the Hotel América. Ask hotel desk clerks or the tourism office for a schedule. These are second-class buses, which stop frequently, prolonging the trip well beyond the normal 1-hour travel time.

CITY LAYOUT   Los Mochis contains no central plaza, and streets run northwest to southeast and southwest to northeast.

[FastFACTS] LOS MOCHIS

The telephone **area code** for Los Mochis is **668.** Changing money outside of Los Mochis is difficult, so stock up on pesos before boarding the train. Most places in the canyons do not accept credit cards.

Exploring Los Mochis

For most travelers, Los Mochis is a stopover en route to somewhere else. There isn't much here, but the town is pleasant, and you can enjoy some excellent seafood. The **Viajes Flamingo** travel agency, on the ground floor of the Hotel Santa Anita (© **668/812-1613,** -1929), arranges a city tour, hunting and fishing trips, and a harbor tour around **Topolobampo Bay.** The harbor tour is fun. The agency is open Monday through Saturday from 8:30am to 1pm and 3 to 6:30pm. The boat ride is really just a spin in the bay and not especially noteworthy, although the bay is pretty and dolphins often show up.

Where to Stay

Hotel Corintios   Behind a campy entrance with Greek columns and mirrored glass are two stories of rooms with ample light, carpeted floors, and adequate space for two comfortable double beds and luggage. The bathrooms are midsize and are neatly finished, but with poor lighting. The junior suites come with a king-size bed.

Obregón 580 Poniente, 81200 Los Mochis, Sin. www.hotelcorintios.com. © **01-800/690-3000** in Mexico, or 668/818-2300. Fax 668/818-2277. 59 units. 587 pesos double; 720 pesos junior suite. Rates include continental breakfast. AE, MC, V. Free parking. **Amenities:** Restaurant; Jacuzzi; room service; smoke-free rooms. *In room:* A/C, TV, Wi-Fi.

Hotel Las Fuentes   Among the inexpensive hotels in town, I like this one the best. The rooms are cheerful and clean, and the staff is helpful. Rooms come with one or two double beds, and the cost varies accordingly. Bathrooms are midsize with okay elbowroom and counter space. The hotel is 5 minutes from downtown on one of the main arteries.

Blvd. Adolfo López Mateos 1251-A Norte, 81220 Los Mochis, Sin. www.hotellasfuentes.com. ☎ **668/818-8871**, -8172. Fax 668/818-8871. 50 units. 490–550 pesos double. AE, MC, V. Free secure parking. **Amenities:** Restaurant; bar; room service. *In room:* A/C, TV, Wi-Fi.

Hotel Santa Anita   The Santa Anita is the choice of most travelers going to the canyon; not only is it a comfortable, quiet hotel, but it offers reliable transportation to and from the train station. The rooms are modern and well furnished but vary a good deal in size. All are carpeted and most come with two double beds. They also come with good air-conditioning, lots of English-speaking channels on the TV, and tap water purified for drinking. There are two bars, one with live music at least 1 day a week.

Leyva, at the corner of Hidalgo (Apdo. Postal 159), 81200 Los Mochis, Sin. www.santaanitahotel.com. ☎ **800/896-8196** in the U.S., or 668/818-7046. Fax 668/812-0046. 116 units. 1,337 pesos double. AE, MC, V. Free parking. **Amenities:** Restaurant; bar; transportation to and from the train station; room service; smoke-free rooms. *In room:* A/C, TV, hair dryer, Wi-Fi.

Where to Eat

El Farallón ★★ SEAFOOD   If you like seafood, there's no reason to eat anywhere else in Los Mochis. You can order seafood cooked any way you want. Try a Mexican style such as *al ajillo*, with toasted *guajillo* chiles. If you're hungry, I recommend the *mariscada* for two or more, which comes with a cold and a hot platter of a variety of fish and shellfish. Try *calamares* (squid), the cheapest thing on the platter. Forget about those rubbery rings fried up in other restaurants; because the squid get to be giant-size in this region's waters, the meat comes in big, tender chunks. One of my favorites is *machaca*, made with either shrimp or smoked marlin (cooked in a reduced fish stock, which is mild and satisfying). The atmosphere is casual, the air-conditioning functions with gusto, and the white-tiled dining area is simply furnished.

Obregón, at Angel Flores. ☎ **668/812-1428.** Main courses 160–380 pesos. AE, MC, V. Daily 8am–11pm.

El Taquito 🍴 MEXICAN   Any time of the day or night, El Taquito serves standard Mexican fare at a good price. With orange booths and Formica tables, the cafe looks like an American fast-food place. Tortilla soup comes in a large bowl, and both breakfast and main-course portions are quite generous.

Leyva at Barrera. ☎ **668/812-8119.** Breakfast 44–72 pesos; main courses 60–85 pesos. AE, DC, MC, V. Daily 24 hr. From the Hotel Santa Anita, turn left on Leyva, cross Hidalgo, and go 1 block; it's on your right.

Restaurante España STEAK/SEAFOOD   This Spanish-style restaurant is a favorite among downtown professionals, who feast on large plates of paella (available Thurs and Sun after 1pm; at other times, it's made to order, which takes 45 min.). The decor is upscale for Los Mochis, with a splashing fountain in the dining room and heavy, carved-wood tables and chairs.

Obregón 525 ☎ **668/812-2221.** Breakfast 60–70 pesos; main courses 90–130 pesos. AE, MC, V. Mon–Sat 7:30am–11pm; Sun 9am–7pm.

CHIHUAHUA: THE EASTERN TERMINUS ★

341km (211 miles) S of El Paso; 440km (273 miles) NW of Torreón

Chihuahua, a city of wide boulevards and handsome buildings, is the capital of the state of Chihuahua, the largest and richest in Mexico. The wealth comes from mining, timber, cattle raising, *maquiladoras* (assembly plants for export goods), and tourism. The city has grown a lot in the last 30 years, thanks mainly to an increase in manufacturing plants, and has lost its frontier feeling. But the historic center of Chihuahua retains much of its character and holds a few museums and buildings worth visiting, including the house where Pancho Villa once lived.

Essentials

GETTING THERE & DEPARTING **By Plane** **Continental** (© 800/523-3273 in the U.S., or 01-800/900-5000 in Mexico) has nonstop service to and from Houston on a 50-seat jet. **Aeroméxico/Aerolitoral** (© 800/237-6639 in the U.S., or 614/415-6303) flies direct from El Paso, Phoenix, Guadalajara, Hermosillo, Mexico City, Monterrey, Torreón, Tijuana, Culiacán, La Paz, and Los Mochis, with connecting flights from Los Angeles and San Antonio. **American Airlines** (© 800/433-7300 in the U.S. or 01-800/904-6000 in Mexico) has nonstop service to/from Dallas.

Transportes Terrestre (© 614/420-3366) controls minivan service from the airport and charges 78 to 95 pesos per person. Taxis from town charge 170 pesos for up to four people.

By Train The **Chihuahua al Pacífico** (© 614/439-7212; fax 614/439-7208) leaves Chihuahua daily for Los Mochis by way of the Copper Canyon country. The complete train schedule and the train route appear in "The Copper Canyon Train & Stops Along the Way," earlier in this chapter. In that section, you'll find information on purchasing tickets. It's easier to go through a travel agency than to deal directly with the company. The train is scheduled to leave at 6am daily. To get to the station in time, it's best to arrange transportation through one of the travel agencies recommended under "Fast Facts," below. They pick up clients taking the train each morning.

By Car **Hwy. 45** leads south from Ciudad Juárez, **Hwy. 16** south from Ojinaga, and **Hwy. 49** north from Torreón. For the drive to Creel, see "Getting There & Departing" under "Stop 5: Creel," earlier in this chapter.

By Bus The **Terminal de Autobuses (bus station)** is on Avenida Juan Pablo II, 8km (5 miles) northeast of town en route to the airport. Buses leave hourly for major points inland and north and south on the coast. Transportes Chihuahuenses, the big local line, offers first-class service to Ciudad Juárez every half-hour; the trip takes 4 hours. Transportes del Norte and Autobuses Estrella Blanca also run buses hourly from the border through Chihuahua to points south. Omnibus de México has *servicio ejecutivo* (deluxe service) from Juárez, Mexico City, and Monterrey. Futura/Turistar also has deluxe service to Monterrey and Durango.

For travel to Creel, look for the Estrella Blanca line. Buses leave every 2 hours from 6am to 6pm. Direct buses make the trip in 4 hours.

VISITOR INFORMATION For basic info, visit the **Tourist Information Center** (© 614/410-1077 or 614/429-3596), Calle Aldama at Carranza in the Government Palace, just left of the altar and murals dedicated to Father Hidalgo. It's open Monday through Friday from 10am to 5pm and Saturday from 10am to 3pm.

CITY LAYOUT The town center is laid out around the **Plaza Principal,** bounded by avenidas Libertad and Victoria (which run northeast-southwest) and Avenida Independencia and Calle 4 (which run northwest-southeast). The **cathedral** is at the southwest end of the plaza, and the city offices are on the northeast end. If you're

Chihuahua

0 330 feet
0 100 meters

Bus

J.D. Palomino

Escudero
To Ciudad Juárez
Holiday Inn
Hotel & Suites
Restaurante
Todo de Maíz

J.E. Múñoz

G. Conde

De Marzo
Reforma
Progreso
Revolución

Calle 10
Bus

Julian Carrillo

Calle 6
Calle 4
Calle 2
Calle 3

Hotel Parador
Chihuahua

Niños Héroes

Av. Universidad

Posada Tierra
Blanca
Trias

Av. Ocampo

Av. Independencia

Doblado

Juárez

Libertad

Calle 7
Calle 9
Calle 13

Calle 5

Hidalgo's
Dungeon

Quality Inn
Chihuahua
San Francisco

Catedral
Plaza Principal

Victoria

Palacio del
Gobierno

Aldama

Escorza

Guerrero

Av. V. Carranza

Calle 10

Morelos

Allende

G. Farias

Coronado

Lallave

Centro Cultural
Quinta Gameros

Calle 7

Parque
Lerdo

Paseo Bolívar

Irigoyen

To Chihuahua al
Pacifico Railway

To Museo de la Revolución

Mina

UNITED STATES

Chihuahua

MEXICO

Mexico
City

0 500 mi
0 500 km

standing on Independencia with the cathedral on your left, odd-numbered streets and blocks will be to your right, and even-numbered streets and blocks to your left.

GETTING AROUND   Local buses run along main arteries beginning at the central plaza. Taxis are readily available. If you want to see the sights and have only 1 day, take a tour (see "Exploring Chihuahua," below).

[Fast FACTS] CHIHUAHUA

The telephone area code is **614.** If you have waited to purchase train tickets and make canyon hotel reservations, contact **Turismo al Mar,** Calle Berna 2202, Colonia Mirador, 31270 Chihuahua, Chih. (✆ **614/410-9232** or 614/416-5950; fax 614/416-6589). **Clínica del Parque** is at Pedro Leal del Rosal and de la Llave (✆ **614/415-7411**). For medical emergencies, call ✆ **614/411-8141.**

Exploring Chihuahua

To see Chihuahua's sights in 1 day, consider taking a 3-hour city tour; English-speaking guides are available. Three recommended agencies are **Torre del Sol,** Independencia 116-2 (✆ **614/415-7380**), in the Hotel Palacio del Sol; **Turismo al Mar** (see "Fast Facts," above); and **Viajes Rojo y Casavantes** in the Quality Inn Chihuahua San Francisco (see below) and at Vicente Guerrero 1207 (✆ **614/415-4636;** fax 614/415-5384). Any of these will pick you up at your hotel. A half-day city tour includes visits to the museums, the churches, the colonial aqueduct, the state capitol building, the state penitentiary, and more. A 7-hour trip to the Mennonite village near Cuauhtémoc costs about 350 pesos per person, with a minimum of four people. Unless you have a particular interest in cheese making or the Mennonites, it's not worth your time.

SIGHTS IN TOWN

Hidalgo's Dungeon   Father Miguel Hidalgo y Costilla was a priest in Dolores, Guanajuato, when he started the War of Independence on September 16, 1810. Six months later, he was captured by the Spanish, brought to Chihuahua, and thrown in a dungeon for 98 days. He was then shot along with his lieutenants, Allende, Aldama, and Jiménez. The four were beheaded, and their heads hung in iron cages for 9½ years on the four corners of the Alhóndiga granary in Guanajuato (see chapter 6) as examples of the fate revolutionaries would meet. In this cell, Hidalgo lived on bread and water before his execution. The night before his death, he wrote a few words on the wall with a piece of charcoal to thank his guard and the warden for the good treatment they gave him. A bronze plaque commemorates his final message.

In the Palacio Federal, Av. Juárez at Guerrero. No phone. Admission 12 pesos. Tues–Sun 10am–6pm. From Plaza Principal, walk on pedestrian-only Calle Libertad for 3 long blocks to Guerrero, turn left,

Staying Safe

Though not as much in the headlines as its neighboring city, Ciudad Juárez, the city of Chihuahua has become increasingly violent. Tourists are not being targeted, but several bystanders (locals) have been wounded or killed in attacks on police and government officials. Also, carjacking is on the rise. You can reduce your risk by not driving a rental car in the city and staying indoors at night.

and walk to corner of Juárez; turn right and go a half-block; museum entrance is on the right, below the post office.

Museo de la Revolución ★★ 🏛 The Revolution Museum is Pancho Villa's house, where Luz Corral de Villa, Pancho Villa's widow, lived until her death in 1981. Exhibits include Villa's weapons, some personal effects, lots of period photos, and the 1922 Dodge in which he was shot in 1923 (you'll see the bullet holes). It's best to see the place with a guide who can add lots of biographical details about this larger-than-life character. Ask about Villa's opinions on marriage and about the total number of his offspring and grandchildren.

Calle 10 no. 3014 (at Méndez). ✆ **614/416-2958.** Admission 30 pesos. Tues–Sat 9am–1pm and 3–7pm. Bus: Colonia Dale (runs west on Juárez, then south on Ocampo); exit at corner of Ocampo and Méndez.

Palacio del Gobierno The Palacio del Gobierno is a magnificent, ornate structure dating in part from 1890; the original building, the Jesuit College, was built in 1718. A colorful, expressive mural encompasses the first floor of the large central courtyard and tells the history of the area around Chihuahua from the time of the first European visitation through the Revolution. In the far-right corner, note the scene depicting Benito Juárez flanked by Abraham Lincoln and Simón Bolívar, liberator of South America. In the far-left rear courtyard are a plaque and altar commemorating the execution in 1811 of Miguel Hidalgo, the father of Mexican independence; the plaque marks the spot where the hero was executed in the old building, and the mural portrays the scene.

Av. Aldama (btw. Guerrero and Carranza). ✆ **614/410-6324.** Free admission. Daily 8am–10pm. With the cathedral on your right, walk along Independencia 1 block, turn left on Aldama, continue 2 long blocks, and cross Guerrero; entrance is on the left.

Quinta Gameros ★★ Quinta Gameros is a neoclassical, French Second Empire–style mansion with a beautiful Art Nouveau interior. Built in 1910 for Manuel Gameros, the mansion became a museum in 1961. Pancho Villa used it briefly as a headquarters. The interior walls, floors, and ceilings are lavishly decorated, which inspired the transfer of a beautiful collection of fine Mexican Art Nouveau furnishings from Mexico City to this museum. If you like design and beautiful antiques, especially Art Nouveau, don't miss this place.

Quinta Gameros, Paseo Bolívar 401. ✆ **614/416-6684.** Admission 20 pesos. Tues–Sun 11am–2pm and 4–7pm. Heading away from the Plaza Principal with the cathedral on your right, walk 7 blocks on Independencia to Bolívar, turn right, and walk 1 block; museum is on the right.

Where to Stay

EXPENSIVE

Holiday Inn Hotel and Suites ★ This Holiday Inn offers the most comfortable rooms in the downtown area. All units are suites, with kitchenettes that include stove, refrigerator, and coffeemaker. There's a sitting area, a large writing table, and a choice of one king-size bed or two doubles. Guests have the use of a video library. The hotel staff is helpful and efficient. They can provide a continental breakfast for people heading off on the train, as well as a box lunch. The hotel is a 5-minute walk from downtown.

Calle Escudero 702 (btw. Av. Universidad and Av. de Montes), 31240 Chihuahua, Chih. www.holidayinn. com. ✆ **800/465-4329** in the U.S., or 614/439-0000. Fax 614/414-3313. 74 units. $125 double. Rates include breakfast buffet. AE, MC, V. Free secure parking. **Amenities:** Restaurant; bar; babysitting; fitness room; Jacuzzi; 2 pools (1 indoor); room service; smoke-free rooms; steam room. *In room:* A/C, TV, fridge, hair dryer, Internet, kitchenette.

Quality Inn Chihuahua San Francisco The good location and comfortable midsize rooms are the main attractions here. Don't bother about getting a view; ask for something quiet. Rooms are well furnished. The bathrooms are well equipped and have ample counter space. Bed choices include two doubles, a queen, or a king. Mattresses are firm.

Victoria 409, 31000 Chihuahua, Chih. www.qualityinnchihuahua.com. ℰ**800/847-2546** in the U.S., or 614/439-9000. Fax 614/415-3538. 131 units. 1,140–1,450 pesos double. AE, MC, V. Free covered parking and continental breakfast. From the cathedral, walk to Victoria and turn right; the hotel is 1½ blocks down on your right, before Av. Ocampo. **Amenities:** Restaurant (see review for Degá, below); bar; fitness room; room service; travel agency. *In room:* A/C, TV, hair dryer, Wi-Fi.

MODERATE

Hotel Posada Tierra Blanca This downtown hotel has an attractive large pool area shaded by trees. Rooms are in two- and three-story buildings. They are large and quiet (none have windows facing the street). Bathrooms are midsize with good counter space and better lighting than in most of the hotels in Chihuahua.

Niños Héroes 102, 31000 Chihuahua, Chih. www.posadatierrablanca.com.mx. ℰ **614/415-0000.** 94 units. 720 pesos double. AE, MC, V. Free secure parking. **Amenities:** Restaurant; bar; fitness room; large outdoor pool; room service. *In room:* A/C, TV, Wi-Fi.

INEXPENSIVE

Hotel Parador Chihuahua I like this motel for the price, the downtown location, and the well-maintained rooms. It occupies the interior of a small city block, with the rooms built around the pool and the garden area. The midsize rooms are carpeted and furnished rather plainly. You'll have a choice of one king-size bed or two doubles. Bathrooms are midsize.

Calle 3, no. 304 (btw. Julián Carrillo and Niños Héroes), 31000 Chihuahua, Chih. www.paradorchihuahua. com. ℰ**614/415-0827.** 34 units. 600 pesos double. AE, MC, V. Free secure parking. **Amenities:** Restaurant; bar; small outdoor pool; room service. *In room:* A/C, TV.

Where to Eat

As a large city, Chihuahua has plenty of international restaurants, but I recommend sticking with steakhouses and Mexican cuisine.

Degá MEXICAN/INTERNATIONAL This restaurant bar at the Quality Inn Chihuahua San Francisco (see above) draws both downtown workers and travelers. The breakfast buffet features made-to-order omelets. The steaks and Mexican dishes are well priced; try the *plato mexicano,* a popular dish that comes with a tamal, chiles rellenos, beans, chips, and guacamole. The tortilla soup is another popular favorite here.

In the Quality Inn Chihuahua San Francisco, Calle Victoria 409. ℰ **614/416-7550.** Breakfast 52–99 pesos; breakfast buffet 90 pesos; main courses 85–230 pesos; Sun buffet 190 pesos. AE, MC, V. Daily 7am–11pm.

La Calesa STEAKS/MEXICAN This restaurant is one of the old-style Mexican steakhouses. Not much has changed here—the dining room is open and large, furnished with heavy, solid-wood chairs and tables. Wood paneling covers the walls, and the menus are bound in leather. Most of the steaks are from local ranches. They aren't as tender has most American cuts, but they are a bargain. A pianist entertains diners from 2:30 to 5pm.

Av. Colón 3300, corner of Av. Juárez. ℰ**614/410-1038.** www.lacalesa.com.mx. Steaks 140–280 pesos; Mexican dishes 90–149 pesos. AE, MC, V. Daily 12:30–10pm.

Restaurante Todo de Maíz ★ 🎁 MEXICAN   To eat cheaply and well in Chihuahua is a bit of a trick—unless you dine at this place. When I'm in Chihuahua, I never miss it. Sra. María Matilde Salazar, the owner, is an unabashed leftist, perhaps the only one in Chihuahua. On occasion I've seen her in the plaza getting signatures for petitions. She's also a great cook and maintains quality and freshness by keeping the menu simple. Between 1 and 2:30pm she offers a *comida corrida* that's a bargain. The rest of the time she makes tacos, quesadillas, tostadas, and *peneques* (a local form of *antojito* that's like a *gordita*) all made with corn *masa,* as the restaurant's name suggests. This place is down the street from the Holiday Inn.

Calle Escudero 2103 (btw. calles 21 and 23). ℂ **614/414-5778.** *Comida corrida* 50 pesos; *antojitos* 30-40 pesos. No credit cards. Mon-Fri 9am-5pm; Sat 11am-5pm.

Rincón Mexicano ★ MEXICAN   The Rincón serves great Mexican food and offers a substantial number of choices. Good appetizers include *quesadillas de huitlacoche* (corn empanadas with cheese and corn fungus) for the adventurous, and *chile con asadero* (melted spicy cheese). For a main dish that gives you a little of everything, try *enchiladas tres moles*. As you would expect of a restaurant in Chihuahua, the emphasis is on beef, prepared in very Mexican ways such as *puntas en chile pasado* (beef tips cooked in a dried chile sauce) or *molcajete de res* (fajitas cooked and served in a steaming stone vessel accompanied by tortillas). The interior is easy on the eyes, with muted tones of yellow and orange, good lighting, and tablecloths. A guitar trio occasionally performs soft music in the evenings. The restaurant is a short taxi ride from downtown.

Av. Cuauhtémoc 2224. ℂ **614/411-1510,** -1427. Main courses 80-200 pesos. AE, MC, V. Daily noon-9:30pm.

Chihuahua After Dark

The nightlife in Chihuahua has seen better times. The killings and carjackings have dampened the locals' appetite for nightlife. If your hotel has live music, you're best off staying put. At the **Quality Inn Chihuahua San Francisco,** there's live music Monday through Saturday, with happy hour from 5 to 8pm. The lobby bar at the **Hotel Palacio del Sol** schedules live entertainment occasionally.

LOS CABOS & BAJA CALIFORNIA

by Joy Hepp

Long before crowds of bikini-clad babes lined the beaches of Los Cabos and adventurous fisherman sought trophies from beyond its shores, Baja California captured the imaginations of adventurous travelers. After conquering mainland Mexico in the 1500s, Spanish conquistador Hernan Cortez was looking for a nice retirement destination. Tales of a paradise called Calafia—which was widely believed to be inhabited solely by wild "Amazon" women—reached Cortez, and so he set out for Baja California to find it. Upon his arrival, Cortez was run off by fierce locals; among them—surprise, surprise—were male warriors. Cortez fled, but others were drawn to this land of azure waters, dramatic landscapes, and diverse wildlife.

Attached mostly to the United States and separated from all but a sliver of Mexico by the Sea of Cortez (Gulf of California), the peninsula consists of one long granite ridge extending about 1,500km (930 miles)—longer than Italy—from Mexico's northernmost city of **Tijuana** to **Cabo San Lucas** at its southern tip. Baja is part Wild West, part country club, part seafaring paradise, part adventure wonderland, and there's room enough for all of its visitors to blaze their own trails. For more detailed coverage of this region, consult *Frommer's Los Cabos & Baja* (Wiley Publishing, Inc.).

Exploring Baja California

The weather in this land of extremes can be sizzling hot in summer, and cold and windy in winter. Winter is often warm enough for watersports, but bring a wet suit for diving and snorkeling, as well as warmer clothes for chilly temperatures. Although Baja's climate varies greatly by season, it is predictable—an important quality for the increasing number of golfers looking for sunny skies. Rainy days are few and far between, with most showers concentrated in September.

THE TWO CABOS   Nearly two million visitors each year—and growing—are lured to Los Cabos (the Capes), the twin towns at the peninsula's southernmost tip. **Cabo San Lucas** holds court on the west, **San José del Cabo** on the east. Connected only by the **Tourist Corridor,**

The Baja Peninsula

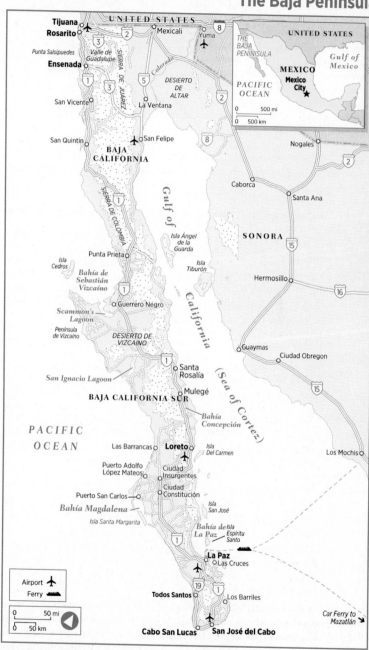

33km (20 miles) of coastline studded with golf courses, luxury resorts, and master-planned communities, the capes could not be more different.

Cabo San Lucas, also known as Land's End, is twofold. Most obviously, she's the rowdy younger sister who takes tequila shots from a holster while dancing on the table chanting, "What happens in Cabo stays in Cabo," and wraps up the night at a local American fast-food joint. The other side of San Lucas is a bling-flashing older brother who frequents swanky clubs, sips champagne in his oceanfront Jacuzzi, or cruises the bay in his luxury yacht. Somewhere in between are the fun-loving aunts and uncles who've come to fish for marlin and/or take a peep at Sammy Hagar.

On the other hand, San José del Cabo, on the eastern side of Baja's tip, is a decidedly more "Mexican" experience. Colorful 18th-century homes–turned–artisan shops, vibrant flowering trees, world-class waves, and exquisite restaurants draw well-tanned West Coast surfers; jolly snowbirds in search of sun and margaritas; celebrities and executives looking for respite from the rat race; and couples and families who wake up early to walk on the beach, go for a swim, take a tour, and spend the afternoon relaxing before enjoying a nice dinner on the town.

Todos Santos, an artistic community on the Pacific side of the coastal curve (1 hr. north of the tip), and Baja's **East Cape** both draw travelers who find that Los Cabos has outgrown them. **La Paz,** capital of Baja Sur, remains an easygoing maritime port skirted by white-sand beaches and a smattering of islands worth exploring.

MID BAJA   Among the highlights of the mid-Baja region are the east coast towns of **Loreto, Bahía Magdalena, Mulegé,** and **Santa Rosalía.** These towns have a much richer cultural heritage than those in Baja Sur. Although Loreto is experiencing growth—driven by a real estate project just outside of town—the remaining east coast towns have all but escaped the tourism boom experienced by the two Cabos.

These mid-Baja towns were the center of the 18th-century Jesuit mission movement. Today they attract travelers who are drawn to Baja's wild natural beauty but find the popularity of Los Cabos a bit overwhelming. This area's natural attractions have made it a center for sea kayaking, sportfishing, diving, and hiking—including excursions to view indigenous cave paintings.

BAJA NORTE   **Tijuana** has the dubious distinction of being the most visited and perhaps most misunderstood town in all of Mexico. Underneath the layers of grit, Tijuana is a true cultural gem with a vibrant art community and fascinating history.

Tranquil **Rosarito Beach** has suffered from the overflow of discordance from its northern neighbor, but locals are holding strong and proud, and there is still a sense of glamour from the days when movie stars made it their playground. Farther south on the Pacific Coast, the lovely port town of **Ensenada** is known for surfing and sportfishing. Tours of nearby inland vineyards (Mexico's wine country) are growing in popularity.

LOS CABOS: RESORTS, WATERSPORTS & GOLF ★★★

The two towns at the southern tip of the rugged Baja Peninsula are grouped together as Los Cabos, although they couldn't be more different. San José del Cabo and Cabo San Lucas are separated not just by 33km (20 miles), but also by distinct attitudes and ways of life. Where Cabo San Lucas mirrors a spirited version of the Los Angeles lifestyle, San José del Cabo remains a traditional, tranquil Mexican small town, although recent gentrification is turning it into the more sophisticated of the two resorts. Because each Cabos has its own character and attractions, we treat them separately; but it's common to stay in one—or in the Corridor between—and make day trips to the other.

The golden days of Los Cabos began when silver-screen greats such as Bing Crosby, John Wayne, and Ava Gardner ventured south in the 1950s. Sportfishing was the first draw, but the transfixing landscape, rich waters, and nearly flawless climate quickly gained the favor of other explorers. The only way to get to the soon-to-be "marlin capital of the world" was by boat or private airplane. As such, Los Cabos was born of exclusivity and extravagance. Fishing remains a lure today, although golf may have overtaken it as the principal attraction. By the early 1980s, the Mexican government realized Los Cabos' growth potential and invested in new highways, airport facilities, golf courses, and marine facilities. Increased air access and the opening of Transpeninsular Hwy. 1 (in 1973) paved the way for booming growth.

Today Los Cabos is not just about marlin and the links. It has become a hub for surfing, hiking, diving, whale-watching, sea kayaking, and spas. And there's always an isolated, wild beach on which to picnic, camp, or simply watch the tide come in.

The road from Cabo San Lucas to San José del Cabo is the centerpiece of resort growth. Known as the "Tourist Corridor," or simply "the Corridor," this four-lane stretch offers cliff-top vistas and an easy ride between the towns, but still has no nighttime lighting and bears too many roadside memorials to count—fair warning that cautious driving is imperative, especially at night. Deluxe resorts and renowned golf courses are here, along with dramatic beaches and coves. The view is especially outstanding in January and February, when gray whales often spout close to shore.

The Los Cabos area is more expensive than other Mexican resorts because luxury is the norm among local hotels, and real estate prices make the San Diego market seem tame. However, a new boom in all-inclusive resorts and off-season travel deals is making Los Cabos vacations more affordable.

You should consider renting a car, even if only for a day or two, because there's too much to see to spend an hour waiting at the bus stop or hundreds of dollars on expensive taxis. For those who like the freedom to explore on their own terms, a rental car is essential, not to mention economical. And to best understand Los Cabos, both capes need your attention.

San José del Cabo

180km (112 miles) SE of La Paz; 33km (20 miles) NE of Cabo San Lucas; 1,760km (1,091 miles) SE of Tijuana

San José del Cabo, with its pastel cottages and narrow streets lined with flowering trees, retains the air of a provincial Mexican town. The main square, adorned with a wrought-iron bandstand and shaded benches, faces the cathedral, which was built on the site of an early mission. San José is becoming increasingly sophisticated, with a collection of noteworthy cafes, art galleries, interesting shops, and intriguing inns adding a newly refined flavor to the downtown area. This is the best choice for those who want to enjoy the paradoxical landscape but still be aware that they're in Mexico.

ESSENTIALS
Getting There & Departing
BY PLANE Aeroméxico (© 800/237-6639 in the U.S., 01-800/021-4000 in Mexico, or 624/146-5098, -5097) flies nonstop from Los Angeles; **American Airlines**

(© 800/433-7300 in the U.S., or 624/146-5300, -5309) flies from Dallas/Ft. Worth, Los Angeles, and Chicago; **US Airways** (© 800/428-4322 in the U.S., or 624/146-5380) operates nonstop flights from Phoenix; **Alaska Airlines** (© 800/252-7522 in the U.S., or 624/146-5100, -5101) flies from Los Angeles, Portland, San Diego, Seattle, Denver, and San Francisco; **Continental** (© 800/523-3273 in the U.S., or 624/146-5080) flies nonstop from Houston; **Delta** (© 800/241-4141 in the U.S., or 624/146-5005) has flights from Atlanta, Cincinnati, and New York; **Frontier** (© 800/432-1359 in the U.S., or 624/146-5421) has nonstop service from Denver, and connecting flights through Kansas City, Los Angeles, Atlanta, Sacramento, and San José; **United Airlines** (© 800/538-2929 in the U.S., or 624/146-5433) flies nonstop from Los Angeles, Chicago, San Francisco, and Denver; and **Virgin America** (© 877/359-8474 in the U.S., or 650/762-7005) flies from San Francisco.

BY CAR   From San Diego, drive south on Hwy. 1. Night driving is inadvisable, so the drive takes about 2½ days. From La Paz, take Hwy. 1 south; the drive takes 3 to 4 hours. Or take Hwy. 1 south just past the village of San Pedro, and then take Hwy. 19 south (a less winding road) through Todos Santos to Cabo San Lucas, where you pick up Hwy. 1 east to San José del Cabo. From Cabo San Lucas, it's a half-hour drive to San José.

BY BUS   The **Terminal de Autobuses (bus station),** on Valerio Gonzalez, a block east of Hwy. 1 (© **624/143-7880**), is open daily from 5:30am to 8pm.

Orientation

ARRIVING   Los Cabos International Airport (© **624/146-5111**) serves both Cabos and the Corridor in between. San José is 13km (8 miles) from the airport, and Cabo San Lucas is a 48km (30-mile) drive. Los Cabos has experienced rapid growth in recent years, which enabled the construction and modernization of its three terminals. Be sure to request the correct terminal when you head home. Upon arriving, pass Customs and baggage claim, and turn right once you exit the sliding doors. Ask for the shuttle desk while breezing past the timeshare booths that hawk free amenities in exchange for attending their sales pitch presentation. You'll have plenty of encounters with timeshare salespeople—especially in Cabo San Lucas—so feel free to head straight for a taxi or shuttle if you want to get to the beach in a hurry. At about $10 to $17 per person, depending on the location of your hotel, shuttles are the most economic transportation option. **Josefinos** (© **624/146-5354**) is located in the airport. A private van for up to five passengers is $85 and may be able to whisk away your large group more quickly than a regular shuttle. Taxis charge about $30 to San José and upward of $70 to San Lucas.

It's helpful to have a car in Los Cabos, and car rental is very affordable when booked online in advance. However, the major car rental agencies all have counters at the airport, open during flight arrivals for last-minute booking. **Avis** (© **800/331-1212** in the U.S., or 624/146-0201) is open daily 6am to 10pm; **Budget** (© **800/527-0700** in the U.S., 624/146-5333 at the airport, or 624/143-4190 in Cabo San Lucas) is open daily 8am to 9pm; **Hertz** (© **800/654-3131** in the U.S., 624/146-1803 in San José del Cabo, or 624/105-1428 in Cabo San Lucas) is open daily 8am to 8pm; and **National** (© **800/328-4567** in the U.S., 624/146-5022 at the airport, or 624/142-2424 in San José del Cabo) is open daily 8am to 8pm.

VISITOR INFORMATION   San José's city tourist information office (©/fax **624/142-3310**, -9628) is in the old post office building on Zaragoza at Mijares. It offers maps, free local publications, and basic information about the area. It's open Monday through Friday from 8:30am to 3pm. Prior to arrival, contact the **Los**

San José del Cabo

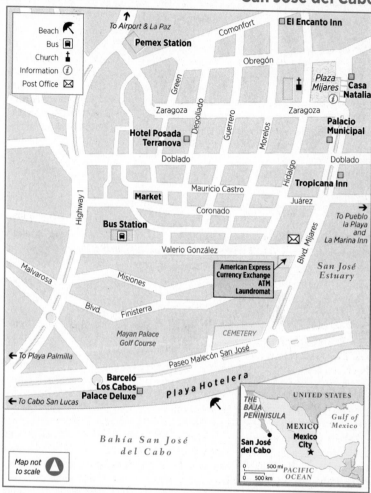

Beach ↖
Bus 🚏
Church ✝
Information ⓘ
Post Office ✉

To Airport & La Paz ↑

Comonfort

☐ El Encanto Inn

Pemex Station

Obregón

Green

Degollado

Zaragoza

Guerrero

Morelos

Plaza
Mijares ⓘ

✝

**Casa
Natalia** ☐

Zaragoza

**Hotel Posada
Terranova** ☐

**Palacio
Municipal** ☐

Doblado

Doblado

Mauricio Castro

Hidalgo

Tropicana Inn ☐

Highway 1

Market

Coronado

Juárez

→
To Pueblo
la Playa
and
La Marina Inn

Bus Station 🚏

Valerio González

✉

Blvd. Mijares

*San José
Estuary*

Malvarosa

Misiones

Blvd.

Finisterra

American Express
Currency Exchange
ATM
Laundromat

Mayan Palace
Golf Course

CEMETERY

← To Playa Palmilla

Paseo Malecón San José

**Barceló
Los Cabos
Palace Deluxe** ☐

P l a y a H o t e l e r a

← To Cabo San Lucas

☂

*Bahía San José
del Cabo*

UNITED STATES

THE
BAJA
PENINSULA

*Gulf of
Mexico*

MEXICO

San José
del Cabo

Mexico
City
★

PACIFIC
OCEAN

0 ___ 500 mi
0 ___ 500 km

Map not
to scale ▲

19

LOS CABOS & BAJA CALIFORNIA | Los Cabos: Resorts, Watersports & Golf

Cabos Tourism Board (© **866/567-2226** in the U.S., or 624/143-4777; www.
visitloscabos.travel).

CITY LAYOUT San José del Cabo sprawls from the airport halfway to San Lucas,
but two main areas are most enticing to visitors: **Downtown,** or *el centro,* has restaurants, shopping, sophisticated inns, and traditional budget hotels, while the **hotel
zone** is lined with all-inclusive resorts along the beach. **Zaragoza** is the main street
leading from the highway into town; **Paseo San José** runs parallel to the beach and
is the principal boulevard of the hotel zone. The 1.6km-long (1 mile) **Bulevar
Mijares** connects the two areas and is the center of most tourist activity in San José.

GETTING AROUND There is no local bus service between downtown and the
beach, but it's about a 30-minute walk from the center of downtown to the sand, and

taxis (📞 624/142-0580) connect the two for about $6 each way. For day trips to **Cabo San Lucas,** ask your concierge if your hotel has a daily shuttle, or just catch a **bus** (see "Getting There & Departing," above) or a cab.

[FastFACTS] SAN JOSÉ DEL CABO

Area Code The local telephone area code is **624.**

Banks Banks exchange currency during business hours, which are generally Monday through Friday from 8:30am to 6pm, and Saturday from 10am to 2pm. There are several major banks with ATMs on Zaragoza between Morelos and Degollado and in the downtown.

Consular Agency The **Canadian** office is at Plaza José Green, Local 9, Blvd. Mijares s/n (📞 **624/142-4333**), open Monday to Friday, 9:30am to 12:30pm.

Drugstores Farmacía Las Palmas, Carretera Transpeninsular Km 31, Plaza Las Palmas near the Scotiabank (📞 **624/146-9077**), is open daily from 8am to 10pm.

Emergencies Dial 📞 **066,** or the local police number at City Hall: 📞 **624/142-0361.**

Hospital Amerimed Hospital is at Plaza Cabo Ley, Paseo de las Misiones Residencial Club de Golf (📞 **624/105-8550;** www.amerimed.com.mx).

Internet Access Around here, Internet cafes have about as much shelf

life as your average reality television star. Most hotels provide some sort of Wi-Fi and/or provide a computer for guest use. Your best bet is to ask your concierge or the front desk.

Post Office The *correo,* Bulevar Mijares 1924, at Valerio Gonzalez (📞 **624/142-0911**), is open Monday through Friday from 8am to 6pm, Saturday from 9am to noon. Mail Boxes Etc., Plaza Las Palmas Km 31 (📞 **624/142-4355**), is open Monday through Friday from 8:30am to 5:30pm and Saturday from 9am to noon.

OUTDOOR ACTIVITIES: BEACHES, SPORTS & MORE

Although the water activities hub is on Cabo San Lucas's Medano Beach, San José is tops for outdoor adventure, and its relaxed pace also makes it an ideal place to unwind in the sand. From quiet coves to advanced surf breaks and untouched beaches to a living estuary, San José has relaxation and adventure by land and by sea.

ADVENTURE TOURS Tío Sports (📞 624/143-3399; www.tiosports.com) arranges a variety of land- and water-based adventure and nature tours, including popular ATV tours to La Candelaria; parasailing; and kayak, catamaran, snorkeling, and diving trips. **Baja Wild** (📞 624/172-6300; www.bajawild.com) is ideal for a wide range of adventure, as they offer every excursion imaginable in Los Cabos, from rock climbing to kayaking, hiking to jeep safaris, ATV rides, and more. **Baja Outback** (📞 624/142-9200; www.bajaoutback.com) provides single-day and multiday adventure tours throughout southern Baja. Armed with a naturalist guide and an expedition guide, who provide information and offer driving instruction over the two-way radios that connect each Hummer in the caravan, you take the wheel of your own H2 Hummer and discover mountain, desert, and sea. The websites have current prices.

BEACHES The best beach safe for swimming is **Palmilla Beach ★★★**, which fronts the glitzy One&Only Palmilla resort 8km (5 miles) west of San José. With its rocky coves, soft sand, and visible sea life, this beach has been home to fishermen for centuries and is the preeminent picnic destination for Mexican families on Sunday

Although this area is ideal for watersports, occasional strong currents and undertows can make swimming dangerous at most **beaches in San José**, the **Tourist Corridor**, and **Cabo San Lucas**. Check conditions before entering the surf. Swimming is generally safe at **Palmilla Beach** (see "Beaches," above), though it, too, can be rough. The safest area beach for swimming is **Medano Beach** in Cabo San Lucas.

afternoons. Past the rock formations, the beach curves east and the culminating swim is well worth the pebble-strewn stroll. Locals agree there's just something about the water on the other side of the rocks. Perfect for swimming, the water in Palmilla Bay has a sort of magic unlike anywhere else, and when you emerge, you'll feel it for yourself. To reach Playa Palmilla, enter the lush Palmilla community at Km 27.5 on the highway, take the road toward the beach, and then take the fork to the left (without entering the hotel grounds) and park in the lot.

Estero San José, a natural freshwater estuary on which the ancient Pericúe Indians built their civilization centuries ago, has at least 270 species of birds and is on the east end of the hotel zone. The estuary is a protected ecological reserve and merits a sunset beach walk from the Hotel Presidente InterContinental to the river mouth where the spring-fed estuary meets the Sea of Cortez.

For a list of other beaches worth exploring if you have a rental car, see "Outdoor Activities: Fishing, Golf & More," under "Cabo San Lucas," later in this chapter.

FISHING   The least expensive way to enjoy deep-sea fishing is to pair up with another angler and charter a *panga*, a 7m (23-ft.) skiff used by local fishermen, from Pueblo la Playa, the beach near the new Puerto Los Cabos Marina. Several *panga* fleets offer 6-hour sportfishing trips, usually from 6am to noon, for $210 to $550. Two or three people can split the cost. For information, visit the fishermen's cooperative in Pueblo la Playa (no phone) or contact **Gordo Banks Pangas** (© 624/142-1147; www.gordobanks.com). For larger charter boats, you'll depart from the marina in Cabo San Lucas (see "Outdoor Activities: Fishing, Golf & More," under "Cabo San Lucas," later in this chapter).

GOLF   Los Cabos has become Latin America's leading golf destination, with a collection of top signature courses and others under construction. The lowest greens fees in the area are at the 9-hole **Punta Sur,** Paseo Finisterra 1 (© 624/142-0900, -0901), which is the first right turn east of the yellow Fonatur statue in the highway roundabout. See p. 702 for fees.

HORSEBACK RIDING   Horses can be rented near the Hotel Presidente InterContinental and the Fiesta Inn, and in the Costa Azul Canyon for $20 to $30 per hour. Most people choose to ride on the beach, but a trip up the arroyo also could prove scenic. For a more organized riding experience—English or Western—there's **Cuadra San Francisco Equestrian Center,** Km 19.5, along the Corridor (© 624/144-0160; www.loscaboshorses.com). It's owned by master horseman Francisco Barrena, whose more than 30 years of experience in training horses and operating equestrian schools will comfort any level of rider, as will his expertise in selecting and fitting a horse to riders' skill levels. A 2-hour canyon ride in and around Arroyo San Carlos or Venado Blanco costs $90; a 1-hour ride to the beach or desert is $45. Private tours go for $60 per hour, and equestrian aficionados may schedule a dressage class for $70.

SEA KAYAKING   Guided, ecology-minded **ocean kayak tours** are available through **Cabo Expeditions** (✆ 624/143-2700; www.caboexpeditions.com.mx) and **Cabo Kayak** (✆ 624/143-3399; www.cabokayak.com). Most ocean kayaking tours depart from Cabo San Lucas, curve around the bay toward the Arch, and break for snorkeling at Lover's Beach.

SNORKELING & DIVING   **Manta** (✆ 624/144-3871; www.caboscuba.com) and **Amigos del Mar** in Cabo San Lucas (✆ 513/898-054 in the U.S., or 624/143-0505; www.amigosdelmar.com) are two of the most reputable dive operations in Los Cabos. Manta offers everything from advanced dive trips to PADI open-water diver certification. Prices start at $80 for a two-tank dive and at $445 for 3 days of diving. Night dives are $70 per person. The 4-day PADI certification course, which certifies you to scuba-dive anywhere in the world, costs $425. A 3-hour resort course including one shallow dive is $115. Among the area's best dive sites are **Gordo Banks** and **Cabo Pulmo.** Gordo Banks is an advanced dive site where you can see whale sharks and hammerhead sharks. It's a deep dive—27 to 30m (89–98 ft.)—with limited visibility (9–12m/30–39 ft.). Most dives are drift dives, and wet suits are highly recommended. Cabo Pulmo, a protected marine park 72km (45 miles) northeast of San José, has seven sites geared for divers of all experience levels, plus some of the most beautiful stretches of Baja beach, so it never feels crowded. **Cabo Pulmo Beach Resort** (✆ 562/366-0722 in the U.S., or 624/141-0726; www.cabopulmo.com) offers charming rental bungalows to call home in between dives or long walks on the beach.

SURFING ★★   Surfing is becoming one of the hottest trends in the entire destination. **Playa Costa Azul**, at Km 29, on Hwy. 1 just south of San José, has the most popular surfing beaches in the area. The **Costa Azul Surf Shop,** Km 28, Playa Costa Azul (✆ 624/142-2771; www.costa-azul.com.mx), offers surfing lessons, surfboard and snorkeling equipment rentals, and specialized surf excursions to any of the 15 local breaks. Excursions include transportation and a DVD video of the day, and owner Alejandro Olea handcrafts all rental boards. Just $20 a day will get you a board, leash, shade umbrella, beach chair, and car rack. One-hour lessons are $85, and special packages are available. **Cabo Surf Hotel** (✆ 858/964-5117 in the U.S., or 624/142-2666; www.cabosurfhotel.com) offers surf lessons and daily board rentals for $37.

The surf switches sides with the seasons, so the waves break on the eastern side of the peninsula in the spring and summer (Mar–Oct), and the Pacific plays host to surfers in the fall and winter (Nov–Mar). The most popular summer breaks start at Acapulquito and extend up the East Cape, while the hot spot for winter waves is Los Cerritos Beach, south of Todos Santos. As every break has its secret—from rocks covered in sea urchins to territorial locals—your best bet is to hook up with a reputable surf shop or guide to take you to the break that's right for you.

TENNIS   Tennis is available at many resorts throughout Los Cabos, but if you're staying somewhere tennis isn't available, the two courts at the **Punta Sur,** Paseo Finisterra 1 (✆ 624/142-0905), rent for 200 pesos an hour during the day, 230 pesos an hour at night. Call the club to reserve. Club guests also can use the swimming pool.

WHALE-WATCHING   From January through March, migrating gray and humpback whales visit Los Cabos to breed and bear their calves, creating one of Baja's most impressive spectacles. Practically every local tour company advertises whale-watching tours that range from an hour to a half-day. Options include Zodiac-style rafts, sportfishing boats, glass-bottom boats, and cruise catamarans, all of which depart from the Cabo San Lucas Marina and cost $35 to $50, depending on the type of boat and whether the trip includes snacks and beverages. You can also spot whales from the shore; good spots include the beach by the Westin Resort & Spa, at Esperanza Resort in the Punta Ballena community, and along the beaches and cliffs of the Corridor.

SHOPPING

San José is the capes' seat of artisan finery, design boutiques, and hip art galleries, clustered around **Bulevar Mijares** and **Zaragoza.** Start in the main plaza and head northwest toward the historic gallery district for a peek at the paintings and sculptures of Pez Gordo Gallery, the Fine Art Annex, Old Towne Gallery, and Galería de Ida Victoria. Head any other direction from the main plaza for crafts boutiques. The galleries host a festive art walk on Thursday nights from 6 to 9pm during high season. A good place to start out is **Casa Dahlia,** near the corner of Morelos and Zaragoza (✆ **624/685-2642;** www.casadahlia.com), a contemporary gallery and cafe with a great view of the cathedral from the back garden. The following businesses accept credit cards (American Express, MasterCard, and Visa).

Mejicanisimo   This shop sells everything from locally made soaps and Damiana tea to embroidered linens and exquisite Emilia Castillo sterling-silver-embedded porcelain. The luminous owner, Magdalena del Río, supplies most of the area's luxury resorts with their fine Oaxacan embroidery, often used for tablecloths and throw pillows. Right across from the plaza, it can't be missed. Open Monday through Saturday from 9am to 10pm and Sunday 10am to 6pm. Zaragoza, across from the cathedral. ✆ **624/142-3090.**

Necri ★   This shop sells the finest in Talavera ceramics and pewter accessories. Shipping is available. Open Monday through Saturday from 9am to 9pm. Zaragoza at Hidalgo, fronting the giant fig tree in the plaza. ✆ **624/142-2777.** www.necri.com.mx.

SAX   For unusual and well-priced jewelry, visit this lovely shop where two local designers (who also happen to be sisters) create one-of-a-kind pieces using silver, coral, and semiprecious stones. They'll even create a special-request design for you and have it ready in 24 hours. Open Monday through Saturday from 10am to 9pm, closed Sunday. On Mijares next to Casa Natalia. ✆ **624/130-7500,** or 559/316-5375 in the U.S. www.saxstyle.com.

The Shoppes at Palmilla   The ultimate in luxury, style, and home design can be found in San José's opulent shopping center, located on the grounds of the One&Only Palmilla Resort. Among other shops, **Pepita** sells haute couture, **SAX** sells chic designer jewelry, and **Galleria** houses Diamonds International's connoisseur collection; there's even a kiosk that sells gear to support the local humane society. Store hours vary; most are open Monday to Friday 9am to 9pm. Km 27.5 Carretera Transpeninsular. ✆ **624/144-6999.** www.lastiendasdepalmilla.com.

WHERE TO STAY

There's more demand than supply in Baja Sur—especially during the idyllic winter months—so prices tend to be higher than those for equivalent accommodations in other parts of Mexico. It's best to call ahead for reservations. Properties in the beachside hotel zone often offer package deals that bring room rates down to the moderate range, especially during summer months. Check with your travel agent. High season generally denotes December through April, and low season is from May through November. Rates listed below do not include tax, which is 15%, and most resorts in Los Cabos offer free parking—although that, too, is changing.

Expensive

Barceló Los Cabos Palace Deluxe ★★★ ☺ If the aim of an all-inclusive resort is to make guests feel as though they're living in their own luxurious self-contained world, then the Barceló chain's latest offering is on the mark. Located in San José's hotel zone, the Palace Deluxe is home to 619 suites, seven restaurants, seven bars, and four swimming pools—it's a wonder that guests ever make it off the property. The rooms pack as much luxury as the 400-thread-count Egyptian cotton sheets pack comfort, with walk-in closets, custom shower heads, and Italian tile in the bathroom. When the Palace Deluxe opened in December 2009, it was the first resort in Los Cabos to feature swim-up suites. Like most all-inclusive properties, Palace Deluxe is a hit with groups and families, so if you're looking for quiet, this may not be your ideal spot.

Paseo del Malecón 1-5 D, Fonatur Zona Hotelera, 23400 San José del Cabo, B.C.S. www.barcelolos cabos.com. ☏ **800/227-2356** in the U.S., or 624/163-7730. 619 units. $305 junior suite; $373 family suite; $456 master suite. All-inclusive rate based on double occupancy for 2 adults. AE, MC, V. Free parking. **Amenities:** 7 restaurants; 7 bars; basketball court; kids' club; concierge; 4 pools; steam room; sauna; gym; tennis court; theater. *In room:* A/C, TV, MP3 player, Wi-Fi.

Casa Natalia ★★★ 🏨 This acclaimed boutique hotel is exquisite. Owners Nathalie and Loic have transformed a former residence into a beautiful amalgam of palms, waterfalls, and flowers. The inn is a completely renovated historic home that combines modern architecture with traditional Mexican touches. All rooms have sliding glass doors that open onto small private terraces or balconies with hammocks and chairs, shaded by bougainvillea and bamboo. Rooms are equipped with CD and DVD players, along with a small collection of DVDs. The two spa suites each have a private terrace with a whirlpool and hammock. The terraces face a small courtyard pool surrounded by California palms. Casa Natalia offers its guests privacy, style, and romance. It's in the heart of downtown San José, just off the central plaza. The excellent on-site restaurant, **Mi Cocina,** is reviewed in "Where to Eat," below.

Bulevar Mijares 4, 23400 San José del Cabo, B.C.S. www.casanatalia.com. ☏ **888/277-3814** in the U.S., or 624/142-5100. Fax 624/146-7100. 20 units. High season $235 double, $335 spa suite; low season $195 double, $285 spa suite. AE, MC, V. Free parking. No children 13 and under. **Amenities:** Gourmet restaurant; bar; heated outdoor pool w/waterfall and swim-up bar; access and transportation to private beach club; concierge; room service; in-room spa services. *In room:* A/C, fan, TV/DVD, hair dryer, Wi-Fi.

Moderate

El Encanto Inn ★ 🖊 On a quiet street in historic downtown, this charming inn borders a grassy courtyard with a fountain and small pool. It's a relaxing alternative to busy hotels and an excellent value. Rooms are decorated with rustic wood and contemporary iron furniture. Nice-size bathrooms have colorful tile accents. Rooms have two double beds, while suites have king-size beds and a sitting room. The pool area has a *palapa* bar and 14 impeccable poolside suites. These newer suites have minibars and other extras, while all rooms offer DirecTV satellite. Fishing packages and golf and diving outings can be arranged. The inn is a half-block from the church.

Morelos 133 (btw. Obregón and Comonfort), 23400 San José del Cabo, B.C.S. www.elencantoinn.com. ☏ **624/142-0388.** 26 units. $82 double; $105–$240 suite. MC, V. Limited street parking available. **Amenities:** Restaurant; *palapa* bar; small outdoor pool; spa. *In room:* A/C, fan, TV, minibar (in some).

La Marina Inn This clean and friendly courtyard hotel (formerly La Playita Hotel) is ideal for visitors looking for a little bit of "old" San José, as the new Puerto Los Cabos community and marina continue to grow and evolve around it. Steps from a beach that's safe for swimming and the lineup of fishing *pangas* on the new marina, the two stories of sunlit rooms frame a patio with a pool just large enough to allow you to swim laps. Each room is spacious, with high-quality basic furnishings, screened windows, a nicely tiled bathroom, and cable TV. Two large suites on the second floor have full kitchens. The inn's La Marina Café, open from 9am until 5pm, serves killer bloody marys for breakfast and their famous fish tacos all day.

Pueblo la Playa, Apdo. Postal 437, 23400 San José del Cabo, B.C.S. www.lamarinahotel.com. ℰ/fax **624/142-4166.** 27 units. $80 double; $130–$190 suite. MC, V. Free parking. From Bulevar Mijares, follow sign pointing to Pueblo la Playa for about 3km (1¾ miles); hotel is on the left. **Amenities:** Restaurant; bar; kayaks; outdoor pool; Wi-Fi. *In room:* A/C, fan, TV.

Tropicana Inn ★ This hacienda-style hotel, a long-standing favorite in San José, welcomes many repeat visitors. Just behind the Tropicana Bar and Grill, it frames a plant-filled courtyard with a graceful arcade bordering the rooms and inviting swimming pool. Each nicely furnished, medium-size room in the L-shaped building (which has a two- and a three-story wing) has tile floors, two double beds, a window looking out on the courtyard, and a brightly tiled bathroom with shower. Each morning, freshly brewed coffee, delicious sweet rolls, and fresh fruit are set out for hotel guests. There's room service until 10pm from the adjacent Tropicana Bar and Grill (owned by the hotel).

Bulevar Mijares 30 (1 block south of the town square), 23400 San José del Cabo, B.C.S. www.tropicanainn. com.mx. ℰ **624/142-0907,** -1580. Fax 624/142-1590. 40 units. High season $128 and up double; low season $108 and up double. Rates include continental breakfast. AE, MC, V. Free limited parking. **Amenities:** Restaurant/bar; small outdoor pool; room service, Wi-Fi. *In room:* A/C, TV, hair dryer, minibar.

Inexpensive

Hotel Posada Terranova This small family-owned hotel is so famous for its traditional Mexican breakfasts and charming outdoor dining terrace that locals often forget it's even a hotel. While local Mexicans and expats love it for weekend brunch, the budget traveler will love it for its spare decor, clean rooms, soft sheets, ideal location in the center of downtown San José, and, yes, its huevos rancheros and fresh-squeezed OJ in the morning.

Degollado, btw. Doblado and Zaragoza, 23400 San José del Cabo, B.C.S. www.hterranova.com.mx. ℰ **624/142-0534.** Fax 624/142-0902. 25 units. $70 double. Seasonal rates available. Rates include continental breakfast. MC, V. Free parking. **Amenities:** Restaurant; bar; room service. *In room:* A/C, fan, satellite TV, no phone.

WHERE TO EAT
Expensive

Baan Thai ★★ 🍴 PAN-ASIAN Asian food is hard to come by in Los Cabos, and Baan Thai—set in one of San José's lovely historic buildings—does an impressive job of seasoning these flavors with a dash of Mexico. Move beyond traditional Asian starters, such as spring rolls or satay, to one of Baan Thai's more unique offerings, such as Thai pizza topped with curried lamb, or steamed mussels with lemon grass. From there, try entrees such as wok-tossed lobster or five-spice barbecue ribs. An impressive wine list and full bar service are available.

Morelos s/n, 1 block behind the church and plaza. ℰ **624/142-3344.** www.loscabosguide.com/baanthai. Reservations recommended. Main courses 150–400 pesos. MC, V. Mon–Sat noon–10pm.

Don Emiliano ★★★ 🍴 MEXICAN If years of queso dip and fried chimichangas have framed your vision of Mexican food, be prepared for your world to come crashing delightfully down. Sparkling seasonal menus, rooted in Mexican traditions such as Day of the Dead and Independence Day, include rare *mole* sauces and stuffed chiles drenched in walnut cream sauce and pomegranate seeds (*chile en nogada*). On a regular basis, traditional staples such as flavored tamales and grilled farm cheese atop roasted tomatillo salsa grace the menu. The wine list is extensive, with both Mexican and imported wines, and fresh-mint mojitos are in ample supply, served by a warm staff. For nearly a decade, chef Margarita C. de Salinas has been traveling the world preparing gourmet Mexican fare for heads of state, while her son, Angel, holds down the fort with such graciousness and culinary precision it must be a secret family recipe. Try the tasting menu or create your own, but whatever you do, don't miss the locally made *queso corazón* (a local cow's milk cheese) to start.

Bulevar Mijares 27, downtown San José. ☎ **624/142-0266.** www.donemiliano.mx. Reservations recommended. Main courses $20–$30. AE, MC, V. Daily 5:30–10:30pm.

Mi Cocina ★★★ CONTEMPORARY MEXICAN   Widely appreciated as one of Los Cabos' finest restaurants, Mi Cocina doesn't rely solely on the romance of its setting—the food is also superb, creative, and consistently flavorful. Notable starters include steamed baby clams topped with a creamy cilantro sauce and served with garlic croutons, or a healthy slice of Camembert cheese, fried and served with home-made toast and grapes. Among the favorite main courses are the baked baby rack of lamb served with grilled vegetables, and the Provençal-style shrimp served with risotto, roasted tomato, basil, and cilantro-fish consommé. Save room for dessert, such as their famous chocolate-chocolate or crème brûlée. Be adventurous and try one of their special martinis—like the Flor de México, an adaptation of the Cosmo, using Jamaica (hibiscus flower infusion) rather than cranberry juice.

In the Casa Natalia (p. 690), Bulevar Mijares. ☎ **624/142-5100.** www.casanatalia.com/dining.htm. Reservations recommended. Main courses 110–260 pesos. AE, MC, V. Daily 6–10pm (hotel guests only 6:30am–6pm).

Tequila Restaurant ★ MEDITERRANEAN/ASIAN   Contemporary fusion cuisine with a light and flavorful touch is the star attraction here, although the garden setting is lovely, with rustic *equipal* furniture and lanterns scattered among palms and mango trees. Organic produce and good greens are hard to find in these parts, so Tequila's homegrown produce, harvested from owner Enrique Silva's ranch, is a welcome dose of light-and-fresh fare, accompanying almost every entree. Try the shrimp risotto or beef tenderloin in rosemary-cabernet sauce. Other enjoyable options include perfectly seared tuna with cilantro and ginger, and rack of lamb topped with tamarind sauce. The accompanying whole-grain bread arrives fresh and hot with a pesto-infused olive oil, and attentive service complements the meal. Cuban cigars and an excellent selection of tequilas are available, as is an extensive wine list emphasizing California vintages.

Manuel Doblado s/n, near Hidalgo. ☎ **624/142-1155** or -3753. www.tequilarestaurant.com. Reservations recommended. Main courses 120–640 pesos. AE. Daily 7am–10:30pm.

Moderate

Zipper's ★★ MEXICAN/GRILL   If cheeseburgers in paradise is your mission, Zipper's is the real deal. Along the Corridor near San José del Cabo, surfers downing icy Pacíficos and fresh shrimp ceviche merge with fishermen bolting Sauza and fried-fish tacos. However, the not-so-humble cheeseburger is the star of Zipper's gringo-fabulous menu. Service is slow, so pass the time watching pelicans swoop the swells, catching rays in board shorts and bikinis, and blissing out to the Jimmy Buffett–laced Radio Margaritaville, which is Zipper's 24/7 soundtrack. You won't find dance contests and Jet Ski vendors here; located beneath a beachfront *palapa* that faces a surf break of the same name, Zipper's is a stripped-down sensory experience that rivals even the swankiest Los Cabos restaurant—at a slightly lesser price tag.

Km 28.5 on Transpeninsular Hwy., in Playa Costa Azul, just south of San José. ✆ **624/172-6162.** Cheeseburgers and sandwiches $8–$10; main courses $13–$39. No credit cards. Daily 11am–10:30pm.

Inexpensive

Las Guacamayas ★★★ 🏠 TACOS This off-the-beaten-path dive is home to the most delectable tacos in all of Los Cabos. If you can get over the plastic chairs, occasional wandering roosters, and low-hanging fruit trees in the courtyard, which is packed nightly, you'll be mesmerized by this meticulously run hot spot for both gringos and Mexicans. Traditionalists wisely go for the *tacos al pastor*—shaved pork tacos with onion, cilantro, and pineapple in a corn or flour tortilla, but the *quesadillas chilangas*—crispy fried tortillas stuffed with an assortment of fillings—are a blissful indulgence. Pace yourself. The addicting flavors and rock-bottom prices may inspire you to stay all night.

Driving east on Transpeninsular Hwy., turn left at the Pescador street sign. The street winds into the Chamizal neighborhood. Take your 2nd left and look for the neon sign. Guacamayas is on the right side. No phone. Tacos, stuffed potatoes, quesadillas, and more 13–90 pesos. No credit cards. Weekdays 6pm–midnight; till 4am Fri-Sat. Closed Tues.

SAN JOSÉ AFTER DARK

The nightlife in San José is a bit more understated than in San Lucas, but a new crop of swanky clubs, wine bars, and neighborhood hangouts is pumping electronic DJ music till 2 or 3am on the weekends, drawing locals and San José visitors alike. Those intent on bumping and grinding to American music will have better luck in San Lucas.

Baja Brewing Company A new addition to the arts district, this hangout was run by a trio of buddies from Colorado who recognized a need for artisan brews in Baja. In addition to the beers—which run the gamut from the light-bodied Baja Blonde to the Scorpion Negro lager—the pub-style pizzas also make a great late-night snack. Live jazz musicians perform Thursday to Saturday beginning at 10pm. During the daily happy hour from 4 to 8pm, all beers are half-price. Open every day from noon to 2am. Morelos btw. Comonfort and Obregón. ✆ **624/146-9995.** www.bajabrewingcompany.com.

Tommy's Barefoot Cantina Next door to La Marina Inn, Tommy's offers a great mix of seafood and standard favorites, plus occasional live jazz or tropical music. It's open daily from noon to 11pm. On Pueblo La Playa, next door to La Marina Inn. ✆ **624/142-3774.** www.tommysbarefootcantina.com.

Tropicana This bar features American sports events and live mariachi music nightly from 6 to 9pm, with live Mexican and Cuban dance music playing from 9:30pm until about 1am on weekends. Bulevar Mijares. ✆ **624/142-1580.**

The Corridor: Between the Two Cabos

The Corridor between the towns of San José del Cabo and Cabo San Lucas contains some of Mexico's most lavish resorts. Most growth at the tip of the peninsula is occurring along the Corridor, which already has become center stage for championship golf. The five major resort areas are **Palmilla, Querencia, Cabo Real, Cabo del Sol,** and **Punta Ballena,** and each is an enclosed master-planned community sprinkled with multimillion-dollar homes (or the promise of them). All but Punta Ballena have championship golf, and all but Querencia, which is a private residential community, have ultraluxury resorts within their gates. If you plan to explore the

The Two Cabos & the Corridor

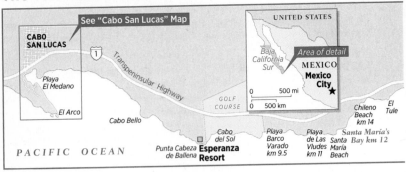

region while staying at a Corridor hotel, you'll need a rental car (available at the hotels) for at least 1 or 2 days. Even if you're not staying here, the beaches and dining options are worth investigating. All hotels listed here offer free parking and qualify as very expensive; quoted rates do not include tax, which is 12% in Baja, and some of the more luxurious resorts also add a 15% service charge to the tab to save guests from having to tip hotel staff. Most resorts offer golf and fishing packages.

WHERE TO STAY

Esperanza ★★★   On a bluff overlooking two small, rocky coves, this luxury resort along Cabo's Corridor amply compensates for the absence of a sandy beach with its pampering services and stylish details. The architecture of this hotel is dramatic, elegant, and comfortable. The casitas and villas spread across 7 hectares (17 acres) are designed to resemble a Mexican village and connect to the resort facilities by stone footpaths. The top-floor suites have handmade *palapa* ceilings and a private outdoor whirlpool spa. All rooms are exceptionally spacious, with woven wicker and tropical wood furnishings, original art, and rugs and fabrics in muted colors with jewel-tone color accents. Terraces are large, extending the living area into the outdoors. All have hammocks and views of the Sea of Cortez. The oversize bathrooms have separate tubs and showers with dual shower heads.

Carretera Transpeninsular Km 7 on Hwy. 1, at Punta Ballena, 23410 Cabo San Lucas, B.C.S. www.esperanza resort.com. ⓒ **866/311-2226** in the U.S., or 624/145-6400. Fax 624/145-6499. 50 suites, 6 villas. High season $950–$1,525 oceanview casita, $1,550–$1,875 beachfront casita, $3,000–$7,000 oceanfront suite; low season $475–$1,125 oceanview casita, $700–$1,675 beachfront casita, $1,800–$4,000 ocean-front suite. AE, MC, V. **Amenities:** Oceanfront restaurant; sushi and ceviche bar; gourmet market; art gallery; babysitting; private beach w/club; concierge; fitness center; golf privileges; outdoor pool; room service; full-service luxury spa; yoga studio w/complimentary daily classes. *In room:* A/C, plasma TV w/ DVD, in-suite bar, hair dryer, Wi-Fi.

Las Ventanas al Paraíso ★★★   With adobe structures and rough-hewn wood accents, the architecture of Las Ventanas provides a soothing complement to the desert landscape. The only color comes from the dazzling *ventanas* (windows) of pebbled rainbow glass handmade by regional artisans. Richly furnished, Mediterranean-style rooms are large (starting at 300 sq. m/3,229 sq. ft.) and appointed with every conceivable amenity, from wood-burning fireplaces, iPods, and aromatherapy turndown service to computerized telescopes for stargazing or whale-watching. Sizable whirlpool tubs overlook each room. Larger suites have extras such as rooftop terraces, sunken

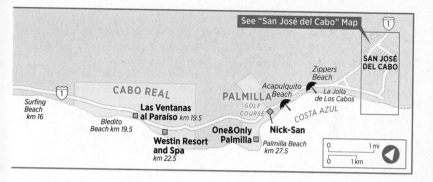

See "San José del Cabo" Map

whirlpools on a private patio, or a personal pool. The surrounding private residences are spacious, with full kitchens, but the rooms and suites have better views. The spa is considered among the best in Mexico, with a focus on holistic healing. The ayurvedic treatment is a one-of-a-kind spiritual experience. With a staff that outnumbers guests by four to one, this is the resort for those who can afford to be seriously spoiled. The 15% service charge is not included in the prices below.

Km 19.5 on Hwy. 1, 23410 San José del Cabo, B.C.S. www.lasventanas.com. © **888/525-0483** or 888/767-3966 in the U.S., or 624/144-2800. Fax 624/144-2801. 61 suites. High season $815 garden-view double, $1,155 oceanview double, $1,340 split-level oceanview suite with rooftop terrace, $1,550 split-level oceanfront suite with rooftop terrace, $3,990–$6,516 luxury suite (1–3 bedrooms); low season $625 garden-view double, $790 oceanview double, $1,000 split-level oceanview suite with rooftop terrace, $1,155 split-level oceanfront suite with rooftop terrace, $2,835–$4,935 luxury suite. Spa Suites packages start at $7,270 for a 4-night program for 2. Spa and golf packages and inclusive meal plans available. AE, DC, MC, V. Free valet parking. **Amenities:** Oceanview restaurant; seaside grill; terrace bar w/live music; fresh juice bar; access to adjoining championship Cabo Real golf course; pet packages, including treats and massages; infinity pool; room service; deluxe European spa w/complete treatment and exercise facilities; sportfishing and luxury yachts; watersports. *In room:* A/C, TV/DVD, MP3 player, hair dryer, minibar, Wi-Fi.

One&Only Palmilla ♨ The One&Only Palmilla is among the most spectacular resort hotels anywhere—certainly within Mexico. Decor features muted desert colors and luxury fabrics, with special extras such as flatscreen TVs with DVD/CD players, and Bose surround-sound systems. Guests receive twice-daily maid service, a personal butler who does everything from unpack your clothes to offer you a poolside iPad, and an aromatherapy menu. Yet unless you're a Fortune 500 CEO or a Hollywood A-lister, staff mostly runs the gamut from indifferent to defiant. The guest-only spa and its 13 private treatment villas are reason to put up with the resort's too-cool attitude. There's also Market, a restaurant by Michelin-starred chef Jean-Georges Vongerichten, that serves Euro-Asian cuisine with Mexican influences. The resort's own championship golf course, designed by Jack Nicklaus, is available for guests. The resort also has two lighted tennis courts, a 600-sq.-m (6,458-sq.-ft.) fitness center, and a yoga garden.

Carretera Transpeninsular Km 7.5, 23400 San José del Cabo, B.C.S. www.oneandonlypalmilla.com. © **866/829-2977** in the U.S., or 624/146-7000. Fax 624/146-7001. 172 units. High season $725 double, $1,050–$3,300 suite; low season $575 double, $1,075–$2,150 suite. AE, MC, V. **Amenities:** 2 restaurants; 2 bars; pool bar; championship Palmilla golf course; 2 infinity pools; room service; deluxe European spa w/complete treatment and exercise facilities; sportfishing; watersports; yoga garden. *In room:* A/C, TV/DVD, CD player, hair dryer, minibar.

Westin Resort & Spa, Los Cabos ★★ ☺   The hotel sits at the end of a long paved road atop a seaside cliff. Vivid terra-cotta, yellow, and pink walls rise against a landscape of sandstone, cacti, and palms, with fountains and gardens lining the long pathways from the lobby to the rooms. The rooms, all of which are ocean view, are sleek and spacious, with fluffy Heavenly Beds and walk-in showers separate from the bathtubs. The seaside 18-hole putting green, first-rate fitness facility, and freshly renovated La Cascada restaurant set this property apart from other Corridor resorts. Plus, it's one of the best options along the corridor for families; it is smoke-free and offers a wealth of activities for children—not to mention Heavenly Dog Beds.

Hwy. 1 Km 22.5, 23400 San José del Cabo, B.C.S. www.westin.com/loscabos. ⓒ **800/228-3000** in the U.S., or 624/142-9000. Fax 624/142-9010. 243 units. High season $344 oceanview double, $750 suite; low season 25% discount. AE, DC, MC, V. **Amenities:** 4 restaurants; 2 bars; babysitting; children's activities; concierge; full fitness center and spa; nearby Palmilla and Cabo Real golf courses; 18-hole putting course; 3 outdoor pools; room service; 2 tennis courts. *In room:* A/C, TV, Internet, hair dryer, minibar.

WHERE TO EAT

Nick-San ★★★ JAPANESE/SUSHI   If you eat one meal out in Los Cabos, do it at Nick-San. This dining experience is so superb, it may shift your worldview. Owned by Masayuki Niikura, Angel Carbajal, and his sister, Carmen Carbajal, who started their sushi dynasty 12 years ago at the original Nick-San in downtown Cabo San Lucas, the newer and swankier outpost at Las Tiendas de Palmilla ensures a taste of teppanyaki nirvana on both ends of the Corridor. The fire of Mexico meets traditional Japanese ingredients in such delicacies as tuna tostada, locally caught sea bass sashimi, and lobster with curried cream sauce. Because the entire menu is too delectable to pick one thing, let someone else make the decision for you: Ask for the chef's tasting plate and, whatever you do, do not miss the lobster tempura roll or the sashimi. Just be sure to let your server know when you've had enough or the plates will keep on coming. By the time the check rolls around, you'll be so enamored it won't even faze you.

The Shoppes, Hwy. 1, Km 27.5 ⓒ **624/144-6262,** -6263. www.nicksan.com. Reservations required except at the bar. Sashimi, rolls, and main courses 100–550 pesos. MC, V. Tues–Sun 12:30–10:30pm.

Cabo San Lucas

183km (113 miles) S of La Paz; 33km (20 miles) W of San José del Cabo; 1,792km (1,111 miles) SE of Tijuana

The hundreds of luxury hotel rooms along the Corridor north of Cabo San Lucas have transformed this formerly rustic and rowdy outpost. Although it retains boisterous nightlife, Cabo San Lucas is no longer the simple town Steinbeck wrote about. Once legendary for big-game fish, Cabo San Lucas now draws more people for its nearby world-class fairways and greens. This has become Mexico's most elite resort destination. Travelers enjoy a growing roster of adventure-oriented activities, as well as sumptuous spa services, and the nightlife is as hot as the desert in July. A collection of popular restaurants and bars along Cabo's main street stay open and active until the morning's first fishing charters head out to sea. Despite the growth in diversions, Cabo remains more or less a one-stoplight town, with almost everything along the main strip.

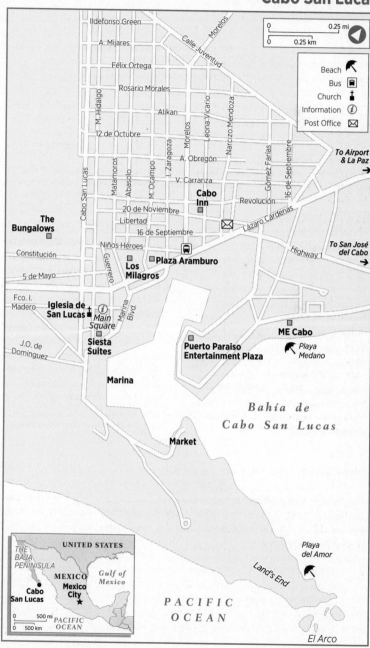

Cabo San Lucas

Map Legend
- Beach
- Bus
- Church
- Information
- Post Office

0.25 mi
0.25 km

Ildefonso Green
A. Mijares
Félix Ortega
Rosario Morales
Alikan
12 de Octubre
A. Obregón
V. Carranza
20 de Noviembre
Libertad
16 de Septiembre
Niños Héroes
Constitución
5 de Mayo
Fco. I. Madero
J.O. de Domínguez

Calle Juventud
Morelos
Leona Vicario
Narciso Mendoza
Gómez Farías
16 de Septiembre
Revolución
Lázaro Cárdenas
Highway 1

Cabo San Lucas
M. Hidalgo
Matamoros
Abasolo
M. Ocampo
I. Zaragoza
Morelos
Guerrero
Marina Blvd.

To Airport & La Paz →
To San José del Cabo →

Cabo Inn
The Bungalows
Los Milagros
Plaza Aramburo
Iglesia de San Lucas
Main Square
Siesta Suites
ME Cabo
Playa Medano
Puerto Paraiso Entertainment Plaza
Marina
Market

Bahía de Cabo San Lucas

Playa del Amor
Land's End
El Arco

PACIFIC OCEAN

Baja Peninsula inset:
THE BAJA PENINSULA
UNITED STATES
MEXICO
Gulf of Mexico
Cabo San Lucas
Mexico City
PACIFIC OCEAN
500 mi
500 km

ESSENTIALS
Getting There & Departing

BY PLANE   For information, see "Getting There & Departing," under San José del Cabo.

BY CAR   From La Paz, the best route is **Hwy. 1** south past San Pedro, and then **Hwy. 19** south through Todos Santos to Cabo San Lucas, a 2-hour drive.

BY BUS   The **bus terminal** is on Héroes at Morelos; it is open daily from 7am to 10pm. Buses go to La Paz every 2 hours starting at 7:15am, with the last departure at 8:15pm. To and from San José, the more convenient and economical **Suburcabos** public bus service runs every 15 minutes and costs 25 pesos, though the routes tend to be meandering, and thus time-consuming.

Orientation

ARRIVING   At the airport, either buy a ticket for a *colectivo* (shuttle) from **Josefinos** (✆ 624/146-5354), the authorized transportation booth inside the building (about $15), or arrange for a rental car, the most economical way to explore the area. Up to four people can share a private taxi, which costs about $65. If you're the chatty type, make friends with fellow travelers on your flight and share a taxi.

VISITOR INFORMATION   The **Los Cabos Tourism Office** (✆ 624/146-9628) is in San José, in the Plaza San José, Locs. 3 and 4, and is open daily from 8am to 3:30pm. The English-language ***Los Cabos Guide, Los Cabos News, Destino Los Cabos,*** and the irreverent and extremely entertaining ***Gringo Gazette*** are distributed free at most hotels and shops, and have up-to-date information on new restaurants and clubs. The Gazette's website now features an amusing and informative video section at www.gringogazette.tv. If you fall so deeply in love with Los Cabos to want to own a piece of it, the ***Baja Real Estate Guide*** is a great place to start (www.bajarealestate guide.com).

> **Information, Please**
>
> The many "visitor information" booths along the street in Cabo are actually timeshare sales booths, and their staffs will pitch a visit to their resort in exchange for discounted tours, rental cars, or other giveaways. Don't sign up unless you feel like sitting through a daylong sales pitch.

CITY LAYOUT   The small town spreads out north and west of the harbor of **Cabo San Lucas Bay,** edged by foothills and desert mountains to the west and south. The main street leading into town from the airport and San José del Cabo is **Lázaro Cárdenas;** as it nears the harbor, **Bulevar Marina** branches off from it and becomes the main artery that curves around the waterfront.

GETTING AROUND   Taxis are easy to find but expensive, in keeping with the high cost of everything else. Expect to pay about $30 to $45 for a taxi between Cabo and the Corridor hotels.

For day trips to San José del Cabo, take the Suburcabos (see "Getting There & Departing," above) or a cab. You'll see car-rental specials advertised in town, but before signing on, be sure you understand the total price after insurance and taxes are added. Rates can run between $30 and $75 per day, with insurance an extra $10 per day. One of the best and most economical agencies is **Advantage Rent-A-Car** (✆ 624/146-5500, or ✆/fax 624/143-0466), on Lázaro Cárdenas between Leona

Vicario and Morelos. VW sedans rent for $50 per day, and weekly renters receive 1 free day. A collision-damage waiver will add $22 per day to the price. If you pick up the car downtown, you can return it to the airport at no extra charge.

[FastFACTS] CABO SAN LUCAS

Area Code The telephone area code is **624.**

Consular Agency A U.S. office is at Blvd. Marina Local C-4 (② **624/143-3566**), open Monday to Friday, 9am to 2pm.

Currency Exchange Banks exchange currency during normal business hours. Currency-exchange booths, throughout Cabo's main tourist areas, aren't as competitive, but they're more convenient. ATMs are widely available and even more convenient, dispensing pesos—and, in some cases, dollars—at bank exchange rates.

Drugstore **American Pharmacy,** in the Puerto Paraiso Mall next to the marina (② **624/143-0000**), stocks a wide selection of toiletries and medicine. It's open daily from 9am to 10pm and accepts Master-Card and Visa.

Emergencies & Hospital In Cabo, **Amerimed** (② **624/105-8500;** www.amerimed-hospitals.com) is a 24-hour, American-standards clinic with bilingual physicians and emergency air evacuation services that accepts major credit cards. Most of the larger hotels have a doctor on call. Dial ② **066** for emergency assistance.

Internet Access **Hemingway's** (② **624/143-9845**), across from Cabo Wabo, is a cigar and tequila lounge that provides Wi-Fi access.

Post Office The *correo* is at Lázaro Cárdenas between Medano and Gomez Farías (② **624/143-0048**), on the highway to San José del Cabo, east of El Squid Roe. It's open Monday through Friday from 9am to 5pm, Saturday from 9am to 3pm.

OUTDOOR ACTIVITIES: FISHING, GOLF & MORE

Although superb sportfishing put Cabo San Lucas on the map, there's more to do than drop your line and wait for the Big One. For most cruises and excursions, try to make fishing reservations at least a day in advance; keep in mind that some trips require a minimum number of people. Most sports and outings can be arranged through a travel agency; fishing can also be arranged directly at one of the fishing-fleet offices at the marina. The marina is on the south side of the harbor.

Besides fishing, there are kayak trips ($65 for a sunset trip around the Arch rock formation; $40 for morning trips) and boat trips to Los Arcos or uninhabited beaches. All-inclusive daytime or sunset cruises are available on a variety of boats, including a restored pirate ship. Many of these trips include snorkeling, and serious divers have great underwater venues to explore.

Between January and March, whale-watching is extremely popular. Guided ATV tours take you down dirt roads and canyons to an ancient Indian village. And then there's the challenge of world-class golf, a major attraction of Los Cabos.

For a complete rundown of what's available, look to **Book Cabo** (② **624/142-9200;** www.bookcabo.com). It offers tours from the best local companies, and you can book ahead online. Most businesses in this section are open daily from 10am to 2pm and 4 to 7pm.

ATV TRIPS Expeditions on ATVs to visit La Candelaria, an Indian pueblo in the mountains, are available through travel agencies. A 200kg (440-lb.) weight limit per two-person vehicle applies. Most guided tours cost around $45 per person on a

Before swimming in the open water, *check if conditions are safe.* Undertows and large waves are common. **Medano Beach,** close to the marina and town, is the principal beach that's safe for swimming. The ME Cabo resort on Medano Beach has a roped-off swimming area to protect swimmers from personal watercraft and boats. Colored flags to signal swimming safety aren't generally found in Cabo, and neither are lifeguards, so be aware.

single vehicle, or $60 for two riding on one ATV. The vehicles are also available for rent ($35 for 3 hr.).

BEACHES All along the curving sweep of sand known as Medano Beach, on the east side of the bay, you can rent snorkeling gear, boats, WaveRunners, kayaks, and sailboards. You can also take windsurfing lessons. This is the town's main beach and is a great place for safe swimming, happy-hour imbibing, and people-watching from one of the many outdoor restaurants along its shore.

Beach aficionados may want to rent a car (see "Getting Around," above) and explore the five more remote beaches and coves between the two Cabos: Playa Palmilla, Chileno, Santa María, Barco Varado, and Lover's Beach. Beaches other than Medano are not considered safe for swimming, although many people don't heed the warning. Experienced snorkelers may wish to check them out, but other visitors should go for the view only. Always check at a hotel or travel agency for directions and swimming conditions. Although a few travel agencies run snorkeling tours to some of these beaches, there's no public transportation: Your options for beach exploring are to rent a car or have a cab drop you off at the beach of your choice.

CRUISES **Glass-bottom boats** leave from the town marina daily every 45 minutes between 9am and 4pm. They cost about $15 for a 1-hour tour, which passes sea lions and pelicans on its way to the famous **El Arco (the Arch)** at Land's End, where the Pacific and the Sea of Cortez meet. Boats drop you off at Playa de Amor; make sure you confirm with your driver which boat will pick you up—it's usually a smaller one run by the same company that ferries people back at regular intervals—and when. Check the timing to make sure you have the correct boat, or expect an additional $10 charge for boarding the boat of an eager competitor.

A number of **daylong** and **sunset cruises** come in a variety of boats and catamarans. They cost $30 to $50 per person, depending on the boat, duration of cruise, and amenities. A sunset "booze cruise" on the 13m (43-ft.) catamaran *Pez Gato* (© 624/143-3797; www.pezgatocabo.com) departs from the Tesoro Resort dock (Dock no. 4, 50m/164 ft. from the main dock) between 4:30 and 5:30pm, depending on the season. A 2-hour cruise costs $30 and includes an open bar and appetizers. The seasonal (winter) whale-watching tour leaves at 10:30am and returns at 1:30pm. It costs $30 and includes open bar and snacks. Similar boats leave from the marina and the Tesoro Resort. Check with travel agencies or hotel tour desks.

DRIVING TOURS A uniquely "Cabo" experience is offered by **Baja Outback** (© 624/142-9200; www.bajaoutback.com) via their caravan-style Hummer Adventures. You drive these luxury Hummer H2s along a dusty trail paved by local ranchers to cruise desert and beachfront terrain in style, while learning about the surrounding area through expert guides. Communication links as many as 10 vehicles in the caravan, allowing you to listen to the narrations of the guide. There's a choice of several routes and itineraries, which include treks to Todos Santos, the East Cape, Santiago and Cañón de la Zorra, and Rancho la Verdad. Tours depart at 9am and return at 3pm, with prices ranging from $135 to $183, depending upon the route, and include lunch. Visa, MasterCard, and American Express are accepted, and you must have your valid driver's license. Special group rates are also available.

If this sounds too tame, **Wide Open Baja Racing Experience** (© 949/340-1155 in the U.S., or 624/143-4170; office in Plaza Nautica; www.wideopenbaja. com) gives you the chance to drive actual Chenowth Magnum race cars through Baja's varied terrain with twists, turns, sand washes, and plenty of bumps for thrill seekers. Drivers meet up across from the bullring in Cabo for a training session before the "arrive and drive" tours. Prices range from $595 to $1,095 for the half- to 1-day trips. Wide Open Baja also offers multiday tours driving race vehicles through Cabo, Ensenada, and the entire Baja Peninsula starting at $1,295 per day.

GOLF   Los Cabos has become the golf capital of Mexico, and although most courses are along the Corridor, people look to Cabo San Lucas for information about this sport in Baja Sur. The master plan for Los Cabos golf calls for a future total of 207 holes. Fees listed below are for 18 holes, including golf cart, water, club service, and tax. Summer rates are about 25% lower, and many hotels offer golf packages.

Specialty tour operator **Golf Adventures** (© 800/841-6570 in the U.S.; www. golfadventures.com) offers golf packages to Los Cabos, which includes accommodations, greens fees, and other amenities.

The 27-hole course at the **Palmilla Golf Club** (© 624/144-5250; www.palmilla gc.com; daily 7am–7pm) was Mexico's first Jack Nicklaus Signature layout, on 360 hectares (889 acres) of dramatic oceanfront desert. The course has two back-nine

---

La Candelaria

Converting from a painter to a potter may not seem like much of a life change, but for Lorena Hankins of Portland, Oregon, the change was less about what she was doing than where she was doing it. For 16 years, Hankins has lived in the ranch community of La Candelaria, a ruggedly beautiful village on the interior route from Cabo San Lucas to Todos Santos, and she has become famous for her pottery made in the ancient traditional style, which involves digging up clay during a specific cycle of the moon—a technique she learned from her sister-in-law.

La Candelaria is a two-horse town, but it's worth a stop on your way to Todos Santos to check out Hankins's

pottery and to inquire about local mythology. Described in *National Geographic,* the old pueblo is known for the practice of white and black witchcraft, but the locals chuckle at the mention of *brujería.*

It's possible to get to La Candelaria on your own, but the road is sandy and bumpy, and if you're in a rental car with a "no off-roading clause," you probably don't want to risk it. **Baja Outback** (© 624/142-9200; www.bajaoutback.com) can help you arrange a tour via Humvee. Lush with palms, mango trees, and bamboo, the settlement gets its water from an underground river that emerges at the pueblo, and you'll get a chance to take it all in on a daylong excursion.

options, with high-season greens fees of $220, lower after 1pm, and low-season greens fees between $130 and $180; guests at some hotels pay discounted rates.

Just a few kilometers away is another Jack Nicklaus Signature course, the 18-hole Ocean Course at **Cabo del Sol,** the posh resort development in the Corridor (© **866/231-4677** in the U.S.; www.cabodelsol.com). The 7,100-yard Ocean Course is known for its challenging three finishing holes, and greens fees start at $180 in the low season and range to $355 for the high season. Tom Weiskopf designed the new 18-hole Desert Course, for which greens fees are $160 in high season, and $130 in low season. Desert Course twilight play starts at $99.

The 18-hole, 6,945-yard course at **Cabo Real,** by the Meliá Cabo Real Hotel in the Corridor (© **877/795-8727** in the U.S., or 624/144-1200; www.caboreal.com; daily 6:30am–6pm), was designed by Robert Trent Jones, Jr., and features holes that sit high on mesas overlooking the Sea of Cortez. Fees run $280 for 18 holes. After 3pm, rates drop to $140 in the low season and $180 in the high season.

An 18-hole course designed by Roy Dye is at the **Cabo San Lucas Country Club,** formerly the Raven Club (© **877/496-1367** in the U.S., or 624/143-4653; fax 624/143-5809; www.golfincabo.com). The entire Dye-designed course overlooks the juncture of the Pacific Ocean and Sea of Cortez, including the famous rocks of Land's End. It includes a 607-yard, par-5 7th hole. High season greens fees are $185 for 18 holes, $155 for the noon rate, and $95 after 2pm. In summer, greens fees drop to $109 for 18 holes and $79 after 10:30am.

The lowest greens fees in the area are at the 9-hole **Punta Sur** (© **624/142-0900,** -0901), in San José del Cabo (see above). Greens fees are just 1255 pesos for 18 holes with equipment.

HORSEBACK RIDING You can rent **horses** through **Rancho Colín** (© **624/143-3652**) for $40 per hour; the 2-hour desert-and-beach trail ride is $70; and the 3½-hour tour through the mountains is $80. If you're interested in a sunset ride with a view of the Sea of Cortez, be sure to call ahead to make sure you book the right time. The ranch is open daily from 8am to noon and 2 to 5pm, and is across from the Hotel Club Las Cascadas. For information on the highly recommended **Cuadra San Francisco Equestrian Center,** see p. 687.

SNORKELING & DIVING Several companies offer snorkeling; a 2-hour cruise to sites around El Arco is $30, and a 4-hour trip to Santa María is $55, including gear. Among the beaches visited on different trips are Playa de Amor, Santa María, Chileno, and Barco Varado. Snorkeling trips start at around $45 per person; contact **Book Cabo** (© **624/142-9200;** www.bookcabo.com). For scuba diving, contact **Manta Diving** (© **624/144-3871;** www.caboscuba.com) and **Amigos del Mar** in Cabo San Lucas (© **813/898-0547** in the U.S., or 624/143-0505; www.amigosdelmar.com). Dives are along the wall of a canyon in San Lucas Bay, where you can see the cascading sand falls by Anegada Rock. There are also scuba trips to Santa María Beach and more distant places, including Gordo Banks and Cabo Pulmo. Prices start at $50 for a one-tank dive and from $415 for 3 days of diving in high season and $375 in summer. Night dives are $70 per person. Snorkeling trips to the coral outcropping at Cabo Pulmo start at $100. You'll need a wet suit for winter dives. A 5-hour resort course is available for $100, and open-water certification is $450.

SPORTFISHING To make your own arrangements, go to the marina on the south side of the harbor, where you'll find several fleet operators with offices near the docks. *Panga* fleets offer the best deals; 5 hours of fishing for two or three people costs $200 to $450, plus a 20% tip. But talk with the captains at the marina—you might be able to negotiate a better deal. Try **Pisces Fleet,** in the Cabo Maritime Center, behind Tesoro Resort and next to Captain Tony's on the marina (© **619/819-7983** in the U.S., or 624/143-1288; www.piscessportfishing.com; daily 10am–4pm; Visa and MasterCard accepted), or **Minerva's** (© **624/143-1282;** www.minervas.com; daily 6am–8pm; American Express, MasterCard, and Visa accepted), on the corner of Bulevar Marina and Madero. A day on a fully equipped cruiser with captain and guide starts at around $445 for up to four people. For deluxe trips with everything including licenses aboard a 9.3m (31-ft.) boat, you'll have to budget around $1,100. If you're traveling in your own vessel, you'll need a fishing permit, which you can get at Minerva's Baja Tackle. Depending on the size of the boat, it will cost $37 to $109 per month. Daily permits for individuals ($13) and weekly and monthly permits are also available. Visit www.conapescasandiego.org for info on permits and fishing rules and regulations.

surf & SLEEP

If you can't get enough of the surf, stay where wave-riding is the specialty and not just another activity. The Los Cabos area has two outposts that cater to surfers, one along Los Cabos Corridor and the other on the Pacific coast, near Todos Santos.

The **Cabo Surf Hotel** (© **858/964-5117** in the U.S., or 624/142-2666; www.cabosurfhotel.com) has 16 beachfront rooms in a secluded, gated boutique resort. It's 13km (8 miles) west of San José del Cabo, across from the Querencia golf course, on Playa Acapulquito, which is the most popular surfing beach in Los Cabos. Along with a choice of rooms and suites, it has an oceanfront terrace restaurant, surf shop, and the Mike Doyle Surf School, which offers day lessons and instruction. Rates range from $265 to $310 for a double and $290 to $625 for suites and villas. Promotional rates are available during summer months, which is optimal for surfers who seek the Sea of Cortez's summertime swells.

The **Pescadero Surf Camp** (© **612/130-3022** or 612/134-0480; www.pescaderosurf.com) is a sparse Pacific getaway at Km 64 on Hwy. 1

toward Todos Santos. Eight pool-front casitas start at $30, and the two-story suite rents for $60 a night; camping spots are available for $10. Although it's 1km (⅔ mile) from the beach, this surf camp is a comfortable step up from the beach camping that's a way of life for most surf mongers, and in the winter, when the waves—and sometimes winds—are at their strongest, it's nice to have a roof overhead. The property's pool has a BYOB swim-up bar that's ideal for cooling off between surf excursions, and a large outdoor kitchen provides a space to prepare your own meals. Owner Jaime Dobies also offers 1½-hour lessons for $50, board rental for $20 a day, Boogie and skim board rental for $10 a day, and daylong guided surf safaris starting at $100 per person. He also repairs boards, should your baby get dinged in action.

Of course, if you're coming to Baja strictly for the surf, you may join the other hard-core wave-riders and camp along the sugary beaches of the East Cape in the summer and the Pacific in the winter. Most beaches—especially the ones fronting secluded surf breaks—are safe and accommodating for overnight stays.

The fishing here lives up to its reputation: Bringing in a 100-pound marlin is routine, although decades of pressure on Sea of Cortez fisheries should inspire you to release your prized catch. Angling is good all year, though the catch varies with the season. Sailfish and wahoo are best from June through November; yellowfin tuna, May through December; yellowtail, January through April; black and blue marlin, July through December. Striped marlin and dorado, or mahimahi, are prevalent year-round.

SURFING Stellar surfing can be found from November through April all along the Pacific beaches north and west of town, and the East Cape is the ultimate North American surfing destination from May through October. (Also see "Surfing" in "San José del Cabo," earlier in this chapter, for details on Costa Azul and East Cape breaks.)

The areas to the east and west of Los Cabos, known as the East Cape and the Pacific side, respectively, have yet to face the onslaught of development that's so rapidly changed the tip. An hour-long drive up the western coast to the little towns of Pescadero and Todos Santos can be a great surf journey, as can a summer trek up the Sea of Cortez coastline toward Cabo Pulmo. Your best bet is to visit **www.costa-azul. com.mx/areas_maps.htm** for a detailed look at the different breaks, excursions, rental equipment, and lessons available.

Many beach breaks are ride-worthy at different times, depending on the wave conditions, but a vicious shore break and strong undertow characterize much of the beach around Todos Santos. The ocean's unruliness has helped keep industrial tourism at bay, but it also means you have to hunt a little harder to find playful waves.

WHALE-WATCHING Whale-watching cruises are the best way to get up close and personal with nature's majestic seafaring mammals. See "Whale-Watching in Baja," p. 728, for information on the excursions, which operate between January and March.

A BREAK FROM SPORTS: EXPLORING CABO SAN LUCAS

FESTIVALS & EVENTS **October 12** is the festival of the patron saint of Todos Santos, a town about 105km (65 miles) north. **October 18** is the feast of the patron saint of Cabo San Lucas, celebrated with a fair, feasting, music, and other special events.

HISTORIC CABO SAN LUCAS Watersports and outright partying are Cabo's main attractions, but there are also a few cultural and historical points of interest. The Spanish missionary Nicolás Tamaral established the **Iglesia de San Lucas (Church of San Lucas)** on Calle Cabo San Lucas, close to the main plaza, in 1730. A large bell in a stone archway commemorates the completion of the church in 1746. The Pericúe Indians, who resisted Tamaral's demands that, among other things, they practice monogamy, eventually killed him in a violent uprising (there's even a painted tile depiction of the event on the front of the church). Buildings on the streets facing the main plaza are gradually being renovated to house restaurants and shops, and the picturesque block has the most Mexican ambience in town.

DAY TRIPS Most local and hotel travel agencies book day trips to the city of **La Paz;** they cost around $70, including beverages and a tour of the countryside along the way. Usually there's a stop at the weaving shop of Fortunato Silva, who spins his own cotton and weaves it into wonderfully textured rugs and textiles. Day trips are also available to **Todos Santos** ($70), with a guided walking tour of the mission, museum, Hotel California, and various artists' homes.

SHOPPING

San José has the better shopping of the two towns, when it comes to quality and uniqueness, but if you're after a beer-themed T-shirt, Cabo San Lucas can't be topped. Nevertheless, the **Puerto Paraíso Entertainment Plaza** (✆ 624/144-3000; www.puertoparaiso.com) does have a selection of designer clothing stores, knickknack shops, and swimwear boutiques. Opened in 2002, this is now the focal point for locals' entertainment and tourists' exploration. It's a truly world-class mall, complete with free parking, movie theaters, a video arcade, a food court, and various restaurants, not the least of which is **Ruth's Chris Steak House,** adjacent to the marina (✆ 624/144-3232; www.ruthschris.com.mx; daily 1–11:30pm). With more than 50,000 sq. m (538,195 sq. ft.) of air-conditioned space on three levels, it's a shame much of the mall is still empty. A new addition to the Paraiso is a high-end section called **Luxury Avenue,** which features ritzy outlets for brands such as Hermès, Fendi, and Swarovski. The plaza is located marina-side, between the Plaza Bonita Mall and Marina Fiesta Resort—you can't miss it if you try. Most other shops in Cabo are on or within a block or two of Boulevard Marina and the plaza.

The following specialty stores stand out among the crowd:

El Callejón   This has Cabo San Lucas's best selection of fine Mexican furniture and decor items, plus gifts, accessories, tableware, fabrics, and lamps. Open Monday through Friday 10am to 7pm and Saturday 9am to 4pm. Hidalgo 2518 near 12 de Octubre in front of La Fonda Restaurant. ✆ **624/143-3188.**

J & J Habanos   J & J is Cabo's largest cigar shop, selling premium Cuban and fine Mexican cigars—it even has a walk-in humidor. They also sell fine tequila and espresso. Open Monday through Saturday 9am to 10pm, Sunday 9am to 9pm. Madero btw. Bulevar Marina and Guerrero. ✆ **624/143-6061,** -3839. www.jnjhabanos.com.

100% Mexico   If you're looking for authentic craftsmanship, a good place to start is 100% Mexico. All of the items in the store—including Oaxacan weavings, Pueblan Talavera, and lacquered boxes from Guerrero—are certified by *Fondo Nacional Para El Fomento de las Artesans* (FONART), Mexico's national foundation for the development of artisans. Open daily from 9am to 9pm. Near the main entrance of Plaza Paraíso. ✆ **624/105-0443.**

Ultrafemme   Mexico's largest duty-free shop has an excellent selection of fine jewelry and watches, including Rolex, Cartier, Omega, TAG Heuer, Tiffany, and Tissot; perfumes, including Lancôme, Chanel, Armani, Carolina Herrera; and other gift items, all at duty-free prices. Open daily 10am to 9:30pm. On the 1st floor of the Luxury Avenue section of Puerto Paraíso. ✆ **624/145-6090.** www.ultrafemme.com.

WHERE TO STAY

High-season prices are in effect from December to Easter. Several hotels offer package deals that significantly lower the nightly rate. Budget accommodations are scarce, but the number of small inns and B&Bs is growing; several notable ones have opened in recent years. Because most of the larger hotels are well maintained and offer packages through travel agents, I will focus on smaller, unique accommodations.

Expensive

ME Cabo ★★   If you've come to Cabo to party, this is your place. The ME Cabo is Sol Meliá's foray into hip, making it Cabo's hottest hot spot. Party-ready rooms, an adult-focused floor called "The Level," and the swank Nikki Beach help to stake a glam claim on this beachfront property, which is geared toward those who'd rather party than relax. Its location on Medano Beach is central to any other action you may want to seek, but with Nikki Beach and Passion Club, you'll find plenty right here (see "Cabo San Lucas After Dark," below. Rooms are awash in fiery red and white, with a sleek, contemporary decor. All suites have ocean views and private terraces looking across to the famed El Arco. Master suites have a separate living room area. Guests gather by the beachfront pool, where oversize daybeds perfectly accommodate this lounge atmosphere.

Playa El Medano s/n; 23410 Cabo San Lucas, B.C.S. www.me-cabo.com. ℰ **624/145-7800.** Fax 624/143-0420. 150 units. High season $355–$459 double, $1,079 chic suite, $1,579 loft suite; low season $266–$389 double, $1,009 chic suite, $1,509 loft suite. AE, MC, V. Free parking. **Amenities:** Restaurant; bar/dance club; beach club; concierge; Jacuzzi; 2 outdoor pools; room service. *In room:* A/C, TV/DVD, Nintendo, hair dryer, minibar, Wi-Fi (in some).

Moderate

The Bungalows Hotel ★ 👬   This is one of the most special places to stay in Los Cabos. Each "bungalow" is a charming retreat decorated with authentic Mexican furnishings. Terra-cotta tiles, hand-painted sinks, wooden chests, blown glass, and other creative touches make you feel as if you're a guest at a friend's home rather than a hotel. Each room has a kitchenette, purified water, DVD player, and designer bedding. Rooms surround a lovely heated pool with cushioned lounges and tropical gardens. A brick-paved breakfast nook serves a gourmet breakfast with fresh-ground coffee and fresh juices. A 100% smoke-free environment, it is 5 blocks from downtown Cabo.

Miguel A. Herrera s/n, in front of Lienzo Charro, 23410 Cabo San Lucas, B.C.S. www.cabobungalows. com. ℰ/fax **624/143-5035,** -0585. 16 units. High season $95–$150 suite, $115–$185 bungalow; low season $75–$95 suite, $95–$115 bungalow; year-round $175 honeymoon suite. Extra person $20. Rates include full breakfast. AE, V. Street parking available. **Amenities:** Breakfast room; concierge; outdoor pool. *In room:* A/C, TV/VCR, fridge, kitchenette.

Los Milagros Hotel   The elegant whitewashed two-level buildings containing the 12 suites and rooms of Los Milagros (the Miracles) border either a grassy garden area or the small tile pool. Rooms contain contemporary iron beds with straw headboards, buff-colored tile floors, and artistic details. Some units have kitchenettes, the master suite has a sunken tub, and there's coffee service in the mornings on the patio. Evenings are romantic: Candles light the garden and classical music plays. Request a room in one of the back buildings, where pomegranate trees buffer others' conversations. It's just 1½ blocks from the Giggling Marlin and Cabo Wabo.

Matamoros 116, 23410 Cabo San Lucas, B.C.S. www.losmilagros.com.mx. ℰ/fax **718/928-6647** in the U.S., or 624/143-4566. 12 units. $85 double; $100 kitchenette suite; $125 master suite. Ask about summer discounts, group rates, and long-term discounts. No credit cards, but payable through PayPal. Free secure parking. **Amenities:** Small outdoor pool. *In room:* A/C, TV, Wi-Fi.

Inexpensive

Cabo Inn ★★ 👬   This three-story hotel on a quiet street is a real find, and it keeps getting better. It offers a rare combination of low rates, extra-friendly management, and great, funky style. Rooms are basic and very small, with either two twin beds or one queen; although this was a bordello in a prior incarnation, everything is kept new and updated, from the mattresses to the minifridges. Muted desert colors add a spark of personality. The rooms surround a courtyard where you can enjoy satellite TV, a barbecue grill, and free coffee. The third floor has a rooftop terrace with *palapa* and a small swimming pool. A large fish freezer is available, and most rooms have kitchenettes. The hotel is just 2 blocks from downtown and the marina. A lively restaurant next door will even deliver pitchers of margaritas and dinner to your room.

20 de Noviembre and Leona Vicario, 23410 Cabo San Lucas, B.C.S. www.caboinnhotel.com. ℂ/fax **619/819-2727** in the U.S., or 624/143-0819. 23 units. $58 double; $79 triple; $90–$120 *palapa* suite. No credit cards. Street parking. **Amenities:** Barbecue; small rooftop pool; communal TV; Wi-Fi. *In room:* A/C, fridge.

Siesta Suites   Reservations are a must at this immaculate, small inn that's popular with return visitors. (It's especially popular with fishermen.) The very basic rooms have white-tile floors and white walls, kitchenettes with seating areas, refrigerators, and sinks. The mattresses are firm, and the bathrooms are large and sparkling clean. Rooms on the fourth floor have two queen-size beds each. The accommodating proprietors offer free movies and VCRs, a barbecue pit and outdoor patio table on the second floor, and a comfortable lobby with a TV. They also arrange fishing trips. Weekly and monthly rates are available. The hotel is 1½ blocks from the marina, where parking is available.

Calle Emiliano Zapata btw. Guerrero and Hidalgo, 23410 Cabo San Lucas, B.C.S. www.cabosiestasuites. com. ℂ **866/271-0952** in the U.S., or 624/143-2773. 20 suites. $64–$76 suite; $400–$500 weekly rates. AE, MC, V. Parking available at marina. **Amenities:** Barbecue pit; outdoor pool. *In room:* A/C, TV, fan, VCR, fridge, kitchenette (in some).

WHERE TO EAT

It's not uncommon to pay a lot for mediocre food in Cabo, so try to get some unbiased recommendations. If people are only drinking and not dining, take that as a clue—many seemingly popular places are long on party atmosphere but short on food. Prices may decrease the farther you walk inland. The absolute local favorite is **Tacos Gardenia's** (no phone), a bare-bones eatery on Paseo Pescadores (same street as McDonald's) that serves Cabo San Lucas's best tacos. It's open from 8am to 5pm and closed Mondays. Streets to explore for other good restaurants include Hidalgo and Lázaro Cárdenas, plus the marina at the Plaza Bonita. Note that many restaurants automatically add the tip (15%) to the bill; make sure you ask.

Very Expensive

Edith's Restaurante ★★★ SEAFOOD/STEAKS/MEXICAN   Prices may seem over-the-top and reservations hard to come by, but once you sit down at one of Edith Jiménez's cheerful tables, you will see you're paying for an exquisite meal and a great time. Lanterns light the open-air way, and bouquets of fresh lilies always perfume the entrance and washrooms. No detail is overlooked and, without exception, everyone in the house is in full celebration mode. You will be, too, after a celestial pitcher of margaritas or a bottle from Edith's carefully stocked cellar. While the lobster, shrimp, seafood, and steak combinations are worth every last penny, the grilled tuna is beyond compare when it comes to quality and value. And if Mexican food is what you crave, both the Tampiqueña and the Pancho Villa offer a magnanimous sampling of some of Mexico's most prized traditional dishes, which are abundant enough for two, especially when kicked off with the squash blossom quesadillas or a Caesar salad.

Camino a Playa Medano. ℂ **624/143-0801.** www.edithscabo.com. Reservations strongly recommended. Main courses $20–$70. MC, V. Daily 5–10pm.

Expensive

Nick-San ★★ JAPANESE/SUSHI   This is the original branch of exceptional Japanese cuisine and sushi in Los Cabos. Now joined by a second location in the Corridor near San José, Nick-San's innovative flavors have two splendid homes. See p. 696 for menu details.

Bulevar Marina, Plaza de la Danza, Loc. 2. © **624/143-2491.** www.nicksan.com. Reservations recommended. Sashimi, rolls, and main courses 95–500 pesos. MC, V. Daily 11:30am–10:30pm.

Moderate

La Dolce ITALIAN   This restaurant is the offspring of Puerto Vallarta's La Dolce Vita, with authentic Italian thin-crust, brick-oven pizzas, fresh pasta dishes, and other specialties. Most of its business is from local customers, underscoring the attention to detail and reasonable prices. The simple menu also features sumptuous calzones and delightful starters, plus great salads. This is the best late-night dining option, and there's also an equally loved branch on the main square in San José del Cabo that's open from 2 to 11pm.

M. Hidalgo and Zapata s/n. © **624/143-4122** or -9553. www.restaurantladolce.com. Reservations recommended. Main courses 110–260 pesos. MC, V. Tues–Sun 5–11pm.

Mi Casa Restaurant ★ MEXICAN   The building's vivid cobalt-blue facade is your first clue that this place celebrates Mexico, and the menu confirms that impression. This is one of Cabo's most renowned Mexican restaurants. Traditional specialties such as *manchamanteles* (literally, "tablecloth stainers"), *cochinita pibil*, and *chiles en nogada* are menu staples. Fresh fish is prepared with delicious seasonings from throughout Mexico. Especially pleasant at night, the restaurant's tables, scattered around a large patio, are set with colorful cloths, traditional pottery, and glassware. It's across from the main plaza.

Calle Cabo San Lucas (at Lazaro Cardenas). © **624/143-1933.** www.micasarestaurant.com. Reservations recommended. Main courses 130–330 pesos. MC, V. Mon–Sat 11am–3pm; daily 5:30–10:30pm.

Inexpensive

Cafe Canela ★ COFFEE/PASTRY/LIGHT MEALS   This cozy, tasty cafe and bistro is a welcome addition to the Cabo Marina boardwalk. Espresso drinks or fruit smoothies and muffins are good eye-openers for early risers. Enjoy a light meal or a tropical drink either inside or on the bustling waterfront terrace. The appealing menu also offers breakfast egg wraps, salads (such as curried chicken salad with fresh fruit), sandwiches (such as blue-cheese quesadillas with smoked tuna and mango), and pastas—all reasonably priced. Full bar service is also available.

Marina boardwalk, below Tesoro Resort. © **624/143-3435.** Breakfast 59–120 pesos; lunch and dinner main courses 85–290 pesos. AE, MC, V. Daily 6am–7pm.

Early Bird's MEXICAN/COFFEE/LIGHT FARE   There are several decent restaurants along the new section of the Marina near Puerto Paraiso, and any one of them would probably suffice. However, if you're looking for a no-nonsense place that offers good value, head to Early Bird's. It has been around for years as a place for fishermen to gear up for their journey. It's open all day and offers great tacos (three for 71 pesos). They also offer boxed lunches with a sandwich, fruit, and other snacks for only 130 pesos. There's also a convenience store inside in case you need to stock your in-room minifridge.

Marina Boardwalk, Puerta 5. © **624/143-5603.** Snacks starting at 15 pesos. MC, V. Daily 5am–10pm.

Mocambo's ★ SEAFOOD   The location of this long-standing Cabo favorite is not inspiring—it's basically a large cement building—but the food definitely is. The place is always packed, generally with locals tired of high prices and small portions. Ocean-fresh seafood is the order of the day, and the specialty platter can easily serve four people. The restaurant is 1½ blocks inland from Lázaro Cárdenas.

Av. Leona Vicario and 20 de Noviembre. ℰ **624/143-2122.** www.mariscosmocambo.com. Main courses 110–410 pesos. MC, V. Daily noon–10pm.

CABO SAN LUCAS AFTER DARK

Cabo San Lucas is the nightlife capital of Baja. After-dark fun starts with the casual bars and restaurants on Bulevar Marina or facing the marina, and transforms into a tequila-fueled dance club scene after midnight. You can easily find a happy hour with live music and a place to dance or a Mexican fiesta with mariachis.

MEXICAN FIESTAS & THEME NIGHTS   Some larger hotels have weekly fiesta nights and other buffet-plus-entertainment theme nights that can be fun as well as a good buy. Check travel agencies and the following hotels: the **Solmar** (ℰ **624/143-3535**) and the **Finisterra** (ℰ **624/143-3333**). Prices range from $25, not including drinks, tax, and tips, to $50, which covers everything, including an open bar with national drinks. Otherwise, **Mi Casa** (ℰ **624/143-1933;** see "Where to Eat," above) is a veritable Mexican theme night every night.

SUNSET WATCHING   A good place to watch the sunset is at the **Pueblo Bonito Sunset Beach hotel**—where nothing obstructs the setting sun—on the Pacific side of San Lucas (ℰ **624/142-9797**).

HAPPY HOURS, CLUBS & HANGOUTS   If you shop around, you can usually find an *hora feliz* (happy hour) somewhere in town between noon and 7pm. The most popular places to drink and carouse until all hours are long-standing favorites such as the Nowhere Bar, the Giggling Marlin, El Squid Roe, and the Cabo Wabo Cantina.

A place to enjoy a more refined setting is **Hemingway's** (ℰ **624/143-9845**), a cigar lounge that features nightly live guitar or jazz music and where the mojitos are gaining fame and are the consummate beverage to complete a night out. It's open Monday through Saturday from 10am to 10pm.

Cabo Wabo Cantina   Owned by Sammy Hagar (formerly of Van Halen) and his Mexican and American partners, this "cantina" packs in youthful crowds, especially when rumors (frequent and frequently false, just to draw a crowd) fly that a surprise appearance by a vacationing musician is imminent. One of Cabo's few air-conditioned dance venues, it's especially popular in the summer months. The house band, Cabo, plays hard-rock covers every night. For snacks, the Taco Wabo, just outside the club's entrance, stays up late, too. The cantina is open from 10am to 2am. Vicente Guerrero at Lázaro Cárdenas. ℰ **624/143-1188.** www.cabowabocantina.com.

El Squid Roe 📷   El Squid Roe is one of the late Carlos Anderson's inspirations, and it still attracts wild, fun-loving crowds of all ages with its two stories of nostalgic decor. The eclectic food is far better than you'd expect from such a party place and, as fashionable as blue jeans, you can't come to Cabo without a visit here. Skin-to-win is the theme as the dancing on tables moves into high gear around 9pm. The scene is mostly tourists jerking to American hip-hop from early evening to around midnight, and at 1am, the local Mexican crowd—just getting their night started—flow in, and the hips don't stop shaking until first light. Bar open daily from 9pm to 4am. Bulevar Marina, opposite Plaza Bonita. ℰ **624/143-0655.** www.elsquidroe.com.

Nikki Beach This haven of the hip in the ME Cabo hails from South Beach, Miami. White-draped lounge beds scatter the outdoor area, under a canopy of umbrellas, surrounding a pool, and overlooking Cabo's best swimming beach. A teak deck offers covered dining. The music is the latest in electronic, house, and chill, with visiting DJs often playing on weekend nights. Sundays feature the signature beach brunch. It's a great choice for catching rays during the day while sipping tropical drinks, but its real appeal is the nocturnal action. Open Sunday to Wednesday from 11am to 1am (food service stops at 11pm), and Thursday to Saturday from 11am to 3am (food service stops at 1am). On the beach at the ME Cabo resort, on Medano Beach. ✆ **624/145-7800.** www.nikkibeach.com.

Passion Club ME Cabo's most recent contribution to Cabo's growing high-end nightlife scene is Passion, arguably the most aphrodisiacal club in San Lucas. Champagne cocktails, the house music of resident and guest DJs, and a low-lit atmosphere prime Los Cabos' jet set for dancing and partying as long as they want. Open Sunday to Wednesday from 10am to 2am and Thursday to Saturday from 10am to 4am. In the ME Cabo resort, on Medano Beach. ✆ **624/145-7800.** www.me-cabo.com/ThePassionClub.html.

TODOS SANTOS: A CREATIVE OASIS ★★★

68km (42 miles) N of Cabo San Lucas

Although Todos Santos is well past its off-the-beaten-path days, it's still a favorite among bohemian types looking either for regional up-and-coming artists or simply a piece of art that makes them feel good—and it's a prime destination among those simply weary of the Cancún-ization of Cabo San Lucas.

The art and artistry created here—from the kitchen to the canvas—is of an evolved type that seems to care less about commercial appeal than quality. This makes it more of a draw. Not to be overlooked are the arts of agriculture, masonry, and weaving created by some of the town's original residents. From superb meals at **Café Santa Fe** to an afternoon browsing at **El Tecolote Libros,** Todos Santos is intriguing to its core.

Not only is the town a cultural oasis in Baja, it's an oasis in the true sense of the word—in this desert landscape, Todos Santos enjoys an almost continuous water supply from the peaks of the Sierra de la Laguna mountains. It's just over an hour's drive up the Pacific coast from Cabo San Lucas; you'll know you've arrived when the arid coastal scenery suddenly gives way to verdant groves of palms, mangos, avocados, and papayas.

During the Mission Period of Baja, this oasis valley was deemed the only area south and west of La Paz worth settling due to its reliable water supply. In 1723, an outpost mission was established, followed by the full-fledged Misión Santa Rosa de Las Palmas in 1733. At the time, the town was known as Santa Rosa de Todos Santos; eventually shortened to its current name, it translates as "All Saints."

Over the next 200 years, the town alternated between prosperity and difficulty. Its most recent boom lasted from the mid–19th century until the 1950s, when the town flourished as a sugar-cane production center and began to develop a strong cultural core. Many of the buildings now being restored and converted into galleries, studios, shops, and restaurants were built during this era. It wasn't until the 1980s that a paved road connected Todos Santos with La Paz, and tourism began to draw new attention to this tranquil town.

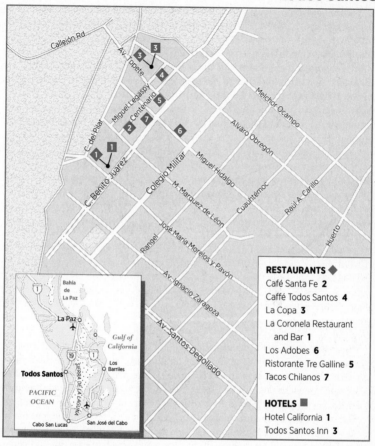

RESTAURANTS ◆

Café Santa Fe **2**
Caffé Todos Santos **4**
La Copa **3**
La Coronela Restaurant
  and Bar **1**
Los Adobes **6**
Ristorante Tre Galline **5**
Tacos Chilanos **7**

HOTELS ■

Hotel California **1**
Todos Santos Inn **3**

The demand for the town's older colonial-style structures by artists, entrepreneurs, and foreign residents has resulted in a real-estate boom, and new shops, galleries, and cafes crop up continuously. The coastal strip south of Todos Santos—once the exclusive hideaway of impassioned surfers—has plans for development, so visit soon, before this perfect stretch of beach and desert changes. For the casual visitor, Todos Santos is easy to explore in a day, but a few tranquil inns welcome guests who want to stay a little longer.

What to See & Do

During the **Festival Fundador** (usually the second week of Oct)—a celebration of the founding of the town in 1723—streets around the main plaza fill with food, games, and wandering troubadours. Many of the shops and the Café Santa Fe close from the end of September through the festival. A new **Arts Festival,** in February, seems to be gaining importance. It includes film festivals, dance and music performances, and more. For up-to-date information on events and festivals, visit www.todossantos.cc.

Todos Santos has at least half a dozen galleries, including the noted **Galería de Todos Santos,** corner of Topete and Legaspi (© **612/145-0500;** www.galeriade todossantos.com), which features a changing collection of works by regional artists. It's open daily from 11am to 4pm (closed Sun May–Nov).

El Tecolote Libros ★★★ (© **612/145-0295**), though tiny, is one of the best bookstores in Mexico. It carries an exceptional selection of Latin American literature, poetry, children's books, and reference books centering on Mexico. Both English and Spanish editions, new and used, are in stock, along with maps, magazines, cards, and art supplies. Information on upcoming writing workshops and local reading groups is also posted here. The shop is at the corner of Hidalgo and Juárez. It's open Monday through Saturday from 10am to 4:30pm, and Sunday from noon to 3pm.

In keeping with the organic and artesian feel is **Heartsease** (© **612/118-8002**), a spa boutique that sells all-natural soaps and skin-care products created by Canadian expat Gwenn McDonald. Look for items like castor oil conditioner, mini perfumes, and after-sun balm; either McDonald or an employee can explain the healing effects. A masseuse offers services on the premises. It's on Juarez between Hidalgo and Topete.

If you want to venture out into the nearby natural treasures, **Todos Santos Eco Adventures** (© **612/145-0780;** www.tosea.net) can arrange a wide variety of day trips including bird-watching, cliff hiking, and horseback riding. Owner Sergio Jauregui has spent the last decade exploring Baja and is quite knowledgeable about all things local.

Where to Stay

Todos Santos Inn ★★   This elegant place to stay is in a historic house that has served as a general store, cantina, school, and private residence. Now under new ownership, it retains its air of casual elegance, with luxurious white bed linens, netting draped romantically over the beds, Talavera tile bathrooms, antique furniture, and high, wood-beamed ceilings. Two rooms and four suites border a lush courtyard terrace, pool, and garden. Rates depend on the room and the season, and breakfast is included in the room rate. The suites are air-conditioned but have neither television nor telephone; the hotel offers free Wi-Fi. The hotel's wine bar, **La Copa,** is open to the public Tuesday through Saturday from 5 to 9pm and has an excellent selection of California and other imported wines.

Calle Legaspi 33, btw. Topete and Obregón. www.todossantosinn.com. © **612/145-0040.** 8 units. $125–$325 double. Rates include full breakfast. MC, V. **Amenities:** Restaurant; bar. *In room:* A/C, no phone, Wi-Fi.

Hotel California   This hotel has been the stuff of legends—and the verdict is still out as to whether it's the source of inspiration for the Eagles' song of the same name. A few years back, it was a dilapidated guesthouse, but after an extensive renovation, it's now the hippest place to stay in the area. Think Philippe Starck in the desert—the decor is a fusion of jewel-tone colors with eclectic Mexican and Moroccan accents. Each room features a different decor, but all of it is high style, with rich hues and captivating details. Most rooms have an outdoor terrace or seating area. On the ground floor, you'll find the lobby and the low-lit library— with deep blue walls, a profusion of candles, and tin stars—as well as a small outdoor pool with sun chairs. Also at ground level is the **Emporio** boutique, which is well worth a visit for its rugs, jewelry, and glass lanterns; **La Coronela Restaurant and Bar** (open daily 7am–11pm) is the nocturnal hot spot, with live guitar, jazz, and blues on Saturday evenings. The recently added tequila bar is a small, decadently decorated spot, with red and black settees and an extensive selection of tequilas, including their own Hotel California label.

Calle Juárez, corner of Morelos. www.hotelcaliforniabaja.com. © **612/145-0525,** -0522. Fax 612/145-0288. 11 units. $110–$215 double. Rates include full breakfast. MC, V. **Amenities:** Restaurant; bar; outdoor pool. *In room:* A/C, Wi-Fi.

Where to Eat

The best no-nonsense option in Todo Santos is **Tacos Chilanos** (no phone), an authentic taco stand located on Topete near the corner of Centenario. Look for a red-and-white awning with a set of plastic tables on the sidewalk. A bean-and-cheese burrito served in a crispy, fresh flour tortilla costs 13 pesos, and a *carne asada* torta is 30 pesos. It's open from 9am to 9pm every day except Sunday.

Café Santa Fe ITALIAN   Much of the attention the town has received in recent years can be directly attributed to this outstanding restaurant. Owners Ezio and Paula Colombo refurbished a large stucco house across from the plaza, creating an exhibition kitchen, several dining rooms, and a lovely courtyard adjacent to a flowering garden. The excellent northern Italian cuisine emphasizes local produce and seafood; try ravioli stuffed with spinach and ricotta in a Gorgonzola sauce, or ravioli with lobster and shrimp, with an organic salad. In high season, the wait for a table at lunch can be long.

Calle Centenario 4. © **612/145-0340.** Reservations recommended. Main courses 180–500 pesos. MC, V. Wed–Mon noon–9pm. Closed Sept–Oct.

Caffé Todos Santos COFFEE/LIGHT FARE   A more casual option, and a magical place to start the day, is this garden setting. The bowl-size caffé latte can be accompanied by a freshly baked croissant or one of the signature cinnamon buns. Lunch or a light meal may include a frittata, a hearty sandwich on home-baked bread, or a fish filet wrapped in banana leaves with coconut milk.

Calle Centenario 33. © **612/145-0300.** Main courses 60–130 pesos. No credit cards. Tues–Sat 7am–9pm; Sun 7am–5pm; Mon 7am–2pm.

Los Adobes MEXICAN   If you prefer a gourmet Mexican experience, go to Los Adobes, in Hidalgo, and dine in a *palapa*-covered courtyard. Here, the margaritas and the *sopa tarasca,* a decadent purée of white beans, chipotle peppers, and cream, are excellent.

Calle Hidalgo s/n, btw. Calle Juarez and Calle Colegio Militar. © **612/145-0203.** www.losadobesde todossantos.com. Reservations recommended. Main courses 165–245 pesos. MC, V. Mon–Sat 9am–9pm; Sun 9am–5pm.

Ristorante Tre Galline ITALIAN   This restaurant is giving Café Santa Fe a run for its money. When an earthquake destroyed Magda Valpiani's family restaurant in northern Italy, she and her husband, Angelo Dal Bon, took it as a sign to set out on a new adventure. They packed a shipping container to the brim with their personal treasures—virgin olive oil, fine Italian wines, table settings, and an authentic pasta machine—headed to Mexico, and signed the papers for their new restaurant within hours of stepping into the former art gallery. Their restaurant is truly a force of nature. I'm still thinking about the sweet potato tortellini with butter and almond sauce, and the tiramisu with fresh mascarpone.

Corner of Calle Topete and Calle Juarez. © **612/145-0274.** Reservations recommended. Main courses 140–260 pesos. No credit cards. Mon–Sat 10am–9pm.

LA PAZ: PEACEFUL PORT TOWN ★★

176km (109 miles) N of Cabo San Lucas; 195km (121 miles) NW of San José del Cabo; 1,544km (957 miles) SE of Tijuana

La Paz means "peace," and the feeling seems to float on the ocean breezes of this provincial town. Despite being an important port, home to almost 200,000 inhabitants and the capital of the state of Baja California Sur, it remains slow paced and relaxed. Beautiful deserted beaches just minutes away complement the lively beach and palm-fringed *malecón* (seaside boulevard) that front the town center. The easygoing city is the guardian of "old Baja" atmosphere, and it has an unmistakable air of outdoor adventure, thanks to the ubiquity of skilled anglers, competitive freedivers, Baja 1000 racers, recreational (as in noncommercial) spear fishermen, a marina full of large yachts, and kayak rental agencies.

Adventurous travelers enjoy countless options, including hiking, rock climbing, diving, fishing, and sea kayaking. Islands and islets sit just offshore, once hiding places for looting pirates but now magnets for kayakers and beachcombers. You can even camp overnight, posh safari style, at **Baja Camp** (www.bajacamp.com), on Espíritu Santo, or swim with sea lions on Los Islotes. The best time for camping is from June through September.

The University of Southern Baja California adds a unique cultural presence that includes museums and a theater and arts center. The surrounding tropical desert diversity and pandemic wildlife are also compelling reasons to visit. Despite its name, La Paz has historically been a place of conflict between explorers and indigenous populations. Beginning in 1535, Spanish conquistadors and Jesuit missionaries arrived and exerted their influence on the town's architecture and traditions. From the time conquistadors saw local Indians wearing pearl ornaments, mass pearl harvesting lasted through the late 1930s, when all the pearls eventually were wiped out. John Steinbeck immortalized a local legend in his novella *The Pearl*.

La Paz is ideal for anyone nostalgic for Los Cabos the way it used to be—and it has the breathtaking sunsets not always visible at Baja's tip. From accommodations to taxis, it's also one of Mexico's most outstanding beach-vacation values and a great place for family travelers. However, as is the case throughout Mexico, development activity in the areas immediately surrounding La Paz may change this in the coming years, so plan a visit now to experience the pearl of La Paz in its natural state.

Essentials

GETTING THERE & DEPARTING

BY PLANE Both **Alaska Airlines** (© 800/252-7522 in the U.S.) and **Delta** (© 800/241-4141 in the U.S.) have nonstop flights from Los Angeles. **Aeroméxico** (© 800/237-6639 in the U.S., or 612/122-0091, -0093, -1636) flies from Mexico City and other points within Mexico as does **Volaris** (© 01-800/122-8000 in Mexico). The airport is 18km (11 miles) northwest of town along the highway to Ciudad Constitución and Tijuana. Airport *colectivos* (around 120 pesos) run only from the airport to town, not vice versa, and a group shuttle is around 250 pesos. **Taxi** service (around 350 pesos) is available as well. Most major rental-car agencies have booths inside the airport, including **Budget** (✆ 612/124-6433 or 612/122-7655), **Avis** (✆ 612/124-6312), and **Alamo** (✆ 612/122-6262, -6260).

BY CAR From San José del Cabo, **Hwy. 1** north is the more scenic route, and it passes through a mountain town called San Bartolo, where heavenly homemade macaroons made of thick, fresh-cut coconut and pralines made from *cajeta* (goat's-milk caramel) are well worth the slightly longer drive; a faster route is heading east of Cabo San Lucas and then north to **Hwy. 19** through Todos Santos. A little before San Pedro, Hwy. 19 rejoins Hwy. 1 and runs north into La Paz; both trips takes 2½ to 3 hours. From northern Baja, Hwy. 1 south is the only choice.

BY BUS The **Central Camionera** (main bus station) is at Jalisco and Héroes de la Independencia, about 25 blocks southwest of the center of town; it's open daily from 6am to 10pm. Bus service operates from the south (Los Cabos, 2½–3½ hr.) and north (as far as Tijuana). It's best to buy your ticket in person the day before, though reservations can be made over the phone at the bus station in your point of origin. Taxis are available in front of the station.

All routes north and south, as well as buses to Pichilingue, the ferry pier, and close to outlying beaches, are available through the **Transportes Aguila** station, sometimes called the beach bus terminal, on the *malecón* at Álvaro Obregón and Cinco de Mayo (✆ **612/122-7898**). The station is open daily from 6am to 10pm. Buses to Pichilingue depart seven times a day from 8am to 5pm and cost 25 pesos one-way. Local buses arrive at the **beach station,** along the *malecón*. Taxis line up out front of both.

BY FERRY **Baja Ferries** serves La Paz from Topolobampo (the port for Los Mochis) daily at 11:30pm, and the return trip to Topolobampo leaves La Paz at 3pm daily. Tickets are available at the Baja Ferries office in La Paz, on the corner of Allende and Marcelo Rubio (✆ **612/123-6600,** -1313), or at any Banamex banks throughout Mexico (make payable to Baja Ferries, SA de CV, account #7145468 sucursal 001). The local office is open daily 8am to 6pm. To make reservations from the U.S., call ✆ **800/884-3107.**

The ferry departs for Topolobampo daily at 11:30pm and arrives in La Paz 6 hours later. The ferries can carry 1,000 passengers, and accommodate vehicles and trucks. Passengers pay one fee for themselves (790 pesos for a seat, 395 pesos for children ages 3–11, or 760 pesos for a cabin with four beds and one bathroom) and another for their vehicles (1,050 pesos). The ferries offer restaurant and bar service, as well as a coffee shop and live music, and a hot meal is included in the cost of the ticket. Access for those with disabilities is offered as well. Passengers are asked to arrive 3 hours prior to departure time. Information and schedules are available at **www.bajaferries.com**. Taxis meet each ferry and cost about 100 pesos to downtown La Paz.

Warning: Although La Paz remains calm, the drug war has escalated in other regions of Mexico. The state of Culiacan has emerged as one of the centers of dangerous activities. If you are planning to travel to Topolobampo, use caution and your best judgment.

ORIENTATION

VISITOR INFORMATION The most accessible visitor information office is on the corner of Álvaro Obregón and Nicolas Bravo (✆ **612/122-5939** or 612/124-0100; turismo@gbcs.gob.mx or turismo@lapaz.cromwell.com.mx). It's open daily from 8am to 8pm. The extremely helpful staff speaks English and can supply information on La Paz, Los Cabos, and the rest of the region. The official website of the La Paz Tourism Board is **www.vivalapaz.net**.

CITY LAYOUT   Although La Paz sprawls well inland from the *malecón* (Paseo Álvaro Obregón), you'll probably spend most of your time in the older, more congenial downtown section within a few blocks of the waterfront. The main plaza, **Plaza Pública,** or Jardín Velasco, is bounded by Madero, Independencia, Revolución, and Cinco de Mayo.

GETTING AROUND   Because most of what you'll need in town is on the *malecón,* between the tourist information office and the Hotel Los Arcos, or a few blocks inland from the waterfront, it's easy to get around La Paz on foot. Public buses go to some of the beaches north of town (see "Beaches & Sports," below). To explore the many beaches within 80km (50 miles) of La Paz, your best bet is to rent a car or hire a taxi. There are several car-rental agencies on the *malecón.*

FESTIVALS & EVENTS   February features the biggest and best **Carnaval/ Mardi Gras** in Baja, as well as a 4- to 5-week **Festival of the Gray Whale** (starting in late Jan or early Feb, sometimes extending into early Mar). On May 3, **a festival** celebrates the city's founding by Cortez in 1535 and features *artesanía* exhibitions from southern Baja. An annual **marlin-fishing tournament** is in August; **other fishing tournaments** occur in September and November. On November 1 and 2, the **Day of the Dead,** altars are on display at the Anthropology Museum.

[FastFACTS] LA PAZ

Area Code   The telephone area code is **612.**

Banks   Banks generally exchange currency during normal business hours: Monday through Friday from 9am to 6pm, Saturday from 10am to 2pm. ATMs are readily available and offer bank exchange rates on withdrawals.

Drugstore   One of the largest pharmacies is **Farmacorama,** 16 de Septiembre in the Centro (⊘ **612/122-4920**). It's open 7:30am to 10:30pm 7 days a week.

Emergencies   Dial ⊘ **066** for emergency assistance, or ⊘ **060** for the police.

Hospitals   The two hospitals in the area are **Hospital Especialidades Médicas,** at Km 4.5 on the highway toward the airport (⊘ **612/ 124-0400**), and **Hospital Juan María de Salvatierra** (⊘ **612/122-1496**), Nicolás Bravo 1010, Col. Centro. Both are open 24 hours, and the former offers access to emergency air evacuation.

Internet Access   In the fleeting world of Internet cafes, your best bet is to scan the *malecón* or ask your hotel concierge for their recommendations. However, **Omni Services,** on the *malecón,* Álvaro

Obregón 460-C, close to Burger King (⊘ **612/123- 4888;** www.osmx.com), doubles as an Internet center and a real estate agency, offering Internet access, Wi-Fi, faxing, and long-distance VoIP phone service to the U.S. and Canada for 3 pesos per minute. It also offers hookups for laptops, color printers, and copiers.

Post Office   The *correo,* 3 blocks inland at Constitución and Revolución de 1910 (⊘ **612/122-0388**), is open Monday through Friday from 8am to 5pm, Saturday from 8am to 1pm.

Beaches & Sports

La Paz combines the un-self-conscious bustle of a small capital port city with the charm of resort Mexico and beautiful, isolated beaches not far from town. Well on its way to becoming the undisputed adventure-tourism capital of Baja, it's the starting point for whale-watching, diving, sea kayaking, climbing, and hiking tours throughout the peninsula. For those interested in day adventures, travel agencies in major hotels or along the *malecón* usually can arrange all of the above, plus beach tours, sunset cruises, and visits to the sea lion colony. Agencies in the United States that specialize in Baja's natural history also book excursions (see "Tours," in chapter 2).

BEACHES   Within a 10- to 45-minute drive from La Paz lie some of the loveliest beaches in Baja. Many rival those of the Caribbean, with their clear, turquoise water. The beach bordering the *malecón* is the most convenient in town. Although the sand in the Bay of La Paz is soft and white and the water appears turquoise and gentle, locals don't generally swim there. Because of the commercial port, the water is not considered as clean as those at the very accessible outlying beaches. With colorful playgrounds dotting the central beachfront and numerous open-air restaurants that front the water, it's best for a casual afternoon of post-sightseeing lunch and play.

The best beach nearby is immediately north of town at **La Concha Beach Resort;** nonguests may use the hotel restaurant and bar, and rent equipment for snorkeling, diving, skiing, and sailing. It's 10km (6¼ miles) north of town on the Pichilingue Highway at Km 5.5. The other beaches are all farther north of town, but midweek you may have these distant beaches to yourself.

For more information about beaches and maps, check at the tourist information office on the *malecón*.

CRUISES   A popular and very worthwhile cruise is to **Isla Espíritu Santo** and **Los Islotes.** You visit the largest sea lion colony in Baja, stunning rock formations, and remote beaches, with stops for snorkeling, swimming, and lunch. If conditions permit, you may even be able to snorkel beside the sea lions. (**Note:** Remember, sea lions are wild animals. Blowing bubbles in your face is their sign of warning, not of play, so steer clear of the giant bulls—who can be quite protective of their females—and let the curious babies come to you.) Boat and bus tours are available to **Puerto Balandra,** where bold rock formations rising up like humpback whales frame pristine coves of crystal-blue water and ivory sand. **Viajes Lybs,** Independencia 1045 (© 612/128-4882; www.lybs.com.mx), and other travel agencies can arrange these all-day trips, weather permitting. Price is around $80 per person.

ECOTOURS   A wide selection of ecotours and adventure activities are available through **Baja Quest** and **Grupo Fun Baja** (© 612/106-7148; www.funbaja. com). In addition to diving excursions (the company's specialty), they offer a "cactus tour" of the interior as well as a tour of downtown La Paz. **DeSea Baja** (© 310/691-8040 in the U.S., or 612/121-5100; www.deseabaja.com) offers driving tours in rental vehicles equipped for off-road adventures.

SCUBA DIVING   Scuba-diving trips are best June through September. Fernando Aguilar's **Club Cantamar,** Obregón 1665-2 (© 612/122-1826; fax 612/122-3296; www.clubcantamar.com), arranges them. Rates start at $105 per person for a daylong three-tank dive, including transportation and food.

Also of note is **DeSea Baja** (✆ 612/121-5100; www.deseabaja.com), a complete tour company with expertise in diving and sportfishing. Prices are $130 for two-tank dives, including equipment, or $147 for three. They also offer private boats with guides for underwater photo or video diving, and private dive masters or instructors for yachts or charters. DeSea also offers **freediving,** including instruction from internationally renowned freediving instructors Aharon and Maria Teresa (MT) Solomon. Courses include yoga-based breathing exercises, mental control, and the physiology of breath hold. Beginning through advanced instruction is available, as are **live-aboard charters** and **spearfishing** excursions.

SEA KAYAKING   Kayaking in the many bays and coves near La Paz is a paddler's dream, and because some of the area's special sites for swimming and snorkeling are accessible only by kayak, daylong or multiday trips can't be beat. In the waters near La Paz, the water clarity gives the sensation of being suspended in the air. Bring your own equipment, or let the local companies take care of you. Several companies in the U.S. (see "Tours," in chapter 2) can book trips in advance. Locally, **Mar y Aventuras** (**Sea and Adventures;** ✆ 612/123-0559 in Mexico, or 406/522-7596 in the U.S.; fax 612/122-3559; www.kayakbaja.com) arranges extended kayak adventures. Multiday trips start at $575.

SPORTFISHING   La Paz, justly famous for its sportfishing, attracts anglers from all over the world. Its waters are home to more than 850 species of fish. The most economical approach is to rent a *panga* boat with a captain and equipment. It costs 1,250 pesos for 3 hours, but you don't go very far out. Super *pangas,* which have a shade cover and comfortable seats, start at around 1,800 pesos for two persons. Larger cruisers with bathrooms start at 4,000 pesos.

You can arrange sportfishing trips locally through hotels and tour agencies. **La Paz Sportfishing** (✆ 612/141-6403 in Mexico, or 310/691-8040 in the U.S.; www.lapazsportfishing.com) has rates starting at $80 pesos a day for two people, $40 for each additional person. David Jones, of the **Fishermen's Fleet** (✆ 612/122-1313 in Mexico, or 408/884-3932 in the U.S.; fax 612/125-7334; www.fishermensfleet.com), uses popular *panga* fishing boats. David is professional, speaks English, and truly understands area fishing. The average price is 2,600 pesos for the boat, and the price usually includes beer, soft drinks, breakfast, and lunch, as well as vacuum packing and freeze drying of your catch.

WHALE-WATCHING   Between January and March, and sometimes as early as December, 3,000 to 5,000 gray whales migrate from the Bering Strait to the Pacific coast of Baja. The main whale-watching spots are **Laguna San Ignacio** (on the Pacific near San Ignacio), **Magdalena Bay** (on the Pacific near Puerto López Mateos—about a 2-hr. drive from La Paz), and **Scammon's Lagoon** (near Guerrero Negro).

Most tours originating in La Paz go to Magdalena Bay, where the whales give birth to their calves in calm waters. Several companies arrange whale-watching tours that originate in La Paz or other Baja towns or in the United States; 12-hour tours from La Paz start at around 1,200 pesos per person, including breakfast, lunch, transportation, and an English-speaking guide. Make reservations at **Viajes Lybs** (see above).

A Break from the Beaches: Exploring La Paz

Most tour agencies offer city tours of all the major sights. Tours last 2 to 3 hours, include time for shopping, and cost around 150 pesos per person.

When Cortez landed here on May 3, 1535, he named it Bahía Santa Cruz. It didn't stick. In April 1683, Eusebio Kino, a Spanish Jesuit, arrived and dubbed the place Nuestra Señora de la Paz (Our Lady of Peace). It wasn't until November 1, 1720, however, that Jaime Bravo, another Jesuit, set up a permanent mission. He used the same name as his predecessor, calling it the Misión de Nuestra Señora de la Paz. The mission church stands on La Paz's main square, on Revolución between Cinco de Mayo and Independencia.

The Anthropology Museum   The museum features large, though faded, color photos of Baja's prehistoric cave paintings. There are also exhibits on various topics, including the geological history of the peninsula, fossils, missions, colonial history, and daily life. All information is in Spanish.

Altamirano and Cinco de Mayo. ℰ/fax **612/122-0162** or 612/125-6424. Admission 31 pesos. Daily 9am-6pm.

Cactus Sanctuary ★   This 50-hectare (124-acre) natural reserve features 1,000m (3,280 ft.) of marked pathways and self-guided tours with information about the plants and animals of La Paz's desert region. Fifty unique areas have been identified, which you can explore. Route maps and guided tours are available, as well as descriptive signs for many of the plants. There's a surprising amount of wildlife to see here, from the myriad types of cacti, many of which are endemic to Baja California, to the numerous plants and animals that support this unique ecosystem. The sanctuary is in the Ejido El Rosario; go to the Ejido's main office (the *delegación*), and they will provide you with a key to enter the reserve.

Ejido El Rosario. ℰ **612/124-0245** (Dr. Hector Nolasco). hnolasco@cibnor.mx. 20 pesos donation to enter. No fixed hours. 45 min. south of La Paz; take Hwy. 1 toward the town of El Triunfo; drive 10 min. inland along a dirt road.

El Teatro de la Ciudad   The city theater is the cultural center, with performances by visiting and local artists. Bookings include small ballet companies, experimental and popular theater, popular music, and an occasional classical concert or symphony. Av. Navarro 700. ℰ **612/125-0486.**

Serpentarium ★   This mostly open-air natural museum offers plenty of opportunities to observe various species of reptiles that inhabit the region's ecosystem, including snakes, turtles, iguanas, lizards, and crocodiles. It's on the corner of Calle Brecha California and Calle La Posada. To get there, go to the southernmost point of the *malecón* at Calle Abasolo, where the last streetlights are, and just before the beach you'll see an unpaved street—that's Brecha California. If you're going with a group, e-mail **cobra293@hotmail.com** to make a reservation.

Calles Brecha California and La Posada. ℰ **612/123-5731.** 80 pesos adults, 50 pesos children. Daily 10am-4pm.

Shopping

La Paz has little in the way of folk art or other treasures from mainland Mexico. The dense cluster of streets behind the **Hotel Perla,** between 16 de Septiembre and Degollado, is full of small shops, some tacky, others quite upscale. In this area, there is also a very small but authentic **Chinatown,** dating from the time when Chinese laborers were brought to settle in Baja. Serdán from Degollado south is home to dozens of sellers of dried spices, piñatas, and candy. Stores carrying crafts, folk art, clothing, handmade furniture, and accessories lie mostly along the *malecón* (Paseo Obregón) or within 1 or 2 blocks. The **municipal market,** at

Revolución and Degollado, has little of interest to visitors. Something you're sure to notice if you explore around the central plaza is the abundance of stores selling electronic equipment. This is because La Paz is a principal port for electronic imports to Mexico from the Far East and therefore offers some of the best prices in Baja and mainland Mexico.

Allende Books   When you accidentally drop your beach read in the ocean (as happens to even the most seasoned traveler), this is the place to pick out a new one. Allende Books is relatively small, but its selection is cheeky and includes recent English-language bestsellers as well as local publications, including a Todos Santos cookbook. Open Monday to Saturday 10am to 1pm and 4 to 8pm. Independencia 518 near Serdán and Guillermo Prieto. ℂ **612/125-9114.** www.allendebooks.com.

Antigua California   This shop manages to stay in business as others come and go. It carries a good selection of folk art from throughout Mexico. It's open Monday to Saturday from 9:30am to 8:30pm, Sunday from 10:30am to 2:30pm. Paseo Álvaro Obregón 220, at Arreola. ℂ **612/125-5230.**

Artesanías Cuauhtémoc (The Weaver)   For beautiful hand-woven table-cloths, place mats, rugs, and other textiles, it's worth the long walk or taxi ride to this unique shop. Fortunato Silva, an elderly gentleman, weaves wonderfully textured cotton textiles from yarn he spins and dyes himself. He charges far less than what you'd pay for equivalent artistry in the U.S. Open Monday through Saturday from 10am to 3:30pm and 6 to 7pm. On the corner of Abasolo and Oaxaca, btw. Jalisco and Nayarit. ℂ **612/122-4575.**

Ibarra's Pottery   Here you not only shop for tableware, hand-painted tiles, and decorative pottery, but you can also watch it being made. Each piece is individually hand-painted or glazed, and then fired. Open Monday to Saturday from 9am to 3pm. You can call ahead to schedule a tour. Guillermo Prieto 625, btw. Torre Iglesias and República. ℂ **612/122-0404.**

Where to Stay

Grand Plaza La Paz ★   This all-suite hotel offers travelers a comfortable sense of U.S. standards and modern conveniences. It's considered the best option for business travelers to the area, one of the few in town with a full business center, Internet access, and meeting space. Vacationers will also enjoy the hotel's location on the marina, as well as its pleasant pool area. The clean, modern, and well-equipped rooms on three floors offer either views to the bay or overlooking the courtyard pool, with a choice of king-size or two double beds. Five different kinds of suites have a private balcony, and all have ocean views. The hotel is at the northern end of town, 5.6km (3½ miles) from downtown, at the Marina Fidepaz.

Lote A Marina Fidepaz, P.O. Box 482, 23090 La Paz, B.C.S. www.grandplazalapaz.com. ℂ **866/357-9711** in the U.S., or 612/124-0830, -0833. Fax 612/124-0837. 54 suites. Suites $99 and up. AE, DC, MC, V. Free guarded parking. **Amenities:** Restaurant; 2 bars; concierge; fitness center; outdoor pool; room service; sauna; squash court; whirlpool; Wi-Fi (in lobby). *In room:* A/C, TV, hair dryer.

Hotel Mediterrane ★   Simple yet stylish, this unique inn mixes Mediterranean with Mexican, creating a cozy place for couples or friends to share. All rooms face an interior courtyard and are decorated with white-tile floors and *equipal* furniture, with colorful Mexican serapes draped over the beds. Some rooms have minifridges. All have VCRs. Its location is great—just a block from the *malecón*. The adjacent **La**

Pazta restaurant (see "Where to Eat," below) is one of La Paz's best. Rates include use of kayaks and bicycles for exploring the town. This is a gay-friendly hotel.

Allende 36, 23000 La Paz, B.C.S. www.hotelmed.com. ©/fax **612/125-1195.** 9 units. $65 and up double; $95 suite. Extra person $100. Weekly discounts available. AE, MC, V. Street parking. *In room:* A/C, TV/VCR, no phone, Wi-Fi.

La Concha Beach Club Resort ★

Five kilometers (3 miles) north of downtown La Paz, this resort's setting is perfect: on a curved beach ideal for swimming and watersports. All rooms face the water and have double beds, balconies or patios, and small tables and chairs. Condos with full kitchens and one or three bedrooms are available on a nightly basis in the high-rise complex next door. They're worth the extra price for a perfect family vacation stay, although no children 13 and younger are allowed in the condos. The hotel offers scuba, fishing, and whale-watching packages.

Carretera Pichilingue Km 5, 23010 La Paz, B.C.S. www.laconcha.com. © **800/999-2252** in the U.S., or 612/121-6161. 113 units. $115 and up double. AE, DC, MC, V. Free guarded parking. **Amenities:** Restaurant (w/theme nights); 2 bars; beach club w/scuba program; babysitting; Jacuzzi; beachside pool; room service; free twice-daily shuttle to town; complete watersports center w/WaveRunners, kayaks, and paddleboats. *In room:* A/C, TV, Internet, minibar.

Posada de Las Flores ★

Owner Giuseppe Marceletti has continued the tradition of hospitality in this elegant B&B (formerly Posada Santa Fe), the best bet for travelers looking for a more refined place to stay in La Paz. Each room is individually decorated with high-quality Mexican furniture and antiques, hand-loomed fabrics, and exquisite artisan details. Bathrooms are especially welcoming, with marble tubs and thick towels. Breakfast is served from 8 to 11am daily, and complimentary wake-up coffee service is available on request. Telephone, fax, and Internet service are available through the office. It's at the northern end of the *malecón*.

Álvaro Obregón 440, 23000 La Paz, B.C.S. www.posadadelasflores.com. © **619/378-0103** in the U.S., or 612/125-5871. 8 units. High season $180 double, $290 suite; low season $150 double, $250 suite. Rates include full breakfast. MC, V. Street parking. No children 11 and younger accepted. **Amenities:** Hospitality desk; Internet; small outdoor pool. *In room:* A/C, TV, hair dryer, minibar.

Where to Eat

Although La Paz is not known for culinary grandeur, it has an assortment of small, pleasant restaurants. In addition to the usual seafood and Mexican dishes, you can find Italian, French, Spanish, Chinese, and vegetarian offerings. Restaurants along the *malecón* tend to be more expensive than those a few blocks inland. For an authentic Baja experience, head to **Palapa Azul ★ (© 612/122-1801**), just outside of town where the bus lets off on Tecolote beach. It's packed with hungry crowds on weekends, but if you make it early enough, you can get a head start on their famed oysters that are so fresh they still move when you squirt lime on them.

MODERATE

Buffalo Bar-B-Q ★★ ARGENTINE/GRILL   Indoor seating plays second fiddle to the outdoor courtyard, which fronts a fiery grill on which prime cuts are turned into delicacies. The hamburgers are big and flavorful, and come in so many delectable styles—from the special-sauced New Mexico burger to the standard cheeseburger—that a carnivore may just call this heaven. Otherwise, Buffalo Bar-B-Q's stellar steaks, ribs, and wine list are a worthy tribute to the chef's Argentine roots.

Madero 1240 (near the corner of Cinco de Mayo and Constitución). © **612/128-8755.** www.buffalolapaz.com. Hamburgers and main courses 80–250 pesos. AE, MC, V. Wed-Mon 4pm–11pm.

La Pazta ★ ITALIAN/SWISS   The trendiest restaurant in town, La Pazta gleams with black-lacquered tables and white tile. The aromas of garlic and espresso float in the air. The menu features local fresh seafood in items such as pasta with squid in wine-and-cream sauce, and crispy fried calamari. There's also homemade lasagna, baked in a wood-fired oven. La Pazta's daytime cafe is appealing for breakfast, too. The restaurant is in front of the Hotel Mediterrane, 1 block inland from the *malecón*.

Allende 36. ☏ **612/125-1195.** www.hotelmed.com. Breakfast 20–40 pesos; main courses 150–275 pesos. AE, MC, V. Cafe Thurs–Tues 7am–11pm; restaurant Thurs–Tues 4–11pm.

INEXPENSIVE

El Quinto Sol VEGETARIAN   Not only is this La Paz's principal health food market, but it's a cheerful, excellent cafe for fresh-fruit *licuados* (smoothies), *tortas,* daily vegetarian lunch specials, and ice cream made from in-season fruit. Tables sit beside oversize wood-framed windows with flowering planters in the sills. Sandwiches are served on whole-grain bread—also available for sale—and the potato tacos are an excellent way for vegetarians to indulge in a Mexican staple. Owner Marta Alonso also offers free nightly meditation classes to clients.

Av. Independencia and B. Domínguez. ☏ **612/122-1692.** Main courses 20–75 pesos. No credit cards. Mon–Sat 8am–4pm; store hours 8am–9pm.

La Paz After Dark

A night in La Paz logically begins at a bar or cafe along the *malecón* as the sun sinks into the sea. A favorite ringside seat at dusk is a table at **La Terraza,** next to the Hotel Perla (☏ 612/122-0777). La Terraza makes good schooner-size margaritas. **Carlos 'n' Charlie's La Paz-Lapa** (☏ 612/122-9290) has live music on weekends; and on the second-floor terrace above is **Casa de Villa,** where current pop music commingles with young *Paceños,* or La Paz locals, till late. **La Cabaña** nightclub (☏ 612/122-0777), in the Hotel Perla, features Latin rhythms. It opens at 9pm; a cover on weekends varies depending on the event. **Las Varitas,** Independencia and Domínguez (☏ 612/125-2025), is where you'll hear Latin rock, ranchero, and salsa. It's open from 9pm to 3 or 4am, with cover charges around 55 pesos. *Note:* Covers may rise or fall.

MID-BAJA: LORETO, MULEGÉ & SANTA ROSALIA

Halfway between the resort sophistication of Los Cabos and the frontier exuberance of Tijuana lies Baja's midsection, an area rich in history and culture. The indigenous cave paintings here are a UNESCO World Heritage Site, and the area was home to numerous Jesuit missions in the 1700s. These days, mid-Baja is known for its sea kayaking, freediving, sportfishing, off-road racing, and hiking.

Overlooked by many travelers (except avid sportfishers), **Loreto** is a rare gem that sparkles under the desert sky. The purple hues of the Giganta Mountains meet the indigo waters of the Sea of Cortez, providing a spectacular backdrop of natural contrasts for the historic town. **Mulegé** is, literally, an oasis in the Baja desert. The only freshwater river (Río Mulegé) in the peninsula flows through town. And the port town of **Santa Rosalía,** while a century or so past its prime, makes a worthy detour, with its pastel clapboard houses and unusual steel-and-stained-glass church, designed by Gustave Eiffel (of Eiffel Tower fame).

The Lower Baja Peninsula

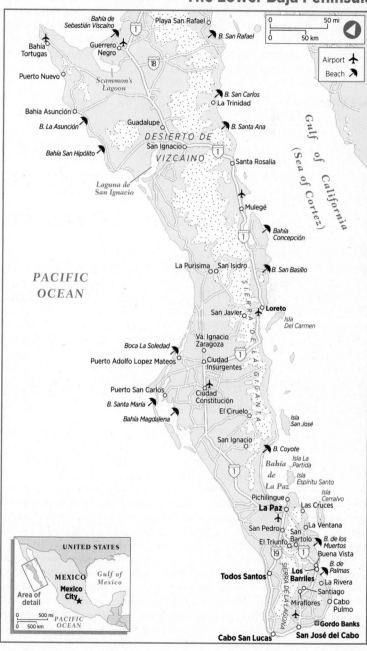

| 0 | 50 mi |
| 0 | 50 km |

Airport ✈
Beach ↗

Playa San Rafael
B. San Rafael
Bahía de Sebastián Viscaíno
Guerrero Negro
Bahía Tortugas
Puerto Nuevo
Scammon's Lagoon
B. San Carlos
La Trinidad
Bahía Asunción
B. La Asunción
Guadalupe
DESIERTO DE
B. Santa Ana
Bahía San Hipólito
San Ignacio
VIZCAINO
Santa Rosalía
Laguna de San Ignacio
Gulf of California (Sea of Cortez)
Mulegé
Bahía Concepción
PACIFIC OCEAN
La Purisima
San Isidro
B. San Basilio
SIERRA DE LA GIGANTA
San Javier
Loreto
Isla Del Carmen
Va. Ignacio Zaragoza
Boca La Soledad
Puerto Adolfo Lopez Mateos
Ciudad Insurgentes
Puerto San Carlos
Ciudad Constitución
B. Santa María
El Ciruelo
Bahía Magdalena
Isla San José
San Ignacio
B. Coyote
Isla La Partida
Bahía de La Paz
Isla Espíritu Santo
Pichilingue
Isla Cerralvo
La Paz
Las Cruces
San Pedro
La Ventana
El Triunfo
San Bartolo
B. de los Muertos
Buena Vista
B. de Palmas
Todos Santos
Los Barriles
La Rivera
SIERRA DE LA LAGUNA
Santiago
Miraflores
Cabo Pulmo
Gordo Banks
Cabo San Lucas
San José del Cabo

UNITED STATES
Gulf of Mexico
MEXICO
Mexico City
Area of detail
PACIFIC OCEAN
500 mi
500 km

It's far enough from the polished tourism gem of Los Cabos that the people's smiles are more sincere, and you rarely hear the timeshare salesman's grating "Hola, amiga" as you walk the streets. But plans may be in the works to change that. Developers north of the border are snapping up spots in Ensenada Blanca Bay and Loreto Bay. Mid-Baja is still a decade or more from being a hot spot for anyone besides adventurers, racing teams, and RV caravans, but the plans are there. If you want a glimpse of the Wild West, now is the time to visit Loreto, Mulegé, Santa Rosalía, and San Ignacio.

The region is also a popular launch for whale-watching. To find out when, where, and how to view the gentle giants, see p. 728, "Whale-Watching in Baja."

Loreto & the Offshore Islands

389km (241 miles) NW of La Paz; 533km (330 miles) N of Cabo San Lucas; 1,125km (698 miles) SE of Tijuana

The center of the Spanish mission effort during colonial times, Loreto was the first capital of the Californias and the first European settlement in the peninsula. Founded on October 25, 1697, it was selected by Father Juan María Salvatierra as the site of the first mission in the Californias. (California, at the time, extended from Cabo San Lucas to the Oregon border.) He held Mass beneath a figure of the Virgin of Loreto, brought from a town in Italy bearing the same name. For 132 years, Loreto served as the state capital, until an 1829 hurricane destroyed most of the town. The capital moved to La Paz the following year.

During the late 1970s and early 1980s, the Mexican government saw in Loreto the possibility for another megadevelopment along the lines of Cancún, Ixtapa, or Los Cabos. It invested in a golf course and championship tennis facility, modernized the infrastructure, and built an international airport and marina facilities at Puerto Loreto, several kilometers south of town. The economics, however, didn't make sense, and few hotel investors and even fewer tourists came. In the past 2 years, however, this effort has been revitalized, and the area is seeing a welcome influx of flights, as well as the addition of its first new hotel in years, a sprawling Inn at Loreto Bay, which has had three different owners in as many years. The Loreto Bay residential development has been a major source of drama for the area as each new developer promises completion of the project. The best place to stay up to date with the saga is **www.nopolonews.com**.

The *Loretanos,* Loreto-born Mexicans, are friendly and helpful; unlike the swarms of proprietary tourists that dominate the peninsula's northern and southern reaches, the mid-Baja region attracts a more unassuming set of visitors, and locals play the part of gracious hosts. Canadian and American expatriates who've settled in Loreto may be a bit more aloof with tourists, and who can blame them? They settled here when there was nothing, and they can't help but want it to stay that way for as long as possible.

The main reason to come here is to see Loreto's historic center on the Sea of Cortez and the five islands just offshore, but the Sierra de la Giganta mountains offer a wealth of opportunities for exploration as well. The reefs around Isla Coronado are home to schools of giant grouper, and beachgoers won't find a bay more beautiful than the one on Coronado's north side. Puerto Escondido shelters a growing yachting community; it's so lovely that most of the sailboats stay put year-round. Kayakers launch here for trips to Isla del Carmen and Isla Danzante or down the remote mountain coast to La Paz; history buffs head for the mountains to visit some of the oldest Jesuit missions.

ESSENTIALS

The **Loreto International Airport** (© 613/135-0499, -0498) is 6km (3¾ miles) southwest of town. **Taxis** (© 613/135-0047) are readily available and charge about $20 for the 10-minute ride to Loreto. It is serviced by **Alaska Airlines** (© 800/252-7522 from Los Angeles. Loreto's Terminal de Autobuses, or **bus station** (© 613/135-0767), is on Salvatierra and Paseo Tamaral, a 10-minute walk from downtown. It's open 24 hours. The 5-hour trip from La Paz costs 300 pesos.

The city **tourist information office** (© 613/135-0411) is in the southeast corner of the Palacio de Gobierno building, across from the town square. It offers maps, local free publications, and other basic information about the area. It's open Monday through Friday from 8am to 3pm. Information, which may be outdated, is also available at **www.gotoloreto.com** and **www.loreto.com**.

Salvatierra is the main street that runs northeast, merging into Paseo Hidalgo, which runs toward the beach. Calle de la Playa, also known as the Malecón, parallels the water; along this road you'll find many hotels, seafood restaurants, fishing charters, and the marina. Most of the town's social life revolves around the central square, the old mission, and the Malecón. The local telephone area code is **613.**

WHAT TO SEE & DO

The Sea of Cortez is the star in Loreto, and the five islands just offshore make for some of the best kayaking, sailing, diving, and fishing in North America. Freediving, too, is becoming more popular. Loreto is the nearest major airport and city to **Bahía de Magdalena (Magdalena Bay),** the southernmost of the major gray whale–calving lagoons on the Pacific coast of Baja. For more information on popular whale-watching spots and tour operators, see "Whale-Watching in Baja," below.

Misión Nuestra Señora de Loreto was the first mission in the Californias, started in 1699. The original Virgen de Loreto, brought to shore by Padre Kino in 1697, is on display in the church's 18th-century gilded altar. The mission is on Salvatierra, across from the central square. Adjacent to the mission church and of equal or greater interest is the **Museo de las Misiones,** Salvatierra 16 (© 613/135-0441). It has a small but complete collection of historical and anthropological exhibits from the Jesuit mission period. The museum is open Tuesday through Sunday from 9am to 1pm and 1:45pm to 6pm. Admission is 30 pesos.

One of this region's greatest treasures is actually located 2 hours into its interior. The **Misión San Javier** is truly a sight to behold. Completed in 1759 near a mountain stream that still flows through a tiny mountain village, it's the only one of the missions in the Californias that has never been restored and still maintains its original grandeur. Its walls and foundation are made up of stone from a nearby quarry. The hour-long drive through the Sierra de la Giganta mountains involves a long dirt road, but the views of sweeping auburn and gold cliffs and canyon are reminiscent of the Grand Canyon or Sedona in Arizona. You'll encounter all manner of desert inhabitants, including cacti, *vaqueros,* and *burros* along the way.

WHERE TO STAY

In general, accommodations in Loreto are the kind you used to find all over Mexico: inexpensive and unique, with genuine, friendly owner-operators. And as mid-Baja is a mecca for RV explorers, **Rivera Del Mar RV Park & Camping** (☎ 613/135-0718; www.riveradelmar.com) has deluxe hookups just 2 blocks from the beach. The rates quoted below do not include the 12% tax. Parking is free at all hotels in mid-Baja. Also of note, as people fall in love with Loreto and build their dream homes there, vacation-rental properties are on the rise, and Kathy and Hector at **Rentals Loreto** (☎ 613/135-2505; www.rentalsloreto.com) have the best selection in town. Gorgeous beachfront homes that sleep up to eight can go for a max of $170 a night and most also rent by the week.

La Damiana Inn ★★ 🏠 The location of the La Damiana Inn—in the heart of town on Calle Madero—is reason enough to book a reservation, but the warmth of color, style, and ownership make it the best accommodations value in Loreto. Debora Simmons lovingly operates this former family home, built in 1917. Today its five rooms, all equipped with air-conditioning and ceiling fans, offer a blend of twin, queen, and king-size beds that provide cozy resting places when you're not exploring the area. Wi-Fi throughout the hotel, laundry facilities, a shared living room, kitchen use, and free cuddles from two friendly house dogs are the perks that make La Damiana Inn seem like the home of a gracious friend. Pets welcome upon prior approval.

Madero, btw. Hidalgo and Jordan, Centro, 23880 Loreto, B.C.S. www.ladamianainn.com. ☎ **613/135-0356.** 5 units. $62 double; $75 suite. No credit cards (traveler's checks accepted). **Amenities:** Bikes; library; phone for local calls; TV; Wi-Fi. *In room:* A/C, fan, no phone.

Posada de Las Flores ★★★ The most luxurious place to stay in Loreto conveniently sits adjacent to the main square, in the heart of historic Loreto. The first thing you'll notice upon entering is a constant shift and sparkle of light—this is because a swimming pool sits atop the ceiling. Every room is beautifully decorated with fine Mexican arts and crafts, including heavy wood doors, Talavera pottery, painted tiles, candles, and Mexican scenic paintings. The colors and decor of the hotel are nouveau-colonial Mexico, with wood and tin accents. Large bathrooms have thick white towels and bamboo doors, with Frette bathrobes hanging in the closet. Every detail has been carefully selected, including the down comforters and numerous antiques tucked into corners. This hotel exudes class and refinement, from the general ambience to the warm polish of its employees.

Salvatierra and Francisco I. Madera, Centro, 23880 Loreto, B.C.S. www.posadadelasflores.com. ☎ **619/378-0103** in the U.S., or 613/135-1162. Fax 613/135-1099. 15 units. High season $180 double, $290 suite; low season $150 double, $250 suite. Rates include continental breakfast. MC, V. Street parking. Children 11 or younger not permitted. **Amenities:** Breakfast restaurant; hospitality desk; rooftop glass-bottom pool. *In room:* A/C, TV, hair dryer, minibar, Wi-Fi.

WHERE TO EAT

Dining in Loreto affords surprising variety, given the small size and laid-back nature of the town. However, don't expect anything fancy, even at the nicest restaurant. Big flavors come in humble packages in Loreto. In addition to the following hubs, the cinnamon rolls at Mediterraneo, on the *malecón*; the grilled porterhouse at **El Nido**, on Salvatierra; and the fried-shrimp tacos at **Tacos el Rey,** on Benito Juárez, are all meals that will add flavor to your stay in Loreto.

Augie's Bar ★ PIZZA/BAR Located on the *malecón*, this is the preeminent happy-hour hot spot for the gringo community. Augie, who hales from the California video arcade business and does fun for a living, offers dancing lessons to patrons after they've had six drinks—and he keeps good on his promise. With TV sports of all kinds, ocean views, fabulous margaritas, tortilla pizzas that drive the town crazy, and an upstairs terrace that showcases Loreto's big-sky sunsets, this is the place to be after 4pm any day of the week.

On the corner of the Malecón and Zaragoza. ⓒ **613/100-0086.** Pizza 50-100 pesos. No credit cards. Daily 7am-11pm.

Café Olé LIGHT FARE   The breezy Café Olé is the best option for breakfast. Try eggs with *nopal* cactus or the hot cakes. For lunch, standards such as burgers and fries, as well as tacos and some Mexican dishes are on the menu, as are fresh-fruit smoothies, or *licuados*.

Madero 14. ⓒ **613/135-0496.** Breakfast 20-50 pesos; sandwiches 20-35 pesos. No credit cards. Mon-Sat 7am-10pm; Sun 7am-2pm.

Del Borracho ★ BURGERS/SANDWICHES   If you're a *Three Amigos* fan from way back, Mike and Andrea Patterson's tribute to the obscure bar in the classic comedy will not disappoint. The movie often plays on loop in the background of this wooden saloon outside of town, while chili dogs, milkshakes, sandwiches, and burgers make the rounds among a happy-bellied crowd that's chugging draft beer. The only place in town to serve Modelo Light and Modelo Negro on draft, Del Borracho's real claim to fame is the 35-peso bowl of clam chowder that comes with a side of Andrea's homemade bread; of note for sports fans, Del Borracho has the *NFL Sunday Ticket*.

.5km (⅓ mile) down the road to San Javier, 3.2km (2 miles) south of Loreto. ⓒ **613/137-0112.** Main courses 30-100 pesos. No credit cards. Daily sunrise-sunset.

LORETO AFTER DARK

Although selection is limited, Loreto after dark offers a place for almost every nightlife preference. Happy hour starts in the late afternoon and ends shortly after sundown at bars like **Augie's Bar** (see above). Cocktails, music, and tapas flow into the wee hours at **Mike's Bar** on Paseo Hidalgo. In addition, as is the tradition throughout Mexico, Loreto's central plaza offers a **free concert** when there's a cruise ship in port. However, Loretanos and their families are so hospitable that the best party may be the one to which you're unexpectedly invited. In Loreto, magic is bound to happen.

Santa Rosalia

61km (38 miles) N of Mulegé

Located in an *arroyo* (dry streambed) north of Mulegé, Santa Rosalía looks more like an old Colorado mining town than a Mexican port city. Founded by the French in 1855, the town has a European ambience combined with a distinctly Mexican culture. Pastel clapboard houses surrounded by picket fences line the streets, giving the town its nickname—*ciudad de madera* (city of wood). The large harbor and rusted ghost of a copper-smelting facility dominate the central part of town bordering the waterfront. The town was a copper-mining center for years, and a French outfit operated here from 1885 until 1954, when the Mexicans regained the use of the land. Problems plagued the facility, which closed permanently in 1985.

Today Santa Rosalía (pop. 14,000) is known for its man-made harbor—the recently constructed Marina Santa Rosalía, complete with concrete piers, floating docks, and full docking accommodations for up to a dozen ocean liners. Because this is the prime entry point of manufactured goods into Baja, the town abounds with auto parts and electronics stores, along with shops selling Nikes and sunglasses. The town has no real beach to speak of and few recreational attractions.

EXPLORING SANTA ROSALÍA

The principal attraction in Santa Rosalía is the **Iglesia de Santa Bárbara,** a structure of galvanized steel designed by Gustave Eiffel (of Eiffel Tower fame) in 1884. It was created for the 1889 Paris World Expo, then transported here section by section and reassembled in 1897. Its somber gray exterior belies the beauty of the intricate stained-glass windows as viewed from inside.

The other sight to see is the former Fundación del Pacífico, or **Museo Histórico Minero de Santa Rosalía.** Located in a landmark wooden building, it houses a permanent display of artifacts from the days of Santa Rosalía's mining operations. It's open Monday through Friday from 8am to 2pm. Admission is free.

However, the city itself is the main attraction. Wooden saloons, wraparound verandas, and mountainous terrain make for a paradoxical contrast to the Mexicans milling in the streets. You can't get lost in this grid of one-way streets, so even if you're on your way someplace else, a 15-minute drive through Santa Rosalía is a must. Here,

 # whale-watching IN BAJA

Few sights inspire as much reverence as close contact with a whale in its natural habitat. The various protected bays and lagoons on Baja's Pacific coast are the preferred winter waters for migrating gray whales as they journey south to mate and give birth to their calves. These whales are known to be so friendly and curious that they frequently come up to the boats and stay close by, and sometimes even allow people to pet them.

The experience is particularly rewarding in the protected areas of the **El Vizcaíno Biosphere Reserve,** where you can easily see many whales. This area encompasses Guerrero Negro, Laguna San Ignacio, Bahía Magdalena, and the famous **Laguna Ojo de Liebre**—also known as **Scammon's Lagoon.**

Because these protected waters offer ideal conditions for gray whales during the winter, the neighboring towns have developed the infrastructure and services to accommodate whale-watchers. Whale-watching season generally runs

from January to March. But remember that the colder the water, the farther south the whales migrate, so check on water temperatures and whale sightings before you plan your expedition. The temperature on the boat can be cool, so bring a jacket.

Although you can fly from Los Cabos and La Paz, **Loreto** is the best place to launch a whale-watching journey, as it has a well-developed tourist infrastructure and a number of lovely resort hotels. Trips take you by road to Bahía Magdalena, where you board a skiff to get up close to the gentle giants. **Las Parras Tours** (© **613/135-1010;** www.mexonline. com/lasparras.htm) offers excellent tours. Prices for package trips from Loreto run around 900 to 1,000 pesos per person for a daylong trip. San Diego-based **Baja Expeditions** (© **800/843-6967** in the U.S., or 612/125-3828; www.bajaex.com) runs longer-term expeditions, which cost upward of $2,995 per person for a multiday trip.

in this thriving ghost town, you won't find hacienda-style architecture or red-tile roofs, but you will find the best bakery in Baja. **El Boleo,** at Avenida Obregón at Calle 4 (*©* **615/152-0310**), has been baking French baguettes since the late 1800s, but I recommend the pitahaya, a dense sweetbread stuffed with a kind of almond paste. It's 3 blocks west of the church and is open from 8am to 9pm Monday to Saturday, and Sunday 9am to 2pm.

WHERE TO STAY & EAT

Dining is limited in the small town of Santa Rosalía, but lunch at **El Muelle** restaurant, on Obregón, right across from the central plaza, is superb. The tacos, enchiladas in spicy fresh tomato sauce, and breaded fish bathed in peppers and cheese are all good reasons to visit, but the main draw is the creamy chipotle–smoked tuna dip that comes with chips before the meal. Follow it up with dessert bread from El Boleo.

Hotel Francés   Founded in 1886, the Hotel Francés once set the standard of hospitality in Baja Sur, welcoming European dignitaries and hosting the French administrators and businessmen of the mining operations. Today it has a worn air of elegance but retains its position as the most welcoming accommodations in Santa Rosalía. Rooms are in the back, with wooden porches and balconies overlooking a small courtyard pool. Each room has individually controlled air-conditioning, plus windows that open for ventilation. Floors are wood planked, and the small bathrooms are beautifully tiled. You have a choice of two double beds or one king. Telephone service is available in the lobby. The popular restaurant serves breakfast until noon.

Calle Jean Michel Cousteau s/n, 23920 Santa Rosalía B.C.S. *©*/fax **615/152-2052.** 16 units. 700 pesos double. Rates include breakfast. No credit cards. Free parking. **Amenities:** Restaurant (7am–noon); small courtyard pool. *In room:* A/C, TV, no phone, Wi-Fi.

TIJUANA & ROSARITO BEACH

Northern Baja California is not only Mexico's most infamous border crossing, it also claims to be the birthplace of the original Caesar salad and the margarita. Long notorious as a hard-partying 10-block border town, **Tijuana** has cleaned up its act a bit on its way to becoming a full-scale city. A growing number of sports and cultural attractions now augment the legendary shopping experience and wild nightlife. **Rosarito Beach,** of *Titanic* fame, remains a more tranquil resort town; the decidedly laid-back atmosphere makes it easy to enjoy its miles of beachfront.

Tijuana: Bawdy Border Town

In northern Baja, 26km (16 miles) south of San Diego, the first point of entry from the West Coast of the U.S. is infamous Tijuana—a town that continues to delude travelers into thinking that a visit there means they've been to Mexico. An important border town, Tijuana is renowned for its hustling, carnival-like atmosphere.

Tijuana has been hit hard by Mexico's drug violence, and, unfortunately, tourism there has suffered. Nowadays you're most likely going to visit either on your way to another destination or for a day trip. However, vineyards associated with the expanding wine industry are nearby, and an increasing number of cultural offerings have joined the traditional sporting attractions of greyhound racing, jai alai, and bullfights.

Although Tijuana has the reputation for being a carefree party playground, now more than ever it's important to use common sense while visiting. The U.S. Department of State first issued a Travel Advisory in February 2009, after a heightened amount of violence by drug gangs along the U.S.-Mexico border in cities such as Ciudad Juarez, Chihuahua City, and Tijuana. This advisory is still in effect. While most of the people targeted in the attacks were involved in law enforcement or the drug trade, the violence has come close to innocent bystanders in some instances. One shootout in Tijuana caused a kindergarten to be shut down, and another caused a high-speed chase that ended with a truck crashing into the airport. The U.S. Department of State offers the following advice to travelers who still wish to travel to

Tijuana and other border cities: "Travelers should leave their itinerary with a friend or family member not traveling with them, avoid traveling alone, and should check with their cellular provider prior to departure to confirm that their cell phone is capable of roaming on GSM or 3G international networks. Do not display expensive-looking jewelry, large amounts of money, or other valuable items."

Despite these shake-ups, however, life goes on in Tijuana as in any other large metropolitan city—even the State Department's advisory mentions that thousands of people cross the border every day without incident. Locals are still very proud of their city's culture and welcome visitors with open arms. They also advise you, however, to say no to illegal drugs of any kind.

You are less likely to find the Mexico you may be expecting here—no charming town squares and churches, no women in colorful embroidered skirts and blouses, no bougainvillea spilling out of every crevice. Tijuana has an urban culture and a profusion of U.S.-inspired goods and services, and its collection of world-class restaurants still warrants at least a day trip for the adventurous.

ESSENTIALS

A visit to Tijuana requires little in the way of formalities—people who stay less than 72 hours in the border zone do not need a tourist card. If you plan to stay longer, a tourist card is required in addition to a passport. If you're staying 7 days or less, tourist cards are free from the border crossing station or from any immigration office; they cost a small fee for more than 7 days.

From downtown San Diego, you have the option of taking the **bright-red trolley** headed for San Ysidro and getting off at the last stop, San Ysidro (it's nicknamed the Tijuana Trolley for good reason). From here, follow the signs to walk across the border, or hop one of the buses (© **664/685-1470**), which are located next to the trolley station. It's simple, quick, and inexpensive; the one-way fare is about $2. The last trolley leaving for San Ysidro departs downtown San Diego around midnight; the last returning trolley from San Ysidro is at 1am. On Saturday, the trolley runs 24 hours.

Once you're in Tijuana, it's easy to get around by taxis, which are still relatively safe compared to those in Mexico City. Cab fares from the border to downtown average 50 pesos; you can also hire a taxi to Rosarito for about 200 pesos one-way.

Tijuana

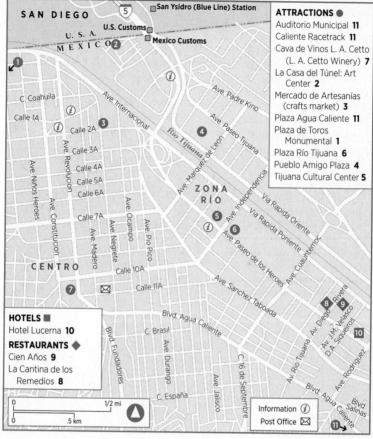

ATTRACTIONS ●
Auditorio Municipal **11**
Caliente Racetrack **11**
Cava de Vinos L. A. Cetto
(L. A. Cetto Winery) **7**
La Casa del Túnel: Art
Center **2**
Mercado de Artesanías
(crafts market) **3**
Plaza Agua Caliente **11**
Plaza de Toros
Monumental **1**
Plaza Río Tijuana **6**
Pueblo Amigo Plaza **4**
Tijuana Cultural Center **5**

HOTELS ■
Hotel Lucerna **10**
RESTAURANTS ◆
Cien Años **9**
La Cantina de los
Remedios **8**

Information ⓘ
Post Office ✉

San Ysidro (Blue Line) Station
SAN DIEGO
U.S. Customs
Mexico Customs
U.S.A.
MEXICO
ZONA RÍO
CENTRO

The Tijuana airport (☎ 664/607-8200) is about 8km (5 miles) east of the city. To drive to Tijuana from the U.S., take I-5 or 805 south to the Mexican border at San Ysidro. The drive from downtown San Diego takes about a half-hour, or you can leave your car in a San Ysidro parking lot and walk the 20 minutes to Avenida Revolución.

Tijuana's **Central Camionera de Autobuses,** Blvd. Lázaro Cárdenas y Río Alamar (☎ 664/621-2982; 24 hr.), is home to several regional lines including **Autotransportes Baja California** (**ABC;** ☎ 01-800/0520-222 in Mexico; www.abc.com.mx), which serves destinations throughout Baja; **Estrella Blanca** (☎ 01-800/507-5500 in Mexico; www.estrellablanca.com.mx), which takes you throughout Mexico; and **Crucero** (☎ 800/231-2222 in the U.S.; www.crucero-usa.com), Greyhound's Mexican affiliate.

LOS CABOS & BAJA CALIFORNIA Tijuana & Rosarito Beach

19

For **tourist information,** visit the Centro Cultural Tijuana, Paseo de los Héroes and Mina (© 664/687-9600). It's in the Zona Río, the principal shopping and dining district, adjacent to the Tijuana River. For more information, visit the Tijuana Tourism board's official website, **www.tijuanaonline.org.**

There are major banks with ATMs and *casas de cambio* (money-exchange houses) all over Tijuana, but you can easily come here—or to Rosarito and Ensenada, for that matter—without changing money, because dollars are accepted everywhere.

The **Canadian Consulate** is at Germán Gedovius 10411-101, Condominio del Parque, Zona Río (© 664/684-0461; Mon–Fri 9:30am–12:30pm). The **U.S. Consulate** is at Av. Tapachula 96, Col. Hipodromo (© 664/622-7400; Mon–Fri 8am–4:45pm).

EXPLORING TIJUANA

For many visitors, Tijuana's main event is the bustling **Avenida Revolución,** which was constructed in 1889. Beginning in the 1920s, American college students, servicemen, and hedonistic tourists discovered this street as a center for illicit fun. Some of the original attractions—gambling, back-alley cockfights (now illegal), and girlie shows—have fallen by the wayside, with drinking and shopping the main order of business these days—although even these activities have fallen off recently due to the dismal headlines. You'll find the action between calles 1 and 9; the landmark Jai Alai Frontón Palace anchors the southern portion. If you don't want to navigate the area on your own, the **Tijuana Convention & Visitors' Bureau** (© 664/607-3097; www.tijuanaonline.org) offers a 1-hour guided walking tour of the city, and **Eco Baja Tours** (www.ecobajatours.com) offers a selection of tours, including visits to the Guadalupe Valley, La Bufadora, and Tecate.

If you're looking to see a different side of Tijuana, the best place to start is the **Centro Cultural Tijuana (Tijuana Cultural Center),** Paseo de los Héroes and Mina Zona Río (© 664/607-3097, ext. 9650; www.cecut.gob.mx). You'll easily spot the ultramodern Tijuana Cultural Center complex, which houses an IMAX theater, the museum's permanent collection of Mexican artifacts, and a gallery of visiting exhibits. The center is open daily from 9am to 9pm. Admission to the permanent exhibits is free, there's a 46-peso charge for the special-event gallery, and tickets for IMAX films are 46 pesos for adults and 26 pesos for children.

 ARTE DE LA frontera

The Casa del Túnel: Art Center ("House of the Tunnel") is built on the former site of a clandestine smuggling tunnel that went underneath the U.S.-Mexico border wall, allowing smugglers to carry contraband items between the two countries out of view of the authorities. Today, the tunnel is long gone, and the building is now home to a thriving art and cultural center, part of the Consejo Fronterizo de Arte y Cultura (COFAC; Border Council of Arts and Culture). On a recent visit, the Casa featured a photo exhibition on Che Guevara's time in Cuba and a sculpture of a white Mustang riddled with bullet holes. The building's third-floor patio and workspace features sweeping city vistas as well as a bird's-eye view of the border-crossing bridge. For more information, contact **La Casa del Túnel: Art Center,** Chapo Márquez 133, at © 664/682-9570 in Mexico, or 323/574-9197 in the U.S.

The fertile valleys of northern Baja produce most of Mexico's finest wines and export many high-quality vintages to Europe. For an introduction to Mexican wines, stop into **Cava de Vinos L. A. Cetto (L. A. Cetto Winery),** Av. Cañón Johnson 2108, at Avenida Constitución Sur (📞 **664/685-3031,** ext. 128, or 664/638-1644; www.lacetto.com). Shaped like a wine barrel, this building's facade is made from old oak aging barrels—call it inspired recycling. Guided tours run Monday through Saturday from 10am to 1:30pm and 5pm; it's open Saturday from 10am to 4pm.

Tijuana's biggest attraction is **shopping.** People come to take advantage of low prices on a variety of merchandise—terra-cotta and colorfully glazed pottery, woven blankets and serapes, embroidered dresses and sequined sombreros, onyx chess sets, beaded necklaces and bracelets, silver jewelry, leather bags and *huarache* sandals, rain sticks, Cuban cigars, and Mexican liquors. Many Americans view Tijuana as a way to purchase inexpensive prescription drugs and bring them back across the border. Be aware—authorities have cracked down and are making surprise arrests of foreigners purchasing drugs without valid prescriptions from a Mexican doctor.

If a marketplace atmosphere and spirited bargaining are what you're looking for, head to **Mercado de Artesanías (crafts market),** Calle 2 and Avenida Negrete. Here vendors of pottery, clayware, clothing, and other handicrafts fill an entire city block. Shopping malls are as common in Tijuana as in any big American city; you shouldn't expect to find typical souvenirs there, but shopping alongside residents and other intrepid visitors is often more fun than feeling like a sitting-duck tourist. One of the biggest, and most convenient, is **Plaza Río Tijuana,** Paseo de los Héroes 96 at Avenida Independencia, Zona Río (📞 **664/684-0402). Plaza Agua Caliente** (📞 **664/681-7777),** at Bulevar Agua Caliente 4558, Col. Aviación, is a more upscale shopping center and, in addition to fine shops and restaurants, is known for its emphasis on health and beauty, with day spas, gyms, and doctors' offices found in abundance here. A comprehensive selection of shopping options is listed at **www. tijuanaonline.org/EN/Visitors/Shopping.php.**

OUTDOOR ACTIVITIES & SPECTATOR SPORTS

BULLFIGHTING   Whatever your opinion, bullfighting has a prominent place in Mexican heritage and is even considered an essential element of the culture. The skill and bravery of matadors is linked with cultural ideals regarding *machismo,* and some of the world's best perform in Tijuana. As in Spain, however, the bulls die. The season runs late spring to early fall (usually May to early Oct), with events held on Sunday at 4:30pm. Ticket prices range from 100 to 300 pesos; the premium seats are on the shaded side of the arena, available at the bullring or in advance from San Diego's **Five Star Tours** (📞 **619/232-5049** in the U.S. or 664/622-2203). **Plaza de Toros Monumental,** also called Bullring-by-the-Sea (📞 **664/680-1808;** www.plaza monumental.com), is 10km (6¼ miles) west of downtown on Hwy. 1-D (before the first toll station); it's at the edge of the ocean and the California border.

LUCHA LIBRE   Although Jack Black made the flamboyant fighters popular with American filmgoers with his 2006 movie *Nacho Libre,* Mexicans have always had a fondness for great masked fighters like El Santo and Rey Misterio. The matches, which feature up to five different bouts, are spectacular. The *luchadores* are equal parts athlete, actor, and boogeyman, and audience members are never shy about joining in with jeers and taunts. **Auditorio Municipal** (📞 **664/250-9015),** at Diaz Ordaz 12421, hosts fights just about every Friday night at 8:30pm. Ticket prices start at $5 and vary depending on the popularity of the fight.

TURISTA LIBRE   One of the best ways to take in Tijuana's charm is to participate in a **Turista Libre** (www.turistalibre.com) tour. American Midwest native Derrick Chinn lives in Tijuana and commutes regularly to nearby San Diego. He started arranging Turista Libre trips for friends and fellow San Diegans in order to show them the parts of the city that drew him in. Chinn has taken groups on field trips to local markets, on a double-decker bus around town, to the circus, and on graffiti art tours. One-day tours occur once a month and prices vary depending on the event.

A PLACE TO STAY

Hotel Lucerna   Once the most chic hotel in Tijuana, Lucerna now feels slightly worn, though it still has personality. The flavor is Mexican colonial—wrought-iron railings and chandeliers, rough-hewn heavy wood furniture, brocade wallpaper, and traditional tiles. The hotel is in the Zona Río, away from the noise and congestion of downtown, so a quiet night's sleep is easily attainable. All of the rooms in the five-story hotel have balconies or patios. Hotel rates in Tijuana are subject to a 12% tax.

Av. Paseo de los Héroes, 10902 Zona Río, Tijuana. © **664/633-3900.** 168 units. $85 double; $175–$360 suite. AE, MC, V. Free parking. **Amenities:** Coffee shop; outdoor pool; room service. *In room:* A/C, satellite TV, hair dryer.

WHERE TO EAT

Cien Años MEXICAN   This elegant and gracious Zona Río restaurant offers artfully blended Mexican flavors (tamarind, poblano chile, mango) in stylish presentations. If you're interested in haute cuisine for breakfast, lunch, or dinner, stop here; the buzz around Tijuana is all about this place.

José María Velazco 1407, Zona del Río. © **888/534-6088,** or 619/819-5097 in the U.S., or 664/634-3039, -3794. www.cien.info. Main courses $10–$25. AE, MC, V. Mon-Thurs 8am-11pm; Fri-Sat 8am-midnight; Sun 8am-10pm.

La Cantina de los Remedios MEXICAN   This is one of Tijuana's most festive atmospheres, wildly popular with Mexicans and Americans alike for its typical Mexican cuisine and courtyard atmosphere. Another highlight is its all-inclusive menu option, which has made it a hit in seven other cities throughout Mexico. For one price, guests can enjoy an appetizer, soup or salad, main course, dessert, and cocktail. Here the drink menu is extensive, inspiring the name *los remedios,* or "the remedies."

Av. Diego Rivera 19 718, Zona del Río. © **664/634-3065.** www.losremedios.com.mx. Average meal $15–$20. MC, V. Mon-Thurs 1pm-1am; Fri-Sat 1pm-2am; Sun 1-10pm.

TIJUANA AFTER DARK

Avenida Revolución is the city's nightlife center, often compared with Bourbon Street in New Orleans during Mardi Gras—though here the blowout is year-round.

Zona Río and Plaza Fiesta are more geared toward late-night dining and dance-clubbing than tequila swilling and barhopping. Although the nightlife scene changes regularly, a very popular dance club is **Baby Rock,** Diego Rivera 1482, Zona Río (© **664/634-2404**), a cousin to Acapulco's lively Baby O, which features everything from Latin rock to rap. It's open from 9pm to 3am, with a cover charge of $12 on Saturday.

Also popular in Tijuana are sports bars, which feature wagering on events in the United States, as well as races from Tijuana's Caliente track. The most popular cluster is in the Pueblo Amigo and Vía Oriente areas and around Plaza Rio Tijuana in the

A NORTHERN BAJA spa sanctuary

One of Mexico's best-known spas is in northern Baja, just 58km (36 miles) south of San Diego. The **Rancho La Puerta** ★★ occupies 1,200 hectares (2,964 acres) of lush oasis surrounded by pristine countryside, which includes a 2.5-hectare (6¼-acre) organic garden and La Cocina Que Canta, a spa cuisine cooking school that opened in 2007. Cottages accommodate up to 150 guests per week, and the ranch has a staff of almost 400. Each cottage has its own patio garden and is decorated with Mexican folk art. Inside the rooms are spacious living-room-size seating areas, desks, CD players, hair dryers, robes, and safes, and most rooms have fireplaces.

Three swimming pools, four tennis courts, five hot tubs, saunas, steam rooms, and 11 gyms for aerobic and restorative classes are only part of the facilities. Separate men and women's health centers offer the full range of spa services. Hiking trails surround the resort, and a labyrinth that is a full-size replica of the ancient labyrinth found in Chartres Cathedral allows for moving meditation.

There are also several lounges and shared spaces, including the library, with thousands of books to browse and read, an evening movie lounge, a recreation room, and for those who can't conceive of totally disconnecting, the E-center, with 24-hour access to e-mail and Internet.

Rancho La Puerta runs weeklong programs—Saturday through Saturday—emphasizing a mind/body/spirit philosophy, and certain weeks throughout the year are geared specifically to one topic; Specialty Week themes range from couples to Pilates and dance to meditation. Prices are $2,835 to $4,720 for the week most of the year. Included in the rates are all classes, meals, evening programs, and use of facilities. Personal spa services cost extra. You may be able to book shorter stays (3 nights or more), and rates may be prorated on a nightly basis.

For reservations or to request a brochure, visit **www.rancholapuerta.com**, call ✆ **800/443-7565** in the U.S., or fax 858/764-5560. American Express, MasterCard, and Visa are accepted.

Zona Río, a center designed to resemble a colonial Mexican village. **Señor Frog's** (✆ **664/682-4964**; no cover) is in **Pueblo Amigo Plaza,** which is just off of Paseo Tijuana. Pueblo Amigo Plaza is less than 3km (1¾ miles) from the border, a short taxi ride, or—during daylight hours—a pleasant walk.

Like any international metropolis, Tijuana is home to a variety of different music scenes. One of its most vibrant is folk/alternative. One of Mexico's most popular singers, **Julieta Venegas,** got her start here and still calls on it for inspiration. Up-and-coming songstress **Carla Morrison** hails from Tecate and has cut her teeth at some of Tijuana's most popular clubs. If you want a chance to discover the area's next big talent, your best bet is to check out **El Lugar Del Nopal** (✆ **664/685-4964**; www.lugardelnopal.com), a cultural space that hosts concerts along with film viewings and art shows. If you want to find out more about local concerts, **La Guia Tijuana** has comprehensive listings of the best events around town at www.facebook.com/LaGuiaTijuanaFB.

Rosarito Beach: Baja's First Beach Resort

Just 29km (18 miles) south of Tijuana and a complete departure in ambience, Rosarito Beach is a tranquil, friendly beach town. Hollywood has played a major part in Rosarito's recent renaissance—it was the location for the soundstage and filming of the Academy Award–winning *Titanic*. The beaches between Tijuana and Rosarito are also known for excellent surf breaks.

GETTING THERE   Two roads run between Tijuana and Ensenada (the largest and third-largest cities in Baja): the scenic, coast-hugging toll road (**Hwy. 1-D,** marked *cuota,* costs $2.40), and the free but slower public road (**Hwy. 1,** marked *libre*). Both roads pass through Rosarito Beach. Alternatively, you can take a shuttle from the last trolley stop in San Ysidro. **Mexicoach** (© **619/428-9517** in the U.S., or 664/685-1470 in Mexico; www.mexicoach.com) offers shuttle rides for about $20 round-trip.

WHAT TO SEE & DO

If you have only a few hours to spend in Rosarito Beach, that's still enough time to have a swim or a horseback ride at the beach, shop for souvenirs, and dine on fish tacos or tamales from one of the family-run stands along **Bulevar Benito Juárez,** the town's main (and only) drag. The dozen or so blocks of Rosarito north of the Rosarito Beach Hotel are packed with stores typical of Mexican border towns: curio shops, cigar and *licores* (liquor) stores, and *farmacías.*

Die-hard Baja fans still make it to the most popular spot in town: **Papas & Beer** (© **661/612-0444;** www.papasandbeer.com). It's a relaxed come-as-you-are club on the beach, a block north of the hotel. It's great fun, with outdoor tables and a bar surrounding a sand volleyball court. The **Rosa and Rita** karaoke bar (© **800/343-8582** in the U.S., or 661/612-0144 in Mexico), in the Rosarito Beach Hotel, attracts a slightly more mature crowd, with live music and karaoke on Friday and Saturday.

WHERE TO STAY & EAT

Rosarito Beach Hotel & Spa   This family-owned resort had its glamorous heyday in the 1920s and is currently defined by glaring nighttime neon and party-mania.

SURFING, northern baja STYLE

Undoubtedly, the most famous surf spot in all of Mexico is **Killers**, at Todos Santos Island. This was the location of the winning wave in the 1997–98 K2 Challenge (a worldwide contest to ride the largest wave each winter—and be photographed doing it). Killers is a very makeable wave for confident, competent surfers. To get there, you need a boat. You can get a lift from the local *panga* (skiff) fleet, for about $200 for the day. That's pretty much the going rate, and the tightly knit Ensenada *pangueros* aren't eager to undercut each other. It's about 15km (9¼ miles) out to the island; there you'll anchor and paddle into the lineup. You must bring everything you'll need—food, drink, sunscreen, and so on.

Other less radical and easier-to-reach spots include the rocky **Popotla** break, south of Rosarito, where you'll walk to the beach through the Popotla trailer park. **Calafia,** just a few kilometers south of Rosarito, has a reeling right point that can get very heavy. **San Miguel** is the point break just south of the final tollbooth on the highway into Ensenada. It's an excellent wave but generally crowded.

The Upper Baja Peninsula

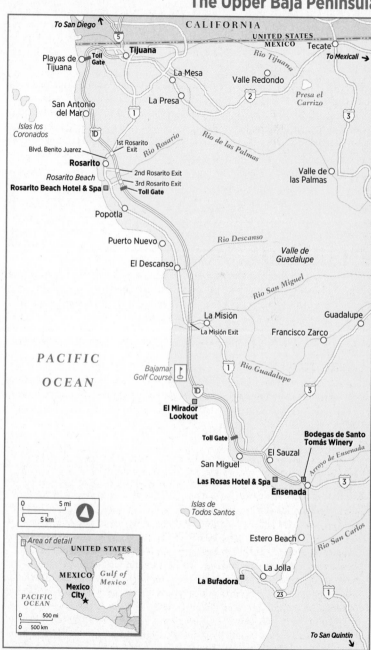

The Torres family changed the hotel's image yet again with the addition of a 17-story condo hotel that opened in the summer of 2008. The new addition features sleek and modern furnishing and suites that include full kitchens. Despite the resort's ever-changing personality, its unique artistic construction and lavish decoration remain on the original property. It has a wide, family-friendly stretch of beach. The stately home of the original owners has been transformed into the full-service **Casa Playa Spa,** where massages and other treatments are only slightly less costly than in the U.S. You'll pay more for a room with an ocean view, and more for the newer, air-conditioned units in the tower; the older rooms in the poolside building have only ceiling fans, but they prevail in the character department, with hand-painted trim and original tile. The mansion's dining room (Chabert's Restaurant) charges top dollar for Continental cuisine; Azteca is a casual Mexican restaurant in the main building.

Bulevar Benito Juárez, Zona Centro, 22710 Rosarito, B.C. www.rosaritobeachhotel.com. ℭ **800/343-8582** in the U.S. or 661/612-1111. 500 units. $79–$139 double; $159–$459 suite. 2 children younger than 12 stay free in parent's room. Packages available. MC, V. Free parking. **Amenities:** 2 restaurants; bar; playground; 2 outdoor pools; wading pool; racquetball court; room service; spa; Wi-Fi (in some common areas). *In room:* A/C (in some), fan (in some), TV.

ENSENADA: PORT OF CALL

134km (83 miles) S of San Diego; 109km (68 miles) S of Tijuana

Ensenada is an attractive town on a lovely bay, surrounded by sheltering mountains. About 40 minutes from Rosarito, it's the kind of place that loves a celebration—be it for a bicycle race or a seafood festival.

GETTING THERE & INFORMATION   After passing through the final tollgate, **Hwy. 1-D** curves sharply toward downtown Ensenada.

The **Tourist and Convention Bureau booth** (ℭ **800/310-9678** in the U.S. or 646/178-8588 in Mexico; www.enjoyensenada.com) is at the western entrance to town, where the waterfront-hugging Bulevar Lázaro Cárdenas—aka Bulevar Costero—curves away to the right. It's open Tuesday through Sunday from 9am to 5pm. Taxis park along López Mateos.

Exploring Ensenada

While Ensenada is technically a border town, one of its appeals is its multilayered vitality. The bustling port consumes the entire waterfront—beach access can be found only north or south of town—and the Pacific fishing trade and agriculture in the fertile valleys surrounding the city dominate the economy.

Even part-time oenophiles should visit the **Bodegas de Santo Tomás Winery ★★**, Av. Miramar 666, at Calle 7 (ℭ **646/178-3333;** www.santo-tomas.com), the oldest winery in Mexico, and the largest in Baja. It uses old-fashioned methods of processing grapes, first cultivated from Spanish varietals in 1888, in the lush Santo Tomás Valley, where a Dominican mission of the same name was founded almost a century earlier. Tours in English run every hour from 9am to 5pm Monday through Saturday and from 10am to 4pm Sunday. The tour is free, and if you wish to follow it up with a tasting, 80 pesos gets you a sampling of three white wines, and the 160-peso option includes six older or high-priced wines and two reserves.

For a complete list of other nearby wineries and tour information, visit www.enjoy ensenada.com/english/wineries.jsp.

Ensenada's equivalent of Tijuana's Avenida Revolución is crowded **Avenida López Mateos,** roughly parallel to Bulevar Lázaro Cárdenas (Bulevar Costero); the highest concentration of shops and restaurants is between avenidas Ruiz and Castillo. Compared to Tijuana, there is more authentic Mexican art and craftwork in Ensenada. And Ensenada is home to a thriving adventure subculture: off-road racers, surfers, kayakers, and more flock to Ensenada in search of their adrenaline fix.

South of the city, 45 minutes by car along the rural Punta Banda peninsula, is one of Ensenada's major attractions: **La Bufadora,** a natural sea spout in the rocks. With each incoming wave, water is forced upward through the rock, creating a geyser whose loud grunt gave the phenomenon its name (it means "buffalo snort"). From downtown Ensenada, take Avenida Reforma (Hwy. 1) south to Hwy. 23 west. La Bufadora is at the end of the road. Once parked (about $2 per car in crude dirt lots), you must walk downhill to the viewing platform, at the end of a 270m (886-ft.) pathway lined with souvenir stands. Also, **Picacho del Diablo,** the 3,046m (10,154-ft.) mountain located in the Sierra de San Pedro Mártir national park, draws hikers and backpackers eager to scale its two-pronged peak about 129km (80 miles) south of Ensenada.

Where to Stay

Las Rosas Hotel & Spa   One of the most modern hotels in the area, Hotel Las Rosas still falls short of most definitions of luxurious, yet the pink oceanfront hotel 3km (1¾ miles) outside Ensenada is the favorite of many Baja aficionados. It offers most of the comforts of an upscale American hotel—which doesn't leave room for much Mexican personality, but surfers will appreciate the view of Todos Santos Island. The atrium lobby is awash in pale pink and sea foam green, a color scheme that pervades throughout. Some rooms have fireplaces, Wi-Fi, and/or in-room whirlpools, and all have balconies overlooking the pool and ocean. One of the resort's main photo ops is the swimming pool that overlooks the Pacific and features a vanishing edge. If you want to maintain the highest comfort level possible, this would be your hotel of choice.

Hwy. 1, 3km (1¾ miles) north of Ensenada. www.lasrosas.com. ℭ **866/447-6727** in the U.S., or 646/174-4310. 48 units. $80–$164 double; $105–$203 suite. MC, V. Free parking. **Amenities:** Restaurant; cocktail lounge; cliff-top hot tub; small workout room; outdoor pool; room service; full-service spa; tennis court. *In room:* Fan, TV, hair dryer, Wi-Fi (in some).

Where to Eat

El Rey Sol ★ FRENCH/SEAFOOD   If you've been to Ensenada without eating at El Rey Sol, you'd better not tell a local. *Ensenadenses* are as proud of this family-run French restaurant as they are of their festivals, and after one taste of the clams au gratin, chateaubriand bouquetière, or mango charlotte, you will understand why. El Rey Sol, which opened in 1947, also offers a selection of traditional Mexican plates for dinner, as well as coffee and French pastries at the sidewalk cafe during the day.

Av. Lopez Mateos 1000. ℭ **646/178-1733.** www.elreysol.com. Reservations recommended on weekends. Main courses $10–$25. AE, MC, V. Daily 7:30am–10:30pm.

Ensenada After Dark

Just like in *Casablanca*, where "everyone goes to Rick's," everyone's been going to **Hussong's Cantina**, Av. Ruiz 113, near Avenida López Mateos (© **646/178-3210**; www.cantinahussongs.com), since the bar opened in 1892. Not much has changed—the place still sports Wild West–style swinging saloon doors, a long bar to slide beers along, and strolling mariachis bellowing above the din. While the crowd (a pleasant mix of tourists and locals) at Hussong's can really whoop it up, they're amateurs compared to those who frequent **Papas & Beer**, Avenida Ruiz near Avenida López Mateos (© **646/174-0145**; www.papasandbeer.com), across the street. A tiny entrance leads to the upstairs bar and dance club. The music is loud and the hip young crowd is here to party.

PLANNING YOUR TRIP TO MEXICO

By Shane Christensen

Planning your trip to Mexico is the first step in what promises to be a fascinating journey. Mexico's geographic and cultural diversity make this country among the world's most interesting to visit. Climate, food, dress, dialect, and social norms often differ markedly from one region to the next: You may be surprised at how a trip to Baja California or the Pacific Coast will differ from an excursion to the Caribbean; how distinctive the Mexican culture is on the U.S. border, compared to the Central American border; and how liberal Mexico City seems compared to the conservative colonial cities surrounding it.

A little planning can make the difference between a bum trip and a great journey. What's the best way to get there? How much should you plan to spend? What safety or health precautions should you take? This chapter answers these and other questions.

In addition to these basics, I highly recommend taking a little time to learn about the culture and traditions of Mexico. It will help enrich even the simplest seaside getaway. See chapter 2, "Mexico in Depth," to get started.

Travelers to Mexico should be aware of security concerns in a number of parts of the country and take precautions to maximize their safety. For the most part, Mexico is safe for travelers who steer clear of drugs and those who sell them, but visitors should still exercise caution in unfamiliar areas and remain aware of their surroundings at all times. Much of the worst drug-related violence has occurred in the border region. See "Safety," later, for more details, and visit the U.S. Department of State's website, www.travel.state.gov, for up-to-date information on travel to Mexico.

GETTING THERE
By Plane

Mexico has dozens of international and domestic airports throughout the country. Among the major airports and their airport codes are Mexico City (MEX), Cancún (CUN), Acapulco (ACA), Guadalajara (GDL), Puerto

Vallarta (PVR), Ixtapa/Zihuatanejo (ZIH), and Los Cabos (SJD). There is one major Mexican airline, Aeroméxico, and a handful of newer, low-cost carriers.

ARRIVING AT THE AIRPORT

Immigration and Customs clearance at Mexican airports is generally efficient. Expect longer lines during peak seasons, but you can usually clear immigration and customs within a half hour. For more about what to expect when passing through Mexican Customs, see "Customs" in "Fast Facts: Mexico," later in this chapter.

By Car

Driving is not the cheapest way to get to Mexico, but it is a convenient way to see the country. Even so, you may think twice about taking your own car south of the border once you've pondered the bureaucracy involved and the security situation across areas you're planning to travel. One option is to rent a car once you arrive and tour around a specific region. Rental cars in Mexico generally are clean and well maintained, although they are often smaller than rentals in the U.S., may have manual rather than automatic transmission, and are comparatively expensive due to pricey mandatory insurance. Discounts are often available for rentals of a week or longer, especially when you make arrangements in advance online or from the United States. Be careful about estimated online rates, which often fail to include the price of the mandatory insurance. (See "Car Rentals," below, for more details.)

If, after reading the section that follows, you have additional questions or you want to confirm the current rules, call your nearest Mexican consulate or the Mexican Government Tourist Office. (You can find the contact information for each in the "Fast Facts" section later in this chapter, under "Embassies & Consulates" and "Visitor Information," respectively.) Although travel insurance companies generally are helpful, they may not have the most accurate information. To check on road conditions or to get help with any travel emergency while in Mexico, call ✆ **55/5089-7500** in Mexico City, which is staffed by English-speaking operators.

In addition, check with the **U.S. Department of State** (www.state.gov) for warnings about dangerous driving areas.

CAR DOCUMENTS

To drive your car into Mexico beyond 25km (16 miles), you'll need a **temporary car-importation permit,** which is granted after you provide a required list of documents (see below). The permit can be obtained after you cross the border into Mexico

Carrying Car Documents

You must carry in the car at all times your temporary car-importation permit, tourist permit (see "Car Documents," above), and, if you purchased it, your proof of Mexican car insurance. The temporary car-importation permit papers are valid for 6 months to a year, while the tourist permit is usually issued for 30 days. It's a good idea to overestimate the time you'll spend in Mexico so that if you have to (or want to) stay longer, you'll avoid the hassle of getting your papers extended. Whatever you do, don't overstay either permit. Doing so invites heavy fines, confiscation of your vehicle (which will not be returned), or both. Remember that 6 months does not necessarily equal 180 days—be sure to return before the earlier expiration date.

through Banco del Ejército (Banjercito) officials with Mexican Customs (*aduanas*), or at Mexican consulates in Austin, San Francisco, Phoenix, Albuquerque, Chicago, Houston, Dallas, Los Angeles, Sacramento, and San Bernardino. For more information, call © **877/210-9469** in the U.S. or visit www.banjercito.com.mx.

The following requirements for border crossing were accurate at press time:

o **Passport.**
o **A valid driver's license,** issued outside of Mexico.
o **Current, original car registration and a copy of the original car title:** If the registration or title is in more than one name and not all the named people are traveling with you, a notarized letter from the absent person(s) authorizing use of the vehicle for the trip is required; have it ready. The registration and your credit card (see below) must be in the same name. If the car is leased or rented, be sure to have a copy of the contract.
o **Original immigration documentation:** Likely a tourist card (see "Visas," p. 763).
o **Processing fee and posting of a bond:** You have three options for covering the car-importation fee: pay $29 at the border, pay $39 in advance at a Mexican consulate, or prepay $49 online at www.banjercito.com.mx. If you apply online, it takes about 2 weeks before you can go into the Banjercito office to get your permit. You will generally need a credit card to make this payment. Mexican law requires the posting of a bond at a Banjercito office to guarantee the export of the car from Mexico within a time period determined at the time of the application. For this purpose, American Express, Visa, or MasterCard credit card holders will be asked to provide credit card information; others make a cash deposit of $200 to $400, depending on the make/model/year of the vehicle. To recover this bond or avoid credit card charges, go to any Mexican Customs office immediately before leaving Mexico.

If you receive your documentation at the border, Mexican officials will make two copies of everything and charge you for the copies. For up-to-the-minute information, a great source is the Customs office in Nuevo Laredo, or *Módulo de Importación Temporal de Automóviles, Aduana Nuevo Laredo* (© **867/712-2071**).

Important reminder: Someone else may drive, but the person (or relative of the person) whose name appears on the car-importation permit must *always* be in the car. (If stopped by police, a nonregistered family member driving without the registered driver must be prepared to prove familial relationship to the registered driver—no joke.) Violation of this rule subjects the car to impoundment and the driver to imprisonment, a fine, or both. You can drive a car with foreign license plates only if you have a foreign (non-Mexican) driver's license.

MEXICAN AUTO INSURANCE (SEGUROS DE AUTO)

Liability auto insurance is legally required in Mexico. U.S. insurance is invalid; to be insured in Mexico, you must purchase Mexican insurance. Any party involved in an accident who has no insurance may be sent to jail and have his or her car impounded until all claims are settled. U.S. companies that broker Mexican insurance are commonly found at the border crossing, and several quote daily rates.

You can also buy car insurance through **Sanborn's Mexico Insurance,** P.O. Box 52840, 2009 S. 10th, McAllen, TX (© **800/222-0158;** fax 800/222-0158 or 956/686-0732; www.sanbornsinsurance.com), in daily, monthly, or yearly time periods. The company has offices at all U.S. border crossings. Its policies cost the same as the competition's do, but you get legal coverage (attorney and bail bonds if needed), roadside assistance, and for a premium, vandalism protection. You also get a detailed guide for your proposed route. Most of the Sanborn's border offices are open Monday through Friday; a few are staffed on Saturday and Sunday. **AAA** auto club (www.aaa.com) also sells insurance.

RETURNING TO THE U.S. WITH YOUR CAR

You *must* return the car documents you obtained when you entered Mexico when you cross back with your car, or within 180 days of your return. (You can cross as many times as you wish within the 180 days.) If the documents aren't returned, serious fines are imposed (50 pesos for each day you're late), your car may be impounded and confiscated, or you may be jailed if you return to Mexico. You can only return the car documents to a Banjercito official on duty at the Mexican *aduana* building *before* you cross back into the United States. Some border cities have Banjercito officials on duty 24 hours a day, but others do not; some do not have Sunday hours. See www.mex bound.com/mexican-vehicle-permits.php for a listing of office hours.

By Ship

Numerous cruise lines serve Mexico. Some (such as Carnival and Royal Caribbean) cruise from California to the Baja Peninsula and ports of call on the Pacific coast, or from Houston or Miami to the Caribbean (which often includes stops in Cancún, Playa del Carmen, and Cozumel). Several cruise-tour specialists sometimes offer last-minute discounts on unsold cabins. One such company is **CruisesOnly** (☎ 800/278-4737; www.cruisesonly.com).

By Bus

Greyhound (☎ 800/231-2222; www.greyhound.com), or its affiliates, offers service from around the United States to the Mexican border, where passengers disembark, cross the border, and buy a ticket for travel into Mexico. Many border crossings have scheduled buses from the U.S. bus station to the Mexican bus station. We've listed bus arrival information in each applicable section of this book.

GETTING AROUND

By Plane

Until recently, Mexico had two large private national carriers, but Mexicana closed operations and filed for bankruptcy in 2010. Now, only **Aeroméxico** remains (☎ 800/237-6399 in the U.S., or 01-800/021-4000 in Mexico; www.aeromexico. com), in addition to several low-cost carriers. Aeroméxico offer extensive connections to the United States as well as within Mexico.

Low-cost carriers include **Interjet** (☎ 866/285-9525 in the U.S., or 01-800/011-2345 in Mexico; www.interjet.com.mx) and **Volaris** (☎ 866/988-3527 in the U.S., or 01-800/122-8000 in Mexico; www.volaris.com.mx). In each applicable section of this book, we've mentioned regional carriers with all pertinent telephone numbers.

Because major airlines may book some regional carriers, check your ticket to see if your connecting flight is on a smaller carrier that may use a different airport or counter.

Mexico charges an **airport tax** on all departures. Passengers leaving the country on international flights pay about $24 or the peso equivalent. It has become a common practice to include this departure tax in your ticket price. Taxes on each domestic

You can get point-to-point driving directions in English for anywhere in Mexico from the website of the Secretary of Communication and Transport. The site will also calculate tolls, distance, and travel time. Go to http://aplicaciones4.sct.gob.mx/ sibuac_internet and click on "Rutas punto a punto" in the left-hand column. Then select the English version.

departure within Mexico are around $17, unless you're on a connecting flight and have already paid at the start of the flight.

By Car

Many Mexican roads are not up to North American and European standards of smoothness, hardness, width of curve, grade of hill, or safety markings. Driving at night is dangerous: The roads are rarely lit; trucks, carts, pedestrians, and bicycles usually have no lights; and you can hit potholes, animals, rocks, dead ends, or uncrossable bridges without warning. The spirited style of Mexican driving sometimes requires keen vision and reflexes. Be prepared for new customs, as when a truck driver flips on his left turn signal when there's not a crossroad for many kilometers. He's probably telling you the road's clear ahead for you to pass.

GASOLINE   There's one government-owned brand of gas and one gasoline station name throughout the country—**Pemex** (Petroleras Mexicanas). There are two types of gas in Mexico: *magna* 87-octane unleaded and *premio* 93 octane. In Mexico, fuel and oil are sold by the liter, which is slightly more than a quart (1 gal. equals about 3.8L). Many franchise Pemex stations have bathroom facilities and convenience stores—a great improvement over the old ones. Gas stations accept credit and debit cards for gas purchases, and a small tip—5 to 10 pesos—is expected for full-service.

TOLL ROADS   Mexico charges relatively high tolls for its network of new toll roads, so they are less used. Generally, though, using toll roads cuts travel time. Older toll-free roads are generally in good condition, but travel times tend to be longer as these roads pass directly through small towns and villages.

BREAKDOWNS   If your car breaks down on the road, help might already be on the way. Radio-equipped green repair trucks, run by uniformed English-speaking officers, patrol major highways during daylight hours (usually 8am–6pm). These **Angeles Verdes/Green Angels** perform minor repairs and adjustments for free, but you pay for parts and materials. To contact them in Mexico, dial ✆ **078.** For more information, see www.sectur.gob.mx.

Your best guide to repair shops is the Yellow Pages. For repairs, look under *Automóviles y Camiones: Talleres de Reparación y Servicio;* auto-parts stores are under *Refacciones y Accesorios para Automóviles.* To find a mechanic on the road, look for the sign TALLER MECÁNICO. Places called *vulcanizadora* or *llantera* repair flat tires, and many are open 24 hours a day on the most traveled highways.

MINOR ACCIDENTS   When possible, many Mexicans drive away from minor accidents, or try to make an immediate settlement, to avoid involving the police. If the police arrive while the involved persons are still at the scene, the cars will probably be confiscated and both parties will likely have to appear in court. Both parties may also be taken into custody until liability is determined. Foreigners who don't speak fluent Spanish are at a distinct disadvantage when trying to explain their version of the event. Three steps may help the foreigner who doesn't wish to do as the Mexicans do: If you were in your car, notify your Mexican insurance company, whose job it is to intervene on your behalf. If you were in a rental car, notify the rental company immediately and ask how to contact the nearest adjuster. If all else fails, ask to contact the nearest Green Angel, who may be able to explain to officials that you are covered by insurance. See "Mexican Auto Insurance," in "Getting There," earlier in this chapter.

CAR RENTALS　You'll get the best price if you reserve a car on the Internet. Cars are easy to rent if you are 25 or older and have a major credit card, valid driver's license, and passport with you. Without a credit card, you must leave a cash deposit, usually a big one. One-way rentals are usually simple to arrange but more costly.

Car rental costs are high in Mexico because cars are more expensive. The condition of rental cars has improved greatly over the years, and newer cars are increasingly common. You pay the least for a manual car without air-conditioning. Prices may be considerably higher if you rent around a major holiday. Also double-check charges for insurance—some companies will increase the insurance rate after several days. Always ask for detailed information about all charges you will be responsible for. Also make sure the vehicle is in good shape and has been properly serviced before driving away.

Car-rental companies often charge on a credit card in U.S. dollars.

Deductibles　Be careful—these vary greatly; some are as high as $2,500, which comes out of your pocket immediately in case of damage.

Insurance　Insurance comes in two parts: **Collision and damage** insurance covers your car and others if the accident is your fault, and **personal accident** insurance covers you and anyone in your car. Note that insurance may be invalid if you have an accident while driving on an unpaved road. Although some international credit cards include as a benefit collision and damage coverage, they almost never include liability.

Damage　Inspect your car carefully and note every damaged or missing item, no matter how minute, on your rental agreement, or you may be charged.

By Taxi

Taxis are the preferred way to get around almost all of Mexico's resort areas. Fares for short trips within towns are generally preset by zone, and are quite reasonable compared with U.S. and European rates. For longer trips or excursions to nearby cities, taxis can generally be hired for around $15 to $20 per hour, or for a negotiated daily rate. A negotiated one-way price is usually much less than the cost of a rental car for a day, and a taxi travels much faster than a bus. For anyone who is uncomfortable driving in Mexico, this is a convenient, comfortable alternative. A bonus is that you have a Spanish-speaking person with you in case you run into trouble. Many taxi drivers speak at least some English. For safety reasons, *sitio* (radio) taxis should be used rather than *libre* taxis off the street. Your hotel can assist with the arrangements.

By Bus

Mexican buses run frequently, are readily accessible, and can transport you almost anywhere you want to go. Taking the bus is common in Mexico, and the executive and first-class coaches can be as comfortable as business class on an airplane. Buses are often the only way to get from large cities to other nearby cities and small villages. Don't hesitate to ask questions if you're confused about anything, but note that little English is spoken in bus stations.

Dozens of Mexican companies operate large, air-conditioned, Greyhound-type (or better) buses between most cities. Classes are *segunda* (second), *primera* (first), and *ejecutiva* (deluxe), which goes by a variety of names. Deluxe buses often have fewer seats than regular buses, show movies, are air-conditioned, and make few stops. Many run express from point to point. They are well worth the few dollars more. In rural areas, buses are often of the school-bus variety, with lots of local color.

Whenever possible, buy your reserved-seat ticket, often using a computerized system, a day in advance on long-distance routes and especially before holidays.

For each relevant destination, we list bus arrival and contact information. The following website provides reservations and bookings for numerous providers throughout Mexico: www.ticketbus.com.mx/wtbkd/autobus.jsp.

HEALTH

For the latest info on health risks when traveling to Mexico, and what to do if you get sick, consult the U.S. Department of State's website (www.travel.state.gov), the CDC website (www.cdc.gov), or the World Health Organization website (www.who.int).

General Availability of Healthcare

In most of Mexico's resort destinations, you can usually find healthcare that meets U.S. standards. Care in more remote areas is limited. Standards of medical training, patient care, and business practices vary greatly among medical facilities in beach resorts throughout Mexico. Cancún has first-rate hospitals, for example, but other cities along the Caribbean coast often do not. In recent years, some U.S. citizens have complained that certain healthcare facilities in beach resorts have taken advantage of them by overcharging or providing unnecessary medical care. On the other hand, Mexican doctors often spend more time with patients than doctors do north of the border, and may be just as good for less cost. Only rudimentary healthcare is generally available in much of Chiapas, Tabasco, and the Yucatán.

Prescription medicine is broadly available at Mexico pharmacies, and many drugs that in the U.S. require a prescription can be obtained in Mexico simply by asking. However, be aware that you may still need a copy of your prescription or may need to obtain a prescription from a local doctor.

Common Ailments

SUN/ELEMENTS/EXTREME WEATHER EXPOSURE Mexico is synonymous with sunshine; much of the country is bathed in intense sunshine for much of the year. Avoid excessive exposure, especially in the tropics where UV rays are more dangerous. The hottest months in Mexico's south are April and May, but the sun is intense most of the year.

DIETARY RED FLAGS Travelers' diarrhea—often accompanied by fever, nausea, and vomiting—used to attack many travelers to Mexico. (Some in the U.S. call this "Montezuma's revenge," but you won't hear it called that in Mexico.) Widespread improvements in infrastructure, sanitation, and education have greatly diminished this ailment, especially in well-developed resort areas. Most travelers make a habit of drinking only bottled water, which also helps to protect against unfamiliar bacteria. In resort areas, and generally throughout Mexico, only purified ice is used. If you do come down with this ailment, nothing beats Pepto Bismol, readily available in Mexico. Imodium is also available in Mexico and is used by many travelers for a quick fix. A good high-potency (or "therapeutic") vitamin supplement and even extra vitamin C can help; yogurt is good for healthy digestion.

Because dehydration can quickly become life-threatening, be careful to replace fluids and electrolytes (potassium, sodium, and the like) during a bout of diarrhea. Drink Pedialyte, a rehydration solution available at most Mexican pharmacies, or natural fruit juice, such as guava or apple (stay away from orange juice, which has laxative properties), with a pinch of salt added.

The U.S. Public Health Service recommends the following measures for preventing travelers' diarrhea: **Drink only purified water** (boiled water, canned or bottled beverages, beer, or wine). Choose food carefully. In general, avoid salads (except in first-class restaurants), uncooked vegetables, undercooked protein, and unpasteurized milk or milk products, including cheese. **Choose food that is freshly cooked and still hot.** Avoid eating food prepared by street vendors. In addition, something as simple as clean hands can go a long way toward preventing an upset stomach.

HIGH-ALTITUDE HAZARDS Travelers to certain regions of Mexico occasionally experience **elevation sickness,** which results from the relative lack of oxygen and the decrease in barometric pressure that characterizes high elevations (more than 1,500m/5,000 ft.). Symptoms include shortness of breath, fatigue, headache, insomnia, and even nausea. Mexico City is at 2,240m (7,349 ft.) above sea level, and a number of other central and southern cities, such as San Cristóbal de las Casas, are as high as or even higher than Mexico City. At high elevations, it takes about 10 days to acquire the extra red blood corpuscles you need to adjust to the scarcity of oxygen. To help your body acclimate, drink plenty of fluids, avoid alcohol, and don't overexert yourself during the first few days. If you have heart or lung trouble, consult your doctor before traveling to places above 2,400m (7,872 ft.).

BUGS, BITES & OTHER WILDLIFE CONCERNS Mosquitoes and gnats are prevalent along the coast and in the Yucatán lowlands. *Repelente contra insectos* (insect repellent) is a must, and you can buy it in most pharmacies. If you'll be in these areas and are prone to bites, bring along a repellent that contains the active ingredient DEET. Another good remedy to keep the mosquitoes away is to mix citronella essential oil with basil, clove, and lavender essential oils. If you're sensitive to bites, pick up some antihistamine cream from a drugstore at home.

Most readers won't ever see an *alacrán* (scorpion). But if one stings you, go immediately to a doctor. The one lethal scorpion found in some parts of Mexico is the *Centruroides,* part of the *Buthidae* family, characterized by a thin body, thick tail and triangular-shaped sternum. Most deaths from these scorpions result within 24 hours of the sting as a result of respiratory or cardiovascular failure, with children and elderly people most at risk. Scorpions are not aggressive (they don't hunt for prey), but they may sting if touched, especially in their hiding places (which can include shoes). In Mexico, you can buy scorpion-toxin antidote at any drugstore. It is an injection, and it costs around $25. This is a good idea if you plan to camp in a remote area, where medical assistance can be several hours away. Note that not all scorpion bites are lethal, but a doctor's visit is recommended regardless.

TROPICAL ILLNESSES You shouldn't be overly concerned about tropical diseases if you stay on the normal tourist routes and don't eat street food. However, both dengue fever and cholera have appeared in Mexico in recent years. Talk to your doctor or to a medical specialist in tropical diseases about precautions you should take.

Over-the-Counter Drugs in Mexico

Antibiotics and other drugs that you'd need a prescription to buy in the States are often available over the counter in Mexican pharmacies. Mexican pharmacies also carry a limited selection of common over-the-counter cold, sinus, and allergy remedies. Contact lenses can be purchased without an exam or prescription.

You can protect yourself by taking some simple precautions: Watch what you eat and drink; don't swim in stagnant water (ponds, slow-moving rivers, or wells); and avoid mosquito bites by covering up, using repellent, and sleeping under netting. The most dangerous areas seem to be on Mexico's west coast, away from the big resorts.

On occasion, coastal waters from the Gulf of Mexico can become contaminated with rapid growth in algae (phytoplankton), leading to a phenomenon known as harmful algal bloom or a "red tide." The algal release of neurotoxins threatens marine life and can cause rashes and even flulike symptoms in exposed humans. Although red tides happen infrequently, you should not enter the water if you notice a reddish-brown color or are told there is a red tide.

SAFETY

Mexico is one of the world's great travel destinations and millions of visitors travel safely here each year. Yet drug-related violence and widespread media coverage of Mexico's insecurity have severely impacted its tourism industry. Mexican drug-trafficking organizations have been engaged in brutal fights against each other for control of trafficking routes, and the Mexican government has deployed military troops and federal police across the country. Much of the worst drug-related violence has occurred in the border region. In a late 2010 travel warning, the U.S. Department of State urged U.S. citizens to defer unnecessary travel to Michoacán and Tamaulipas, and to parts of Chihuahua (particularly Ciudad Juarez), Sinaloa, Durango, and Coahuila. The state of Guerrero, including Acapulco, has been affected by drug-related violence. The level of violence in Monterrey has also increased, and there have been numerous incidents of violence in the city of Cuernavaca, near Mexico City. The Mexican government is working hard to protect visitors to major tourist destinations, which do not experience anything like

ONE MORE AUTHOR GIVES HIS TWO CENTS:
safety in mexico

Stories of murder and mayhem are making all the headlines about Mexico these days. Stories of assassinations, kidnappings, and shootouts sell newspapers but are of no help evaluating the risk in traveling through the country. They are newsworthy in that they document the gravity of the problem Mexico faces in gaining control of its borders and ensuring public safety. But the best way to understand the risk of traveling in Mexico is to read the U.S. Department of State travel warnings (www.travel.state.gov).

The current situation has changed the way I travel in two ways beyond the usual precautions—such as not flashing a lot of money, not wearing an expensive watch, keeping aware of my surroundings, and not driving on the highway at night. These changes boil down to two objectives: Avoid being in the wrong place at the wrong time, and avoid the possibility of mistaken identity. The **first** is largely met by not lingering in Mexico's northern border states (including Durango and the interior of Sinaloa), where most violence occurs. The **second** minimizes any risk of being held up or nabbed by kidnappers, and it is achieved by looking as much like a tourist as possible. Kidnappers in Mexico don't target tourists. They have targeted resident foreigners with family in Mexico or businesspeople who have associates because they need someone to demand a ransom from. The risk here is from small-time gangs who act opportunistically. (Serious kidnappers aren't a threat because they won't do anything without planning and surveillance.) In the last few years, small-time gangs have increased. The best way I know of to avoid this risk is not to carry a briefcase or satchel. What's more, by hauling around a backpack, you will automatically escape scrutiny because businesspersons in Mexico never use them. The backpack (mochila) in Mexico is a strong cultural identifier. It's associated with students and counterculture types, so much so that the word mochilero has come to describe hippies.

–David Baird

the levels of violence and crime reported in the border region and along major drug-trafficking routes, mainly in the north.

In most places, it's uncommon for foreign visitors to face anything worse than petty crime. The risk of pickpockets and petty theft rises considerably during the winter high tourist season. Always use common sense and exercise caution when in unfamiliar areas. Leave valuables and irreplaceable items in a safe place, or don't bring them at all. Use hotel safes when available. Avoid driving alone, especially at night. You can generally trust a person you approach for help or directions, but be wary if someone approaches you offering the same. The more insistent a person is, the more cautious you should be. Stay away from areas where drug dealing and prostitution occur.

The U.S. and Mexico share a border more than 3,000km (nearly 2,000 miles) long and Americans comprise the vast majority of tourists to Mexico. Due to this close and historically intertwined relationship, we recommend that all travelers read the **U.S. Department of State travel advisories/warnings for Mexico** (www.travel.state. gov). The U.S. Department of State encourages its citizens to use main roads during daylight hours, stay in well-known tourist destinations and tourist areas with better security, cooperate fully with Mexican military and other law enforcement checkpoints, and provide an itinerary to a friend or family member not traveling with them.

For emergency numbers, see "Emergencies," later in this chapter.

Crime in Mexico City

Violent crime is also serious in the capital. Do not wear fine jewelry or expensive watches, or display any other obvious signs of wealth. If you do not have local friends who can help guide you around the city, ask your hotel staff to help point you in the right direction. Muggings are common by day and by night. Theft is even common at the Benito Juárez International Airport, where items such as briefcases, cameras, or laptops are common targets. To avoid theft upon arrival, incoming passengers in need of pesos should use the exchange counters or ATMs in the arrival/departure gate area, where access is restricted, rather than changing money after passing through Customs. Metro (subway) robberies are frequent in Mexico City.

Avoid the use of the **green Volkswagen Beetle** and **libre taxis,** many of which have been involved in "pirate" robberies, muggings, and kidnappings. These taxis are also common in incidents where passengers are "hijacked" and released only after they are forced to withdraw the limit on their ATM bank cards. Always use official airport or radio taxis (called *sitios*) instead. Tourists and residents alike should avoid driving alone at night anywhere in the city.

Crime in Resort Towns

A significant number of rapes have been reported in Cancún and other resort areas, usually at night or in the early morning. Women should not walk alone late at night. Drug-related violence has increased in Acapulco and Mazatlán. Although this violence is not targeted at foreign residents or tourists, visitors in these areas should be vigilant in their personal safety. Armed street crime is a serious problem in all the major cities. Some bars and nightclubs, especially in resort cities such as Cancún, Cabo San Lucas, Mazatlán, Acapulco, and Tijuana, can be havens for drug dealers and petty criminals.

The U.S. Department of State offers specific safety and security information for travelers on spring break in Mexico: www.travel.state.gov/travel/cis_pa_tw/spring_break_mexico/spring_break_mexico_5014.html. It is also advised that you should not hike alone in backcountry areas nor walk alone on less-frequented beaches, ruins, or trails.

Kidnapping

Kidnapping, including the kidnapping of non-Mexicans, continues to occur at alarming rates. Although visitors are less likely to be targeted, those who believe they are being targeted for kidnapping or other crimes should notify Mexican law enforcement and their respective embassy or consulate, and should consider returning to their home country immediately. The U.S. Department of State states the following: "So-called express kidnappings, that is, attempts to get quick cash in exchange for the release of an individual, have occurred in almost all of Mexico's large cities and appear to target not only the wealthy but also the middle class. Kidnapping in Mexico has become a lucrative business, whether the kidnappings are actual or "virtual." A common scam throughout Mexico is "virtual" kidnapping by telephone, in which the callers typically speak in a distraught voice in a ploy to elicit information about a potential victim and then use this knowledge to demand ransom for the release of the supposed victim. In the event of such a call, it is important to stay calm, as the vast majority of the calls are hoaxes. Do not reveal any personal information; try to speak with the victim to corroborate his/her identity; and contact the local police as well as the Embassy or nearest consulate." Also avoid hailing taxis on the street and use *sitio* (radio) taxis instead. It can be useful to travel with a working cellphone, as well. This is good advice for all travelers to Mexico.

Highway Safety

Travelers should exercise caution while traveling Mexican highways, avoiding travel at night and using toll (*cuota*) roads rather than the less secure free (*libre*) roads whenever possible. Fully cooperate with all official checkpoints, the number of which has increased, when traveling on Mexican highways.

Bus travel should take place during daylight hours on first-class conveyances. Although bus hijackings and robberies have occurred on toll roads, buses on toll roads have a markedly lower rate of incidents than second-class and third-class buses that travel the less secure "free" highways.

Bribes & Scams

As is the case around the world, there are the occasional bribes and scams in Mexico, targeted at people believed to be naive, such as telltale tourists. For years, Mexico was known as a place where bribes—called *mordidas* (bites)—were expected; however, the country is rapidly changing. Frequently, offering a bribe today, especially to a police officer, is considered an insult, and it can land you in deeper trouble.

Many tourists have the impression that everything works better in Mexico if you "tip"; however, in reality, this only perpetuates the *mordida* tradition. If you are pleased with a service, feel free to tip. But you shouldn't tip simply to attempt to get away with something illegal or inappropriate—whether it is evading a ticket that's deserved or a car inspection as you're crossing the border.

Whatever you do, **avoid impoliteness;** you won't do yourself any favors if you insult a Mexican official. Extreme politeness, even in the face of adversity, rules Mexico. In Mexico, gringos have a reputation for being loud and demanding. By adopting the local custom of excessive courtesy, you'll have greater success in negotiations of any kind. Stand your ground, but do it politely.

As you travel in Mexico, you may encounter several types of **scams,** which are typical throughout the world. One involves some kind of a **distraction** or feigned commotion. While your **attention is diverted,** for example, a pickpocket makes a grab for your wallet. In another common scam, an unaccompanied child pretends to be lost and frightened and takes your hand for safety. Meanwhile the child or an accomplice plunders your pockets. A third involves **confusing currency.** A shoeshine boy, street musician, guide, or other individual might offer you a service for a price that seems reasonable—in pesos. When it comes time to pay, he or she tells you the price is in dollars, not pesos. Be very clear on the price and currency when services are involved. An ATM scam involves **ATMs** in questionable locations where card numbers are "skimmed" and information is copied, money stolen, or cards fraudulently charged.

TIPS ON ACCOMMODATIONS
Mexico's Hotel Rating System

The hotel rating system in Mexico is called "Stars and Diamonds." Hotels may qualify to earn one to five stars or diamonds. Many hotels that have excellent standards are not certified, but all rated hotels adhere to strict standards. The guidelines relate to service, facilities, and hygiene more than to prices.

Five-diamond hotels meet the highest requirements for rating: The beds are comfortable, bathrooms are in excellent working order, all facilities are renovated regularly, infrastructure is top-tier, and services and hygiene meet the highest international standards.

Five-star hotels usually offer similar quality, but with lower levels of service and detail in the rooms. For example, a five-star hotel may have less luxurious linens or, perhaps, room service during limited hours rather than 24 hours.

Four-star hotels are less expensive and more basic, but they guarantee cleanliness and basic services such as hot water and purified drinking water. Three-, two-, and one-star hotels are at least working to adhere to certain standards: Bathrooms are cleaned and linens are washed daily, and you can expect a minimum standard of service. Two- and one-star hotels generally provide bottled water rather than purified water.

Hotel Chains

In addition to the major international chains, you'll run across a number of less-familiar brands as you plan your trip to Mexico. They include the following:

o **Brisas Hotels & Resorts** (www.brisashotelonline.com): These were the hotels that originally attracted jet-set travelers to Mexico. Spectacular in a retro way, these properties offer the laid-back luxury that makes a Mexican vacation so unique.

o **Fiesta Americana and Fiesta Inn** (www.posadas.com): Part of the Mexican-owned Grupo Posadas company, these hotels set the country's midrange standard for facilities and services. They generally offer comfortable, spacious rooms and traditional Mexican hospitality. Fiesta Americana hotels offer excellent beach-resort packages. Fiesta Inn hotels are usually more business-oriented. Grupo Posadas also owns the more luxurious Caesar Park hotels and the eco-oriented Explorean hotels.

o **Hoteles Camino Real** (www.caminoreal.com): Hoteles Camino Real remains Mexico's premier hotel chain with beach resorts, city hotels, and colonial inns scattered throughout the country. Its beach hotels are traditionally located on the best beaches in the area. This chain also focuses on the business market. The hotels are famous for their vivid and contrasting colors.

o **Quinta Real Grand Class Hotels and Resorts** (www.quintareal.com): These hotels are noted for architectural and cultural details that reflect their individual regions. At these luxury properties, attention to detail and excellent service are the rule. Quinta Real is the top-line Mexican hotel brand.

House Rentals & Swaps

House and villa rentals and swaps are becoming more common in Mexico, but no single recognized agency or business provides this service exclusively for Mexico. In

Mexico lends itself beautifully to the concept of small, private hotels in idyllic settings. They vary in style from grandiose estate to palm-thatched bungalow. **Mexico Boutique Hotels** (✆ 877/278-8018; www.mexicoboutiquehotels.com) specializes in smaller places to stay with a high level of personal attention and service. Most options have less than 50 rooms, and the accommodations consist of entire villas, *casitas,* bungalows, or a combination.

the preceding chapters, we have provided information on independent services that we have found to be reputable.

You'll find the most extensive inventory of homes at **Vacation Rentals by Owner** (**VRBO;** www.vrbo.com). They have thousands of homes and condominiums worldwide, including a large selection in Mexico. Another good option is **VacationSpot** (✆ **888/903-7768;** www.vacationspot.com). It has fewer choices, but the company's criteria for adding inventory is much more selective and often includes on-site inspections. They also offer toll-free phone support.

[Fast FACTS] MEXICO

Business Hours   Most businesses in larger cities are open between 9am and 7pm; in smaller towns they may close between 2 and 4pm. Many close on Sunday. In resort areas, stores commonly open in the mornings on Sunday, and shops stay open late, until 8 or even 10pm. Bank hours are Monday through Friday from 9 or 9:30am to anywhere between 3 and 7pm. Banks open on Saturday for at least a half-day.

Car Rental   See "By Car" under the "Getting There" section, earlier in this chapter.

Cellphones   See "Mobile Phones," later in this section.

Crime   See "Safety," earlier in this chapter.

Customs   Mexican Customs inspection has been streamlined. At most points of entry, tourists are requested to press a button in front of what looks like a traffic signal, which alternates on touch between red and green. Green light and you go through without inspection; red light and your luggage or car may be inspected. If you have an unusual amount of luggage or an oversized piece, you may be subject to inspection anyway. Passengers that arrive by air will be required to put their bags through an X-ray machine, and then move to the kiosk and push a button to determine whether their luggage will be selected for any further inspection.

What You Can Bring into Mexico   When you enter Mexico, Customs officials will be tolerant if you are not carrying illegal drugs or firearms. Tourists are allowed to bring in their personal effects duty-free. A laptop computer, camera equipment, and sports equipment that could feasibly be used during your stay are also allowed. The underlying guideline is: Don't bring anything that looks as if it's meant to be resold in Mexico. Those entering Mexico by air or sea can bring in gifts worth a value of up to $300 duty-free, except alcohol or tobacco products. The website for Mexican Customs *(Aduanas)* is **www.aduanas.sat.gob.mx**.

Disabled Travelers   Mexico presents a challenging course to travelers in wheelchairs or on crutches. At airports, you may encounter steep stairs before finding a well-hidden elevator or escalator—if one exists. Airlines will often arrange wheelchair assistance to the baggage area. Porters are generally available to help with luggage at airports and large bus stations, once you've cleared baggage claim.

Mexican airports are upgrading their services, but you may still occasionally board from a remote position, meaning you either descend stairs to a bus that ferries you to the plane, which you board by climbing stairs, or you walk across the tarmac to your plane and ascend the stairs. Deplaning presents the same problem in reverse.

Escalators (and there aren't many in the country) are often out of order. Stairs without handrails abound. Few restrooms are equipped for travelers with disabilities; when one is available, access to it may be through a narrow passage that won't accommodate a wheelchair or a person on crutches. Many deluxe hotels (the most expensive) now have rooms with bathrooms designed for people with disabilities. Those traveling on a budget should stick with one-story hotels or hotels with elevators. Even so, there will probably still be obstacles somewhere. Generally speaking, no matter where you are, someone will lend a hand, although you may have to ask for it.

Doctors   Any embassy or consulate staff in Mexico from an English-speaking country can provide a list of area doctors who speak English. If you get sick in Mexico, consider asking your hotel concierge to recommend a local doctor—even his or her own. Some hotels even have in-house medical personnel. You can also try the emergency room at a local hospital or urgent care facility. Mexican doctors may not always have access to the latest technologies, and the quality of medical facilities varies, but they usually spend considerable time with patients and charge much less than their North American counterparts. Before choosing a doctor, you can ask for his or her qualifications and where he or she was trained.

Also see "Hospitals," later in this section.

Drinking Laws   The legal drinking age in Mexico is 18; however, asking for ID or denying purchase is extremely rare. Grocery stores sell everything from beer and wine to national and imported liquors. You can buy liquor 24 hours a day, but during major elections, dry laws often are enacted by as much as 72 hours in advance of the election—and they apply to tourists as well as local residents. Mexico does not have laws that apply to transporting liquor in cars, but authorities are beginning to target drunk drivers more aggressively. It's a good idea to drive defensively.

It's illegal to drink in the street; but many tourists do. If you are getting drunk, you shouldn't drink in the street, because you are more likely to get stopped by the police.

Driving Rules   See "By Car" under "Getting Around," earlier in this chapter.

Electricity   The electrical system in Mexico is 110 volts AC (60 cycles), as in the United States and Canada. In reality, however, it may cycle more slowly and overheat your appliances. To compensate, select a medium or low speed on hair dryers. Many older hotels still have electrical outlets for flat two-prong plugs; you'll need an adapter for any plug with an enlarged end on one prong or with three prongs. Adapters are available in most Mexican electronics stores. Many better hotels have three-hole outlets (*trifásicos* in Spanish). Those that don't may loan adapters, but to be sure, it's always better to carry your own.

Embassies & Consulates   Citizen services provided by country missions include passports, notaries, lists of doctors and lawyers, regulations concerning marriages in Mexico, emergency preparedness information, and other valuable assistance. Contrary to popular belief, your embassy cannot get you out of jail, provide postal or banking services, or fly you home if you run out of money. Consular officers provide advice on most matters and problems, however. Most countries have an embassy in Mexico City, and many have consular offices or representatives in the provinces.

It is a good idea to register with your embassy or consulate when visiting Mexico. The Smart Traveler Enrollment Program (STEP) is a free service provided by the U.S. government to U.S. citizens who are traveling to, or living in, a foreign country. STEP allows them to enter information about their upcoming trip abroad so that the Department of State can better assist them in an emergency, and also allows Americans residing abroad to obtain routine information from the nearest U.S. embassy or consulate. Visit https://travelregistration.state.gov.

The Embassy of **Australia** in Mexico City is at Rubén Darío 55, Col. Polanco (*(C)* **55/1101-2200;** www.mexico.embassy.gov.au). It's open Monday through Thursday from 9:30am to noon.

The Embassy of **Canada** in Mexico City is at Schiller 529, in Polanco (*(C)* **55/5724-7900,** or for emergencies 01-800/706-2900; http://mexico.gc.ca); it's open Monday through Friday from 9am to 1pm and 2 to 5pm. The website above also lists consulates and consular agencies in Mexico.

The Embassy of **Ireland** in Mexico City is at Cda. Bl. Manuel Avila Camacho 76, 3rd floor, Col. Lomas de Chapultepec (*(C)* **55/5520-5803;** www.irishembassy.com.mx). It's open Monday through Thursday from 8:30am to 5pm, and Friday from 8:30am to 1:30pm.

The Embassy of **New Zealand** in Mexico City is at Jaime Balmes 8, 4th Floor, Col. Los Morales, Polanco (*(C)* **55/5283-9460;** www.nzembassy.com/mexico). It's open Monday through Thursday from 8:30am to 2pm and 3 to 5:30pm, and Friday from 8:30am to 2pm.

The Embassy of the **United Kingdom** in Mexico City is at Río Lerma 71, Col. Cuauhtémoc (*(C)* **55/1670-3200;** http://ukinmexico.fco.gov.uk/en). It's open Monday through Thursday from 8am to 4pm and Friday from 8am to 1:30pm.

The Embassy of the **United States** in Mexico City is at Paseo de la Reforma 305, next to the Hotel María Isabel Sheraton at the corner of Río Danubio (*(C)* **55/5080-2000**); hours are Monday through Friday from 8:30am to 5:30pm. Visit http://mexico.usembassy.gov for information related to U.S. Embassy services. A U.S. consulate is at Calle 60 No. 338 K x 29 y 31, Col. Acala Martin, Mérida (*(C)* 999/942-5700). In addition, there are consular agencies in Cancún (*(C)* 998/883-0272) and Cozumel (*(C)* 987/872-4574).

Emergencies   In case of emergency, dial *(C)* **066** from any phone within Mexico. Dial *(C)* **065** for the Red Cross. For police emergency numbers, turn to the "Fast Facts" sections in each of the individual chapters. The 24-hour Tourist Help Line in Mexico City is *(C)* **01-800/987-8224** in Mexico, or 55/5089-7500, or simply dial *(C)* **078.** The operators don't always speak English, but they are always willing to help.

Family Travel   Children are considered the national treasure of Mexico, and Mexicans will warmly welcome and cater to your children. Many parents were reluctant to bring young children into Mexico in the past, primarily due to health concerns, but I can't think of a better place to introduce children to the exciting adventure of exploring a different culture. One of the best destinations for kids is Cancún. Hotels can often arrange for a babysitter.

Before leaving, ask your doctor which medications to take along. Disposable diapers cost about the same in Mexico but are of poorer quality. You can get Huggies Supreme and Pampers identical to the ones sold in the United States, but at a higher price. Many stores sell Gerber's baby foods. Dry cereals, powdered formulas, baby bottles, and purified water are easily available in midsize and large cities or resorts.

Only the largest and most luxurious hotels provide cribs. However, rollaway beds are often available. Child seats or high chairs at restaurants are common. Consider bringing your own car seat; they are not readily available for rent in Mexico.

To locate accommodations, restaurants, and attractions that are particularly kid-friendly, refer to the "Kids" icon throughout this guide.

Gasoline   See "By Car" under the "Getting Around" section, earlier in this chapter.

Hospitals   Many hospitals have walk-in clinics for emergency cases that are not life-threatening; you may not get immediate attention, but you won't pay emergency room prices. The quality varies, but is often quite high, especially in resort towns.

See also "Emergencies" and "Embassies & Consulates," above.

Insurance   For travel to Mexico, you may have to pay all medical costs upfront and be reimbursed later. Before leaving home, find out what medical services your health insurance covers. To protect yourself, consider buying medical travel insurance.

For information on traveler's insurance, trip cancellation insurance, and medical insurance while traveling, please visit www.frommers.com/tips.

Internet & Wi-Fi   Mexico's largest airports offer Wi-Fi access provided for a fee by Telcel's Prodigy Internet service. Most five-star hotels now offer Wi-Fi in the guest rooms for free or for a fee. Hotel lobbies often have Wi-Fi as well. To find public Wi-Fi hotspots in Mexico, go to **www.jiwire.com**; its Hotspot Finder holds the world's largest directory of public wireless hotspots.

Many large Mexican airports have Internet kiosks, and quality Mexican hotels usually have business centers with Internet access. You can also check out such copy stores as **FedEx Office** or **OfficeMax**, which offer computer stations with fully loaded software (as well as Wi-Fi).

Language   Spanish is the official language in Mexico. English is spoken and understood to some degree in most tourist areas. Mexicans are very accommodating with foreigners who try to speak Spanish, even in broken sentences. See chapter 21 for a glossary of simple phrases for expressing basic needs.

Legal Aid   Embassies and consulates can often provide a list of respected lawyers in the area who speak English.

LGBT Travelers   Mexico is a conservative country, with deeply rooted Catholic religious traditions. Public displays of same-sex affection are rare and still considered surprising for men, especially outside of urban or resort areas. Women in Mexico frequently walk hand in hand, but anything more crosses the boundary of acceptability. However, gay and lesbian travelers are generally treated with respect and should not experience harassment, assuming they give the appropriate regard to local customs.

On December 21, 2009, Mexico City became the first Latin American jurisdiction to legalize same-sex marriage, and 14th overall after the Netherlands, Belgium, Spain, Canada, South Africa, Norway, Sweden, and six U.S. jurisdictions.

While much of Mexico is socially conservative, Cancún and Playa del Carmen are not. Popular with many gay travelers, both coastal resorts offer gay-friendly accommodations, bars, and activities. For more information, visit MexGay Vacations at www.mexgay.com. Information about gay-friendly accommodations is available at www.gayplaces2stay.com.

Mail   Postage for a postcard or letter varies by destination; it may take from a few weeks to over a month to arrive. The price for registered letters and packages depends on the weight. The recommended way to send a package or important mail is through FedEx, DHL, UPS, or another reputable international mail service.

Medical Requirements   See "Health," p. 747.

Mobile Phones   **Telcel** is Mexico's expensive, primary cellphone provider. It has upgraded its systems to GSM and offers good coverage in much of the country, including the major cities and resorts. Most Mexicans buy cellphones without a specific coverage plan and then pay as they go or purchase prepaid cards with set amounts of air-time credit. These cellphone cards with scratch-off pin numbers can be purchased in Telcel stores as well as many newspaper stands and convenience stores.

Many North American and European cellphone companies offer networks with roaming coverage in Mexico. Rates can be very high, so check with your provider before committing to making calls this way. An increasing number of Mexicans, particularly among the younger generation, prefer the less expensive rates of **Nextel** (www.nextel.com.mx), which features a range of service options. **Cellular Abroad** (www.cellularabroad.com) offers cellphone rentals and purchases as well as SIM cards for travel abroad. Whether you rent or purchase the cell-phone, you need to purchase a SIM card that is specific for Mexico.

Money & Costs   In general, the southern region of Mexico is considerably cheaper than not just most U.S. and European destinations but also many other parts of Mexico, although prices vary significantly depending on the specific location. The most expensive destinations are those with the largest number of foreign visitors, such as Cancún and Los Cabos. The least expensive are those off the beaten path and in small rural villages, particularly in the poorer states. In the major cities, prices vary greatly depending on the neighborhood. As you might imagine, tourist zones tend to be more expensive.

The currency in Mexico is the peso. Paper currency comes in denominations of 20, 50, 100, 200, and 500 pesos. Coins come in denominations of 1, 2, 5, 10, and 20 pesos, and 20 and 50 **centavos** (100 centavos = 1 peso). The current exchange rate for the U.S. dollar, and the one used in this book, is 12 pesos; at that rate, an item that costs 12 pesos would be equivalent to $1.

Many establishments that deal with tourists, especially in coastal resort areas, quote prices in U.S. dollars. To avoid confusion, they use the abbreviations DLLS. for dollars and M.N. (*moneda nacional,* or national currency) or M.X.P. for Mexican Pesos. **Note:** Establishments that quote their prices primarily in U.S. dollars are listed in this guide with U.S. dollars.

Getting change is a problem. Small-denomination bills and coins are hard to come by, so start collecting them early in your trip. Shopkeepers and taxi drivers everywhere always seem to be out of change and small bills; that's doubly true in markets. There seems to be an expectation that the customer should provide appropriate change, rather than the other way around.

Don't forget to have enough pesos to carry you over a weekend or Mexican holiday, when banks are closed. Because small bills and coins in pesos are hard to come by in Mexico, the $1 bill is very useful for tipping. **Note:** A tip of U.S. coins, which cannot be exchanged into Mexican currency, is of no value to the service provider.

Casas de cambio (exchange houses) are generally more convenient than banks for money exchange because they have more locations and longer hours; the rate of exchange may be the same as at a bank or slightly lower. Before leaving a bank or exchange-house window, count your change in front of the teller before the next client steps up. Also, most major hotels will change money for you.

Large airports have currency-exchange counters that often stay open whenever flights are operating. Though convenient, they generally do not offer the most favorable rates. The bottom line on exchanging money: Ask first, and shop around. Banks generally pay the top rates.

Banks in Mexico have expanded and improved services. Except in the smallest towns, they tend to be open weekdays from 9am until 5pm, and often for at least a half day on Saturday. In larger resorts and cities, they can generally accommodate the exchange of dollars (which used to stop at noon) anytime during business hours. Some, but not all, banks charge a 1% fee to exchange traveler's checks. But you can pay for most purchases directly with traveler's checks at the establishment's stated exchange rate. Don't bother with personal checks drawn on a U.S. bank—the bank will wait for your check to clear, which can take weeks, before giving you your money.

Travelers to Mexico can easily withdraw money from ATMs, called *cajeras,* in most major cities and resort areas. The U.S. Department of State recommends caution when you're using ATMs in Mexico, stating that they should only be used during business hours and in large protected facilities, but this pertains primarily to Mexico City, where crime remains a significant problem. In most resorts in Mexico, the use of ATMs is perfectly safe—just use the same precautions you would at any ATM. However, beware of using ATMs in dubious locations as there have been reports of people having their card numbers "skimmed" (where information is copied and monies stolen or cards fraudulently charged). The ATM exchange rate is generally more favorable than at *casas de cambio*. Most machines offer Spanish/English menus and dispense pesos, but some offer the option of withdrawing dollars.

THE VALUE OF THE MEXICAN PESO VS. OTHER POPULAR CURRENCIES

Pesos	US$	Can$	UK£	Euro (€)	Aus$	NZ$
100	8.30	8.20	5.18	6.15	8.28	10.96

Frommer's lists exact prices in the local currency (unless rates are given in U.S. dollars). The currency conversions quoted above were correct at press time. However, rates fluctuate, so before departing consult a currency exchange website such as **www.oanda.com/convert/ classic** to check up-to-the-minute rates.

In Mexico, Visa, MasterCard, and American Express are the most accepted cards. You'll be able to charge most hotel, restaurant, and store purchases, as well as almost all airline tickets, on your credit card. Most Pemex gas stations now accept credit card purchases for gasoline, though this option may not be available everywhere and often not at night—check before you pump. Generally you receive the favorable bank rate when paying by credit card. However, be aware that some establishments in Mexico add a 5% to 7% surcharge when you pay with a credit card. This is especially true when using American Express. Many times, advertised discounts will not apply if you pay with a credit card.

> **Money Matters**
>
> The **universal currency sign ($)** is sometimes used to indicate pesos in Mexico. The use of this symbol in this book, however, denotes U.S. currency.

Beware of hidden credit-card fees while traveling. Check with your credit or debit card issuer to see what fees, if any, will be charged for overseas transactions. Recent reform legislation in the U.S., for example, has curbed some exploitative lending practices. But many banks have responded by increasing fees in other areas, including fees for customers who use credit and debit cards while out of the country—even if those charges were made in U.S. dollars. Fees can amount to 3% or more of the purchase price. Check with your bank before departing to avoid any surprise charges on your statement.

For help with currency conversions, tip calculations, and more, download Frommer's convenient Travel Tools app for your mobile device. Go to www.frommers.com/go/mobile and click on the "Travel Tools" icon.

Newspapers & Magazines   The *Miami Herald* is published in conjunction with *El Universal*. You can find it at most newsstands. *The News* is a new English-language daily with Mexico-specific news, published in Mexico City. Newspaper kiosks in larger cities also carry a selection of English-language magazines.

Packing   In general, Mexico is an easy destination to pack for, as weather is consistent and predictable, and the style is casual and accepting. Check forecasts before you go and bring something for cool nights. For more helpful information on packing for your trip, download our convenient Travel Tools app for your mobile device. Go to www.frommers. com/go/mobile and click on the Travel Tools icon.

Passports   See www.frommers.com/tips for help obtaining a passport.

WHAT THINGS COST IN MEXICO	PESOS (US$ WHERE INDICATED)
Cancún beachfront double room, moderate	US$120
Puerto Vallarta beachfront double room, expensive	US$250
Mexico City dinner for one, expensive	300–400
Merida dinner for one, moderate	100–150
Tacos from market or street vendor	20–30
Cozumel two-tank scuba dive	US$70
Admission to most archaeological sites	50
Night dancing in Cancún	US$40
Night dancing in Mazatlan	US$20

Citizens from most countries are required to present a valid passport for entry to Mexico. Citizens from some countries will need a Mexican visa. As of March 1, 2010, all U.S. citizens, including children, have been required to present a valid passport or passport card for travel beyond the "border zone" into Mexico, with the "border zone" defined as an area within 20 to 30km (12–19 miles) of the United States.

All U.S. and Canadian citizens traveling by air or sea to Mexico are required to present a valid passport or other valid travel document to enter or reenter the United States except if returning from a closed-loop cruise. In addition, all travelers, including U.S. and Canadian citizens, attempting to enter the United States by land or sea must have a valid passport or other WHTI compliant document.

 A Few Words About Prices

Many hotels in Mexico—except places that receive little foreign tourism—quote prices in U.S. dollars or in both dollars and pesos. Thus, currency fluctuations are unlikely to affect the prices most hotels charge.

Other valid travel documents (known as WHTI-compliant documents) include the new Passport Card and SENTRI, NEXUS, FAST, and the U.S. Coast Guard Mariner Document. Members of the U.S. Armed Forces on active duty traveling on orders are exempt from the passport requirement. U.S. citizens may apply for the limited-use, wallet-size Passport Card, available for a cost of about $40. The card is valid only for land and sea travel between the U.S. and Canada, Mexico, the Caribbean region, and Bermuda. Beginning March 1, 2010, the Mexican immigration authorities began to accept the passport card for travel into Mexico by air. However, the card is not valid to board international flights in the U.S. or to return to the U.S. from abroad by air. This card is only available to U.S. citizens. For more details on application restrictions, see www.getyouhome.gov. There is also the new "Global Entry" program for frequent travelers, available at www.globalentry.gov.

From our perspective, it's easiest just to travel with a valid passport. Safeguard your passport in an inconspicuous, inaccessible place, like a money belt, and keep a copy of the critical pages with your passport number in a separate place. If you lose your passport, visit the nearest consulate of your native country as soon as possible for a replacement.

Passport Offices

Australia   Australian Passport Information Service (☎ 131-232, or visit www.passports.gov.au).

Canada   Passport Office, Department of Foreign Affairs and International Trade, Ottawa, ON K1A 0G3 (☎ 800/567-6868; www.ppt.gc.ca).

Ireland   Passport Office, Setanta Centre, Molesworth Street, Dublin 2 (☎ 01/671-1633; www.foreignaffairs.gov.ie).

New Zealand   Passports Office, Department of Internal Affairs, 47 Boulcott St., Wellington, 6011 (☎ 0800/225-050 in New Zealand, or 04/474-8100; www.passports.govt.nz).

United Kingdom   Visit your nearest passport office, major post office, or travel agency or contact the Identity and Passport Service (IPS), 89 Eccleston Sq., London, SW1V 1PN (☎ 0300/222-0000; www.ips.gov.uk).

United States   To find your regional passport office, check the U.S. Department of State website (www.travel.state.gov/passport) or call the National Passport Information Center (☎ 877/487-2778) for automated information.

Petrol   See "By Car" under the "Getting Around" section, earlier in this chapter.

Police   Several cities, including Cancún, have a special corps of English-speaking Tourist Police to assist with directions, guidance, and more. In case of emergency, dial ☎ **060** or 066 from any phone within Mexico. For police emergency numbers, turn to "Fast Facts" in the individual chapters.

Safety   See "Safety," earlier in this chapter.

Senior Travel   Mexico is a popular country for retirees. For decades, North Americans have been living indefinitely in Mexico by returning to the border and recrossing with a new tourist permit every 6 months. Mexican immigration officials have caught on, and now limit the maximum time in the country to 6 months within any year. This is to encourage even partial residents to acquire proper documentation.

AIM-Adventures in Mexico, Apartado Postal 31–70, 45050 Guadalajara, Jalisco, is a well-written, informative newsletter for prospective retirees. Subscriptions are $29 to the United States.

Sanborn Tours, 2015 S. 10th St., P.O. Box 936, McAllen, TX 78505-0519 (☎ **800/395-8482;** www.sanborns.com), offers a "Retire in Mexico" orientation tour.

Smoking   In early 2008, the Mexican president signed into law a nationwide smoking ban in workplaces and public buildings, and on public transportation. Under this ground-breaking law, private businesses are permitted to allow public smoking only in enclosed ventilated areas. Hotels may maintain up to 25% of guest rooms for smokers. Violators face stiff fines, and smokers refusing to comply could receive up to 36-hour jail sentences. The law places Mexico—where a significant percentage of the population smokes—at the forefront of efforts to curb smoking and improve public health in Latin America. So before you light up, be sure to ask about the application of local laws in Mexican public places and businesses you visit.

Student Travel   Because Mexicans consider higher education a luxury rather than a birthright, there is no formal network of student discounts and programs. Most Mexican students travel with their families rather than with other students, so student discount cards are not commonly recognized.

The U.S. Department of State offers information designated specifically for students traveling abroad: www.studentsabroad.state.gov.

The website www.hostels.com/mexico offers a list of hostels in Acapulco, Cancún, Guadalajara, Guanajuato, Mérida, Mexico City, Oaxaca, Playa del Carmen, Puerto Escondido, Puebla, San Cristobal las Casas, San Miguel de Allende, and Zacatecas, among other locations.

Taxes   Mexico has a value-added tax of 16% (*Impuesto de Valor Agregado,* or IVA; pronounced *Ee*-bah) on most everything, including restaurant meals, bus tickets, and souvenirs. (Exceptions are in Cancún, Cozumel, and Los Cabos, where the IVA is 11%; as ports of entry, they receive a break on taxes.) Hotels charge the usual 16% IVA, plus a locally administered bed tax of 3% (in most areas), for a total of 19%. In Cancún, Cozumel, and Los Cabos, hotels charge the 11% IVA plus 3% room tax, for a total of 14%. The prices quoted by hotels and restaurants do not necessarily include IVA. You may find that upper-end properties (three or more stars) often quote prices without IVA included, while lower-priced hotels include IVA. Ask to see a printed price sheet and ask if the tax is included.

Telephones   Mexico's telephone system is slowly catching up with modern times. Most telephone numbers have 10 digits. Every city and town with telephone access has a two-digit (Mexico City, Monterrey, and Guadalajara) or three-digit (everywhere else) area code. In Mexico City, Monterrey, and Guadalajara, local numbers have eight digits; elsewhere, local numbers have seven digits. To place a local call, you do not need to dial the area code. Many fax numbers are also regular phone numbers; ask whoever answers for the fax tone *("me da tono de fax, por favor").*

The country code for Mexico is 52.

To call Mexico:

1. Dial the international access code: 011 from the U.S. and Canada; 00 from the U.K., Ireland, or New Zealand; or 0011 from Australia.
2. Dial the country code: 52.
3. Dial the two- or three-digit area code, then the eight- or seven-digit number. For example, if you wanted to call the U.S. consular agent in Acapulco, the entire number would be 011-52-744-484-0300. If you wanted to dial the U.S. embassy in Mexico City, the entire number would be 011-52-55-5080-2000.

To make international calls: To make international calls from Mexico, dial 00, then the country code (U.S. and Canada 1, U.K. 44, Ireland 353, Australia 61, New Zealand 64). Next, dial the area code and number. For example, to call the British Embassy in Washington, you would dial 00-1-202-588-7800.

To call a Mexican cellular number: From the same area code, dial 044 and then the number. To dial the cellular phone from anywhere else in Mexico, first dial 01, and then the three-digit area code and the seven-digit number. To place an international call to a cellphone (e.g., from the U.S.), you now must add a 1 after the country code: for example, 011-52-1 + 10-digit number.

For directory assistance: Dial (*C*) **040** if you're looking for a number inside Mexico. **Note:** Listings usually appear under the owner's name, not the name of the business, and your chances of finding an English-speaking operator are slim.

For operator assistance: If you need operator assistance in making a call, dial (*C*) **090** to make an international call, and (*C*) **020** to call a number in Mexico.

Toll-free numbers: Numbers beginning with 800 within Mexico are toll-free, but calling a U.S. toll-free number from Mexico costs the same as an overseas call. To call an 800 number in the U.S., dial 001-880 and the last seven digits of the toll-free number. To call an 888 number in the U.S., dial 001-881 and the last seven digits of the toll-free number. For a number with an 887 prefix, dial 882; for 866, dial 883.

Time   Central Time prevails throughout most of Mexico, including the Yucatán, Tabasco, and Chiapas. The states of Baja California Sur, Chihuahua, Nayarit, Sinaloa, and Sonora fall in the Mountain Time Zone, while Baja California uses Pacific Time. All of Mexico observes **daylight saving time.**

Tipping Most service employees in Mexico count on tips for the majority of their income, and this is especially true for bellboys and waiters. Bellboys should receive the equivalent of 5 to 15 pesos per bag; waiters generally receive 10% to 15%, depending on the level of service. It is not customary to tip taxi drivers, unless they are hired by the hour or provide touring or other special services.

Toilets Public toilets are not common in Mexico, but an increasing number are available, especially at fast-food restaurants and Pemex gas stations. These facilities and restaurant and club restrooms commonly have attendants, who expect a small tip (about 5 pesos).

VAT See "Taxes" earlier in this section.

Visas For detailed information regarding visas to Mexico, visit the **National Immigration Institute** at http://embamex.sre.gob.mx/usa.

American and Canadian tourists are not required to have a visa or a tourist card for stays of 72 hours or less within the border zone (20–30km/12–19 miles from the U.S. border). For travel to Mexico beyond the border zone, all travelers from Australia, Canada, New Zealand, the U.K., and the U.S., among others, can get their visas upon arrival. Many other countries require a preapproved visa, although as of May 1, 2010, non-U.S. citizens with valid U.S. visas may enter Mexico with the U.S. visa, and do not have to obtain a Mexican visa. For the latest requirements, please check **www.inm.gob.mx/index.php**. Once in Mexico, all travelers must be in possession of a tourist card, also called Tourist Migration Form. This document is provided by airlines or by immigration authorities at the country's points of entry. Be careful not to lose this card, as you will be required to surrender it upon departure and you will be fined if you lose it.

Your tourist card is stamped on arrival. If traveling by bus or car, ensure that you obtain such a card at the immigration module located at the border and have it stamped by immigration authorities at the border. If you do not receive a stamped tourist card at the border, ensure that, when you arrive at your destination within Mexico, you immediately go to the closest National Institute of Immigration office, present your bus ticket, and request a tourist card. Travelers who fail to have their tourist card stamped may be fined, detained, or expelled from the country.

An immigration official will determine the number of days you can remain in Mexico. Do not assume that you will be granted the full 180 days. An extension of your stay can be requested for a fee at the National Institute of Immigration of the Ministry of the Interior or its local offices.

If you plan to enter Mexico by car, please read the vehicle's importation requirements (p. 742).

Note on travel of minors: Mexican law requires that any non-Mexican citizen under the age of 18 departing Mexico without both parents must carry notarized written permission from the parent or guardian who is not traveling with the child to or from Mexico. This permission must include the name of the parent, the name of the child, the name of anyone traveling with the child, and the notarized signature(s) of the absent parent(s). The U.S. Department of State recommends that permission include travel dates, destinations, airlines, and a summary of the circumstances surrounding the travel. The child must be carrying the original letter (not a facsimile or scanned copy), and proof of the parent/ child relationship (usually a birth certificate or court document) and an original custody decree, if applicable. Travelers can also contact the Mexican Embassy or closest Mexican Consulate for more current information.

Visitor Information The **Mexico Tourism Board** (© **800/44-MEXICO** in the U.S., or 01-800/006-8839 or 078 from within Mexico; www.visitmexico.com) is an excellent source for general information; you can request brochures and get answers to the most common questions from the exceptionally well-trained, knowledgeable staff. You can also call the Cancún location at ☏ **998/884-8073.**

The **Mexican Government Tourist Board's** main office is in Mexico City (☏ **55/5278-4200**). Satellite offices in the U.S. are in Chicago (☏ **312/228-0517**), Houston (☏ **713/772-2581**), Los Angeles (☏ **213/739-6336**), Miami (☏ **786/621-2909**), and New York (☏ **212/308-2110**). In Canada, you may call the Toronto office at ☏ **416/925-0704;** and in the United Kingdom, offices are in London (☏ **020/7488-9392**).

The **Chiapas Tourism Board** is at Blvd. Belisario Dominguez 950, CP29060 Tuxtla Gutiérrez, Chiapas (☏ **961/613-9396**). The **Quintana Roo Tourist Board** is at Carr. a. Calderitas 622, CP77010 Chetumal, Quintana Roo (☏ **983/835-0860**). The **Tabasco Tourism Board** is at Av. Los Rios s/n, Tabasco 2000, CP86035 Villahermosa, Tabasco (☏ **993/316-5134**). The **Yucatán Tourism Board** is at Calle 59 No. 514, Centro, CP97000 Mérida, Yucatán (☏ **999/924-9389**).

The **Mexican Embassy** in **Canada** is at 45 O'Connor St., Suite 1000, Ottawa, ON, K1P 1A4 (☏ **613/233-8988;** fax 613/235-9123). Consulate offices are at 2055 rue Peel, Bureau 1000, Montreal, QC, H3A 1V4 (☏ **514/288-2502**); Commerce Court West, 199 Bay St., Suite 4440, Toronto, ON, M5L 1E9 (☏ **416/368-2875**); and 411-1177 W. Hastings St., 4th Floor, Vancouver, BC, V6E 2K3 (☏ **604/684-1859**).

The **Mexican Embassy** (Consular Section) in the **United Kingdom** is at 16 Georges St., London, W1S1FD (☏ **020/7499-8586**).

The **Mexican Embassy** in the **United States** is at 1911 Pennsylvania Ave. NW, Washington, DC 20006 (☏ **202/736-1600**).

Water   Tap water in Mexico is generally not potable and it is safest to drink purified bottled water. Some hotels and restaurants purify water, but you should ask rather than assume this is the case. Use ice with caution as it may also come from tap water.

Women Travelers   Women do not frequently travel alone in Mexico, including driving alone on the highways. Walking on the street could net you a catcall, and walking alone at night is not advisable except in well-protected tourist areas. I've known people who have had uncomfortable experiences in crowded places such as subways. In general, though, Mexicans are extremely gracious, and will help a woman carry heavy items, open doors, and provide information, among other courtesies.

SURVIVAL SPANISH

Most Mexicans are very patient with foreigners who try to speak their language; it helps a lot to know a few basic phrases. Included here are simple phrases for expressing basic needs, followed by some common menu items.

ENGLISH-SPANISH PHRASES

English	Spanish	Pronunciation
Good day	**Buen día**	Bwehn *dee*-ah
Good morning	**Buenos días**	*Bweh*-nohs *dee*-ahs
How are you?	**¿Cómo está?**	*Koh*-moh eh-*stah*
Very well	**Muy bien**	Mwee byehn
Thank you	**Gracias**	*Grah*-syahs
You're welcome	**De nada**	Deh *nah*-dah
Goodbye	**Adiós**	Ah-*dyohs*
Please	**Por favor**	Pohr fah-*bohr*
Yes	**Sí**	See
No	**No**	Noh
Excuse me	**Perdóneme**	Pehr-*doh*-neh-meh
Give me	**Déme**	*Deh*-meh
Where is . . . ?	**¿Dónde está . . . ?**	*Dohn*-deh eh-*stah*
the station	**la estación**	lah eh-stah-*syohn*
a hotel	**un hotel**	oon oh-*tehl*
a gas station	**una gasolinera**	*oo*-nah gah-soh-lee-*neh*-rah
a restaurant	**un restaurante**	oon res-tow-*rahn*-teh
the toilet	**el baño**	el *bah*-nyoh
a good doctor	**un buen médico**	oon bwehn *meh*-dee-coh
the road to . . .	**el camino a/hacia**	el cah-*mee*-noh ah/*ah*-syah
To the right	**A la derecha**	Ah lah deh-*reh*-chah
To the left	**A la izquierda**	Ah lah ees-*kyehr*-dah
Straight ahead	**Derecho**	Deh-*reh*-choh
I would like	**Quisiera**	Key-*syeh*-rah
I want . . .	**Quiero**	*Kyeh*-roh
to eat	**comer**	koh-*mehr*
a room	**una habitación**	*oo*-nah ah-bee-tah-*syohn*

English	Spanish	Pronunciation
Do you have . . . ?	**¿Tiene usted . . . ?**	Tyeh-neh oo-*sted*
a book	**un libro**	oon *lee*-broh
a dictionary	**un diccionario**	oon deek-syoh-*nah*-ryoh
How much is it?	**¿Cuánto cuesta?**	*Kwahn*-toh *kweh*-stah
When?	**¿Cuándo?**	*Kwahn*-doh
What?	**¿Qué?**	Keh
There is (Is there . . . ?)	**(¿)Hay (. . . ?)**	Eye
What is there?	**¿Qué hay?**	Keh eye
Yesterday	**Ayer**	Ah-*yer*
Today	**Hoy**	Oy
Tomorrow	**Mañana**	Mah-*nyah*-nah
Good	**Bueno**	*Bweh*-noh
Bad	**Malo**	*Mah*-loh
Better (best)	**(Lo) Mejor**	(Loh) Meh-*hohr*
More	**Más**	Mahs
Less	**Menos**	*Meh*-nohs
No smoking	**Se prohibe fumar**	Seh proh-*ee*-beh foo-*mahr*
Postcard	**Tarjeta postal**	Tar-*heh*-tah poh-*stahl*
Insect repellent	**Repelente contra insectos**	Reh-peh-*lehn*-teh *cohn*-trah een-*sehk*-tohs

MORE USEFUL PHRASES

English	Spanish	Pronunciation
Do you speak English?	**¿Habla usted inglés?**	*Ah*-blah oo-*sted* een-*glehs*
Is there anyone here who speaks English?	**¿Hay alguien aquí que hable inglés?**	Eye *ahl*-gyehn ah-*kee* keh ah-*bleh* een-*glehs*
I speak a little Spanish.	**Hablo un poco de español.**	*Ah*-bloh oon *poh*-koh deh eh-spah-*nyohl*
I don't understand Spanish very well.	**No (lo) entiendo muy bien el español.**	Noh (loh) ehn-*tyehn*-doh mwee byehn el eh-spah-*nyohl*
The meal is good.	**Me gusta la comida.**	Meh *goo*-stah lah koh-*mee*-dah
What time is it?	**¿Qué hora es?**	Keh *oh*-rah ehs
May I see your menu?	**¿Puedo ver el menú (la carta)?**	*Pweh*-doh vehr el meh-*noo* (lah *car*-tah)
The check, please.	**La cuenta, por favor.**	Lah *kwehn*-tah pohr fa-*borh*
What do I owe you?	**¿Cuánto le debo?**	*Kwahn*-toh leh *deh*-boh
What did you say?	**¿Mande?** (formal)	*Mahn*-deh
	¿Cómo? (informal)	*Koh*-moh
I want (to see) . . .	**Quiero (ver) . . .**	*kyeh*-roh (vehr)
a room	**un cuarto** or **una habitación**	oon *kwar*-toh, *oo*-nah ah-bee-tah-*syohn*
for two persons	**para dos personas**	*pah*-rah dohs pehr-*soh*-nahs
with (without) bathroom	**con (sin) baño**	kohn (seen) *bah*-nyoh

English	Spanish	Pronunciation
We are staying here only . . .	**Nos quedamos aquí solamente . . .**	Nohs keh-*dah*-mohs ah-*kee* soh-lah-*mehn*-teh
one night.	**una noche.**	*oo*-nah *noh*-cheh
one week.	**una semana.**	*oo*-nah seh-*mah*-nah
We are leaving . . .	**Partimos (Salimos) . . .**	Pahr-*tee*-mohs (sah-*lee*-mohs)
tomorrow.	**mañana.**	mah-*nya*-nah
Do you accept . . . ?	**¿Acepta usted . . . ?**	Ah-*sehp*-tah oo-*sted*
traveler's checks?	**cheques de viajero?**	*cheh*-kehs deh byah-*heh*-roh

NUMBERS

English	Spanish	Pronunciation
1	**uno**	(ooh-noh)
2	**dos**	(dohs)
3	**tres**	(trehs)
4	**cuatro**	(kwah-troh)
5	**cinco**	(seen-koh)
6	**seis**	(sayes)
7	**siete**	(syeh-teh)
8	**ocho**	(oh-choh)
9	**nueve**	(nweh-beh)
10	**diez**	(dyehs)
11	**once**	(ohn-seh)
12	**doce**	(doh-seh)
13	**trece**	(treh-seh)
14	**catorce**	(kah-tohr-seh)
15	**quince**	(keen-seh)
16	**dieciséis**	(dyeh-see-sayes)
17	**diecisiete**	(dyeh-see-syeh-teh)
18	**dieciocho**	(dyeh-syoh-choh)
19	**diecinueve**	(dyeh-see-nweh-beh)
20	**veinte**	(bayn-teh)
30	**treinta**	(trayn-tah)
40	**cuarenta**	(kwah-ren-tah)
50	**cincuenta**	(seen-kwen-tah)
60	**sesenta**	(seh-sehn-tah)
70	**setenta**	(seh-tehn-tah)
80	**ochenta**	(oh-chehn-tah)
90	**noventa**	(noh-behn-tah)
100	**cien**	(syehn)
200	**doscientos**	(do-syehn-tohs)
500	**quinientos**	(kee-nyehn-tohs)
1,000	**mil**	(meel)

TRANSPORTATION TERMS

English	Spanish	Pronunciation
airport	**Aeropuerto**	Ah-eh-roh-*pwehr*-toh
flight	**Vuelo**	*Bweh*-loh
rental-car agency	**Arrendadora de autos**	Ah-*rehn*-da-doh-rah deh *ow*-tohs
bus	**Autobús**	Ow-toh-*boos*
bus or truck	**Camión**	Ka-*myohn*
lane	**Carril**	Kah-*reel*
nonstop (bus)	**Directo**	Dee-*rehk*-toh
baggage (claim area)	**Equipajes**	Eh-kee-*pah*-hehss
intercity	**Foraneo**	Foh-rah-*neh*-oh
luggage storage area	**Guarda equipaje**	*Gwar*-dah eh-kee-*pah*-heh
arrival gates	**Llegadas**	Yeh-*gah*-dahss
originates at this station	**Local**	Loh-*kahl*
originates elsewhere	**De paso**	Deh *pah*-soh
Are seats available?	**Hay lugares disponibles?**	Eye loo-*gah*-rehs dis-pohn-*ee*-blehss
first class	**Primera**	Pree-*meh*-rah
second class	**Segunda**	Seh-*goon*-dah
nonstop (flight)	**Sin escala**	Seen ess-*kah*-lah
baggage claim area	**Recibo de equipajes**	Reh-*see*-boh deh eh-kee-*pah*-hehss
waiting room	**Sala de espera**	*Sah*-lah deh ehss-*peh*-rah
toilets	**Sanitarios**	Sah-nee-*tah*-ryohss
ticket window	**Taquilla**	Tah-*kee*-yah

DINING TERMINOLOGY

MEALS

desayuno Breakfast.
comida Main meal of the day, taken in the afternoon.

cena Supper.

COURSES

botana A small serving of food that accompanies a beer or drink, usually served free of charge.

entrada Appetizer.

sopa Soup course. (Not necessarily a soup—it can be a dish of rice or noodles, called *sopa seca* [dry soup].)

ensalada Salad.

plato fuerte Main course.

postre Dessert.

comida corrida Inexpensive daily special usually consisting of three courses.

menú del día Same as *comida corrida*.

DEGREE OF DONENESS

término un cuarto Rare, literally means one-fourth.

término medio Medium rare, one-half.

término tres cuartos Medium, three-fourths.

bien cocido Well done.

Note: Keep in mind, when ordering a steak, that *medio* does not mean "medium."

MISCELLANEOUS RESTAURANT TERMINOLOGY

cucharra Spoon.

cuchillo Knife.

la cuenta The bill.

plato Plate.

plato hondo Bowl.

propina Tip.

servilleta Napkin.

tenedor Fork.

vaso Glass.

IVA Value-added tax.

fonda Strictly speaking, a food stall in the market or street, but now used in a loose or nostalgic sense to designate an informal restaurant.

POPULAR MEXICAN DISHES

a la tampiqueña (Usually *bistec a la t.* or *arrachera a la t.*) A steak served with several sides, including but not limited to an enchilada, guacamole, rice, and beans.

adobo Marinade made with chiles and tomatoes, often seen in adjectival form *adobado/adobada*.

albóndigas Meatballs, usually cooked in a chile chipotle sauce.

antojito Literally means "small temptation." It's a general term for tacos, tostadas, quesadillas, and the like, which are usually eaten for supper or as a snack.

arrachera Skirt steak, fajitas.

arroz Rice.

bistec Steak.

bolillo Small bread with a crust much like a baguette.

buñuelos Fried pastry dusted with sugar. Can also mean a large, thin, crisp pancake that is dipped in boiling cane syrup.

cajeta Thick caramel sauce made from goat's milk.

calabaza Zucchini squash.

caldo tlalpeño Chicken and vegetable soup, with rice, chile chipotle, avocado, and garbanzos. Its name comes from a suburban community of Mexico City, Tlalpan.

caldo xochitl Mild chicken and rice soup served with a small plate of chopped onion, chile serrano, avocado, and limes, to be added according to individual taste.

camarones Shrimp. For common cooking methods, see ***pescado.***

carne Meat.

carnitas Slow-cooked pork dish from Michoacán and parts of central Mexico, served with tortillas, guacamole, and salsa or pickled jalapeños.

cebolla Onion.

cecina Thinly sliced pork or beef, dried or marinated, depending on the region.

ceviche Fresh raw seafood marinated in fresh lime juice and garnished with chopped tomatoes, onions, chiles, and sometimes cilantro.

chalupas poblanas Simple dish from Puebla consisting of handmade tortillas lightly fried but left soft, and topped with different chile sauces.

chayote Spiny squash boiled and served as an accompaniment to meat dishes.

chilaquiles Fried tortilla quarters softened in either a red or a green sauce and served with Mexican sour cream, onion, and sometimes chicken *(con pollo)*.

chile Any of the many hot peppers used in Mexican cooking, in fresh, dried, or smoked forms.

chile ancho A dried chile poblano, which serves as the base for many varieties of sauces and *moles*.

chile chilpotle (or **chipotle**) A smoked jalapeño dried or in an *adobo* sauce.

chile en nogada Chile poblano stuffed with a complex filling of shredded meat, nuts, and dried, candied, and fresh fruit, topped with walnut cream sauce and a sprinkling of pomegranate seeds.

chile poblano Fresh pepper that is usually dark green in color, large, and not usually spicy. Often stuffed with a variety of fillings (chile relleno).

chile relleno Stuffed pepper.

chivo Kid or goat.

cochinita pibil Yucatecan dish of pork, pit-baked in a *pibil* sauce of *achiote*, sour orange, and spices.

col Cabbage. Also called *repollo*.

consomé Clear broth, usually with rice.

cortes Steak; in full, it is *cortes finas de carne* (fine cuts of meat).

cuitlacoche Variant of *huitlacoche*.

elote Fresh corn.

empanada For most of Mexico, a turnover with a savory or sweet filling. In Oaxaca and southern Mexico, it is corn *masa* or a tortilla folded around a savory filling and roasted or fried.

empanizado Breaded.

enchilada A lightly fried tortilla, dipped in sauce and folded or rolled around a filling. It has many variations, such as enchiladas suizas (made with a cream sauce), enchiladas del portal or enchiladas placeras (made with a predominantly *chile ancho* sauce), and enchiladas verdes (in a green sauce of tomatillos, cilantro, and chiles).

enfrijoladas Like an enchilada, but made with a bean sauce.

enmoladas Enchiladas made with a *mole* sauce.

entomatadas Enchiladas made with a tomato sauce.

escabeche Vegetables pickled in a vinegary liquid.

flan Custard.

flautas Tortillas that are rolled up around a filling (usually chicken or shredded beef) and deep-fried; often listed on a menu as *taquitos* or *tacos fritos*.

gorditas Thick, fried corn tortillas, slit open and stuffed with meat or cheese.

horchata Drink made of ground rice, melon seeds, ground almonds, or coconut and cinnamon.

huazontle A vegetable vaguely comparable to broccoli, but milder in taste.

huitlacoche Salty and mild-tasting corn fungus that is considered a delicacy.

jitomate Tomato.

lechuga Lettuce.

limón A small lime. Mexicans squeeze them on everything from soups to tacos.

lomo adobado Pork loin cooked in an *adobo*.

masa Soft dough made of corn that is the basis for making tortillas and tamales.

menudo Soup made with beef tripe and hominy.

milanesa Beef cutlet breaded and fried.

mole Any variety of thick sauce made with dried chiles, nuts, fruit or vegetables, and spices. Variations include *m. poblano* (Puebla style, with chocolate and sesame), *m. negro* (black *mole* from Oaxaca, also with chocolate), and *m. verde* (made with herbs and/or pumpkinseeds, depending on the region).

pan Bread. A few of the varieties include *p. dulce* (general term for a variety of sweet breads), *p. de muerto* (bread made for the Day of the Dead holidays), and *p. Bimbo* (packaged sliced white bread).

panuchos A Yucatecan dish of *masa* cakes stuffed with refried black beans and topped with shredded turkey or chicken, lettuce, and onion.

papas Potatoes.

papadzules A Yucatecan dish of tortillas stuffed with hard-boiled eggs and topped with a sauce made of pumpkinseeds.

parrillada A sampler platter of grilled meats or seafood.

pescado Fish. Common ways of cooking fish include *al mojo de ajo* (pan seared with oil and garlic), *a la veracruzana* (with tomatoes, olives, and capers), and *al ajillo* (seared with garlic and fine strips or rings of *chile guajillo*).

pibil See *cochinita pibil.* When made with chicken, it is called *pollo pibil.*

picadillo Any of several recipes using shredded beef, pork, or chicken and onions, chiles, and spices. Can also contain fruit and nuts.

pipián A thick sauce made with ground pumpkinseeds, nuts, herbs, and chiles. Can be red or green.

poc chuc A Yucatecan dish of grilled pork with onion marinated in sour orange.

pollo Chicken.

pozole Soup with chicken or pork, hominy, lettuce, and radishes, served with a small plate of other ingredients to be added according to taste (onion, pepper, lime juice, oregano). In Jalisco it's red (*p. rojo*), in Michoacán it's clear (*p. blanco*), and in Guerrero it's green (*p. verde*). In the rest of Mexico, it can be any one of these.

puerco Pork.

quesadilla Corn or flour tortillas stuffed with white cheese and cooked on a hot griddle. In Mexico City, it is made with raw *masa* folded around any of a variety of fillings (often containing no cheese) and deep-fried.

queso Cheese.

res Beef.

rompope Mexican liqueur, made with eggs, vanilla, sugar, and alcohol.

salbute A Yucatecan dish like a *panucho*, but without bean paste in the middle.

sopa azteca Tortilla soup.

sopa tarasca A blended soup from Michoacán made with beans and tomatoes.

sope Small fried *masa* cake topped with savory meats and greens.

tacos al pastor Small tacos made with thinly sliced pork marinated in an *adobo* and served with pineapple, onion, and cilantro.

tamal (Not "tamale.") *Masa* mixed with lard and beaten until light and folded around a savory or sweet filling, and encased in a cornhusk or a plant leaf (usually corn or banana) and then steamed. *Tamales* is the plural form.

taquitos See *flautas.*

tinga Shredded meat stewed in a chile chipotle sauce.

torta A sandwich made with a bolillo.

Index

A

INDEX